OpenSolaris™ Bible

Nicholas A. Solter
Gerald Jelinek
David Miner

WILEY

Wiley Publishing, Inc.

OpenSolaris™ Bible

Published by
Wiley Publishing, Inc.
10475 Crosspoint Boulevard
Indianapolis, IN 46256
www.wiley.com

Copyright © 2009 by Wiley Publishing, Inc., Indianapolis, Indiana

Published simultaneously in Canada

ISBN: 978-0-470-38548-7

Manufactured in the United States of America

10 9 8 7 6 5 4 3 2

Library of Congress Cataloging-in-Publication Data:

Solter, Nicholas, 1977-
   OpenSolaris bible / Nicholas Solter, Gerald Jelinek, David Miner.
      p. cm.
   Includes index.
   ISBN 978-0-470-38548-7 (paper/website)
   1.   OpenSolaris (Electronic resource) 2.   Operating systems
(Computers) 3.   Open source software.   I. Jelinek, Gerald.   II. Miner,
David.   III. Title.
   QA76.76.O63S6526 2009
   005.3 — dc22

                               2008049814

For general information on our other products and services or to obtain technical support, please contact our Customer Care Department within the U.S. at (800) 762-2974, outside the U.S. at (317) 572-3993 or fax (317) 572-4002.

Library of Congress Cataloging-in-Publication Data is available from the publisher.

Wiley also publishes its books in a variety of electronic formats. Some content that appears in print may not be available in electronic books.

To my children, Kai and Katja. — Nicholas Solter

To my wife, Sarah, who had no idea we would be moving when I was in the middle of this book, but who was always encouraging and supportive. — Jerry Jelinek

I dedicate this book to my wife, Kris. I hope she doesn't regret telling me, while I was considering participating, that I won't regret having written it! — Dave Miner

About the Authors

Nicholas Solter has worked at Sun Microsystems for more than eight years in the areas of high availability and distributed systems. In his work on the Solaris Cluster product, he has implemented clustering support for core Solaris features such as Zones and SMF. He was the technical lead in open sourcing the Solaris Cluster product and is currently leading the effort to run Solaris Cluster on the OpenSolaris distribution.

In addition to his work at Sun, Nicholas has experience in the computer game industry at Digital Media International and Electronic Arts. He is also the lead author of *Professional C++* (Wrox) and has taught C++ at the college level.

Nicholas studied computer science at Stanford University, where he earned bachelor of science (with distinction) and master of science degrees, with a concentration in systems. When not working, he enjoys spending time with his family, playing basketball, reading, and playing in the Colorado snow (having been deprived of winters growing up in Southern California).

Gerald Jelinek has been an engineer at Sun Microsystems for a total of almost 20 years, although not contiguously. He currently works on the Zones virtualization subsystem in OpenSolaris. In the past, he has worked on a wide variety of projects, including system installation, JumpStart, printing, a variety of system administration tools, and the Solaris Volume Manager. A little-known fact is that he personally assembled the various project bits and burned the Solaris 2.0 golden CD. In addition to Sun, Gerald has worked at several other companies.

Gerald graduated from Washington University in St. Louis with a B.S. in computer science, and from the University of Colorado with an M.S. in computer science. He and his wife, Sarah, spend most of their free time fixing up the 85-year-old house they recently moved into.

David Miner has been an engineer at Sun Microsystems for nearly two decades. He is presently the lead for the Caiman installer project and co-lead for the OpenSolaris distribution. During his time at Sun he has worked primarily in the areas of system administration and networking and has been a significant contributor to a variety of projects in both fields, including the Solaris admintool and sysidtool, PC-NFS, the Solaris DHCP server and DHCP Manager management tool, and the Service Management Facility (SMF). Prior to Sun, Dave worked at Prime Computer on TCP/IP networking.

David graduated from Michigan State University with a B.S. (with honors) in computer science. In his spare time, Dave is an avid golfer and hoopster. He and his wife, Kris Corwin, are the adoptive parents of a small pack of retired racing greyhounds.

Credits

Executive Editor
Bob Elliott

Development Editor
Maryann Steinhart

Technical Editor
Peter Baer Galvin

Production Editor
Dassi Zeidel

Copy Editor
Luann Rouff

Editorial Manager
Mary Beth Wakefield

Production Manager
Tim Tate

Vice President and Executive Group Publisher
Richard Swadley

Vice President and Executive Publisher
Barry Pruett

Project Coordinator, Cover
Lynsey Stanford

Proofreader
Josh Chase, Word One

Indexer
Ted Laux

Cover Illustration
Joyce Haughey

Cover Designer
Michael E. Trent

Acknowledgments

Many people contributed directly and indirectly to this book. We would first like to thank Bob Elliot, executive editor at Wiley, for letting us write this book, and our agent, David Fugate of LaunchBooks Literary Agency, for helping to make the project possible. Our editors, Maryann Steinhart, Dassi Zeidel, and Luann Rouff, excellently guided us through the writing and revision process, while Peter Baer Galvin provided invaluable technical feedback and corrections.

Additionally, we would like to thank the following people, who reviewed one or more chapters: Alexandre Chartre, Bonnie Corwin, Thorsten Früauf, Moinak Ghosh, Susan Kamm-Worrell, and John Levon. Thank you, also, to Steve McKinty for providing the content on Open HA Cluster Geographic Edition. Any remaining errors are, of course, our own.

A special thanks goes to Sanjay Nadkarni, who provided the camera Dave used in completing the examples in Chapter 5 during a trip to Sun's Broomfield campus.

We also want to acknowledge the thousands of engineers over the past 40 years who have contributed to the code that is now OpenSolaris. Additionally, we would like to recognize Sun Microsystems' courageous step of open sourcing the Solaris operating system to create OpenSolaris, and the combined wisdom and numerous contributions of the OpenSolaris community. Although we are employees of Sun and members of the OpenSolaris community, the contents of this book are our own, and do not necessarily reflect the views of these entities.

Finally, we would like to thank our respective spouses, Sonja Solter, Sarah Jelinek, and Kris Corwin, for bearing with us through this process and tolerating our long nights and weekends spent on this book.

Contents at a Glance

Contents at a Glance

Part VI

Contents

Contents

Part II

Part III

Contents

Part IV

Contents

Part V

Contents

Contents

Introduction

Welcome to *OpenSolaris Bible*! This book provides an introduction and tutorial on one of the newest open source operating systems: OpenSolaris. Based on the enterprise-class Solaris operating system from Sun Microsystems with roots in UNIX dating back to 1969, and chock-full of exciting new features such as ZFS, Zones, SMF, and DTrace, OpenSolaris was released to the open source community in 2005. Since then, Sun and the OpenSolaris community have added significant virtualization features, such as xVM Hypervisor and VirtualBox; created a new network packaging model called IPS; rewritten the installer; and created a brand-new Live CD distribution. Whether you're looking for a new laptop, workstation, development platform, or server, it's worth your while to read this book and take OpenSolaris for a spin.

This book is a comprehensive resource on using OpenSolaris. By the time you have completed the book, you'll know how to install, use, administer, develop on, and deploy OpenSolaris. In fact, you'll become a power user, conversant in advanced troubleshooting with FMA, SMF, DTrace, and more. In addition, you'll understand how to use virtualization technologies with OpenSolaris to optimize your physical hardware.

Additionally, *OpenSolaris Bible* contains the following features:

- **Practical, hands-on advice**. As active software developers who use OpenSolaris every day, the authors have included hands-on usable information. Unlike some books that address only theory, this book contains practical tips and tricks that you can immediately put into practice.

- **Concrete examples**. The book is full of specific examples — including exact command lines and screenshots — that walk you through the tasks you need to accomplish. These examples are all well tested.

- **Cutting-edge information**. As active contributors to OpenSolaris, the authors provide cutting-edge details about rapidly evolving features such as IPS, xVM Hypervisor, VirtualBox, and more.

- **Candid insider tips**. As both Sun Microsystems employees and OpenSolaris community leaders, the authors are in an ideal position to explain OpenSolaris to you.

Who Should Read This Book

Perhaps you've heard about the ZFS file system, DTrace, or one of the other novel features in OpenSolaris and are eager to try out the operating system to see what all the fuss is about; or maybe you're an experienced UNIX or Linux user who wants to explore one of the newest open source operating systems on the block. You might be a disgruntled Windows user interested in moving into the wonderful world of open source software; or perhaps you're already an experienced OpenSolaris user who would like to move to the next level or learn about a feature that you haven't had the chance to try yet. This book has something for you, regardless of your background or familiarity with OpenSolaris.

The only prerequisite for reading this book is that you have some experience with UNIX or Linux. That could be with any UNIX/Linux variant, such as Solaris, HP-UX, NetBSD, MacOS X, Ubuntu, Red Hat Linux, and so on. The key point is that you should be familiar with the basic UNIX/Linux model: You should know what a shell is, and be familiar with the concepts of users, processes, file systems, network interfaces, and the like. If you've used only Microsoft Windows, the UNIX model represents a paradigm shift; and you will find it easier to approach once you've read an introductory book on UNIX or Linux, such as *UNIX for Dummies* by John R. Levine and Margaret Levine Young. However, Chapter 3 of this book provides a whirlwind introduction to basic OpenSolaris user and administrator concepts, so if you're in doubt, skim through that chapter to decide whether this book is appropriate for you.

Programming experience is not a prerequisite for this book. You can read the book even if you've never written a C program or shell script in your life.

How This Book Is Organized

OpenSolaris Bible contains 24 chapters, divided into six parts. Although the book is organized so that you can start with Chapter 1 and read straight through to Chapter 24, if you're like the authors of this book you are unlikely to tackle a technical book that way. Instead, you may want to jump straight to the sections that most interest you, or use the book as a reference for whatever task you currently have at hand. For example, if virtualization is the hot topic for you right now, you might want to jump straight to Part V. To that end, this book has been carefully designed such that each chapter more or less stands on its own. Chapters that reference material in other parts of the book contain cross-references where appropriate, so you'll always know where to look for more information.

Part I: Introduction to OpenSolaris

Part I provides a crash course in OpenSolaris. Chapter 1 introduces the OpenSolaris operating system and open source community, and contrasts it with other popular operating systems such as Linux. Chapter 2 describes the various distributions available and shows you how to obtain and install the OpenSolaris distribution from Sun. Chapter 3 concludes Part I with a tour of the

OpenSolaris operating environment, from the GNOME desktop to the bash shell, from using vim, to system administration. If you're new to OpenSolaris, Part I is the place to start. This part assumes no prior experience with OpenSolaris. Even if you're experienced with Linux or Solaris and are tempted to jump straight to a more advanced topic, you should skim this section to ensure that you're up to speed on the latest developments in OpenSolaris and how it differs from other popular operating systems.

Part II: Using OpenSolaris

Part II provides the details of using OpenSolaris as a desktop or workstation system. Chapter 4 begins Part II by covering the GNOME desktop and the various applications available to you for accessing the Internet, listening to music, and so on. Chapter 5 continues to describe how to use your OpenSolaris box as a desktop machine by connecting printers and other peripherals, such as USB devices. Chapter 6 concludes Part II by describing how to obtain additional software and how to upgrade your OpenSolaris system. Even if you're planning to use OpenSolaris only as a server, you should familiarize yourself with the software management discussion in Chapter 6.

Part III: OpenSolaris File Systems, Networking, and Security

Part III delves into the details of OpenSolaris administration. Any OpenSolaris user or administrator needs to understand how to use disk storage, how to network OpenSolaris machines, and how to take advantage of the OpenSolaris security features. Chapter 7 starts Part III with an introduction to using disks with OpenSolaris, including disk naming, formatting, and partitioning; the UFS file system; and the Solaris Volume Manager. Chapters 8 and 10 present details on the ZFS file system and Network File System (NFS), respectively. Chapter 9 provides a detailed look at OpenSolaris networking, while Chapter 10 also includes information on the NIS and LDAP directory services. Chapter 11 concludes Part III with a thorough discussion of the OpenSolaris security features, including Role-Based Access Control, IP Security, and Kerberos.

Part IV: OpenSolaris Reliability, Availability, and Serviceability

Part IV describes the reliability, availability, and serviceability features of OpenSolaris. Computer systems can and will fail at both the hardware and software level. How an operating system handles these failures determines its suitability as a robust platform. OpenSolaris, based on the enterprise-class Solaris operating system from Sun, provides significant robustness in the form of what computer scientists sometimes call RAS: reliability, availability, and serviceability. This part opens with fault management and service management, in Chapters 12 and 13, respectively. These features combine to implement OpenSolaris' predictive self-healing, which provides significant robustness in the presence of both hardware and software faults. Chapters 14 and 15 describe the serviceability aspects of OpenSolaris, including the innovative dynamic tracing (DTrace) facility. The part concludes with Chapter 16, on clustering OpenSolaris machines together for increased availability of the system as a whole.

Part V: OpenSolaris Virtualization

Part V covers the various technologies available to use with OpenSolaris to share the computing resources of a single physical machine among multiple users, processes, and even operating systems. Chapter 17 presents on overview of virtualization terms and concepts. Chapter 18 describes OpenSolaris resource management techniques for virtualizing resources within a single operating system instance. Chapter 19 covers the Zones OS-level virtualization feature in OpenSolaris. Chapters 20 and 21 describe the xVM and Logical Domains hypervisor-based virtualization approaches on x86 and SPARC hardware, respectively, that enable you to run multiple operating system instances on a single physical machine. Chapter 22 concludes Part V with a look at VirtualBox, an easy-to-use virtualization software application that can run on a variety of host operating systems, including OpenSolaris, and can support OpenSolaris as a guest operating system. VirtualBox is your best bet for trying out OpenSolaris, even if you don't have a physical machine available on which to install it. If that's the case, you might want to jump to Chapter 22 after reading Part I.

Part VI: Developing and Deploying on OpenSolaris

Part VI concludes *OpenSolaris Bible* with a thorough look at deploying web services and using OpenSolaris as a development platform. Chapter 23 shows you how to use the web stack applications available on OpenSolaris, such as the Apache web server, MySQL, PostgreSQL, Apache Tomcat, and others. Chapter 24 presents the various development and debugging tools available on OpenSolaris, including the Java Development Kit, the Sun Studio Compiler Collection, NetBeans, the GNU Compiler Collection, and various source code management systems such as Mercurial. If you're a developer considering OpenSolaris as your platform, Chapter 24 has all the background information you need.

Conventions Used in This Book

There are many different organizational and typographical features throughout this book designed to help you get the most from the information.

Text styles

This book uses a number of conventions to present the material clearly and consistently:

- New terms are *italicized* when they are introduced.
- Keyboard strokes are shown like this: Ctrl+K.
- Nested menu options are listed in order of selection, separated with arrows, like this: Applications→Graphics→Image Editor
- Code, commands, URLs, filenames, and file listings are all printed in a monospace font like this: `www.opensolaris.com`.

■ When an example includes both input and output, the same monospace typography is
used, but input is presented in bold type to distinguish the two. Here's an example of a
command with both input and output:

```
$ echo "Hello, world"
Hello, world
```

Command prompts

The book shows two different prompts for shell commands. A root shell is shown with the pound
sign (#), whereas a non-root shell is shown with the dollar sign ($). Here's an example of a root
shell command:

```
# svcadm enable network/physical:default
```

Here's an example of a user shell command:

```
$ date
Tue Jul 29 13:11:10 MDT 2008
```

Note that OpenSolaris allows certain non-root users to execute privileged commands. This capability is discussed further in Chapters 3 and 11.

Icons

The following items are used to call your attention to points that are particularly important:

 Notes provide additional, ancillary information that is helpful, but somewhat outside
of the current presentation of information.

 Tips generally are used to provide information that can make your work
easier — special shortcuts or methods for doing something easier than the norm.

 This information is important and is set off in a separate paragraph with a special
icon. Cautions provide information about things to watch out for, whether simply
inconvenient or potentially hazardous to your data or systems.

CROSS-REF Cross-references point you to other places in the book where you can find related or
additional material.

Hardware Architecture

Throughout the text the term x86 is used to refer generally to both 32-bit and 64-bit AMD or
Intel hardware architectures. SPARC refers to 64-bit systems with either sun4u or sun4v pro-
cessor class CPUs unless specifically noted. This is primarily only an issue in Chapter 21 on
LDoms.

Manual Page References

System commands are sometimes written in the body of the text such that they refer to the appropriate manual page for that command. For example, svcs(1) means the svcs command, which is documented in section 1 of the manual pages. OpenSolaris includes the traditional UNIX man(1) command, which can be used to display the manual page for a command. Thus, the following example displays the manual page for the svcs(1) command:

```
$ man svcs
```

Resources

Most of the chapters include a "Resources" section at the end that provides suggestions for more information — for example, URLs to project pages, other reference books, or pointers to the source code.

What's on the Companion Website

The companion website for *OpenSolaris Bible*, at www.wiley.com/go/opensolaris contains the source code for the programming examples in Chapters 15 and 24, as well as an up-to-date errata list.

Minimum Requirements

To install and try out OpenSolaris on bare metal, you need a desktop or laptop machine with the following minimum requirements:

- Intel or AMD 32-bit or 64-bit Pentium III or faster processor
- 512MB RAM
- 10GB free hard disk space
- CD or DVD drive

If you intend to download OpenSolaris from the Internet, you need a reasonably high-speed Internet connection and a CD burner to burn the image to a CD. Alternately, you can order a free CD from http://opensolaris.com.

OpenSolaris does not work perfectly with every off-the-shelf laptop or desktop machine. Use the device detection tool described in Chapter 2 to determine whether your hardware will work.

OpenSolaris in a virtual machine

If, instead of running on bare metal, you want to run OpenSolaris in VirtualBox, VMware, or on other virtualization software, you need at least 1GB of RAM, but you won't need a CD/DVD drive or a CD burner. You also won't need to worry about hardware compatibility and the device detection tool.

Other requirements

A few of the topics in this book require hardware other than the minimum listed here. Logical Domains, described in Chapter 21, require a sun4v SPARC processor. Running virtual machines under xVM, VirtualBox, or Logical Domains generally requires more than 512MB of RAM; and Solaris Cluster Express, described in Chapter 16, requires additional disk space and RAM.

Where to Go from Here

While reading this book, the authors strongly suggest that you "play along at home" by downloading and installing the free OpenSolaris distribution from http://opensolaris.com.

After reading the book, you should be a confident user and administrator of OpenSolaris. If you have clarifying questions or queries about topics not covered in this book, please feel free to ask the OpenSolaris community at http://opensolaris.org. Chapter 1 contains a list of helpful mailing lists and forums.

Despite our best efforts to ensure the correctness of all the material in this book, you might uncover a mistake as you're reading. If you do find a bug, please report it at www.wiley.com/go/opensolaris.

We hope you find this book useful, and that you enjoy using OpenSolaris as much as we do!

Part I

Introduction to OpenSolaris

Chapter 1

What Is OpenSolaris?

You probably wouldn't have picked up this book if you hadn't at least heard of OpenSolaris or Solaris, but even if you've poked around OpenSolaris or used Solaris for years, you might be confused about what, exactly, OpenSolaris is. Is it an operating system, an open source code base, an open source community, or a distribution? How is it different from Solaris? How is it different from Linux? Is it really open source?

This chapter answers those questions and more. Even if you're an experienced Solaris user, this chapter may be useful in helping you understand OpenSolaris and its differences from Solaris. On the other hand, if you're already involved in OpenSolaris, you might still want to skim this chapter to learn a bit about the history of OpenSolaris and Solaris with which you might not be familiar.

Introduction to OpenSolaris

OpenSolaris is an open source operating system, similar in scope to GNU/Linux and BSD, but descended from the proprietary Solaris operating system from Sun Microsystems. The authors of this book find it helpful to think of OpenSolaris as divided into three distinct but related aspects: the code, the distributions, and the community.

OpenSolaris code

OpenSolaris is the open source version of Sun Microsystems' Solaris operating system, but OpenSolaris consists of code for much more than just the core operating system — it includes source for installers, desktops, layered software such as Open High Availability Cluster, documentation, test frameworks and test suites, and much more. OpenSolaris is millions of lines of source code in tens of thousands of source files.

You can browse the source code online at http://src.opensolaris.org.

If you're familiar with the Linux world, you can think of this aspect of OpenSolaris as similar to kernel.org, but with source code for much more than just the operating system kernel.

NOTE Some parts of Solaris are legally encumbered, such that they cannot be open sourced. Thus, OpenSolaris does not contain the source code for the complete Solaris operating system.

OpenSolaris distributions

Unless you're an operating systems developer, source code doesn't do you much good. Most people want a running operating system, not a bunch of code. While you can theoretically build a running system from the source, if all you want to do is run OpenSolaris, it's much easier to install one of the OpenSolaris binary distributions. Luckily, there are several of them, including Solaris Express, Shillix, BeleniX, NexentaCore, and MartUX. This book focuses on the OpenSolaris distribution from Sun Microsystems, confusingly also named OpenSolaris. (The OpenSolaris distribution from Sun is available from http://opensolaris.com.)

NOTE Sun Microsystems owns the trademark for the term OpenSolaris. Thus, distributions from outside Sun are allowed to use the term only by following the OpenSolaris Trademark Policy. See http://opensolaris.org/os/trademark.

The various OpenSolaris distributions are comparable to the various Linux distributions such as Ubuntu, Red Hat, and SUSE Linux.

CROSS-REF Chapter 2 describes OpenSolaris distributions in more detail.

OpenSolaris community

The OpenSolaris community consists of the activity around the OpenSolaris source code and distributions, including design and development of new features, bug fixes, advocacy and evangelism, distribution building, discussions, and much more. The development community, centered at http://opensolaris.org, hosts the source code and provides resources for projects such as web space, mailing lists, and source code repositories. This community supports active development, similar to the Apache community.

A more user-centered community built around the OpenSolaris binary distribution from Sun can be found at http://opensolaris.com.

Both of these OpenSolaris communities are sponsored by Sun Microsystems. However, non-Sun employees are encouraged to participate at all levels, from using the distributions to writing kernel code.

The section "Getting Involved in OpenSolaris" near the end of this chapter provides more information about the OpenSolaris communities.

OpenSolaris Features

OpenSolaris contains a rich feature-set that makes it suitable for a wide variety of uses, from running a personal desktop or laptop to providing web services to hosting enterprise-class databases with stringent availability requirements. OpenSolaris contains far too many features to list here, but an overview of the key differentiators can help you start to evaluate its usefulness. For more details on these features and many others, read the rest of this book! Here are some of the OpenSolaris highlights:

- Support for multiple hardware architectures, including both SPARC and 32-bit and 64-bit x86-based systems. OpenSolaris also performs well in many industry benchmarks.
- High scalability. OpenSolaris runs on both single processor machines and multiprocessor systems with hundreds of CPUs and terabytes of RAM.
- Innovative file system and volume manager support. Solaris uses a Virtual File System (VFS) layer so that different file systems can be plugged in on top of it relatively easily. In addition to the standard Unix File System (UFS), OpenSolaris includes the Solaris Volume Manager (SVM) and the new ZFS.
- Networking features, including a kernel-level, high-performance TCP/IP stack, IPv6 support, IPsec, Network Auto-Magic (NWAM) for automatic detection and configuration of network interfaces, and IP Network Multipathing (IPMP) for fault tolerance and load balancing.
- Complex resource management, including processor pools, physical memory controls, and a fair share scheduler.
- Sophisticated security, including role-based access control (RBAC), configurable privileges, and trusted extensions.
- Rich observability and debugging support, including myriad system monitoring tools, the Modular Debugger (MDB), and the dynamic tracing facility (DTrace).
- Predictive self-healing features in the form of the Fault Management Architecture (FMA) and Service Management Facility (SMF). They work together to detect hardware and software faults and take appropriate action.
- Multiple forms of virtualization. In addition to the operating-system-level virtualization of Solaris Zones, OpenSolaris offers support for xVM Hypervisor, Logical Domains (LDoms), and VirtualBox, and runs in VMware and other virtualization frameworks.
- Sophisticated 64-bit fully preemptable kernel. The OpenSolaris kernel is also modular — device drivers can be installed without requiring a system reboot, and features can be configured without recompiling the kernel. The virtual memory subsystem uses demand paging for greater performance and less memory usage. The process scheduling

system supports multiple scheduling classes, including timeshare, real time, interactive, fair share, and fixed priority.

- Full POSIX compliance with a rich application programming API, including support for 64-bit applications.
- Integrated AMP stack (Apache, MySQL, PHP) for running web services.

With all of these features in mind, let's take a look at open source software.

The "Open" in OpenSolaris

As implied by the "open" in the name, OpenSolaris is open source software. The general meaning of open source is that the source code is available for anyone to look at. However, the details vary, and in fact OpenSolaris is not open source in exactly the same way as Linux, Apache, MySQL, BSD, Perl, Java, or most other open source software with which you might be familiar. To understand the details of the OpenSolaris open source model, it's helpful to first review and define some open source software basics.

Open source software basics

In the traditional closed source model of software development, companies or developers distribute only running programs in the form of binaries. Users cannot look at the source code from which those binaries were compiled. In the open source model, as its name implies, anyone can view, modify, compile, and even redistribute the source code for the programs. More specifically, the Open Source Initiative, a respected authority and advocate for open source software, specifies 10 criteria that software must fulfill in order to be open source, including the following:

- **Free redistribution** — Anyone can sell or give away the software by itself or as part of an aggregate distribution.
- **Source code** — Source must be available for all distributions.
- **Derived works** — Anyone can modify the code and redistribute it.
- **No discrimination** — The code must be available to anyone for any "field of endeavor."

The complete list is available at `http://opensource.org/docs/osd`. It's important to remember that open source software, despite sometimes being called free software, is not required to be free of charge. Think of the "free" in free software as referring to free speech, rather than free beer. Thus, companies or individuals can sell programs built from open source code.

> **NOTE** Other terms for open source software include *free software* and *free and open source software* (FOSS).

This book uses the term open source software not to emphasize any particular software philosophy but because the authors think it's the clearest term.

Open source licenses

All open source code is available under an open source license, which defines the terms of use. Different open source projects choose different licenses. Some licenses with which you might be familiar are the GNU General Public License version 2 (GPLv2), under which Linux is available, and the BSD license, under which OpenBSD, NetBSD, and other BSD variants are available.

The major difference between the licenses is their requirements regarding *derivative works,* or modifications to the source code. Specifically, if someone who is not the original author takes some open source code and changes it by adding newly written code, removing code, or combining it with other code, is she required to release the new code under the original license, or can she use a different license? Based on this criterion, there are three categories of open source licenses:

- **Strong copyleft licenses** require that any derived code stay under the original license. Therefore, if a developer adds some code to a file under a copyleft license, then that new file must also be released under the original license. A strong copyleft license is project-based, rather than file-based. That is, all source files in a project must be under the same license. This requirement generally means that code under a strong copyleft license cannot link (either statically or dynamically) with code under a non-strong copyleft license. Another way of looking at it is that every piece of code that strong copyleft licensed code touches must also be under that license. For this reason, strong copyleft licenses are sometimes called *viral licenses.* Thus, you cannot generally combine code under a strong copyleft license with code under other licenses. The best-known strong copyleft license is the GNU General Public License (GPL), both versions 2 and 3. The Linux kernel, the GNU tools, Java, and a multitude of other software projects use the GPL.

- **Weak copyleft licenses** are nearly identical to strong copyleft licenses except that they're file-based instead of project-based. That is, modifications to a file must be released under the original license, but that file can be combined in a project with code under a different license. As a result, weak copyleft licenses are not viral in the same way as strong copyleft licenses. The Mozilla Public License (MPL), under which the Mozilla Firefox browser is licensed, is a weak copyleft license.

- **Non-copyleft licenses** do not require derived works to stay under the original license. They do not even require derived code to be released under any open source license. Thus, someone could take an open source project under a non-copyleft license and use it as a basis for a proprietary product. The BSD license is the best-known example of a non-copyleft license.

While these differences can seem esoteric, a quick glance at the discussions in various open source communities shows that the debate can become quite passionate. Some people, particularly in the Linux and GNU communities, feel strongly that only strong copyleft licenses are "true" open source licenses because they best protect the original author. Others feel that non-copyleft licenses, such as the BSD license, are preferable because they give the most freedom to developers creating derived works. Still others find weak copyleft licenses to be a reasonable compromise.

Open source licenses generally include provisions to distribute binary executables built from the source. The licenses usually require that the source code be made available with the binary executables, or be made available upon request. For example, both the Linux source and the Linux distributions are available under the GPLv2.

OpenSolaris licenses

The OpenSolaris source code is heterogeneous in its open source licenses and the predominant license may be unfamiliar to you.

Common Development and Distribution License

The majority of the OpenSolaris source code is available under the Common Development and Distribution License (CDDL), pronounced "cuddle." Written by Sun explicitly for OpenSolaris, this license has been officially approved by the Open Source Initiative (OSI) as a legitimate open source license. It's a weak copyleft license like the MPL (which it resembles) in that it requires derivative works to maintain the same license on a per-file basis, but does not require all the files in a project to be under the CDDL.

Because the CDDL is copyleft, changes to the source code itself must be released under the CDDL as well. It is hoped that any such changes are contributed back to the OpenSolaris community itself, but that is not a requirement. However, because the CDDL is weak copyleft, instead of strong copyleft, whole pieces of it may be incorporated into projects under different licenses, including proprietary projects. This aspect of the license has allowed OpenSolaris features such as DTrace and ZFS to be ported to other operating systems such as Mac OS X 10.5. (DTrace and ZFS are covered in Chapters 15 and 8, respectively.)

NOTE The GPLv2 is incompatible with the CDDL because the GPLv2 requires all code in the project to be under the GPL. Thus, porting OpenSolaris features to Linux is significantly more complicated than porting to other systems.

Because the Solaris code base contained some open source and third-party code even before it was open sourced by Sun, not all the OpenSolaris code is under the CDDL. Parts of it are licensed under the BSD license and other open source licenses. Each source file contains a header comment specifying the license for that file.

Binary distributions under the CDDL

It's sometimes perplexing that some binary distributions of OpenSolaris are available under the CDDL. Isn't the CDDL a source code license? Yes, it is. However, like many other open source licenses, the CDDL permits binary executables built from source code under the license to be distributed under the CDDL. Thus, distributions of OpenSolaris may be distributed under the CDDL.

As if things weren't confusing enough with the source code licenses, OpenSolaris also uses another binary license called the OpenSolaris Binary License (OBL). Binaries under this license are freely redistributable, and can be used for running and developing OpenSolaris. Binaries released under the OBL include build tools, parts of Solaris that cannot be open sourced (and so aren't under the CDDL), and binaries built from proprietary code.

Open development

Open source software is generally, but not always, developed as part of a community in an open development process. In open development, developers can collaborate in public forums, participants need not all work for the same company, and there is freedom to pursue projects that might not fit within the scope of a single company's business needs.

The opposite of an open development process is a proprietary development process, in which a company or individuals write the code on their own, with their particular business needs in mind, and without interacting with people outside their group.

NOTE Eric S. Raymond's seminal article, "The Cathedral and the Bazaar," compares these two software development models. You can read the article at www.catb.org/~esr/writings/cathedral-bazaar/cathedral-bazaar.

Although the Solaris operating system was originally developed in a proprietary development model, the OpenSolaris community is intended to support an open development model. Consequently, you will find many active developers, discussions, and ongoing projects at www.opensolaris.org.

What open source OpenSolaris means to you

At this point you might be wondering what the open source and open development aspects of OpenSolaris mean for you. On the open source side, while the specific terms of the licenses and the legal requirements can be complicated, the important thing to remember is that you can always look at the OpenSolaris source code. That may not be too useful if you only want to run an OpenSolaris distribution, but if you're a developer or advanced system administrator, studying the OpenSolaris code can be a valuable proposition.

On the other hand, the open development aspects of OpenSolaris should interest everyone. The OpenSolaris community is a great place to ask for help, contribute suggestions, participate in discussions, and in general influence the direction of OpenSolaris!

The History of OpenSolaris

The history of OpenSolaris, and even some of the source code, dates back to 1969. In that year, Ken Thompson at AT&T Bell Laboratories wrote the first version of the UNIX operating system. UNIX was designed from the beginning to be multi-user and multi-tasking, with an interactive shell that would still look familiar to any UNIX or Linux user today. Over the next few years, Thompson and Dennis Ritchie continued refining UNIX, which was used mostly inside Bell Labs. However, in the mid to late 1970s, UNIX versions 6 and 7 were distributed fairly widely, and used by various academic and government institutions, including the University of California at Berkeley.

Because of the lenient license terms in early versions of AT&T's UNIX, other organizations began significantly customizing and enhancing it. This work led to several major branches of UNIX, the most relevant of which to OpenSolaris was the Berkeley Software Distribution (BSD). In 1978, Bill Joy and others at Berkeley added virtual memory, demand paging, and other embellishments to UNIX Version 7 to create a version of UNIX called 3BSD. Joy and others continued enhancing BSD UNIX over the next few years, adding the familiar TCP/IP networking stack, the C shell, the VI editor, and other key features.

In 1982, Bill Joy co-founded Sun Microsystems and by 1984 had used BSD UNIX as the basis for the SunOS operating system that ran Sun's workstations. In the meantime, AT&T continued developing its line of UNIX, calling it System V, and other companies created their own branches, such as Microsoft's Xenix (which later became SCO UNIX).

In the late 1980s, Sun and AT&T began work on a joint project to remerge several popular variants of UNIX to create System V Release 4. The result, completed in 1990, contained the best features from AT&T's earlier System V Release 3, Sun's SunOS, 4.3BSD, and Xenix 5, including TCP/IP support, the Network File System (NFS), the Unix File System (UFS), and the Virtual File System (VFS) interface. Additionally, System V Release 4 (SVR4) fully complied with the Portable Operating System Interface (POSIX) standard, which defines an application programming interface, utilities, and other aspects of an operating system. Theoretically, a program written to POSIX interfaces can run on any POSIX-compliant operating system. In 1992, SVR4 became the basis of Sun's new operating system, Solaris 2.0.

> **NOTE** "Solaris" technically refers to the entire operating environment, including the graphical user interface. The kernel itself is still called SunOS. However, this book uses Solaris in the colloquial sense to refer to both the entire operating environment and the kernel.

In the years since, Sun has continually enhanced Solaris with features such as the kernel slab memory allocator, multithreaded kernel and multithreaded process support, 64-bit kernel and process support, Solaris doors inter-process communication, and many others. The most recent release of Solaris, Solaris 10, introduced several exciting new features such as a dynamic tracing facility (DTrace), the Service Management Facility (SMF), Zones, and the ZFS file system.

In 2005, Solaris became the first mature proprietary operating system to go open source when Sun released the source code as OpenSolaris. The open sourced code was basically the source for Solaris 10, which had been first released approximately five months earlier. Since then, some of the active development in OpenSolaris has been backported and released in Solaris 10 updates, but much of it is currently unique to OpenSolaris. It's important to note that backports of OpenSolaris features to Solaris 10 can only be done by Sun because the Solaris 10 source code is not open source.

In summary, OpenSolaris's development path has not been exactly straightforward. As an open source operating system based on a closed-source operating system that in turn is related to several other open source and closed source operating systems, OpenSolaris can be confusing. If nothing else, this history should help you understand why there are so many AT&T and University of California Berkeley copyrights in the OpenSolaris source code.

Comparing OpenSolaris to Other Operating Systems

So how does OpenSolaris compare to other open source and proprietary operating systems? Let's take a look.

OpenSolaris and Solaris

OpenSolaris is an open source code base, community, and distribution. Solaris is a proprietary product from Sun Microsystems. The two are not synonymous, but they are intertwined. First of all, OpenSolaris was seeded from the Solaris code base around the time of Solaris 10. However, the OpenSolaris code base has subsequently diverged from the Solaris 10 code base, so the latest update of Solaris 10 is significantly different from OpenSolaris.

> **NOTE**   Solaris is a product from Sun, whereas OpenSolaris is an open source code base, community, and distribution.

Confusingly, Sun does release a distribution of OpenSolaris called OpenSolaris. This distribution is not the same as the Solaris 10 product. For one thing, unlike Solaris 10, the OpenSolaris distribution is available free of charge and is fully redistributable. This book focuses primarily on the OpenSolaris distribution.

> **CROSS-REF**   The OpenSolaris distribution and other distributions are described in Chapter 2.

In the future, Sun will likely release a version of the Solaris product with long-term support that is based on a more recent OpenSolaris snapshot. This model will be similar to the way Red Hat Enterprise Linux is based on the open source Fedora code base.

OpenSolaris and Linux

Linux and OpenSolaris are both open source UNIX-like operating systems. They can support identical user interfaces, such as GNOME, run many identical applications, such as Apache, MySQL, Mozilla Firefox, and OpenOffice, and support identical tools such as the GNU compiler tools, Java, Perl, Python, Ruby, and others. But the two operating systems have significant differences in their histories, licensing, distribution models, and underlying implementations.

History

Although UNIX-like, the Linux source code is not descended from the original AT&T or BSD UNIX code. Linus Torvalds and others created it independently in the early 1990s. Because

Linux is not based on the original AT&T UNIX, BSD, SVR4, or any other form of UNIX, it does not have any kernel code in common with OpenSolaris. Linux was open source from the beginning, and was developed following a community development model.

Conversely, OpenSolaris was open sourced in whole based on the mature Solaris operating system, which was developed in large part in a proprietary development model. Partly because of this history, Linux has a much larger development community than does OpenSolaris. Linux also has many more distributions, from several different vendors.

Licensing

The Linux kernel uses the GNU General Public License version 2 (GPLv2), which is incompatible with the CDDL used by OpenSolaris because of the GPL's viral nature, as described earlier in this chapter. Thus, code cannot be ported between the OpenSolaris kernel and the Linux kernel. However, both OpenSolaris and Linux can run userland programs distributed under the GPL and other licenses, which is why they can appear to be quite similar.

Distributions

The Linux kernel, user applications, tools, and libraries are developed separately and then packaged together into distributions, which some in the free software community refer to as GNU/Linux because of the combination of the GNU tools and the Linux kernel. Some of the well-known distributions include Ubuntu, Red Hat Enterprise Linux, SUSE Linux, and Debian GNU/Linux.

OpenSolaris is more of a monolithic model, in which many of the userland tools, libraries, and applications are part of OpenSolaris itself. However, OpenSolaris distributions also use a significant amount of third-party open source software such as GNOME, Firefox, OpenOffice, and more.

Technical differences

Some of the most apparent differences between Linux and OpenSolaris derive from the fact that OpenSolaris is a variant of UNIX System V Release 4, while Linux is not. One of the most noticeable results of Linux not being based on SVR4 is that it doesn't use SVR4 packaging. Linux packaging varies between distributions, but lately it has tended toward a model whereby packages can be easily downloaded and installed dynamically from a network package repository. Interestingly, OpenSolaris has recently introduced a more Linux-like packaging approach called the Image Packaging System (IPS).

> **NOTE** OpenSolaris contains many of the same GNU tools found on Linux. Historically, these were in /usr/gnu/bin/ and /usr/sfw/bin/, but are moving to /usr/bin/ when possible. Because of conflicts, some commands are still in /usr/gnu/bin/ and /usr/sfw/bin/.

Additionally, the Linux and OpenSolaris kernels differ significantly in the areas of scheduling, virtual memory, file systems, and others. For more details, consult one of the references listed in the "Resources" section at the end of this chapter.

OpenSolaris and BSD

Because OpenSolaris is based on Solaris, which is based in part on BSD, OpenSolaris and BSD have significant similarities in their code. The main differences are threefold. First, BSD has been developed in the open, like Linux, and so has diverged substantially from Solaris. Interestingly, the BSD community has split into three main camps such that there are now three different BSD-based operating systems: OpenBSD, NetBSD, and FreeBSD.

Second, BSD is not based on SVR4. In fact, OpenSolaris is the only open source UNIX System V Release 4–based operating system.

> **NOTE** Historically, Solaris contains the SVR4-style tools in /usr/bin, while its BSD-style tools are in /usr/ucb/. However, in OpenSolaris the BSD-style tools are moving to /usr/bin when possible. Because of conflicts, a few tools remain in /usr/ucb/.

Finally, unlike the CDDL used for OpenSolaris and the GPL used for Linux, the BSD license is a non-copyleft license. This lenient license does not force modifications and enhancements to be contributed back to the "commons."

Interestingly, Mac OS X is a variant of UNIX based on the Mach operating system, which itself is based on BSD. However, Mac OS contains a distinctive Macintosh user interface, hiding the details of the underlying UNIX operating system from most of its users. Apple has ported some OpenSolaris features, such as DTrace and ZFS to Mac OS X, and has released the source code of the core operating system as the Darwin Open Source Project.

Getting Involved in OpenSolaris

As you read this book and use OpenSolaris, we encourage you to become involved in the Open-Solaris community. There are a number of ways to do so, from trying out a distribution to contributing code. A good starting point is http://opensolaris.org/os/participate.

Running OpenSolaris

The best way to get started with the OpenSolaris community is to actually try out OpenSolaris. In fact, playing with OpenSolaris simultaneously with reading this book will significantly enhance your learning experience.

> **NOTE** The OpenSolaris distribution from Sun, related documentation, and user help forums are available from http://opensolaris.com. Chapter 2 contains more information about the OpenSolaris distribution from Sun as well as other distributions available.

While using OpenSolaris, you can enhance your community involvement in two ways. First, if you encounter a problem, ask questions on the community discussion lists and forums. Several relevant discussion lists are introduced in the next section. Second, if you find a bug, report it at http://defect.opensolaris.org (for problems with the OpenSolaris distribution from Sun) or http://bugs.opensolaris.org (for other issues) so that it can be tracked and fixed. You can also request enhancements.

Participating in discussion lists

The OpenSolaris communities feature a plethora of forums and mailing lists on a variety of topics. www.opensolaris.com contains user-oriented forums on the OpenSolaris distribution from Sun, while www.opensolaris.org contains developer-oriented mailing lists. If you're just searching for a particular piece of information, you can read the list archives online. However, to begin to get a feel for the OpenSolaris communities and the day-to-day issues and questions, consider subscribing to the mailing lists to receive e-mails directly. Some useful lists include the following:

- opensolaris-help@opensolaris.org — This list is a great resource for general questions about "getting, building, and installing OpenSolaris."

- opensolaris-announce@opensolaris.org — This is a moderated list for general community announcements. It's useful for keeping track of the major OpenSolaris happenings.

- ogb-discuss@opensolaris.org — The public mailing list for the OpenSolaris Governing Board. Although theoretically for "governance" issues, the list seems to be a catch-all for any sort of controversy in the community, and is therefore a good way to track current "hot" issues.

- advocacy-discuss@opensolaris.org — The mailing list for the Advocacy community. This is useful to understand what sort of outreach and marketing efforts are going on for OpenSolaris.

TIP Many new community members are tempted to subscribe to opensolaris-discuss@opensolaris.org. We do not recommend that list because it's high-traffic without much useful content.

Additionally, you can subscribe to more focused lists in your areas of interest. For example, if you are interested in Sun's OpenSolaris distribution, subscribe to indiana-discuss@opensolaris.org. If you are interested in high-availability clusters, subscribe to ha-clusters-discuss@opensolaris.org. If you are interested in DTrace, subscribe to dtrace-discuss@opensolaris.org.

CAUTION You may have heard the phrase, "There are no stupid questions." That's not entirely true in the OpenSolaris community. As in many online technical communities, some people have little patience for redundant, off-topic, or trivial questions. To avoid possible embarrassment, search this book, the mailing list archives, relevant FAQs, and other resources before asking anything on the discussion lists.

Finding OpenSolaris user groups

OpenSolaris user groups connect people in similar geographic areas for face-to-face meetings, from Adelaide, Australia, to New York City to Warangal, India. They are a good way to meet other OpenSolaris users and enthusiasts, and to learn more about cutting-edge topics. If you live in a large metropolitan area, chances are good that you can find an OpenSolaris user group in your area.

Each user group is independently run, so check out the individual group for mailing lists, upcoming meetings, and other resources. The complete list can be found at `http://opensolaris.org/os/community/advocacy/usergroups/ug-leaders`.

If there is no OpenSolaris user group in your area, consider starting one! You can find instructions for doing so at `http://opensolaris.org/os/community/advocacy/usergroups`.

Contributing to OpenSolaris

The best way to increase your involvement in the OpenSolaris community is to start participating in relevant development discussions. These usually occur on mailing lists at `opensolaris.org`. You can find a complete list of mailing lists at `http://opensolaris.org/os/discussions`.

If you're interested in contributing code or other tangibles to the OpenSolaris community effort, consult the instructions at `http://opensolaris.org/os/communities/participation` for the current process.

OpenSolaris Development Process

Although you may not be interested in contributing code to OpenSolaris, it can be interesting and useful to understand how the operating system is developed. Before delving into the process, it helps to understand the OpenSolaris source-code layout. The OpenSolaris code base is divided into major areas, called *consolidations*, each of which has its own source-code repository. The core OpenSolaris consolidation is Operating System/Networking (ON), which contains the operating system kernel, userland libraries, and tools. Other consolidations include Developer Product Tools (Dev Pro), Documentation (Docs), and Globalization Support (G11N). You'll find a list of consolidations at `http://opensolaris.org/os/downloads`.

> **NOTE** Unlike some open source projects, OpenSolaris does not have a notion of "committers" or a select group of people who are permitted to integrate code. Anyone can integrate code into OpenSolaris as long as they follow the process and have submitted a signed Sun Contributor Agreement. See `http://sun.com/software/opensource/contributor_agreement.jsp` for details.

OpenSolaris allows two different paths for source code development, depending on whether the code is destined for an official consolidation such as ON.

If the code is not destined for an official consolidation, then no standard development process must be followed. Anyone can start an OpenSolaris project and create a code repository or post code as a tarball on the project page.

However, code developed in that way will not become part of the OpenSolaris code base. If you want your code to become part of the OpenSolaris code base, you must follow a rigorous development process to integrate it into a consolidation. This process evolved from the internal process that Sun Microsystems required for integration into Solaris. Although it varies by repository, the process generally includes the following:

- **Initiation** — Propose a project.

- **Architecture review** — The architecture is generally reviewed by an *Architecture Review Committee* (ARC). Projects destined for ON are mostly reviewed by the Platform Software Architecture Review Committee (PSARC), projects destined for Open HA Cluster are reviewed by the Cluster Architecture Review Committee (CLARC), and projects destined for the desktop area are generally reviewed by the Layered Software Architecture Review Committee (LSARC). See the Architecture Processes and Tools Community Group at `http://opensolaris.org/os/community/arc` for more information.

- **Design** — Prepare written documentation about the code design of your project.

- **Development** — Write, test, and debug the code.

- **Code reviews** — Each area has different requirements regarding the number of code reviewers, but a good rule of thumb is to obtain reviews from at least two people, at least one of whom is a known expert in that area.

- **Integration approval** — Every project must be approved for integration by the C-Team. Currently, the C-Team is Sun-internal only, but it is moving to become more open.

- **File request to integrate (RTI)** — This is the formal mechanism for obtaining the final integration approval.

- **Integrate**

As you can see, this process is not for the fainthearted; but it's the price to pay to keep Open-Solaris at the same level of quality as the Solaris product on which it was based, and it's not too extreme compared with the process in other open source projects. For example, the Linux kernel contribution process, although different in style, is similarly rigorous.

> **NOTE** Various parts of the development process moved from Sun internal to OpenSolaris at different times. To allow external contributions before the source code repository offered direct-commit access from outside Sun, OpenSolaris used a request/sponsor model in which a Sun employee sponsored an external contributor.

For more information on the OpenSolaris development process, see the complete process in the ON Community Group: `http://opensolaris.org/os/community/on`.

Resources

The user-oriented site on the OpenSolaris distribution from Sun is `http://opensolaris.com`. It provides binary downloads and contains documentation and help forums. The documentation is located at `http://opensolaris.com/learn`.

The developer site for the OpenSolaris community is at `http://opensolaris.org`. It contains useful mailing lists, user group details, and a plethora of information about past and current development projects. You can start with `http://opensolaris.org/os/participate`.

The Trademark Policy can be found at `http://opensolaris.org/os/trademark`.

The OpenSolaris source code can be browsed at `http://src.opensolaris.org`.

You can file bugs at `http://defect.opensolaris.org` and `http://bugs.open solaris.org`.

The Open Source Initiative web page (`http://opensource.org`) contains much useful information on open source code, including the text of all the licenses mentioned in this chapter.

For general information on operating systems, consult *Operating System Concepts* by Abraham Silberschatz, Peter Baer Galvin, and Greg Gagne (Wiley, 2005).

For details on the Solaris and OpenSolaris implementation, see *Solaris Internals: Solaris 10 and OpenSolaris Kernel Architecture* by Richard McDougall and Jim Mauro (Prentice Hall, 2006).

For more information on using and administering Linux, see the *Linux Bible* by Christopher Negus (Wiley, 2005).

For details on the Linux implementation, see *Understanding the Linux Kernel (Third Edition)* by Daniel Bovet and Marco Cesati (O'Reilly, 2006).

You can find the Sun Contributor Agreement at `http://sun.com/software/opensource/contributor_agreement.jsp`.

The Architecture Review Process and development process are documented at `http://open solaris.org/os/community/arc/` and `http://opensolaris.org/os/community/on`.

Summary

This chapter introduced OpenSolaris, described its three main aspects, enumerated some of the salient OpenSolaris features, explained its licensing, related some of its history, contrasted OpenSolaris with several familiar operating systems, explained the OpenSolaris development process, and described how to get involved in the community. Now you're ready to learn more about the OpenSolaris distributions in Chapter 2 and to jump into a crash course on OpenSolaris in Chapter 3.

Chapter 2

Installing OpenSolaris

A surprisingly large number of distributions are derived from the OpenSolaris source base, given the relative youth of the Open-Solaris community. This chapter covers the basics of the distributions created through mid-2008:

- Solaris Express Community Edition (SXCE)
- Schillix
- BeleniX
- NexentaCore
- MartUX
- MilaX
- OpenSolaris

The OpenSolaris distribution is specifically created for users new to the OpenSolaris community and technology, and is a special focus of this book. After getting a feel for what the other OpenSolaris-based distributions are about and the reasons why you might be interested in them, you'll walk through the process of downloading, installing, and updating OpenSolaris. By the end of this chapter you should have a clear idea about which OpenSolaris-based distribution is likely to be right for you; and if you've chosen OpenSolaris itself, you'll have a working installation to use to explore further. (If you find the multiple meanings of OpenSolaris confusing, you may find it helpful to review Chapter 1.)

IN THIS CHAPTER

Overview of OpenSolaris distributions

Determining hardware compatibility with OpenSolaris

Downloading OpenSolaris and burning a CD

Booting the OpenSolaris live CD

Installing OpenSolaris on hardware

Installing OpenSolaris in a VMware virtual machine

> **TIP** In addition to the download site for each distribution, a community-run mirror of all of the redistributable distribution downloads is provided at `http://genunix.org`.

Solaris Express Community Edition

Solaris Express Community Edition (commonly abbreviated SXCE) is the "original" OpenSolaris distribution. Releases of SXCE began with the establishment of the OpenSolaris community in 2005. It is available for both x86 and SPARC processor platforms. SXCE is targeted specifically at developers who want to participate in the development of OpenSolaris, giving them access to the same development platform used by Sun's own engineering staff. SXCE is distributed as a free download from Sun's website. Its license is limited: while the software is free to use, it may not be put into production. Additionally, the images may not be mirrored or otherwise redistributed outside of the organization to which the license is granted. Within the images, the individual software components in the SXCE distribution are provided in the form of SVR4 packages. SXCE is not a pure open source distribution in that it includes components that are closed source and proprietary to it; most of the examples of these components are drivers for which Sun does not have licensing permission to offer for redistribution. In short, it is a hybrid of open and closed source components.

How SXCE Is Developed

SXCE offers the clearest view into how Solaris has historically been developed by making Sun's development snapshots of the Solaris release under development, which is code-named Nevada, directly available to the OpenSolaris community.

For many years, Solaris releases have been developed on a two-week build cycle. This means that every two weeks, each consolidation contributing software to the distribution provides its current binary packages to the release management, or Product, team. The Solaris Release Engineering organization then uses a set of custom-built tools to assemble the packages into the media formats used to release the software. These include CDs, DVDs, and pre-built network installation images (only the CD and DVD images are released outside of Sun).

Once the images have been built, they are passed along to various test organizations for validation; after the build passes a basic set of tests, it is released within Sun. Releases to the community generally follow within a few days, after any necessary legal and regulatory approvals are obtained. These biweekly releases are not a supported product, but instead are considered test builds for the next release of Solaris, so each version of SXCE is referred to by a build number starting from 1. Nevada has had by far the longest development cycle of any Solaris release since Solaris 2.0, well past three years at this writing.

For a time, Sun offered a stabilized version of SXCE known as Solaris Express Developer Edition (SXDE). It provided a simplified installer, additional software such as an AMP (Apache/MySQL/PHP) stack, and developer tools such as NetBeans and Sun Studio. You may still see references to SXDE, but it has been replaced by the OpenSolaris distribution described later in this chapter.

Users obtain SXCE by downloading media images from the Sun download center. This distribution is available to the community as a DVD ISO image. Installing the release requires downloading the ISO image, burning it to media, and then booting from the DVD and installing the distribution to disk. The installation media is a bootable version of Solaris, but it's designed strictly for installation and some limited disaster recovery, not for a general evaluation of the distribution.

To upgrade from one build of SXCE to another, it is necessary to download the entire media image. Then you have two options: burn the image to optical media and boot from the media to upgrade, or mount the media image as an ISO file system and then use a technology known as Live Upgrade to copy the already installed version of Solaris and then upgrade that copy, all while the original installed version of Solaris remains running and usable for normal operation. Live Upgrade is generally the preferred option if the system has sufficient free disk space to use it because system downtime is minimized and the impact of a failed upgrade or any other serious problem with the new build is minimized, as the system can always be booted back into the original image should it be necessary. SXCE also supports both forms of upgrade from older versions of Solaris, not just older releases of SXCE.

> **NOTE** Downloads of Solaris Express Community Edition are available from `http://opensolaris.org/os/downloads`.

Schillix

Schillix holds a special claim to fame as the first OpenSolaris distribution created from the OpenSolaris source code. As its creators, Jörg Schilling and Fabian Otto, proudly note on the project home page (`http://schillix.berlios.de`), the first version of Schillix was released just a week after the public opening of the OpenSolaris community in June 2005. Truth be told, they didn't do all of the work in a week; a closed pilot of the OpenSolaris community enabled them to get a head start on building this new distribution. Nonetheless, Schillix rightfully deserves respect for blazing the trail for other non-Sun distributions.

Schillix is a pure open source operating system, consisting entirely of open source components. It is distributed under a license that allows free redistribution, and is available only for the x86 platform.

Schillix is distributed as a downloadable DVD ISO image, which boots into a text-based live DVD environment, enabling users to test drive the distribution without any more commitment than burning a DVD; even less than that is possible by booting the ISO image under some other operating system using any one of a number of virtualization tools.

> **NOTE** A *live CD* or *live DVD* is a CD or DVD that's designed to boot into an operating system and run directly from the CD or DVD without altering the computer's hard drive. A live CD is often used to demonstrate an operating system to new users, usually with

an installation option, but a live CD is also very useful as a toolkit for recovery and repair of systems that have been damaged in some way that makes them unable or unsafe to boot.

Schillix uses the SVR4 packaging system, just as Solaris Express does, but it adds the `pkg-get` utility developed by the Blastwave project. This utility allows for easy, automatic download and installation of software from an extensive repository of pre-built open source software packaged by the Blastwave project maintainers for Solaris and OpenSolaris. Thus, while the system provided on the Schillix media is fairly basic, it is easily extended to include a full desktop such as GNOME and myriad other utilities. The other unique attribute of Schillix is that it includes Jörg's own set of utilities, which have been developed over the last 20 years; these include the popular CD authoring tools `mkisofs` and `cdrecord`, also provided in the other OpenSolaris distributions and many Linux distributions, as well as improved versions of utilities such as `make`, `tar`, and `cpio`.

Schillix has been updated irregularly, as its developers find the time to make improvements. It remains a very basic distribution, lacking an integrated desktop environment and requiring a complex, manual installation process. It's probably best suited to users who like to get under the hood and build a distribution from the ground up, understanding how the pieces are put together.

In addition to being the first non-Sun distribution, Schillix was also the first OpenSolaris distribution to provide a live CD, a feature that is now common across distributions.

BeleniX

BeleniX is another pure open source distribution based on the OpenSolaris source code. Led by Moinak Ghosh, BeleniX was created primarily by a group of engineers in India, many of whom are Sun employees. Because it is substantially a product of India, this distribution has achieved quite a bit of local notoriety, made minor celebrities of its developers, and created a lot of interest in OpenSolaris among that country's technology community. As with Schillix, BeleniX has a license that allows for free redistribution, and it is available only for x86 platforms.

From a technical standpoint, BeleniX has made a substantial contribution to advancing the OpenSolaris technology. While Schillix created the first OpenSolaris live CD, BeleniX took the basic concepts and developed them to the point where its performance and functionality rival the well-known Linux live CD distributions. BeleniX developed the techniques used to compress the CD's contents and optimize its layout to achieve acceptable boot performance. The team also adapted the live CD to run from a USB flash drive and developed session persistence for it. With this capability, you have the option of carrying around a fully usable OpenSolaris computing environment without carrying a computer.

Additionally, BeleniX was the first to offer the KDE and Xfce desktops as part of an OpenSolaris distribution. The BeleniX team has also been a substantial contributor in porting additional desktop technologies from the GNOME and X.Org projects to OpenSolaris, helping

OpenSolaris to take advantage of developments in those communities in as timely a fashion as Linux distributions. Finally, they've pioneered the porting and development of disk partition management tools from Linux and BSD distributions, enabling a simpler experience in installing OpenSolaris alongside other operating systems on a single system.

BeleniX continues to be under active development, releasing updates periodically. Because many of the technologies developed in BeleniX are being incorporated into the OpenSolaris code base as part of the development of the OpenSolaris distribution, the focus of BeleniX has shifted somewhat to being a KDE-oriented derivative of the OpenSolaris distribution. The collaboration across these distributions is only natural given the strong shared Sun engineering influence, and should help accelerate the evolution of OpenSolaris technologies. If your preferred desktop on other operating systems is not GNOME, you may well find that BeleniX will be your favorite OpenSolaris distribution.

NOTE More information on BeleniX, including downloads, can be found at `http://belenix.org`.

NexentaCore

NexentaCore is an OpenSolaris distribution with a substantial twist: It fuses the OpenSolaris kernel and utilities with the GNU Project's utilities (these are available in the Solaris and OpenSolaris distributions, but not as complete a set or as the default environment) and the Debian Linux-developed packaging technology APT (Advanced Packaging Tool). The result is a rich operating system that feels in many ways like a version of Ubuntu Linux (the best-known of the Debian-based Linux distributions and the direct source for many of the packages available for NexentaCore), but with the underlying core of OpenSolaris. NexentaCore is available only for x86 platforms, and is provided with a license that allows for free redistribution.

The Nexenta team initially produced a desktop-oriented distribution known as NexentaOS, but has subsequently focused on the NexentaCore distribution, which is designed to be a stable foundation platform on which specialized distributions can be built. The team put this foundation to use in building a storage appliance (called NexentaStor) that leverages ZFS and the attributes of NexentaCore to provide a very simple yet powerful NAS (network-attached storage) appliance.

Although NexentaCore is itself a small distribution (a single CD) with low memory requirements (256MB is the stated requirement), the distribution's decision to leverage the Ubuntu software repository makes a large selection of software available. The system installed from the CD boots to a text console, from which adding software is a simple matter of using the `aptitude` command to select and install packages from the Nexenta repository. The APT system automatically resolves dependencies of packages that are selected for installation and includes them in the process.

Beyond these standard capabilities of APT, the Nexenta team has integrated the power of the ZFS file system. NexentaCore uses ZFS as its default file system for the installed operating system; and by melding it with APT, it has provided something that the Debian family of Linux distributions lacks: a truly safe software upgrade and rollback paradigm, enabling users to back out of a failed or unsatisfactory upgrade and return to a known state with a new command called apt-clone. This is conceptually similar to the Live Upgrade capability described earlier for Solaris Express, but based on the ZFS file system, simplifying and speeding up many aspects of the implementation. A substantial benefit of this capability is that it frees users to experiment with newer versions of software, safe in the knowledge that recovering from failure will be simple and straightforward. As the Nexenta APT repositories provide stable, testing, and unstable versions of packages, users have a great deal of opportunity to take advantage of apt-clone.

Another interesting attribute of the NexentaCore distribution is an outgrowth of the hybrid GNU/OpenSolaris environment it provides. The default installation places the GNU utilities in the normal executable search path, which means that the command-line environment generally feels quite Linux-like. However, for those who prefer a more traditional Solaris feel, that's easily available by merely setting the SUN_PERSONALITY environment variable to 1, and the view presented to the user switches seamlessly to one familiar to Solaris users. It's a clever way to provide both choice and compatibility.

NexentaCore has an active development community and is updated frequently. Outside of the Solaris Express and OpenSolaris distributions, it is probably the most polished of the OpenSolaris distributions, feeling like a professional product. If you have experience with Debian Linux distributions, starting with NexentaCore may help you make a very smooth transition to the OpenSolaris community.

NOTE More information on NexentaCore, including downloads, can be found at http://nexenta.org

MartUX

Created by Martin Bochnig, MartUX is, first and foremost, a distribution designed to appeal to SPARC devotees because it was the first non-Sun distribution available for SPARC. One capability it provides that is not available with Solaris Express is that it can run on systems with the original UltraSPARC 1 64-bit processor, found in systems such as the now-ancient Ultra 1 workstations. MartUX runs on these processors in 64-bit mode, which Sun never supported. Note that 32-bit SPARC support is not available in the OpenSolaris kernel sources.

Providing an open source distribution on SPARC turns out to be a fairly difficult problem to solve. That's because the drivers for most SPARC graphics devices are proprietary to Sun and not available for free use by other distributions. In several cases, the X.Org X server can support these devices as strictly X Window displays, but the system must be run with a serial console. Partly because of this issue, MartUX remains a prototype, primarily of interest to those who would like to hack on a very rough distribution and figure out how it works, or die-hard owners of old SPARC systems who would like to use them with the latest OpenSolaris technologies. This prototyping has proven valuable to the broad community, however; the significant effort Martin Bochnig has invested, for instance, has resulted in much better driver support for the SPARC graphics chips in the X.Org X Window server. He has also been a major contributor to the Fully Open X project, doing the majority of the work required to port it to SPARC hardware. These changes are important because supporting SPARC in the X.Org server enables SPARC to benefit much more completely from the work done in the X community.

The MartUX DVD image makes use of the compression and I/O scheduling enhancements developed by the BeleniX team for their live CD, and thus provides reasonable performance. The DVD image also includes a large collection of software from the Blastwave project repository. In addition to the SPARC focus discussed here, MartUX is available for x86 systems as well, but x86 users new to OpenSolaris will likely find the other distributions discussed in this chapter an easier introduction to the OpenSolaris community. Recently, Martin and others have launched a derivative of MartUX and the OpenSolaris distribution called Natamar, which appears to be the project's focus of development.

NOTE More information on MartUX, including downloads, can be found at `http://martux.org`.

MilaX

One of the newer OpenSolaris distributions is MilaX. Created by Alexander Eremin, this distribution fills a previously unexplored niche in the OpenSolaris universe, that of the minimal distribution. Modeled on small Linux distributions such as Damn Small Linux, MilaX provides the core OpenSolaris technology in a more lightweight wrapper, eschewing the fully integrated desktop environments such as GNOME and KDE for a simpler X Window desktop and a more restricted selection of included software. MilaX supports both x86 and SPARC; the SPARC edition does not provide a graphical desktop at this writing. All of the MilaX software is freely redistributable.

MilaX's approach to constructing a distribution offers two principal benefits:

- A small initial download
- Support for lower-cost hardware with limited memory capacity

That makes it a great "starter" distribution for those new to OpenSolaris. It's also especially well suited for running in a virtual machine such as VMware or VirtualBox. Finally, it's a handy rescue CD for use when you have trouble booting your system's installed OS, because it boots quickly with limited resource requirements yet includes a rich set of system tools.

MilaX is freely redistributable, and has been regularly updated since its initial release in early 2008. You can download it from its website at `http://milax.org`.

OpenSolaris

The last distribution from the OpenSolaris universe to be discussed here is OpenSolaris. Initially known as Project Indiana, OpenSolaris is an aggregation of the core OpenSolaris code with several key projects that are under development. OpenSolaris is heavily supported by Sun's engineering organization, and it is expected to provide the basis for the successor release to Solaris 10.

History of the OpenSolaris distribution

The core idea of the OpenSolaris distribution is that, while Solaris is in many ways the most advanced UNIX operating system, some aspects of it had become quite dated. For example, the software packaging system, known as SVR4 Packaging, was state-of-the-art 20 years ago but has become outdated. It not only lacks enhanced features such as network repositories that are common in newer packaging systems, but also has become increasingly creaky as its implementation was modified to deal with features such as Zones that extended it in ways that its original design could not possibly have anticipated. The patching system layered on top of SVR4 Packaging suffers from similar issues.

Similarly, the installation software was based on a design from the early 1990s; and the user experience, along with the look and feel, were based on network and GUI technologies, as well as assumptions about users, that are no longer in touch with current trends. Requiring users to download an image that was several gigabytes in size, burn it to media, and then install it to a system before they could even try out the software meant that only the most devotedly interested users would ever run Solaris. Potential users who had heard about it from the media or a friend would usually not make it to the point where they'd actually install Solaris and become users. Having to repeat the experience to obtain newer versions only added to users' frustration. Simpler ways to obtain, try, and use OpenSolaris were necessary if the technology was to attract a growing number of users in the increasingly crowded open source operating systems market.

In addition, because many utilities had only been updated for conformance to standards such as POSIX, the command-line user environment felt much like a relic of the UNIX of the early 1990s; meanwhile, those same utilities on Linux and BSD platforms had gained additional features. All told, users who were new to Solaris would often describe the experience as familiar, but uncomfortable, in the way that going back to one's childhood neighborhood may be familiar yet uncomfortable because none of the people you remember live there anymore.

By mid-2007, OpenSolaris-sponsored projects to address many of these shortcomings in Solaris were starting to bear fruit in the form of working prototypes that were functional enough to use within the development community. However, the projects were still far from integrating into the Solaris Express releases. Additionally, a rising issue within the OpenSolaris community was user confusion about distributions; many users from Linux backgrounds come to the OpenSolaris community site expecting to download a distribution called OpenSolaris, but instead find the list of distributions discussed earlier in this chapter. Because the names are mostly unfamiliar, and many users have a difficult time understanding the differences between the distributions, they were left to choose between Solaris Express, with Sun's name behind it, and a cast of other distributions they'd likely never heard of before. No matter what choice they made, they were likely to find a less comfortable and polished system than the most popular Linux distributions, and were often left decidedly unimpressed with OpenSolaris.

To address these problems, Sun decided to release a new distribution with the installation, packaging, and modernization technologies that were under development. By using the Open-Solaris name for the released distribution, new users to the community would find what they were looking for: a distribution named OpenSolaris that represented the work of the community with a polished, easy-to-use, and supported product that would make their introduction to the community as simple as possible. The goal was to establish this distribution as the reference for the community, and to base the next version of Solaris on it, effectively turning the relationship between OpenSolaris and Solaris inside out. The use of the OpenSolaris name for the distribution proved to be a controversial topic within the community, due to the trademark restrictions that Sun had originally placed on the name. This confusion spawned a project to develop trademark guidelines that allow the use of the OpenSolaris name by other distributions.

As mentioned earlier, this effort was initially established under Project Indiana to distinguish it from the Nevada code name already in use for the next version of Solaris. The first preview of OpenSolaris was released in October 2007, and it was a solid success, with thousands of down-loads in the first week; a second preview was released in February 2008. The first supported release arrived in May 2008, and the second in November 2008, with subsequent releases expected approximately every six months. Sun offers paid support by its support organization for these OpenSolaris releases; see the opensolaris.com site for information on the support products. Between each release, development builds are made available, approximately every two weeks, in synchronization with SXCE builds. The OpenSolaris distribution is provided under a license that allows for free redistribution. The releases so far support only x86 systems, but SPARC support is anticipated in 2009.

What OpenSolaris includes

OpenSolaris consists of open source and a few freely redistributable binary components produced by the various OpenSolaris communities and projects. It includes the following major components:

- The OpenSolaris kernel, networking, and command-line utilities from the OS/Net community. The OpenSolaris distribution's version of this code is virtually identical to that included in the other distributions.

- The X Window System from the Fully Open X (FOX) project. The OpenSolaris version differs from the version used in Solaris Express, which includes drivers and other legacy components that are not available under redistributable license terms.

- The GNOME desktop from the Desktop community. The primary difference between the OpenSolaris version of GNOME and that used in Solaris Express is the removal of Sun proprietary branding and trademark elements.

- The Image Packaging System (IPS) from the project of the same name
- The installer from the Caiman project
- The live CD technology from the Live Media project
- Modifications to the default user environment designed to increase familiarity for users coming from Linux or BSD distributions

These technologies and projects are discussed in more detail later in this book. The remainder of this chapter focuses on how to download and install OpenSolaris.

CROSS-REF   Chapter 3 provides a crash course in using OpenSolaris once you have it installed.

Will OpenSolaris run on my hardware?

Because of the tremendous diversity of x86-based computer systems that are available, one common question is whether a particular operating system can support your hardware. The last thing you, as a user, want to do is spend a great deal of time or money downloading or purchasing an operating system only to find out that it won't run on your computer.

If you already have the OpenSolaris live CD, perhaps the best answer is to just stick it in your system and try to boot from it. There really is nothing like just trying out the system to determine whether it works. In addition, the CD includes the Device Detection Utility; if you boot the CD and run this utility, it provides a complete report of the OpenSolaris device support for your system. If you don't have the media yet, aren't sure that OpenSolaris is likely to run on your system, and would like to have an answer before you spend the time downloading OpenSolaris, then consider the following options to perhaps save some time.

First, if you have virtual machine technology such as VirtualBox or VMware available, you'll likely find that OpenSolaris runs satisfactorily with it. In the case of those two virtual machine technologies, this book walks you through the process of creating an OpenSolaris virtual machine, booting, and installing within it. Other virtual machine technologies such as Parallels for Mac OS, Xen, or KVM also generally support OpenSolaris guests.

The next best option is to use the Sun Device Detection Tool, which provides you with a custom and complete answer for your specific system. This tool does have some limitations, however, that can prevent it from being an answer for everyone. First, you must be running Windows (2000, 2003, XP, or Vista), a Linux distribution with a 2.6 kernel, or Solaris. You must also have a Java Runtime Environment (JRE) installed on your system. If you meet those two requirements, then running this tool will, in just a couple of minutes, give you a detailed list of the hardware devices on your system, and an answer as to whether OpenSolaris has the drivers necessary to support your hardware. It can be time well spent because its device database is updated frequently and includes pointers to third-party drivers that may not be included in the OpenSolaris media (for licensing or other reasons).

If you can't use the Device Detection Tool, then the traditional answer to hardware support questions has been lists of compatible systems and components that you can search. That can be a tedious process and requires you to know a great deal about your system's hardware, including technologies, manufacturers, speeds, and so on. It's probably best regarded as your last resort in terms of determining system compatibility, but it can be a useful resource if you're in the market for a peripheral device and the vendor doesn't necessarily specify support for OpenSolaris.

> **NOTE** The Sun Device Detection Tool can be accessed at `http://sun.com/bigadmin/hcl/hcts/device_detect.jsp`.

Sun's hardware compatibility list for the Solaris family of operating systems is available on the BigAdmin website at `http://sun.com/bigadmin/hcl/search.jsp`.

Downloading OpenSolaris

The first noticeable difference between OpenSolaris and Solaris Express is how you obtain it. OpenSolaris is distributed as a single live CD image, in the manner of Ubuntu Linux; the live CD's design and implementation are based on the work pioneered in the Schillix and BeleniX distributions. Thus, as with any live CD, you have the possibility of a complete try-before-you-buy experience, which enables you to evaluate how well the distribution works on your system before the potential disruption of making any commitment of disk space to it. In addition to the live CD, OpenSolaris can be installed over a network using an automated installer. This technology is under development as of this writing, so you should consult the OpenSolaris documentation for information.

Beyond the image format, the other immediately noticeable difference from Solaris Express is that OpenSolaris is available from sites other than Sun's own download center. You'll find it mirrored at a number of other sites for traditional HTTP and FTP downloads, and you can also obtain it through the BitTorrent file-sharing system. These new options are possible because OpenSolaris contains only software that's licensed to be freely redistributed. Conversely, Solaris Express contains a number of components that are under more restrictive licenses that may require Sun to maintain distribution records for the software, and therefore can't be made available other than through Sun's download center.

> **NOTE** Download locations for OpenSolaris are available on the distribution's website: `http://opensolaris.com`.

You can use your web browser or programs such as `wget` or `ftp` to retrieve the image from the URLs provided on the download page. Downloads through BitTorrent are also provided. Once you have downloaded the CD ISO image for OpenSolaris, you have several options for trying it out.

If you have a virtual machine technology available that can host OpenSolaris as a guest operating system, then you often can use the ISO image directly to boot OpenSolaris in a virtual machine; this generally does not require actually burning the ISO image to media. Later in this chapter you will walk through the booting and installation process using VMware. Chapter 22 explains how to install OpenSolaris as a VirtualBox guest.

The traditional approach, which is always possible, is to burn the ISO image to a CD and then boot your system from it. On most Linux and OpenSolaris distributions, selecting the ISO image file from the desktop's file browser program (such as Nautilus in GNOME desktops) presents a menu option to write the ISO image to a disc; select it and follow the prompts, if any. From a shell command prompt, most distributions provide the cdrecord command for burning CDs. For example, assuming the OpenSolaris ISO image is named OpenSolaris.iso, the following procedure would discover the correct device number for the CD drive and then use that device number to burn the CD:

```
$ cdrecord --scanbus
scsibus9:
    9,0,0    900) 'MATSHITA' 'DVD-RAM UJ-841S ' '1.40' Removable CD-ROM
    9,1,0    901) *
    9,2,0    902) *
    9,3,0    903) *
    9,4,0    904) *
    9,5,0    905) *
    9,6,0    906) *
    9,7,0    907) *
$ cdrecord dev=9,0,0 OpenSolaris.iso
```

On Windows and Mac systems, use your favorite CD burning program to burn the CD image; if it offers the option to burn a bootable CD, rather than a data CD, be sure to burn a bootable CD.

Booting the OpenSolaris CD

Now that you've burned the OpenSolaris ISO image to CD, the next step is to boot it and try it out. Shut down your currently running operating system, make sure the OpenSolaris CD is inserted into your system's CD drive, and then boot your system. Depending on your system's BIOS settings, you may need to press a special key such as Esc or F12 to select the CD, rather than the hard drive, as the boot device. If you've done that successfully, you should be greeted with a screen that resembles Figure 2-1.

Sharp-eyed Linux users will recognize this screen as a fairly standard GNU GRUB (GRand Unified Bootloader) menu. OpenSolaris uses GRUB as its primary boot loader, which enables its boot menu to also directly boot Linux and BSD operating systems and indirectly boot Windows by invoking the Windows boot loader.

> **TIP** If you plan to install OpenSolaris as a dual-boot system with another operating system that also uses GRUB, save your existing GRUB menu configuration to a USB memory stick that has a DOS file system format, or print it out, so that you can merge the menu entries from the other operating system with the OpenSolaris GRUB menu after you have finished installing OpenSolaris.

Selecting the first item in the boot menu boots OpenSolaris to a graphical desktop. This is usually the option you'll want. If you don't want a graphical desktop for some reason (this may be necessary if the graphical desktop is unable to automatically start on your system), select the second item, which boots OpenSolaris to a text-only mode, where you can log in.

The Boot from Hard Disk item on the menu merely skips attempting to boot from the CD and instead starts the boot process from your system's primary hard disk. The final two menu items enable assistive technology for those with visual impairment; see the OpenSolaris website for information on their use. The remainder of this walk-through assumes you've chosen the first item and will boot to a graphical desktop.

FIGURE 2-1

Boot screen from the OpenSolaris CD

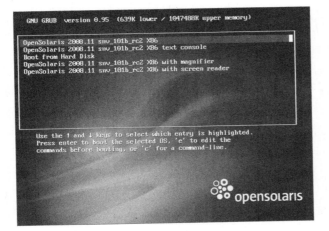

Using GRUB with OpenSolaris

To boot any operating system on the x86 processor platform, a relatively simple program called a *boot loader* is required to enable the transition from the machine's BIOS to the operating system kernel. For OpenSolaris, and many Linux distributions, GRUB serves as that boot loader. The OpenSolaris version of GRUB contains all of the features of the GRUB version used in Linux distributions, but it also contains several extensions that are not available in the main GRUB distribution. The extensions that are of the most interest to users of OpenSolaris distributions are related to automatic selection of 32- or 64-bit kernels, and support for ZFS. You normally do not need to deal with these extensions directly; selecting the desired entry from the main GRUB menu is usually all you need to do to boot OpenSolaris.

An example OpenSolaris GRUB menu entry would be as follows:

```
title OpenSolaris 2008.11 snv_100 X86
kernel$ /platform/i86pc/kernel/$ISADIR/unix -B $ZFS-BOOTFS
```

continued

continued

```
module$ /platform/i86pc/$ISADIR/boot_archive
```

Automatic selection between 32- and 64-bit kernels is enabled by two new commands, `kernel$` and `module$`, that extend the standard `kernel` and `module` commands, respectively. The new commands can expand simple tokens within the parameters supplied to them, whereas the standard commands do not. The OpenSolaris menu items contain a `$ISADIR` token that expands to `amd64` on 64-bit systems, and to the empty string on 32-bit systems, meaning that the same menu entry can be used on either type of system and automatically select the correct kernel. If you need to boot a 64-bit system in 32-bit mode for some reason, use the GRUB command-line editor and remove the `$ISADIR` tokens and you'll boot a 32-bit kernel.

ZFS boot support is flagged by providing the `-B $ZFS-BOOTFS` option to the `kernel` or `kernel$` commands. In the preceding example, GRUB would locate a ZFS pool on the first disk in the system and read the pool's `bootfs` property to determine the name of the ZFS dataset within which the kernel (and module) can be found. You can also use another new GRUB command, `bootfs`, to specify the ZFS dataset; usually this is necessary only if you need to boot from a different dataset temporarily for system maintenance or repairs.

Because these extensions are not likely to be present in the version of GRUB supplied with Linux distributions, always use the version of GRUB supplied with OpenSolaris as your primary system boot loader if you have multiple operating systems installed on your system. See the installation walk-through in this chapter for tips on merging Linux and OpenSolaris GRUB menu entries.

For basic documentation on the common features of GRUB, refer to the GRUB project's website, `http://gnu.org/software/grub/grub-legacy.en.html`.

After the OpenSolaris kernel begins running and starts loading the system services, you'll be prompted to select the keyboard layout used by your system. Figure 2-2 shows an example of the display for selecting the keyboard. You need only enter the number corresponding to your keyboard's layout. US-English is the default value.

After you select the keyboard layout, OpenSolaris next prompts you to select the language for the desktop from the list of languages supplied on the CD. Once a language is selected, Open-Solaris completes booting, auto-configures the X Window graphics system, and starts a GNOME desktop. At this point, you can try out the desktop, viewing the menu items and starting and running applications. Chapter 3 presents a crash course in OpenSolaris, and Chapter 4 presents an overview of the OpenSolaris desktop if you'd like to explore it more deeply. If you have a network interface connected, either wired or wireless, OpenSolaris will attempt to automatically configure it, although the success of this depends on OpenSolaris having a device driver available for your system's network hardware.

CROSS-REF   See Chapter 9 for more information about OpenSolaris networking.

FIGURE 2-2

OpenSolaris keyboard layout selection screen

```
Preparing live image for use
Done mounting Live image
USB keyboard
 1. Albanian                    22. Latvian
 2. Belarusian                  23. Macedonian
 3. Belgian                     24. Malta_UK
 4. Bulgarian                   25. Malta_US
 5. Croatian                    26. Norwegian
 6. Czech                       27. Polish
 7. Danish                      28. Portuguese
 8. Dutch                       29. Russian
 9. Finnish                     30. Serbia-And-Montenegro
10. French                      31. Slovenian
11. French-Canadian            32. Slovakian
12. Hungarian                   33. Spanish
13. German                      34. Swedish
14. Greek                       35. Swiss-French
15. Icelandic                   36. Swiss-German
16. Italian                     37. Taiwanese
17. Japanese-type6             38. TurkishQ
18. Japanese                    39. TurkishF
19. Korean                      40. UK-English
20. Latin-American             41. US-English
21. Lithuanian
To select the keyboard layout, enter a number [default 41]:_
```

Installing OpenSolaris

Once you've booted OpenSolaris to the desktop as described in the previous section, double-click the Install OpenSolaris icon to start the installer. Figure 2-3 shows the first screen of the installation.

This welcome screen provides a link to the release notes for the distribution. Clicking the link launches the Firefox web browser to load the release notes page from the OpenSolaris website, so you need network access to display the notes. Selecting Next advances the installer to the disk selection and partitioning screen.

Disk partitioning in an OpenSolaris installation

The Disk screen (see Figure 2-4) displays the disks found on the system, including any removable hard disks or USB disks.

Note that the recommended and minimum sizes for installation are displayed at the very top. The recommended size is typically several times larger than the minimum size. Its value is chosen to allow for local storage of your own files, installation of additional software after the operating system installation, and later updates of OpenSolaris. Updates of OpenSolaris require additional space because the update process always uses a copy of the OS for its work, enabling you to roll back to a prior version if the update is a problem for any reason.

CROSS-REF See Chapter 6 for more details on updates and OpenSolaris software management.

Selecting a size smaller than what is recommended may leave you with insufficient space for your work or prevent you from updating OpenSolaris later. Unless you're fairly experienced in operating system installations, using the recommended size generally gives you the most satisfying result.

FIGURE 2-3

Initial screen of the OpenSolaris installation

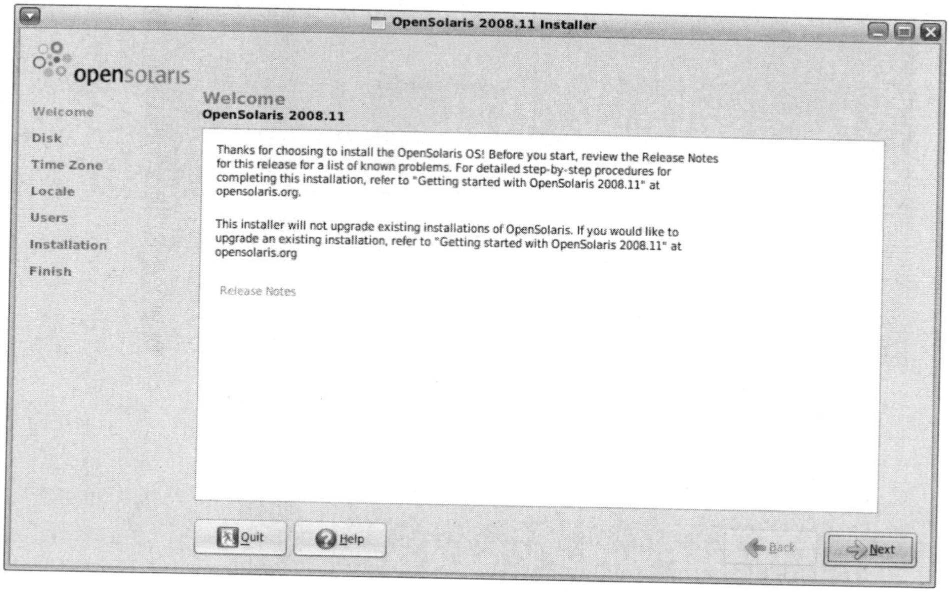

The disks are displayed across the top to enable you to select the disk that will be used for installation. Point your mouse at a disk in the display to get a more detailed description of it, including manufacturer and device names, which sometimes can be necessary to help differentiate between similar disks. After you choose the disk you want, use the bottom half of the screen to select the partition to use. Partitioning is a means of parceling out portions of the disk for different uses; for example, to have multiple operating systems (perhaps Windows, Linux, and OpenSolaris) installed and available to boot at different times, you would typically assign a partition to each operating system. On x86 systems, the partitioning standard allows up to four primary partitions to be created on each disk; Linux can use multiple partitions for different portions of its installation, but OpenSolaris can use only one partition on each disk.

NOTE Linux users may also be accustomed to installing multiple distributions in different partitions. However, the limitation of using only one partition on each disk means that you must install multiple OpenSolaris distributions into the same partition, allowing them to either share the same ZFS pool or use different slices within the partition. This book does not cover this topic, so see the OpenSolaris Installation and Packaging community, http://opensolaris.org/os/community/install, for information.

If you're going to use the entire disk for OpenSolaris, select the Use the whole disk radio button. To use only part of the disk and have an available partition entry and space, select Partition the disk, and then set up a partition for OpenSolaris to use. Any existing partitions on the disk are displayed. To assign a partition to OpenSolaris, set that partition's partition type to Solaris and select a size at least as large as the minimum size; if you select a partition that is smaller than the minimum size, you cannot proceed beyond this screen.

FIGURE 2-4

Disk selection and partitioning screen

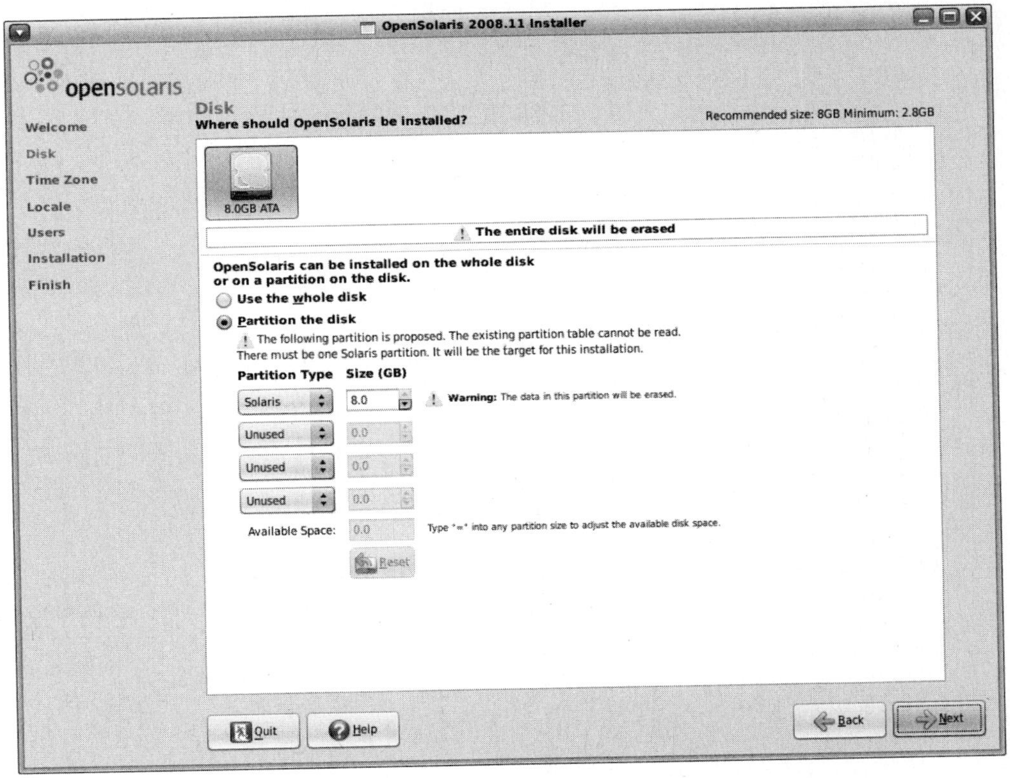

If you don't have a partition of at least the minimum size available, you may need to shrink the size of one or more existing partitions. Two types of repartitioning can be done: destructive and non-destructive.

CAUTION The OpenSolaris installation program can do only destructive repartitioning. It warns you if any changes you make to the partitioning will result in a destructive change to an existing partition.

Destructive partitioning means that if you change the size of a partition, the existing contents of that partition (and possibly others that are adjacent to it on the disk) will no longer be readable. Non-destructive repartitioning requires more advanced software that can understand the format of the file system contained within the partition and shrink it into a smaller space without losing any files, allowing the free space to be reallocated to another partition.

If your system only has Windows on it, there will typically be a fairly large amount of empty space on the Windows partition that can be reclaimed and used for other partitions because in most installations the entire disk will have been allocated to Windows. Windows Vista offers a built-in utility to shrink its partitions, whereas older versions of Windows require a third-party tool. If you have spare space from a Linux distribution installation, your distribution may well include the GNU `parted` utility and possibly the graphical interface for it, known as GParted. Otherwise, you can download it from `http://gparted.sourceforge.net`. The latest versions of the GParted live CD can also safely shrink Vista partitions — and usually more completely than Vista's own shrinking tool.

NOTE For instructions on shrinking Windows Vista partitions, search for "Can I repartition my hard disk?" at `http://windowshelp.microsoft.com`.

GParted doesn't list OpenSolaris or Solaris as a partition type that it will create, so any new partitions you create for OpenSolaris using GParted should be created as unformatted; the OpenSolaris installer will format the partition correctly once you select it.

You may notice that, unlike many other operating systems, the OpenSolaris installer allows you to select only a single partition for OpenSolaris, and doesn't require you to specify the file systems to associate with partitions. That's because OpenSolaris uses the ZFS file system for all of its storage, and ZFS uses a pooled storage model. The partition you create is set up as a pool, and the OpenSolaris installer creates a number of ZFS file systems in it to install the operating system. You can easily create additional file systems for your data within that pool at any time after OpenSolaris is installed and running.

CROSS-REF See Chapter 8 for a detailed discussion of ZFS.

Configuring the time, time zone, language, and users

Once you've provided the necessary disk space for the OpenSolaris installation, you need to configure the system's clock and time zone on the Time Zone, Date and Time screen (see Figure 2-5). To specify the time zone, either click on the appropriate location on the map that's displayed or select by region and location from the menus on this screen. If the date and time require adjustment, you can either enter them directly into the text fields or use the spin buttons next to the text fields to adjust their values. Clicking Next immediately sets the system time to the selected value.

On the installer's next screen, Locale, you select the default language for the installed system, as shown in Figure 2-6. Here you have the opportunity to select a language on the installed system other than the one used during installation; the default value selected in this screen is the language you selected during the CD boot process.

The next screen, Users (see Figure 2-7), enables you to set the system's root password, create a user account, and provide the name by which the system will be known.

FIGURE 2-5

Set the time and time zone.

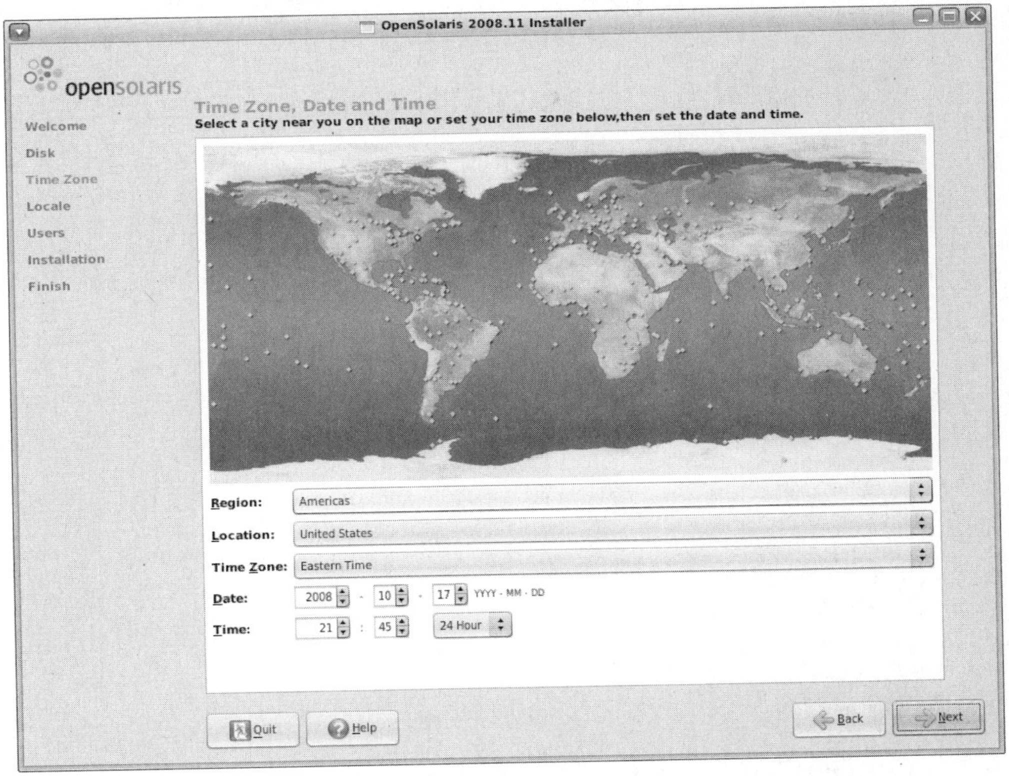

The user account that you create during installation is a special account that has administrative access to the computer, provided by the OpenSolaris security technology known as Role-Based Access Control. Create a user account here and OpenSolaris also makes the root account a *role*, which is a special type of account that is not available for login. This provides an extra layer of system security by ensuring that only user accounts with administrative access can become root. You can choose to not create a user account during installation, in which case the root account is not made into a role and is available for direct login.

CROSS-REF See Chapter 3 for a quick introduction to, and Chapter 11 for detailed information on, Role-Based Access Control and other OpenSolaris security features.

NOTE Experienced UNIX and Linux users will note that there's no option at installation to set details of the user account, such as the user ID number or group memberships. If necessary, these values can be modified after installation using the desktop administration tools included with the system. Chapter 3 discusses this and other basic administration topics.

The computer name set on this screen is the name by which the system knows itself, and the name it advertises on the local network to other systems that are running discovery protocols such as multicast DNS (see Chapter 9 for more on OpenSolaris networking). The name selected is not registered into centralized naming services such as DNS or LDAP; such registrations must be made by the administrators of those services.

FIGURE 2-6

Select the language support.

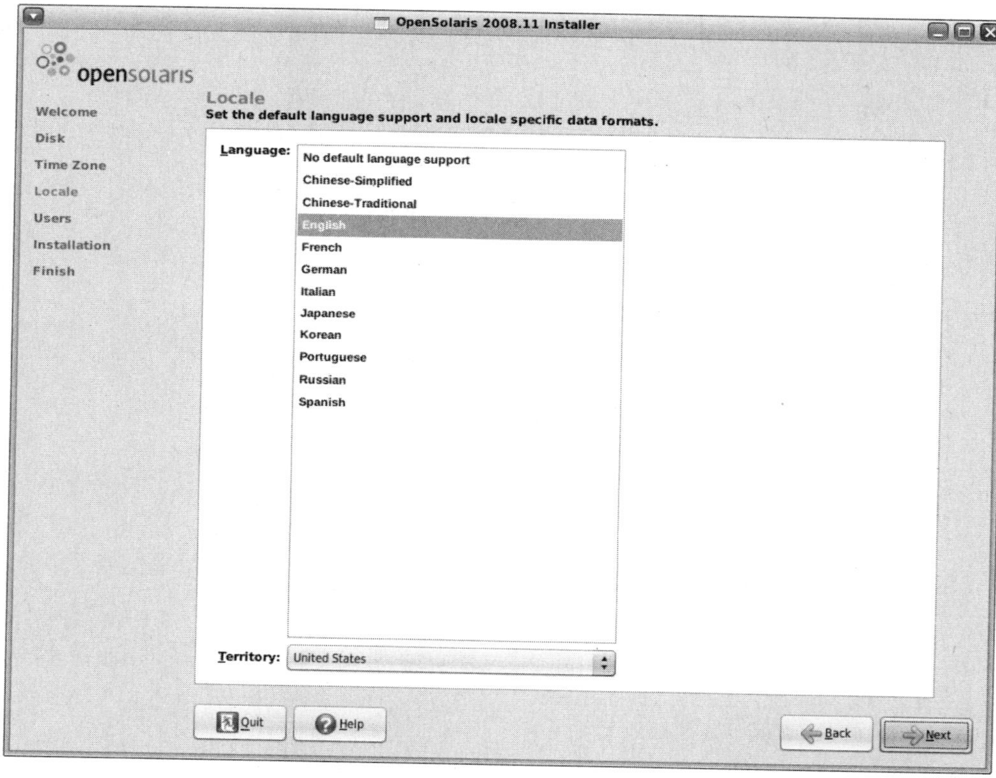

Click Next to display the Installation screen. Here you review the selections you've made before starting the actual installation process. The screen looks much like the one shown in Figure 2-8.

When you're satisfied with your selections, click Install to start the installation process; prior to this point no changes have been made to your system's permanent storage. Once you initiate the installation, a progress screen displays as the installation proceeds. On most systems the installation process takes roughly twenty minutes. During this time, the installer is copying the contents of the live CD onto the provided disk partition. When the installation process completes, the Finish screen is displayed, indicating the success or failure of the installation. The installer also offers the option to display the installation log, should there be a problem or you're just curious about what happened during the installation. The installation log is also saved on the installed system at /var/sadm/system/logs/install_log, should you need to reference it later. Clicking the Reboot button causes the system to reboot and start using OpenSolaris.

FIGURE 2-7

Create root and user accounts.

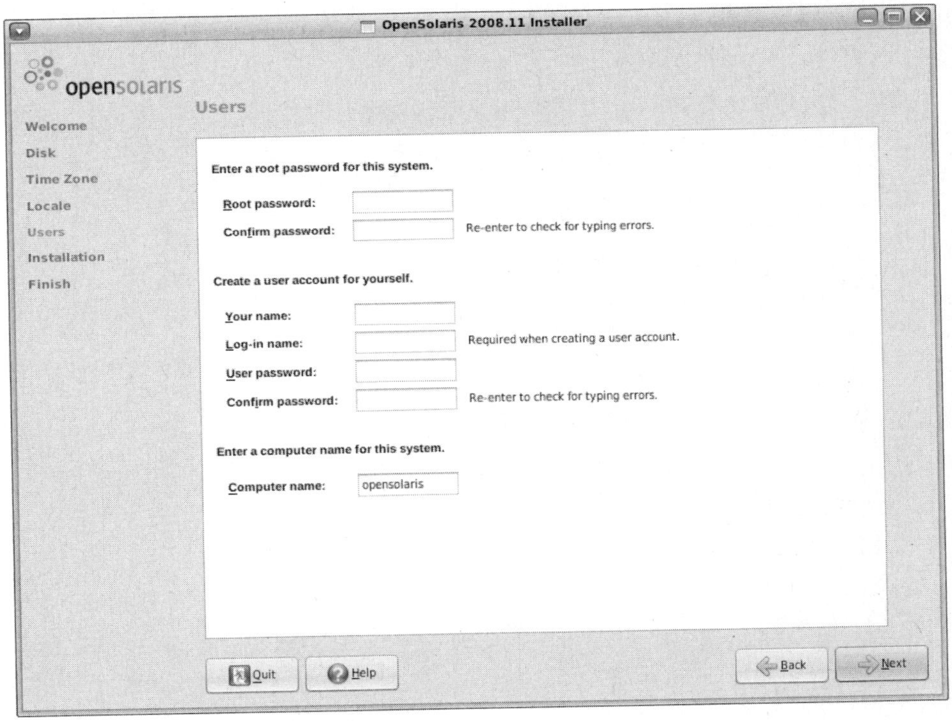

Troubleshooting installation

There are several points at which you might run into trouble installing OpenSolaris. The first potential problem can occur when booting the OpenSolaris CD. As mentioned in the instructions for booting the CD, you need to select the CD as the preferred boot device in your BIOS. Most BIOSs allow a one-time selection by pressing a key at boot and then selecting from a menu using the arrow keys on the keyboard, but you may have to go into your BIOS menu to ensure that booting from CD is enabled, and that it is preferred over the hard disk. Unfortunately, the method for doing this varies across BIOS implementations, so we can't offer general instructions, but your system's manuals should be helpful in sorting this out.

If you're trying to boot from the CD but it fails to bring up the GRUB menu shown earlier in this chapter, you most likely have a bad CD. This happens much more often than you might think — burning CDs is notoriously prone to failure. First, ensure that the ISO image you downloaded wasn't corrupted by comparing its checksum with the one published on the download site. To help make the CD burning process more reliable, try to leave your computer alone while it's burning the CD, as it is necessary to send data to the CD at a constant rate during the burning process. If you've tried both of those suggestions and still have unreliable results, you might check your computer vendor's support site for BIOS or firmware updates (bugs in CD and DVD drives are not at all unheard of).

FIGURE 2-8

Review your choices.

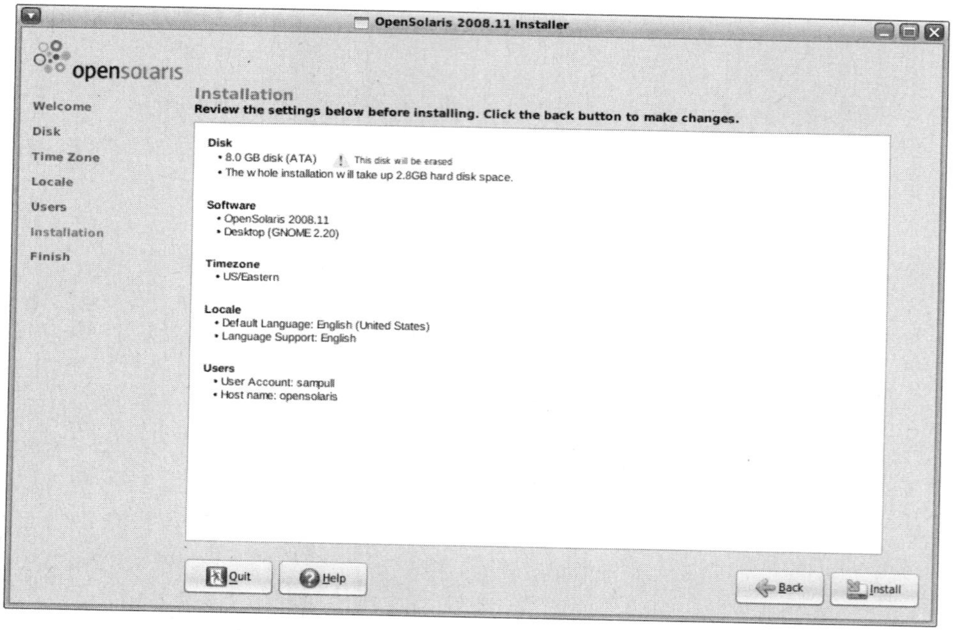

If you do get the GRUB menu and can start booting OpenSolaris but it hangs while booting and doesn't present a login prompt, you may have a device driver problem. Consulting the release notes page for OpenSolaris, which are linked from the download page, should be your first step in case there's a known issue and solution that matches your problem. If there isn't such a release note, consulting the support forums on opensolaris.com or sending mail to the OpenSolaris help mailing list, opensolaris-help@opensolaris.org, should connect you to experts who can assist in diagnosing your problem. To get answers as quickly as possible, send as much detail as you can about the type of system, the version of OpenSolaris, and any messages displayed on the screen.

OpenSolaris may manage to partially boot but run into a problem that it prevents it from completely booting. At that point it displays a message that says "Requesting System Maintenance Mode" and then prompts you for the root password. The CD's root password is opensolaris, so enter it and you should be logged in as root to a shell prompt. From there you're generally troubleshooting why a critical service did not start, which requires you to work with the Service Management Facility (SMF) to diagnose the problem.

CROSS-REF See Chapter 13 for instructions on how to troubleshoot with SMF.

A graphical desktop failing to display usually points to problems with the X Window system display drivers, which may not support your system's display hardware, especially if it's very new or very old. Because diagnosis is difficult and the supported devices change very frequently, the best advice in this situation is to contact opensolaris-help@opensolaris.org with the details of the problem.

Finally, if you have a graphical desktop that looks correct but you are having trouble running the installation program, you can first consult the installation log, which can be found at the pathname /tmp/install_log during the live CD session. Consulting the release notes may also be helpful here, but your best source of help at this point is likely to be the Installation and Packaging community, http://opensolaris.org/os/community/install, which will connect you directly with the developers of the installation software.

Booting OpenSolaris

Assuming your installation of OpenSolaris succeeded, a reboot of the system brings up a GRUB menu with graphics similar to the menu shown on the live CD. If it brings up the live CD's menu again, this means the system's device boot order is choosing the CD first, and you should either eject it and reboot the system, or select the Boot from Hard Disk menu item, which takes you to the hard disk's GRUB menu. Its first, and default, selection is to boot OpenSolaris; if you select it or allow it to time out, it will boot OpenSolaris for the first time. During this initial boot, the operating system may take a moment to configure various system services, but before long you are presented with the login screen (see Figure 2-9).

Enter the username and password that you provided to the installer. You'll be presented with a GNOME desktop that is virtually identical to the desktop on the live CD. Once you've reached the desktop, the first thing to do is start a terminal window (select Accessories➤Terminal on the desktop menu) and ensure that your system's software database is updated. In the terminal, type the following:

```
# pkg refresh
# pkg list -a
FMRI                                                STATE      UFIX

NAME (AUTHORITY)                        VERSION       STATE      UFIX
BRCMbnx                                 0.5.11-0.99   installed  ----
FSWfontconfig-devel-docs                0.5.11-0.99   known      ----
FSWxorg-client-docs                     0.5.11-0.99   installed  ----
FSWxorg-client-programs                 0.5.11-0.99   installed  ----
FSWxorg-clientlibs                      0.5.11-0.99   installed  ----
FSWxorg-data                            0.5.11-0.99   installed  ----
```

```
FSWxorg-devel-docs              0.5.11-0.99        installed    ---- ·
FSWxorg-fonts                   0.5.11-0.99        installed    ----
FSWxorg-headers                 0.5.11-0.99        known        ----
FSWxwpft                        0.5.11-0.99        installed    ----
   ...
```

FIGURE 2-9

OpenSolaris login screen

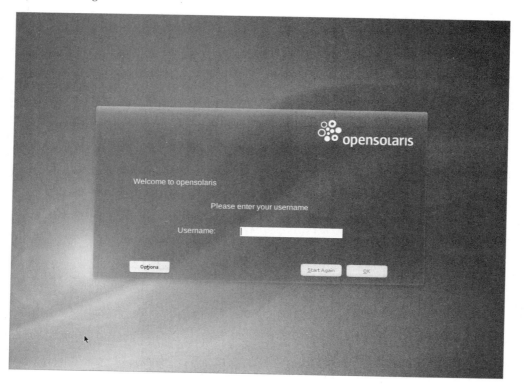

The `pkg refresh` command updates the system's local catalog of software available in the repository. Always do this immediately after installation to ensure that the system is synchronized with the software listing from the package servers; you'll likely want to do it periodically thereafter so that you're always operating from current information when deciding which versions of software to install.

CROSS-REF See Chapter 6 for more information on OpenSolaris software management.

The `pkg list -a` command displays the list of all software available from the openso-laris.org package repository, including whether it's installed on your system (STATE column value is installed) or available for download and installation (STATE column value is known). The listing is very long. One package that many users will want to install for working on documents is OpenOffice; it can be installed with a simple command:

```
# pkg install openoffice
```

> **TIP** To locate the package containing a particular program of interest — gcc, for example — use the command `pkg search -lr gcc`, which searches both the locally installed software and the package repositories.

At this point, take a breath and congratulate yourself — you've got a running OpenSolaris system!

> **TIP** If you have previously saved a GRUB menu configuration from other operating systems that are also installed on the system, this would be a good time to use a text editor such as `gedit` to merge those entries with the OpenSolaris GRUB menu. You'll find the OpenSolaris GRUB menu at `/rpool/boot/grub/menu.lst`. If you have placed your saved menu on a USB stick, inserting the stick into a USB port causes OpenSolaris to mount it and display a Nautilus file browser window with the contents of the stick. The stick will be mounted under `/media`.

Installing OpenSolaris in a virtual machine

If you're interested in running OpenSolaris but aren't ready to make it your primary operating system, one particularly convenient approach is to use a desktop virtualization program. Another benefit to this approach is that while OpenSolaris might not directly support your system hardware, the virtual machine that the virtualization program provides generally emulates hardware that's well-supported by OpenSolaris.

The virtualization options available to you depend on what primary operating system you run, but two of the more popular are VirtualBox, which is a free, open source virtualization program from Sun that runs on nearly every popular desktop operating system, and VMware Workstation, a proprietary product of VMware, Inc., that runs on Windows and Linux; VMware also offers its similar Fusion product for Mac OS users.

> **CROSS-REF** For detailed information on using VirtualBox, including procedures for installing OpenSolaris as a guest in VirtualBox, see Chapter 22.

This section assumes that you already have VMware Workstation 6 installed on your system; if not, you can obtain it free from VMware's website: `http://vmware.com`.

Installing OpenSolaris as a VMware virtual machine is a simple process. Once you've started VMware Workstation, the main window presents several options. Select Create A New Virtual

Machine. This starts the New Virtual Machine wizard, which walks you through the process of creating the virtual machine.

The first screen of the wizard offers two options for creating a virtual machine: Typical and Custom. The Typical virtual machine has a fairly standard set of devices and configuration options. For the Custom option, you specify the details yourself. OpenSolaris generally works well without requiring any custom settings, so selecting Typical is a good choice. The main reason you might choose Custom is if you know that you want to assign a larger amount of RAM than the default 512MB that will be assigned, although you can always change this later so don't feel compelled to choose the Custom path right now. Click Next when you're done with this screen.

Now you need to select a type of guest operating system. Choose Sun Solaris; and for the version, select either Solaris 10 or Solaris 10 64-bit, depending on whether your host operating system is 32-bit or 64-bit (if VMware offered an OpenSolaris option you'd select that, but because it doesn't, Solaris 10 is the closest option). Click Next, and then supply a name for the virtual machine and a location to store its virtual disk image. VMware suggests defaults for these values; accepting them may be the simplest option.

The next screen requires you to choose the virtual machine's type of network connection. Usually either Bridged Networking or Network Address Translation is a good choice; the main difference is whether you want the virtual machine to obtain its own address from the host system's network (bridged networking) or use the host operating system's network address (network address translation). If you can easily obtain additional addresses on the host system's network, bridged networking may be a more convenient option. If you select "Use host-only networking" or "Do not use a network connection," OpenSolaris won't be able to contact any package repositories and you'll likely find it difficult to install additional software into the virtual machine.

The final screen of the wizard enables you to specify the size of the virtual disk assigned to the machine. OpenSolaris recommends at least 8GB of disk space, so select at least that much space here. Allowing VMware to split the disk into 2GB files enables the virtual machine to be created more quickly, and generally won't affect its performance, so you may want to select that option. After you click Finish, VMware pauses briefly while it creates the virtual machine, after which you are returned to the main window, shown in Figure 2-10.

Your next step depends on whether you are going to boot OpenSolaris from a physical CD or from a downloaded ISO image file. If you're using an ISO image file, select the virtual machine and then select Edit Virtual Machine Settings. In the dialog that is displayed, select the CD-ROM device in the Hardware listing, select the Use ISO Image radio button, and either enter the path to the ISO file or use the Browse button to browse the file system to find the ISO image. Make sure that the Connect at power on box is checked so that the virtual machine can boot from the virtual CD.

Finally, select the virtual machine in the list and click the Power On button. This should start the boot process for the virtual machine, and you can now follow the directions from the "Booting the OpenSolaris CD" section earlier in the chapter.

FIGURE 2-10

VMware Workstation main window

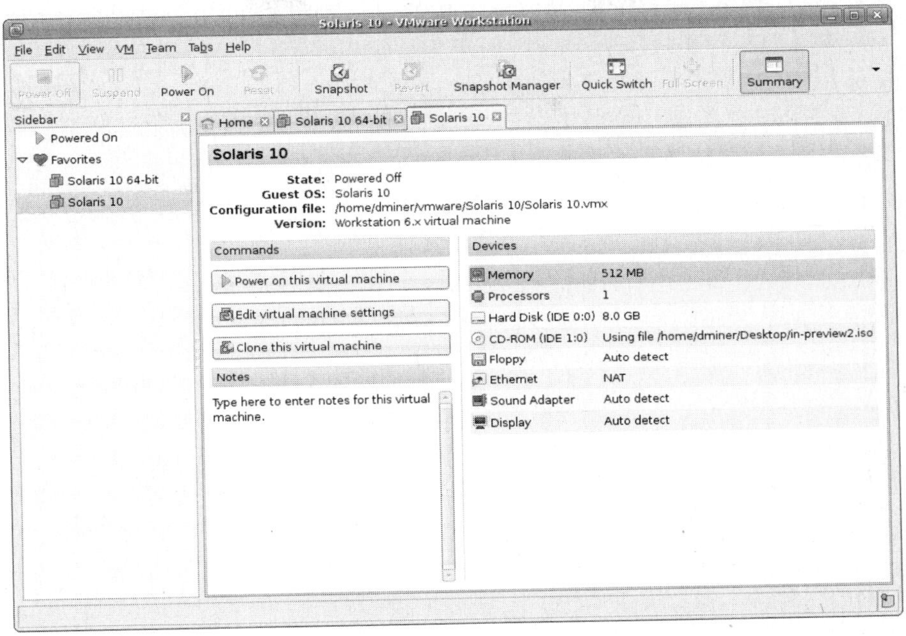

Resources

Most of the distributions discussed in this chapter can be downloaded from http://genunix.org.

Downloads, documentation, and support forums for the OpenSolaris distribution are available at http://opensolaris.com.

Solaris Express Community Edition can be downloaded from http://opensolaris.org/os/downloads.

Schillix information and downloads are available at http://schillix.berlios.de.

BeleniX information and downloads are available at http://belenix.org.

Nexenta downloads and documentation can be found at http://nexenta.org.

Information on MartUX and Natamar, including downloads, can be found at http://martux.org.

MilaX information is available from http://milax.org.

Summary

This chapter gave you a brief introduction to each of the OpenSolaris-based distributions, pointing out the unique contributions each has made to the OpenSolaris community and highlighting the reasons why you might be interested in each of them. If you chose the OpenSolaris distribution, you've walked through how to verify that OpenSolaris will run on your system, how to download the distribution, and how to boot and install it both to physical hardware and VMware Workstation. You should, at this point, have a working installation of OpenSolaris and be ready to dive in. Chapter 3 provides a crash course on the most common administration tasks you might be interested in as a new user. Later chapters explore the various technologies in OpenSolaris in much greater detail.

Chapter 3

OpenSolaris Crash Course

I t's time to jump in and start using OpenSolaris. This chapter provides a whirlwind tour of the OpenSolaris operating environment, including an overview of the GNOME desktop and an introduction to the OpenSolaris command line, focusing on the `bash` shell. You'll learn how to leverage the OpenSolaris internationalization features, how to get online, and how to use the new Image Packaging System to obtain the software you need. The chapter concludes with an overview of OpenSolaris system administration. Although this chapter provides an introduction to many aspects of OpenSolaris, most of the content in this chapter is discussed in more detail in subsequent chapters.

This chapter is aimed at the beginning and intermediate user. If you're already familiar with OpenSolaris, you can probably skip it and move right into Part II of the book. If you're an experienced UNIX or Linux user, you might still want to skim this chapter to bring yourself up to date on the differences between those platforms and OpenSolaris.

Note that this chapter, and, with a few exceptions, most of this book, focuses on the OpenSolaris distribution from Sun. However, much of the information is applicable to other distributions as well.

IN THIS CHAPTER

Discovering the desktop

Using the command line

Switching languages and locales

Getting online

Adding software

Developing on OpenSolaris

Connecting remotely

System administration

Discovering the Desktop

After installing, booting, and logging in to OpenSolaris as described in Chapter 2, you are presented with a desktop, as shown in Figure 3-1.

This graphical user interface is the GNOME desktop, the default windowing environment in OpenSolaris. GNOME should be familiar to you if you're coming from Red Hat, Fedora, Ubuntu, or many other Linux distributions. Even if you've never used GNOME before, it's pretty intuitive, so you should be able to find your way around relatively quickly.

FIGURE 3-1

The GNOME desktop is the default windowing environment in OpenSolaris.

Overview

As shown in Figure 3-1, the default GNOME interface on OpenSolaris consists of two gray panels lining the top and bottom of your screen, separated by a large blue desktop area.

The panels contain menus, application launcher icons, and other tools. The top panel on the left contains three menus (Applications, Places, System) and several icons. From left to right, the icons can be used to launch a file browser, launch the Mozilla Firefox web browser, launch the Mozilla Thunderbird e-mail client, launch the graphical package manager, open a command-line terminal, and search for files. Later sections in this chapter cover most of these applications and tools in more detail. On the right, the top panel contains the battery/AC power indicator, two network status monitors, the volume control, and a clock. Mouse-over or click on the various tools to access more information or change settings.

The bottom panel lists all the open windows, including minimized windows. On the far right, you can select from among the four different workspaces. The following section on managing windows provides more detail on these workspaces. The bottom panel also contains a trash can, which functions similarly to the Recycle Bin on Windows.

The large desktop area is empty in Figure 3-1 except for a few icons, which are present in the default configuration. However, the desktop can also show application windows, icons for volumes such as CDs and USB sticks, and any files or folders in your Desktop directory.

Managing windows

GNOME on OpenSolaris uses the Metacity window manager. Each graphical user interface application that you run opens one or more windows on the desktop. Figure 3-2 shows Mozilla Firefox and a command-line terminal window open.

FIGURE 3-2

GNOME applications open one or more windows on the desktop.

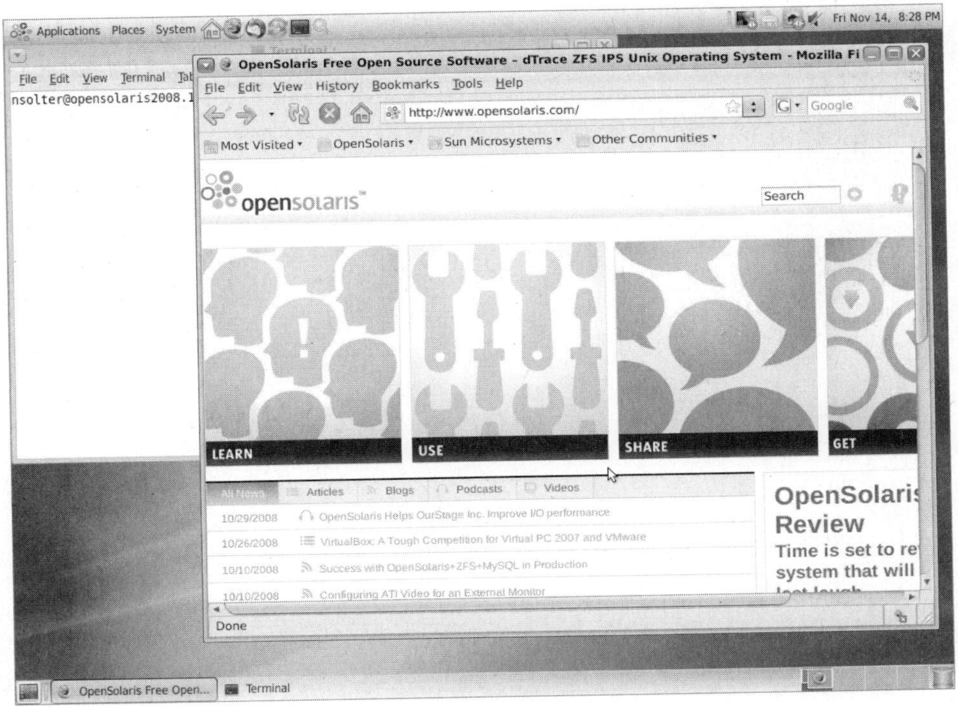

If you're familiar with Microsoft Windows XP, you should feel right at home. As in XP, each window has three buttons on the top right that, from left to right, enable you to minimize, maximize, or close the window. Each window also generally has its own menu for the specific application.

Only one window at a time has the focus, which means it accepts keyboard input. There are a few ways you can switch between windows in the default configuration. First, you can use the mouse to click on the window that you want to have the focus. Second, you can click on the name of the window you want on the bottom panel. Finally, you can use the Alt+Tab keyboard shortcut to cycle through the windows. This shortcut is the same as the default in Windows XP. The button on the far left of the bottom panel minimizes all windows.

CROSS-REF The window focus behavior is configurable. See Chapter 4 for details.

One nice feature of Metacity is the capability to navigate between multiple virtual desktops. These workspaces give you more desktop space and enable you to run multiple applications without cluttering up a single desktop with windows. If you're familiar with Macs, *workspaces* in GNOME are quite similar to *spaces* on the Mac. Each of the four boxes at the far right of the bottom panel represents a workspace. You can switch between workspaces by clicking on the box of the workspace you want, or you can cycle through them with the Ctrl+Alt+Right Arrow and Ctrl+Alt+Left Arrow keyboard shortcuts. You can move applications between workspaces by clicking and dragging their little icons in the four boxes on the right of the bottom panel.

Navigating files and directories

GNOME uses the Nautilus file browser. To open a file browser, click the File Browser icon on the top panel or select Places ➤ Home Folder, Places ➤ Desktop, or one of the other locations in the Places menu. Once you have a Nautilus browser open, you can navigate to any of the directories on your system. The Nautilus browser is shown in Figure 3-3.

You can drag and drop files between directories (called *folders* in Nautilus), create new folders, delete folders and files, and, in short, do pretty much anything you can do in Windows Explorer.

Media that you've inserted, such as a USB stick or a DVD, will show up both in the Places menu and as icons on the desktop. You can browse that media with Nautilus by double-clicking the desktop icon or selecting it from the Places menu. Most media also cause GNOME to automatically open a Nautilus File Browser window.

TIP Eject CDs and DVDs from the system by right-clicking on the volume's icon on the desktop and selecting Eject. Similarly, always unmount a USB volume by right-clicking on its icon and selecting Unmount Volume before pulling out the USB stick. (Chapter 5 covers peripheral devices in detail.)

Select Places ➤ Network to bring up a Nautilus browser showing file systems that are remotely accessible, automatically detecting available Samba shares, NFS shares, and even Windows workgroups.

FIGURE 3-3

The Nautilus file browser enables you to browse the files and directories on your system.

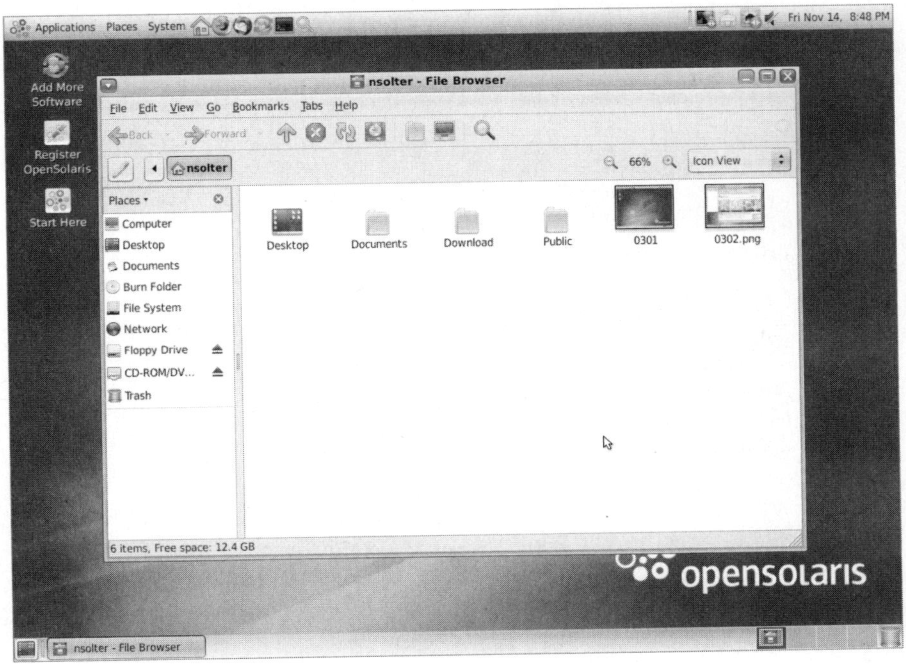

CROSS-REF   See Chapter 10 for details on CIFS and NFS.

Using the Internet

OpenSolaris comes with the Mozilla Firefox web browser, which you can use to browse the World Wide Web. You can launch it by clicking the Firefox icon on the top panel or by selecting Applications ➤ Internet ➤ Firefox Web Browser.

TIP   OpenSolaris does not include the Adobe Flash player, which is necessary for viewing many websites. Install it by navigating your browser to
`http://adobe.com/products/flashplayer` and clicking the Download Now button.
Select Solaris x86 or Solaris SPARC as appropriate for your platform, and click the yellow "Agree
and install now" button. Select Save to Disk from the window that pops up and save it in your
home directory. Next, open a terminal window, as described later in the section "The OpenSolaris
Command Line," and execute the following commands:

```
$ cd ~
$ mkdir .mozilla/plugins
```

```
$ bunzip2 flash_player_9_solaris_x86.tar.bz2
$ tar -xvf flash_player_9_solaris_x86.tar
x flash_player_9_solaris_r125_x86, 0 bytes, 0 tape blocks
x flash_player_9_solaris_r125_x86/flashplayer.xpt, 856 bytes,
 2 tape blocks
x flash_player_9_solaris_r125_x86/libflashplayer.so, 6733812
 bytes, 13152 tape blocks
$ mv flash_player_9_solaris_r125_x86/* .mozilla/plugins/
```

Finally, exit Firefox and restart it. Flash should now be working.

OpenSolaris also includes two popular e-mail clients: Thunderbird and Evolution. Both are found in the Applications ➤ Internet menu. You can also launch Thunderbird from its icon, directly to the right of the Firefox icon.

For your instant messaging needs, OpenSolaris includes the Pidgin Internet Messenger program, which you can launch from Applications ➤ Internet ➤ Pidgin Internet Messenger. Pidgin enables you to talk on any of your favorite chat networks, such as AIM, MSN, Google Talk, IRC, and others.

Office suite

The primary office suite for OpenSolaris is OpenOffice.org. It's not installed by default, but you can add it through the graphical Package Manager or the command line as described a little later in the section "Adding Software."

Once OpenOffice.org is installed, you can use its Writer, Calc, and Impress components to do word processing, spreadsheets, and presentations, respectively. These applications all show up under the Applications ➤ Office menu. The first time you launch one of them, OpenOffice.org takes you through a configuration and registration process. OpenOffice.org also includes additional tools for preparing graphics and equations for documents, and for interfacing with databases.

You can read PDF files with the Evince document viewer, which should launch automatically if you download a PDF with Firefox. You can launch it manually from Applications ➤ Office ➤ Evince Document Viewer.

Multimedia

OpenSolaris includes several audio and video multimedia applications — including Rhythmbox music player and Totem Movie Player — under Applications ➤ Sound & Video.

For image editing, you can use the Gnu Image Manipulation Program (GIMP) which is available in the package repository in the SUNWgnome-img-editor package. To just view photos, use the Image Viewer or Image Organizer in the Applications ➤ Graphics menu.

CROSS-REF Chapter 4 explores the multimedia capabilities of OpenSolaris in more detail.

Printers and peripherals

OpenSolaris supports most USB-based printers and peripherals, such as webcams, mp3 players, and the like. Generally, OpenSolaris can auto-detect and configure them, but occasionally you will have to configure them manually. OpenSolaris also supports network printers, and peripherals connected via older technology such as serial ports.

CROSS-REF See Chapter 5 for details on using printers and peripherals with OpenSolaris.

Customizing GNOME

You can customize many aspects of the GNOME interface. Most of the customization preferences can be accessed through System ➤ Preferences. For example, to change the screensaver, select System ➤ Preferences ➤ Screensaver.

One customization of particular interest is the Visual Effects feature. These effects use the Compiz compositing window manager. To enable them, select System ➤ Preferences ➤ Appearance, choose the Visual Effects tab, and select one of the options. If you come from a Mac world, the visual effects should make you feel somewhat at home — they include functionality similar to Exposé on the Mac.

You can also add menu items, launchers, icons, and other tools to the panels and desktop.

CROSS-REF Chapter 4 provides more details on customizing GNOME.

Logging out and shutting down

To log out the current user, select System ➤ Log Out <*username*> ... . This brings up a confirmation dialog to ensure that you really want to log out before actually doing so. Once you log out, you are presented with the login screen again.

To shut down or reboot the computer, select System ➤ Shut Down ... . A pop-up window enables you to Restart, Cancel, or Shut Down.

If you're going to be away from your computer, select System ➤ Lock Screen to start the screensaver and require your password before allowing access again.

CROSS-REF This section was just an introduction to the GNOME desktop. The remainder of this chapter focuses on the command line. For more details on the OpenSolaris graphical user interface, see Chapter 4.

Using the Command Line

If you're like the authors of this book, the first thing you generally want to do in any windowing environment is find your way to a command line. You can open a command line terminal by clicking the command line terminal icon on the top panel or by right-clicking on the desktop and selecting Open Terminal from the pop-up menu.

> **TIP** Like many Linux systems with which you might be familiar, OpenSolaris includes support for *Virtual Console* (VC), also called *Virtual Terminal* (VT). This feature enables you to switch between multiple text consoles without the windowing system, or between the windowing system and various text consoles. As of this writing, only the former option (switching between multiple text consoles) is available. Consult the vt(7I) man page for details.

Shells

The user that you created in the OpenSolaris installer is assigned the GNU Bourne-Again Shell (BASH) by default. If you're familiar with Linux, you'll feel right at home with bash on OpenSolaris. If you've used Solaris Express or Solaris 10 in the past, this may be a change for you. If you prefer a different shell, OpenSolaris includes several other options, as shown in Table 3-1.

TABLE 3-1

OpenSolaris Shells

Shell	Path	Comments
Bourne-Again Shell	/usr/bin/bash	Default for user created by installer and for root role
Korn Shell	/usr/bin/ksh	Korn Shell 93 (not the older Korn Shell 88 that ships with Solaris 10)
C Shell	/usr/bin/csh, /usr/bin/tcsh	Standard C shell and enhanced C shell
POSIX-compliant Shell	/usr/xpg4/bin/sh	POSIX-compliant shell; quite similar to Korn Shell 88
Z Shell	/usr/bin/zsh	Z Shell

> **NOTE** The Z Shell (zsh) and the enhanced C Shell (tcsh) are not installed on your system by default. To use them you must install the SUNWzsh and SUNWtcsh packages from the network package repository. See the "Adding Software" section later in this chapter for details on installing packages from the package repository.

The system shell, /bin/sh, is now Korn Shell 93, not the old Bourne shell you find on Solaris Express, Solaris 10, and previous releases. /usr/bin/jsh (the job-control shell) also is a symlink to Korn Shell 93.

You can, of course, change your shell. To try one out, simply type the path of the shell you want to use. To change your default shell, consult the section "System Administration" later in this chapter.

To exit a shell, use exit or logout.

> **TIP** To get system console output, launch a terminal from your shell using /usr/X11/bin/xterm -C &.

The remainder of this section assumes you have some familiarity with a command-line environment, so it doesn't explain every detail about the shell or about navigating your environment. It also assumes use of the bash shell, although many of the features discussed apply to the C shell and Korn shell as well.

Both bash and the UNIX command-line environment are quite prevalent and popular, so you can find plenty of information about them elsewhere if you're a beginner. For example, most introductory Linux books contain a good overview of bash. For details on bash and the other shells available in OpenSolaris, consult one of the references listed in the "Resources" section.

This section focuses on the user side of things. For administration, consult the section "System Administration" later in this chapter.

Executing commands

As with all shells, you enter commands to the bash command prompt followed by a carriage return (the Enter key on your keyboard). The $ in the following examples is the command prompt. Everything else on that line is what the user types:

```
$ echo ''Hello, world''
Hello, world
```

You can execute multiple commands on a single line by separating them with a semicolon:

```
$ touch file1
$ rm file1; ls file1
file1: No such file or directory
```

If you end a command line with a backslash, bash lets you continue the command on the next line. This feature is useful for entering lengthy commands:

```
$ touch \
> file1
$ ls file1
file1
```

One particularly nice feature of bash is command-line editing. You can edit your command line in place before executing it. Use the left and right arrows to move the cursor
back and forth on the line, to delete characters with the backspace, and to enter text as
normal. You can also use keystrokes for moving around the line, editing the line, and even
cutting and pasting text within the line. For example, Alt+F and Alt+B move forward
and backward, respectively, on a word-by-word, instead of character-by-character, basis.
The Bash Reference manual at www.faqs.org contains a useful list of editing keystrokes:
http://faqs.org/docs/bashman/bashref_81.html.

> **TIP**   The bash command-line editing keystrokes are in many cases identical to the corre-
> sponding keystrokes in the emacs text editor, with Alt used instead of the Meta (Esc)
> character in emacs. For example, Ctrl+K to cut ("kill") to the end of the line and Ctrl+Y to paste
> ("yank") are the same as in emacs.

Another nifty feature of bash command-line editing is automatic completion. If you press the
Tab key with the cursor at the end of a partially completed word, bash attempts to complete it
as a command, filename, environment variable, or other entity depending on context. If multiple options are available, bash first completes the word up to the divergence, and then a second
Tab presents a list of all the options. For example, to get a list of all the commands in your path
that start with "fil," type **fil** and press Tab twice:

```
$ file<tab><tab>
file            file-roller  filesync
$ file
```

bash first completed the word up to file (because there were no commands starting with fil
that didn't have an e next), and then provided a list of possibilities with the second Tab.

Here's an example of the context-sensitive nature of the completion:

```
$ ls
file1  file2  file3  otherfile
$ ls file<tab><tab>
file1  file2  file3
$ ls file
```

Note that the tab autocomplete for file shows only those files in the directory beginning with
the string file. In this case, bash completed file as a filename in the working directory, not
as a command.

> **TIP** $? holds the exit status of the most recent command executed. Print it with the echo
> command:

```
$ date
Fri Jul 18 15:22:23 MDT 2008
$ echo $?
0
$ ls nothere
```

```
nothere: No such file or directory
$ echo $?
2
```

Shell History

bash keeps a history of all the commands you execute. Unlike some other shells, this history is kept on a per-user basis, not on a per-session basis. This means that the history is persistent between login sessions, and represents an aggregation of the commands executed from all your login sessions. Type the history command to see the complete history of commands:

```
$ history
    1  ls
    2  ls -a
    3  pwd
    4  whoami
    5  touch testfile
    6  which gcc
    7  which cc
    8  rm testfile
    9  history
```

Give history an integer argument to see only that number of previous commands:

```
$ history 2
   12  date
   13  history 2
```

To execute a command in the history, use !<command number>. To execute the previous command, use the !! shortcut:

```
$ !4
whoami
test
$ date
Fri Jul 18 15:03:58 MDT 2008
$ !!
date
Fri Jul 18 15:03:59 MDT 2008
```

> **TIP** Rather than use the history command to generate a list of commands, use the up arrow on your keyboard to iterate backward through the command history. Once you've moved backward into the history, you can use the down arrow to iterate forward. After you find a command with the arrows, you can edit it and execute it. You can also use Ctrl+R to search (backward) through the history.

The history is stored in the .bash_history file in your home directory. The number of commands saved in the history is controlled by the HISTSIZE environment variable, with 500 as the default. See the next section for details on environment variables.

Environment variables

Like most shells, bash stores some information in special variables known to the shell called *environment variables*. You can view a complete list of the currently defined environment variables with declare:

```
$ declare
BASH=/usr/bin/bash
BASH_ARGC=()
BASH_ARGV=()
BASH_LINENO=()
BASH_SOURCE=()
BASH_VERSINFO=([0]=''3'' [1]=''2'' [2]=''25'' [3]=''1''
[4]=''release'' [5]=''i386-pc-solaris2.11'')
BASH_VERSION='3.2.25(1)-release'
COLUMNS=80
    ...
```

You can print the values of the environment variables using the echo or printf commands, accessing the value of the variable by prefixing it with the usual $ character:

```
$ echo $SHELL
/bin/bash
$ printf ''$PATH\n''
/usr/bin
```

Set the value of an environment variable with an assignment statement. The following example sets the shell history size to 1,000:

```
$ echo $HISTSIZE
500
$ HISTSIZE=1000
$ echo $HISTSIZE
1000
```

CAUTION Environment variable values are not persistent between sessions. To set up your environment consistently between login sessions, add your changes to the .bashrc file. See the section on Customizing Bash with .bashrc later in this chapter.

You can create your own environment variables by setting them to a value:

```
$ MYVAR=test
$ echo $MYVAR
test
```

Usually when you set an environment variable you also want to export it to make it available to child shells and processes:

```
$ export MYVAR
```

You can capture the output from a command in an environment variable using back-ticks:

```
$ TIME=`date`
$ echo $TIME
Fri Jul 18 16:24:31 MDT 2008
```

Command paths

Other than the built-in shell commands such as `declare` and `set`, all the commands you execute are located in various directories on your system. Table 3-2 lists the principal directories containing commands.

`/bin` is a symbolic link to `/usr/bin`, but `/sbin` is an independent directory from `/usr/sbin`.

You can execute commands by providing an absolute path or a relative path. With an absolute path, the shell looks for the command in the given path. With a relative path, bash tries to find it in one of the directories specified in your PATH environment variable. The PATH is a colon-separated list of directories in the order they should be searched. The first match is the one that is executed.

Use the `which` command to see which version of a command you are executing based on your path:

```
$ which grep
/usr/gnu/bin/grep
$ which xterm
/usr/X11/bin/xterm
$ which which
/usr/bin/which
```

The user created by the installer is set up with the following path:

```
$ echo $PATH
/usr/gnu/bin:/usr/bin:/usr/X11/bin:/usr/sbin:/sbin
```

Note that `/usr/gnu/bin` is first. If there are two versions of a command, one in `/usr/gnu/bin` and one in `/usr/bin`, the GNU version is executed by default.

The working directory (.) is not in the path for security purposes. If it were, an attacker could place a malicious program with the same name as a standard command somewhere in a writable directory such as `/tmp`. If you happened to be in the `/tmp` directory and you tried to execute the command, you would actually execute the malicious program. To execute something in your working directory, you must specify it explicitly with `./`. Therefore, using absolute paths to commands is generally safer because you know exactly which version of a command you're executing. Administrators should generally use absolute paths, although for brevity this book uses mostly relative paths. See Chapter 11 for more security topics.

TABLE 3-2

OpenSolaris Command Directories

Directory	Description
/usr/bin	The default directory for commands; contains utilities such as grep and tr, applications such as firefox and thunderbird, shells such as bash and zsh, and myriad other commands
/usr/ccs/bin	Traditionally System V development tools, but these have mostly moved to /usr/bin
/usr/gnu/bin	The GNU versions of commands; slightly different versions of many of them are also found in /usr/bin
/usr/sbin	The system tools, commands, and daemons, such as zfs, dumpadm, in.routed, and others. These are generally privileged commands.
/usr/sfw/bin	Traditionally the Sun Freeware (mostly GNU) tools, but almost all of these have been moved to /usr/bin, with symlinks left here; or symlinks have been added to /usr/bin
/usr/ucb	Traditionally the BSD tools, but these have been moved to /usr/bin, with only a few symlinks left here
/usr/X11/bin	X11 commands, such as xterm, xhost, and others
/usr/openwin/bin; /usr/X/bin; /usr/X11R6/bin	Aliases for /usr/X11/bin
/usr/xpg4/bin	Versions of some of the tools that adhere to the POSIX standard, where the versions in /usr/bin don't
/bin	Alias for /usr/bin
/sbin	System tools and utilities required for booting and possibly recovering the system if /usr is not mounted. These are generally privileged commands.

To change your path, set the PATH environment variable. If you just want to add a directory to the path, be sure to include the old version of the PATH on the right-hand side of the assignment. For example, use the following to add the Sun Studio Express directory to the end of your path:

```
$ PATH=$PATH:/opt/SunStudioExpress/bin
$ echo $PATH
/usr/gnu/bin:/usr/bin:/usr/X11/bin:/usr/sbin:/sbin:/opt/SunStudioExpress/bin
```

As mentioned earlier, however, setting an environment variable in this manner is not persistent across sessions. To set your PATH persistently, set it in .bashrc, discussed later in this chapter.

CROSS-REF Sun Studio Express and other development tools are covered in detail in Chapter 24.

The MANPATH environment variable works similarly to the PATH, specifying where the man command should look for manual pages. The MANPATH in the user created by the installer is as follows:

```
$ echo $MANPATH
/usr/gnu/share/man:/usr/share/man:/usr/X11/share/man
```

You can set the MANPATH in .bashrc as well, but OpenSolaris now contains an enhancement to the man command that enables it to find man pages based on the PATH, without an explicit MANPATH.

TIP The man pages for many of the common commands are not included in the OpenSolaris distribution for legal reasons, but you can find them online at http://docs.sun.com/app/docs/coll/40.17.

Managing files

As on most UNIX-like systems, each user on OpenSolaris has a home directory. Your home directory path is stored in the HOME environment variable. You can also use the tilde character (~) to navigate to your home directory or to another user's home directory. The tilde alone implies the current user's home directory. The following code shows how to navigate to home directories:

```
$ cd ~
$ pwd
/export/home/nsolter
$ cd ~test
$ pwd
/export/home/test
```

This example also demonstrates that the pwd command shows your current working directory.

As usual, you can use regular expressions when referring to files on the file system. For example, to list all the files in the current directory starting with file, use the following:

```
$ ls file*
file1   file2   file3
```

Files on OpenSolaris have an owner, a group, and traditional UNIX permissions associated with them.

NOTE The concepts of users and groups are discussed later in the section "System Administration."

Each file can be assigned an owner and a group, and read, write, and execute permissions on the basis of owner, group, and all. Use `ls -l` to see the permissions:

```
$ ls -l file1
-rw-r--r-- 1 nsolter staff 0 2008-07-17 14:43 file1
```

This output shows that the file owner is `nsolter` and the file group is `staff`. The 10-character string on the far left shows the permissions. From left to right, the first character indicates whether the file is special in any way, such as a directory or link. The - means it's a regular file. The next three characters are the read, write, and execute permissions for owner. The three following characters are the three permissions for group, and the final three are the permissions for all users. A - means the permission is not granted. In this case, you can see that the owner is granted read and write access on `file1`, group and all are granted read access, and no one is granted execute permissions. Note that execute permissions for a directory actually means list permissions.

You can change the owner and group of a file with the `chown` command, although by default users lack the `file_chown_self` privilege that allows you to change the ownership. Thus, the following example is run as the root role (see the section "Running privileged commands" later in this chapter for details):

```
# chown test:mygroup file1
# ls -l file1
-rw-r--r-- 1 test mygroup 0 2008-07-17 14:43 file1
```

You can change permissions on a file with the `chmod` command. Although `chmod` can take a symbolic permissions argument, it's typically used with an octal (or base eight) representation of the permissions. To understand what that means, consider each permission flag as a single bit, either on or off. The combined read, write, and execute permissions for each of user, group, or all are thus composed of three bits. Three bits in binary can represent the decimal numbers 0 through 7, which can be represented by a single octal digit. The permissions are always represented, left to right, as read, write, and execute, in that order. Considering execute the least significant bit, you can translate any configuration of these three permissions to a single octal digit according to Table 3-3.

Each octal number represents the permissions for one of user, group, or all. The `chmod` command sets the permissions for all three at once, with three octal numbers representing, from left to right, user, group, and all. For example, to set the permissions of `file2` to read, write, and execute for owner, to read and execute for group, and to just read for all, use the following command:

```
$ chmod 754 file2
$ ls -l file2
-rwxr-xr-- 1 nsolter staff 0 2008-07-17 15:10 file2
```

When you create a new file or directory, the permissions are 666 (read and write) for a file and 777 (all permissions) for a directory, minus the permissions specified in your *user file creation mode mask* ("umask" for short). You can view your umask value by running the umask command:

```
$ umask
0022
```

TABLE 3-3

OpenSolaris File Permissions

Permissions	Binary	Octal
- - -	000	0
- - x	001	1
- w -	010	2
- wx	011	3
r - -	100	4
r - x	101	5
rw -	110	6
rwx	111	7

A umask value of 0022 specifies write permissions for both group and all. Recall that the umask permissions are subtracted from the full permissions, so with a umask of 0022, when you create a file it will have read/write permissions for owner, and read-only permissions for group and all. For example, you can create a file called umasktest and examine its permissions:

```
$ touch umasktest
$ ls -l umasktest
-rw-r--r-- 1 nsolter staff 0 2008-07-20 13:01 umasktest
```

You can set the umask value for the current shell with the umask command:

```
umask 022
```

To set it persistently, add it to your .bashrc file (described later).

CROSS-REF OpenSolaris also supports finer-grained access control lists (ACLs) on files. Consult Chapter 11 for details.

Redirection

As with most shells, bash supports redirection of command input and output and piping of command output with the usual symbols:

- command > file directs the standard output of the command to a file, overwriting the contents of the file if it exists.
- command >> file directs the standard output of the command to a file, appending the contents to the file.
- file < command gives the contents of file to command as standard input.
- command1 | command2 gives the standard output of command1 to command2 as its standard input.

Here are some examples of command redirection and piping:

```
$ date > test.out
$ cat test.out
Fri Jul 18 16:43:26 MDT 2008
$ date >> test.out
$ cat test.out
Fri Jul 18 16:43:26 MDT 2008
Fri Jul 18 16:43:36 MDT 2008
$ ls -l | wc -l
      5
```

> **TIP** The > symbol redirects only standard output, not standard error. As shown in the following example, you can redirect standard error with 2>, because standard error is always represented by file descriptor 2.

```
$ ls notfound > test.out
notfound: No such file or directory
$ ls notfound > test2.out 2> test2.out
$ cat test2.out
notfound: No such file or directory
```

Job control

The bash shell provides job control functionality similar to the C Shell. To run a job in the background, add an ampersand (&) to the end of the line:

```
$ ./long-running &
[1] 1018
```

The [1] means that this is job number 1 in your shell. If you start another job, it receives a different number:

```
$ ./myjob &
[2] 1021
```

You can list all the current jobs with the jobs command:

```
$ jobs
[1]-  Running                ./long-running &
[2]+  Running                ./myjob &
```

To bring a job to the foreground, use fg. To suspend the running foreground job, press Ctrl+Z. To put a suspended job in the background, use bg:

```
$ fg %1
./long-running
^Z
[1]+  Stopped              ./long-running
$ bg %1
[1]+ ./long-running &
```

The fg and bg commands without arguments apply to the job most recently acted on, denoted with a + next to it in the output from jobs.

Customizing Bash

You can customize your bash shell persistently by adding configuration settings to the .bashrc file in your home directory. The initial user created by the installer has a .bashrc that sets the PATH, MANPATH, and command prompt, which are the three most typical things to set in a .bashrc. PATH and MANPATH were discussed earlier in the section "Command Paths." Here's what the settings look like in the .bashrc:

```
export PATH=/usr/gnu/bin:/usr/bin:/usr/X11/bin:/usr/sbin:/sbin
export MANPATH=/usr/gnu/share/man:/usr/share/man:/usr/X11/share/man
```

To set the command prompt, set the PS1 environment variable. You can use whatever text you want, plus some special character macros that expand to specific values depending on context. Table 3-4 lists a few of these macros. For a complete list, see http://faqs.org/docs/bashman/bashref_74.html#SEC81.

For example, to set your prompt to username:working directory $, you could use the following:

```
PS1='\u:\W\$ '
```

Now your prompt might look like this if you're in your home directory:

```
nsolter:~$
```

TABLE 3-4

Bash Command Prompt Macros

Macro	Meaning
\d	Current date
\h	Hostname
\t or \T	Time in 24-hour or 12-hour format
\u	Username
\w	Current working directory
\W	Base name of the working directory
\$	$, unless effective ID is 0 (root), in which case #

CAUTION The .bashrc file is not executed for all login shells, specifically not for remote sessions. If you want to execute it in all cases, create a .bash_profile in your home directory that looks like this:

```
if [ -f ~/.bashrc ]; then
. ~/.bashrc
fi
```

You can, of course, add configurations other than these three to .bashrc, such as setting a CLASSPATH environment variable for Java programming.

NOTE The /etc/profile file is executed for all users for each new shell before the .bash_profile and .bashrc. Among other things, /etc/profile sets a default umask for all users.

Text editors

OpenSolaris includes the vim text editor, which is an improved version of the original vi text editor. You can use vim directly, or run vi, which launches vim in vi-compatibility mode.

In addition to vim, OpenSolaris includes the standard utilities cat, more, and less for quickly viewing file contents. Consult their man pages, all in section 1, for details.

TIP If you're an emacs fan, you can install it from the package repository. Install the SUNWgnu-emacs-gtk package for the graphical version or SUNWgnu-emacs-nox for the basic tty text-based version. See the section "Adding Software" later in this chapter for details on installing additional software from the package repository.

The remainder of this section focuses on vim.

If you're a regular UNIX or Linux user, it's pretty hard to avoid using vi or vim at least once in a while, so you're probably already familiar with at least its basic functionality. However, if you're coming from a different computing environment or if, like one of the authors, you stubbornly use emacs whenever possible, you might not be completely comfortable with vi and vim. Thus, this section provides a basic tutorial on the vim editor. Most of the commands, with the exception of the visual mode, apply to vi as well.

NOTE   This tutorial on vim is not comprehensive. A good cheat sheet can be found at http://fprintf.net/vimCheatSheet.html.

You can launch vim with one or more filenames:

```
$ vim vimtest
```

You'll then see something like this:

```
~
~
~
~
~
~
```

The tildes represent lines in the file that do not yet exist.

TIP   If vim displays errors about "terminal entries" or "terminal capabilities," your TERM environment variable is probably set incorrectly. If you don't know your terminal type, setting TERM to vt100 is usually a safe bet. See the terminfo(4) man page for all the gory details.

The first point to understand about vim is that it is a modal editor. When editing a file, you are always in one of command, insert, or visual mode. You start in command mode, from which you can execute various commands such as searching, cutting and pasting, saving, and quitting. To enter insert mode, use i, a, or another similar command, after which anything you type will be inserted into the file. To return to command mode press the Esc key. Esc is the only command that works in insert mode.

Similarly, to enter visual mode, use the v command. In visual mode you can select text to cut or copy. Return to command mode with the Esc key.

General commands

Table 3-5 lists some of the commands for working with files in vim.

TABLE 3-5

vim General Commands

Command	Description
:w	Saves file. Use :w! to override read-only settings, if you have appropriate permissions.
:q	Quits the editor. Use :q! to exit without saving changes to the file.
ZZ	Saves changes and exits
u	Undoes the previous action
Esc	Enters command mode
Ctrl+G	Displays the filename, modification status, and current line number

Inserting text

As mentioned earlier, you insert text primarily in input mode. There are a few different ways to enter input mode, as described in Table 3-6. You can also search and replace text.

Navigating and searching

In command mode you can quickly get where you want in a file. vim's navigation commands are described in Table 3-7.

Cutting and pasting

vim, of course, provides mechanisms for cutting and pasting text. Table 3-8 describes the commands.

Repeating commands

The vim editor allows most commands to be preceded with a number. The command is then repeated that number of times. For example, to delete the next 10 lines, enter 10dd.

Running privileged commands

Traditionally, UNIX has two access control levels: regular users and the privileged user, also called *superuser*, with login name root. The root user is always assigned user ID 0, and can do essentially anything he or she wants. Regular users are restricted from performing system and administrative actions.

If you're coming from the Linux world you might be familiar with sudo, which allows regular users with appropriate privileges to access privileged commands. OpenSolaris has a similar model, implemented with Role-Based Access Control (RBAC).

TABLE 3-6

vim Insertion Commands

Command	Description
i	Inserts text starting to the left of the cursor. Enters insert mode.
a	Inserts text starting to the right of the cursor. Enters insert mode.
o	Inserts a newline below the cursor and inserts text starting in that newline. Enters insert mode.
O	Inserts a newline above the cursor and inserts text starting in that newline. Enters insert mode.
r	Replaces the current character with the next character typed
R	Enters input mode, but overwrites characters instead of inserting
:g/string/s//newstring/g	Replaces every occurrence of string in the file with newstring. Without the trailing g, substitutes only the first occurrence on each line. Without the s in the middle, replaces string only on the current line.

TABLE 3-7

vim Navigation Commands

Command	Description
Arrow Keys	Moves the cursor around the file one character/line at a time
^	Moves the cursor to the beginning of the current line
$	Moves the cursor to the end of the current line
Ctrl+D, Ctrl+U	Moves down and up in the file, one-half page at a time
/string	Searches forward for the occurrence of the string. Enter to search again. You may use regular expressions in the string.
?string	Searches backward for the string
nG	Jumps to line number n in the file. G alone jumps to the last line in the file.

NOTE If you prefer sudo, you can install it from the network package repository. See the "Adding Software" section later in this chapter for details on the network package repository, and Chapter 11 for more information on sudo.

TABLE 3-8

vim Cutting and Pasting Commands

Command	Description
x	Deletes the current character
dd	Deletes the entire line
v	Enters visual mode to select text by moving the cursor
y	Copies ("yanks") text selected in visual mode
d	Deletes (cuts) text selected in visual mode
p	Pastes text most recently deleted or copied
Esc	Exits visual mode (returns to command mode)

If you created a user during OpenSolaris installation, the installer configured your system such that root is a role instead of a regular user. The implication of that change is that you can no longer log in as root. Instead, if you really want the power of root, you can assume the root role by first logging in as a user who has been assigned that role and then su-ing to root. To check whether your user has been assigned the root role, use the roles command:

```
$ roles
root
$ su
Password:
#
```

However, there's an easier and safer way to administer the system. The user created by the installer is assigned the Primary Administrator profile, which means that she can perform most administrative actions. The trick is that she can't execute them directly. Like on Linux with sudo, you must explicitly indicate that you want to execute a privileged command by prefixing the command with pfexec. If you forget the pfexec, you'll be warned that the operation is privileged. Here's an example:

```
$ usermod -s /usr/bin/bash test
UX: usermod: ERROR: Permission denied.
$ pfexec usermod -s /usr/bin/bash test
$
```

To check your profiles, use the profiles command.

NOTE To avoid showing pfexec repeatedly, the examples in the rest of this book run privileged commands from a root shell. In those examples, the prompt is shown as the pound sign (#) instead of the usual dollar sign ($). Generally, however, avoid adopting the root role if possible because it can lead to accidentally doing something harmful to the system.

If you didn't create a user in the installer, then root is not a role, and no user is assigned the Primary Administrator profile. Thus, you'll need to explicitly log in as root, or su to root, to administer the system.

CROSS-REF Chapter 11 covers RBAC, pfexec, and other security features of OpenSolaris in much more detail.

Switching Languages and Locales

Although most of the examples in this book show OpenSolaris using American English and the American formats for dates and such, OpenSolaris includes comprehensive internationalization support. If you live in a region other than the United States or natively speak a language other than American English, you might be more comfortable working in a different *locale*. The locale is more than just the language. It also includes the formats for date and time, monetary conventions, decimal formatting style, and other location-specific items.

There are a few different ways to switch locales in OpenSolaris. First, as shown in Chapter 2, you select the default language and locale during installation. After installation, you can select a locale for each GNOME session, set the locale for each terminal session, or change the default system locale.

Changing locale in GNOME

You can select a different language before logging in to GNOME. On the login screen, click the Options button on the lower left, and then click Select Language from the pop-up menu. Select the language you want and click the Change Language button (see Figure 3-4).

The first time you select a different language, you're asked if you want to restart the login screen with the chosen language. Subsequent changes automatically restart the login screen. You then see the login screen in the new language. Figure 3-5 shows the screen in Simplified Chinese.

When you log in, you're asked (in the new language) if you want to make this language setting your default. Select this option if you do indeed want this language to be that user's default.

CAUTION Selecting the language as your default sets it for that user only. Logging in as a different user uses the system default language, so the login screen always starts in the system default language. Also, setting the per-user default language this way applies only to GNOME. If that same user logs in via ssh or another text-based mechanism, she will use the system default language.

You'll also be asked if you want to change the names of the standard folders in your home directory to use the new language.

FIGURE 3-4

GNOME lets you select a language from the login screen.

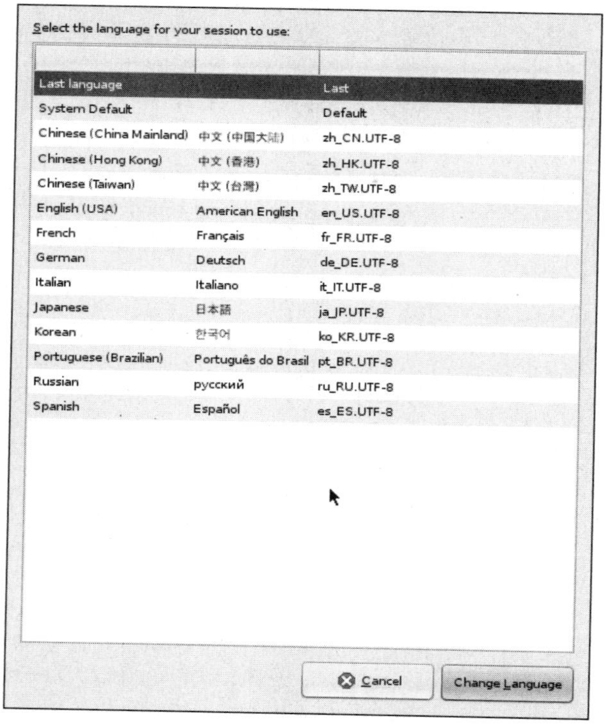

Select the language for your session to use:

Last language		Last
System Default		Default
Chinese (China Mainland)	中文 (中国大陆)	zh_CN.UTF-8
Chinese (Hong Kong)	中文 (香港)	zh_HK.UTF-8
Chinese (Taiwan)	中文 (台灣)	zh_TW.UTF-8
English (USA)	American English	en_US.UTF-8
French	Français	fr_FR.UTF-8
German	Deutsch	de_DE.UTF-8
Italian	Italiano	it_IT.UTF-8
Japanese	日本語	ja_JP.UTF-8
Korean	한국어	ko_KR.UTF-8
Portuguese (Brazilian)	Português do Brasil	pt_BR.UTF-8
Russian	русский	ru_RU.UTF-8
Spanish	Español	es_ES.UTF-8

❌ Cancel   Change Language

FIGURE 3-5

The GNOME login screen in simplified Chinese.

Changing locale in a terminal session

The locale in each terminal session is controlled by several environment variables, which are listed in Table 3-9.

TABLE 3-9

Locale Environment Variables

Environment Variable	Description
LANG	General language specification; when in doubt, set this one
LC_ALL	Language setting; overrides LANG and other LC_ variables
LC_COLLATE	Specifies the character collation sequence
LC_CTYPE	Specifies character width and other character settings
LC_MESSAGES	Specifies the message database to use
LC_MONETARY	Specifies symbols and formats related to money
LC_NUMERIC	Specifies the delimiter for decimals and thousands
LC_TIME	Specifies date and time formats

Each of these variables can be set to a language specification. For example, the language specification for German looks like de_DE.UTF-8. You can see all the locales available on your system by looking in /usr/lib/locale:

```
$ ls /usr/lib/locale
C             en_GB.UTF-8  es_CR.UTF-8  es_SV.UTF-8  fr.UTF-8     ru_RU.UTF-8
common        en_IE.UTF-8  es_EC.UTF-8  es_UY.UTF-8  iso_8859_1   ru.UTF-8
de_AT.UTF-8   en_MT.UTF-8  es_ES.UTF-8  es_VE.UTF-8  it_IT.UTF-8  sk_SK.UTF-8
de_CH.UTF-8   en_NZ.UTF-8  es_GT.UTF-8  es.UTF-8     it.UTF-8     sv_SE.UTF-8
de_DE.UTF-8   en_US.UTF-8  es_MX.UTF-8  fr_BE.UTF-8  ja_JP.UTF-8  sv.UTF-8
de_LU.UTF-8   es_AR.UTF-8  es_NI.UTF-8  fr_CA.UTF-8  ko_KR.UTF-8  zh_CN.UTF-8
de.UTF-8      es_BO.UTF-8  es_PA.UTF-8  fr_CH.UTF-8  ko.UTF-8     zh_HK.UTF-8
en_AU.UTF-8   es_CL.UTF-8  es_PE.UTF-8  fr_FR.UTF-8  POSIX        zh_TW.UTF-8
en_CA.UTF-8   es_CO.UTF-8  es_PY.UTF-8  fr_LU.UTF-8  pt_BR.UTF-8  zh.UTF-8
```

Each directory name listed is a valid setting for the environment variables listed in Table 3-9.

You can use the locale command to check your current locale:

```
$ locale
LANG=en_US.UTF-8
LC_CTYPE=''en_US.UTF-8''
LC_NUMERIC=''en_US.UTF-8''
```

```
LC_TIME=''en_US.UTF-8''
LC_COLLATE=''en_US.UTF-8''
LC_MONETARY=''en_US.UTF-8''
LC_MESSAGES=''en_US.UTF-8''
LC_ALL=
```

To set the overall locale, change the LANG variable. The following example shows the changed output of the date command after changing locale:

```
$ date
Tue Jul 29 13:11:10 MDT 2008
$ LANG=fr_CH.UTF-8
$ date
mardi, 29 juillet 2008 13.12:02h MDT
```

You can, of course, set any of the LC_ variables individually to different language settings if you want, but it's usually best to set just LANG.

TIP   Setting LANG or another environment variable at the command line is not persistent across login sessions. To set your locale persistently, set the environment variable in your .bashrc file.

Changing the default system locale

You can set the default system locale, which then applies to both GNOME sessions and terminal sessions, unless the user explicitly sets a different locale. The system locale is set in the /etc/default/init file. That file sets the LANG environment variable to the locale you specified in the installer. Simply change the LANG variable to the locale you want as the new default. For example, to set the default system locale to German, set LANG in /etc/default/init as follows:

```
LANG=de_DE.UTF-8
```

NOTE   You must reboot the system in order for the LANG setting in /etc/default/init to take effect.

Changing keyboard layout and input languages

The default keyboard layout is based on the default system locale that you selected during installation. However, if you write in more than one language, it's useful to be able to switch between different input languages. To configure this feature, first select System ➤ Preferences ➤ Input Methods. On the dialog's General tab, make sure that Use Input Method Switcher Application is selected as the Input Method Status and switcher placement. Also, under the Languages/Scripts tab, add all languages you plan to use from the Available Languages/Scripts to the right-hand Languages/Scripts to Input.

Once you've set up your preferences, you can switch your keyboard layout/input language at any time by selecting the desired language in the language switcher, which shows up on the right side of the top panel, directly to the left of the power monitor.

Installing additional languages

If your preferred locale isn't one of the default languages installed, you can install additional languages from the `pkg.opensolaris.org` package repository by following the instructions in "Adding Software" later in this chapter. The easiest way to install a language is to install the package named `SUNWlang-<language>`. For example, Polish language support package is `SUNWlang-pl`.

Getting Online

Unless you're planning on traveling back in time a few decades, you probably want to connect your OpenSolaris box to some sort of network. OpenSolaris includes the Network AutoMagic (NWAM) service to configure your computer's network interfaces automatically, but if you want more control, you can configure your network connections manually.

Network AutoMagic

NWAM starts automatically when your system boots and attempts to connect your computer to a network using DHCP.

CROSS-REF If you're new to UNIX networking, see Chapter 9 for details about network interfaces, DHCP, NWAM, and other networking topics.

NWAM attempts wired connections first, if available. If it connects successfully, it provides a notification telling you the name of the interface configured and the IP address obtained from the DHCP server. There's nothing you need to do to connect to a wired network that supports DHCP; NWAM takes care of everything automatically.

NOTE NWAM often connects to the network before you've logged in to the GNOME desktop, so you usually won't see this notification.

If no wired interface is available and your computer has a wireless network interface, it attempts to connect to a wireless network. In that case, NWAM presents a list of detected wireless networks and you can select the one to which you want to connect, entering the security key if required.

Manual network configuration

Although NWAM is quite convenient for getting your system online quickly and without complicated configuration, the service is somewhat limited in its capabilities. For example, you can't easily configure static IP addresses. Thus, for advanced administration, you need to use manual methods to configure your networking. To switch to manual configuration, select System ➤ Administration ➤ Network. A pop-up window will inform you that the system is currently configured to manage the network automatically. Click the Manual button to change the configuration. A Network Settings dialog similar to the one shown in Figure 3-6 will appear.

FIGURE 3-6

Use the networking configuration GUI to configure your interfaces manually.

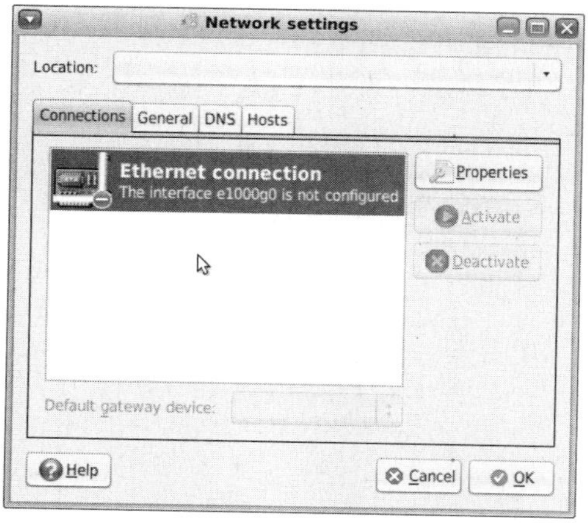

CROSS-REF This section covers the OpenSolaris networking GUI. For details on the commands and configuration files, see Chapter 9.

By default, none of the interfaces are active. To activate an interface, select it in the box and then click the Properties button on the right. The dialog shown in Figure 3-7 will appear.

Check Enable This Connection; and if you want the connection to be persistent, check Activate on Boot. Then, in the Connection Settings section, choose either DHCP or Static IP address for the configuration. If you select Static IP, fill in the IP address and the Gateway address, which is usually the address of the external-facing router on your LAN. The subnet mask should be filled in automatically. If this is a wireless interface, fill in the Wireless settings information as well. Finally, click OK. Your network connection should now be configured.

Depending on the information — if any — that OpenSolaris was able to obtain from the DHCP server on your network, you may need to fill in other networking information. You specify the hostname and domain name on the General tab, and Domain Name Servers on the DNS tab. On the Hosts tab, you fill in hostname/IP address mappings for files-based resolution. Consult your network administrator or Internet service provider (ISP) for the domain and DNS settings. You generally shouldn't need to modify the hostname and files-based host mappings.

CROSS-REF Chapter 9 explains DNS and the uses of the other settings mentioned here.

If you ever want to switch back to NWAM, you can select System ➤ Administration ➤ Network again. The dialog that appears will give you the option to switch back to automatic network configuration. Alternatively, you can run the following two commands:

```
# svcadm disable network/physical:default
# svcadm enable network/physical:nwam
```

FIGURE 3-7

Activate an interface via the Interface Properties dialog.

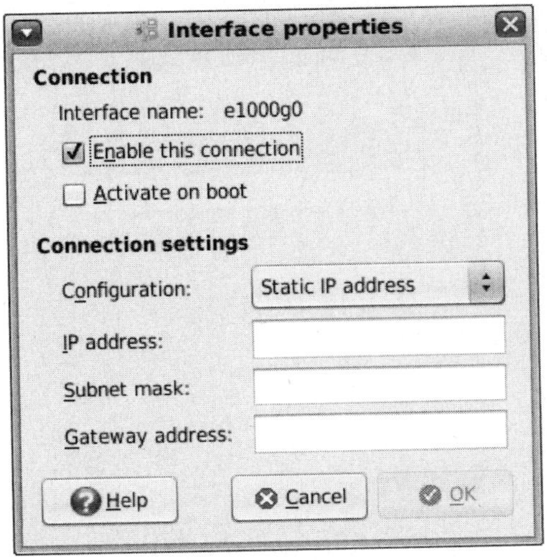

Troubleshooting network connections

To determine whether your network connection is working, open a Firefox browser and try to connect to your favorite web page. If it's not working, and you're using NWAM, try restarting the NWAM service:

```
# svcadm restart nwam
```

This action should force NWAM to try to disconnect from and reconnect to the network. Give it a few minutes, especially if connecting over a wireless network.

If the network connection still isn't working, run ifconfig -a to determine whether your interface has an assigned IP address:

```
# ifconfig -a
...
pcn0: flags=201004843<UP,BROADCAST,RUNNING,MULTICAST,DHCP,IPv4,CoS>
mtu 1500 index 4
        inet 192.168.1.101 netmask ffffff00 broadcast 192.168.1.255
        ether 0:c:29:a2:4:9
...
```

If no IP address is shown for your interface in the inet field, give NWAM a bit more time to work. If nothing happens after restarting NWAM, switch to manual networking, as previously described.

If ifconfig shows an IP address but the connection still isn't working, you'll need to use some of the more sophisticated debugging techniques discussed in Chapter 9.

If your network interface isn't shown, OpenSolaris might not have drivers for it. To check, run the driver detection tool by selecting Applications ➤ System Tools ➤ Device Driver Utility. This tool quickly tells you whether you have the drivers for your particular network interface cards.

CROSS-REF   Chapter 5 explains where you might find missing drivers for your network interfaces.

Adding Software

The OpenSolaris distribution included on the LiveCD provides a comfortable desktop environment, but because of space limitations necessarily omits a multitude of useful software. However, the new OpenSolaris Image Packaging System (IPS) enables you to install additional applications from the OpenSolaris network package repositories quite easily.

As mentioned in Chapter 2, OpenSolaris has replaced the old System V packaging with IPS. The new packaging system is based on the concept of a network package repository. If you're familiar with APT or Yum from the Linux world, you should feel right at home with IPS. As with other network-based packaging systems, in IPS the packages are served from various network repositories. Instead of downloading software in gzip format or the like, unpacking it, and installing it, installing from IPS is a simple one-step process. You interact with IPS by using the new pkg command.

Finding and installing software

Before searching for or installing software, always refresh your local copy of the software catalog from the repository first:

```
# pkg refresh
```

Next, you can search for software you want using pkg search. This command enables you to search for the names of packages containing specific binaries or files, so you must know the name of at least one of the files in the package if you want to find it.

By default, pkg search searches only the software installed on your system. To search the network repositories, use pkg search -r.

For example, to find OpenOffice.org, you can search for the file named openoffice:

```
# pkg search -r openoffice
INDEX      ACTION    VALUE                        PACKAGE
basename   dir       opt/openoffice.org/share/registry/res/en-US/org/openoffice
  pkg:/openoffice@0.5.11-0.79
basename   dir       opt/openoffice.org2.4/share/registry/modules/org/openoffice
  pkg:/openoffice@2.4.0-0.86
```

```
basename   dir       opt/openoffice.org2.4/share/registry/modules/org/openoffice
pkg:/openoffice@2.4.0-0.86
...
```

These results from `pkg search` are somewhat confusing because there appears to be more than one package containing OpenOffice.org, such as `pkg:/openoffice@0.5.11-0.79` and `pkg:/openoffice@2.4.0-0.86`. However, the different packages are actually just different versions of the same package. Everything after the @ in the package name represents the version. When you want to install the package, you usually don't need to worry about the version. IPS automatically uses the version that matches the rest of your system. Just reference the part of the package name before the @. You can omit the `pkg:/` as well.

CROSS-REF IPS package versioning is discussed in Chapter 6.

To ensure that the `openoffice` package is the one you want, use `pkg info`. Like `pkg search`, `pkg info` takes a `-r` option to indicate that you want the information from the repository:

```
# pkg info -r openoffice
          Name: openoffice
       Summary: OpenOffice.org 2.4
         State: Not installed
     Authority: opensolaris.org (preferred)
       Version: 2.4.0
 Build Release: 5.11
        Branch: 0.86
Packaging Date: Wed Jul  9 08:35:00 2008
          Size: 420.6 MB
          FMRI: pkg:/openoffice@2.4.0,5.11-0.86:20080709T083500Z
```

The `Name` field in the `pkg info` output is the package name, not the filename that you searched for with `pkg search`. In this example, the package name and the filename are identical, but that's not always the case.

When you're sure you have the package you want, you can install it with `pkg install`:

```
# pkg install openoffice
DOWNLOAD              PKGS        FILES      XFER (MB)
Completed             1/1     4220/4220  420.64/420.64

PHASE                         ACTIONS
Install Phase               4798/4798
PHASE                           ITEMS
Reading Existing Index            9/9
Indexing Packages                 1/1
```

To uninstall software, use `pkg uninstall`:

```
# pkg uninstall openoffice
PHASE                         ACTIONS
```

```
Removal Phase                           5290/5290
PHASE                                        ITEMS
Reading Existing Index                        9/9
Indexing Packages                             1/1
```

Alternative repositories

IPS enables you to specify the package *authority* from which you want to install software. The default authority is opensolaris.org, which is served by the repository at the URL http://pkg.opensolaris.org/release. You can list the authorities with pkg authority:

```
# pkg authority
AUTHORITY                      URL
opensolaris.org (preferred)    http://pkg.opensolaris.org/release/
```

Although pkg.opensolaris.org/release/ contains quite a bit of software, it doesn't have everything you might need or want. For example, as of this writing, it doesn't include the X Multimedia System (XMMS) media player. A few additional repositories with useful software include the following:

- Sunfreeware: http://pkg.sunfreeware.com:9000
- OpenSolaris development repository: http://pkg.opensolaris.org/dev
- OpenSolaris Contrib repository: http://pkg.opensolaris.org/contrib

NOTE Sun also provides additional repositories that include software that can't be included with pkg.opensolaris.org for legal reasons or that is available only to customers with support contracts. Consult opensolaris.com for current information on these options.

To add an authority, use pkg set-authority, specifying the URL of the repository and the authority name by which you want to refer to it. In addition, always run pkg refresh after adding an authority:

```
# pkg set-authority -O http://pkg.sunfreeware.com:9000 sunfreeware.com
# pkg refresh
# pkg authority
AUTHORITY                      URL
opensolaris.org (preferred)    http://pkg.opensolaris.org/release/
sunfreeware.com                http://pkg.sunfreeware.com:9000/
```

Now pkg search and pkg install will search and install from both repositories. You don't need to specify a specific authority to search or install from in each command. Here's an example:

```
# pkg search -r xmms
INDEX       ACTION     VALUE            PACKAGE
basename    file       opt/sfw/bin/xmms  pkg:/IPSFWxmms@0.5.11-5.7
```

After confirming with `pkg info` that IPSFWxmms is the package you want, you can install it:

```
# pkg info -r IPSFWxmms
            Name: IPSFWxmms
         Summary: xmms - X MultiMedia System
           State: Not installed
       Authority: sunfreeware.com
         Version: 0.5.11
   Build Release: 5.11
          Branch: 5.7
  Packaging Date: Wed May  7 04:13:32 2008
            Size: 5.1 MB
            FMRI: pkg://sunfreeware.com/IPSFWxmms@0.5.11,5.11-5.7:20080507T041332Z
# pkg install IPSFWxmms
PHASE                                   ITEMS
Indexing Packages                     579/579
DOWNLOAD                     PKGS         FILES      XFER (MB)
Completed                    2/2       135/135      6.30/6.30

PHASE                                 ACTIONS
Install Phase                         307/307
Reading Existing Index                    9/9
Indexing Packages                         2/2
```

> **TIP** As of this writing, the IPSFWxmms package is dependent on the SUNWGtk package but it doesn't declare that dependency. In order to use xmms, you also need to install the SUNWGtk package with the following command:

```
# pkg install SUNWGtk
DOWNLOAD                     PKGS        FILES       XFER (MB)
Completed                    2/2        50/50       0.63/0.63

PHASE                                 ACTIONS
Install Phase                         135/135
PHASE                                   ITEMS
Reading Existing Index                    9/9
Indexing Packages                         2/2
```

After installing both packages, xmms can be run from /opt/sfw/bin/xmms.

> **NOTE** In the rest of the book, the output from `pkg install` is generally omitted for brevity.

You can remove an authority with `pkg unset-authority`:

```
# pkg unset-authority sunfreeware.com
# pkg authority
```

```
AUTHORITY                          URL
opensolaris.org (preferred)        http://pkg.opensolaris.org/release
```

CROSS-REF The Image Packaging System and OpenSolaris software management are covered in detail in Chapter 6.

Developing on OpenSolaris

OpenSolaris provides a comprehensive development environment for anything from systems software to web applications, using languages from Java to Fortran to Python.

To get started with Java development, you need the JDK, available in the SUNWj6dev package:

```
# pkg install SUNWj6dev
```

To get started with C and C++ development, you want either the Sun Studio compiler collection or the GNU compiler collection (GCC). Install ss-dev to obtain the Sun Studio compiler collection:

```
# pkg install ss-dev
```

The Sun Studio compilers and tools are now available in /opt/SunStudioExpress/bin.

To obtain GCC, install the gcc-dev package:

```
# pkg install gcc-dev
```

The GNU compilers and tools are now available in /usr/bin.

To code using an integrated development environment (IDE), install NetBeans:

```
# pkg install netbeans
```

Launch it with /usr/netbeans/bin/netbeans, or select Applications ➤ Developer Tools ➤ NetBeans IDE.

CROSS-REF Chapter 24 describes Sun Studio, NetBeans, and the other development and debugging tools available on OpenSolaris for a variety of languages in much more detail.

Connecting Remotely

OpenSolaris employs a *secure-by-default* configuration, such that the only way to connect to the system remotely is with the Secure Shell (ssh).

TIP We recommend that you maintain the secure-by-default configuration and do not attempt to enable other network services, because they can expose your system to security threats.

From another OpenSolaris, UNIX/Linux-based system, or Mac OS X, you should be able to just type `ssh` at the terminal, providing a hostname or IP address. The first time you connect to a system, you'll see a warning about host authenticity, which you can safely ignore:

```
$ ssh 192.168.1.101
The authenticity of host '192.168.1.101 (192.168.1.101)' can't be established.
RSA key fingerprint is ac:36:67:dd:d0:7d:fe:76:c8:56:42:ff:db:df:ca:34.
Are you sure you want to continue connecting (yes/no)? yes
Warning: Permanently added '192.168.1.101' (RSA) to the list of known hosts.
Password:
Last login: Thu Jul 31 13:38:01 2008 from 192.168.1.105
Sun Microsystems Inc.   SunOS 5.11      snv_93  January 2008
$
```

To connect from Windows, you can download and install an open source `ssh` client, such as PuTTY, which is available from `http://chiark.greenend.org.uk/~sgtatham/putty`.

CROSS-REF Chapter 9 covers the various network services available, and Chapter 11 explains the secure-by-default settings and the `ssh` service in more detail.

System Administration

The material in this chapter so far has focused on the use, rather than the administration, of OpenSolaris. A crash course on the system, however, wouldn't be complete without a look at the system from an administration perspective. Although you can perform some administrative tasks using a GUI, to really understand the system, you need to get down-and-dirty with the command line. Thus, this section focuses on CLI administration.

System information

OpenSolaris provides some useful tools for discovering information about the hardware and software of your system. A good starting place is `uname -a`, which provides, in order, the operating system name, the hostname, the operating system release level, the operating system version, the machine hardware class, the processor type, and the platform name. Here is the `uname -a` output of OpenSolaris build 99 on a 32-bit Intel machine (OS0805 is the hostname):

```
$ uname -a
SunOS OS0805 5.11 snv_99 i86pc i386 i86pc Solaris
```

The operating system release and version information that `uname` provides is listed in the `/etc/release` file:

```
# cat /etc/release
              OpenSolaris 2008.11 snv_99 X86
    Copyright 2008 Sun Microsystems, Inc.  All Rights Reserved.
```

```
Use is subject to license terms.
Assembled 08 October 2008
```

TIP For an overview of your system's hardware and peripherals, run the Device Driver
utility (System ➤ Administration ➤ Device Driver Utility).

For more details on the hardware, use the `prtconf` command:

```
# prtconf
System Configuration: Sun Microsystems  i86pc
Memory size: 512 Megabytes
System Peripherals (Software Nodes):
 ...
```

The `isainfo` command prints further details about the instruction set architecture of the
system:

```
# isainfo -v
32-bit i386 applications
        ahf sse3 sse2 sse fxsr mmx cmov sep cx8 tsc fpu
```

For processor information, run `psrinfo`:

```
# psrinfo -pv
The physical processor has 1 virtual processor (0)
  x86 (GenuineIntel 6E8 family 6 model 14 step 8 clock 1600 MHz)
      Intel(r) CPU       T2050  @ 1.60GHz
```

The `prtdiag` command gives detailed information about hardware, including diagnostic information when appropriate.

For more detailed fault information, run `fmadm faulty`.

For live information about process resource usage, use `prstat`. This command gives you a continuously refreshing snapshot of system activity, as this example shows:

```
   PID USERNAME  SIZE   RSS STATE  PRI NICE      TIME  CPU PROCESS/NLWP
  1213 root     5684K 3104K cpu0    59    0   0:00:00 0.2% prstat/1
   690 root     9248K 4444K sleep   59    0   0:00:00 0.1% sshd/1
   641 nsolter   135M   24M sleep   59    0   0:00:06 0.0% gnome-panel/1
   676 nsolter    79M   18M sleep   59    0   0:00:03 0.0% clock-applet/1
   668 nsolter  7708K 4000K sleep   59    0   0:00:03 0.0% gvfs-trash/1
   644 nsolter   153M   39M sleep   49    0   0:00:07 0.0% nautilus/1
   692 nsolter  8648K 2348K sleep   59    0   0:00:01 0.0% sshd/1
  1036 nsolter   138M   23M sleep   59    0   0:00:06 0.0% users-admin/1
   223 root     7804K 3756K sleep   59    0   0:00:02 0.0% nscd/33
  1073 root     5532K 2564K sleep   59    0   0:00:00 0.0% bash/1
   424 root     5096K 1948K sleep   59    0   0:00:00 0.0% automountd/4
   543 root       53M   36M sleep   59    0   0:00:21 0.0% Xorg/1
```

```
 1196 root       9232K 4436K sleep   59    0   0:00:00 0.0% sshd/1
 1189 root       9232K 4440K sleep   59    0   0:00:00 0.0% sshd/1
  631 nsolter    9404K 5268K sleep   59    0   0:00:01 0.0% xscreensaver/1
 1198 newuser    8648K 2332K sleep   59    0   0:00:00 0.0% sshd/1
    9 root         12M   11M sleep   59    0   0:00:17 0.0% svc.configd/20
   92 root       4788K 1544K sleep   59    0   0:00:00 0.0% dhcpagent/1
  110 daemon     8880K 4456K sleep   59    0   0:00:00 0.0% kcfd/3
  368 daemon     2908K 1868K sleep   59    0   0:00:00 0.0% avahi-daemon-br/1
  570 root       5868K 2008K sleep   59    0   0:00:00 0.0% sendmail/1
Total: 77 processes, 213 lwps, load averages: 0.01, 0.02, 0.02
```

CROSS-REF Chapter 14 describes the tools for obtaining system information in more detail. Chapter 12 covers OpenSolaris fault management.

Processes and services

As with most operating systems, running programs in OpenSolaris are called *processes*. OpenSolaris also adds a higher-level abstraction called a *service*, which can be a collection of related processes. You'll generally manage your system at the service level, but sometimes you'll need to deal with the actual processes.

Processes

Each process is assigned a unique numeric ID, called the process ID (PID). You can view the currently running processes with the ps command. The e option tells ps to list all processes, not just the processes owned by the user executing ps, while the f option instructs ps to give the "full" listing, including the owner, parent PID, and start time:

```
# ps -ef
     UID   PID  PPID  C  STIME TTY      TIME CMD
    root     0     0  0 10:38:57 ?      0:01 sched
    root     1     0  0 10:38:58 ?      0:00 /sbin/init
    root     2     0  0 10:38:58 ?      0:00 pageout
    root     3     0  0 10:38:58 ?      0:03 fsflush
    root   403     1  0 10:39:41 ?      0:00 /usr/lib/inet/inetd start
    root     7     1  0 10:39:02 ?      0:04 /lib/svc/bin/svc.startd
    root     9     1  0 10:39:03 ?      0:12 /lib/svc/bin/svc.configd
    root   134     1  0 10:39:22 ?      0:00 /usr/lib/picl/picld
    root   488     1  0 10:39:44 ?      0:02 /usr/lib/fm/fmd/fmd
    root    23     1  0 10:39:09 ?      0:00 /lib/inet/nwamd
   dladm    14     1  0 10:39:07 ?      0:00 /sbin/dlmgmtd
    root   559     1  0 10:39:57 ?      0:00 /usr/lib/sendmail -bl -q15m
  daemon   126     1  0 10:39:20 ?      0:01 /usr/lib/crypto/kcfd
    root   412     1  0 10:39:42 ?      0:00 /usr/lib/utmpd
   smmsp   556     1  0 10:39:52 ?      0:00 /usr/lib/sendmail -Ac -q15m
 nsolter   578   569  0 10:45:52 ?      0:01 /usr/bin/gnome-session
    root   511     1  0 10:39:45 ?      0:00 /usr/perl5/bin/perl /usr/lib/intrd
    ...
```

The ps command can provide additional information, such as process priority, process state, and so on. Consult the man page for details.

CROSS-REF   **Chapter 14 covers tools and utilities related to processes.**

Signals

You'll occasionally need to terminate a process that is stuck or misbehaving. To kill a running process, use the kill command to send it a signal. Most processes will die with SIGTERM, signal number 15, which is the default signal sent by kill. Here's an example:

```
# ps | grep sleep
   986 pts/3        0:00 sleep
# kill 986
[1]+  Terminated                sleep 400
# ps | grep sleep
```

However, occasionally you might need to send SIGKILL, which is signal number 9:

```
$ ps | grep killtest
   755 pts/3        0:00 killtest
$ kill 755
$ ps | grep killtest
   755 pts/3        0:00 killtest
$ kill -s SIGKILL 755
$
[1]+  Killed                   ./killtest
$ ps | grep killtest
```

Many system processes restart with SIGHUP, signal number 1. To restart a process that accepts SIGHUP, send it signal number 1.

TIP   **Run kill -l for a complete list of signals and their numbers:**

```
# kill -l
 1) SIGHUP        2) SIGINT       3) SIGQUIT      4) SIGILL
 5) SIGTRAP       6) SIGABRT      7) SIGEMT       8) SIGFPE
 9) SIGKILL      10) SIGBUS      11) SIGSEGV     12) SIGSYS
13) SIGPIPE      14) SIGALRM     15) SIGTERM     16) SIGUSR1
17) SIGUSR2      18) SIGCHLD     19) SIGPWR      20) SIGWINCH
21) SIGURG       22) SIGIO       23) SIGSTOP     24) SIGTSTP
25) SIGCONT      26) SIGTTIN     27) SIGTTOU     28) SIGVTALRM
29) SIGPROF      30) SIGXCPU     31) SIGXFSZ     32) SIGWAITING
33) SIGLWP       34) SIGFREEZE   35) SIGTHAW     36) SIGCANCEL
37) SIGLOST      38) SIGXRES     41) SIGRTMIN    42) SIGRTMIN+1
43) SIGRTMIN+2   44) SIGRTMIN+3  45) SIGRTMAX-3  46) SIGRTMAX-2
47) SIGRTMAX-1   48) SIGRTMAX
```

To kill a job running in the foreground, press Ctrl+C. That sends the TERM signal to the process.

CAUTION Don't kill random processes on your system just because you don't know what they're doing. Many arcane-sounding processes are actually imperative for the correct functioning of OpenSolaris.

Proc tools

The *proc tools*, or *ptools*, are a useful collection of utilities for working with processes. pgrep returns the process ID of processes matching the search criteria provided. pkill works just like pgrep but also sends the resultant processes a signal, as shown in the following example:

```
# pgrep init
1
# pkill sleep
[1]+  Terminated              sleep 100
```

CAUTION The pkill command matches every process containing the string supplied, so in this example all processes with the string "sleep" will be sent the signal.

The remaining proc tools provide information about running processes. For example, pldd shows the dynamically linked libraries used by the running process:

```
# pldd `pgrep syslog`
469:    /usr/sbin/syslogd
/lib/libc.so.1
/lib/libnsl.so.1
/usr/lib/locale/en_US.UTF-8/en_US.UTF-8.so.3
/usr/lib/locale/common/methods_unicode.so.3
/lib/libscf.so.1
/lib/libuutil.so.1
```

This example also demonstrates how pgrep is often used in conjunction with the other ptools. Recall that the backticks cause the expression inside to be evaluated and return the standard output from that expression.

Other useful proc tools include pstack, pflags, and pfiles. Consult the proc(1) man page for more details.

CROSS-REF See Chapter 14 for more discussion about the proc tools.

Resource management and scheduling classes

Like in all modern multiprogramming operating systems, the physical processors, memory, and other resources are shared among the various processes running on the OpenSolaris system. OpenSolaris provides many capabilities to customize the way in which these various resources are shared, including six different scheduling classes, projects, resource caps, resource pools, processor sets, and others.

CROSS-REF Chapter 18 covers OpenSolaris resource management, including scheduling classes.

Services

Most operating systems use the concept of processes, and most have tools similar to those mentioned so far in this section. OpenSolaris is unique in the UNIX world, however, in its addition of the service concept, called the *Service Management Facility* (SMF). While a service in OpenSolaris is generally anything that can be started or stopped, it's usually a process or a collection of processes that work together to provide a service. OpenSolaris provides a common mechanism for defining, starting, and stopping services, replacing the UNIX rc scripts, and for managing the services, obviating the need to manage them at the process level. The service concept also allows for unified property management, theoretically replacing ad hoc text-based configuration files. However, you'll find that OpenSolaris is still replete with text-based configuration files.

You can view the services on your system with the svcs command:

```
# svcs
STATE           STIME    FMRI
legacy_run      11:27:41  lrc:/etc/rc2_d/S20sysetup
legacy_run      11:27:41  lrc:/etc/rc2_d/S47pppd
 ...
online          11:27:14  svc:/system/power:default
online          11:27:14  svc:/system/picl:default
online          11:27:15  svc:/network/ipsec/policy:default
online          11:27:15  svc:/milestone/network:default
online          11:27:16  svc:/network/npiv_config:default
online          11:27:17  svc:/system/device/fc-fabric:default
online          11:27:17  svc:/milestone/devices:default
online          11:27:18  svc:/network/initial:default
 ...
```

The state of legacy_run indicates that the service is started by the old init mechanism. svcs without arguments lists only online services. To view all services, use svcs -a.

Most of the system daemons you're accustomed to using on UNIX are now represented by services. For example, syslogd is now the system-log service:

```
# svcs system-log
STATE           STIME    FMRI
online          11:27:39  svc:/system/system-log:default
```

> **TIP** The -x option to svcs shows services that are degraded in some way:
>
> ```
> # svcs -x
> svc:/network/device-discovery/printers:snmp (Hardware Abstraction
>   Layer network attached device discovery)
>  State: maintenance since Thu Jul 31 12:35:45 2008
> Reason: Start method failed repeatedly, last exited with status 1.
>    See: http://sun.com/msg/SMF-8000-KS
>    See: /var/svc/log/network-device-discovery-printers:snmp.log
> Impact: This service is not running.
> ```

The output from `svcs -x` gives you a log file in `/var/svc/log`, where you can look for further detail.

Services go through a life cycle, starting in the disabled state. You can enable a service with the `svcadm enable` command. For example, to enable the ftp daemon, run the following:

```
# svcadm enable network/ftp
# svcs ftp
STATE          STIME    FMRI
online         12:39:14 svc:/network/ftp:default
```

Similarly, you disable a service with `svcadm disable`:

```
# svcadm disable network/ftp
# svcs ftp
STATE          STIME    FMRI
disabled       12:40:04 svc:/network/ftp:default
```

Restart a service with `svcadm restart`:

```
# pgrep syslogd
965
# svcadm restart system-log
# pgrep syslogd
986
```

You can change property values of a service with `svccfg`. After setting a property, you always need to refresh the service with `svcadm refresh`, and sometimes restart it with `svcadm restart`, as the following example shows:

```
# svccfg -s system-log setprop config/log_from_remote = true
# svcadm refresh system-log
# svcprop -p config/log_from_remote system-log
true
# svcadm restart system-log
```

Users, groups, and roles

OpenSolaris, like most UNIX and Linux variants, employs the concept of a *user*, which is an account that provides access to the system. Each user has a login name, a password, and other attributes. A *group* is basically a collection of users. When you install OpenSolaris, the installer gives you an option to create an initial user. Using either the GUI or the command line, you can easily add additional users, delete users, or modify user attributes.

CROSS-REF In organizations, user accounts are generally stored in a network naming service such as NIS or LDAP. See Chapter 10 for details on these options. The examples in this chapter apply only to local users.

As described in the section "Running Privileged Commands" earlier in this chapter, the root user is made a role on OpenSolaris if you create a user account in the installer. A role can be thought of as a special kind of user. The main difference between a user and a role is that you cannot log in directly as a role. You must first log in as a user who is assigned that role, and then you can su to that role. (Roles and other security topics are described in greater detail in Chapter 11.)

Configuration files

Each user and role has a username, password, default shell, home directory, rights profiles, and other properties. The user and role information is divided between /etc/passwd, /etc/shadow, and /etc/user_attr. The group information is stored in /etc/group.

CROSS-REF Chapter 11 describes the user configuration files in more detail.

The users and groups GUI

OpenSolaris provides a GUI tool for managing users and groups. Select System ➤ Administration ➤ Users and Groups, and you'll see a dialog similar to the one shown in Figure 3-8.

FIGURE 3-8

You can manage users and groups in this OpenSolaris GUI.

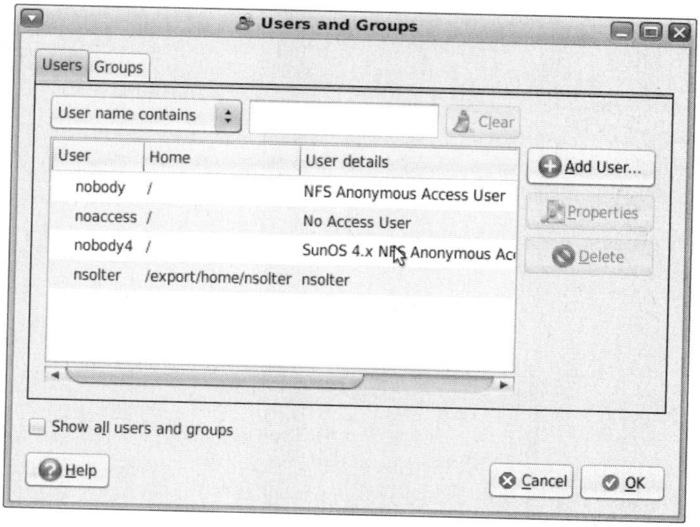

With this utility, you can add users and groups, delete users and groups, and modify properties of users and groups, including assigning rights profiles (called *user privileges* in the GUI). You cannot manage roles with the GUI.

Managing users, groups, and roles with the command line

You can add a user with `usermod`, supplying attributes with various flags. You must explicitly create the home directory and assign the password in separate commands. For example, to create a user `newuser` with shell `/usr/bin/bash` and home directory `/export/home/newuser`, execute the following commands:

```
# mkdir /export/home/newuser
# useradd -s /usr/bin/bash -d /export/home/newuser newuser
# chown newuser:staff /export/home/newuser
# passwd newuser
New Password:
Re-enter new Password:
passwd: password successfully changed for newuser
```

Similarly, you create a role with `roleadd`.

The `usermod` and `rolemod` commands modify the properties of users and roles, respectively:

```
# usermod -s /usr/bin/csh newuser
```

Finally, `userdel` and `roledel` delete users and roles.

Similarly, `groupadd`, `groupmod`, and `groupdel` manage groups.

CROSS-REF Chapter 11 describes rights profiles, roles, and their interaction with users in more detail.

Utilities

A few utilities enable you to see who's currently online on the system, and who has recently been online. The `who` command shows you who's logged in:

```
# who
nsolter    console    2008-07-31 11:32 (:0)
nsolter    pts/3      2008-07-31 11:39 (192.168.1.105)
test       pts/2      2008-07-31 13:38 (192.168.1.105)
newuser    pts/4      2008-07-31 13:38 (192.168.1.105)
```

The `w` command gives a bit more information:

```
# w
  1:38pm  up  2:12,  4 users,  load average: 0.02, 0.02, 0.02
User    tty         login@ idle  JCPU  PCPU  what
nsolter console  11:32am 26:53                /usr/bin/ctrun -l child -i none
nsolter pts/3    11:39am          9          w
test    pts/2     1:38pm   1                  -bash
newuser pts/4     1:38pm   1                  -csh
```

Finally, the last command shows you a history of logins:

```
# last
newuser  pts/4      192.168.1.105    Thu Jul 31 13:38    still logged in
newuser  sshd       192.168.1.105    Thu Jul 31 13:38    still logged in
test     pts/2      192.168.1.105    Thu Jul 31 13:38    still logged in
test     sshd       192.168.1.105    Thu Jul 31 13:38 - 13:38  (00:00)
nsolter  pts/3      192.168.1.105    Thu Jul 31 11:39    still logged in
nsolter  sshd       192.168.1.105    Thu Jul 31 11:39 - 13:38  (01:58)
reboot   system boot                 Thu Jul 31 11:26
reboot   system down                 Wed Jul 30 12:11
...
```

Storage and file systems

The OpenSolaris directory structure is set up much like the standard System V configuration, which should be somewhat familiar to you if you've used other System V, BSD, or even Linux systems. The main difference between OpenSolaris and these other systems is that OpenSolaris uses ZFS, the innovative file system first introduced in Solaris 10.

Disks and ZFS

In OpenSolaris, disk device names show up in the file system under /dev/dsk, for block-level access, and /dev/rdsk, for raw byte-level access. The names are created by the disk device driver, and usually follow the format c#t#d#s#. As in most operating systems, you rarely need to modify the disk devices directly. Instead, you use the abstraction of the file systems that are built on top of the devices.

OpenSolaris is the first operating system to make ZFS available as the root file system. ZFS has two primary concepts: *pools* and *datasets*. A ZFS storage pool, called a *zpool*, is a collection of physical storage from which you carve out datasets, which are either file systems or volumes. ZFS volumes are called *zvols*. The OpenSolaris installer creates a single pool, called rpool (for "root pool"), using the disk space you configure during installation. You can see this pool with zpool list:

```
# zpool list rpool
NAME    SIZE    USED    AVAIL    CAP   HEALTH   ALTROOT
rpool   7.44G   3.73G   3.71G    50%   ONLINE   -
```

The installer also creates several ZFS file systems out of the rpool, including the following:

- The root file system, mounted at /
- The home directories, mounted at /export/home

You can view all the ZFS file systems with zfs list.

NOTE /var, /usr, and /opt are part of the root file system; they are not separate file systems.

The installer also creates separate swap and dump zvols from the rpool. Both /tmp and /var/run are mounted on swap. You can view the partitions using the interactive format command.

CROSS-REF See Chapter 7 for general information on disks and file systems, and Chapter 8 for details on ZFS.

Mirroring the root pool

One unique feature of ZFS is its built-in support for providing data redundancy through mirroring. A data mirror is simply a copy of the data on another device. If any block on either of the physical devices fails, you can still access the data from the other device. Because the root file system is so important, consider mirroring it so that you can still use your system even if your primary physical hard drive fails.

Mirroring in ZFS occurs at the zpool level. In the installer, you specified the disk device on which OpenSolaris should be installed. In this example, the rpool zpool was created on slice c3d0s0, which you can see in the output of zpool status:

```
# zpool status rpool
  pool: rpool
 state: ONLINE
 scrub: none requested
config:

        NAME        STATE     READ WRITE CKSUM
        rpool       ONLINE       0     0     0
          c3d0s0    ONLINE       0     0     0

errors: No known data errors
```

NOTE A *slice* in OpenSolaris is another name for a partition. See Chapter 7 for details on slices and partitions.

Suppose you have another physical disk on which you can access slice 0 with the name c3d1s0. You can add this disk slice as a mirror on rpool with a single command:

```
# zpool attach -f rpool c3d0s0 c3d1s0
```

CAUTION ZFS boot does not work with EFI labeled disks. Before adding the new disk as a mirror, use fdisk -B to create a single fdisk partition and then use format to create VTOC slices inside the fdisk partition. Here's what the partitions of the disk used in this example look like:

```
format> fdisk
         Total disk size is 4095 cylinders
```

```
             Cylinder size is 4096 (512 byte) blocks

                                                    Cylinders
         Partition   Status     Type          Start    End    Length %
         =========   ======   ===========    ======   ===    ======  ===
             1       Active    Solaris2          1     4094    4094   100
      ...
      partition> print
      Current partition table (original):
      Total disk cylinders available: 4092 + 2 (reserved cylinders)

      Part        Tag   Flag   Cylinders     Size          Blocks
        0        root   wm    257 - 4091    7.49GB    (3835/0/0) 15708160
        1  unassigned   wm      0             0       (0/0/0)           0
        2      backup   wu      0 - 4091    7.99GB     4092/0/0) 16760832
        3  unassigned   wm      0             0       (0/0/0)           0
        4  unassigned   wm      0             0       (0/0/0)           0
        5  unassigned   wm      0             0       (0/0/0)           0
        6  unassigned   wm      0             0       (0/0/0)           0
        7  unassigned   wm      0             0       (0/0/0)           0
        8        boot   wu      0 -    0     2.00MB   (1/0/0)        4096
        9  alternates   wm      1 -    2     4.00MB   (2/0/0)        8192
```

If you give ZFS the whole disk it will relabel it with EFI labeling, so give it only a single slice, as shown here. (Chapter 7 explains disk labels, partitions, slices, and names.)

After adding a mirror, ZFS automatically starts a resilver operation, which is just a sync of the data from the original disk to the new mirror:

```
# zpool status
  pool: rpool
 state: ONLINE
status: One or more devices is currently being resilvered.  The pool will
        continue to function, possibly in a degraded state.
action: Wait for the resilver to complete.
 scrub: resilver in progress for 0h0m, 0.03% done, 4h43m to go
config:

        NAME        STATE     READ WRITE CKSUM
        rpool       ONLINE       0     0     0
          mirror    ONLINE       0     0     0
            c3d0s0  ONLINE       0     0     0
            c3d1s0  ONLINE       0     0     0

errors: No known data errors
```

After the resilver completes, you'll have a mirror of your root file system:

```
# zpool status
  pool: rpool
```

```
state: ONLINE
scrub: resilver completed after 0h16m with 0 errors on Tue Aug  5
       21:48:41 2008
config:

        NAME       STATE    READ WRITE CKSUM
        rpool      ONLINE     0    0     0
          mirror   ONLINE     0    0     0
            c3d0s0 ONLINE     0    0     0
            c3d1s0 ONLINE     0    0     0

errors: No known data errors
```

In order to be able to boot from the new mirror when the primary disk fails, you need to run `installgrub` (on x86 systems) or `installboot` (on SPARC systems) to install the boot information. On an x86 system, this would look like the following:

```
# installgrub -mf /boot/grub/stage1 /boot/grub/stage2 \
  /dev/rdsk/c3d1s0
stage1 written to partition 0 sector 0 (abs 4096)
stage2 written to partition 0, 265 sectors starting at 50 (abs 4146)
stage1 written to master boot sector
```

CROSS-REF   Chapter 8 describes ZFS mirroring and other, more efficient, techniques for increasing the availability of your ZFS storage system.

File system layout

Table 3-10 shows the important directories on your system.

TABLE 3-10

System Directories

Mountpoint	Description
/	The root of the file system
/bin	Symbolic link to /usr/bin
/boot	Boot files and utilities
/dev	Provides file system access to devices. See Chapter 7 for details
/etc	Contains system configuration files; discussed in various chapters throughout the book
/export/home	User home directories; on a separate file system from root
/lib	Libraries needed for boot, before /usr might be mounted

TABLE 3-10	(continued)
Mountpoint	**Description**
/opt	Location for extra or third-party software
/proc	procfs; provides file system access to live process information. See Chapter 7 for details.
/rpool/boot/grub	Contains the GRUB menu and splash screen. See Chapter 6 for details.
/sbin	Administrative commands needed for boot, before /usr might be mounted
/tmp	Mounted on swap device; contents not persistent across boots
/usr	Contains most commands and shared object libraries. See Table 3-2 earlier in this chapter for details of command locations within /usr.
/var	Typically used for live runtime information such as logs, statistics, and core files. Both the system and applications use /var.

Log files

As a system administrator, it's imperative to be able to find the log files that you need. Table 3-11 lists the locations of some commonly used log files.

TABLE 3-11	
Log Files	
Name	**Location**
System log	/var/adm/messages and /var/log/syslog
SMF logs	/var/svc/log/
su log	/var/adm/sulog

CROSS-REF See Chapters 11 and 14 for more information on OpenSolaris logs.

Booting and shutting down

There are a few different commands to shut down or reboot the computer from the shell, including shutdown, init, and reboot. These commands are all privileged, so they must be run by the root role or by a user with the required privileges using pfexec.

The most polite way to shut down or reboot is with the shutdown command because it broadcasts a shutdown warning message to all users. shutdown takes an *init state* argument, which is a number from 0 to 6, s, or S. The states 1–4 correspond to the old run levels, while s or S goes to single-user mode. Use 5 to shut down, and 6 to reboot. Here's an example:

```
# shutdown -i 5

Shutdown started.    Sat Jul 19 17:21:30 MDT 2008

Broadcast Message from root (pts/6) on OS0805 Sat Jul 19 17:21:30
The system OS0805 will be shut down in 1 minute
```

Alternatively, you can use init, which also takes an init state argument, and immediately transitions to the requested state:

```
# init 6
```

Finally, to reboot quickly and without notice to users, you can use the reboot command. This command is generally not recommended on a multi-user system.

Managing boot environments

The combination of ZFS and the Image Packaging System on OpenSolaris provides a powerful mechanism for upgrading and rolling back your system. OpenSolaris uses the concept of a *boot environment*, which is a complete image of the system. When you upgrade your system, Open-Solaris automatically creates a new boot environment so that you can roll back to the old image in case anything goes wrong. You manage the boot environments with the beadm command. For example, to list your available boot environments, run beadm list:

```
# beadm list

BE            Active Mountpoint Space Policy Created
----          ------ ---------- ----- ------ -----
opensolaris   NR     /          2.36G static 2008-12-01 17:03
opensolaris-1 -      -          57.0K static 2008-12-01 17:55
```

 Chapter 6 describes boot environments and beadm in great detail.

Managing GRUB and the OpenSolaris boot archive

OpenSolaris on an x86-based system uses the GNU GRand Unified Bootloader (GRUB) as its bootloader, as described in Chapter 2. You can use GRUB to manage multiple operating system installations on the same physical machine.

TIP   Instead of setting up bare-metal installations of multiple operating systems on the same machine, install a single host operating system, such as OpenSolaris, and use VirtualBox or some other virtualization technology to run the other operating systems as virtual machines. Part V of this book details the various virtualization technologies available on OpenSolaris.

Because GRUB is well-documented elsewhere, this book does not cover it in detail. However, you should know a few things about OpenSolaris and GRUB. First, the OpenSolaris GRUB menu can be found in /rpool/boot/grub/menu.lst. Second, you must use the version of GRUB that comes with OpenSolaris to boot OpenSolaris. The Linux GRUBs do not know how to boot OpenSolaris.

You can use the bootadm command to set the location of the GRUB menu. See the man page for details. (Chapter 2 discusses some of the new OpenSolaris GRUB enhancements, and Chapter 6 provides additional information on GRUB.)

When GRUB launches OpenSolaris, it loads into memory a ramdisk image of the key kernel modules and data called the OpenSolaris *boot archive*. You won't usually need to do anything with the boot archive directly, but if the system is not shut down cleanly, sometimes it can become corrupted. OpenSolaris provides no failsafe boot mode, but sometimes you can get a shell in system maintenance mode. You'll then need to use the bootadm command to update the boot archive. Generally, to fix a corrupted boot archive from system maintenance mode, run the following:

```
# svcadm clear system/boot-archive
# bootadm update-archive
```

If you can't even get a shell in system maintenance mode, you'll need to boot into a different boot environment and run the following commands (substituting the name of your corrupted boot environment for opensolaris in the first and last command):

```
# beadm mount opensolaris /mnt
# bootadm update-archive -R /mnt
# beadm unmount opensolaris
```

Then reboot your system.

> **TIP**   If that still doesn't fix the problem, repeat the three commands in the previous example but remove the files /mnt/platform/i86pc/boot_archive and /mnt/platform/i86pc/amd64/boot_archive before running bootadm to force it to recreate the entire boot archive.

Consult the bootadm(1M) man page for more details on the bootadm command.

> **NOTE**   Booting on SPARC-based systems is somewhat similar to x86 in that it uses a boot archive that is maintained with bootadm. However, SPARC does not use GRUB or supply an interactive menu to select the OS to boot. Instead, you can discover the bootable OpenSolaris instances using boot -L from the Open Boot Prom (OBP). Consult the boot(1M) man page for more information.

Resources

Most of the topics in this chapter are discussed in further detail elsewhere in the book, so this section provides just a sampling of the resources available.

A great reference for the UNIX command line is *UNIX System V: A Practical Guide* by Mark G. Sobell (Addison-Wesley, 1994).

References for Bash abound. Most Linux books contain a section, and there is plenty of information online. Here are a few pointers:

- The Bash Manual is at `http://faqs.org/docs/bashman/bashref.html`.
- *The Linux Bible, 2008 Edition* by Christopher Negus (Wiley, 2005).
- *Learning the Bash Shell* by Cameron Newham (O'Reilly, 1998).

For `vim`, try these:

- `www.fprintf.net/vimCheatSheet.html`
- *Learning the vi and vim Editors* by Arnold Robbins, et al. (O'Reilly, 2008).

For internationalization, see the article at `http://docs.sun.com/app/docs/coll/767.3?l=en`.

The OpenSolaris man pages can be found at `http://docs.sun.com/app/docs/coll/40.17`.

The SMF Quickstart Guide is located at `http://sun.com/bigadmin/content/selfheal/smf-quickstart.jsp`.

The ZFS Administration Guide (`http://opensolaris.org/os/community/zfs/docs/zfsadmin.pdf`) covers ZFS boot and mirroring the root zpool.

A good article about Solaris and GRUB can be found at `http://sun.com/bigadmin/features/articles/grub_boot_solaris.jsp`.

The OpenSolaris Virtual Console project details are available at `http://opensolaris.org/os/project/vconsole`.

Summary

This chapter provided a crash course in the OpenSolaris distribution. By reading this chapter you familiarized yourself with the GNOME desktop and the OpenSolaris command line, specifically the `bash` shell and the `vim` text editor. You learned how to use `pfexec` to run privileged commands, how to switch languages and locales, how to connect your OpenSolaris machine to the network, and how to install additional IPS-based packages from the network repositories. You took a peek at some of the features OpenSolaris offers as a development platform and learned how to connect to OpenSolaris with the secure shell. The chapter concluded with an overview of OpenSolaris system administration, including system information, processes and services, users and groups, storage and file systems, ZFS, GRUB, and other topics related to booting and shutting down your system.

This chapter concludes Part I of this book, but it is hoped that it has whetted your appetite for more information about OpenSolaris. Part II dives into the details of using the OpenSolaris desktop, attaching printers and peripherals, and adding software.

Part II

Using OpenSolaris

Chapter 4

The Desktop

The crash course in Chapter 3 provided a brief introduction to the OpenSolaris desktop environment, which is based on the GNOME desktop project. If you're not already familiar with GNOME, at least skim through the desktop section of Chapter 3 before reading this chapter, which explores the desktop further. This chapter describes the applications included in the desktop on the OpenSolaris distribution's Live CD. Additional applications are provided in the pkg.opensolaris.org package repository, so if you are interested in an application that isn't already on your desktop, check the repository to see if it's available.

NOTE While the OpenSolaris distribution includes GNOME, other desktop environments can be used with OpenSolaris. The most prominent alternative to GNOME is the KDE desktop. If you're interested in KDE, you may want to try the BeleniX distribution covered in Chapter 2, which is similar to the OpenSolaris distribution but replaces GNOME with KDE.

Desktop Customization

Chapters 2 and 3 introduced the basics of the GNOME desktop, including how to log in, log out, shut down the system, switch between workspaces, and navigate the menus. To make your desktop really work for you, though, you'll want to customize it.

Desktop session

The set of desktop programs that you have running at any given time is known as a *session*. When you log in, GNOME starts a session (Chapter 3 describes the programs in the default session, which is what you use initially). Use the Sessions preferences dialog to display and modify the programs that are part of your session. Open the dialog by selecting System➤Preferences➤Sessions. You can configure your GNOME session to operate in one of two modes:

- Start a specific set of programs every time you log in. This is the default behavior.
- Restore the set of programs that were running when you logged out of your previous session. You can select this behavior from the Session Options tab by checking the box for Automatically Remember Running Applications When Logging Out.

If you choose to have a specific set of programs started at login, you can customize that set of programs in two different ways:

- Start the desktop programs you normally like to use, and then click the Remember Currently Running Applications button on the Session Options tab of the dialog. This saves the current state of the desktop as your default session.
- Use the Startup Programs tab in the Sessions dialog to add to or delete from the session startup list. This can be useful if you have non-GNOME desktop programs that you'd like to run when your desktop session starts, as only desktop programs can be recognized and remembered by the first option.

> **TIP**   One common program you may want to add to your session is ssh-add, which stores your decrypted ssh private key with the ssh-agent daemon. Using ssh-agent, you can log in via ssh to other systems without re-authenticating yourself directly to each system. To add this program to your session, click the Add button on the Startup Programs tab. In the dialog that appears, provide a name such as **ssh-add**, and specify /usr/bin/ssh-add as the command to run. Click OK. The next time you log in, a dialog will prompt you to enter your ssh passphrase to decrypt your ssh private key.

Locking the session

One important security feature of the desktop is its capability to lock your session while you're away from the system, which helps prevent a malicious user or prankster from creating havoc in your name. It's especially important to lock your desktop if your login has any privileged access to the system because the potential damage is obviously much greater. Desktop session locking on OpenSolaris is provided by the xscreensaver(1) command. Normally this starts when you log in and runs in the background, automatically locking your session after it's been idle for a while, but you can also manually lock the session using the desktop menu item System➤Lock Screen. Once the session is locked, you must enter your password to unlock the session and resume work.

> **NOTE**   You can also enter the root password to unlock a user's locked session. This provides administrators with an emergency override should a locked desktop need to be accessed.

In addition to locking your session, xscreensaver also includes functions to manage the display's power consumption and can run a variety of screensaver programs. (If you use a CRT display, a screensaver helps prevent an image of your desktop from being permanently burned into the display, thus saving your screen. Now that LCDs have largely replaced CRTs, this function is unnecessary, but many users like their screensavers and use them to personalize their systems.)

To configure xscreensaver's behavior, select System➤Preferences➤Screensaver. Consider shortening the period of idle time before the screen is automatically locked because the default is 15 minutes, a rather long time for your system to be idle and unattended.

Customizing the panel

The default desktop session contains two panels. The panel across the top of the screen includes the Applications, Places, and System menus, launchers for commonly used applications such as the Firefox web browser, the Thunderbird e-mail client, Package Manager, and Terminal, and a notification area at the far right with icons for power management, volume control, and so on. The panel at the bottom provides the workspace selector at the far right, with most of the space used by a window list that enables you to switch between active windows by clicking buttons for each window on the panel.

Each panel is configurable; you access its configuration options by right-clicking on the panel and selecting Properties. The Properties dialog enables you to change the edge of the screen to which the panel is attached and to increase or reduce its size. You can choose the Autohide option, which keeps the panel hidden unless you move the mouse pointer to the edge of the screen, at which time the panel is made fully visible; this is most useful on systems with limited screen real estate, such as a laptop. You can also configure the panel to display hide buttons, which enables you to manually hide the panel when it isn't needed. The Background tab enables you to customize the panel's color and opacity, or select a background image for it to display.

More interesting than configuring the panel properties is the capability to customize the items displayed on it. Right-click on the panel and select Add to Panel to open a dialog offering a selection of GNOME panel *applets*, or miniature applications, that can be added to the panel. Some of these are quite useful, such as displaying a clock, monitoring the system or network, showing the weather for a chosen location, or providing an electronic version of a Post-It note. You can also add a custom launcher, which is an icon on the panel that directly launches a specified application when you click it. The Firefox and Thunderbird icons on the standard panel are launchers; you may want to add launchers for other applications that you frequently use.

You can add or delete panels by right-clicking on a panel and then selecting New Panel or Delete This Panel, respectively. You can add as many panels as you want; they are automatically spread around the edges of the screen. Deleting a panel is allowed unless it is the last panel. The right-click context menu of any item enables you to remove it from the panel, modify its properties, or, if it is a menu, edit the menu items.

Customizing your desktop's appearance

All X Window-based desktops require the use of a window manager to provide basic window behaviors such as switching focus, resizing, stacking, minimizing, maximizing, and terminating an application window. As discussed in Chapter 3, the OpenSolaris GNOME desktop uses Metacity as its default window manager. Metacity is a relatively simple window manager with limited configuration options; as a result, it performs well on older systems and new GNOME users find it easy to get started with the desktop.

The configuration options for Metacity can be accessed via System➤Preferences➤Windows. The item most commonly configured is the Window Selection behavior; the default configuration requires you to click the left mouse key in a window to assign focus to that window. By checking the box labeled Select Windows When The Mouse Moves Over Them, you can change this behavior so that you only need to move the mouse pointer within the boundary of a window to assign focus to it.

OpenSolaris includes an additional window manager, Compiz, that you may want to use. Compiz relies on hardware acceleration of 3D graphics operations to provide a much richer visual experience than the simple 2D graphics that Metacity uses. However, this means that Compiz is only usable if your system has a video card that can provide the required hardware acceleration. Fortunately, you don't need to spend time determining this. If you're interested in trying Compiz, select System➤Preferences➤Appearance. Once the Appearance Preferences dialog is displayed, select the Visual Effects tab, shown in Figure 4-1.

You can select from four options. None uses Metacity as the window manager; the other options use Compiz. The difference between the last three options — Normal, Extra, and Custom — is the specific Compiz behaviors that are configured. To see if your hardware supports Compiz, just select one of those options. That will start Compiz immediately, which may take a few seconds. If your hardware can support Compiz, a confirmation dialog asks whether you want to keep the new settings. Otherwise, an error dialog is displayed stating that desktop visual effects could not be enabled.

Try the Normal, Extra, and Custom options to find the setting you like best. If you select Custom and click the Preferences button, the CompizConfig Settings Manager starts (also accessed directly via System➤Preferences). You can modify an extensive set of configuration settings for Compiz to achieve a highly custom desktop experience. Some of these merely customize the desktop's appearance, but you can also customize application windows (e.g., you can specify windows that can't be minimized or that have a fixed size, and these can use matching rules based on window attributes to apply to specific types of windows or applications). See the Compiz Fusion website, `http://compiz-fusion.org`, for detailed configuration information.

NOTE You can use any X Window manager on OpenSolaris; check the various software repositories for others that may already be built for OpenSolaris. You can also see the X Window manager information site, `http://xwinman.org`, about other managers. (For an introduction to the basic concepts of the X Window system, see the X(1) man page.)

The Visual Effects tab of the Appearance Preferences dialog

Other preferences

This section describes several other aspects of your desktop, such as screen resolution, fonts, and themes, that you can configure through System≻Preferences.

Screen resolution

The display resolution is selectable using System≻Preferences≻Screen Resolution. By default, GNOME selects the highest resolution that your display reports it can support. To use a different resolution, simply adjust the settings in this dialog.

You can also use the xrandr command to adjust screen resolution and other attributes. This command uses the X server's Resize and Rotate extension to modify display configuration on-the-fly. The most likely scenario in which you would use this command is when you plug an external projector into a laptop, because you normally need to reconfigure the X server to access the additional display device. Using xrandr, you can reconfigure the X server on-the-fly, without restarting your X session. You can also use this extension to rotate the display or run mirror-image displays. See the xrandr(1) man page for details.

TIP If your system has an NVIDIA display adapter, you can use the device-specific tool provided by NVIDIA to configure the features of the display. To access it, select Applications≻System Tools≻NVIDIA X Server Settings. Consult the tool's online help for assistance in using it.

Fonts

To adjust the fonts used by your desktop and applications, select System➤Preferences➤ Appearance. In the dialog that appears, select the Fonts tab and choose your preferred font for each class of font used in GNOME. You can also use the Rendering selections on this tab to adjust the specific drawing behavior used in rendering the fonts to the screen. Depending on the specifics of your system, one of the options is likely to be more aesthetically pleasing than the others. Experiment with the selections to see what fits you and your system best.

> **NOTE** The system's font configuration is collected into a series of cache files so that the applications perform well in locating fonts. These caches are updated by the `application/font/fc-cache` SMF service; see the `fc-cache(1M)` man page and the `fontconfig` user document at `/usr/share/doc/fontconfig/fontconfig-user.html` for more information. Chapter 13 provides more details on SMF.

Themes

The GNOME desktop uses a *theme* to configure its visual appearance. A theme specifies the way in which controls and window borders are drawn, the colors used for the desktop and window elements, the set of icons, and the style of mouse pointer displayed. OpenSolaris defaults to a theme called Nimbus, which is custom-designed to give OpenSolaris a distinctive appearance. However, several other themes are available; select System➤Preferences➤Appearance and open the Theme tab. Some of the themes are designed for users with specific accessibility requirements, such as higher contrast or larger print. You can also acquire additional themes and add them to the system, or even design your own, either by combining elements from the installed themes or by building your own from scratch. The GNOME Artwork and Themes website at `http://art.gnome.org` is a good resource for additional themes.

Desktop Sharing

One useful X Window feature is the capability to direct an application's display to a remote system. The OpenSolaris desktop can remotely display the entire desktop as well, using the VNC (Virtual Network Computing) protocol. You might use this feature to remotely troubleshoot a system problem, or to demonstrate a program to colleagues who work in different locations.

To enable and configure desktop sharing, select System➤Preferences➤Desktop Sharing. The Remote Desktop Preferences dialog, shown in Figure 4-2, opens.

Check the Allow Other Users To View Your Desktop option to share your desktop display. You can share it in a view-only mode, or you can allow remote users to control the desktop. You can also configure the security settings, such as confirming any attempts to access the desktop, and a password that must be used to access the desktop remotely. The Advanced tab enables you to configure the network port used to access the display, some additional security settings, and the notification display when this feature is active.

FIGURE 4-2

Enable desktop sharing via the Remote Desktop Preferences dialog.

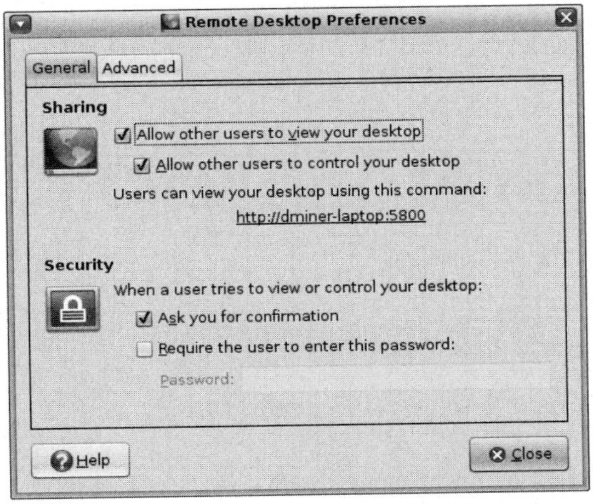

Once desktop sharing is enabled, you can connect to the display using the web browser on a remote system by entering the URL displayed in the Preferences dialog. This requires that the remote system have a Java runtime installed because the remote display from a web browser uses a Java applet. Alternatively, you can connect directly to the desktop with a VNC client such as vncviewer(1), which is included in OpenSolaris and most other UNIX and Linux operating systems. A free Windows VNC client can be downloaded at http://realvnc.com/products/free/4.1/winvncviewer.html. To connect using a VNC viewer, use the system's name or IP address and 0 for the display number — for example, the following connects to a desktop shared by the system krissy:

```
$ vncviewer krissy:0
```

In addition to the desktop sharing capability of GNOME, OpenSolaris includes the Xvnc server, which is a virtual X server that is accessed using the VNC protocol. You might want to use this if you install OpenSolaris on a system that doesn't have a graphics display, like many rack-mounted server systems. You can use the Xvnc server to run a desktop session on such a system, and access it from your laptop or desktop system's VNC client.

The default OpenSolaris installation provides the Xvnc server in the package SUNWxvnc. Two configuration steps are required to enable the Xvnc server and configure GNOME to use it:

CAUTION Be aware that if you restart gdm while logged into a GNOME session on the system, your session will be terminated, so it's usually a better idea to ssh into the system to perform these steps.

1. Configure the GNOME Display Manager, gdm, to provide login services over TCP sessions by adding the following four lines to the gdm configuration file, /etc/X11/gdm/custom.conf:

```
[xdmcp]
Enable=true
[security]
DisallowTCP=false
```

2. Enable the xvnc service and restart gdm (re-read the cautionary note preceding these steps first):

```
# svcadm enable xvnc-inetd
# svcadm restart gdm
```

Now, assuming the system is named krissy, you can use the following vncviewer command to connect to Xvnc and log in to your GNOME desktop:

```
$ vncviewer krissy:5900
```

> **NOTE** OpenSolaris also provides the rdesktop(1) client for the Remote Desktop Protocol, which is used to remotely display a Microsoft Windows desktop. rdesktop can also be used to remotely access VirtualBox virtual machines when the VM is configured for RDP access. See Chapter 22 for more information about VirtualBox.

Internet Applications

The most common use for a computer today is to access Internet services. OpenSolaris provides applications for the most popular Internet services — web browsing, e-mail, and instant messaging — as well as for Internet telephony and video conferencing.

> **CROSS-REF** See Chapter 5 for information on using the Ekiga telephony and video conferencing application.

Web browsing with Firefox

OpenSolaris provides Firefox as its standard web browser. Figure 4-3 shows the opensolaris.com home page rendered in Firefox 3.

Firefox is available for all major operating systems and works nearly identically on each one. If you've used it before, you'll find it quite familiar on OpenSolaris.

Firefox bookmarks are populated initially with content related to OpenSolaris, including the following:

- The OpenSolaris community site, opensolaris.org
- A feed of community members' blog postings

- Documentation and screencasts for common tasks on OpenSolaris
- The OpenSolaris defect tracking website, `defect.opensolaris.org`
- The OpenSolaris source code browser, `src.opensolaris.org`

FIGURE 4-3

Firefox is the standard web browser for OpenSolaris.

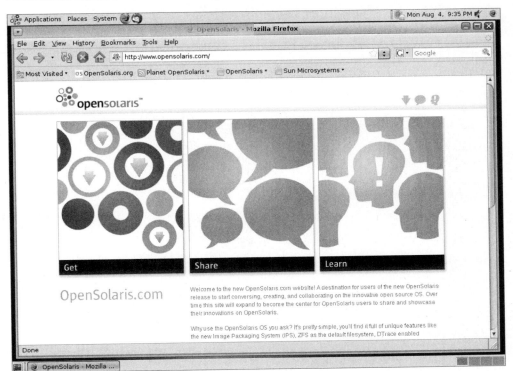

Firefox is a tremendously extensible browser, which is one reason for its popularity, and its `addons.mozilla.org` website offers a remarkable list of extensions for customizing its behavior and adding functionality. If you use Firefox on multiple systems, one extension you may want to try is the Foxmarks bookmark synchronization extension, which can synchronize your bookmarks across all of your systems.

NOTE On OpenSolaris, your Firefox settings are stored in the `.mozilla` subdirectory of your user account's home directory.

A couple of GNOME desktop preferences relate to web browsing: If you need to use a network proxy for Internet access, configure that in the Network Proxy Preferences dialog

(System➤Preferences➤Network Proxy). While Firefox has its own configurable network proxy settings, its default is to read this from the desktop preferences. Configuring proxies in the desktop preferences makes them available to all desktop applications, which is usually more desirable.

In addition, if you prefer to install and use a different web browser such as Opera, you can configure the GNOME desktop to use it anytime you attempt to access a website from a GNOME application. Select System➤Preferences➤Preferred Applications, and configure a custom web browser command to invoke instead of the default use of Firefox.

Because Firefox is so well known and there is little about it that is unique to OpenSolaris, it is not covered further here. See the "Resources" section at the end of this chapter for additional materials on Firefox.

E-mail and calendar

Electronic mail (e-mail) has long been one of the most important applications for the Internet, and many e-mail clients have been developed over the years, including text clients, graphical clients, and clients embedded in other programs such as the Emacs text editor. OpenSolaris includes two graphical e-mail clients in the distribution, Evolution and Thunderbird. They provide similar features:

- Access to e-mail accounts using POP (Post Office Protocol) or IMAP (Internet Mail Access Protocol)
- Sending e-mail using SMTP (Simple Mail Transfer Protocol)
- Mail filtering, including junk mail filters
- Local and web-based calendars
- Local and LDAP address books
- Encrypted connections using SSL or TLS
- Display and composition of both plain text and HTML messages
- Disconnected operation

Choosing one is mostly a matter of personal taste, likely to be influenced by secondary factors such as availability on other platforms.

Thunderbird development is managed by the same community as Firefox, and its look and feel is similar to that of Firefox. Many of the add-ons for Firefox can also be used with Thunderbird, which can be appealing to those who make extensive use of add-ons. Thunderbird is also available on Linux, Windows, and Mac OS X. To start Thunderbird, either click its icon on the main panel or select Applications➤Internet➤Thunderbird Mail and News.

Evolution is the official e-mail client for the GNOME desktop, so you can expect to find it on other platforms that use GNOME, whereas Thunderbird isn't necessarily included in the default installation of those platforms. However, current versions of Evolution are not available for Mac OS X or Windows. Evolution's appearance was designed to be quite similar to the Microsoft

Outlook e-mail client, so if you have a Windows background, you may find it comfortingly familiar. To start Evolution, select Applications➤Internet➤Evolution Mail and Calendar.

NOTE   For what it's worth, all three of the authors primarily use Thunderbird.

If you aren't familiar with either mail client, then just try each one for a few days. The setup process for each client is similar: The first time you start it you are taken through a configuration wizard to set up access to an e-mail account. The example that follows demonstrates configuring Evolution to access a Google Gmail account using IMAP and SMTP. Many people use the web interface to Gmail quite happily, but if you have other e-mail accounts, such as for your workplace, that you'll be accessing using a desktop client, you may find it more convenient to use it with a public mail service such as Gmail as well.

TIP   You can get help with configuring many mail applications for use with Gmail at the Gmail Help Center, http://mail.google.com/support.

Evolution's setup assistant greets you with a welcome screen that doesn't require entering any data. Click Forward. The next screen offers to restore a saved configuration if you have one. Assuming you don't, click Forward. The next screen, shown in Figure 4-4, enables you to configure your name and e-mail address. You can make this your default account, or, if you'll have multiple accounts and want to use a different account as your default, just uncheck the box and configure a subsequent account as your default.

FIGURE 4-4

You can choose your default account on Evolution's Identity configuration screen or later.

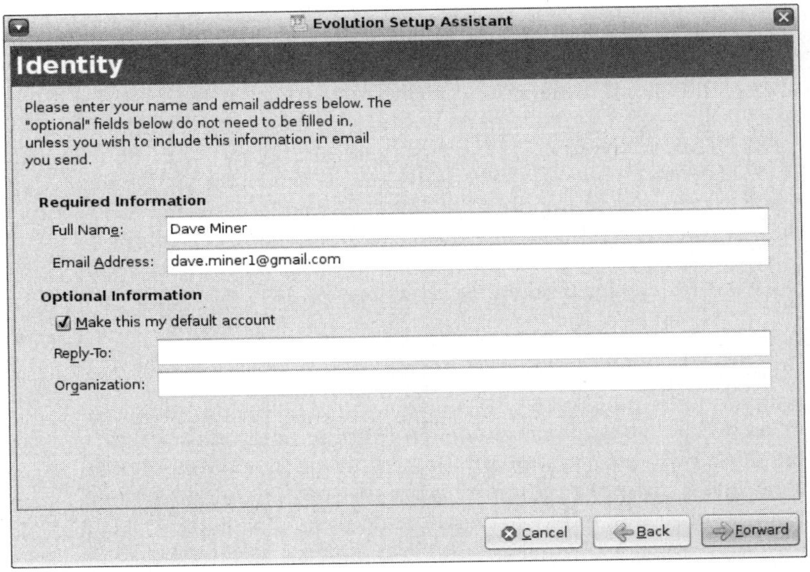

FIGURE 4-5

Configure how you receive incoming mail.

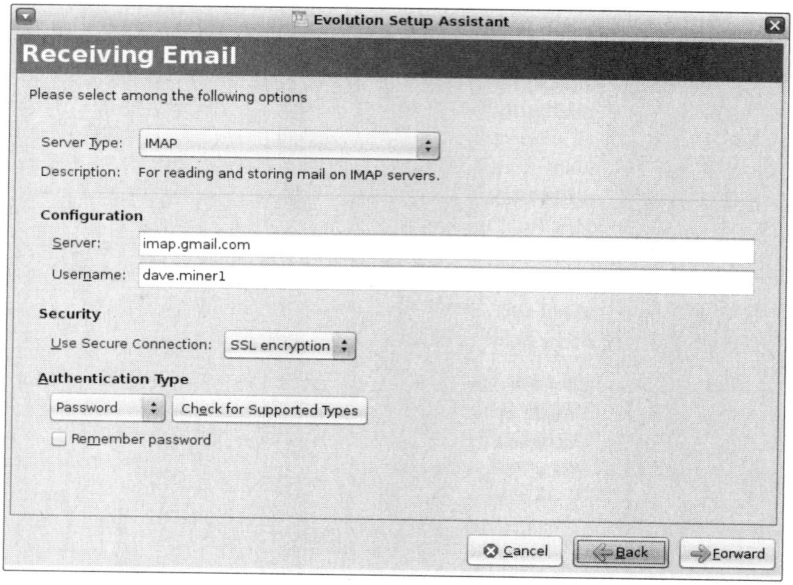

Use the next screen to configure how you'll receive e-mail for the account. Figure 4-5 shows the settings for using IMAP.

Many servers require the use of encryption to access your e-mail to ensure that the contents are not subject to interception in transit from the mail server to your mail client. If you can't access your e-mail after creating the account and authenticating with your password, the most likely problem is an incorrect encryption setting, so be sure to select the correct option for your mail server. Most mail servers support Password authentication, but it's a good idea to use the Check for Supported Types button to have Evolution contact your IMAP server and attempt to determine which types of authentication it allows.

CROSS-REF See Chapter 11 for information on TLS and SSL encryption.

The next screen in the setup assistant, shown in Figure 4-6, enables you to configure Evolution's behavior regarding e-mail retrieval.

You'll almost certainly want Evolution to check for new messages periodically; if your mail server has server-side filtering that places new messages into mailboxes other than your Inbox, you'll also want to have it check for new messages in all folders, rather than just the Inbox. The other settings here are not often changed from their defaults. With junk mail such a common problem, you might be wondering why the Check New Messages For Junk Contents box isn't enabled. That's recommended by Google, which does server-side junk mail filtering for you.

FIGURE 4-6

Decide how often you want to get new messages and other receiving options.

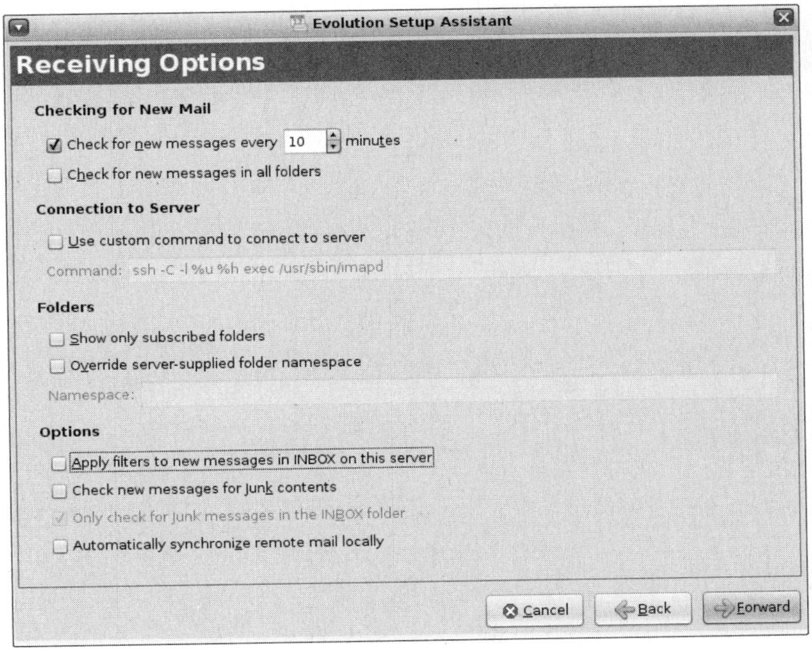

The other important piece of configuration for an e-mail account is sending mail, shown in Figure 4-7.

SMTP is the standard protocol for sending e-mail on the Internet. Many providers require encryption for sending mail, and you'll need to authenticate using Password or some other form of authentication. As with receiving mail, Evolution can contact the server and display the supported authentication types. The encryption type can differ between receiving mail and sending mail.

The final two steps of the wizard enable you to configure a name to be used for this account in Evolution's account list, and the time zone in which you reside. After completing the wizard, Evolution displays its main window, where you are prompted for your password to access the e-mail account and view the contents of your mailbox.

Once you've decided on your e-mail client, ensure that it's selected as your mail reader in the Preferred Applications settings (System➤Preferences➤Preferred Applications) so that it's used automatically when a mailto link is selected in Firefox or other applications. Each client, when started, offers to configure itself as the preferred mail client if it's not already.

FIGURE 4-7

Configure your options for sending e-mail here.

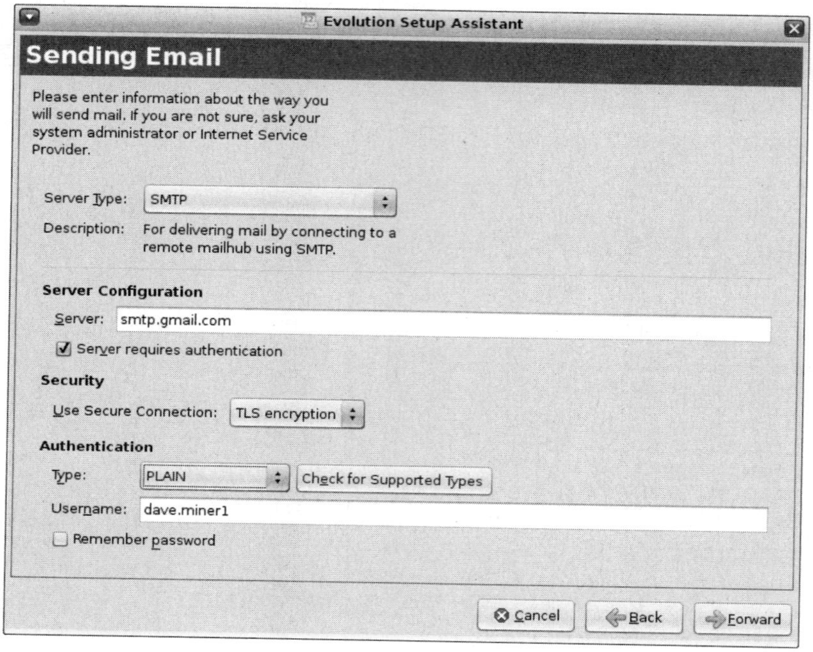

Instant messaging

One of the most popular applications on the Internet is *instant messaging* (IM), also called text chat, chat rooms, or IRC (Internet Relay Chat). Instant messaging and chat rooms enable you to carry on real-time conversations with one or more people, providing a more immediate inter-action than is possible with e-mail. Instant messaging applications also provide an option that reflects "presence," which enables you to set a status that others can see to determine whether you're available for a conversation. The OpenSolaris desktop provides the Pidgin client, which can be used with many instant messaging services, including AOL, Google, MSN, and Yahoo, among others.

> **NOTE** If you're interested only in IRC, the xchat application is available in the pkg.opensolaris.org repository as the package SUNWxchat.

To start using Pidgin, select Applications➤Internet➤Pidgin Instant Messenger. The first time you run Pidgin, you are prompted to add an account for a messaging service. Figure 4-8 shows cre-ating an account for the irc.freenode.net public IRC service.

Once you've created an account, Pidgin displays the Buddy List window (see Figure 4-9).

FIGURE 4-8

Create an account on Pidgin's Add Account dialog.

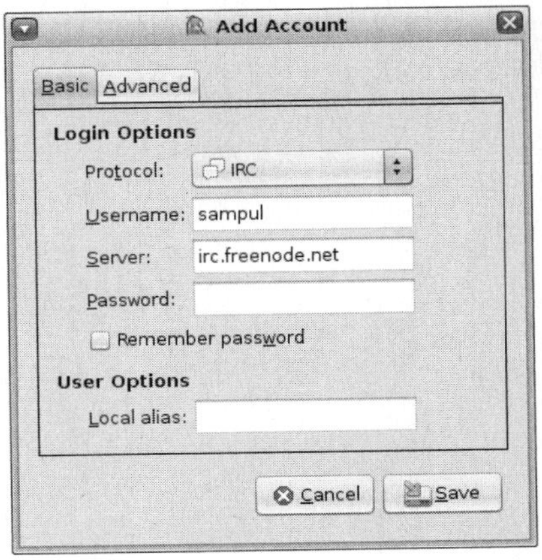

FIGURE 4-9

Pidgin's main menu is at the top of the Buddy List.

This window has the main menu for Pidgin across the top, the center section displays your saved chat rooms and IM buddies, while the bottom section contains a drop-down control for setting your status, and a display for your buddy icon (see Pidgin help for information on that). To connect to your IM accounts, click on the status drop-down and select Available. You'll be automatically connected to your IM accounts; and if any of them requires a password, you'll be prompted for it. You can select other statuses from this drop-down too (e.g., you can let others know that you're away from the computer or don't want to be bothered, or you can add your own custom status messages).

Once you've connected to an IM or IRC service such as `irc.freenode.net`, you can join a chat room, such as #opensolaris, which is dedicated to general discussion of OpenSolaris. To join a chat room, select Buddies➤Join a Chat in the Pidgin menu, select your IRC account, and then enter the room name, if you know it, or click the Room List button to get a list of chat rooms and select the one you want to join. You'll then see a conversation window like the one shown in Figure 4-10.

FIGURE 4-10

The largest pane in Pidgin's conversation window displays the "chat."

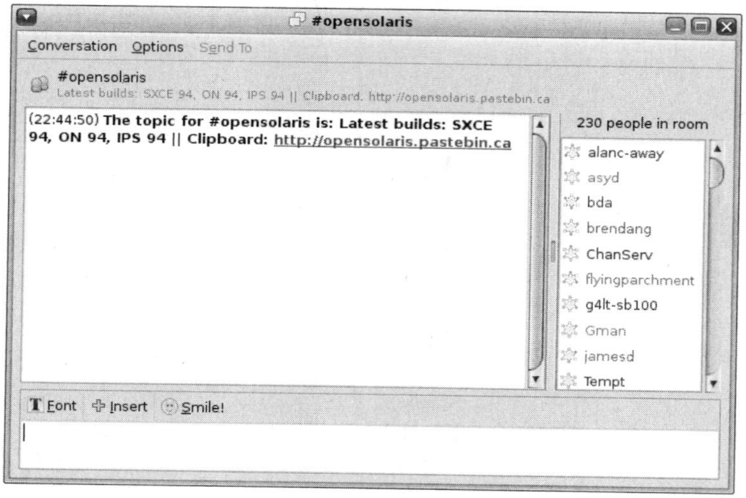

The window is divided into four sections. Below the menu bar, the top area provides the name of the chat room and the room's current topic. Below that, the left side of the screen displays the conversation, while the right side displays a list of people currently in the room. The bottom portion of the display is a text area where you enter any messages you want to post into the room's conversation. Just type your message into this area, press Enter, and your message appears in the conversation window. You can use the formatting buttons immediately above the text area to format your text or insert special content such as links or smileys (also called *emoticons*).

> **NOTE** Private conversations with buddies use a similar conversation window; the main difference is that it lacks the list of people in the room.

The menus in the Buddy List window provide access to additional features of Pidgin. You can configure buddies for IM accounts, or chats that you'd like to save in your configuration and automatically join, using the Add Buddy and Add Chat items on the Buddies menu. Manage your IM accounts through the Accounts menu — create additional accounts and enable or disable existing accounts as needed. Use the Tools menu to configure various aspects of Pidgin, including your preferences, privacy, and security features, and to enable and configure plug-ins, which extend the functionality of Pidgin and enable you to customize it to your liking.

This section has provided only a brief introduction to Pidgin. For more information consult its online help and its project home page, `http://pidgin.im`.

Media Applications

A popular use for computers these days is to listen to music or watch videos. Like other operating systems, the OpenSolaris desktop includes applications for accessing and managing digital audio and video.

Digital Media Codecs

The main problem with using media applications on OpenSolaris and other free operating systems is obtaining the proper software, known as a *codec* (short for coder/decoder), to decode the media files you want to use. The OpenSolaris GNOME desktop includes a framework called *GStreamer* for media encoding and decoding, and all codecs are written as plug-ins for this framework.

OpenSolaris includes plug-ins for raw formats such as WAV and AU, as well as the free compressed file formats FLAC and Ogg Vorbis; and video decoding for the Theora format. However, most commercial audio is distributed in MP3 format, and video is usually distributed in the MPEG-2, MPEG-4, or WMV format. Because each of these formats is controlled by a patent holder that requires royalties for each decoder distributed, OpenSolaris cannot include those plug-ins in the freely redistributable base OS. As of this writing, you can either build your own plug-ins from source code or purchase them from a commercial supplier. The only commercial supplier for OpenSolaris codecs is Fluendo (`www.fluendo.com`).

If you're interested in building your own codecs, the source is available through the spec-files-extra project at Sourceforge (`http://pkgbuild.sourceforge.net/spec-files-extra`). Experience with building software on OpenSolaris should be considered a prerequisite for pursuing this path, though, because it's fairly complex.

Audio

The primary audio application for the OpenSolaris desktop is Rhythmbox (select Applications➤Sound and Video➤Rhythmbox Music Player). Rhythmbox can manage and play all of your

119

digital audio — you can think of it as the GNOME version of iTunes. Figure 4-11 shows the main window of Rhythmbox.

FIGURE 4-11

Rhythmbox is the OpenSolaris desktop's principal audio application.

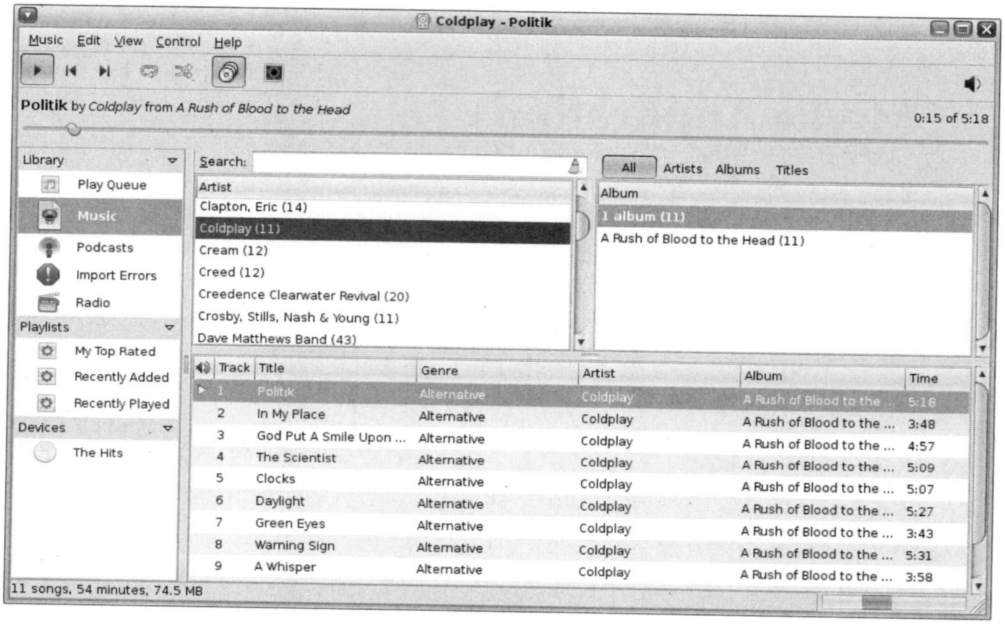

NOTE The pkg.opensolaris.org software repository also includes the Songbird music player, in the package SUNWsongbird.

Immediately below the menu and toolbar is a display area showing the currently playing track, including a slider control showing the track's progress. Drag this slider to move forward or backward within the track. Use the controls in the toolbar to pause, move forward and backward between tracks, or enable the repeat and random play modes.

The left side of the window is called the *side pane*; you can control its visibility using View➤Side Pane. It provides access to various sections of your music library, organized by sources: Music, Podcasts, and Radio. The Play Queue shows any items you've queued for playing. This pane also provides access to any playlists, including those that it automatically maintains: tracks that you've rated highly, recently added tracks, and recently played tracks. Below the playlists, any removable music devices, such as your MP3 player or a CD, are displayed. If your device is connected but not displayed, select Music➤Scan Removable Media to have Rhythmbox rescan for the device.

TIP   If your MP3 player still isn't recognized after a rescan by Rhythmbox, you may need to add a file to the MP3 player's storage in order for Rhythmbox to recognize it. See the Rhythmbox FAQ at `http://live.gnome.org/Rhythmbox/FAQ` for specific instructions.

The right side of the main window is used to browse or search the portion of your music library that you selected in the left pane. You can select tracks to play immediately, add to your play queue, and copy to your MP3 player, or you can reorganize your music library.

By default, Rhythmbox is configured to look for your music files in the Music directory under your home directory. If you stored them in a different path, select Edit➤Preferences and in the Music tab, enter the correct location. You can also specify how the library should be structured and how tracks are named. Once you close the Preferences dialog, Rhythmbox will scan that directory and load all of the music files into its browsing display.

Rhythmbox can be used to import (rip) tracks from your music CDs into your library as audio files. The tracks on commercial CDs are automatically identified using an Internet CD identification database known as MusicBrainz (`http://musicbrainz.org`). Right-click the CD in the side pane and select Copy To Library to have the CD ripped directly into your music library. Select the details of the encoding format used in the import process using the Preferred Format item on the Music tab of the Preferences dialog.

Any of the audio codec formats installed into the GStreamer framework mentioned earlier can be used with Rhythmbox, which means you can choose a variety of lossy or lossless encoding formats when ripping CDs. Rhythmbox defaults to the Ogg Vorbis format to provide more compact music files, but because storage capacities have climbed in recent years, many users now prefer to use lossless formats such as FLAC. You can also create audio CDs using Rhythmbox by right-clicking on a playlist and selecting Create Audio CD.

NOTE   OpenSolaris also includes a specialized CD ripping application called Sound Juicer (accessed via Applications➤Sound & Video➤CD Ripper). While it offers a few additional options for ripping specific tracks, the functionality of Rhythmbox is typically all you need to rip CDs.

To access Internet radio stations, select Music➤New Internet Radio Station, enter the URL of the station, and then select the station in the browsing pane to listen to it.

Rhythmbox can also be used to download and play podcasts. Select Music➤New Podcast Feed, and enter the URL of the podcast's XML feed. Rhythmbox checks the podcast feeds at a frequency you specify in the Podcasts tab of its Preferences dialog, and displays any new episodes. You can select an episode you want to hear, have Rhythmbox download it, and then listen.

OpenSolaris includes two other audio applications: the sound recorder and the volume control. Use the sound recorder to record audio using your computer's built-in microphone (if it has one) or an external microphone such as on a USB headset. It can record in any of the audio formats for which you have GStreamer plug-ins. The volume control application provides functionality to mix multi-track audio if your hardware supports it, as well as control the output volume. Access both via Applications➤Sound & Video.

Video

OpenSolaris includes the Totem Movie Player application as its primary video player. As discussed earlier, essentially all of the commercial video formats are proprietary and require that you obtain additional GStreamer plug-ins to display video.

Once you have the necessary plug-ins, Totem is easy to use. Inserting a DVD into your DVD drive causes Totem to start and attempt to play the DVD. Similarly, video files you download from the Internet should automatically start Totem for playback.

Graphics Applications

OpenSolaris includes several desktop applications that can be used to create, view, edit, and organize images.

Screenshots

It's common to take a snapshot of a window or an entire desktop to illustrate a program or to provide data for diagnosing a problem. The GNOME desktop provides a tool for capturing screenshots, which can be accessed via Applications➤Graphics➤Save Screenshot. In the dialog that appears, select whether to capture the entire desktop or just a single window. You can specify a delay before the screenshot is taken, which enables you to select the correct window or perhaps display a specific menu item or other artifact of the program that can't be statically displayed before selecting the screenshot application. Once the screenshot is taken, another dialog shows a thumbnail image of the screenshot and enables you to save the screenshot to a file in PNG (Portable Network Graphics) format.

> **TIP** You can bypass hunting through the GNOME menus and take a screenshot directly using keyboard shortcuts. Pressing the Print Screen or PrtSc key captures the full desktop, while Alt+PrtSc captures the current window. The exact label for this key varies among system vendors. If your keyboard doesn't have this key, you can use the Keyboard Shortcuts preferences tool (accessed via System➤Preferences➤Keyboard Shortcuts) to configure a different shortcut.

The authors made heavy use of this tool to create the figures used throughout the book.

Viewing images

For simple image browsing and viewing, you can use the Eye of GNOME (eog) image viewer. Select Applications➤Graphics➤Image Viewer, or type the eog command in a terminal. Once you've opened an image, you can zoom in, flip, or rotate it, and save the resulting image. For more advanced manipulation of the image, select File➤Open With➤GIMP Image Editor or File➤Open With➤Image Organizer. (There's more information about these tools a little later in the chapter.)

When you open an image in eog, it also makes any other images in the same directory available as an image collection; you can move from image to image within the collection using the left and right arrow buttons in the eog toolbar. Eog displays small thumbnail images of each image in the collection if you select View➤Image Collection. That enables you to skim through the images and find ones you'd like to display. Finally, select View➤Slideshow to have eog display the images as a slideshow. The parameters for the slideshow are configured in the eog Preferences dialog, accessed via Edit➤Preferences.

Organizing and editing images

If you have an interest in digital photography, you'll rapidly accumulate photos and need a way to organize them. OpenSolaris includes the gThumb image organizer program, which can be started by selecting Applications➤Graphics➤Image Organizer.

Once you've started gThumb, it functions as a specialized file browser for image files. The left pane in the interface displays directories, and the right pane previews images in the current directory. Figure 4-12 shows gThumb browsing a directory with several images.

Using gThumb, you can do many basic photo editing tasks. For example, double-click on an image and the display changes to show only that image. Use the items on the Image and Tools menus to perform tasks such as rotate or scale the image, edit the color map, or convert the image to a different format. You can also add comments to each image.

FIGURE 4-12

Organize your photos with the gThumb image organizer program.

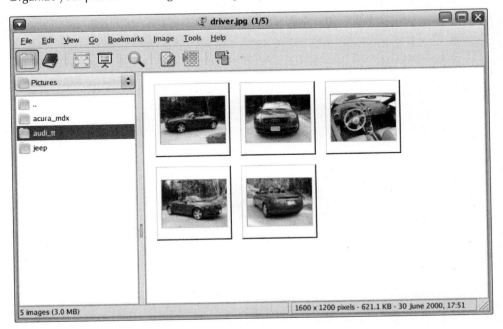

FIGURE 4-13

A photo album created in gThumb.

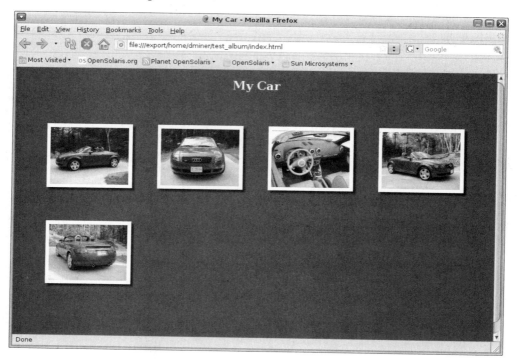

You can organize your photos in multiple ways using gThumb. You can assign multiple categories to each image, and you can create catalogs, which function like playlists on MP3 players. You can search based on the image filename, comment, date, place, and any categories you've assigned.

Select Create Web Album to create web albums of your photos to publish. Figure 4-13 shows an example.

gThumb can also import images from your camera, similar to the functionality of the gtkam digital camera browser; just select the File➤Import Photos menu item. You can create copies of images on a CD as well by selecting File➤Write to CD. Finally, gThumb can be used to display slideshows (select View➤Slide Show).

CROSS-REF   See Chapter 9 for information on using the gtkam digital camera browser program with your digital camera.

For advanced image editing and drawing, the OpenSolaris package repository includes the GNU Image Manipulation Program (GIMP). It's a full-featured image editing application developed by the open source community as an open source equivalent to proprietary programs such as Adobe Photoshop that are usually available only on Windows and Mac OS. Once you have installed the SUNWgnome-img-editor package, start GIMP by selecting Applications➤Graphics➤GIMP Image Editor. You can edit existing graphics files or create new ones from scratch. It provides a multi-layer model for image manipulation that enables you to perform virtually any type of transformation to an image and to merge images into composite images. Graphic manipulation and photo retouching are specialized topics beyond the scope of this book; for more information, we recommend starting with the resources at http://gimp.org to develop skills in this area.

System Administration

Currently, most system administration tasks in OpenSolaris are performed using command-line tools, but a few graphical configuration and monitoring tools are included with the desktop.

NOTE Additional graphical management tools are being developed by the Visual Panels project (http://opensolaris.org/os/project/vpanels).

Users and groups

As mentioned in Chapter 3, the Users and Groups tool is used to manage user accounts and UNIX group identities (select System➤Administration➤Users and Groups). To add a user, click the Add User button. The dialog shown in Figure 4-14 appears.

The Account tab displayed is quite similar to the user account creation step in the OpenSolaris installer. The main difference is that the program can generate a random user password if requested. To customize the user, select the Advanced tab, shown in Figure 4-15.

The Advanced settings are based on the profile that's selected; each profile specifies the user's home directory, shell, group, and privileges, as well as the numeric range to use in generating the user ID. You can modify any of these values as necessary, but the profile provides initial settings that should be appropriate for most users.

CROSS-REF See Chapter 11 for details about the user privileges available for assignment in the tool, which are properly known as execution or rights profiles.

You can create, modify and delete the user profiles used in the Users and Groups tool by clicking the Edit User Profiles button. If you frequently create users with similar attributes, such as default group membership or home directory path, you'll likely want to create additional user profiles to consistently define those attributes.

You can manage group memberships by selecting the Groups tab, where you can add, modify, or delete groups, including the users who are members of each group.

FIGURE 4-14

Add a user account here.

FIGURE 4-15

Advanced settings for user accounts

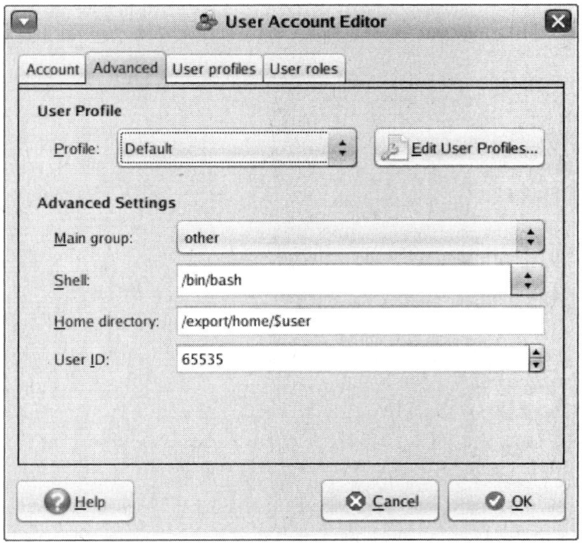

Keyring Manager

One problem all computer users face today is how to remember a plethora of passwords, as many services require entering a password to gain access. Ideally, you want to use separate passwords for each application or service, but it's impractical for a person to remember more than a few unique passwords. For your convenience, the desktop offers the Keyring Manager application, which other applications can use to store and retrieve passwords. It's modeled as keys on a keyring and is secured with a single password that must be provided to read any of the passwords stored in the keyring. This enables you to use unique passwords per service, reducing the risk of disclosure of any single service password, but it requires you to choose an especially strong and secure password to secure the keyring.

> **NOTE** Firefox can store website passwords for you, but it uses its own key store, rather than the GNOME keyring.

Usually, you won't need to interact directly with the Keyring Manager application; instead, keyring-enabled applications store and retrieve the passwords on your behalf — you only need to provide your keyring password to authorize the operation. This is how Pidgin, for example, saves any passwords for your IM service if you allow it to do so. However, you may occasionally need to perform maintenance on the keyring, perhaps to change an obsolete password (although applications using the keyring usually do that on your behalf). If so, run the Keyring Manager by selecting System➤Administration➤Keyring Manager.

> **CAUTION** Surprisingly, the current version of Keyring Manager included in OpenSolaris doesn't include an option to change the master password for a keyring, so don't forget your master password. If you do, your best option is to remove the keyring file, `~/.gnome2/keyrings/default.keyring`, so that it will be recreated when you store passwords in it, but be aware that this also deletes all of the passwords stored on the keyring.

Disk Usage Analyzer

The Disk Usage Analyzer tool can be used to provide a graphical display of your disk space usage. To start it, select Applications➤System Tools➤Disk Usage Analyzer. Once the main window appears, use the toolbar icons to select a folder or file system to scan. After the scan, the window will look similar to the one shown in Figure 4-16.

The left pane in the window displays a table of the folders within the selected folder or file system (in this case, /usr was selected). You can sort the table by any column in ascending or descending order by clicking on the column's heading. The right pane displays a usage map for the selected folder; as you select different folders within the table, the map changes to display the usage within that folder. If you hover the mouse pointer over any colored area of the map, it displays a tooltip identifying the folder corresponding to the map segment, along with the folder's size. The map's center section represents the folder at the top level of the scan, with folder subtrees extending out radially. This can help you quickly find the major space consumers within a directory tree.

FIGURE 4-16

The Disk Usage Analyzer has a sortable table in the left pane and a usage map in the right.

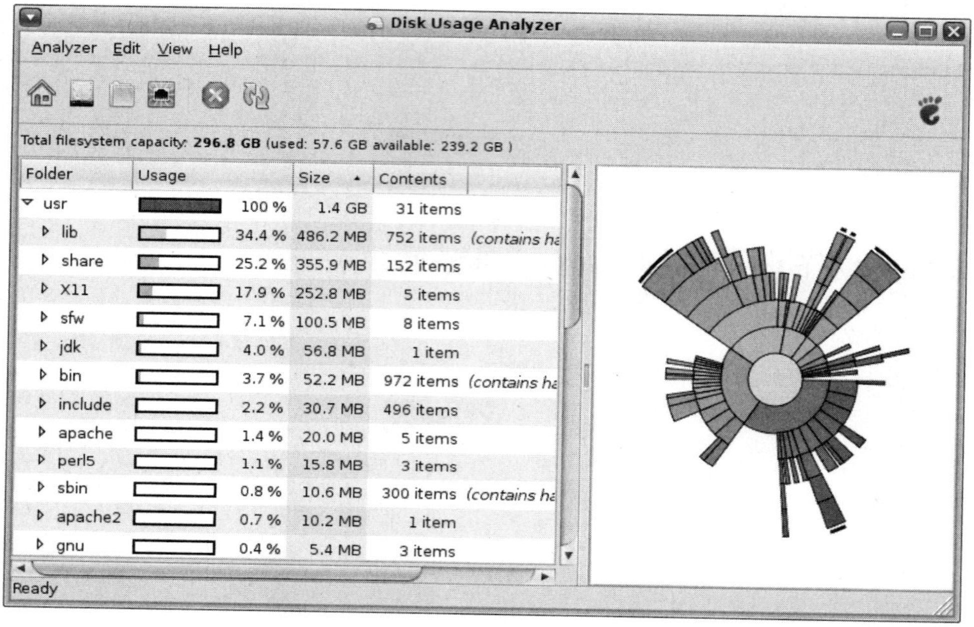

CAUTION Currently, the Disk Usage Analyzer is not aware of ZFS. Because each file system in ZFS shows free space within the pool as its own free space, the Disk Usage Analyzer can greatly overestimate the total file system capacity. The ZFS pool containing the /usr file system in Figure 4-16 actually had only 6.6GB of free space when this example was generated, but it contained approximately 40 datasets, so the free space was multiplied many times over its true capacity. In addition, the dataset containing /usr in this example has compression enabled, which is not reported by the Disk Usage Analyzer. Be aware of this when estimating space usage if you move data from a compressed dataset to a noncompressed dataset. See Chapter 8 for more information on ZFS.

Log File Viewer

The Log File Viewer application (Applications➤System Tools➤Log File Viewer) enables you to browse the various system and service log files, displaying and filtering the messages recorded in them. The window's left pane displays a list of the various log files on OpenSolaris; once you select a file, its contents are displayed in the right pane. You can use the calendar in the lower-left pane to display messages from a specific date, and select the View➤Filter menu item to filter any log messages to those that are of interest.

FIGURE 4-17

System Monitor displays system performance information.

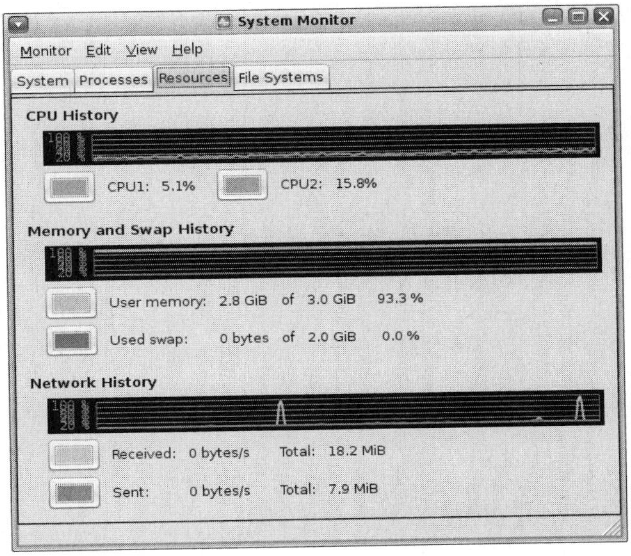

CROSS-REF See Chapter 14 for information on the system logs, and Chapter 13 for information on the service logs listed under `/var/svc/log`.

Performance Monitor

The Applications≻System Tools≻Performance Monitor menu item starts the System Monitor application, which provides information about the processes running on your system, usage of CPU, memory, and networking, and space usage of your file systems. The data available through this application is essentially the same as you'd obtain using the `prstat`, `vmstat`, `mpstat`, `netstat`, and `df` commands, presented in a more attractive and understandable format. Figure 4-17 shows a sample display from this application.

CROSS-REF See Chapter 14 for more information on system monitoring.

Power management and statistics

Power consumption of computer systems is a hot topic, and the OpenSolaris desktop includes the GNOME Power Manager to assist you in managing your system's power consumption. Power Manager is started as part of the default session, and the notification area on the right side of the panel includes an icon for power management status; hover the mouse pointer over the icon to check battery charge status if you're using a laptop. You can configure Power Manager using

System➤Preferences➤Power Management, controlling display brightness and CPU performance when on battery and AC power, as well as the behavior when closing the lid of a laptop. You can also configure the icon displayed in the notification area and behavior of the system when the power button is pressed.

TIP   **If you're running OpenSolaris on a desktop system that does not have CPU frequency scaling capability, you may want to remove Power Manager from your session because it has no function to perform. You can check this using the following command:**

```
$ kstat -m cpu_info -i 0 -s supported_frequencies_Hz
```

If the output shows only a single value for supported_frequencies_Hz, **then CPU frequency scaling is not available.**

Power Manager also provides graphical displays of the system's power behavior, which can be accessed by selecting Applications➤System Tools➤Power Statistics; you may need to enable this menu item using the menu preferences, accessed by selecting System➤Preferences➤Main Menu. See the tool's online help for explanation of the different graphs available.

CROSS-REF   **See Chapter 5 for more information on OpenSolaris power management.**

Other Applications

The OpenSolaris desktop includes several other tools for specific tasks, which can be found on the Applications➤Accessories menu:

- **Archive Manager** — Enables you to archive groups of files into a single file, or extract files from an archived file, including compressed archives

- **Calculator** — A desktop calculator with scientific and financial modes

- **Character Map** — A graphical interface for entering characters from other scripts into your documents

- **PDA Synchronization** — A tool for synchronizing calendar, contact, and e-mail data with a personal digital assistant (PDA)

- **Text Editor** — A graphical text editor with extensions that can help with viewing and writing code in a variety of languages

OpenSolaris also includes several accessibility features in the base OS that enable the system to be used by those with physical or visual impairments. Accessibility is a major area in which Sun has contributed to the GNOME community, so these features work well on OpenSolaris. The accessibility features include an onscreen keyboard, predictive text entry, and a screen reader and magnifier application. An Accessibility community group was recently created in the Open-Solaris community to provide a forum for advancing this work further.

Troubleshooting

There are two phases of desktop startup problems you might run into: X server startup problems, which prevent you from seeing a graphical login screen, leaving you at a text console login prompt, and GNOME session startup problems, whereby you see the graphical login screen and your password is authenticated, but the GNOME session doesn't start and returns you to the login screen. This section describes some basic troubleshooting steps you can take to determine what's wrong.

> **NOTE** Unlike Linux and BSD UNIX systems, OpenSolaris does not by default enable multiple virtual consoles. Therefore, after the GNOME login screen has started, you can't switch back to a text console login with keystrokes such as Ctrl+Alt+F1. The OpenSolaris Virtual Console project at http://opensolaris.org/os/project/vconsole is working to add this feature to OpenSolaris. See the project web site and the vt(7I) man page for information on virtual console support.

X server startup

Unlike some operating systems that use X, OpenSolaris does not create a configuration file for the X server, instead relying on the X server's auto-configuration capability to find and load the correct display driver and configure it to use your monitor at its optimal resolution. However, this auto-configuration process can fail, so you may need to resort to examining the X server logs and creating a configuration file.

The X server log is located at /var/log/Xorg.0.log; the log from the previous startup is automatically renamed to /var/log/Xorg.0.log.old, so you can compare them to help identify any problems. One common source of problems is using an older monitor that doesn't provide Extended Display Identification Data (EDID) settings for the X server to use. If you're not getting the resolution you expect from auto-configuration, this is very likely to be the problem, and you need to create a configuration file.

The X server configuration file you create must be placed at /etc/X11/xorg.conf. Configuring X is fairly complex, so the best way to start is to use the server's auto-configuration capability to generate a configuration file. First, log in to a text console session because X cannot already be running. If you're already logged into an X desktop, you can disable the GNOME Display Manager:

```
# svcadm disable gdm
```

This immediately terminates your X session and returns you to the console login prompt. From there, log in and start X using the following:

```
# /usr/X11/bin/Xorg -configure
```

This command creates the file /xorg.conf.new. You can then edit this file to customize your configuration and then copy it to /etc/X11/xorg.conf when you're ready to use it. Finally, you need to re-enable GDM to start a new X session:

```
# svcadm enable gdm
```

> **TIP** If your system has an NVIDIA graphics interface, you can use the NVIDIA X Server Settings tool (Applications≻System Tools) to create a configuration file that can exploit the NVIDIA driver's unique features.

GNOME session startup

If you see the graphical login screen and your username and password are accepted, but you can't log into your desktop, there are a few steps you can try to identify the problem.

First, select a different session from the login screen. Click the Options button and then choose Select Session. In the dialog that appears, you can choose from several sessions. The default is your last session, normally the GNOME session, which is also shown in the list, so choosing either of these options usually provides the same result.

> **NOTE** Your last session is stored in the file .dmrc in your home directory.

The other selections on the Sessions dialog enable you to try various troubleshooting options. The Failsafe GNOME session starts GNOME but does not use any of your session customizations, so if you suspect that something you've configured in your session preferences is the problem, try this option to help you confirm that. The Failsafe Terminal session doesn't start GNOME at all, but instead starts the X server and then starts only an xterm terminal, with no window manager. This is a good fallback if the failsafe GNOME session fails because it allows you to work around problems with GNOME components such as the session manager or the window manager. The final session you can select is one that runs an Xclient script; this is often useful for those who want to use older X window managers that aren't integrated into the GNOME desktop structure.

Once you log in to one of the failsafe sessions, examine the .xsession-errors file in your home directory to determine what might be causing the error. This file captures the standard error stream from all of the programs started by the GNOME session manager, so the cause of a failure to start the GNOME desktop is likely be found here.

Resources

General information on GNOME can be found at its home page, http://gnome.org.

Information on the X.org X server used in OpenSolaris is available at http://x.org.

Information on the Compiz window manager can be found at two sites, `http://compiz.org` and `http://compiz-fusion.org`.

A comprehensive directory of X window managers is available at `http://xwinman.org`.

Additional GNOME themes can be downloaded from `http://art.gnome.org`.

The GIMP image editor documentation is available at `http://gimp.org`.

The Pidgin instant messaging client project is hosted at `http://pidgin.im`.

Information on both Firefox and Thunderbird is available through `http://mozilla.com`.

Summary

In this chapter you learned how to configure the OpenSolaris GNOME desktop, explored many of the more prominent applications, and learned how to troubleshoot basic X and GNOME problems. You should now have a comfortable OpenSolaris desktop configuration and be ready to move on to exploring the rest of OpenSolaris in greater depth.

Chapter 5

Printers and Peripherals

I f your computer system consisted solely of a CPU, disk drive, keyboard, and display, it would be useful, of course, but many other devices can be used to extend the tasks your system is capable of performing. The generic term used in the computer industry for these devices is *peripherals*.

Printers and scanners enable you to convert between electronic and paper documents. Digital cameras enable you to record and share images of all types. Webcams and audio headsets enable you to use the Internet for cheap video conferencing and telephony. When equipped with all of these devices, your computer system becomes an essential tool for many parts of your life. In this chapter, you'll learn how to use these and other peripherals with OpenSolaris.

CROSS-REF Storage devices are discussed in Chapter 7.

Printing

Printers are among the oldest type of peripherals for computer systems. During the era of mainframes and batch processing, users didn't directly interact with computer systems often; instead, programs were submitted on media such as tape or punch cards, executed, and the results written to other media or printed on a *line printer*. Modern computer systems are interactive, of course, and mostly use printers that are based on laser or ink-jet technologies that can produce high-resolution graphics and color not imagined with the old line printers. However, the terminology associated with line printers persists in UNIX-type systems with commands such as lp, lpr, and lpq. OpenSolaris retains the legacy printing system designed in the days of line printers, updated to provide improved ease of use and support for a wide range of printing devices.

Automatic printer configuration with Presto

The most recent work in OpenSolaris printing comes from the Presto project, http:// opensolaris.org/os/project/presto/, which is developing automatic printer configuration capabilities. You may have already encountered it if you've booted the OpenSolaris live CD on a system with an attached printer.

Configuring locally attached printers

Figure 5-1 shows the dialog that is displayed when an attached printer is detected by Presto.

FIGURE 5-1

Presto printer configuration dialog

When OpenSolaris detects that a printer is attached to the system, this dialog enables the user to configure the printer. In this case, the printer is attached to the system via the USB interface, and OpenSolaris is able to use USB's device description properties to determine its manufacturer and model number. OpenSolaris has a driver for this printer model, so that is supplied as the suggested configuration for the printer queue, but you can select an alternative manufacturer or model if necessary. See the section "PPD (PostScript Printer Description) management" later in this chapter for more details on OpenSolaris printer driver support. You can also specify a different name for the printer and provide a description that will be useful to you and your users in identifying the printer's characteristics. Finally, you can specify that this queue should be the default queue for your system, meaning that any print jobs not sent to a specific printer queue will be directed to this one.

Once you're satisfied with the configuration of the printer, click the Add button to configure the queue.

CROSS-REF The Add Printer Queue dialog shown in Figure 5-1 is provided by the `ospm-applet` application, which is part of the default GNOME desktop session. See Chapter 4 for more information on the GNOME desktop.

NOTE If your printer is attached using the older parallel port technology, Presto will not automatically detect it. See the section "Manual printer configuration" later in this chapter.

Configuring network-attached printers

Presto works very well for configuring USB printers, which is now the technology used to attach virtually all printers directly to computer systems. However, an increasing number of printers now sold can be attached to wired or wireless networks and accept print jobs directly from any system on the network. If you have this type of printer on your network, Presto can automatically configure it as well, although the configuration process operates somewhat differently from that of an attached USB printer.

In the case of USB, Presto receives a notification from the kernel as soon as a printer is plugged into the system; this triggers a query of the device properties from the printer, the results of which are then used to populate the Add Printer Queue dialog shown in the previous section. Most systems have only one or two printers directly attached, so these dialogs are not distracting. However, a large number of network printers can be detected, so displaying the Add Printer Queue dialog when each is found would likely be annoying to users. In addition, most network printers do not announce their presence; to detect them, Presto must use a polling mechanism to query the network. It is not desirable to have every system on your network polling the network constantly to detect printers, as this generates some load on the network and the printers.

To detect network printers, Presto supplies an SMF service, `svc:/network/device- discovery/printers:snmp`, which implements polling for network-attached printers. This service is disabled by default on OpenSolaris but can be enabled using the following command:

```
# svcadm enable printers:snmp
```

CROSS-REF Chapter 13 describes SMF service management.

Once enabled, this service sends a broadcast SNMP message to the local network; most network-attached printers will respond to this message. OpenSolaris print servers do not normally respond to this message because they are not configured to advertise printers via

SNMP. Presto automatically creates a print queue for each printer that responds, and displays a notification icon in the GNOME message tray. The SNMP discovery service continues to broadcast messages periodically and add queues as additional responses are received. The default interval between messages is 60 seconds, but you can control this by modifying the config/interval property of the service. For example, to modify the interval to five minutes, use the following commands:

```
# svccfg -s printers:snmp setprop config/interval=integer: 300
# svcadm refresh printers:snmp
# svcadm restart printers:snmp
```

Manual printer configuration

If your printer is one that can't be configured automatically using Presto, perhaps because your print server doesn't advertise its printers using SNMP, or you have more complex printing needs than the automatic configuration tools support, then you'll need to configure your printing manually. OpenSolaris provides two printing subsystems, including graphical and command-line tools for managing printers in each printing system; this section provides guidance in selecting and using a printing system on OpenSolaris.

Before you begin, it's helpful to understand a few basic concepts in the OpenSolaris printing model. Each printer is attached to a port, which can be USB, a parallel port, a serial port, or an address on the network. Each printer has one or more queues associated with it; you can use multiple queues to offer different options, such as single-sided or duplex printing, print quality, or size of paper. In this chapter, the term "printer" is generally used because most of the time a printer has only a single queue associated with it, but a queue is in fact the object that is configured. You can also group related printers into a class, enabling them to behave as a virtual print service.

> **NOTE** Printer classes are not discussed in this book; consult the OpenSolaris documentation for specific information on configuring printer classes.

To print a document, a user must submit a job to a queue, which may transmit the job to a remote system if the printer is not directly attached to the local system. In processing the job, the print server will apply one or more filters, which convert the document into a format that the printer can understand and apply to paper. Finally, each printer has a driver associated with it, which is used by the operating system to communicate with the printer.

Selecting a print service

Your first decision in setting up printing is to select the print service your system will use. OpenSolaris continues to offer the traditional System V UNIX LP subsystem, which has been a part of Solaris since the early 1990s. More recently, the CUPS (Common UNIX Printing System) printing system has been added to OpenSolaris. The CUPS system has been ported to most UNIX-like platforms and is now sponsored by Apple.

The two print systems offer similar capabilities; both have graphical or web-based interfaces for configuration, and share similar, though not identical, command-line interfaces. The principal difference between them at this writing is that the automatic configuration capabilities of Presto work only with the LP system, not CUPS, though it's expected that CUPS will be supported in the future. Which one should you choose? Most likely, your choice is best based on familiarity: If you have used CUPS on Linux (and found it acceptable), then using CUPS on OpenSolaris will offer a similar experience. If your background is primarily with earlier versions of Solaris, then the LP system may be more to your liking. If you're not familiar with either one, then we recommend CUPS, as its web-based administrative interface is more comprehensive than the graphical utilities included for the LP system, and it provides better support for setting options such as duplex printing on print queues. In addition, the knowledge that you'll gain will be more portable to other systems, such as Linux and Mac OS X.

If you decide to use CUPS, you may need to first install it from the OpenSolaris package repository using the following command:

```
# pkg install SUNWcups
```

You can check, and select, the print service configured for your system using the print-service command. Use the following to query the currently configured service:

```
# print-service -q
active print service: lp
```

The preceding means that the traditional SVR4 LP system is configured as the print service. The -s option is used to select the print service:

```
# print-service -s cups
disabling LP services ...
enabling CUPS services ...
# print-service -s lp
disabling CUPS services ...
enabling LP services ...
```

The print-service command disables the SMF services associated with the print service that is no longer being used, and enables those associated with the selected service; you cannot run both systems simultaneously, as they will attempt to use the same network ports, and the conflicts can result in a system that behaves strangely.

If you already have print queues configured in the currently active print system, the -m option can migrate them when you switch the services:

```
# print-service -s cups -m
disabling LP services ...
enabling CUPS services ...
```

CAUTION The queue migration performed by print-service is only a basic migration of printer names and ports. If you have configured special printing options on the queues in the old service, you will likely need to edit the queue configuration in the new service to replicate the same options.

The `print-service` command also offers the `-e` option to export the printer queue configuration to a file, and the `-i` option to import an exported configuration file. Again, this is only a basic migration of printer names and ports, and may require modification.

The following sections provide information on configuring and operating printers for each print system.

Using the LP system

If you've chosen the LP system for printing, the easiest way to begin configuring your printer is with the Solaris Print Manager, which is run using the command `/usr/sbin/printmgr` or by selecting System ➤ Administration ➤ Print Manager from the GNOME desktop menus. Figure 5-2 displays a screenshot of the initial display for `printmgr`.

FIGURE 5-2

Print Manager initial display

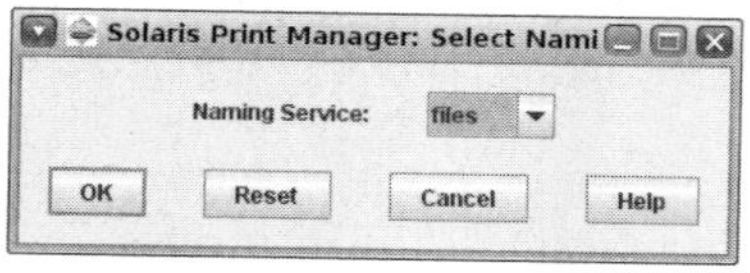

OpenSolaris can share print queue configuration information across multiple systems using naming services, but unless you already have a naming service set up, select files, which means that your actions in `printmgr` will affect only the local system. The printers you configure with `printmgr` will be listed in `/etc/printers.conf`.

CROSS-REF   Naming services are discussed in Chapter 10.

Once you've selected the naming service, `printmgr`'s main window is displayed, as shown in Figure 5-3.

From the `printmgr` main screen, you can configure options to the program using the Print Manager menu; add, modify, and remove printers using the Printer menu; and use the Tools menu to search for printers. The Print Manager default options — Use PPD Files and Use Local-host For Printer Server — usually should not be modified because they offer the best results.

TIP   One useful option that isn't selected by default is the Show Command-Line Console option. If you select this option, `printmgr` will display, in a separate window, the actual commands it is using to perform printer configuration; this can help you learn how to use the lp commands. All commands are recorded in the console automatically, even if the window is not being displayed, so you can display it after the operations have completed to see the detailed record.

FIGURE 5-3
_____

Print Manager main window

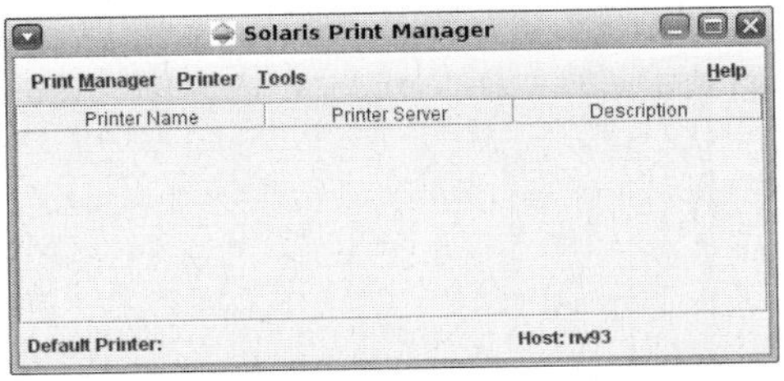

Configuring a local printer

To configure a local printer with printmgr, select Printer ➤ New Attached Printer. This will display the dialog shown in Figure 5-4.

In this example dialog, the printer is attached to the parallel port (/dev/ecpp0), and a generic PostScript printer is being used. Parallel ports are accessed using the ecpp(7D) driver; if you have a printer attached to a serial port, select from the serial devices listed, which will have names such as /dev/term/a or /dev/term/b, because serial printers are accessed using terminal devices. See the section "Serial ports" later in this chapter for more information on serial devices.

Select the Printer Make first, and then the Printer Model selections will be filtered to those that are within that make. Once you select the Printer Model, a driver will automatically be filled in as recommended; if other drivers correspond to this model, they are offered as additional selections in the Printer Driver menu. See the section "PPD management" later in this chapter for more details on how printer drivers are selected.

One selection you may want to customize is the Banner field; this controls whether an identifying banner is printed for each print job. If you are sharing the printer in an office with multiple users, you'll probably want to always print a banner so that users can identify their documents, but for a private printer in your home or office, disabling the printing banners saves paper and ink or toner.

Usually, leave the Fault Notification selection as Write to Superuser, because that causes printer faults to be displayed on the system console and in the main system log, /var/adm/messages. Alternatively, you can have fault notifications e-mailed instead, or disable notification entirely.

The Default Printer selection is important. If you specify this printer as the default, then any print jobs not specifically directed to another printer will be sent to this printer.

You can also customize the user access list. By default, all users have access to a newly added printer, but if you want to restrict this printer to specific users, then select the All item in the User Access List and press Delete. Then type the username of a user who is allowed access and click Add; repeat this for each user who should have access.

FIGURE 5-4

New Attached Printer dialog

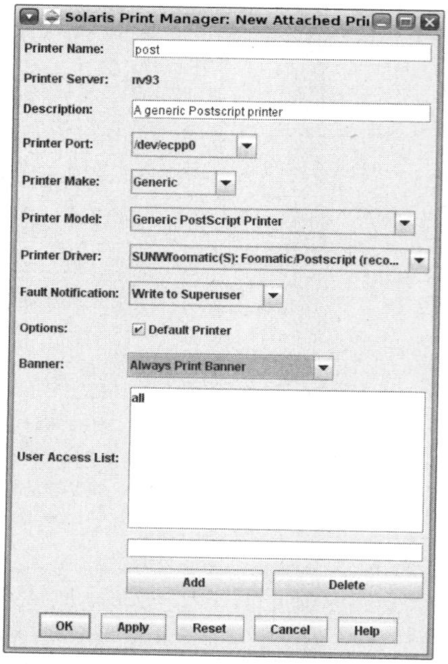

When you're satisfied with the printer configuration, click OK to add the printer. If you display the command-line console, it shows the commands that correspond to this operation:

```
# /usr/sbin/lpadmin -p post -s localhost -v /dev/ecpp0 -m standard_foomatic
-A write -n /usr/share/ppd/SUNWfoomatic/Generic/Generic-PostScript_Printer-
Postscript.ppd.gz -o banner=always -I postscript -u allow:all
# /usr/sbin/lpadmin -p post -D "A generic postscript printer"
# /usr/sbin/lpadmin -d post
# /usr/bin/enable post
# /usr/sbin/accept post
```

The lpadmin command is the primary command used to configure print queues; it configures the device or connection type, filters, content types, and access control. You can consult the man page for details on all of the options available in lpadmin. The enable and accept commands are discussed in the section "Managing print queues and jobs" later in this chapter.

If all goes well, you'll see the printer listed in the printmgr main window. Test that the printer is configured correctly by printing a test document; for the printer in this example, a command such as the following sends a brief text file to the printer:

```
$ lp -d post /etc/motd
```

If the printer is capable of printing PostScript, it's a good idea to also test printing a PostScript file to ensure that the filters are operating correctly.

> **TIP** If you've configured a local printer on OpenSolaris and want to configure a Linux client to print to it, then configure the Linux print queue to use a printer type of Generic PostScript. In this configuration, the Linux client will convert its content to PostScript prior to sending to the OpenSolaris server, which can then convert it to the correct format for the printer.

Configuring a network printer

OpenSolaris can also use network-attached printers. To configure such a printer, select print-mgr ➤ Printer ➤ New Network Printer. The dialog displayed is very similar to the New Attached Printer dialog; the only difference is that the Printer Port field is replaced by two fields, Destination and Protocol.

There are three protocol options, and the protocol selected determines the format of the destination:

- **BSD** — The destination is the hostname or IP address of the printer and the queue name, separated by a colon. For example, netprinter:default.

- **TCP** — The destination is the hostname or IP address of the printers and a port number, separated by a colon. For example, netprinter:515.

- **URI** — The destination is a URI address for the printer. For example, a printer that understands the Internet Printing Protocol might be addressed with the URI ipp://netprinter/printers/default. You can use an smb URI to print to Windows printers if you have smbspool(1M) installed. This is part of Samba, which is available as the SUNWsmba package; see its man page for information on the smb URI format. You can also use an lpd URI, but that's exactly the same as specifying the BSD protocol.

CROSS-REF See Chapter 10 for more information on OpenSolaris interoperability with Windows networking.

You can consult the printer's documentation to determine which protocol it supports and the port number or queue name. As with a local printer, you should print a test job to verify that the printer is configured correctly.

Submitting print jobs

Most desktop applications on OpenSolaris include printing their output as a standard menu item, which is usually the easiest way to submit a print job. Otherwise, you can use the lp command to submit files for printing, as shown in examples throughout this section. OpenSolaris also includes the lpr command for compatibility with BSD command interfaces; consult its man page for usage information if you're not already familiar with it.

Checking printer status

The lpstat command is used to view the status of the print system and queues. When issued with no options, lpstat displays the status of any print jobs you have submitted. A system status summary is provided by lpstat -s:

```
$ lpstat -s
scheduler is running
system default printer: post
device for post: /dev/ecpp0
```

You can view the status of a single printer as follows:

```
$ lpstat -p post
printer post idle. enabled since Tue Jul 15 00:11:53 2008. available.
```

To view a printer's complete configuration, add the -l option:

```
$ lpstat -p post -l
printer post idle. enabled since Tue Jul 15 00:11:53 2008. available.
    Form mounted:
    Content types: application/postscript
    Description: A generic postscript printer
    Printer types: unknown
    Connection:
    Interface: /usr/lib/lp/model/standard_foomatic
    PPD: /usr/share/ppd/SUNWfoomatic/Generic/Generic-
PostScript_Printer-Postscript.ppd.gz
    After fault: continue
    Users allowed:
        (all)
    Forms allowed:
        (none)
    Media supported:
```

```
            Letter
            A4
            11x17
            A3
            A5
            B5
            Env10
            EnvC5
            EnvDL
            EnvISOB5
            EnvMonarch
            Executive
            Legal
        Banner required
        Character sets:
            (none)
        Default pitch:
        Default page size:
        Default port setting:
        Options:
```

See the section "PPD management" later in this chapter for information on the Interface, PPD, and Media supported sections of the `lpstat` output.

Configuring a print client

If you already have a print server configured to support the BSD or IPP protocol and want to configure OpenSolaris as a client to submit print jobs, you can do this easily using `printmgr`. Select Printer ➤ Add Access to Printer, and a simple dialog box with three fields is displayed. You must enter the printer name, and the name or IP address of the print server. You can supply an optional description, as well as select whether this printer will be the system default. Viewing the command-line console output, you'll see that this is equivalent to a simple `lpadmin` command. For example, to add access to the printer `docprint` on the server `printserv`, the command is as follows:

```
# lpadmin -p docprint -s printserv -D ''test printer''
```

You can then print to this printer using the following:

```
$ lp -d docprint /etc/motd
```

Managing print queues and jobs

Once you have configured printer queues, several commands are available to manage the queues and jobs. Table 5-1 summarizes these commands; consult the man page for each for more information. Note that print queues created by Print Manager or Presto are enabled as part of the configuration process — you do not need to explicitly enable the queue or accept jobs unless you disable or reject a queue.

TABLE 5-1	

Print Queue Management Commands

Command	Description
accept	Allow print jobs to be queued
cancel	Cancel a print job
disable	Disable a printer
enable	Enable a printer
lpmove	Move print jobs between queues
reject	Disallow print jobs from being queued

In addition, you can configure the default printer for the system using lpadmin; use the following to designate the printer "snoopy" as your default:

```
# lpadmin -d snoopy
```

It's unlikely that you would need to do so, but should you need to restart the LP print service, its name is application/print/server, and it can be restarted using svcadm:

```
# svcadm restart application/print/server
```

 **Two additional SMF services for LP are** application/print/rfc1179 **and** application/print/ipp-listener. **They receive submitted jobs from other systems using the RFC 1179 (lpd) or IPP printing protocols, respectively. These are automatically restarted if you restart** application/print/server.

Using CUPS

If you've enabled CUPS as your printing system, you can manage it using its built-in web management interface. If you enter the address http://localhost:631 into the location bar of Firefox, you'll see a page similar to that shown in Figure 5-5.

Because CUPS on OpenSolaris is essentially identical to CUPS on Linux and other systems, this book does not cover its use; consult its included documentation and the references in the "Resources" section of this chapter for further information.

NOTE **The default configuration for CUPS listens only on the loopback interface. Use the web management interface to enable remote systems to access your CUPS service.**

FIGURE 5-5

CUPS administration page

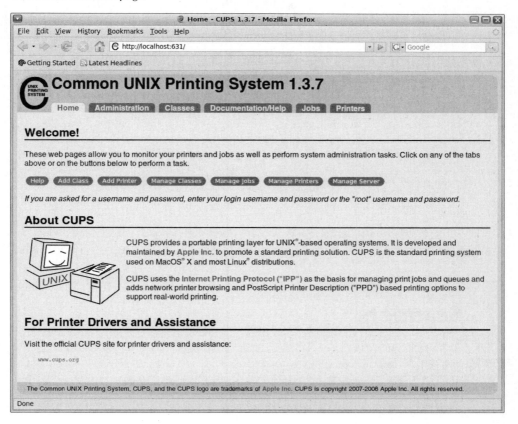

PPD management

Regardless of whether you are using LP or CUPS as your print system, output to your printer will in most cases be formatted by the foomatic-rip(1) print filter, which is called by the standard_foomatic interface program shown earlier in the lpstat example output in the section "Checking printer status." This filter program converts PostScript and other file formats into the printer's native representation. To convert all forms of data into a variety of printer output languages, foomatic-rip uses a repository of printer descriptions, known as the PostScript Printer Description (PPD) repository. Each model of printer is represented by a PPD file in the repository; the PPD file provides all the information required by foomatic-rip to produce printable output for that specific printer model.

If you acquire a printer for which OpenSolaris does not have a PPD file, you may find one on the manufacturer's website, or on the OpenPrinting website, http://openprinting.org/printer_list.cgi. Once you have downloaded the PPD file, you must use the ppdmgr command to install it into the OpenSolaris PPD repository so that foomatic-rip can use it. For example, to install the FastPrinter.ppd file into the system, use ppdmgr -a:

```
# ppdmgr -a FastPrinter.ppd
```

You can then configure the printer — either manually using printmgr or automatically with Presto. OpenSolaris maintains a cache of the descriptive information from each PPD, stored in the file /var/lp/ppd/ppdcache, so these user interfaces can efficiently list the available PPDs. This cache is automatically updated when you add a PPD file with ppdmgr. Additionally, because PPD files can be installed directly into the PPD repository by packages, OpenSolaris provides an SMF service, application/print/ppd-cache-update, which automatically updates the ppdcache table each time the system is booted. You can restart the service to have it run without rebooting the system:

```
# svcadm restart ppd-cache-update
```

You may also need to acquire a driver for printers not yet supported by the distribution; you can contact the manufacturer, check with the OpenSolaris printing community, or check the OpenPrinting website for information on driver availability.

Scanners

Scanning support for OpenSolaris and many other platforms is provided by the SANE (Scanner Access Now Easy) project; its main website is http://sane-project.org. SANE supports a vast number of devices, including parallel, SCSI, and USB scanners, as well as digital still and video cameras, from a variety of manufacturers. The SANE website provides detailed information on devices supported by the software.

You can install SANE from the pkg.opensolaris.org software repository using the following command:

```
# pkg install SUNWsane-frontend SUNWsane-backend
```

CROSS-REF   Chapter 6 provides information on installing packages from the OpenSolaris package repository.

Once SANE is installed, you can use the sane-find-scanner command to verify that your device is recognized, and then use the scanimage command or xscanimage graphical user interface to retrieve images from your scanner. SANE can also be used as a plug-in to the GIMP to provide integrated image capture and editing. See the man pages for these commands for further details.

USB Devices

The Universal Serial Bus (USB) has become the most common means of attaching peripheral devices to computer systems. Over the past 10 years, USB has made obsolete the separate serial, parallel, keyboard, and mouse ports that were found on PCs for many years, resulting in simpler and more flexible PC designs and reducing cable clutter for users. The original USB 1.1 standard provided for fairly slow data transfer speeds suitable for replacing those devices. The more recent USB 2.0 standard increased the transfer speed sufficiently for use as an interface for bandwidth-intensive applications such as disk storage, video transfer, and networking. OpenSolaris supports a wide variety of USB devices, the details of which are discussed in the following sections.

NOTE OpenSolaris also includes support for USB's principal competitor technology, IEEE 1394 (also commonly known as FireWire). However, FireWire is typically found only in data storage and digital video devices, and is not covered in this book. See Sun's *System Administration Guide: Devices and File Systems*, http://docs.sun.com/app/docs/doc/819-2723, for more information.

Keyboards and mice

OpenSolaris supports USB keyboards and mice. You can even have multiple keyboards and mice connected simultaneously, and OpenSolaris will multiplex the input from all of them, a function provided by the virtualkm(7D) driver. Note that OpenSolaris also retains support for the older PS/2 standard for keyboard and mouse devices, and virtualkm will multiplex them with USB devices. You can view the type of keyboard used on your system using the kbd command:

```
$ kbd -t
USB keyboard
```

The kbd command supports several configuration options, including the layout. Persistent settings are stored in /etc/default/kbd, from which they are read during system boot. Some keyboards support auto-detection of their layout, but the inexpensive keyboards on most systems do not provide this, so you usually need to manually configure the layout.

CROSS-REF See Chapter 3 for more information on configuring keyboard layout.

Mice are usually auto-configured by the X Window System during startup, but can be manually configured using a /etc/X11/xorg.conf X server configuration file.

CROSS-REF See Chapter 4 for information on configuring the X server.

MP3 players

Because MP3 music players support the USB Mass Storage protocol, connecting one to Open-Solaris will cause it to be automatically mounted under the /media directory, similar to USB disk drives. After it is mounted, you can access the tracks as files and use the standard file utilities to transfer tracks to and from the player. This functionality will work with any MP3 player.

If you have an Apple iPod, the gtkpod program provides a more complete interface for managing its various functions; it is located in the Blastwave package repository, as the package IPSgtkpod.

CROSS-REF See Chapter 6 for information on installing packages from alternative repositories.

Webcams

One of the more interesting types of USB peripherals is the *webcam*, a video camera that connects to your computer's USB port and provides video (and often audio, if the device includes a microphone) input capabilities. Current USB webcams support the USB Video Class 1.1 specification, and OpenSolaris provides the usbvc(7D) device driver to interface with devices compliant with that specification. If your system has a built-in webcam, it's likely connected internally via USB and thus usable with OpenSolaris.

The primary application for webcams is low-cost video conferencing over the Internet using the Session Initiation Protocol (SIP). The OpenSolaris GNOME desktop includes the Ekiga video conferencing and voice-over-IP (VOIP) application. You can use Ekiga to conduct video conferences with anyone else on the Internet who also has a webcam and software that supports the SIP protocol, or you can place Internet phone calls. You may need to first install the Ekiga application from the OpenSolaris package repository. At this writing, it is found in the package SUNWgnome-meeting.

Connect your webcam to one of your USB ports and verify that the usbvc driver attaches to it. You should see a message similar to the following in the system log, /var/adm/messages:

```
Jul 17 20:28:43 dminer-laptop usba: [ID 912658 kern.info] USB 2.0 interface-
association (usbia46d,8cb.config1.0) operating at hi speed (USB 2.x) on
USB 2.0 root hub: video@0, usbvc0 at bus address 2
```

You can also verify that the device links are created:

```
$ ls -l /dev/video0
lrwxrwxrwx   1 root     root           10 Jul 17 20:28 /dev/video0 -> usb/video0
$ ls -l /dev/usb/video0
lrwxrwxrwx   1 root     root           66 Jul 17 20:28 /dev/usb/video0 ->
../../devices/pci@0,0/pci1179,1@1d,7/miscellaneous@7/video@0:usbvc
```

If all appears well with the devices, you can start Ekiga from the GNOME menu: Applications ➤ Internet ➤ Video Conference. The first time you run Ekiga, it starts a wizard interface to walk you through the initial configuration process. As part of the configuration process, Ekiga offers the option to obtain a free `ekiga.net` SIP account; by creating an account, you can call, and receive calls from, other `ekiga.net` users. This is not required, though, because Ekiga can be used with any SIP conferencing service.

NOTE The most well-known Internet telephony and video service is Skype, but unfortunately Skype is not available for OpenSolaris. Because Skype uses proprietary protocols, you cannot place calls to (or receive calls from) Skype users with Ekiga.

You can also use Ekiga for direct connection between two systems without a SIP service, if the two systems can be directly connected to each other, as is often the case on an organization's internal network. To use direct connection on the Internet, both systems must have public IP addresses, not private addresses used behind firewalls that provide Network Address Translation (NAT). If your system is connected via NAT, you need to use a service such as `ekiga.net` for video conferencing.

CROSS-REF See Chapter 9 for information on NAT and firewalls.

Other portions of Ekiga's configuration process include detecting whether your network is using NAT and configuring the audio and video devices. Usually, Ekiga detects these automatically and you only need to confirm the settings it suggests; you can consult its online help for assistance if you run into trouble. The last step of the wizard is a confirmation screen that displays all of the settings you'll be using (see Figure 5-6).

FIGURE 5-6

Ekiga configuration

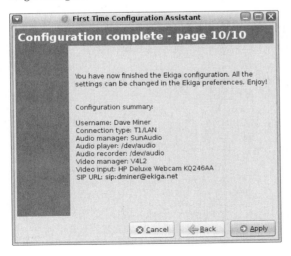

FIGURE 5-7

Ekiga's main window

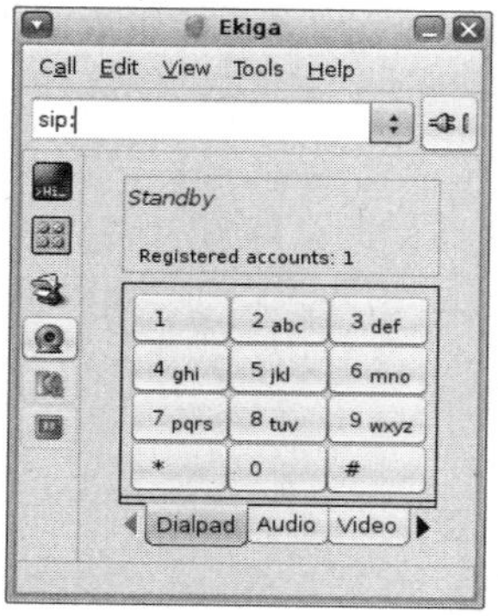

After you apply the configuration, you'll see Ekiga's main window, which should look similar to Figure 5-7.

The main menu bar includes Call, Edit, View, Tools, and Help menus. The Call menu includes commands to place a call, as well as options for setting your status for receiving calls:

- **Available** — You are available for calls, but are prompted to answer before an incoming call is connected.
- **Auto Answer** — Incoming calls are connected automatically.
- **Do Not Disturb** — Incoming calls are blocked.
- **Forward** — Incoming calls are forwarded to a different SIP host, which is configured in your preferences.

The Call menu also includes menu items to control calls that are in progress.

The Edit menu includes items to configure Ekiga, configure your preferences, and manage your SIP accounts. The View menu items can be used to modify the display settings. The Tools menu enables you to manage your address book, open the Chat window (Ekiga can be used for text chats, too), view the call and session diagnostic logs, and configure a PC-to-phone account, which you can use to call a telephone number using Ekiga.

Below the menu bar is a text field into which you enter the address you're calling. Next to it is a button to initiate the connection after you've entered an address. After you're in a call, you click this button to disconnect. The left side of the window displays a series of icons — from top to bottom, they perform the following functions:

- Open the text chat window
- Toggle the display of the tabbed controls at the bottom of the window

- Open the address book
- Toggle display of the current image from the local camera. When not in a call, you can click this button to activate the camera, and its stream will be displayed in the center of the window.
- Mute audio toggle
- Pause video toggle

The center of the main window is used to display the local or remote video, or both, depending on the settings selected in the View menu; you can also choose to display the local and remote video in separate windows. The lower part of the main window provides a set of tabs with controls to adjust the audio and video and view statistics for a call in progress, as well as a graphical dialing pad for dialing phone numbers using the mouse.

> **TIP** Before you attempt to place or receive any calls with Ekiga, select Edit ➤ Preferences, choose Network Settings from the list on the left of the Preferences window, and ensure that the Network Interface option is set to listen on your actual network interface and not on the localhost (127.0.0.1) address (because that address won't allow you to make or receive calls with another system).

If you don't have anyone specific to call, you can perform a simple echo test with Ekiga by calling the address sip:500@ekiga.net. This mirror service reflects back the audio and video you are sending, enabling you to verify and adjust your camera settings. It also gives you some idea of the latency between you and the ekiga.net SIP service. If your network is operating well, there should be very little delay between the sent and received video images. Once you have your camera adjusted and working, start calling your friends!

You can obtain much more information about Ekiga from its main project site, http://ekiga.org.

Digital cameras

OpenSolaris supports most digital cameras available today — thanks, in part, to the flexibility of the cameras. Digital cameras often offer two options for communication over USB: the USB Mass Storage protocol or the USB Picture Transfer Protocol (PTP). When a camera is connected as a mass storage device, you see messages similar to the following in the system log, /var/adm/messages:

```
Jul 16 22:04:45 dminer-laptop usba: [ID 912658 kern.info] USB 1.10 device
(usb4b0,304) operating at full speed (USB 1.x) on USB 1.10 root hub:
storage@1, scsa2usb3 at bus address 2
Jul 16 22:04:45 dminer-laptop usba: [ID 349649 kern.info]   NIKON  DSC
COOLPIX L4
Jul 16 22:04:45 dminer-laptop genunix: [ID 936769 kern.info] scsa2usb3 is
/pci@0,0/pci1179,1@1d,2/storage@1
Jul 16 22:04:45 dminer-laptop genunix: [ID 408114 kern.info]
/pci@0,0/pci1179,1@1d,2/storage@1 (scsa2usb3) online
```

```
Jul 16 22:04:45 dminer-laptop scsi: [ID 193665 kern.info] sd7 at
scsa2usb3: target 0 lun 0
Jul 16 22:04:45 dminer-laptop genunix: [ID 936769 kern.info] sd7 is
/pci@0,0/pci1179,1@1d,2/storage@1/disk@0,0
Jul 16 22:04:45 dminer-laptop genunix: [ID 408114 kern.info]
/pci@0,0/pci1179,1@1d,2/storage@1/disk@0,0 (sd7) online
```

When a camera that supports PTP is attached, you see messages such as the following in /var/adm/messages:

```
Jul 16 22:08:24 dminer-laptop usba: [ID 912658 kern.info] USB 1.10 device
(usb4b0,305) operating at full speed (USB 1.x) on USB 1.10 root hub:
image@1, usb_mid3 at bus address 2
Jul 16 22:08:24 dminer-laptop usba: [ID 349649 kern.info]    NIKON  DSC
COOLPIX L4-PTP
Jul 16 22:08:24 dminer-laptop genunix: [ID 936769 kern.info] usb_mid3 is
/pci@0,0/pci1179,1@1d,2/image@1
Jul 16 22:08:24 dminer-laptop genunix: [ID 408114 kern.info]
/pci@0,0/pci1179,1@1d,2/image@1 (usb_mid3) online
Jul 16 22:08:24 dminer-laptop usba: [ID 349649 kern.info] usba:    no
driver found for interface 0 (nodename: 'image') of NIKON  DSC COOLPIX L4-PTP
```

These two examples are the same camera; its setup menu offers a choice between Mass Storage or PTP mode. In Mass Storage mode, the camera appears to be a pluggable disk drive, similar to a USB memory stick or a hard drive in a USB enclosure. When attached in this mode, the camera presents itself as a PCFS file system and is automatically mounted into the file system under the /media directory. The pictures stored on the camera are located in one or more directories under the camera's mount point; for example:

```
$ ls /media/NO_NAME/DCIM/118NIKON
DSCN1207.JPG  DSCN1240.JPG  DSCN1266.JPG  DSCN1293.JPG  DSCN1319.JPG
DSCN1209.JPG  DSCN1241.JPG  DSCN1267.JPG  DSCN1294.JPG  DSCN1320.JPG
DSCN1211.JPG  DSCN1242.JPG  DSCN1268.JPG  DSCN1295.JPG  DSCN1321.JPG
DSCN1212.JPG  DSCN1243.JPG  DSCN1269.JPG  DSCN1296.JPG  DSCN1322.JPG
```

You can use image viewing and editing programs to view and edit the files, and copy them from the camera using standard utilities such as cp and mv.

CROSS-REF   See Chapter 4 for information on image viewing and editing tools.

To access a camera that uses PTP, you need to use the gtkam graphical interface or the gphoto2 command. To start gtkam from the GNOME menus, select Applications ➤ Graphics ➤ Gtkam Digital Camera Browser. Once started, select Camera ➤ Add Camera; and in the dialog that displays, click the Detect button to have gtkam automatically detect the camera model. If it fails, then you can manually select the model and port. Then click OK and gtkam will initialize the camera, which may take some time. Figure 5-8 shows the display during the initialization process.

FIGURE 5-8

Adding a camera in gtkam

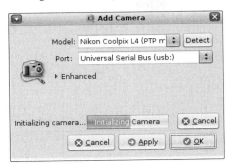

FIGURE 5-9

Browsing a camera in gtkam

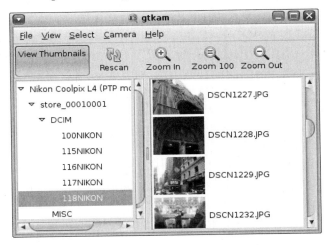

Once the camera is initialized, you can browse thumbnails of the photos stored on the camera, view individual photos, and copy or delete the photos. Figure 5-9 shows gtkam's main window browsing a camera's photo storage. See the gtkam man page and online help for more information.

Once you have transferred photos from your camera to your computer, you will probably want to create digital photo albums to organize and display them. The gThumb program included in the OpenSolaris desktop provides a simple photo album capability; see Chapter 4 for more information on it. For more sophisticated photo albums, we recommend the excellent open source JAlbum software (`http://jalbum.net`), which is a powerful tool for organizing and sharing digital photo albums.

Audio

Audio support in OpenSolaris has historically been weak, but it's rapidly improving. In part, this is because of greater standardization by manufacturers on the interfaces for audio devices; but OpenSolaris is also, as of this writing, in the process of overhauling its audio framework by integrating the Open Sound System (OSS) framework. The OSS framework includes a much richer set of sound interfaces and extensive driver support (see the project page at `http://opensolaris.org/os/project/opensound` for information on OSS). If you have USB audio devices, such as speakers or a headset, you should be able to use them successfully with OpenSolaris because the USB Audio Class specification is supported by the `usb_ac(7D)` driver. If you attach a USB headset, for example, you'll see a series of messages in the system log, `/var/adm/messages`, as the USB drivers bind to it. As a result, built-in or USB audio devices should work automatically.

OpenSolaris provides the simple command-line utilities `audioplay(1)` and `audiorecord(1)` for playing and recording uncompressed audio formats such as AU, AIFF, and WAV. The GNOME desktop also includes a sound recording application. Started by selecting Applications ➢ Sound and Video ➢ Sound Recorder, it supports additional recording formats, including FLAC, Ogg, and Speex. You can easily test that your audio devices are working correctly using these applications.

CROSS-REF   Chapter 4 covers the playing of MP3 and other audio and video formats.

Serial Devices and Modems

Before high-speed Internet access over DSL and cable technologies became widespread, a great deal of Internet traffic was transmitted between systems using phone-line modems connected to serial ports. These technologies are still used for some low-bandwidth applications such as console access to server systems.

Serial ports

For many years, it was standard for PCs to include two serial ports, which might be used to dial in or out with a modem, or to connect a terminal server to provide console access to the PC, once the operating system was configured to use a serial port as its console. OpenSolaris retains some legacy configuration from this era, such as the port monitor configuration displayed with pmadm(1M), shown here:

```
# pmadm -l
PMTAG         PMTYPE      SVCTAG       FLGS ID        <PMSPECIFIC>
zsmon         ttymon      ttya           u  root      /dev/term/a I -
/usr/bin/login - 9600 ldterm,ttcompat ttya login: - tvi925 y  #
zsmon         ttymon      ttyb           u  root      /dev/term/b I -
/usr/bin/login - 9600 ldterm,ttcompat ttyb login: - tvi925 y  #
```

This configuration shows two ports, ttya and ttyb, attached to the serial devices
/dev/term/a and /dev/term/b. With this default configuration, users can log in via
the serial port if a device such as a terminal or terminal server is connected to the serial port
and configured with a speed of 9,600 bits per second. Consult pmadm(1M) and related man
pages for more details on port monitor configuration.

> **NOTE** If your system has serial ports, the first port is accessed at the device /dev/term/a,
> the second is /dev/term/b, and so on.

You can also connect out over a serial port using the tip(1) command. The /etc/remote file
defines systems to which you can connect using tip. The most useful entry in the default
/etc/remote is hardwire:

```
hardwire:&bsol;
    :dv=/dev/term/b:br#9600:el=^C^S^Q^U^D:ie=%$:oe=^D:
```

Typing the command **tip hardwire** will connect you to whatever device is connected to the system's second serial port, which is the device /dev/term/b. If this port is in turn connected via
a cable to the serial console of another OpenSolaris (or Linux) system, then it's possible to log in
on that system to perform administrative tasks. For example:

```
$ tip hardwire
connected

badboy console login: dminer
Password:
Last login: Thu Jul 10 22:28:03 from krissy
{badboy} ~.
[EOT]
```

As shown, you can type the character sequence ~. to terminate the tip session. Other special
tilde sequences are available within tip; type ~? during a tip session for help with them.

Consult the tip(1) and remote(4) man pages for more information on connecting over serial
ports.

USB-to-serial converters

While serial ports are disappearing from newer systems, you may still need to connect to an
older system over its serial port. Devices known as USB-to-serial converters are sold by several
manufacturers for this application, and OpenSolaris includes drivers for several common ones.

Current information on supported devices is available on the Solaris USB FAQ referenced in the "Resources" section at the end of this chapter. The following example demonstrates connecting a Keyspan USA-19HS converter, configuring it to connect to the console port of a Sun server, and starting a console session using tip. First, the system log /var/adm/messages shows the converter being connected to the system:

```
Jul 11 19:44:21 dminer-laptop usba: [ID 912658 kern.info] USB 1.10 device
(usb6cd,121) operating at full speed (USB 1.x) on USB 1.10 root hub:
device@1, usbsksp0 at bus address 2
Jul 11 19:44:21 dminer-laptop usba: [ID 349649 kern.info]    Keyspan, a
division of InnoSys Inc.  USA-19H
Jul 11 19:44:21 dminer-laptop genunix: [ID 936769 kern.info] usbsksp0 is
/pci@0,0/pci1179,1@1d/device@1
Jul 11 19:44:21 dminer-laptop genunix: [ID 408114 kern.info]
/pci@0,0/pci1179,1@1d/device@1 (usbsksp0) online
```

A device link for the converter is automatically created in devfs, as shown here:

```
$ ls -l /dev/cua/*
lrwxrwxrwx  1 root     root            48 Jul 11 19:44 /dev/cua/1 ->
../../devices/pci@0,0/pci1179,1@1d/device@1:0,cu
lrwxrwxrwx  1 root     root            32 Feb  6 18:08 /dev/cua/a ->
../../devices/isa/asy@1,3f8:a,cu
```

The device path for /dev/cua/1 corresponds to the device path listed in the system log entry. To use this device with tip, you must add an entry such as the following to /etc/remote:

```
cua1:dv=/dev/cua/1:br#9600:el=^C^S^Q^U^D:ie=%$:oe=^D:
```

This is just a copy of the hardwire entry shown in the previous section, with the device name changed to reference the converter. Now it's possible to connect to the converter port and access the server's console:

```
$ tip cua1
connected

netra console login: dminer
Password:
Last login: Thu Jul 10 22:28:03 from china
{netra}
```

If you disconnect the converter, a message similar to the following appears in the system log:

```
Jul 11 19:51:48 dminer-laptop genunix: [ID 408114 kern.info]
/pci@0,0/pci1179,1@1d/device@1 (usbsksp0) offline
```

Disconnecting the converter also automatically removes the /dev/cua link for it.

USB-to-serial converters can also be used as login ports, but to do so you need to add a port monitor using the pmadm command. Consult the *System Administration Guide: Advanced Administration*, at http://docs.sun.com/app/docs/doc/819-2380, for information.

Modems

Unfortunately, OpenSolaris is unable to support the modems that are included in recent desktop and laptop systems, which are commonly known as *softmodems*. These modems are designed to provide only a simple hardware interface to the telephone network, with most of the signal and protocol processing functions pushed up to the operating system driver. This means that the manufacturer of the modem generally must either publish the specifications for the hardware or provide the driver. Few of the manufacturers write drivers for any operating system other than Windows, so most modern modems work only with that OS (hence, another term for these modems is *Winmodems*). If you need to use a modem with OpenSolaris, you may be able to locate a PC Card modem for a laptop's PC Card slot that can be used. Otherwise, you need to find a modem that can work with a serial interface and then connect it to your computer's serial port. However, most recent systems have eliminated the serial ports, so you likely need a USB-to-serial converter as well, and then connect the modem to the converter.

Once you have a hardware modem that will work with OpenSolaris, you can use the PPP software to connect to your ISP. The OpenSolaris PPP implementation is not covered in this book. For assistance, consult the OpenSolaris documentation, specifically the *System Administration Guide: Network Services* (see `http://docs.sun.com/app/docs/doc/819-1634`).

Network Interfaces

Most modern computer systems come with an Ethernet interface as a standard feature, and laptops usually include an IEEE 802.11 (WiFi) network interface. OpenSolaris includes drivers for many of the common network interface cards and is continually adding more, so your system's interfaces are likely to be supported automatically; you can use the Device Driver Utility discussed in Chapter 2 to verify this. If they are not supported, you may be able to locate a third-party driver by checking the manufacturer's website. Some community developers have also written drivers that are not integrated with OpenSolaris. The most notable of these is the free driver collection written by Masayuki Murayama, which can be found at `http://homepage2.nifty.com/mrym3/taiyodo/eng`.

If you can't find a driver for your built-in network interfaces, you can likely purchase a PCI or PC Card network interface for which a driver is available, either as part of the OS or from other sources. These are generally not expensive.

Another networking technology for which some support is available in OpenSolaris is the wireless broadband, or 3G network, technologies provided by the mobile phone networks. The OpenSolaris Wireless Wide Area Network project, `http://opensolaris.org/os/project/wwan`, has developed drivers for several of the USB and PC Card devices that are used to connect to these networks. They operate somewhat like modems, in that PPP is used to manage the connection to the provider. You usually need to perform an initial registration and setup process for these networks using Windows, after which you can use OpenSolaris to connect at any time.

One additional characteristic of network interface drivers is that, unlike many other types of drivers, they often have tunable properties that can be used to alter their behavior to improve their operation or performance. The Brussels project on OpenSolaris has extended the dladm(1M) command to provide a standard interface for configuring the interface properties using the subcommands show-linkprop, set-linkprop, and reset-linkprop. You can view the tunable properties of your network interfaces using show-linkprop:

```
#  dladm show-linkprop
LINK        PROPERTY         VALUE   DEFAULT   POSSIBLE
e1000g0     speed            100     --        --
e1000g0     autopush         --      --        --
e1000g0     zone             --      --        --
e1000g0     duplex           full    --        half,full
e1000g0     state            up      up        up,down
e1000g0     adv_autoneg_cap  1       1         1,0
e1000g0     mtu              1500    1500      --
e1000g0     flowctrl         bi      bi        no,tx,rx,bi
e1000g0     adv_1000fdx_cap  1       1         1,0
e1000g0     en_1000fdx_cap   1       1         1,0
e1000g0     adv_1000hdx_cap  0       1         1,0
e1000g0     en_1000hdx_cap   0       1         1,0
e1000g0     adv_100fdx_cap   1       1         1,0
e1000g0     en_100fdx_cap    1       1         1,0
e1000g0     adv_100hdx_cap   1       1         1,0
e1000g0     en_100hdx_cap    1       1         1,0
e1000g0     adv_10fdx_cap    1       1         1,0
e1000g0     en_10fdx_cap     1       1         1,0
e1000g0     adv_10hdx_cap    1       1         1,0
e1000g0     en_10hdx_cap     1       1         1,0
wpi0        channel          14      --        --
wpi0        powermode        ?       off       off,fast,max
wpi0        radio            ?       on        on,off
wpi0        speed            --      --        1,2,5.5,6,9,11,12,18,24,
                                               36,48,54
wpi0        autopush         --      --        --
wpi0        zone             --      --        --
wpi0        state            down    up        up,down
wpi0        mtu              1500    1500      --
```

The system in this example has both a wired interface, e1000g0 (an Intel Gigabit Ethernet device) and a wireless interface, wpi0 (an Intel WiFi interface). As shown, each has several properties that can be configured, and show-linkprop provides a view of the default values, as well as the possible values, for each one. Configuring these properties is uncommon, however, so this book doesn't cover it further, but you can consult the dladm man page for more information on link property configuration.

CROSS-REF Additional information on network interface configuration may be found in Chapter 9.

Power Management and UPSs

Power management is an increasingly important issue in computing today as electricity costs continue to increase, and it's an area of active development in OpenSolaris. The Power Management community, `http://opensolaris.org/os/community/pm`, sponsors several projects to provide a variety of power management capabilities, including CPU power management, system suspend and resume, and power management policies for servers.

If you are using a laptop with OpenSolaris, you're probably most interested in OpenSolaris support for suspend and resume of the system, so that you can shut your system off for transport from home to office, for example, and pick up right where you left off when you turn the system back on. As of this writing, OpenSolaris has only limited support for suspend and resume, due to the need to update device drivers to re-initialize correctly when the system is resumed. All SPARC desktops, and recent Sun x86 desktops, are capable of suspend and resume, and support for additional systems, including laptops, is in progress. The Suspend/Resume project is performing this work, and you can track its progress at `http://opensolaris.org/os/project/suspend-resume`. If your system is capable of being suspended, you can select the Suspend option on the GNOME System Shutdown dialog (select System ➤ Shut Down in the GNOME menus).

A logical question at this point is how to determine whether your system is suspend-capable. As of this writing, the best answer is to try it. If you attempt to suspend and it fails, look at `/var/adm/messages` to determine which driver(s) rejected the suspend request. If the system fails to resume after a suspend, you may also be able to use `/var/adm/messages` to determine which drivers failed to resume. Beyond that, consulting the OpenSolaris community and project mailing lists is likely necessary to obtain additional help.

Server power management is also an increasingly important topic, and the OpenSolaris community would like its operating system to be known as the most power-efficient on the market. The Tesla project, `http://opensolaris.org/os/project/tesla`, is the hub for server power management development activity in the OpenSolaris community.

Configuring power management

Power management on OpenSolaris is configured using the file `/etc/power.conf`. Its default entries are as follows:

```
device-dependency-property removable-media /dev/fb
autopm                     default
autoS3                     default
# Auto-Shutdown            Idle(min)      Start/Finish(hh:mm)    Behavior
autoshutdown               30             9:00 9:00              noshutdown
cpupm enable
cpu-threshold 1s
```

The device-dependency-property entry instructs the system to keep any removable media devices, such as CD drives or memory card readers, powered on if the system's display device and monitor (represented by the device /dev/fb) are powered on.

The autopm entry controls whether device power management is enabled; it can have the value enabled, disabled, or default. If the value is default, the behavior depends on the type of system. If the system is a desktop or laptop system, devices are power-managed, but if it's a server, they are not. See the power.conf(4) man page for details on how the system determines whether it uses a server or desktop/laptop policy.

The autoS3 entry controls suspend-to-ram capability on x86 systems. As with autopm, the default value depends on system type. When enabled, this allows the system to automatically suspend itself if all power-managed devices have gone into their lowest power state, meaning the system is completely idle.

You can use the autoshutdown entry to have suspend-capable systems suspend automatically when the system has been idle for a specified period of time during certain periods of the day. The noshutdown value in the default configuration disables this feature. It's most useful for office desktops, which can suspend overnight while idle.

The cpupm entry controls CPU power management. CPU power management is possible on x86 processors that include Intel's Enhanced SpeedStep or AMD's PowerNow! technologies. The default configuration enables CPU power management whenever the hardware supports it. You can also control the threshold time for CPU power stepping using a cpu-threshold entry. The default configuration uses a one-second threshold. This means that if the CPU has performed no work in the last second, it is slowed one step, repeating until it reaches its lowest power state. You can use a threshold value of always-on to always run the CPU at full power.

If you make any changes to /etc/power.conf, you must run the pmconfig(1M) command to update the running system with the configuration specified in the file.

Uninterruptible power supply (UPS)

Another aspect of power management is ensuring that you don't lose power at an inopportune time; or that if you have a power interruption, you can perform an orderly shutdown of your system to avoid data loss or corruption. OpenSolaris's use of ZFS as its standard file system greatly reduces your risk of such problems due to its inherent design characteristics, so this isn't as critical an issue as it once was, but allowing a system time to shut down before power vanishes is certainly still a good idea.

You can use any uninterruptible power supply (UPS) with OpenSolaris to provide protection against a brief power glitch — to ensure the system doesn't go down due to a momentary interruption from events such as a lightning strike, for instance. However, to automatically perform an orderly shutdown before the UPS battery is drained, you need to connect the system to the UPS using a USB or serial connection, and then install software that can interface with the UPS to interpret its signals and initiate a system shutdown. Some manufacturers provide support for

Solaris and OpenSolaris in their proprietary software; check the Solaris Hardware Compatibility List (see the link in the "Resources" section at the end of this chapter) and your UPS vendor's website for information on vendor support.

The best-known open source project for UPS software is Network UPS Tools (see http://networkupstools.org). As of this writing, these tools have not been packaged for OpenSolaris, so download the source and compile them yourself. Consult the project's website for further details.

CROSS-REF Chapter 24 provides information on developing software on OpenSolaris.

Device Drivers

Like most other operating systems, OpenSolaris uses kernel modules known as *device drivers* to communicate with both the internal and the peripheral devices attached to the system. Having the right device drivers is critical if you're going to use all of your computer system's capabilities. OpenSolaris strives to have device drivers for as many devices as possible, but not all devices are supported. Chapter 2 presented several options for determining whether your devices are supported, so your first step is to run one of those tools if you have a question about device support.

OpenSolaris uses a special type of file system called the *device file system*, or devfs, to provide raw access to the devices on the system. You generally don't need to interact with devfs, nor do you often need to delve into the details of device support, but you can use the prtdiag(1M) and prtconf(1M) commands to examine this information when necessary.

CROSS-REF See Chapter 7 for information on devfs, and Chapter 14 for more information on prtdiag and prtconf.

One concept that is useful to understand is the mechanism by which OpenSolaris associates device drivers with devices. This is controlled by the contents of the file /etc/driver_aliases. Each device driver on the system registers the identifiers for the devices it supports into this database when the driver package is installed. This is just an ordinary text file, so you can view its contents with cat or more. Here's an excerpt:

```
npe "pciex_root_complex"
pcie_pci "pciexclass,060400"
pcie_pci "pciexclass,060401"
kb8042 "pnpPNP,303"
mouse8042 "pnpPNP,f03"
vgatext "pnpPNP,900"
vgatext "pciclass,000100"
vgatext "pciclass,030000"
vgatext "pciclass,030001"
bscbus "SVI0101"
```

```
pseudo zconsnex
st "scsiclass,01"
sgen "scsa,08.bfcp"
sgen "scsa,08.bvhci"
mpt "pci1000,30"
mpt "pci1000,50"
 ...
```

CAUTION   Although /etc/driver_aliases is a text file, do not edit it directly because if it is corrupted in any way, your system may fail to boot. If modifications to the driver_aliases file are necessary, they must be made using the add_drv(1M) and rem_drv(1M) commands.

A more detailed discussion of device drivers is beyond the scope of this book. If the topic is of interest to you, see the OpenSolaris Device Drivers community at http://opensolaris.org/os/community/device_drivers for more information and resources.

Resources

A number of printing resources are available:

- The Sun documentation is found in the *System Administration Guide: Solaris Printing*, at http://docs.sun.com/app/docs/doc/819-7761.
- The OpenSolaris Printing community has more information on a variety of printing topics at http://opensolaris.org/os/community/printing.
- Find full information on CUPS at http://cups.org.
- A useful note on how to enable duplex printing is available at http://sun.com/bigadmin/content/submitted/duplex_printing.html.

A primary source of information about using USB devices with OpenSolaris is the USB FAQ, hosted at http://sun.com/io_technologies/usb/USB-Faq.html.

The JAlbum software for digital photo albums is available from http://jalbum.net.

The main information page for Ekiga video conferencing is http://ekiga.org.

Details on the Open Sound System (OSS) are available at http://opensound.com.

Sun maintains an OpenSolaris Hardware Compatibility List at http://sun.com/bigadmin/hcl/search.jsp.

Masayuki Murayama's collection of open source network interface drivers is hosted at http://homepage2.nifty.com/mrym3/taiyodo/eng/.

Development of drivers for 3G cellular data networking is hosted at the Wireless Wide-Area Networking project, `http://opensolaris.org/os/project/wwan`.

Additional documentation from Sun related to topics from this chapter can be found here:

- *System Administration Guide: Advanced Administration* at `http://docs.sun.com/app/docs/doc/819-2380`.
- *System Administration Guide: Devices and File Systems* at `http://docs.sun.com/app/docs/doc/819-2723`.

Device driver development activity in OpenSolaris is hosted by the Device Drivers community, `http://opensolaris.org/os/community/device_drivers`.

OpenSolaris power management development is managed by the Power Management community, `http://opensolaris.org/os/community/pm`.

Summary

In this chapter, you learned how to set up and manage printers on OpenSolaris, including switching between the two printing systems offered. You explored the details of device support for a variety of peripheral devices, including multimedia devices such as webcams, digital cameras, and MP3 players. You also learned about the OpenSolaris interfaces for managing traditional serial devices and modems, as well as USB-to-serial converters. Finally, you were introduced to the power management functions available and under development in OpenSolaris, and the commands used to explore the system's device configuration.

Chapter 6

Software Management

Once you've installed an operating system, you'll most likely need to add software that wasn't installed initially. It's also likely that you'll soon want to upgrade your installed software to obtain new functionality or fixes for bugs that are causing problems or that present a security threat. Software management is one of the most common administrative tasks that you'll perform on your system, so it's critical to understand the tools available.

As mentioned in earlier chapters, one of the key features of OpenSolaris is a new software management system: the Image Packaging System (IPS). Chapter 3 presented a basic introduction to the `pkg` command; in this chapter, you'll learn more about IPS and software management on OpenSolaris.

NOTE IPS can be used on operating systems other than OpenSolaris, but such usage is beyond the scope of this book. See the IPS project site at `http://opensolaris.org/os/project/pkg` for information.

Package Management

Like other operating systems, software for OpenSolaris is distributed in the form of a *package*. Oversimplified a bit, a package is a bundle of files that is installed to provide a specific function, such as word processing. Once upon a time, software packages were large and standalone, which meant that installing a package was a simple operation of copying the files from the bundle onto your system.

However, modern systems contain hundreds or thousands of packages linked together by dependencies, so typically you'll need to install multiple packages to obtain the functionality you want. Modern package managers understand and follow the package dependencies for you and automatically install any required packages, so this process usually remains a simple operation from the user's point of view, even though the underlying process is often quite complex.

IPS concepts

To use IPS effectively, you must understand several important concepts and terms. In IPS, the components that make up a package are called *actions*; each action expresses an operation that IPS applies to the system when installing or removing a package. The actions making up each package are collected into a *manifest*. Each package can evolve through a series of *versions*. Table 6-1 summarizes the actions supported by IPS.

TABLE 6-1

IPS Package Actions

Action	Description
depend	Defines a dependency on another package
directory	Creates a directory in the file system
driver	Registers a device driver
file	Creates a file in the file system
group	Defines a group in /etc/group
hardlink	Creates a hard link in the file system
legacy	Defines package data for the SVR4 legacy packaging system
license	Stores a license associated with the package
link	Creates a symbolic link in the file system
set	Defines a package attribute
user	Defines a user in /etc/passwd

Each IPS package is published by an *authority*, which is a name associated with a specific URL you configure. The packages published by each authority are listed in a *catalog*, and each authority distributes its packages using a *repository*, which is a server that resides either on a local system, on some other system on your network, or on the Internet. Multiple *mirrored* repositories can be used to optimize package download performance for users in different networks or geographical locations.

CROSS-REF See Chapter 3 for examples of installing packages from multiple authorities.

An IPS package is always installed into an *image*; each image can contain only a single version of any one package. An image can obtain packages from multiple authorities, one of which is designated as the *preferred authority*, meaning it is the default authority for any pkg commands that do not specify an authority explicitly. There are several types of images:

- **Full** — A standalone image typically containing an installed instance of an operating system. The OpenSolaris distribution's Live CD is a full image, as is a system installed using it.

- **Partial** — Linked to a full image. Partial images are used to install and manage OpenSolaris zones.

- **User** — Dependent on a full image. User images enable users to install their own versions of packages that differ from the versions installed in a full image.

CROSS-REF Zones are discussed in Chapter 19.

Each image contains data about the packages installed in it, including an *index* of the package information and actions that can be searched using the Package Manager and pkg command. For full and partial images, the package data is stored in the directory /var/pkg. For user images, the package data is stored in the directory .org.opensolaris.pkg in the root of the image.

Unlike most other package systems, a key aspect of the design of IPS is its emphasis on safe package installation and updates. In IPS terms, safety means that operations can be rolled back, enabling you to return your system to a prior state should a package operation have undesirable effects on its stability, performance, or usability. The safety of IPS is accomplished by leveraging the capabilities of the ZFS file system to create a snapshot of the file system prior to package operations. If you are updating the system using the pkg image-update command, a clone based on that snapshot is created and the package operations are applied to the clone, ensuring that the prior system state can be easily restored by rolling back to the snapshot. The clone is called a *boot environment*. A boot environment is also created if a pkg install or pkg uninstall operation fails. If this happens, pkg displays instructions for reverting your system to that boot environment. See the section "Boot Environment Management" later in this chapter for more details.

CROSS-REF Chapter 8 describes the features of the ZFS file system, including snapshots and clones.

Package names and versions

All packaging systems provide some type of a naming and versioning scheme so that users can identify their software. The naming and versioning provided by IPS is key to its ability to resolve dependencies and upgrade packages as new versions are released.

The canonical form of a package name in IPS is in the form of a Fault Managed Resource Identifier (FMRI), which is a naming scheme for system resources introduced as part of the Fault

Management Architecture in Solaris 10. FMRIs are also used to identify hardware components and system services in OpenSolaris.

CROSS-REF FMRIs and fault management are described in Chapter 12.

The FMRI for an IPS package is of the following form:

```
pkg://authority/name@version
```

For example, the full FMRI for a version of the Sun Studio Express package in the opensolaris.org repository is as follows:

```
pkg://opensolaris.org/sunstudioexpress@0.2008.5,5.11-0.86:20080430T211032Z
```

Fortunately, you'll rarely need to use the entire FMRI in referring to a package. Usually you can use just the name portion as an argument to the pkg command to install, uninstall, or view a package, and IPS will use the correct version (which is usually the newest version when installing, or the installed version when uninstalling) from your preferred authority. Because it's sometimes necessary to specify an exact version if you need to install a package that's not the newest, it's useful to understand the meaning of the version portion of the name. It's defined to be of the following form:

```
component_version,build_version-branch_version:timestamp
```

The version of the sunstudioexpress package just shown is interpreted as follows:

- **Component Version.** 0.2008.5. This version is based on the component's project version. Many projects provide packages that are portable across platforms, so the version string defined by that project is normally used as the component version.

- **Build Version.** 5.11. This specifies which version of OpenSolaris the package contents were built on. Because OpenSolaris provides forward compatibility, this version indicates the oldest version of OpenSolaris on which this package can be expected to run. As of this writing, all releases of OpenSolaris are based on version 5.11 of the operating system. Solaris 10 was version 5.10.

- **Branch Version.** 0.86. The branch is normally used to indicate a development build number, or a maintenance release number in the case of packages updated to provide specific fixes, such as a security patch.

- **Timestamp.** 20080430T211032Z. This specifies the date and time when the package was published into the repository. Each time the package is published into the repository, it has a different timestamp, even if other portions of the version are identical.

An IPS package that defines only dependency actions is known as a *group package*, as it's used to provide a shortcut to install a set of otherwise unrelated packages that are needed to provide a function. An example is the hpc-dev package; its manifest demonstrates what a group package looks like:

```
$ pkg contents -rm hpc-dev
set name=fmri value=pkg:/hpc-dev@0.5.11,5.11-0.86:20080504T074641Z
```

```
set name=authority value=opensolaris.org
set name=description value="HPC Application Development cluster"
depend fmri=pkg:/SUNWj6dmo@0.5.11-0.86 type=require
depend fmri=pkg:/SUNWsvn@1.4.3-0.86 type=require
depend fmri=pkg:/SUNWj6cfg@0.5.11-0.86 type=require
depend fmri=pkg:/SUNWj6rt@0.5.11-0.86 type=require
depend fmri=pkg:/SUNWcvs@1.12.13-0.86 type=require
depend fmri=pkg:/SUNWj6rtx@0.5.11-0.86 type=require
depend fmri=pkg:/SUNWj6man@0.5.11-0.86 type=require
depend fmri=pkg:/SUNWgmake@3.81-0.86 type=require
depend fmri=pkg:/SUNWj6dvx@0.5.11-0.86 type=require
depend fmri=pkg:/SUNWmercurial@0.9.5-0.86 type=require
depend fmri=pkg:/SUNWsprot@0.5.11-0.86 type=require
depend fmri=pkg:/sunstudioexpress@0.2008.05-0.86 type=require
depend fmri=pkg:/clustertools@7.1-0.86 type=require
depend fmri=pkg:/SUNWj6dev@0.5.11-0.86 type=require
depend fmri=pkg:/SUNWj6dmx@0.5.11-0.86 type=require
```

IPS defines another type of group package called an *incorporation*, which is used to tie compatible package versions together, ensuring that the set of all such packages that are installed are updated in lockstep. As of this writing, an incorporation called entire is used to tie the Open-Solaris operating system packages together for update purposes. See the pkg(5) man page for more information on incorporations.

Installing packages with Package Manager

Chapter 3 described the basic procedure for installing a package using the pkg(1) command, including refreshing the catalog using the pkg refresh command, searching for a package using pkg search, and installing a package using pkg install. In addition to the pkg command, OpenSolaris includes a graphical interface for software management: the Package Manager. You can start the Package Manager using the GNOME menu item System ➤ Administration ➤ Package Manager. Its main window is shown in Figure 6-1.

This window consists of several elements, most of which will be familiar if you've used tools such as Synaptic on Linux distributions. The menu bar and tool bar items enable you to refresh the catalog, update all packages, install or update a package, or remove a package. To the right of the toolbar is a drop-down menu for selecting the repository; opensolaris.org is the default repository for the OpenSolaris distribution, but other distributions might have a different default. The left pane and the drop-down menu above it enable you to select the categories of packages that are of interest, while the right pane displays the packages in the selected category, including name, status, and description. The Show drop-down menu enables you to further filter the packages displayed in the right pane: only packages that are installed, not installed, or that have updates available. The Search box enables you to filter the packages by searching the package index for specific strings. Finally, the bottom pane displays details about the package selected in the right pane; tabs organize this information into general information about the package, its contents, and its dependencies.

FIGURE 6-1

The Package Manager is used to manipulate IPS packages.

To install a package, use the searching and filtering capabilities to display the name of the package, and then click the checkbox to the left of the package name to select it. Then select Package ➤ Install/Update, or click the Install/Update icon on the toolbar. Package Manager then downloads the package and any packages that it depends on, and installs them. You can also select multiple packages (or all packages, using Edit ➤ Select All) and have them installed simultaneously.

Removing packages

Of course, you may also want to remove packages. This is just as easy as installing. To remove a package in the Package Manager, select the package by clicking its checkbox and then select Package ➤ Remove, or click the Remove icon in the toolbar. From the command line, you can use `pkg uninstall`:

```
# pkg uninstall SUNWwbsup

Creating Plan \
pkg: Cannot remove 'pkg:/SUNWwbsup@0.5.11,5.11-0.95:20080807T161553Z' due to
the following packages that depend on it:
  pkg:/SUNWpkgcmds@0.5.11,5.11-0.95:20080807T160715Z
  pkg:/SUNWswmt@0.5.11,5.11-0.95:20080807T161311Z
  pkg:/slim_install@0.1,5.11-0.95:20080807T163254Z
  pkg:/SUNWgui-install@0.5.11,5.11-0.95:20080807T154707Z
  pkg:/SUNWinstall-libs@0.5.11,5.11-0.95:20080807T160313Z
```

Clearly, removing a package won't always be simple because many packages have dependent packages, and IPS blocks the removal of a package that has installed dependents. You can, however, cause a package and all of its dependents to be removed by adding the -r option:

```
# pkg uninstall -r SUNWwbsup
```

In addition, you can use the -n option to simulate an uninstall, and the -v option to obtain more verbose output from the pkg command; these options can also be used with pkg install.

Viewing, verifying, and searching packages

As shown earlier, you can use Package Manager to view and search packages, the same capabilities available using the pkg command.

You can easily check the state of a package using pkg list:

```
$ pkg list SUNWtoo
NAME (AUTHORITY)                    VERSION       STATE      UFIX
SUNWtoo                             0.5.11-0.95   installed  ----
$ pkg list netbeans
pkg: no matching packages installed
```

If the package is installed, its version and state are displayed; if it's not installed, then you see the preceding error message (you can include packages that are not installed using pkg list -a). If the package is not associated with the image's preferred authority, then the package's authority is displayed in parentheses next to the package name. The UFIX column provides a concise display of additional state information for the package. The U column means that the catalog shows the package is upgradeable to a later version from that authority. F indicates that the package version has been frozen by the administrator and must remain at the installed version; this is used to ensure that upgrades that are incompatible with a critical package cannot be applied to the image. I indicates that the package is part of an incorporation, which means the package will be upgraded if the incorporation is upgraded. X means that the package has an exclusion with another package, meaning that the two packages cannot both be installed.

> **NOTE** As of this writing, the frozen, incorporate, and exclusion capabilities are not yet implemented in IPS.

If you enter the `pkg list` command without a package name, then it displays information about all installed packages, or all known packages if the `-a` option is specified.

To view the details about a package, use `pkg info`:

```
$ pkg info SUNWtoo
            Name: SUNWtoo
         Summary: Programming Tools
           State: Installed
       Authority: opensolaris.org (preferred)
         Version: 0.5.11
   Build Release: 5.11
          Branch: 0.95
  Packaging Date: Thu Aug  7 16:14:29 2008
            Size: 1.2 MB
            FMRI: pkg:/SUNWtoo@0.5.11,5.11-0.95:20080807T161429Z
```

Note that the information is broken down from the package FMRI to include Version, Build Release, Branch, and Packaging Date. You can also display this information for packages that are not installed by using the `-r` option to `pkg info`; this causes the information to be retrieved from the repository. An additional option to `pkg info` displays the license for a package (the output is not shown for brevity):

```
$ pkg info --license SUNWzfs
```

You can view the contents of a package using `pkg contents` (some of the output has been omitted for brevity):

```
$ pkg contents SUNWtoo
PATH
usr
usr/bin
usr/bin/amd64
usr/bin/amd64/elfwrap
usr/bin/amd64/gcore
usr/bin/amd64/ld
usr/bin/amd64/ldd
usr/bin/amd64/plimit
usr/bin/amd64/pvs
    ...
```

The default display shows only the package's file, directory, hard link, and link actions, which are the objects that one would traditionally think of as a package's contents. You can obtain the complete set of actions for a package using `pkg contents -m`:

```
$ pkg contents -m SUNWtoo
set name=fmri value=pkg:/SUNWtoo@0.5.11,5.11-0.95:20080807T161429Z
license e9e74f0dd7ea1ec725fd34c9c371a3c5389269bc license=SUNWtoo.copyright pkg
.size=10824 transaction_id=1218125669_pkg%3A%2FSUNWtoo%400.5.11%2C5.11-0
```

```
.95%3A20080807T161429Z

set name=authority value=opensolaris.org
set name=description value="Programming Tools"
depend fmri=pkg:/SUNWcsl@0.5.11-0.95 type=require
depend fmri=pkg:/SUNWcs@0.5.11-0.95 type=require
dir group=sys mode=0755 owner=root path=usr
dir group=bin mode=0755 owner=root path=usr/bin
dir group=bin mode=0755 owner=root path=usr/bin/amd64
dir group=bin mode=0755 owner=root path=usr/bin/i86
dir group=bin mode=0755 owner=root path=usr/ccs
dir group=bin mode=0755 owner=root path=usr/ccs/bin
dir group=bin mode=0755 owner=root path=usr/ccs/bin/amd64
dir group=bin mode=0755 owner=root path=usr/ccs/lib
dir group=bin mode=0755 owner=root path=usr/lib
dir group=bin mode=0755 owner=root path=usr/lib/abi
dir group=bin mode=0755 owner=root path=usr/lib/amd64
dir group=bin mode=0755 owner=root path=usr/lib/ld
dir group=bin mode=0755 owner=root path=usr/lib/ld/amd64
dir group=bin mode=0755 owner=root path=usr/lib/link_audit
dir group=bin mode=0755 owner=root path=usr/lib/link_audit/amd64
file a7ae9ddfd45463f398ffb9aea9e42fd818bb6155 elfarch=i386 elfbits=64 elfhash
=808e638647834d1c02f335c0e6755013a78a1925 group=bin mode=0555 owner=root path
=usr/bin/amd64/elfwrap pkg.size=34096
file 6f1aad1188e2f33fecf4e90e88a3f105f3354be5 elfarch=i386 elfbits=64 elfhash
=506c3e4353dabcb45c36770dca895710c034fd12 group=bin mode=0555 owner=root path
=usr/bin/amd64/gcore pkg.size=19256
...
```

Again, the output has been abridged for brevity, but you can see that this output provides all of the actions included in the package, and much more detail about each action, including a recorded hash for each file action that can be used to verify that the installed file matches the expected contents. This enables you to check your installed packages using pkg verify:

```
$ pkg verify SUNWtoo
```

You can also check all packages by omitting the package name. Any files, directories, hard links, or links that do not match the recorded hashes are reported, and pkg exits with status 1 if the package fails to verify cleanly. Verification can be helpful if your system is behaving in an unusual manner because it enables you to check whether your software has been corrupted or tampered with. If any errors are reported by pkg verify, you can use the pkg fix command to correct them.

Support for searching packages is provided through the pkg search command, as shown in this example:

```
$ pkg search xvm
INDEX      ACTION    VALUE                    PACKAGE
```

```
groupname  group  xvm                            pkg:/SUNWxvm@3.1-0.95
basename   dir    var/svc/manifest/system/xvm pkg:/SUNWxvm@3.1-0.95
basename   dir    var/svc/manifest/system/xvm pkg:/SUNWlibvirt@0.5.11-0.95
username   user   xvm                            pkg:/SUNWxvm@3.1-0.95
```

The output displays the packages that contain actions matching the search token. As shown in the output, multiple action types can match a search token, and all matching values are printed. Recall from Chapter 3 that you can also search your configured repositories by adding the -r option. Use -s to search a repository that is not one of your configured repositories:

```
$ pkg search -s http://pkg.sunfreeware.com:9000 pine
INDEX      ACTION  VALUE             PACKAGE
basename   file    opt/sfw/bin/pine  pkg:/IPSFWpine@0.5.11-5.7
basename   file    opt/sfw/bin/pine  pkg:/IPSFWpine@0.5.11-5.7
basename   file    opt/sfw/bin/pine  pkg:/IPSFWpine@0.5.11-5.7
```

The pkg.sunfreeware.com repository contains three instances of the IPSFWpine@0.5.11-5.7 package with different timestamps, which is why the same entry appears three times in the example output.

Searches on your local system use an index to provide good performance. This index is normally maintained by IPS automatically; as each package is installed or uninstalled, the index is updated, which is noted in the output from pkg install and pkg uninstall. If the index is corrupted, a search request will generate a message instructing you to rebuild the index; you can do so with the following command:

```
# pkg rebuild-index
PHASE                                          ITEMS
Indexing Packages                             583/583
```

Rebuilding the complete index normally takes just a minute or two.

The package catalog that is cached by IPS from each authority is normally updated automatically as you install, uninstall, and update packages. It is also updated regularly by the application/pkg/update SMF service. You can update the local catalog cache using pkg refresh:

```
# pkg refresh
```

SVR4 Packaging and IPS

From Solaris 2.0 through Solaris 10, all of the Solaris operating system software, as well as many applications, were delivered using a packaging technology known as SVR4 (short for System V Release 4) Packaging. This packaging system was developed by AT&T and Sun as part of the System V Release 4 project in the late 1980s. See Chapter 1 for more information on the history of OpenSolaris.

continued

continued

OpenSolaris continues to provide this packaging system so that applications that have been packaged using it can be installed on OpenSolaris. Because an SVR4 package can express dependencies on other SVR4 packages, IPS provides the `legacy` action so that an IPS package that provides the same functionality as a legacy SVR4 package can declare this equivalence. When installing a package that includes a legacy action, IPS creates the same package metadata in the SVR4 package database that the SVR4 package would have provided, so that SVR4 packages that depend on the package will install normally. As a result, you can run the SVR4 `pkginfo(1)` command on a freshly installed OpenSolaris system to see a list of SVR4 packages. However, you can't remove those packages. If you attempt to do so with `pkgrm(1M)`, it fails with an error message that indicates the package is not correctly installed. SVR4 packages that are installed using `pkgadd` can be removed with `pkgrm`, however.

If you have prior experience with Solaris 10 or earlier releases, you may have encountered the patching system it used, which was layered on top of SVR4 packages. With IPS, all updates are delivered as packages, rather than patches — the capabilities that the Solaris patching system provided are embedded in the IPS design.

Updating Your Software

New versions of software appear with great frequency, and you'll likely want to update your system to the latest versions, whether to obtain fixes to bugs you're encountering or to use new features. OpenSolaris offers both graphical and command-line update tools.

The availability of updates depends on the authorities you have configured. If the preferred authority of `opensolaris.org` is set to the OpenSolaris distribution's release repository, `http://pkg.opensolaris.org/release`, updates are provided for each release, as well as important free updates, such as security updates. The OpenSolaris distribution also offers the `http://pkg.opensolaris.org/dev` repository, which provides each development build of the distribution, normally at two-week intervals. If you are interested in using the OpenSolaris development updates, you can reset your preferred repository using `pkg set-authority`:

```
# pkg set-authority -O http://pkg.opensolaris.org/dev opensolaris.org
# pkg refresh
```

Remember that `pkg refresh` is necessary to obtain the updated package catalog from the repository you have configured. Other package authorities provide updates according to whatever schedules and policies suit their purpose.

You also use the set-authority subcommand to configure access to additional package repositories. For example, the `http://pkg.opensolaris.org/contrib` repository provides a collection of open source packages that are not supported by Sun. Other repositories hosted at `http://pkg.sun.com` provide access to software that requires registration and support updates for OpenSolaris and other Sun software products.

To perform an update, the OpenSolaris desktop includes an Update Manager application (select System ➤ Administration ➤ Update Manager). Figure 6-2 shows the Update Manager window.

The top half of the window shows packages for which updates are available; the bottom half shows details about the selected package. If updates are available, click Update All to install them. A new boot environment will be created based on the current one, and the package updates applied to it. See the section "Boot Environment Management" later in this chapter for more information.

FIGURE 6-2

Use Update Manager for easy software updates.

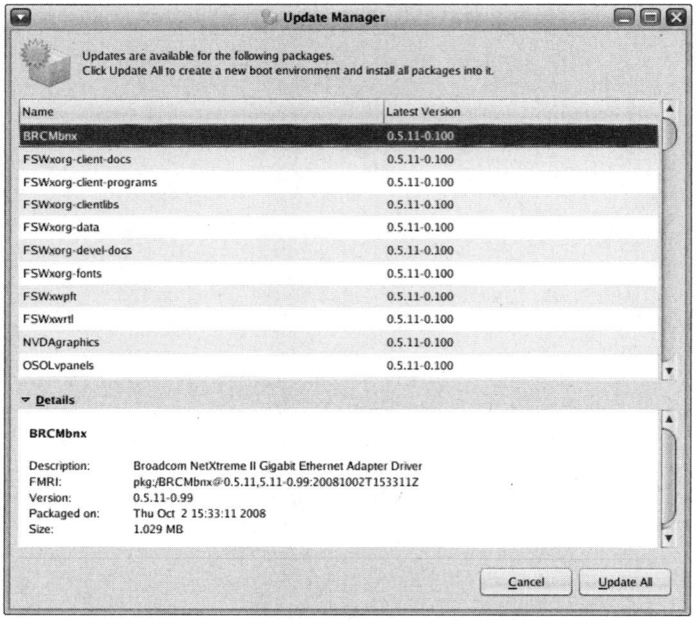

You can also check for available updates, and update the system, using the command-line tools. As discussed earlier, the pkg list command lists the packages for which updates are available:

```
$ pkg list
NAME (AUTHORITY)                          VERSION        STATE      UFIX
BRCMbnx                                   0.5.11-0.86    installed  u---
FSWxorg-fonts                             0.5.11-0.86    installed  u---
NVDAgraphics                              0.5.11-0.86    installed  u---
SUNW1394                                  0.5.11-0.86    installed  u---
SUNWDTraceToolkit                         0.5.11-0.86    installed  u---
```

```
SUNWPython                              2.4.4-0.86      installed  u---
SUNWPython-extra                        0.5.11-0.86     installed  u---
SUNWTcl                                 8.4.14-0.86     installed  u---
SUNWTiff                                0.5.11-0.86     installed  u---
SUNWTk                                  8.4.14-0.86     installed  u---
SUNWa2ps                                4.13-0.86       installed  u---
SUNWaac                                 0.5.11-0.86     installed  u---
SUNWacc                                 0.5.11-0.86     installed  u---
...
```

You can update just a single package and its dependents to the most recent version using `pkg install`; you don't need to specify a version because the most recent version is the default. To update all of your packages to the most recent version, use the `pkg image-update` command. Here is a sample update session:

```
# pkg image-update
Checking that SUNWipkg (in '/') is up to date ...
DOWNLOAD                            PKGS       FILES       XFER (MB)
Completed                          544/544 26632/26632 1560.96/1560.96

PHASE                                    ACTIONS
Removal Phase                           7668/7668
Update Phase                          22607/22607
Install Phase                         12666/12666
PHASE                                     ITEMS
Reading Existing Index                     8/8
Indexing Packages                        544/544
stage1 written to partition 0 sector 0 (abs 4096)
stage2 written to partition 0, 266 sectors starting at 50 (abs 4146)
A clone of opensolaris exists and has been updated and activated. On next boot
the Boot Environment opensolaris-1 will be mounted on '/'. Reboot when ready to
switch to this updated BE.

-------------------------------------------------------------------------

NOTE: Please review release notes posted at:
      http://opensolaris.org/os/project/indiana/resources/relnotes/200811/x86
-------------------------------------------------------------------------
```

NOTE As of this writing, you must manually update `SUNWipkg` (the package that contains IPS) to its current version before running `pkg image-update`. If you don't, `pkg` exits with an error, instructing you to update it. The command to update it is `pkg install SUNWipkg`.

Be sure to review the release notes listed in the preceding message, especially if you are updating to a development build of the OpenSolaris distribution, because additional manual steps may be required to ensure that your system operates correctly after the update.

As shown in the output, a new boot environment is created and activated as part of the update process. The name of the boot environment is automatically generated, but you can rename it (see the next section).

Boot Environment Management

As discussed earlier in this chapter, each time you upgrade the operating system using `pkg image-update`, a new boot environment (often abbreviated as BE, hence the name of the `beadm` command used in managing them) is created, ensuring that you can easily switch back to the prior version if necessary. You can also create boot environments for your own uses, such as configuring a system to run different operating systems and applications with just a reboot. Thus, you need to know a bit about managing boot environments to fully exploit OpenSolaris' capabilities.

NOTE   Solaris 10 and earlier versions of Solaris also incorporate the concept of a boot environment, as part of the Live Upgrade technology that can be used to upgrade or patch Solaris. The boot environment concept in OpenSolaris is similar to, but different from, the boot environments used with Live Upgrade. The commands used for each are different, and currently the Live Upgrade and OpenSolaris boot environments do not interact in any way.

A boot environment consists of one or more datasets in the ZFS root pool; each dataset directly under the pool's `ROOT` dataset is defined as a boot environment. Thus, you should not directly create your own datasets under this dataset using the `zfs` command. In addition, on x86 systems, an entry for each boot environment is created in the GRUB menu, enabling you to select the desired boot environment during system boot.

CROSS-REF   See Chapter 8 for more information on ZFS.

Three possible states can apply to a boot environment:

- **Active** — The system is currently booted from this BE.
- **Active on Reboot** — This BE will be used to boot the system at the next reboot.
- **Mounted** — The BE's datasets are mounted at some path in the active BE.

These states are not exclusive. Most of the time your currently active BE will be active on reboot as well. The active BE is also mounted, obviously, as the root file system.

When you install the OpenSolaris distribution, the initial boot environment that is created is named `opensolaris`; it is also activated, of course. There isn't anything special about this BE name, though, and you can name a boot environment virtually anything you want — the only restriction is that the name must be a valid ZFS dataset name because the boot environment name is also the name of the root dataset for the boot environment. OpenSolaris creates a snapshot of the `opensolaris` boot environment at installation time. (A boot environment snapshot is just a ZFS snapshot of each file system that's part of the boot environment.)

Viewing boot environments

You can use the `beadm list` command to view your boot environments:

```
$ beadm list
BE          Active Mountpoint Space Policy Created
--          ------ ---------- ----- ------ -------
```

```
b95              -      -        71.5K static 2008-08-22 22:35
opensolaris NR     /        2.50G static 2008-08-22 21:53
```

The BE listing shows the name of each boot environment, whether it is active, its mount point (if currently mounted), disk space used, retention policy, and creation date. The Active column denotes the currently active boot environment with an N, and the BE that will be active on reboot with R. If neither state applies to the BE, a hyphen is displayed in this column. The listing displays all BEs that are present in all ZFS pools attached to the system.

> **NOTE** The retention policy information is intended to allow the system to automatically clean up old boot environments and snapshots, but the automatic clean-up feature is not currently implemented.

To list the datasets owned by each BE, add the -d option:

```
$ beadm list -d
BE/Dataset                  Active Mountpoint Space Policy Created
----------                  ------ ---------- ----- ------ -------
b95
    rpool/ROOT/b95          -      -          71.5K static 2008-08-22 22:35
opensolaris
    rpool/ROOT/opensolaris NR     /           2.50G static 2008-08-22 21:53
```

Note that this listing doesn't include all of the file systems and volumes on the system, which are shown here:

```
# zfs list -t filesystem,volume
NAME                   USED   AVAIL  REFER  MOUNTPOINT
rpool                  3.34G  7.43G  61K    /rpool
rpool/ROOT             2.50G  7.43G  18K    legacy
rpool/ROOT/b95         71.5K  7.43G  2.49G  legacy
rpool/ROOT/opensolaris 2.50G  7.43G  2.49G  legacy
rpool/dump             349M   7.43G  349M   -
rpool/export           694K   7.43G  19K    /export
rpool/export/home      676K   7.43G  658K   /export/home
rpool/swap             512M   7.88G  49.6M  -
```

The /export and /export/home file systems are shared across all boot environments in the pool; this sharing is also applied to the dump and swap volumes, named rpool/dump and rpool/swap in the preceding example. This means that no matter which of the boot environments you are booted from, the same space is used for swap and dump, and /export and /export/home refer to the same file systems. Therefore, users' home directories persist across all BEs.

Your installation of the OpenSolaris distribution may not have swap or dump volumes. Creation of the swap and dump volumes is dependent on the amount of disk space you allocate for installing OpenSolaris. If it's less than the recommended amount, then dump and swap volumes may not be created, as they are not required for OpenSolaris to operate correctly, and the installer's first priority is to allocate sufficient space for your software. See Chapter 7 for information about swap space, and Chapter 24 for information about crash dumps.

Usually, you'll want your file systems that contain data to be shared across boot environments. If so, then create additional file systems under `rpool`, `rpool/export`, or `rpool/export/home`. However, if you need to create additional file systems that you do not want shared across boot environments, create those file systems under the boot environment's root file system (e.g., `rpool/ROOT/b95` or `rpool/ROOT/opensolaris` in the previous example) so that they will be specifically associated with that boot environment.

You can list just the snapshots for each BE using `beadm list -s`:

```
$ beadm list -s
BE/Snapshot              Space Policy Created
-----------              ----- ------ -------
b95
opensolaris
    opensolaris@b95      30.0K static 2008-08-23 22:13
    opensolaris@install  2.90M static 2008-08-22 22:22
```

The `opensolaris@b95` snapshot was used as the basis for the b95 boot environment, as shown by using the `zfs` command to view the root dataset's `origin` property:

```
$ zfs get origin rpool/ROOT/b95
NAME            PROPERTY  VALUE                          SOURCE
rpool/ROOT/b95  origin    rpool/ROOT/opensolaris@b95     -
```

The section "Creating and destroying boot environments" later in this chapter provides more information on snapshots.

Activating and renaming boot environments

You can specify which boot environment will be active on reboot using the `beadm activate` command:

```
# beadm activate b95
```

When you activate a BE, the pool's `bootfs` property is set to the activated BE's root dataset; and its ZFS datasets are promoted so that they are no longer dependent on their origin snapshots and datasets, which allows you to delete the snapshots and datasets associated with the inactive boot environments if you no longer need them. In addition, on x86 systems the GRUB menu will be modified so that the activated BE's menu entry is made the default.

The promotion of the ZFS datasets has an interesting effect: The disk space accounting will charge the space for all snapshots to the newly active BE. To see this, compare the listings before and after the BE b95 is activated:

```
# beadm list
BE           Active Mountpoint Space Policy Created
--           ------ ---------- ----- ------ -------
```

```
b95           -        -        71.5K static 2008-08-22 22:35
opensolaris NR        /         2.50G static 2008-08-22 21:53
# beadm activate b95
# beadm list
BE           Active Mountpoint Space Policy Created
--           ------ ---------- ----- ------ -------
b95          R        -        2.50G static 2008-08-22 22:35
opensolaris N        /         1.75M static 2008-08-22 21:53
```

As mentioned earlier, boot environments can be renamed; use the `beadm rename` command:

```
# beadm rename b95 b95-1
# beadm list -d
BE/Dataset              Active Mountpoint Space Policy Created
----------              ------ ---------- ----- ------ -------
b95-1
    rpool/ROOT/b95-1        -        -        80.5K static 2008-08-23 22:13
opensolaris
    rpool/ROOT/opensolaris NR       /         2.50G static 2008-08-22 21:53
```

As shown, the BE's root dataset is renamed to the new name. On x86 systems, the GRUB menu item for the boot environment is renamed to the new name.

> **NOTE** You cannot rename the currently active boot environment, as the ZFS datasets making up the boot environment must be remounted to be renamed, and that is not possible while the system is booted from them.

Creating and destroying boot environments

You can create additional BEs using `beadm create`:

```
# beadm create altbe
# beadm list
BE           Active Mountpoint Space Policy Created
--           ------ ---------- ----- ------ -------
altbe        -        -        72.5K static 2008-08-23 21:53
b95          R        -        2.50G static 2008-08-22 22:35
opensolaris N        /         1.91M static 2008-08-22 21:53
```

Unlike a BE created automatically by `pkg image-update`, this newly created BE is not activated; either append the `-a` option to `beadm create` or use `beadm activate` to make it active on the next reboot. Remember that a snapshot of the current BE is taken to serve as the basis for the clones making up the new BE. This snapshot is named using the name of the new BE, so creating a new BE named `testbe` will create a snapshot of the current BE called `@testbe`.

> **NOTE** Keep in mind that a snapshot is a read-only copy of a file system at a point in time, whereas a clone is a writable copy of a snapshot.

You can create a boot environment in a ZFS pool that is different from the current BE's pool by adding the -p option to beadm create. If you have a second pool named bigpool, you can create the new BE as follows:

```
# beadm create -p bigpool testbe
```

Creating a BE in a different pool takes some time because rather than create a clone in the same pool, which is virtually instantaneous, beadm must actually copy the ZFS datasets using ZFS's send and receive dataset capability.

You can create a boot environment based on a boot environment other than the currently active BE using beadm create -e:

```
# beadm create -e b95 altbe
```

The altbe environment will be created based on the current contents of BE b95. You can also specify a snapshot of a BE to be used as the source, by including the snapshot name in the BE specification:

```
# beadm create -e b95@install altbe
```

You can create a snapshot of a BE using beadm create by specifying the snapshot name:

```
# beadm create altbe@testsnap
```

This creates a snapshot with the provided snapshot name for each dataset that's a component of the BE.

You can also set ZFS properties on a BE's datasets at creation time using the -o option to beadm create. For example, you can create the BE's datasets as compressed using the following command:

```
# beadm create -o compression=on altbe
```

Any ZFS dataset property may be set using this option. See Chapter 8 or the zfs(1M) man page for a list of the ZFS dataset properties.

Of course, you also need to be able to destroy BEs to free the disk space they occupy; this can be done using beadm destroy:

```
# beadm destroy altbe
Are you sure you want to destroy altbe? This action cannot be undone (y/[n]): y
```

You can force the destroy operation to not prompt by adding the -F option to the command. This is most useful for scripting; we don't recommend getting into the habit of using -F interactively, as it's all too easy to destroy a boot environment accidentally.

NOTE   Be aware that the destroy operation also destroys the ZFS snapshots from which the boot environment is cloned, unless those snapshots have other dependent clones, in which case they cannot be destroyed until those clones are promoted to remove the dependency.

You can destroy a specific snapshot by specifying the snapshot name to `beadm destroy`:

```
# beadm destroy altbe@testsnap
```

Mounting boot environments

Finally, if you need to correct a problem with a boot environment or compare files between boot environments, you can mount and unmount BEs using `beadm mount` and `beadm unmount`:

```
# beadm mount b95 /b95
# beadm list
BE          Active Mountpoint Space Policy Created
--          ------ ---------- ----- ------ -------
altbe       -      -          71.5K static 2008-08-24 21:19
b95         -      /b95       79.5K static 2008-08-23 22:13
opensolaris NR     /          2.50G static 2008-08-22 21:53
# ls /b95
bin    COPYRIGHT etc    kernel  lost+found net      proc   save   tmp
boot   dev       export lib     media      opt      root   sbin   usr
cdrom  devices   home   LICENSE mnt        platform rpool  system var
# beadm unmount b95
```

CAUTION Currently, you must be careful to always unmount a mounted boot environment before rebooting the system; otherwise, an attempt to boot from that BE will cause the system to panic because the datasets' `mountpoint` properties will be set to an incorrect value.

Managing a Package Repository

IPS packages are published to, and installed from, repository servers that are accessed over a network. You may be completely satisfied using the repositories provided by the OpenSolaris community, Sun, or other software providers and community members, as the extensive list of packages provided by the various repositories is likely to meet your needs. However, if you're a software developer or a system administrator, you may want to run your own repository for development purposes, to distribute your custom packages using your own servers, or to provide a local mirror of a repository to optimize performance and network utilization.

NOTE Mirroring has recently been implemented; see the IPS documentation for instructions on setting up a mirror repository.

An IPS repository is provided by the SMF service `application/pkg/server`. This service is disabled by default, so to start using it you first need to enable it:

```
# svcadm enable application/pkg/server
```

This starts the IPS server, which is the daemon program `pkg.depotd(1M)`. The service configuration is specified by the service's SMF properties, which are members of the `pkg` application property group. The properties are described in Table 6-2.

TABLE 6-2

Application/pkg/server SMF Properties

Property Name	Description
content_root	Path to server's static web content; defaults to /usr/share/lib/pkg
inst_root	Path to repository storage; defaults to /var/pkg/repo
log_access	Pathname of access log; defaults to no access log for SMF service, stdout if run from a terminal
log_errors	Pathname of error log; defaults to stderr, meaning the errors appear in the SMF service log
port	Network port for repository; defaults to 80
proxy_base	Base URL for the server; used for reverse proxy configurations with a web server. The default value is empty.
socket_timeout	Seconds to wait for client response before closing the connection; defaults to 60 seconds
threads	Number of threads used to serve requests; defaults to 10

CROSS-REF See Chapter 13 for more information on managing SMF services.

For example, to configure the IPS server to use port 8000, use the svccfg command, and then svcadm to refresh and restart the server:

```
# svccfg -s application/pkg/server setprop pkg/port = 8000
# svcadm refresh application/pkg/server
# svcadm restart application/pkg/server
```

TIP We recommend that you modify the inst_root property to use a pathname that's outside of the boot environment's datasets. That way, the repository is not cloned in each boot environment. For example, you can create a dataset called rpool/export/repo mounted at /export/repo and then modify the inst_root property to this value.

You can view the status of your repository server by connecting to it with your web browser. The status page from pkg.opensolaris.org/release is shown in Figure 6-3.

Using the web interface, you can view statistics for a repository and browse information about each package, which is the same information you can obtain from the command line using pkg info and pkg contents.

TIP The IPS repository also provides an RSS feed of package updates to the repository at the path /feed. For the opensolaris.org repository, the URL is thus http://pkg.opensolaris.org/release/feed. This enables you to use the Live Bookmarks feature of Firefox or another RSS reader to track updates to repositories, providing an alert to packages you may want to install or update.

A web browser can be used to view the IPS repository status.

Once you have a repository running, the next task is publishing packages into it, which is done using the pkgsend(1) command. See its man page for basic information. Chapter 24 provides a detailed example of building an IPS package and publishing it into a repository.

IPS also provides the pkgrecv(1) command to copy a package from an IPS repository in a format that allows it to be modified and then republished using pkgsend. See the man page for more information.

NOTE If you're familiar with other packaging systems, you may have noticed that there is no on-disk format specified for an IPS package. The IPS designers intend to provide such a format in the near future, but it does not currently exist.

Building Your Own Distribution

Rather than use the OpenSolaris software management tools to manage your own installation of the OpenSolaris distribution, you may want to build your own custom distribution based on its packages. This is possible because, as described in Chapter 1, the core technology in

OpenSolaris is freely redistributable. The tools used to construct the OpenSolaris distribution, called the Distribution Constructor, are also open source and available for you to use in constructing your own distribution. This topic is beyond the scope of this book, but to explore further, install the Distribution Constructor using the following command:

```
# pkg install SUNWdistro-const
```

Once this package is installed, consult the `distro_const(1M)` man page and the documentation links it provides to get started building your own distribution. You can also consult the Distribution Community group, `www.opensolaris.org/os/community/distribution/`, for assistance. The builders of most of the distributions discussed in Chapter 2 are members of this community group.

> **NOTE**   If you do build a custom distribution that you'd like to redistribute, be aware that you need to conform to the OpenSolaris trademark and branding guidelines, which are maintained by the Trademark and Branding project, `http://opensolaris.org/os/project/branding/`.

Resources

The Image Packaging System development is hosted at `http://opensolaris.org/os/project/pkg`.

The boot environment management utilities and Distribution Constructor are products of the Caiman installer project, `http://opensolaris.org/os/project/caiman`.

The Distributions community group provides resources for distribution creators; its home page is `http://opensolaris.org/os/community/distribution`.

Summary

This chapter introduced the concepts underlying the innovative new packaging system in Open-Solaris, the Image Packaging System (IPS), and demonstrated how to perform many of the common software management tasks using both the graphical Package Manager and the `pkg` command, including updating to a new release of the operating system and managing multiple boot environments. You also learned how to create a package repository and obtain the tools needed to build your own distribution. You're ready to manage the software on an OpenSolaris system!

Part III

OpenSolaris File Systems, Networking, and Security

Chapter 7

Disks, Local File Systems, and the Volume Manager

OpenSolaris includes support for a variety of storage devices and local file systems, as well as a traditional volume manager. This chapter describes these capabilities, with the exception of ZFS, which is described in the next chapter. Network file system support is described in Chapter 10.

Although data is usually stored on disk, it is generally accessed through a file system, hiding device-specific details. OpenSolaris provides file system support through a pluggable framework so that a variety of file systems can be used concurrently and applications are unaware of the type of underlying file system on which their data actually resides. Applications simply access files and directories through the standard POSIX APIs, while the kernel transparently manages the low-level access using the file system–specific code. New file systems can be introduced at any time without affecting existing application code.

This chapter describes the general disk storage support provided in OpenSolaris and focuses on the local file systems that applications use to store data. However, because of the flexible nature of the file system interface in UNIX, and the way that UNIX has traditionally exposed services such as networking through the file system API, OpenSolaris also provides access to a variety of other services as if they were true file systems. This way, those services can be accessed using the familiar file APIs, even though the underlying service may be quite different. One example is the Process File System, procfs, which is a pseudo-file system that actually provides access to all of the running processes on the system. This file system is described in the proc(4) man page. Some of the other nontraditional file systems are used for contracts, ctfs(7fs), or kernel modules, objfs(7fs). You can learn more about these types of file systems on their man pages.

The file systems described in this chapter are the more traditional local file systems used for data storage. Because of its close relationship with disks and standard file systems, the Solaris Volume Manager (SVM) is also discussed.

Disks

Before delving into the specifics of each file system, you need to first understand how storage is managed on OpenSolaris. Although most data is still commonly stored on traditional *hard disk drives*, a variety of other media are treated by the system as if they were a standard disk. This includes DVD drives, USB sticks, and system memory. Modern disks present a logical view of the device as a sequential array of disk *blocks*, normally 512 bytes in size. Each block is individually addressable, but it is up to the operating system and file system to manage accesses down to the individual byte level within a block. In addition to exposing blocks, older disks exposed the concept of *heads*, *tracks*, and *cylinders*. These concepts still persist, but this data is usually fabricated and no longer has any actual relationship to the underlying physical hardware.

Disk device names

All disks have a name under the /dev/dsk and /dev/rdsk subdirectories. Because disks can be accessed at both the block level and the individual byte level, each disk is exposed with two different names. The block-level access is made through the /dev/dsk name, and the byte-level access, which is known as *raw* access, is made through the /dev/rdsk name (hence the "r"). Some commands must be used with the block name, while others must be used with the raw name. These restrictions are described as each command is discussed.

Although OpenSolaris has a convention for naming individual disks, it is not always followed by third-party device drivers, so you should not make any assumptions about how a disk will be named. For disks managed by a driver that is part of OpenSolaris, the name is normally of the following form:

    c#t#d#s#

The name has up to four parts, with an embedded hex number for each part. A typical example would be the name c0t0d0s0 or even c1t01000003BA4E5E2000002A0047FA3E22d0s2. The t# portion of the name is optional and might not be present with some disks, depending on the driver that manages the device. The meanings of each part of the name are controller (c), target (t), disk (d), and slice (s).

Another common style of disk name that you will encounter follows a form similar to the ctds name but instead of the s# component, it ends with a p# component. An example would be c0t0d0p0. The meaning of this part of the name is partition (p). Both slices and partitions are described in the next section.

As previously mentioned, the name is created by the device driver for the specific disk and might not follow this convention. You don't need to worry about the exact style of the name — just understand that each disk has specific names in the file system, which you use to access and manage that disk. Depending on what you're doing, different paths and names are used for the same device.

If you have many disks attached to your system, it can be confusing to determine which name is associated with each disk. The format command, described below, is probably the easiest tool to display the list of disks on the system. The prtconf command can also be used to display a detailed view of the configuration of the system, which includes the layout of the system buses and the devices attached to each bus. The dev_link property in the output shows the /dev/dsk name for each disk, but you still need a detailed understanding of the system's hardware configuration to understand the output. This example shows a portion of the prtconf output:

```
$ prtconf -v
...
    sd, instance #18
...
        Device Minor Nodes:
            dev=(27,1152)
                dev_path=/pci@5,0/pci1022,7450@4/pci108e,534d@4,1/sd@0,0:a
                    spectype=blk type=minor
                    dev_link=/dev/dsk/c2t0d0s0
                    dev_link=/dev/sd144a
                dev_path=/pci@5,0/pci1022,7450@4/pci108e,534d@4,1/sd@0,0:a,raw
                    spectype=chr type=minor
                    dev_link=/dev/rdsk/c2t0d0s0
                    dev_link=/dev/rsd144a
    ...
```

Notice the two dev_link properties in the output. Use the /dev/dsk property; the other link is for legacy naming.

Formatting and labeling

Before creating a file system on a disk, you must *format* and *label* it. Formatting is a low-level process that writes data onto the disk so that it is usable by the disk controller. Modern disks are normally preformatted, but OpenSolaris includes the format command, which can be used if a disk must be reformatted. Labeling enables you to divide a disk into logical sections, or partitions, each of which can be used by a different operating system or file system. Both the fdisk and format commands can be used to label a disk As described in the following sections, you typically use both fdisk and format on x86-based systems, but only format on SPARC-based systems.

fdisk

The fdisk labeling goes back to the early days of MS-DOS and is the common disk label used on x86 machines. This label enables you to divide a disk into four different *partitions*, each of which can be used by a different operating system or file system on the same machine. When only a single OS is installed, it is common to have a single fdisk partition that spans the entire disk.

The OpenSolaris fdisk command is named after this style of label and is used to manage these labels. The command takes the name of the device to partition:

```
# fdisk /dev/rdsk/c2t0d0p0
                Total disk size is 8924 cylinders
                Cylinder size is 16065 (512 byte) blocks

                                                 Cylinders
         Partition  Status   Type            Start   End    Length    %
         =========  ======   =============   =====   ===    ======   ===
            1       Active   Solaris2           1    8923    8923    100

SELECT ONE OF THE FOLLOWING:
     1. Create a partition
     2. Specify the active partition
     3. Delete a partition
     4. Change between Solaris and Solaris2 Partition IDs
     5. Exit (update disk configuration and exit)
     6. Cancel (exit without updating disk configuration)
```

You can see that this disk has a single fdisk partition, used for OpenSolaris, and spans the entire disk. If there is free space on the disk, then you can use fdisk to allocate a new partition using some or all of that space. If there is no free space but you still want to use the disk, then you need to shrink an existing partition to create some free space (as discussed in Chapter 2).

CAUTION   Shrinking an fdisk partition that is in use by another OS or file system can cause data loss if you are not careful.

In the preceding example, the fdisk partition type is Solaris2. OpenSolaris actually supports two different types, and you can use option 4 in the fdisk program to switch back and forth. The Solaris type is used for legacy compatibility. You use that type only if you have an older version of Solaris installed on the system.

Each fdisk partition on a disk is named in the file system using the c#t#d#p# style of name. For example, the first fdisk partition of the c0t0d0 disk will have the name c0t0d0p1. Each disk also has a p0 name, which is used to access the entire disk, as shown earlier in the fdisk command example. You always use the p0 name with the fdisk command because you are operating on the whole disk, not on an individual fdisk partition.

format

The format command is used to manage VTOC-style disk labels. VTOC stands for Volume Table of Contents. This is the label style that has been used since the early SunOS releases; it predates Solaris support for fdisk-style labels. This style of label allows a disk to be divided into eight slices on SPARC or 10 slices on x86.

> **NOTE** On x86 systems, the last two slices are used for system information, the boot block and alternate cylinder information, and are not directly partitioned by the user. This leaves eight usable slices on both SPARC and x86.

This label is normally used on its own, on disks attached to SPARC systems, or indirectly, by being placed inside of a Solaris2 fdisk partition, on x86. That is, on x86 it is standard to have an fdisk-style label on the disk for compatibility with the BIOS boot loader and other operating systems, and to have a VTOC-style label inside of the fdisk partition being used by OpenSolaris. Unlike the fdisk label, the VTOC-style label is not normally used to provide support for multiple operating systems. Confusingly, VTOC labeling is also called *partitioning*, so it is easy to get mixed up when talking about fdisk and VTOC labels, especially because they are both used to divide a disk into logically separate chunks. However, the term "slice" is commonly used when referring to VTOCs.

The device for each VTOC slice on a disk is named using the c#t#d#s# style of name. For example, the first VTOC slice of the c0t0d0 disk will have the name c0t0d0s0. Use the s# name with various commands to refer to the specific slice on which the command will operate.

> **NOTE** VTOC slices are numbered beginning with 0. With fdisk, partition 0 refers to the whole disk, and partition 1 is the first partition used to store data. When using a VTOC, there is no requirement for a slice that refers to the whole disk, although by convention, slice 2 is usually set up to span the full disk. To add to the confusion, a new style of label, called an *EFI* label (because it is part of the Extensible Firmware Interface definition), can be used in place of either the fdisk or VTOC labels. This label also enables a disk to be divided into multiple partitions, and is required for disks larger than the 2TB upper limit with fdisk and VTOC-style labels. The format command can manage both VTOC and EFI labeled disks. Slice names in the file system are also represented using the c#t#d#s# style of name when an EFI label is in use.

The format command discovers all of the disks on the system and prints a simple menu to start:

```
# format

Searching for disks ... done

AVAILABLE DISK SELECTIONS:
       0. c1t15d0 <DEFAULT cyl 8938 alt 2 hd 255 sec 63>
          /pci@5,0/pci1022,7450@4/pci108e,534d@4/sd@f,0
       1. c2t0d0 <DEFAULT cyl 8921 alt 2 hd 255 sec 63>
          /pci@5,0/pci1022,7450@4/pci108e,534d@4,1/sd@0,0
Specify disk (enter its number):
```

After you choose a disk, you are presented with another menu that enables you to perform a variety of disk management tasks:

```
FORMAT MENU:
        disk       - select a disk
        type       - select (define) a disk type
        partition  - select (define) a partition table
        current    - describe the current disk
        format     - format and analyze the disk
        repair     - repair a defective sector
        label      - write label to the disk
        analyze    - surface analysis
        defect     - defect list management
        backup     - search for backup labels
        verify     - read and display labels
        save       - save new disk/partition definitions
        inquiry    - show vendor, product and revision
        volname    - set 8-character volume name
        !<cmd>     - execute <cmd>, then return
        quit
format>
```

The most common task is `partition`, which enables you to define VTOC or EFI slices on the disk. To manage EFI labels, the `format` command must be invoked with the expert flag (`-e`).

CAUTION   It is rare for x86 or SPARC systems to include firmware that can boot from an EFI labeled disk. Use EFI labels only if you know your hardware can boot from disks with that style of label or for secondary disks from which you don't need to boot. Check the documentation for your system if you are in doubt about its capability to boot from an EFI labeled disk.

Removable media

Support for removable media, such as DVD, CD-ROM, USB stick, SD Card, or floppy, is provided by additional services and commands in OpenSolaris. The `rmvolmgr` is a system service that monitors removable drives and automatically mounts media when it is inserted. This daemon is managed by the `system/filesystem/rmvolmgr` SMF service. In some cases, particularly with floppy drives, there is no way for the `rmvolmgr` to detect when a drive has been inserted. You can use the `volcheck` command to check for new media. To unmount and eject removable media, you can use the `eject` command. In some cases, drives cannot actually eject the media — you have to use the physical eject button after the command has been run.

CAUTION   Even if the system cannot automatically eject the media, such as with a USB stick, run the `eject` command. This ensures that the file system is properly unmounted before you physically remove the media; otherwise, you risk losing data.

In most cases, when removable media is inserted, the `rmvolmgr` is configured to bring up the Gnome `Nautilus` file browser or the `Sound Juicer` music player.

 Gnome applications, as well as procedures to customize the graphical user interface, are described in Chapter 4.

You can also access the device through its mount point in the file system. The default mount point is /media but rmvolmgr also creates links named /cdrom, /floppy, and /rmdisk, as necessary.

Formatting removable media is handled differently from fixed media drives. You must use the format -e command, or the rmformat command, to format removable media. The rmformat command with no options displays all of the removable media devices attached to the system:

```
# rmformat
Looking for devices ...
     1. Logical Node: /dev/rdsk/c6t0d0p0
        Physical Node: /pci@0,0/pci1022,7460@6/pci108e,534d@3,
2/storage@4/disk@0,0
           Connected Device:            USB DISK 25X       PMAP
           Device Type: Removable
        Bus: USB
        Size: 123.0 MB
        Label: <None>
        Access permissions: Medium is not write protected.
     2. Logical Node: /dev/rdsk/c0t1d0p0
           Physical Node: /pci@0,0/pci-ide@7,1/ide@1/sd@1,0
           Connected Device: AOPEN    DUW1608/ARR      A04b
           Device Type: DVD Reader/Writer
        Bus: IDE
        Size: <Unknown>
        Label: <Unknown>
        Access permissions: <Unknown>
     3. Logical Node: /dev/rdsk/c14t0d0p0
           Physical Node: /pci@0,0/pci8086,2448@1e/pci1179,1@b,
3/sdcard@0/disk@0,0
           Connected Device: OSOL    SD Memory Card
           Device Type: Removable
           Bus: <Unknown>
           Size: 1.9 GB
           Label: <None>
           Access permissions: Medium is not write protected.
```

Here, the first device is a USB stick, the second is a DVD burner, and the third is an SD card. You can also see the device name that OpenSolaris has assigned to each of these drives in the Logical Node entry. You would use that name to run rmformat on the device. The rmformat command includes a variety of options for formatting different types of removable media. See the man page for more details.

CROSS-REF You may need to install the SUNWsdcard package to enable support for an SD card. See Chapter 6 for information on installing software.

RAM disk

OpenSolaris includes support for RAM disks — that is, disks whose only storage is system memory and whose contents are lost when the system shuts down. However, in many cases, the tmpfs file system described later in this chapter provides the same performance benefits and is easier to manage. You manage RAM disks using the ramdiskadm command. This example creates a 100MB RAM disk named memdisk:

```
# ramdiskadm -a memdisk 100m
/dev/ramdisk/memdisk
```

The command outputs the device name, which can then be used just like a standard disk device.

lofi

The loopback file driver, lofi, enables you to use a regular file as if it were a block device. For example, if you have an ISO image file of a CD-ROM that you have downloaded, you can use lofi to mount the file just as if it were an actual CD-ROM disk. The mount command, which is described in more detail later in the section "File System Management," can normally be used to mount the file directly, as shown in this example:

```
# mount -F hsfs /home/myhome/sxde.iso /mnt
```

Behind the scenes, mount uses the lofi driver. On old releases of OpenSolaris, or if you need to create the device without mounting it, use the lofiadm command to create a lofi device directly. This example shows the use of the lofiadm command to first set up the file as a device before mounting it, instead of directly mounting the file:

```
# lofiadm -a /home/myhome/sxde.iso
/dev/lofi/1
```

The new device is named /dev/lofi/1 and can be used like a regular disk. Here the lofi device is being mounted:

```
# mount -F hsfs /dev/lofi/1 /mnt
```

The lofi driver can perform decompression on-the-fly, which is used to support the live CD, and there is an OpenSolaris project to add encryption.

SANs

Storage area networks (SANs) are a popular enterprise-grade approach to provisioning storage onto a server. In this configuration, the disks reside on the SAN instead of being directly attached to the system. The benefits of a SAN are that the storage devices can be easily shared, provisioned, and reprovisioned among the servers. The drawback is that expensive SAN networking gear and a *host bus adapter* (HBA) are required because SANs are generally Fibre

Channel-based. SANs are usually contrasted with *network-attached storage* (NAS). In a SAN, disks are accessed at the block level, just as if they were locally attached. With NAS, access is at the file level using a file system that is explicitly network-aware, such as NFS or CIFS. Also, with NAS, the underlying network technology is much less of a factor than in a SAN because NAS has been used for decades on industry standard networks, ranging from 10Mbs Ethernet on up.

CROSS-REF Network file systems are discussed in Chapter 10.

OpenSolaris includes drivers for a variety of Fibre Channel HBAs. Adding SAN-based storage is primarily a SAN configuration operation, which is outside of the scope of this book. You should follow the HBA-specific documentation included with your hardware.

By using iSCSI, described in the following section, you can achieve similar capabilities as with a Fibre Channel-based SAN, but using standard TCP/IP networking.

iSCSI

The SCSI specification defines a disk protocol that has traditionally been used for locally connected, high-performance disk drives. The iSCSI protocol encapsulates the SCSI protocol inside the standard TCP/IP protocol, enabling block-level storage access across the network. iSCSI offers similar benefits to those seen in a traditional SAN, but using industry standard networking protocols and NICs. However, to use iSCSI in production, you most likely need at least one dedicated 1Gbs NIC and fast network access to the remote storage to achieve acceptable performance.

The SCSI specification uses the terms *target* and *initiator*. For the purposes of this chapter, think of the target as a disk drive, and the initiator as the client computer using the disk. OpenSolaris supports both an iSCSI target and initiator, so you can use OpenSolaris as a server to provide storage to iSCSI clients or as a client system to use iSCSI storage on the network.

CROSS-REF To use iSCSI, you may need to install either the target or the initiator software, depending on how you want to configure the system. The target is in the SUNWiscsitgt package and the initiator is in the SUNWiscsi package. See Chapter 6 for information on installing software.

The following example walks through the steps to configure an iSCSI target and initiator. For clarity, the system prompts are shown as `target#` on the host providing the SCSI target disk and `init#` on the host using the remote disk. OpenSolaris provides two commands — `iscsitadm`, which is used to manage iSCSI targets, and `iscsiadm`, which is used to manage iSCSI initiators.

Configuring the target

On the target system, you first create a directory where the storage will reside, and then use the iscsitadm command to define the configuration:

```
target# mkdir /export/home/disks
target# iscsitadm modify admin -d /export/home/disks
target# iscsitadm create target -z 5g mytarget
target# iscsitadm list target
Target: mytarget
    iSCSI Name: iqn.1986-03.com.sun:02:8f23a58f-337f-6989-d09f-
d4fb7bb3dfae.mytarget
    Connections: 0
```

In this case, the storage will reside under the /export/home/disks directory. The first iscsitadm command defines that as the default directory. The second iscsitadm command creates a new target that is 5GB in size, named mytarget. This target will be a file in the file system that is used as a disk by the initiator. The final command shows the new target configuration.

An SMF service provides support for iSCSI targets. This service is named system/iscsitgt:default and is automatically enabled when you configure the first target device.

Configuring the Initiator

On the initiator system you use the iscsiadm command to configure access to the remote storage. The initiator can discover remote storage in various ways. This example shows the simplest case. First, you specify the IP address of the target system (192.168.0.1 for this example):

```
init# iscsiadm add discovery-address 192.168.0.1
init# iscsiadm modify discovery -t enable
init# iscsiadm list discovery
Discovery:
        Static: disabled
        Send Targets: enabled
        iSNS: disabled
init# iscsiadm list target
Target: iqn.1986-03.com.sun:02:8f23a58f-337f-6989-d09f-
d4fb7bb3dfae.mytarget
        Alias: mytarget
        TPGT: 1
        ISID: 4000002a0000
        Connections: 1
```

The target device is now visible — look at the disks available on the system: a new disk named c1t01000003BA4E5E2000002A0047FA3E22d0 is now visible. The exact name will vary based on your system and network configuration.

```
init# ls /dev/dsk
c0t0d0s0
```

```
c0t0d0s1
c0t0d0s2
c0t0d0s3
c0t0d0s4
c0t0d0s5
c0t0d0s6
c0t0d0s7
c1t01000003BA4E5E2000002A0047FA3E22d0s0
c1t01000003BA4E5E2000002A0047FA3E22d0s1
c1t01000003BA4E5E2000002A0047FA3E22d0s2
c1t01000003BA4E5E2000002A0047FA3E22d0s3
c1t01000003BA4E5E2000002A0047FA3E22d0s4
c1t01000003BA4E5E2000002A0047FA3E22d0s5
c1t01000003BA4E5E2000002A0047FA3E22d0s6
c1t01000003BA4E5E2000002A0047FA3E22d0s7
```

Using the iSCSI disk

Now you can create a file system on this disk, just as if it were a locally attached device (the procedure to create a file system is described in more detail later in this chapter):

```
init# newfs /dev/rdsk/c1t01000003BA4E5E2000002A0047FA3E22d0s2
newfs: construct a new file system /dev/rdsk
/c1t01000003BA4E5E2000002A0047FA3E22d0s2: (y/n)? y
/dev/rdsk/c1t01000003BA4E5E2000002A0047FA3E22d0s2:
      10485120 sectors in 32766 cylinders of 4 tracks, 80 sectors
        5119.7MB in 256 cyl groups (128 c/g, 20.00MB/g, 2560 i/g)
super-block backups (for fsck -F ufs -o b=#) at:
 32, 41072, 82112, 123152, 163872, 204912, 245952, 286992, 327712,
 368752,
 10076352, 10117392, 10158112, 10199152, 10240192, 10281232,
 10321952,
 10362992, 10404032, 10445072
```

On the target system you can monitor the performance of the target devices:

```
target# iscsitadm show stats
                     operations    bandwidth
device               read  write   read  write
--------------------  ----- -----   ----- -----
mytarget              339   664    17M    83M
```

Finally, on the initiator, you can set up the vfstab entry and mount the file system you just created. vfstab is used for persistently managing file system mounts, and is described in detail in the section "Mounting and unmounting file systems" later in this chapter.

```
init# mount /remotespace
init# df -hl
Filesystem              size   used   avail capacity  Mounted on
```

```
/dev/dsk/c0t0d0s0        7.5G    5.1G    2.3G    70%    /
/devices                   0K      0K      0K     0%    /devices
/dev                       0K      0K      0K     0%    /dev
ctfs                       0K      0K      0K     0%    /system/contract
proc                       0K      0K      0K     0%    /proc
mnttab                     0K      0K      0K     0%    /etc/mnttab
swap                     976M    688K    976M     1%    /etc/svc/volatile
objfs                      0K      0K      0K     0%    /system/object
sharefs                    0K      0K      0K     0%    /etc/dfs/sharetab
fd                         0K      0K      0K     0%    /dev/fd
swap                     976M     32K    976M     1%    /tmp
swap                     976M     88K    976M     1%    /var/run
/dev/dsk/c0t0d0s7         20G     20M     19G     1%    /export/home
/dev/dsk/c1t01000003BA4E5E2000002A0047FA3E22d0s2
                         4.9G    5.0M    4.9G     1%    /remotespace
```

Advanced iSCSI administration

There are some limitations to using iSCSI in OpenSolaris. An iSCSI device cannot currently be used as a boot device or a dump device.

CROSS-REF   In OpenSolaris, a dump device is used to save a crash dump if the system panics. The crash dump is necessary for postmortem analysis to determine the cause of the panic and fix the bug. See Chapter 24 for more information.

The previous example walked through setting up a simple iSCSI configuration. Because the disk traffic will be going over the network, it is recommended that you configure additional security for your iSCSI devices. One option is to use IP Security (IPsec) for the network traffic. This provides both authentication and encryption of the data. Alternatively, you can use the built-in iSCSI support for either the Challenge Handshake Authentication Protocol (CHAP) or the Remote Authentication Dial In User Service (RADIUS) protocol for authenticating remote access, although neither of these actually encrypts the data.

CROSS-REF   See Chapter 11 for details on configuring IPsec.

This section only scratches the surface of using iSCSI. Consult the man pages and documentation for more information about a variety of other advanced topics for configuring and managing iSCSI.

I/O Multipathing

Because SANs are generally used in enterprise-grade server configurations, multipathing is usually described in that context. Multipathing can be configured anytime you have more than one path to access your disks. In a SAN configuration, this is done by adding multiple HBAs to the server. Using multipathing enables the system to maintain access to its storage, even if an HBA fails. In OpenSolaris, I/O multipathing is also sometimes called MPxIO.

OpenSolaris includes the scsi_vhci(7D) driver, which manages multipathing. If multipathing were not enabled, the same disk would show up more than once in the device tree because each path to the disk looks like a separate instance. With multipathing enabled, the device tree on the system is restructured so that the separate instances are removed and a single instance appears instead. If you look at a system in this state, you'll notice that these disks appear under the /device/scsi_vhci subdirectory. Multipath support is enabled by default in OpenSolaris. If necessary, you must disable it by reconfiguring the driver for your HBA. You can also use the mpathadm command to view information about the multipath configuration.

When using iSCSI, you can configure multipathing using the standard OpenSolaris networking features such as IPMP or link aggregation. You can also use the scsi_vhci multipathing driver, which is useful if you are using a mix of iSCSI and Fibre Channel-based devices.

> **CROSS-REF** IPMP and link aggregation are described in Chapter 9.

Remote replication

Remote replication of data is used when disaster recovery is important. This is typically in large server configurations. This type of configuration is outside the scope of this book, but OpenSolaris includes support for remote replication using the "Sun StorageTek Availability Suite 4.0" software. The project, documentation, and source code are available on OpenSolaris.org.

> **CROSS-REF** When using ZFS, you can also use the send and receive operations to replicate a file system to another machine. See Chapter 8 for more information.

Other Disk Utilities

The prtvtoc command can be used to print the VTOC label for a disk:

```
# prtvtoc /dev/rdsk/c0t0d0s0
* /dev/rdsk/c0t0d0s0 partition map
*
* Dimensions:
*     512 bytes/sector
*      63 sectors/track
*     255 tracks/cylinder
*   16065 sectors/cylinder
*    8923 cylinders
*    8921 accessible cylinders
*
* Flags:
*   1: unmountable
*  10: read-only
*
*                          First     Sector    Last
* Partition  Tag  Flags    Sector    Count     Sector   Mount Directory
        0      2    00    1076355  10249470  11325824
        1      3    01      16065   1060290   1076354
```

```
   2      5     00            0 143315865 143315864
   5      0     00     11325825  52436160  63761984
   6      0     00     63761985  79537815 143299799
   7      0     00    143299800     16065 143315864
   8      1     01            0     16065     16064
```

The fmthard command can format a disk in a non-interactive way, although the format command is usually preferable.

The iostat command is used to monitor disk I/O activity. It supports a variety of options, but on a system with more than a couple of disks, the -nx options are the most useful. The output displays one line for each disk, showing reads and writes per second (r/s, w/s), KB read and written per second (kr/w, kw/s), wait queue length (wait), average number of active operations (actv), average time in the wait queue in milliseconds (wsvc_t), average service time for active operations in milliseconds (asvc_t), percent of the time wait queue is not empty (%w), and percent of time the disk is busy (%b). The number 5 in the example specifies the output interval in seconds; updated statistics are reported every five seconds:

```
# iostat -nx 5
                    extended device statistics
    r/s    w/s    kr/s    kw/s wait  actv wsvc_t asvc_t  %w  %b device
    0.0    0.0     0.0     0.0  0.0   0.0    0.0    0.0    0   0 c0t0d0
   15.0  208.6   230.5  4455.3  0.0  10.0    0.0   44.9    0  38 c0t1d0
   12.4  203.0   177.6  4314.7  0.0  12.8    0.0   59.2    0  46 c0t2d0
...
```

CROSS-REF   See Chapter 14 for more information about iostat. The iostat(1M) man page describes all of the options and the output format in detail. DTrace, described in Chapter 15, enables unprecedented observability into the dynamic behavior of disk I/O. You can use the DTrace toolkit, which is listed in Chapter 15's "Resources" section, to get several pre-built DTrace programs for disk I/O analysis.

OpenSolaris includes a sophisticated *dynamic reconfiguration* (DR) capability. This functionality is beyond the scope of this chapter, but one of the things DR can be used for is to reconfigure I/O devices. See the cfgadm(1M) command for more information.

One further command that can be useful with disks, as well as in a variety of other contexts, is the dd command. This command is used for converting and copying files; and because disks look just like files in the file system, the command can be used to copy and convert raw disk images. It includes a variety of arcane options, which are described on the man page.

NOTE   The dd command options are unusual and differ from the typical command-line syntax. The abbreviation stands for "data definition" and traces its roots all the way back to the IBM Job Control Language (JCL) used in the punch card era.

File System Management

The specific commands used to create each type of file system are described later in the chapter, in each file system-specific section. Once the file systems have been created, they are normally managed using a common set of commands that work across all types of file systems.

Mounting and unmounting file systems

Once a file system has been created, the mount command is used to make the file system accessible to the system:

```
# mount /dev/dsk/c0t0d0s7 /export/home
```

The mount command accepts a variety of options, including various file system-specific options, but in the simplest case you specify the slice to mount and the directory on which the file system will be mounted. Once a file system is mounted, the directory is referred to as the *mount point*. You can see from the disk path name in the example that the mount command must be used with a block device. The umount command can be used with either the disk name or the mount point to unmount a file system:

```
# umount /export/home
```

A file system cannot be unmounted of it is busy — that is, if an application is using a file within the file system or if a process's current working directory is within the file system. In this case, you need to determine which process is preventing the unmount. The lsof tool is the common command in Linux to perform this task. While this command is not part of OpenSolaris, there is a port that you can download and build. Because it relies on undocumented kernel implementation details, it is easily broken and may not always work. Instead, OpenSolaris includes the fuser command, which provides similar information:

```
# umount /export/home
umount: /export/home busy
# fuser /dev/dsk/c0t0d0s7
/dev/dsk/c0t0d0s7:    29212c
```

This output tells you that pid 29212 is using this mount point as its current working directory. You can read about all of the options and the output format on the fuser(1M) man page.

CROSS-REF   The pfiles command, described in Chapter 14, enables you to observe all of the files that a specific process is using.

Manual mounts using the mount command do not persist across reboots. Instead, the entries in the /etc/vfstab file are used to manage persistent mounts. This is a simple ASCII file that you edit to add any mounts that should be done when the system boots. Each mount has a one-line entry in this file, with seven columns, using the following format:

```
Device      Device     Mount     File       fsck     Mount      Mount
to Mount    to fsck    Point     System     pass     at Boot    Options
                                 Type
```

This is a sample entry for the /export/home file system used in the preceding example:

```
/dev/dsk/c0t0d0s7   /dev/rdsk/c0t0d0s7   /export/home   ufs   2   yes   -
```

The block device is listed first, followed by the raw device, which is used to check the file system for errors. The fsck command is described later in the "UFS" section. The next columns specify the mount point, the type of file system, the fsck pass, whether the file system should be mounted when the system boots, and, finally, any mount options. Because there are no mount options, a dash (-) is used as a placeholder in this entry.

After an entry exists in the file, you can just use the mount point with the mount command:

```
# mount /export/home
```

A variety of SMF milestones are used during boot to mount various file systems:

```
system/filesystem/minimal
system/filesystem/root
system/filesystem/usr
system/filesystem/local
```

See the service definitions and methods to understand what each milestone does.

CROSS-REF SMF is described in Chapter 13.

Monitoring file systems

Although there are a variety of commands for interacting with the file system, the most useful general-purpose commands for monitoring are df, du, and fsstat.

The df command displays each mounted file system, along with statistics about its usage:

```
$ df -hl
Filesystem             size   used   avail  capacity  Mounted on
/dev/dsk/c0t0d0s0      5.2G   3.7G   1.5G    71%      /
...
swap                   1.0G   520K   1.0G    1%       /tmp
/dev/dsk/c0t0d0s7      22G    706M   21G     4%       /export/home
```

The du command shows space usage from any point in the file system:

```
$ du -sh book
174M    book
```

The fsstat command displays information about each type of file system or about file systems at specific mount points:

```
$ fsstat /
  new   name  name  attr   attr lookup rddir   read  read  write  write
 file  remov  chng   get    set    ops   ops    ops bytes    ops  bytes
15.6K  10.8K   717  4.95M  2.68K  29.7M  142K  1.11M 1.26G   241K   221M /
```

The fsstat command supports a variety of options for monitoring file system activity in different ways. See the man page for full details.

File systems and shutting down

For better performance, most file systems buffer some of their data in kernel memory, delaying the actual writes to disk. The fsflush process is a system process (it runs inside the kernel) that periodically writes cached data out to disk. You'll notice this process in the output of the ps command. This means that an improper shutdown, such as turning off the system power, can leave the file system in an inconsistent state. This situation, and how to recover from it, is described in more detail in the "UFS" section of this chapter. The ZFS file system does not suffer from this problem. To ensure that all file system data is in a valid state, always perform an orderly shutdown using the init or shutdown commands. The sync command has also been used in the past to ensure that file system data has been written to disk, but an orderly shutdown does this automatically.

devfs

Devices in OpenSolaris are named in the file system, just like regular files. You have seen examples of this with the disks named under /dev/dsk. Devfs is responsible for the entries under /dev and /devices. This file system is primarily managed by the running operating system and requires limited administrative attention. You'll notice a devfs entry in the vfstab and a daemon named devfsadmd.

The devfsadm command can be used to manage the namespace under /dev. The most common usage is to simply run the command to cause any devices that have been dynamically added to the system to appear in the file system. You can check the other options on the man page.

UFS

The *Unix File System (UFS)* has been the primary file system used on OpenSolaris, and its predecessor, Solaris, for more than 25 years. The roots of this file system trace back to the Berkeley Fast File System developed by Marshall Kirk McKusick and Bill Joy for the BSD project in the early 1980s. This file system has been continuously enhanced over the years to reach its current maturity. Its longevity is a testament to the strength of its basic design. However, the UFS file system has been showing its age and is being phased out in favor of ZFS, which is the default file system on OpenSolaris, and is described in the next chapter. For most new installations you should consider using ZFS, although a large base of legacy installed UFS file systems will continue to be in use for many years.

Creating a UFS File System

The newfs command is used to create a new UFS file system on a block device slice:

```
# newfs /dev/dsk/c0t0d0s7
newfs: /dev/rdsk/c0t0d0s7 last mounted as /export/home
newfs: construct a new file system /dev/rdsk/c0t0d0s7: (y/n)? y
Warning: 1392 sector(s) in last cylinder unallocated
/dev/rdsk/c0t0d0s7:     46342800 sectors in 7543 cylinders of 48
tracks, 128 sectors
        22628.3MB in 472 cyl groups (16 c/g, 48.00MB/g, 5824 i/g)
super-block backups (for fsck -F ufs -o b=#) at:
 32, 98464, 196896, 295328, 393760, 492192, 590624, 689056, 787488,
 885920,
Initializing cylinder groups:
........
super-block backups for last 10 cylinder groups at:
 45418272, 45516704, 45615136, 45713568, 45812000, 45910432,
 46008864,
 46107296, 46205728, 46304160
```

The command prompts for confirmation and then emits a variety of bookkeeping messages as the file system is being created.

CAUTION   Creating a new file system on a slice is a destructive operation. Any data previously on the slice will be lost. It is common for VTOC slice 2 to span the entire disk, so creating a file system on that slice can wipe out data on all of the other slices on the disk.

The newfs command is a simplified front end to the mkfs command. Several options can be used to tune the file system in various ways. These are described on the mkfs_ufs(1M) man page. In most cases, you won't need to use these options, but a few might be useful. Use the -T option if you are creating a file system that you expect to later grow to be larger than 1TB. Growing a UFS file system is described in the section "The Volume Manager" later in this chapter. Another option is -C num, which specifies the maximum number of blocks that should be allocated contiguously. In particular, this option is often set on a file system that will be used with a database, where it is known in advance that data will be primarily written in contiguous chunks. The tunefs command can be used to adjust some of these options after the file system has been created.

Logging

One of the traditional problems with UFS is that its file system metadata, the data about the file system itself, is written in separate operations at different locations on the disk. Thus, it is possible for this data to be out of sync if the system goes down unexpectedly, before all of these writes have been completed. This leaves the file system in a corrupted state, which you would need to repair before the file system can be mounted. In the worst case, serious data loss can occur.

Logging is a solution to this problem and is one of the features added to UFS over the years. With logging, the metadata operations are grouped into a transaction that is written to a log. If the system goes down, then the log can be replayed when the system boots, restoring the file system to a consistent state. Any incomplete transactions are discarded. A beneficial side effect is that performance is also improved, because metadata writes are grouped and written in one operation.

Logging is on by default, but you can disable it if necessary with the `nologging` mount option.

UFS Mount Options

All of the UFS-specific mount options are described on the `mount_ufs(1M)` man page. A few of the options you might have an occasion to use are as follows:

- `noatime` — Disables recording of file access times. If you are not interested in tracking access times, then using `noatime` can provide a small performance boost.
- `quota` — Enables disk-space quotas, as described shortly
- `forcedirectio` — Provides a performance boost for certain applications, such as databases

Checking and Repairing a UFS File System

UFS includes a variety of mechanisms, such as logging, to keep file systems consistent. However, sometimes a file system will become corrupted and need to be fixed before it can be used. The `fsck` command is used to check a file system and, optionally, to try to repair it. This command is normally run automatically, if necessary, when the system boots. If you need to run it manually to repair a file system, specify the raw slice.

```
# fsck /dev/rdsk/c0t0d0s7
** /dev/rdsk/c0t0d0s7
** Last Mounted on
** Phase 1 - Check Blocks and Sizes
** Phase 2 - Check Pathnames
** Phase 3a - Check Connectivity
** Phase 3b - Verify Shadows/ACLs
** Phase 4 - Check Reference Counts
** Phase 5 - Check Cylinder Groups
```

```
2 files, 9 used, 22820199 free (7 frags, 2852524 blocks,
 0.0% fragmentation)
```

This is the output on a clean file system. Do not run this on a device that hosts a file system that is already mounted; and do not run this command unless it is necessary. For example, on a multi-terabyte file system, it can take a very long time (many hours or days) to complete. The output of the command varies depending on the type of corruption that has occurred, but this example also shows how fsck can repair a file system:

```
# fsck /dev/rdsk/c0t0d0s7
** /dev/rdsk/c0t0d0s7
BAD SUPERBLOCK AT BLOCK 16: MAGIC NUMBER WRONG

LOOK FOR ALTERNATE SUPERBLOCKS WITH MKFS? y

LOOK FOR ALTERNATE SUPERBLOCKS WITH NEWFS? y

FOUND ALTERNATE SUPERBLOCK 98464 WITH NEWFS

USE ALTERNATE SUPERBLOCK? y

FOUND ALTERNATE SUPERBLOCK AT 98464 USING NEWFS
If filesystem was created with manually-specified geometry, using
auto-discovered superblock may result in irrecoverable damage to
filesystem and user data.

CANCEL FILESYSTEM CHECK? n

** Last Mounted on
** Phase 1 - Check Blocks and Sizes
** Phase 2 - Check Pathnames
** Phase 3a - Check Connectivity
** Phase 3b - Verify Shadows/ACLs
** Phase 4 - Check Reference Counts
** Phase 5 - Check Cylinder Groups

UPDATE STANDARD SUPERBLOCK? y

2 files, 9 used, 22820199 free (7 frags, 2852524 blocks,
 0.0% fragmentation)

***** FILE SYSTEM WAS MODIFIED *****
```

The corruption on this file system was simple and easy to fix, but you may be faced with a seriously corrupted file system that causes fsck to emit a seemingly unending series of prompts. If you are not a UFS expert, and you just want fsck to try its best to fix things, use the -y option to let fsck take its default repair action in all cases.

As you look around mounted UFS file systems, you will notice a lost+found directory at the top level of each file system. This directory is where fsck puts any files it finds during a repair operation that have become disconnected from any directory. In the worst case, you might be able to look through these lost files and recover some of your data, although this can be hit or miss. Don't remove the lost+found directory, as fsck depends on it.

Quotas

UFS provides support for quotas, whereby disk space can be limited on a per-user basis. To use quotas, the file system must first be mounted using the quota option, as described earlier. Use this option in the vfstab so that quotas for the specified file system are enabled each time the system boots.

The following example sets up quotas for the /export/home file system. Each file system that will use quotas must have a file named quotas at the top level of the file system. The file should be read-only and owned by root:

```
# cd /export/home
# touch quotas
# chmod 600 quotas
```

Next, use the edquota command to edit the quotas for a user. This command brings up an editor where you can specify the user's quota for each file system that is set up for quotas:

```
# edquota sarah
```

Because only one file system is set up with quotas, this is the one-line entry you would see in the file:

```
fs /export/home blocks (soft = 0, hard = 0) inodes (soft = 0, hard = 0)
```

This shows the entry for the /export/home file system. You specify the user's total space limits in the blocks soft and hard entries, in units of 1,024 byte blocks. The inodes limits are used to set the total number of files that a user can have. The soft limit is used to warn users when they exceed the limit, but the operation still succeeds. The hard limit cannot be exceeded and causes the operation to fail.

You can use the -p option to quickly set up quotas for a number of users. See the edquota(1M) man page for more information.

After all of the quotas are set up, turn on quotas using the quotaon command with the -a option:

```
# quotaon -a
```

The quota command with the -v option shows the usage for a specified user:

```
# quota -v sarah
Disk quotas for sarah (uid 100):
Filesystem     usage  quota  limit    timeleft  files  quota  limit    timeleft
/export/home    113   1000   2000                  2     50     50
```

In this example, the soft space limit was set to one thousand 1,024-byte blocks, or approximately 1MB, and the hard space limit was set to 2,000 blocks, or about 2MB. The number of files was limited to 50. The user is already using 113 blocks.

Once quotas are enabled, any command by which the user attempts to exceed his or her quota will fail, as the following example shows. Note the warning when the soft limit is exceeded, and the error when the hard limit is reached:

```
$ cd /export/home/sarah
$ mkfile 2m f1
quota_ufs: Warning: over disk limit (pid 29832, uid 100, inum 6,
 fs /export/home)
quota_ufs: over hard disk limit (pid 29832, uid 100, inum 6, fs /export/home)
f1: initialized 2023424 of 2097152 bytes: Disc quota exceeded
```

In addition to the `quota` command, you can use the `repquota` command to report on quotas by file system:

```
# repquota /export/home
                  Block limits               File limits
User       used  soft  hard  timeleft   used  soft  hard  timeleft
sarah  --  1993  1000  2000               2    50    50
```

You can read more information about UFS quotas in the *OpenSolaris System Administration Guide, Volume 2*, Chapter 29, "Managing Quotas (Tasks)."

Backup, Snapshots, and Restore

The `ufsdump` program is used for backing up UFS file systems — for both full and incremental dumps. An incremental dump enables you to back up only those files that have changed since the last incremental or full dump. The next example shows a full back up of the root file system. Because an explicit dump device is not specified, `ufsdump` writes to the /dev/rmt/0 device, which is the name of a magnetic tape device on OpenSolaris. Your backup device may be different. If so, you can specify an explicit device using the -f option.

```
# ufsdump -0cu /
```

The argument -0 means take a level-0, or full, dump. The -c argument specifies that the defaults for a cartridge tape device should be used, and the -u option means that a dump record should be written to /dev/dumpdates, recording that a successful dump was taken.

A file system should be dumped only when it is unmounted, or mounted read-only, so that no changes occur while the dump is taking place. To dump a critical file system such as root, you need to boot the system to single-user mode so that root is mounted read-only. Because dumps can take a long time, this will have a significant effect on the availability of the system. Instead, you can create a snapshot of the file system using the `fssnap` command and use that as the source of the dump. The following example creates a snapshot of the root file system:

```
# fssnap -F ufs -o bs=/export/home/snap /
/dev/fssnap/0
```

This snapshot takes just a few seconds to create; and once it is complete, the root file system can be modified while a dump of the snapshot is taken. The fssnap_ufs(1M) man page describes all of the options for UFS snapshots. This example uses the -o bs option to specify a backing-store for the snapshot. The snapshot is created as a temporary file in that directory. You can now run the same dump as above, but using the snapshot as a raw device:

```
# ufsdump -0cu /dev/rfssnap/0
```

Once the dump is finished, you can delete the snapshot:

```
# fssnap -d /
Deleted snapshot 0.
```

CAUTION   UFS snapshots are not persistent across reboots.

The ufsrestore program is used to restore from your backups. The exact sequence of commands you need to run depends on your dump strategy and how many incremental dumps you need to restore, along with the level-0 dump.

Restoring a critical file system such as root is the most complex task, because you presumably can no longer just boot from the original device. In this case, you first need to boot from an alternate device, such as the OpenSolaris Live-CD or from an image on the net. Once you are running, you need to create a UFS file system, and then you can use ufsrestore just as you would if you were restoring a noncritical UFS file system:

```
# newfs /dev/dsk/c0t0d0s0
# mount /dev/dsk/c0t0t0s0 /a
# cd /a
# ufsrestore -rv
```

In this example, you are recreating the root file system from scratch while running on another image, so you first need to make a file system, mount it, and finally restore it.

As with ufsdump, the command defaults to the /dev/rmt/0 device, or you can use the -f option to specify an alternate dump file such as a different tape drive or other device. The ufsrestore command restores dumps into the current directory and includes a variety of options for interactive restores, as well as other features.

Restoring the root file system has additional complexity that you won't see with other file systems. Specifically, the information needed to boot the system also needs to be put in place.

Because the boot block is not part of the root file system, it won't be included in the UFS dump. The procedure to install the boot block varies from SPARC to x86. On SPARC you use the installboot program:

```
# installboot /usr/platform/`uname-i`/lib/fs/ufs/bootblk /dev/rdsk/c0t0d0s0
```

On x86 you use installgrub:

```
# installgrub /boot/grub/stage1 /boot/grub/stage2 /dev/rdsk/c0t0d0
```

See the man pages for more details on these commands, as well as the various possibilities for restoring individual files or directories from incremental backups.

> **NOTE**   OpenSolaris includes a variety of other programs for archiving and managing files, including the tar(1), gtar(1), pax(1), and cpio(1) commands.

Swap Space

Swap space is not really a file system, but because it is related to storage and can be specified in the vfstab, it is described here. The system's physical memory, combined with its swap space, defines the *anonymous memory* available to the system. The swap space is used when there is pressure on physical memory, and some of the in-core memory must be paged out to disk. In general, if this occurs often, then system performance will be noticeably degraded. In that case, consider adding more physical memory to the system or moving some of the workload to a different machine. However, in some cases it is beneficial to be able to swap out some of the in-core pages, so you should almost always configure some swap space. When you have insufficient anonymous memory, the most common symptom is that either existing processes or new applications you try to start will begin to fail with out of memory errors. Adding swap space will alleviate this symptom, but with the performance penalty already mentioned.

> **CROSS-REF**   This chapter describes the traditional way to configure swap by using a disk slice or file. When using ZFS as the root file system, then both the swap device and the system dump device are configured to use a zvol in the root pool. See Chapter 8 for more information on ZFS, and Chapter 24 for more information on configuring dump.

Swap space can be either an unused disk slice or a file. By convention, the installer usually sets up slice 1 on your boot disk as a swap device. This would be a typical entry in the vfstab:

```
/dev/dsk/c0t0d0s1   -    - swap - no -
```

If you want to use additional slices for swap, you can add the entries into the vfstab, but they don't take effect until the system reboots. To dynamically add swap space, use the swap command. With the -l option, it prints the swap space currently configured:

```
# swap -lh
swapfile              dev    swaplo  blocks    free
```

```
/dev/dsk/c0t0d0s1   27,1153     4K    518M    457M
/dev/dsk/c0t1d0s1   27,2113     4K    1.2G    1.1G
```

The `-s` option prints a one-line summary, which is helpful to check overall usage:

```
# swap -sh
total: 800M allocated + 85M reserved = 884M used, 1.6G available
```

CROSS-REF The `vmstat` command, described in Chapter 14, can be used to dynamically monitor swap space usage.

Use the `-a` option to add additional space, and the `-d` option to delete space. The next example creates a 100MB file to be used for swap space and dynamically adds it:

```
# mkfile 100m /export/swp
# swap -a /export/swp
# swap -lh
swapfile               dev     swaplo   blocks    free
/dev/dsk/c2t0d0s1    27,1153     4K      518M     457M
/dev/dsk/c1t15d0s1   27,2113     4K      1.2G     1.1G
/export/swp             -        4K      100M     100M
```

This additional swap space would not be persistent across reboots unless you also added it to the `vfstab`.

A common question is, "How much swap space should be configured?" The answer obviously varies based on the amount of physical memory and the workload running on the system. Your application vendor may recommend a specific amount of swap. With the larger amount of physical memory on modern systems, the old rule of thumb to use twice the physical memory is usually no longer valid. If you have 8GB, 16GB, or even more physical memory, then having twice that in swap space doesn't make sense. With larger memory configurations, and no other factors, having swap set between one-third to half of physical memory is generally a good guideline. The OpenSolaris installer defaults to half of physical memory, with an upper bound of 32GB and a lower bound of 0.5GB. You can easily add more swap space later if needed.

However, a swap device can also be used for system crash dumps if there is a panic. If possible, configuring a separate dump device is preferable because it will speed reboots after a panic. (See Chapter 24, as well as the `dumpadm(1M)` man page, for information on configuring a dump device and dump content.) If you are also using your swap device as a dump device, ensure that it is large enough to hold a system dump, whose size increases with the size of physical memory even though compression is used. In this case, having swap configured for half or more of physical memory may be required. Generally, larger memory systems are used in server configurations where uptime is a factor, so a dedicated dump device makes more sense because post-panic rebooting is much faster. Remember that dumping into swap doesn't apply when using ZFS root on OpenSolaris, as described earlier, so dump size is not a factor when sizing swap in that case.

Other Local File Systems

OpenSolaris includes a variety of other local file systems.

pcfs

The pcfs file system is used to mount traditional file systems used on the Windows operating system. These file systems include FAT12, which is used on floppies, and FAT16 or FAT32 file systems. In addition to floppies, this type of file system is common on other removable media such as USB sticks. Although the removable media volume manager will automatically handle mounts on removable media, if you must manually mount one of these file systems, simply use the -F pcfs option on the mount command. The mkfs -F pcfs command with the raw device is used to create a pcfs on a disk. The options are described on the mkfs_pcfs(1M) man page. Support for other common Windows file systems, such as ntfs, is not part of a standard OpenSolaris installation, but open source utilities and projects on the OpenSolaris.org website provide some support.

hsfs

The hsfs file system supports the High Sierra and ISO 9660 file systems commonly used on CD-ROMs. Again, the removable media volume manager normally automatically handles mounts of removable media, but you can use the -F hsfs option on the mount command if you need to manually mount this file system. Remember that the file system must be mounted read-only. The mount_hsfs(1M) man page describes the options.

You cannot use the mkfs command to create one of these file systems because this type of file system resides on read-only media. Instead, a special utility called mkisofs is used to create hsfs file systems. You can then use the cdrecord or cdrw commands to burn data in this format, if your system is equipped with a DVD or CD-ROM writable drive.

tmpfs

The tmpfs file system resides in anonymous memory — that is, in physical memory and swap space. This file system is similar in concept to a RAM disk, but it is at the file system level instead of the device level. As such, it is easier to manage because you don't actually have to create a file system; the tmpfs file system manages that automatically. As with a RAM disk, the contents of this file system are not preserved across reboots. A tmpfs file system is most often used as the mount point for /tmp because /tmp is defined not to be preserved across reboots. By using a memory-based file system for /tmp, activities such as compilation, which create many short-lived temporary files, can be significantly sped up. Although tmpfs is usually mounted on /tmp, additional mounts can be placed anywhere. The /var/run file system is another common tmpfs mount point. All tmpfs mounts share the same anonymous memory as the backing store. The swap device name is used when mounting tmpfs.

Because tmpfs shares anonymous memory with other applications, it reduces the available physical memory and swap space for running applications. All of the tmpfs-specific mount options are described on the mount_tmpfs(1M) man page. In particular, the size option limits the amount of anonymous memory used by a particular mount:

```
# mount -F tmpfs -o size=10m swap /foo
```

lofs

The lofs file system is not a true file system but is instead the loop-back file system. It enables you to mount a directory or file someplace else within the system's directory tree, making that part of the tree visible in more than one place. There are no lofs-specific mount options, but the generic options, such as read-only, can be used. The following example mounts / under /export/home/foo as a read-only mount:

```
# mount -F lofs -o ro / /export/home/foo
```

The lofs file system is used by various other parts of the system, such as Zones, described in Chapter 19.

SAM-QFS

SAM-QFS (Storage Archive Manager/Quick File System) is a high-end, enterprise-level file system and archiving solution that can be used with OpenSolaris. Like ZFS, QFS integrates volume management support into the file system. In addition, QFS can be used in a clustered configuration to provide shared data access. SAM provides transparent data archiving support and is integrated with QFS, so the two components automatically work together. Configuring and managing SAM-QFS is outside the scope of this book, but OpenSolaris includes this software. The project, along with its source code, is available on OpenSolaris.org.

FUSE

FUSE stands for "file system in user space." This file system is actually a shim layer that allows new file systems to run as user-level applications instead of having to be integrated into the kernel. The OpenSolaris FUSE project is working to port FUSE from the BSD version. Using FUSE enables support for new file systems that cannot be integrated into the kernel for various reasons, speeds porting of some file systems, and simplifies the development of new file systems. The current status of the project, as well as the source, is available at http://opensolaris.org/os/project/fuse/. A variety of popular file systems can be used with FUSE, including versions of ntfs and ext2.

The Volume Manager

A volume manager is used to create a composite storage device out of a collection of disks. OpenSolaris includes the Solaris Volume Manager (SVM), which provides this feature. Using SVM, you can take a set of disks and make a larger volume, either by concatenating the disks together or by striping across the disks. You can either mirror disks or use RAID-5 for redundancy. You can also use SVM as a component in a clustered configuration to provide redundant access to data for improved uptime.

> **NOTE** Because SVM is a traditional volume manager, it works at the disk-block level and presents pseudo-devices that look like standard disks. A file system, such as UFS, must be created on top of one of these volumes, just as you would with a standard disk. The ZFS file system, described in the next chapter, actually incorporates the functionality of a volume manager with the file system, providing the features of both in an integrated way that enables them to work better than when the functionality is implemented as separate layers. In general, you either choose ZFS, which is preferred, or use UFS with SVM, but you typically won't mix the use of ZFS and SVM on the same system.

SVM uses the term *metadevice* as the name for the volumes it provides. All of the SVM commands use `meta` as a prefix. This section provides a brief overview on configuring and using SVM, but you should consult the manual to fully understand all of the features.

Creating the metadb

SVM stores its configuration data in metadbs (metadevice databases). Metadbs must be stored on a raw slice. If you plan to use SVM when installing your system, set aside a small slice of about 10MB on several disks, for your metadbs. For proper behavior, SVM should be configured with at least three metadbs on three different disks. If one of the disks fails, SVM needs to find the configuration on another disk. SVM also uses a quorum algorithm to validate the metadbs, so if you have only two disks and one fails, SVM cannot be sure that the visible metadb is actually correct. In this situation, the system will boot to single-user so that you can manually verify the configuration and delete the bad metadb. However, by having three different metadbs on three different disks, any one disk can fail, and SVM can still have a metadb quorum with the other two disks.

This example assumes three different disks that have been partitioned with a 10MB slice 7 for storing the metadbs. You must use the `-f` flag when you are creating the first metadb. Notice that you don't need to specify the full disk path name:

```
# metadb -af c0t0d0s7
# metadb -a c0t1d0s7
# metadb -a c0t2d0s7
```

You can also place more than one metadb on a slice. While this will not help if the disk fails, it can be used for redundancy if some of the blocks on the disk where a metadb is stored go bad.

Creating a metadevice

Now that the metadbs have been created, you can create metadevices. A metadevice is a pseudo-device that appears just like a regular disk to the code layered above it, such as file system code, but uses real disks underneath. In this example, you create a simple mirror for the UFS file system `/export/home` on `c0t0d0s6` and `c0t1d0s6`. SVM mirrors are composed of metadevices, so the first step is to create a simple one-stripe metadevice on each slice. Because you are creating a mirror and SVM works at the block level, both the c0t0d0s6 and c0t1d0s6 slices must be partitioned so that they are the exact same number of blocks in size:

```
# metainit d1 1 1 c0t0d0s6
d1: Concat/Stripe is setup
# metainit d2 1 1 c0t1d0s6
d2: Concat/Stripe is setup
```

This command creates metadevices named d1 and d2. There is only one stripe and one slice in each device. If you have enough disks, you could concatenate or stripe several slices into one larger, nonredundant metadevice, and use that to build your mirror.

Now that you have created the underlying metadevices, you can create a one-sided mirror using the -m option:

```
# metainit metaexport -m d1
metaexport: Mirror is setup
```

Here, you created a mirror named metaexport, on top of the d1 metadevice. This example also shows that you can use your own logical names for your metadevices. This mirror has only one side, so now you attach the other metadevice to make a two-way mirror:

```
# metattach metaexport d2
metaexport: submirror d2 is attached
```

Once a side has been attached to a mirror, the mirror must be resynced so that both sides are block-for-block identical. It does not matter that there is no data on this metadevice yet; SVM works at the block level, so it must mirror each block. This is one example where the tighter integration that ZFS provides between the file system and volume management features is a big improvement. Resyncing a mirror can take a long time, depending on the size of the mirror. You can use the metastat command to monitor the progress:

```
# metastat -c
metaexport      m   25GB d1 d2 (resync-9%)
    d1          s   25GB c0t1d0s6
    d2          s   25GB c0t0d0s6
```

The -c option prints condensed output. You can see that metaexport is a mirror, composed of the d1 and d2 metadevices, and that resyncing is 9% complete. Once the resync has finished, the mirror will be redundant and loss of one of the disks will not cause data loss. You don't need to wait for mirror resyncs to complete before using the metadevice. That bookkeeping is handled transparently by the SVM code.

Now you can create a file system on the mirror and set up the vfstab entry. Metadevices reside under the /dev/md subdirectory and have both block and raw names, just like real disks:

```
# newfs /dev/md/rdsk/metaexport
newfs: construct a new file system /dev/md/rdsk/metaexport: (y/n)? y
```

```
Warning: 5056 sector(s) in last cylinder unallocated
/dev/md/rdsk/metaexport:        54154304 sectors in 8815 cylinders
   of 48 tracks, 128 sectors
        26442.5MB in 551 cyl groups (16 c/g, 48.00MB/g, 5824 i/g)
super-block backups (for fsck -F ufs -o b=#) at:
   32, 98464, 196896, 295328, 393760, 492192, 590624, 689056, 787488,
   885920,
Initializing cylinder groups:
..........
super-block backups for last 10 cylinder groups at:
   53186208, 53284640, 53383072, 53481504, 53579936, 53678368,
   53776800, 53875232, 53973664, 54072096
```

This is the entry in the vfstab:

```
/dev/md/dsk/metaexport /dev/md/rdsk/metaexport /export/home  ufs  2  yes  -
```

Other commands and features

The metastat command is used to display the configuration. You already saw the condensed output earlier. Here is the full output for the configuration you just created:

```
# metastat
metaexport: Mirror
     Submirror 0: d1
       State: Okay
     Submirror 1: d2
       State: Okay
     Pass: 1
     Read option: roundrobin (default)
     Write option: parallel (default)
     Size: 54154305 blocks (25 GB)

d1: Submirror of metaexport
    State: Okay
    Size: 54154305 blocks (25 GB)
    Stripe 0:
        Device        Start Block  Dbase        State Reloc Hot Spare
        c0t0d0s6            0       No           Okay  Yes

d2: Submirror of metaexport
    State: Okay
    Size: 54154305 blocks (25 GB)
    Stripe 0:
        Device        Start Block  Dbase        State Reloc Hot Spare
        c0t1d0s6            0       No           Okay  Yes

Device Relocation Information:
Device   Reloc  Device ID
```

```
c0t0d0     Yes     id1,sd@SSEAGATE_ST336607LSUN36G_3JA6EFT100007418CACF
c0t1d0     Yes     id1,sd@SSEAGATE_ST336607LSUN36G_3JA6EEA200007418KWQB
```

This output shows all of the components of the d1 and d2 metadevices and indicates that they are themselves components of the metaexport mirror metadevice. The State column shows that each component is working properly. If there were a problem with one of the disks in one of the submirrors, it would print with an error status. You can see that the mirror will perform reads in a round-robin fashion, from one side to the other, which improves performance. You can also see that writes to both sides of the mirror are done in parallel. If the mirror were configured with hot-spare disks and one of those disks was spared in, that would be displayed in the Hot Spare column. The Device Relocation Information shows the device ID for each disk in the configuration. Device IDs are used so that SVM can keep track of disks, even if they are recabled and show up on the system with a new c#t#d# name.

Although this example used only a single slice on each side of the mirror, because d1 and d2 are metadevices, you can add additional slices to those devices and grow their size later. This enables you to grow the size of the mirror as well. OpenSolaris includes the growfs command, which you can use to grow the size of a UFS file system if the underlying storage has increased in size. You can see how building your file system on top of a volume, instead of directly on a slice, gives you this flexibility. However, there is no way to shrink a UFS file system if the size of the underlying volume is reduced. Reducing the size of a volume that is hosting a UFS file system will leave that file system corrupted and unusable.

In addition to the simple mirror shown in the example, SVM supports RAID-5 stripes, soft partitions, hot spares, and metasets, which are used in clustered configurations to manage volume failover across nodes. If you plan to use SVM, consult the documentation to learn more about these features.

Resources

The Network Storage project delivers Fibre Channel and iSCSI support, along with a variety of other low-level storage software. That project is at http://opensolaris.org/os/project/nws. The I/O multipathing project is at http://opensolaris.org/os/project/mpxio. Remote replication is part of the Sun StorageTek Availability Suite project at http://opensolaris.org/os/project/avs. The UFS community at http://opensolaris.org/os/community/ufs includes pointers to source code and a discussion of UFS-related topics. The original Berkeley Fast File System paper is available at http://cs.berkeley.edu/~brewer/cs262/FFS.pdf, as well as several other sites.

File system projects for compatibility with other operating systems include the ext3 project at http://opensolaris.org/os/project/ext3 and ntfs reader at http://sourceforge.net/projects/mount-ntfs.

Although they are not described in this chapter, databases have a close relationship with storage and file systems. The community at http://opensolaris.org/os/community/databases

provides discussions and resources for using databases on OpenSolaris. The Volume Manager community at http://opensolaris.org/os/community/volume_manager provides resources for the SVM. Other projects covered in this chapter include SAM-QFS, http://opensolaris.org/os/project/samqfs, and FUSE, http://opensolaris.org/os/project/fuse.

Summary

This chapter described how disk storage is managed and configured on OpenSolaris, including how to format disks and how disk devices appear on the system. It introduced general file system concepts and described a variety of local file systems. In particular, it explained UFS and swap space, which are commonly used on many systems. It briefly covered other available local file systems, and then examined the Solaris Volume Manager's features and basic configuration.

The next chapter describes ZFS, the preferred alternative to UFS and SVM. However, many of the basic concepts described in this chapter, such as disk fundamentals, monitoring disk I/O, and the details of other file systems besides UFS, are helpful even when using ZFS.

Chapter 8

ZFS

One of the unique features of OpenSolaris is the ZFS file system. Most likely, one of the main reasons you're interested in OpenSolaris is because of the fame that this powerful, yet easy-to-use, file system has gained.

The motivation behind ZFS is to make available to everyone the flexibility of the pooled storage model that large-scale storage systems provide, but without the complex administration and high cost of those storage systems. By integrating management of the disks and the file systems together, ZFS tries to make your storage as self-managing as your system's memory. ZFS is designed to scale to extremely large quantities of data by using 128-bit data addressing and dynamically scaling its metadata, rather than using the fixed scales demanded by UFS and other file systems of its generation, which weren't designed for terabyte and larger scales.

ZFS provides high performance through a fully parallel design with an I/O pipeline that's modeled on the concepts of CPU instruction pipelines. By using a transactional, copy-on-write update model, ZFS ensures that its data is always consistent on disk. ZFS computes a checksum on every data and metadata block, and because its checksums cover the entire data path and are stored separately from the data being checksummed, it can detect data corruption caused by any element of the storage subsystem, not just disk errors. As a result, there is no need for a traditional file system checking and repair utility such as `fsck`, and inexpensive disks can provide similar reliability to high-priced storage systems.

IN THIS CHAPTER

ZFS pools

Mirroring

RAID Z

ZFS file systems

ZFS volumes

ZFS encryption

ZFS versioning

In addition to scalability, performance, and reliability, ZFS also provides advanced features such as built-in compression and encryption, constant-time snapshots and clones of file systems, fast and easy data replication, and a simple, logical administrative model that makes the power of ZFS available to anyone.

ZFS's unique feature set also provides a powerful base for building the OpenSolaris software management functions described in Chapter 6.

ZFS Basics

Conceptually, ZFS is extremely simple. Disks are assigned to *pools*, and *datasets* are carved out of the pools. There are two primary types of datasets: *file systems* and *volumes*. A volume provides a virtual device, which can be accessed as either a block device or a raw character device, whereas a file system is just a directory hierarchy for organizing and storing files. The two objects, pools and datasets, each have an administration command: zpool for pools, and zfs for datasets. If you're using the OpenSolaris distribution, you already have a ZFS pool and some file systems and volumes created, so start by examining them to get a basic idea of what ZFS looks like.

First, use the zpool command to list the pools available:

```
$ zpool list

NAME      SIZE    USED    AVAIL    CAP   HEALTH   ALTROOT
backup    278G    33.4G   245G     12%   ONLINE   -
rpool     17.5G   2.58G   14.9G    14%   ONLINE   -
scratch   37.2G   26.7G   10.6G    71%   ONLINE   -
```

This system has three different pools. The default name for the pool created by the OpenSolaris distribution's installer to hold the system software is rpool, although any name could be used. (Pools from which a system can boot are called *root pools*, hence rpool.) You can use the command zpool status to see more details about pools. With no additional arguments it displays the status of all pools, or you can specify the name of a specific pool, such as rpool:

```
$ zpool status rpool
  pool: rpool
 state: ONLINE
 scrub: none requested
config:

        NAME        STATE     READ WRITE CKSUM
        rpool       ONLINE       0     0     0
          c9d0s0    ONLINE       0     0     0

errors: No known data errors
```

The most immediately interesting piece of information in the status display is the config section, which displays the devices that make up the pool. This pool is a simple one, created from a single disk slice.

A pool is also a file system, and by default it is mounted on the system at the mount point */poolname*. Use the zfs command to examine the pool's file system:

```
$ zfs list rpool
NAME    USED   AVAIL  REFER  MOUNTPOINT
rpool   2.58G  14.7G  49.5K  /rpool
```

The amount of space used and available is displayed in the columns labeled USED and AVAIL, respectively. The REFER column displays the amount of data accessible within the specific file system, while the USED value is the sum of the space used by this file system and all of its subsidiary file systems. To list all of those subsidiaries, add a simple -r option to the zfs list command:

```
$ zfs list -r rpool
NAME                                USED   AVAIL  REFER  MOUNTPOINT
rpool                               2.58G  14.7G  49.5K  /rpool
rpool@install                       16K    -      49.5K  -
rpool/ROOT                          2.57G  14.7G  18K    none
rpool/ROOT@install                  0      -      18K    -
rpool/ROOT/opensolaris              2.57G  14.7G  2.00G  legacy
rpool/ROOT/opensolaris@install      113M   -      1.94G  -
rpool/ROOT/opensolaris/opt          479M   14.7G  479M   /opt
rpool/ROOT/opensolaris/opt@install  79K    -      3.61M  -
rpool/export                        52K    14.7G  19K    /export
rpool/export@install                15K    -      19K    -
rpool/export/home                   18K    14.7G  18K    /export/home
rpool/export/home@install           0      -      18K    -
```

This listing has several interesting entries. First, you might wonder what all of the entries with the string @install at the end are; these are *snapshots* of the file systems that were taken at the conclusion of the OpenSolaris installation process. A snapshot is a third distinct type of dataset that is a read-only copy of either a file system or a volume at a particular point in time. Later in this chapter, you'll learn more details about using and creating ZFS snapshots; but for now, it's enough to understand that these particular @install snapshots save the original copy of every file that was initially installed on the system. Your listing may not include the snapshots, depending on the value of the pool's listsnapshots property. You can add the option -t all to ensure that snapshots are included in the listing.

Another interesting entry in this listing is the rpool/ROOT file system. This is a special file system name that is created by the OpenSolaris distribution's installation software to contain the root file system for each instance of OpenSolaris installed within a root pool. By convention, each file system immediately under rpool/ROOT is expected to be a bootable installation of OpenSolaris.

CROSS-REF See Chapter 6 for details on managing OpenSolaris software.

Managing ZFS Pools

To use ZFS as your file system, you first need to create a pool. This section demonstrates creating and managing common pool configurations.

TIP   One particularly fast and cheap way to experiment with ZFS is to use flash memory devices. The examples in this section demonstrate different ways to create and manage pools and file systems using USB flash memory.

A simple single-device pool (using a disk device at /dev/dsk/c11t0d0p0) named tank is created with the following:

```
# zpool create tank c11t0d0p0
# zpool status tank
  pool: tank
 state: ONLINE
 scrub: none requested
config:

        NAME          STATE      READ WRITE CKSUM
        tank          ONLINE        0     0     0
          c11t0d0p0   ONLINE        0     0     0

errors: No known data errors
# zpool list tank
NAME   SIZE    USED   AVAIL    CAP  HEALTH   ALTROOT
tank   3.81G   92.5K  3.81G     0%  ONLINE   -
```

As shown here, it's not necessary to specify the full path to the device; zpool is smart enough to fill that in for you. Note also that creating this pool is quite fast — just a few seconds.

CROSS-REF   OpenSolaris disk device names are discussed in Chapter 7.

When creating ZFS pools, it's preferable to assign the whole disk to ZFS, rather than just a partition. When ZFS is managing the entire disk, it enables the disk's built-in write cache, which improves the I/O performance to that disk. However, at this writing you cannot use an entire disk for a root pool. ZFS labels disks using an EFI label that is not understood by current system firmware, so the system cannot boot from the disk. If you need to add more storage to this pool, you can do so very easily, again with the zpool command:

```
# zpool add tank c7t0d0p0
# zpool status tank
  pool: tank
 state: ONLINE
 scrub: none requested
config:

        NAME          STATE      READ WRITE CKSUM
```

```
    tank        ONLINE     0    0    0
      c11t0d0p0 ONLINE     0    0    0
      c7t0d0p0  ONLINE     0    0    0

errors: No known data errors
# zpool list tank
NAME    SIZE   USED   AVAIL   CAP  HEALTH  ALTROOT
tank    7.62G  114K   7.62G   0%   ONLINE  -
```

Both devices are now listed in the pool configuration and the capacity of the pool has increased to include the space on the second device. This type of pool is known as a *concatenation*.

Destroying a pool is also simple:

```
# zpool destroy tank
# zpool status tank
cannot open 'tank': no such pool
```

If you inadvertently destroy a pool, don't panic! You can get it back if the devices haven't been reused. Use zpool import -D <poolname> to re-import the pool. See the section "Migration" later in this chapter for more details.

CAUTION   Unfortunately, ZFS cannot currently remove a device from a pool that is a concatenation. To remove the devices from such a pool, you must destroy the pool. It's better to configure most pools as mirrors or Raid Zs, which are covered in the next two sections, so that you can replace failed devices without loss of data.

Mirrors

In ZFS (as well as in traditional volume managers), a *mirror* is a storage pool in which a copy of each block is written to each device that is a part of the mirror. This redundancy provides the most basic type of storage protection: If one device in the mirror fails, the other device (or devices, if the mirror is more than a two-way mirror) can continue to provide service. A ZFS mirror, however, provides a higher level of data protection than a traditional volume manager. Both types handle failed devices in essentially the same way, but ZFS is capable of detecting a single bad block error via the checksum that it stores with each piece of data. If such an error occurs, ZFS automatically checks the other devices in the mirror; and if it finds one that has good data, it uses the good copy to attempt to repair the bad block.

CROSS-REF   See Chapter 7 for information on the Solaris Volume Manager (SVM).

Converting a single-device pool to a mirror is quite easy:

```
# zpool status tank
  pool: tank
 state: ONLINE
 scrub: none requested
config:
```

```
NAME            STATE     READ WRITE CKSUM
  tank          ONLINE      0    0    0
    c7t0d0p0    ONLINE      0    0    0

errors: No known data errors
# zpool attach tank c7t0d0p0 c11t0d0p0
# zpool status tank
  pool: tank
 state: ONLINE
 scrub: resilver completed with 0 errors on Sat Mar 29 12:56:25 2008
config:

NAME            STATE     READ WRITE CKSUM
  tank          ONLINE      0    0    0
    mirror      ONLINE      0    0    0
      c7t0d0p0  ONLINE      0    0    0
      c11t0d0p0 ONLINE      0    0    0

errors: No known data errors
```

One notable item in the status listing is the scrub status (see the section "Data scrubbing" later in this chapter for more about what this means). Once a device is attached to a mirror, ZFS automatically initiates a *resilver*, the process of duplicating all of the existing pool data onto the mirror device. Because this pool was empty, the resilver required no time to complete, but even in the case of a large pool, the ZFS resilver will often be much faster than that of the mirror devices provided by traditional block-level volume managers such as Solaris Volume Manager. This optimization is possible because the integrated design of ZFS enables the device layer to duplicate only blocks that actually contain file system data, rather than also duplicating all of the free blocks, which is necessary when the volume manager and file system are effectively black boxes to each other.

> **TIP** Because it's so easy to convert a single-device pool to a mirror with ZFS, the OpenSolaris distribution's installer doesn't ask you to spend time creating complex disk configurations at installation. If your system has multiple disks, it's highly recommended that you use `zpool attach` to convert your OpenSolaris root pool to a mirrored configuration. See Chapter 3 for an example.

You can also create the pool as a mirror initially, using a longer form of the `create` subcommand:

```
# zpool create tank mirror c7t0d0p0 c11t0d0p0
```

Detaching a device from a mirror is simple as well:

```
# zpool detach tank c11t0d0p0
# zpool status tank
  pool: tank
 state: ONLINE
```

```
    scrub: none requested
config:

        NAME          STATE     READ WRITE CKSUM
        tank          ONLINE       0     0     0
          c7t0d0p0    ONLINE       0     0     0

errors: No known data errors
```

You can also replace one device with another in a single operation:

```
# zpool status tank
  pool: tank
 state: ONLINE
 scrub: resilver completed with 0 errors on Sat Mar 29 13:42:44 2008
config:

        NAME          STATE     READ WRITE CKSUM
        tank          ONLINE       0     0     0
          mirror      ONLINE       0     0     0
            c10t0d0p0 ONLINE       0     0     0
            c7t0d0p0  ONLINE       0     0     0

errors: No known data errors
# zpool replace tank c7t0d0p0 c11t0d0p0
```

While the replacement is in progress, the pool status shows it:

```
$ zpool status tank
  pool: tank
 state: ONLINE
 scrub: resilver completed with 0 errors on Sat Mar 29 13:45:06 2008
config:

        NAME            STATE     READ WRITE CKSUM
        tank            ONLINE       0     0     0
          mirror        ONLINE       0     0     0
            c10t0d0p0   ONLINE       0     0     0
            replacing   ONLINE       0     0     0
              c7t0d0p0  ONLINE       0     0     0
              c11t0d0p0 ONLINE       0     0     0

errors: No known data errors
```

Once the replacement is completed, the pool status reflects the new configuration:

```
$ zpool status tank
  pool: tank
 state: ONLINE
```

```
scrub: resilver completed with 0 errors on Sat Mar 29 13:45:06 2008
config:

    NAME            STATE     READ WRITE CKSUM
    tank            ONLINE       0     0     0
      mirror        ONLINE       0     0     0
        c10t0d0p0   ONLINE       0     0     0
        c11t0d0p0   ONLINE       0     0     0

errors: No known data errors
```

You can also take a device offline, which might be necessary to perform maintenance on it:

```
# zpool offline tank c11t0d0p0
# zpool status tank
  pool: tank
 state: DEGRADED
status: One or more devices has been taken offline by the administrator.
    Sufficient replicas exist for the pool to continue functioning in a
    degraded state.
action: Online the device using 'zpool online' or replace the device with
    'zpool replace'.
 scrub: resilver completed with 0 errors on Sat Mar 29 14:39:57 2008
config:

    NAME            STATE     READ WRITE CKSUM
    tank            DEGRADED     0     0     0
      mirror        DEGRADED     0     0     0
        c10t0d0p0   ONLINE       0     0     0
        c11t0d0p0   OFFLINE      0     0     0

errors: No known data errors
```

As you can see, the pool goes into a degraded state, with the reason reported in the status. The action entry provides advice on operations that can be performed to return the pool to the normal online state.

ZFS also automatically detects devices that have been disconnected, placing them in the offline state:

```
$ zpool status tank
  pool: tank
 state: DEGRADED
 scrub: resilver completed with 0 errors on Sat Mar 29 14:47:05 2008
config:

    NAME            STATE     READ WRITE CKSUM
    tank            DEGRADED     0     0     0
      mirror        DEGRADED     0     0     0
```

```
          c10t0d0p0  ONLINE      0    0    0
          c11t0d0p0  REMOVED     0    0    0

  errors: No known data errors
```

Once the device is reattached, it's automatically detected and brought online, and the mirror automatically resilvered.

RAID Z

While mirrors are an effective means of increasing the availability of data in a storage system, they are an expensive solution. The capacity of the mirror is the size of a single device in the mirror, so a two-way mirror effectively doubles the per-bit storage cost. A mirror can negatively affect performance because it's necessary to write a copy of the data to each device. It's often desirable to increase reliability at a lower cost in terms of both money and performance, so the storage industry developed techniques for spreading the data across multiple disks (called *striping*) and using mathematical techniques to detect and correct errors (called *parity checking*). With such a configuration, costs are lower than in a mirror configuration of equivalent capacity, while enabling the system to tolerate errors in one or two devices simultaneously, thus offering essentially the same level of reliability as a two- or three-way mirror. This technique is called RAID 5 or RAID 6 (a standard mirror is known as RAID 1). ZFS offers its own flavor of RAID 5, called RAID Z.

> **NOTE** The acronym RAID stands for Redundant Arrays of Inexpensive Disks. A good introduction to RAID concepts can be found at http://en.wikipedia.org/wiki/RAID.

Creating a RAID Z pool is just as simple as creating a mirror:

```
# zpool create tank raidz c7t0d0p0 c11t0d0p0 c10t0d0p0
# zpool status tank
  pool: tank
 state: ONLINE
 scrub: none requested
config:

        NAME         STATE     READ WRITE CKSUM
        tank         ONLINE      0    0    0
          raidz1     ONLINE      0    0    0
            c7t0d0p0   ONLINE      0    0    0
            c11t0d0p0  ONLINE      0    0    0
            c10t0d0p0  ONLINE      0    0    0

  errors: No known data errors
```

This example created a RAID Z pool with three disks, capable of sustaining a single drive failure because it is a raidz1 (single-parity) pool, as shown in the output. Note that raidz is a synonym for raidz1. To create a double-parity pool, enabling the pool to sustain two drive failures without data loss, you can use a type of raidz2. Currently, these are the only two types of RAID Z pools.

In other respects, a RAID Z pool is managed similarly to a mirror; however, the `attach` and `detach` subcommands can only be used on mirrors, not on RAID Z devices. As a result, you must create a pool as `raidz` initially, not convert it later. Replacing a device in a RAID Z pool is supported, of course.

It's common to create far more complex pool configurations that consist of multiple RAID Z groupings on larger storage servers such as a Sun x4500 server. The *ZFS Best Practices Guide* at `http://solarisinternals.com/wiki/index.php/ZFS_Best_Practices_Guide` provides examples and recommendations for such configurations; we recommend consulting it if you're planning a large ZFS deployment.

Spare devices

To run a truly reliable storage system, plan for disks to fail. Mirrors and RAID Z are an essential part of a reliability strategy, but configuring spare devices (also called *hot spares*) buys an extra bit of assurance. If a device in a pool fails, ZFS automatically replaces the failed disk using a device from the list of available spares. A ZFS pool can have any number of spare devices assigned, and you can share spare devices between multiple pools. Spares may be configured at pool creation time or added later. The following configures a spare at pool creation:

```
# zpool create tank mirror c7t0d0p0 c10t0d0p0 spare c11t0d0p0
# zpool status tank
  pool: tank
 state: ONLINE
 scrub: none requested
config:

        NAME          STATE     READ WRITE CKSUM
        tank          ONLINE       0     0     0
          mirror      ONLINE       0     0     0
            c7t0d0p0  ONLINE       0     0     0
            c10t0d0p0 ONLINE       0     0     0
        spares
          c11t0d0p0   AVAIL

errors: No known data errors
```

To add a spare after a pool exists, use the `add` subcommand:

```
# zpool add tank spare c11t0d0p0
```

When a replacement is in use, the spare is brought online into the pool and marked in use (here, the failure was caused by disconnecting the disk):

```
$ zpool status tank
  pool: tank
 state: DEGRADED
status: One or more devices are faulted in response to persistent errors.
        Sufficient replicas exist for the pool to continue functioning in a
        degraded state.
```

```
action: Replace the faulted device, or use 'zpool clear' to mark the device
        repaired.
 scrub: resilver completed with 0 errors on Thu Apr  3 20:33:04 2008
config:

        NAME             STATE     READ WRITE CKSUM
        tank             DEGRADED     0     0     0
          mirror         DEGRADED     0     0     0
            c7t0d0p0     ONLINE       0     0     0
            spare        DEGRADED     0     0     0
              c10t0d0p0  FAULTED      0     0     0  too many errors
              c11t0d0p0  ONLINE       0     0     0
        spares
          c11t0d0p0      INUSE     currently in use

errors: No known data errors
```

Once the faulted device is repaired, you can use the `clear` subcommand to request that it be brought back online, enabling the pool to exit the degraded state:

```
# zpool clear tank
# zpool status tank
  pool: tank
 state: ONLINE
 scrub: resilver completed with 0 errors on Thu Apr  3 20:37:32 2008
config:

        NAME             STATE     READ WRITE CKSUM
        tank             ONLINE       0     0     0
          mirror         ONLINE       0     0     0
            c7t0d0p0     ONLINE       0     0     0
            spare        ONLINE       0     0     0
              c10t0d0p0  ONLINE       0     0     0
              c11t0d0p0  ONLINE       0     0     0
        spares
          c11t0d0p0      INUSE     currently in use

errors: No known data errors
```

Once you're satisfied that the original device is functioning properly, you can return the spare to the available spare list using the `detach` subcommand. The `status` subcommand then displays the spare as available, as shown here:

```
# zpool detach tank c11t0d0p0
# zpool status tank
  pool: tank
 state: ONLINE
 scrub: resilver completed with 0 errors on Thu Apr  3 20:37:32 2008
config:
```

```
NAME              STATE     READ WRITE CKSUM
tank              ONLINE       0     0     0
  mirror          ONLINE       0     0     0
    c7t0d0p0      ONLINE       0     0     0
    c10t0d0p0     ONLINE       0     0     0
  spares
    c11t0d0p0     AVAIL

errors: No known data errors
```

> **NOTE** ZFS will not automatically detach a spare device from use after it has been brought online in a pool; you need to do this manually after you've repaired and verified a failed device.

Data scrubbing

Another reliability feature of ZFS pools is data scrubbing. One problem with traditional file systems is that the reliability of any data that's not referenced by the system's normal operation is unknown; you may have errors that are silently lying in wait to be found when the data is actually needed. To combat this hazard, ZFS provides a data-scrubbing feature to verify the integrity of every block of data in a pool. During a scrub operation, ZFS reads each block and verifies it against its checksum. If it finds an error on a device that is part of a mirror or raidz device, ZFS attempts to repair the block; otherwise, the error is reported. A scrub is initiated on a pool named tank as follows:

```
# zpool scrub tank
```

You can observe the progress of the scrub operation using zpool status:

```
$ zpool status tank
  pool: tank
 state: ONLINE
 scrub: scrub in progress, 9.21% done, 0h41m to go
config:

	NAME              STATE     READ WRITE CKSUM
	tank              ONLINE       0     0     0
	  mirror          ONLINE       0     0     0
	    c7t0d0p0      ONLINE       0     0     0
	    c10t0d0p0     ONLINE       0     0     0
	  spares
	    c11t0d0p0     AVAIL

errors: No known data errors
```

Scrubbing runs at a low priority relative to other I/O, so it should not interfere with the operation of the pool. However, a scrub operation that is in progress can be stopped if necessary. For example, here's how to stop a scrub on the pool named `tank`:

```
# zpool scrub -s tank
# zpool status tank
  pool: tank
 state: ONLINE
 scrub: scrub stopped with 0 errors on Fri Apr  4 22:45:52 2008
config:

        NAME            STATE     READ WRITE CKSUM
        tank            ONLINE       0     0     0
          mirror        ONLINE       0     0     0
            c7t0d0p0    ONLINE       0     0     0
            c10t0d0p0   ONLINE       0     0     0
        spares
          c11t0d0p0     AVAIL

    errors: No known data errors
```

As discussed earlier, a resilver of a mirror is effectively the same as a scrub, so you'll see the results of a resilver reported in the scrub status if your pool is a mirror.

Migration

ZFS pools can be easily migrated from system to system; unlike most file systems, migration is supported even if the two systems are of different instruction-set architecture endianness (byte ordering), such as SPARC and x86. ZFS makes this possible by using an adaptive endianness scheme to store data. Each block has its endianness recorded when written, and if the system reading the data does not have the same endianness as the data block, ZFS automatically swaps the data bytes to the host endianness.

NOTE Migration of a pool between systems of different endianness is possible only if ZFS is given the use of entire disk devices to build the pool. This is because the use of only a portion of a disk requires using a Solaris VTOC disk label, which is endian-specific. When ZFS uses an entire disk device, it labels the disk with an endian-neutral EFI label, enabling the label to be read by systems of opposite endianness. Chapter 7 covers disk devices and labeling.

ZFS records the hostname and hostid of the system that owns the pool in the pool's private data structures, so to ready a pool to be moved, use the `export` subcommand to release the ownership:

```
# zpool export tank
# zpool status tank
cannot open 'tank': no such pool
```

Once the storage is attached to the new system, use the `import` subcommand to make the pool accessible to OpenSolaris. You can use `import` with no arguments to find the pools that are available for import:

```
# zpool import
  pool: tank
    id: 3244598400197407233
 state: ONLINE
action: The pool can be imported using its name or numeric
 identifier.
config:

        tank            ONLINE
          raidz2        ONLINE
            c7t0d0p0    ONLINE
            c11t0d0p0   ONLINE
            c10t0d0p0   ONLINE
```

Then use the pool name or id to import it:

```
# zpool import tank
# zpool status tank
  pool: tank
 state: ONLINE
 scrub: none requested
config:

        NAME            STATE     READ WRITE CKSUM
        tank            ONLINE       0     0     0
          raidz2        ONLINE       0     0     0
            c7t0d0p0    ONLINE       0     0     0
            c11t0d0p0   ONLINE       0     0     0
            c10t0d0p0   ONLINE       0     0     0

errors: No known data errors
```

You can also use the `-a` option, rather than specify a pool name, to import all pools that the system can find on its attached storage devices.

If a pool you attempt to import wasn't exported from its owning system, the import will fail with a message that it appears to be in use by another system. If that's the case, you can use the `-f` option to the `import` subcommand to force the import to proceed — this is quite helpful for unplanned storage migrations in case of catastrophic system failure.

If you are attempting to import a pool and you have an existing pool with the same name, the import will fail. However, you can rename the pool as it is importing to resolve the conflict:

```
# zpool import tank frank
```

 **To rename a pool that is currently in use, you first export it** (zpool export) **and then use** zpool import **to provide its new name, as the preceding example shows.**

The import subcommand has several other options that are infrequently used; they are discussed in the zpool(1M) man page.

Pool properties

ZFS pools have a number of properties that can be viewed and modified using the get and set subcommands. To view all of the properties, use the special property name all:

```
$ zpool get all tank
NAME   PROPERTY      VALUE              SOURCE
tank   size          1.91G              -
tank   used          92.5K              -
tank   available     1.91G              -
tank   capacity      0%                 -
tank   altroot       -                  default
tank   health        ONLINE             -
tank   guid          15434063680586116038  -
tank   version       10                 default
tank   bootfs        -                  default
tank   delegation    on                 default
tank   autoreplace   on                 local
tank   cachefile     -                  default
tank   failmode      wait               default
```

The properties whose source is listed as a hyphen (-) are read-only properties used to report status of the pool. Otherwise, the SOURCE column indicates whether the property is the default value or is locally set on the pool. Table 8-1 briefly summarizes the pool properties.

The properties detailing the size and space usage of the pool should be self-explanatory. The remainder of this section describes some of the more interesting properties in greater detail. Consult the zpool(1M) man page for reference information on all of the pool properties.

The version property is discussed later in this chapter in the section "ZFS Versioning." The delegation property is used to enable the delegated administration feature for the ZFS datasets within this pool (more about this feature later in the chapter).

The autoreplace property controls whether the system can automatically replace a device that is a member of the pool with a new device found in the same location. Its default setting is off, meaning the administrator must manually replace any devices using the replace subcommand described earlier in this chapter. To set the autoreplace property value, use zpool set:

```
$ zpool set autoreplace=on tank
$ zpool get autoreplace tank
NAME   PROPERTY      VALUE      SOURCE
tank   autoreplace   on         local
```

TABLE 8-1

Pool Properties

Property	Description
altroot	Directory under which pool datasets are mounted
autoreplace	Indicates whether automatic device replacement is allowed
available	Storage space available in a pool
bootfs	Default bootable dataset
cachefile	File used to cache pool configuration
capacity	Percentage of space used
delegation	Indicates whether dataset delegation is available in pool
failmode	System's reaction to pool failure
guid	Global unique identifier for this pool, generated at creation
health	System's assessment of pool's health, such as ONLINE, DEGRADED, or OFFLINE
listsnapshots	Controls whether snapshots are included in default output from zfs list
size	Size of a pool
used	Storage space used in a pool
version	Pool version

The failmode property defines how the system should react to a failure of the pool. The default value of wait causes all I/O to the pool to be blocked until the pool is returned to health. Other possible values are panic, which causes the system to generate a crash dump on pool failure, and continue, which generates an I/O error on any write requests but allows reads to any devices that are online. The default value is probably the best compromise for most pools because panic makes the system somewhat more brittle, and continue can lead to situations in which applications can access data that might be stale.

The listsnapshots property controls the behavior of the zfs command when listing the datasets in a pool. If set to off, the default value, then snapshots are not included in the zfs list output. Setting it to on includes snapshots in dataset listings. The -t option to zfs list can be used to override this setting.

The altroot and cachefile properties are typically used in manipulating pools and datasets during system installation; they are set as a result of using the -R or -c options to zpool import. The bootfs property is used by the ZFS booting support in the kernel to locate the correct dataset to mount as the root file system. The OpenSolaris version of GRUB also offers a `bootfs` command, which is used to override the property when you want to boot a different root file system within the pool.

CROSS-REF See Chapter 6 for more information on OpenSolaris software management, including booting of alternate root file systems.

Pool history

Good system administrators keep detailed records on what is changed, and when, on their systems in order to help analyze problems and reconstruct system state when failures occur. They also configure system auditing to record who is responsible for changes, which is especially important when multiple staff have administrative rights; this also helps detect the activities of intruders.

CROSS-REF Chapter 11 discusses the OpenSolaris auditing facility.

ZFS provides a pool history feature to record significant events affecting pools, which you can access using the `zpool history` command. The pool history is implemented as a 128KB ring buffer within the pool, which means it will eventually wrap around and overwrite events, so you can't rely on it to maintain a full history over time — that's the realm of the auditing facility. When investigating a system problem, though, you'll often find that some recent change has triggered the problem. Data ring buffers are quite effective aids to an administrator investigating a problem, yet they impose little cost because their bounded size eliminates the need to manage them as an additional entity, unlike a full-blown system auditing or logging feature. This sort of limited-capacity telemetry recorder is common in many systems where reconstructing recent events is important, such as the well-known "black boxes" used to record airliner data.

The pool history for `tank` can be viewed using the following:

```
$ zpool history tank
History for 'tank':
2008-04-11.18:03:15 zpool create tank c11t0d0p0
2008-04-11.19:17:59 zpool set replace=on tank
```

One detail to note about the pool history implementation is that the pool creation record is never overwritten; thus, you can always determine when the pool was created.

You can use the `-l` option to include the username, zone, and hostname in the output of each record. The `-i` option includes internal event records, such as the following:

```
$ zpool history -i tank
History for 'tank':
2008-04-11.18:03:15 zpool create tank c11t0d0p0
2008-04-11.19:17:58 [internal pool property set txg:901] autoreplace 1 tank
2008-04-11.19:17:59 zpool set replace=on tank
```

Monitoring ZFS performance

There are many resources for monitoring general system I/O performance, such as the iostat(1M) command. These resources are also generally useful with ZFS, but ZFS also provides a very simple I/O performance monitoring capability, the zpool iostat command. To simply report a snapshot in time for all pools in the system, use the following:

```
$ zpool iostat
                capacity      operations     bandwidth
pool         used  avail    read  write    read  write
----------   -----  -----   -----  -----   -----  -----
backup       30.9G   247G      0      0      56     15
rpool        2.61G  14.9G      0      0    6.04K  14.0K
scratch      29.8G  7.48G      0      0     346   9.22K
----------   -----  -----   -----  -----   -----  -----
```

This system is a lightly loaded desktop, so the statistics are unimpressive. The following shows one pool on a more heavily loaded server:

```
$ zpool iostat tank
                capacity      operations     bandwidth
pool         used  avail    read  write    read  write
----------   -----  -----   -----  -----   -----  -----
tank         2.72T  3.15T     210    410    902K  4.05M
```

Most often, you'll probably want to use an interval argument to have the statistics reported every few seconds — this example reports every five seconds — continuing until you break out with ˆC:

```
$ zpool iostat tank 5
                capacity      operations     bandwidth
pool         used  avail    read  write    read  write
----------   -----  -----   -----  -----   -----  -----
tank         2.72T  3.15T     210    410    902K  4.05M
tank         2.72T  3.15T      22    307   61.4K  11.9M
tank         2.72T  3.15T      81    216    118K  5.54M
tank         2.72T  3.15T      16    229   82.2K  6.20M
tank         2.72T  3.15T      50    299    263K  7.85M
tank         2.72T  3.15T      13    246   86.9K  2.48M
```

If you want to collect only a specific number of samples, you can add one more argument to specify the sample count:

```
$ zpool iostat tank 5 12
```

This example would report the statistics for the pool every five seconds for one minute.

You can also get detailed information for each device in a pool by adding the -v option:

```
$ zpool iostat -v
                capacity      operations     bandwidth
```

pool	used	avail	read	write	read	write
rpool	3.11G	131G	0	0	2.71K	2.02K
c7t0d0s0	3.11G	131G	0	0	2.71K	2.02K
space	10.1G	268G	1	4	25.2K	130K
mirror	10.1G	268G	1	4	25.2K	130K
c7t3d0p0	-	-	0	2	17.1K	130K
c7t4d0p0	-	-	0	2	16.9K	130K

ZFS can be configured with additional devices reserved for some of its internal operations to increase performance for some workloads. See the zpool(1M) man page for details on log and cache devices for more information.

CROSS-REF More detailed performance analysis can be performed using the DTrace environment, which is discussed in Chapter 15. Further information on system monitoring is provided in Chapter 14.

ZFS Datasets

As discussed briefly at the beginning of this chapter, data in ZFS is stored in entities called datasets, which can be either file systems or volumes, and snapshots can be used to retain a point-in-time copy of either a file system or a volume. In this section, you'll learn more about managing each of these dataset types.

ZFS file systems

Once you've configured a pool in which to store your data, the next step is to configure the file systems that will actually organize the data. In a traditional file system such as UFS, you would create a partition using fdisk and/or format; format a file system within it using a command such as newfs; and then create directories within the file system to place data files. The same can be done with ZFS, of course, although adhering strictly to traditional file system management practices won't enable you to take full advantage of ZFS.

CROSS-REF Management of UFS and other OpenSolaris file systems is discussed in Chapter 7.

In ZFS, file systems can be plentiful, as they're not limited by the scarcity of resources such as partitions. Instead, they are easy and fast to create, and are best thought of as administrative control points, more like a souped-up version of a directory than a traditional file system. Because ZFS offers many features at the file system level, strongly consider creating a file system, rather than a directory, when you need an additional container for storing a set of files. By doing so, you'll have the option to apply different ZFS property settings, such as compression, to each file system and to delegate administrative access to the file systems to individual users so that they, too, can take advantage of ZFS features, such as snapshots and clones, as they need them.

When you create a pool, you also implicitly create a file system with the same name as the pool:

```
# zpool create tank
# zfs list tank
NAME   USED  AVAIL  REFER  MOUNTPOINT
tank   105K  1.87G    18K  /tank
# ls /tank
#
```

Because the pool was just created, its file system is empty. While you could use the pool this way, usually you'll want to create additional file systems within the pool to organize the data:

```
# zfs create tank/fish
# zfs list -r tank
NAME        USED  AVAIL  REFER  MOUNTPOINT
tank        130K  1.87G    19K  /tank
tank/fish    18K  1.87G    18K  /tank/fish
```

As you can see, the -r option to zfs list recursively displays the information on all datasets that are children of the specified dataset. Destroying a file system is simple:

```
# zfs destroy tank/fish
```

However, you can't destroy the file system associated with the pool:

```
# zfs destroy tank
cannot destroy 'tank': operation does not apply to pools
use 'zfs destroy -r tank' to destroy all datasets in the pool
use 'zpool destroy tank' to destroy the pool itself
```

As suggested in this error message, the -r option to zfs destroy destroys a dataset and all of its children. If you don't specify -r and the dataset contains child datasets, then the operation will fail:

```
# zfs create tank/fish/pacific
# zfs destroy tank/fish
cannot destroy 'tank/fish': filesystem has children
use '-r' to destroy the following datasets:
tank/fish/pacific
```

This behavior shouldn't be surprising — it's similar to that of rmdir when you attempt to remove a directory.

It's also easy to rename a file system:

```
# zfs list -r tank
NAME        USED  AVAIL  REFER  MOUNTPOINT
tank        156K  1.87G    19K  /tank
tank/fish    38K  1.87G    20K  /tank/fish
```

```
tank/fish/pacific    18K  1.87G    18K  /tank/fish/pacific
# zfs rename tank/fish/pacific tank/pacific
# zfs list -r tank
NAME                USED  AVAIL  REFER  MOUNTPOINT
tank                156K  1.87G    19K  /tank
tank/fish            20K  1.87G    20K  /tank/fish
tank/pacific         18K  1.87G    18K  /tank/pacific
```

> **NOTE** You can rename a file system only within its pool; to move a file system from one pool to another, see the section "Data replication and backups" later in this chapter.

As shown in the examples so far, by default, a ZFS file system is automatically mounted as soon as it's created; also by default, its pathname is constructed by preceding the file system name with / so that it's mounted relative to the root of the system. This behavior can be modified, however, by setting the values of the canmount and mountpoint properties on the file system. See the section "Dataset properties" later in this chapter for more details on managing dataset properties.

ZFS volumes

Most of the time, you'll use ZFS just for storing files, so you'll deal mostly with file systems. Sometimes, though, the system requires a basic block or character device in which to store data. In a traditional Solaris storage and file system hierarchy, you would typically create a separate partition at the disk level, and then access the block or character device nodes associated with the partition using a device path such as /dev/dsk/c0d0s3. However, partitioning the disk in this way is directly counter to the ZFS design principle of pooling the available storage devices in order to use the available storage as efficiently as possible. Thus, ZFS provides another type of dataset, the volume, which presents itself to the system as a disk device that can be accessed as either a block or character device.

When you install OpenSolaris, it automatically creates two ZFS volumes to be used as the swap and crash dump devices. The swap device serves as the overflow area for the system's main memory, while the dump device is used to save the contents of the system's memory when the operating system panics. These volumes are named rpool/swap and rpool/dump, respectively:

```
$ zfs list rpool/swap rpool/dump
NAME         USED  AVAIL  REFER  MOUNTPOINT
rpool/dump   512M  15.9G    16K  -
rpool/swap   768M  15.9G    16K  -
```

In this case, the system has a 768MB swap volume available for use, and a 512MB dump volume.

> **CROSS-REF** See Chapter 7 for more information on swap devices, and Chapter 24 for information on dump devices.

243

You can create additional volumes using zfs create by adding the -V option to specify that the dataset is a volume, rather than a file system. For example, the following creates a 50MB volume named testvol in the tank pool:

```
# zfs create -V 50m tank/testvol
# zfs list -r tank
NAME            USED   AVAIL  REFER  MOUNTPOINT
tank            50.2M  1.83G  21K    /tank
tank/fish       18K    1.83G  18K    /tank/fish
tank/pacific    18K    1.83G  18K    /tank/pacific
tank/testvol    50M    1.87G  16K    -
```

As you can see, volumes are listed along with file systems by zfs list. Note that the space configured for the volume is immediately allocated exclusively to the volume dataset and is unavailable to the rest of the datasets in the pool. You can configure the volume as a *sparse* volume, for which storage space will be allocated only as it is actually used, by adding the -s option to the create subcommand. However, that's not advisable because software that uses storage devices directly is often unprepared to encounter an "out of space" error, which can occur when you create a sparse volume and force it to compete with other datasets for space — as a result, the software may fail with unreliable results.

To access a volume's device nodes, prefix the volume name with /dev/zvol/dsk for the block device node, and /dev/zvol/rdsk for the character device node:

```
$ ls -l /dev/zvol/*/tank/testvol
lrwxrwxrwx  1 root    root        35 Apr 13 21:40 /dev/zvol/dsk/tank
/testvol -> ../../../../devices/pseudo/zfs@0:4c
lrwxrwxrwx  1 root    root        39 Apr 13 21:40 /dev/zvol/rdsk/tank
/testvol -> ../../../../devices/pseudo/zfs@0:4c,raw
```

Just as with file systems, you can easily rename a volume:

```
# zfs list -r tank
NAME            USED   AVAIL  REFER  MOUNTPOINT
tank            50.2M  1.83G  21K    /tank
tank/fish       18K    1.83G  18K    /tank/fish
tank/pacific    18K    1.83G  18K    /tank/pacific
tank/testvol    50M    1.87G  16K    -
# zfs rename tank/testvol tank/fish/volume
# zfs list -r tank
NAME               USED   AVAIL  REFER  MOUNTPOINT
tank               50.2M  1.83G  21K    /tank
tank/fish          50.0M  1.83G  18K    /tank/fish
tank/fish/volume   50M    1.87G  16K    -
tank/pacific       18K    1.83G  18K    /tank/pacific
```

To destroy a volume, use zfs destroy:

```
# zfs destroy tank/fish/volume
```

Common uses of ZFS volumes include serving as the backing store for iSCSI targets, or as the storage for xVM guest domains.

CROSS-REF See Chapter 7 for information on iSCSI. See Chapter 20 for information on xVM.

ZFS snapshots

The third, and last, type of dataset is the snapshot. As discussed earlier in this chapter, a snapshot is merely a point-in-time copy of its base dataset, which can be either a file system or a volume. Snapshots are useful in their own right, as they provide an exceptionally efficient and convenient means of saving the state of a dataset for later reference or recovery. They also provide the basis for other ZFS features, such as cloning and copying datasets, which are discussed in subsequent sections. Understanding and using snapshots is important in leveraging the full capabilities of ZFS.

Snapshots are very fast to create in ZFS, in part because they use a copy-on-write design. Rather than replace a data block in place when new data is written to it, a new block is allocated and the data written there, and then the parent is updated to reference the new block, with the old block freed once it is no longer referenced, and so on up the tree structure that ZFS uses to track block references. As a result, taking a snapshot merely requires creating a reference to the root of the block tree (known as the *überblock*) at that point in time, which prevents it or any block within its tree from being freed. Paradoxically, a snapshot actually speeds up file system operation, because there's no need to free blocks that have been overwritten! Figure 8-1 shows the block tree when a snapshot has been created and new blocks written. The snapshot root and all blocks it points to are immutable, while the live dataset points to the modified blocks written within it, as well as unmodified blocks from the snapshot.

FIGURE 8-1

A ZFS block tree with snapshot and new blocks

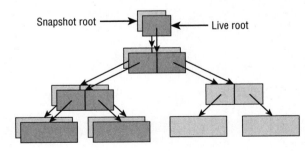

To create a snapshot, use the `zfs snapshot` command. Because a snapshot is based on a file system or volume dataset, the snapshot is named using the name of the base dataset, followed

by the @ character, and then the snapshot name. You can create a snapshot named today for
the tank/fish dataset with the following command:

```
# zfs snapshot tank/fish@today
# zfs list -r tank/fish
NAME               USED   AVAIL  REFER  MOUNTPOINT
tank/fish          50.0M  1.83G  18K    /tank/fish
tank/fish@today    0      -      18K    -
tank/fish/pacific  18K    1.83G  18K    /tank/fish/pacific
tank/fish/volume   50M    1.87G  16K    -
```

Like the other dataset types, you can rename a snapshot:

```
# zfs rename tank/fish@today tank/fish@trip
# zfs list -r tank/fish
NAME               USED   AVAIL  REFER  MOUNTPOINT
tank/fish          50.1M  1.83G  19K    /tank/fish
tank/fish@trip     16K    -      18K    -
tank/fish/pacific  18K    1.83G  18K    /tank/fish/pacific
tank/fish/volume   50M    1.87G  16K    -
```

The data contained in a file system snapshot is directly accessible only if the base dataset's
snapdir property is set to the value visible. When this is the case, the snapshot can be
accessed via the file system's .zfs/snapshot directory; in the example, that would be as
follows:

```
$ ls -ld /tank/fish/.zfs/snapshot/trip
drwxr-xr-x   2 root      root              2 Apr 13 21:05 /tank/fish
/.zfs/snapshot/trip
```

CAUTION   In most instances, it is better to access the contents of a file system snapshot by creating a clone, rather than making the snapshot directory visible. That's because the
snapshot directory is included if you attempt to use traditional UNIX utilities such as cp, tar, or
cpio to copy the file hierarchy under a file system; backup software that is not aware of ZFS may
also capture the snapshot data if it is exposed in this way. See the following section, "ZFS clones,"
for more information.

You can return a dataset to its state as a particular snapshot using the rollback subcommand:

```
# zfs rollback tank/fish@trip
```

One point to understand is that a snapshot of a given dataset applies only to that dataset, not
to any subsidiary datasets; as a result, in our example, the rollback of tank/fish would not
return tank/fish/pacific to a prior state because no snapshot of it was created. However,
it's easy to create snapshots of an entire dataset hierarchy at once by adding -r to the snapshot
command:

```
# zfs snapshot -r tank@today
# zfs list -r tank
```

```
NAME                      USED   AVAIL  REFER  MOUNTPOINT
tank                      50.2M  1.83G  19K    /tank
tank@today                0      -      19K    -
tank/fish                 50.1M  1.83G  19K    /tank/fish
tank/fish@trip            16K    -      18K    -
tank/fish@today           0      -      19K    -
tank/fish/pacific         18K    1.83G  18K    /tank/fish/pacific
tank/fish/pacific@today   0      -      18K    -
tank/fish/volume          50.0M  1.87G  16K    -
tank/fish/volume@today    0      -      16K    -
```

You can't rollback the entire hierarchy at once, but rolling back each dataset in the hierarchy can be done individually if needed.

If there are multiple snapshots of a dataset, an attempt to rollback to any snapshot other than the most recent will fail:

```
# zfs rollback tank/fish@trip
cannot rollback to 'tank/fish@trip': more recent snapshots exist
use '-r' to force deletion of the following snapshots:
tank/fish@today
```

As the error message indicates, using the -r option destroys the more recent snapshots. The next section discusses clones, but a similar error will occur if there is a clone of one of those snapshots:

```
# zfs rollback -r tank/fish@trip
cannot rollback to 'tank/fish@trip': clones of previous snapshots exist
use '-R' to force deletion of the following clones and dependents:
tank/todays-fish
```

You need to be aware of pool space when using snapshots. While they consume no space initially, they increase the overall space usage in the pool, as each modification to the base dataset consumes additional blocks in the pool without releasing any blocks that are referenced only by the snapshot. As a result, some housekeeping cleanup of snapshots on a regular basis may be required to avoid filling a pool. When you no longer need a snapshot, use zfs destroy to delete the snapshot:

```
# zfs destroy tank/fish@trip
```

NOTE One popular use of snapshots is to set up an automatic snapshot service, which can help protect you from the common problem of mistakenly deleting a file that you really need. Sometimes you can get the file from a backup, but all too often, backups haven't been done recently enough to capture the current contents of the file, or it takes a long time to get a file restored from backup, or the backup turns out to be corrupt. ZFS can't protect you from all of these problems, but by taking frequent snapshots you can often avoid these common mistakes. OpenSolaris includes an automatic snapshot capability in the SUNWzfs-auto-snapshot package, which can snapshot datasets at several different frequencies. OpenSolaris also includes a feature known as "time slider," which provides management tools for the automatic snapshot service and integration with the GNOME file browser, Nautilus, to view and retrieve the files in ZFS snapshots; this is in the package SUNWgnome-time-slider. Consult the OpenSolaris documentation for details on this feature.

ZFS clones

While snapshots of a ZFS dataset are quite useful in their own right, they have one limitation: they're read-only. Sometimes, what you really want is a copy of a dataset that you can then modify. That's what ZFS clones provide, as they are a full read-write dataset that is based on a snapshot of another dataset.

To create a clone, you first need to take a snapshot of a dataset, and then you create the clone from the snapshot. Using the tank pool, which already has some snapshots, you can create a clone:

```
# zfs list -r tank/fish
NAME                    USED   AVAIL   REFER   MOUNTPOINT
tank/fish               50.1M  1.83G    19K    /tank/fish
tank/fish@trip           16K     -      18K    -
tank/fish@today            0     -      19K    -
# zfs clone tank/fish@today tank/todays-fish
# zfs list -r tank
NAME                    USED   AVAIL   REFER   MOUNTPOINT
tank                    50.3M  1.83G    21K    /tank
tank/fish               50.1M  1.83G    19K    /tank/fish
tank/fish@trip           16K     -      18K    -
tank/fish@today            0     -      19K    -
tank/todays-fish           0   1.83G    19K    /tank/todays-fish
```

In general, you won't notice any difference between a clone and an ordinary dataset. The only way to tell that a dataset is a clone is by the presence of an origin property:

```
# zfs get origin tank/todays-fish
NAME               PROPERTY   VALUE              SOURCE
tank/todays-fish   origin     tank/fish@today    -
```

Because a clone is dependent on the original dataset and snapshot from which it was created, you can't destroy the original snapshot and dataset:

```
# zfs destroy tank/fish@today
cannot destroy 'tank/fish@today': snapshot has dependent clones
use '-R' to destroy the following datasets:
tank/todays-fish
```

However, ZFS provides a way out of this quandary: by *promoting* the clone dataset. The effect of a promotion is that the dependency is reversed, so the original dataset is now the dependent:

```
# zfs promote tank/todays-fish
# zfs list -r tank
```

```
NAME                         USED   AVAIL  REFER  MOUNTPOINT
tank                         50.3M  1.83G    21K  /tank
tank@today                     16K      -    19K  -
tank/fish                    50.0M  1.83G    19K  /tank/fish
tank/todays-fish               35K  1.83G    19K  /tank/todays-fish
tank/todays-fish@trip          16K      -    18K  -
tank/todays-fish@today           0      -    19K  -
# zfs get origin tank/fish
NAME        PROPERTY  VALUE                   SOURCE
tank/fish   origin    tank/todays-fish@today  -
```

As you can see, the promotion also moves any snapshots of the original dataset to the promoted clone. As the original dataset no longer has any dependents, it can now be destroyed:

```
# zfs destroy tank/fish
```

It may not be immediately obvious, but a clone can be created only within the same pool as its original dataset. If you try to create the clone in a different pool, you'll receive an error:

```
# zfs clone tank/todays-fish@trip rpool/fish-trip
cannot create 'rpool/fish-trip': source and target pools differ
```

Dataset replication and backups

As noted previously, a rename or clone of a dataset cannot cross the boundary of a pool. However, ZFS offers another highly efficient means of moving data between pools, and, indeed, between systems. With traditional file system such as UFS you can use a byte-level copying utility such as dd(1M) to copy data from one disk device to another. Utilities such as dd can be very fast because there is no need for the utility to conform to all of the file system implementation semantics; it just copies bytes between raw devices. However, this is also dd's weakness. Because it is copying a device, not a file system, it doesn't understand which portions are in use and which are free, so it must copy everything. With a large storage device that may not be very full, this can obviously be quite inefficient.

ZFS provides a low-level, file-system-aware copying capability in the zfs send and zfs receive commands. These commands operate at the block level, but because zfs send understands the file system, it includes only blocks that are in use. It's also capable of performing incremental copies, including only the differences between one snapshot and another. This feature enables you to efficiently maintain backup copies of datasets.

ZFS doesn't actually send a dataset, but instead sends a snapshot of a dataset, so it's always sending a self-consistent version of the dataset. Thus, the first step in sending the dataset is to take a snapshot; you then supply that snapshot name to zfs send:

```
# zfs snapshot tank/fish@trip
# zfs send tank/fish@trip
```

However, this is not a very useful example, as it just dumps the snapshot to standard output; you can, of course, use shell redirection to send it to a file, or pipeline it through standard OpenSolaris utilities. Most often, you'll pipeline a zfs send with a zfs receive to create a copy of the dataset in some other pool. The following copies a dataset snapshot from one pool to another on the same system:

```
# zfs send tank/fish@trip | zfs receive newpool/crab@trap
```

This will create the new dataset newpool/crab@trap as a complete copy of the tank/fish@trip snapshot.

Moving data from one pool to another on the local system is useful, but often you'll want to copy to some other system. A good solution is to use ssh as the remote transport, which ensures that the data will be encrypted during transmission between the systems:

```
# zfs send tank/fish@trip | ssh faraway zfs receive backup_tank/fish
```

This copies the snapshot to backup_tank/fish@trip on the system faraway.

Both of these examples copied an entire dataset as of a given snapshot; but if you followed the recommendation earlier in this chapter and used datasets in place of directories for organizing data, you'll likely want to replicate a hierarchy of datasets at a point in time. As shown earlier, you can use zfs snapshot -r to create snapshots of a dataset and all of its descendants at once; using zfs send -R you can send all of those snapshots in one stream:

```
# zfs send -R tank@today | zfs receive -d backup
```

The -d option enables zfs receive to create any necessary file systems within the backup pool to replicate the sent file system hierarchy.

If you're replicating a dataset on a regular basis, you'll almost certainly want to use incremental sends so that you only transfer changes that have occurred since the last common snapshot, as this greatly reduces the amount of data that must be sent. To do this, you must specify the base snapshot against which the incremental changes can be computed. The choice you need to make is whether to have zfs send include any other intermediate snapshots between the two endpoints; depending on your choice, you'll use either the -i or -I option to zfs send. The following example demonstrates sending only the endpoints with -i:

```
# zfs snapshot scratch/pkg@a
# zfs send scratch/pkg@a | zfs receive backup/pkg
# zfs list -r backup/pkg
NAME             USED    AVAIL    REFER   MOUNTPOINT
backup/pkg       19K     239G     19K     /backup/pkg
backup/pkg@a     0       -        19K     -
# zfs snapshot scratch/pkg@b
# zfs snapshot scratch/pkg@c
# zfs list -r scratch/pkg
```

```
NAME                    USED   AVAIL   REFER   MOUNTPOINT
scratch/pkg              42K   5.25G     19K   /scratch/pkg
scratch/pkg@a              0       -     19K   -
scratch/pkg@b              0       -     19K   -
scratch/pkg@c              0       -     19K   -
# zfs send -i scratch/pkg@a scratch/pkg@c | zfs receive backup/pkg
# zfs list -r backup/pkg
NAME                    USED   AVAIL   REFER   MOUNTPOINT
backup/pkg               19K    239G     19K   /backup/pkg
backup/pkg@a               0       -     19K   -
backup/pkg@c               0       -     19K   -
```

As shown here, the copy to the backup pool did not replicate the @b snapshot. Compare this to the use of -I to include the intermediate snapshots (note that it's necessary to first roll the destination dataset back to the snapshot that matches the base snapshot used on the send side):

```
# zfs rollback -r backup/pkg@a>
# zfs send -I scratch/pkg@a scratch/pkg@c | zfs receive backup/pkg
# zfs list -r backup/pkg
NAME                    USED   AVAIL   REFER   MOUNTPOINT
backup/pkg               19K    239G     19K   /backup/pkg
backup/pkg@a               0       -     19K   -
backup/pkg@b               0       -     19K   -
backup/pkg@c               0       -     19K   -
```

In this case, the @b snapshot was included in the send stream and created on the receive pool.

Dataset properties

Like pools, datasets use properties to report statistics and configure the dataset's behavior; previous sections of this chapter mentioned a couple of dataset properties. While pools have a small set of properties, all of which are defined by the ZFS implementation, datasets have two types of properties: native and user. Both types of property are set using zfs set, and retrieved with zfs get.

One feature of properties that is very convenient and important to understand is that a dataset automatically inherits properties from its parent dataset, unless specifically overridden. The root dataset in a pool inherits its properties from the implementation-defined default values. The properties that are used to provide statistics on a dataset are not inherited, of course. If you have set a property locally on a dataset and wish to revert it to being inherited from the parent, use the zfs inherit command to specify the property that should be inherited:

```
# zfs inherit mountpoint tank/fish
```

When you list properties with zfs get, the default display format includes the SOURCE column, which identifies from where the property's value came. Table 8-2 lists the possible source values.

TABLE 8-2

Property Source Values

Value	Description
-	No source; used only for read-only properties
default	Implementation-defined default value
inherited	Inherited from an ancestor dataset
local	Set locally on this dataset
temporary	Set only for the duration of this mount

Native properties

Native properties are the properties defined by the ZFS implementation; these are the properties that report statistics and control behavior. As not all of the native properties apply to all types of datasets, Tables 8-3 and 8-4 provide a quick reference to the native properties applicable to file systems and volumes, respectively. The properties applicable to a snapshot depend on whether it is a snapshot of a file system or a volume; in either case, the snapshot will have only a subset of the properties of its base dataset's type. The zfs(1M) man page documents all of the native properties in detail.

To set a property, use zfs set:

```
# zfs set readonly=on tank/fish
```

You can then retrieve the property with zfs get:

```
# zfs get readonly tank/fish
NAME            PROPERTY  VALUE       SOURCE
tank/fish       readonly  on          default
```

When writing scripts, you'll often want to use the -H and -o options to get just the value of a property:

```
$ zfs get -H -o value readonly tank/fish
on
```

Most of the native properties can be set at any time; however, a few must be set at the time the dataset is created (casesensitivity, normalization, and utf8only). To set a property when a dataset is created, use the -o option to zfs create:

```
# zfs create -o utf8only=on tank/test
```

The next few sections describe some of the more important native properties.

TABLE 8-3

File System Properties

Property	Description
aclinherit	Inheritance of ACL entries
aclmode	Modification of ACLs in a chmod(2) operation
atime	Whether access times of files are updated when read
available	Space available to the file system
canmount	Whether the file system is mountable
casesensitivity	Case sensitivity of filename matching
checksum	Checksum algorithm for data integrity
compression	Compression algorithm
compressratio	Compression ratio achieved
copies	Number of data copies stored
creation	Time the file system was created
devices	Whether device nodes can be opened
exec	Whether processes can be executed
mounted	Whether the file system is mounted
mountpoint	Mount point for the file system
nbmand	Use of nonblocking mandatory locks with CIFS
normalization	Use Unicode-normalized filenames in name comparisons
origin	Snapshot on which a clone is based
primarycache	Controls whether ZFS data and metadata are cached in the primary cache
quota	Limit on space that the file system can consume
readonly	Whether the file system can be modified
recordsize	Suggested block size for files
referenced	Amount of data accessible within the file system
refquota	Space limit for this file system
refreservation	Minimum space guaranteed to the file system
reservation	Minimum space guaranteed to the file system and descendants

TABLE 8-3 *(continued)*

Property	Description
secondarycache	Controls whether ZFS data and metadata are cached in the secondary cache
setuid	Allow setuid file execution
shareiscsi	Export volumes within the file system as iSCSI targets
sharenfs	Share the file system via NFS
sharesmb	Share the file system via CIFS
snapdir	Whether the .zfs directory is visible
type	Type of dataset
used	Space consumed by the file system and descendants
usedbychildren	Space freed if children of the file system were destroyed
usedbydataset	Space freed if snapshots and refreservation were destroyed, and contents of the file system were deleted
usedbyrefreservation	Space freed if the refreservation was removed
usedbysnapshots	Space freed if all snapshots of the file system were destroyed
utf8only	Use only UTF-8 character set for filenames
version	On-disk version of the file system
vscan	Whether to scan regular files for viruses
xattr	Whether extended attributes are enabled
zoned	Whether the file system is managed from a nonglobal zone

TABLE 8-4

Volume Properties

Property	Description
available	Space available to the volume
checksum	Checksum algorithm for data integrity
compression	Compression algorithm
compressratio	Compression ratio achieved
copies	Number of data copies stored
creation	Time the volume was created

TABLE 8-4	(continued)
Property	**Description**
origin	Snapshot on which the clone is based
primarycache	Controls whether ZFS data and metadata are cached in the primary cache
readonly	Whether the volume can be modified
referenced	Amount of data accessible within the volume
refreservation	Minimum space guaranteed to the volume
reservation	Minimum space guaranteed to the volume and descendants
secondarycache	Controls whether ZFS data and metadata are cached in the secondary cache
shareiscsi	Export the volume as an iSCSI target
type	Type of dataset
used	Space consumed by the volume and descendants
usedbychildren	Space freed if children of the volume were destroyed
usedbydataset	Space freed if snapshots and refreservation were destroyed, and contents of the volume were deleted
usedbyrefreservation	Space freed if the refreservation was removed
usedbysnapshots	Space freed if all snapshots of the volume were destroyed
volblocksize	Block size of the volume
volsize	Logical size of the volume

CROSS-REF Information related to a number of the native properties is covered elsewhere in this book. See Chapter 19 for information on the zoned property and integration between zones and ZFS. See Chapter 7 for information on iSCSI. See Chapter 11 for information on access control lists (ACLs). See Chapter 10 for information on the NFS and CIFS network file systems.

Mountpoint

The mountpoint property is used to control where a dataset is mounted in the file system. As mentioned earlier, the default mount point for a file system is computed by prepending / to the dataset name, so the default mount point for the dataset tank/fish would be /tank/fish. If you want a file system to be mounted at a completely different location, you can set the mountpoint property to have it mounted at any path you like:

```
# zfs set mountpoint=/space/mars tank/fish
```

Combined with property inheritance, this makes it very easy for you to reorganize your file system layout as your needs change.

There are two special values for the `mountpoint` property:

- `legacy` — The file system will not be mounted automatically by ZFS, but can be mounted using an entry in `/etc/vfstab` or using the `mount -F zfs` command.
- `none` — The file system cannot be mounted.

Compression

One useful feature of ZFS is integrated data compression, controlled by setting the `compression` property. Compression is not enabled by default, but if your system has limited disk space, you can make it go farther by enabling compression on your datasets (it can be used for either file systems or volumes). You may also want to use compression if your system has fairly fast CPUs in comparison to its disks, as is often the case with modern laptops, especially multi-core systems. ZFS offers a choice of compression algorithms and levels:

- `lzjb` — A compression algorithm that provides a decent level of compression (typically reducing space consumption by not quite half) and does not significantly affect performance
- `gzip-N` — Uses the same compression as the `gzip(1)` command, with N replaced by a value in the range 1 to 9. Larger numbers offer better compression, but cost more in performance, especially when writing.
- `gzip` — The same as `gzip-N`, with N equal to 6
- `on` — Uses the default compression value, which is currently the same as `lzjb`
- `off` — No compression

 A change in the compression setting applies only to data that is written after the change. You often will want to set the compression value at dataset creation time to ensure that it is applied to all of the data in the dataset.

Copies

Earlier in this chapter, you saw how to set up mirror and RAID Z pools to increase the reliability of your data storage. However, if your pool only has a single disk, or is a concatenation, you can't use either of those techniques. In this situation, you can use the `copies` property to cause ZFS to make multiple copies of each block of data. You can set the `copies` value to either 2 or 3 and ZFS will spread an extra copy or two of your data in different areas of the disk, which can improve its resilience against a failure in an area. It won't help you if the disk completely fails, however.

Of course, creating multiple copies also doubles or triples the amount of space required to store your data, so do so only when you have plenty of disk space. One way to offset this overhead is to use copies and compression together — you'll pay less in space to get the additional reliability that the `copies` feature provides.

TIP Like the `compression` property, a change in the `copies` property applies only to data written after the property is changed.

Quotas and reservations

Like CPU time and memory, disk space is a system resource that often requires management to ensure that it is used fairly. ZFS provides quotas and reservations to assist you in apportioning disk space. Unlike UFS, which provides quotas that apply to a user, ZFS applies quotas and reservations to a dataset; by setting permissions on the dataset's directory so that only a specific user can write to a dataset, you can achieve an effect similar to the UFS quota system. Another difference between UFS and ZFS quotas is that ZFS does not offer the "soft" quota limits that UFS does.

CROSS-REF See Chapter 7 for information on UFS quotas. See Chapter 18 for information on resource management for CPU and memory resources.

The `quota` property sets a limit on the total space that can be consumed by a dataset and all of its children; you can also set quotas on the child datasets, but such specific quotas will not enable more space to be consumed than an inherited quota would enable.

The `reservation` property specifies the minimum amount of space guaranteed to a dataset and its children; any other datasets in the pool will not be allowed to consume space that would leave less than this amount of space for the dataset. Additionally, ZFS offers the `refreservation` property, which specifies the minimum amount of space guaranteed to a specific dataset, and does not reserve space for any children of the dataset.

User properties

User properties have no effect on how a ZFS dataset behaves; they are provided so that users can add locally meaningful information to datasets or identify datasets for some other purpose such as archiving. User properties are distinguished from native properties by including a colon character in the name; other rules about their syntax are detailed in the `zfs(1M)` man page. Because there is no central authority that allocates names of user properties, it's recommended that you prefix any user properties you create with a unique identifier such as your reversed domain name (`com.sun` is reserved for Sun's use, for example). This limits the likelihood of a naming conflict between different programs that use user properties. For example, you might create a user property to record the department that owns a dataset:

```
# zfs set :department=sales tank/prospects
# zfs get :department tank/prospects
NAME              PROPERTY      VALUE          SOURCE
tank/prospects    :department   sales          local
```

Like native properties, user properties are inherited by a dataset from its ancestor.

ZFS encryption

Encryption support for ZFS is under development and is expected to appear in OpenSolaris in the near future. The design has been reviewed and approved; and the materials, including the command changes expected, may be viewed in the architecture case directory, which is available at `http://opensolaris.org/os/community/arc/caselog/2007/261`.

To briefly summarize the expected features, encryption is performed at the dataset level; thus, both file systems and volumes can be encrypted, including the swap and dump volumes. You must specify that a dataset is to be encrypted when you create the dataset, so that all data in the dataset will have encryption applied to it. This means that you need to move data in existing datasets into new datasets to encrypt it; the most efficient means of doing this is with `zfs send` and `zfs receive`. You do not need to move data to a new pool, though, because existing pools can be upgraded with `zpool upgrade` to obtain support for the encryption feature. See the section "ZFS Versioning" later in this chapter for more information on upgrading pools.

The encryption implementation uses a randomly generated per-dataset key that is never changed to perform the actual data encryption. The encryption key is then itself encrypted, or *wrapped*, with a key that you specify. You can use a different wrapping key for each dataset, or use a common wrapping key for multiple (or all) datasets in a pool. Keys can be stored in hardware encryption devices or standard file-based storage devices, or can be supplied interactively as a passphrase. AES is the only encryption algorithm initially supported. Delegation of encryption features is also supported, so you can allow users to encrypt their own datasets if desired.

Encryption of data is a complex topic. We recommend consulting the ZFS documentation, including the `zfs(1M)` and `zpool(1M)` man pages, for detailed information before attempting to use the ZFS encryption feature.

ZFS Delegated Administration

If your system has multiple users, you may want to make use of ZFS's delegated administration features to allow them to manage their own ZFS datasets. You have a choice of two techniques for delegating administration; the appropriate one to use depends on the scope of the power you wish to delegate.

If you want to share administration of the ZFS pools, or all of the ZFS datasets on the system, you can assign RBAC (role-based access control) profiles that allow that capability to a user. If you want to share administrative access to pools, this is your only choice. The ZFS storage management profile allows administration of all pools on the system, while the ZFS File System Management profile allows administration of all datasets on the system. To assign the storage management profile to user `jack`, use the `usermod` command:

```
# usermod -P "ZFS Storage Management" jack
```

CROSS-REF   See Chapter 11 for more information on RBAC.

Often, though, you may wish to delegate administration of the datasets more finely, so that a user has administrative-level access to only certain datasets. To support this administrative model, ZFS provides the `zfs allow` and `zfs unallow` commands, which assign administrative access at the dataset level to a user or group. The permissions can be specified quite precisely, so that users can modify only certain properties, or perform only specific administrative operations on a dataset. Also, like properties, the delegated administration permissions can be inherited by a dataset's descendants. As a simple example, you can assign user `jack` the capability to create and destroy child datasets of the dataset `tank/jack`, as well as the capability to take snapshots of the dataset, as follows:

```
# zfs allow jack create,destroy,mount,snapshot tank/jack
```

The following displays the delegated permissions on the dataset:

```
# zfs allow tank/jack
-------------------------------------------------------------
Local+Descendent permissions on (tank/jack)
     user jack create,destroy,mount,snapshot
-------------------------------------------------------------
```

If no permissions are delegated for a dataset, then the attempt to display them produces no output.

You can revoke a permission with `zfs unallow`:

```
# zfs unallow jack snapshot tank/jack
```

This change would prevent user `jack` from taking any snapshots.

This is just a taste of what's possible with the delegated administration capability. Consult the `zfs(1M)` man page for more details on the delegations that are possible.

ZFS Versioning

Many types of software use the concept of *versioning* to enable the software to evolve over time yet still retain compatibility with older data. Solaris has leaned heavily on versioning as a mechanism to enable it to provide the compatibility guarantees for which it is well known, while allowing innovation in the operating system to proceed.

ZFS has two levels of versioning, at both the pool and dataset levels. If a pool is formatted using an older version, `zpool status` notes that in the pool's status entry:

```
$ zpool status
  pool: backup
 state: ONLINE
status: The pool is formatted using an older on-disk format.  The pool can
        still be used, but some features are unavailable.
action: Upgrade the pool using 'zpool upgrade'.  Once this is done, the
        pool will no longer be accessible on older software versions.
 scrub: none requested
config:

        NAME        STATE     READ WRITE CKSUM
```

```
              backup      ONLINE     0     0     0
              c8t0d0      ONLINE     0     0     0

errors: No known data errors
```

You can examine the versions of your pools and datasets with the zpool and zfs upgrade commands:

```
$ zpool upgrade
This system is currently running ZFS pool version 10.

All pools are formatted using this version.
$ zfs upgrade
This system is currently running ZFS filesystem version 3.

The following filesystems are out of date, and can be upgraded.  After being
upgraded, these filesystems (and any 'zfs send' streams generated from
subsequent snapshots) will no longer be accessible by older software versions.


VER   FILESYSTEM
---   ------------
 2    rpool/space
 2    rpool/space/dc
 2    rpool/space/dc/zones
 2    rpool/space/dc/zones/dctest
 2    rpool/space/dc/zones/dctest/root
 1    rpool/space/dminer
 2    rpool/space/hg
 1    rpool/space/hg-clones
 1    rpool/space/iso
 2    rpool/space/iso/preview1
 2    rpool/space/iso/preview2

 1    rpool/space/live
 2    rpool/space/pkg
 1    rpool/space/sw
 2    rpool/space/zones
 2    rpool/space/zones/test
```

> **TIP** Use the -v option to zpool upgrade or zfs upgrade to print details about the differences between the versions of pools and datasets.

Use the following to upgrade a specific pool to the most current version supported by your system:

```
# zpool upgrade backup
This system is currently running ZFS pool version 10.
```

```
Successfully upgraded 'backup' from version 8 to version 10
```

Similarly, the following upgrades a dataset:

```
# zfs upgrade rpool/space/iso
1 filesystems upgraded
```

You can use the `-a` option rather than a specific pool or dataset name to upgrade all of your pools or datasets. You can also use the `-V` option to choose a specific version to which the pool or dataset should be upgraded.

NOTE Pool and dataset versions are independent of each other; you can use the most current dataset version in a pool that has an older version, and vice versa.

Generally, it's a good idea to upgrade your pools and datasets to the most current version — otherwise, you may find some features to be unavailable; for example, hot spare devices weren't introduced until pool version 3, but if you need to move a pool or dataset to a system that supports only an older version of ZFS, make sure you don't upgrade that pool or dataset to a later version. Also, be aware that you cannot downgrade a pool or dataset from a newer to an older version, so it's important to exercise some caution in upgrading.

TIP When you create a pool or dataset, it is, by default, created as the most current version supported by your system. You may specify that an older version be used by setting the version property at creation:

```
# zpool create -o version=4 oldtank c7t0d0p0
```

Resources

The ZFS community at `opensolaris.org` provides a wealth of detailed information on ZFS: `http://opensolaris.org/os/community/zfs`.

The BigAdmin page on ZFS has a number of articles on various ZFS topics: `www.sun.com/bigadmin/topics/zfs`.

Jeff Bonwick, the principal inventor of ZFS, provides background on some of the ideas behind ZFS in his blog: `http://blogs.sun.com/bonwick`.

The Solaris Internals website has an extensive guide to ZFS best practices: `http://solarisinternals.com/wiki/index.php/ZFS_Best_Practices_Guide`.

The source code for ZFS is available via the ONNV repository at `opensolaris.org`, in the following subdirectories:

- Core file system: `usr/src/uts/common/fs/zfs/`
- Commands: `usr/src/cmd/zfs` and `usr/src/cmd/zpool`
- GRUB implementation of ZFS for booting: `usr/src/grub/grub-0.95/stage2/fsys_zfs.c`

Summary

This chapter introduced the features of ZFS, including pools, file systems, volumes, and snapshots. Uses of some of the important properties were described. Techniques for efficiently transferring and backing up datasets, monitoring performance, and delegating administration were demonstrated.

Chapter 9

Networking

In the last twenty years, the Internet has become the predominant application for computer systems, whether providing services such as a website, or consuming them, such as a client system running a web browser. Indeed, Sun's venerable slogan, "The Network Is the Computer," well expresses how vital networking capability has become in computing. As a result, all modern operating systems include a TCP/IP protocol stack and standard networking services that enable users to construct their own branch local area networks, aggregate them into organization-wide wide area networks, and connect to the global Internet. This chapter tackles the major networking features included in OpenSolaris.

IN THIS CHAPTER

Network interfaces

Network Auto-Magic (NWAM)

IP multipathing

Link aggregation

DNS, DHCP, and NTP

inetd

Routing

Firewalls

Network troubleshooting

> **NOTE** This chapter assumes that you have a basic knowledge of Internet networking, such as the format of an IP address. If you're not an experienced Internet user already, you might find it helpful to consult an introductory text or article, such as http://en.wikipedia.org/wiki/IP_Address, that explains the basic concepts.

Network Interfaces

To communicate over a network, the first thing you need is a connection to it. As on other UNIX-like systems, OpenSolaris models a connection to the network as a *network interface*.

> **NOTE** Historically, a network interface was provided as a separate printed-circuit board to be installed into a computer. As a result, network interfaces are commonly referred to as NICs,

for "network interface card," even though today most network interfaces are built into the system at the factory. Another term that's occasionally used for a network interface is *network adapter*.

On OpenSolaris, network interfaces exist at two layers: the *link* (also called *data-link*) layer, and the IP layer. These layers correspond to layers 2 and 3 of the OSI model. When sending data, the IP layer is responsible for formatting data from a transport such as TCP into datagrams for transmission on the Internet, and for selecting source and destination IP addresses that can be used to send the datagram. The source IP address selected corresponds to one of the network interfaces. The datagram is passed to the link layer, which translates the IP addresses into MAC (Media Access Control, also commonly called Ethernet) addresses, and transmits the message on the physical network medium. The process of receiving data operates in reverse, with the link layer collecting messages and passing them up to the IP layer, which in turn passes them to the transport.

Networking Concepts and Standards

In order for heterogeneous computer systems to communicate over a network, they must have a common understanding of how to interpret each other's signals, which are called *protocols*. This requires the creation of documents known as *standards*, which provide protocol specifications to developers of networking hardware and software. The standards and protocols use a theoretical model of networking known as the *OSI seven-layer model*. A brief summary of this model can be found at http://en.wikipedia.org/wiki/OSI_model, as well as any standard networking text.

Standards for link and MAC layers are primarily developed by cooperative industry efforts sponsored by the IEEE, a professional association that has its roots in electrical and electronics engineering. The predominant networking standards produced by it are known as IEEE 802, which includes specifications for the Ethernet and Wi-Fi technologies.

The Internet itself is governed by a cooperative international effort under an organization known as ICANN, the Internet Corporation for Assigned Names and Numbers. The standards that ICANN uses to enable Internet interoperability are developed by another organization, the Internet Engineering Task Force (IETF), which publishes its technical specifications as a series of documents known as Requests for Comment (RFCs). The networking features in OpenSolaris are primarily designed to implement the standards developed by the IEEE and the IETF.

The simplest form of a network interface is a physical Ethernet port built into your system. Another common network interface is a Wi-Fi wireless network radio transmitter/receiver, also often built into modern systems, especially laptops. However, not all interfaces are tied directly to a hardware component because OpenSolaris includes network virtualization technology, including loopback interfaces, logical interfaces, tunnels, and virtual NICs. Network interfaces can also be constructed as composites of multiple physical devices using link aggregation and multipathing. The following sections introduce you to the gamut of network interfaces supported on OpenSolaris.

Displaying IP interfaces

If you're using the OpenSolaris distribution, you likely already have several network interfaces configured on your system. That's because OpenSolaris configures the system to use a technology known as Network Auto-Magic (commonly called NWAM, pronounced "en-wham"), which is designed to automatically detect and configure any network interfaces available on your system using DHCP, the Dynamic Host Configuration Protocol. The OpenSolaris Live CD also uses this technology to provide automatic network access when the CD is booted. You will learn more about NWAM and DHCP later in this chapter.

Like other UNIX-based systems, IP network interfaces on OpenSolaris are configured and displayed using the ifconfig(1M) command. You can list the IP interfaces on your system using ifconfig -a:

```
$ ifconfig -a
lo0: flags=2001000849<UP,LOOPBACK,RUNNING,MULTICAST,IPv4,VIRTUAL> mtu 8232
 index 1
    inet 127.0.0.1 netmask ff000000
e1000g0: flags=201000802<BROADCAST,MULTICAST,IPv4,CoS> mtu 1500 index 8
    inet 0.0.0.0 netmask 0
wpi0: flags=201004843<UP,BROADCAST,RUNNING,MULTICAST,DHCP,IPv4,CoS> mtu 1500
 index 9
    inet 192.168.1.30 netmask ffffff00 broadcast 192.168.1.255
lo0: flags=2002000849<UP,LOOPBACK,RUNNING,MULTICAST,IPv6,VIRTUAL> mtu 8252
 index 1
    inet6 ::1/128
```

The output of ifconfig is a bit dense but it contains a lot of information, so it's worthwhile to spend a little time learning to understand it. Each IP interface's data begins in column 0 with its name, and additional lines of output related to that interface are indented, so the preceding listing shows four IP interfaces, named lo0, e1000g0, wpi0, and lo0.

OpenSolaris defaults to naming the interfaces based on the name of the *driver*, the piece of software that controls the hardware. The e1000g driver is used for Intel's Gigabit Ethernet hardware, for example, while the wpi driver is used for Intel's 3945 Wi-Fi hardware. OpenSolaris then appends an instance number, starting at zero, to the driver name to distinguish each piece of hardware; for example, if you have two e1000g interfaces, they would be named e1000g0 and e1000g1. This is somewhat different from Linux, for example, which usually bases interface names on generic names such as eth for all Ethernet interfaces, irrespective of the drivers used to control them.

NOTE **You can rename network interfaces to fit your own needs. See the BigAdmin article** at http://sun.com/bigadmin/sundocs/articles/vnamingsol.jsp **for information on using this feature.**

If you're wondering why there are two interfaces named lo0, rather than lo0 and lo1, a clue to the answer is found in the first token on the second line of output for each interface. This token is the protocol family for the interface; inet represents ordinary IP (also called IPv4, or IP version 4) interfaces, while inet6 represents IPv6 (IP version 6) interfaces. The flags field contains IPv4 for the first instance, and IPv6 for the second instance. OpenSolaris provides separate IP interface instances for each of the IP protocol families, which is why you see two interfaces named lo0. This is different from Linux, which models the two protocol families as multiple addresses on the same interface.

> **NOTE** IPv4 is the standard address format used on the Internet at present, although IPv6 addressing is expected to eventually replace it as the standard because IP version 4 addresses are becoming a scarce commodity. However, IPv6 is not currently widely deployed, so this book does not cover using IPv6 with OpenSolaris. For more information on IPv6 and OpenSolaris, consult the *Solaris IP Services Administration Guide* at http://docs.sun.com/app/docs/doc/819-3000.

Another question that probably arises from the ifconfig -a output is why, if your system has only two network interfaces, does ifconfig list more than that? As you might discern from the string LOOPBACK in the flags section of the output, the lo0 interface is a *loopback interface* used by the system to connect to itself without the need for any physical networking hardware. This makes it a *virtual interface*, which is also expressed in the flags field by the string VIRTUAL.

> **NOTE** The addresses used for loopback interfaces (127.0.0.1 for IPv4, ::1 for IPv6) are reserved for loopback by the IP protocol standards approved by the IETF. It is an error to attempt to assign them to a physical interface.

You can examine the IP configuration for a particular interface by specifying the interface name as the single argument to ifconfig:

```
$ ifconfig wpi0
wpi0: flags=201004843<UP,BROADCAST,RUNNING,MULTICAST,DHCP,IPv4,CoS> mtu 1500
   index 9
     inet 192.168.1.30 netmask ffffff00 broadcast 192.168.1.255
```

Several other portions of the output bear closer examination. The flags field displays a numeric value, followed by a series of symbolic values that interpret the numeric value. The flags UP and RUNNING are normally displayed for interfaces that have an address assigned and are capable of sending and receiving packets. The DHCP flag indicates that DHCP was used to obtain the address assigned to this interface. The second line of output shows the details of the interface's address configuration: its address (preceded with the inet keyword because this is an IPv4 interface), its netmask, and the broadcast address for the network. The interface's address is the single most important piece of information in the entire ifconfig output because it is used by other systems to communicate with this system.

Contrast the preceding output with that for e1000g0:

```
$ ifconfig e1000g0
```

```
e1000g0: flags=201000802<BROADCAST,MULTICAST,IPv4,CoS> mtu 1500 index 8
        inet 0.0.0.0 netmask 0
```

This interface is not up or running, and does not have an address assigned, as evidenced by the value 0.0.0.0 for the address. As a result, it is not usable for communication at this time.

> **NOTE** The MULTICAST and CoS flags, as well as other flag values not shown in these examples, are described in the ifconfig(1M) man page.

Configuring interfaces automatically with NWAM

NWAM is designed to automatically configure physical network interfaces on the system without any configuration actions by the user. It does so by bringing up each network interface and attempting to configure it using DHCP. The version of NWAM currently included in Open-Solaris is designed to configure only a single network interface at a time. By default, NWAM prefers wired interfaces to wireless, so it attempts to configure a wired interface first; if that fails, then NWAM attempts to configure any wireless interfaces. Switching between wired and wireless networks is as simple as unplugging or plugging in the Ethernet cable; NWAM automatically detects the cable being connected or disconnected and takes the appropriate action. This extends to wireless networks as well; if you're connected to a wireless network and the connection is lost, perhaps because you moved out of range of the base station, NWAM rescans for wireless networks and attempts to connect to another network.

NWAM isn't the right answer for every situation at this time. Because it brings only one interface online at a time, you wouldn't use it on systems where you want to run multiple interfaces simultaneously, such as running your system as a router, using availability and performance features such as IP multipathing (IPMP) and link aggregation, or clustering with private interconnects. Many server configurations require one or more of these features, which are explored later in this chapter.

> **NOTE** Some wired Ethernet drivers do not provide the notifications needed by NWAM to automatically switch between wired and wireless networking. The NWAM project has collected information about driver support for link status notifications at http://opensolaris.org/os/project/nwam/prototype/dl_note_link/. All OpenSolaris wireless drivers support the mechanisms that NWAM uses to detect signal loss.

Enabling NWAM

As mentioned earlier, the OpenSolaris distribution, by default, uses Network Auto-Magic (NWAM) to configure its network interfaces. You can use SMF's svcs command to verify that you're using NWAM:

```
$ svcs nwam
STATE        STIME    FMRI
online       10:33:36 svc:/network/physical:nwam
```

If the state is online, you're using NWAM; if the state is disabled, you're not. However, if your system is a desktop or laptop system that is not being used as a server, then consider using

NWAM because you will spend less time setting up and maintaining your system's network configuration.

CROSS-REF   See Chapter 13 for details on SMF.

If your system is not using NWAM and you want to switch to NWAM, use the following two commands:

```
# svcadm disable network/physical:default
# svcadm enable network/physical:nwam
```

You can also switch to NWAM by selecting System ➤ Administration ➤ Network from the GNOME desktop.

CAUTION   Switching from manual configuration to NWAM causes any running network interfaces to shut down and restart, which likely terminates any active network connections. Be especially careful not to do this if you're connected to the system over the network!

Interacting with NWAM

After NWAM configures an interface, it displays a notification pop-up in the desktop notification area if you're logged in to the console and have the NWAM Manager applet configured as part of your GNOME desktop (it's included in the default session). NWAM also displays a notification when an interface is deconfigured due to loss of connection. If you're not running a graphical desktop on the system console, NWAM proceeds silently. Often, when the system is rebooted, NWAM has a network connection up and running before you log in and can see its notifications.

Wireless networks require special handling by NWAM. Because it's impolite — and illegal in some jurisdictions — to connect to a network that you don't have permission to use, NWAM presents a list of wireless networks that its scans detect, from which you can choose an appropriate network. This happens only if none of the scanned networks is recognized as *known*, which means that they have been previously connected to by your system. The known networks are recorded in /etc/nwam/known_wifi_nets, which contains entries such as the following:

```
rover    0:40:5:ca:b4:56
```

The first column in each entry is the SSID (or name) of the Wi-Fi network, and the second is the MAC address of the access point you've connected to; both must match for a network to be considered known. If no known networks are found, the NWAM notification pop-up instructs you to right-click on the NWAM Manager icon. Once you do, the NWAM Manager presents the menu shown in Figure 9-1. (If user interaction is required to select a network but no user is logged in to a graphical desktop on the system console, NWAM does not connect and tries again in a few minutes.)

In the menu's top section you select the interface you want to use, overriding NWAM's automatic behavior. You can also configure the relative priority of the interfaces, perhaps to make wireless interfaces preferred over wired. The third section of the menu lists the wireless networks found by scanning: Click on one to select it. The bottom portion enables you to join a network that wasn't found by scanning, or to manage the known wireless networks list. It's sometimes necessary to use Join Unlisted Wireless Network because wireless networks can be configured to not broadcast their availability, which prevents NWAM from automatically discovering them.

FIGURE 9-1

NWAM Manager's pop-up menu enables you to control NWAM's operation.

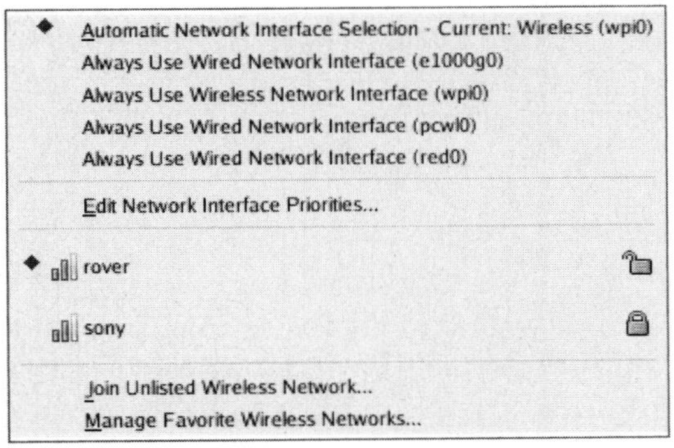

TIP Configuring a Wi-Fi network to not broadcast its SSID is sometimes recommended as a security measure, but it tends to add more inconvenience for legitimate users than security against illegitimate ones because the SSID can be easily obtained by watching legitimate traffic. If you need a secure wireless network, use WPA (Wi-Fi Protected Access) to control access to your network, and, potentially, IP security as well. WEP (Wired Equivalent Privacy) is not recommended because flaws in its design allow its encryption to be easily broken. See your wireless access point or wireless router's documentation for instructions on configuring WPA. IP security (IPsec) is discussed in Chapter 11.

If you select a network that uses encryption (both WEP and WPA are supported), an additional dialog prompts you to enter the encryption key needed to access the network. After entering the key once, it's stored on the system in a secure location for future use, so you don't need to reenter it every time you connect to the network.

Once NWAM connects to a network, it attempts to use the configuration parameters provided by the DHCP server to update the system configuration. Currently, the default behavior of NWAM is limited to updating the DNS and name service switch configuration if the DHCP server has supplied DNS configuration information. If DNS servers are supplied, NWAM uses the script /lib/svc/method/net-svc (the start method for the svc:/network/service:default SMF service) to update /etc/resolv.conf and /etc/nsswitch.conf to use this DNS configuration.

For instance, if the DHCP server supplies a DNS domain of example.com and a DNS server address of 192.168.1.7, /etc/resolv.conf is updated as follows:

```
domain example.com
nameserver 192.168.1.7
```

The hosts and ipnodes entries in /etc/nsswitch.conf will read as follows:

```
hosts: files dns
ipnodes: files dns
```

NWAM allows for some customization of its behavior, including specifying the preference order for interfaces and providing more complex actions when interfaces are configured and deconfigured. You can even use NWAM to configure static addresses on your network interfaces, but that is rarely done with the current implementation and is therefore not recommended. Because NWAM's features are under active development, consult the nwamd(1M) man page and the project page at www.opensolaris.org/os/project/nwam/ for current information on customizing NWAM.

Troubleshooting NWAM

If you think you're using NWAM but your system doesn't seem to be able to reach any other systems on the network, there are several steps you can take to diagnose and correct the problem.

First, verify that NWAM is in the online state, using the svcs command shown earlier. If its state is shown as disabled, follow the procedure in the section "Enabling NWAM" to ensure it's enabled. If it's in the offline or maintenance state, then something more serious is wrong with your system; use the svcs -x command and the SMF troubleshooting procedures in Chapter 13 to determine what services are causing the problem.

If NWAM is online, your next step is to examine the network interfaces with ifconfig -a, as described earlier. If you have no interfaces other than the loopback interface, then either you don't have any network interfaces on your system (which is unlikely) or you don't have the necessary interface drivers. See Chapter 5 for information on checking your hardware for driver support and obtaining drivers.

If the ifconfig output shows no interfaces with an IP address, and no interfaces have the DHCP flag indicating that NWAM is attempting to configure them with DHCP, wait a few minutes for NWAM to make another attempt to configure the interfaces. If you have already done this, then restart NWAM:

```
# svcadm restart nwam
```

Again, give NWAM a few minutes after restarting to try to bring up your network interfaces. If the `ifconfig -a` output shows that DHCP is being attempted on one of the interfaces, use the `netstat -D` command to examine what's happening with DHCP:

```
$ netstat -D
Interface  State         Sent  Recv  Declined  Flags
e1000g0    SELECTING      5     0        0
```

Output similar to this — in which the interface is in the `SELECTING` state and has a `Recv` value of 0 (no packets have been received) — most likely means that you have a connection problem. If the interface is a wired network, the problem is likely a disconnected cable or a more serious network infrastructure failure (e.g., a switch, router, or server that is down). If it's a wireless network, you may have an incorrect encryption key, or again, there could be a network infrastructure failure. You can use tools such as `ping` or `snoop` to investigate further. See the "Troubleshooting" section later in this chapter.

Configuring interfaces manually

If you've decided that NWAM isn't for you, OpenSolaris offers a manual method to configure network interfaces, which has been in use since Solaris 2.0. Using manual configuration, you still have the option to configure your system with static addresses or use DHCP, and you can use all of OpenSolaris' other networking features. Chapter 3 described how to use the GNOME Network Manager application to manually configure network interfaces; in this section you'll learn how to manipulate the underlying configuration files directly.

NOTE Some information sources recommend that you use the `sys-unconfig(1M)` program to reconfigure network interfaces. Be aware that `sys-unconfig` deconfigures several aspects of your system, such as the root password and ssh server key, and halts your system. You then need to boot the system and answer a series of questions to reconfigure it. We don't recommend this approach to system reconfiguration because it is likely to disrupt your system in ways that will be at least as time-consuming to fix as the manual procedures outlined here, which try to avoid modifying the system unnecessarily.

If you're currently using NWAM and want to switch to manual configuration, you must disable NWAM and enable the manual configuration service, `network/physical:default`, as follows:

```
# svcadm disable network/physical:nwam
# svcadm enable network/physical:default
```

CAUTION Switching from NWAM to manual configuration causes any running network interfaces to shut down. This likely terminates any active network connections, so avoid switching if you're connected to the system over the network.

Next, decide whether you're going to use DHCP or a static address to configure each interface, and then follow one of the subsequent procedures accordingly. First, however, you need to know the name of the interface you want to configure. You can obtain the full list of available links using the dladm show-link command (you'll learn more about the dladm command in a subsequent section):

```
# dladm show-link
LINK            CLASS    MTU     STATE    OVER
e1000g0         phys     1500    up       --
e1000g1         phys     1500    up       --
```

Note that this example uses a different system than the examples in the previous section on NWAM. The important output here is the LINK column, because these are the device names that you can use to configure IP interfaces. This system has two e1000g links: e1000g0 and e1000g1. The procedures in the next section will configure these interfaces for use with IP, but before you can configure an IP interface in any way you must use the plumb subcommand of ifconfig to create an IP interface attached to a link:

```
# ifconfig e1000g0 plumb
```

You can verify that the interface is properly plumbed with ifconfig:

```
$ ifconfig e1000g0
e1000g0: flags=201000842<BROADCAST,RUNNING,MULTICAST,IPv4,CoS> mtu 1500 index 2
    inet 0.0.0.0 netmask 0
```

Configuring a DHCP interface

Once you've plumbed an IP interface, you can configure it with DHCP using the dhcp subcommand of ifconfig. For example, the following configures e1000g0 using DHCP:

```
# ifconfig e1000g0 dhcp start
```

This command normally pauses for a few seconds while the DHCP transaction completes, and then exits with no output. You can verify it completed successfully by checking the interface's configuration with ifconfig:

```
$ ifconfig e1000g0
e1000g0: flags=201004843<UP,BROADCAST,RUNNING,MULTICAST,DHCP,IPv4,CoS> mtu
1500 index 2
    inet 10.0.2.15 netmask ffffff00 broadcast 10.0.2.255
```

If there's a problem completing the DHCP transaction, you may see output similar to the following:

```
# ifconfig e1000g0 dhcp start
ifconfig: e1000g0: wait timed out, operation still pending ...
```

If this occurs you need to investigate the problem using netstat, snoop, and possibly other tools. See the "Troubleshooting" section of this chapter for suggestions.

At this point, you have a running DHCP interface but only until you next reboot the system. If you want this interface to be persistently configured, you must create two empty files, /etc/hostname.*interface* and /etc/dhcp.*interface*, replacing *interface* with the name of the link. The network/physical:default service uses the presence of these files as a signal to configure the interface on the next reboot. The following command configures the e1000g0 interface persistently:

```
# touch /etc/hostname.e1000g0 /etc/dhcp.e1000g0
```

The empty /etc/hostname.e1000g0 file causes the interface to be plumbed, and the empty /etc/dhcp.e1000g0 file causes DHCP to be started on the interface.

Stop DHCP on an interface using ifconfig, using one of the following two commands:

```
# ifconfig e1000g0 dhcp release
# ifconfig e1000g0 dhcp drop
```

The difference between the two commands is that a release sends a packet to the DHCP server informing it that your system is no longer using the address, whereas drop just stops DHCP on the interface without informing the DHCP server. Generally, it's better to use release so that the DHCP server can reuse the address for other clients immediately; otherwise, it must wait until the lease on the address expires. See the section "Dynamic Host Configuration Protocol" later in this chapter for more information on address leases.

To permanently deconfigure an interface after you've stopped it using one of these commands, just remove both the hostname.*interface* and dhcp.*interface* files:

```
# rm /etc/hostname.e1000g0 /etc/dhcp.e1000g0
```

> **NOTE** OpenSolaris also supports configuring network interfaces using the Reverse Address Resolution Protocol (RARP), an older protocol still used in some environments. As RARP has very limited capabilities and is primarily of historical interest, it is not covered here. Consult the ifconfig(1M) man page for information on using RARP.

Configuring a static IP interface

If your network doesn't use DHCP, or you're configuring a system that will be an important part of your infrastructure, such as a server or a router, then you can configure the IP interfaces with static addresses. To configure an IP interface temporarily with a static address, use ifconfig:

```
# ifconfig e1000g0 inet 192.168.1.20/24
```

This assigns the IPv4 address 192.168.1.20 to the interface, with the first 24 bits specified as the network portion of the address (an IPv6 address can be assigned instead by replacing the inet protocol family token with inet6 and supplying a properly formatted IPv6 address). You can display the result with ifconfig:

```
$ ifconfig e1000g0
e1000g0: flags=201000842<BROADCAST,RUNNING,MULTICAST,IPv4,CoS> mtu 1500 index 3
    inet 192.168.1.20 netmask ffffff00 broadcast 192.168.1.255
```

The 24-bit prefix specification results in a netmask of ffffff00 and a broadcast address of 192.168.1.255. This interface is not yet online, though, because it is missing the UP flag; this can be included at the same time the address is assigned by adding the up token to the end of the ifconfig command, but it was intentionally omitted to enable you to check the interface configuration first, which is recommended. Once you're satisfied that the interface is configured properly, you can bring it up using ifconfig:

```
# ifconfig e1000g0 inet up
```

As with the examples configuring a DHCP interface, the ifconfig command configures an interface only temporarily, so it is lost when the system is rebooted unless you configure it persistently. The persistent configuration for a statically addressed interface is stored in /etc/hostname.*interface*; unlike the DHCP case, this file is not empty but contains fragments of the ifconfig command required to configure the interface. To make the simple configuration of e1000g0 demonstrated earlier persistent, use the echo command or your favorite editor to place the following in /etc/hostname.e1000g0:

```
192.168.1.20/24
```

This is all that's necessary to configure the interface because the network/physical:default start method script, /lib/svc/method/net-physical, will prepend ifconfig *interface* inet to the contents of the /etc/hostname.*interface* file to construct the ifconfig command that's executed to configure the interface during system boot. Note that the /etc/hostname.*interface* file can have multiple lines; each line will cause network/physical:default to execute a separate ifconfig command against the interface, in the order they are listed in the file. One subtlety when using a multi-line host-name.*interface* file is that you must add the up command to one of the commands to bring the interface up; see the section "Logical interfaces" later in this chapter for examples of a multi-line file.

In most cases, you need to perform two additional tasks to complete your static network configuration:

- Configure routing so that you can connect to systems beyond your local network. See the section "Routing" later in this chapter.
- Configure the DNS resolver so that your system can translate hostnames to IP addresses. See the section "Configuring the DNS resolver" later in this chapter.

When configuring a local static address, it is also helpful to configure a mapping between the IP address and a name in the local /etc/inet/hosts file. This isn't strictly required, but names are friendlier to use, easier to type, and can help in recognizing systems when troubleshooting problems.

CROSS-REF See Chapter 10 for information on name service configuration.

To deactivate a statically addressed interface, use `ifconfig` to mark the interface as down:

```
# ifconfig e1000g0 inet down
```

The IP address remains set on the interface when you mark it down. You can remove the `/etc/hostname.`*interface* file to prevent the interface from being configured on the next boot.

Configuring a Wi-Fi interface

If the interface you're configuring manually is a Wi-Fi (also known by its standards name, IEEE 802.11) interface, then there is more to be done before you can configure it with IP. For a standard wired Ethernet interface, usually all that's necessary to configure its data link is to plug in a cable between your system and the network switch; but in the case of Wi-Fi, you need to provide the driver with the information necessary to establish the connection over the airwaves, because often there is more than one Wi-Fi network that is reachable from a particular location. The `dladm(1M)` command is the OpenSolaris interface for configuring data links, and it includes the functions needed to configure a Wi-Fi link.

First, use `dladm scan-wifi` to display the available Wi-Fi networks at your location:

```
# dladm scan-wifi
LINK      ESSID          BSSID/IBSSID      SEC    STRENGTH    MODE   SPEED
wpi0      sony           0:1:4a:10:ac:4c   wep    weak        g      54Mb
wpi0      rover          0:21:29:63:a8:85  none   excellent   g      54Mb
```

For each access point that is seen, `dladm` displays the data link name, the ESSID (also called the network name), the BSSID (which is the network address of the access point), the security mode (`none`, `wep`, or `wpa`), an indication of the signal strength, the IEEE 802.11 mode (which can be a, b, g, or n) and the speed at which the network is operating. If you have a choice, select a network with the appropriate security mode, the best strength, and the best speed.

Next, use `dladm connect-wifi` to establish the connection, specifying the ESSID of the desired network:

```
# dladm connect-wifi -e rover wpi0
```

No output is returned if the connection is established successfully. You can verify the status using `dladm show-wifi`:

```
# dladm show-wifi
LINK      STATUS        ESSID      SEC    STRENGTH    MODE   SPEED
wpi0      connected     rover      none   weak        g      36Mb
```

To switch networks once connected, you first need to disconnect, using `dladm disconnect-wifi`:

```
# dladm disconnect-wifi wpi0
# dladm show-wifi
LINK        STATUS           ESSID              SEC   STRENGTH  MODE  SPEED
wpi0        disconnected     --                 --    --        --    --
```

If the network to which you want to connect is using WEP or WPA for security, you must create the security key required to access that network; consult your network administrator if you don't already know the key. Security keys are managed by additional `dladm` subcommands: `create-secobj`, `show-secobj`, and `delete-secobj`. To create a key, specify its class (which must be either `wep` or `wpa`) and provide a name — `dladm` prompts for the actual key value, which is obscured during entry and must be entered twice, with matching values:

```
# dladm create-secobj -c wep sony-key
provide value for 'sony-key': *****
confirm value for 'sony-key': *****
```

Use `show-secobj` to list the security objects known to `dladm`:

```
# dladm show-secobj
OBJECT            CLASS
sony-key          wep
```

Note that there is no way for `dladm` to display the actual value of the key; and if you need to change a key, you must delete it and recreate it. After a key is created, you can use it to connect to a secure network by specifying the key name with the `-k` option to `connect-wifi`:

```
# dladm connect-wifi -k sony-key -e sony wpi0
# dladm show-wifi
LINK        STATUS           ESSID              SEC   STRENGTH  MODE  SPEED
wpi0        connected        sony               wep   weak      g     36Mb
```

Once you have the Wi-Fi link successfully connected, you can proceed to configure it using DHCP or a static IP address by following the procedures described earlier.

Logical interfaces

As with systems such as Linux, you can associate multiple IP addresses with a single physical interface in OpenSolaris. Doing so requires creating a *logical interface*, which is just an additional address tied to a physical interface. Historically, one significant use of logical interfaces has been to add more addresses to a physical network when the initially configured IP address space has been exhausted. In that situation, you can use logical interfaces to configure an additional IP network on the same physical network. In OpenSolaris, the most common current uses are for

IP multipathing, covered in the next section, and to provide distinct IP addresses for nonglobal zones without dedicating physical interfaces to the zones.

CROSS-REF Zones are discussed in Chapter 19.

You can add a logical interface to a physical interface using ifconfig's addif subcommand. For example, use the following to add the address 10.1.3.17/22 to the e1000g0 physical interface:

```
# ifconfig e1000g1 addif 10.1.3.17/22
Created new logical interface e1000g1:1
# ifconfig -a
lo0: flags=2001000849<UP,LOOPBACK,RUNNING,MULTICAST,IPv4,VIRTUAL> mtu 8232
 index 1
    inet 127.0.0.1 netmask ff000000
e1000g0: flags=201004843<UP,BROADCAST,RUNNING,MULTICAST,DHCP,IPv4,CoS> mtu 1500
 index 2
    inet 10.0.2.15 netmask ffffff00 broadcast 10.0.2.255
e1000g1: flags=201000843<UP,BROADCAST,RUNNING,MULTICAST,IPv4,CoS> mtu 1500
 index 3
    inet 192.168.1.20 netmask ffffc00 broadcast 192.168.3.255
e1000g1:1: flags=201000842<BROADCAST,RUNNING,MULTICAST,IPv4,CoS> mtu 1500
 index 3
    inet 10.1.3.17 netmask ffffc00 broadcast 10.1.3.255
lo0: flags=2002000849<UP,LOOPBACK,RUNNING,MULTICAST,IPv6,VIRTUAL> mtu 8252
 index 1
    inet6 ::1/128
```

As shown here, the logical interface's name is constructed using the physical interface's name as the base, appending a colon and an instance number. Note that the logical interface is not brought up automatically — you need to mark it as up for it to be usable:

```
# ifconfig e1000g1:1 up
# ifconfig -a
lo0: flags=2001000849<UP,LOOPBACK,RUNNING,MULTICAST,IPv4,VIRTUAL> mtu 8232
 index 1
    inet 127.0.0.1 netmask ff000000
e1000g0: flags=201004843<UP,BROADCAST,RUNNING,MULTICAST,DHCP,IPv4,CoS> mtu 1500
 index 2
    inet 10.0.2.15 netmask ffffff00 broadcast 10.0.2.255
e1000g1: flags=201000843<UP,BROADCAST,RUNNING,MULTICAST,IPv4,CoS> mtu 1500
 index 3
    inet 192.168.1.20 netmask ffffc00 broadcast 192.168.3.255
e1000g1:1: flags=201000843<UP,BROADCAST,RUNNING,MULTICAST,IPv4,CoS> mtu 1500
 index 3
    inet 10.1.3.17 netmask ffffc00 broadcast 10.1.3.255
```

```
lo0: flags=2002000849<UP,LOOPBACK,RUNNING,MULTICAST,IPv6,VIRTUAL> mtu 8252
    index 1
       inet6 ::1/128
```

To make the logical interface persistent across reboots, you can add the addif command to the hostname.*interface* file; for example, /etc/hostname.e1000g1 for the preceding configuration:

```
192.168.1.20/22 up
addif 10.1.3.17/22 up
```

To deconfigure a logical interface, use the removeif subcommand to remove the address from the physical interface. To remove the logical interface previously created, use the following:

```
# ifconfig e1000g1 removeif 10.1.3.17
```

To remove it from the persistent configuration, you must remove the line that adds it from the hostname.*interface* file.

IP multipathing

One unique networking feature of OpenSolaris is a technology called *IP network multipathing* (*IPMP*). When you group interfaces together with IPMP, OpenSolaris provides enhanced failure detection for each interface in the group and can move IP addresses from failed interfaces to working ones, which enables network traffic to continue uninterrupted while you repair the problem, improving network reliability and availability. This is conceptually similar to the I/O multipathing used with storage technologies such as Fibre Channel that provide multiple connections to storage devices — hence the name.

CROSS-REF See Chapter 7 for information on I/O multipathing.

IPMP can also automatically restore service on a failed interface once it has been repaired. IPMP enables interfaces in groups to be either *active* or *standby*: an active interface is up and usable for IP traffic, whereas a standby interface is brought up only to replace an active interface. If more than one interface in the group is configured as active, IPMP can spread network traffic over the interfaces, improving overall network performance. The load-spreading performed by IPMP applies only to outgoing traffic, and is per-connection: Once an interface is selected for transmitting to a specific address and port number, all traffic for that destination is transmitted on the same interface.

TIP Unless there are incremental financial costs associated with using additional interfaces, or there is a wide disparity in performance between the interfaces, it's generally best to configure all interfaces as active. The examples in this section focus on all-active configurations. Consult the OpenSolaris documentation for information on configuring standby interfaces.

There are several technical requirements to use IPMP:

■ You must have two or more physical interfaces connected to the same subnet. The interfaces may use the same driver, but that is not required.

- You cannot use different media types, such as Ethernet and InfiniBand, in the same group, although that is rarely an issue because Ethernet is so prevalent.

- The interfaces do not need to be the same speed; you can group a 100 Mb Ethernet interface with a 1 Gb Ethernet interface, for example.

- You must use static IP addresses with IPMP; IPMP's operation is not compatible with using DHCP to configure your network interfaces.

- Finally, you cannot use NWAM with IPMP because the two features conflict with each other.

> **TIP** All interfaces in an IPMP group must have unique MAC addresses to ensure that each interface's traffic is separately distinguishable on the network. This is usually an issue only on SPARC systems, which are often configured by default to share a single MAC address across all interfaces. You can verify this using the `eeprom` command to examine the OpenBoot firmware's `local-mac-address?` setting:
>
> ```
> # eeprom local-mac-address?
> local-mac-address?=false
> ```
>
> If the value is false, you need to modify it to true, which is also done with the `eeprom` command:
>
> ```
> # eeprom local-mac-address?=true
> ```
>
> You must reboot the system after this change for it to take effect.

One last note: You can have multiple IPMP groups on a system, though each interface (including any standby interfaces) can be a member of only one group. The examples in this section show only a single group on the system.

Before you proceed to configure an IPMP group, you need to make one decision: will it use *active* (also called *probe-based*) failure detection or only *passive* (or *link-based*) failure detection? When configured to use active failure detection, the IPMP daemon, `in.mpathd`, sends periodic probe packets to a probe target address that's configured for each interface; the probe address is usually the router for the IP network, though any system connected to the link can be the probe target. If `in.mpathd` doesn't receive a response to the probes for a configurable period of time, the interface is considered failed and IPMP begins a failover operation.

Passive failure detection is implemented by `in.mpathd` monitoring the interface's RUNNING flag; most OpenSolaris network drivers are designed to set this flag when the link is detected to be active, and to clear the flag when a link failure is detected. This detection is primarily useful for quickly detecting a failure or disconnection of the network cable, or a failure of the switch to which the interface is connected. Passive detection, however, is unable to detect whether there is a failure further along the network link, such as between the switch and the router.

Passive detection is always used by IPMP when the driver supports it (to determine this, you need to read the driver documentation or experiment with disconnecting cables and checking the interface flags with `ifconfig`). If the driver doesn't support it, then you must configure active detection. The main disadvantage of active detection is that you must configure additional IP addresses, called *test addresses*, on each network interface; these addresses are used exclusively for `in.mpathd`'s probes. If IP addresses are in short supply, then you may need to make use of IPv4 private addresses; see the OpenSolaris documentation for information on this option.

Another slight disadvantage of active failure detection is that it adds a small amount of additional traffic to the local network, as `in.mpathd` will send an ICMP echo request probe from each test address to the target address roughly once every 1–2 seconds. This load is almost unmeasurable on gigabit-speed Ethernet networks, though, unless you have an unusually large number of systems running IPMP.

We recommend configuring active failure detection if possible, as you'll get more complete failure detection and thus better reliability.

> **TIP**   If your network supports IPv6, you can avoid assigning IPv4 test addresses; `in.mpathd` can use the IPv6 link-local address as its test address when this is available. See the OpenSolaris documentation for more on this option.

Configuring an IPMP group with passive failure detection

Creating a group that uses only passive failure detection is simple. In this example, two interfaces are configured on the system:

```
$ ifconfig -a
lo0: flags=2001000849<UP,LOOPBACK,RUNNING,MULTICAST,IPv4,VIRTUAL> mtu 8232
 index 1
        inet 127.0.0.1 netmask ff000000
elxl0: flags=201000843<UP,BROADCAST,RUNNING,MULTICAST,IPv4,CoS> mtu 1500 index 4
        inet 192.168.1.11 netmask ffffff00 broadcast 192.168.1.255
nfo0: flags=201000843<UP,BROADCAST,RUNNING,MULTICAST,IPv4,CoS> mtu 1500 index 5
        inet 192.168.1.21 netmask ffffff00 broadcast 192.168.1.255
lo0: flags=2002000849<UP,LOOPBACK,RUNNING,MULTICAST,IPv6,VIRTUAL> mtu 8252
 index 1
        inet6 ::1/128
```

The `elxl0` and `nfo0` interfaces are both connected to the 192.168.1.0 network. To create an IPMP group, just assign an interface to a group using the `group` subcommand to `ifconfig`:

```
# ifconfig elxl0 group mygroup
# ifconfig nfo0 group mygroup
# ifconfig -a
lo0: flags=2001000849<UP,LOOPBACK,RUNNING,MULTICAST,IPv4,VIRTUAL> mtu 8232
 index 1
        inet 127.0.0.1 netmask ff000000
elxl0: flags=201000843<UP,BROADCAST,RUNNING,MULTICAST,IPv4,CoS> mtu 1500 index 4
```

```
        inet 192.168.1.11 netmask ffffff00 broadcast 192.168.1.255
        groupname mygroup
        ether 0:10:5a:0:f8:89
nfo0: flags=201000843<UP,BROADCAST,RUNNING,MULTICAST,IPv4,CoS> mtu 1500 index 5
        inet 192.168.1.21 netmask ffffff00 broadcast 192.168.1.255
        groupname mygroup
        ether 0:e0:4c:ba:37:69
lo0: flags=2002000849<UP,LOOPBACK,RUNNING,MULTICAST,IPv6,VIRTUAL> mtu 8252
 index 1
        inet6 ::1/128
```

The group is automatically created as soon as an interface is assigned to it, and disappears when no interfaces are assigned. Also, once an interface is placed in a group, ifconfig automatically starts in.mpathd to monitor the group, if needed; the system runs only one in.mpathd process to monitor all IPMP groups.

As with all ifconfig commands, the group it creates is not persistent and will vanish when the system is rebooted. To make this configuration persistent, you must add the group subcommand to each interface's /etc/hostname.*interface* file. For the preceding configuration, the contents of the files are as follows:

```
$ cat /etc/hostname.elxl0
192.168.1.11/24 group mygroup
$ cat /etc/hostname.nfo0
192.168.1.21/24 group mygroup
```

To remove an interface from an IPMP group, specify an empty group name to ifconfig:

```
# ifconfig elxl0 group ""
```

Of course, to permanently remove the interface from the group, remove the group subcommand from the interface configuration file.

Configuring active failure detection

Using active failure detection with an IPMP group requires a bit more configuration work. For each interface in the group, you must add a logical interface that in.mpathd can use for its probes, and mark the logical interface as reserved for this purpose so that it will be left in place when in.mpathd starts a failover operation. This is done using the deprecated and -failover options to ifconfig. The deprecated option sets the DEPRECATED flag, which prevents IP from using the interface for ordinary network traffic. The -failover option sets the NOFAILOVER flag, preventing the interface from participating in failover.

Continuing with the last example, the following commands create the logical interfaces and mark them for IPMP usage:

```
# ifconfig elxl0 addif 192.168.1.70/24 up deprecated -failover
Created new logical interface elxl0:1
```

```
# ifconfig nfo0 addif 192.168.1.71/24 up deprecated -failover
Created new logical interface nfo0:1
```

The resulting interface configuration appears as follows:

```
# ifconfig -a
lo0: flags=2001000849<UP,LOOPBACK,RUNNING,MULTICAST,IPv4,VIRTUAL> mtu 8232
 index 1
        inet 127.0.0.1 netmask ff000000
elx10: flags=201000843<UP,BROADCAST,RUNNING,MULTICAST,IPv4,CoS> mtu 1500 index 2
        inet 192.168.1.11 netmask ffffff00 broadcast 192.168.1.255
        groupname mygroup
        ether 0:10:5a:0:f8:89
elx10:1: flags=209040843<UP,BROADCAST,RUNNING,MULTICAST,DEPRECATED,IPv4
,NOFAILOVER,CoS> mtu 1500 index 2
        inet 192.168.1.70 netmask ffffff00 broadcast 192.168.1.255
nfo0: flags=201000843<UP,BROADCAST,RUNNING,MULTICAST,IPv4,CoS> mtu 1500 index 3
        inet 192.168.1.21 netmask ffffff00 broadcast 192.168.1.255
        groupname mygroup
        ether 0:e0:4c:ba:37:69
nfo0:1: flags=209040843<UP,BROADCAST,RUNNING,MULTICAST,DEPRECATED,IPv4
,NOFAILOVER,CoS> mtu 1500 index 3
        inet 192.168.1.71 netmask ffffff00 broadcast 192.168.1.255
lo0: flags=2002000849<UP,LOOPBACK,RUNNING,MULTICAST,IPv6,VIRTUAL> mtu 8252
 index 1
        inet6 ::1/128
```

To make this configuration persistent, the /etc/hostname.*interface* files contain the following:

```
$ cat /etc/hostname.elx10
192.168.1.11/24 group mygroup up
addif 192.168.1.70/24 deprecated -failover up
$ cat /etc/hostname.nfo0
192.168.1.21/24 group mygroup up
addif 192.168.1.71/24 deprecated -failover up
```

To remove a test address and disable active failure detection, delete the logical interface's address using the removeif subcommand to ifconfig, as shown earlier. To remove it permanently, delete the addif command from the interface configuration file.

IPMP in action

To close this discussion on IPMP, the next example demonstrates what happens when IPMP detects a failure. In this case, the cable was disconnected from the nfo0 interface. First, in the system log /var/adm/messages, the following messages were recorded:

```
Jun 19 14:02:13 compaq nfo: [ID 104132 kern.info] NOTICE: nfo0:
 link down detected: status:7849<100_BASEX_FD,100_BASEX,10_BASE_FD
,10_BASE,MFPRMBLSUPR,CANAUTONEG,EXTENDED>
Jun 19 14:02:13 compaq nfo: [ID 311469 kern.info] nfo0: restarting
 auto-negotiation
Jun 19 14:02:21 compaq in.mpathd[156]: [ID 594170 daemon.error] NIC failure
 detected on nfo0 of group mygroup
Jun 19 14:02:21 compaq in.mpathd[156]: [ID 832587 daemon.error] Successfully
 failed over from NIC nfo0 to NIC elxl0
```

CROSS-REF See Chapter 14 for more information on system logging.

This is a rather unusual case because although the nfo driver detected the link failure, it did not clear the interface's RUNNING flag, so the failure was not detected by in.mpathd until several seconds later when its probes did not receive responses. The failover happened very quickly, within a second, once in.mpathd detected the failure, which is typical. The resulting interface configuration is as follows:

```
# ifconfig -a
lo0: flags=2001000849<UP,LOOPBACK,RUNNING,MULTICAST,IPv4,VIRTUAL> mtu 8232
 index 1
        inet 127.0.0.1 netmask ff000000
elxl0: flags=201000843<UP,BROADCAST,RUNNING,MULTICAST,IPv4,CoS> mtu 1500 index 2
        inet 192.168.1.11 netmask ffffff00 broadcast 192.168.1.255
        groupname mygroup
elxl0:1: flags=209040843<UP,BROADCAST,RUNNING,MULTICAST,DEPRECATED,IPv4
,NOFAILOVER,CoS> mtu 1500 index 2
        inet 192.168.1.70 netmask ffffff00 broadcast 192.168.1.255
elxl0:2: flags=201000843<UP,BROADCAST,RUNNING,MULTICAST,IPv4,CoS> mtu 1500
 index 2
        inet 192.168.1.21 netmask ffffff00 broadcast 192.168.1.255
nfo0: flags=219000842<BROADCAST,RUNNING,MULTICAST,IPv4
,NOFAILOVER,FAILED,CoS> mtu 0 index 3
        inet 0.0.0.0 netmask 0
        groupname mygroup
nfo0:1: flags=219040843<UP,BROADCAST,RUNNING,MULTICAST,DEPRECATED,IPv4
,NOFAILOVER,FAILED,CoS> mtu 1500 index 3
        inet 192.168.1.71 netmask ffffff00 broadcast 192.168.1.255
lo0: flags=2002000849<UP,LOOPBACK,RUNNING,MULTICAST,IPv6,VIRTUAL> mtu 8252
 index 1
        inet6 ::1/128
```

An additional logical interface, elx10:2, was created on the surviving interface, the address from nfo0 was moved to it, and the FAILED flag was set on nfo0. Users of the system were entirely unaware of the interface failure and the failover process. Once the cable was reconnected to nfo0, IPMP automatically moved the interface back, as shown in the log and interface configuration here:

```
$ tail /var/adm/messages
...
Jun 19 14:11:58 compaq nfo: [ID 455749 kern.info] nfo0: auto-negotiation done,
 advert:5e1<PAUSE,100BASE_TX_FD,100BASE_TX,10BASE_T_FD,10BASE_T>,
 lpable:45e1<PAUSE,100BASE_TX_FD,100BASE_TX,10BASE_T_FD,10BASE_T>,
 exp:1<LPCANAN>
Jun 19 14:11:58 compaq nfo: [ID 103695 kern.info] nfo0: Link up: 100Mbps full
 duplex with symmetric flow control
Jun 19 14:12:13 compaq in.mpathd[156]: [ID 299542 daemon.error] NIC repair
 detected on nfo0 of group mygroup
Jun 19 14:12:13 compaq in.mpathd[156]: [ID 620804 daemon.error] Successfully
 failed back to NIC nfo0
$ ifconfig -a
lo0: flags=2001000849<UP,LOOPBACK,RUNNING,MULTICAST,IPv4,VIRTUAL> mtu 8232
 index 1
        inet 127.0.0.1 netmask ff000000
elx10: flags=201000843<UP,BROADCAST,RUNNING,MULTICAST,IPv4,CoS> mtu 1500 index 2
        inet 192.168.1.11 netmask ffffff00 broadcast 192.168.1.255
        groupname mygroup
elx10:1: flags=209040843<UP,BROADCAST,RUNNING,MULTICAST,DEPRECATED,IPv4
,NOFAILOVER,CoS> mtu 1500 index 2
        inet 192.168.1.70 netmask ffffff00 broadcast 192.168.1.255
nfo0: flags=201000843<UP,BROADCAST,RUNNING,MULTICAST,IPv4,CoS> mtu 1500 index 3
        inet 192.168.1.21 netmask ffffff00 broadcast 192.168.1.255
        groupname mygroup
nfo0:1: flags=209040843<UP,BROADCAST,RUNNING,MULTICAST,DEPRECATED,IPv4
,NOFAILOVER,CoS> mtu 1500 index 3
        inet 192.168.1.71 netmask ffffff00 broadcast 192.168.1.255
lo0: flags=2002000849<UP,LOOPBACK,RUNNING,MULTICAST,IPv6,VIRTUAL> mtu 8252
 index 1
        inet6 ::1/128
```

If for some reason all of the interfaces fail, IPMP can detect that. You'll see a message like the following in the log for a failure such as disconnecting the switch to which the interfaces are connected:

```
Jun 19 14:18:50 compaq in.mpathd[156]: [ID 168056 daemon.error] All Interfaces
 in group mygroup have failed
```

Once the switch is plugged back in, the following messages appear in the log:

```
Jun 19 14:19:24 compaq in.mpathd[156]: [ID 299542 daemon.error] NIC repair
  detected on elxl0 of group mygroup
Jun 19 14:19:24 compaq in.mpathd[156]: [ID 620804 daemon.error] Successfully
  failed back to NIC elxl0
Jun 19 14:19:24 compaq in.mpathd[156]: [ID 237757 daemon.error] At least 1
  interface (elxl0) of group mygroup has repaired
Jun 19 14:19:24 compaq in.mpathd[156]: [ID 299542 daemon.error] NIC repair
  detected on nfo0 of group mygroup
Jun 19 14:19:24 compaq in.mpathd[156]: [ID 620804 daemon.error] Successfully
  failed back to NIC nfo0
```

IPMP can do a great deal to improve your network reliability, especially when used on critical infrastructure systems. To further explore IPMP, consult the OpenSolaris documentation, specifically the *System Administration Guide: IP Services*, at http://docs.sun.com/app/docs/doc/819-3000.

Link aggregation

Another network interface technology supported by OpenSolaris is *link aggregation*, which is a standard defined by IEEE 802.3ad. Linux distributions often refer to this technology as *Ethernet bonding*.

Like IPMP, link aggregation groups interfaces together to improve network performance and reliability. Unlike IPMP, link aggregation is done at the link layer, rather than at the IP layer; this means that an aggregation uses only a single IP address, and it can be used with dynamic IP addresses provided by DHCP. Aggregations do not use the active probe-based failure detection that IPMP groups can provide, but they can be configured to use the Link Aggregation Control Protocol (LACP) to provide link failure detection.

Aggregations require that each interface's driver support link up/down notification, and that each interface operates with the same duplex, although identical speeds and drivers are not required. Unlike IPMP, the load-spreading behavior of an aggregation may be configured and may provide better balance than IPMP for some traffic patterns. IPMP and link aggregation are not mutually exclusive; you can create multiple aggregations and then assign the aggregated interfaces to an IPMP group.

> **NOTE** Aggregations cannot be used with Network Auto-Magic at this time. You must disable NWAM and manually configure IP interfaces if aggregations are in use.

As aggregations are a link-layer entity, you use the dladm(1M) command to manage them. Use the create-aggr subcommand to create an aggregation:

```
# dladm create-aggr -l e1000g0 -l e1000g1 aggr0
```

This command creates an aggregation named aggr0, formed using the physical links e1000g0 and e1000g1. You must first ensure that none of the physical links is plumbed at the IP layer — otherwise, dladm displays an error message stating that the devices are in use and fails; if this happens, use the ifconfig unplumb command to remove the IP plumbing of the interface. You can view the resulting set of links using dladm show-link:

```
# dladm show-link
LINK        CLASS    MTU    STATE    OVER
e1000g0     phys     1500   up       --
e1000g1     phys     1500   up       --
aggr0       aggr     1500   up       e1000g0 e1000g1
```

As you can see, an aggregation is a different class of link and is formed over other links. Unlike ifconfig, objects configured using dladm are persistent by default, so this aggregation will appear on the next reboot (to create a temporary aggregation, perhaps to test out this feature, you can use the -t option to dladm create-aggr). You can view details of the aggregation using dladm show-aggr:

```
# dladm show-aggr
LINK            POLICY   ADDRPOLICY           LACPACTIVITY   LACPTIMER   FLAGS
aggr0           L4       auto                 off            short       -----
```

See the dladm(1M) man page for details on the aggregation settings. In particular, if you are using a switch that supports LACP, you likely need to change the LACPACTIVITY setting to ensure proper operation with the switch. By adjusting the policy settings, you can control the aggregation's load-spreading behavior.

With the aggregation created, you can use it just like a physical link to configure IP interfaces on top of. Of course, you need to start by plumbing the aggregation interface; here, it's configured using DHCP:

```
# ifconfig plumb aggr0
# ifconfig aggr0 dhcp start
# ifconfig -a
lo0: flags=2001000849<UP,LOOPBACK,RUNNING,MULTICAST,IPv4,VIRTUAL> mtu 8232
  index 1
        inet 127.0.0.1 netmask ff000000
aggr0: flags=201004843<UP,BROADCAST,RUNNING,MULTICAST,DHCP,IPv4,CoS> mtu 1500
  index 2
        inet 192.168.1.11 netmask ffffff00 broadcast 192.168.1.255
lo0: flags=2002000849<UP,LOOPBACK,RUNNING,MULTICAST,IPv6,VIRTUAL> mtu 8252
  index 1
        inet6 ::1/128
```

As you know, to make this configuration persistent, you create the hostname.aggr0 and dhcp.aggr0 files:

```
# touch /etc/hostname.aggr0 /etc/dhcp.aggr0
```

Use the add-aggr and remove-aggr subcommands to add interfaces to and remove interfaces from an aggregation once it's been created. delete-aggr deletes the aggregation entirely. See dladm(1M) for details.

Configuring virtual LAN interfaces

Virtual LAN technology (VLAN) enables you to create multiple logical link-layer networks on a single physical network link by tagging packets at the link layer with an identifier, which enables intelligent network switches to isolate the traffic on the different VLANs. In other words, the physical network behaves as if it were multiple physical networks, as the traffic on each network is not visible to the others. OpenSolaris network interfaces can be configured to recognize and use VLAN tagging by creating VLANs using the dladm(1M) command.

Use dladm create-vlan to create a VLAN interface:

```
# dladm create-vlan -l e1000g0 -v 2 red0
```

This creates a VLAN over the e1000g0 physical interface, using a tag of 2, named red0. The tag value isn't special; just ensure that it is a number between 1 and 4094, and that all systems and switch ports that are meant to be part of the same VLAN use the same tag value.

To view the link, use dladm show-link:

```
# dladm show-link red0
LINK          CLASS   MTU     STATE    OVER
red0          vlan    1500    down     e1000g0
```

You can examine the VLAN link properties using dladm show-vlan:

```
# dladm show-vlan red0
LINK          VID      OVER           FLAGS
red0          2        e1000g0        -----
```

Once the link is created, you can plumb and configure an IP interface. Here's a simple example of configuring the OpenSolaris IP interface using DHCP:

```
# ifconfig red0 plumb
# ifconfig red0
red0: flags=201000842<BROADCAST,RUNNING,MULTICAST,IPv4,CoS> mtu 1500 index 13
    inet 0.0.0.0 netmask 0
    ether 8:0:27:2f:10:81
# ifconfig red0 dhcp start
```

Remember that the switch port to which the physical interface is connected must be configured to accept an identical VLAN tag — otherwise, the network traffic is dropped by the switch. Consult your switch's documentation for instructions.

A VLAN link can be deleted using dladm delete-vlan.

Configuring a virtual NIC

Yet another type of network interface supported by OpenSolaris is a *virtual NIC*. A virtual NIC is similar to a logical interface in that it's tied to a specific physical interface, but it differs in that it's a link-layer entity, rather than an IP entity, and can reserve specific resources such as buffers and priority queues from the physical NIC. The `vnic` driver is included in current releases of OpenSolaris but is used only by virtualization software such as xVM and VirtualBox.

CROSS-REF See Chapter 22 for information on VirtualBox, and Chapter 20 for information on xVM.

OpenSolaris support for virtual NICs is still under development by the Crossbow project and is not yet a published interface, so this book does not cover it. The goal of Crossbow is to provide complete virtual IP protocol stacks from the link layer up as a basis for network resource management. For more information, see the project website at `http://opensolaris.org/os/project/crossbow/`.

Configuring IP tunnels

An additional type of network interface on OpenSolaris is the *IP tunnel*. A tunnel is, essentially, a virtual point-to-point interface used to connect two networks over a third network, without that third network being directly aware that it is making that connection. Point-to-point interfaces connect only two systems; they're like a private line, as opposed to Ethernet or other broadcast networks that operate as party lines, with many systems talking and listening. The most common use for a tunnel is to create a virtual private network (VPN) between multiple physical locations of an organization over the public Internet. This is highly attractive for a company because it avoids the high costs of leasing physical lines to connect sites, a practice common in the 1980s and early 1990s. VPNs are also often used to provide access to the company's computing resources to employees who are working at home or traveling. This is likely where you'll encounter IP tunnels, though most VPN software manages the tunneling automatically, without you even being aware that the tunnel is being used. If you display the network interface list using `ifconfig -a` while a VPN is running on OpenSolaris, you may see a tunnel interface similar to the `ip.tun0` interface shown here:

```
lo0: flags=2001000849<UP,LOOPBACK,RUNNING,MULTICAST,IPv4,VIRTUAL> mtu 8232
  index 1
       inet 127.0.0.1 netmask ff000000
elxl0: flags=201004843<UP,BROADCAST,RUNNING,MULTICAST,DHCP,IPv4,CoS> mtu 1500
  index 3
       inet 192.168.1.11 netmask ffffff00 broadcast 192.168.1.255
nfo0: flags=201004843<UP,BROADCAST,RUNNING,MULTICAST,DHCP,IPv4,CoS> mtu 1500
  index 4
       inet 192.168.1.21 netmask ffffff00 broadcast 192.168.1.255
ip.tun0: flags=10010008d1<UP,POINTOPOINT,RUNNING,NOARP,MULTICAST,IPv4
,FIXEDMTU> mtu 1366 index 5
```

```
        inet tunnel src 192.168.1.21 tunnel dst 192.168.5.223
        tunnel hop limit 60
        inet 10.16.24.12 --> 10.16.22.19 netmask ffffffff
lo0: flags=2002000849<UP,LOOPBACK,RUNNING,MULTICAST,IPv6,VIRTUAL> mtu 8252
  index 1
        inet6 ::1/128
```

As you can see, a tunnel interface has several additional parameters:

- Tunnel source and destination, which are the Internet addresses of the systems at each end of the tunnel

- Tunnel hop limit, which can be used to limit the number of network links any tunneled packets may traverse. The default value is 60.

- Source and destination addresses, which are the addresses of each end of the tunnel. These are addresses on the networks that are being connected.

The following ifconfig commands were used to create this tunnel:

```
# ifconfig ip.tun0 plumb
# ifconfig ip.tun0 10.16.24.12 10.16.22.19 tsrc 192.168.1.21 tdst 192.168.5.223
# ifconfig ip.tun0 up
```

You can create a /etc/hostname.ip.tun0 file to persistently configure such a tunnel — in this case, as follows:

```
10.16.24.12 10.16.22.19 tsrc 192.168.1.21 tdst 192.168.5.223 up
```

For traffic to flow over a tunnel, you must configure both ends of it. On the other end, you must perform a similar configuration process, but reverse the two pairs of source and destination addresses:

```
# ifconfig ip.tun0 plumb
# ifconfig ip.tun0 10.16.22.19 10.16.24.12 tsrc 12.168.5.223 tdst 192.168.1.21
# ifconfig ip.tun0 up
```

At this point, you should have a tunnel that can pass traffic between the two systems. To route packets for other systems, you need to configure each system as a router. See the section "Configuring a dynamic router" later in this chapter for information.

Configuring and securing a VPN is a complex topic beyond the scope of this book. The OpenSolaris documentation provides good examples in the *System Administration Guide: IP Services*, http://docs.sun.com/app/docs/doc/819-3000.

CROSS-REF Chapter 11 provides information on using the IPsec security technology in OpenSolaris.

PPP and PPP over Ethernet

If you need to connect to a network using the Point-to-Point Protocol (PPP), OpenSolaris is up to the task. PPP is typically used for the following types of network links:

- Dial-up networking using a modem over the phone network
- Leased lines
- Wireless wide-area networks (WWAN), such as the high-speed 3G cellular data networks
- Digital subscriber line (DSL), which uses a variant known as PPP over Ethernet (PPPoE). Usually a router purchased or rented from the ISP (Internet service provider) provides the PPPoE function.

OpenSolaris includes PPP software, based on the open source ANU PPP implementation, which is also used on Linux, BSD, and other commercial UNIX systems. Because PPP is currently used by a relatively small percentage of users, this book does not cover PPP configuration. For assistance, consult the OpenSolaris documentation, specifically the *System Administration Guide: Network Services* available at `http://docs.sun.com/app/docs/doc/819-1634`. See also the "Resources" section at the end of this chapter for recommended books on PPP.

CROSS-REF See Chapter 5 for additional information about using dial-up and WWAN modems with OpenSolaris.

Network Services

Once you have successfully configured a network interface, you'll likely want to connect to another system, perhaps to check your favorite website or blog, read your e-mail, or IM a friend or colleague. These tasks all require using services on the network. In this section, you'll learn about a few of the networking services in OpenSolaris that are critical to using it on the Internet.

Domain Name System

All systems on the Internet are reachable using an IP address, but IP addresses — like phone numbers — are not very easy for humans to remember. Most people can remember the names of many more people than they can their numbers. Hence, the phone book and address book were created, and, more recently, online versions of these tools. Similarly, once the Internet grew beyond the first few dozen sites in the 1980s, it was clear that users needed the capability to refer to sites by name in order to use the Internet.

At first this was solved by creating the `hosts` file, which is simply a text file that associates a name with an IP address, and copying that `hosts` file to all of the sites on the Internet so that they could refer to each other by name. OpenSolaris, like almost all operating systems, includes a `hosts` file, which is stored at `/etc/inet/hosts` and contains a couple of entries by default.

If you installed your system with the name `opensolaris`, then the `hosts` file contains the following (the block comment at the beginning has been omitted for brevity):

```
::1        localhost
127.0.0.1    opensolaris opensolaris.local localhost loghost
```

Recall from earlier in this chapter that the `::1` and `127.0.0.1` addresses are the IPv6 and IPv4 loopback interfaces on your system, so you can connect to your own system using `opensolaris`, `opensolaris.local`, `localhost`, or `loghost`. You can add entries to the file for other systems as well.

Introduction to DNS

The problem with the `hosts` file, of course, was that copying it to each and every system on the Internet wasn't practical once the Internet grew to a few thousand hosts and kept growing; the `hosts` file was always out of date, and an increasing amount of time was spent copying it. A better approach was needed, so Internet researchers invented the Domain Name System (DNS), which became the directory service of the Internet.

The core idea of the DNS is to organize the names into a hierarchy and delegate the management of a portion of the hierarchy to an organization that owns that piece; the organization is then free to further register names and delegate authority within its hierarchy as needed. Each level of the hierarchy is called a *domain*. For example, there are top-level domains such as com, edu, mil, org, us, uk, zh, and so on, which are created through an international standards process. Organizations can register a second-level domain with a registrar that's designated for each top-level domain, and then create their own names within their domain. Examples of second-level domains include sun.com, opensolaris.org, and wiley.com.

The registrars and organizations are responsible for running (or hiring another organization to run) a DNS server that can translate a name within their domain of authority into an IP address. Each system on the Internet then runs a DNS client, commonly known as a *resolver*, which can perform lookups from the DNS servers. The OpenSolaris distribution includes both DNS resolver and DNS server software, which are based on the Internet Systems Consortium's BIND software, used on virtually all UNIX-like systems. If you're already accustomed to this software on other platforms, you'll find OpenSolaris familiar in this respect. The following sections demonstrate how to configure your own DNS resolver and DNS server on OpenSolaris.

NOTE DNS can store and retrieve other types of information beyond IP addresses, but this book does not cover that topic. See the "Resources" section at the end of this chapter for additional materials on DNS.

Configuring the DNS resolver

The OpenSolaris DNS resolver is configured using the file `/etc/resolv.conf`, which is the same file used on Linux and most other UNIX systems. If you're using DHCP to configure your network interfaces, either via NWAM or a manual configuration, you probably won't need to configure the DNS resolver at all, as the DHCP server is usually configured to provide the DNS domain and list of DNS servers appropriate for your network. If you're not using DHCP, or your DHCP server doesn't supply DNS configuration data, then you need to create your own `resolv.conf` file to use DNS. The most basic `resolv.conf` contains a `nameserver` statement:

```
nameserver 192.168.1.7
```

This simple configuration relies on a single DNS server at IP address 192.168.1.7 to help you resolve DNS queries. If that name server is unavailable for some reason, you won't be able to look up any addresses in DNS. You can list additional DNS servers in `resolv.conf`, and the DNS resolver will try them in the order listed:

```
nameserver 192.168.1.7
nameserver 10.2.3.34
```

Note that the name servers listed do not need to be on your local network. Consult your network administrator for the list of DNS servers that can be used on your network.

While this configuration will work, it's not the most usable one because you are forced to type the full DNS domain name of any system you want to contact, such as `file-server.example.com`. Providing full domain names for systems that you contact frequently, especially those in your local domain, can be tedious. You can use the `search` parameter to provide a list of domains that the resolver will automatically append to any name passed to it, enabling you to use short names in your applications. For example, in the `example.com` domain you might have the following `resolv.conf`:

```
search example.com
nameserver 192.168.1.7
nameserver 10.2.3.34
```

NOTE You can use the `domain` parameter, rather than the `search` parameter, in `resolv.conf`, though `domain` allows only a single domain to be listed, whereas `search` allows up to six domains. Be careful when using the search feature, as the time required to resolve a DNS query can increase quite a bit when you search multiple domains.

See the next section for information on testing your resolver configuration.

One last thing you may need to do if you're setting up your own DNS resolver configuration is to enable DNS lookups in the OpenSolaris name service switch.

CROSS-REF See Chapter 10 for information on the name service switch.

To enable the system to use DNS for all IP address lookups, edit `/etc/nsswitch.conf` and ensure that the `hosts` (and `ipnodes`, if you're using IPv6) entries contain the `dns` keyword, such as this:

```
hosts: files dns
ipnodes: files dns
```

A few other parameters can be supplied in resolv.conf but are not discussed here. See the resolv.conf(4) man page for more information.

> **NOTE** You may notice when perusing the SMF service configuration that OpenSolaris includes a service called svcs:/network/dns/client:default. **This service is an implementation detail related to OpenSolaris name services and SMF service dependencies and doesn't actually do anything at this writing. Do not disable or remove this service yourself because doing so may interfere with future operation of the DNS resolver.**

DNS troubleshooting

OpenSolaris supplies a special command, dig(1M), for troubleshooting DNS lookups. If you've configured your DNS resolver in /etc/resolv.conf, then you can use dig to look up a domain name such as www.opensolaris.com and see the gory details of the DNS response:

```
$ dig www.opensolaris.com

; <<>> DiG 9.3.4-P1 <<>> www.opensolaris.com
;; global options:  printcmd
;; Got answer:
;; ->>HEADER<<- opcode: QUERY, status: NOERROR, id: 1734
;; flags: qr rd ra; QUERY: 1, ANSWER: 2, AUTHORITY: 4, ADDITIONAL: 4

;; QUESTION SECTION:
;www.opensolaris.com.           IN      A

;; ANSWER SECTION:
www.opensolaris.com.   22082   IN      CNAME   opensolaris.com.
opensolaris.com.       22082   IN      A       72.5.124.83

;; AUTHORITY SECTION:
opensolaris.com.         16723   IN      NS      ns8.sun.com.
opensolaris.com.         16723   IN      NS      ns1.sun.com.
opensolaris.com.         16723   IN      NS      ns2.sun.com.
opensolaris.com.         16723   IN      NS      ns7.sun.com.

;; ADDITIONAL SECTION:
ns1.sun.com.             159128  IN      A       192.18.128.11
ns2.sun.com.             159128  IN      A       192.18.99.5
ns7.sun.com.             159128  IN      A       192.18.43.15
ns8.sun.com.             159128  IN      A       192.18.43.12

;; Query time: 3 msec
;; SERVER: 192.168.1.7#53(192.168.1.7)
;; WHEN: Fri Jun 20 14:46:02 2008
;; MSG SIZE  rcvd: 207
```

The output of dig is broken down into several sections that correspond to details of the DNS protocol. The QUESTION section shows the type of query you supplied — in this case, an A (or address lookup) for `www.opensolaris.com`; address queries are the default unless you specify a different type on the command line.

The `ANSWER` section displays the answer to the query. This answer contained two parts: a `CNAME` record, which indicates that the name `www.opensolaris.com` is actually an alias for the true name `opensolaris.com`, and an `A` (or address) record for `opensolaris.com` that supplies its IP address.

The `AUTHORITY` and `ADDITIONAL` sections provide additional data that the resolver can use to improve its performance in resolving additional names within the `opensolaris.com` domain: a list of name servers in the `AUTHORITY` section, and the addresses for those servers in the `ADDI-TIONAL` section.

Note that each record in the output includes a number; that number is a cache timeout in seconds for the record, telling the resolver how long the data is guaranteed by the server to be usable. If the resolver chooses to cache this data for future reference, it must discard it when the cache timeout expires. This caching greatly reduces the amount of DNS traffic on the Internet and improves performance in looking up frequently requested data.

`dig` is a very flexible, powerful command-line DNS client. Make an extra effort to become familiar with it if you're running a DNS server because it will be your best tool to begin testing and troubleshooting any DNS problems, as demonstrated in the next section.

Configuring a DNS server

If you've registered your own DNS domain, or have been delegated a domain to manage within your organization, you'll need a DNS server to respond to queries for your domain's IP addresses. This section demonstrates how to configure a single DNS server for a domain.

> **TIP**   If you've registered your own domain, you can easily find services, likely from the registrar you used, that will provide DNS hosting for your domain for a small fee. We suggest exploring this option unless you're interested in taking on this responsibility yourself.

The DNS server on OpenSolaris is provided by the `named(1M)` daemon, which is run under the SMF (Service Management Facility) service instance `svc:/network/dns/server:default`. The OpenSolaris version of `named` has been enhanced to interact well with SMF, by using SMF service properties to configure options that on other operating systems must be set by editing the `init` scripts used to start the service. These are described in the `named` man page.

> **CROSS-REF**   SMF is discussed in Chapter 13.

To configure `named`, you organize the data it will supply, such as name and IP address mappings, into zone files, and then provide the list of zones in its main configuration file, which by default is `/etc/named.conf`. On OpenSolaris you may want to consider relocating the configuration file, along with the zone files, to a ZFS dataset that will be shared between boot environments so that the DNS configuration remains consistent across system updates. The example demonstrates this by placing the data in /export/named. Note that the term "zones" in the named configuration has nothing to do with the Zones virtualization feature of OpenSolaris.

CROSS-REF See Chapter 6 for details on OpenSolaris boot environments. See Chapter 8 for details on ZFS.

To begin the DNS server configuration process, create the ZFS dataset that will contain the configuration files:

```
# zfs create rpool/export/named
```

This dataset will be mounted at /export/named. You can then create the master named.conf file by editing /export/named/named.conf using your favorite editor. Here's an example file:

```
options {
    directory "/export/named";
};

zone "example.com" {
    type master;
    file "example";
};

zone "1.168.192.in-addr.arpa" {
    type master;
    file "192.168.1";
};
```

NOTE A complete description of the syntax of the named.conf and zone data files is beyond the scope of this book. Consult the BIND 9.5 Administrator Reference Manual at http://isc.org/sw/bind/arm95 for detailed documentation.

This sample file begins with an options clause identifying the directory in which other files referenced in the configuration can be found. You can set other options, but this configuration doesn't require any others. The first zone clause specifies that this server is a master server for the domain example.com, and that the data for this zone is found in the example file, which is in /export/named. This zone data is used to map names in the example.com domain to IP addresses.

The second zone clause specifies that this server is a master server for the 1.168.192.in-addr.arpa domain. Unless you have some knowledge of DNS already, this domain name must look quite strange. Briefly, DNS reserves the in-addr.arpa domain for mapping addresses to names; the subdomains within it are the reversed form of the IP address for the network. This convention is specified in the DNS standards and is known to all resolvers so that when a system attempts to retrieve the name that corresponds to an IP address, the resolver automatically reverses the address and looks it up in the `in-addr.arpa` domain. The implication of BIND's design is that when you assign a name to an IP address that will be published in DNS, you must update both zone files for forward (name-to-address) and reverse (address-to-name) resolution to provide consistent results.

Here is the sample zone file for the `example.com` domain:

```
$TTL 86400
@       IN      SOA     ns.example.com. sam.example.com. (
                        2008062001      ; serial
                        10800   ; refresh
                        3600    ; retry
                        3600000 ; expire
                        86400 ) ; minimum

@               NS      ns.example.com.

ns              A       192.168.1.1
www             A       192.168.1.2
mail            A       192.168.1.3
sleepy          A       192.168.1.4
stuffy          A       192.168.1.5
```

This zone file begins by using a `$TTL` directive to set the time-to-live (TTL) in seconds for each record in the file that does not specify an explicit TTL value. The value used here, 86400, equals 24 hours. Generally, a value of a day or so is reasonable, as it enables clients to cache the data for some time and reduces the load on your network and DNS servers. If you have a scheduled renumbering or renaming of systems on your network, then you can lower this value as the changes approach so that clients will not cache stale data past the transition date.

The next record is the `SOA`, or Start of Authority, record, which defines some basic data about the domain that can be used in resolving problems with DNS lookups for data in the zone. The @ token in the first field is translated by BIND as the zone name that was declared for this file in `named.conf`. The remaining fields of the record specify, in order, the following:

- The master name server for the zone (`ns.example.com`)
- The e-mail address of the administrative contact for this zone, with the first period replacing the @ symbol that normally separates a user's mailbox from its domain name. Thus, the e-mail address would be `sam@example.com`
- A serial number (by convention this is usually the date the file was updated plus a sequence number) and TTL values specific to this record. Unless you have a good understanding of DNS, just use the preceding TTL values in your own zones — they're quite common.

The next record is the NS, or nameserver, record, which declares that ns.example.com is a name server for example.com. If you have more than one name server for a zone, list a NS record for each name server.

The remaining records in the file are A, or address, records for each named system in the domain. If a system has more than one address, by virtue of having multiple physical or logical interfaces, you can list an A record for each address associated with the name.

Here's the sample zone file for the 1.168.192.in-addr.arpa domain:

```
$TTL 86400
@        IN       SOA      ns.example.com. sam.example.com. (
                           2008062001      ; serial
                           10800   ; refresh
                           3600    ; retry
                           3600000 ; expire
                           86400 ) ; minimum

@        NS       ns.example.com.

1        PTR      ns.example.com.
2        PTR      www.example.com.
3        PTR      mail.example.com.
4        PTR      sleepy.example.com.
5        PTR      stuffy.example.com.
```

Here, the in-addr.arpa zone file is very similar to the example.com zone file. It includes identical SOA and NS records (though this is not strictly required; you could have different owners and name servers for the in-addr.arpa zone); the difference is entirely in the remaining records, all PTR records, which are the record type used to map an IP address to a domain name.

You can verify that your zone files are correct before proceeding using the named-checkzone command:

```
# named-checkzone example.com /export/named/example
zone example.com/IN: loaded serial 2008062001
OK
# named-checkzone 1.168.192.in-addr.arpa /export/named/192.168.1
zone 1.168.192.in-addr.arpa/IN: loaded serial 2008062001
OK
```

Next, you must configure the dns/server service in SMF to use the configuration files in /export/named:

```
# svccfg -s dns/server:default
svc:/network/dns/server:default> setprop options/configuration_file
=/export/named/named.conf
svc:/network/dns/server:default> exit
```

```
# svcadm refresh dns/server
# svcadm enable dns/server
```

Now that the server has been started, you can use `dig` to verify that it's working. First, confirm that name-to-address translation is working by looking up the address record for one of the hostnames in the domain; using the `@localhost` argument directs `dig` to contact the DNS server running on this system, rather than any server that may be configured in your system's `/etc/resolv.conf`:

```
# dig @localhost stuffy.example.com

; <<>> DiG 9.3.4-P1 <<>> @localhost stuffy.example.com
; (2 servers found)
;; global options:  printcmd
;; Got answer:
;; ->>HEADER<<- opcode: QUERY, status: NOERROR, id: 1988
;; flags: qr aa rd ra; QUERY: 1, ANSWER: 1, AUTHORITY: 1, ADDITIONAL: 1

;; QUESTION SECTION:
;stuffy.example.com.                    IN      A

;; ANSWER SECTION:
stuffy.example.com.        86400    IN      A       192.168.1.5

;; AUTHORITY SECTION:
example.com.              86400    IN      NS      ns.example.com.

;; ADDITIONAL SECTION:
ns.example.com.           86400    IN      A       192.168.1.1

;; Query time: 27 msec
;; SERVER: 127.0.0.1#53(127.0.0.1)
;; WHEN: Fri Jun 20 16:21:25 2008
;; MSG SIZE  rcvd: 85
```

In this case, the name was resolved successfully. Next, verify that the address-to-name mapping is working by looking up the PTR record associated with one of the addresses using the `in-addr.arpa` domain:

```
# dig @localhost 2.1.168.192.in-addr.arpa. ptr

; <<>> DiG 9.3.4-P1 <<>> @localhost 2.1.168.192.in-addr.arpa. ptr
; (2 servers found)
;; global options:  printcmd
;; Got answer:
;; ->>HEADER<<- opcode: QUERY, status: NOERROR, id: 213
;; flags: qr aa rd ra; QUERY: 1, ANSWER: 1, AUTHORITY: 1, ADDITIONAL: 1

;; QUESTION SECTION:
```

```
;2.1.168.192.in-addr.arpa.    IN    PTR

;; ANSWER SECTION:
2.1.168.192.in-addr.arpa.  86400   IN    PTR    www.example.com.

;; AUTHORITY SECTION:
1.168.192.in-addr.arpa.    86400   IN    NS     ns.example.com.

;; ADDITIONAL SECTION:
ns.example.com.            86400   IN    A      192.168.1.1

;; Query time: 20 msec
;; SERVER: 127.0.0.1#53(127.0.0.1)
;; WHEN: Fri Jun 20 16:21:49 2008
;; MSG SIZE  rcvd: 104
```

If this works as well, then your domain is operating correctly. You can proceed to configure the clients in your domain to use your DNS server by updating `resolv.conf` on each client. You can also configure additional servers, known as *slave* or *secondary servers*, which replicate the data from the master server; see the BIND documentation for instructions. Finally, if you're running a DHCP server, update the configuration that it provides to DHCP clients to include the DNS domain name and name server address.

> **NOTE** You can also configure the BIND DNS server to accept dynamic DNS updates from DHCP servers so that system name and address associations can be formed dynamically based on the system names desired by individual users. Consult the BIND manual and your DHCP server documentation for details about enabling dynamic updates.

Multicast DNS

OpenSolaris includes a second DNS implementation, known as *multicast DNS*, so called because the participating systems send *IP multicast* packets to the network to resolve names. An IP multicast packet uses a special IP network address (the 224.0.0.0 network) that will be sent to all of the systems on a network link. The IP addresses you normally use are known as *unicast addresses* because they are destined for only a single system. Multicast DNS (mDNS) is of interest because it enables you to create a network in which systems can find one another by name, without the need to set up and manage a centralized DNS server such as BIND. Such networks are often called *ad hoc networks*. This is especially attractive in home and small office networks, or any situation for which you would like to use system names but don't want to bother with the management effort of a standard DNS server. Unlike standard DNS, each system participating in multicast DNS must be running the multicast DNS service, but the multicast DNS service requires almost no configuration.

In addition to hostname-to-IP address resolution, multicast DNS can be used to locate other services on the network, such as printers, though OpenSolaris does not yet use it for this purpose. Multicast DNS is included on a wide variety of systems, including Linux and Apple's

Mac OS X. Apple refers to the technology as *Bonjour* and uses it extensively. Apple also supplies multicast DNS software for Windows, called Bonjour for Windows; you can get it from `http://apple.com/support/downloads/bonjourforwindows.html`.

Configuring multicast DNS is a simple, two-step process. First, enable the `network/dns/multicast` service:

```
# svcadm enable network/dns/multicast
```

This starts the multicast DNS daemon, `mdnsd(1M)`. Then, edit `/etc/nsswitch.conf` to add `mdns` to the `hosts` (and `ipnodes`, if using IPv6) search list:

```
hosts: files mdns dns
ipnodes: files mdns dns
```

Your system will now advertise itself as *hostname*`.local`; the `.local` top-level domain is reserved for the use of mDNS. You can verify that your system is advertising itself correctly using the `getent` command. If your system is named `celtic` and has IP address 192.168.1.30, you can look it up as `celtic.local`:

```
$ getent hosts celtic.local
192.168.1.30 celtic.local.
```

If the output is as shown, then your mDNS service is operating correctly, and you can look up any other systems on your local network that have mDNS configured by using the `.local` domain name.

OpenSolaris also includes the `dns-sd(1M)` command, which is used to both advertise and look up services using mDNS. You can use it to make your own mDNS-capable applications. For more information on multicast DNS, see `http://multicastdns.org`.

Dynamic Host Configuration Protocol

When widespread deployment of IP networks in organizations began in the 1990s, configuring those systems into the network with little or no administrative effort became an important problem to solve to make the network deployments cost-effective. The IETF developed the Dynamic Host Configuration Protocol (DHCP) as the primary solution to that problem.

The core principle in DHCP's design is that a DHCP server has a pool of addresses that it *leases* to clients for a specified time period upon request. Along with an address lease, a DHCP server can also provide a set of configuration parameters, called *options*, which the client can use to operate correctly on the network. Roughly 100 options have been standardized through the IETF; commonly used options include a default router, DNS servers, NTP servers, and network boot servers. Vendors of networking equipment, as well as individual organizations, can also define custom options for their own purposes.

OpenSolaris includes both a DHCP client and a DHCP server whose implementations are custom to OpenSolaris. This section describes the use of both.

Using the DHCP client

As demonstrated earlier in this chapter, the DHCP client is automatically used to configure interfaces when NWAM is used for network interface configuration. You can also choose to use DHCP for manually configured interfaces. The OpenSolaris DHCP client is implemented by the dhcpagent(1M) daemon; dhcpagent is automatically started when ifconfig is used to configure a DHCP interface, and the single daemon process then manages all DHCP-configured interfaces on the system. The dhcpagent daemon also automatically exits when there are no longer any interfaces under DHCP control running on the system. Thus, it's unlikely that you'll have a need to directly manage the dhcpagent process.

You can configure some behavior of dhcpagent by modifying the parameters specified in its configuration file, /etc/default/dhcpagent. The parameters are documented extensively in the file's comments. In most situations, you won't need to modify the default values, but if your system is frequently shut down and moved from one network to another while powered off, such as a laptop, then set the value of RELEASE_ON_SIGTERM to yes, as this ensures that your system operates correctly when moved from one network to another. If you move your system to a different network while it is powered off and the RELEASE_ON_SIGTERM setting is the default value, no, then your client will attempt to continue using its address from the original network if that address's lease has time remaining. If this happens, your client will almost certainly be unable to communicate with the new network; should that occur, you need to issue the command ifconfig *interface* dhcp release followed by ifconfig *interface* dhcp start to recover.

Another useful feature of dhcpagent is its capability to run a script when the state of the interface changes, such as when an address lease is acquired, extended, or released, or it expires. You can use this feature by creating a script called /etc/dhcp/eventhook; the script must be owned and executable by root; otherwise, dhcpagent will ignore it. See the dhcpagent man page for a skeletal eventhook script that you can extend for your own purposes.

> **NOTE** If you are using Network Auto-Magic (NWAM), use its scripting mechanisms, rather than dhcpagent's eventhook, to perform custom actions when interfaces are started and stopped. See the nwamd(1M) man page for details on NWAM profiles and scripting.

A final useful feature of dhcpagent is the method used to retrieve DHCP options supplied by the server. This is especially helpful if you're supplying an eventhook script or using NWAM profiles to reconfigure aspects of your system, but it's also a troubleshooting tool whenever you're using DHCP for interface configuration. All of the options included in the DHCP server's lease to the client are stored by dhcpagent. You can then use the dhcpinfo(1) command to query dhcpagent for any option, and dhcpinfo will print its value to standard output.

When using dhcpinfo, you can request option values by option code number or by the more mnemonic option names that OpenSolaris defines in /etc/dhcp/inittab; this file is documented in the dhcp_inittab(4) man page. For example, if you are running DHCP on the interface wpi0, you can retrieve the DNS domain name using either of the following invocations of dhcpinfo (note that dhcpinfo is stored in /sbin, which may not be in your PATH environment variable, so the example uses the full pathname to the executable):

```
$ /sbin/dhcpinfo -i wpi0 DNSdmain
example.com
$ /sbin/dhcpinfo -i wpi0 15
example.com
```

Configuring a DHCP server

If you're already familiar with the Internet Systems Consortium's (ISC) DHCP server from other platforms, then you can use it on OpenSolaris; you need to download the source from ISC directly at http://isc.org or obtain a pre-built package from the sunfree-ware.com package repository. See Chapter 6 for information on installing packages from repositories.

Otherwise, you can use the OpenSolaris implementation of the DHCP server. The first step is to ensure that the software is installed. You can install it with the following command:

```
# pkg install SUNWdhcs SUNWdhcsb
```

Once the DHCP server is installed, you can proceed to configure it. For this task, you have two options: the dhcpconfig(1M) command, or the DHCP Manager, dhcpmgr(1M), which is a graphical configuration tool for the DHCP server. If you want to use the DHCP Manager, you must also install its package:

```
# pkg install SUNWdhcm
```

If you'd like to configure the server using the DHCP Manager, run /usr/sadm/admin/bin/dhcpmgr; this will begin a wizard-style step-by-step procedure that creates an initial configuration for the DHCP server. However, this section explains how to configure the DHCP server using the command-line tools.

CROSS-REF An example configuration session using DHCP Manager can be found in Chapter 24.

To create the initial DHCP server configuration, use dhcpconfig -D. There are two required options that specify how and where the DHCP server data will be stored. The -p option specifies the path in which to place the configuration files, and the -r option specifies the format to use for the files: SUNWfiles uses a text file format, and SUNWbinfiles uses a binary file format. SUNWbinfiles is recommended, as it provides better performance. It's also recommended that you place the file storage in a separate ZFS dataset that can be shared across OpenSolaris boot environments.

NOTE The DHCP server also offers the option to store data in the NIS+ name service, but NIS+ has been deprecated by Sun and may be removed from a future release. Thus, new installations using NIS+ are discouraged.

For example, the following commands configure a DHCP server on the system named opensolaris to use SUNWbinfiles and store the data in /export/dhcp:

```
# zfs create rpool/export/dhcp
# dhcpconfig -D -r SUNWbinfiles -p /export/dhcp
Created DHCP configuration file.
Created dhcptab.
Added "Locale" macro to dhcptab.
Added server macro to dhcptab - opensolaris.
DHCP server started.
```

The DHCP configuration file is stored at /etc/inet/dhcpsvc.conf; see its man page, dhcpsvc.conf(4). View and edit its contents using dhcpconfig -P. After this configuration is created, it appears as follows:

```
# dhcpconfig -P
DAEMON_ENABLED TRUE
RESOURCE SUNWbinfiles
RUN_MODE server
PATH /export/dhcp
CONVER 1
```

The initial dhcpconfig output also refers to creating the dhcptab file and adding macros to it. A macro is just an administrative mechanism used by the DHCP server to group related options; dhcptab is the configuration file where the macros are stored. When supplying leases to clients, the server also supplies options in its replies, and clients can use those options to configure themselves. The clients see only a list of options and are unaware of the macro mechanism used on the server. The dhtadm command is used to manage the contents of dhcptab; to view it, use dhtadm -P:

```
# dhtadm -P
Name                     Type          Value
==================================================
opensolaris              Macro         :Include=Locale:Timeserv=10.0.2.15:LeaseTim
=86400:LeaseNeg:DNSdmain
="example.com":DNSserv=10.0.2.3:
Locale                   Macro         :UTCoffst=-18000:
```

This provides the most basic DHCP configuration, with a macro that's named the same as the DHCP server's hostname, and a Locale macro that defines the local time offset against UTC time. The DNS information was taken from /etc/resolv.conf on this system; if the DHCP server is not configured for DNS, then this information won't be added to the server macro. The LeaseTim and LeaseNeg options specify that leases are good for 24 hours (86400 seconds) and that the leases are negotiable, which means they can be extended at the client's request. You can modify the default lease duration, but it is highly unlikely that you'll want to change the leases to be non-negotiable, as that disrupts systems that stay on the network for longer than the initial lease duration; they'll be forced to disconnect from the network for at least a few seconds at the expiration of the lease to negotiate a new one.

Now that you have a simple set of configuration values for DHCP clients, you need to provide the DHCP server with a set of addresses that it can lease to the clients. Before you can do that, however, you must ensure that the DHCP server's /etc/inet/netmasks table (or the NIS netmasks map, if the server is configured to use NIS for name service lookups) contains the correct network mask for each network on which the server will provide address leases. The server in this example is using a 24-bit network mask on the 10.0.2.0 network, so the netmasks entry would be as follows:

```
10.0.2.0     255.255.255.0
```

Now you're ready to create DHCP addresses — with the pntadm command. You must start by creating a DHCP network table for each network on which the server leases addresses. For the 10.0.2.0 network, this is done as follows:

```
# pntadm -C 10.0.2.0
```

The network table is empty initially. To create addresses, use pntadm -A:

```
# pntadm -A 10.0.2.20 -m opensolaris
```

The -m option specifies a dhcptab macro to associate with this address. To view the contents of the network table, use pntadm -P:

```
# pntadm -P 10.0.2.0
Client ID  Flags  Client IP  Server IP  Lease Expiration  Macro  Comment
00         00     10.0.2.20  10.0.2.15  Zero                     opensolaris
```

As you can see, the table has a number of columns, which the dhcp_network(4) man page describes. Here's a brief summary:

- Client ID is the client to which the address was last assigned; each DHCP client provides an identifier that must be unique on a network. Usually this is based on the MAC address of the network interface. Because this is a new address that hasn't yet been assigned, it has the value 00.

- Flags is used to specify various properties of the IP address; it could be manually assigned to a specific Client ID, or it may be unusable.

- Client IP is the address being leased.

- Server IP is the IP address of the DHCP server.

- Lease Expiration is the date and time when the lease expires; because the address has yet to be assigned, this has the value zero.

- The Macro field associates the address with a macro from the dhcptab table; usually this should be the name of the server macro, though it's not required to be.

- Comment can be used by the administrator to record notes or other identifying information for this address.

TIP You can use dhtadm to create additional macros that the DHCP server will use automatically when constructing the set of options supplied in lease responses to clients. A network macro, named the same as the network address, is automatically used for all clients on that network; this macro often contains a default router option so that clients can reach systems on other networks. The DHCP Manager's Network Wizard automatically does this for you. You can also create macros that are associated with a specific client ID or a specific vendor's clients to customize the configuration for a particular client or class of clients. See the dhcptab(4) man page for information about the macros that are processed in responding to a client's lease request.

Now that you have an address available for lease, you can start up a system that is a DHCP client and it should obtain this address from your DHCP server. Before it offers an address to a client, the DHCP server uses ICMP echo requests to verify that the address is not in use. If the server receives a response, it marks the address as disabled in the network table and attempts to find another address to offer to the client. If the server has no more available addresses, you'll see messages such as the following in your system log:

```
Jun 24 21:15:56 opensolaris in.dhcpd[803]: [ID 603263 daemon.notice] No more
    IP addresses on 192.168.2.0 network (01080027440630)
```

Monitor the DHCP server's logs and periodically scan the DHCP network tables for addresses that have been marked unusable to ensure that addresses are available. You can use tools such as ping and snoop, described later in this chapter, to troubleshoot any unusable addresses and reenable them using pntadm -M once you've resolved any conflicts. Add more addresses as needed using pntadm, and delete addresses from the DHCP configuration using pntadm -D.

The DHCP server is managed as the SMF service svc:/network/dhcp-server, which executes in.dhcpd(1M). In addition to using the svcadm command to control the service, you can use dhcpconfig -S -e to enable the server, and dhcpconfig -S -d to disable it. To unconfigure the server, use dhcpconfig -U.

This section has only scratched the surface of the DHCP server's capabilities; see the OpenSolaris documentation for much more information about the DHCP server.

File Transfer Protocol

The File Transfer Protocol (FTP) is one of the earliest Internet applications and is commonly supported by IP systems. OpenSolaris includes both the FTP client program, ftp, and the server, in.ftpd. The FTP server is managed by SMF as the service svc:/network/ftp. This service is disabled by default in OpenSolaris because SSH, which is enabled by default, includes the sftp program that performs a similar file transfer function using SSH as the transport, thus providing encryption of the data while in transit. The OpenSolaris FTP server implementation is based on the WU-FTP daemon originally developed at Washington University and commonly used on current operating systems.

One popular application of FTP is to set up an anonymous FTP service, which allows for public download of content from the server. This service is often used for distributing large files such as CD or DVD images, as FTP can transfer these more efficiently than HTTP. You can set up an anonymous FTP service using `ftpconfig(1M)`. As with other services, it's recommended that you place the FTP service data in a ZFS dataset that is shared across OpenSolaris boot environments, as shown in the following example:

```
# zfs create rpool/export/ftp
# ftpconfig /export/ftp
Creating user ftp
Updating directory /export/ftp
```

This sets up the anonymous FTP server directory and user account, which appears like this:

```
# ls /export/ftp
bin  dev  etc  lib  pub  usr
# grep ftp /etc/passwd
ftp:x:102:1:Anonymous FTP:/export/ftp:/bin/true
```

When running a public anonymous FTP server, you should disable non-anonymous FTP access to help protect any other user accounts from attack via FTP; you can do so by adding the following entry to `/etc/ftpd/ftpaccess`:

```
# echo 'defaultserver    deny    *' >>/etc/ftpd/ftpaccess
```

At this point the service is ready for use, so you can enable it:

```
# svcadm enable ftp
```

Any files you want to distribute via anonymous FTP can be copied to `/export/ftp/pub`; users can then log in to the FTP service using the `ftp` account, supply their e-mail address as a password, and download files from `/pub`.

Network Time Protocol

All modern operating systems provide a clock to record the time of events in logs, place a timestamp on files, and provide job-scheduling functions, among other uses. However, some hardware and operating systems are better at keeping time than others, and if you aren't careful, your systems can easily end up with clocks that differ by seconds or minutes, possibly even hours. *Clock skew*, the name for this condition, can cause significant operational problems, as many administrative operations are scheduled to occur at specific times. Accurate timekeeping can be especially important in security protocols, which often use cryptographic algorithms that depend on accurate clocks to prevent replay attacks.

The Network Time Protocol (NTP) was developed to provide accurate time to an operating system from highly accurate clock sources and to synchronize the clocks of other systems on a network to systems that have accurate clocks. OpenSolaris, like most operating systems, includes the open source NTP reference implementation, developed cooperatively through a project hosted at the University of Delaware. A great deal of information on the protocol and project is available from its main website, `http://ntp.org`. As of this writing, OpenSolaris includes NTP version 3 software, while the documentation on the `ntp.org` website is primarily based on the more recent version 4.

On OpenSolaris, the NTP configuration is stored in the file `/etc/inet/ntp.conf`. You can get full details on the configuration options available in this file by reviewing the `xntpd(1M)` man page, which is the name of the executable daemon program. To configure your system to use the U.S.A. public servers specified on the `ntp.org` website, create the `ntp.conf` file with the following contents:

```
driftfile /var/ntp/ntp.drift
server 0.us.pool.ntp.org
server 1.us.pool.ntp.org
server 2.us.pool.ntp.org
server 3.us.pool.ntp.org
server pool.ntp.org
```

Once you've done that, simply enable the SMF service for NTP:

```
# svcadm enable network/ntp
```

You can use the `ntpq` command to verify that NTP has found servers and is working, as follows:

```
# ntpq -p
```

remote	refid	st	t	when	poll	reach	delay	offset	disp
NTP.MCAST.NET	0.0.0.0	16	-	-	64	0	0.00	0.000	16000.0
+mail.ggong.info	tick.ucla.edu	2	u	223	256	377	90.81	0.952	1.45
+server.donkeyfl	bonehed.lcs.mit	2	u	41	256	377	22.78	-1.585	1.24
-mirror	ntp-2.gw.uiuc.e	3	u	13	512	377	47.74	11.288	2.73
-sulaco.textdriv	clock.isc.org	2	u	590	1024	357	60.87	-11.906	0.64
*8.15.10.42	clock.xmission.	2	u	181	256	377	23.96	1.341	0.32

The last server listed is preceded with an asterisk (*), which means that it has been selected for synchronization and thus NTP is working properly. See the `ntpq(1M)` man page for information on interpreting the details of this table.

If you are operating a home or small office network, configure just one server system this way, and then use it as your own local time server, configuring any other clients to reference it, to prevent overloading the public NTP servers. In addition, consider making your server available as part of the public NTP server pool — instructions are included on the `support.ntp.org` site referenced earlier.

> **CROSS-REF** See Chapter 11 for an example of configuring a group of related systems as NTP peers for Kerberos.

Mail service

Electronic mail, or e-mail, is one of the oldest Internet applications, dating to the earliest days of the Internet. OpenSolaris, like other UNIX-like systems, includes e-mail software with the operating system. Specifically, OpenSolaris includes the sendmail(1M) transport agent, and both command-line clients such as mailx(1) and the graphical desktop mail clients Evolution and Thunderbird.

> **CROSS-REF** See Chapter 4 for information on Evolution and Thunderbird.

By default, sendmail on OpenSolaris is configured to operate only as a client, which means that processes on your system can use it to send outgoing messages, but no messages will be accepted from other systems for delivery. This configuration is preferred for most systems because it minimizes the likelihood that your system can be exploited as a conduit for the scourge of Internet junk mail or spam.

> **TIP** If you're configuring your system as a mail server, then also configure it as a DNS client, described earlier in this chapter.

To configure your system as a mail server, you must first verify that your system's hostname can be resolved correctly in the name services using the check-hostname program:

```
$ check-hostname
Hostname mailman OK: fully qualified as mailman.example.com
```

This is the output you'll see if the system name is configured properly; if the configuration is incorrect, check-hostname provides a recommended change to the system configuration, which you should make and then rerun check-hostname to verify. Once check-hostname is satisfied, you must convert sendmail's configuration to allow for remote mail service by modifying the config/local_only property of the sendmail SMF service:

```
# svccfg -s svc:/network/smtp:sendmail setprop config/local_only=false
# svcadm refresh svc:/network/smtp:sendmail
```

The sendmail configuration files are stored in /etc/mail/cf. The standard configuration supplied with OpenSolaris is suitable for most sites to begin using. Consult the sendmail documentation for information on customizing the sendmail configuration for your site's purposes.

At this point, the service is configured and can be restarted:

```
# svcadm restart svc:/network/smtp:sendmail
```

If you are going to run a mail service that is connected to the Internet, we recommend that you investigate mail-filtering software so that you can cope with the spam that will inevitably find your server. See the sendmail documentation for information on integrating mail filtering with sendmail.

Finally, consider installing POP or IMAP mailbox server software so that users can efficiently access their mailboxes with the mail client of their choice. OpenSolaris does not include POP or IMAP software as of this writing, but open source, as well as commercial, software for this purpose is easy to find. The pkg.sunfreeware.com repository includes an open source mail server in the IPSFWimap package.

HTTP

The vast majority of websites and Internet applications used today communicate using the Hypertext Transport Protocol (HTTP), making it the most important application protocol in networking. Versions of the Apache HTTP server, Sun's HTTP server, and all of the popular web application environments such as application servers and servlet engines are available as part of OpenSolaris. Chapter 23 provides details on installing and using these packages, as well as related software such as MySQL.

OpenSolaris also includes the Firefox web browser as part of the standard desktop, which is discussed in Chapter 4.

inetd

If you're familiar with UNIX or Linux operating systems, you've probably encountered the super-server known as inetd. The function of inetd is to provide a single process that listens on a set of network ports and, when data is received on that port, to invoke a service that can process the received data. This enables infrequently used services to be started only when needed, minimizing the number of processes running and system memory consumed. Constraining system resources can be helpful as a simple resource-management strategy.

CROSS-REF More sophisticated OpenSolaris resource management capabilities are described in Chapter 18.

In Solaris 10, inetd was converted to a delegated restarter in the SMF framework. It continues to provide the on-demand service invocation function, but now it's integrated with SMF so that the inetd services can be managed like any other OpenSolaris service.

CROSS-REF SMF is discussed in Chapter 13.

For those familiar with inetd on other platforms, the most noticeable effect of this change is that /etc/inetd.conf is no longer used to configure inetd services. OpenSolaris retains an inetd.conf file, but it is provided only to enable packages that expect to add a service to inetd.conf to continue to do so. Once an inetd.conf entry is added, you must convert the service definition from inetd.conf to an SMF service manifest. Fortunately, OpenSolaris provides the inetconv utility to automatically perform this conversion and import the generated SMF service manifest; the auto-import can be disabled if you want to customize the service definition after its conversion but prior to import. See the `inetconv(1M)` man page for details about using `inetconv` if you encounter a package that installs an `inetd.conf` entry. Inetd checks the `inetd.conf` file when it starts and will print a message such as the following if `inetd.conf` has been modified:

```
Jun 26 19:36:21 testsys inetd[3353]: [ID 702911 daemon.warning] Configuration
file /etc/inet/inetd.conf has been modified since inetconv was last run.
"inetconv -i /etc/inet/inetd.conf" must be run to apply any changes to
the SMF
```

Because `inetd` services are also SMF services, you can use the SMF administration commands such as `svcadm`, `svccfg`, and `svcprop` to manage them. In addition, a special command is provided for managing `inetd` services, `inetadm`, which duplicates some functions of `svcadm`: You can enable an `inetd` service using `inetadm -e` and disable it with `inetadm -d`. It also provides several options that are specific to `inetd` services.

When invoked with no options, `inetadm` displays the status of all `inetd`-managed services, as shown here:

```
ENABLED    STATE        FMRI
disabled   disabled     svc:/application/x11/xfs:default
disabled   disabled     svc:/application/x11/xvnc-inetd:default
disabled   disabled     svc:/application/print/rfc1179:default
disabled   disabled     svc:/network/finger:default
disabled   disabled     svc:/network/telnet:default
disabled   disabled     svc:/network/shell:default
disabled   disabled     svc:/network/shell:kshell
disabled   disabled     svc:/network/rexec:default
disabled   disabled     svc:/network/talk:default
disabled   disabled     svc:/network/ftp:default
disabled   disabled     svc:/network/nfs/rquota:default
disabled   disabled     svc:/network/swat:default
disabled   disabled     svc:/network/security/ktkt_warn:default
disabled   disabled     svc:/network/rpc/spray:default
disabled   disabled     svc:/network/rpc/rex:default
enabled    online       svc:/network/rpc/gss:default
disabled   disabled     svc:/network/rpc/metamh:default
disabled   disabled     svc:/network/rpc/rusers:default
disabled   disabled     svc:/network/rpc/metamed:default
disabled   disabled     svc:/network/rpc/mdcomm:default
disabled   disabled     svc:/network/rpc/rstat:default
enabled    online       svc:/network/rpc/smserver:default
disabled   disabled     svc:/network/rpc/wall:default
disabled   disabled     svc:/network/rpc/meta:default
disabled   disabled     svc:/network/login:eklogin
disabled   disabled     svc:/network/login:klogin
disabled   disabled     svc:/network/login:rlogin
disabled   disabled     svc:/network/comsat:default
```

```
disabled   disabled        svc:/network/stlisten:default
disabled   disabled        svc:/network/stdiscover:default
disabled   disabled        svc:/application/cups/in-lpd:default
```

The properties of inetd services are handled in a slightly different fashion from standard SMF services. There is a set of property defaults attached to the inetd service itself that each of its services inherits unless you override them. You can display these defaults using inetadm -p:

```
$ inetadm -p
NAME=VALUE
bind_addr=""
bind_fail_max=-1
bind_fail_interval=-1
max_con_rate=-1
max_copies=-1
con_rate_offline=-1
failrate_cnt=40
failrate_interval=60
inherit_env=TRUE
tcp_trace=FALSE
tcp_wrappers=FALSE
connection_backlog=10
```

Consult the inetd(1M) man page for details about these properties. You can modify any of these default properties using inetadm -M. For example, the following limits the connection rate for all nowait services to 10 connections per second:

```
# inetadm -M max_con_rate=10
# inetadm -p
NAME=VALUE
bind_addr=""
bind_fail_max=-1
bind_fail_interval=-1
max_con_rate=10
max_copies=-1
con_rate_offline=-1
failrate_cnt=40
failrate_interval=60
inherit_env=TRUE
tcp_trace=FALSE
tcp_wrappers=FALSE
connection_backlog=10
```

The properties of an individual service can be displayed using inetadm -l:

```
$ inetadm -l rexec
SCOPE    NAME=VALUE
         name="exec"
         endpoint_type="stream"
```

```
                          proto="tcp6only,tcp"
                          isrpc=FALSE
                          wait=FALSE
                          exec="/usr/sbin/in.rexecd"
                          user="root"
          default  bind_addr=""
          default  bind_fail_max=-1
          default  bind_fail_interval=-1
          default  max_con_rate=10
          default  max_copies=-1
          default  con_rate_offline=-1
          default  failrate_cnt=40
          default  failrate_interval=60
          default  inherit_env=TRUE
          default  tcp_trace=FALSE
          default  tcp_wrappers=FALSE
          default  connection_backlog=10
```

Table 9-1 describes the per-service properties. See the inetd(1M) man page for details about the inheritable properties.

TABLE 9-1

inetd Service Properties

Property Name	Description
name	Service name, used to specify the port or RPC program number on which inetd will listen. Must be available in the /etc/services table for non-RPC services, in the /etc/rpc table for RPC services.
endpoint_type	Socket type, usually stream for TCP services, dgram for UDP services, tli for RPC services
proto	Protocols for service: tcp for TCPv6, tcp6only for TCPv6
isrpc	True for RPC services
wait	True for wait services, which inetd must handle specially. A service that has endpoint_type dgram must be a wait service.
exec	Executable path inetd invokes when data is received for this service
user	User identity from /etc/passwd to use when running the executable

Any of the properties, including the inherited defaults, can be modified on any inetd service using inetadm -m:

```
# inetadm -m rexec max_con_rate=-1
# inetadm -l rexec
```

```
SCOPE     NAME=VALUE
          name="exec"
          endpoint_type="stream"
          proto="tcp6only,tcp"
          isrpc=FALSE
          wait=FALSE
          exec="/usr/sbin/in.rexecd"
          user="root"
default   bind_addr=""
default   bind_fail_max=-1
default   bind_fail_interval=-1
          max_con_rate=-1
default   max_copies=-1
default   con_rate_offline=-1
default   failrate_cnt=40
default   failrate_interval=60
default   inherit_env=TRUE
default   tcp_trace=FALSE
default   tcp_wrappers=FALSE
default   connection_backlog=10
```

The functionality of the `tcp_wrappers` property is discussed in the next section.

OpenSolaris As a Router or Firewall

In addition to behaving as a network client and server, OpenSolaris can also serve as a network router and firewall. Many organizations purchase dedicated special-purpose hardware to perform these functions, but OpenSolaris' functionality might be suitable for your environment.

Routing

When computer systems are attached to the same physical network, they can communicate with each other directly by sending packets on the network medium, whether it's wired or wireless. When the systems are attached to different networks, an intermediate system, called a *router*, must be used to forward data from one network to another. On the Internet, there can be several, perhaps dozens, of routers along the path from one system to another. In order for your system to exchange data with other networks across a router, it must be aware that the router exists, and know for which networks the router can accept traffic for forwarding, as not all routers can accept traffic for all destinations. You must configure routing in some way, regardless of whether your system will operate as a router — otherwise, it can only contact systems on the same network. In addition, if your system is to operate as a router, it must be configured to forward packets; otherwise, any traffic directed to it by systems for routing will be discarded.

IP forwarding

By default, OpenSolaris is configured to not provide forwarding of IP packets, because most systems do not operate as routers, but instead are end systems connected to only a single network at a time; you should not enable forwarding unless your system is configured as a router. You can view your system's forwarding configuration using the routeadm(1M) command:

```
$ routeadm -p ipv4-forwarding
persistent=disabled default=disabled current=disabled
```

To enable forwarding, use routeadm -e:

```
# routeadm -e ipv4-forwarding
# routeadm -p ipv4-forwarding
persistent=enabled default=disabled current=disabled
```

Note that the persistent configuration was changed to enabled, but it isn't yet the current, running configuration. To make the persistent configuration current, use routeadm -u:

```
# routeadm -u
# routeadm -p ipv4-forwarding
persistent=enabled default=disabled current=enabled
```

You can also disable IPv4 forwarding using routeadm -d, and apply it with routeadm -u:

```
# routeadm -d ipv4-forwarding
# routeadm -p ipv4-forwarding
persistent=disabled default=disabled current=enabled
# routeadm -u
# routeadm -p ipv4-forwarding
persistent=disabled default=disabled current=disabled
```

Static IP routing

Static routing, so called because the routes are not changed automatically in response to routing protocol messages, is the most basic type of routing on OpenSolaris. Static routing is configured with the route command. To add a route, use route add, supplying the destination system or network and the address of the next-hop router:

```
# route add net 192.168.2.0/24 10.0.2.10
add net 192.168.2.0: gateway 10.0.2.10
```

You can verify the route is installed using route get, supplying the address of the network or a system on the network:

```
# route get 192.168.2.0
   route to: 192.168.2.0
destination: 192.168.2.0
       mask: 255.255.255.0
    gateway: 10.0.2.10
  interface: e1000g0
      flags: <UP,GATEWAY,DONE,STATIC>
 recvpipe  sendpipe  ssthresh     rtt,ms rttvar,ms  hopcount        mtu     expire
        0         0         0          0         0         0       1500          0
```

Delete a route using `route delete`:

```
# route delete 192.168.2.0/24 10.0.2.10
delete net 192.168.2.0: gateway 10.0.2.10
```

Verify the deletion with `route get`:

```
# route get 192.168.2.0
192.168.2.0: not in table
```

> **TIP** Routes configured with the `route` command are temporary and will be lost when the system is rebooted. Configuration of persistent static routes must be done using the `/etc/gateways` file, in combination with enabling the `in.routed` daemon via the `svc:/network/routing/route:default` service. See `gateways(4)` for details on static route configuration, and the example later in this section to set up `in.routed`.

However, even after deleting the route, systems on that network may still be reachable, as demonstrated by the following:

```
# route get 192.168.2.1
   route to: 192.168.2.1
destination: default
       mask: default
    gateway: 10.0.2.2
  interface: e1000g0
      flags: <UP,GATEWAY,DONE,STATIC>
 recvpipe sendpipe ssthresh   rtt,ms rttvar,ms hopcount      mtu    expire
        0        0        0        0        0        0     1500        0
```

What's going on here? The answer is that the system has a configured default router, which is the router of last resort. If no more specific route to a network can be found, the default router is used. OpenSolaris, like all systems with IP networking, maintains a routing table in the kernel, which is used to assign outgoing traffic to the correct interface. You can view the routing table with the `netstat -r` command. The routing table on an OpenSolaris client system usually appears similar to the following table:

```
$ netstat -r
Routing Table: IPv4
  Destination          Gateway           Flags  Ref   Use    Interface
-------------------- -------------------- ----- ----- ---------- ---------
default              10.0.2.2             UG      1        0 e1000g0
10.0.2.0             10.0.2.15            U       1        3 e1000g0
opensolaris          opensolaris          UH      1      315 lo0

Routing Table: IPv6
  Destination/Mask     Gateway                    Flags Ref  Use  If
-------------------- --------------------         ----- --- ------- -----
localhost            localhost                    UH    1       0 lo0
```

You may be wondering how that default route was configured. If you configure a network interface using DHCP, and the DHCP server supplies a `Router` option in its response, then the OpenSolaris DHCP client automatically installs that default route into the kernel. If you're using static IP address configuration, you can create the file `/etc/defaultrouter`, which lists the addresses of any default routers, one per line, and these routes are added during system boot; see `defaultrouter(4)` for more information.

Note that you can have more than one default route, or more than one route to any destination; in a well-designed network, this will often be the case. The following example routing table shows a system that is routing between three different networks using static routes (the `-n` option to `netstat` prevents it from translating IP addresses to names):

```
# netstat -nr

Routing Table: IPv4
  Destination          Gateway            Flags  Ref    Use      Interface
-------------------- -------------------- ----- ----- ---------- ---------
default              68.189.244.1         UG       1   12510876 dmfe1
default              10.10.10.254         UG       1   8772019
10.10.10.0           10.10.10.1           U        1       4618 dmfe1:2
68.189.244.0         68.189.244.104       U        1       6567 dmfe1
192.168.1.0          192.168.1.7          U        1      53697 dmfe0
224.0.0.0            192.168.1.7          U        1          0 dmfe0
127.0.0.1            127.0.0.1            UH       2       2565 lo0
```

Dynamic IP routing

Static routes can be useful, but administrators must update them when the network topology changes. To ease the maintenance burden, a number of routing protocols have been developed for the Internet, with names such as RIP, BGP, and OSPF. If you're setting up a network of any appreciable size, strongly consider using dynamic routing.

The OpenSolaris distribution includes two dynamic routing packages. The simple `in.routed` daemon is installed as part of the default installation in package `SUNWroute` and is managed under the SMF service `svc:/network/routing/route:default`; it uses the RIP protocol to exchange routes between routers. A much more powerful routing service, known as Quagga, is available from the OpenSolaris package repository under the name `SUNWquagga`. You can install it using the following command:

```
# pkg install SUNWquagga
```

Quagga is an open source project hosted at `http://quagga.net`. It provides a sophisticated routing service that runs on UNIX systems and includes support for current versions of RIP, BGP, and OSPF. To use RIP as your routing protocol, you can use either `in.routed` or Quagga; otherwise, you need to use Quagga. This book does not cover Quagga configuration details.

Configuring a dynamic router

You can view the routing service configuration with routeadm; the following default output displays the configuration for both routing and forwarding services:

```
# routeadm
             Configuration   Current        Current
                    Option   Configuration  System State
          --------------------------------------------------------
             IPv4 routing    disabled       disabled
             IPv6 routing    disabled       disabled
          IPv4 forwarding    disabled       disabled
          IPv6 forwarding    disabled       disabled

         Routing services    "route:default ripng:default"

Routing daemons:

                     STATE   FMRI
                    online   svc:/network/routing/ndp:default
                  disabled   svc:/network/routing/ripng:default
                  disabled   svc:/network/routing/ripng:quagga
                  disabled   svc:/network/routing/rdisc:default
                  disabled   svc:/network/routing/route:default
                  disabled   svc:/network/routing/legacy-routing:ipv4
                  disabled   svc:/network/routing/legacy-routing:ipv6
                  disabled   svc:/network/routing/zebra:quagga
                  disabled   svc:/network/routing/rip:quagga
                  disabled   svc:/network/routing/ospf:quagga
                  disabled   svc:/network/routing/ospf6:quagga
                  disabled   svc:/network/routing/bgp:quagga
```

This system has the Quagga package installed, but for this example you enable only the standard in.routed routing service. First, modify the routing services setting to include only route:default (the ripng:default service is used for routing IPv6 packets, which is not part of this example):

```
# routeadm -s routing-svcs="route:default"
```

Next, enable IPv4 routing and forwarding, and apply the configuration to the system:

```
# routeadm -e ipv4-forwarding
# routeadm -e ipv4-routing
# routeadm -u
```

You can view the routing configuration using routeadm:

```
# routeadm
             Configuration   Current        Current
                    Option   Configuration  System State
```

```
  ----------------------------------------------------------------
          IPv4 routing     enabled               enabled
          IPv6 routing     disabled              disabled
      IPv4 forwarding      enabled               enabled
      IPv6 forwarding      disabled              disabled

      Routing services     "route:default"

Routing daemons:

                 STATE     FMRI
                online     svc:/network/routing/ndp:default
              disabled     svc:/network/routing/ripng:default
              disabled     svc:/network/routing/ripng:quagga
              disabled     svc:/network/routing/rdisc:default
                online     svc:/network/routing/route:default
              disabled     svc:/network/routing/legacy-routing:ipv4
              disabled     svc:/network/routing/legacy-routing:ipv6
              disabled     svc:/network/routing/zebra:quagga
              disabled     svc:/network/routing/rip:quagga
              disabled     svc:/network/routing/ospf:quagga
              disabled     svc:/network/routing/ospf6:quagga
              disabled     svc:/network/routing/bgp:quagga
```

IP routing configuration and management is a fairly complex topic that extends well beyond the scope of this book. To manage RIP effectively, not to mention the more advanced protocols such as BGP and OSPF, you will definitely need to spend some time learning about the details of their configuration. For this, you can consult the in.routed(1M) and quagga(8) man pages and the Quagga documentation. See also the "Resources" section at the end of this chapter for references.

Configuring a firewall with IP filter

Systems connected to the Internet need to be protected against a variety of attacks against any network services they are running. Chapter 11 discusses the extensive array of security features built into OpenSolaris, but one concept in networking security that's particularly important is the idea of *defense in depth*. The Secure by Default (SBD) feature limits the set of network services on OpenSolaris that is enabled by default, and thus vulnerable to attack. However, a second level of security can be provided through the use of a *firewall*. The function of a firewall is to block network traffic from reaching any applications or services unless explicitly allowed. All modern operating systems include some form of firewall software, and they all operate on the same basic principle: Packets that are received or sent on a network interface are inspected, the contents of each packet are compared against a set of rules, and the packet is blocked or passed based on the matching rules. Thus, even if you have a network service running on your system, you can use a firewall to restrict who may use it to only a select group of systems or networks, and you can use the firewall to restrict what outgoing traffic may be sent.

The OpenSolaris firewall function is provided by the IP Filter software, an open source implementation that is also included on variants of BSD UNIX and can be used on most other UNIX-like operating systems, including Linux. IP Filter provides two closely related features: packet filtering and Network Address Translation (NAT). NAT is a technique that enables multiple systems to appear to share a single IP address. It's commonly used on the public Internet by individuals or small organizations to set up a private network that can access the Internet within the home or office. However, rather than obtain a block of public IP addresses, which can be expensive, only a single IP address for the organization's router is purchased from the Internet service provider. That address is shared by the router's software with the systems inside the private network. Virtually all modern routers include NAT software. Note that you can run a filtering firewall without using NAT, and vice versa, but often you will run both. On OpenSolaris, for most purposes, the Secure by Default configuration installed makes it unnecessary to run a filtering firewall on each system. However, if you need to enable additional network services on your system, consider running a filtering firewall.

> **NOTE** A simplified firewall configuration capability for OpenSolaris is currently under development.

The example in this section uses both filtering and NAT together, on a system configured as an IPv4 router; see the "Routing" section for examples of routing configuration. This example uses a system with the following network interface configuration:

```
# ifconfig -a
lo0: flags=2001000849<UP,LOOPBACK,RUNNING,MULTICAST,IPv4,VIRTUAL> mtu 8232
 index 1
    inet 127.0.0.1 netmask ff000000
e1000g0: flags=201104843<UP,BROADCAST,RUNNING,MULTICAST,ROUTER,IPv4
,CoS> mtu 1500 index 2
    inet 10.0.2.15 netmask ffffff00 broadcast 10.0.2.255
    ether 8:0:27:2f:10:81
e1000g1: flags=201100843<UP,BROADCAST,RUNNING,MULTICAST,ROUTER,IPv4
,CoS> mtu 1500 index 3
    inet 192.168.2.1 netmask ffffff00 broadcast 192.168.2.255
    ether 8:0:27:36:98:af
```

The e1000g0 interface is connected to the public network, while the e1000g1 interface is connected to the private network.

IP Filter is disabled by default on OpenSolaris and requires configuration before it can be enabled and used. First, configure the packet filtering rules, which are stored in the configuration file /etc/ipf/ipf.conf. Here is an example ipf.conf:

```
#
# ipf.conf
#
# IP Filter rules to be loaded during startup
#
# See ipf(4) manpage for more information on
```

```
# IP Filter rules syntax.
#
# Filter set for firewalled router between external net and internal

# Block everything from outside network by default
block in log on e1000g0 all
block return-rst in log on e1000g0 proto tcp from any to any

# Allow ssh and http in
pass in quick on e1000g0 proto tcp from any to e1000g0/32 port = 22
pass in quick on e1000g0 proto tcp from any to e1000g0/32 port = 80

# Allow any connections initiated from this system or the private network
pass out quick on e1000g0 proto tcp/udp from 192.168.2.0/24 to any keep state
pass out quick on e1000g0 proto icmp from 192.168.2.0/24 to any keep state
pass out quick on e1000g0 proto tcp/udp from 10.0.2.15/32 to any keep state
pass out quick on e1000g0 proto icmp from 10.0.2.15/32 to any keep state
```

Complete documentation of the `ipf.conf(4)` syntax is provided in its man page. Conceptually, each rule is specified as follows:

```
action direction filter
```

A number of actions can be specified, but most often the action is either `block` or `pass`. A blocked packet is discarded unless otherwise specified, whereas a passed packet is forwarded up the networking stack. The direction must be either `in` or `out`, corresponding to whether the packet is being received or sent, respectively. The filter specifies packet characteristics that must be matched to apply the action; you can filter based on a network interface, an IP address, a protocol, or a port number.

The most important thing to understand about IP Filter's filtering behavior is that it will match each packet against the entire set of filter rules in the order they appear in the file, and the last matching rule will be applied. This complete matching can be short-circuited, however, using the `quick` option to a filter, which means that if the rule is matched to a packet, then the matching process concludes and the action specified by the rule is taken immediately.

The preceding rule set is designed to block incoming traffic from the external network (network 10.0.0.0, on `e1000g0`) except for the explicitly permitted services. Outgoing traffic originating from either the internal 192.168.2.0 network or the local system is permitted. A detailed explanation of each section of the rule set follows.

The first section applies the default blocking rules:

```
# Block everything from outside by default
block in log on e1000g0 all
block return-rst in log on e1000g0 proto tcp from any to any
```

The first rule blocks all packets received on `e1000g0`; the log option in the rule causes each packet to be recorded in IP Filter's packet log device, which can be monitored using the `ipmon` utility. The second rule applies an alternate blocking behavior for any TCP traffic received on e1000g0. The `return-rst` option to the action in this rule causes IP Filter to generate a reply packet that has the TCP reset flag set. The other end of the connection interprets such a response as a refused connection, which is friendlier than just dropping the packet; a lack of response causes the other end to keep retrying, perhaps indefinitely, because the lack of response may indicate that the network is disrupted in some way, or that the end system is down. Both the resulting user experience and extra network load are undesirable.

The next section of the rule set allows incoming traffic on the e1000g0 interface for services that are to be visible to the outside network:

```
# Allow ssh and http in
pass in quick on e1000g0 proto tcp from any to e1000g0/32 port = 22
pass in quick on e1000g0 proto tcp from any to e1000g0/32 port = 80
```

The only two services allowed in are `ssh` and `http`, which use these ports. Note the use of the `quick` option to each of these actions, ensuring that no further filtering will be applied.

> **TIP** The port and protocol for most standard services can be found by consulting the `/etc/services` file. See `services(4)` for more information.

The final section of the rule set restricts outgoing traffic to the outside network:

```
# Allow any connections initiated from this system or the private network
pass out quick on e1000g0 proto tcp/udp from 192.168.2.0/24 to any keep state
pass out quick on e1000g0 proto icmp from 192.168.2.0/24 to any keep state
pass out quick on e1000g0 proto tcp/udp from 10.0.2.15/32 to any keep state
pass out quick on e1000g0 proto icmp from 10.0.2.15/32 to any keep state
```

As no restrictions are desired on either this system or any of the systems on the inside network, the four rules allow any traffic to be sent to any recipient. The `keep state` option to the filters is critical, because IP Filter recognizes responses to outgoing traffic and allows it to pass, even though the other rules restricting incoming traffic would cause it to be blocked.

> **CAUTION** Internet addresses can be faked, or spoofed. Do not rely exclusively on IP address filtering, but make your traffic filters as specific as possible, so that they limit your network's vulnerability to spoofing attacks.

If the 192.168.2.0 network is registered in the external network's routing tables so that systems on that network can reach it, then the preceding filtering would be sufficient to protect the internal network while allowing it to communicate. However, it's more likely that the internal network is a private address space that is not visible to the external network. In that case, it's necessary to configure this system as a NAT gateway to convert the addresses on the internal network into addresses on the gateway system, so that the external network responses can be routed back. The NAT configuration is placed in `/etc/ipf/ipnat.conf`, and for this example configuration the NAT rules are very simple:

```
# Simple NAT configuration
```

```
map dmfe1 192.168.2.0/24 -> 10.0.2.15/32 portmap tcp/udp 40000:60000
map dmfe1 192.168.2.0/24 -> 10.0.2.15/32
```

The first rule causes all TCP and UDP traffic from the internal network to be remapped into the gateway's port range between 40000 and 60000. This potentially restricts the number of simultaneous connections from each of those addresses, but unless you have an unusually active inside network connecting to many outside hosts, such a configuration will likely be sufficient; you can extend the port range if needed. The second rule causes ICMP traffic to have only its source address rewritten. See ipnat.conf(4) for details on the NAT configuration options available with IP Filter.

Once you have created the configuration files for IP Filter, you can enable it with the svcadm command:

```
# svcadm enable ipfilter
```

If you modify the IP Filter configuration, you can reload the configuration using svcadm:

```
# svcadm refresh ipfilter
```

IP Filter includes several management and monitoring commands:

- ipf(1M) is used to manage the filter rules.
- ipnat(1M) is used to manage the NAT rules.
- ipfstat(1M) can be used to view filtering statistics.
- ipmon(1M) can be used to view the packet filter logs.

Consult the man pages for each of these commands for more information on their usage and options.

TCP Wrappers

In addition to IP Filter, OpenSolaris includes an alternate network access control technology, called *TCP Wrappers*. It can be used to monitor an incoming request for a specific service and apply access control based on the client's address. If your requirements for service access control are met by TCP Wrappers, it may be preferable to IP Filter because it imposes a cost only on the services configured to use it. By contrast, a network packet filter such as IP Filter must inspect every packet entering the system to provide protection, which can affect performance on very busy systems. See the tcpd(1M) man page for general information on TCP Wrappers.

The most common use of TCP Wrappers is to provide network access control for inetd services. You can enable TCP Wrappers support for either a single inetd service or for all inetd services using inetadm. To enable TCP Wrappers for all inetd services, use inetadm -M:

```
# inetadm -M tcp_wrappers=TRUE
# inetadm -p
```

```
NAME=VALUE
bind_addr=""
bind_fail_max=-1
bind_fail_interval=-1
max_con_rate=-1
max_copies=-1
con_rate_offline=-1
failrate_cnt=40
failrate_interval=60
inherit_env=TRUE
tcp_trace=FALSE
tcp_wrappers=TRUE
connection_backlog=10
```

To enable TCP Wrappers for only a single service, such as telnet, use inetadm -m:

```
# inetadm -m telnet tcp_wrappers=true
# inetadm -l telnet
SCOPE     NAME=VALUE
          name="telnet"
          endpoint_type="stream"
          proto="tcp6"
          isrpc=FALSE
          wait=FALSE
          exec="/usr/sbin/in.telnetd"
          user="root"
default   bind_addr=""
default   bind_fail_max=-1
default   bind_fail_interval=-1
default   max_con_rate=-1
default   max_copies=-1
default   con_rate_offline=-1
default   failrate_cnt=40
default   failrate_interval=60
default   inherit_env=TRUE
default   tcp_trace=FALSE
          tcp_wrappers=TRUE
default   connection_backlog=10
```

TCP Wrappers is configured by a pair of files, /etc/hosts.allow and /etc/hosts.deny. To deny access to telnet to all hosts except those in the local DNS domain (example.com for this example), use the following rules:

1. Configure /etc/hosts.deny to deny all clients:

   ```
   in.telnetd: ALL
   ```

2. Configure /etc/hosts.allow to allow example.com:

   ```
   in.telnetd: .example.com
   ```

TCP Wrappers is capable of extensive access control checks and can invoke additional commands when a protected service is accessed. Consult the hosts_access(4) man page for detailed information.

Troubleshooting

Modern networks are very complex, with many components involved in shepherding packets from one system to another. In spite of this complexity, networks are quite reliable, especially when technologies such as IPMP and redundant routers are used to eliminate single points of failure. Nonetheless, failures occur, and being able to diagnose the root cause is an important skill. OpenSolaris provides several tools to investigate networking problems. In earlier sections of this chapter you learned about some protocol-specific tools such as dig; in this section you'll learn about the basic tools that can be used to observe TCP/IP network behavior.

netstat

The netstat command has long been a standard diagnostic tool for networking problems on UNIX systems. Earlier sections of this chapter demonstrated the use of netstat for examining DHCP transactions and routing tables, but other options can be used to examine active connections and statistics for the protocols or interfaces.

Coincidentally, when readying this chapter, I was the victim of a serious network failure due to a lightning strike. Once the ISP's network had recovered after a number of hours and the cable modem had reconnected, the system was unable to obtain an address using DHCP. A brief investigation led to the diagnosis. First, the output of netstat -D indicated that the DHCP operation was in progress, but no replies had been received:

```
# netstat -D
Interface   State        Sent  Recv  Declined  Flags
dmfe1       SELECTING      23    0          0  [BUSY]
```

Inspecting the interface more completely with netstat -i:

```
# netstat -i -I dmfe1
Name  Mtu  Net/Dest   Address    Ipkts  Ierrs Opkts  Oerrs Collis Queue
dmfe1 1500 0.0.0.0    0.0.0.0      0      0     0      25    0     0
```

The lack of any statistics other than output errors (Oerrs) indicates a serious problem: neither incoming nor outgoing packets are being transmitted, and all packets being transmitted are causing errors. This indicates an issue with the link, which the output of ifconfig also confirms:

```
# ifconfig dmfe1
dmfe1: flags=201104803<UP,BROADCAST,MULTICAST,DHCP,ROUTER,IPv4,CoS> mtu 1500
   index 3
```

```
inet 0.0.0.0 netmask ff000000
ether 0:3:ba:c:14:d8
```

The lack of the RUNNING flag on the interface indicates that the driver is not detecting an active link, and inspection of the system (an old Sun Netra X1) confirmed that the link LED for the interface was not lit. Swapping cables and connecting the cable modem to a different system, as well as a different cable modem to this system, led to the ultimate diagnosis, which turned out to be two failures: a failed network interface on the cable modem and a failed network interface on the OpenSolaris system.

ping and traceroute

Two more network diagnostic commands commonly found on UNIX systems are ping and traceroute. Both use ICMP, the Internet Control Message Protocol, to diagnose Internet connectivity.

Ping is used to determine the reachability of another system and the round-trip time for traffic to it; the latter measures *network latency*, the time required for a packet to reach its destination, which is a key determining factor in network performance. On OpenSolaris, ping with no options merely determines reachability:

```
$ ping www.yahoo.com
www.yahoo.com is alive
```

On Linux systems, ping with no options sends a request once per second and reports statistics; to obtain the equivalent behavior on OpenSolaris, you must use the -s option:

```
$ ping -s www.charter.net
PING www.charter.net: 56 data bytes
64 bytes from 64-192-190-12.wcg.net (64.192.190.12): icmp_seq=0. time=25.183 ms
64 bytes from 64-192-190-12.wcg.net (64.192.190.12): icmp_seq=1. time=23.589 ms
64 bytes from 64-192-190-12.wcg.net (64.192.190.12): icmp_seq=2. time=23.872 ms
64 bytes from 64-192-190-12.wcg.net (64.192.190.12): icmp_seq=3. time=23.958 ms
64 bytes from 64-192-190-12.wcg.net (64.192.190.12): icmp_seq=4. time=24.643 ms
64 bytes from 64-192-190-12.wcg.net (64.192.190.12): icmp_seq=5. time=24.032 ms
64 bytes from 64-192-190-12.wcg.net (64.192.190.12): icmp_seq=6. time=25.617 ms
64 bytes from 64-192-190-12.wcg.net (64.192.190.12): icmp_seq=7. time=23.677 ms
64 bytes from 64-192-190-12.wcg.net (64.192.190.12): icmp_seq=8. time=23.770 ms
64 bytes from 64-192-190-12.wcg.net (64.192.190.12): icmp_seq=9. time=24.023 ms
64 bytes from 64-192-190-12.wcg.net (64.192.190.12): icmp_seq=10. time=24.033 ms
64 bytes from 64-192-190-12.wcg.net (64.192.190.12): icmp_seq=11. time=23.551 ms
64 bytes from 64-192-190-12.wcg.net (64.192.190.12): icmp_seq=12. time=24.049 ms
64 bytes from 64-192-190-12.wcg.net (64.192.190.12): icmp_seq=13. time=25.062 ms
64 bytes from 64-192-190-12.wcg.net (64.192.190.12): icmp_seq=14. time=23.909 ms
^C
----www.charter.net PING Statistics----
```

```
15 packets transmitted, 15 packets received, 0% packet loss
round-trip (ms)  min/avg/max/stddev = 23.551/24.198/25.617/0.628
```

Widely variable round-trip times or loss of a significant percentage of packets can indicate network instability that may require further investigation. If so, traceroute should be the next tool you use — it can help determine which hop on the path between the systems is at fault:

```
$ traceroute -n www.charter.net
traceroute: Warning: Multiple interfaces found; using 192.168.1.7 @ dmfe0
traceroute to www.charter.net (64.192.190.12), 30 hops max, 40 byte packets
 1  192.168.1.1  0.727 ms  0.570 ms  0.568 ms
 2  10.85.0.1  11.802 ms  6.751 ms  7.431 ms
 3  172.20.15.49  8.366 ms  9.028 ms  9.630 ms
 4  172.20.15.26  10.062 ms  10.917 ms  9.239 ms
 5  65.124.189.105  17.112 ms  17.192 ms  17.229 ms
 6  205.171.30.93  17.281 ms  16.962 ms  15.410 ms
 7  67.14.5.162  16.831 ms  17.030 ms  15.154 ms
 8  63.237.128.170  25.031 ms  25.261 ms  23.441 ms
 9  * * *
10  * * *
```

In this case the destination system isn't responding to the ICMP requests used by traceroute (apparently it's configured not to do so), but all of the hops prior to that point are operating correctly.

Snoop

When diagnosing network problems, it's often useful, and sometimes necessary, to directly inspect the network traffic; for this OpenSolaris includes the snoop command as its packet capture and decoding utility. You can use snoop in two ways: The first is to display captured packets in real time, while the second is to capture packets to a file and then decode them later. For detailed problem analysis, capturing to a file is usually the preferred option; real-time display is most useful for quick inspection of whether traffic of a certain type is arriving or being sent.

Here is the simplest use of snoop to capture and display traffic in real time:

```
# snoop
Using device dmfe0 (promiscuous mode)
client-30.2great.com -> netra        TCP D=22 S=61598 Ack=1351882141
  Seq=1438228666 Len=0 Win=32806 Options=<nop,nop,tstamp 647025 9391886>
    clint-19 -> proxy-outbound-32b.kewr0.s.vonagenetworks.net UDP D=10000
S=5061 LEN=625
      clint -> clint-19     ICMP Redirect (for host proxy-outbound-32b.kewr0
.s.vonagenetworks.net to linksys.2great.com)
    clint-19 -> proxy-outbound-32b.kewr0.s.vonagenetworks.net UDP D=10000
S=5061 LEN=625
```

```
proxy-outbound-32b.kewr0.s.vonagenetworks.net -> clint-19    UDP D=5061
  S=10000 LEN=457
```

In this mode, `snoop` selects the first physical network interface, places it in promiscuous mode to capture all traffic seen by the interface, and displays a summarized interpretation of the highest-level protocol that it can recognize in the packet. If you have multiple network interfaces, you can specify the interface using the -d option. To capture to a file, use the `-o` option and specify the filename:

```
# snoop -d dmfe0 -o /tmp/trace
Using device dmfe0 (promiscuous mode)
14
```

While capturing to a file, `snoop` displays the count of packets captured. You can then inspect the capture file using `snoop -i`:

```
# snoop -i /tmp/trace
...
20   0.08831        clint -> ntp.LogicX.net NTP  client [st=3]
(2008-07-01 21:56:56.92521)
21   0.01776 ntp.LogicX.net -> clint        NTP   server [st=2]
(2008-07-01 21:56:56.92329)
22   0.83377        clint -> clint-30.2great.com TCP D=61598 S=22 Push
Ack=1438231354 Seq=1351886317 Len=64 Win=32806 Options=<nop,nop,tstamp
9490373 745420>
23   0.06050 clint-30.2great.com -> clint        TCP D=22 S=61598
Ack=1351886381 Seq=1438231354 Len=0 Win=32806 Options=<nop,nop,tstamp
745521 9490373>
```

These examples captured and displayed all traffic on an interface. It's usually more useful to include some filtering, either to the packets captured or to the packets displayed. For example, the following captures only DHCP traffic:

```
# snoop -d dmfe0 dhcp
Using device dmfe0 (promiscuous mode)
        hugo -> nitro          DHCP/BOOTP DHCPREQUEST
        nitro -> hugo          DHCP/BOOTP DHCPACK
```

You can specify filters based on source or destination IP address (using hostnames, if that is more convenient), a protocol such as TCP or UDP, port number, MAC address, or packet length, among other packet characteristics. See the `snoop(1M)` man page for details about the filter expressions. You can also display more detailed output using the `-V` and `-v` options, which decode the packet more completely. Finally, the `-x` option can be used to dump the raw bytes from the packet for a truly detailed inspection. See the man page for a more detailed description of these options and more examples of using `snoop`.

NOTE If you prefer to use a graphical interface for network traffic inspection, you can obtain the Wireshark, also known as Ethereal, program from the `sunfreeware.com` package repository; see `http://sunfreeware.com` for information.

SNMP

The Simple Network Management Protocol (SNMP) can be used to diagnose networking problems on remote systems. This book does not cover SNMP, but OpenSolaris does include an SNMP agent based on the Net-SNMP distribution; for more information on the agent, see the project's home page at `www.net-snmp.org` and the `snmpd(1M)` man page. The OpenSolaris agent is managed by SMF as the service `svc:/application/management/sma:default`.

Resources

Current projects in OpenSolaris networking can be tracked via the Networking community's website, `http://opensolaris.org/os/community/networking`.

Renaming of network interfaces is discussed in an article at `http://sun.com/bigadmin/sundocs/articles/vnamingsol.jsp`.

Sun's main documentation on network interface administration can be found in the *IP Services Administration Guide* at `http://docs.sun.com/app/docs/doc/819-3000`.

Sun documents many of the Solaris network services in the *System Administration Guide: Network Services* at `http://docs.sun.com/app/docs/doc/819-1634`.

The Internet Systems Consortium (ISC) website at `http://isc.org` provides source code and documentation for the BIND DNS server and the ISC DHCP server.

The main site for information on multicast DNS is `http://multicastdns.org`.

A good overview of the DHCP protocol and user information for the ISC DHCP server can be found in *The DHCP Handbook, Second Edition*, by Ralph Droms and Ted Lemon (Sams, 2002).

Detailed guidance in configuring and managing a mail server with `sendmail` is available in *sendmail, Fourth Edition*, by Bryan Costales, Claus Assmann, George Jansen, and Gregory Shapiro (O'Reilly, 2007).

For more information on PPP, consult *Using and Managing PPP*, by Andrew Sun (O'Reilly, 1999), and *PPP Design, Implementation, and Debugging, Second Edition*, by James D. Carlson (Addison-Wesley, 2000).

Information on the Quagga routing suite is available at its website, `http://quagga.net`.

Extensive information on the Network Time Protocol is available at `http://ntp.org`.

For further reading on TCP/IP, see *Internetworking with TCP/IP, Vol. 1, Fifth Edition*, by Douglas E. Comer (Prentice Hall, 2005).

Summary

In this chapter, you've learned how OpenSolaris network interfaces are configured and managed, including the new Network Auto-Magic (NWAM) capability for automatic configuration, and you explored features such as IPMP that are unique to OpenSolaris. You also were introduced to some of the more commonly used network services on OpenSolaris, including DNS, DHCP, FTP, NTP, routing, and firewalls. Finally, you learned about some of the most useful network troubleshooting tools on OpenSolaris.

Chapter 10

Network File Systems and Directory Services

The motivation for creating computer networks is to share information. In Chapter 9, you learned how to use the basic Internet protocols to transfer information between systems using programs such as `ftp`. However, copying files from system to system creates the problem of efficiently distributing copies and keeping them consistent. File synchronization programs exist, but it's usually more convenient to store files centrally and access them just like a file that's stored on a local disk, a concept known as a *network file system*. Sun long ago created the Network File System (NFS) to provide exactly this service. Microsoft created the Common Internet File System (CIFS) to provide similar functionality for the Windows operating system. OpenSolaris includes both client and server software for both NFS and CIFS.

In most networks of any size it's also desirable to share and synchronize system configuration data, such as user accounts, among systems. Again, it's possible to use synchronization software to distribute files such as `/etc/passwd` among a set of systems, but such a solution doesn't scale well. It's also possible to use a network file system for this purpose, but most uses of such configuration data involve searching for only a specific entry. Clearly, in such cases, having each system open a large data set and search it does not scale to an appreciable number of systems. Such solutions also limit the possibility to improve performance through caching of frequently obtained results, so the *naming service* was invented. Think of naming services as special-purpose databases that use a key value to retrieve a complete record.

The most well-known naming service is the Domain Name System (DNS) used by systems connected to the Internet to translate domain names to Internet Protocol (IP) addresses, but others have been created to solve this problem for other types of administrative data. Sun designed the Network Information Service (NIS) to provide an easy-to-use naming service for small-to-medium size environments. For environments that require an enterprise-level directory service, OpenSolaris offers the standard Lightweight Directory Access Protocol (LDAP), which was developed to provide greater flexibility and scalability than NIS can offer. Windows offers the Active Directory service for enterprise deployments, which is based on LDAP, but with proprietary extensions; OpenSolaris can work as a client of Active Directory services, but not as a server.

This chapter describes how to use the NFS, CIFS, and NIS services on OpenSolaris. A brief discussion of LDAP concludes the chapter.

CROSS-REF DNS is discussed in Chapter 9.

Introduction to NFS

The Network File System (NFS) has been the standard network file system in the UNIX industry since the 1980s, and its protocol standards are published and maintained by the Internet Engineering Task Force (IETF), which is responsible for all Internet standards. Designed originally for sharing files between UNIX systems, NFS has been ported to virtually every operating system over the last 20 years and continues to be enhanced. Sun originated this technology and continues to be a leader in its development. The NFS protocol has several versions, known as versions 2, 3, and 4, with additional versions under development. Clients and servers typically negotiate the best NFS version automatically, but be aware of the versions supported by your systems because mismatched versions can be a source of interoperability problems. OpenSolaris supports versions 2 through 4 of the NFS protocol.

As mentioned, the idea behind NFS is to make files that are stored on one system (the server) available on another system (the client) directly through the client's file system hierarchy. This means that you can use the shell's cd command to access directories on the server, and any file utilities such as more or editors such as vi to access or edit the files. As with the local file systems described in Chapters 7 and 8, this requires that the client *mount* the file system before accessing it to locate files or read or write data. Additionally, before any clients can mount a file system, the server must *share* the file system. This chapter describes the administrative tasks required to share and access files via NFS.

Introduction to CIFS

The Common Internet File System (CIFS) — also called Server Message Block (SMB), the name of the original protocol created by IBM on which CIFS is based — is the file-sharing mechanism commonly used between Windows clients and servers. It also provides printer-sharing services, though they are not currently included in the OpenSolaris CIFS implementation. While NFS can be used on both Windows clients and servers, it is not part of the standard Windows product. Because many installations have many more Windows systems than UNIX systems, the burden often falls on the UNIX systems to provide interoperability with the Windows file sharing.

Several commercial products have appeared over the years to address the need for file sharing between UNIX systems and Windows, with varying degrees of success. A major difficulty for these products has been a lack of access to details about the required Windows protocols. Another significant problem is that a number of facets of the protocols are highly dependent on Windows-specific behavior that can be difficult to emulate on a non-Windows operating system.

The most well-known solution for Windows file-sharing interoperability is the open source project called Samba, which has been developed by reverse-engineering the Windows networking and file-sharing protocols. It has been available on Solaris and OpenSolaris for many years. While quite successful, the Samba project is entirely a user-level implementation of the file-sharing function. Coupled with its design for cross-platform portability, this means that Samba is not as well integrated into the OpenSolaris file system interfaces and management model as one might like. To integrate CIFS more completely with OpenSolaris and to provide a higher level of interoperability with Windows services such as Active Directory, Sun has developed an implementation of CIFS functionality for OpenSolaris through the OpenSolaris CIFS Server, CIFS Client, and Winchester projects. If your background is with Linux or BSD UNIX, you may already be familiar with Samba and feel comfortable with its management. If so, then you may want to install the Samba package and use it in much the same way. Samba is available in the OpenSolaris package repository; see Chapter 6 for information on installing additional packages. This chapter focuses on the CIFS implementation developed by the preceding projects and included in OpenSolaris.

> **NOTE** This chapter uses the terms SMB and CIFS interchangeably. In all cases, the reference is to the native file-sharing protocols used by versions of the Microsoft Windows operating system.

The native CIFS service provides CIFS file sharing, but does not include CIFS printer sharing. If your requirements include CIFS printer sharing, you may prefer to use the Samba package. However, modern Windows clients can also be configured to use UNIX printer protocols by adding Print Services for UNIX, so this limitation may not be important.

Managing File Sharing

Since Solaris 2.0, Solaris has used the `share` command to share a directory, and OpenSolaris continues to provide this command as a basic interface. However, sharing wasn't easy to manage, as any shares set up with the `share` command are not persistent, lasting only until the system is rebooted. To set up a persistent share, users were required to edit the file `/etc/dfs/dfstab` and insert appropriate share commands, and then use the `shareall` command to activate sharing from the persistent configuration (or reboot, at which time the `shareall` command would be automatically executed). When ZFS was introduced, it included properties to manage sharing of its data sets and the zfs share and zfs unshare commands to start and stop the sharing during a particular session; this improves the management of sharing but is a ZFS-specific solution.

CROSS-REF ZFS is discussed in detail in Chapter 8.

To provide a more uniform interface to manage file sharing, OpenSolaris includes two new commands, sharemgr and sharectl. Using sharemgr, you can set up *share groups* to configure sharing of multiple file systems or directories with common properties. The sharectl command is used to configure the properties of a file sharing service, such as NFS or CIFS.

Installing sharing packages

Depending on your distribution, the NFS or CIFS services may need to be installed. On the OpenSolaris distribution, the NFS service is provided by the SUNWnfss package; you can verify whether it is installed with the following command:

```
# pkg list SUNWnfss
NAME (AUTHORITY)                        VERSION        STATE      UFIX
SUNWnfss                                0.5.11-0.86    known      ----
```

If the output of pkg list shows the package in the known state, then it must be installed using the pkg install command to enable the NFS service:

```
# pkg install SUNWnfss
```

The CIFS service is in a different package, SUNWsmbs, which must be installed to enable it.

Share groups and sharemgr

File sharing can be easily managed by using the share groups that are configured using sharemgr. Using share groups, you can create a common configuration for a set of shares, and then start or stop sharing that group as a unit. Usually, you set up a share group for any set of files that you want to share with a common policy, such as read-only for all users, or read-write for only a particular set of users.

You can list the share groups configured on a system with the sharemgr list command:

```
$ sharemgr list
default
zfs
```

As shown here, OpenSolaris is automatically configured with two basic share groups: default and zfs. The default group is meant to hold legacy NFS shares that have been previously configured in /etc/dfs/dfstab; the zfs group contains any ZFS datasets that have been shared by setting the sharenfs or sharesmb properties using the zfs command.

Sharing directories

To share a directory, no matter what local file system it is on, first create an additional share group in which to place the shared directory (assuming you don't already have an appropriate group created), and then add the directory to the share group. Using the `default` group is possible but not advised because you'd be mixing up legacy shares from `/etc/dfs/dfstab` with your standard shares. For example:

```
# sharemgr create test
# sharemgr list -v
default enabled nfs
test    enabled smb nfs
zfs     enabled
# sharemgr add-share -r share-example -s /shared/example test
# sharemgr show -v test
test
    share-example=/shared/example
```

This example share is now available to both CIFS and NFS clients, as that is the default for share groups created using `sharemgr` when both services are installed on the system. Because the shares in this group are available via CIFS, you must supply a resource name with the `-r` option to `add-share`, as the resource name is used by CIFS clients to access the share. To make the share group available to only one of the protocols, create it specifying only a single protocol:

```
# sharemgr create -P nfs nfsgroup
# sharemgr list -v
default enabled nfs
test    enabled smb nfs
zfs     enabled
nfsgroup enabled nfs
```

Alternatively, if you already have the group created and want to remove a protocol from it, use the `-P` option to `sharemgr delete`:

```
# sharemgr delete -P nfs test
# sharemgr list -v
default    enabled nfs
test       enabled smb
zfs        enabled
nfsgroup   enabled nfs
```

Specify no protocol argument to `delete` to remove the group completely:

```
# sharemgr delete nfsgroup
# sharemgr list -v
default    enabled nfs
test       enabled smb
zfs        enabled
```

You can remove a share from a share group using the `remove-share` subcommand, specifying either the share path with `-s` or the resource name (if assigned) with `-r`. You can use either of the following two commands to remove the share added in the example:

```
# sharemgr remove-share -s /shared/example test
# sharemgr remove-share -r share-example test
```

Shares can also be moved from one group to another; simply specify the new group, and the share's existing group will be automatically located and updated:

```
# sharemgr move-share -s /shared/example nfsgroup
# sharemgr show -vp nfsgroup
nfsgroup nfs=()
            share-example=/shared/example
```

As shown in these examples, each share group is automatically enabled once it has been created. You can control whether a particular share group is enabled using the `enable` and `disable` subcommands:

```
# sharemgr disable test
# sharemgr list -v
default enabled nfs
test    disabled        smb
zfs     enabled
```

The `enable` and `disable` subcommands control the *persistent state* of the share group — that is, if you disable a share group, then it remains disabled across system reboots. You can also control the current state of the group using the `start` and `stop` subcommands:

```
# sharemgr start test
# sharemgr stop test
```

> **TIP**　The `start` and `stop` subcommands operate only on enabled share groups; attempting to start or stop a disabled share group has no effect but it doesn't produce an error message. Generally, you should use `enable` and `disable` to manage the state of share groups persistently; `start` and `stop` are intended primarily for use by the SMF services that activate and deactivate file sharing.

The properties that can be set through `sharemgr` are described in its man page. Most of the properties relate to security topics; see the section "NFS security" later in this chapter for examples of property manipulation with `sharemgr`.

The properties that apply to sharing the directories in the group with NFS are independent of the properties that apply to sharing via CIFS, although currently no properties apply to CIFS shares.

> **NOTE**　When creating share groups, you may notice that `sharemgr` automatically creates an SMF service instance that corresponds to each share group. These SMF services

are named using the FMRI pattern `svc:/network/shares/group:`*groupname*, where *groupname* is replaced by the name of the group. These service instances should be viewed as an implementation detail that you can essentially ignore, as they are managed automatically, based on your use of `sharemgr`. The only effect that you need to be aware of is that group names must be valid SMF instance names. See Chapter 13 for more information on SMF.

Sharing ZFS datasets

You can also use `sharemgr` to manage the sharing of ZFS datasets, in much the same way as the earlier examples demonstrated for directories. Recall that you can also choose to use the `zfs` command to directly manipulate the `sharenfs` and `sharesmb` properties on the dataset. In that case, `sharemgr` represents the share as a subgroup of the automatically created `zfs` share group. In addition, each ZFS dataset inherits its properties from its parent, so multiple datasets are often shared by setting properties only on a parent dataset. Any dataset that inherits its `sharenfs` and `sharesmb` properties from its parent is a member of the parent's share group:

```
# zfs set sharesmb=off space
# zfs set sharenfs=on space
# zfs set sharesmb=on space/test
# zfs get -r sharesmb space
NAME                PROPERTY   VALUE            SOURCE
space               sharesmb   off              local
space/nfs_test      sharesmb   off              inherited from space
space/test          sharesmb   on               local
# zfs get -r sharenfs space
NAME                PROPERTY   VALUE            SOURCE
space               sharenfs   on               local
space/nfs_test      sharenfs   on               inherited from space
space/test          sharenfs   on               inherited from space
# sharemgr show -vp zfs
zfs
    zfs/space nfs=()
    /space
    /space/nfs_test
    zfs/space/test nfs=() smb=()
    space_test=/space/test
```

You can also manipulate the `zfs` share group properties with `sharemgr`, and `sharemgr` will update the dataset properties to record the settings:

```
# sharemgr set -P nfs -S sys -p ro="*" zfs/space
# sharemgr show -vp zfs
zfs
    zfs/space nfs=() nfs:sys=(ro="*")
    /space
    /space/nfs_test
    zfs/space/test nfs=() smb=() nfs:sys=(ro="*")
    space_test=/space/test
```

```
# zfs get -r sharenfs space
NAME                PROPERTY  VALUE         SOURCE
space               sharenfs  sec=sys,ro    local
space/nfs_test      sharenfs  sec=sys,ro    inherited from space
space/test          sharenfs  sec=sys,ro    inherited from space
```

Here, the sharenfs property's value has been modified to contain the security settings specified to the sharemgr command in the format that would be used with the share command. This demonstrates that you can use the zfs or sharemgr commands interchangeably to manage sharing of ZFS datasets.

> **TIP** When creating ZFS datasets that will be shared with CIFS, strongly consider setting the casesensitivity property to either insensitive or mixed, as most CIFS clients expect the file system to be case insensitive, unlike UNIX systems, which use a case-sensitive file system. See the ZFS documentation for more information on this property setting.

Configuring sharing services with sharectl

Besides using sharemgr to manage share groups, it's sometimes necessary to configure the sharing service. OpenSolaris includes a new command for this purpose, sharectl(1M). Using it, you can view the status of the file sharing services and manipulate properties that control how the sharing services operate.

Use the following to view the status of the file sharing services:

```
# sharectl status
smbfs    disabled client
smb      online
nfs      online
```

In this case, the server has both CIFS and NFS services enabled and online, but it is not using the CIFS client, which is disabled. Disabling the CIFS service would result in the following:

```
# svcadm disable smb/server
# sharectl status
smbfs    disabled client
smb      disabled
nfs      online
```

Note that sharectl doesn't allow you to directly enable or disable the service — that occurs automatically as you create and delete share groups with sharemgr — but you can use the SMF command svcadm to disable the service directly if necessary.

The configuration properties of the NFS service can be viewed with sharectl get:

```
# sharectl get nfs
listen_backlog=32
```

```
protocol=ALL
servers=16
lockd_listen_backlog=32
lockd_servers=20
lockd_retransmit_timeout=5
grace_period=90
server_versmin=2
server_versmax=4
client_versmin=2
client_versmax=4
server_delegation=on
nfsmapid_domain=
max_connections=-1
```

The properties listed are described in detail in the NFS man page, nfs(4) and are stored in the file /etc/default/nfs. In general, the default property settings for the NFS service provide good performance and interoperability with most other NFS implementations and won't often need to be changed. If it is necessary to tune any of them, you can use sharectl set to modify the properties of the service. For example, some of your clients may have interoperability bugs with NFS version 4 but no bugs with NFS version 3. While it's usually preferable to obtain a fix for the clients, it may be necessary to restrict the server to advertising version 3 as its maximum version. Using sharectl, this is easily done:

```
# sharectl set -p server_versmax=3 nfs
# sharectl get -p server_versmax nfs
server_versmax=3
# svcadm restart nfs/server
```

You must use svcadm to restart the NFS service for the change to take effect.

The CIFS service also has a number of properties, again viewable with sharectl get:

```
# sharectl get smb
system_comment=
max_workers=64
netbios_scope=
lmauth_level=4
keep_alive=5400
wins_server_1=
wins_server_2=
wins_exclude=
signing_enabled=false
signing_required=false
restrict_anonymous=false
pdc=
ads_site=
ddns_enable=false
autohome_map=/etc
```

The properties are stored in the SMF repository as properties of the smb/server service. See the smb(4) man page for a detailed explanation of the SMB properties; most of them are used only when integrating your CIFS server with Windows servers, not in the workgroup mode described in the following section. As with the NFS properties, you can use sharectl set to modify the SMB server properties, and you need to restart the smb/server service for the changes to take effect.

Configuring the CIFS service in workgroup mode

The OpenSolaris CIFS service can run in one of two modes: workgroup or domain. This book does not address configuring the CIFS service in domain mode because that mode requires Windows Active Directory domains and services to be configured, a topic beyond the scope of this book. The procedures to configure the CIFS service in domain mode are documented in the *OpenSolaris CIFS Administration Guide* at http://docs.sun.com/app/docs/doc/820-2429.

By default, the CIFS service runs in workgroup mode as a member of a default workgroup called WORKGROUP. This is also the name of the default workgroup used by Windows clients, so you can likely just use this default workgroup to interoperate with standard Windows clients in many smaller networks. If you do need to change the workgroup name, use the smbadm command. For example, if your workgroup were named engineering, then the command to join that workgroup would be as follows:

```
# smbadm join -w engineering
```

The next step in configuring the CIFS service is to modify the OpenSolaris Pluggable Authentication Module (PAM) to enable SMB password encryption for user accounts. This is necessary because the encryption for CIFS passwords uses a different algorithm than the default UNIX password encryption used for standard OpenSolaris user accounts. Add the following to the end of /etc/pam.conf:

```
other    password  required  pam_smb_passwd.so.1    nowarn
```

CROSS-REF More information on PAM can be found in Chapter 11.

Once PAM is configured, you must set (or reset) the password of each user who will access the server's CIFS shares so that the CIFS-encrypted version of the password can be stored. To do this, either run the passwd command as root, specifying the username, or have each user log in to the CIFS server and run the passwd command. The following sets the password for user sam:

```
# passwd sam
New Password:
Re-enter new Password:
passwd: password successfully changed for sam
```

Once you've completed these steps, SMB shares from your server can be accessed by users on CIFS clients using the passwords entered, which will be the same passwords used to log in to the user account on the CIFS server. If you have the CIFS client software installed as well (which is highly recommended if you are running a CIFS server), you can verify that passwords and shares are correctly configured and working using the `smbutil` command:

```
$ smbutil view //sam@localhost
Password:
Share          Type        Comment
--------------------------------
space_test     disk
example        disk

2 shares listed from 2 available
```

> **CAUTION** The encrypted SMB passwords for users are stored separately from the UNIX passwords, in the file `/var/smb/smbpasswd`. Do not modify this file directly — instead, use the `passwd` command. However, several administrative tools from the open source world may directly modify `/etc/passwd`, so consult their documentation to ensure correct operation with the OpenSolaris CIFS server when considering their use.

Automatic sharing of user home directories with CIFS

The OpenSolaris CIFS server includes a special feature to ease the sharing of any home directories located on the server. This mechanism is not enabled by default but is easily enabled by creating the file `/etc/smbautohome` and adding entries to it. The `smbautohome(4)` man page discusses the complete set of options, which include how to use this feature with Active Directory domains. For a simple workgroup server such as the example in the previous section, the best solution is probably to configure the `smbautohome` function to automatically share the home directories listed in the `passwd` table in your configured name services. This enables you to manage your OpenSolaris system in a UNIX-centric fashion, while the CIFS service does the hard work. The following simple command appends the required entry to `/etc/smbautohome` to enable this type of home directory sharing:

```
# echo "+nsswitch" >>/etc/smbautohome
```

Advanced CIFS server topics

Basic statistical information on the CIFS server is maintained by the drivers and can be viewed using the `smbstat(1M)` command. For example, use the following to view basic information on the number of clients and files being accessed:

```
# smbstat -i
SMB Info:
state       open_files  connections sessions
2           0           1           1
```

The OpenSolaris CIFS server has some additional features that are useful in more complex Windows integration environments but they are beyond the scope of this book.

One important feature is *identity mapping*, which is used to convert between Windows and UNIX user identities in evaluating a user's access privileges to files and directories shared by the CIFS server. The default mode of operation for the CIFS service is to use an *ephemeral* mapping of Windows users to UNIX users; in this case, the Windows user and group identities are automatically converted to UNIX uids and gids, which are not retained across restarts of the CIFS server. You can, however, configure rules for mapping identities between the environments using the idmap(1M) command, which allows for better security coordination between UNIX and CIFS identities. See the man page and the OpenSolaris documentation for more information.

The CIFS server also provides the capability to automatically perform virus scans on files as the CIFS clients access them. This feature is not enabled by default and requires a virus-scanning engine, usually on a Windows server, as the products available to perform this function seldom run on non-Windows servers. See the vscanadm(1M) and vscand(1M) man pages for more information.

Accessing Files with NFS

Once you have a server that is sharing files over NFS, you can access those files from an NFS client. As mentioned earlier, before you can access files, you first must *mount* an NFS share within your system's local file system hierarchy. There are multiple ways to do this on OpenSolaris. Before you can mount a share, you need to know its name. If you don't know what shares are available from a server, you can use the showmount command to discover them. The following lists NFS shares from the server nfssrv:

```
$ showmount -e nfssrv
export list for nfssrv:
/shared/def     (everyone)
/space          (everyone)
/space/nfs_test (everyone)
/space/test     (everyone)
```

The (everyone) portion of the listing indicates that the share is mountable by any client. If it's restricted to only certain clients, that is reported too. For example, if these shares were restricted to only the clients on the 192.168.1.0 IP network, then the output would look like the following:

```
$ showmount -e nfssrv
export list for nfssrv:
/shared/def     @192.168.1
/space          @192.168.1
/space/nfs_test @192.168.1
/space/test     @192.168.1
```

If the server does not have NFS services running, then you'll see an error similar to the following:

```
$ showmount -e nfssrv
showmount: nfssrv: RPC: Program not registered
```

Manual NFS mounts

On an OpenSolaris client, the simplest way to mount an NFS share is to use the `mount` command, specifying the share to be mounted and the local directory on which it should be mounted. If the server `nfssrv` is sharing the directory `/space/test` and you want to access the files within it at the local directory `/mnt`, then the following `mount` command will do the trick:

```
# mount -F nfs nfssrv:/space/test /mnt
```

This mount is a temporary mount, and is lost once the client is rebooted, but it will remain mounted until that time or until it is manually unmounted. To make the mount persistent, so that it will be remounted after a system reboot, add an entry to `/etc/vfstab`:

```
nfssrv:/space/test  -   /mnt  nfs  -  yes  -
```

As noted in Chapter 7, the format of `/etc/vfstab` is as follows:

Device to Mount	Device to fsck	Mount Point	File System Type	fsck Pass	Mount at Boot	Mount Options

For NFS mounts, `fsck` is not used because the server is responsible for file system integrity, so those two fields are specified as placeholders using the value dash (`-`). The device to mount is specified using the server:path format (the server portion can be specified using its hostname or IP address). In this example, no mount options are specified; instead, it uses the client's default values, so a placeholder value is used for the options as well. Once an entry is created in `/etc/vfstab`, you can mount it using only the mount point name:

```
# mount /mnt
```

You must enable the NFS client service to cause the NFS mount to occur at boot:

```
# svcadm enable nfs/client
```

Mounting NFS file systems specified in the local `/etc/vfstab` is the only function of the `nfs/client` service, so it can be safely disabled if you're not using them. This service is delivered as disabled by default on OpenSolaris because no persistent NFS mounts are created during system installation.

If you no longer want an NFS share to be mounted, use the umount command to terminate the mount:

```
# umount /mnt
```

Note that an unmount will fail if any files on the file system are open, or if the current working directory of a process is within the file system. You can force the unmount by adding the -f option to the umount command:

```
# umount /mnt
nfs umount: /mnt: is busy
# umount -f /mnt
```

CAUTION Forcibly unmounting a file system can cause service failures and data corruption, so do so only in emergency situations.

If the mount was persistent by virtue of being recorded in /etc/vfstab, then you need to remove the entry from /etc/vfstab to prevent the mount from returning after the system is rebooted.

If you have multiple persistent NFS mounts in /etc/vfstab, you can mount or unmount all of them at once using mountall and umountall:

```
# mountall -F nfs
# umountall -F nfs
```

Alternately, you can manipulate the nfs/client SMF service to mount and unmount all NFS mounts — enabling the service mounts all NFS mounts; disabling it unmounts them:

```
# svcadm enable nfs/client
# svcadm disable nfs/client
```

CROSS-REF See Chapter 13 for details on SMF and the svcadm command.

Mounting NFS shares with the automounter

As you've seen, it's possible to mount NFS shares using entries in your system's local /etc/vfstab, but this method doesn't scale very well if you need to mount an NFS share on more than a few clients, which in all but the smallest networks is likely to be the case. In addition, you usually can't just synchronize copies of /etc/vfstab across multiple systems because unless your systems are identical models of the same hardware, it's highly likely that they don't use the same device paths for other file systems, such as the root (/) file system, that can be mounted using /etc/vfstab. Also, if you have a large number of clients and a server (or many servers) with a large number of shares, having all of those clients mounting all of the shares all of the time can consume extra resources on each system to maintain active mounts for each client. It's unlikely that all of the clients would need to access all of the shares simultaneously.

To improve NFS's capability to scale with the number of clients, servers, and shares, a separate facility called the *automounter* was developed. The premise of the automounter is to mount a share from a server only when it's accessed by the client; that is, the share is automatically mounted on demand. Once the client is no longer referencing the share, it can be automatically unmounted. By separating the configuration of mounts controlled by the automounter from those configured in /etc/vfstab, it is possible to share the configuration among multiple clients. Usually the shared configuration is stored using the NIS or LDAP naming services, which are discussed later in this chapter. In this section, you'll learn how to configure the automounter using local files on the client; the same principles can be extended to configure the automounter in the naming service.

The primary configuration file for the automounter is the file /etc/auto_master. Its default contents in OpenSolaris are as follows:

```
+auto_master
/net          -hosts          -nosuid,nobrowse
/home         auto_home       -nobrowse
```

The +auto_master entry instructs the automounter to insert the entries from an auto_master map from the system's network name service as if it occurred at that point in the file. If you aren't using any network naming service, then no entries will be inserted.

The remainder of the auto_master file is formatted as three fields: a *mount point*, a *map name*, and an optional list of *mount options*. The mount point specifies a directory name within the client's file system under which all of the entries in the specified map name will be mounted. This mount point is set up as an autofs mount point within the kernel. The autofs file system works by trapping access to any pathnames assigned to it within the kernel; if that pathname isn't already available on the file system, then the pathname is forwarded by the kernel to the automount daemon, automountd, to look up the path in the automount maps, and, if it's found, to attempt to mount it. The automount map name is located in any name services that the system is configured to use. In the local file system, the map is a file under /etc with the specified name, so the preceding entry for /home will be looked up in /etc/auto_home. With the NIS name service, any underscores in the map name are replaced with a period, so the map name would be auto.home.

Any mount options specified in an auto_master entry are applied by default to all mount points included in the referenced map; but if an entry within the referenced map contains specific mount options, those options override the defaults specified in auto_master. For example, the entry for /net specifies -nosuid, which means that the setuid bit on any files accessed through this mount point will be ignored.

If you add entries to auto_master on a running system, you need to restart the autofs SMF service for the new automount mount points to take effect:

```
# svcadm restart autofs
```

The /net entry is a special entry; the map name -hosts means that the client can access any NFS share on any NFS server that can be reached using a hostname or IP address. For example, if the server nfssrv with IP address 192.168.2.4 is sharing /space/archives, then an NFS client with this /net entry can access that share using the name /net/nfssrv/space/archives or /net/192.168.2.4/space/archives.

The /home entry is an example of a more typical auto_master entry, as it specifies a mount point and a map name. By convention, each user's home directory in OpenSolaris is accessed using the pathname /home/*username*; the home directory for user sam would be accessed at /home/sam. This is configured by adding an entry to /etc/auto_home, referencing the server on which sam's home directory is stored. If the home directory is on nfssrv, at pathname /space/sam, then the entry in /etc/auto_home would be as follows:

```
sam   nfssrv:/space/sam
```

Once this entry exists, simply cd to /home/sam, or access the files in /home/sam, as if they were on a local disk.

Like the auto_master map, you can specify mount options on each entry in an automount map. If you wanted to have sam's home directory mounted using only NFS version 3 or earlier, you could add the option as follows:

```
sam   -vers=3   nfssrv:/space/sam
```

> **TIP**   A number of additional capabilities are available in automount maps, such as specifying multiple locations, as well as variable substitutions based on the client's hardware and OS version. There is even an executable form, whereby a script may be run to generate an automount entry dynamically when accessed. See the automount(1M) man page for details.

NFS security

Most often, you'll want to use share groups to set up common security settings for a group of shares. For example, by default, NFS shares are shared read-write, and are shared with a weak authentication method, AUTH_SYS, which essentially requires the server to trust the user id and group id credentials presented by the client. This obviously leaves the data fairly unprotected, which may be acceptable in an otherwise secure network, but few networks are. NFS can use other, stronger security modes, including Kerberos and Diffie-Hellman. These stronger security modes require that the server authenticate each user itself, rather than trust the client. Kerberos authentication can also encrypt the data during transmission, ensuring confidentiality, whereas if you use Diffie-Hellman, you need to separately configure IP security (IPsec) to encrypt data during transmission.

> **NOTE**   The available NFS security modes are described in the nfssec(5) man page. Kerberized NFS, IPsec, and general security topics in OpenSolaris are discussed in Chapter 11.

Controlling read and write access

Using a strong authentication mode for NFS is advisable but it's not always the only option. Some data may be best protected by sharing it read-only, with write access reserved to only the server system and perhaps a few well-secured, trusted clients. You can use sharemgr to modify the properties of the group to share the group read-only for all clients like so:

```
# sharemgr set -P nfs -S sys -p ro="*" test
# sharemgr show -pv test
test smb=() nfs:sys=(ro="*")
    share-example=/shared/example
    space-test=/space/test
    st2=/space/test2
    st3=/space/test3
```

The following grants read-write access to the client knox.fort.mil:

```
# sharemgr set -P nfs -S sys -p rw=knox.fort.mil test
# sharemgr show -vp test
test smb=() nfs:sys=(ro="*" rw="knox.fort.mil")
    share-example=/shared/example
    space-test=/space/test
    st2=/space/test2
    st3=/space/test3
```

You might also allow read-write access to any clients that are configured to use Diffie-Hellman authentication, which provides strong authentication and is quite trustworthy:

```
# sharemgr set -P nfs -S dh -p rw="*" test
# sharemgr show -vp test
test smb=() nfs:sys=(ro="*" rw="knox.fort.mil") nfs:dh=(rw="*")
    share-example=/shared/example
    space-test=/space/test
    st2=/space/test2
    st3=/space/test3
```

As shown in the output of sharemgr show, the different NFS security modes are configured independently. The NFS protocol negotiates a security mode between the client and server based on the capabilities of each and the security modes specified by the share on the server and the mount on the client.

Configuring Diffie-Hellman authentication

To use Diffie-Hellman authentication, both client and server must have access to each other's public keys, which leads to the problem of distributing the keys. While it's possible to replicate the file used to store the keys (/etc/publickey) on each system, it really isn't a viable solution when more than a few machines are involved. It's best to use a name service such as NIS or LDAP to store the keys, which allows all systems configured to use the name service to obtain the keys as needed with little administrative overhead. Later in this chapter you'll learn the basics for setting up the name service; the example here assumes that NIS has already been configured.

First, you need to create Diffie-Hellman keys for the NFS server's root account, as well as for any users who need authenticated access. To configure the root key for nfssrv, run newkey on the NIS master server:

```
nismaster# newkey -h nfssrv -s nis
Adding new key for unix.nfssrv@test.domain.
Enter nfssrv's root login password:
Please confirm nfssrv's root login password:
```

Next, add a key for each user, again on the NIS master. For user sam:

```
nismaster# newkey -u sam -s nis

WARNING:
The publickey entry in /etc/nsswitch.conf is "publickey:nis files".
It should be "publickey: nis"; add 'files' if you want the
'nobody' key.

Adding new key for unix.102@test.domain.
Enter sam's login password:
Please wait for the database to get updated ...
```

This warning can be safely ignored because nis is included in the list of publickey data sources, and it's advisable to include files as well so that the nobody key is available. Now that you've created the keys, rebuild the NIS maps:

```
nismaster# cd /var/yp; make
```

At this point, the keys are published to the entire NIS domain. Now you must log in as root to the NFS server and load the cached, decrypted copy of its private key. This key is stored in the file /etc/.rootkey file, which is readable only by root. This step is necessary so that the system can re-enable the Diffie-Hellman authentication mechanism after reboot without requiring input from an administrator to decrypt the system key. Before you can do that, though, you must enable the keyserv daemon, which holds decrypted copies of the users' private keys on the local system. This design is used to protect the secret keys from discovery by nonprivileged users.

```
nfssrv# svcadm enable keyserv
nfssrv# keylogin -r
Password:
Wrote secret key into /etc/.rootkey
```

Finally, user sam must ensure that his private key is decrypted on the client he's logged into. This can be done either by running keylogin within a session that's already logged in or by logging out and then back in, as the keylogin process is performed automatically during login. At this point, sam will be strongly authenticated for any NFS operations.

> **TIP** You must also ensure that the keyserv service is enabled on any client systems that are expected to access shared directories using Diffie-Hellman authentication.

NFS monitoring and troubleshooting

If your system is configured as an NFS server, then you should see the following SMF services online:

```
$ svcs '*nfs*'
STATE        STIME     FMRI
disabled     Apr_25    svc:/network/nfs/client:default
online       Apr_25    svc:/network/nfs/rquota:default
online       Apr_25    svc:/network/nfs/status:default
online       Apr_25    svc:/network/nfs/mapid:default
online       Apr_25    svc:/network/nfs/nlockmgr:default
online       Apr_25    svc:/network/nfs/server:default
online       Apr_25    svc:/network/nfs/cbd:default
```

Normally you don't need to directly manipulate any of these services, as sharemgr enables and disables them as needed. As noted earlier, the nfs/client service needs to be enabled only if you have NFS mounts configured in your /etc/vfstab. The nfs/cbd service is not related to the NFS server but to the NFS client; it is automatically enabled when an NFSv4 mount is done either by the mount command or by the automounter.

> **TIP** If user accounts are unable to read or write files, then investigate the NFS identity mapping done by the nfsmapid service. This should work automatically when systems are in the same DNS domain, but can be overridden to deal with unusual situations. Consult the nfs(4) man page for details on the identity mapping implementation.

The nfsstat(1M) command can be used to examine various counters that are maintained by the NFS implementation regarding the operations it performs, both client and server. See the man page for more information.

Accessing Files with CIFS

If your network includes servers that are sharing files using CIFS, which may be either Windows servers, OpenSolaris servers configured to share files with the CIFS server, or other UNIX or Linux servers that are sharing files with Samba, then you can use the OpenSolaris CIFS client to access those files.

The OpenSolaris CIFS client is implemented as a standard OpenSolaris file system called the smbfs. This means that, as with NFS or any local file system, you use the standard OpenSolaris mount command to mount a share from the CIFS server onto a local directory on the client and then access it as a seamless part of the file system. For example, to mount the share example from server smbsrv on the directory /mnt, the command is as follows:

```
# mount -F smbfs //sam@smbsrv/example /mnt
Password:
```

Note two differences between smbfs mounts and most other mounts, though. The first is the somewhat unusual-looking name used to specify the resource to mount (discussed in the sidebar later in this section). A second difference is that you will likely be prompted for the password of the user identity used for the mount (user sam in the example). Password prompts can be avoided; see the sidebar, "CIFS Resource Names and Passwords," for ways to do this.

This mount then shows up as a standard file system in listings from utilities such as mount or df:

```
$ df -h
Filesystem           Size  Used Avail Use% Mounted on
rpool/ROOT/opensolaris
                     3.5G  2.3G  1.2G  66% /
swap                 519M  808K  518M   1% /etc/svc/volatile
/usr/lib/libc/libc_hwcap3.so.1
                     3.5G  2.3G  1.2G  66% /lib/libc.so.1
swap                 518M  8.0K  518M   1% /tmp
swap                 518M   68K  518M   1% /var/run
rpool/ROOT/opensolaris/opt
                     1.2G  5.1M  1.2G   1% /opt
rpool/export         1.2G   21K  1.2G   1% /export
rpool/export/home    1.2G  507K  1.2G   1% /export/home
rpool                1.2G   57K  1.2G   1% /rpool
rpool/ROOT           1.2G   18K  1.2G   1% /rpool/ROOT
//sam@smbsrv/example 6.8G  4.9G  2.0G  72% /mnt
```

Unmounting the SMB file system is done using the umount command to specify the mount point or resource name that should be unmounted, just as with any other file system. The following unmounts the preceding mount:

```
# umount /mnt
```

Just as with NFS or other file systems, a mount command creates a temporary mount that is lost when the system reboots. Likewise, umount will fail if the file system is in use by any process; you can use the -f option to forcibly unmount the file system. You can add smbfs mounts to /etc/vfstab, but you need to ensure that the system's root user has access to appropriate passwords by adding them to the root user's .nsmbrc file (normally this is /root/.nsmbrc on OpenSolaris distributions), which is discussed in the sidebar, "CIFS Resource Names and Passwords."

> **TIP**　If your environment makes extensive use of CIFS, you might want to allow ordinary users to mount CIFS shares for themselves. To enable this functionality for all users,

add the SYS_MOUNT privilege to the Basic Solaris User rights profile by appending the following two lines to /etc/security/exec_attr:

```
Basic Solaris \
User:solaris:cmd:::/usr/lib/fs/smbfs/mount:privs=sys_mount
Basic Solaris \ User:solaris:cmd:::/usr/lib/fs/smbfs/umount:privs
=sys_mount
```

See Chapter 11 for details on rights profiles.

You can also mount CIFS shares with the automounter, in a manner similar to that used for mounting NFS shares. However, CIFS share mounts are restricted to being used only in a *direct* automounter map, which is a type that was not discussed earlier, though it can be used for NFS mounts as well. The examples earlier showed the use of indirect maps. The difference is that each entry in a direct map places a single mount on a full pathname in the NFS or CIFS client. By contrast, each entry in an indirect map provides a mount on a subdirectory of a top-level directory that is configured for the map as a whole. To add a direct map to the automounter configuration, add an entry similar to the following to /etc/auto_master:

```
/- auto_direct -intr
```

The special key /- in /etc/auto_master specifies that the entry is for a direct map. After adding this entry, create the /etc/auto_direct file and add entries for each directory that will be mounted using the automounter, as shown in this example:

```
/example  -noprompt,fstype-smbfs  //cifssrv/example
```

This adds a direct map entry for a CIFS share that allows anonymous access, which would be configured on the server. This is the most common scenario for which you might want to use the automounter with CIFS shares. If the share doesn't allow anonymous access, you must not use the noprompt option in the automounter map; and you must create a user and password for use in accessing the share in root's .nsmbrc file. See the following sidebar.

CIFS Resource Names and Passwords

The resource names used to access CIFS shares have the following general format:

```
//[workgroup;][user[:password]@]server/share
```

Items in brackets ([]) are optional. Thus, the most basic specification of a CIFS resource is as follows:

```
//server/share
```

continued

continued

When this simple format is used, the username will be the name of the OpenSolaris user running the mount command. The workgroup is either the standard default name of workgroup or the name of the default domain specified in the user's .nsmbrc file; you need to specify the workgroup only if the server is a member of a workgroup other than the one that would be obtained by the default or by using the .nsmbrc file settings. If the server is using Active Directory authentication, then the workgroup must be the name of the Active Directory domain in which the user account is defined. Otherwise, it must be the name of the workgroup configured on the server. If you do specify the workgroup name, be careful to use shell quoting to prevent the shell from interpreting the semicolon as a command separator.

Password prompts in mounting smbfs file systems can be avoided in one of three ways: including the password on the mount command, using the smbutil login command, or placing an obscured version of the password in the user's .nsmbrc file. We do not recommend placing passwords on the command line, as it can be viewed using utilities such as ps or pargs, which compromises security. The most secure option is to use the smbutil login command, which loads the password into the smbfs driver, where it is used when needed. This is approximately as secure as the stronger authentication options used with NFS, but it can be inconvenient because a system reboot requires another smbutil login to reload the password into the driver. Therefore, saving a password into the .nsmbrc file in your home directory offers a fairly good balance between security and convenience. To do this, use the smbutil crypt command to generate an obscured version of the password. Then add an entry containing it to the default section of your .nsmbrc file, and ensure that the .nsmbrc file is readable only by you. Here's an example:

```
$ smbutil crypt
Password:
$$17650017577695e
```

Next, edit $HOME/.nsmbrc and add the password to the default section:

```
[default]
password=$$17650017577695e
```

Finally, ensure that the .nsmbrc file is readable only by you:

```
$ chmod 600 $HOME/.nsmbrc
```

Once you've done this, you should no longer be prompted for passwords when mounting SMB shares, and your access to those shares is authenticated, although not as strongly as with the more secure options in NFS. You can also create different password entries for specific servers or shares, and specify a different username if your OpenSolaris login name is not the same as your login name on the CIFS server. For example, suppose the CIFS server is named cifssrv, the user is sam, and the preceding password hash is the correct one for sam. You can create the following entries in .nsmbrc:

```
[cifssrv]
user=sam
password=$$17650017577695e
```

OpenSolaris Naming Services

OpenSolaris offers several naming services, which can be used to assist an administrator in managing a network of computer systems. NIS and LDAP are the primary naming services in current use, but the local configuration files on the system are also modeled as a naming service in the OpenSolaris system architecture. In this section, you'll learn how to use these naming services. Before diving into the details of configuring a naming service, it's helpful to understand some of the OpenSolaris infrastructure that's used to knit the naming services together with the rest of the system.

NOTE Sun developed, and OpenSolaris continues to include, the NIS+ naming service, which was intended to be a successor to NIS. Unlike NIS and, more recently, LDAP, it failed to catch on with other operating systems and remained essentially proprietary to Solaris. Sun considers NIS+ deprecated and discourages its use in new installations. As a result, this book does not cover NIS+, although it is currently still a part of OpenSolaris, and you will see references to it in Sun's official documentation.

The name service switch

As it is usually necessary to use multiple naming services to operate a system that's connected to a network, Sun developed a technology known as the *name service switch* to enable administrators to control how the various naming services are used in looking up information. The name service switch consists of two components: a configuration file, /etc/nsswitch.conf, and a set of library calls, commonly called the getXbyY calls (e.g., gethostbyname(3C)), which use the configuration specified in /etc/nsswitch.conf to retrieve information from the naming services. After you install the OpenSolaris distribution, the default contents of /etc/nsswitch.conf appear as follows (the header comments have been omitted for brevity):

```
passwd:     files
group:      files
hosts:      files
ipnodes:    files
networks:   files
protocols:  files
rpc:        files
ethers:     files
netmasks:   files
bootparams: files
publickey:  files
# At present there isn't a 'files' backend for netgroup;  the system will
#   figure it out pretty quickly, and won't use netgroups at all.
netgroup:   files
automount:  files
aliases:    files
services:   files
printers:   user files
```

```
auth_attr:   files
prof_attr:   files
project:     files

tnrhtp:      files
tnrhdb:      files
```

This file specifies, for each type of information, such as password or printer data, which name services should be used to look up the information, and the order in which they should be used. You may need to edit this file to customize how your system behaves. We recommend consulting the nsswitch.conf(4) man page for detailed information on constructing nss-witch.conf entries. In addition, OpenSolaris ships example files for each name service as /etc/nsswitch.*nameservice*, such as /etc/nsswitch.nis for NIS, that you can use as a starting point.

CAUTION OpenSolaris does not support using both NIS and LDAP naming services simultaneously on a client.

Name service caching with nscd

One issue early in Solaris' development was that a large number of programs would frequently look up data in name services, such as translating uids to usernames when listing a directory with the ls -l command, and would suffer performance problems from repeatedly translating the same information. They would also excessively load the name servers with what amounted to duplicate requests. Clever coding in the programs can overcome this, but that places a burden on the developer of any program that needs to look up data in a name service to develop appropriate caching strategies — and the quality of such algorithms varies widely. To provide a consistent, high-quality solution to this problem for the entire operating system, OpenSolaris includes the *name service cache* service, which provides a fast, centralized clearinghouse for name service lookups. You can see it running on your OpenSolaris system with the svcs command:

```
$ svcs -p name-service-cache
STATE          STIME    FMRI
online         16:02:42 svc:/system/name-service-cache:default
               16:02:42     254 nscd
```

Several of the name service lookup functions have been implemented to channel their requests through the name service cache. You probably won't need to manage the name service cache, as it generally goes about its business transparently, but you can consult the nscd(1M) and nscd.conf(4) man pages for more detailed information.

TIP Some older Solaris references may recommend disabling the name service cache, but recent work on it has made that advice obsolete; we do not recommend disabling the name service cache. Changes to the name service switch configuration file /etc/nsswitch.conf are seen automatically by nscd and take effect immediately. If you suspect that it isn't using the correct configuration, restart the service as follows:

```
# svcadm restart name-service-cache
```

Troubleshooting name service lookups

Occasionally, you might run into problems with your system not obtaining correct information from its name services. The first step in troubleshooting name service problems on a client is to use the getent(1M) command to simulate lookups from the command line. getent calls the various getXbyY lookup functions that work through the name service switch and the name service cache, so it effectively simulates the results obtained by other programs using those functions, enabling you to start diagnosing the source of any problems. For example, you can test hostname-to-IP address translation for a system named indy using the following command:

```
$ getent hosts indy
192.168.0.1        indy
```

Each name service also offers specific commands that can be used to help debug problems; those commands are discussed in the sections on each name service that follow.

NIS

The Network Information Service (NIS) is a relatively simple naming service developed in the 1980s by Sun to provide a more convenient means of administering workgroups of UNIX work-stations. It was ported to all of the major UNIX variants over the years, as well as to Linux, so it is widespread in organizations with significant UNIX operating system populations.

Unlike more recent naming services such as LDAP, NIS does not present a hierarchical namespace; instead, each NIS domain is an administrative entity without any capability to work in combination with other NIS domains. Thus, larger organizations with multiple sites and multiple administrative boundaries will likely not run NIS servers but instead use LDAP as their naming service. Each domain has a single *master server* (generally called *master*) that stores the domain's data and responds to client queries. Additionally, a domain may have slave servers (usually called *slaves*) that hold duplicate copies of the domain data and respond to client queries. All updates to the domain's data must be made on the master and then pushed to the slaves.

In NIS, the data is organized into *maps*, which are really just simple databases that have only a single search key. They are implemented using a very simple underlying database technology known as dbm or ndbm. Details about ndbm can be found in its man page, ndbm(3C); its limited capabilities and implementation details also constrain the scalability of NIS as a name service. In addition to the ndbm limitations, the protocol used to replicate data between master and slave servers requires sending the complete contents of the new maps from the master to each slave, rather than just the differences from the prior version of the map. This means that updates can take quite some time to propagate between the master and slave servers, so you may not be able to have more than a few slaves.

Generally speaking, NIS is best suited to networks on a single site, used with maps that contain at most a few thousand entries per map. However, NIS is very easy to set up and manage, so if its limitations are acceptable for your uses, it's far easier to start using than a more powerful name service such as LDAP.

The NIS maps are generated from standard OpenSolaris text configuration files using the make(1S) command. This command must be run to load updates made to the text configuration files into the dbm tables that underlie the NIS maps and notify the NIS server daemon. OpenSolaris includes a Makefile that is used to drive the conversion of the files into NIS maps. (The NIS maps and data files are listed later in this chapter, in Table 10-1.)

CAUTION Confusingly, the commands and daemons related to managing the NIS service begin with the yp prefix, not the nis prefix, which is instead used for managing the NIS+ service. This is because the original name of the NIS service was the Yellow Pages service; the name was changed because of trademark conflicts, but references to YP still exist in some command output and documentation.

Configuring a NIS client

Some information sources recommend using the sys-unconfig(1M) program to reconfigure your system to a NIS client. Be aware that sys-unconfig will deconfigure a number of aspects of your system, such as the root password and ssh server key, and then halt your system. You then need to boot the system and answer a series of questions to reconfigure the system. We do not recommend this approach to system reconfiguration because it will likely disrupt your system in ways that will be at least as time-consuming to fix as the more manual procedures outlined here, which attempt to avoid modifying the system unnecessarily.

If you already have a NIS domain that you'd like to configure your client to use, you can do so quite easily. One question you need to consider is whether your client should be configured to locate a NIS server automatically using network broadcasts or be configured to use a specific set of NIS servers. The broadcast option is less secure but easier to maintain, but it also requires that the NIS servers be directly reachable on any network link to which your system is connected (in other words, there cannot be an IP router between the client and the server). We recommend using the broadcast option if your network's topology supports it, though both are described here.

CAUTION We do not currently recommend configuring a mobile client such as a laptop as a NIS client if that client won't always be connected to a network with the NIS service. The OpenSolaris projects Network Auto-Magic and Duckwater are designed to make the system work better with transient network and name service configurations. See the "Resources" section at the end of this chapter for references to Duckwater. Network Auto-Magic is discussed further in Chapter 9. Using NIS on mobile clients may be recommended once those projects are delivered.

Configuring hostnames for NIS servers

The first step in configuring a NIS client is to ensure that the client will be able to translate the hostname of the NIS server(s) to IP addresses, and vice versa. If your system is already configured to use DNS to resolve IP addresses, then you've met this requirement. This approach is best, as most clients need to use DNS to access the Internet. You can verify this by checking the hosts entry in /etc/nsswitch.conf:

```
$ grep ^hosts /etc/nsswitch.conf
hosts: files dns
```

As this example contains the string dns, you are already using DNS for IP address resolution; but if DNS is not included in the output, then you need to either configure the system as a DNS client or add entries for the NIS servers to your local /etc/inet/hosts file.

CROSS-REF Configuring a DNS client is discussed in Chapter 9.

If you need to add an entry to /etc/inet/hosts, ask your NIS administrator or some other user to provide the name and address of the NIS server(s). If you have one server with the name nismaster and its address is 192.168.0.1, then you can add this entry to /etc/inet/hosts as follows:

```
# echo "192.168.0.1    nismaster" >>/etc/inet/hosts
```

Repeat this command with the name and address of any additional NIS servers you may use.

Configuring the NIS domain name

The next step is to configure the system's NIS domain name. You must configure it both in the kernel and in the system's /etc/defaultdomain configuration file so that it can be loaded again on the next reboot. As the domainname(1M) command can be used to both set the kernel value and display it, the following example shows how to configure the system's domain as test.domain:

```
# domainname test.domain
# domainname >/etc/defaultdomain
```

Configuring the NIS client

Now you must decide whether to use broadcasts to locate the NIS servers, or configure a specific list on your client. If you had to add local /etc/inet/hosts entries as described earlier in this chapter, then we recommend using a configured server list.

To do so, use the ypinit command:

```
# ypinit -c
```

```
In order for NIS to operate sucessfully, we have to construct a list of the
NIS servers.  Please continue to add the names for YP servers in order of
preference, one per line.  When you are done with the list, type a <control D>
or a return on a line by itself.
  next host to add:  nismaster
  next host to add:
The current list of yp servers looks like this:

nismaster

Is this correct?  [y/n: y]  y
# svcadm enable nis/client
# ypwhich
nismaster
```

To use broadcasts to locate servers, use the following command sequence:

```
# mkdir /var/yp/binding/`domainname`
# svcadm enable nis/client
# ypwhich
nismaster
```

If `ypwhich` prints a server name and not an error message, then your client has successfully joined the NIS domain.

Configuring the name service switch

Once your client has joined the NIS domain, you can start using NIS to look up usernames and other data, but you need to configure the name service switch to use NIS. The best way to do this is to use one of the example files that are shipped with OpenSolaris as a starting point and edit it as needed. The file `/etc/nsswitch.nis` is an example file that configures your client to use NIS for all naming service lookups; it will still use local files as a preferred source for some information. Start by copying the sample file into place:

```
# cp /etc/nsswitch.nis /etc/nsswitch.conf
```

You could use this file as is, but we do not recommend doing so. The sample file's default configuration will cause your client to use only NIS for IP address resolution, which is rarely desirable. Most clients prefer local files in case you need to add special entries. In addition, you'll almost certainly want to use DNS to resolve IP addresses so that you can access the entire Internet directly. Thus, unless your NIS administrator has provided other instructions, edit `/etc/nsswitch.conf` and modify the `hosts` and `ipnodes` entries so that they appear as shown here:

```
hosts: files dns
ipnodes: files dns
```

At this point, your system should be using NIS to look up usernames, groups, and so on. You can use the `getent` command to verify that it's working correctly. For example, if you know that user `sam` is listed in the NIS `passwd` map but not in your local `/etc/passwd` file, you can confirm that his username is found using the following:

```
$ getent passwd sam
sam:PUwTFalsenB2U:12345:10:Sam Pull:/home/sam:/bin/ksh
```

If NIS and the name service switch were not working correctly, this command would return either no output or an error message.

Configuring a NIS master server

Before you begin configuring a NIS server, you may need to install the NIS server package. You can check with the following command:

```
$ svcs nis/server
svcs: Pattern 'nis/server' doesn't match any instances
STATE          STIME    FMRI
```

This output indicates that the NIS server package is not installed. You can install it as follows:

```
# pkg install SUNWyp
```

Once you have this package installed, you can proceed with configuring the NIS service.

Configuring NIS map data

To start configuring your NIS master server, collect the data files used in generating the NIS maps into a separate working directory. While this step is not strictly required, it is a good idea from an administrative point of view, as it enables you to segregate the domain data in the maps from the configuration of the NIS master. In the example that follows, this data is collected into a directory called `/export/nismaster` using a separate ZFS dataset. This is a good location to use on the OpenSolaris distribution because it will be shared across multiple OpenSolaris boot environments.

CROSS-REF Management of OpenSolaris boot environments is discussed in Chapter 6. ZFS is discussed in Chapter 8.

Start by creating the ZFS dataset, which will be automatically mounted at `/export/nismaster` by virtue of it inheriting its mount point from its parent, the `rpool/export` dataset:

```
# zfs create rpool/export/nismaster
```

Next, collect the data files for the NIS maps by copying each of the files listed in Table 10-1 to the `/export/nismaster` directory.

TABLE 10-1

NIS Map Data Files

File	NIS Maps
/etc/auto_home	auto.home
/etc/auto_master	auto.master
/etc/bootparams	bootparams
/etc/ethers	ethers.byaddr, ethers.byname
/etc/group	group.bygid, group.byname
/etc/inet/hosts	hosts.byaddr, hosts.byname
/etc/inet/ipnodes	ipnodes.byaddr, ipnodes.byname
/etc/mail/aliases	mail.aliases, mail.byaddr
/etc/netgroup	netgroup, netgroup.byuser, netgroup.byhost
/etc/netid	netid.byname
/etc/netmasks	netmasks.byaddr
/etc/networks	networks.byaddr, networks.byname
/etc/passwd	passwd.byname, passwd.byuid
/etc/project	project.byname, project.byprojid
/etc/protocols	protocols.byname, protocols.bynumber
/etc/publickey	publickey.byname
/etc/rpc	rpc.bynumber
/etc/security/audit_user	audit_user
/etc/security/auth_attr	auth_attr
/etc/security/exec_attr	exec_attr
/etc/security/prof_attr	prof_attr
/etc/services	services.byname, services.byservicename
/etc/shadow	passwd.byname, passwd.byuid
/etc/timezone	timezone.byname
/etc/user_attr	user_attr

> **NOTE** Notice that multiple maps are generated from some of the files — this is how NIS works around the fact that dbm databases can have only a single search key, while many of the configuration files have multiple search keys. Each search key is accommodated by generating a corresponding map using it as a key, so that, for example, NIS can be used to translate a username into a uid and vice versa.

Once you've finished copying the files, edit the /var/yp/Makefile to instruct it to use the files in /export/nismaster. Change the following entries in the Makefile to the values shown:

```
DIR =/export/nismaster
INETDIR=/export/nismaster
RBACDIR=/export/nismaster
PWDIR =/export/nismaster
ALIASES = /export/nismaster/aliases
```

Creating the NIS master server

Now that you've collected the data files and modified the Makefile, it's time to configure the NIS master. You must first configure its domain name. For example, to configure the domain test.domain, use the following:

```
# domainname test.domain
# domainname >/etc/defaultdomain
```

Once the domain is configured, use ypinit(1M) to configure the master server. If you know that you will be configuring additional slaves, make sure that their hostnames are available and enter them in the list of servers when prompted by ypinit. Don't worry if you think you may need to add a slave later but aren't sure what system it will be; the procedure for adding slaves in the next section shows you how to do this. The following example shows how to configure just the master without any slaves:

```
# ypinit -m

In order for NIS to operate sucessfully, we have to construct a list of the
NIS servers.  Please continue to add the names for YP servers in order of
preference, one per line.  When you are done with the list, type a <control D>
or a return on a line by itself.
  next host to add:  nismaster
  next host to add:  ^D
The current list of yp servers looks like this:

nismaster

Is this correct?  [y/n: y]  y

Installing the YP database will require that you answer a few questions.
Questions will all be asked at the beginning of the procedure.
```

```
Do you want this procedure to quit on non-fatal errors? [y/n: n] n
OK, please remember to go back and redo manually whatever fails.  If you
don't, some part of the system (perhaps the yp itself) won't work.
The yp domain directory is /var/yp/test.domain
There will be no further questions. The remainder of the procedure should take
5 to 10 minutes.
    ...
```

Assuming that the `ypinit` command succeeded, you should be able to verify that the NIS services are online:

```
$ svcs network/nis/*
STATE          STIME     FMRI
online         16:42:21  svc:/network/nis/xfr:default
online         16:42:21  svc:/network/nis/server:default
online         16:42:21  svc:/network/nis/update:default
online         16:42:21  svc:/network/nis/passwd:default
online         16:42:21  svc:/network/nis/client:default
```

Additionally, your server should be bound to itself as the NIS server, which you can check with the `ypwhich` command:

```
$ ypwhich
nismaster
```

This completes the NIS master initial configuration process.

Configuring a NIS slave server

To increase the reliability of your NIS service, it's best to configure at least one slave server so that the NIS service remains available for lookups even if the master server is unavailable, whether because of a planned maintenance operation or an unplanned failure.

To add a slave, first verify that the slave is already listed in the `ypservers` map. If it isn't, add it. To display the map contents, use `ypcat -k`:

```
$ ypcat -k ypservers
nismaster
```

In this case, only the master has been configured. That means you need to add the slave to the `ypservers` map. However, unlike the other maps in a NIS domain, the `ypservers` map does not have a text file from which it is generated. Therefore, you must update it directly using the `makedbm` command, which generates the dbm database files that the NIS service uses as its storage medium. You need to log in to the NIS master and assume the root role. The first step is to convert the `ypservers` dbm file to a text file:

```
# makedbm -u /var/yp/`domainname`/ypservers >/tmp/ypservers
# cat /tmp/ypservers
YP_LAST_MODIFIED 1212266517
```

```
YP_MASTER_NAME nismaster
nismaster
```

Now that you have a text file, you can append the new slave to it. If the name of the slave were nisslave, the command is as follows:

```
# echo "nisslave" >>/tmp/ypservers
# cat /tmp/ypservers
YP_LAST_MODIFIED 1212266517
YP_MASTER_NAME nismaster
nismaster
nisslave
```

The next step is to convert the text file back to dbm format and verify that the slave is listed:

```
# makedbm /tmp/ypservers /var/yp/`domainname`/ypservers
# ypcat -k ypservers
nismaster
nisslave
```

This completes the work necessary on the master to add the slave. Now you need to log in to the slave and become root to configure it as a slave. First you must configure the slave as a NIS client using the procedure described earlier. Once the slave has been configured as a client, you can proceed to configure it as a slave server:

```
# ypinit -s nismaster


Installing the YP database will require that you answer a few questions.
Questions will all be asked at the beginning of the procedure.

Do you want this procedure to quit on non-fatal errors? [y/n: n]  n
OK, please remember to go back and redo manually whatever fails.  If you
don't, some part of the system (perhaps the yp itself) won't work.
The yp domain directory is /var/yp/test.domain
There will be no further questions. The remainder of the procedure should take
a few minutes, to copy the data bases from nismaster.
Transferring audit_user ...
Transferring user_attr ...
Transferring prof_attr ...
Transferring exec_attr ...
Transferring auth_attr ...
Transferring ageing.byname ...
Transferring auto.home ...
Transferring auto.master ...
Transferring netmasks.byaddr ...
Transferring netid.byname ...
Transferring publickey.byname ...
```

```
        Transferring mail.byaddr ...
        Transferring mail.aliases ...
        Transferring protocols.byname ...
        Transferring services.byservicename ...
        Transferring services.byname ...
        Transferring rpc.bynumber ...
        Transferring networks.byaddr ...
        Transferring networks.byname ...
        Transferring ipnodes.byname ...
        Transferring ipnodes.byaddr ...
        Transferring hosts.byaddr ...
        Transferring hosts.byname ...
        Transferring group.bygid ...
        Transferring group.byname ...
        Transferring passwd.byuid ...
        Transferring protocols.bynumber ...
        Transferring ypservers ...
        Transferring passwd.byname ...

        nisslave's nis data base has been set up

        without any errors.
```

Verify that the NIS service is online on the slave server:

```
$ svcs nis/server
STATE          STIME    FMRI
online         22:54:53 svc:/network/nis/server:default
```

Managing NIS maps

Once your NIS servers are up and running, the main regular task in managing them is updating the maps. The most common updates are the `passwd` and `shadow` files to add, delete, or modify user accounts (users can modify their own passwords using the `passwd` command). If you followed the procedures recommended earlier, you need to edit the files stored in `/export/nismaster` to make any necessary changes. After you've done that, you need to rebuild the NIS maps to include the changes, which is done by running the following command:

```
# cd /var/yp
# make
```

If any slaves are configured, the new maps are pushed to them immediately. Pushing NIS maps can be a time-consuming process, so in many sites it is preferable to have the map updates done at scheduled times, such as noon and midnight or another time that makes sense based on domain size and update frequency. This is usually done by creating a `cron(1M)` job script, which is used to execute the preceding `make` command on the defined update schedule. Note that because the push is sequential to each slave and clients may be bound to different servers, not all clients will see changes simultaneously.

Leaving a NIS domain

If your system is a member of a NIS domain and you'd like to revert your system to using only its local configuration files as the name service, you can do so quite easily. Some documentation recommends using the `sys-unconfig` command, but we believe that `sys-unconfig` affects too many other aspects of your system configuration. Use the following procedure to revert a client from NIS to local files:

```
# cp /etc/nsswitch.files /etc/nsswitch.conf
# svcadm disable nis/client
# rm /var/yp/binding/`domainname`
# domainname ''
# rm /etc/defaultdomain
```

This procedure first configures the name service switch to ignore NIS and use only local files, which is important to do first so that disabling the NIS client and removing its configuration will not cause system processes to hang while attempting to look up data in NIS. If you want to revert to files plus DNS for IP address resolution, then copy `/etc/nsswitch.dns` to `/etc/nsswitch.conf`.

If your system is also a NIS slave, you need to modify the NIS master's `ypservers` map to remove the slave from the map; otherwise, the NIS master server can't completely push any map updates. See "Configuring a NIS Slave Server" earlier in the chapter for instructions on editing the `ypservers` map. You also need to disable the NIS service on the slave:

```
# svcadm disable nis/server
```

Removing a NIS master results in destroying the NIS domain. If you need to move the master to a different server, copy the data files and `/var/yp/Makefile` to the new master server, configure it as before, and then reconfigure the clients and slaves as needed.

LDAP

As you've seen, NIS provides a very capable workgroup-level naming service. However, its limited scalability proved to be a problem as computing environments grew ever larger in the 1990s. Large enterprises need to manage large system and user bases, with a large number of applications, yet simultaneously keep their IT costs low. This meant that a more capable directory service was required. The computer industry developed the Lightweight Directory Access Protocol (LDAP) standard as a directory service protocol to meet those requirements. It is based on earlier work known as the X.500 Directory Access Protocol that was developed by telephony standards bodies; the most significant difference initially was that LDAP uses TCP/IP as its communication protocol, though X.500 directories subsequently adopted TCP/IP too.

LDAP is designed to provide a comprehensive corporate directory of people, organizations, computer systems, printers, and indeed any object about which one might want to record information. As a result, it has a complex means of describing and organizing data, called a *schema*, which can be standardized across systems and enterprises so that multiple applications can reuse the directory data. The most common application for LDAP is to provide a corporate personnel address book and a standardized single-sign-on service across a corporation's computer systems and applications.

LDAP has been the subject of an extensive standardization effort, so interoperability between directories is possible but achieving a usable, cross-platform LDAP directory environment can be quite challenging and depends to some extent on the specific LDAP server you are using, as your server may not include specific schema definitions that are needed by a particular type of client. A detailed discussion of such issues is beyond the scope of this book. Note that ease of use for LDAP on OpenSolaris is a subject of several active projects; see the "Resources" section at the end of this chapter for more information.

OpenSolaris as an LDAP server

To use OpenSolaris as an LDAP server, you need to acquire LDAP server software, as the distribution does not currently include it in the standard installation. If you have a Linux background, you may be familiar with the OpenLDAP server software, which is commonly used on Linux platforms. It's also available for OpenSolaris from the `pkg.opensolaris.org` repository. To install OpenLDAP, install the OpenLDAP package:

```
# pkg install SUNWopenldap
```

> **CROSS-REF** More information on package installation, the Image Packaging System, and software repositories is available in Chapter 6.

Once you have installed the OpenLDAP software, consult the documentation installed under `/usr/share/doc/openldap`, the example configuration files in `/etc/openldap`, and the man pages for detailed configuration information.

Another open source LDAP server to consider is the OpenDS server, which is based on technology that Sun open sourced in 2006 and is under continuing development. The project offers prebuilt versions of the directory server that may be downloaded from its website, `http://opends.org/`. The server is primarily written in Java, so it runs on virtually any operating system. The OpenDS package offers a very simple, graphical setup program that will have your LDAP server up and running in just a couple of minutes.

Sun also offers an LDAP directory server as part of its Java Enterprise System. OpenSolaris is designed to support use of this server; see `http://docs.sun.com/app/docs/coll/1224.4` for details about installing and configuring the Sun Java System Directory Server.

OpenSolaris as an LDAP client

OpenSolaris can also be configured as an LDAP client using the `ldapclient(1M)` utility, which is included in the basic installation. If your LDAP server administrator has configured the server to support profile-based configuration, configuring an LDAP client is easy using `ldapclient`. If the default configuration profile on the LDAP server is to be used, and the server's IP address is 10.1.2.3, you can configure your LDAP client as follows:

```
# ldapclient init 10.1.2.3
```

This retrieves an LDAP configuration profile and stores the resulting configuration in files under /var/ldap. It also enables the ldap/client SMF service and copies /etc/nsswitch.ldap to /etc/nsswitch.conf to switch the system to use LDAP as its preferred name service. You need to modify /etc/pam.conf to add pam_ldap(5) as an authentication module if you want to use LDAP for user authentication. See its man page for more information.

Other, more complex client configuration scenarios are possible; consult the ldapclient man page for directions.

> **TIP** As with NIS, we recommend using DNS, rather than LDAP, for IP address resolution, so edit /etc/nsswitch.conf and modify the hosts and ipnodes entries to search files and dns, rather than LDAP.

If your computing environment is predominantly Microsoft Windows, you'll likely find that the Microsoft Active Directory is already implemented in your environment, so you may want to focus on using OpenSolaris as an Active Directory client; see "Resources" at the end of this chapter for references that can assist with this. You may also want to investigate configuring the Evolution mail and calendar client to use Active Directory as its address book and calendar storage; see Chapter 4 for information on Evolution.

Resources

The OpenSolaris NFS community is home to a number of projects under development in NFS; see the community page at http://opensolaris.org/os/community/nfs.

A how-to guide for setting up Solaris 10 and OpenSolaris as clients of a Microsoft Active Directory server is available from the Sun BigAdmin site at http://sun.com/bigadmin/features/articles/kerberos_s10.jsp.

Current troubleshooting information for the CIFS service is maintained at http://genunix.org/wiki/index.php/Solaris_CIFS_Service_Troubleshooting.

Several OpenSolaris projects are underway to improve OpenSolaris name service usability, management, and interoperability:

- The Duckwater project, http://opensolaris.org/os/project/duckwater, is focused on ease-of-use improvements for LDAP and general name service configuration.
- The Sparks project, http://opensolaris.org/os/project/sparks, is providing enhancements to the name service switch and name service cache.

- The Winchester project, `http://opensolaris.org/os/project/winchester`, is working to improve interoperability between OpenSolaris and Windows Active Directory.

An older reference that is useful, primarily for NIS, which has changed little in many years, is *Managing NFS and NIS* by Hal Stern, Mike Eisler, and Ricardo Labiaga (O'Reilly, 1999).

For a focused introduction to LDAP, you may want to investigate *LDAP System Administration* by Gerald Carter (O'Reilly, 2003).

Summary

This chapter introduced the file-sharing services included in OpenSolaris, NFS, and CIFS, and showed how you can configure OpenSolaris to both share its files and access the files of other systems over each service, allowing you to exchange files seamlessly with virtually any other system you may encounter. Additionally, the OpenSolaris naming service infrastructure was discussed, including the name service switch and cache, and procedures for configuring your system as either a NIS client or server were demonstrated. Finally, you learned the steps involved in obtaining and installing LDAP server software, as well as configuring OpenSolaris as an LDAP client.

Chapter 11

Security

There are two kinds of people in the computer world: those who care about security and those who should care about security. From large companies to small companies to government systems to your personal home network, computer systems can be compromised. Luckily, OpenSolaris contains numerous security features to protect against and ameliorate various forms of attacks. Unfortunately, many of the features are not enabled by default because they would affect performance or usability of the system. If you want your OpenSolaris system to be safe, you must take active steps to secure it. This chapter will help you put the appropriate security measures in place.

Security Overview

Computer attacks are varied and numerous. You've probably read about some of the infamous ones, such as the theft of over 45 million customer credit and debit card numbers from the T. J. Maxx company in 2006 and 2007 by hackers who cracked the wireless network in one of the stores and used it as a gateway to the central database. But computer attacks don't need to be direct. Someone could break into your system by calling one of your users on the telephone and convincing him to provide his password. An attacker could even snoop your wireless network to obtain access to data without ever breaking into a computer.

The intent of the attacks varies as well. Some attacks are purely malevolent, such as viruses and worms meant only to cause damage. Other attacks, such as breaking into a system to steal proprietary or customer data, are clearly for financial gain. Still other attacks use your system as only a platform from which to launch a denial of service, phishing, or other attack on different systems or users. You must protect your computer systems against all forms of attacks, occurring at any time.

Furthermore, attackers need not be experts in computer work. A multitude of free and open source tools can aid anyone with basic computer skills in carrying out some fairly complex attacks. No one is immune, including the authors of this book. One of the authors recounts the following incident with some embarrassment but also with the hope of preventing you from making a similar mistake. A few years ago, among other computers in his home network, he had a machine running an older version of Solaris. Because his home network sat behind a router that implemented Network Address Translation, the IP addresses and hostnames of the individual machines were not exposed. Feeling that this rudimentary level of security was sufficient, he didn't configure a software firewall or otherwise secure the Solaris machine in any way.

One morning, after logging into the Solaris box, the author noticed that his shell prompt looked a little different than usual. With a bit of poking, he discovered two interesting changes to his system. First, a new daemon was running that he didn't recognize. Second, he found a bunch of new files installed in an out-of-the-way path. The daemon turned out to be a *backdoor access program*, providing return access to the attacker. The new files were a *root kit*, a bunch of tools for taking over a system once it has been compromised. The shell appeared different because the root kit had tried to mess with it to hide the new backdoor access daemon. Luckily for the author, the root kit was for a slightly different variant of UNIX, so it didn't operate effectively, leaving the clues that he was able to uncover.

Fortunately, OpenSolaris provides substantial security measures that could have prevented this attack or made it easier to detect, including secure by default, role-based access control, privileges, ipfilter, logs, and auditing. This chapter explores these techniques and others that will help you maintain effective security.

Being a global security citizen

The single most important mechanism to maintain security of your system is to stay up-to-date with security fixes. You can keep on top of known security flaws in a number of ways. For example, the United States Computer Emergency Readiness Team (US-CERT) tracks computer security flaws of all kinds. You can subscribe by e-mail or RSS to receive timely updates about vulnerabilities and alerts. Following the Sun security alerts and discussions about news of OpenSolaris vulnerabilities is another way to stay informed. The Sun Alert and Security Discussion on the Sun Developer Network is a good source to check periodically.

Another important part of being a global security citizen is reporting any security flaws you find. The quicker everyone is aware of a problem, the quicker a patch can be generated, and the less time there will be for a malicious user to exploit the flaw. The "Resources" section at the end of this chapter contains pointers to websites where you can report security problems.

Organization of this chapter

The remainder of this chapter is organized around several broad levels of security, with some additional topics, such as Kerberos, at the end. The four main aspects of security are as follows:

- **Preventing unauthorized access** — By using secure authentication techniques and disabling unneeded network services, you can prevent unauthorized access to your systems. Topics include pluggable authentication modules, password management, and secure by default.

- **Limiting the damage** — Even if an attacker breaks into the system, proper security practices can limit the attacker's damage. Topics include role-based access control, privileges, and file system access control lists.

- **Ensuring secure communication** — Attackers can also cause damage without breaking into your system directly, by eavesdropping or snooping, so it is vital to protect communications between machines. Topics include secure shell and IP security.

- **Detecting attacks** — Despite your best efforts, your system may still be compromised. Tools to detect these attacks include logs and auditing.

Terminology

A few terms used throughout this chapter require some explanation. First, many people incorrectly refer to computer attackers as *hackers*. The term hacker, however, simply refers to someone who is skilled with computers, and can have a positive or negative connotation. Thus, some people prefer to call computer attackers *crackers* or *black-hats*. In this book we call them *attackers*.

Similarly, the term *hacking* can have either positive or negative connotations, and does not necessarily imply nefarious activity.

Finally, the term *harden* is commonly employed among security mavens to describe the process of securing a system against attackers. A *hardened* system is one to which all necessary security precautions have been applied.

Preventing Unauthorized Access

Most computer attacks involve gaining access, or attempting to gain access, to a computer system. Attackers can accomplish this in a multitude of ways, from cracking account passwords to exploiting flaws in a network service. Your first goal in security is to prevent unauthorized access.

Secure access relies on user authentication. Authentication is the process of determining that someone is the person he or she claims to be. Authentication is imperative when someone first accesses the system.

User education and physical security

Unfortunately, the best authentication security can be defeated by any user who simply lets slip his or her password or is tricked into giving the attacker direct access to his or her system. The process of gaining access to a computer system through nontechnical means is called *social engineering*.

Furthermore, even if you harden your OpenSolaris system and set it up with secure authentication and educate your users, an attacker could still break in if she obtains physical access to the system. For example, if you leave your logged-in system unattended, an attacker can merely sit down in front of the computer and start typing. In this case, an attacker would need only minutes in an account to install a Trojan horse that would allow future remote access.

User education, social engineering, and physical security in general are beyond the scope of this book. However, here are a few tips. Make sure you have a documented security policy and educate your users about the policy. Instruct users to never give their passwords to anyone and never write them down, to always log out or bring up a password-protected screensaver when they step away from their desks, and to never leave laptops unattended. For more information on these topics, consult one of the general security references listed in the "Resources" section at the end of this chapter.

Pluggable Authentication Modules (PAM)

OpenSolaris uses *Pluggable Authentication Modules (PAM)* for a generalized authentication framework. Although you don't need to worry about — or even notice — PAM most of the time, it actually underlies all the authentication mechanisms in OpenSolaris. Thus, it's important to have a general understanding of PAM before delving into the various authentication mechanisms available.

PAM enables authentication, account management, session management, and password management to be centralized into pluggable modules instead of distributed throughout the various programs (such as `login`, `passwd`, `sshd`, and others) that need these capabilities. For example, instead of looking up passwords directly to authenticate users, the login program calls a generic library function, `pam_authenticate()`, which in turn calls into one or more modules to actually perform the authentication. In a simple file-based password scheme, the PAM library might load a module to check passwords in `/etc/shadow`. In a Kerberized system, the PAM library might load a module to request a ticket from the Kerberos Key Distribution Center. Deciding which modules to use is based on a configuration file. That way, there is a clear separation between the authentication entry points, such as login, and the authentication mechanisms, such as Kerberos, described later in this chapter. Because of this level of indirection, a system administrator can change the authentication mechanism for the system in one central configuration file without changing any settings in the programs that use the authentication.

Additionally, PAM allows multiple modules to be specified for a single service and type. This feature is called *module stacking*. For example, you might want password authentication to check Kerberos first, and then, only if that authentication fails, check the local password files.

The PAM configuration is centralized in the /etc/pam.conf file. The best way to understand the syntax of the file is through examples. Here are example entries for the login service:

```
login   auth requisite    pam_authtok_get.so.1
login   auth required     pam_dhkeys.so.1
login   auth required     pam_unix_cred.so.1
login   auth required     pam_unix_auth.so.1
login   auth required     pam_dial_auth.so.1
```

These entries stack five different modules for the login authentication functionality. The modules are processed in the order they appear in the file. All five modules must return success, as indicated by the requisite and required keywords. The difference between requisite and required is that failure of a requisite module terminates processing immediately, whereas failure of a required module allows the rest of the modules to be processed before returning failure overall.

Note that the actual password-checking is performed in the pam_unix_auth module. The first module, pam_authtok_get, just prompts the user for username and password. The second module, pam_dhkeys, handles Diffie-Hellman key exchange, if in use. pam_unix_cred checks the user's credentials and privileges, and pam_dial_auth is only relevant for dial-up connections.

> **TIP** Each module listed in /etc/pam.conf has an associated man page, which you can read for details about that module's policies and functionalities.

Now that you've seen an example, take a look at the syntax of /etc/pam.conf. Each line of the file consists of the following elements, in order:

1. Service name — The name of the service, which in the preceding example is login. other serves as the default for all services not explicitly listed.

2. Module type — One of the four functionalities provided:

   - auth: Authenticates users and sets up their credentials
   - account: Checks if users' accounts are valid, including checking roles and password expiration
   - session: Manages login sessions
   - password: Changes user passwords

3. Control flag — Specifies how this module fits into the stacking. In addition to requisite and required, other common control flags are sufficient and optional. sufficient causes success to be returned to the service immediately if the module returns success, skipping any remaining modules. optional modules count if they succeed but are ignored if they fail.

4. Module path — The name of the module itself.

5. Options — This field enables you to pass options directly to the module. These options are module-specific. For example, as shown in the section on Kerberos later in this chapter, you can pass the expire_pw option to the pam_krb5_migrate module to force users to create new passwords the next time they log in and are migrated to Kerberos.

Here's the default authentication stack for all services not explicitly mentioned in /etc/pam.conf, as specified by the other service name:

```
other    auth requisite        pam_authtok_get.so.1
other    auth required         pam_dhkeys.so.1
other    auth required         pam_unix_cred.so.1
other    auth required         pam_unix_auth.so.1
```

This is identical to the login stack, except that pam_dial_auth is missing. That's because it's only relevant to the login and ppp service, not other kinds of logins, such as dtlogin and rlogin.

The defaults for the account module type are as follows:

```
other    account requisite     pam_roles.so.1
other    account required      pam_unix_account.so.1
```

pam_roles checks the role-based access control (RBAC) configuration to verify that the user is allowed to take the specified role. RBAC is described in detail later in this chapter.

pam_unix_account checks for password expirations and other account access details.

The defaults for the session type use only a single module:

```
other    session required      pam_unix_session.so.1
```

This module basically just updates /var/adm/lastlog, which is used to determine the last time the user logged in.

Finally, the defaults for password, which come into play when a password is updated, are a bit more complicated:

```
other    password required     pam_dhkeys.so.1
other    password requisite    pam_authtok_get.so.1
other    password requisite    pam_authtok_check.so.1
other    password required     pam_authtok_store.so.1
```

pam_dhkeys handles the Diffie-Hellman key exchange, while pam_authtok_get queries the user for the new password, and pam_authtok_store actually sets the new password. The most interesting module here is pam_authtok_check, which verifies that the newly entered password meets certain criteria, such as minimum length. The next section describes these checks in more detail.

Password management

Even in the most rudimentary security model, every account in your system must have a password. An account without a password allows anyone to log in as that user!

CROSS-REF Chapter 3 describes basic user and password creation and management.

OpenSolaris supports four different password management schemes:

- **Local Files** — This default model places encrypted passwords in /etc/shadow. This option is not network-aware, so each user must have a separate account on each system.

- **NIS** — This option stores the user account and password information in a central Network Information Service repository, enabling access to be configured simultaneously for multiple networked machines.

- **NIS+ (Network Information Service Plus)** — Because NIS+ is deprecated, password management with NIS+ is not covered in this book.

- **LDAP** — This option stores user account and password information in a central LDAP directory tree, enabling access to be configured simultaneously for multiple networked machines.

CROSS-REF Chapter 10 covers NIS and LDAP trade-offs, setup, and configuration.

On a specific machine, you specify the desired password database in the passwd field of /etc/nsswitch.conf. This field lists password databases in the order they should be checked. Always list "files" first so that local settings on the machine can override the directory server. To use files for all passwords, use the following default passwd line:

```
passwd: files
```

To specify NIS for passwords, use this line:

```
passwd: files nis
```

To specify LDAP, use the following:

```
passwd: files ldap
```

CROSS-REF Chapter 10 discusses /etc/nsswitch.conf in more detail.

CAUTION Even if you use a directory server for user accounts, always store the root password in the local files instead of in the directory server, and use unique root passwords for each machine. If you store the root password in the directory server, an attacker who cracks the root password or obtains root access on one machine can then access any machine in your network. In addition, always place files first in the passwd entry so that a problem with the network or name service won't prevent you from accessing a system if necessary.

Behind the scenes, password setting and checking use PAM to implement standardized checks across different system entry points. See the section "Pluggable Authentication Modules (PAM)" earlier in this chapter for more details.

Why Aren't There Any Passwords in /etc/passwd?

In the traditional UNIX model, /etc/passwd stores login names, User ID numbers (UIDs), login shells, encrypted passwords, and a few other fields. When a user attempts to log in, the given password is encrypted and compared to the stored password. If they match, the user is logged in. However, /etc/passwd must be world-readable in order for commands such as ls, which map UIDs to login names or vice-versa, to function properly. Although the passwords are encrypted with a one-way function that theoretically protects the passwords, the availability of the encrypted versions is still a security risk because an attacker can run a password-cracking program against the encrypted passwords to discover the passwords themselves. Thus, OpenSolaris stores the actual encrypted passwords in /etc/shadow, which is readable only by root, and the login program runs as a setuid root executable to access it.

Strong passwords

Traditionally, Solaris passwords are encrypted with the crypt_unix algorithm, which, among other limitations, silently limits the passwords to eight characters in length. However, the Open-Solaris distribution uses the stronger SHA256 algorithm by default. You can change the default encryption algorithm by editing the /etc/security/policy.conf configuration file. The following line lists the allowed algorithms:

```
CRYPT_ALGORITHMS_ALLOW=1,2a,md5,5,6
```

Confusingly, algorithms 1 and 2a refer to the MD5 and Blowfish algorithms, respectively, which are compatible with Linux and BSD. The "md5" option is a stronger version of MD5 that is not compatible with Linux and BSD. The 5 and 6 options represent the SHA256 and SHA512 algorithms respectively. Finally, although not listed, __unix__ is a valid option to revert to the old crypt_unix algorithm.

To change the default algorithm, you must change the CRYPT_DEFAULT line. For example, to use the Linux and BSD-compatible MD5 algorithm, change the CRYPT_DEFAULT entry in /etc/security/policy.conf as follows:

```
CRYPT_DEFAULT=1
```

That's it! No reboot is needed. However, existing passwords are not converted to the new encryption format until they are changed. See the man page policy.conf(4) for more information about the configurations in /etc/security/policy.conf.

CAUTION LDAP can be configured to encrypt passwords using either the client's settings in /etc/security/policy.conf and /etc/default/passwd or the

LDAP server settings. To use the client settings, do not use the `pam_ldap` module or the `pam_authtok_store server_policy` option in /etc/pam.conf.

Additional password settings can be configured in /etc/default/passwd. These settings enforce password security. For example, you can set the minimum password length from its default of six characters by modifying the PASSLENGTH field:

```
PASSLENGTH=8
```

Now users will not be allowed to create passwords of fewer than eight characters:

```
$ passwd
passwd: Changing password for test1
Enter existing login password:
New Password:
passwd: Password too short - must be at least 8 characters.
Please try again
```

The /etc/default/passwd file contains several other useful tunable parameters, as described in Table 11-1.

See the pam_authtok_check(5) and passwd(1) man pages for more information.

> **CAUTION** The HISTORY flag applies only to passwords stored in local files.

Password aging

Forcing users to change their passwords periodically is considered good security policy because it limits the amount of time in which an attacker could benefit from a snooped or cracked password. The downside is that users are more likely to forget their passwords, or to write them down to remember them.

> **CAUTION** NIS does not support password aging.

If you decide to implement password aging, you have several options. First, you can set aging on a per-account basis using the passwd command with the -x option:

```
# passwd -x 90 nick
passwd: password information changed for nick
```

User nick's password is now set to expire in 90 days. When you use password aging, specify a minimum number of days between password changes, with the -n option, and the number of days to warn the user before the password expires, with the -w option:

```
# passwd -n 10 -w 15 -x 90 nick
passwd: password information changed for nick
```

TABLE 11-1

Tunables in /etc/default/passwd

Tunable	Description
PASSLENGTH	Minimum length of passwords
HISTORY	Number of previous passwords to store and disallow users from repeating
MINDIFF	Minimum number of characters at the beginning of the password that must be different from the previous characters
MINALPHA / MINNONALPHA/MINDIGIT/ MINSPECIAL	Minimum numbers of alphabetic, non-alphabetic, numeric, and special characters in the password
MINUPPER / MINLOWER	Minimum numbers of uppercase and lowercase characters in the password
MAXREPEATS	Number of allowed characters repeating in a row in the password
WHITESPACE	Boolean property specifying whether whitespace is allowed in the password
DICTIONLIST	Specifies a list of words on which the password is not allowed to be based
DICTIONBDIR	Specifies the directory in which to store the password dictionary
MAXWEEKS / MINWEEKS	Password aging; discussed in the next section

When the age limit of the password falls under the warning time, nick will be warned:

```
login as: nick
Password:
Your password will expire in 10 days.

Last login: Sun Mar  9 22:55:34 2008 from 192.168.1.100
Sun Microsystems Inc.    SunOS 5.11      snv_83  January 2008
$
```

When the age limit of the password is reached, nick will be forced to change his password the next time he logs in:

```
login as: nick
Password:
Warning: Your password has expired, please change it now.

New Password:
Re-enter new Password:
```

```
sshd-kbdint: password successfully changed for nick

Last login: Sun Mar  9 22:36:56 2008 from 192.168.1.100
Sun Microsystems Inc.   SunOS 5.11      snv_83  January 2008
$
```

> **TIP** Disable password aging for an account by setting the days-to-age with the `passwd`
> `-x` option to `-1`.

Managing aging on a per-account basis can be useful if specific accounts need different aging policies, although it's often more convenient to configure a systemwide aging policy. To set aging for all accounts, use the `/etc/default/passwd` configuration file discussed in the previous section to set the `MINWEEKS` and `MAXWEEKS` parameters.

> **CAUTION** Setting `MINWEEKS` and `MAXWEEKS` in `/etc/default/passwd` does not affect preex-
> isting accounts.

Remote logins

By default, OpenSolaris does not allow remote logins as root. This policy is useful because it requires anyone logging in as root to first login as a non-root user, and then `su` to root, providing a trail in the logs that makes root logins easier to track. The section on logs later in this chapter describes the various password and login logs that you should be aware of as an administrator.

You can adjust this policy by setting or commenting out the `CONSOLE` line in `/etc/default/login`:

```
# If CONSOLE is set, root can only login on that device.
# Comment this line out to allow remote login by root.
#
CONSOLE=/dev/console
```

Additionally, only allow remote logins over a secure service such as `ssh`. Disable insecure services such as `telnet` and `rlogin`. These insecure services are actually disabled by default in the standard OpenSolaris service configuration. The section "Secure by Default" later in this chapter explains how to disable unsafe network services. Kerberos, a useful tool for authentication within intranets, is described in detail at the end of this chapter.

Firewalls

Even if attackers can't gain access to a user account, they could still do significant damage by exploiting flaws in network services, finding open ports, or otherwise accessing the system in unexpected ways. To prevent these kinds of attacks, run a firewall that inspects incoming and outgoing packets, and filters out unwanted packets according to various rules.

>  Because of its networking specificity, the `ipfilter` security feature of OpenSolaris
> is covered in Chapter 9.

Secure by Default (SBD)

OpenSolaris contains quite a few network services, many of which are insecure for various reasons, such as allowing plain-text logins. Even those that aren't inherently insecure provide potential access points for attackers. These unneeded services include rlogin, telnet, finger, ftp, and others. You should disable all unused network services, or configure them to accept connections only from localhost. That may sound like an arduous task, but OpenSolaris makes it easy with *Secure by Default (SBD)*.

Because of Secure by Default, an OpenSolaris installation out-of-the-box runs only one network service that is not limited to local connections — ssh, which provides a mechanism to remotely administer the machine. Most of the other services, such as rlogin, telnet, finger, and ftp are not running. Those that still run, such as rpcbind, sendmail, and X server, are configured to accept connections only from localhost.

If you ever need to return to this pristine state, simply run the following command:

```
# netservices limited
```

NOTE As of this writing, the netservices command on the OpenSolaris distribution produces warnings about services that don't exist. You can safely ignore the warnings.

The opposite of netservices limited is netservices open. This option enables most network services (see Table 11-2 for a complete list):

```
# netservices open
```

CAUTION netservices open can expose you to serious security risk! Do not use netservices open on a production or Internet-facing machine.

In addition to the two extremes of netservices limited and netservices open, you can manually open or close specific services using SMF. Behind the scenes, netservices limited uses an SMF profile to disable the services shown in Table 11-2.

To selectively run any of these services, simply enable them with svcadm and perform any other configuration required by that particular service. For example, to allow ftp connections to your machine, run svcadm enable ftp. The following example checks the state of the ftp service, enables it, and then verifies that it is enabled:

```
# svcs ftp
STATE          STIME    FMRI
disabled       16:43:47 svc:/network/ftp:default
# svcadm enable ftp
# svcs ftp
STATE          STIME    FMRI
online         16:43:59 svc:/network/ftp:default
#
```

TABLE 11-2

Network Services Disabled by Default

Service	SMF FMRI
NFS status daemon	network/nfs/status
NFS lockd	network/nfs/nlockmgr
NFS client	network/nfs/client
NFS server	network/nfs/server
NFS rquotad	network/nfs/rquota
NFS v4 callback daemon	network/nfs/cbd
NFS ID mapping	network/nfs/mapid
CIFS client	network/smb/client
DHCP server	network/dhcp-server
Network Time Protocol	network/ntp
Reverse Address Resolution Protocol	network/rarp
Service Location Protocol	network/slp
Kerberos	network/security/kadmin network/security/krb5_prop network/security/krb5kdc
SNMP	application/management/sma
Seaport	application/management/seaport
Solstice Enterprise Agent	application/management/snmpdx
Internet print protocol	application/print/ipp-listener
Line printer daemon	application/print/rfc1179
Finger	network/finger
FTP	network/ftp
Remote Login	network/login:rlogin network/login:klogin network/login:eklogin
Remote Shell	network/shell:default network/shell:kshell
Telnet	network/telnet
UUCP	network/uucp
CHARGEN	network/chargen

TABLE 11-2 *(continued)*

Service	SMF FMRI
Daytime	network/daytime
Discard	network/discard
Echo	network/echo
Time	network/time
Comsat (biff) server	network/comsat
Remote execution	network/rexec
Talk	network/talk
Service Tag Discovery Probe	network/stdiscover
Service Tag Listener	network/stlisten
SVM communication	network/rpc/mdcomm
Kernel statistics server	network/rpc/rstat
Network Username server	network/rpc/rusers
SVM remote metaset	network/rpc/meta
SVM remote mediator	network/rpc/metamed
SVM remote multihost disk	network/rpc/metamh
OCF server	network/rpc/ocfserv
Remote Execution Service	network/rpc/rex
Spray packets	network/rpc/spray
Write to All Users (wall)	network/rpc/wall
X font server	application/x11/xfs

To selectively disable services you don't need, use `svcadm disable`. It's best to start in the hardened state and selectively enable services you need, rather than start with all services enabled and selectively disable the ones you don't need.

CROSS-REF Chapter 13 discusses SMF and service management in more detail.

In addition to disabling the services listed in Table 11-2, `netservices limited` configures some services, such as `rpcbind`, to accept connections only from `localhost`. Configuring services to accept only local connections is slightly trickier than simply disabling them, and involves setting SMF properties. Each service that can be configured in this way has an SMF property that can be used to specify local connections only. Unfortunately, the property names are not consistent; some are Boolean properties where `true` means remote connections are allowed, while others are Boolean properties where `false` means remote connections are allowed. Table 11-3 lists the services and their properties:

TABLE 11-3

Network Services Configured to Accept Local Connections Only

Service	SMF FMRI	SMF Property	Property Type and Values
Syslog	`system/system-log`	`config/log_from_remote`	Boolean: `false` for local only; `true` for remote
rpcbind	`network/rpc/bind`	`config/local_only`	Boolean: `true` for local only, `false` for remote
X Server	`application/x11/x11-server`	`options/tcp_listen`	Boolean: `false` for local only, `true` for remote
sendmail	`network/smtp:sendmail`	`config/local_only`	Boolean: `true` for local only, `false` for remote

You can check the values of these service properties with the `svcprop` command, and set them with the `svccfg` command. The following example checks whether the `syslog` service allows remote connections, specifies that it should allow remote connections, and verifies the setting:

```
# svcprop -p config/log_from_remote system-log
false
# svccfg -s system-log setprop config/log_from_remote=true
# svcadm refresh system-log
# svcprop -p config/log_from_remote system-log
true
# svcadm restart system-log
```

You must refresh the service with `svcadm refresh` before the property change takes effect.

> **TIP** The list of services enabled and disabled by default changes as new services are added to the OpenSolaris code base. For the definitive list, see the `/var/svc/profile/generic_limited_net.xml` file on your system.

Thinking Like an Attacker

When hardening your system, it's a good idea to test it from the outside by thinking like an attacker. The best way to perform this exercise is to use some of the same tools that attackers use for port scanning and vulnerability detection. Popular, free port-scanning tools include the following:

- Unix utilities, including `netstat`, `traceroute`, and `ping`

- Network Mapper (Nmap) — This powerful open source tool has appeared in movies such as *The Bourne Ultimatum* and *The Matrix Reloaded*. Nmap can be found in the OpenSolaris distribution in the `SUNWnmap` package. You can download the source code for other distributions and build it yourself, or you can run it from Linux or Microsoft Windows.

- The Network Vulnerability Scanner (Nessus) — This powerful vulnerability detection tool is no longer open source, but (as of this writing) it is still free to download and use. Unfortunately, there doesn't appear to be a version for OpenSolaris on x86, but you can run it on OpenSolaris on SPARC, Linux, or other operating systems.

See the "Resources" section at the end of this chapter for links.

Limiting the Damage

Despite your best efforts to prevent unauthorized access, your system may still experience security breaches. It is imperative that you are prepared for these potential break-ins by configuring your system to limit the damage as much as possible. Even if an attacker compromises a user account or exploits a flaw in a network service, proper use of security measures can prevent a bad situation from becoming disastrous. A side benefit of preparing your system to expect the worst is that you protect it from clueless or incompetent users and prevent poorly written processes from inadvertently damaging the system.

Role-based access control

The traditional UNIX security model has only two access control levels: regular users with limited access and the aptly named *superuser*, or root user, with complete system access. The main problem with this model is the power of root. Attackers who obtain root access can perform whatever malicious activities they can imagine. Alternatively, a clueless admin who needs root access for one specific activity could inadvertently misconfigure the system, mess up security settings, delete files, or damage the computer in some other way. Moreover, because there's no other way to delegate administration, multiple people often end up knowing the root password and accessing the root account, providing increased opportunities for attackers to break in.

When delegating administrative tasks, users almost never need the full power of root. Instead, they usually need access to only a handful of commands to perform their administrative tasks. The approach of assigning to users only the exact authorizations they need for their particular tasks is the principle of *least privilege*. Several solutions are available in the UNIX and Linux world to implement this principle.

One implementation of least privilege with which you might be familiar is *sudo*. This software, used by Ubuntu Linux and Mac OS X, among others, enables users to "do" certain actions as superuser. These actions can usually be individually assigned to specific users, enabling the desired fine-grained control over administrative authorizations.

> **TIP** Sudo is available on OpenSolaris in the SUNWsudo package. You can install it from the network repository with the following command:
>
> ```
> # pkg install SUNWsudo
> ```

Natively, however, OpenSolaris takes a slightly different approach, using *role-based access control* (RBAC) to implement least privilege for users.

RBAC terminology

Before delving into the details of RBAC, it's important to understand the terminology. RBAC introduces three new concepts:

- **Authorization** — A fine-grained capability for a specific task. For example, solaris.smf.modify.framework allows a user to enable and disable SMF services.
- **Rights profile** — A grouping of authorizations. For example, the Cron Management Rights Profile allows management of at and cron jobs by including the solaris.jobs.* and solaris.smf.manage.cron authorizations. Rights profiles can also contain commands that must be run as specific user IDs or with certain security privileges.
- **Role** — A special account on the system. Similar to a user, except that you cannot log in directly to a role. Roles can be assigned authorizations and rights profiles, and are assigned to specific users.

Using RBAC

As explained in Chapter 3, the OpenSolaris distribution from Sun makes root itself a role, gives the initial user account the Primary Administrator rights profile, and assigns the root role to the initial user account.

385

NOTE   If you don't create a user account in the installer, the OpenSolaris distribution does not make root a role.

The benefit of making root a role is that the only way to access the root account is to first log in as a user assigned the root role. Even if attackers managed to obtain the root password, they couldn't access the root role without first accessing another account with that role assigned. Thus, making root a role adds an extra level of security to your system. However, as explained later in this section, the Primary Administrator role is quite powerful, basically giving root capabilities. Therefore, when using the OpenSolaris distribution, protect the initial user account as you would root.

There are two different ways to use RBAC as a user with the Primary Administrator role. The first, as described in Chapter 3, is to prefix privileged commands with the `pfexec` command. For example, if you try to create a file in `/etc` without `pfexec`, the command is rejected. With `pfexec`, the command succeeds:

```
$ touch /etc/blah
touch: cannot touch `/etc/blah': Permission denied
$ pfexec touch /etc/blah
$ ls /etc/blah
/etc/blah
```

If you grow tired of using `pfexec`, you can run multiple commands from a *profile shell*, which is a special version of the shell that understands RBAC, obviating the need to execute `pfexec` explicitly. For example, you can use `pfcsh` as follows:

```
$ pfcsh
% touch /etc/newfile
```

TIP   The OpenSolaris distribution provides `sh` and `csh` versions of the profile shell, called `pfsh` and `pfcsh`, respectively. Other distributions of OpenSolaris, such as Solaris Express, also provide a `ksh` version, `pfksh`, which is not in the OpenSolaris distribution because of redistribution restrictions. Currently, there is no `bash` version of the profile shell.

Authorizations

Now that you understand the terminology and how to use RBAC as initially configured, it's time to delve into the details. An authorization is a fine-grained capability for a specific task. All authorizations are listed in the `/etc/security/auth_attr` file. Here is a short listing from that file:

```
# tail /etc/security/auth_attr
solaris.smf.value.servicetags:::Change Service Tag Service Property Values
::help=StValue.html
solaris.smf.value.smb:::Change Values of SMB Service Properties::help=
SmfValueSMB.html
```

```
solaris.smf.value.tnd:::Change Trusted Network Daemon Service Property Values
::help=ValueTND.html
solaris.smf.value.vscan:::Change Values of VSCAN Properties::help=
SmfValueVscan.html
solaris.snmp.:::SNMP Management::help=AuthSnmpHeader.html
solaris.snmp.read:::Get SNMP Information::help=AuthSnmpRead.html
solaris.snmp.write:::Set SNMP Information::help=AuthSnmpWrite.html
solaris.system.:::Machine Administration::help=SysHeader.html
solaris.system.date:::Set Date & Time::help=SysDate.html
solaris.system.shutdown:::Shutdown the System::help=SysShutdown.html
```

The first field in each entry is the authorization name. As an administrator, you won't need to create or change the authorizations themselves, and you should not modify /etc/security/auth_attr.

Keep in mind that authorization names are not inherently meaningful. Each program that requires authorizations must explicitly check for that authorization name. For example, here's the code in the lpset command that checks for the solaris.print.admin authorization:

```
if (chkauthattr("solaris.print.admin", pw->pw_name) == 1)
    return (1);    /* "solaris.print.admin" is authorized */
```

You can view the authorizations for the current user by running the auths command. Here are the authorizations for a normal user:

```
$ auths
solaris.device.cdrw,solaris.profmgr.read,solaris.jobs.user,solaris
.mail.mailq,solaris.device.mount.removable,solaris.admin.usermgr.read
,solaris.admin.logsvc.read,solaris.admin.fsmgr.read,solaris.admin
.serialmgr.read,solaris.admin.diskmgr.read,solaris.admin.procmgr.user
,solaris.compsys.read,solaris.admin.printer.read,solaris.admin
.prodreg.read,solaris.admin.dcmgr.read,solaris.snmp.read,solaris
.project.read,solaris.admin.patchmgr.read,solaris.network.hosts
.read,solaris.admin.volmgr.read
```

Here are the authorizations for root:

```
# auths
solaris.*
```

As expected, and as expressed with the wildcard *, root has every possible authorization.

You can assign authorizations directly to users using the usermod command. For example, suppose you want to allow user test to enable and disable SMF services. Without the solaris.smf.modify.framework authorization, test can't do that:

```
$ auths | grep smf
$ /usr/sbin/svcadm disable telnet
svcadm: svc:/network/telnet:default: Permission denied.
```

As root, or as a user with the `solaris.grant` authorization, you can assign the `solaris.smf.modify.framework` authorization to user `test`:

```
# usermod -A solaris.smf.modify.framework test
```

> **CAUTION** If your user information is stored in a directory server such as NIS or LDAP, you cannot assign or modify authorizations or profiles (discussed in subsequent sections) with `usermod`.

Now user `test` can enable and disable SMF services:

```
$ auths | grep smf
solaris.smf.modify.framework,solaris.device.cdrw,solaris.profmgr.
read,solaris.jobs.user,solaris.mail.mailq,solaris.device.mount.
removable,solaris.admin.usermgr.read,solaris.admin.logsvc.read,
solaris.admin.fsmgr.read,solaris.admin.serialmgr.read,solaris.
admin.diskmgr.read,solaris.admin.procmgr.user,solaris.compsys.
read,solaris.admin.printer.read,solaris.admin.prodreg.read,
solaris.admin.dcmgr.read,solaris.snmp.read,solaris.project.read,
solaris.admin.patchmgr.read,solaris.network.hosts.read,solaris.
admin.volmgr.read
$ svcs telnet
STATE          STIME    FMRI
online         13:21:45 svc:/network/telnet:default
$ /usr/sbin/svcadm disable telnet
$ svcs telnet
STATE          STIME    FMRI
disabled       13:21:49 svc:/network/telnet:default
```

> **CAUTION** The `-A` option to `usermod` replaces the current authorizations that aren't part of an assigned rights profile with the new list, rather than add the authorization to the existing list.

One question you might have at this point is how to determine which authorizations are required for which actions. The answer, unfortunately, is basically trial and error. There's no explicit mapping that you can look up, and the command man pages don't provide the specific authorizations.

Despite the capability to assign authorizations directly to users, it's best to avoid that in favor of the bigger picture: rights profiles and roles. For one thing, messing around with individual authorizations is annoying and difficult to track. Moreover, simply assigning the appropriate authorization to a user is often not enough to allow that user to perform the desired action, because the necessary application or script itself may check user IDs or privileges to run. These user ids and privileges are assigned as part of a rights profile. Finally, as mentioned, it's not always clear which authorization is required for which action. The predefined rights profiles include the necessary authorizations for the higher-level goals. For all of these reasons, it's best to work on the level of rights profiles and roles, rather than directly assign authorizations.

Rights profiles

A rights profile is a collection of authorizations along with a list of commands that can be run with different user IDs or special privileges by users or roles assigned to that rights profile. The rights profile information is split between /etc/security/prof_attr, which lists the authorizations, and /etc/security/exec_attr, which lists the commands. For example, consider the File System Management rights profile. The entry in /etc/security/prof_attr looks like this:

```
File System Management:::Manage, mount, share file systems:profiles=
SMB Management,VSCAN Management;auths=solaris.smf.manage.autofs,
solaris.smf.manage.shares.*, solaris.smf.value.shares.*,solaris.
admin.fsmgr.*,solaris.admin.diskmgr.*,solaris.admin.volmgr.*;help=
RtFileSysMngmnt.html
```

The fields in this entry are colon-separated. The first field in the entry, File System Management, is the name of the profile. The next field that's filled is just a human-readable description. The final field sets the properties. One property of particular interest is the profiles property, which allows a profile to be layered on other profiles. In this case, the File System Management profile incorporates the SMB Management and VSCAN profiles. The second property of particular interest is the auths property, which specifies the specific authorizations from /etc/security/auth_attr that are part of this rights profile. In this case, you can see several file-system-related authorizations listed, which is expected because this is the File System Management rights profile.

The second half of the rights profile description is in /etc/security/exec_attr. Here are a few of the many File System Management entries from that file:

```
File System Management:solaris:cmd:::/sbin/mount:privs=sys_mount
File System Management:solaris:cmd:::/usr/sbin/quotacheck:uid=0;gid=sys
File System Management:suser:cmd:::/usr/bin/eject:euid=0
File System Management:suser:cmd:::/usr/bin/mkdir:euid=0
```

Each entry in this file starts with the profile name. In all of these cases, the final field lists a command and any security attributes that must accompany it. For example, the /usr/bin/mkdir command is listed with an effective uid of 0. The /sbin/mount command is listed with the sys_mount privilege. Because of these security attributes, non-root users assigned this rights profile can run these commands, which will execute with the appropriate privileges. Process privileges are discussed later in this chapter.

OpenSolaris comes with quite a few interesting rights profiles already defined, from Apache 22 Administration to Project Management to ZFS File System Management. Three profiles deserve particular examination:

- **Basic Solaris User** — Contains the default authorizations and commands required by any user of the system, including read access to many facilities, read/write access to the CD/DVD device, and others.

- **Primary Administrator** — Essentially grants superuser capabilities, including all authorizations and the capability to run any command as uid 0. As mentioned earlier, this profile is assigned to the user created by the OpenSolaris installer.

- **All** — Grants access to all commands. To prevent overriding the security and privilege settings on commands in other profiles, this profile should generally be listed last in a user's profile list.

To examine the rights profiles of a particular user, run the `profiles` command:

```
$ profiles
Basic Solaris User
All
```

As you can see, by default a standard user account contains two profiles: Basic Solaris User and All. These are assigned in the /etc/security/policy.conf file:

```
AUTHS_GRANTED=solaris.device.cdrw
PROFS_GRANTED=Basic Solaris User
```

This file lists the authorizations and profiles granted by default to all users. You might be wondering where the All profile comes from. The Basic Solaris User profile includes the All profile, so listing only the Basic Solaris User draws in the All profile after the Basic Solaris User profile (recall that the order is important!)

Assigning and using profiles

Now that you understand the basics of profiles, you can assign them to users. For example, suppose you want to allow the user `test` to configure and administer zones. With only the default profiles and authorizations, `test` can't create a zone:

```
$ /usr/sbin/zonecfg -z myzone
WARNING: you do not have write access to this zone's configuration file;
going into read-only mode.
```

You can assign the Zone Management profile to user `test` with the `usermod` command:

```
# usermod -P "Zone Management" test
```

> **CAUTION** The -P option to usermod replaces current profiles that aren't part of the default assignment in /etc/security/policy.conf with the new list, rather than add the profiles to the existing list.

Now user `test` should be able to create a zone. However, `test` still cannot run `zonecfg` directly in a normal shell:

```
$ profiles
Zone Management
Basic Solaris User
```

```
All
$ /usr/sbin/zonecfg -z myzone
WARNING: you do not have write access to this zone's
configuration file;
going into read-only mode.
```

What's going on? Doesn't the Zone Management profile provide the capability to create zones? It does, but it requires an extra step. Note that zonecfg is listed in /etc/security/exec_attr as follows:

```
Zone Management:solaris:cmd:::/usr/sbin/zonecfg:uid=0
```

Because zonecfg requires special privileges to run, it must be executed from a profile shell. As explained earlier, there are two ways to execute privileged commands. The first way is to actually run the shell, and then execute the zonecfg command from inside it. This example uses the pfsh shell:

```
$ pfsh
$ /usr/sbin/zonecfg -z myzone
myzone: No such zone configured
Use 'create' to begin configuring a new zone.
zonecfg:myzone> create
zonecfg:myzone> set zonepath=/test/myzone
zonecfg:myzone> exit
$ exit
$
```

The second way is to execute a privileged command directly with pfexec:

```
$ pfexec /usr/sbin/zonecfg -z myzone
myzone: No such zone configured
Use 'create' to begin configuring a new zone.
zonecfg:myzone> create
zonecfg:myzone> set zonepath=/test/myzone
zonecfg:myzone> exit
$
```

For convenience, you can configure a role with a profile shell as the default shell and assign the rights profiles to that role to avoid dealing explicitly with profile shells.

Creating profiles

You can, of course, create, modify, and delete profiles. The easiest way is to directly modify /etc/security/prof_attr and /etc/security/exec_attr. For example, here's an entry from /etc/security/prof_attr to create a new profile that combines a few random authorizations:

```
myprofile:::Test Profile:auths=solaris.network.wifi.config;solaris.smf.manage.
cron;solaris.jobs.admin
```

Here's the entry from /etc/security/exec_attr to give that profile the capability to execute zonecfg as uid 0:

```
myprofile:solaris:cmd:::/usr/sbin/zonecfg:uid=0
```

Now you can assign this profile to a user:

```
# usermod -P myprofile test
```

This enables the user to perform the actions allowed by the profile:

```
$ profiles
myprofile
Basic Solaris User
All
$ pfexec /usr/sbin/zonecfg -z myzone
myzone: No such zone configured
Use 'create' to begin configuring a new zone.
zonecfg:myzone> create
zonecfg:myzone> set zonepath=/test/myzone
zonecfg:myzone> exit
$
```

To delete the profile, simply remove the entries from exec_attr and prof_attr.

Roles

A role is an identity on the system similar to a user. Like a user, a role can be assigned authorizations and rights profiles. Given that a role is so similar to a user, you might be wondering why you should use roles. Here are a few advantages:

- Roles must be explicitly assigned to users. To log in as that role, you must first log in as one of the users with that role assigned, then su to the role. Even an attacker who gains a role password cannot log in as that role unless the attacker also gains access to a user account with that role assigned.

- A role can be assigned a profile login shell, avoiding the need to run the shell explicitly or use pfexec to access commands allowed by assigned profiles.

- Roles can be assigned to more than one user, centralizing the assignments of authorizations and profiles.

Now that you understand the benefits of roles, you are ready to learn how to use them. The first step is to create a role, with the roleadd command. This example adds a role for zone administration, assigning the pfsh profile shell and the Zone Management profile to it:

```
# roleadd -s /usr/bin/pfsh -P "Zone Management" zoneadm
# passwd zoneadm
New Password:
Re-enter new Password:
passwd: password successfully changed for zoneadm
```

Roles are created in the same namespace as users, so you can't use a username or userID for a role that's already been used for a user. Adding a role creates an entry in /etc/passwd just like it does for a user, and a fairly self-explanatory entry in /etc/user_attr:

```
# grep zoneadm /etc/passwd
zoneadm:x:109:1::/home/zoneadm:/usr/bin/pfsh
# grep zoneadm /etc/user_attr
zoneadm::::type=role;profiles=Zone Management
```

You can delete and modify roles with roledel and rolemod, respectively. Use rolemod -P to assign profiles to the role. You can also assign authorizations directly to the role with rolemod -A.

CAUTION If your user information is stored in a directory server such as NIS or LDAP, you cannot assign or modify roles with rolemod.

As mentioned, only users with roles assigned can use those roles. Without assigning the role to anyone, it can't be used:

```
$ su zoneadm
Password:
Roles can only be assumed by authorized users
su: Sorry
$
```

You can assign roles with the usermod command:

```
# usermod -R zoneadm test
```

Now user test can su to the zoneadm role. You can use the roles command to view the roles assigned to a user. The following example verifies that this user is assigned the zoneadm role, switches to that role, and then executes zonecfg to create a zone:

```
$ roles
zoneadm
$ su zoneadm
Password:

$ /usr/sbin/zonecfg -z myzone
myzone: No such zone configured
Use 'create' to begin configuring a new zone.
zonecfg:myzone> create
zonecfg:myzone> set zonepath=/test/myzone
zonecfg:myzone> exit
$
```

TIP You cannot log in directly as a role. You must always log in to a user account with that role assigned and su to the role.

Making root a role

As described earlier, the OpenSolaris distribution makes root a role if you create a user in the installer. If you're using a different distribution, or you didn't create an initial user and you now want to make root a role by hand, you can do so easily with `usermod`:

```
# usermod -K type=role root
# grep root /etc/user_attr
root::::type=role;auths=solaris.*,solaris.grant;profiles=Web Console
Management,All;lock_after_retries=no;clearance=admin_high;min_label=
admin_low
```

> **CAUTION** You must assign the root role to at least one user; otherwise, you'll never be able to log in as root again!

```
# usermod -R root test
```

You can use this technique to move any user to a role. To move a role back to a user, you must use `rolemod` instead:

```
# rolemod -K type=normal root
```

Privileges

As discussed earlier in the chapter, role-based access control (RBAC) implements the policy of least privilege for users in OpenSolaris. Privileges in OpenSolaris essentially do the same thing, but at the process level.

setuid

Before delving into OpenSolaris privileges, it's helpful to understand the old way of solving the problem of running processes with more permissions than the user who runs them. The *Set User ID (setuid)* capability in UNIX enables a process to run with the permissions of the executable file's owner instead of the permissions of the user who executes it. A setuid executable that runs with root permissions is called *setuid root*. Traditionally, setuid is the only mechanism available to run commands that require more privileges than the user executing the command has. Thus, many commands in OpenSolaris, such as `passwd` and `rlogin`, run with setuid, usually setuid root.

Setuid root programs, however, are security risks. A process running as root has virtually unlimited power. If it's compromised, through a bug, buffer-overflow attack, or some other technique, the attacker can do unlimited damage.

Furthermore, although most processes that run as root need only a handful of additional capabilities, the all-or-nothing model gives them far more privileges than they need, creating security risks. Consider a process that needs to communicate over a privileged network port.

In the all-or-nothing model, this process would need to run as root, giving it a multitude of unneeded capabilities, such as write access to all files on the system, fork and exec privileges, access to devices, and more. If attackers compromised this process, perhaps via a bug in the applications, they could use it to perform any malicious activities they desired.

> **TIP** Because setuid root programs can be so dangerous, and are so well-loved by attackers, periodically scan your system for new setuid root programs. The Basic Audit Reporting Tool (BART) described later in this chapter can help with this task.

Privileges overview

The privileges mechanism in OpenSolaris provides a safer alternative to the all-or-nothing model of running processes as setuid root. Processes can instead be assigned fine-grained privileges for specific activities. For example, the process that needs access to a privileged port would require the PRIV_NET_PRIVADDR privilege. Assigning the requisite privileges to a command in a rights profile provides several benefits. First, only users or roles assigned that rights profile can execute it. Second, and most important, the command can be assigned the least privileges it needs to run properly, instead of the unlimited privileges of root.

OpenSolaris, coming from the traditional UNIX model, hasn't transitioned completely to privileges, so you'll still see quite a few setuid programs and daemons running as root. However, some commands have transitioned to use privileges, or have at least become part of rights profiles specifying that they run as uid 0 instead of being setuid root explicitly. Furthermore, a few system daemons now run as user daemon instead of user root, with the appropriate privileges.

> **TIP** To list all the privileges in OpenSolaris, run ppriv -lv, or look at the privileges(5) man page.

To enhance security further, processes that are privilege-aware can discard the privileges with which they were started but no longer need. For example, after daemonizing, a process could drop the PRIV_PROC_FORK and PRIV_PROC_EXEC privileges such that, even if the process were compromised, it wouldn't be capable of doing as much damage.

Although privileges apply principally to processes, they can also be assigned directly to users. Processes started by those users inherit the specified privileges from them. Unlike authorizations, privileges are enforced at the kernel level, so no profile shell or su to a role is needed.

> **CROSS-REF** By default, zones have restricted privileges. However, they are configurable. Consult Chapter 19 for details on privileges and zones.

Viewing privileges

You can use the ppriv command to view your shell's current privileges:

```
$ ppriv $$
755:    -bash
```

```
flags=<none>
        E: basic
        I: basic
        P: basic
        L: all
```

This output requires some explanation. Table 11-4 summarizes the four privilege sets for each process.

TABLE 11-4

Process Privilege Sets

Set	Description
Effective	Privileges the process is current using (currently "in effect")
Inheritable	Privileges that are passed across a call to exec
Permitted	Privileges the process is currently allowed to use.
Limit	Maximum privileges that the process would ever be allowed to assume

The output from ppriv uses E, I, P, and L to refer to the Effective, Inheritable, Permitted, and Limit sets, respectively. The effective, inheritable, and permitted sets are all basic, while the limit set is all. The basic set, as the name implies, reflects fundamental privileges that all processes generally need. The all set, also as the name implies, reflects all privileges on the system. To see an explicit list of privileges instead of the basic and all shorthands, use the -v option to ppriv:

```
$ ppriv -v $$
755:    -bash
flags=<none>
        E: file_link_any,proc_exec,proc_fork,proc_info,proc_session
        I: file_link_any,proc_exec,proc_fork,proc_info,proc_session
        P: file_link_any,proc_exec,proc_fork,proc_info,proc_session
        L: contract_event,contract_observer,cpc_cpu,dtrace_kernel,
dtrace_proc,dtrace_user,file_chown,file_chown_self,file_dac_execute,
file_dac_read,file_dac_search,file_dac_write,file_downgrade_sl,file_
flag_set,file_link_any,file_owner,file_setid,file_upgrade_sl,
graphics_access,graphics_map,ipc_dac_read,ipc_dac_write,ipc_owner,
net_bindmlp,net_icmpaccess,net_mac_aware,net_privaddr,net_rawaccess,
proc_audit,proc_chroot,proc_clock_highres,proc_exec,proc_fork,proc_
info,proc_lock_memory,proc_owner,proc_priocntl,proc_session,proc_
setid,proc_taskid,proc_zone,sys_acct,sys_admin,sys_audit,sys_config,
sys_devices,sys_ip_config,sys_ipc_config,sys_linkdir,sys_mount,sys_
net_config,sys_nfs,sys_res_config,sys_resource,sys_smb,sys_suser_
```

```
compat,sys_time,sys_trans_label,win_colormap,win_config,win_dac_
read,win_dac_write,win_devices,win_dga,win_downgrade_sl,win_
fontpath,win_mac_read,win_mac_write,win_selection,win_upgrade_sl
```

Running ppriv as root shows the following:

```
# ppriv $$
728:    sh
flags=<none>
        E: all
        I: basic
        P: all
        L: all
```

As expected, the root shell has all privileges. Interestingly, though, the inheritable set is only basic. That's a security measure to prevent even those processes running with root privileges from spawning other processes with those same privileges.

You can also view the privilege sets on a currently running process with ppriv:

```
# ppriv `pgrep syslogd`
488:    /usr/sbin/syslogd
flags=<none>
        E: all
        I: basic
        P: all
        L: all
```

Another useful feature of ppriv is the -D option, which causes it to specify exactly which privileges are missing for a desired operation. Use it with -e to execute a command under ppriv. For example, users by default can't chown files:

```
$ ls -l testfile
-rw-r--r--   1 test      other           0 Mar 26 11:08 testfile
$ chown nsolter testfile
chown: testfile: Not owner
$ ppriv -eD chown nsolter testfile
chown[892]: missing privilege "file_chown_self" (euid=108, syscall
= 16) needed at tmp_setattr+0x5e
chown: testfile: Not owner
```

Now you know that you need the file_chown_self privilege to change ownership of a file. The truss command also prints the missing privileges for an operation:

```
$ truss chown nsolter testfile
 ...
chown("testfile", 101, -1)                    Err#1 EPERM [file_chown_self]
 ...
```

Privileges and RBAC

As described earlier, rights profiles can contain commands that run with specific security attributes. One of those attributes could be simply running as uid or euid root. However, you can also specify finer-grained privileges. For example, consider the entry for the mount command in /etc/security/exec_attr:

```
File System Management:solaris:cmd:::/sbin/mount:privs=sys_mount
```

This line says that the mount command should run with the extra sys_mount privilege when executed by a user assigned the File System Management rights profile. Recall that users must execute privileged commands via a profile shell or with pfexec.

This technique is the preferred way to use process privileges. Rather than assign privileges directly to users or roles, you specify commands with security privileges as part of a rights profile. That rights profile can then be assigned to a user or role.

Assigning privileges to users and roles

Although it's not the preferred way to use privileges, you can assign them directly to users and roles with the usermod and rolemod commands. This is sometimes useful for quickly modifying a user's or role's privileges for testing purposes, but adding unneeded privileges can be a security risk and removing necessary privileges can make user accounts unusable. Instead of assigning privileges directly to users and roles, it's better to assign privileges to processes via rights profiles, as described previously.

Restricted shell

If you're concerned about clueless users inadvertently damaging the system in some way, you can assign a *restricted shell* to them instead of a standard shell. The restricted shell, /usr/lib/rsh, prohibits changing directories, setting the PATH, using / in path or command names, and redirecting output. It's not too fun to use, but it can be useful for severely limiting a user. You can set the login shell for a user with usermod:

```
# usermod -s /usr/lib/rsh test
```

Now user test can't do too much:

```
$ cd /
cd: restricted
$ /usr/bin/passwd
/usr/bin/passwd: restricted
```

Most users shouldn't need to be assigned a restricted shell. However, you should also strongly encourage all users to avoid putting the current directory in their paths. Users with a dot (.) in their paths are at risk for Trojan horse commands that could be placed in a public directory, and then executed unknowingly instead of the desired command if that directory were the working directory.

Access control lists

By employing the requisite file system security measures, you can limit an attacker's ability to access files, even if your system is compromised in some way.

Traditional UNIX file permissions allow you to grant read, write, and execute access at three different levels: to the file owner, to the group, and to "the world." To protect files from nefarious attackers, users should not grant write and execute access to anyone except themselves. A world-readable, writable, or executable file can be accessed by anyone with access to the system, so an attacker who breaks in to any account could access that file. However, sometimes you need to grant access to files for various reasons. Because the traditional UNIX file permissions are fairly coarse, OpenSolaris implements finer-grained access control lists (ACLs) for its file systems. Unfortunately, ACLs differ between UFS and ZFS/NFSv4.

CROSS-REF See Chapters 7, 8, and 10 for coverage of UFS, ZFS, and NFS, respectively.

UFS access control lists

UFS ACLs add the capability to specify permissions on a per-user and per-group basis. For example, for a specific file, you could give read and write permissions to one user and read-only permissions to another user. Or you could give execute permissions to one group, except for one user in that group.

Use `getfacl` to see the ACLs on a UFS file:

```
$ getfacl accltest

# file: accltest
# owner: nsolter
# group: staff
user::rw-
group::r--              #effective:r--
mask:r--
other:r--
```

The user, group, and other lines are simply the standard owner, group, and "all other" file permissions. The mask is the maximum permissions for any user other than the owner. By setting the mask, you can reduce the permissions, which are represented by the effective permissions listed in the right column of this output.

You can use `setfacl` to set ACLs on a UFS file. The following example removes read permissions from group and other, giving read permissions only to user `test` for the `accltest` file:

```
$ setfacl -m group::---,other:---,user:test:r-- accltest
$ getfacl accltest

# file: accltest
```

```
# owner: nsolter
# group: staff
user::rw-
user:test:r--              #effective:r--
group::---                 #effective:---
mask:r--
other:---
```

Note that `group` is followed by two colons, but `other` only one colon. With the `-m` option to `setfacl`, you can specify selected ACL entries. Use `-s` to set all ACL entries.

As another example, you could give the `staff` group read permissions, except for user `test`. This example also shows that you can use the octal representation for permissions instead of the symbolic representation:

```
$ setfacl -m group::4,user:test:0 accltest
$ getfacl accltest

# file: accltest
# owner: nsolter
# group: staff
user::rw-
user:test:---              #effective:---
group::r--                 #effective:r--
mask:r--
other:---
```

You can also set default ACLs on a directory, which apply to any file created in that directory:

```
$ setfacl -m default:user::6,default:group::0,default:other:0.
$ getfacl.

# file: .
# owner: nsolter
# group: staff
user::rwx
group::r-x                 #effective:r-x
mask:r-x
other:r-x
default:user::rw-
default:group::---
default:other:---
$ touch defaulttest
$ getfacl defaulttest

# file: defaulttest
# owner: nsolter
# group: staff
user::rw-
```

```
group::---                    #effective:---
mask:---
other:---
```

To delete ACLs, use the -d option to setfacl:

```
$ setfacl -d user:test accltest
$ getfacl accltest

# file: accltest
# owner: nsolter
# group: staff
user::rw-
group::r--                    #effective:r--
mask:r--
other:---
```

> **NOTE** In our experience, UFS ACLs are not commonly used, so to avoid confusing your fellow users, employ them only when strictly necessary.

ZFS access control lists

In addition to providing the finer-grained user-level controls in UFS ACLs, ZFS provides finer-grained permissions. Instead of just read, write, and execute, the NFSv4 specification includes all of the following permissions:

```
read_data          read_xattr          delete_child
list_directory     write_xattr         read_acl
write_data         execute             write_acl
add_file           read_attributes     write_owner
append_data        write_attributes    synchronize
add_subdirectory   delete
```

However, synchronize and append_data are not supported on OpenSolaris; and note that some of the permissions, such as list_directory, add_subdirectory, and delete_child, are applicable only to directories. Most of the permissions are self-explanatory, but consult the chmod(1) man page for a detailed description of each of these permissions.

> **NOTE** ZFS uses the same ACLs as NFSv4 and CIFS. See Chapter 10 for details on NFS and CIFS.

ZFS permissions also have a concept of allow or deny. Each permission is explicitly allowed or denied. The remainder of this section shows ZFS ACL examples.

Use /usr/bin/ls -v to view ZFS ACLs:

```
$ /usr/bin/ls -v accltest
-rw-r--r--   1 nsolter  staff         15 Apr  1 13:58 accltest
```

```
0:owner@:execute:deny
1:owner@:read_data/write_data/append_data/write_xattr/write_attributes
    /write_acl/write_owner:allow
2:group@:write_data/append_data/execute:deny
3:group@:read_data:allow
4:everyone@:write_data/append_data/write_xattr/execute/write_attributes
    /write_acl/write_owner:deny
5:everyone@:read_data/read_xattr/read_attributes/read_acl/synchronize
    :allow
```

As shown in ACL entry 1, the file owner is explicitly allowed to read, write, and append data, write attributes, extended attributes and ACLs, and change the file owner. However, the file owner is denied execution permissions in ACL entry 0. Entries 2 and 3 deny write and execute permissions for the group, but allow read permissions. Entries 4 and 5 deny write and execute permissions, but allow read permissions for everyone who is not the owner or in the group.

> **CAUTION**   The GNU versions of `ls` and `chmod` do not understand ZFS ACLs. You must use `/usr/bin/ls` and `/usr/bin/chmod`, not the GNU versions `/usr/gnu/bin/ls` and `/usr/gnu/bin/chmod` to view and modify ZFS ACLs. Because `/usr/gnu/bin` is first in your path by default, you may need to explicitly list the full path for `ls` and `chmod` to get the `/usr/bin` versions.

You can modify ZFS file ACLs with the `/usr/bin/chmod` command. To remove all permissions from `group` and `other` and give read permissions to user `test`, use the following commands:

```
$ /usr/bin/chmod 600 accltest
$ /usr/bin/chmod A+user:test:read_data:allow accltest
$ /usr/bin/ls -v accltest
-rw-------+  1 nsolter  staff           0 Apr  1 17:46 accltest
    0:user:test:read_data:allow
    1:owner@:execute:deny
    2:owner@:read_data/write_data/append_data/write_xattr/write_attributes
        /write_acl/write_owner:allow
    3:group@:read_data/write_data/append_data/execute:deny
    4:group@::allow
    5:everyone@:read_data/write_data/append_data/write_xattr/execute
        /write_attributes/write_acl/write_owner:deny
    6:everyone@:read_xattr/read_attributes/read_acl/synchronize:allow
```

The first command uses the shortcut of setting the file permissions to 600, which ZFS automatically translates into the appropriate ACLs for owner, group, and everyone. The second command explicitly adds the `read_data` permission for the `test` user.

If instead you want to give everyone read permissions except for user `test`, run the following commands:

```
$ /usr/bin/chmod 644 accltest
$ /usr/bin/ls -v accltest
-rw-r--r--+  1 nsolter  staff           0 Apr  1 18:00 accltest
```

```
        0:user:test::deny
        1:user:test:read_data:allow
        2:owner@:execute:deny
        3:owner@:read_data/write_data/append_data/write_xattr/write_attributes
            /write_acl/write_owner:allow
        4:group@:write_data/append_data/execute:deny
        5:group@:read_data:allow
        6:everyone@:write_data/append_data/write_xattr/execute/write_attributes
            /write_acl/write_owner:deny
        7:everyone@:read_data/read_xattr/read_attributes/read_acl/synchronize
            :allow
$ /usr/bin/chmod A1- accltest
$ /usr/bin/chmod A0=user:test:read_data:deny accltest
$ /usr/bin/ls -v accltest
-rw-r--r--+  1 nsolter  staff           0 Apr  1 18:00 accltest
        0:user:test:read_data:deny
        1:owner@:execute:deny
        2:owner@:read_data/write_data/append_data/write_xattr/write_attributes
            /write_acl/write_owner:allow
        3:group@:write_data/append_data/execute:deny
        4:group@:read_data:allow
        5:everyone@:write_data/append_data/write_xattr/execute/write_attributes
            /write_acl/write_owner:deny
        6:everyone@:read_data/read_xattr/read_attributes/read_acl/synchronize
            :allow
```

This example first uses the standard UNIX permissions to give everyone read permissions. Then it removes entry 1 in the ACL list, which gives read permissions to user test, with this command:

```
$ /usr/bin/chmod A1- accltest
```

Finally, it changes entry 0 to deny read permissions for user test:

```
$ /usr/bin/chmod A0=user:test:read_data:deny accltest
```

Note that the test user can still list the file attributes and the ACLs on the file, because read_attributes and read_acl are not denied.

ZFS also provides a compact permissions format. To see permissions in this format, use ls -V:

```
$ /usr/bin/ls -V accltest
-rw-r--r--+  1 nsolter  staff           0 Apr  1 18:00 accltest
            user:test:r------------:-------:deny
               owner@:--x----------:-------:deny
               owner@:rw-p---A-W-Co-:-------:allow
               group@:-wxp---------:-------:deny
               group@:r------------:-------:allow
            everyone@:-wxp---A-W-Co-:-------:deny
            everyone@:r-----a-R-c--s:-------:allow
```

In this format, each permission is represented by a single unique character, in order, from read_data (r) to synchronize (s). You can use this shorthand in the chmod command line as well. For example, to give user test the read_data, read_xttr, read, read_attributes, and read_acl permissions, you can use the following:

```
$ /usr/bin/chmod A0=user:test:raRc:allow accltest
$ /usr/bin/ls -v accltest
-rw-r--r--+ 1 nsolter  staff        0 Apr  1 18:00 accltest
    0:user:test:read_data/read_xattr/read_attributes/read_acl:allow
    1:owner@:execute:deny
    2:owner@:read_data/write_data/append_data/write_xattr/write_attributes
        /write_acl/write_owner:allow
    3:group@:write_data/append_data/execute:deny
    4:group@:read_data:allow
    5:everyone@:write_data/append_data/write_xattr/execute/write_attributes
        /write_acl/write_owner:deny
    6:everyone@:read_data/read_xattr/read_attributes/read_acl/synchronize:allow
```

As with UFS, ZFS supports ACLs on directories. Unlike UFS, ZFS also supports four different inheritance flags: file_inherit, dir_inherit, inherit_only, and no_propagate. These flags can be specified on directories, and applied to files and subdirectories created within those directories. The file_inherit and dir_inherit flags specify that files and subdirectories created in that directory should inherit the permissions of that directory. The inherit_only flag means that the specified permissions apply only to subdirectories and files, not to the directory itself. Finally, no_propagate means that the permissions inheritance should not apply transitively to files and subdirectories within subdirectories.

Note that the behavior of the inheritance flags is moderated by the aclinherit property on the ZFS dataset. See Chapter 8 for details on ZFS dataset properties.

Encrypted files

Another way to protect your files against attackers who obtain access to your user account, or even to root, is to encrypt them. You can use the encrypt and decrypt commands to encrypt and decrypt your files, respectively. First, use encrypt -l to see a list of available algorithms and their keysizes:

```
$ encrypt -l
Algorithm       Keysize:  Min   Max (bits)
------------------------------------------
aes                       128   128
arcfour                     8   128
des                        64    64
3des                      192   192
```

To encrypt a file, you need a key, which you can generate with the `pktool` command and store it in a file:

```
$ pktool genkey keystore=file outkey=filekey keytype=generic \
keylen=192
```

Finally, encrypt the file:

```
$ encrypt -a 3des -k filekey -i test.txt -o test.encrypted.txt
```

If you don't specify a key, you'll be prompted for a passphrase, which is converted into a key.

You can decrypt the file with the `decrypt` command:

```
$ decrypt -a 3des -k filekey -i test.encrypted.txt -o \
test.decrypted.txt
```

> **NOTE** Consult the `pktool(1)`, `encrypt(1)`, and `decrypt(1)` man pages for more information on these tools. The OpenSolaris cryptography framework takes advantage of special cryptography hardware if it is found on the system.

Encrypting individual files by hand can get tiresome. Luckily, there is a project in progress to provide encryption support for ZFS datasets.

> **CROSS-REF** To learn more about ZFS encryption, consult Chapter 8, "ZFS."

Message digests

OpenSolaris provides several tools for manually calculating message digests and message authentication codes (MACs). A *message digest*, also called a *hash* or a *checksum*, is simply a number that is uniquely generated from a file. The mathematical algorithms used in hash computation make it extremely unlikely that different files would generate the same hash. These digests are useful for verifying file or message integrity.

A message authentication code is like a digest, but protected with a key, such that it can provide message authentication.

If you come from a Linux background, you're probably familiar with `/usr/bin/md5sum`, `/usr/bin/sha1sum`, and the other Secure Hash Algorithm (SHA) digests such as `/usr/bin/sha224sum` and so on. OpenSolaris also includes the traditional `digest` command, which provides functionality similar to `md5sum` and friends.

Additionally, OpenSolaris provides the `mac` command for key-protected authentication.

Consult the man pages for these commands, all in section 1, for details.

Preventing user stack execution

In addition to protecting access to regular files, you must consider executable files. Most legitimate programs have no need to execute code off their stack. However, attackers can exploit executable stacks for buffer overflows and other similar attacks. Unfortunately, the default behavior in OpenSolaris is to mark each program's stack as executable. However, you can change this behavior by adding the following two lines to /etc/system and rebooting the system:

```
set noexec_user_stack=1
set noexec_user_stack_log=1
```

The first line makes the user stacks non-executable, while the second specifies that attempts to execute code off the stack should be logged. With these changes, stacks are not executable, thus preventing many of these kinds of attacks.

CAUTION   On rare occasions, stack execution is required by legitimate programs. Although we recommend disabling this feature, be aware that if you come across an application that requires it, you'll need to enable it.

Zones and resource management

Two related OpenSolaris features, zones and resource management, are useful for limiting user and process damage to your system. Zones can serve as security containers, isolating malicious users or rogue processes, while effective resource management can provide similar protection even in the global zone.

CROSS-REF   The security applications of zones and resource management are discussed in Chapters 19 and 18, respectively.

Ensuring Secure Communication

Even if attackers are unable to attack your OpenSolaris system directly, they could still gain important information by eavesdropping or snooping your network communication between machines. Furthermore, snooping the networking communication is a great way to obtain passwords and other information that enables the attacker to break into the system.

Attackers can also interfere with your network communication by modifying packets as they go by, or by resending, or *replaying*, certain packets.

Communication over the network is secure only if it guarantees confidentiality, authenticity, and integrity. Confidentiality means that no one between the sender and intended recipient of the data can read the data. Confidentiality is enabled through encryption. The process of encryption mangles the message in such a way that only the intended recipient can unmangle, or decrypt, it. Thus, encryption protects the secrecy of your communication. The encryption algorithms are generally public, but each individual or machine uses different *keys*. There are two basic forms of encryption in use today:

- **Symmetric, or shared-key, encryption** — Uses the same key to both encrypt and decrypt messages. Symmetric encryption is usually quick, but the downside is the problem of key distribution. Because both the sender and the recipient of a message need the shared key, there's a bootstrapping problem of getting that shared key to both parties in a secure fashion. Well-known symmetric encryption algorithms are 3DES and Blowfish.

- **Asymmetric, or public-key, encryption** — Uses different keys for encryption and decryption. A user or machine can freely distribute a public key, which anyone can use to encrypt a message that only the intended user or machine can then decrypt with its private key. This technique avoids the bootstrapping key distribution problem but generally results in performance that is significantly below that of symmetric encryption. A common compromise is to use public key encryption to securely exchange a shared key, which is then used for the remainder of the transaction. Well-known public key algorithms are Diffie-Hellman and RSA.

Authenticity means that the recipient can securely verify the sender. Authentication is usually obtained through digital signatures, in which the sender uses his or her private key to produce a hash or digest of the message that only the sender could produce.

Data integrity means that the information is not modified en route. Integrity is usually provided by including digests, or secure checksums, of the message that can be verified by the recipient. Digest algorithms, like encryption algorithms, are public, but use a shared secret key (or public/private key pairs) to provide security. Well-known digest algorithms include MD5 and SHA.

There are basically two levels at which secure communication can be implemented: the application level and the network level. Application-level support can be implemented in an ad hoc fashion by each application type, or it can implement a standard. The most widely known standards are the Secure Socket Layer (SSL) and its successor, the Transport Layer Security (TLS). For example, communication between a web browser and a web server, or between an e-mail client and an e-mail server, often use SSL or TLS. The key aspect of application-level security is that it must be provided by each application independently. The Secure Shell, discussed in more detail in the next section, is one of the most useful applications employing application-level security.

NOTE Technically speaking, SSL and TSL implement security at the socket layer, which is right below the application layer; but the implementation is usually part of the application itself, rather than something at the network layer that can apply to all applications, which is why this book categorizes it as application-level security.

An alternative to application-level security is network-level security — specifically, Internet Protocol (IP)-level security. Security at this level protects all IP network traffic (which is almost everything of interest) between the systems implementing it. With IP-level security, there is no need for individual applications to implement their own forms of encryption and integrity. OpenSolaris' implementation of IP security is discussed later in this chapter.

Secure Shell

The Secure Shell (SSH) provides a secure alternative to `telnet`, `rlogin`, `rsh`, `ftp`, and other clear-text network services. If you've ever used the `ssh` command to log in to a remote machine, you've used the Secure Shell network service. As described in the "Secure by Default" section earlier in this chapter, the SSH service is the only network service enabled by default in Open-Solaris to allow connections from remote machines. OpenSolaris currently provides an implementation of version 2 of the SSH protocol (SSH-2).

> **NOTE** It's possible to use `telnet`, `rlogin`, and other similar services in a more secure fashion with Kerberos covered later in this chapter.

Basic use of `ssh` is quite straightforward. On the server, make sure that the `ssh` service is online:

```
# svcs ssh
STATE          STIME    FMRI
online         10:19:56 svc:/network/ssh:default
```

If it's not running, enable it using the SMF techniques described in Chapter 13.

On the client machine, you can use the `ssh` command to obtain a secure remote shell on the server:

```
$ ssh mendelssohn
Password:
Last login: Sat Mar 29 10:23:09 2008 from 192.168.1.101
Sun Microsystems Inc.   SunOS 5.11      snv_83  January 2008
$
```

> **NOTE** The first time you connect to a remote machine, you'll see the following:
>
> ```
> The authenticity of host 'mendelssohn (192.168.1.120)' can't be established.
> RSA key fingerprint is 85:71:ee:5e:03:9f:a1:52:1e:67:1c:26:7d:4a:c1:7a.
> Are you sure you want to continue connecting (yes/no)? yes
> Warning: Permanently added 'mendelssohn,192.168.1.120' (RSA) to
> the list of known hosts.
> ```
>
> That's normal and expected. You can usually just answer "yes" unless you're concerned about the authenticity of the machine in question.

Non-password-based authentication

If you want to get fancy, there are a few different ways to set up your systems such that `ssh` authenticates automatically instead of prompting for passwords. One method, described later in this chapter, is to use Kerberos. A second mechanism, which must be implemented by the superuser or someone assigned the Primary Administrator role, authenticates at the host level instead of the user level.

> **CAUTION** Host-level authentication is generally considered to be less secure than user-level authentication.

To configure host-level authentication, follow these steps:

1. On the server machine, add the following property to /etc/ssh/sshd_config (or change it from no to yes):

   HostbasedAuthentication yes

2. Set the same property, HostbasedAuthentication, to yes in the /etc/ssh/ssh_config files on each client that will be authenticated to this server.

3. Create a file on the server machine /etc/shosts.equiv, and add to it all the client machines, one per line. The hostnames should be fully qualified.

4. Add the SSH public key for each client machine to the /etc/ssh/ssh_known_hosts file on the server. The SSH public key is found in /etc/ssh/ssh_host_dsa_key.pub. You can copy it from the client to the server using scp, which is described in more detail later.

5. Restart the SSH service on the server:

   ```
   # svcadm restart ssh
   ```

With these changes, you can now ssh into the server from the configured clients without entering a password:

```
$ ssh mendelssohn
Last login: Sat Mar 29 11:31:05 2008 from chopin.example.com
Sun Microsystems Inc.    SunOS 5.11       snv_83  January 2008
$
```

> **NOTE** Host-based authentication requires DNS to be configured properly for the machines in your network. Consult Chapter 10 for instructions on setting up DNS.

The final method for avoiding password-based authentication is user-based public key authentication. This method requires each user to generate a public/private key pair. The following example shows the configuration for SSH authentication from the client machine chopin to the server machine mendelssohn, and assumes the user has separate home directories on the two machines, rather than a single network-accessible home directory. The first step is to generate the public/private key pair with the ssh-keygen command on the client machine. You can generate either rsa or dsa keys, specified with the -t flag. The differences between the two algorithms are beyond the scope of this book. Consult a cryptography book listed in the "Resources" section at the end of this chapter for more information.

```
$ ssh-keygen -t dsa
Generating public/private dsa key pair.
Enter file in which to save the key (/export/home/nsolter/.ssh/id_dsa):
Enter passphrase (empty for no passphrase):
Enter same passphrase again:
Your identification has been saved in /export/home/nsolter/.ssh/id_dsa.
Your public key has been saved in /export/home/nsolter/.ssh/id_dsa.pub.
The key fingerprint is:
ab:80:31:81:32:51:16:b9:de:5a:48:9b:61:f5:d1:c0 nsolter@chopin
```

The public key must go into the user's ~/.ssh/authorized_keys file on the server machine. To do this, on the server machine, create the directory if it doesn't already exist:

```
$ mkdir ~/.ssh
```

Then copy the public key from the client machine. You can use the scp command described in the next section:

```
$ scp ~/.ssh/id_dsa.pub mendelssohn:.ssh/id_dsa_chopin.pub
Password:
id_dsa.pub          100% |*****************************|   601          00:00
```

Finally, put the key into the ~/.ssh/authorized_keys file on the server machine:

```
$ cat ~/.ssh/id_dsa_chopin.pub >> ~/.ssh/authorized_keys
```

Now you can ssh from the client machine to the server machine using your public/private keys instead of your password:

```
$ ssh mendelssohn
Enter passphrase for key '/export/home/nsolter/.ssh/id_dsa':
Last login: Sat Mar 29 11:31:07 2008 from chopin.example.com
Sun Microsystems Inc.   SunOS 5.11      snv_83  January 2008
$
```

Sadly, you haven't made your life much easier because you've just substituted the dsa key passphrase for the account password. However, if you must log into multiple machines on which you have accounts with different passwords, you can set up your ssh configurations on each machine to allow public/private key authentication. That way, you can ssh to any of those machines by typing only your key passphrase, instead of the separate account password for each machine.

To avoid entering even your key passphrase, use the ssh authentication agent to store your private keys:

```
$ ssh-agent /bin/bash
$ ssh-add
Enter passphrase for /export/home/nsolter/.ssh/id_dsa:
Identity added: /export/home/nsolter/.ssh/id_dsa (/export/home
```

```
/nsolter/.ssh/id_dsa)
$ ssh mendelssohn
Last login: Sat Mar 29 11:34:49 2008 from chopin.example.com
Sun Microsystems Inc.   SunOS 5.11      snv_83  January 2008
$
```

The first command, ssh-agent, starts the authentication agent. You must specify a shell to start
it in so that the environment variables are set up properly. The second command, ssh-add,
adds your keys from ~/.ssh/. Now, whenever you ssh to a machine configured with your
public key, ssh obtains the private key from the ssh-agent instead of prompting you for the
passphrase. Some users like to configure their login scripts to start the ssh authentication agent
automatically.

> **TIP** If you're using the OpenSolaris distribution, you'll find that the default GNOME session starts ssh-agent for you automatically.

If you want to remove your keys, run ssh-add -D:

```
$ ssh-add -D
All identities removed.
$ ssh mendelssohn
Enter passphrase for key '/export/home/nsolter/.ssh/id_dsa':
Last login: Sat Mar 29 11:57:48 2008 from chopin.example.com
Sun Microsystems Inc.   SunOS 5.11      snv_83  January 2008
$
```

Now you're back to entering your passphrase with each ssh connection.

Secure copy and FTP

The secure copy command, scp, is layered on top of ssh. You can use it to copy files to or
from a remote host over a secure connection. The following example copies the test file from
chopin to mendelssohn:

```
$ scp test.txt mendelssohn:test.txt
test.txt              100% |*****************************|    0       00:00
```

> **NOTE** scp uses the same authentication mechanisms as ssh. In the example, the user has configured the ssh authentication agent to use non-password-based authentication without entering a passphrase. See the previous section for details.

Secure copy is a secure alternative to the File Transfer Protocol (FTP), but the user interface
might be unfamiliar. If you prefer the traditional FTP interface, you can use sftp, which is also
layered on top of ssh:

```
$ sftp mendelssohn
Connecting to mendelssohn ...
sftp> put test.txt
```

```
Uploading test.txt to /export/home/nsolter/test.txt
test.txt                              100%   0    0.0KB/s   00:00
sftp> quit
$
```

SSH Tunneling

Another useful feature of ssh is *tunneling*, also called *port forwarding*. You can use tunneling
to run any TCP-based network service through ssh, enabling you to run a nonsecure service
in a secure manner. To take a trivial example, you can enable a secure telnet by forwarding an
unused local port to port 23 on the server:

```
$ ssh -L 9876:mendelssohn:23 mendelssohn
Last login: Sat Mar 29 13:47:19 2008 from mendelssohn.exa
Sun Microsystems Inc.   SunOS 5.11      snv_83  January 2008
$
```

In a second shell, you can obtain a secure telnet connection to the mendelssohn server by connecting to localhost port 9876:

```
$ hostname
chopin
$ telnet localhost 9876
Trying 127.0.0.1 ...
Connected to localhost.
Escape character is '^]'.
login: nsolter
Password:
Last login: Sat Mar 29 13:49:10 from chopin.example.com
Sun Microsystems Inc.   SunOS 5.11      snv_83  January 2008
$ hostname
mendelssohn
```

> **NOTE** To use ssh tunneling, port forwarding must be enabled on the server by setting
> AllowTcpForwarding yes in /etc/ssh/sshd_config.

One of the most useful capabilities of ssh tunneling is X11 forwarding, which you can use to
run GUI applications from a remote machine on your desktop in a secure manner. ssh provides
a convenience option, -X, to use X11 forwarding. Simply connect to the remote machine with
the -X option and launch X11 applications:

```
$ ssh -X mendelssohn
Last login: Sat Mar 29 13:52:56 2008 from mendelssohn.exa
Sun Microsystems Inc.   SunOS 5.11      snv_83  January 2008
$/usr/X11/bin/xterm &
[1] 714
$
```

ssh sets up a proxy X11 server on the remote host and sets the shell DISPLAY to connect to it. Assuming you're running an X11 server on the client, with this example, an xterm window should pop up.

To use X11 forwarding, it must be enabled on the server by setting X11Forwarding yes in /etc/ssh/sshd_config.

> **TIP** To improve the performance of SSH X11 forwarding, use the -C option to ssh to compress the data sent across the network.

Because you can run any network service securely with ssh, ssh tunneling is sometimes called a "poor man's virtual private network (VPN)." However, IPsec, described in the next section, provides an easier way to implement a VPN.

IP security

IP security (IPsec) implements network security at the IP level. TCP and UDP traffic running on top of IP is protected, so any application built on top of TCP or UDP benefits from the security without any modifications. These applications don't care, or even need to know, that their underlying networking communication is being encrypted and/or authenticated. Because pretty much every network application of interest uses the TCP or UDP protocols, IPsec can protect basically every network communication on your system. IPsec works with both IPv4 and IPv6. This chapter shows examples of IPv4 only.

IPsec is actually two different protocols:

- **Authentication Header (AH)** — Provides authentication, integrity, and protection against replays
- **Encapsulating Security Payload (ESP)** — Provides encryption, authentication, integrity, and protection against replays

You can use the protocols individually or in tandem. Note that although ESP seems to provide a superset of the functionality provided by AH, ESP actually provides slightly less authentication than AH provides. That's because ESP encrypts and authenticates the IP payload, but not the IP header. AH, however, authenticates some fields of the IP header.

IPsec uses the concept of a *Security Association* (SA), which defines the secure connection between two machines. Note that SAs are unidirectional, so secure communication between two machines requires two SAs (one in each direction).

IPsec requires shared keys between the participating machines. Managing these shared keys manually could be a logistical nightmare. Luckily, OpenSolaris provides an implementation of the Internet Key Exchange (IKE) protocol, which shares the keys automatically. The rest of this section shows you how to configure IPsec using IKE for key management.

Key management configuration

IPsec relies on shared keys, so before configuring IPsec you must set up your key exchange. OpenSolaris provides an implementation of IKE, so that is the recommended key exchange method. Unfortunately, there's a bootstrapping problem in that IKE itself needs to communicate securely and with integrity between machines. IKE allows several methods to implement this security. The simplest is a *preshared key*, which is a fancy way of saying the administrator must manually generate a key and ensure that both participating machines know its value.

> **NOTE** If you're a glutton for punishment, you can manage the IPsec keys manually instead of using IKE. See `ipseckey(1M)` for details.

To configure IKE with preshared keys, first create `/etc/inet/ike/config` on each machine. You can start with `/etc/inet/ike/config.sample`:

```
# cp /etc/inet/ike/config.sample /etc/inet/ike/config
# chmod 644 config
```

The only part of this file you need to modify is the rules. Delete all the text in the file below this comment:

```
### Now some rules ...
```

Now add a new rule for the two machines that will be exchanging keys. For example, to configure IKE to exchange keys between two machines, one named `mendelssohn`, with IP address 192.168.1.120, and one named `chopin`, with IP address 192.168.1.130, add the following rule to `/etc/inet/ike/config` on `mendelssohn`:

```
{
    label "mendelssohn to chopin"
    local_addr 192.168.1.120
    remote_addr 192.168.1.130
    p1_xform
    {auth_method preshared  oakley_group 5  auth_alg md5  encr_alg 3des }
    p2_pfs 5
}
```

You can use whatever name you want as the label.

In `/etc/inet/ike/config` on `chopin`, add a similar rule, just reversing the `local_addr` and `remote_addr`:

```
{
    label "chopin to mendelssohn"
    local_addr 192.168.1.130
    remote_addr 192.168.1.120
    p1_xform
    {auth_method preshared  oakley_group 5  auth_alg md5  encr_alg 3des }
    p2_pfs 5
}
```

Verify the syntax of the configuration file on each machine with the following command:

```
# /usr/lib/inet/in.iked -c -f /etc/inet/ike/config
in.iked: Configuration file /etc/inet/ike/config syntactically checks out.
```

Next, create a shared key. You can use the pktool command to generate a key. The key must be identical on both machines, so run this command on only one of the machines to generate a single key, and then copy the key to the other machine:

```
# pktool genkey keystore=file outkey=ikekey keytype=generic keylen=128 print=y
     Key Value ="b60cb44978e470dc6af3936186d39d9a"
```

Now add this key to /etc/inet/secret/ike.preshared. The entry should look like this on mendelssohn (IP address 192.168.1.120):

```
{ localidtype IP
localid 192.168.1.120
remoteidtype IP
remoteid 192.168.1.130
key b60cb44978e470dc6af3936186d39d9a
}
```

It should look like this on chopin (IP address 192.168.1.130):

```
{ localidtype IP
localid 192.168.1.130
remoteidtype IP
remoteid 192.168.1.120
key b60cb44978e470dc6af3936186d39d9a
}
```

Note that, as implied by the term "shared key," the keys must be identical on the two machines.

CAUTION Use scp or another encrypted transfer mechanism to transfer the shared key from the machine on which you generate it to the machines that will use it.

If the ike service is not yet running, enable it:

```
# svcadm enable ike
# svcs ike
STATE          STIME      FMRI
online         11:42:07   svc:/network/ipsec/ike:default
```

Otherwise, just refresh and restart the service:

```
# svcadm refresh ike
# svcadm restart ike
```

Now IKE should be set. You can verify that the shared keys are correct on each node with ikeadm. You'll probably need to change the privilege level of the ike service first. Don't forget to change it back when you're finished!

```
# svccfg -s ike setprop config/admin_privilege=keymat
# svcadm refresh ike
# svcadm restart ike
# ikeadm dump preshared

PSKEY: For <unspecified> exchanges
PSKEY: Pre-shared key (16 bytes): b60cb44978e470dc6af3936186d39d9a/128
LOCIP: Address:
LOCIP: AF_INET: port 0, 192.168.1.120 (mendelssohn.example.com).
REMIP: Address:
REMIP: AF_INET: port 0, 192.168.1.130 (chopin.example.com).

Completed dump of preshared keys

# svccfg -s ike setprop config/admin_privilege=base
# svcadm refresh ike
# svcadm restart ike
```

NOTE   You can also configure IKE to use public key certificates for authentication, which scale better than preshared keys. Consult the ikecert(1M) and ike.config(4) man pages for more details.

Basic IPsec configuration

Now that you have IKE configured, you can set up IPsec between the two nodes. On each machine, create /etc/inet/ipsecinit.conf. You can start with the sample provided, which contains only comments:

```
# cp /etc/inet/ipsecinit.sample /etc/inet/ipsecinit.conf
# chmod 644 /etc/inet/ipsecinit.conf
```

Add a single line specifying the policy for communication between mendelssohn and chopin. On mendelssohn, add the following sample policy, which uses both the AH and ESP protocols (the details of the policy configuration are explained below):

```
{laddr mendelssohn raddr chopin} ipsec {auth_algs any encr_algs any sa shared}
```

On chopin, add the identical policy, with only the laddr and raddr entries reversed:

```
{laddr chopin raddr mendelssohn} ipsec {auth_algs any encr_algs any sa shared}
```

CAUTION   /etc/inet/ipsecinit.conf is read before default routes are established or naming services are started. Also, it's a bad idea to rely on an insecure name service for IPsec name resolution, so ensure that all hostnames can be resolved through local files, or use only IP addresses in the configuration file.

Now restart the ipsec/policy service (or enable it if it's not yet enabled):

```
# svcadm restart ipsec/policy
```

As a final step, verify that the traffic between the two machines is indeed being encrypted and authenticated. You can use snoop to view the packet details. Just run snoop in one terminal window, and then cause some traffic to be sent between the nodes with ping or some other command. Here's the snoop output of a ping from mendelssohn to chopin with the preceding IPsec configuration:

```
# snoop -v chopin
Using device iwi0 (promiscuous mode)
ETHER:  ----- Ether Header -----
ETHER:
ETHER:  Packet 1 arrived at 13:40:11.43546
ETHER:  Packet size=146 bytes
ETHER:  Destination=0:18:de:3e:14:19,
ETHER:  Source     =0:16:6f:3c:64:7b,
ETHER:  Ethertype=0800 (IP)
ETHER:
IP:   ----- IP Header -----
IP:
IP:   Version=4
IP:   Header length=20 bytes
IP:   Type of service=0x00
IP:         xxx. ....=0 (precedence)
IP:         ...0 ....=normal delay
IP:         .... 0...=normal throughput
IP:         .... .0..=normal reliability
IP:         .... ..0.=not ECN capable transport
IP:         .... ...0=no ECN congestion experienced
IP:   Total length=132 bytes
IP:   Identification=54498
IP:   Flags=0x0
IP:         .0.. ....=may fragment
IP:         ..0. ....=last fragment
IP:   Fragment offset=0 bytes
IP:   Time to live=255 seconds/hops
IP:   Protocol=51 (AH)
IP:   Header checksum=6219
IP:   Source address=192.168.1.120, mendelssohn.example.com
IP:   Destination address=192.168.1.130, chopin.example.com
IP:   No options
IP:
AH:   ----- Authentication Header -----
AH:
```

```
AH:    Next header=50 (ESP)
AH:    AH length=4 (24 bytes)
AH:    <Reserved field=0x0>
AH:    SPI=0xc028b0ab
AH:    Replay=21
AH:    ICV=30121c4fe669c4240e662b90
AH:
ESP:    ----- Encapsulating Security Payload -----
ESP:
ESP:    SPI=0x8f571059
ESP:    Replay=21
ESP:        ....ENCRYPTED DATA....
```

As you can see, this packet contains both an AH section and an ESP section because the IPsec policy you specified includes both those protocols.

Configuring IPsec policy

You can indicate specific IPsec policies in the /etc/inet/ipsecinit.conf file. For example, to use only ESP with the Blowfish encryption algorithm and the md5 authentication algorithm, change the policy line on mendelssohn to the following:

```
{laddr mendelssohn raddr chopin} ipsec {encr_algs blowfish encr
_auth_algs md5 sa shared}
```

Make the same changes on chopin, and then restart the ipsec/policy service on each node:

```
# svcadm restart ipsec/policy
```

You can verify the policies in effect by running the ipsecconf command:

```
# ipsecconf -l
#INDEX 60
{ laddr mendelssohn.example.com/32 raddr chopin.example.com/32
dir out } ipsec { encr_algs blowfish-cbc(128..448) encr_auth
_algs hmac-md5(128) sa shared }
 ...
```

Finally, running snoop on a ping confirms that only ESP, not AH, is being used:

```
# snoop -v chopin
Using device iwi0 (promiscuous mode)
ETHER:    ----- Ether Header -----
ETHER:
ETHER:    Packet 1 arrived at 14:57:3.09929
ETHER:    Packet size=134 bytes
ETHER:    Destination=0:18:de:3e:14:19,
ETHER:    Source      =0:16:6f:3c:64:7b,
ETHER:    Ethertype=0800 (IP)
```

```
ETHER:
IP:    ----- IP Header -----
IP:
IP:    Version=4
IP:    Header length=20 bytes
IP:    Type of service=0x00
IP:         xxx. ....=0 (precedence)
IP:         ...0 ....=normal delay
IP:         .... 0...=normal throughput
IP:         .... .0..=normal reliability
IP:         .... ..0.=not ECN capable transport
IP:         .... ...0=no ECN congestion experienced
IP:    Total length=120 bytes
IP:    Identification=61700
IP:    Flags=0x0
IP:         .0.. ....=may fragment
IP:         ..0. ....=last fragment
IP:    Fragment offset=0 bytes
IP:    Time to live=255 seconds/hops
IP:    Protocol=50 (ESP)
IP:    Header checksum=4604
IP:    Source address=192.168.1.120, mendelssohn.example.com
IP:    Destination address=192.168.1.130, chopin.example.com
IP:    No options
IP:
ESP:   ----- Encapsulating Security Payload -----
ESP:
ESP:   SPI=0x7279a2f6
ESP:   Replay=3
ESP:      ....ENCRYPTED DATA....
```

TIP   To find out which encryption and authentication algorithms are available on your system, run the `ipsecalgs` command.

You can also specify IPsec policy on a per-port basis. For example, to secure only telnet traffic, you could add rport 23 to the previous example:

```
{laddr mendelssohn raddr chopin rport 23} ipsec {encr_algs
blowfish encr_auth_algs md5 sa shared}
```

You can also use the ipsecconf command to make temporary policy changes that persist until the next ipsec/policy service restart or system reboot. However, that is not recommended when using the ipsec/policy SMF service to manage IPsec. Instead, make changes to the configuration file as described earlier. Consult the ipsecconf(1M) man page for more detailed options if you're curious.

CROSS-REF   As described in Chapter 9, you can use IPsec in tunnel mode to implement a virtual private network (VPN).

Detecting Attacks

As a final line of defense, configure your system so that it can detect attacks if and when they occur. Assume your system will be broken into despite your best efforts at security, and prepare accordingly. If you are never attacked, great; but if you are, you'll notice quickly and will be able to fix the problems instead of letting Trojan horses and root kits linger.

Logs

Your OpenSolaris system can be configured to log quite a bit of useful information, some of it relevant to security. Unfortunately, it's not all logged to the same place, and some features must be explicitly enabled before you can use them.

System log

The system log is the first place to look for information. The `syslogd` daemon, under control of the `system/system-log:default` service, logs various system events. Configurable in `/etc/syslog.conf`, the default is to send error, alert, and some lower-priority messages to `/var/adm/messages` and to console. Although these messages are not usually security related, you should monitor them to detect anything unusual. For example, if your IPsec policy is misconfigured, you might see a message like this in the system log:

```
Mar 31 10:35:34 mendelssohn ip: [ID 468610 kern.error] ipsec_check
_global_policy: Dropping the datagram because the incoming packet
is secure, but the recipient expects clear; Source 192.168.001.130,
Destination 192.168.001.120.
```

Some system log messages are also sent to `/var/log/syslog`.

> **CAUTION**   One of the first things attackers might do after gaining access to your system is to modify the system log and other logs to attempt to hide their traces. One technique to make this log modification less likely is to configure the `system-log` service to send log messages to a remote host. Consult the `syslog.conf(4)` man page for details on this configuration.

Login logs

Information about logins to your system is quite useful in detecting malicious activity. OpenSolaris logs all successful logins and logouts from the system in `/var/adm/wtmpx`. This file is in binary format, but you can use the `last` command to view the logins. For example, here are the recent logins for user `test`:

```
# last test
test      pts/5      chopin.example.com  Mon Mar 31 11:14 - 11:14  (00:00)
test      pts/4      192.168.1.101       Mon Mar 31 11:13    still logged in
test      sshd       192.168.1.101       Mon Mar 31 11:13    still logged in
test      pts/2      chopin.example.com  Sat Mar 29 14:43 - 14:43  (00:00)
```

```
test      sshd          chopin.example.com Sat Mar 29 14:43 - 14:43  (00:00)
test      pts/2         chopin.example.com Sat Mar 29 14:38 - 14:43  (00:04)
test      sshd          chopin.example.com Sat Mar 29 14:38 - 14:43  (00:04)
...
wtmp begins Tue Mar  4 14:56
```

The /var/adm/sulog records all uses of su, both successful and failed. If you've set up your system to disallow root logins remotely, or, even better, made root a role, then every attempt to become root will be logged in /var/adm/sulog. Here are some sample entries from /var/adm/sulog:

```
SU 03/31 11:39 - pts/5 test-root
SU 03/31 11:39 + pts/5 test-root
```

The - or + in the fourth column indicates failure or success, respectively.

By default, OpenSolaris does not log all failed login attempts. However, numerous failed logins can be an indication that someone is attempting to crack a password. To enable the failed login log, first add the following lines to /etc/default/login:

```
SYSLOG=YES
SYSLOG_FAILED_LOGINS=0
```

Note that SYSLOG=YES should already be in the file by default, and SYSLOG_FAILED _LOGINS=5 is in the file by default but commented out. These two lines specify that all failed logins should be logged.

Next, specify in /etc/syslog.conf where the failed logins should be logged:

```
auth.notice      /var/adm/authlog
```

Finally, create the file /var/adm/authlog that you specified in /etc/syslog.conf with owner root, group sys, and 600 permissions, and refresh the system-log service so that the changes take effect:

```
# touch /var/adm/authlog
# ls -l /var/adm/authlog
-rw-r--r--  1 root     root             0 Mar 31 11:11 /var/adm/authlog
# chmod 600 /var/adm/authlog
# chgrp sys /var/adm/authlog
# ls -l /var/adm/authlog
-rw-------  1 root     sys              0 Mar 31 11:11 /var/adm/authlog
# svcadm refresh system-log
```

Now failed login attempts are logged to /var/adm/authlog:

```
Mar 31 11:14:04 mendelssohn login: [ID 143248 auth.notice] Login
failure on /dev/pts/5 from chopin.example.com
```

SMF logs

As described in Chapter 13, SMF services each have their own log in /var/svc/log, named after their FMRI. In addition to providing useful debugging information when something goes wrong, the logs for security services in particular can provide useful security information. For example, messages like the following in the ipsec/policy log in /var/svc/log/network-ipsec-policy:default.log are a good indication that IPsec is not functioning on your system:

```
[ Mar  4 16:15:51 Executing start method ("/usr/sbin/ipsecconf -q -a
/etc/inet/ipsecinit.conf"). ]
Policy configuration file (/etc/inet/ipsecinit.conf) does not exist.
IPsec policy not configured.
[ Mar  4 16:15:51 Method "start" exited with status 0. ]
```

Security service logs

In addition to the general logs and SMF logs just described, various security services log information in different places. For example, IKE logs information in /var/log/in.iked.log. Kerberos, by default, logs information about tickets in /var/krb5/krb5.log. Read the documentation for whatever services you're using, and check the logs periodically to ensure that everything looks fine.

Basic Audit Reporting Tool

Auditing takes logging to the next level, recording not only error conditions and boundary cases, but tracking even "normal" system and user events, commands, actions, and file system modifications. By employing auditing, you can keep a record of all system, user, and file system activity, providing an essential resource in detecting malicious activity on the system. OpenSolaris provides two auditing services: the Basic Audit Reporting Tool (BART) and general Solaris Auditing. This section discusses BART; the next section discusses Solaris Auditing.

Although it's fairly simple, the BART is quite useful for detecting changes to files on your system. It can do two things: catalog information about files on your system and compare catalogued information generated at different times. By default, BART catalogs all attributes of all files, including creation time, permissions, and size. The recommended way to use BART is to create a snapshot of your file system immediately after system installation. Then, periodically compare the current system to that snapshot (or to more recent snapshots) to detect any suspicious changes, such as a new setuid root file.

> **TIP** The OpenSolaris distribution creates an @install snapshot of ZFS file systems at install time. You can access this snapshot in the /.zfs/snapshot/install directory of each file system. See Chapter 8 for more about ZFS snapshots.

BART uses the term *manifest* to describe the catalogued file system information. Don't confuse a BART manifest with an SMF manifest, described in Chapter 13; they're not related.

BART doesn't cross file system boundaries, but works on both UFS and ZFS file systems. If you have both UFS and ZFS file systems on your machine, you need to generate separate manifests for each.

Creating BART manifests

Create a snapshot of your system using the `bart` command:

```
# bart create -R / > /var/bart/bart-baseline-manifest
```

`bart create` spits its output to `stdout` by default, so you must redirect it to a file to save it. The manifest contains single-line entries for each file or directory, including hidden files. For example, here's the entry for `/etc/passwd` on a UFS file system:

```
/etc/passwd F 1063 100644 user::rw-,group::r--,mask:r--,other
:r-- 47eade28 0 3 ddb6fea9b46e925e73c7c1369e1d90a5
```

The fields for a regular file are, in order, as follows: filename, file type (F for "file"), size, file permissions, ACLs, modification time (in seconds since January 1, 1970), UID of the file owner, UID of the group, and checksum of the contents. For comparison, here's the entry for `/etc/passwd` on a ZFS file system:

```
/etc/passwd F 765 100644 owner@:execute:deny,owner@:read_data/write
_data/append_data/write_xattr/write_attributes/write_acl/write_owner
:allow,group@:write_data/append_data/execute:deny,group@:read_data
:allow,everyone@:write_data/append_data/write_xattr/execute/write
_attributes/write_acl/write_owner:deny,everyone@:read_data/read
_xattr/read_attributes/read_acl/synchronize
:allow 47e96ee6 0 3 b17ca5b685481e6cc7e3c559598d4f34
```

Consult the `bart_manifest(4)` man page for more details about the format of this file.

Comparing BART manifests

You can compare your snapshot manifest to your baseline manifest using the `bart compare` command:

```
# bart compare /var/bart/bart-baseline-manifest \
/var/bart/bart-snapshot > /var/bart/bart-report
```

As with the `bart create` command, you must redirect the output to a file. This comparison report lists all differences between the two manifests, with the original called `control` and the changes called `test`. For example, the report just generated shows the following entry for `/etc/shadow`:

```
/etc/shadow:
  mode  control:100400  test:100444
  acl   control:user::r--,group::---,mask:---,other:---  test:user::r--,
group::r--,mask:r--,other:r —
```

Note the changes to the mode: The permissions have changed from 400 (readable only by root) to 444 (readable by everyone). That's not good! Another change in this report is as follows:

```
/usr/bin/trojanhorse:
  add
```

There's evidently a new file /usr/bin/trojanhorse since the baseline. A closer look at that file shows that it's a setuid root executable:

```
# ls -l /usr/bin/trojanhorse
-r-sr-xr-x   1 root      bin              264 Mar 31 12:33 /usr/bin/trojanhorse
```

There definitely appears to be some malicious activity on this system!

Customizing BART reports

The BART report generated in the previous section had some bogus entries, including the following:

```
/var/bart/bart-snapshot:
  add
/var/ntp/ntpstats/loopstats:
  size  control:3706  test:4658
  mtime  control:47f1286f  test:47f12f6f
  contents  control:9061f8a6921cb4111f4e2765b9fb6330  test:b3918953395b65bc3b
c7dc8d7864aec9
```

The first, bart-snapshot, is the new manifest generated by the second bart create command. The second, loopstats, is dynamic Network Time Protocol (NTP) information. Neither of those really needs to be flagged in the report. Luckily, you can customize your reports by setting up a rules file. Here's a rules file to ignore all files in /var/bart and to ignore the size, mtime, and contents attributes of files in /var/ntp/ntpstats:

```
# cat /var/bart/bartrules
CHECK all

/var/bart
IGNORE all

/var/ntp/ntpstats
IGNORE size mtime contents
```

The rules in a BART rules file are processed in order, with later rules modifying earlier rules. This file contains three rules. Note that the first rule says to check everything. Without that first rule, the exclusion rules that follow would be the only rules, and so nothing outside /var/bart and /var/ntp/ntpstats would be checked. See the bart_rules(4) man page for more details about the format of the rules file.

Now that you've created a rules file, you can use it to modify your manifest comparison:

```
# bart compare -r /var/bart/bartrules bart-baseline-manifest bart-snapshot
/etc/shadow:
  mode  control:100400  test:100444
  acl  control:user::r--,group::---,mask:---,other:---  test:user
::r--,group::r--,mask:r--,other:r--
/usr/bin/trojanhorse:
  add
```

Now the report shows only the two differences of real interest.

You can also employ a rules file when generating the manifests originally with `bart create`. However, you can only compare manifests that were generated with the same rules.

> **TIP** If you have a large collection of machines, consider automating BART and collecting BART manifests onto a central security server. Glen Brunette describes how to do that in the blog post at `http://blogs.sun.com/gbrunett/entry/automating_solaris _10_file_integrity`.

Solaris Auditing

Solaris Auditing, provided as part of the Solaris Basic Security Module, enables your OpenSolaris system to record a wide variety of system and user events, commands, and other actions. Auditing is highly configurable, enabling administrators to select exactly the events in which they are interested.

Turning on auditing

To turn on auditing, you first need to enable the Basic Security Module (BSM). To do so, run the `/etc/security/bsmconv` script and reboot your system:

```
# /etc/security/bsmconv
This script is used to enable the Basic Security Module (BSM).
Shall we continue with the conversion now? [y/n] y
bsmconv: INFO: checking startup file.
bsmconv: INFO: turning on audit module.
bsmconv: INFO: initializing device allocation.

The Basic Security Module is ready.
If there were any errors, please fix them now.
Configure BSM by editing files located in /etc/security.
Reboot this system now to come up with BSM enabled.
# init 6
```

Once the system comes up, specify your audit configuration in `/etc/security/audit_control`. Here's a sample `/etc/security/audit_control` file:

```
dir:/var/audit
flags:lo,as,ss
```

```
minfree:20
naflags:lo
```

The first line specifies the directory in which binary audit records should be stored. You can specify multiple directories, in order of preference.

> **CAUTION** Audit records can eat up a lot of disk space quickly. Consider creating a separate ZFS file system with quotas and reservations for your audit records. See Chapter 8 for details on ZFS. You can also periodically delete old audit data files in /var/audit.

The second line in the sample /etc/security/audit_control, flags, specifies which *event classes* should be audited. An event class is a predefined collection of audit events. For example, the lo class includes login and logout events. The event classes are defined in /etc/security/audit_class and the events themselves in /etc/security/audit_event. The sample /etc/security/audit_control audits the lo, as, and ss classes, to collect information on login or logout, systemwide administration, and system state changes.

Note that the flags line specifies events to be logged that can be attributed to a specific user. The naflags line lists classes to audit for events that are "non-attributable" to a specific user.

> **TIP** Run bsmrecord to view a user-friendly list of audit events in a given class. For example, use the following to see the events in the lo class:

```
# bsmrecord -c lo
...
terminal login
    program     /usr/sbin/login         See login(1)
                /usr/dt/bin/dtlogin     See dtlogin
    event ID    6152                    AUE_login
    class       lo                      (0x00001000)
        header
        subject
        [text]                          error message
        return

login: logout
    program     various                 See login(1)
    event ID    6153                    AUE_logout
    class       lo                      (0x00001000)
        header
        subject
        [text]                          "logout" username
        return
...
```

The minfree line specifies, as a percentage of free space in the file system storing the audit records, a threshold at which the audit_warn script is invoked. See the audit_control(4), audit_class(4), and audit_event(4) man pages for more information on the syntax and contents of these configuration files.

The final step to turn on auditing is to enable the auditd service:

```
# svcadm enable auditd
# svcs auditd
STATE          STIME    FMRI
online         14:26:50 svc:/system/auditd:default
```

Now audit information for the event classes you specified are stored in /var/audit/.

Reviewing audit data

The audit system stores audit data in binary format, so you can't just read the files directly. Instead, use a combination of the auditreduce and praudit commands to view events. For example, to view all audit events for user test, run the following:

```
# auditreduce -u test | praudit -s
file,2008-03-31 15:31:55.000 -06:00,
header,69,2,AUE_ssh,,mendelssohn.example.com,2008-03-31 15:31
:55.366 -06:00
subject,test,test,other,test,other,1150,1231787470,2434 71168
192.168.1.101
return,success,0
...
file,2008-03-31 15:32:51.000 -06:00,
```

The selection command, auditreduce, filters the audit records, in this case retrieving all records attributable to user test. However, auditreduce produces binary output. Luckily, praudit takes binary input in standard input and converts it to a (supposedly) human-readable format. The records are bracketed by file entries, showing the timestamp of the first and last entries in the log. The records themselves are a little obscure. The example record is the login, via ssh, for the test user. Use bsmrecord to find details on the expected fields for each record type.

> **TIP** Use the -x option to praudit to get output in XML format, which includes name tags for fields:

```
# auditreduce -u test | praudit -x | head -11
<?xml version='1.0' encoding='UTF-8' ?>
<?xml-stylesheet type='text/xsl' href='file:///usr/share/lib/xml
/style/adt_record.xsl.1' ?>

<!DOCTYPE audit PUBLIC '-//Sun Microsystems, Inc.//DTD Audit V1
//EN' 'file:///usr/share/lib/xml/dtd/adt_record.dtd.1'>

<audit>
<file iso8601="2008-03-31 15:31:55.000 -06:00"></file>
```

```
<record version="2" event="login - ssh" host=
"mendelssohn.example.com" iso8601="2008-03-31 15:31:55.366 -06:00">
<subject audit-uid="test" uid="test" gid="other" ruid="test" rgid
="other" pid="1150" sid="1231787470" tid="2434 71168 192.168.1.101"/>
<return errval="success" retval="0"/>
</record>
```

As another example, suppose you want to know who restarted the `ipsec/policy` daemon. You can use `auditrecord` to select all records of event `AUE_smf_restart` and FMRI `ipsec/policy`:

```
# auditreduce -m AUE_smf_restart -o fmri=ipsec/policy | praudit -x
<?xml version='1.0' encoding='UTF-8' ?>
<?xml-stylesheet type='text/xsl' href='file:///usr/share/lib/xml
/style/adt_record.xsl.1' ?>

<!DOCTYPE audit PUBLIC '-//Sun Microsystems, Inc.//DTD Audit V1
//EN' 'file:///usr/share/lib/xml/dtd/adt_record.dtd.1'>

<audit>
<file iso8601="2008-03-31 16:07:20.000 -06:00"></file>
<record version="2" event="restart service instance" host
="mendelssohn.example.com" iso8601="2008-03-31 16:07:20.150 -06:00">
<subject audit-uid="nsolter" uid="root" gid="root" ruid="root" rgid
="root" pid="1300" sid="2762192639" tid="14146 5632 192.168.1.101"/>
<use_of_authorization>solaris.smf.manage.ipsec</use_of_
authorization>
<fmri>svc:/network/ipsec/policy:default/:properties/restarter
_actions/restart</fmri>
<return errval="success" retval="0"/>
</record>
<file iso8601="2008-03-31 16:07:20.000 -06:00"></file>
</audit>
```

You can see that it was user `nsolter`, operating as `root`. This example demonstrates that audit records are tracked under the original user login ID, even if that user `su`'s to a different user, or even to root. This feature provides another incentive for disallowing direct logins as root.

Auditing on a per-user basis

Instead of recording audit data for all users, you can choose to audit only specific users. For example, to audit user `test` instead of every user, add the following entry to `/etc/security/audit_user`:

```
test:lo,as,ss
```

Remove the flags from `/etc/security/audit_control`, so the complete file looks like this:

```
dir:/var/audit
flags:
minfree:20
naflags:lo
```

Note that you leave the `naflags` in the `/etc/security/audit_control` file because they have no meaning for specific users (by definition, they are not attributable to any user).

Finally, restart the `auditd` service so that the changes take effect:

```
# svcadm restart auditd
```

Now only the `test` user is audited for the `lo`, `as`, and `ss` event classes.

Syslogging audit events

In addition to generating binary audit records, the audit system can produce human-readable syslog entries. To configure this feature, first add a `plugin` entry to `/etc/security/audit_control`:

```
plugin:name=audit_syslog.so.1; p_flags=lo,ss
```

The `p_flags` in this entry specify the subset of classes being audited that should additionally be syslogged.

Next, specify in `/etc/syslog.conf` where audit messages should be logged:

```
audit.notice       /var/adm/auditlog
```

Create the `auditlog` file:

```
# touch /var/adm/auditlog
```

Finally, refresh the `system-log` service and restart the `auditd` service:

```
# svcadm refresh system-log
# svcadm restart auditd
```

Here are sample login and svcadm restart events from the `/var/adm/auditlog`:

```
# tail /var/adm/auditlog
Mar 31 16:21:52 mendelssohn audit: [ID 702911 audit.notice] login
- ssh ok session 2933273505 by test as test:other from 192.168.1
.101 proc_uid bin
Mar 31 16:22:12 mendelssohn audit: [ID 702911 audit.notice] restart
service instance ok session 2994180326 by nsolter as root
:root from 192.168.1.101 proc_uid bin uauth solaris.smf.manage.ipsec
```

Auditing security features

Some of the security features discussed earlier in this chapter can be audited by selecting certain auditing classes. For example, to audit Kerberos, select the ap class. To audit profile shell commands, select the ua or as classes. To audit role login or logout, select the lo class. Consult the documentation or man page for the feature of interest to determine the correct auditing class.

Configuring audit policy

You can tune auditing options with the auditconfig command. However, any changes made with auditconfig are temporary, and do not persist across a reboot. To make permanent configuration changes, add the appropriate auditconfig commands to the /etc/security/audit_startup file.

For a list of policy options, run auditconfig -ls policy. The most interesting policy option is perzone. If that option is not set, auditing is conducted on a systemwide basis, with a single audit record stored according to the global zone configuration. If you set perzone, however, each zone can run its own auditd service, and configure and record auditing information on a per-zone basis.

Turning off auditing

To disable auditing on your system, run the /etc/security/bsmunconv script and reboot. Unless you run it at the single-user level, the script will give you a warning:

```
# /etc/security/bsmunconv
bsmunconv: ERROR: this script should be run at run level S.
Are you sure you want to continue? [y/n] y
This script is used to disable the Basic Security Module (BSM).
Shall we continue the reversion to a non-BSM system now? [y/n] y
bsmunconv: INFO: removing c2audit:audit_load from /etc/system.
bsmunconv: INFO: stopping the cron daemon.

The Basic Security Module has been disabled.
Reboot this system now to come up without BSM.
# init 6
```

Virus scanning

Computer viruses are another form of attack on your system. OpenSolaris provides a virus-scanning service, VSCAN, that works with third-party scan engines. Because it requires non-open-source scan engines, and is useful mostly for scanning Windows file systems, configuration is beyond the scope of this book. However, you can read the vscand(1M) and vscanadm(1M) man pages for more details.

> **NOTE** Most of the supported scan engines are for SPARC hardware only.

Kerberos

Kerberos, originally developed at the Massachusetts Institute of Technology (MIT), is an authentication system useful for managing a network of machines. It enables users to authenticate on one machine in the network and thereafter access services or log in to other machines in the network without additional authentication. It's quite handy and is widely deployed within intranets.

Kerberos implements authentication using the concept of *tickets*. When users first authenticate themselves, they are granted a *ticket-granting ticket* (TGT) from the *key distribution center* (KDC). Whenever a user subsequently attempts to use a service that requires authentication, Kerberos sends the TGT to the KDC requesting a ticket for that particular service. This interaction is invisible to users; after one authentication, they can use the services with Kerberos performing additional ticket-granting behind the scenes.

The network of computers participating in the Kerberos authentication is called the Kerberos *realm*. Think of the realm as similar to a domain; in fact, Kerberos realms are often synonymous with domains of the same name.

Users in Kerberos are called *principals*. Confusingly, services, such as NFS, and machines are also principals. Users must have a Kerberos account, which means they must have a Kerberos principal name and password. You can use PAM to configure automatic UNIX user accounts to Kerberos principal mappings.

OpenSolaris provides an implementation of the KerberosV5 protocol. However, the OpenSolaris distribution doesn't include the Kerberos packages in the initial install, so you first need to install them on each computer that you want to Kerberize:

```
# pkg install SUNWkdc
```

Now you can configure Kerberos in your network.

NOTE Kerberos needs to be able to map hostnames to IP addresses and vice versa for hosts in your domains, and to assemble the fully qualified domain name from the `hostname` and `domainname` commands. Thus, DNS or another naming service must be configured properly. See Chapter 9 for more information about DNS.

Clock synchronization

Kerberos requires the participating computers to keep their clocks synchronized. The easiest way to maintain consistent clocks is to use the Network Time Protocol (NTP) service available on OpenSolaris.

CROSS-REF Chapter 9 provides an overview of the Network Time Protocol and an example of configuring your system to synchronize its clock with an external NTP server.

NTP can be configured in a number of different ways. Typically, computers are synchronized with an external NTP server to keep their clocks accurate. However, Kerberos cares only that the participating machines are consistent among themselves regarding the concept of the correct time. Thus, for Kerberos' purposes, you can use a simpler symmetric configuration that makes each host a peer of the others.

Additionally, set up your NTP service to use authentication. (Given that this is the security chapter, you didn't really think you'd get away without authentication, did you?) NTP uses symmetric key authentication, meaning that identical keys must be replicated on each host.

Here are the steps for configuring a network of machines to synchronize their clocks in "symmetric active" mode with MD5-based authentication.

First, create a keys file in /etc/inet/ntp.keys on each host. Each line of the file declares one key and contains three entries: key number, key type, and the key itself. The key number is any number you choose starting from 1. There are several different types; this example uses M for MD5. The MD5 keys are eight-character strings. Here is an example /etc/inet/ntp.keys file defining one key:

```
123 M DeMoPaSs
```

The keys must be identical on each host.

> **CAUTION**   Your /etc/inetn/ntp.keys file should be readable only by root to prevent non-root users from viewing the plain-text keys. Be sure to chmod the file to 600 or 400.

Next, create your NTP configuration file in /etc/inet/ntp.conf on each node. Here is an example ntp.conf:

```
server 127.127.1.0

peer 192.168.1.106 key 123 prefer
peer 192.168.1.107 key 123
peer 192.168.1.108 key 123
# Add additional peer entries for all the machines to be kerberized

enable auth
statsdir /var/ntp/ntpstats/
filegen peerstats file peerstats type day enable
filegen loopstats file loopstats type day enable
filegen clockstats file clockstats type day enable

# authentication settings
keys /etc/inet/ntp.keys
trustedkey 123
```

These settings require a bit of explanation. The server line specifies that the machine should use itself as the time server, meaning it will take its initial idea of time from its internal clock.

The following `peer` lines list all the other machines in the network as peers. You should replace the IP addresses in this example with the IP addresses or hostnames of the machines in your own network. The `key 123` part of the line indicates that communication with those peers should be encrypted with that key number. Finally, one of the peers is listed as the preferred one.

The `enable auth` line enables authentication. The next four lines specify statistics logging. The final two lines specify the location of the `ntp.keys` file you created earlier, and declare that key number 123 is a trusted key.

The final step is to start the NTP service. Run the following on each node:

```
# svcadm enable ntp
```

> **TIP** The Network Time Protocol doesn't correct clock times immediately. It may take a few hours for the clocks on your machines to synchronize.

Setting up the key distribution center

After synchronizing clocks, the second task to get Kerberos running on your network is to configure the key distribution center (KDC). Although you could create all the configuration files by hand, OpenSolaris provides a nice utility called `kdcmgr` to set up the KDC. Run the following command as root on the machine that will be your KDC (substituting your desired administrator username and your desired realm):

```
# kdcmgr create master

Starting server setup
------------------------------------------------------
Enter the Kerberos realm: example.com

Setting up /etc/krb5/kdc.conf.

Setting up /etc/krb5/krb5.conf.

Initializing database '/var/krb5/principal' for realm 'EXAMPLE.COM',
master key name 'K/M@EXAMPLE.COM'
You will be prompted for the database Master Password.
It is important that you NOT FORGET this password.
Enter KDC database master key:
Re-enter KDC database master key to verify:

Enter the krb5 administrative principal to be created: nick/admin

Authenticating as principal nick/admin@EXAMPLE.COM with password.
WARNING: no policy specified for nick/admin@EXAMPLE.COM; defaulting to no policy
```

```
Enter password for principal "nick/admin@EXAMPLE.COM":
Re-enter password for principal "nick/admin@EXAMPLE.COM":
Principal "nick/admin@EXAMPLE.COM" created.

Setting up /etc/krb5/kadm5.acl.

--------------------------------------------------
Setup COMPLETE.
```

TIP   If you see an error message like one of the following from kdcmgr, you probably don't have DNS configured properly:

```
# kdcmgr

yourhostname.example.com  is unreachable, exiting.
--------------------------------------------------
Setup FAILED.
```

```
# kdcmgr
Error: can not determine full hostname (FQHN).  Aborting
Note, trying to use hostname and domainname to get FQHN.
```

NOTE   If you'd rather set up the configuration files and perform the other configuration steps by hand, see the detailed instructions in the *System Administration Guide: Security Services* Solaris book listed in the "Resources" section at the end of this chapter.

Setting up the Kerberos clients

Now you need to configure the client machines in your network. Don't get confused by the use of the word "client." Even if these machines will be servers of various sorts, they're clients of the Kerberos key distribution center. Every machine that will participate in your Kerberos network must be configured as a client. OpenSolaris provides an interactive script, kclient, for this purpose. Run the script as follows, substituting your realm, the hostname of your KDC, and the administrative principal, all of which you specified while configuring the KDC:

```
# kclient

Starting client setup

--------------------------------------------------
Do you want to use DNS for kerberos lookups ? [y/n]: n
        No action performed.
Enter the Kerberos realm: example.com
Specify the KDC hostname for the above realm: mendelssohn
```

```
Note, this system and the KDC's time must be within 5 minutes of each other for
Kerberos to function.  Both systems should run some form of time
synchronization system like Network Time Protocol (NTP).

Setting up /etc/krb5/krb5.conf.

Enter the krb5 administrative principal to be used: nick/admin
Obtaining TGT for nick/admin ...
Password for nick/admin@EXAMPLE.COM:

Do you have multiple DNS domains spanning the
Kerberos realm EXAMPLE.COM ? [y/n]: n
        No action performed.

Do you plan on doing Kerberized nfs ? [y/n]: n
        No action performed.

host/tchaikovsky.example.com entry already exists in KDC database.
host/tchaikovsky.example.com entry already present in keytab.

Do you want to copy over the master krb5.conf file ? [y/n]: n
        No action performed.

-----------------------------------------------------
Setup COMPLETE.
```

> **NOTE** As with setting up the Key Distribution Center, you can perform the configuration steps by hand. See the System Administration Guide: Security Services book listed in the "Resources" section for more detail.

Starting Kerberized services

OpenSolaris provides Kerberos-aware (kerberized) versions of the ftp, rlogin, rcp, rsh, rdist, ssh, and telnet services. Configure these services on machines in your Kerberos realm as follows:

> **CAUTION** Kerberized network services other than ssh enforce secure authentication only — they don't enforce encrypted session traffic for privacy.

- ftp — Specify that the in.ftpd daemon should be started with the -K option, which allows only authenticated connections:

```
# inetadm -m svc:/network/ftp:default exec="/usr/sbin/in.ftpd -K"
# svcadm restart ftp
```

- rlogin — Disable the insecure network/login:rlogin service and enable either or both of the login:klogin or login:eklogin services:

```
# svcadm disable network/login:rlogin
# svcadm enable network/login:klogin
# svcadm enable network/login:eklogin
```

- rcp, rsh, and rdist — Disable the network/shell:default service and enable the shell:kshell service:

```
# svcadm disable network/shell:default
# svcadm enable network/shell:kshell
```

- ssh — No changes necessary; ssh supports Kerberos by default.

- telnet — Specify that the telnet daemon should be started with the -a user option:

```
# inetadm -m svc:/network/telnet:default \
exec="/usr/sbin/in.telnetd -a user"
# svcadm restart network/telnet:default
```

CROSS-REF Chapters 3 and 13 describe svcadm and other service management commands. Chapter 9 describes inetadm and inetd.

Creating Kerberos accounts

Every user in your system who will use Kerberos must be registered as a Kerberos principal, which is basically a user of the Kerberos service. Your users might become confused keeping track of different Kerberos and OpenSolaris usernames, so it's a good idea to create a principal name for each user that is identical to his or her username. A side benefit of this approach is that Kerberos automatically maps principal names to OpenSolaris usernames, so if a user has a Kerberos ticket under the principal nsolter and tries to rlogin to a server where he has access under the username nsolter, Kerberos will automatically map the Kerberos principal nsolter to the username nsolter and give him access.

CAUTION A Kerberos principal account alone is not enough to access services on a machine in the Kerberos realm. Users can access services on a machine via Kerberos only if they have a valid OpenSolaris user account on that machine. Instead of duplicating user accounts across machines, it's best to store accounts in a directory service such as NIS or LDAP. See Chapter 10 for more information on directory services.

You can create Kerberos principals with the kadmin command. The following command, run on the KDC master, creates a principal nsolter and verifies that it was created:

```
# kadmin -p nick/admin
Authenticating as principal nick/admin with password.
Password for nick/admin@EXAMPLE.COM:
kadmin:  addprinc nsolter
WARNING: no policy specified for nsolter@EXAMPLE.COM; defaulting to no policy
```

```
Enter password for principal "nsolter@EXAMPLE.COM":
Re-enter password for principal "nsolter@EXAMPLE.COM":
Principal "nsolter@EXAMPLE.COM" created.
kadmin: list_principals
...
nick/admin@EXAMPLE.COM
nsolter@EXAMPLE.COM
kadmin: quit
```

This manual approach could quickly become tiresome if you have more than a handful of users on your system. An alternative is to configure PAM to create Kerberos principals automatically for your users when they next log in, as described shortly in the section "Configuring PAM for Kerberos."

Managing tickets

The first action every Kerberos user needs to take when logging into a system is to obtain a ticket. As described in the next section, you can use PAM to configure your system so that users obtain tickets automatically upon login. However, if your system isn't set up to obtain tickets automatically, or if you prefer manual control, you can also manage your tickets directly using kinit, klist, and kdestroy. For example:

```
login as: nsolter
Using keyboard-interactive authentication.
Password:
Last login: Mon Mar 17 13:25:11 2008 from 192.168.1.101
Sun Microsystems Inc.   SunOS 5.11     snv_83   January 2008
$ klist -f
klist: No credentials cache file found (ticket cache FILE:/tmp/krb5cc_101)
$ kinit
Password for nsolter@EXAMPLE.COM:
$ klist -f
Ticket cache: FILE:/tmp/krb5cc_101
Default principal: nsolter@EXAMPLE.COM

Valid starting             Expires              Service principal
03/17/08 13:59:48  03/17/08 21:59:48  krbtgt/EXAMPLE.COM@EXAMPLE.COM
        renew until 03/24/08 13:59:48, Flags: RIA
$ kdestroy
$ klist -f
klist: No credentials cache file found (ticket cache FILE:/tmp/krb5cc_101)
```

> **TIP** If you see an error like the following, you probably don't have a Kerberos principal set up that maps to the username for which you're attempting to obtain a ticket:
>
> ```
> $ kinit
> kinit(v5): Client not found in Kerberos database while getting
> initial credentials
> ```

Using Kerberized services

Once you have a ticket, you can access Kerberized services running on other machines in the realm without needing to re-authenticate yourself. For example, ssh automatically detects your ticket and logs you in without prompting for a password:

```
$ ssh mendelssohn
Last login: Mon Mar 17 15:57:37 2008 from tchaikovsky.example
Sun Microsystems Inc.   SunOS 5.11     snv_83  January 2008
$
```

For all the other Kerberized services, special options to the commands are required.

CAUTION Kerberized services don't require encrypted session traffic for privacy, only secure authentication. For privacy, you should always use ssh or add the -x option to the other network commands for encrypted sessions.

Use ftp with the -x option, for instance, to specify that it should use both authentication and encryption:

```
$ ftp mendelssohn
Connected to mendelssohn.example.com.
220 mendelssohn.example.com FTP server (Version wu-2.6.2+Sun) ready.
Name (mendelssohn:nsolter):
530 Must perform authentication before identifying USER.
Login failed.
ftp> quit
221 Goodbye.
$ ftp -x mendelssohn
Connected to mendelssohn.example.com.
220 mendelssohn.example.com FTP server (Version wu-2.6.2+Sun) ready.
334 Using AUTH type GSSAPI; ADAT must follow
GSSAPI accepted as authentication type
GSSAPI authentication succeeded
200 PROT P ok.
Name (mendelssohn:nsolter):
232 User nsolter logged in.
Remote system type is UNIX.
Using binary mode to transfer files.
ftp>
```

You can use rsh and rcp with -a and -x to specify authentication and encryption:

```
$ rsh mendelssohn date
mendelssohn.example.com: Connection refused
$ rsh -ax mendelssohn date
This rsh session is using encryption for all data transmissions.
Mon Mar 17 16:12:06 MDT 2008
```

The `rlogin` command supports `-x` and `-A` to specify encryption and authentication:

```
$ rlogin -Ax mendelssohn
connected with Kerberos V5
This rlogin session is using encryption for all data transmissions.
Last login: Mon Mar 17 16:06:29 from tchaikovsky.example
Sun Microsystems Inc.   SunOS 5.11      snv_83  January 2008
$
```

You can `telnet` to another machine using the `-x` option to specify encryption and authentication:

```
$ telnet -x mendelssohn
Trying 192.168.1.120 ...
Connected to mendelssohn.example.com.
Escape character is '^]'.
Waiting for encryption to be negotiated ...
[ Kerberos V5 accepts you as ``nsolter@EXAMPLE.COM`` ]
done.
Last login: Mon Mar 17 15:51:16 from tchaikovsky.example
Sun Microsystems Inc.   SunOS 5.11      snv_83  January 2008
$
```

If you attempt to connect to a remote machine running only Kerberized services without these special options, your connection will be rejected:

```
$ telnet mendelssohn
Trying 192.168.1.120 ...
Connected to mendelssohn.example.com.
Escape character is '^]'.
Connection to mendelssohn.example.com closed by foreign host.
```

Also, if you attempt to connect without a valid ticket, your connection will be rejected:

```
$ telnet -x mendelssohn
Trying 192.168.1.120 ...
Connected to mendelssohn.example.com.
Escape character is '^]'.
Waiting for encryption to be negotiated ...

Authentication negotiation has failed, which is required for
encryption.  Good-bye.
```

Kerberized NFS

In addition to the network services described earlier, Kerberos can enable secure Network File System (NFS) access.

CROSS-REF You can also run NFS over Secure RPC without using Kerberos. See Chapter 10 for details on NFS and Secure RPC.

To configure Kerberized NFS, first add a Kerberos principal for nfs, specifying the name of the server that will be the NFS server (in this case. chopin):

```
# kadmin -p nick/admin
Authenticating as principal nick/admin with password.
Password for nick/admin@EXAMPLE.COM:
kadmin:  addprinc nfs/chopin.example.com
WARNING: no policy specified for nfs/chopin.example.com@EXAMPLE.COM;
defaulting to no policy
Enter password for principal "nfs/chopin.example.com@EXAMPLE.COM":
Re-enter password for principal "nfs/chopin.example.com@EXAMPLE.COM":
Principal "nfs/chopin.example.com@EXAMPLE.COM" created.
kadmin:  quit
```

On the machine that will be the NFS server, add the nfs principal to the keytab:

```
# kadmin -p nick/admin
Authenticating as principal nick/admin with password.
Password for nick/admin@EXAMPLE.COM:
kadmin:  ktadd nfs/chopin.example.com
Entry for principal nfs/chopin.example.com with kvno 3. encryption type
AES-128 CTS mode with 96-bit SHA-1 HMAC added to keytab WRFILE:
/etc/krb5/krb5.keytab.
Entry for principal nfs/chopin.example.com with kvno 3. encryption type Triple
DES cbc mode with HMAC/sha1 added to keytab WRFILE:/etc/krb5/krb5.keytab.
Entry for principal nfs/chopin.example.com with kvno 3. encryption type
ArcFour with HMAC/md5 added to keytab WRFILE:/etc/krb5/krb5.keytab.
Entry for principal nfs/chopin.example.com with kvno 3. encryption type DES
cbc mode with RSA-MD5 added to keytab WRFILE:/etc/krb5/krb5.keytab.
kadmin:  quit
```

Verify that the entry is in the keytab:

```
# klist -k
Keytab name: FILE:/etc/krb5/krb5.keytab
KVNO Principal
---- --------------------------------------------------------------------
   3 host/chopin.example.com@EXAMPLE.COM
   3 host/chopin.example.com@EXAMPLE.COM
   3 host/chopin.example.com@EXAMPLE.COM
   3 host/chopin.example.com@EXAMPLE.COM
   3 nfs/chopin.example.com@EXAMPLE.COM
   3 nfs/chopin.example.com@EXAMPLE.COM
   3 nfs/chopin.example.com@EXAMPLE.COM
   3 nfs/chopin.example.com@EXAMPLE.COM
```

On the NFS server and any machines that will be NFS clients, uncomment the following three lines in /etc/nfssec.conf:

```
krb5          390003  kerberos_v5   default -           # RPCSEC_GSS
krb5i         390004  kerberos_v5   default integrity   # RPCSEC_GSS
krb5p         390005  kerberos_v5   default privacy     # RPCSEC_GSS
```

On the NFS server, share your files, specifying one of the three Kerberos security modes listed in /etc/nfssec.conf. This example shares /export/shared manually with the share command:

```
# share -F nfs -p -o sec=krb5 /export/shared
# share
-                    /export/shared   sec=krb5   ""
```

On the NFS client machines, mount the file system, also specifying the Kerberos security mode:

```
# mount -F nfs -o sec=krb5 chopin:/export/shared /mnt
```

If you're using the automounter, you can add the sec option to the appropriate entry in /etc/auto_master.

Now users on the NFS clients can access the NFS-mounted files only if they are authenticated by Kerberos:

```
$ klist -f
Ticket cache: FILE:/tmp/krb5cc_101
Default principal: nsolter@EXAMPLE.COM

Valid starting          Expires              Service principal
04/02/08 16:36:12  04/03/08 00:36:12  krbtgt/EXAMPLE.COM@EXAMPLE.COM
        renew until 04/09/08 16:36:12, Flags: FRIA
04/02/08 16:36:34  04/03/08 00:36:12  nfs/chopin.example.com@EXAMPLE.COM
        renew until 04/09/08 16:36:12, Flags: FRAT
$ ls /mnt
testfile
$ kdestroy
$ klist -f
klist: No credentials cache file found (ticket cache FILE:/tmp/krb5cc_101)
$ ls /mnt
/mnt: Permission denied
$
```

Configuring PAM for Kerberos

You can use the pam_krb5 and pam_krb5_migrate PAM modules to do the following:

- Configure your system to obtain tickets for users automatically when they first log in
- Create Kerberos principals automatically for users who don't already have them

■ Change both the UNIX and Kerberos passwords simultaneously when the user changes his or her password

To implement that functionality, make the following changes to /etc/pam.conf on each client machine:

1. Add pam_krb5.so.1 and pam_krb5_migrate.so.1 to the auth stack for each non-kerberized service, and change pam_unix_auth in the stack to requisite instead of required. Note that the pam_krb5_migrate entry has an expire_pw option to force users to change their passwords when they are migrated to Kerberos. This example assumes that login is the only authentication service that is explicit:

```
#
# login service
#
login   auth requisite          pam_authtok_get.so.1
login   auth required           pam_dhkeys.so.1
login   auth required           pam_unix_cred.so.1
login   auth sufficient         pam_krb5.so.1
login   auth requisite          pam_unix_auth.so.1
login   auth optional           pam_krb5_migrate.so.1 expire_pw


#
# Default definitions for Authentication management
# Used when service name is not explicitly mentioned for
# authentication
#
other   auth requisite          pam_authtok_get.so.1
other   auth required           pam_dhkeys.so.1
other   auth required           pam_unix_cred.so.1
other   auth sufficient         pam_krb5.so.1
other   auth requisite          pam_unix_auth.so.1
other   auth optional           pam_krb5_migrate.so.1 expire_pw
```

CAUTION   **Don't add the Kerberos PAM modules to the authentication stacks for Kerberized services such as** krlogin, krsh, **and** ktelnet.

2. Add pam_krb5.so.1 to the default account management stack:

```
# Default definition for Account management
# Used when service name is not explicitly mentioned for
# account management
#
other   account requisite       pam_roles.so.1
other   account required        pam_krb5.so.1
other   account required        pam_unix_account.so.1
```

3. Add `pam_krb5.so.1` to the default password management stack:

```
#
# Default definition for Password management
# Used when service name is not explicitly mentioned for
# password management
#
other    password required    pam_dhkeys.so.1
other    password requisite   pam_authtok_get.so.1
other    password requisite   pam_authtok_check.so.1
other    password sufficient  pam_krb5.so.1
other    password required    pam_authtok_store.so.1
```

4. Add two entries to the `/etc/pam.conf` file on the KDC:

```
k5migrate auth required pam_unix_auth.so.1
k5migrate account required pam_unix_account.so.1
```

5. Finally, add two entries for each client machine to the access control list in `/etc/krb5/kadm5.acl` on the KDC:

```
host/tchaikovsky.example.com@EXAMPLE.COM U root
host/tchaikovsky.example.com@EXAMPLE.COM ui *
```

After modifying the access control list, you must restart the `kadmin` service:

```
# svcadm restart network/security/kadmin
```

> **TIP** For more information on the Kerberos PAM modules, see the `pam_krb5(5)` and `pam_krb5_migrate(5)` **man pages.**

With these changes to `/etc/pam.conf`, users who already have Kerberos principals in the realm will obtain tickets automatically when they log in:

```
login as: nsolter
Using keyboard-interactive authentication.
Password:
Last login: Mon Mar 17 15:03:26 2008 from 192.168.1.101
Sun Microsystems Inc.   SunOS 5.11     snv_83  January 2008
$ klist -f
Ticket cache: FILE:/tmp/krb5cc_101
Default principal: nsolter@EXAMPLE.COM

Valid starting              Expires              Service principal
03/17/08 15:04:29  03/17/08 23:04:29  krbtgt/EXAMPLE.COM@EXAMPLE.COM
        renew until 03/24/08 15:04:29, Flags: RIA
```

 Logins may take perceptibly longer with Kerberos than without because of the extra encryption and network traffic.

When users without existing Kerberos principals log in, they are migrated to Kerberos and prompted to change their passwords:

```
login as: ktest
Using keyboard-interactive authentication.
Password:

User `ktest' has been automatically migrated to the Kerberos realm EXAMPLE.COM


Your Kerberos password has expired.


Warning: Your password has expired, please change it now.

New Password:
Re-enter new Password:
Kerberos password successfully changed


Last login: Mon Mar 17 14:20:53 2008 from 192.168.1.101
Sun Microsystems Inc.   SunOS 5.11      snv_83  January 2008
$
```

CAUTION If you're using local files to store passwords, then Kerberos will update the password for the Kerberos principal on the machine to which the user is logging in, but not on other machines in the realm.

Kerberos logs

One of the benefits of using Kerberos is that it logs on the KDC each ticket that is issued. Configurable in /etc/krb5/krb5.conf, the default log location is /var/krb5/kdc.log. The following example entries show that user nsolter obtained a ticket-granting ticket and an NFS ticket:

```
Apr 02 16:36:12 mendelssohn krb5kdc[360](info): AS_REQ (5 etypes
{17 16 23 3 1})
 192.168.1.125: ISSUE: authtime 1207175772, etypes {rep=17 tkt=17 ses=17},
nsolt
er@EXAMPLE.COM for krbtgt/EXAMPLE.COM@EXAMPLE.COM
Apr 02 16:36:34 mendelssohn krb5kdc[360](info): TGS_REQ (5 etypes
{17 16 23 3 1}
) 192.168.1.125: ISSUE: authtime 1207175772, etypes {rep=17 tkt=17 ses=17},
nsol
ter@EXAMPLE.COM for nfs/chopin.example.com@EXAMPLE.COM
```

Enhancing Kerberos availability

In the Kerberos configuration so far, the KDC is a single point of failure. There are a couple ways to increase the availability of the service. You may recall that the command you used to create the KDC was kdc create master. As implied by the "master," you can also create slave KDCs, which contain a copy of the KDC database, and you can issue tickets. You can create a slave KDC with the interactive kdcmgr create slave command:

```
# kdcmgr create slave

Starting server setup
-------------------------------------------------------
Enter the Kerberos realm: example.com
What is the master KDC's host name?: mendelssohn

Setting up /etc/krb5/kdc.conf.

Setting up /etc/krb5/krb5.conf.

Enter the krb5 administrative principal to be used: nick/admin
Obtaining TGT for nick/admin ...
Password for nick/admin@EXAMPLE.COM:

Setting up /etc/krb5/kadm5.acl.

Setting up /etc/krb5/kpropd.acl.

Waiting for database from master ...
...
Waiting for database from master ...
kdb5_util: Cannot find/read stored master key while reading master key
kdb5_util: Warning: proceeding without master key
Enter KDC database master key:

-------------------------------------------------------
Setup COMPLETE.
```

Another mechanism to increase the availability of the KDC is to run it on a high-availability cluster, using the OpenSolaris Open High Availability Cluster software.

CROSS-REF Chapter 16 describes Open High Availability Cluster in more detail.

Trusted Extensions

Trusted Extensions (TX), as the name implies, is an extension to the basic OpenSolaris security features. TX was originally a separate product, called Trusted Solaris 8, but it has been integrated into Solaris 10 and OpenSolaris. TX provides *mandatory access control*, implemented through *labels*. With TX, everything on the system is labeled, and each user has a specific clearance, or label range. TX is most useful for implementing hierarchical security models, such as that employed by the United States military, with top secret, secret, confidential, and unclassified security levels.

A full treatment of Trusted Extensions is beyond the scope of this book. For more details, consult one of the references in the next section.

Resources

The T.J. Maxx credit-card theft is described at `http://arstechnica.com/news.ars/post/20070506-blame-for-record-breaking-credit-card-data-theft-laid-at-the-feet-of-wep.html`.

The following books cover general security and cryptography concepts:

- *Counter Hack Reloaded: A Step-by Step Guide to Computer Attacks and Effective Defens*es, *Second Edition*, by Ed Skoudis with Tom Liston (Prentice Hall, 2006). Provides detailed descriptions of computer attack techniques and tools, and how to protect against them.

- *Cryptography and Network Security: Principles and Practice*, by William Stallings (Prentice Hall, 1999). Contains solid explanations of cryptographic algorithms, plus various security protocols discussed in this chapter, including Kerberos, IPsec, and SSL.

- *Cryptography: Theory and Practice*, by Douglas R. Stinson (CRC Press, 1995). For the mathematically inclined, this book provides a rigorous treatment of cryptography.

- *Applied Cryptography: Protocols, Algorithms, and Source Code in C*, by Bruce Schneier (Wiley, 1996). If you want to get down-and-dirty with the source code for the cryptographic algorithms, this is your book. Bruce Schneier also writes a great security blog, though lately it focuses more on anti-terrorism security, rather than computer security: `http://schneier.com/blog`.

You can track and report OpenSolaris security problems at the following:

- United States Computer Emergency Readiness Team (US-CERT) — `http://us-cert.gov`.

- The Sun Solve Security page — Contains links to Sun security alerts, among other pages: `http://sunsolve.sun.com/show.do?target=security/sec`.

- Sun Alert and Security Discussion Forum — `http://forum.java.sun.com/forum.jspa?forumID=839`.

The OpenSolaris community security resources include the following:

- OpenSolaris security community group — Contains links to useful presentations, Sun blueprints, and other documentation and explanations that you might not find elsewhere.

It also hosts several "unofficial" projects, such as Trusted Extensions, PAM, and Secure by Default: http://opensolaris.org/os/community/security.

■ The OpenSolaris security mailing list — security-discuss@opensolaris.org.

■ Various official OpenSolaris projects, including of particular interest:

▨ Flexible Mandatory Access Control — A joint project with the United States National Security Agency: http://opensolaris.org/os/project/fmac.

▨ Forensic Tools — http://opensolaris.org/os/project/forensics.

▨ Kerberos — http://opensolaris.org/os/project/Kerberos.

▨ OpenSolaris Security Audit — http://opensolaris.org/os/project/audit.

▨ Solaris Security Toolkit — The Solaris Security Toolkit, formerly called the Jump-Start Architecture and Security Scripts (JASS) toolkit, provides a simplified means to secure, harden, and audit Solaris. There is work in progress to open source the code and provide a Security Toolkit for OpenSolaris. This toolkit will be quite useful when it's available for OpenSolaris. You can track its status on the OpenSolaris security toolkit project page: https://opensolaris.org/os/project/jass.

The official Sun documentation includes the following:

■ *System Administration Guide: Security Services* — Covers most of the topics in this chapter: http://docs.sun.com/app/docs/doc/819-3321?l=en.

■ *System Administration Guide: IP Services* — Covers IPsec: http://docs.sun.com/app/docs/doc/819-3000?l=en.

■ *System Administration Guide: Network Services* — Contains a section on the Network Time Protocol: http://docs.sun.com/app/docs/doc/819-1634?l=en.

■ *Solaris Trusted Extensions Collection* — Several books on Trusted Extensions: http://docs.sun.com/app/docs/coll/175.12?l=en.

■ *Solaris ZFS Administration Guide* — Includes coverage of ACLs in ZFS: http://docs.sun.com/app/docs/doc/817-2271?l=en.

■ Sun Security Blueprints — Dozens of medium-length (15–50 page) tutorials on various security topics: http://sun.com/blueprints/browsesubject.html#security.

Pointers to other useful security articles (not necessarily by Sun or OpenSolaris folks) can be found on Sun's BigAdmin site: http://sun.com/bigadmin/collections/security.html.

Some useful tools for thinking like an attacker include the following:

■ Network Mapper (Nmap) — http://nmap.org.

■ The Network Vulnerability Scanner (Nessus) — http://nessus.org/nessus.

Finally, the OpenSolaris source code can be an invaluable resource for learning more about OpenSolaris security features. The security-related source code is all over the place, so the easiest approach is to use the source code search tool at http://src.opensolaris.org/source/ to find the code for a particular security feature.

Summary

This chapter provided a tour of the OpenSolaris security features. You learned about preventing unauthorized access with Pluggable Authentication Modules (PAM), passwords, and Secure By Default. You read about limiting attacker damage with role-based access control (RBAC), privileges, and access control lists, among other topics. To protect network communication, you learned about secure shell and IP Security (IPsec). The chapter further explained that logs and auditing are imperative for detecting intrusions. It also included a detailed tutorial on networked authentication with Kerberos. Finally, it provided a brief overview of Trusted Extensions (TX).

Part IV

OpenSolaris Reliability, Availability, and Serviceability

Fault Management

Computer systems can fail in myriad ways. Computer hardware suffers from physical limitations and wear and tear that limit its lifetime. From disks to processors to network cards, it's not a question of whether your hardware will fail, it's a question of when. Although software doesn't have the same physical limitations as hardware, it has its own share of problems. Bugs in applications, device drivers, file systems, system software, and any other software component can cause diverse kinds of failures.

Luckily, OpenSolaris provides substantial infrastructure for reliability, availability, and serviceability (RAS) in the presence of these inevitable faults. *Predictive self-healing*, described in this chapter and Chapter 13, provides a unified approach to fault management and service management in OpenSolaris. The observability tools, presented in Chapter 14, enable administrative monitoring and troubleshooting. In addition, the innovative Dynamic Tracing facility (DTrace), covered in Chapter 15, enables administrators to troubleshoot complex problems on live systems. Finally, the layered Open High Availability Cluster software, described in Chapter 16, enables you to group multiple physical OpenSolaris machines to obtain even higher availability of your system as a whole.

IN THIS CHAPTER

Predictive self-healing

Fault management overview

Fault management commands

Using fault management

Predictive Self-Healing

Traditionally, UNIX systems handle hardware and software faults in an ad hoc manner without much, if any, automated detection or repair. At best, the system logs a message for the user. The administrator is responsible for the detection, isolation, diagnosis, and repair of a problem. For example, if a CPU starts showing problems, the administrator needs to decide whether it's a transitory or permanent problem, and whether to disable or replace it. If a system daemon dies, the administrator is responsible for detecting the failure and restarting the application.

OpenSolaris takes a different approach, providing a unified infrastructure for predictive self-healing in the presence of failures. Three principal innovations are involved in predictive self-healing on OpenSolaris:

- **Unified error-handling channels, fault management, and service management** — OpenSolaris manages both faults and services in a unified fashion, providing a single event channel for all error reports, a Fault Manager component that interprets the events, and a Service Manager component that monitors software services.

- **Automated recovery when possible** — The OpenSolaris predictive self-healing framework can automatically restart software daemons that die, and automatically deconfigure some hardware components that fail.

- **Unified knowledge base articles** — Faults are assigned unique identifiers that can be used by administrators to look up the problem and solution on the Predictive Self-Healing Knowledge Article Web website.

Fault management is necessarily inexact, and thus must employ heuristic algorithms to determine when a service or hardware component is really faulted, rather than transitively failing or simply appearing to fail because of a problem in another area. For example, suppose the system sees an unaligned memory reference. That could be due to either a hardware memory error or a software bug. If it happens just once, a good heuristic algorithm is unlikely to flag it as a hardware error, but if it occurs consistently on memory references from different programs, it's more likely to be a hardware problem.

Fault managed resource identifiers

As part of the predictive self-healing framework, each hardware and software resource on the system is identified by a unique *Universal Resource Identifier (URI)* called a *Fault Managed Resource Identifier (FMRI)*.

CROSS-REF Chapter 6 introduces FMRIs and describes their use in IPS package names.

For hardware components, the FMRI for the motherboard might look like the following:

```
hc://:product-id=TECRA-M3:chassis-id=36019791H:server-id=mendelssohn
/motherboard=0
```

The FMRI for a processor might look like this:

```
hc://:product-id=TECRA-M3:chassis-id=36019791H:server-id=mendelssohn
/motherboard=0/chip=0/cpu=0
```

For software services, the FMRI for the Secure Shell service looks like this:

```
svc:/network/ssh:default
```

The FMRI for the Internet Key Exchange (IKE) service looks like this:

```
svc:/network/ipsec/ike:default
```

CROSS-REF   Chapter 13 explains how OpenSolaris service management uses FMRIs.

Fault management versus service management

OpenSolaris divides predictive self-healing into two areas: fault management and service management. The Fault Manager primarily handles hardware failures, while the Service Manager handles software service failures. This chapter focuses on fault management; Chapter 13 covers service management.

Fault Management Overview

OpenSolaris fault management is an extensible framework to unify fault handling. Starting from the bottom of the fault management stack, OpenSolaris defines an event protocol for error events. Participating components called *error handlers*, generally hardware drivers, are instrumented to generate error reports (ereports) in the event protocol format when something goes wrong. This telemetry data is picked up by the Fault Management Daemon (FMD).

NOTE   The FMD is itself managed by the Service Management Facility under the FMRI `svc:/system/fmd:default`. See the `fmd(1M)` man page for more information.

The FMD diagnoses problems based on the ereports, and then generates *fault events* or *fault diagnoses*. You can think of the error reports as the symptoms of a problem, and the fault events as the diagnoses of the problem. Put another way, the fault is the problem and the errors are the symptoms of that problem. There is not necessarily a one-to-one mapping between ereports and fault diagnoses. Often, multiple error reports are explained by a single fault diagnosis.

In addition to generating fault diagnoses, the FMD can take action to notify an administration via system log messages or SNMP traps. Furthermore, the FMD can actually perform automated repairs when appropriate.

FMD pluggable modules

The FMD itself is just a generic framework for pluggable modules. These modules implement the logic to actually diagnose problems and take corrective actions. There are two types of modules: *diagnosis engines* and *agents*. Diagnosis engines diagnose problems, whereas agents take corrective actions or issue notifications.

The main hardware diagnosis engine supplied on OpenSolaris is eft. This diagnosis engine is a collection of fault trees written in the Eversholt fault diagnosis language. Don't worry if you've never heard of Eversholt: Invented at Sun, it is used primarily for Solaris and OpenSolaris fault management. There is also a ZFS diagnosis engine, which diagnoses faults in ZFS.

CROSS-REF   Chapter 8 describes ZFS in detail.

OpenSolaris has a number of agent modules, including the following:

- cpumem-retire and io-retire: The CPU/Memory Retire Agent and I/O Retire Agent are responsible for deconfiguring failed hardware.
- syslog-msgs: Logs fault diagnoses to the system log
- snmp-trapgen: Generates SNMP traps for fault diagnoses
- zfs-retire: The ZFS Retire Agent takes care of any automated ZFS actions.

NOTE   The OpenSolaris Fault Management Architecture (FMA) theoretically allows multiple fault managers to co-exist on the system. Thus far, the FMD is the only fault manager supplied natively by OpenSolaris.

Knowledge articles

Each fault management case has a Universal Unique Identifier (UUID). Cases usually correspond to a single diagnosis. Furthermore, each diagnosis has a unique Sun Message Identifier, with a corresponding web page at http://sun.com/msg. The articles on the Sun Knowledge Article website are called, appropriately enough, Knowledge Articles.

The Sun Message Identifier shows up in system log entries, fault logs, and some command outputs. For example, zpool status -x includes a Knowledge Article pointer in the see entry:

```
# zpool status -x
  pool: testpool
 state: UNAVAIL
status: One or more devices could not be opened.  There are insufficient
        replicas for the pool to continue functioning.
action: Attach the missing device and online it using 'zpool online'.
   see: http://www.sun.com/msg/ZFS-8000-3C
 scrub: none requested
config:
```

```
NAME                        STATE    READ WRITE CKSUM
testpool                    UNAVAIL     0     0     0  insufficient replicas
  /export/home/fma/fma-zfs  UNAVAIL     0     0     0  cannot open
```

 SMF Services, described in Chapter 13, also have Knowledge Articles for error conditions and faults, included in the `svcs -x` command output.

Fault management hardware support

The overarching goal of OpenSolaris fault management is to handle every fault through the framework. However, the generation of error reports and fault diagnoses are fairly hardware-specific, so fault handling with this framework has not been implemented yet for all the possible hardware and software components. That means your particular hardware might not be monitored as part of this framework.

That said, active work is under way to supply generic fault handlers for classes of architecture. For example, the Generic Machine Check Architecture project aims to integrate x86 processors that implement the Machine Check Architecture (MCA) into the OpenSolaris fault management framework. Other recent projects include support for the UltraSPARC T1 and T2 systems.

Fault Management Commands

The OpenSolaris fault management framework provides three main commands for administrators: `fmadm`, `fmdump`, and `fmstat`. This section examines those commands in turn, plus some additional commands.

NOTE General OpenSolaris administration does not require you to use these commands because important faults are logged to the system log.

fmadm

The `fmadm` command provides administrative control over the FMD. The most useful option is `faulty`, which lists the resources that are currently faulted. For example:

```
# fmadm faulty
--------------- ------------------------------------------  --------------  ---------
TIME            EVENT-ID                                    MSG-ID          SEVERITY
--------------- ------------------------------------------  --------------  ---------
Apr 07 16:09:32 c870f49c-d6b9-c3b4-e4ac-d6db0eaf2cc5        ZFS-8000-D3     Major

Fault class : fault.fs.zfs.device
```

455

```
Description : A ZFS device failed.  Refer to http://sun.com/msg/ZFS-8000-D3 for
              more information.

Response    : No automated response will occur.

Impact      : Fault tolerance of the pool may be compromised.

Action      : Run 'zpool status -x' and replace the bad device.
```

You can also use the fmadm config option to see the list of modules currently loaded:

```
# fmadm config
MODULE                VERSION STATUS   DESCRIPTION
cpumem-retire         1.1     active   CPU/Memory Retire Agent
disk-transport        1.0     active   Disk Transport Agent
eft                   1.16    active   eft diagnosis engine
fmd-self-diagnosis    1.0     active   Fault Manager Self-Diagnosis
io-retire             2.0     active   I/O Retire Agent
snmp-trapgen          1.0     active   SNMP Trap Generation Agent
sysevent-transport    1.0     active   SysEvent Transport Agent
syslog-msgs           1.0     active   Syslog Messaging Agent
zfs-diagnosis         1.0     active   ZFS Diagnosis Engine
zfs-retire            1.0     active   ZFS Retire Agent
```

The fmadm command also gives you the capability to manually load and unload modules, and to repair, flush, and perform other actions on the FMD. You won't normally need to use these capabilities, and you can consult the fmadm(1M) man page for more information.

fmstat

The fmstat command provides statistics from the fault management modules:

```
# fmstat
module              ev_recv ev_acpt wait   svc_t  %w  %b  open solve  memsz  bufsz
cpumem-retire         1       0    0.0      1.9    0   0    0     0      0      0
disk-transport        0       0    0.0    866.6    0   0    0     0     32b     0
eft                   3       3    0.0      7.3    0   0    1     1    1.4M     0
fmd-self-diagnosis    0       0    0.0      0.1    0   0    0     0      0      0
io-retire             0       0    0.0      0.1    0   0    0     0      0      0
snmp-trapgen          1       0    0.0      9.9    0   0    0     0     32b     0
sysevent-transport    0       0    0.0   2494.7    0   0    0     0      0      0
syslog-msgs           1       0    0.0      9.8    0   0    0     0      0      0
zfs-diagnosis         2       2    0.0     11.2    0   0    0     0      0      0
zfs-retire            0       0    0.0      0.1    0   0    0     0      0      0
```

The ev_recv column shows the number of events received by that module; the ev_acpt column shows the number of events accepted; and so on.

You can obtain more statistics on specific modules with the -m and -a options, as shown here:

```
# fmstat -m zfs-diagnosis -a
            NAME VALUE           DESCRIPTION
    fmd.accepted 2               total events accepted by module
    fmd.buflimit 10M             limit on total buffer space
    fmd.buftotal 280b            total buffer space used by module
   fmd.caseclosed 0             total cases closed by module
    fmd.caseopen 2              cases currently open by module
   fmd.casesolved 1             total cases solved by module
     fmd.ckptcnt 2              number of checkpoints taken
  fmd.ckptrestore true          restore checkpoints for module
    fmd.ckptsave true           save checkpoints for module
    fmd.ckpttime 47739944ns      total checkpoint time
    fmd.ckptzero false          zeroed checkpoint at startup
    fmd.debugdrop 0             dropped debug messages
     fmd.dequeued 8             total events dequeued by module
   fmd.dispatched 8             total events dispatched to module
 fmd.dlastupdate 8719972828434ns hrtime of last event dequeue completion
     fmd.dropped 0              total events dropped on queue overflow
       fmd.dtime 91213668ns      total processing time after dequeue
    fmd.loadtime 65059846749ns   hrtime at which module was loaded
     fmd.memlimit 10M            limit on total memory allocated
     fmd.memtotal 336b           total memory allocated by module
   fmd.prdequeued 4             protocol events dequeued by module
    fmd.snaptime 8719972838765ns hrtime of last statistics snapshot
     fmd.thrlimit 8             limit on number of auxiliary threads
     fmd.thrtotal 0             total number of auxiliary threads
        fmd.wcnt 0              count of events waiting on queue
 fmd.wlastupdate 8719972828434ns hrtime of last wait queue update
    fmd.wlentime 74653491ns      total wait length * time product
       fmd.wtime 74642323ns      total wait time on queue
    fmd.xprtlimit 256            limit on number of open transports
    fmd.xprtopen 0              total number of open transports
   fmd.xprtqlimit 1024           limit on transport event queue length
```

fmdump

The fmdump command enables you to examine the error reports and fault diagnoses directly from the error logs. fmdump without any options shows a one-line entry for each fault diagnosis:

```
# fmdump
TIME                 UUID                                     SUNW-MSG-ID
Apr 07 16:09:32.1724 c870f49c-d6b9-c3b4-e4ac-d6db0eaf2cc5 ZFS-8000-D3
Apr 11 15:06:09.9541 00ef1a80-6f5f-44cd-ef4f-fb0e7265963c INTEL-8000-PR
```

You can examine the ZFS diagnosis in more detail by specifying its UUID along with the `-v` option:

```
# fmdump -v -u c870f49c-d6b9-c3b4-e4ac-d6db0eaf2cc5
TIME                    UUID                                    SUNW-MSG-ID
Apr 07 16:09:32.1724 c870f49c-d6b9-c3b4-e4ac-d6db0eaf2cc5 ZFS-8000-D3
    100%  fault.fs.zfs.device

        Problem in: zfs://pool=c8e108872ea709c3/vdev=39d1cbdfa50ff878
           Affects: zfs://pool=c8e108872ea709c3/vdev=39d1cbdfa50ff878
               FRU: -
          Location: -
```

Note that this diagnosis also appears in the system log:

```
Apr  7 16:09:32 mendelssohn fmd: [ID 441519 daemon.error] SUNW-MSG-ID:
ZFS-8000-D3, TYPE: Fault, VER: 1, SEVERITY: Major
Apr  7 16:09:32 mendelssohn EVENT-TIME: Mon Apr  7 16:09:32 MDT 2008
Apr  7 16:09:32 mendelssohn PLATFORM: TECRA M3, CSN: 36019791H, HOSTNAME:
mendel ssohn
Apr  7 16:09:32 mendelssohn SOURCE: zfs-diagnosis, REV: 1.0
Apr  7 16:09:32 mendelssohn EVENT-ID: c870f49c-d6b9-c3b4-e4ac-d6db0eaf2cc5
Apr  7 16:09:32 mendelssohn DESC: A ZFS device failed.  Refer to http:
//sun.com/msg/ZFS-8000-D3 for more information.
Apr  7 16:09:32 mendelssohn AUTO-RESPONSE: No automated response will occur.
Apr  7 16:09:32 mendelssohn IMPACT: Fault tolerance of the pool may be
compromised.
Apr  7 16:09:32 mendelssohn REC-ACTION: Run 'zpool status -x' and replace the
bad device.
Apr  7 16:09:38 mendelssohn zfs: [ID 664491 kern.warning] WARNING: Pool
'testpoo l' has encountered an uncorrectable I/O error. Manual intervention is required.
```

To examine the error reports that led to the diagnoses, use the `-e` option to `fmdump`:

```
# fmdump -e
TIME                 CLASS
Apr 07 16:09:31.9644 ereport.fs.zfs.vdev.open_failed
Apr 07 16:09:32.0801 ereport.fs.zfs.data
Apr 09 11:00:22.8596 ereport.fs.zfs.vdev.open_failed
Apr 09 11:00:22.8596 ereport.fs.zfs.zpool
Apr 10 13:35:55.7876 ereport.fs.zfs.vdev.open_failed
Apr 10 13:35:55.7876 ereport.fs.zfs.zpool
Apr 11 14:29:26.5469 ereport.fs.zfs.vdev.open_failed
Apr 11 14:29:26.5469 ereport.fs.zfs.zpool
Apr 11 15:06:08.9454 ereport.cpu.intel.l0icache_uc
Apr 11 15:06:09.9499 ereport.cpu.intel.l0icache_uc
Apr 11 15:06:10.9597 ereport.cpu.intel.l0icache_uc
```

To see the full event, use the -V option. Use the -c option to specify a specific event class:

```
# fmdump -V -e -c ereport.fs.zfs.vdev.open_failed
TIME                              CLASS
Apr 07 2008 16:09:31.964478474 ereport.fs.zfs.vdev.open_failed
nvlist version: 0
        class = ereport.fs.zfs.vdev.open_failed
        ena = 0x6dc76ba22d900001
        detector = (embedded nvlist)
        nvlist version: 0
                version = 0x0
                scheme = zfs
                pool = 0xc8e108872ea709c3
                vdev = 0x39d1cbdfa50ff878
        (end detector)

        pool = testpool
        pool_guid = 0xc8e108872ea709c3
        pool_context = 0
        vdev_guid = 0x39d1cbdfa50ff878
        vdev_type = file
        vdev_path = /export/home/fma/fma-zfs
        parent_guid = 0xc8e108872ea709c3
        parent_type = root
        prev_state = 0x1
        __ttl = 0x1
        __tod = 0x47fa9b9b 0x397cc60a
...
```

Other fault management commands

You can see the topology, or view, of a system's fault-management-enabled resources with the fmtopo command. Note the nonstandard path of fmtopo:

```
# /usr/lib/fm/fmd/fmtopo
TIME              UUID
Apr 10 17:13:27 fef22410-0f28-cf16-ec0b-cfd1f23e7574

hc://:product-id=TECRA-M3:chassis-id=36019791H:server-id=mendelssohn
/motherboard=0

hc://:product-id=TECRA-M3:chassis-id=36019791H:server-id=mendelssohn
/motherboard=0/chip=0

hc://:product-id=TECRA-M3:chassis-id=36019791H:server-id=mendelssohn
/motherboard=0/chip=0/cpu=0

hc://:product-id=TECRA-M3:chassis-id=36019791H:server-id=mendelssohn
/motherboard=0/hostbridge=0
```

```
hc://:product-id=TECRA-M3:chassis-id=36019791H:server-id=mendelssohn
/motherboard=0/hostbridge=0/pciexrc=0
 ...
```

For more details, use -P to see the resource properties:

```
# /usr/lib/fm/fmd/fmtopo -P all hc://:product-id=TECRA-M3:chassis-id=
36019791H:server-id=mendelssohn/motherboard=0/chip=0/cpu=0
TIME                  UUID
Apr 10 17:20:48 7d6c4f8f-a7cb-ea99-a552-c0369e9a9afb

hc://:product-id=TECRA-M3:chassis-id=36019791H:server-id=mendelssohn
/motherboard=0/chip=0/cpu=0
  group: protocol                    version: 1   stability: Private/Private
    resource       fmri      hc://:product-id=TECRA-M3:chassis-id=36019791 ...
    ASRU           fmri      cpu:///cpuid=0
    FRU            fmri      hc://:product-id=TECRA-M3:chassis-id=36019791 ...
  group: authority                   version: 1   stability: Private/Private
    product-id     string    TECRA-M3
    chassis-id     string    36019791H
    server-id      string    mendelssohn
  group: cpu-properties              version: 1   stability: Private/Private
    cpuid          uint32    0x0
    chip_id        int32     0
    core_id        int32     0
    clog_id        int32     0
    pkg_core_id    int32     0
```

You can also specify a different topology scheme, such as cpu, in which case you will see different names for the same resources. For example, the CPU in the previous example can be named with the cpu schema:

```
# /usr/lib/fm/fmd/fmtopo -s cpu
TIME                  UUID
Apr 14 13:47:18 54ac989a-f456-49f0-9e19-e2224ffa0484

cpu:///cpuid=0
```

Additional fault management commands include /usr/lib/fm/fmd/fminject and /usr/lib/fm/fmd/fmsim, which can be used to inject and simulate faults, respectively. Consult the *Fault Management Daemon Programmer's Reference Manual* (FMDPRM) listed in the "Resources" section at the end of this chapter for more details.

Using Fault Management

The fault management framework logs faults to the system log, usually configured as /var/adm/messages, by default, so you generally don't need to interact with the framework directly. As an administrator, you only need to monitor the system log for errors, look up the referenced knowledge base article, and take the recommended corrective action, if required.

Alternatively, you can configure your system to send SNMP traps for fault events to whatever management framework you're using. For more details, consult the documentation on the Fault Management Community Group website referenced in the "Resources" section at the end of this chapter.

If you're curious, you can sometimes use the fault management commands directly to obtain more information. For example, suppose you see a message like the following in your system log:

```
Apr 11 15:06:09 mendelssohn fmd: [ID 441519 daemon.error] SUNW-MSG-ID:
 INTEL-8000-PR, TYPE: Fault, VER: 1, SEVERITY: Major
Apr 11 15:06:09 mendelssohn EVENT-TIME: Fri Apr 11 15:06:09 MDT 2008
Apr 11 15:06:09 mendelssohn PLATFORM: TECRA M3, CSN: 36019791H, HOSTNAME:
 mendelssohn
Apr 11 15:06:09 mendelssohn SOURCE: eft, REV: 1.16
Apr 11 15:06:09 mendelssohn EVENT-ID: 00ef1a80-6f5f-44cd-ef4f-fb0e7265963c
Apr 11 15:06:09 mendelssohn DESC: A level 0 Instruction Cache on this cpu is
 faulty. Refer to http://sun.com/msg/INTEL-8000-PR for more information.
Apr 11 15:06:09 mendelssohn AUTO-RESPONSE: The system will attempt to offline
 this cpu to remove it from service.
Apr 11 15:06:09 mendelssohn IMPACT: Performance of this system may be affected.
Apr 11 15:06:09 mendelssohn REC-ACTION: Schedule a repair procedure to replace
 the affected CPU.  Use 'fmadm faulty' to identify the module.
```

The preceding message seems to indicate a problem with one of the system's CPUs. The first thing to do is look at the supplied web page for a knowledge base article: http://sun.com/msg/INTEL-8000-PR. If you want more information, however, start with fmadm faulty:

```
# fmadm faulty
--------------- ------------------------------------ --------------- ---------
TIME            EVENT-ID                             MSG-ID          SEVERITY
--------------- ------------------------------------ --------------- ---------
Apr 11 15:06:09 00ef1a80-6f5f-44cd-ef4f-fb0e7265963c INTEL-8000-PR   Major

Fault class : fault.cpu.intel.l0icache
Affects     : cpu:///cpuid=0
                   degraded but still in service
```

```
FRU        : hc://:product-id=TECRA-M3:chassis-id=36019791H:server-id=
mendelssohn/motherboard=0/chip=0

Description : A level 0 Instruction Cache on this cpu is faulty.  Refer to
             http://sun.com/msg/INTEL-8000-PR for more information.

Response   : The system will attempt to offline this cpu to remove it from
             service.

Impact     : Performance of this system may be affected.

Action     : Schedule a repair procedure to replace the affected CPU.  Use
             'fmadm faulty' to identify the module.
```

> **NOTE** FRU stands for **field replaceable unit**, a component that can be replaced easily.

To obtain even more information from your system about the error, check out the actual fault log for messages with the unique EVENT-ID listed in the fmadm faulty output:

```
# fmdump -v -u 00ef1a80-6f5f-44cd-ef4f-fb0e7265963c
TIME                 UUID                                 SUNW-MSG-ID
Apr 11 15:06:09.9541 00ef1a80-6f5f-44cd-ef4f-fb0e7265963c INTEL-8000-PR
   100%   fault.cpu.intel.l0icache

          Problem in: hc://:product-id=TECRA-M3:chassis-id=36019791H:server-id=
mendelssohn/motherboard=0/chip=0/cpu=0
             Affects: cpu:///cpuid=0
                 FRU: hc://:product-id=TECRA-M3:chassis-id=36019791H:server-id=
mendelssohn/motherboard=0/chip=0
            Location: -
```

There is only one message (a fault summary) that still doesn't give you much more information. To see the actual error events that caused the fault manager to generate the fault, look at the raw error log with fmdump -e. This example uses the -t option to fmdump to find only those errors that were part of this particular problem:

```
# fmdump -e -t 15:06
TIME                 CLASS
Apr 11 15:06:08.9454 ereport.cpu.intel.l0icache_uc
Apr 11 15:06:09.9499 ereport.cpu.intel.l0icache_uc
Apr 11 15:06:10.9597 ereport.cpu.intel.l0icache_uc
```

For more detail, use the -V option to fmdump. This example looks only at the final ereport, using the -t option to fmdump to specify it:

```
# fmdump -V -e -t 15:06:10
Apr 11 2008 15:06:10.959775322 ereport.cpu.intel.l0icache_uc
nvlist version: 0
        detector = (embedded nvlist)
        nvlist version: 0
                version = 0x0
                scheme = hc
                hc-list = (array of embedded nvlists)
                (start hc-list[0])
                nvlist version: 0
                        scheme =
                        hc-name = motherboard
                        hc-id = 0
                (end hc-list[0])
                (start hc-list[1])
                nvlist version: 0
                        scheme =
                        hc-name = chip
                        hc-id = 0
                (end hc-list[1])
                (start hc-list[2])
                nvlist version: 0
                        scheme =
                        hc-name = cpu
                        hc-id = 0
                (end hc-list[2])

        (end detector)

        compound_errorname = ICACHEL0_ERR_ERR
        IA32_MCG_STATUS1 = 0x0
        machine_check_in_progress = 0
        bank_number = 0x0
        bank_msr_offset = 0x404
        IA32_MCi_STATUS = 0xe200000000000100
        overflow = 1
        error_uncorrected = 1
        error_enabled = 0
        processor_context_corrupt = 1
        error_code = 0x100
        class = ereport.cpu.intel.l0icache_uc
```

```
ena = 0x20b23e0000000001
__ttl = 0x1
__tod = 0x47ffd2c2 0x3935025a
```

That's probably more detail than you wanted, but it can be helpful in some cases.

Resources

The most important resource for OpenSolaris fault management is the Knowledge Article Web at `http://sun.com/msg`. This collection of articles, each referenced by a unique Sun Message Identifier, provides important information about various problems.

The OpenSolaris Fault Management Community Group, at `http://opensolaris.org/os/community/fm`, contains an overview of OpenSolaris fault management, pointers to documentation and relevant blog entries, and a list of fault management projects. Interesting projects include the following:

- Generic Machine Check Architecture Improvement: `http://opensolaris.org/os/project/generic-mca`
- Events Registry: `http://opensolaris.org/os/project/events-registry`

Although aimed at Fault Management Daemon module developers, the *Fault Management Daemon Programmer's Reference Manual* (FMD PRM) is useful for understanding various aspects of the fault management architecture on OpenSolaris.

The source code for the Fault Management Daemon, various fault management commands, and the plug-in modules lives in `usr/src/cmd/fm/`. You can browse it at `http://src.opensolaris.org/source/xref/onnv/onnv-gate/usr/src/cmd/fm`.

Summary

This chapter introduced the OpenSolaris approach to fault management and explained how predictive self-healing is a combination of fault management and service management. By reading this chapter, you learned about the OpenSolaris fault management framework and the commands for interacting with the framework, including `fmadm`, `fmstat`, and `fmdump`. You also saw examples of ZFS and CPU faults handled through the fault framework.

Chapter 13

Service Management

S ince the first versions of UNIX in 1969, one of the core abstractions in the operating system is the *process*, used to provide multi-programming and scheduling of system resources. Open-Solaris, of course, continues to use the process for essentially the same purposes as earlier versions of UNIX. However, beginning with Solaris 10, a higher-level abstraction called a *service* has become central to the system administration model. Chapter 3 briefly introduced the idea of services and the most basic commands used to manipulate them. Chapter 12 described fault management, which together with service management, provides the predictive self-healing feature of OpenSolaris. In this chapter, you'll gain an in-depth understanding of OpenSolaris service management and learn how to develop your own services.

Processes and Services

Considering the deep roots of the process model in UNIX and the commonality it represents with other operating systems, it's logical to ask why OpenSolaris has added the concept of a service to the system. After all, a service is implemented in terms of processes, so what does the service provide that a process doesn't?

The highly oversimplified answer to this question is that not all processes are equally important. After all, a process is created to execute almost every command that you type to a command shell, but many of those processes are born, execute, and die in a matter of milliseconds. Some, such as a text editor, a web browser, or an e-mail client, last much longer, but even those longer-lasting processes are only of interest to the user who launched them because they don't provide a function to any other user of the system. As a result, most processes don't require any management — their management is handled automatically by the system as a by-product of each user's interaction with the process.

Other processes, however, can be of great importance to every user of a system. For example, a routing daemon such as in.routed is responsible for monitoring the network for routing messages to determine the paths for sending network traffic to other systems. If it fails, your system will likely become unable to communicate with any systems that are not on the local network. Worse, it may be quite some time before anyone realizes there's a problem with the system because the network might continue to function without change, and failures may affect only some communications or users. Diagnosing and correcting such problems immediately can be much less difficult and less costly than doing so long after the fact. In response, many larger enterprises install monitoring tools to detect failures as soon as possible, but such tools can be expensive, and they usually still require action by an administrator to restart the failed process.

In addition, the increasing complexity of applications means that nearly all meaningful work done on a system involves communication between multiple processes. Even serving a typical web page can involve an HTTP server, an application server, and a database server; if any one of those processes fails, the entire website fails. If that website is how a business makes money, that failure is costing it money every second it continues.

The sheer number of system and application services available increases yearly and is compounded by the trend toward consolidating applications on single systems to increase efficiency and utilization of those systems. Consider also that virtualization technologies enable even further consolidation, and it becomes apparent that it's very desirable for the operating system to provide more assistance than it traditionally has in ensuring that the applications are running as much as possible. That is the core problem the Service Management Facility (SMF) is designed to solve.

Beyond that, the designers of the SMF recognized two related problems that had to be solved to present a complete solution: providing a consistent administration model for managing system services, and a mechanism for delivering service descriptions so that the system can understand the service relationships — for example, the preceding scenario in which multiple services implement a website.

SMF versus UNIX init

A problem that has traditionally dogged UNIX systems has been a lack of consistency regarding how different "services" are started, stopped, and managed. System V UNIX took some tentative

continued

continued

steps toward standardizing this aspect of the system with the concept of init scripts. The premise of init scripts was that each script is responsible for starting a daemon or performing some other task needed to start or stop the system. The scripts were organized into directories based on the system's run-level. A numerical sequencing of the scripts within each directory controlled the order in which they would be executed, and a prefix character specified whether a script was used to start or stop its daemon. Because it was typically convenient to use the same script for both starting and stopping, it would receive a single command argument of `start` or `stop` to specify which function was desired. This was how Solaris through Solaris 9 was booted, and Linux adopted the same system. For example, the `/etc/rc2.d` directory in Fedora 8 has the following contents:

```
K01smartd                    K75netfs           S09isdn
K01smolt                     K75udev-post       S10network
K02avahi-daemon              K84btseed          S11auditd
K02haldaemon                 K84bttrack         S12restorecond
K02NetworkManager            K85rpcgssd         S13rpcbind
K02NetworkManagerDispatcher  K85rpcidmapd       S15mdmonitor
K05atd                       K86nfslock         S25pcscd
K05saslauthd                 K87irqbalance      S26rsyslog
K10psacct                    K87multipathd      S27messagebus
K15httpd                     K88wpa_supplicant  S44acpid
K20nfs                       K89dund            S50bluetooth
K24irda                      K89netplugd        S55sshd
K50netconsole                K89pand            S80sendmail
K69rpcsvcgssd                K89rdisc           S85gpm
K72autofs                    K91capi            S90ConsoleKit
K73setroubleshoot            K95firstboot       S90crond
K73winbind                   K95kudzu           S97yum-updatesd
K73ypbind                    S00microcode_ctl   S98cups
K74lm_sensors                S06cpuspeed        S99anacron
K74nscd                      S08ip6tables       S99local
K74ntpd                      S08iptables
```

This system has obviously worked well enough to survive basically intact for 20 years, but it has problems.

First, while designed as a modular architecture for starting and stopping a system, init is flawed as a solution to that problem. It's strictly sequential, which means the boot process remains very linear, even as systems become increasingly parallel with multiple processors and threads. There's no provision for a service to signal a problem in a way that can stop the parade of services beyond

continued

continued

it. Nor is there a provision for handling a service that hangs in its start process, so a problem or bug with one fairly irrelevant service can prevent important services from starting. Longtime Solaris users have certainly seen this happen when a NIS server is unreachable during system boot, for instance.

Second, because starting and stopping individual services wasn't the primary design center, there's very little management functionality offered. While you can try to execute one of these scripts individually after the system is booted to start or stop the corresponding function, there's no general guarantee that it will work correctly when run outside of the init framework. Each script can be called with a `start` or `stop` argument, but there's no consistency specified beyond that. An occasional service might offer a `restart` option, but very few do. There's no standard way to determine the state of a service after it starts. Unless you pore over scripts and source code, it's basically impossible to tell which services have dependencies on each other. Some information can be inferred from the sequencing within the run-level directories, but the forced linearity of the naming scheme means that the dependencies are only approximate. Service configuration is not standardized — each is responsible for defining and implementing its own configuration store.

Finally, the method for diagnosing service problems is specific to each service. All of these deficiencies in the init system are corrected by SMF's dependency system and the commands it provides to monitor, configure, and manage the services.

SMF By Example

Before diving further into the theory, concepts, and gritty details of SMF, take a look at an example service that is available on virtually any platform: the Secure Shell (SSH) daemon, `sshd`. Start by looking at the files included in the ssh server package using the `pkg` command:

```
$ pkg contents -t file SUNWsshd
PATH
etc/ssh/sshd_config
lib/svc/method/sshd
usr/lib/ssh/sftp-server
usr/lib/ssh/sshd
var/svc/manifest/network/ssh.xml
```

CROSS-REF Details of browsing and managing packages can be found in Chapter 6. The capabilities and uses of ssh are discussed in Chapter 11.

Of the files in the listing, `/etc/ssh/sshd_config`, `/usr/lib/ssh/sftp-server`, and `/usr/lib/ssh/sshd` are similar to the files you'd find in a Linux package such as `openssh-server` on Fedora 8. The other two files, however, are decidedly unfamiliar. First, look at the `ssh.xml` file, which is shown in Listing 13-1.

LISTING 13-1

---

ssh service manifest

```
$ cat /var/svc/manifest/network/ssh.xml
<?xml version="1.0"?>
<!DOCTYPE service_bundle SYSTEM "/usr/share/lib/xml/dtd/service_bundle.dtd.1">
<!--
    CDDL HEADER START

    The contents of this file are subject to the terms of the
    Common Development and Distribution License, Version 1.0 only
    (the "License").  You may not use this file except in compliance
    with the License.

    You can obtain a copy of the license at usr/src/OPENSOLARIS.LICENSE
    or http://www.opensolaris.org/os/licensing.
    See the License for the specific language governing permissions
    and limitations under the License.

    When distributing Covered Code, include this CDDL HEADER in each
    file and include the License file at usr/src/OPENSOLARIS.LICENSE.
    If applicable, add the following below this CDDL HEADER, with the
    fields enclosed by brackets "[]" replaced with your own identifying
    information: Portions Copyright [yyyy] [name of copyright owner]

    CDDL HEADER END

    Copyright 2004 Sun Microsystems, Inc.  All rights reserved.
    Use is subject to license terms.

    ident    "@(#)ssh.xml    1.8    05/06/10 SMI"

    NOTE:  This service manifest is not editable; its contents will
    be overwritten by package or patch operations, including
    operating system upgrade.  Make customizations in a different
    file.
-->

<service_bundle type='manifest' name='SUNWsshdr:ssh'>

<service
    name='network/ssh'
    type='service'
    version='1'>

    <create_default_instance enabled='false' />
```

```
<single_instance />

<dependency name='fs-local'
    grouping='require_all'
    restart_on='none'
    type='service'>
    <service_fmri
        value='svc:/system/filesystem/local' />
</dependency>

<dependency name='fs-autofs'
    grouping='optional_all'
    restart_on='none'
    type='service'>
    <service_fmri value='svc:/system/filesystem/autofs' />
</dependency>

<dependency name='net-loopback'
    grouping='require_all'
    restart_on='none'
    type='service'>
    <service_fmri value='svc:/network/loopback' />
</dependency>

<dependency name='net-physical'
    grouping='require_all'
    restart_on='none'
    type='service'>
    <service_fmri value='svc:/network/physical' />
</dependency>

<dependency name='cryptosvc'
    grouping='require_all'
    restart_on='none'
    type='service'>
    <service_fmri value='svc:/system/cryptosvc' />
</dependency>

<dependency name='utmp'
    grouping='require_all'
    restart_on='none'
    type='service'>
    <service_fmri value='svc:/system/utmp' />
</dependency>

<dependency name='config_data'
    grouping='require_all'
    restart_on='restart'
    type='path'>
```

```
    <service_fmri
        value='file://localhost/etc/ssh/sshd_config' />
</dependency>

<dependent
    name='ssh_multi-user-server'
    grouping='optional_all'
    restart_on='none'>
        <service_fmri
            value='svc:/milestone/multi-user-server' />
</dependent>

<exec_method
    type='method'
    name='start'
    exec='/lib/svc/method/sshd start'
    timeout_seconds='60'/>

<exec_method
    type='method'
    name='stop'
    exec=':kill'
    timeout_seconds='60' />

<exec_method
    type='method'
    name='refresh'
    exec='/lib/svc/method/sshd restart'
    timeout_seconds='60' />

<property_group name='startd'
    type='framework'>
    <!-- sub-process core dumps shouldn't restart session -->
    <propval name='ignore_error'
        type='astring' value='core,signal' />
</property_group>

    <property_group name='general' type='framework'>
            <!-- to start stop sshd -->
            <propval name='action_authorization' type='astring'
                    value='solaris.smf.manage.ssh' />
    </property_group>

<stability value='Unstable' />

<template>
    <common_name>
        <loctext xml:lang='C'>
        SSH server
```

```
            </loctext>
        </common_name>
        <documentation>
            <manpage title='sshd' section='1M' manpath='/usr/share/man' />
        </documentation>
    </template>

</service>

</service_bundle>
```

While it's possible to define a service directly using the svccfg command, normally you will find that services are defined by an XML file called a *manifest* because it is more convenient, maintainable, and reliable to deliver service definitions using such a mechanism, rather than as a scripted set of commands.

The service manifest

Let's walk through the ssh manifest section-by-section to understand how a service is defined. After the XML version header, the very first item is as follows:

```
<!DOCTYPE service_bundle SYSTEM "/usr/share/lib/xml/dtd/service_bundle.dtd.1">
```

This clause tells the XML parser that the document is a *service bundle*, and its format is defined by the DTD file, service_bundle.dtd.1. The rest of the manifest contents are required to be in the format described by the DTD.

> **TIP** The SMF DTD is extensively commented and is a useful resource in understanding SMF, especially when developing your own service definitions.

Service declaration

The next section (ignoring comments) is the basic service declaration:

```
<service_bundle type='manifest' name='SUNWsshdr:ssh'>

<service
    name='network/ssh'
    type='service'
    version='1'>

    <create_default_instance enabled='false' />

    <single_instance />
```

First, the service_bundle element's type attribute defines which type of service bundle this document contains — in this case, a manifest, which is the most common type. Another type is the profile, described later in this chapter. The name attribute, by convention, is used to record the name of the package in which this service is delivered — in this case, SUNWsshdr.

Next, the actual service declaration begins, defining the service name. The full name of the service is known as a service FMRI (short for Fault Managed Resource Identifier). The actual FMRI for the ssh service is written as svc:/network/ssh, but the prefix does not need to be written in the manifest because it's implied by being part of a service declaration.

CROSS-REF See Chapter 12 for more on fault management and FMRIs.

The type attribute defines this as a service; other possibilities are restarter and milestone. The version attribute allows for service versioning, which is currently not used in SMF; all service manifests shipped in OpenSolaris have a version attribute set to 1. Eventually, versions may be used to enable services to change in future releases of OpenSolaris while maintaining compatibility for services written for older releases. See later sections of this chapter for details on restarters and milestones.

The last two elements of this section, create_default_instance and single_instance, define an actual *instance* of a service, which is necessary for the service to run. This can be a confusing aspect of SMF because while you generally talk about services running, in fact you are normally referring to an instance of a service. Most services will have a single instance, named default, and that instance is what the create_default_instance element defines; the FMRI for the instance will be svc:/network/ssh:default.

The enabled attribute indicates whether this instance should be enabled or disabled immediately after the instance is defined. In most cases the manifest declares the service to be disabled by default. This is based on an OpenSolaris architecture best practice, which suggests that only service instances that are required to boot and initialize the system should be enabled by default, with all others disabled to reduce the system's vulnerability to attack. This has the additional benefit of reducing system load by limiting the number of unneeded processes started on the system. The services that are enabled by default are typically those used to configure the system after installation.

CROSS-REF See Chapter 11 for more information on OpenSolaris security policies.

The single_instance element notifies SMF that only one instance of this service can be online at a time. Few of the early services have had multiple instances, but because SMF is incorporated further into the design of other subsystems, multiple instances of services are starting to appear. The most notable example in OpenSolaris is the network/physical service, which has both default and nwam instances to support the traditional Solaris networking configuration (the default instance) and the automatic configuration from the Network Auto-Magic project (the nwam instance).

CROSS-REF Network configuration is discussed in Chapter 9.

Dependencies

One of the core principles of SMF is that services are related to each other by dependencies. Each service declares its dependencies in its manifest, and ssh is fairly typical in this respect, having a number of dependencies. Here's a look at just one of them:

```
<dependency name='fs-local'
    grouping='require_all'
    restart_on='none'
    type='service'>
    <service_fmri
        value='svc:/system/filesystem/local' />
</dependency>
```

Each dependency has a name attribute. By convention, dependencies are named based on the service to which the dependency refers, as is the case here, though it used an abbreviated form.

The grouping attribute is the key attribute in the dependency, specifying how critical the dependency is to this service. The require_all grouping used here is the most common type of dependency. It represents a "hard" dependency — one that must come online before this service can be started. There are other types of dependency groupings, though:

- require_any — At least one service in the grouping must come online in order for this service to come online.

- optional_all — All services in the grouping must be online, disabled, or in maintenance. Essentially, this means that if the dependency is enabled, it should be started prior to this service, but this service should be brought online regardless of the result of starting the dependency. This is useful in cases where your service can provide additional functionality or behave differently if the dependency is available, but can function correctly without it. The ssh service uses this grouping for the autofs service dependency because many users have their home directories located on automounted file systems, which aren't available until after the autofs service is online.

- exclude_all — If any of the services in the grouping are online, this service may not be brought online.

The restart_on attribute specifies how SMF should propagate changes in the state of the dependency to this service. In this case, the value none specifies that no change in the state of the dependency will cause this service to be automatically restarted; the result of this setting is that the dependency applies only for initial startup of this service. Other possible values are as follows:

- error — Restart if the dependency fails
- restart — Restart if the dependency restarts
- refresh — Restart if the dependency restarts or is refreshed

TIP When writing your own service manifests, include a comment with each dependency recording why the dependency exists, so that future service maintainers understand why it's there. Unlike the ssh manifest, most system manifests do contain at least some comments on their dependencies.

The `type` and `service_fmri` attributes together specify that this dependency is on another service, and the FMRI of that service. Compare that setting to another of ssh's dependencies:

```
<dependency name='config_data'
    grouping='require_all'
    restart_on='restart'
    type='path'>
    <service_fmri
        value='file://localhost/etc/ssh/sshd_config' />
</dependency>
```

Rather than specify a dependency on another service, this dependency is on a file — in this case, the sshd configuration file; if the file does not exist, ssh will not be brought online.

NOTE You will not currently see path dependencies used very often. While it seems like a good idea for services that have such configuration files, the current SMF implementation makes it less attractive than it appears. If the configuration file doesn't exist, the service is left in the offline state, and other services that have optional (rather than required) dependencies on that service will be brought online. More often, the desired behavior is for the service whose configuration file is missing to go to the maintenance state, which blocks any services that depend on it from being brought online. To achieve this behavior, the service's start method should check for the file's existence and exit with the code 96 (SMF_EXIT_ERR_CONFIG).

Additionally, there is no monitoring of the file for changes, so the service cannot be notified of updates to the file. An efficient file event monitoring capability has recently been added to OpenSolaris, but SMF does not yet make use of it to monitor file dependencies.

Dependents

In addition to defining the service's dependencies, the manifest can also define its dependents. There is no difference between how SMF treats these two methods of defining the dependency relationships between services, so why would you use a `dependent` element in one service's manifest and a `dependency` in the other's?

The SMF community recommends that when writing a service manifest, you directly define all of the dependencies you are aware of by using `dependency` elements. However, if the developer of a service realizes that some other services need to depend on it and he does not have the ability to modify and deliver the dependent service's manifest at the same time as his service, he should use a `dependent` element in his service manifest to create the correct dependency relationship. The ssh manifest has a single dependent element:

```
<dependent
    name='ssh_multi-user-server'
```

```
            grouping='optional_all'
            restart_on='none'>
                <service_fmri
                    value='svc:/milestone/multi-user-server' />
        </dependent>
```

Like the `dependency` element, the `dependent` element has `name`, `grouping`, and `restart_on` attributes that work in the same fashion, and it includes a `service_fmri` element that identifies the dependent service. It lacks a `type` attribute, because declaring a file as being a dependent would make no sense and no other types of dependencies are supported by SMF. The `ssh` manifest's use of `dependent` also demonstrates another reason why it's useful: when a service has optional dependencies on a large set of services, which is the case for milestones such as `multi-user-server`. Milestones are discussed later in this chapter.

Listing all of those optional dependencies would lead to a very large service manifest, and may lead to extra work in maintaining the dependencies due to the need to update multiple service manifests if the dependencies change. Using a `dependent` element in the `ssh` manifest keeps its relationships local to the single manifest, simplifying the developer's maintenance of the `ssh` service.

Methods

The next section of the service manifest makes the crucial connection between the SMF service definition and the programs that are run to provide the service. These are the method declarations from the `ssh` manifest:

```
<exec_method
    type='method'
    name='start'
    exec='/lib/svc/method/sshd start'
    timeout_seconds='60'/>

<exec_method
    type='method'
    name='stop'
    exec=':kill'
    timeout_seconds='60' />

<exec_method
    type='method'
    name='refresh'
    exec='/lib/svc/method/sshd restart'
    timeout_seconds='60' />
```

Each `exec_method` element defines a different action that can be taken on the service. The `ssh` service defines the three method types that are standard across most SMF services:

- `start` — To bring the service online. Required.

■ stop — To take the service offline. Required.

■ refresh — To reload the service's configuration without an interruption of the service. Optional.

Each method declaration is required to have the type, name, exec, and timeout_seconds attributes.

The exec attribute defines the command that should be run for that method. This is often the full pathname of an executable program, but two special tokens may also appear. The ssh stop method demonstrates the first token, :kill. This token directs SMF to send processes that are part of the service a signal; the mechanism SMF uses to track those processes is discussed later in this chapter. SIGTERM is the default, although any signal can be sent by adding it as an option to the :kill token. The other special token is :true, which can used in a required method declaration to instruct SMF that no action is to be taken for this method on the service. You most often see :true used as the stop method for services that are transient in nature.

The timeout_seconds attribute provides a boundary for the expected execution time on the method. If the method does not exit within the duration specified, SMF will terminate the method and retry it, until a retry limit is reached, at which point the service is placed into a maintenance state. The retry limit for all services at this time is three method failures in a row, or a restart rate of greater than once per second, and it is not configurable.

Property groups

The next section of the ssh manifest contains two property_group elements:

```
<property_group name='startd'
    type='framework'>
    <!-- sub-process core dumps shouldn't restart session -->
    <propval name='ignore_error'
      type='astring' value='core,signal' />
</property_group>

<property_group name='general' type='framework'>
    <!-- to start stop sshd -->
    <propval name='action_authorization' type='astring'
        value='solaris.smf.manage.ssh' />
</property_group>
```

Both of the property groups have a type of framework, meaning that they are property groups defined by SMF to be usable on any service. A property_group element may contain propval elements, each of which is used to set the value of a single-valued property; the property element is available to set the value of list-valued properties.

A service may also define property groups with a type of application, which the service will use to store configuration values for its own use. Because ssh has a configuration file that it uses on multiple platforms, it doesn't use application property groups, although the contents of its configuration file, /etc/ssh/sshd_config, could easily be modeled using SMF properties. More complex service configuration languages, such as that used by the ipfilter firewall, are less likely to be candidates for modeling with SMF property groups.

The ignore_error property in the first property group element is used to alter how SMF treats some failures in this service. In this case, the property includes a list of two values:

- core — SMF will not restart the service if it produces a core dump.
- signal — SMF will not restart the service if a subprocess of the service exits due to a signal from a process that is not part of the service, such as a kill signal sent by an administrator.

The service will be restarted if all of its processes exit.

The action_authorization property in the second property group is used to delegate some administrative tasks on the service using the OpenSolaris role-based access control (RBAC) framework. By specifying a value for the action_authorization property, users who are assigned that authorization (solaris.smf.manage.ssh in this example) will have the capability to use svcadm to modify the state of this service.

CROSS-REF   See Chapter 11 for details on assigning authorizations using RBAC.

Stability and templates

The last section of the service manifest contains information describing the service for developers and administrators:

```
<stability value='Unstable' />

<template>
    <common_name>
        <loctext xml:lang='C'>
        SSH server
        </loctext>
    </common_name>
    <documentation>
        <manpage title='sshd' section='1M' manpath='/usr/share/man' />
    </documentation>
</template>
```

The stability element is often confusing to those new to OpenSolaris. You might assume that it's making a comment on how well the service works, but that's not the case. Instead, it relates to the OpenSolaris architectural review process as defined by the Architecture Process and Tools community and governed by the Architecture Review Committees (ARCs).

CROSS-REF   The ARCs and the OpenSolaris development process are described in Chapter 1.

In this realm, the term *stability* describes the conditions under which an interface may be changed in an incompatible fashion. The interface in this case reflects the names of the service, instances, and properties defined within the manifest. The stability values are defined by a document known as the Interface Taxonomy, which is maintained by the ARCs; the value used here, Unstable, means that the name of the service, any instances, or any property groups, are subject to change in a minor release of OpenSolaris. A separate document called the Release Taxonomy defines what constitutes a minor release.

> **NOTE** The Architecture Process and Tools community at www.opensolaris.org/os/community/arc/ publishes both the Interface Taxonomy and the Release Taxonomy.

The template element provides a place for the service developer to include some very basic information about the service, which can be displayed by the SMF management tools. While it's desirable for the service name to be as descriptive as possible, the common_name element is used to provide a name in ordinary language that should be clear to a user. Its documentation element provides a pointer to the manual page describing the service, which can be accessed using the man command. This element can also contain a link to web-based documentation resources, though the ssh service hasn't provided one. The SMF community has additional work in progress to expand the template section to enable service authors to provide more information about the properties and values. This work will enable the configuration tools to provide more assistance to users by improving the documentation and validation of properties.

> **TIP** When writing your own service manifest, it's usually not a good idea to start from a blank file and write it from scratch. Instead, find an existing service that is similar to your new one and use its manifest as a starting point, modifying it for your new service's purposes. The Easy Tools project, at http://opensolaris.org/os/project/phpEasyTools/, is also developing a tool to simplify manifest construction.

Service method script

Now let's turn our attention to the other part of this service, the method script. Not all services use a script as their start method, but a substantial percentage do. Listing 13-2 shows the ssh method script, /lib/svc/method/sshd.

LISTING 13-2

ssh method script

```
#!/sbin/sh
#
# Copyright 2008 Sun Microsystems, Inc.  All rights reserved.
# Use is subject to license terms.
#
# ident    "@(#)sshd    1.4    04/11/17 SMI"

SSHDIR=/etc/ssh
KEYGEN="/usr/bin/ssh-keygen -q"
```

```
PIDFILE=/var/run/sshd.pid

# Checks to see if RSA, and DSA host keys are available
# if any of these keys are not present, the respective keys are created.
create_key()
{
    keypath=$1
    keytype=$2

    if [ ! -f $keypath ]; then
        grep "^HostKey $keypath" $SSHDIR/sshd_config > /dev/null 2>&1
        if [ $? -eq 0 ]; then
            echo Creating new $keytype public/private host key pair
            $KEYGEN -f $keypath -t $keytype -N ''
            return $?
        fi
    fi

    return 0
}

# This script is being used for two purposes: as part of an SMF
# start/stop/refresh method, and as a sysidconfig(1M)/sys-unconfig(1M)
# application.
#
# Both, the SMF methods and sysidconfig/sys-unconfig use different
# arguments..

case $1 in
    # sysidconfig/sys-unconfig arguments (-c and -u)
'-c')
    create_key $SSHDIR/ssh_host_rsa_key rsa
    create_key $SSHDIR/ssh_host_dsa_key dsa
    ;;

'-u')
    # sys-unconfig(1M) knows how to remove ssh host keys, so there's
    # nothing to do here.
    :
    ;;

    # SMF arguments (start and restart [really "refresh"])
'start')
    if [ -f /.livecd ] && [ ! -f $SSHDIR/ssh_host_rsa_key ]; then
        create_key $SSHDIR/ssh_host_rsa_key rsa
        create_key $SSHDIR/ssh_host_dsa_key dsa
    fi
    /usr/lib/ssh/sshd
    ;;
```

```
'restart')
    if [ -f "$PIDFILE" ]; then
        /usr/bin/kill -HUP `/usr/bin/cat $PIDFILE`
    fi
    ;;

*)
    echo "Usage: $0 { start | restart }"
    exit 1
    ;;
esac

exit $?
```

This method script shouldn't look all that unfamiliar if you're a Linux user; the /etc/init.d/sshd script in Fedora 8 contains similar operations, including generating the keys, starting the daemon, and using the sshd.pid file to find the right process to signal when reloading the configuration. This similarity demonstrates that adapting a service written for a platform lacking SMF will often not require many changes in the service itself, as the SMF manifest can be used to define the service so that it uses existing code to start and stop itself. In fact, for many daemon services, you may not need to write a method script at all, as the daemon can just be run directly as the service start method, and the SMF :kill method token can be used to stop the service or send a SIGHUP signal to refresh it.

Service management commands

While the system is running, you can manage and monitor services using a set of service management commands. This section demonstrates each of these in turn. Table 13-1 lists the SMF commands.

TABLE 13-1

Service Management Commands

Command	Tasks
svcs	Displays service status and dependencies; diagnoses service problems
svcadm	Manages service state
svccfg	Configures service properties; imports service manifests
svcprop	Retrieves service properties

svcs

The svcs(1m)command provides a monitoring interface for SMF. Its most basic form, without any options, displays the state of all of the currently enabled services, as shown in the example in Listing 13-3.

LISTING 13-3

Example service listing

```
$ svcs
STATE          STIME     FMRI
legacy_run     Mar_03    lrc:/etc/rcS_d/S99punchclean
legacy_run     Mar_03    lrc:/etc/rc2_d/S20sysetup
legacy_run     Mar_03    lrc:/etc/rc2_d/S47pppd
legacy_run     Mar_03    lrc:/etc/rc2_d/S72autoinstall
legacy_run     Mar_03    lrc:/etc/rc2_d/S73cachefs_daemon
legacy_run     Mar_03    lrc:/etc/rc2_d/S81dodatadm_udaplt
legacy_run     Mar_03    lrc:/etc/rc2_d/S89PRESERVE
legacy_run     Mar_03    lrc:/etc/rc2_d/S98deallocate
legacy_run     Mar_03    lrc:/etc/rc3_d/S50apache
disabled       Mar_03    svc:/system/xvm/xend:default
disabled       Mar_03    svc:/system/xvm/console:default
disabled       Mar_03    svc:/system/xvm/domains:default
disabled       Mar_03    svc:/system/xvm/store:default
online         Mar_03    svc:/system/svc/restarter:default
online         Mar_03    svc:/network/loopback:default
online         Mar_03    svc:/system/identity:node
online         Mar_03    svc:/system/filesystem/root:default
online         Mar_03    svc:/system/scheduler:default
online         Mar_03    svc:/system/boot-archive:default
online         Mar_03    svc:/system/filesystem/usr:default
online         Mar_03    svc:/system/keymap:default
online         Mar_03    svc:/system/device/local:default
online         Mar_03    svc:/system/filesystem/minimal:default
online         Mar_03    svc:/system/coreadm:default
online         Mar_03    svc:/system/identity:domain
online         Mar_03    svc:/system/rmtmpfiles:default
online         Mar_03    svc:/system/resource-mgmt:default
online         Mar_03    svc:/system/cryptosvc:default
online         Mar_03    svc:/system/power:default
online         Mar_03    svc:/system/sysevent:default
online         Mar_03    svc:/network/ipsec/ipsecalgs:default
online         Mar_03    svc:/system/device/fc-fabric:default
online         Mar_03    svc:/network/ipsec/policy:default
online         Mar_03    svc:/milestone/devices:default
online         Mar_03    svc:/milestone/network:default
online         Mar_03    svc:/system/picl:default
online         Mar_03    svc:/network/initial:default
online         Mar_03    svc:/system/manifest-import:default
```

```
online          Mar_03     svc:/network/service:default
online          Mar_03     svc:/network/dns/client:default
online          Mar_03     svc:/milestone/name-services:default
online          Mar_03     svc:/milestone/single-user:default
online          Mar_03     svc:/application/print/ppd-cache-update:default
online          Mar_03     svc:/network/routing-setup:default
online          Mar_03     svc:/network/routing/ndp:default
online          Mar_03     svc:/network/routing/route:default
online          Mar_03     svc:/system/filesystem/local:default
online          Mar_03     svc:/system/cron:default
online          Mar_03     svc:/system/sysidtool:net
online          Mar_03     svc:/system/boot-archive-update:default
online          Mar_03     svc:/network/rpc/bind:default
online          Mar_03     svc:/application/opengl/ogl-select:default
online          Mar_03     svc:/network/shares/group:default
online          Mar_03     svc:/system/sysidtool:system
online          Mar_03     svc:/network/shares/group:zfs
online          Mar_03     svc:/milestone/sysconfig:default
online          Mar_03     svc:/system/sac:default
online          Mar_03     svc:/system/utmp:default
online          Mar_03     svc:/network/inetd:default
online          Mar_03     svc:/system/console-login:default
online          Mar_03     svc:/system/dbus:default
online          Mar_03     svc:/system/postrun:default
online          Mar_03     svc:/network/rpc/gss:default
online          Mar_03     svc:/network/rpc/smserver:default
online          Mar_03     svc:/network/security/ktkt_warn:default
online          Mar_03     svc:/system/avahi-bridge-dsd:default
online          Mar_03     svc:/system/filesystem/autofs:default
online          Mar_03     svc:/system/dumpadm:default
online          Mar_03     svc:/network/ntp:default
online          Mar_03     svc:/system/system-log:default
online          Mar_03     svc:/network/ssh:default
online          Mar_03     svc:/network/dns/multicast:default
online          Mar_03     svc:/application/font/fc-cache:default
online          Mar_03     svc:/system/fmd:default
online          Mar_03     svc:/milestone/multi-user:default
online          Mar_03     svc:/system/intrd:default
online          Mar_03     svc:/application/graphical-login/gdm:default
online          Mar_03     svc:/system/hal:default
online          Mar_03     svc:/system/filesystem/rmvolmgr:default
online          Mar_03     svc:/milestone/multi-user-server:default
online          Mar_03     svc:/network/physical:nwam
online          Mar_03     svc:/system/name-service-cache:default
online          22:05:02   svc:/system/zones:default
```

You can use the svcs -a option to display a similar listing that includes all services known to the system, including those that are disabled.

> **TIP** Listing 13-3 shows several disabled services, even though the `-a` option wasn't specified. They are listed because they are only temporarily disabled. On the next boot of the system, these services will revert to being enabled.

You can easily check the state of a single service by specifying its name as an argument to `svcs`, such as for `ssh`:

```
$ svcs ssh
STATE          STIME   FMRI
online         19:40:42 svc:/network/ssh:default
```

The default listing of a service shows its current state, the time it entered that state (in the `STIME` column), and its fully qualified FMRI. If you specify the `-o` option, you can control the columns displayed (several others are possible) and the order in which they are displayed. This feature is most often used in scripts. This example demonstrates another feature of `svcs`, and all of the SMF commands: It automatically expands a partial service name to its full FMRI so that you don't need to provide the entire proper name of a service. In the case of a command such as `svcadm`, which would modify a service's configuration or state, the expansion of the name must yield a unique FMRI; otherwise, the operation is rejected and an error message is generated stating that the pattern matches multiple service instances. For `svcs`, the expansion works in all cases because it is only displaying information; multiple matches will just yield information on all of them.

You can use `svcs -l` to see a more detailed listing of a service's status. Again looking at `ssh`:

```
$ svcs -l ssh
fmri         svc:/network/ssh:default
name         SSH server
enabled      true
state        online
next_state   none
state_time   Thu Mar 06 19:40:42 2008
logfile      /var/svc/log/network-ssh:default.log
restarter    svc:/system/svc/restarter:default
contract_id  64
dependency   require_all/none svc:/system/filesystem/local (online)
dependency   optional_all/none svc:/system/filesystem/autofs (online)
dependency   require_all/none svc:/network/loopback (online)
dependency   require_all/none svc:/network/physical (multiple)
dependency   require_all/none svc:/system/cryptosvc (online)
dependency   require_all/none svc:/system/utmp (online)
dependency   require_all/restart file://localhost/etc/ssh/sshd_config (online)
```

This long listing repeats the information shown in the short listing earlier, and adds much more detail. You should recognize the dependencies and the name from the manifest. One item of particular interest is the log file; the default system restarter provides a log file for each of its services. If you look at the log file, you'll see that the restarter logs an entry every time it executes one of the service's methods, including the exit status of the method. The standard output and standard error file descriptors from the service methods are also captured and recorded in the log file, though many services use a specific log or the system log service, syslog, to record log information. See the section "Restarters" later in this chapter for information on the contract_id.

> **TIP** You can display just the dependencies of a service by using svcs -d. You can also display the dependents of a service using svcs -D.

Another useful option is svcs -p, which is used to display the processes associated with a service. Looking again at the ssh service:

```
$ svcs -p ssh
STATE          STIME    FMRI
online         22:33:33 svc:/network/ssh:default
               22:33:33    1246 sshd
```

In this case, process 1246 is the only process associated with the service; it's the main ssh listening daemon, waiting for incoming ssh connections. You won't see any active ssh sessions associated with the service. Because of the way that sshd spawns each session, the individual sessions are independent of the ssh service. This feature enables the ssh service to be restarted without terminating any active sessions. If multiple processes are associated with a service, they will all be listed; the hal service (which provides a hardware abstraction layer for the GNOME desktop) shows an example of multiple processes for a service:

```
$ svcs -p hal
STATE          STIME    FMRI
online         19:40:44 svc:/system/hal:default
               19:40:40     480 hald
               19:40:40     481 hald-runner
               19:40:42     518 hald-addon-netw
               19:40:43     528 hald-addon-acpi
               19:40:43     535 hald-addon-stor
```

The final option to explore in the svcs command is svcs -x. If any service is not in the normal state (online for enabled services, offline for disabled services), svcs -x should be the first step in diagnosing the problem. An example of ssh in a failure state might look like the following:

```
$ svcs -x
svc:/network/ssh:default (SSH server)
 State: maintenance since Sun Mar 09 19:37:50 2008
Reason: Restarting too quickly.
   See: http://sun.com/msg/SMF-8000-L5
   See: sshd(1M)
   See: /var/svc/log/network-ssh:default.log
Impact: This service is not running.
```

To investigate the problem further, start by inspecting the log file listed in the svcs -x output. The manual page listed is also likely to be helpful. In addition, don't overlook the first reference, to the web page `http://sun.com/msg/SMF-8000-L5`. This is a Sun knowledge article that provides help in diagnosing the root cause of the failure you're experiencing. Consulting this article will provide the latest information and recommended procedures to repair the problem. Once you've investigated and corrected the problem, you can ask SMF to bring the service back to its intended state with the `svcadm` command.

svcadm

The `svcadm(1m)` command is used to manipulate the state of services. Seven subcommands are available within it. The `enable` and `disable` subcommands are the ones you'll most commonly use; they set the permanent desired state of the service. SMF will immediately attempt to transition the service from whatever state it is currently in to the desired state. If the service is not running, enabling it will cause it to immediately start, provided its dependencies are met; if dependencies are not met, it will remain offline and you can use `svcs -x` to diagnose the problem. The enabled or disabled state can be set temporarily, rather than permanently, by using the `-t` option; a temporary setting applies only until the next time the system is booted.

```
# svcs ssh
STATE          STIME    FMRI
online         Mar_21   svc:/network/ssh:default
# svcadm disable ssh
# svcs ssh
STATE          STIME    FMRI
disabled       22:32:35 svc:/network/ssh:default
# svcadm enable ssh
# svcs ssh
STATE          STIME    FMRI
online         22:32:42 svc:/network/ssh:default
```

> **TIP** Many experienced UNIX or Linux users are accustomed to stopping services such as `ssh` by merely using the `kill` or `pkill` command to directly terminate the daemon process. In the case of OpenSolaris with SMF, you might be confused by the fact that the daemon won't seem to die. This is a simple demonstration of how SMF changes the system model to one in which services just keep going, like the Energizer Bunny. It won't take long to retrain yourself to use `svcadm disable` to stop services instead.

One important detail to understand about all of the `svcadm` subcommands is that they act asynchronously. That is, the SMF infrastructure is notified of the new desired state of the service, and then the command exits; the service may take some time to reach the desired state after the command has completed. The `enable` and `disable` subcommands can operate synchronously if you specify the `-s` option, which causes the command to wait until the service has reached the desired state.

The `restart` subcommand is used to transition a service that is online to the offline state, and then return it to the online state. This means that the service's `stop` method will be run, followed by its `start` method. If any services that depend on this service have requested to be restarted if it restarts, then they will also be restarted in the same fashion.

The `refresh` subcommand causes the service's `refresh` method, if any, to be executed. Before the method is executed, the service's configuration in the SMF repository is also updated to capture any changes that have been saved in the repository but not yet applied to the service.

> **TIP** One common mistake is to modify a service's configuration using `svccfg` and then use `svcadm restart` to restart the service without using `svcadm refresh` to ensure that the configuration has been applied.

The `clear` subcommand notifies SMF that the administrator has corrected the condition that caused a service to be placed in a maintenance state. The service's restarter will attempt to start the service. Working from the example in the previous section, you can use this option to bring `ssh` back online:

```
# svcs ssh
STATE          STIME    FMRI
maintenance    19:37:50 svc:/network/ssh:default
# svcadm clear ssh
# svcs ssh
STATE          STIME    FMRI
online         19:56:49 svc:/network/ssh:default
```

It's possible, however, that the service may still have difficulty and be placed back into a maintenance state. If this occurs, you need to dig in using `svcs -x` to locate and examine the service log files, and use documentation resources such as the knowledge base and documents from the OpenSolaris communities to diagnose the root cause of the problem.

The `mark` subcommand enables the administrator to manually place a service into the maintenance state; it's rare to actually do this other than when you're developing services.

The `milestone` subcommand provides a way to temporarily enable all of the services that are dependencies of the specified milestone, and disable all others. This subcommand is presently somewhat restricted; it operates only for the special milestones `none`, `single-user`, `multiuser`, `multi-user-server`, and `all`, which are discussed more fully later in this chapter.

svccfg

The `svccfg(1m)` command provides all of the basic functionality required to configure SMF services. Using `svccfg`, you have direct access to the configuration of each service in the repository, and if you have the required authorization, you can modify the service configuration. You can use `svccfg` in an interactive session by entering `svccfg` with no arguments to a shell prompt:

```
$ svccfg
svc:> help
General commands:    help set repository end
Manifest commands:    inventory validate import export archive
Profile commands:    apply extract
```

```
Entity commands:        list select unselect add delete
Snapshot commands:      listsnap selectsnap revert
Property group commands: listpg addpg delpg
Property commands:      listprop setprop delprop editprop
Property value commands: addpropvalue delpropvalue setenv unsetenv
svc:>
```

`svccfg` can also be used in a non-interactive mode; some subcommands require selecting a service or instance FMRI, which is done by specifying the `-s` option — for example, to view the properties of the `ssh` service:

```
$ svccfg -s ssh listprop
fs-local                        dependency
fs-local/entities               fmri    svc:/system/filesystem/local
fs-local/grouping               astring require_all
fs-local/restart_on             astring none
fs-local/type                   astring service
fs-autofs                       dependency
fs-autofs/entities              fmri    svc:/system/filesystem/autofs
fs-autofs/grouping              astring optional_all
fs-autofs/restart_on            astring none
fs-autofs/type                  astring service
net-loopback                    dependency
net-loopback/entities           fmri    svc:/network/loopback
net-loopback/grouping           astring require_all
net-loopback/restart_on         astring none
net-loopback/type               astring service
net-physical                    dependency
net-physical/entities           fmri    svc:/network/physical
net-physical/grouping           astring require_all
net-physical/restart_on         astring none
net-physical/type               astring service
cryptosvc                       dependency
cryptosvc/entities              fmri    svc:/system/cryptosvc
cryptosvc/grouping              astring require_all
cryptosvc/restart_on            astring none
cryptosvc/type                  astring service
utmp                            dependency
utmp/entities                   fmri    svc:/system/utmp
utmp/grouping                   astring require_all
utmp/restart_on                 astring none
utmp/type                       astring service
config_data                     dependency
config_data/entities            fmri    file://localhost/etc/ssh/sshd_config
config_data/grouping            astring require_all
config_data/restart_on          astring restart
config_data/type                astring path
general                         framework
general/action_authorization    astring solaris.smf.manage.ssh
```

```
general/entity_stability            astring   Unstable
general/single_instance             boolean   true
dependents                          framework
dependents/ssh_multi-user-server    fmri      svc:/milestone/multi-user-server
startd                              framework
startd/ignore_error                 astring   core,signal
start                               method
start/exec                          astring   "/lib/svc/method/sshd start"
start/timeout_seconds               count     60
start/type                          astring   method
stop                                method
stop/exec                           astring   :kill
stop/timeout_seconds                count     60
stop/type                           astring   method
refresh                             method
refresh/exec                        astring   "/lib/svc/method/sshd restart"
refresh/timeout_seconds             count     60
refresh/type                        astring   method
tm_common_name                      template
tm_common_name/C                    ustring   "SSH server"
tm_man_sshd                         template
tm_man_sshd/manpath                 astring   /usr/share/man
tm_man_sshd/section                 astring   1M
tm_man_sshd/title                   astring   sshd
```

If you compare the properties of the ssh service to the service manifest listed earlier in this chapter, you'll see that all of the data from the manifest is recorded as properties of the service. Each dependency is represented as a property group using the name of the dependency as the name of the property group. Each method definition is also represented as a property group, again using the method name as the property group name.

NOTE As shown in the svccfg listprop **command output, the notation used to refer to properties resembles UNIX pathname notation. If you equate a property group to a directory, and a property value to a file within that directory, the notation will seem quite natural.**

The setprop subcommand is used to set the value of a property; you must first select a service or instance with the select subcommand, and then use setprop to modify a property value. For example, the following modifies the timeout of the ssh stop method:

```
# svccfg
svc:> select network/ssh
svc:/network/ssh> listprop stop/timeout_seconds
stop/timeout_seconds   count    60
svc:/network/ssh> setprop stop/timeout_seconds=30
svc:/network/ssh> listprop stop/timeout_seconds
stop/timeout_seconds   count    30
svc:/network/ssh> exit
```

The exit subcommand terminates an interactive svccfg session. Any changes made during the session are written immediately to the repository. To apply the changed values in the repository to the service, you must refresh the service using svcadm refresh.

An SMF manifest is converted to property groups in the repository using the svccfg import subcommand, and the export subcommand can be used to translate a service from its repository representation back into a service manifest. A related subcommand is archive, which can be used to dump the entire repository for disaster recovery purposes, as it dumps the persistent properties of the services, not the transient state.

svcprop

The svcprop(1m) command is provided primarily as a programmatic interface for retrieving property values from scripts. The following example retrieves a property value such as the timeout on the start method:

```
$ svcprop -p start/timeout_seconds ssh
60
```

You can also use the -q option just to test the existence of a property. This will result in svcprop exiting with a zero exit code if the property exists, a nonzero code if it doesn't.

Another option available in svcprop is to request that it wait for a value to change before printing it, which can be done using the -w option. The most common use of this option is to wait for a service to move to the online or offline state when it's not possible or desirable to use the -s option to svcadm enable or svcadm disable. Because the service's state is stored in the restarter/state property, the following command can be used to wait for it to change:

```
$ svcprop -w -p restarter/state ssh
```

Once the property changes state, svcprop will print its value and exit.

SMF Machinery

At this point you've had a chance to explore how a service is defined and how it can be configured and monitored. Having explored the surface of SMF, now it's time to take apart its machinery and see how it works.

Restarters

The core of the SMF machinery is the concept of a *restarter*. A restarter is a process or, more properly, a service, that is responsible for monitoring and restarting other services. UNIX has actually had a form of a restarter since the very beginning, and it exists on all versions of UNIX-derived systems: the init(1m) process, which is the process that the kernel has always started first and assigned the PID 1, and which has been responsible for starting all of the other processes used to boot the system and manage transitions between run-levels. init also serves as the default parent process for any process that has remained running after its parent process has exited, as shown by the PPID column in a process listing:

```
UID   PID  PPID  C   STIME TTY        TIME CMD
root    0     0  0 23:22:59 ?         0:01 sched
root    1     0  0 23:23:02 ?         0:00 /sbin/init
root    2     0  0 23:23:02 ?         0:00 pageout
root    3     0  0 23:23:02 ?         1:16 fsflush
root  121     1  0 23:23:17 ?         0:00 /usr/lib/picl/picld
root    7     1  0 23:23:05 ?         0:02 /lib/svc/bin/svc.startd
root    9     1  0 23:23:05 ?         0:06 /lib/svc/bin/svc.configd
root  354     1  0 23:23:25 ?         0:01 /usr/lib/dbus-daemon --system
root   18     1  0 23:23:08 ?         0:01 /lib/inet/nwamd
root  399   359  0 23:23:25 ?         0:00 /usr/lib/saf/ttymon
root   73     1  0 23:23:12 ?         0:01 devfsadmd
root  412     1  0 23:23:26 ?         0:00 /usr/lib/autofs/automountd
root   85     1  0 23:23:15 ?         0:00 /usr/lib/sysevent/syseventd
root  510   508  0 23:23:30 ?         0:00 /usr/sbin/gdm-binary
```

In OpenSolaris, init continues to serve as the default parent process, but the function of starting all boot processes and managing run-level transitions has been ceded to a new process, svc.startd(1m), which is the *master restarter* for the system. You can see it in the preceding process listing. This change means that all services on the system, unless declared otherwise, have svc.startd as their restarter.

More properly, the master restarter is the service identified by the FMRI svc:/system/svc/restarter:default, and svc.startd is merely the process that implements that service, but you'll more often see references to svc.startd as the master restarter. If svc.startd fails for any reason, init is responsible for restarting it.

> **TIP** To declare an alternate restarter for a service, the service manifest must include the restarter element, which has as its value the FMRI of the service that will serve as the restarter.

Referring to svc.startd as the master restarter might imply that there are other types of restarters, and that's a correct assumption. SMF provides the concept of a *delegated restarter*, which is simply a service that provides restarting for other services. Why have delegated restarters? The simple reason is because some sets of services can benefit from more common functionality from a restarter. Rather than have svc.startd grow ever more complex to meet those demands, it instead provides a delegation model that enables it to hand off the task of directly managing those services to the delegated restarter, which can then communicate the status of the services back to svc.startd. This delegation enables svc.startd to focus on the two core tasks of maintaining the *service graph* for the entire system and providing a standard set of restart actions for all services.

The service graph is the construct used by svc.startd to represent the state of each service in the system, as well as its relationship to other services. It is simplest to accurately track this information if svc.startd maintains the states and merely parcels out the tasks of starting and stopping services to the delegated restarters. This division of labor makes it necessary for the delegated restarters to communicate changes in the state of any services they manage to svc.startd, because changes in the status of one service might require actions against another service based on dependency relationships.

CROSS-REF   The only delegated restarter currently included in OpenSolaris is inetd, which manages several of the networking services. See Chapter 9 for more on inetd and networking services.

The restart actions available on a standard service are the methods, which you have already seen defined in the service manifest. The methods shown in the ssh manifest are those defined by svc.startd. Delegated restarters can define additional methods for their services; this is true of inetd, which defines several alternative methods.

Methods also have additional attributes that you haven't yet encountered, provided by the method_context element. This element enables a service author to specify in detail the execution environment in which the method should run. Attributes that can be specified include the user, groups, privileges, RBAC profile, environment variables, working directory, project, and resource pool with which to execute the method.

One question you might have at this point is how svc.startd tracks the states of all the service processes it spawns. That depends on the service because svc.startd supports three different service models for its services, selected by setting the value of the startd/duration property on the service.

The first two are fairly simple to explain. A wait service is one that has only a single process that should be restarted anytime it exits; currently, no services in OpenSolaris use this model. A transient service either does not spawn any long-lived processes or does not want to have svc.startd manage any of its long-lived processes. This type of service will not have any processes associated with it when listed with svcs -p, for example:

```
$ svcprop -p startd/duration device/local
transient
$  svcs -p device/local
STATE          STIME    FMRI
online         Mar_10   svc:/system/device/local:default
```

Most of the transient services perform simple tasks such as mounting file systems or configuring network interfaces.

The third type of service is a contract service; if a service doesn't have a specific setting for the startd/duration property, then it will be a contract service. The obvious question here is, what does a contract mean? A fairly detailed answer can be found by reading the process(4) man page on OpenSolaris, but for SMF's purposes it's sufficient to understand that its restarters use process contracts to track the status of processes and receive notifications when they exit. Essentially, the contract subsystem in the kernel offloads some of the bookkeeping that svc.startd would need to perform to track all of the processes it spawns. Prior to the introduction of contracts, some of the same features could be gained by using the waitpid function, but contracts provide greater efficiency and features not possible in the waitpid model.

The contract terms that are specified by svc.startd when it runs the service's start method tell the kernel which events for the service are of interest to svc.startd. The default contract terms specify that svc.startd wants to be notified if any of the following are true:

- The service encounters a hardware error
- Any process in the service receives a signal from a process outside the service, which causes it to exit
- Any process in the service produces a core file
- All processes in the service exit

Under the default terms, svc.startd will attempt to restart the service if any of these conditions occur. As shown in the ssh service manifest, these terms can be modified by setting the startd/ignore_error property. Most services function best under the default contract terms, though.

> **NOTE** You can use the ctstat(1) and ctwatch(1) commands to observe the active contracts and events on the system. The ctrun(1) command is used to execute a command in a separate contract from its parent process. See the man pages for these tools for more information.

SMF repository

In addition to restarters, another piece of the SMF machinery that you haven't seen yet is the *repository*. Simply, the SMF repository is a database that is used to store all of the service definitions and properties known to SMF; it can be found at /etc/svc/repository.db. However, it's not really quite that simple, because while there's a database underlying it, the database is not directly exposed. All access to the repository is mediated by a daemon called svc.configd(1m); and the service configuration library, libscf(3lib), is used to read and write values in the repository. This library is used by all of the SMF commands presented thus far, as well as svc.startd and any other restarters, to access the repository.

There are several reasons why the repository is managed via svc.configd. First, svc.configd can provide a performance boost by implementing an in-memory caching layer so that transaction rates aren't bounded by system I/O performance and aren't competing directly with other I/O needs. By routing all access to the repository this way, the cache is maximally effective. Second, svc.configd can provide automatic, intelligent notification to svc.startd when the types of properties that have special meaning to svc.startd are modified, thereby lessening its impact on the system by avoiding the need to poll for changes. Third, using svc.configd provides fine-grained access permissions for all data in the repository; SMF uses the RBAC systemwide mechanism for delegating administrative tasks, as you saw in the ssh service manifest.

Obviously, the repository, svc.configd, and svc.startd represent critical failure points in the SMF machinery, so you might wonder how OpenSolaris maintains a high level of reliability. The answer, of course, in the case of svc.configd is that svc.startd uses the contract subsystem to monitor its health. There's a dedicated thread in svc.startd whose only job is to notice an exit of svc.configd and start a new process to take its place. As mentioned earlier, svc.startd is automatically restarted by init on failure, and it ensures that it can pick up its state in such a case by storing the state of each service in the repository. Each service has a restarter property group that is used for bookkeeping purposes by svc.startd:

```
$ svcprop -p restarter ssh
restarter/logfile astring /var/svc/log/network-ssh:default.log
restarter/contract count 64
restarter/start_pid count 418
restarter/start_method_timestamp time 1205708475.901372000
restarter/start_method_waitstatus integer 0
restarter/auxiliary_state astring none
restarter/next_state astring none
restarter/state astring online
restarter/state_timestamp time 1205708475.903837000
```

The state, next_state, and contract properties are the most critical element of the restarter property group, as they enable a restart of svc.startd to rebuild the service graph and continue operation correctly. The contract subsystem enables contracts to be *adopted*, so by recording the state of the service and the contract that was associated with any online services, svc.startd allows for its replacement instance to pick up where it left off by notifying the kernel of the contracts it is adopting. The recorded start_method_timestamp similarly enables a replacement restarter to recognize whether a service's in-progress start method has timed out and requires corrective action.

The reliability of the repository is somewhat dependent on the natural implementation of the database, which is, of course, designed to maintain its integrity. However, because it can't completely protect itself against failures in the storage subsystem, its reliability is partially based on keeping automatic backups. If you look at /etc/svc, you'll see several copies of the repository:

```
$ ls -l /etc/svc
total 57620
lrwxrwxrwx  1 root    root            31 Mar 11 08:14 repository-boot -> repository
-boot-20080311_081406
-rw-------  1 root    root       3529728 Feb 15 19:57 repository-boot-20080215_195720
-rw-------  1 root    root       3529728 Feb 15 20:35 repository-boot-20080215_203514
-rw-------  1 root    root       3529728 Feb 15 20:40 repository-boot-20080215_204043
```

```
-rw-------  1 root   root    3529728 Mar 11 08:14 repository-boot-20080311_081406
lrwxrwxrwx  1 root   root         42 Dec 31 16:52 repository-manifest_import ->
repository-manifest_import-20071231_165230
-rw-------  1 root   root    2609152 Apr 23  2006 repository-manifest_import
-20060423_192650
-rw-------  1 root   root    2669568 Jul 31  2006 repository-manifest_import
-20060731_223346
-rw-------  1 root   root    2939904 Nov 24  2006 repository-manifest_import
-20061124_184442
-rw-------  1 root   root    3529728 Dec 31 16:52 repository-manifest_import
-20071231_165230
-rw-------  1 root   sys     3529728 Mar 11 08:14 repository.db
drwxr-xr-x  3 root   sys       11520 Mar 12 21:04 volatile
```

The `repository.db` file is the repository currently in use. As you might surmise from the names of the other repository files here, a copy is made on each reboot of the system, and each time the `manifest-import` service finds new services to import. The `repository-boot` symlink points to the most recent boot-time copy, and the `repository-manifest-import` symlink points to the most recent copy made by `manifest-import`.

Of course, the system may be unable to boot due to corruption in the repository or other fatal errors in the SMF services. If this happens, the boot process will stop, state that it needs to enter System Maintenance Mode, and prompt you for the root password. Once you've logged in, there's a cheat sheet for recovery stored at `/lib/svc/share/README`. The instructions there will help you determine the problem and, it is hoped, repair the system.

> **TIP** Recovery instructions are also in the Sun knowledge base, at `www.sun.com/msg/SMF-8000-QD`.

The manifest-import service

This chapter earlier described use of the `svccfg import` command to convert an XML service manifest into its representation in the SMF repository. You might be wondering at this point how the repository is populated with all of the service manifests that are delivered as part of the system. If you were paying close attention to the first boot of the system, you would have seen a progress message like the following displayed during the boot process:

```
Loading smf(5) service descriptions: 120/120
Loaded 120 smf(5) service descriptions
```

These messages are emitted by the service `system/manifest-import`, which is responsible for importing all of the service manifests under the `/var/svc/manifest` directory hierarchy. On subsequent boots of the system, the `manifest-import` service re-scans the `/var/svc/manifest` hierarchy and imports any new or updated manifests.

> **TIP** More details about the SMF bootstrapping process are available in the man page `smf_bootstrap(5)`.

One interesting thing to understand is that the `manifest-import` service is really just another SMF service; you can find its manifest at `/var/svc/manifest/system/manifest-import.xml`. However, that raises an obvious chicken-and-egg conundrum: If `manifest-import` is the service that imports the manifests, and it's one of those services, then how does it get started to begin with?

The answer is in the directory `/lib/svc/seed`. There you'll find two files, `global.db` and `nonglobal.db`. These are the *seed repositories* for the global zone and nonglobal zones, respectively.

CROSS-REF The OpenSolaris zones technology is described in Chapter 19.

The seed repository is a prebuilt SMF repository that contains just enough of the service graph imported to boot the system (or nonglobal zone) to the point where the `manifest-import` service starts and imports the rest of the manifests. The seed repository is built as part of the OS/Net consolidation's build process and delivered to `/lib/svc/seed` as part of the system packaging. The installer (or the `zoneadm install` process in the case of a nonglobal zone) is then responsible for copying the seed repository to `/etc/svc/repository.db` so that the initial boot of the system (or zone) happens correctly. On the OpenSolaris distribution's Live CD, the entire repository has been prebuilt by running the `manifest-import` service during the CD construction process.

Milestones and init compatibility

Another element of the SMF machinery is the *milestone*. A milestone is a service, but it isn't designed to offer functionality of its own. Instead, it provides a means of establishing conveniently aggregated dependencies. Several special milestones provided in the SMF implementation are designed to preserve compatibility with the old `init` script operations (described earlier in this chapter). If you look at the default service listing from `svcs`, you'll see a number of services whose FMRIs look oddly reminiscent of the `init` script names. Here's an excerpt that demonstrates these FMRIs:

```
$ svcs
STATE          STIME    FMRI
legacy_run     16:10:04 lrc:/etc/rcS_d/S99punchclean
legacy_run     16:10:18 lrc:/etc/rc2_d/S20sysetup
legacy_run     16:10:18 lrc:/etc/rc2_d/S47pppd
legacy_run     16:10:18 lrc:/etc/rc2_d/S72autoinstall
legacy_run     16:10:18 lrc:/etc/rc2_d/S73cachefs_daemon
legacy_run     16:10:18 lrc:/etc/rc2_d/S81dodatadm_udaplt
legacy_run     16:10:18 lrc:/etc/rc2_d/S89PRESERVE
legacy_run     16:10:18 lrc:/etc/rc2_d/S98deallocate
legacy_run     16:10:21 lrc:/etc/rc3_d/S50apache
disabled       16:10:08 svc:/system/xvm/console:default
disabled       16:10:10 svc:/system/xvm/store:default
disabled       16:10:10 svc:/system/xvm/xend:default
disabled       16:10:10 svc:/system/xvm/domains:default
```

```
online          16:09:48 svc:/system/svc/restarter:default
online          16:09:50 svc:/network/loopback:default
online          16:09:51 svc:/system/identity:node
```

As shown in the listing, the first nine services have an FMRI that begins with the string
`lrc:`. This special FMRI denotes that the service is a "legacy run control" script. Each
of them corresponds to a script in the `/etc/rc*.d` directories. Thus, for example,
the service `lrc:/etc/rc2_d/S47pppd` is the service that corresponds to the script
`/etc/rc2.d/S47pppd`. This is visible evidence of how SMF continues to provide compatibility
with the `init` scripts that have long been used in booting Solaris.

It's important to understand that these legacy services are really only pseudo-services as far as
SMF is concerned. They show up in the `svcs` listing because SMF's designers felt this would
be helpful to administrators in at least viewing what was started when the system booted. However, the simple listing indicating that the service started and the time at which it started is all
SMF will tell you about it; none of the other SMF commands — indeed, none of the other `svcs`
options — will operate on the legacy services:

```
# svcs lrc:/etc/rc2_d/S47pppd
STATE          STIME    FMRI
legacy_run     16:10:18 lrc:/etc/rc2_d/S47pppd
# svcs -l lrc:/etc/rc2_d/S47pppd
svcs: Operation not supported for legacy service 'lrc:/etc/rc2_d/S47pppd'
# svcprop lrc:/etc/rc2_d/S47pppd
svcprop: Operation not supported for legacy service 'lrc:/etc/rc2_d/S47pppd'
# svccfg -s lrc:/etc/rc2_d/S47pppd
svccfg: Operation not supported for legacy service 'lrc:/etc/rc2_d/S47pppd'
# svcadm disable lrc:/etc/rc2_d/S47pppd
svcadm: Operation not supported for legacy service 'lrc:/etc/rc2_d/S47pppd'
```

To manage legacy services, you need to use the legacy commands such as `ps` and `kill`, and
execute the `init` script directly. This should provide some motivation to convert any legacy services you've written to SMF so you can take advantage of all the SMF functionality.

Returning to the topic on which we started this section, you might wonder how these services
were started because SMF mostly seems to want nothing to do with them. This is where the
standard milestones come in. SMF provides a set of milestones that correspond to the old UNIX
run-levels:

```
$ svcs '*-user*'
STATE          STIME    FMRI
online         16:10:04 svc:/milestone/single-user:default
online         16:10:18 svc:/milestone/multi-user:default
online         16:10:21 svc:/milestone/multi-user-server:default
```

The `single-user` milestone is equivalent to the S, or single-user, run-level, while the
`multi-user` milestone is equivalent to run-level 2, or multi-user, and the `multi-user-server`
milestone is equivalent to run-level 3, multi-user plus networking services.

> **NOTE** Although milestones are equivalent to the UNIX run-levels in terms of the services that are run, you must use the `init` command to set the system's run-level; the `svcadm milestone` command does not change `init`'s view of the system's run-level.

Let's look at the `multi-user` milestone to see how it works. Begin by displaying the `start` method's properties:

```
$ svccfg -s multi-user listprop 'start/*'
start/exec              astring  "/sbin/rc2 start"
start/restart_on        astring  external_fault
start/timeout_seconds   count    1800
start/type              astring  method
```

As you can see, when the milestone is started, it executes the program `/sbin/rc2`. It also has a very long timeout: 1,800 seconds, or one-half hour, which should be plenty of time for all of the legacy scripts in `/etc/rc2.d` to run. The `restart_on` value for the milestone is an unusual one, `external_fault`. This value tells `svc.startd` that the milestone may be restarted only if the method exits due to a hardware error or a signal from some other process, and may not be restarted if it times out. This is necessary because the legacy scripts were never written with the expectation that they might be run more than once; if they don't complete within the time-out, the milestone will be placed into maintenance state and any dependent services will remain offline until the problem is corrected. Each of the run-level milestones works similarly.

> **NOTE** If you look at `/sbin/rc2`, you'll see that the rc scripts are actually run using a special program, `/lib/svc/bin/lsvcrun`. You can look at the source at `http://src.opensolaris.org` if you're interested in how legacy service handling in SMF works.

Another feature of these milestones is that they can be used as "target" milestones for booting the system, as well as with the `svcadm milestone` command. When booting OpenSolaris, you can use the options `-m milestone=<milestone-name>` to have the system boot with some services disabled; this option is supplied either to the OBP `boot` command on SPARC systems, or to the `kernel$` command in GRUB on x86 systems. This option will cause `svc.startd` to only start the graph of services that are dependencies of the specified milestone.

Two additional specially defined milestones can be used similarly: `none` and `all`. The `all` milestone is the usual default milestone to which the system is booted, whereby all enabled services are brought online. The `none` milestone specifies that only the master restarter (`svc.startd`) is to be enabled. This is sometimes useful for letting you log into and debug a system with serious service-related problems. The procedure in this case is to boot to the `none` milestone, log in as root, and then use the `svcadm milestone all` command to allow SMF to proceed with starting other services. While the services are starting, you can observe them using the `svcs` command, or use tools such as `truss` or `dtrace` to observe system or process activity.

> **TIP** `svc.startd` has two properties configurable with `svccfg` that can be useful in diagnosing system boot problems. The first, `options/boot_messages`, controls the verbosity of the boot process. The default setting, `quiet`, prints very few messages to the console during boot. Change its value to `verbose`, and `svc.startd` prints a message to the console

as each service is started. This property can also be set for a single boot by supplying the `-m ver-bose` option to the boot command line.

The second property, `options/logging`, controls the verbosity of `svc.startd` in its logging. This can have the value `quiet` (the default), `verbose`, or `debug`. A detailed explanation of these values is available in the man page for `svc.startd`.

Several other milestones, listed in Table 13-2, are defined by the standard OpenSolaris services. They can't be used as target milestones for booting, but they are useful as convenient dependencies for other services, as they signal certain capabilities in the boot process. For example, if you have a service that needs to be able to look up values in whatever name service the system is using, but is not dependent on a specific type of name service such as LDAP or NIS, you can specify a dependency on the `name-services` milestone and be assured that the system's configured name services will be online before your service is started.

TABLE 13-2

Capability Milestones

Milestone	Capability
devices	Hardware devices configured
network	IP networking running
name-services	Name service clients online
sysconfig	Initial system configuration completed

Profiles

Yet one more element of SMF's machinery is another type of service bundle known as the *profile*. As discussed earlier in this chapter, the SMF community recommends that only services that are critical to starting the system to the point of importing manifests should be enabled by default in their manifests, while all other services should be delivered disabled. That, of course, raises the question of how all of the services that are online after the system is installed are enabled. Profiles are the answer to that question. In SMF parlance, a profile is an XML service bundle that contains a listing of service instances and the value of the `general/enabled` property for each service instance.

The system profiles are delivered in `/var/svc/profile`:

```
$ ls /var/svc/profile
generic.xml              name_service.xml      ns_nisplus.xml
generic_limited_net.xml  ns_dns.xml            ns_none.xml
generic_open.xml         ns_files.xml          platform.xml
inetd_generic.xml        ns_ldap.xml           platform_none.xml
inetd_upgrade.xml        ns_nis.xml
```

After the `manifest-import` service has imported all of the service manifests during initial boot, it applies the `generic.xml` profile, which isn't actually a profile but a symlink to `generic_limited_net.xml`. This profile is the default service profile for all OpenSolaris systems, and is intended to provide a quite secure network configuration. The purpose of this profile is to allow network access to the system only via `ssh`; other enabled network services are configured to respond only to requests from the local system, not remote systems. Also provided is the `generic_open.xml` profile, which can be applied to set the system to have most network services open for remote requests, which was the default configuration for Solaris through Solaris 10.

CROSS-REF   See Chapter 11 for more information on OpenSolaris network security profiles.

The other profiles in `/var/svc/profile` are included by the generic profiles to configure some specific subsets of the SMF services. You can inspect each of these profiles to see how they work. You can also write your own profiles and use the `svccfg apply` command to apply a profile appropriate for your system's configuration.

Customizing SMF Services

To close your tour of SMF, it's important to understand some of the best practices that you should follow in customizing SMF on your own systems. The first thing to keep in mind when you think about customizing SMF is that the service manifests are not meant to be edited by users or administrators. They are delivered as read-only files in their packages, and any updates that are delivered in those packages will overwrite your edits to the manifests. Thus, while it might seem natural to edit a manifest file and re-import it to change a setting for a service or to introduce a new dependency, never do so because it will be lost on an upgrade.

Instead, you can modify a service property directly in the repository using `svcadm` or `svccfg`. SMF automatically maintains historical information about service instances in the form of saved *snapshots* of the service properties. By comparing the state of instances in the repository to the saved snapshot taken when the service was imported, SMF can detect your customizations and preserve them even if the service is modified by a new manifest shipped as part of an updated package.

NOTE   The Snapshots section of `smf(5)` describes the snapshots that are taken. You can also access snapshotted values of properties using the `-s` option to the `svcprop` command or using `svccfg`.

Similarly, never edit service method scripts because they are almost always delivered by the packages as read-only files, and they'll be overwritten on any upgrade of the package. To modify a service method, make a copy of the script and edit it. Then use `svccfg` to modify the service properties to point the service at your modified method. Here's an example of modifying the ssh service's start method:

```
# cp /lib/svc/method/sshd /lib/svc/method/sshd-local
<edit /lib/svc/method/sshd-local and make your changes>
# svccfg -s ssh setprop
svc:/network/ssh> setprop start/exec = "/lib/svc/method/sshd-local start"
svc:/network/ssh> exit
# svcadm refresh ssh
```

The next time the ssh service is started, the new method script will be run.

If you would prefer to have a manifest in which your alternate value is stored, another option is to create an alternate instance of the service, such as svc:/network/ssh:local to replace the standard instance, svc:/network/ssh:default. Probably the easiest way to do this is to copy the manifest for the standard instance, edit it, import it, and then enable it and disable the standard instance. The steps would be similar to the following:

```
# cp /var/svc/manifest/network/ssh.xml /var/svc/site/ssh.xml
<edit /var/svc/site/ssh.xml and create ssh:local instance>
# svccfg import /var/svc/site/ssh.xml
# svcadm disable svc:/network/ssh:default
# svcadm enable svc:/network/ssh:local
```

Resources

The OpenSolaris SMF community continues to actively develop SMF; its home page is at http://opensolaris.org/os/community/smf.

Sun's BigAdmin site contains a collection of articles about SMF that can be accessed from http://sun.com/bigadmin/content/selfheal.

The source code for SMF can be found in the OS/Net consolidation source tree; the bulk of the code is located under usr/src/cmd/svc.

Summary

This chapter explained how the introduction of the SMF service as a first-class administrative object is a natural evolution of the UNIX process model. It examined the ssh service to explain how SMF services are defined. The chapter also introduced the SMF commands and machinery, and used them to demonstrate common tasks. Finally, it provided recommendations for the best way to customize SMF services to meet your system's needs.

Chapter 14

Monitoring and Observability

System management can be broadly divided into two main tasks: configuration and monitoring. The configuration and monitoring capabilities of the various OpenSolaris subsystems are described in the individual chapters in this book. System-wide hardware fault handling is described in Chapter 12 on FMA, and system-wide software service management is covered in Chapter 13 on SMF. However, some system monitoring capabilities don't fit neatly into a specific subsystem. This chapter describes these various tools and procedures.

Because there is such a broad range of different utilities, this chapter may feel a bit eclectic. The sections group the various utilities into general categories, but because many different utilities are introduced, each utility is not described in complete detail. To learn more about all of the options and features of a particular tool, consult the man page for that utility.

Although the predefined utilities described in this chapter can be used for many day-to-day monitoring and troubleshooting tasks, you will occasionally encounter a complex problem that cannot be understood using these tools. OpenSolaris includes the innovative DTrace facility, which can be used to programmatically monitor and analyze problems in a way that many other operating systems cannot match — although because OpenSolaris is open source, DTrace has been ported to other operating systems. Chapter 15 is devoted to DTrace. Use DTrace whenever you have a complex monitoring problem that can't be understood using the standard system utilities.

Getting System Configuration Information

The first task when monitoring a system or analyzing a problem is to understand the system configuration. OpenSolaris includes a variety of tools that can be used to obtain information about the configuration. The uname command will indicate what version of OpenSolaris is in use and the system's architecture:

```
$ uname -a
SunOS myhost 5.11 snv_98 i86pc i386 i86pc
```

> **NOTE** On x86 systems, the processor type is always reported as i386, even if running on a 64-bit Intel or AMD-based system.

Use either the sysdef or prtconf commands to output detailed information about the hardware configuration and device tree. A full understanding of the prtconf output requires detailed knowledge of hardware, but this command is frequently used to determine how much physical memory is on the system:

```
$ prtconf
System Configuration:  Sun Microsystems  i86pc
Memory size: 32256 Megabytes
System Peripherals (Software Nodes):

i86pc
    scsi_vhci, instance #0
    isa, instance #0
        lp, instance #0 (driver not attached)
        asy, instance #0 (driver not attached)
        asy, instance #1 (driver not attached)
        pit_beep, instance #0
    pci, instance #1
        pci1022,7460, instance #1
            pci108e,534d, instance #0
            pci108e,534d, instance #1
            pci108e,534d, instance #2
                mouse, instance #0
    ...
```

Here, the second line of output shows that the system has 32GB of memory.

The prtdiag command is used to print a simpler view of the hardware configuration, along with diagnostic information about failed components on the system:

```
$ prtdiag
System Configuration: Sun Microsystems Sun Fire X4600
BIOS Configuration: American Megatrends Inc. 080012  07/10/2006
BMC Configuration: IPMI 1.5 (KCS: Keyboard Controller Style)
```

```
==== Processor Sockets ======================================

Version                            Location Tag
-----------------------------      --------------------------
Dual Core AMD Opteron(tm) Processor 885 CPU 1
Dual Core AMD Opteron(tm) Processor 885 CPU 2
Dual Core AMD Opteron(tm) Processor 885 CPU 3
Dual Core AMD Opteron(tm) Processor 885 CPU 4
Dual Core AMD Opteron(tm) Processor 885 CPU 5
Dual Core AMD Opteron(tm) Processor 885 CPU 6
Dual Core AMD Opteron(tm) Processor 885 CPU 7
Dual Core AMD Opteron(tm) Processor 885 CPU 8


==== Memory Device Sockets ======================================

Type     Status Set Device Locator        Bank Locator
-------  ------ --- -------------------    --------------------
DDR      in use 0   DIMM0                  BANK0
DDR      in use 0   DIMM1                  BANK1

==== On-Board Devices ======================================
 LSI serial-ATA #1
 Gigabit Ethernet #1
 Gigabit Ethernet #2
 ATI Rage XL VGA


==== Upgradeable Slots ======================================
ID  Status    Type             Description
--- --------  ---------------  --------------------
0   in use    PCI-X            PCIX SLOT0
1   available PCI-X            PCIX SLOT1
2   available other            PCIExp SLOT2
3   available other            PCIExp SLOT3
4   available other            PCIExp SLOT4
5   available other            PCIExp SLOT5
6   available other            PCIExp SLOT6
7   available other            PCIExp SLOT7
```

This example, on an X64 machine, shows the BIOS version and indicates that the system has eight dual-core AMD CPUs, and two populated memory banks. Finally, information about on-board devices, as well as devices on the bus, is listed.

> **NOTE** On x86 systems, prtdiag depends on BIOS support for the System Management BIOS (SMBIOS) image; some systems may not provide this support, in which case prtdiag will display little information. You can see the raw SMBIOS data with the smbios(1M) command.

The output on a SPARC system appears differently, as the following abbreviated example illustrates:

```
$ prtdiag
System Configuration:  Sun Microsystems  sun4v Sun Fire(TM) T1000
Memory size: 8064 Megabytes

================================ Virtual CPUs ================================

CPU ID Frequency Implementation        Status
------ --------- --------------------- -------
0      1000 MHz  SUNW,UltraSPARC-T1    on-line
1      1000 MHz  SUNW,UltraSPARC-T1    on-line
...
23     1000 MHz  SUNW,UltraSPARC-T1    on-line

========================= IO Configuration =========================

                 IO

Location Type Slot Path                               Name              Model
-------- ---- ---- --------------------------------- --------------    ------
MB/NET0  PCIE MB   /pci@7c0/pci@0/network@4           network-pci14e4,1668
MB/NET1  PCIE MB   /pci@7c0/pci@0/network@4,1         network-pci14e4,1668
MB/NET2  PCIX MB   /pci@7c0/pci@0/pci@8/network@1     network-pci108e,1648
MB/NET3  PCIX MB   /pci@7c0/pci@0/pci@8/network@1,1 network-pci108e,1648
MB/PCIX  PCIX MB   /pci@7c0/pci@0/pci@8/scsi@2        scsi-pci1000,50   LSI,1064
...
```

The psrinfo command is used to print detailed information about the processors on the system:

```
$ psrinfo -pv
The physical processor has 2 virtual processors (0 1)
   x86 (AuthenticAMD 20F12 family 15 model 33 step 2 clock 2613 MHz)
      Dual Core AMD Opteron(tm) Processor 885
The physical processor has 2 virtual processors (2 3)
   x86 (AuthenticAMD 20F12 family 15 model 33 step 2 clock 2613 MHz)
      Dual Core AMD Opteron(tm) Processor 885
...
The physical processor has 2 virtual processors (14 15)
   x86 (AuthenticAMD 20F12 family 15 model 33 step 2 clock 2613 MHz)
      Dual Core AMD Opteron(tm) Processor 885
```

This shows details about the eight AMD processors, including that each runs at 2.6 GHz. You can also use the isainfo command to get a detailed list of the various low-level processor features available:

```
$ isainfo -v
64-bit amd64 applications
```

```
        ahf sse3 sse2 sse fxsr amd_3dnowx amd_3dnow amd_mmx mmx cmov amd_sysc
        cx8 tsc fpu
32-bit i386 applications
        ahf sse3 sse2 sse fxsr amd_3dnowx amd_3dnow amd_mmx mmx cmov amd_sysc
        cx8 tsc fpu
```

> **NOTE** The isa in the isainfo **command stands for Instruction Set Architecture.**

The modinfo command indicates which kernel modules are loaded:

```
$ modinfo
 Id       Loadaddr   Size Info Rev Module Name
  0 fffffffffb800000 17bde6   -   0 unix ()
  1 fffffffffb906ea0 28f638   -   0 genunix ()
  3 fffffffffbb40000   5f10   1   1 specfs (filesystem for specfs)
  4 fffffffffbb45e70   4790   3   1 fifofs (filesystem for fifo)
  5 fffffffff8325000  1b7c0 155   1 dtrace (Dynamic Tracing)
  6 fffffffffbb4a548   5a68  16   1 devfs (devices filesystem 1.19)
  7 fffffffffbb4fd68  10e08  17   1 dev (/dev filesystem 1.6)
  ...
```

A variety of less commonly used commands can provide more information. The prtpicl command prints data used by the Platform Information and Control Library (PICL). This library provides a uniform API for hardware-related data. See the picld(1M) man page for more information. The /usr/X11/bin/scanpci command also prints data about PCI devices. The data from both commands is similar to that obtained with the sysdef or prtconf commands. The lgrpinfo command prints data about *locality groups*. Locality groups are data used by the operating system to represent the Non-Uniform Memory Access (NUMA) characteristics of the hardware.

> **NOTE** **Many modern multiprocessor systems are NUMA. That is, not all processors have the same access time to all memory. Some memory is "closer" to an individual processor than other memory. The operating system uses locality groups as part of its scheduling input to determine the most efficient processor on which to schedule processes. In some cases it is advantageous for an application to be aware of locality groups and explicitly control which processors to use. You might also use this data when you are troubleshooting a performance problem.**

The following example shows a portion of the tree view of the lgrpinfo output on a Sun Fire x4600, which illustrates the differing amounts of memory and access time in each latency group:

```
$ lgrpinfo -Tlcm
0
|-- 10
|   CPUs: 0-13
|   Memory: installed 28G, allocated 26G, free 2.4G
|   Latency: 124
|   `-- 9
```

```
|        CPUs: 0-5
|        Memory: installed 12G, allocated 9.8G, free 1.7G
|        Latency: 91
|        `-- 1
|            CPUs: 0 1
|            Memory: installed 3.5G, allocated 2.8G, free 769M
|            Latency: 61
|-- 12
|    CPUs: 0-15
|    Memory: installed 32G, allocated 30G, free 2.4G
|    Latency: 124
|    `-- 11
|        CPUs: 0-3 6 7 12 13
|        Memory: installed 16G, allocated 14G, free 1.8G
|        Latency: 91
|        `-- 2
|            CPUs: 2 3
|            Memory: installed 4.0G, allocated 3.4G, free 573M
|            Latency: 61
|-- 14
|    CPUs: 0-15
|    Memory: installed 32G, allocated 30G, free 2.4G
|    Latency: 124
|    `-- 13
|        CPUs: 0 1 4 5 8-11
|        Memory: installed 16G, allocated 15G, free 1.4G
|        Latency: 91
|        `-- 3
|            CPUs: 4 5
|            Memory: installed 4.0G, allocated 3.6G, free 431M
|            Latency: 61
|-- 15
|
 ...
```

In node 12 in this output, you can see that the nested nodes 11 and 2 show better latency. That is, node 2, which contains CPUs 2 and 3, has the best relative latency between those two CPUs. Moving up to node 11, the relative latency is less for this node, which contains CPUs 0–3, 6, 7, 12, and 13. Finally, the relative latency is even less at node 12, which contains CPUs 0–15. The lgrpinfo(1) man page describes this output in more detail.

The smbios command can be used to print information from the System Management BIOS on systems that have that feature.

CROSS-REF Chapter 9 describes utilities to gather information about the network configuration. Chapters 7 and 8 describe the utilities to gather information about storage and file systems.

Primary Utilities

This section describes the most common utilities you will use when looking at the overall usage of the system.

CROSS-REF The `netstat` command and other utilities such as `snoop` are used to monitor network activity. Chapter 9 describes these utilities.

uptime

The `uptime` command indicates how long the system has been running since the last reboot. It also prints the system *load average* and is commonly used for a quick one-line view of how busy the system is.

The load average is shown as three numbers, which are the average number of threads in the run queue over the past 1, 5, and 15 minutes. Roughly speaking, these numbers represent the average number of running and runnable threads. If these numbers approximate the number of processors on the system, then the system is 100 percent busy. Numbers consistently greater than the number of processors on the system indicate that the system has more work to do than it can complete. If this condition persists, then either there is a problem that requires further attention or you should consider spreading some of the load to a different system.

The following example for an idle system indicates that the load average values are very low:

```
$ uptime
  6:38pm  up 108 day(s),  3:17,  2 users,  load average: 0.02, 0.01, 0.01
```

The next example, on a busier four-processor system, shows values indicating that the system has more work than it can complete over the past 15-minute interval:

```
$ uptime
  6:39pm  up 160 day(s),  1:45,  1 user,  load average: 11.82, 13.04, 7.55
```

If the system seems sluggish, check the load average; if it is unexpectedly high, use some of the tools described in this chapter to understand what is happening.

ps

The `ps` command is one of the first utilities to use when you want to monitor system activity. The `ps` command has many options to enable you to observe different aspects of the currently running processes. The `-e` and `-f` options are commonly used to get an initial view. The `-e` option requests that all processes should be displayed, and the `-f` option requests a full listing, which provides more data about each process:

```
$ ps -ef
    UID   PID  PPID   C    STIME TTY         TIME CMD
```

```
    root     0    0    0    Apr 30  ?        0:04  sched
    root     1    0    0    Apr 30  ?        0:02  /sbin/init
    root     2    0    0    Apr 30  ?        0:00  pageout
    root     3    0    0    Apr 30  ?        7:54  fsflush
  daemon   602    1    0    Apr 30  ?        0:00  /usr/lib/nfs/nfs4cbd
    ...
```

This output shows you what is running and the user ID of each process. The TIME field shows how much CPU time the process has used; a high value may be an indication of a process that is running out of control. However, in this example, the fsflush process is a system housekeeping process, and not one that you should worry about if the TIME is high.

You can use the -o option to indicate specific elements of the process data you are interested in. This example uses vsz to show the total size of the process, rss to show the *resident set size*, and pmem to show the percent of physical memory that each process is using. These options are helpful when you think the system is experiencing memory pressure and you want to see what processes are using a lot of memory.

```
$ ps -eo user,pid,vsz,rss,pmem,time,args
    USER   PID     VSZ     RSS %MEM   TIME  COMMAND
    root     0       0       0  0.0  00:04  sched
    root     1    2540    1140  0.1  00:02  /sbin/init
    root     2       0       0  0.0  00:00  pageout
    root     3       0       0  0.0  07:57  fsflush
  daemon   602    2756    1576  0.1  00:00  /usr/lib/nfs/nfs4cbd
 gjelinek 2951  159228  133544  6.4  07:23  /usr/X11/bin/Xorg :0 -depth 24
    ...
```

The output shows that the Xorg process size is 159MB of virtual memory, and it is using 133MB of physical memory, which represents more than 6 percent of the system's physical memory.

> **NOTE** OpenSolaris implements *virtual memory* for processes, and resident set size (RSS) is the amount of physical memory that a process is actually using. Some parts of a process are typically not paged in to physical memory and that memory is reported in the overall memory size, but not in the RSS.

You can observe many other process attributes with the ps command — it is well worth the time to study the man page and familiarize yourself with the data that you can obtain using this command.

prstat

The ps command has certain limitations that can be inconvenient. It shows only a snapshot of the current process data, and it can be hard to see the most important data when many processes are running. The `top` command has traditionally been used to monitor the most active processes on a system. OpenSolaris provides a version of this command, but the preferred alternative is the `prstat` command, which provides similar functionality and is built using standard system interfaces, making it more efficient than the `top` command:

```
$ prstat
   PID USERNAME  SIZE   RSS STATE   PRI NICE      TIME  CPU PROCESS/NLWP
  1161 gjelinek  218M  104M sleep    49    0   0:02:13 0.6% soffice.bin/6
  2951 gjelinek  156M  130M sleep    59    0   0:07:37 0.3% Xorg/1
  3346 gjelinek   90M   25M sleep    59    0   0:01:39 0.1% gnome-terminal/2
  3302 gjelinek   72M   14M sleep    59    0   0:00:42 0.1% metacity/1
  3312 gjelinek 3880K 2316K sleep    59    0   0:01:42 0.0% gam_server/28
  4082 gjelinek  323M  124M sleep    49    0   0:08:35 0.0% firefox-bin/9
...
Total: 115 processes, 312 lwps, load averages: 0.04, 0.03, 0.02
```

By default, `prstat` prints a screen of data. It updates its display every five seconds and sorts the running processes by CPU usage so that the highest consumers are shown first. In this example, the `soffice.bin` process is using the most CPU, but only 0.6 percent. If there were a runaway process, its CPU time would be high, and it would be one of the first processes shown in the `prstat` output.

Other useful data, including memory consumption, is also displayed. You can sort the data by different statistics, as this example, sorting on resident set size, shows:

```
$ prstat -s rss
   PID USERNAME  SIZE   RSS STATE   PRI NICE      TIME  CPU PROCESS/NLWP
  2951 gjelinek  156M  130M sleep    59    0   0:07:40 0.3% Xorg/1
  4082 gjelinek  323M  124M sleep    49    0   0:08:36 0.0% firefox-bin/9
  1161 gjelinek  218M  104M sleep    49    0   0:02:22 0.7% soffice.bin/6
  4006 gjelinek  278M   85M sleep    49    0   0:02:45 0.0% thunderbird-bin/8
...
```

It can also be useful on a multi-user system to summarize by user:

```
$ prstat -t
 NPROC USERNAME   SWAP   RSS MEMORY      TIME  CPU
    56 gjelinek   468M  650M    32%   0:26:54 2.3%
    48 root        92M   99M   4.8%   0:00:42 0.0%
     2 lp        1900K 4292K   0.2%   0:00:00 0.0%
     1 dladm      444K  668K   0.0%   0:00:00 0.0%
     8 daemon    9428K   11M   0.5%   0:00:00 0.0%
...
```

Use the `prstat` command when you want to dynamically observe what is using the most resources on the system.

vmstat

In some cases you need a system-wide summary of key activity. You can use several commands to monitor this data, including the `vmstat` command, which provides an overall summary of a variety of virtual memory-related system statistics:

```
$ vmstat 10
 kthr      memory              page              disk          faults      cpu
 r b w   swap   free  re  mf pi po fr de  sr s1 s2 s3 --   in   sy    cs us sy id
 0 0 0 1420872 236664 31 343 96 7 11   0 31  3  3  6  0  607 2868  555  2  1 96
 0 0 0 662624 41700   3  37 162 592 3125 0 5667 87 87 0  0 3011 3595 6988 3 47
 50
 0 0 0 662544 48872   1  17 70  6 29   0 44 88 88 92  0 2196 3753 5815  3 45 51
 0 0 0 662544 42284   4  50 110 734 1640 0 3098 80 80 0 0 2417 5564 6070 4 44 52
 0 1 0 662544 47560   4 100 480 350 2557 0 3740 104 0 128 0 2880 6404 7432 4 43
 54
 0 1 0 662544 45640   3 121 522 0  0   0  0 98 96 126 0 2354 4304 4559  4 45 51
 0 1 0 662544 36264  11 167 651 627 1097 0 2936 105 0 142 0 1780 3861 2345 5 48
 47
 0 2 0 662544 32864  25 179 650 1226 2202 0 4243 111 0 151 0 1972 5498 4515 5 46
 49
 0 2 0 662544 33772  10 237 1252 890 3593 0 6828 126 0 181 0 2161 3664 4215 4 46
 50

 ...
```

The man page explains the meaning of each column in detail. In brief, the `kthr` columns show the number of kernel threads in various states. The `memory` columns show the available swap space and the size of the free list. The `page` columns show a variety of statistics related to paging. The `disk` columns summarize disk operations, up to four disks. The `faults` columns show interrupt and system call trap rates. Finally, the `cpu` columns show CPU time spent executing user-level (`us`) and kernel (`sy`) code, as well as idle time (`id`).

The first line of data is a summary since the system booted. The subsequent lines are a summary for the interval, which in this example was specified as 10 seconds.

The `vmstat` command is primarily used to observe two different aspects of the overall system behavior: CPU utilization and the virtual memory system. The example is slightly hard to read because some of the numbers are large and the columns aren't lined up. Reformatting the `cpu` data on its own, and ignoring the first line of output, results in the following:

```
     cpu
 us sy id
  3 47 50
  3 45 51
  4 44 52
  4 43 54
```

```
4  45  51
5  48  47
5  46  49
4  46  50
```

The CPU data is the total across all of the processors on the system. This example was run on a two-processor system, and you can see that one processor is spending almost 100 percent of its time executing in the kernel (system time averages close to 50 percent, which represents one total CPU), while the other is essentially doing nothing (idle time averages around 50 percent, which represents the second CPU). This is not what you would normally expect to see because typical applications spend the majority of their time either executing in user-level code or idle. You can look at the virtual memory statistics to get a sense of what is happening.

Reformatting the output so that you can focus on the virtual memory-related statistics reveals the following:

```
   memory                     page
 swap     free   re   mf    pi    po    fr   de    sr
662624   41700    3   37   162   592  3125    0  5667
662544   48872    1   17    70     6    29    0    44
662544   42284    4   50   110   734  1640    0  3098
662544   47560    4  100   480   350  2557    0  3740
662544   45640    3  121   522     0     0    0     0
662544   36264   11  167   651   627  1097    0  2936
662544   32864   25  179   650  1226  2202    0  4243
662544   33772   10  237  1252   890  3593    0  6828
```

A detailed explanation of the OpenSolaris virtual memory subsystem is beyond the scope of this book, but this example can be understood with only a few basic concepts. The system has 2GB of physical memory, but the free column shows that only about 32MB–48MB is free. This is not necessarily bad because OpenSolaris tries to efficiently use as much physical memory as it can, but the amount of free memory is a small percentage of the total, so that is one clue. Looking at the page-in (pi) and page-out (po) data, you can see that the amount of paging activity is fairly high. On a typical system these numbers might spike occasionally, but over time they should be consistently small. That is a second clue. Finally, the scan-rate (sr) is also high. The scanner is the part of the VM system that tries to page out pages when there is demand for physical memory. The fact that the scanner is running steadily and scanning a large number of pages in each interval is the final clue and a clear indication that the system is low on memory. This also explains the CPU data shown. The system is spending all of its time trying to reclaim memory for applications to use. In other words, it is thrashing.

Another useful diagnostic from the vmstat command is the length of the run queue in the kthr r column. Although the example does not illustrate this situation, a run queue that is consistently non-0 is an indication that the system has work backed up that it is not completing.

In other words, the system is overloaded, so you should continue to investigate or consider moving some of the work to a different system if the condition persists.

mpstat

The mpstat command provides a summary of processor statistics, broken down by CPU, for the system. This example shows statistics every five seconds on a four-processor system:

```
$ mpstat 5
CPU minf mjf xcal  intr ithr  csw icsw migr  smtx  srw  syscl  usr sys  wt idl
  0 1053   4  417    94   59  129   38   15  4166    0 197917   37  17   0  46
  1 1035   3  391   142  108  121   37   14  4693    0 222818   39  18   0  43
  2 1056   4  394    42    1  128   40   14  4777    0 222863   39  18   0  42
  3 1043   5  442   317  190  155   39   16  1902    0 112913   30  13   0  57
CPU minf mjf xcal  intr ithr  csw icsw migr  smtx  srw  syscl  usr sys  wt idl
  0    0   0    6    16    3   25   11    8  7298    0 627722   54  32   0  13
  1    0   0    2    14    2   16    9    3  6150    0 715774   62  35   0   3
  2    0   0    2    11    1   17    8    5 34685    0 696003   58  37   0   6
  3    1   0   30   289  186  109    8   11  3917    0 167391   14   9   0  76
  ...
```

As with the vmstat command, the first block of output is a summary since the system booted, while subsequent blocks are summaries for the interval.

The various columns are described in the man page. Briefly, you can see major and minor faults, cross-calls, interrupts, context switches, thread migrations, spins on mutexes and locks, the number of system calls, and time spent in various kernel states. These last columns are the same data that is reported by the vmstat command.

You use the mpstat command when you need to get more information about system activity related to CPU utilization. Looking at the CPU utilization numbers first, as you did in the vmstat example, this example shows a typical distribution of user-level, kernel-level, and idle time. Looking at some of the other data, you can see the number of involuntary context switches (icsw) per CPU. The numbers here are low; consistently high numbers would be an indication that there are more runnable threads than processors on which to schedule them. High thread migration (migr) can be the underlying cause of performance problems because the cache on the new processor might not be warmed up for the process.

The mpstat command reports locking statistics in the smtx and srw columns, but the lock-stat command, described shortly, provides better visibility into locking issues.

> **NOTE** The wt column reports the time spent waiting for I/O. Previously, this statistic was always inaccurate and a source of confusion. The software has been changed so that this data is now always reported as 0. This applies not only to the mpstat command, but to all commands that report this data, such as iostat or sar.

iostat

The iostat command is used to obtain I/O statistics. As with the previous commands, you can specify a reporting interval, and the first line shows a summary since the system was booted:

```
$ iostat 5
       tty          sd0           sd1           sd2           sd3          cpu
  tin tout kps tps serv  kps tps serv  kps tps serv  kps tps serv  us sy wt id
    0   66  32   2    7   32   2    3    0   0    0    0   0    0    2  1  0 97
    0   67   9   1    3    9   1    0    0   0    0    0   0    0    3  2  0 95
    3   67 249  61   11  261  61    1    0   0    0    0   0    0   16  6  0 78
    0   16 150  84   12  193  84    4    0   0    0    0   0    0    6 11  0 83
    0   16 194 106    9  192 106    4    0   0    0    0   0    0    6 11  0 83
    0   16 236 105   14  254 105    3    0   0    0    0   0    0    5 10  0 86
    0   16 146  87   12  168  87    3    0   0    0    0   0    0   14 10  0 76
    0   16 172  86   11  212  86    4    0   0    0    0   0    0    4 10  0 86
  ...
```

This example shows I/O for the terminal (tty) and four disks (sd0-sd3). It indicates that shortly after the command was started, the sd0 and sd1 disks began to experience increased I/O. The disk columns are reporting the Kbytes/second (kps), transfers/second (tps) and average service time (serv), in milliseconds, for the four disks. The cpu columns report the same data that you can obtain using the vmstat or mpstat commands.

Another useful option is -D, which reports reads/second (rps), writes/second (wps), and the percentage of disk utilization (util). This percentage indicates how busy the disk is, not how full it is:

```
$ iostat -D 5
       sd0              sd1              sd2              sd3
  rps wps util    rps wps util    rps wps util    rps wps util
    2   1  1.2      2   1  0.5      0   0  0.0      0   0  0.0
    0   0  0.0      0   0  0.0      0   0  0.0      0   0  0.0
    0   0  0.0      0   0  0.0      0   0  0.0      0   0  0.0
   17   0  6.8     17   0  2.1      0   0  0.0      0   0  0.0
  118   0 71.4    118   0 26.1      0   0  0.0      0   0  0.0
  158   0 91.8    158   0 34.0      0   0  0.0      0   0  0.0
  119   0 86.2    118   0 27.6      0   0  0.0      0   0  0.0
  ...
```

Here, I/O to sd0 and sd1 increased shortly after the command was started. The utilization can be used as an initial indicator if you suspect I/O activity is the cause of a performance issue, but you will certainly need to investigate further to determine whether the situation is normal or points to a deeper problem.

One limitation to note in the output is that disk names are reported using internal names, such as sd0 or sd1. This can make it hard to understand which disks are actually experiencing the I/O. Use the -n option to report the names in the standard style:

```
$ iostat -nD 5
  c0t0d0        c0t1d0        c1t0d0        c1t1d0
```

```
rps wps util   rps wps util   rps wps util   rps wps util
  2   1  1.2     2   1  0.5     4   2  2.6     3   2  1.2
 67 117 93.3    67 117 26.7    99 132 98.5    87 139 34.6
 66 113 93.4    65 113 20.7    93 116 98.0    77 116 25.3
 81   0 83.6    81   0 16.6   138   5 95.4   100   0 21.8
 23   0 21.6    23   0  2.8    36   0 24.3    31   0  4.3
```

You can also specify the names of the disks to monitor on the command line, which is useful when the system has many disks and you are interested in only a subset.

Monitoring I/O is a complex task, and the iostat command includes numerous options that enable you to view a variety of statistics. It is worth studying the man page and spending time investigating the various capabilities.

/proc

The previous section described some of the key utilities you can use to understand activity on the system. In particular, the ps and prstat commands are frequently used to observe process activity. However, in some cases you need to delve more deeply into the specifics of an individual process. OpenSolaris provides the /proc pseudo-file system, which is used by various utilities to access data about each running process, along with a set of associated utilities, the proc tools, which enable you to observe and manage various aspects of running processes. Many of these tools can also be used to examine a core file. The proc tools are listed in Table 14-1.

This section doesn't cover all of these tools, but a few examples illustrate some of their capabilities.

NOTE The /proc file system in OpenSolaris is somewhat different from the one in Linux. In OpenSolaris, /proc is used purely to provide visibility and control of running processes, whereas in Linux, /proc also implements a collection of unrelated interfaces. In OpenSolaris, those interfaces are implemented in other ways, not by using /proc.

One very common task is to kill a running process. Using the traditional ps and kill commands, you must use grep or some other matching tool to find the process ID to kill. Many of the proc tools accept user-friendly names to do this. The following example kills all processes named evince:

```
$ pkill evince
```

You can use pgrep to easily find running processes and combine them with another command. This example shows the stack for the Xorg process:

```
# pstack `pgrep Xorg`
2951:    /usr/X11/bin/Xorg :0 -depth 24 -nobanner
-auth /var/dt/A:0-4ga0Wf
 fffffd7fff2da82a __read () + a
```

```
00000000004bf17f _XSERVTransLocalRead () + f
00000000004b557a ReadRequestFromClient () + 14a
000000000048aaea Dispatch () + 2fa
000000000049e035 main () + 495
000000000047a33c _start () + 6c
```

TABLE 14-1

Proc Tools

Tool	Description
pargs	Prints arguments or environment variables
pcred	Prints or sets the effective or real UID and GID
pflags	Prints general proc and signal information
pfiles	Prints information about open files
pgrep	Finds processes by name or other attributes
pkill	Sends a signal to processes specified by name or other attributes
pldd	Prints the dynamic libraries linked into the process
prun	Resumes running the process or specified lightweight process. See pstop.
psig	Prints information about signal handling
pstack	Prints a stack trace for the full process or each lightweight process
pstop	Stops the process or the specified lightweight process. See prun.
ptime	Times the process using microstate accounting
pwait	Waits for the process to end
pwdx	Prints the current working directory

This example shows all open files for Xorg:

```
# pfiles `pgrep Xorg`
2951:   /usr/X11/bin/Xorg :0 -depth 24 -nobanner
-auth /var/dt/A:0-4gaOWf
  Current rlimit: 256 file descriptors
   0: S_IFREG mode:0644 dev:27,1152 ino:23302 uid:0 gid:0 size:30899
      O_WRONLY|O_CREAT|O_TRUNC|O_LARGEFILE
      /var/log/Xorg.0.log
   1: S_IFSOCK mode:0666 dev:318,0 ino:38121 uid:0 gid:0 size:0
```

```
        O_RDWR
      SOCK_STREAM
      SO_REUSEADDR,SO_SNDBUF(49152),SO_RCVBUF(49152)
      sockname: AF_INET6 ::  port: 6000
    2: S_IFREG mode:0644 dev:27,1152 ino:31112 uid:0 gid:0 size:48941
      O_WRONLY|O_CREAT|O_LARGEFILE
      /var/dt/Xerrors
    3: S_IFSOCK mode:0666 dev:318,0 ino:38122 uid:0 gid:0 size:0
      O_RDWR
      SOCK_STREAM
      SO_REUSEADDR,SO_SNDBUF(49152),SO_RCVBUF(49152)
      sockname: AF_INET 0.0.0.0  port: 6000
    4: S_IFSOCK mode:0666 dev:318,0 ino:4417 uid:0 gid:0 size:0
      O_RDWR
      SOCK_STREAM
      SO_SNDBUF(16384),SO_RCVBUF(5120)
      sockname: AF_UNIX /tmp/.X11-unix/X0
    5: S_IFIFO mode:0000 dev:308,0 ino:2634 uid:0 gid:0 size:0
      O_RDWR
  ...
   50: S_IFIFO mode:0000 dev:308,0 ino:64761 uid:6209 gid:10 size:0
      O_RDWR|O_NONBLOCK
   52: S_IFIFO mode:0000 dev:308,0 ino:62309 uid:6209 gid:10 size:0
      O_RDWR|O_NONBLOCK
```

The output has been trimmed, but you can see that Xorg has 53 open files.

Kstats

Internally, OpenSolaris maintains a large number of detailed kernel statistics. Sometimes it is useful to examine this data, although many of the statistics are related to the implementation of specific subsystems and are hard to interpret without a detailed understanding of the code. Many of the commands described in this chapter, as well as elsewhere in this book, use kstats as their underlying source of information. In most cases, using those commands will be preferable to accessing the raw kstat data. Because these statistics are specific to the kernel implementation, the data being maintained can change over time as each subsystem evolves.

You can use the kstat command to select and print kstat data. By default, the command prints all kstats, which is generally too much information and not what is needed; but kstats are organized by module, class, and name, so you can use various options to select the specific data you want — e.g., CPU data is in the cpu module:

```
$ kstat -m cpu
module: cpu                              instance: 0
name:   intrstat                         class:    misc
      crtime                             49.521558236
```

```
        level-1-count                  1895859
        level-1-time                   7619887450
   ...
module: cpu                                 instance: 0
name:   sys                                 class:   misc
   bawrite                       6
   bread                         5337
   ...
module: cpu                                 instance: 0
name:   vm                                  class:   misc
   anonfree                      0
   anonpgin                      0
   ...
module: cpu                                 instance: 1
name:   intrstat                            class:   misc
   crtime                        53.115550131
   level-1-count                 35
   level-1-time                  375708
   ...
module: cpu                                 instance: 1
name:   sys                                 class:   misc
   bawrite                       398
   bread                         7342
   ...
module: cpu                                 instance: 1
name:   vm                                  class:   misc
   anonfree                      0
   anonpgin                      0
   ...
```

This truncated example indicates that the cpu module includes three differently named kstats: intrstat, sys, and vm. This example was run on a two-CPU system, so there are instances of these statistics for each CPU. As previously mentioned, most of the kstats are not explicitly documented, so you need to use the source for the release you are running to truly understand this data.

Other Utilities

In addition to the most commonly used commands described already, OpenSolaris includes other utilities for monitoring the system.

cpustat

The cpustat and cputrack commands provide detailed information about CPUs based on their hardware performance counters. This can be useful in certain low-level troubleshooting situations, although you need in-depth knowledge of the CPU to understand the meaning of this data. You can use the help option (-h) to see a list of the available performance counters. This abbreviated example shows the counters available on an AMD-based system:

```
# cpustat -h
Usage:
  ...
    event[0-3]: FP_dispatched_fpu_ops FP_cycles_no_fpu_ops_retired
                FP_dispatched_fpu_ops_ff LS_seg_reg_load
                LS_uarch_resync_self_modify LS_uarch_resync_snoop
                LS_buffer_2_full LS_retired_cflush LS_retired_cpuid
                DC_access DC_miss DC_refill_from_L2 DC_refill_from_system
                DC_misaligned_data_ref DC_uarch_late_cancel_access
                DC_uarch_early_cancel_access DC_dispatched_prefetch_instr
                DC_dcache_accesses_by_locks BU_memory_requests
                BU_data_prefetch BU_cpu_clk_unhalted IC_fetch IC_miss
                IC_refill_from_L2 IC_refill_from_system
                IC_itlb_L1_miss_L2_hit IC_uarch_resync_snoop
                IC_instr_fetch_stall IC_return_stack_hit
                IC_return_stack_overflow FR_retired_x86_instr_w_excp_intr
    ...
```

> **NOTE** Hardware performance counters are built into the CPU and are used to track various low-level CPU activities. As such, these are CPU-specific and are used primarily for advanced monitoring.

truss

The truss command is frequently used to watch the system call activity of a single process. You can either start a command under truss or attach to a running process, as this example shows:

```
# truss -p 970
/1:     read(4, "\n\0D6FB J\0A002\0CA 6FF".., 96)     = 96
/1:     pollsys(0x094CD310, 8, 0x08046938, 0x00000000)     = 0
/1:     pollsys(0x094CD310, 8, 0x08046938, 0x00000000)     = 0
/1:     pollsys(0x094CD310, 8, 0x08046938, 0x00000000)     = 0
/1:     lwp_unpark(3)           = 0
/3:     lwp_park(0xF929EE58, 0)           = 0
/1:     ioctl(4, FIONREAD, 0x080468AC)     = 0
/1:     pollsys(0x094CD310, 8, 0x08046938, 0x00000000)     = 0
/1:     write(4, " 51804\0D6\bA0021702\0\0".., 2636)     = 2636
/1:     read(4, "1C07D6FB I\0A002 l\0\0\0".., 32)     = 32
/1:     read(4, "1C07D6FB I\0A002 101\0\0".., 32)     = 32
/1:     read(4, 0x08044CC0, 32)           Err#11 EAGAIN
/1:     pollsys(0x080B4420, 1, 0x00000000, 0x00000000)     = 1
/1:     read(4, "0118 NFC\001\0\0\0\0\0".., 32)     = 32
/1:     readv(4, 0x08044C80, 2)           = 1024
/1:     write(4, "9503\n\0D6\bA0021E03A002".., 1472)     = 1472
    ...
```

The truss command is a useful way to get a general overview of what an individual process, or tree of processes, is doing, but running truss on a process adds overhead that can affect the result you are trying to observe. For example, if you diagnosing a timing issue, using truss might cause the timing problem to disappear. In those cases, DTrace, described Chapter 15, might be a preferable solution.

You can use the -f option to truss all children of a command, and various options for timestamps to get a general understanding of how the system call activity of a process is affecting its performance. In addition to tracing system calls, you can also use truss to trace user-level library function calls using the -u option. This example shows the command line to trace the printf calls from libc in addition to the system calls:

```
$ truss -u libc:printf demo
```

intrstat

In rare cases, a system will seem to be busy but no specific process appears to be causing the load. It's possible that the system is experiencing a high number of interrupts. This can happen for various reasons, some of which are normal, but it is also possible that a broken device or defective driver is causing the problem. You can monitor interrupt activity using the intrstat command:

```
# intrstat

      device |   cpu0 %tim      cpu1 %tim
-------------+-------------------------------
      ata#1 |    20  0.1         0  0.0
      ehci#0 |     0  0.0       122  0.0
    nvidia#0 |     0  0.0       122  0.3

      device |   cpu0 %tim      cpu1 %tim
-------------+-------------------------------
  adpu320#1 |     0  0.0         0  0.0
      ata#1 |     0  0.0         0  0.0
      bge#0 |     0  0.0         5  0.0
      ehci#0 |     0  0.0       123  0.0
    nvidia#0 |     0  0.0       123  0.3

    ...
```

By default, the command outputs data every second, but you can configure this with the interval option. The data for each CPU is displayed by column. If you have more than the four CPUs that will fit, the additional data is printed in multiple tables. You can also select specific CPUs using the -c or -C options. In this example there are no problems, but if the number of interrupts and the percentage of time handling those interrupts is consistently high, that might be an indication of a problem requiring further investigation.

The trapstat command, which is only available on SPARC-based systems, enables you to collect statistics about traps:

```
# trapstat
vct name                  |    cpu0     cpu1     cpu2     cpu3
--------------------------+-----------------------------------
 24 cleanwin              |      21        0       44        3
 41 level-1               |       2        1        1        7
 44 level-4               |       0      264        0      276
 46 level-6               |    1013        0        0        0
 4a level-10              |       0        0        0      100
 4d level-13              |       0        1        1        1
 4e level-14              |       3        2        2      102
 60 int-vec               |    1108      386      100      380
 64 itlb-miss             |     177       35      214       56
 68 dtlb-miss             |   11725   417113     8140     6608
 6c dtlb-prot             |       2        0        0        0
 84 spill-user-32         |       1        0        9        0
 8c spill-user-32-cln     |       2        0        8        1
 98 spill-kern-64         |   12007    11107     4214     3390
 a4 spill-asuser-32       |       6        0       48        4
 ac spill-asuser-32-cln   |       8        0      416        0
 c4 fill-user-32          |       1        0        0        0
 cc fill-user-32-cln      |       8        0      374        6
 d8 fill-kern-64          |   10997    10841     4212     3275
108 syscall-32            |       6        0      140        1
127 gethrtime             |       4        0        0        0
```

lockstat

The lockstat command can be used to monitor the kernel's locking behavior on the system. Lock contention can be another cause of unexplained poor performance:

```
# lockstat sleep 30
Adaptive mutex spin: 358 events in 30.043 seconds (12 events/sec)

Count indv cuml rcnt     nsec Lock                 Caller
-------------------------------------------------------------------------------
  130  36%  36% 0.00     2595 0xffffff01480ab080   lwp_unpark+0x32
   78  22%  58% 0.00     3383 0xffffff01480ab080   lookuppnat+0x67
   17   5%  63% 0.00     7732 0xffffff0148ffc050   bge_intr+0x1a8
   16   4%  67% 0.00     2760 0xffffff0148ffc050   bge_chip_factotum+0x62
   13   4%  71% 0.00      726 0xffffff014f16f2c0   polllock+0x31
   10   3%  74% 0.00      926 0xffffff014e81b1c0   polllock+0x31
    8   2%  76% 0.00    11715 0xffffff014f16f2c0   fifo_read+0x4e
    8   2%  78% 0.00     1250 0xffffff01471b4000   callout_execute+0xcf
...
    1   0% 100% 0.00      538 0xffffff014812d680   vn_rele+0x21
```

```
      1   0% 100% 0.00      1149 0xffffff0148d97f50     ohci_allocate_periodic_in
_resource+0x100
-----------------------------------------------------------------------------

Adaptive mutex block: 5 events in 30.043 seconds (0 events/sec)

Count indv cuml rcnt   nsec Lock               Caller
-----------------------------------------------------------------------------
    2  40%  40% 0.00  62847 0xffffff01480ab080   lwp_unpark+0x32
    1  20%  60% 0.00  10250 0xffffff014bf3b1f8   cv_timedwait_sig+0x1e8
    1  20%  80% 0.00  43437 0xffffff01496b84c0   cv_wait_sig_swap_core+0x193
    1  20% 100% 0.00  87939 0xffffff01480ab080   lookuppnat+0x67
-----------------------------------------------------------------------------

Spin lock spin: 2181 events in 30.043 seconds (73 events/sec)

Count indv cuml rcnt    nsec Lock               Caller
-----------------------------------------------------------------------------
 1090  50%  50% 0.00    2041 0xffffff0148ab5b28   disp_lock_enter+0x31
  875  40%  90% 0.00    1888 cpu0_disp           disp_lock_enter+0x31
  152   7%  97% 0.00    1714 0xffffff0148ab5b28   disp_lock_enter_high+0x11
   64   3% 100% 0.00    1627 cpu0_disp           disp_lock_enter_high+0x11
-----------------------------------------------------------------------------

Thread lock spin: 5 events in 30.043 seconds (0 events/sec)

Count indv cuml rcnt    nsec Lock               Caller
-----------------------------------------------------------------------------
    3  60%  60% 0.00     288 cpu0_disp           ts_update_list+0x54
    1  20%  80% 0.00     229 sleepq_head+0xb98    ts_update_list+0x54
    1  20% 100% 0.00     832 0xffffff0148ab5b28   ts_update_list+0x54
-----------------------------------------------------------------------------
```

The lockstat command collects data until the command specified as an argument has completed. You can use sleep, as in the example, to collect data for the specified period of time. This example collected data for 30 seconds.

sar

The system activity reporter (sar) is another utility that can report much of the same data that is reported by the previously described commands. The standard usage is with an interval time and count. This example shows a five-second interval for three iterations:

```
$ sar 5 3
SunOS myhost 5.11 snv_88 i86pc    05/05/2008

19:03:11    %usr    %sys    %wio    %idle
```

```
19:03:16        2        1        0        97
19:03:21        0        1        0        99
19:03:26        8        2        0        90

Average         4        1        0        95
```

Aside from utilization, a variety of options can report additional system data, such as system calls, block device I/O, paging, and run queue length.

One advantage of using sar over the other stat commands is that the output is timestamped. The data can be saved to a file to provide a historical record of activity for later analysis. You can use the system/sar service to handle this automatically. See the sadc(1M) man page for more information about using sar for automatic logging.

CROSS-REF See Chapter 13 for more information on managing services with SMF.

Logs

In addition to using various utilities to view current activity, sometimes you need historical data to get a sense of past activity on the system.

syslog

The primary system log file is normally /var/adm/messages. This file consists of timestamped entries for system message. In addition to the timestamp, each entry is flagged with a tag indicating the severity and the subsystem that generated the message. Here is an example of some entries from the log file:

```
May  4 19:26:10 myhost su: [ID 810491 auth.crit] 'su root' failed for sarah
  on /dev/pts/12
May  5 01:15:03 myhost sendmail[1910]: [ID 702911 mail.crit] My unqualified
  host name (myhost) unknown; sleeping for retry
May  5 05:40:28 myhost ufs: [ID 845546 kern.notice] NOTICE: alloc: /: file
  system full
May  5 07:40:15 myhost ntpdate[7993]: [ID 558275 daemon.notice] adjust time
  server 129.146.228.54 offset -0.003553 sec
```

This shows the timestamp for each entry and the host that generated the entry. This is useful when logging has been configured to a remote host. For local logging, this will simply be the hostname of the system. Next is a tag with the subsystem and severity. The first line was generated by the auth subsystem and the severity is critical. Finally, the rest of the line contains the actual log message. The next three lines were generated by the mail, kernel, and daemon subsystems.

Data in this file is logged through the syslog(3C) facility and the log file is managed by the syslogd. The syslogd can be configured to send various messages to different destinations or to even send all log data to a remote host. The syslogd is configured through the syslog.conf file and managed by the system/system-log SMF service. The syslog.conf(4) man page describes how to configure handling for the various levels of messages.

Most of the messages in the log file are informative and do not indicate a problem. At a minimum, you should review the syslog(3C) man page and track the high-severity log messages.

Log management

Without management, log files grow endlessly and eventually consume all of the free space on the disk. OpenSolaris includes the logadm command, which is a general-purpose utility to rotate logs and prevent this problem. The logadm command is configured by the /etc/logadm.conf file and run by root's crontab entry.

The logadm command is configured to rotate the /var/adm/messages file, along with other log files, on a regular basis so that you don't need to worry about a single file filling the file system. Note that the older /var/adm/messages files are named messages.0, messages.1, and so on. You may need to look in one of these older files if the data you need is not in the current log file. You can customize the logadm.conf file if you need to maintain the log files for longer than the default configuration.

User activity

The system tracks user logins in the /var/adm/utmpx database. Unlike the syslog file, you do not access this file directly. You can use the who or w commands to see a list of users currently logged in. The last command shows a record for each user, indicating when, and for how long, they were logged in. This output will also show when the system was booted:

```
$ last
sarah      console       :0             Sun May  4 18:54   still logged in
reboot     system boot                  Sun May  4 18:50
reboot     system down                  Sun May  4 18:43
sarah      console       :0             Sat May  3 13:44 - down  (1+05:05)
reboot     system boot                  Sat May  3 13:39
reboot     system down                  Sat May  3 13:38
sarah      console       :0             Wed Apr 30 13:36 - down  (3+00:03)
reboot     system boot                  Wed Apr 30 13:30
reboot     system down                  Wed Apr 30 12:34
sarah      console       :0             Mon Apr 21 19:04 - down  (8+18:26)
   ...
```

The /var/adm/sulog file contains a record for each attempt by a user to run the su command. This is particularly useful to monitor which users are su-ing to root.

CROSS-REF   See the "Accounting" section in Chapter 18 and the "Auditing" section in Chapter 11 for information on setting up and using those facilities to track user activity in more detail.

SNMP

The various utilities described up to this point focus on monitoring and observing a single system. In an enterprise setting there are many systems, and it is generally impractical to try to closely monitor each one individually. Instead, enterprise-grade management software is usually deployed to collect data from all of the systems in a distributed fashion. If a problem is observed, the utilities described in the chapter, and elsewhere in this book, can be used to further diagnose the problem.

The Simple Network Management Protocol (SNMP) is a well-established and very common protocol used to enable distributed monitoring and management of networked systems. A full discussion of SNMP management is beyond the scope of this book, but this section offers a brief overview of the SNMP capabilities provided with OpenSolaris. For details, consult the documentation. If your site uses an unbundled system management framework that provides its own agentry, consult the documentation for the product you are using to learn more about configuring its management agents for OpenSolaris.

Within the SNMP framework, an *agent* is a component that resides on the system being managed. A management application communicates with the agents using SNMP to perform the appropriate task. Because a variety of components exist within a complex system, such as a server running OpenSolaris, there can be a number of agents to manage the various subsystems. A *master agent* listens for SNMP requests and dispatches the request to the appropriate sub-agent. SNMP uses a well-defined management information base (MIB) to define the capabilities and attributes for each agent.

OpenSolaris provides the system management agent (SMA) as its master agent. The SMA is based on the Net-SNMP open source project. This agent runs on the standard SNMP network port 161. If another SNMP agent is already running on this port, the SMA won't start. You can check the agent's log file (/var/log/snmpd.log) to see if this is the case.

NOTE   The Net-SNMP project is based at www.net-snmp.org.

If you don't already have the SNMP packages installed, you first need to install them on your system. The following command installs all of the necessary packages:

```
# pkg install SUNWsacom SUNWsmagt SUNWsmcmd SUNWsmmgr
```

The /etc/sma/snmp/snmpd.conf file configures the SMA. You can use this file as a template and customize it for your configuration. The SMA supports the *AgentX* protocol for communicating with sub-agents. See the snmpd.conf(4) man page for information on configuring the agent, and the sma_snmp(5) man page for general information about the SMA. The SMA is managed by the application/management/sma SMF service and must be enabled or restarted after configuration changes have been made. The various MIB definitions shipped with OpenSolaris are delivered in the /etc/sma/snmp/mibs directory. The HOST-RESOURCES-MIB.txt file defines interfaces for managing a host computer, and the SNMPv2-MIB.txt file defines interfaces for accessing information about the SNMP service itself.

> **CAUTION** Enabling SNMP allows remote machines to monitor, and possibly manage, the various OpenSolaris subsystems. You should understand the security implications of SNMP and consider configuring security within SMA to limit the possibility of a remote host gaining access to the system.

Resources

The source for the various stat utilities described in this chapter resides under the usr/src/cmd/stat directory. Most of the other utilities are directly under the usr/src/cmd directory — for example, intrstat, kstat, lockstat, prtconf, prtdiag, ps, syseventd, and uname. The proc tools are under usr/src/cmd/ptools.

The kstat library is under usr/src/lib/libkstat.

The SNMP source is in the SFW consolidation under http://cvs.opensolaris.org/source/xref/sfw/usr/src/cmd/sma/net-snmp.

The SNMP SMA documentation is available at http://docs.sun.com/app/docs/doc/819-6813.

Solaris Performance and Tools by McDougall, Mauro, and Gregg (Prentice Hall, 2007) is an excellent reference devoted to the topic of this chapter.

Summary

This chapter provided an overview of OpenSolaris monitoring and observability. It discussed the various utilities you can use to display the system configuration and view various aspects of system behavior, along with some basic guidelines for troubleshooting. It also described the system log files, which you can use to access historical data. Finally, it introduced SNMP, which is used for distributed monitoring.

Chapter 15

DTrace

The DTrace facility is one of the most innovative capabilities within OpenSolaris. DTrace enables you to observe and understand the dynamic behavior of the entire software system, from the low-level kernel details to high-level application behavior, in ways that were not possible prior to the creation of DTrace.

DTrace is fundamentally different from previous tools. Using DTrace enables you to get a complete view of all of the software running. The software does not have to be instrumented or explicitly built for monitoring. Instead, the standard software that is normally running in production can be observed at any time using DTrace. As such, there is no special application that the software must run under to observe the system's behavior. Instead, if you notice a problem or the system is in a state that needs further investigation, you can immediately start using DTrace to dive into the running system to understand what is happening.

For DTrace to be used in this fashion, on production systems, it is critical that DTrace be safe. This safety is the second key innovation within DTrace. Previous tracing or debugging facilities could not be used on live, production systems without the possibility that the system could be destabilized or even crash. However, use on production systems was one of the key design goals of DTrace and, as such, safety was designed into the facility from the beginning.

DTrace *probes*, which are described later in this chapter, enable you to observe behavior at virtually any point of interest within the system. The number of available probes varies depending on the version of OpenSolaris that you are running, but as an example, the system used to write this chapter includes more than 75,000 probes. However, even with so many probes, they have no runtime impact until enabled, and then only the enabled probes will have any effect, which is minimal. The impact of probes increases linearly with the total number enabled, and once the probes have been disabled, they have no further runtime overhead.

Finally, DTrace includes a programming language that is used to express a variety of tracing behaviors, from simple to highly complex. In this way, you define the appropriate behavior to enable you to understand any aspect of the system, as needed.

Because DTrace is such a sophisticated facility, this chapter can only introduce its basic capabilities. It is hoped that this will whet your appetite to dive in, start using DTrace to gain insight into the behavior your systems and applications, and eventually learn more about this powerful feature within OpenSolaris.

Once you understand this chapter, not only will you know the capabilities of DTrace, but you will also comprehend advanced tracing techniques such as speculative tracing, tracing during boot, and postmortem tracing, and you will have a basic knowledge of application-level tracing in a variety of high-level languages.

Getting Started

Before delving into the full DTrace syntax, it is worth looking at a few simple examples to illustrate the basic capabilities of DTrace and how you might use it to start investigating some aspects of the system.

As described in Chapter 14, OpenSolaris includes the `truss` command, which enables you to trace the system calls made by a process. This command is useful for tracing a single process, or a process and its children, but what if you want to observe all of the system call activity on the system? DTrace is perfect for this sort of task.

As previously mentioned, DTrace includes a programming language to define your tracing behavior. This language is called D and this simple D program will trace all system calls:

```
syscall:::
{
    printf("%d %s %s\n", pid, probefunc, execname);
}
```

The first line of the program specifies the *probes* that will be enabled. Although probes haven't been explained yet, you can easily see that system calls are being specified. The rest of the program, which is the action taken when the probe fires, looks a lot like a one-line C program. As you will see, the D programming language resembles C in several ways. This one-line program will print three different variables: the process ID of the process making the system call (`pid`), the system call name (`probefunc`), and the name of the process (`execname`) making the call. DTrace includes a variety of built-in variables such as these, which are described later in this chapter.

If you type this command into a file named ex1.d and run DTrace as follows, you'll see output similar to the example, although the exact output depends on what processes are active on your system:

```
# /usr/sbin/dtrace -q -s ex1.d
1107 ioctl dtrace
1107 ioctl dtrace
1107 ioctl dtrace
1107 ioctl dtrace
1107 ioctl dtrace
1107 sysconfig dtrace
1107 sysconfig dtrace
1107 sysconfig dtrace
1107 sysconfig dtrace
1107 schedctl dtrace
1107 schedctl dtrace
1107 sigaction dtrace
...
```

The obvious problem here is that dtrace itself is running and the system call tracing of itself is mixed in with any useful data you might collect about other, more interesting processes that are running.

CROSS-REF The examples in this chapter are run as root. However, there are three DTrace-related privileges (dtrace_kernel, dtrace_proc, and dtrace_user) that can be assigned to a user. See Chapter 11 for more information on configuring privileges. The privileges(5) man page describes each of these privileges in more detail.

A simple modification to the program solves this problem:

```
syscall:::
/execname != "dtrace"/
{
    printf("%d %s %s\n", pid, probefunc, execname);
}
```

You can see that the second line of this new program, which is a pattern that will be matched, specifies that the execname should not be dtrace. This part of the probe function is called a *predicate* in the D script language. In this way, you can trace all processes except the dtrace process itself. Running this, your output will now appear more informative:

```
# dtrace -q -s ex2.d
994 ioctl gnome-terminal
994 ioctl gnome-terminal
994 pollsys gnome-terminal
994 pollsys gnome-terminal
994 write gnome-terminal
994 write gnome-terminal
994 ioctl gnome-terminal
```

```
994 ioctl gnome-terminal
994 pollsys gnome-terminal
797 setitimer Xorg
797 setitimer Xorg
797 clock_gettime Xorg
797 clock_gettime Xorg
797 read Xorg
...
```

It may not be immediately obvious, but this second example suffers from the same problem as the first. Although the dtrace process is not being traced, the program is printing to the terminal window and that activity, the terminal emulator process and the window system, still dominate the output.

While you could modify the predicate to exclude more processes, or redirect the command output to a file, DTrace includes a variety of additional capabilities that enable you to hone in on exactly the data in which you are interested.

For the sake of this example, assume that you weren't actually interested in tracing all of the system calls. Instead, what you really wanted to understand is how a certain log file, /var/log/myapp, is getting modified. That is, you know the file is modified at some point, but you don't know what process is actually making the change or why. Tracing the system calls initially seemed like a good way to detect this, but now you can see that there is so much activity on the system that just tracing system calls swamps the data you actually want.

One simple solution is to modify the program to only trace open system calls, as this example shows:

```
syscall::open:entry
{
    printf("%s, %s\n", execname, copyinstr(arg0));
}
```

You can see a few differences in this program. First, the probe line has been modified. Instead of tracing all system calls, only the entry to the open system call is being traced. The action has also been modified to print the process name and the value of the first argument to the system call, arg0, which is the filename passed to the open system call. The syntax for this parameter may seem a bit odd. Because the DTrace probes are running in the kernel, you need to copy the data from the user-level code into the probe's address space. Running this example, you might see something like the following:

```
# dtrace -q -s ex3.d
rcapd, /dev/null
rcapd, /var/run/daemon/rcap.stat.jSaaya
in.routed, /dev/kstat
rcapd, /dev/null
```

```
rcapd, /var/run/daemon/rcap.stat.kSaaya
rcapd, /dev/null
rcapd, /var/run/daemon/rcap.stat.lSaaya
...
```

You could certainly pipe this command through grep to look for the file you are interested in, but that wouldn't leverage the capabilities of DTrace or enable you to use DTrace to explore the behavior further. Instead, you can add a predicate to the program that will do the matching for you:

```
syscall::open:entry
/"/var/log/myapp" == copyinstr(arg0)/
{
     printf("%s, %s\n", execname, copyinstr(arg0));
}
```

In the predicate, which is the new second line in the program, you can see that the matching is being done on the file you are interested in. Running this example produces the following output:

```
# dtrace -q -s ex4.d
myprog, /var/log/myapp
```

There is only a single line of output, which tells you that the process named myprog is the one opening the file; but what if different processes are opening this file and you want to see what any one of them is doing? Now that you know how to select the processes in which you are interested, you can use DTrace to explore the behavior of any process that opens this file. This final example shows how to trace all of the system calls of a process after it opens the log file:

```
syscall::open:entry
/"/var/log/myapp" == copyinstr(arg0)/
{
        self->trace = 1;
}

syscall:::entry
/self->trace/
{
        printf("%s, %s enter\n", execname, probefunc);
}

syscall:::return
/self->trace/
{
        printf("%s, %s exit\n", execname, probefunc);
}
```

This example has three clauses instead of the single clause you have seen up to now. A DTrace program clause is composed of the three parts you have seen in the examples: a probe specification, a predicate, and actions.

The first clause uses a predicate to do the matching, as shown previously. However, instead of just printing the data, it sets a variable. The self name represents the thread being traced. You can set the value of variables on the thread, and then use that data in other parts of the program. The trace variable on the thread is not a special name. You can use any name and DTrace will dynamically create that variable for you. You can also see that the predicates on the other clauses use this new trace variable to determine when the actions on those clauses should run. If the value of trace is nonzero, then the actions will run when the probe fires. Using a thread-local variable this way is a common construct within DTrace programs; you have one clause that does some form of selection and sets some data on the thread, and then other clauses use that data in their predicates or actions. In this case, the second clause will print some data when the system call is entered, and the third clause prints some data when the system call returns.

Running this program shows something like the following:

```
# dtrace -q -s ex5.d
myprog, open enter
myprog, open exit
myprog, write enter
myprog, write exit
myprog, rexit enter
progdemo, open enter
progdemo, open exit
progdemo, close enter
progdemo, close exit
progdemo, write enter
progdemo, write exit
progdemo, open enter
progdemo, open exit
progdemo, write enter
progdemo, write exit
progdemo, close enter
progdemo, close exit
progdemo, rexit enter
```

You can see that the same process shown earlier, myprog, is opening the log file, writing some data, and exiting; but another process named progdemo also opens the file, calls close, write, open, and so on. What is this second process doing? You immediately want to know what files are being opened or closed, what data is being written to what files, and so on. DTrace enables you to easily answer all of these questions, and more, with simple changes to your program. It is common to use DTrace to watch some aspect of the system's behavior, which will give you new ideas or questions about what is going on; and then, with additional enhancements to your program, as this example illustrated, you can refine your tracing to understand exactly what is happening.

Tracing Syntax

The previous examples showed that a DTrace program is made up of one or more clauses, each of which has three parts: a probe specification, a predicate, and actions. In this section, the syntax of each of these components is described in more detail.

NOTE Although this section is just an overview of the programming capabilities in DTrace, it is still long and might seem a bit overwhelming. Remember that most D programs are actually very simple and that you can achieve a great deal of visibility into the behavior of the system with extremely small programs. However, DTrace is capable of tracing to any level of sophistication, as your needs and abilities increase. The best way to use DTrace is to jump in, get your feet wet with simple D programs, and then expand your knowledge as needed.

Program structure

Because clauses are executed in the order you write them, you cannot reference variables that have not yet been declared. For example, the following portion of a program is incorrect:

```
fbt:::entry
/self->t/
{
}

syscall::open:entry
/execname == "myapp"/
{
        self->t = 1;
}
```

Attempting to compile the preceding program results in an error:

```
# dtrace -s ex26.d
dtrace: failed to compile script ex26.d: line 2: self->t has not yet
been declared or assigned
```

Changing the order in which the clauses are written corrects the problem.

Within your program, you can use comments in the C style, as in this example:

```
/*
 * This is a comment.
 */
```

Probes

You have seen that a probe specification is composed of four different fields, delimited by colons (:). This is one of the specifications from an earlier example:

```
syscall::open:entry
```

The four fields in the specification are as follows:

```
provider:module:function:name
```

What is a probe?

Within the system, all of the points of interest that can be traced using DTrace are known as probes. As mentioned in the introduction to this chapter, there are tens of thousands of these probe points on a standard OpenSolaris system. These probes are not normally hard-coded into the software, as you might expect from traditional tracing systems. Instead, the probes are made available by the probe provider. For example, the fbt provider is the *function boundary tracing* provider. This provider enables you to trace virtually every function entry and exit point within the kernel. When new functions are added to the OpenSolaris kernel, developers do not implement any special code to enable DTrace to trace their new functions. The fbt provider knows how to trace the functions automatically.

A key feature of probes is that they have no effect when they are not enabled. That is, the production code running on your system has all of the probe points available, but there is no overhead for these probes until a DTrace program is running. At that time, only the probes that are enabled within the D program actually have any effect. When the DTrace program ends, any probes that were enabled are gone and there is no longer any overhead. Even when probes are enabled they have very little overhead, so the *probe effect* is very low.

> **NOTE** The *probe effect* is something typically seen in traditional tracing systems where the presence of a probe changes the software's behavior. For example, in a program with a race condition, if you added print commands to enable you to see what is happening, the actual presence of the print commands might change the software behavior so that the race condition no longer occurs.

What probes are available?

You can use the -l option to the dtrace command to see a list of all probes. Because there are so many probes, you might want to redirect the output to a file. Looking at the output, you'll see something like the following example, although the exact order of the probes printed will vary:

```
# dtrace -l
   ID   PROVIDER          MODULE                        FUNCTION NAME
    1     dtrace                                                 BEGIN
```

```
    2   dtrace                                              END
    3   dtrace                                              ERROR
    4      fbt          pfil              pfil_list_add entry
    5      fbt          pfil              pfil_list_add return
  ...
```

You can see that each probe has a provider, module, function, and name. These are the four fields of a probe specification described earlier. Within your programs, you use this data to specify exactly which probes should be enabled when the program is running. The earlier examples also demonstrated that each field in the probe specification is optional. This was the probe specification for the first example:

```
    syscall:::
```

This specification enabled every probe delivered by the syscall provider. If you were to use the following probe specification, you could trace virtually every function entry and return point in the kernel:

```
    fbt:::
```

> **NOTE** There are a handful of nonstandard function boundaries where it is unsafe to trace, so the fbt provider will not enable probes at those points.

You can see in the -l listing that the dtrace provider delivers three probes with no specific module or function. These probes are described later in the chapter.

Providers

The exact providers available on your system will vary according to which release of OpenSolaris you are running. However, a set of common, frequently used providers is described in Table 15-1.

There are many other providers that are not described in this chapter. See the DTrace manual at http://docs.sun.com/app/docs/doc/819-3620 for more information on all providers.

You can use the dtrace -l command with the -P option to see a list of probes that are delivered by a specific provider. This example lists the profile probes:

```
# dtrace -l -P profile
   ID   PROVIDER         MODULE           FUNCTION NAME
  480   profile                                    profile-97
  481   profile                                    profile-199
  482   profile                                    profile-499
  483   profile                                    profile-997
  484   profile                                    profile-1999
  485   profile                                    profile-4001
  486   profile                                    profile-4999
  487   profile                                    tick-1
```

```
488   profile                                      tick-10
489   profile                                      tick-100
490   profile                                      tick-500
491   profile                                      tick-1000
492   profile                                      tick-5000
```

TABLE 15-1

Common Providers

Provider	Description
dtrace	Probes for the DTrace framework
fbt	Function boundary tracing. Enables you to trace entry and return of almost every function in the kernel.
io	Probes for disk I/O
lockstat	Probes for observing lock activity. The lockstat command, described in Chapter 14, is actually a DTrace program that uses this provider.
pid	Similar to the fbt provider. Enables you to trace entry and return of any function in a user-level process. You can also trace user-level instructions by address or using an offset within a specific function.
proc	Probes for process-related activity such as creation of a new process or exec-ing a new image
profile	Probes that fire at fixed time intervals. These probes are not defined at any specific point in the code. Instead, they fire after a specified time. This capability is useful for the traditional sampling style of tracing.
sdt	Statically defined tracing. Unlike the other providers, these are for probes that have been explicitly added to the code by developers at key points of interest.
syscall	Probes for entry and return from each system call

The module and function

In addition to the provider and name fields, the other two components of a probe specification are the module and function fields.

The module specifies which kernel module or user library contains the probe. The function specifies which function in the module contains the probe. Both of these are used to narrow the probe selection when there are multiple probes with the same provider and name. Some providers, such as the dtrace or profile providers, don't publish module and function names. However, these fields are commonly used with providers, such as fbt, which publish a large number of probes.

Advanced probe specification

Up to this point you have only seen examples of a probe specification with four simple fields, some of which have been empty. However, you can use a variety of more complex specifications in your clauses. For example, the following specification will enable entry probes for both the read and write system calls:

```
syscall::read:entry, syscall::write:entry
```

In this way, a single clause can use the same predicate and action on multiple probes. The specification does not have to be written on the same line. It could just as easily be written as follows:

```
syscall::read:entry,
syscall::write:entry
```

You can also use wildcards in a probe specification. For example, if you look at the various syscall provider probes, you will see the following functions related to wait:

```
# dtrace -l -P syscall | grep wait
77403    syscall                                    wait entry
77404    syscall                                    wait return
77575    syscall                                 waitsys entry
77576    syscall                                 waitsys return
...
```

If you wanted to trace both wait and waitsys you could use the following probe specification:

```
syscall::wait*:
```

The asterisk (*) provides similar pattern matching to what you see in the shell.

dtrace provider probes

Earlier, in the probe listing, you saw that the dtrace provider publishes three probes: BEGIN, END, and ERROR. These probes are related to the behavior of DTrace itself. The BEGIN probe is used on a clause that should execute before any other probe in your program fires. You would use this for any initialization required in the rest of your program. Likewise, the END probe is used on a clause that should execute when your program is ending. It fires after all other probes have completed firing and DTrace is cleaning up. You could use this probe for printing any data that has been accumulated during the execution of your program. Finally, the ERROR probe can be defined for any error handling required by your program. It will fire if a runtime error is detected while one of the program's clauses is executing.

Predicates

When a D program is running, the specified probes in the program are enabled. When one of these probes is hit, the probe is said to fire. However, as shown in the earlier examples, before the actions are executed, the clause's predicate must evaluate to true. Predicates allow a second level of filtering, beyond the simple probe specification, to determine when the actions should run. If the predicate on a clause evaluates to false, then the clause actions are not executed.

In addition to their role in filtering before a clause's actions are run, predicates are the main flow-of-control construct within D programs. Although much of the DTrace syntax resembles the C programming language, control-flow constructs such as `if-then-else`, `for`, or `while` loops are not available. The primary reason for this omission is the requirement for safety that DTrace offers in production environments. Programs with general-purpose control-flow constructs cannot always be evaluated to determine if they will complete. That is, there is no way to determine whether an arbitrary program will go into an infinite loop on some arbitrary input. Because the probes are executing in the kernel and DTrace must always be safe to use on live systems, the D programming language only offers the more restrictive control flow that predicates provide.

NOTE Although full `if-then-else` control flow is not provided, the C variant using `?:` is available for use within assignment statements in actions. If you are not familiar with the C programming language, the `?:` operator enables you to write a condensed form of `if-then-else` embedded within an assignment statement. The following example sets the variable t to "true" if i is not equal to 0; otherwise, it sets t to "false":

```
t = i != 0 ? "true" : "false";
```

You can also nest `?:` constructs within each side of the conditional, as this example illustrates:

```
suffix = i > 1024 ? (i > 1048576 ? "M" : "K") : "";
```

The true portion of the conditional is a second, nested conditional. More information about the syntax of statements within actions is described later in the "Actions" section.

Predicate syntax

Predicates use the boolean operators provided by DTrace. As you have seen in the examples, a predicate follows the probe specification on the clause and is enclosed within slashes (`//`). The conditional operators are described a little later in the "Actions" section. One of the key points to note is that predicates can be composed of complex conditionals using the boolean and (`&&`) and or (`||`) constructs. Here is a simple example:

```
/self->i > 0 && self->i < 100/
```

Complex control flow

It may seem that the lack of the usual flow-of-control constructs is too limiting for complex programming, but through the use of predicates on multiple clauses, you can achieve similar results. The following trivial example shows a program that iterates until the open system call has been traced ten times, and then exits:

```
dtrace:::BEGIN
{
```

```
        i = 0;
}

syscall::open:entry
/i < 9/
{
        i++;
}

syscall::open:entry
/i == 9/
{
        printf("10 open system calls\n");
        exit(0);
}
```

This program has two clauses with the same probe specification, but with different predicates. This is a common programming construct in DTrace programs. The predicate is used to control which clause action is to be run when the probe fires, with a common variable used as a conditional value in the predicates.

Actions

The set of actions is the third and final component of a clause. These are encased in curly braces ({ }) and use a programming syntax similar to C. The actions define the behavior when a probe fires. Aside from the ability to write complex tracing actions, DTrace includes a variety of sophisticated data structures for collecting and aggregating data in various ways. The functionality described in this section enables you to trace system behavior from the simple to the extremely complex, as your needs dictate.

Although your clauses will frequently have a set of actions associated with them, this portion of the clause is also optional, and you can still obtain useful information with no actions. By default, a clause with no actions traces the enabled probe associated with the clause. The following example uses a thread-local variable to enable tracing of all of the function calls made within the kernel by the myapp program during the processing of the open system call. It uses fbt probes with no actions on those clauses:

```
syscall::open:entry
/execname == "myapp"/
{
        self->t = 1;
}

syscall::open:return
/self->t/
{
        self->t = 0;
}
```

```
fbt:::entry
/self->t/
{
}

fbt:::return
/self->t/
{
}
```

Running the preceding shows the following output:

```
# dtrace -s ex25.d
dtrace: script 'ex25.d' matched 81835 probes
CPU     ID                    FUNCTION:NAME
  1   13743                    open32:entry
  1    7153                     copen:entry
  1   13359                    falloc:entry
  1   16189                   ufalloc:entry
  1   11057              ufalloc_file:entry
  1    6304                   fd_find:entry
  1    6305                  fd_find:return
  1    6306                fd_reserve:entry
  1    6307               fd_reserve:return
  1   11058             ufalloc_file:return
  1   16190                  ufalloc:return
  ...
```

While this is useful, it can be hard to read. Simply adding the -F option to the dtrace command, which nicely formats function call entry and return data, shows the following output:

```
# dtrace -F -s ex25.d
dtrace: script 'ex25.d' matched 81835 probes
CPU FUNCTION
  1  -> open32
  1    -> copen
  1      -> falloc
  1        -> ufalloc
  1          -> ufalloc_file
  1            -> fd_find
  1            <- fd_find
  1            -> fd_reserve
  1            <- fd_reserve
  1          <- ufalloc_file
  1        <- ufalloc
  1        -> kmem_cache_alloc
  1        <- kmem_cache_alloc
  1        -> crhold
```

```
1          <- crhold
1        <- falloc
...
```

This simple example can yield great insight into what an application is doing, without requiring any real coding, and illustrates the power of even simple D programs.

Types and variables

In D programs, variables do not have to be declared before being used. The first time a variable is used, it takes the type of the value assigned. You cannot assign different types to the same variable, so once the variable has a type, subsequent assignments must be of the same type. The supported types are the same as in C: char, int, short, long, and long long. DTrace also supports strings as fixed-size character arrays, similar to C, but instead of declaring a character array, DTrace uses an explicit string type. You can cast an expression to type string or use the stringof operator. The boolean operators work as expected on strings, just as they do on other types. For example, the equivalence operator == does a byte-wise comparison of strings.

Within DTrace programs, you can use typedefs, structures, unions, and enumerations, just as you would in a C program. You can also add the -C option to the dtrace command so that the C preprocessor is run against your D programs, expanding included header files appropriately. In this way sophisticated programs can easily access kernel data structures and variables while tracing.

A set of predefined variables is maintained by DTrace itself. You have already seen examples of three of these — pid, probefunc, and execname. Table 15-2 describes the commonly used built-in variables.

Other, less commonly used, built-in variables are described in the DTrace documentation.

In addition to the standard, built-in variables, you can access kernel data that is not defined in your program. This capability is described in detail in the DTrace manual, but the general technique is to use the backtick (`) to refer to a kernel variable. For example, as the manual describes, you can access the kernel kmem_flags variable in this way:

```
`kmem_flags
```

CROSS-REF See Chapter 24 for more information on kmem_flags.

By default, variables are global to your entire program. The first time a variable is used in an action, its type is set and the variable's value will then be accessible in any clause. Although you don't have to declare variables in D, you can achieve a similar effect by initializing them in your BEGIN clause, if necessary.

In addition to the program's global variables, you can use the thread-local storage that was demonstrated in the earlier examples. As previously described, the self variable refers to the current thread. You can dynamically create new variables that will be thread-specific, just as you do with global variables. That is, the first reference to a thread-local variable will cause it to be created on the thread with the appropriate type.

TABLE 15-2

Predefined DTrace Variables

Variable	Description
arg0-arg9	For entry probes, the first 10 arguments to the function being traced. Each is a 64-bit integer. For return probes, arg1 holds the return value.
errno	Error number from the last system call
execname	Name of the process
pid	ID of the process
probefunc	Function name of the current probe
probemod	Module name of the current probe
probename	Name of the current probe
probeprov	Provider name of the current probe
self	Refers to the current thread. Used for thread-local variables as described in this section.
this	Refers to the current clause. Used for clause-local variables as described in this section.
tid	Thread ID
timestamp	A nanosecond timestamp. This should only be used for relative comparisons to earlier timestamps in the trace.

NOTE Thread-local variables are for use by DTrace itself. That is, this data does not have any relationship to the running thread. Setting a thread-local variable in DTrace has no impact on the actual program data used during the execution of the thread itself. These thread-local variables are only used to store data related to the tracing of the specific thread.

Thread-local variables are used to keep track of tracing data for the thread so that it can be used later in a clause. One common usage is as a boolean that is used to trigger tracing in another clause's predicate. The following example, which is similar to the example in the introduction, shows how a thread-local variable is used to enable tracing of all function calls made during the execution of the open system call:

```
syscall::open:entry
{
        self->t = 1;
}
```

```
syscall::open:return
{
        self->t = 0;
}

fbt:::entry
/self->t/
{
        printf("%s enter\n", probefunc);
}

fbt:::return
/self->t/
{
        printf("%s return\n", probefunc);
}
```

You can see the thread-local variable t is used in the predicates on the fbt clauses. The other key point is that the variable is cleared when the open system call returns. If that were not done, tracing would continue on all functions after the first open system call was made by the thread. Of course, you do not need to restrict yourself to using thread-local variables in this way. You can use them to store any tracing data that is thread-specific.

In addition to global variables and thread-local variables, you can also use clause-local variables. The syntax for these is similar to thread-local variables except that you use this instead of self. Clause-local variables persist across all of the clauses for the same probe, so you can set a variable in one clause and reference its value in another, as this contrived example shows:

```
syscall::open:entry
/execname == "myapp"/
{
        self->t = 1;
        this->myvar = 5;
}

syscall::open:return
/self->t/
{
        self->t = 0;
        printf("open return %d\n", this->myvar);
}
```

Running this program always prints 5 for the value of myvar when the open returns.

In addition to simple scalar variables, DTrace also supports other types such as pointers, scalar arrays, and associative arrays.

Pointers

In D, pointers have a similar syntax to C. That is, an asterisk (*) is used for indirect references through the pointer. Unlike C, pointer usage within a D program is safe. You cannot crash the system you are tracing through an invalid pointer reference. Instead, DTrace will detect this situation and print an error. This simple example attempts to reference through a NULL pointer named nullptr when a system call is entered:

```
dtrace:::BEGIN
{
        nullptr = (int *)NULL;
}

syscall:::entry
{
        printf("%d\n", *nullptr);
}
```

Running this program will quickly return many error messages similar to the following output:

```
dtrace: error on enabled probe ID 186 (ID 77491: syscall::ioctl:entry): invalid
address (0x0) in action #1 at DIF offset 4
```

This error shows DTrace detecting the runtime error and printing the diagnostic error message, but no other ill effect.

Scalar arrays

Scalar arrays in D are similar to arrays in C. They are indexed numerically, with multi-dimensional arrays using multiple brackets to denote each dimension. As in C, the first element begins at 0. This example assigns an integer element in a two-dimensional array:

```
x[1][2] = 5;
```

Associative arrays

If you are not familiar with associative arrays, instead of accessing array elements by a simple numeric index, as you do with scalar arrays, you access the elements by a key. While the key can certainly be a simple integer, it can also be a more complex value. When you specify an expression for an associative array element, the expression forms a key. Any expression that evaluates to that key will refer to the same element. A simple but powerful technique is to use a string as the key. The following example counts all of the system calls made by each running process and then prints the number of system calls made by the Xorg process when the program ends:

```
syscall:::entry
{
        calls[execname]++;
```

```
}

dtrace:::END
{
        printf("%d\n", calls["Xorg"]);
}
```

Elements in the associative array named `calls` are accessed by a string instead of the numeric index you might be used to. In the example, the value of `execname` is used as the index. Although this example shows a simple key, you can use multiple expressions, each of which can be a different type.

Macros

In addition to the built-in variables described earlier, DTrace also provides a set of built-in macros. These are similar to the built-in variables, but their values are defined once, when your program begins to run. An example is the `pid` macro, which will have the value of the process ID for the running D program. Macros are specified using a dollar sign ($) prefix. Table 15-3 describes the built-in macros.

TABLE 15-3

Built-in DTrace Macros

Macro	Description
$[0-9]+	Arguments. See description in the "Macro arguments" section following this table.
$egid	Effective group ID
$euid	Effective user ID
$gid	Real group ID
$pid	Process ID
$pgid	Process group ID
$ppid	Parent process ID
$projid	Project ID
$sid	Session ID
$target	Target process ID. See description in the "Target process ID" section.
$taskid	Task ID
$uid	Real user ID

Macro arguments

Macro arguments are any additional arguments passed along to your program that you specify when you invoke dtrace. For example, the following standalone D program takes the name of a running process as a parameter and traces all system calls made by that process:

```
#!/usr/sbin/dtrace -s
#pragma D option quiet

syscall:::
/execname == $1/
{
        printf("%d %s\n", pid, probefunc);
}
```

You can see the $1 macro used in the predicate on the clause. The first line of the program is explained later in the "Standalone programs" section. The pragma sets the quiet, or -q, option for the program.

> **NOTE** A pragma is a command to the D compiler instead of a D program statement. These can appear anywhere in your program. By using pragma, your program will always use the specified runtime options without you having to remember to run DTrace with specific arguments.

Running this with "Xorg" as the argument results in the following output:

```
# ./ex17.d '"Xorg"'
1938 setitimer
1938 setitimer
1938 read
1938 read
1938 read
1938 read
1938 pollsys
  ...
```

In this example the process name string, "Xorg", is quoted with additional single-quotes so that the shell does not interpret the double quotes.

Target process ID

This macro refers to the specific process ID against which the dtrace program is run. The following example is similar to the previous example but uses the $target macro in the predicate:

```
#!/usr/sbin/dtrace -s
#pragma D option quiet
```

```
syscall:::
/pid == $target/
{
        printf("%s %s\n", probefunc, execname);
}
```

Instead of specifying a process name, a PID is passed to dtrace using the -p option:

```
# ./ex18.d -p 1938
```

The $target macro is filled in with either the -p option for an existing process or the -c option if dtrace is used to invoke the command.

Simple expressions

Within a clause, the actions are a sequence of expressions that are executed in order, just as in a typical program. Each expression is a simple statement or a function call. As already described, there are no if-then-else or loop statements, although the ?: conditional operator is supported. The syntax for a simple statement follows the C language syntax, with each statement terminated by a semicolon (;).

Table 15-4 summarizes the various operators.

Consult the DTrace manual if you are not familiar with the syntax of the various C operators or their precedence. As in C, parentheses can be used to force a specific precedence.

Built-in functions

Many of the built-in functions record data related to the activity being traced. Details about how tracing data is actually recorded are described in the "Buffering" section later in this chapter. In the examples, you have seen the use of the printf function. Table 15-5 lists the built-in data recording functions and provides a brief description of each. The DTrace manual provides full details on the behavior and arguments for each function.

In addition to the data recording functions, Table 15-6 describes a set of general-purpose functions.

Finally, in addition to these functions, DTrace includes a set of *destructive* functions. Ordinarily tracing is not allowed to have any adverse side-effects on the system, and the DTrace infrastructure is rigorous in enforcing this restriction. Because of this constraint, you can be confident when tracing on a live, production system. However, in some cases it is beneficial to actually modify or impact the system in some way during tracing. Referred to as *destructive tracing*, this must be explicitly enabled with the -w command-line option when you run dtrace. When doing destructive tracing, the functions described in Table 15-7 are available.

TABLE 15-4

Operators

Category	Operator	Description
Arithmetic		
	+	addition
	++	increment
	-	subtraction
	- -	decrement
	*	multiplication
	/	division
	%	modulus
Relational		
	<	less than
	<=	less than or equal to
	>	greater than
	>=	greater than or equal to
	==	equal
	!=	not equal
Logical		
	&&	AND
	||	OR
	^ ^	XOR
Bitwise		
	&	AND
	|	OR
	^	XOR
	<<	shift left
	>>	shift right
Assignment		
	=	assign

TABLE 15-4	*(continued)*	
Category	**Operator**	**Description**
	+=	increment and assign
	-=	decrement and assign
	*=	multiply and assign
	/=	divide and assign
	%=	modulo and assign
	|=	OR and assign
	&=	AND and assign
	^=	XOR and assign
	<<=	shift left and assign
	>>=	shift right and assign
Pointer		
	&	address of
	*	dereference a pointer
	->	structure member with pointer
	.	structure member
Other		
	offsetof	offset of a member
	sizeof	the size of the object
	stringof	convert to string
	xlate	translate data type

Aggregations

DTrace includes support for a data type and a set of functions that enable you to aggregate data during tracing. That is, aggregation enables you to combine data from different entities into a new, higher-level entity. Aggregation during tracing has a couple of advantages:

- All of the data does not need to be maintained. Instead, when a new entity is aggregated, the aggregation function is applied, after which the new entity is no longer needed and can be discarded.

- Scaling problems are minimized because entities can be aggregated per-CPU, and then aggregated again when the final data is needed.

TABLE 15-5	

Built-in Data Recording Functions

Function	Description
jstack	An alias for the ustack function. Used for printing Java stack frames.
printa	Similar to printf but used for printing aggregations. See the "Aggregation" section later in the chapter for more details.
printf	Used for formatting and printing variables. Similar to the C printf function.
stack	Prints a kernel stack trace. See ustack for printing user-level stack traces.
trace	Prints the given expression
tracemem	Prints the memory at the given address
ustack	Prints a user-level stack trace. See stack for printing kernel stack traces.

Within a D program, an aggregation data type is used to store the result of an aggregation function. The aggregation data type is similar to the associative array type described earlier; it looks like an array that is indexed by keys. To distinguish the two, the aggregation is prefixed by an ampersand (@), as shown in the examples following Table 15-8. Values are set within an aggregation using one of the aggregating functions listed in Table 15-8.

Because aggregations are such a powerful tool for analyzing the behavior of the system, a number of examples are shown illustrating their use. The first example aggregates the number of system calls by the running process:

```
syscall:::entry
{
        @syscalls[execname] = count();
}
```

In the preceding example, the aggregation is named syscalls, is indexed by execname, and uses the count aggregation function. This syntax may seem a bit confusing. With aggregations there are always two components — the aggregation where the data is stored and the aggregation function itself, which dictates how the data is aggregated. Once an aggregation is defined to be a specific type, based on the function used, then the type is set. You cannot use different aggregation functions to store data into the same aggregation. You would need a second aggregation to store data from a different function. Also, you can only assign the result of an aggregation function to an aggregation. Attempting to assign the result of some other type of expression to an aggregation is an error.

TABLE 15-6

General-Purpose Functions

Function	Description
alloca	Allocates a given number of bytes
basename	Substring of the given string, with any prefix ending in / removed
bcopy	Copies bytes from source to destination
cleanpath	Removes redundant elements from the given path string
copyin	Copies the number of bytes from the given user address into a scratch buffer
copyinstr	Copies a null-terminated string from the given user address into a scratch buffer
copyinto	Copies the number of bytes from the given user address into the given buffer
dirname	Substring of the given path name string, with the last level removed
exit	Stops tracing and ends
msgdsize	See the msgdsize(9) man page.
msgsize	The number of bytes in the message. See the msgdsize(9) man page.
mutex_owned	See the mutex_owned(9) man page.
mutex_owner	Gets the thread of the current owner of the given mutex
mutex_type_adaptive	Returns true if the given mutex is of type MUTEX_ADAPTIVE. See the mutex_init(9F) man page.
progenyof	Returns true if the current process is in the progeny of the given PID
rand	Returns a weak random integer
rw_iswriter	Returns true if the given lock is held or needed by a writer
rw_write_held	Returns true if the given lock is held by a writer
speculation	Reserves a buffer for speculative tracing. See the "Speculative Tracing" section later in the chapter for more information.
strjoin	Concatenates two strings
strlen	Returns the length of the given string

TABLE 15-7

Destructive Tracing Functions

Function	Description
breakpoint	Stops the kernel and transfers to the kernel debugger
chill	Causes DTrace to pause for the given number of nanoseconds. This is useful for inducing timing-related issues.
copyout	Copies the source buffer to the destination buffer in the current process' user-level address space.
copyoutstr	Copies the source string to the destination string in the current process' user-level address space
panic	Panics the system
raise	Sends the given signal to the current process
stop	Stops the current process when it exits the kernel
system	Runs the given program. Similar to the system(3c) function.

TABLE 15-8

Aggregating Functions

Function	Description
avg	Average of the given expressions
count	The number of times the function has been called
lquantize	A linear frequency distribution of the given expressions
max	The maximum value in the given expressions
min	The minimum value in the given expressions
quantize	A power of two frequency distribution of the given expressions
sum	The sum of the given expressions

Running the preceding example for a short time, and then ending the trace, yields the following output:

```
svc.configd                                      1
svc.startd                                       1
fmd                                              2
gnome-volume-man                                 2
```

```
    inetd                                                  2
    utmpd                                                  2
    gconfd-2                                               3
    mapping-daemon                                         4
    ssh-agent                                             12
  ...
    metacity                                            6638
    firefox-bin                                        18607
    Xorg                                               90280
```

DTrace automatically prints the aggregation when it ends. With this simple program you can instantly see which processes are causing the most system call activity during the trace. In this case, the Xorg process dominates all other processes. What if you wanted to see which system calls within all of the processes were the most heavily used? A small change to the previous program enables you to determine that:

```
syscall:::entry
{
        @syscalls[execname, probefunc] = count();
}
```

This just changes the aggregation so that the key is both the process name and the system call that is being probed. Running this program for a short period yields the following result:

```
  ...
    thunderbird-bin                 write              3678
    thunderbird-bin                 pollsys            4390
    thunderbird-bin                 lseek              4841
    dtrace                          ioctl              4930
    thunderbird-bin                 llseek             7139
    Xorg                            writev             7144
    Xorg                            pollsys            7703
    thunderbird-bin                 read              10282
    Xorg                            read              11579
    Xorg                            clock_gettime     35985
```

Here, the Xorg process still performs the most system calls but now you can also see that the clock_gettime system call is the one most heavily used. You can also see that there is some data from DTrace itself within the output and that the output is not formatted very well. You can improve the program by filtering out the DTrace process and adding your own printing code:

```
syscall:::entry
/pid != $pid/
{
        @syscalls[execname, probefunc] = count();
}

dtrace:::END
```

```
{
        printa("%15s %15s %@7u\n", @syscalls);
}
```

The preceding program yields the following output, which is easier to read due to the formatting:

```
        ...
                Xorg            writev   5169
                Xorg           pollsys   5322
   thunderbird-bin               read    5473
                Xorg              read   8558
                Xorg    clock_gettime   28726
```

The predicate on the syscall probe uses a style that you haven't seen before. The $pid macro represents the PID of the process that enabled the probes. By filtering this against the built-in pid variable, you can eliminate tracing the actions of the program itself. Thus, even if you didn't invoke this using the dtrace program, the activity will be filtered out. This technique will be useful later when you see how to build commands that are actually DTrace scripts.

This is also the first example you have seen using the printa function for formatting an aggregation. Note that the keys for the aggregation are the first two items printed. Those correspond to the first two formatting directives. The @ formatting character on the third formatting directive is special; it denotes that the value of the aggregation itself should be used.

Now that you can see which system calls are being heavily used, you are probably thinking that it would be more useful to see which ones are actually taking the most time. You can change the program to aggregate on the average amount of time spent in each system call:

```
syscall:::entry
/pid != $pid/
{
        self->t = timestamp;
}

syscall:::return
/self->t/
{
        @systime[execname, probefunc] = avg(timestamp - self->t);
        self->t = 0;
}

dtrace:::END
{
        printa("%15s %15s %@15u\n", @systime);
}
```

This program keeps track of the time when the system call was entered by using a thread-local variable named t. It also uses the built-in timestamp variable already described. When the system call returns, the program aggregates the average time spent by taking the difference of the current timestamp to the entry timestamp. The program output shows the following:

```
    ...
         xscreensaver          pollsys          105489062
                rcapd       rusagesys          216732902
      multiload-applet         pollsys          252354894
                 java    lwp_cond_wait         420329502
       gnome-settings-d        pollsys          659260503
                xntpd      sigsuspend          999925478
                httpd          pollsys         1009968617
           gam_server       nanosleep         1509901404
             devfsadm        lwp_park         1999974184
       mapping-daemon          pollsys         5009862515
```

Note that there is a completely different set of processes and system calls high on the list. If you are surprised to see so much time in the pollsys system call at the top of the list, you can continue to refine your program to get a better understanding of what is happening. This last aggregation example uses the quantize function to show distribution of time spent in pollsys:

```
syscall::pollsys:entry
/pid != $pid/
{
        self->t = timestamp;
}

syscall::pollsys:return
/self->t/
{
        @dist[execname] = quantize(timestamp - self->t);
        self->t = 0;
}
```

As you can see, the probes have been changed so that only time spent in the pollsys system call is being tracked. Given that, the aggregation has also been changed to only key off of the execname. This produces the following output:

```
    ...
    evince
         value  ------------- Distribution ------------- count
          1024 |                                         0
          2048 |@@@@@@@                                  142
          4096 |                                         7
          8192 |                                         6
         16384 |@@@@@@                                   129
```

```
        32768 |@@@@@@@@@@@@@@@@@@@                      366
        65536 |@                                         23
       131072 |@@                                        38
       262144 |@@                                        34
       524288 |                                           5
      1048576 |                                           9
      2097152 |                                           5
      4194304 |@@                                        38
      8388608 |                                           7
     16777216 |                                           0
     33554432 |                                           2
     67108864 |                                           1
    134217728 |                                           1
    268435456 |                                           1
    536870912 |                                           2
   1073741824 |                                           2
   2147483648 |                                           0

  Xorg
        value ------------- Distribution ------------- count
         1024 |                                           0
         2048 |@@@@@@@@@                                 928
         4096 |@@@@@                                     508
         8192 |@@                                        231
        16384 |@@@@@@@                                   699
        32768 |@@@@                                      374
        65536 |@@                                        224
       131072 |@@@                                       304
       262144 |@                                         152
       524288 |@                                         101
      1048576 |@                                          71
      2097152 |@                                          92
      4194304 |@@@@                                      382
      8388608 |                                          46
     16777216 |                                          36
     33554432 |                                           6
     67108864 |                                           6
    134217728 |                                           3
    268435456 |                                           1
    536870912 |                                           0
```

DTrace automatically prints the frequency distribution histograms for the `dist` aggregation when the program ends. This output is much longer because each entry in the aggregation prints many lines of output. Seeing the data graphed in this way, which collects groups of values along with their counts, may provide more insight or new ideas for further exploration.

This discussion only scratches the surface of the analysis that can be done using aggregations. The DTrace manual includes an extensive discussion of tracing with the various aggregation functions.

The dtrace Command

The dtrace command is the way you typically run your tracing. This command supports many options, only a few of which are described here. You should see the man page for a complete description of each option.

The most common usage of this command is to run your D program using the -s option, as you have seen in previous examples. The quiet option (-q) is also frequently used to suppress the various messages that dtrace normally produces. This was the usage shown with the first example in the chapter:

```
# dtrace -q -s ex1.d
```

You have also seen examples of the -l option for listing probes. As mentioned earlier, you can use the C preprocessor with your programs. This is enabled with the -C option. If your program contains destructive actions, you must use the -w option to enable destructive tracing. The -F option, shown in a previous example, is useful for formatting function and entry return data into easy to read output, as shown in the following example:

```
CPU FUNCTION
  1   -> open32
  1     -> copen
  1       -> falloc
  1         -> ufalloc
  1           -> ufalloc_file
  1             -> fd_find
  1             <- fd_find
 ...
```

Although the discussion up to this point has focused on writing D programs, you can perform basic tracing without writing any program, by specifying probes to the dtrace command on the command line. You can also specify predicates and actions on the command line, although this quickly gets unwieldy for anything more than simple tracing:

```
# dtrace -n syscall::read:entry'/pid != $pid/{trace (execname)}'
```

This example enables the probe for entry on the read system call, specifying a predicate and a simple action. Note that there is no space between the probe specification and the predicate and that the predicate and action are quoted so that the shell does not try to interpret any of the special characters.

The dtrace command accepts a variety of options for tuning the behavior of the running program. Some of these options are described later in the "Buffering" section. For a complete list of options, see the manual.

Advanced Tracing

In addition to the tracing capabilities already described, DTrace includes support for even more sophisticated tracing to handle complex scenarios.

Tracing during boot

DTrace supports the capability to trace during boot through what is known as *anonymous tracing*. Anonymous tracing means that there is no consumer of the tracing data while the tracing is taking place. Any DTrace program can be run anonymously, but only one anonymous trace can be enabled at a time. You use the -A option to the dtrace command to enable an anonymous trace. This sets up the dtrace kernel driver to load as early as possible during boot, and the driver's conf file to configure the tracing. Here is an example of the command:

```
# dtrace -As ex20.d
```

Once you reboot the system, your tracing will take place. Because there is no consumer of the trace data, it is stored in the kernel. After the system boots, you then read the trace data using the -a option. The data can only be read once and the in-kernel storage space is reclaimed after the command is run, so it is a good idea to save the results to a file in case there is more output than expected. The following example shows reading the trace data after the reboot:

```
# dtrace -aeo results.txt
```

The -e option on the command instructs dtrace to exit after completing the request. Once the reboot is done, you disable the anonymous trace using the -A option with no arguments:

```
# dtrace -A
```

Buffering

All tracing output is recorded into a buffer from which the data is later consumed. By default, the data is recorded into the *principal buffer*. The section "Speculative tracing" describes how to record data into speculative buffers. A variety of options are used to tune how DTrace will buffer data. Each DTrace program, or *consumer*, can tune the buffering as appropriate for its behavior.

Principal buffers are allocated per-CPU. Because of the variety of situations in which DTrace can be used, it might not always be possible for the kernel to allocate memory for buffering. In fact, it is always possible that there might not be space for recording trace data. You can tune the policy for handling this situation, based on what you are trying to accomplish. DTrace supports three different policies for buffering: switch, fill, and ring.

switch

The switch policy is the default. With this policy, two buffers are allocated per CPU. Data is recorded into the active buffer until the consumer is ready to read the data. At that point,

DTrace switches the buffers so that data can be read from the originally active buffer while new trace data is recorded into the newly active buffer. The switching is done using a technique that ensures that no trace data is lost while switching or that the system is paused for any reason. This also ensures that the data being read is always in a consistent state. If the active buffer fills before the consumer is ready to read data, then data is dropped. DTrace will increment a counter each time data is dropped and print a message telling you how many times this occurred.

To reduce the chances of dropped data, you can use the switchrate option to tune how often your program will consume the data, and the bufsize option to change the size of the primary buffers. The default switchrate is one second and the default buffer size is 4MB.

In this example, the switchrate is set to cycle twice per second and the buffer size is set to 8 MB:

```
# dtrace -x bufsize=8m -x switchrate=2hz ...
```

You can specify the units for the switchrate in Hz or seconds. You can also set these options within your D program using a pragma, as this example shows:

```
#pragma D option bufsize=8m
#pragma D option switchrate=2hz
```

fill

The fill policy enables you to allocate one buffer per CPU and trace until one of the buffers is full. At that point, all of the recorded data is processed and dtrace will exit. You can use the bufpolicy option to set the buffer policy, and you can use the bufsize option to set the size of the buffer:

```
# dtrace -x bufpolicy=fill -x bufsize=2m ...
```

You can also set the buffering policy using a pragma. DTrace will take special care to reserve space for recording any END probe actions when using the fill policy.

ring

The ring policy is used to record data into a ring buffer so that older data is discarded and only the most recent data is kept. This is similar to a flight data recorder on an airplane and is useful for diagnosing intermittent problems that might take days to occur. To use the ring policy, set the bufpolicy using either the command-line option or a pragma, as shown earlier.

With the ring policy, no data is processed until your D program ends. At that point, each per-CPU buffer is processed in CPU order.

Additional buffer tuning

In addition to the principal buffers, there are buffers for aggregations and speculative tracing, which is described in the following section. As with principal buffers, the default size is 4MB.

These can be tuned using the `aggsize` or `specsize` options in the same way that the `bufsize` is tuned. The number of speculative buffers can be tuned using the `nspec` option. The default value is 1.

You can also tune the buffer's behavior if the system is not able to allocate memory for the requested buffer size. The default policy is `auto`, which means that the requested size is repeatedly cut in half until the allocation succeeds. As an alternative, you can set the policy to `manual`, which means the program will not run if the requested size cannot be met. This policy is tuned through the `bufresize` option.

Speculative tracing

In some cases it is useful to trace activity and then decide later whether the data should be kept or discarded. Within DTrace this is known as *speculative tracing*. This is in contrast to predicates, which filter tracing activity before any actions are run. With speculative tracing, the actions are run, but the decision to keep the data is made later, although you can still also use predicates with speculative tracing.

DTrace provides the functions described in Table 15-9 to support speculative tracing.

TABLE 15-9

Speculative Tracing Functions

Function	Description
commit	Records the data that has been speculatively traced
discard	Discards the data that has been speculatively traced
speculate	Switches the behavior of the rest of the clause so that all tracing is recorded into the given speculation buffer
speculation	Creates a new buffer for recording speculative trace data

To use speculative tracing, you create a new buffer for recording the trace data, and then use the `speculate` function in the appropriate clauses to record the trace data into the buffer. Finally, at the appropriate point, you can decide if the data should be kept or discarded. The following example illustrates tracing all of the functions called during a `write` system call, and then only recording the trace data if the write fails:

```
syscall::write:entry
{
    self->t = speculation();
}
```

```
fbt:::
/self->t/
{
    speculate(self->t);
    trace(probefunc);
}

syscall::write:return
/self->t && errno != 0/
{
    speculate(self->t);
    printf("write failed %d\n", errno);
    commit(self->t);
    self->t = 0;
}

syscall::write:return
/self->t && errno == 0/
{
    discard(self->t);
    self->t = 0;
}
```

Note that a new buffer is created when the write system call is entered. In the fbt probes, the trace data is recorded into the buffer. Finally, when the write system call returns, the predicates on each of the two clauses determine whether the data is kept or discarded.

During speculative tracing, it is possible that no new buffers are available for tracing or that a buffer fills up. You will notice warning messages from dtrace is these cases. You can use the specsize and nspec options, described earlier in the "Buffering" section, to reduce the chances of losing data.

It is also possible for a speculation buffer to be unavailable because it has not yet been committed on all CPUs. To reduce the chances of this, you can increase the rate at which CPUs are cleaned using the cleanrate option, which defaults to 101 Hz.

Postmortem tracing

If the system crashes while you are tracing, you can use DTrace to extract the trace data from the crash dump. This might enable you to determine the cause of the crash, particularly if you were using the ring buffering policy described earlier.

To access DTrace data from within a crash dump, you use the modular debugger mdb command.

CROSS-REF The modular debugger is described in Chapter 24.

Within `mdb`, the `dtrace_state` command shows all of the consumers running when the system crashed. Use the `dtrace_state` command to get the address of the state for a given consumer, and then the `dtrace` dcmd can be used to dump the buffers.

Standalone programs

Up to now, the examples have used the `dtrace` command to run the sample D programs. However, you can write standalone D programs that run on their own by specifying `dtrace` as the command interpreter, just as you do when writing a shell script. The first line of your program must begin like this example:

```
#!/usr/sbin/dtrace -s
```

You can specify additional `dtrace` options besides just the `-s` option, such as `-q`, or `-b`. See the `dtrace(1M)` man page for details on which options make sense in this context. Once you make the file executable, you can run it as you would any other command.

There is a C library, `libdtrace`, but the interfaces within the library are not currently public, so a script file is the preferred solution for creating standalone programs.

User-Level and High-Level Language Tracing

Up to this point the discussion has focused primarily on systemwide tracing or tracing the activity of process within the kernel. However, you can use the capabilities provided by DTrace to achieve the same insight into user-level application code as well.

The pid provider

The `pid` provider enables you to trace function calls within user-level code, just as the `fbt` provider enables you to trace function calls within the kernel.

The `pid` provider actually represents a class of providers, as each running process can have its own `pid` provider. The following example illustrates tracing all function entry points in the process with Process ID 1938:

```
pid1938:::entry
{
        printf("%s %s\n", probefunc, execname);
}
```

For pid probes, the module portion of the probe specification refers to the shared object loaded into the process' address space. The pldd command is one way to see which objects are mapped in:

```
# pldd 1938
1938:    /usr/X11/bin/Xorg :0 -depth 24 -nobanner -auth
/var/dt/A:0-zdaWsb
/lib/amd64/libc.so.1
/usr/X11/lib/X11/xserver/amd64/libXfont.so.1
/lib/amd64/libsocket.so.1
/lib/amd64/libnsl.so.1
/usr/X11/lib/amd64/libXdmcp.so.6
  ...
```

Within the probe specification, you use the base name of the object as the module name — for example, libc.so.1. The .so.1 suffix is optional, so you can also just specify libc.

You can use macros in your D program to make it general-purpose, as shown in this probe specification, which uses the $target macro to dynamically obtain the process ID:

```
pid$target:::entry
```

As previously mentioned, the pid provider also enables you to probe specific instructions. To trace a specific instruction, you specify its offset as the name in the probe specification. The following example prints a user-level stack trace when the instruction "at offset 8 bytes within the z function" is probed. This enables you to see the function call path that led to this instruction:

```
pid$target:a.out:z:8
{
        ustack();
}
```

It is also possible to trace every instruction within a function by omitting the probe name field, as the following probe specification illustrates:

```
pid$target:a.out:z:
```

This can be combined with speculative tracing so that only the code paths that turn out to be relevant are actually reported.

The sdt provider

The *statically defined tracing* (sdt) provider enables you to manually add probes into your applications at points in the code where you know you want to trace. Using the sdt provider is similar to traditional tracing systems, but with all of the advantages of DTrace, such as zero probe

effect when the probes are not enabled and the sophisticated programmatic tools within the
D language.

Developers within the kernel, such as those writing device drivers, can add explicit probes using
DTRACE_PROBE macros as described in the DTrace manual.

More commonly, you will want to add explicit probes into user-level application code. This
enables you to provide probes at points where there is a specific meaning that is useful to
the user tracing the code. In this way, users can trace by something meaningful within the
application instead of simply at the low-level function entry and exit points offered by the pid
provider.

When adding probes to an application, you define the probes in a .d file that is used when com-
piling the application. The following example walks through adding two probes to an application named myapp. This simple application has two functions into which sdt probes will be
added: start_job and join_job. The start_job function takes one argument, the name of
the job to run, and returns a job identifier. Within the function it performs various bookkeeping
and administrative operations before forking the job. The join_job function also does bookkeeping, waits for a job to complete, and returns the job identifier that actually completed.

Start by creating the myprobes.d file with the following contents. For your application, you can
name this file anything you want:

```
provider myapp
{
    probe start_job(string, int);
    probe join_job(int);
};

#pragma D attributes Evolving/Evolving/Common provider myapp provider
#pragma D attributes Evolving/Evolving/Common provider myapp module
#pragma D attributes Evolving/Evolving/Common provider myapp function
#pragma D attributes Evolving/Evolving/Common provider myapp name
#pragma D attributes Evolving/Evolving/Common provider myapp args
```

Within the file, you can see that a provider is defined, which matches the name of the application. Within the provider definition are the declarations for the two probes whose names will
match the functionality described earlier. You can also see that these declarations include the
arguments that the probes will use.

The rest of this file consists of a set of pragmas that define the stability of the various components of the probes. Defining the stability levels informs users of these probes how likely it
is that the implementation will change. This is not unique to your new sdt probes; all of the
probes in DTrace have stability levels associated with them. Probe stability is discussed in greater
depth in the DTrace manual.

> **TIP** You can use the dtrace -v option to print a report of the stability levels of the
> probes used in any of your D programs.

Now that you have written the definition for your new probes, you must modify the application source files in which the probes will be added. First, you must include the following header file:

```
#include <sys/sdt.h>
```

Next you add the probes into the code itself. The following abbreviated code snippet shows the two probes within the two functions described earlier:

```
pid_t
start_job(char *cmd)
{
  ...
    if ((id = vfork()) == 0) {
                (void) execl("/bin/sh", "sh", "-c", cmd,
            (char *)NULL);
        }
    DTRACE_PROBE2(myapp, start_job, cmd, id);

  ...
}

pid_t
join_job()
{
  ...
    while ((pid = waitpid(-1, &status, 0)) && pid != -1)
                ;
    DTRACE_PROBE1(myapp, join_job, pid);
  ...
}
```

You can see the new `DTRACE_PROBE` macros in the existing code. The number on each macro indicates how many additional arguments are used by the probe. The first two arguments are required: the `provider` and `name` fields of the probe. These match the definitions specified in the `myprobes.d` file. In the first case, the two additional arguments, as specified in `myprobes.d`, are also specified, while in the second case only the single additional argument is passed.

Finally, you compile the application. Either the `cc` or `gcc` compiler can be used for this step:

```
$ cc -c myapp.c
$ dtrace -G -32 -s myprobes.d myapp.o
$ cc -o myapp myprobes.o myapp.o
```

The first line simply builds the existing application source file. The second line uses the `dtrace` command with the `-G` option to generate the ELF file with the new probes. This yields the `myprobes.o` file. Finally, the last line links the application with the new probe file. These new build rules can easily be added to your existing `make` files.

You can now use these probes in a D program, just as you have with any other probe. The following simple D program uses an aggregation to count the number of times each probe fired. The probe name is myapp, as you defined in the myprobes.d file. These sdt probes are similar to pid probes in that each process can have its own sdt providers, so you append the process ID, just as you did with the pid probes. You can also see that the action on the start_job clause uses printf to display the two arguments defined for the probe. Arguments on sdt probes are referenced using the arg0-arg9 convention described earlier.

```
myapp$target:::start_job
{
    printf("start_job '%s' %d\n", copyinstr(arg0), arg1);
        @cnt[probefunc] = count();
}

myapp$target:::join_job
{
        @cnt[probefunc] = count();
}
```

User-level data

DTrace includes support for accessing both stack and register data in user-level code.

User-level stack

The ustack function, shown in the pid provider example, is a powerful tool for seeing how a particular point in the code was reached. This function accepts two optional parameters: nframes, the number of stack frames, or stack depth, to record, and strsize, the amount of string space to use for address-to-symbol translation. This second option is only used with Java Virtual Machines and is discussed in the following section, "Tracing Java Programs." The ustackframes dtrace option specifies the number of stack frames to record if nframes is omitted.

When the user-level stack data from ustack is being formatted, it is possible that dtrace will not be able to map the program addresses to the function symbol names. This happens if the process exits before the formatting takes place. In this case, the output will show the addresses only. If you run the program directly using the dtrace -p or -c options, then this situation does not occur. Otherwise, you can use dtrace to stop the process whose stack data you need, as the process is exiting. A procedure for handling this situation is described in the DTrace manual.

User-level registers

DTrace provides the uregs array, which can be used to access user-level register data. The elements in the array vary according to the hardware architecture of the system on which tracing is taking place. The DTrace manual lists the various elements by architecture.

Tracing Java programs

DTrace enables excellent observability into applications implemented in Java.

The jstack function

The ustack function can be used for tracing Java programs, but the jstack function, which is an alias to ustack, provides better results because the jstack function uses reasonable defaults for the nframes and strsize parameters. The strsize option is used to record the strings of the Java class and method names so that those symbolic names appear in the stack trace instead of the program addresses. This example shows a simple Java stack trace when the write system call is probed:

```
syscall::write:entry
/pid == $target/
{
        jstack();
        exit(0);
}
```

Running this to print the Java version string shows the stack trace:

```
# dtrace -s ex23.d -c "java -version"
dtrace: description 'syscall::write:entry' matched 1 probe
 ...
dtrace: pid 7596 has exited
dtrace: 1 jstack()/ustack() string table overflow
CPU     ID                  FUNCTION:NAME
  1     34                    write:entry
            libc.so.1`__write+0x7
            libjvm.so`__1cDhpiFwrite6FipkvI_I_+0xa0
            libjvm.so`JVM_Write+0x36
            libjava.so`writeBytes+0x154
            libjava.so`Java_java_io_FileOutputStream_writeBytes+0x3f
            java/io/FileOutputStream.writeBytes([BII)V
            java/io/FileOutputStream.write([BII)V
            java/io/BufferedOutputStream.flushBuffer()V
            java/io/BufferedOutputStream.flush()V
            java/io/PrintStream.write([BII)V
            sun/nio/cs/StreamEncoder.writeBytes()V
            sun/nio/cs/StreamEncoder.implFlushBuffer()V
            sun/nio/cs/StreamEncoder.flushBuffer()V
            java/io/OutputStreamWriter.flushBuffer()V
            java/io/PrintStream.write(Ljava/lang/String;)V
            java/io/PrintStream.print(Ljava/lang/String;)V
            java/io/PrintStream.println(Ljava/lang/String;)V
            sun
            0xfb202f0d
            0xfb200244
```

```
                 libjvm.so`__1cJJavaCallsLcall_helper6FpnJJavaValue
_pnMmethodHandle_pnRJavaCallArguments_pnGThread__v_+0x1a3
                 libjvm.so`__1cCosUos_exception_wrapper6FpFpnJJavaValue_
pnMmethodHandle_pnRJavaCallArguments_pnGThread__v2468_v_+0x27
                 libjvm.so`__1cJJavaCallsEcall6FpnJJavaValue_
nMmethodHandle_pnRJavaCallArguments_pnGThread__v_+0x2f
                 libjvm.so`__1cRjni_invoke_static6FpnHJNIEnv__
pnJJavaValue_pnI_jobject_nLJNICallType_pnK_jmethodID_pnSJNI_
ArgumentPusher_pnGThread__v_+0x1df
                 libjvm.so`jni_CallStaticVoidMethod+0x154
                 java`JavaMain+0x1d9
                 libc.so.1`_thr_setup+0x70
                 libc.so.1`_lwp_start
```

You might notice the "string table overflow" error message in this example. It means that the default `strsize` parameter to `jstack` did not provide enough space to record all of the symbolic names. Note also that some of the stack frames are only printed as hexadecimal addresses. This is due to the missing symbolic names. Passing an explicit `strsize` to `jstack`, as in the following example, enables the full stack to print, with all of the stack frames resolved to their Java class and method names:

```
jstack(50, 1000);
```

Depending on the complexity of your Java program, you may need to experiment with reasonable values for these parameters so that all of the stack data can be mapped.

hotspot probes

With Java 1.6 or later, DTrace probes have been integrated into the HotSpot Virtual Machine (VM). The `hotspot` provider includes probes for observing the VM itself, threads, class loading, garbage collection, method compilation, monitors, method execution, object allocation, and JNI calls. In all, there are approximately 500 probes delivered by the provider at the time of this writing. Because the monitor and method execution probes currently have an effect on the VM performance, these probes must be enabled with the `ExtendedDTraceProbes` flag on the VM. The rest of the probes do not require a runtime flag to be enabled. If needed, you can either start the VM with this flag or dynamically enable it on a running application using the `/usr/java/bin/jinfo` command.

To see the full list of `hotspot` probes, run the following command while a Java program is running so that the probes are loaded:

```
# dtrace -ln 'hotspot*:::'
   ID  PROVIDER       MODULE                  FUNCTION NAME
13152 hotspot29124    libjvm.so __1cTClassLoadingServiceTnotify_class_loade
d6FpnNinstanceKlass_b_v_ class-loaded
13153 hotspot29124    libjvm.so __1cTClassLoadingServiceVnotify_class_unloa
ded6FpnNinstanceKlass__v_ class-unloaded
13154 hotspot29124    libjvm.so __1cHnmethodbFpost_compiled_method_load_eve
nt6M_v_ compiled-method-load
   ...
```

For the method entry and return probes, Table 15-10 shows their argument values.

TABLE 15-10

Method Probe Arguments

Argument	Description
0	Java thread ID
1	Name of the method's class
2	Length of the class name, in bytes
3	Method name
4	Length of the method name, in bytes
5	String representing the method signature
6	Length of the signature, in bytes

The following simple D program uses the `method-entry` and `method-return` probes, along with the arguments from Table 15-10, to show how to trace Java method entry and return:

```
hotspot*:::method-entry
{
    printf("enter %4s.%s\n", stringof(copyin(arg1, arg2)),
        stringof(copyin(arg3, arg4)));
}

hotspot*:::method-return
{
    printf("return %4s.%s\n", stringof(copyin(arg1, arg2)),
        stringof(copyin(arg3, arg4)));
}
```

Running this program against a simple Java demo gives the following results:

```
# dtrace -qs ex27.d -c "java -XX:+ExtendedDTraceProbes demo"
got 9
enter java/lang/ref/Reference$ReferenceHandler.run
enter java/lang/ref/Reference.access$100
return java/lang/ref/Reference.access$100
enter java/lang/ref/Reference.access$200
return java/lang/ref/Reference.access$200
...
```

The example shows how the `ExtendedDTraceProbes` flag is passed to the VM so that the method entry and return probes are available. Using more sophisticated DTrace programs, you can gain a deep insight into the behavior of your Java applications.

For a complete list of the `hotspot` probes, along with their arguments, see `http://java.sun.com/javase/6/docs/technotes/guides/vm/dtrace.html`.

Tracing programs in other languages

One of the advantages of the open source nature of OpenSolaris is that other projects can extend and incorporate the code with their projects. This has been particularly true for DTrace, which has been extended to enable tracing of applications written in a variety of high-level languages. Using DTrace with these providers enables visibility into the software stack from the lowest to the highest levels.

Perl

Alan Burlison prototyped a provider for Perl. This is described at `http://xray.mpe.mpg.de/mailing-lists/perl5-porters/2005-08/msg00140.html` and at `http://blogs.sun.com/alanbur/entry/dtrace_and_perl`. Richard Dawe then built on this work and provided a Perl patch at `http://rich.phekda.org/perl-dtrace`. The probes are `sub-entry` and `sub-return`.

PHP

Wez Furlong implemented a provider for PHP as a pluggable extension. This work is described in Bryan Cantrill's blog at `http://blogs.sun.com/bmc/entry/dtrace_and_php` and `http://blogs.sun.com/bmc/entry/dtrace_and_php_demonstrated`. The probes are `function-entry` and `function-return`.

Python

John Levon added function entry and return tracing for Python. This work is described in his blog at `http://blogs.sun.com/levon/entry/python_and_dtrace_in_build`. The probes are `function-entry` and `function-return`. He also extended the `ustack` code so that user-level stack traces print correctly. This enhancement is integrated into the Python shipped with OpenSolaris.

Ruby and Ruby on Rails

Joyent has extended Ruby with probes. The project website is at `https://dtrace.joyent.com`. The following Ruby probes have been implemented: `function-entry`, `function-return`, `raise`, `rescue`, `line`, `gc-begin`, `gc-end`, `object-create-start`, `object-create-done`, `object-free`, and `ruby-probe`.

The following Rails probes have also been implemented: `request-start`, `request-done`, `query-start`, `query-done`, `render-start`, `render-done`, `db-start`, and `db-done`. The website provides downloads and documentation.

Others

There is a variety of other activity, including providers for JavaScript, the Bourne shell, and TCL. The DTrace unconference website at `http://wikis.sun.com/display/DTrace/dtrace.conf` provides an overview of some of the people and projects working with DTrace.

Resources

The DTrace community is at `http://opensolaris.org/os/community/dtrace`. This includes links to various projects, documentation, and discussions. DTrace is one of the most widely discussed components within OpenSolaris and many additional resources are available on the net. Bryan Cantrill, one of the creators of DTrace, has an active blog at `http://blogs.sun.com/bmc`. A simple search will also turn up many other good discussions and pages related to DTrace.

Bryan Cantrill, one of the authors of DTrace, has an excellent discussion of DTrace safety and the safety of system instrumentation in general on his blog, at `http://blogs.sun.com/bmc/entry/dtrace_safety`.

Within the source tree, the `dtrace` command is under `usr/src/cmd/dtrace`, and the libraries are under `usr/src/lib/libdtrace` and `usr/src/lib/libdtrace.jni`. The generic kernel components are under `usr/src/uts/common/sys/dtrace.h`, `usr/src/uts/common/sys/dtrace_impl.h`, `usr/src/uts/common/os/dtrace_subr.c`, `usr/src/common/dtrace`, and `usr/src/common/xen/dtrace`.

Platform-specific kernel components are under `usr/src/uts/sparc/dtrace`, `usr/src/uts/sun4/os/dtrace_subr.c`, `usr/src/uts/intel/dtrace`, and `usr/src/uts/i86pc/os/dtrace_subr.c`. The `fbt.c` function under the sparc or intel subdirectories contains the code for instrumenting kernel function boundary tracing.

The DTrace toolkit at `http://opensolaris.org/os/community/dtrace/dtracetoolkit` is an excellent resource that provides a large number of pre-built D programs that can be used to observe a variety of system behavior, including CPU, disk I/O, network I/O, memory, system analysis, and zones tracing. It also includes high-level language examples for Java, JavaScript, Perl, PHP, Python, Ruby, and TCL, as well as a variety of other examples. Extensive documentation is provided. These tools are not only useful in their own right, but also provide a good starting point for learning more about DTrace programming and for building your own programs. This toolkit is included as part of a standard OpenSolaris installation.

The Chime project at `http://opensolaris.org/os/project/dtrace-chime` has implemented a GUI for visualizing DTrace aggregations.

Solaris Performance and Tools by Richard McDougall, Jim Mauro, and Brendan Gregg (Prentice Hall, 2006) includes a discussion of DTrace.

Summary

This chapter provided an overview of the DTrace subsystem. DTrace is one of the key innovations in OpenSolaris. It enables you to achieve unprecedented insight into both systemwide and application-specific behavior. The basic syntax of DTrace programs was introduced, along with the `dtrace` command itself. Various examples illustrating how to refine your tracing to focus on specific issues were presented. Advanced techniques for speculative tracing, tracing during boot, and postmortem tracing were also introduced. Finally, an overview of the various capabilities for high-level language tracing was presented.

Chapter 16

Clustering OpenSolaris for High Availability

OpenSolaris is a solid, highly robust operating system. As described in Chapters 12 and 13, OpenSolaris contains considerable built-in support for reliability and availability in the form of predictive self-healing. Because of hardware and software failures, however, there are limits to the level of availability that a single physical machine can provide, regardless of the robustness of the underlying operating system. To increase the availability of your system beyond the capabilities of a single machine, you can cluster two or more machines together. This chapter describes the Open High Availability Cluster software that you can use to tightly couple multiple machines running OpenSolaris for augmented availability of the system as a whole.

Introduction to High-Availability Clusters

Before delving into the details of the Open High Availability (HA) Cluster software, it's helpful to understand why high availability is important, and why it sometimes makes sense to cluster for high availability.

First, downtime is costly. If you're using OpenSolaris only as a desktop or laptop operating system, you probably aren't too concerned with occasional downtime; but if you're using OpenSolaris to host services such as a web server, a database, or any other service to which clients connect, then obtaining as close as possible to 100 percent uptime is important. Even seconds of downtime are seconds during which no potential clients can access your services. For example, suppose you are running a website based on advertising revenue — when your site is down, no one is clicking on your ads, and you're not making any money.

Second, failures in computer systems are inevitable. In addition to the hardware and software failures discussed in Chapters 12 and 13, there are many other possibilities for failure, from a human tripping over a power cord or flipping the wrong switch, to a natural disaster such as a hurricane or earthquake, to terrorism. With a single physical system, most single points of failure are catastrophic. If your system loses power, its network card fails, or the operating system panics, then your services are no longer accessible. Many larger systems have redundancy in the form of multiple CPUs, multiple network adapters, and other redundant hardware components, but they still have many potential single points of failure — from the motherboard to the single operating system kernel.

High-availability clusters take hardware redundancy to the extreme by providing two or more completely redundant systems, thus avoiding any single points of failure. Cluster software monitors the system and automatically recovers from inevitable failures, minimizing downtime and cost.

Categories of Computer Clusters

Open HA Cluster is a high-availability cluster, which is a specific type of computer cluster. Other common types of computer clusters with which you might be familiar include grid clusters and high-performance computing clusters. Grid clusters, or parallel computing clusters, such as Sun Grid Engine and Beowulf, implement efficient batch queuing systems by distributing the work across many physical nodes. High-performance computing (HPC) clusters are a group of tightly coupled physical systems that work in tandem to provide supercomputing levels of throughput.

Overview of Open High Availability Cluster

Open HA Cluster is the open source code base for the Solaris Cluster enterprise product from Sun Microsystems. The source code and development community are hosted in the HA Clusters community group on OpenSolaris. The Open HA Cluster software tightly couples one or more physical machines running OpenSolaris to provide high availability for server applications. The software itself is tightly integrated with OpenSolaris, with about half the code running in the kernel and half in userland. The cluster uses off-the-shelf hardware; no specialized disks, interconnects, or other hardware is required. Figure 16-1 illustrates a typical cluster architecture.

FIGURE 16-1

A typical cluster architecture consists of two physical nodes with a private cluster interconnect and shared storage.

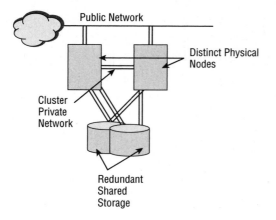

Cluster infrastructure

The Open HA Cluster infrastructure provides many capabilities for monitoring hardware and software components, detecting failures, and taking corrective action, including the following:

■ Frequent messages, called *heartbeats*, between machines to track the nodes currently participating in the cluster, called *cluster membership*, and to detect complete physical machine failures

■ Membership algorithm based on the concept of *quorum* to prevent a *split-brain* scenario, in which a network partition leaves two groups of cluster nodes up but unable to communicate with each other. With correctly configured quorum, only one of the partitions is allowed to continue as the "real" cluster; the machines in the other partition halt themselves.

■ Support for UFS and ZFS as *failover file systems*, whereby the file system is automatically mounted, or the zpool imported, on the node where it is needed

■ A *cluster file system* to provide POSIX-compliant access to shared data on a UFS file system simultaneously from multiple nodes of the cluster, even if the nodes are not physically connected to the storage device

■ *Disk fencing* to prevent machines from accessing shared storage after leaving the cluster

- Highly available network addresses, which are automatically configured on the host where they are needed so that the details of the cluster are transparent to the clients of the services that the cluster is hosting
- Support for volume management with Solaris Volume Manager (SVM) or ZFS
- Integration with OpenSolaris IP Network Multipathing (IPMP) to monitor network addresses and take corrective action when needed
- Disk path monitoring for detection of storage path failures
- Intelligent application monitoring through application-specific monitors
- Disaster recovery with Open HA Cluster Geographic Edition, which provides for a backup cluster at a great physical distance from the primary cluster

CROSS-REF Chapter 7 describes general storage concepts, UFS, and SVM. Chapter 8 covers ZFS. Chapter 9 describes IPMP.

With these capabilities, the cluster is able to quickly detect and recover from any single points of failure, and some double failures, at any of the hardware, operating system, application, and network levels.

Cluster agents

Open HA Cluster provides a general-purpose platform for making OpenSolaris applications highly available, but the cluster software itself is unaware of the specifics of the services it hosts. The cluster provides an abstraction for running a service, treating each specific service as a black box. The intelligence for each specific service takes the form of a cluster *agent*, also called a *data service*. An agent is the "glue" code between the cluster software and the application. The agent knows how to start, stop, and monitor the applications, as well as how to communicate with the cluster — for example, to order a service *failover* to another machine if a problem with the application is detected.

Highly available applications can run on the cluster in one of two modes: failover or scalable. A *failover service* runs on only one machine at a time. If that machine fails for any reason, the service is automatically started on a different machine of the cluster, as shown in Figure 16-2.

Conversely, a *scalable service* runs simultaneously on more than one node at a time, providing greater throughput for servicing client requests. The cluster software serves as a software load balancer between the hosts. If one of the nodes hosting the service fails, client traffic is automatically distributed among the remaining nodes, as shown in Figure 16-3.

Open HA Cluster includes agents for a variety of popular open-source services, including Apache Web Server, Apache Tomcat, PostgreSQL, MySQL, NFS, DNS, Grid Engine, Samba, DHCP, and Kerberos. You can also easily create an agent for other applications using one of several techniques described later in the section "Making Custom Services Highly Available."

FIGURE 16-2

A failover cluster service runs on one machine at a time.

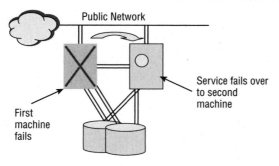

FIGURE 16-3

A scalable cluster service can run on more than one machine simultaneously.

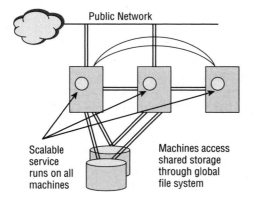

Setting Up a Cluster

Broadly speaking, there are two steps to setting up a cluster: configuring the hardware and installing the software.

Hardware requirements and configuration

Although it uses off-the-shelf hardware, Open HA Cluster has certain specific hardware requirements to provide high availability.

> **TIP** To avoid complex hardware configuration, such as shared storage, quorum devices, and cluster interconnects, start with a single-node cluster and use zones to emulate

physical nodes. While a single-node cluster won't provide high availability, it will help you gain familiarity with the cluster software. See the section "Zones as logical nodes" later in this chapter for details.

Nodes

A cluster consists of one or more physical machines, called *cluster nodes*, each with its own CPU, memory, local storage, and operating system kernel. The cluster supports up to 16 physical nodes and unlimited logical nodes.

CAUTION Cluster nodes must be homogenous in their architecture and OS version. That is, you can't create a cluster consisting of one x86 node and one SPARC node, or one machine running OpenSolaris and another running Solaris 10. Also, builds and patch levels should be the same, although the cluster software doesn't enforce that restriction.

Shared storage

Most server applications use data from disk storage. When running on a cluster, the application needs access to the storage from the node on which it's currently running. Thus, in addition to local storage for each node, your cluster will probably require shared storage accessible from any node. Because the global file system can make storage available even to nodes not directly connected to the storage device, you don't need your disk to be connected to each node of the cluster. However, you should use multihost disk devices, if possible, to connect any storage devices to at least two nodes. Otherwise, the single node to which your disk is connected is a single point of failure for that storage.

NOTE Quorum devices, described in the next section, must be directly connected to two or more nodes.

Furthermore, to protect against disk failures, use multiple disk devices to mirror your data, either with hardware RAID, Solaris Volume Manager (SVM), or RAID Z with ZFS.

In addition to directly connected SCSI devices, you can use storage area networks (SANs) or network-attached storage (NAS) devices with Open HA Cluster.

CROSS-REF Devices, SVM, and SAN are described in Chapter 7. ZFS is covered in Chapter 8.

Quorum device

Open HA Cluster uses the concept of *quorum* to continue running after node failures. As an example of quorum, consider a three-node cluster in which each node gets one vote. Quorum for this cluster would be two votes, so if any one node goes down, the other two nodes could continue to operate. However, this scheme breaks down with a two-node cluster. If each node in a two-node cluster gets one vote and two votes are required for quorum, then the cluster can't survive the loss of one of the nodes. That pretty much defeats the purpose of having a cluster.

If you are wondering why the cluster couldn't require a quorum of just one vote, the answer is that a network partition that left each node up but unable to communicate with the other node would allow each node individually to keep running as a cluster, possibly accessing the shared storage, not knowing the other node was doing the same. In a database application, that could cause severe data corruption.

The solution is to configure a third quorum vote from outside the cluster. Traditionally, in Open HA Cluster you do this with a SCSI device connected to both nodes of the cluster. This *quorum device* is given a tie-breaker vote. In a network partition, whichever node gets to the quorum device first gets the vote and excludes, or *fences out*, the other node by writing a reservation to the device.

NOTE   An active OpenSolaris effort called Project Colorado will, among other features, allow a two-node cluster to run in a *weak membership* mode without a quorum device. The weak membership will tolerate a network partition by allowing both partitions to remain operational. As of this writing, project Colorado is not complete.

An alternative to a physical quorum device is to use a software *quorum server* running on a third host outside the cluster.

Quorum devices are not restricted to two-node clusters. You can use them in larger clusters to provide higher availability in the case of multiple node failures. Consult the documentation for details.

CAUTION   Improper use of quorum devices can actually lead to lower availability. Make sure you follow recommended quorum guidelines.

Private cluster interconnect

Open HA Cluster requires dedicated interconnects between cluster nodes. Each cluster node must have at least one direct connection to each other cluster node. These interconnects require dedicated network adapters because they must not go through the public network. Interconnects are generally configured with switches to reduce the number of adapters and cables required.

NOTE   Project Colorado, mentioned earlier, will also permit private cluster traffic over the public network. Thus, a dedicated private physical interconnect will no longer be required, although it will still be recommended for higher performance and availability.

Although not required, it's highly recommended to configure redundant interconnects between nodes. Otherwise, the network adapter, switch, and cable are all potential single points of failure.

Public network

To provide any sort of useful service, the cluster nodes must be accessible from the public network as well. Each adapter providing service on the public network must be part of an IPMP group, but the IPMP group may contain only a single adapter if that's all you have available. However, multiple adapters in the IPMP group are recommended so that each adapter is not a potential single point of failure.

CROSS-REF   IPMP is covered in Chapter 9.

Local disk file system and partitioning

Beyond the disk space requirements for OpenSolaris, you need approximately 300MB of extra space in your root file system. If you configure /var, /usr, and /opt as separate file systems, you'll need approximately an additional 100MB in root, 100MB in /var, 50MB in /usr, and 50MB in /opt.

You also have the option of creating a separate disk partition for the cluster global devices. To do that, you must create a separate UFS file system of at least 512MB on each node mounted in /globaldevices before you install the cluster software. If you don't create this separate file system, Open HA Cluster will use lofi to mount global devices instead of a separate partition. The only downside of the lofi approach is slightly slower booting.

Here are example cluster-ready partitions using UFS, including a separate partition for the global devices, on a Sun Fire V240 (SPARC) node before the clustering software has been installed:

```
# cat /etc/vfstab
#device          device          mount           FS      fsck    mount   mount
#to mount        to fsck         point           type    pass    at boot options
#
fd       -       /dev/fd fd      -       no      -
/proc    -       /proc   proc    -       no      -
/dev/dsk/c1t0d0s1        -               swap    -       no      -
/dev/dsk/c1t0d0s0        /dev/rdsk/c1t0d0s0      /       ufs     1       no -
/dev/dsk/c1t0d0s3        /dev/rdsk/c1t0d0s3      /globaldevices  ufs     2 yes     -
/devices         -       /devices        devfs   -       no      -
sharefs  -       /etc/dfs/sharetab       sharefs -       no      -
ctfs     -       /system/contract        ctfs    -       no      -
objfs    -       /system/object  objfs   -       no      -
swap     -       /tmp    tmpfs   -       yes     -
# df -hl
Filesystem              size    used    avail capacity Mounted on
/dev/dsk/c1t0d0s0       62G     5.0G    57G     9%      /
/devices                0K      0K      0K      0%      /devices
/dev                    0K      0K      0K      0%      /dev
ctfs                    0K      0K      0K      0%      /system/contract
proc                    0K      0K      0K      0%      /proc
mnttab                  0K      0K      0K      0%      /etc/mnttab
swap                    4.5G    1.7M    4.5G    1%      /etc/svc/volatile
objfs                   0K      0K      0K      0%      /system/object
sharefs                 0K      0K      0K      0%      /etc/dfs/sharetab
```

```
/platform/sun4u-us3/lib/libc_psr/libc_psr_hwcap1.so.1
                        62G    5.0G    57G    9%    /platform/sun4u-us3/lib
/libc_psr.so.1
/platform/sun4u-us3/lib/sparcv9/libc_psr/libc_psr_hwcap1.so.1
                        62G    5.0G    57G    9%    /platform/sun4u-us3/lib
/sparcv9/libc_psr.so.1
fd                      OK     OK      OK     0%    /dev/fd
swap                    5.2G   744M    4.5G   14%   /tmp
swap                    4.5G   88K     4.5G   1%    /var/run
/dev/dsk/c1t0d0s3       997M   1.0M    936M   1%    /globaldevices
```

CROSS-REF Consult Chapter 7 for details on file systems and disk partitioning.

Installing the cluster software

As of this writing, the only binary release of Open HA Cluster is Solaris Cluster Express (SCX), which runs on Solaris Express. Project Colorado, mentioned earlier, will provide a binary distribution of Open HA Cluster on the OpenSolaris binary distribution; as of this writing, the results of that project are not yet available. Thus, this section explains how to install SCX on Solaris Express. The rest of this chapter, including configuring the cluster, applies to both SCX and Project Colorado.

TIP To check whether Open HA Cluster packages are available for the OpenSolaris binary distribution, use the `pkg search -r` command described in Chapters 3 and 6 to search for `clrg`.

Before installing SCX, you must download Solaris Express from the Sun Download Center (`http://sun.com/download/index.jsp`) and install it on each node of the hardware you set up in the previous section. (See Chapter 2 for details on Solaris Express).

CAUTION Each release of Solaris Cluster Express runs only on specific releases of Solaris Express. Check the documentation for the latest SCX to ensure that you install the correct Solaris Express release.

After installing Solaris Express on each node of your cluster, download Solaris Cluster Express from the Sun Download Center (`http://sun.com/download/index.jsp`) and unzip it somewhere handy, such as a network-mounted path accessible from all nodes, or in `/tmp` on each node of the cluster.

Run the interactive installer script in the `Solaris_<platform>` subdirectory of the unzipped installation image, where `<platform>` is either `sparc` or `x86`.

NOTE To run the installer, your working directory must be the directory in which the installer program lives:

```
# unzip -q clusterexpress-20080916-sparc.zip
# cd Solaris_sparc
# ./installer
```

Due to its length, the output from the installer is not shown. When you install the software yourself, simply answer the questions as you are prompted. It's easiest to install everything, including upgrading all the shared components.

Configuring the cluster

Once you've installed the cluster packages, you need to configure the software and set up a cluster. The following example shows the interactive use of the scinstall command to configure a two-node cluster of Sun Fire V240 (SPARC) nodes with SAN storage. The procedure is similar for x86 nodes and other forms of storage. Comments and explanations are interspersed.

Run scinstall from one of your cluster nodes only. This example runs it from the machine named dizzy:

```
# /usr/cluster/bin/scinstall


    *** Main Menu ***

    Please select from one of the following (*) options:

        * 1) Create a new cluster or add a cluster node
          2) Configure a cluster to be JumpStarted from this install server
          3) Manage a dual-partition upgrade
          4) Upgrade this cluster node
          5) Print release information for this cluster node

        * ?) Help with menu options
        * q) Quit

    Option:  1

    *** New Cluster and Cluster Node Menu ***

    Please select from any one of the following options:

          1) Create a new cluster
          2) Create just the first node of a new cluster on this machine
          3) Add this machine as a node in an existing cluster

          ?) Help with menu options
          q) Return to the Main Menu

    Option:  1

    *** Create a New Cluster ***


        This option creates and configures a new cluster.
```

You must use the Java Enterprise System (JES) installer to install the
Sun Cluster framework software on each machine in the new cluster
before you select this option.

If the "remote configuration" option is unselected from the JES
installer when you install the Sun Cluster framework on any of the new
nodes, then you must configure either the remote shell (see rsh(1)) or
the secure shell (see ssh(1)) before you select this option. If rsh or
ssh is used, you must enable root access to all of the new member
nodes from this node.

Press Control-d at any time to return to the Main Menu.

Do you want to continue (yes/no) [yes]? **yes**

NOTE To use the default remote configuration option, you must configure rpcbind on each
node to allow remote connections. See Chapter 11 for details on how to do that.
Alternatively, you can configure rsh or ssh on each node to allow root logins from the primary
node (the one on which you run the scinstall command). See Chapter 11 for details on ssh
configuration.

    >>> Typical or Custom Mode <<<

    This tool supports two modes of operation, Typical mode and Custom.
    For most clusters, you can use Typical mode. However, you might need
    to select the Custom mode option if not all of the Typical defaults
    can be applied to your cluster.

    For more information about the differences between Typical and Custom
    modes, select the Help option from the menu.

    Please select from one of the following options:

        1) Typical
        2) Custom

        ?) Help
        q) Return to the Main Menu

    Option [1]: <**enter**>

    >>> Cluster Name <<<

    Each cluster has a name assigned to it. The name can be made up of any
    characters other than whitespace. Each cluster name should be unique
    within the namespace of your enterprise.

    What is the name of the cluster you want to establish? **jazz**

```
>>> Cluster Nodes <<<

    This Sun Cluster release supports a total of up to 16 nodes.

    Please list the names of the other nodes planned for the initial
    cluster configuration. List one node name per line. When finished,
    type Control-D:

    Node name (Control-D to finish):  bird
    Node name (Control-D to finish):  ^D


    This is the complete list of nodes:

        dizzy
        bird

    Is it correct (yes/no) [yes]?  <enter>


    Attempting to contact "bird" ... done

    Searching for a remote configuration method ... done

    The Sun Cluster framework is able to complete the configuration
    process without remote shell access.


Press Enter to continue: <enter>

  >>> Cluster Transport Adapters and Cables <<<

    You must identify the cluster transport adapters which attach this
    node to the private cluster interconnect.

    Select the first cluster transport adapter for "dizzy":

        1) bge1
        2) bge2
        3) bge3
        4) ce0
        5) ce1
        6) ce2
        7) ce3
        8) Other

    Option:  1

    Will this be a dedicated cluster transport adapter (yes/no) [yes]? <enter>
```

```
Searching for any unexpected network traffic on "bge1" ... done
Verification completed. No traffic was detected over a 10 second
sample period.

Select the second cluster transport adapter for "dizzy":

        1) bge1
        2) bge2
        3) bge3
        4) ce0
        5) ce1
        6) ce2
        7) ce3
        8) Other

Option:  5

Will this be a dedicated cluster transport adapter (yes/no) [yes]? <enter>

Searching for any unexpected network traffic on "ce1" ... done
Verification completed. No traffic was detected over a 10 second
sample period.

Plumbing network address 172.16.0.0 on adapter bge1 >> NOT DUPLICATE ... done
Plumbing network address 172.16.0.0 on adapter ce1 >> NOT DUPLICATE ... done
```

The cluster host IP address itself is configured on bge0, so that does not appear as an option for the private interconnect. Note that the cluster automatically detects the switches and adapters on the second node to which the adapters on the first node are cabled.

```
>>> Quorum Configuration <<<

Every two-node cluster requires at least one quorum device. By
default, scinstall selects and configures a shared disk quorum device
for you.

This screen allows you to disable the automatic selection and
configuration of a quorum device.

You have chosen to turn on the global fencing. If your shared storage
devices do not support SCSI, such as Serial Advanced Technology
Attachment (SATA) disks, or if your shared disks do not support
SCSI-2, you must disable this feature.

If you disable automatic quorum device selection now, or if you intend
to use a quorum device that is not a shared disk, you must instead use
```

```
clsetup(1M) to manually configure quorum once both nodes have joined
the cluster for the first time.

Do you want to disable automatic quorum device selection (yes/no) [no]?  <enter>
```

In addition to SCSI disks, you can use a software quorum server and some NAS devices for quorum.

```
Is it okay to create the new cluster (yes/no) [yes]?  <enter>

During the cluster creation process, sccheck is run on each of the new
cluster nodes. If sccheck detects problems, you can either interrupt
the process or check the log files after the cluster has been
established.

Interrupt cluster creation for sccheck errors (yes/no) [no]?  <enter>
```

The sccheck command is described in more detail later, in the section "Advanced Cluster Administration."

```
Cluster Creation

Log file - /var/cluster/logs/install/scinstall.log.7865

Testing for "/globaldevices" on "dizzy" ... done
Testing for "/globaldevices" on "bird" ... done

Starting discovery of the cluster transport configuration.

The following connections were discovered:

    dizzy:bge1   switch1   bird:bge1
    dizzy:ce1    switch2   bird:ce1

Completed discovery of the cluster transport configuration.

Started sccheck on "dizzy".
Started sccheck on "bird".

sccheck completed with no errors or warnings for "dizzy".
sccheck completed with no errors or warnings for "bird".


Configuring "bird" ... done
Rebooting "bird" ... done

Configuring "dizzy" ... done
Rebooting "dizzy" ...
```

```
Log file - /var/cluster/logs/install/scinstall.log.7865
```

```
Rebooting ...
```

After completing the configuration, `scinstall` automatically reboots both of the cluster nodes, which reboot in cluster mode and form a cluster.

> **TIP** You can also use Solaris JumpStart to install and configure a cluster. See the *Sun Cluster Installation Guide* listed in the "Resources" section for details.

Using the Cluster

The purpose of a high-availability cluster is to provide just that: high availability of services, such as Apache, DNS, NFS, MySQL, or any other service to which clients can connect. As mentioned earlier, Open HA Cluster contains built-in support for many common services. The best way to become familiar with the capabilities of the cluster software is to dive in with some examples.

The first example shows how to make Apache Web Server highly available (HA) in failover mode using a ZFS failover file system to provide access to the data to be served from any of the nodes in the cluster.

Apache Web Server can also be hosted in a scalable mode. The second example shows Apache in scalable mode using the global file system to provide simultaneous access to the shared data from all nodes in the cluster.

Managing services

Before diving into the examples, however, you should understand the concepts that Open HA Cluster uses to manage services. This section provides an overview of service management; more details can be found in the "Advanced Cluster Administration" section later in the chapter.

Every service that the cluster manages is called a *resource*. A resource can be an application, such as Apache Web Server, a network address, a file system, or anything else that can be started and stopped (loosely speaking) on a cluster node.

> **NOTE** The concept of a "resource" in Open HA Cluster is unrelated to the Resource Management features described in Chapter 18.

Each resource on the cluster is managed by a *cluster agent*, also called a *data service*. The agent is responsible for several tasks:

- Starting the resource: For an application, this usually means running a start script or starting a daemon directly.

- Stopping the resource
- Monitoring the resource: The monitoring is specific to the resource. For example, the Apache monitor periodically connects to the port on which the Apache Web Server is listening and issues an HTTP request to verify that Apache is functioning correctly.
- Storing properties of the resource

This agent is represented in the cluster as a *resource type*. Each resource is an instantiation of a resource type. You can have more than one resource of the same resource type simultaneously. If you're familiar with object-oriented programming, think of the resource type as the class, and the resource as the object instantiated from that class.

NOTE   The resource type in Open HA Cluster is similar to an SMF manifest, in that it defines the service. Although the two are not related, you can make an SMF service highly available with the SMF Proxy Resource Type described later in this chapter in the section "Making Custom Services Highly Available."

Resources are grouped together in resource groups, which are the basic unit of failover on the cluster. Resource groups, rather than individual resources, are brought online and offline on various nodes. A resource group that is online on a node is providing services on that node. Usually, when a resource group is online, resources inside that group are online. However, if a resource inside that group is disabled, its dependencies are not met, or it experiences a failure, then it could be offline or faulted while its containing resource group is online.

Failover services are run in failover resource groups. A failover resource group is configured with a list of possible hosts in its `nodelist` property. If the node on which it is running fails or a resource within the resource group fails, the resource group can be stopped on that node and started on a different node in the `nodelist`. You specify the nodes that can host the service in order in the nodelist. For a failover service, the first node is the primary, and others are *secondaries*, or *spares*.

A scalable service runs in a scalable resource group, which runs on one or more nodes in its `nodelist` simultaneously.

Making Apache highly available

Now that you've installed and configured your cluster and learned how the cluster manages services, it's finally time to run a service. The Apache web server is a good service to start with because of its ubiquity and simplicity. Apache basically serves files to clients that connect using the Hypertext Transfer Protocol (HTTP), usually from a web browser such as Mozilla Firefox.

CROSS-REF   Chapter 23 describes Apache configuration on OpenSolaris in more detail.

Making Apache HA requires three steps: configuring storage, configuring networking, and configuring Apache itself.

Configuring failover storage

The Apache service must have access to the files that it's serving from any node on which it's running. You have several options for the type of file system to use. This example demonstrates how to make a ZFS zpool highly available. First, configure a ZFS failover zpool for the files that Apache will serve. The zpool should be on a device or devices accessible from both nodes. You can put the zpool under cluster control as an Open HA Cluster resource so that it will be available on whatever node Apache is running.

Creating a zpool

Open HA Cluster needs a consistent way to refer to devices across different nodes, but because multihost devices can show up with different names on different nodes of the cluster to which they are connected, the local names, such as `c1t2d3s4`, cannot be used. Instead, the cluster manages shared devices with a Device ID (DID) pseudo-device driver, automatically assigning clusterwide unique IDs to each device path.

CROSS-REF ZFS zpools are covered in Chapter 8. Device IDs are described in Chapter 7. Pseudo-device drivers are introduced in Chapter 5.

These IDs can be found in `/dev/did/dsk` and `/dev/did/rdsk` on each cluster node, or listed with the `/usr/cluster/bin/cldevice` command. Use these IDs instead of the ones in `/dev/dsk` and `/dev/rdsk`, respectively, when creating failover file systems.

NOTE ZFS import can find zpools even if the device names are different on different nodes, so when using ZFS for failover file systems, you don't technically need to refer to the devices using the `/dev/did` namespace. However, this example uses `/dev/did` for consistency.

First, use the `cldevice` command on any node of the cluster to find a device:

```
# /usr/cluster/bin/cldevice list -v
DID Device          Full Device Path
----------          ----------------
d1                  bird:/dev/rdsk/c1t1d0
d2                  bird:/dev/rdsk/c1t0d0
d3                  bird:/dev/rdsk/c4t600C0FF000000000092AFF2DEE5F9607d0
d3                  dizzy:/dev/rdsk/c4t600C0FF000000000092AFF2DEE5F9607d0
d4                  bird:/dev/rdsk/c4t600C0FF000000000092AFF2DEE5F9608d0
d4                  dizzy:/dev/rdsk/c4t600C0FF000000000092AFF2DEE5F9608d0
d5                  bird:/dev/rdsk/c4t600C0FF000000000092AFF2DEE5F9609d0
d5                  dizzy:/dev/rdsk/c4t600C0FF000000000092AFF2DEE5F9609d0
d6                  bird:/dev/rdsk/c4t600C0FF000000000092AFF2DEE5F960Ad0
d6                  dizzy:/dev/rdsk/c4t600C0FF000000000092AFF2DEE5F960Ad0
d7                  bird:/dev/rdsk/c4t600C0FF000000000092AFF2DEE5F960Bd0
d7                  dizzy:/dev/rdsk/c4t600C0FF000000000092AFF2DEE5F960Bd0
d8                  bird:/dev/rdsk/c4t600C0FF000000000092AFF2DEE5F960Cd0
d8                  dizzy:/dev/rdsk/c4t600C0FF000000000092AFF2DEE5F960Cd0
d9                  bird:/dev/rdsk/c4t600C0FF000000000092AFF2DEE5F960Dd0
d9                  dizzy:/dev/rdsk/c4t600C0FF000000000092AFF2DEE5F960Dd0
```

```
d10                     bird:/dev/rdsk/c4t600C0FF000000000092AFF00C5B5D707d0
d10                     dizzy:/dev/rdsk/c4t600C0FF000000000092AFF00C5B5D707d0
d11                     bird:/dev/rdsk/c4t600C0FF000000000092AFF00C5B5D708d0
d11                     dizzy:/dev/rdsk/c4t600C0FF000000000092AFF00C5B5D708d0
d12                     bird:/dev/rdsk/c4t600C0FF000000000092AFF00C5B5D709d0
d12                     dizzy:/dev/rdsk/c4t600C0FF000000000092AFF00C5B5D709d0
d13                     bird:/dev/rdsk/c4t600C0FF000000000092AFF00C5B5D70Ad0
d13                     dizzy:/dev/rdsk/c4t600C0FF000000000092AFF00C5B5D70Ad0
d14                     bird:/dev/rdsk/c4t600C0FF000000000092AFF00C5B5D70Bd0
d14                     dizzy:/dev/rdsk/c4t600C0FF000000000092AFF00C5B5D70Bd0
d15                     bird:/dev/rdsk/c4t600C0FF000000000092AFF00C5B5D70Cd0
d15                     dizzy:/dev/rdsk/c4t600C0FF000000000092AFF00C5B5D70Cd0
d16                     bird:/dev/rdsk/c4t600C0FF000000000092AFF00C5B5D70Dd0
d16                     dizzy:/dev/rdsk/c4t600C0FF000000000092AFF00C5B5D70Dd0
d17                     dizzy:/dev/rdsk/c1t1d0
d18                     dizzy:/dev/rdsk/c1t0d0
```

CAUTION   Don't create a zpool using a configured quorum disk because ZFS will relabel the quorum disk with EFI labeling, destroying the quorum information.

To find out which devices (and nodes) are used for quorum, run the `/usr/cluster/bin/clquorum` command on any node of the cluster:

```
# /usr/cluster/bin/clquorum list
d3
bird
dizzy
```

For the zpool, this example uses the pseudo-device d14, which corresponds to `/dev/rdsk/c4t600C0FF000000000092AFF00C5B5D70Bd0`.

Finally, create the zpool using the block device from the DID pseudo-device driver. Run this command on any one node of the cluster to which the shared storage is connected:

```
# zpool create azp /dev/did/dsk/d14
```

TIP   For greater availability, use a RAID Z zpool or mirror your zpool across at least two devices to avoid a single point of storage failure. See Chapter 8 for details on RAID Z and ZFS mirroring.

Making the zpool highly available

Next, configure the cluster to manage the `azp` zpool as a resource using the `HAStoragePlus` resource type. This resource type will import the zpool on whichever node it is online, thus making it available for the Apache service on that node. Run the commands in this section on only one node of the cluster.

First, create the resource group that will contain the failover file system resource (and later the Apache resource as well). clrg is a shorthand form of the clresourcegroup command:

```
# /usr/cluster/bin/clrg create apache-rg
```

> **TIP** The Open HA Cluster commands are in the /usr/cluster/bin directory. You may want to add that directory to your path.

Next, register the HAStoragePlus resource type and create a resource of that type named azp-rs, specifying one *property*: the zpool you created in the previous section (the Zpools property):

```
# /usr/cluster/bin/clrt register HAStoragePlus
# /usr/cluster/bin/clrs create -g apache-rg -t HAStoragePlus -p Zpools=azp\
azp-rs
```

Now you can bring the resource group online and check its status:

```
# /usr/cluster/bin/clrg online -M apache-rg
# /usr/cluster/bin/clrg status

=== Cluster Resource Groups ===

Group Name     Node Name     Suspended     Status
----------     ---------     ---------     ------
apache-rg      bird          No            Online
               dizzy         No            Offline
```

Note that the resource group is online on node bird, and offline on node dizzy. Thus, you should be able to access the zpool from bird, but not from dizzy:

```
bird# hostname
bird
bird# zpool status
  pool: azp
 state: ONLINE
 scrub: none requested
config:

        NAME                                       STATE     READ WRITE CKSUM
        azp                                        ONLINE       0     0     0
          c4t600C0FF000000000092AFF00C5B5D70Bd0    ONLINE       0     0     0

errors: No known data errors
```

So far, so good. Now try it from the other node:

```
dizzy# hostname
dizzy
```

```
dizzy# zpool status
no pools available
```

As expected, you can't access it from dizzy. If you switch the resource group to dizzy, you can then access the file system from that node. To switch the resource group, use the switch -n option to /usr/cluster/bin/clrg:

```
# /usr/cluster/bin/clrg switch -n dizzy apache-rg
# /usr/cluster/bin/clrg status

=== Cluster Resource Groups ===

Group Name        Node Name        Suspended        Status
----------        ---------        ---------        ------
apache-rg         bird             No               Offline
                  dizzy            No               Online

dizzy# hostname
dizzy
dizzy# zpool status
  pool: azp
 state: ONLINE
 scrub: none requested
config:

        NAME                                     STATE    READ WRITE CKSUM
        azp                                      ONLINE      0     0     0
          c4t600C0FF000000000092AFF00C5B5D70Bd0  ONLINE      0     0     0

errors: No known data errors
```

Configuring Apache to use the highly available zpool

Now that your failover file system is working, you need to create your htdocs directory on it and tell Apache to look there instead of its default location.

First, create a new ZFS file system for htdocs and populate it with some test data. Run these commands on the node of the cluster that is currently hosting the storage resource you created in the previous section:

```
# zfs create azp/htdocs
# echo "hello, world" > /azp/htdocs/index.html
# chgrp bin /azp/htdocs/index.html
```

Now, on each node of the cluster, change the Apache configuration file, /etc/apache2/2.2/httpd.conf, to look for htdocs in /azp. The DocumentRoot entry in the file should look like this:

```
DocumentRoot "/azp/htdocs"
```

The first line of the Directory entry should look like this:

```
#
# This should be changed to whatever you set DocumentRoot to.
#
<Directory "/azp/htdocs">
```

If you use CGI scripts, you need to change the ScriptAlias entry in httpd.conf as well.

NOTE To avoid keeping redundant copies of the httpd.conf file on each node, you could put one copy on the failover file system and tell Apache to look there. However, that requires modifying the apachectl script, so this example avoids it.

You could also put the Apache binaries themselves on the failover file system instead of storing them on the local file system of each node, but because they're installed by default on OpenSolaris, you might as well use the local copies.

Test the configuration on the node of the cluster that is currently hosting the apache-rg resource group, so that Apache has access to the zpool. First, make sure Apache starts:

```
# pgrep http
# /usr/apache2/2.2/bin/apachectl start
# pgrep http
2880
2882
2881
2883
2884
2885
2886
```

You can test it using the wget utility. By default, the httpd.conf file specifies that Apache should bind to the localhost address, so you need to test it from the local node (in this case, dizzy):

```
dizzy$ /usr/sfw/bin/wget -q localhost
dizzy$ cat index.html
hello, world
```

Remember to stop Apache after you've tested it:

```
# /usr/apache2/2.2/bin/apachectl stop
```

Now you can switch over the apache-rg resource group to bird so that the zpool is imported on that node and tested on bird. Use the switch -n option to /usr/cluster/bin/clrg:

```
# /usr/cluster/bin/clrg switch -n bird apache-rg
```

If you try to run Apache with this configuration on a node that's not hosting apache-rg, you'll see the following error:

```
# /usr/apache2/2.2/bin/apachectl start
```

595

```
Syntax error on line 106 of /etc/apache2/2.2/httpd.conf:
DocumentRoot must be a directory
```

Configuring logical hostname networking

In order for clients to access the Apache service, it must be available at a specific hostname, which maps to a specific IP address. Clients should be able to use a single hostname regardless of the node in the cluster on which Apache is running at any given time.

Open HA Cluster implements this requirement with a *logical hostname*. The hostname is managed as a cluster resource, and the IP address to which it maps is automatically configured on the node on which the resource is online. This way, the cluster details are hidden from clients, and the cluster appears to clients as a single system. Regardless of the node on which the service is running, clients can connect to the service via the logical hostname.

> **CAUTION**   When configuring your services on the cluster, publicize only the logical hostname, not the physical hostnames of the machines. If clients connect to a physical hostname, they won't be able to access the service if it fails over to another node.

To configure a logical hostname, first pick a hostname and IP address and add it to your DNS mappings. This example uses coltrane, which maps to IP address 10.11.157.87. Note that the IP address must be in a subnet that is configured on an existing IPMP group on your cluster nodes.

Next, use the clreslogicalhostname command to add a logical hostname resource in the apache-rg resource group that you created in the previous section:

```
# /usr/cluster/bin/clreslogicalhostname create -g apache-rg -h coltrane\
  coltrane-rs
```

> **NOTE**   You might see warnings like the following from clreslogicalhostname if you haven't added coltrane to your local network mappings:

```
bird - Could not find a mapping for coltrane in /etc/inet/ipnodes or
      /etc/inet/hosts. It is recommended that a mapping for coltrane be
      added to /etc/inet/ipnodes.
dizzy - Could not find a mapping for coltrane in /etc/inet/ipnodes or
      /etc/inet/hosts. It is recommended that a mapping for coltrane be
      added to /etc/inet/ipnodes.
```

You should add the hostname/IP information in /etc/inet/hosts **in case DNS is down, and configure the subnet in** /etc/inet/netmasks.

Because you added the new resource to a resource group that was already online, it immediately starts up. You can see the result using ifconfig on the node hosting the resource group:

```
# ifconfig -a
...
```

```
bge0: flags=209000843<UP,BROADCAST,RUNNING,MULTICAST,IPv4,NOFAILOVER,CoS>
mtu 1500 index 2
        inet 10.11.157.82 netmask ffffff00 broadcast 10.11.157.255
        groupname sc_ipmp0
        ether 0:14:4f:4d:58:e5
bge0:1: flags=201040843<UP,BROADCAST,RUNNING,MULTICAST,DEPRECATED,IPv4,CoS>
mtu 1500 index 2
        inet 10.11.157.87 netmask ffffff00 broadcast 10.11.157.255
...
```

As you can see, the logical hostname resource has configured IP address 10.11.157.87 (coltrane) as a logical interface on the bge0 adapter to add a separate flow on the physical adapter.

CROSS-REF Chapter 9 covers networking, including interfaces, adapters, DNS, and ifconfig.

One convenient feature of Open HA Cluster logical hostnames is that they automatically configure IPMP, if possible. As shown in the preceding ifconfig output, there's an IPMP group configured for bge0. The cluster software configured this group at configuration time. You can see the details with scstat -i:

```
# /usr/cluster/bin/scstat -i

-- IPMP Groups --

                Node Name        Group    Status      Adapter   Status
                ---------        -----    ------      -------   ------
    IPMP Group: bird             sc_ipmp0 Online      bge0      Online

    IPMP Group: dizzy            sc_ipmp0 Online      bge0      Online
```

Because there was only one adapter in this subnet, the IPMP group contains only the bge0 adapter. If there were other adapters in the subnet, the cluster software would have added those to the group.

When you create a logical hostname, the cluster software puts it in whatever IPMP group is available — in this case, sc_ipmp0.

The final change you need to make to use the logical hostname is to change the ServerName to coltrane in the /etc/apache2/2.2/httpd.conf file on each node:

```
# grep ServerName httpd.conf
# ServerName gives the name and port that the server uses to identify itself.
ServerName coltrane
```

Configuring failover Apache

Now that you've set up the storage and networking, adding the Apache resource itself is the easy part. First, register the resource type:

```
# /usr/cluster/bin/clrt register apache
```

Next, create the `apache` resource. You must specify a few properties with `-p`, including the directory containing the Apache binaries and the port on which it will listen. You also need to specify that the `apache` resource depends on both the `HAStoragePlus` resource, `azp-rs`, and the logical hostname resource, `coltrane-rs`. The `HAStoragePlus` dependency ensures that the cluster framework will always import the zpool on a node before starting the Apache daemon, and will always stop the Apache daemon before exporting the zpool. Similarly, the logical hostname dependency tells the cluster framework that this `apache` resource depends on the `coltrane-rs` logical hostname. Thus, the cluster will always configure the interface on a node before starting the Apache daemon, and will always stop the Apache daemon before unconfiguring the logical hostname:

```
# /usr/cluster/bin/clrs create -g apache-rg -t apache -p Bin_dir=/usr/apache2/2.2/bin\
  -p Port_list=80/tcp -p Resource_dependencies=azp-rs,coltrane-rs apache-rs
```

Because the `apache-rg` resource group is already online, the `apache` resource that you create will start automatically. When the `apache` resource comes online, it starts the Apache daemon.

> **NOTE** Because of the dependency of the `apache-rs` resource on the `azp-rs` HAStoragePlus failover file system resource, the `apache` resource type attempts to validate that the file system is really available. Thus, the `azp-rs` resource must be online on one of the nodes when you create the `apache-rs` resource.

Verify the status with `clrg` and `clrs`:

```
# /usr/cluster/bin/clrg status

=== Cluster Resource Groups ===

Group Name      Node Name     Suspended     Status
----------      ---------     ---------     ------
apache-rg       bird          No            Online
                dizzy         No            Offline

# /usr/cluster/bin/clrs status

=== Cluster Resources ===

Resource Name    Node Name     State       Status Message
-------------    ---------     -----       --------------
azp-rs           bird          Online      Online
                 dizzy         Offline     Offline
```

```
coltrane-rs        bird          Online       Online - LogicalHostname online.
                   dizzy         Offline      Offline

apache-rs          bird          Online       Online - Completed successfully.
                   dizzy         Offline      Offline

# /usr/cluster/bin/clrs show

=== Resources ===

Resource:                                     azp-rs
  Type:                                       SUNW.HAStoragePlus:6
  Type_version:                               6
  Group:                                      apache-rg
  R_description:
  Resource_project_name:                      default
  Enabled{bird}:                              True
  Enabled{dizzy}:                             True
  Monitored{bird}:                            True
  Monitored{dizzy}:                           True

Resource:                                     coltrane-rs
  Type:                                       SUNW.LogicalHostname:2
  Type_version:                               2
  Group:                                      apache-rg
  R_description:
  Resource_project_name:                      default
  Enabled{bird}:                              True
  Enabled{dizzy}:                             True
  Monitored{bird}:                            True
  Monitored{dizzy}:                           True

Resource:                                     apache-rs
  Type:                                       SUNW.apache:4.1
  Type_version:                               4.1
  Group:                                      apache-rg
  R_description:
  Resource_project_name:                      default
  Enabled{bird}:                              True
  Enabled{dizzy}:                             True
  Monitored{bird}:                            True
  Monitored{dizzy}:                           True
```

Now the Apache daemon is running on node bird. You can verify it with wget from any machine that can resolve the coltrane hostname:

```
$ /usr/sfw/bin/wget -q coltrane
```

```
$ more index.html
hello, world
```

The apache resource type monitors the Apache daemon at the process level, the logical hostname resource type monitors the network, the HAStoragePlus resource type monitors the storage, and the cluster infrastructure tracks the health of the node as a whole. You might want to try out various failure scenarios, such as killing the httpd processes, unplugging the public network cable, and halting the entire node. The cluster can recover from all those failures and quickly bring the service back online on the same node or on the other node in the cluster.

Making Apache scalable

The previous example showed how you can make the Apache web server highly available on Open HA Cluster. In that example, Apache ran on only one node at a time, but there's usually no reason why Apache can't run on multiple nodes simultaneously to increase the throughput.

Recall that configuring a service to run in scalable mode consists of three steps: configuring storage, configuring networking, and configuring Apache itself.

CAUTION If you created a failover apache resource group in the previous example, disable and unmanage it before proceeding with this example:

```
# /usr/cluster/bin/clrs list
azp-rs
coltrane-rs
apache-rs
# /usr/cluster/bin/clrs disable azp-rs coltrane-rs apache-rs
# /usr/cluster/bin/clrg offline apache-rg
# /usr/cluster/bin/clrg unmanage apache-rg
```

Configuring global storage

Because scalable Apache will run on both nodes of the cluster simultaneously, both nodes must have access at all times to the htdocs directory. Thus, you can't use the same failover file system as in the previous example. Instead, you can use the *cluster file system* (CFS), also called the *global file system* (GFS) or the *proxy file system* (PxFS).

NOTE Because NFS, described in Chapter 10, is a network file system, you might be wondering why you can't use it instead of the cluster file system. The answer is that NFS was not designed as a cluster file system, and its implementation exhibits problems when the same machine is both a client and a server of the same file system.

Creating a global file system

As the name proxy file system implies, the cluster file system is layered on top of a local file system such as UFS. (Note that the cluster file system cannot run on top of ZFS.) Therefore, to use the cluster file system, you first create a standard UFS file system on a device in the *global namespace*. The global namespace, found in /dev/global/dsk and /dev/global/rdsk, includes the DID pseudo-device names discussed earlier, plus any volumes created on top of those pseudo-devices. The main difference between the /dev/global namespace and the /dev/did namespace is that the global names are valid on any node of the cluster, even on hosts to which the storage is not directly connected.

NOTE /dev/global **is actually a symbolic link to** /global/.devices/node@<node number>/dev/global.

Your first step in configuring a cluster file system is to create a new file system on one of the devices in /dev/global:

```
# newfs /dev/global/rdsk/d15
newfs: construct a new file system /dev/global/rdsk/d15: (y/n)? y
/dev/global/rdsk/d15:   12288 sectors in 2 cylinders of 48 tracks, 128 sectors
        6.0MB in 1 cyl groups (13 c/g, 39.00MB/g, 18624 i/g)
super-block backups (for fsck -F ufs -o b=#) at:
 32,
```

Note again that you specify the device using /dev/global/rdsk, rather than /dev/rdsk or /dev/did/rdsk.

TIP For increased availability, use the Solaris Volume Manager (SVM) with redundancy across multiple physical devices underneath the file system. For simplicity, this example omits the Volume Manager.

On each node in the cluster, create the mount point. It's customary to mount global file systems in /global:

```
# mkdir -p /global/adata
```

Next, add the following entry to /etc/vfstab on each node so that the file system is mounted automatically at boot time. Note the global option, and the use of /dev/global for the devices:

```
/dev/global/dsk/d15    /dev/global/rdsk/d15    /global/adata    ufs    2    yes
    global,logging
```

Finally, on one of the nodes, issue a mount command to mount the file system. You can omit the device and global option in the mount command because of the /etc/vfstab entry:

```
# mount /global/adata
```

Running the mount on any cluster node mounts the file system on all nodes of the cluster.

Configuring Apache to use the cluster file system

Now that you have a file system accessible from all nodes of the cluster simultaneously, you need to set up your htdocs directory and configure Apache to use it.

On one node of the cluster, create the directory and populate it:

```
# mkdir /global/adata/htdocs
# chgrp bin /global/adata/htdocs
# echo "hello, world, from cluster file system" >\
 /global/adata/htdocs/index.html
# chgrp bin /global/adata/htdocs/index.html
```

On each node of the cluster, change the htdocs entry in /etc/apache2/2.2/httpd.conf to point to the htdocs directory on the global file system:

```
DocumentRoot "/global/adata/htdocs"
```

Don't forget to change the Directory entry in /etc/apache2/2.2/httpd.conf as well:

```
<Directory "/global/adata/htdocs">
```

Finally, for testing purposes, change the ServerName back to localhost:

```
# ServerName gives the name and port that the server uses to identify itself.
ServerName 127.0.0.1
```

Verify that Apache can start and serve files from the global file system:

```
# pgrep http
# /usr/apache2/2.2/bin/apachectl start
# pgrep http
29273
29276
29275
29274
29277
29278
29279
dizzy$ /usr/sfw/bin/wget -q localhost
dizzy$ cat index.html
hello, world, from cluster file system
```

Don't forget to stop Apache when you've completed your tests:

```
# /usr/apache2/2.2/bin/apachectl stop
```

Repeat the test on the second node of the cluster. Unlike the previous example, there's no need to switch over a resource group to test the second node.

Configuring scalable networking

With failover Apache, the service was online on only one node at a time, and all network traffic from clients could be directed to that one node. With scalable Apache, however, you want traffic to be load-balanced across all the nodes hosting the service. Open HA Cluster provides this functionality with a *shared address*. The shared address manages a hostname as a resource. When the resource starts on a node, the address is configured on an adapter on that node, just like a logical hostname. However, the cluster networking kernel module intercepts traffic to this IP address and distributes it around the cluster based on the load-balancing policy in effect. In order for applications on the other nodes to bind to that address, the address is configured on the loopback adapter of those nodes.

CROSS-REF Loopback adapters and other networking topics are covered in Chapter 9.

To create a shared address resource, you again need to find a hostname registered with DNS. This example uses `miles`, which maps to IP address `10.11.157.85`.

First, create a resource group to hold the shared address. Unlike with failover Apache, the network resource will go in a different resource group than the Apache resource itself because the network resource needs to run on only one node at a time, whereas the Apache service will run on all nodes simultaneously:

```
# /usr/cluster/bin/clrg create apache-sa
```

Next, add the shared address resource:

```
# /usr/cluster/bin/clressharedaddress create -g apache-sa -h miles miles-rs
```

Finally, bring the resource group online and verify its status:

```
# /usr/cluster/bin/clrg online -M apache-sa
# /usr/cluster/bin/clrg status apache-sa

=== Cluster Resource Groups ===

Group Name      Node Name      Suspended      Status
----------      ---------      ---------      ------
apache-sa       bird           No             Online
                dizzy          No             Offline
```

The resource group is online on node `bird`. As shown in the `ifconfig` output on that node, the address is configured as a logical interface on the `bge0` adapter:

```
# ifconfig -a
...
bge0: flags=209000843<UP,BROADCAST,RUNNING,MULTICAST,IPv4,NOFAILOVER,CoS>
 mtu 1500 index 2
        inet 10.11.157.82 netmask ffffff00 broadcast 10.11.157.255
        groupname sc_ipmp0
        ether 0:14:4f:4d:58:e5
bge0:1: flags=201040843<UP,BROADCAST,RUNNING,MULTICAST,DEPRECATED,IPv4,CoS>
 mtu 1500 index 2
        inet 10.11.157.85 netmask ffffff00 broadcast 10.11.157.255
...
```

As with the logical hostname described earlier, the IPMP configuration occurs automatically behind the scenes.

On node `dizzy`, on which the resource group is offline, the IP address is configured on the loopback adapter `lo0`:

```
# ifconfig -a
lo0: flags=20010008c9<UP,LOOPBACK,RUNNING,NOARP,MULTICAST,IPv4,VIRTUAL>
 mtu 8232 index 1
        inet 127.0.0.1 netmask ff000000
lo0:1: flags=20010088c9<UP,LOOPBACK,RUNNING,NOARP,MULTICAST,PRIVATE,IPv4,
VIRTUAL> mtu 8232 index 1
        inet 10.11.157.85 netmask ffffffff
 ...
```

Your final step to configure the shared address networking is to change the `ServerName` in the `/etc/apache2/2.2/httpd.conf` file on each node to use `miles`:

```
# grep ServerName /etc/apache2/2.2/httpd.conf
# ServerName gives the name and port that the server uses to identify itself.
ServerName miles
```

Configuring scalable Apache

Now that you have global storage and scalable networking configured, you need to add the actual Apache service. First, create the resource group. This command sets the `maximum_primaries` and `desired_primaries` properties to 2, to specify that the resource group should run on two nodes ("primaries") simultaneously:

```
# /usr/cluster/bin/clrg create -p Maximum_primaries=2 -p\
  Desired_primaries=2 apache-scal-rg
```

Now add the Apache resource. As in the failover example, you specify several resource properties, including the directory of the binaries, the port to use, and the resource dependencies. This time you also specify the `scalable` property as `true`, indicating that Apache should be configured in scalable mode:

```
# /usr/cluster/bin/clrs create -g apache-scal-rg -t apache -p\
  Bin_dir=/usr/apache2/2.2/bin -p Resource_dependencies=miles-rs -p\
  scalable=true -p port_list=80/tcp apache-scal-rs
```

Finally, bring the resource group online and verify its status:

```
# /usr/cluster/bin/clrg online -M apache-scal-rg
# /usr/cluster/bin/clrg status apache-scal-rg
```

```
=== Cluster Resource Groups ===

Group Name            Node Name       Suspended      Status
----------            ---------       ---------      ------
apache-scal-rg        bird            No             Online
                      dizzy           No             Online
```

 # /usr/cluster/bin/clrg show apache-scal-rg

```
=== Resource Groups and Resources ===

Resource Group:                               apache-scal-rg
 RG_description:                              <NULL>
 RG_mode:                                     Scalable
 RG_state:                                    Managed
 Failback:                                    False
 Nodelist:                                    bird dizzy

    --- Resources for Group apache-scal-rg ---

    Resource:                                 apache-scal-rs
      Type:                                   SUNW.apache:4.1
      Type_version:                           4.1
      Group:                                  apache-scal-rg
      R_description:
      Resource_project_name:                  default
      Enabled{bird}:                          True
      Enabled{dizzy}:                         True
      Monitored{bird}:                        True
      Monitored{dizzy}:                       True
```

 # /usr/cluster/bin/clrs status apache-scal-rs

```
=== Cluster Resources ===

Resource Name         Node Name       State          Status Message
-------------         ---------       -----          --------------
apache-scal-rs        bird            Online         Online - Completed successfully.
  dizzy            Online       Online - Completed successfully.
```

Now you can test it from any machine that can resolve the miles hostname:

```
$ /usr/sfw/bin/wget -q miles
$ cat index.html
hello, world, from cluster file system
```

Advanced Cluster Administration

The previous examples have given you a taste of the capabilities of Open HA Cluster, but they barely scratch the surface of this powerful software. This section introduces some advanced administration topics.

> **TIP** The cluster commands are located in /usr/cluster/bin, and their man pages in /usr/cluster/man. The commands beginning in cl are described in the 1CL section of the man pages. For an overview of this cluster command set, run the following:

```
# man -M /usr/cluster/man -s 1CL intro
```

Shutting down the cluster

To safely shut down the entire cluster, use the cluster shutdown command:

```
# /usr/cluster/bin/cluster shutdown -g0 -y
```

To shut down or reboot a single node, first *evacuate* all services from the node, which moves them to other nodes of the cluster, and then use the OpenSolaris shutdown command. The following example safely powers off the bird node:

```
# /usr/cluster/bin/clnode evacuate bird
# shutdown -g 0 -y -i 5

Shutdown started.    Thu Oct 16 14:39:18 PDT 2008

Changing to init state 5 - please wait
Broadcast Message from root (pts/1) on bird Thu Oct 16 14:39:18...
THE SYSTEM bird IS BEING SHUT DOWN NOW ! ! !
Log off now or risk your files being damaged
```

> **CAUTION** The reboot and init commands are not safe for shutting down or rebooting cluster nodes; they can lead to node panics. See Chapter 3 for a discussion of the shutdown, reboot, and init commands.

Service management

As introduced earlier in this chapter, Open HA Cluster service management is built around three service objects: resource types, resource groups, and resources. The previous Apache examples demonstrated these objects in action. Now it's time to delve into the advanced administration details.

Resource types

A resource type is defined in a Resource Type Registration (RTR) file. The RTR file is similar to the SMF manifest discussed in Chapter 13 but uses a different format and syntax. RTR files are usually installed in /opt/cluster/lib/rgm/rtreg/ or /usr/cluster/lib/rgm/rtreg.

The RTR file specifies two primary things: the paths for *callback methods* and the resource properties.

The callback methods are binaries or scripts that implement a specific functionality such as starting or stopping the service. For example, the START method should start the service, the STOP method should stop the service, the MONITOR_START method should start a monitor daemon to monitor the service, and so on.

> **NOTE** The rt_callbacks(1HA) **man page describes the various callback methods.**

The RTR file also specifies properties of the resource, including their minimum, maximum, and default values, and when they can be *tuned* or modified.

A complete resource type name consists of a company symbol, such as SUNW, the service name, such as apache, and the resource type version. For example, the complete Apache name is SUNW.apache:4.1. If there is no ambiguity, then you can use just the service name to refer to the resource type.

A complete resource type implementation consists of the RTR file, the callback method binaries, and the monitor, which is usually a long-running daemon started by the MONITOR_START callback and stopped by the MONITOR_STOP callback.

The /usr/cluster/bin/clresourcetype, abbreviated /usr/cluster/bin/clrt, manages resource types on the cluster. You'll generally use this command only to register and unregister resource types. You've already seen an example of this command to register resource types:

```
# /usr/cluster/bin/clrt register HAStoragePlus
```

When registering resource types, clrt looks in the two default paths for RTR files. If the file you want to register is in a nonstandard path, then express the path explicitly with the -f option.

Resource types also have properties. Note that the properties defined in the RTR file apply to resources instantiated from that resource type, not the resource type itself. The resource type properties are a predefined set, most of which is not tunable except in the RTR file itself. Table 16-1 describes the resource type properties.

> **NOTE** The rt_properties(5) **man page describes the resource type properties.**

You can view various levels of detail about the resource types on your system with clrt list and clrt show:

```
# /usr/cluster/bin/clrt list
SUNW.LogicalHostname:2
SUNW.SharedAddress:2
SUNW.HAStoragePlus:6
SUNW.apache:4.1
# /usr/cluster/bin/clrt show apache
```

```
=== Registered Resource Types ===

Resource Type:                              SUNW.apache:4.1
  RT_description:                             Apache Web Server on Sun Cluster
  RT_version:                                 4.1
  API_version:                                2
  RT_basedir:                                 /opt/SUNWscapc/bin
  Single_instance:                            False
  Proxy:                                      False
  Init_nodes:                                 All potential masters
  Installed_nodes:                            <All>
  Failover:                                   False
  Pkglist:                                    SUNWscapc
  RT_system:                                  False
  Global_zone:                                False
```

You can obtain just a list of properties with clrt list-props or modify a property of a resource type with clrt set. The following example sets the RT_system property of the Apache resource type to true:

```
# /usr/cluster/bin/clrt set -p RT_system=true apache
# /usr/cluster/bin/clrt show apache | grep RT_system
  RT_system:                                  True
```

Resource groups

A resource group (RG) is a logical container for resources, and is the unit of failover and switchover between nodes in Open HA Cluster. Resource groups do not manage services directly; they are merely a container for resources, which are described below.

You use the /usr/cluster/bin/clresroucegroup command, abbreviated /usr/cluster/bin/clrg, to manage RGs. For example, you can list the RGs on your system with clrg list:

```
# /usr/cluster/bin/clrg list
apache-sa
apache-scal-rg
apache-rg
```

Resource group life cycles

You create an RG with clrg create:

```
# /usr/cluster/bin/clrg create test-rg
```

Use clrg status to see the RG's status. An RG starts in the unmanaged state, which means the cluster basically ignores it:

```
# /usr/cluster/bin/clrg status test-rg
```

```
=== Cluster Resource Groups ===

Group Name      Node Name      Suspended      Status
----------      ---------      ---------      ------
test-rg         bird           No             Unmanaged
                dizzy          No             Unmanaged
```

TABLE 16-1

Resource Type Properties

Name	Value	Meaning
RT_description	String	Read-only description of the resource type
RT_basedir	Directory path	Read-only path to the location of the callback methods
Single_instance	true or false	Indicates whether more than one resource of this type can exist simultaneously
Init_nodes	RG_primaries or RT_installed_nodes	The list of nodes on which the INIT, FINI, and BOOT methods for resources of this type should be run; either the nodes in the containing resource group's nodelist, or all nodes on which the resource type is allowed to run
Installed_nodes	List of nodes, or all	All the nodes on which the resource type can run; the default is all nodes
Failover	true or false	Indicates whether resources of this type can ever be scalable
API_version	Integer	Read-only; the minimum version of the cluster API required by the resource type
RT_version	String	Read-only; the version of the resource type
Pkglist	List of packages in which this resource type implementation is shipped	Read-only
Global_zone	true or false	Indicates whether resources of this type run methods in the global zone even if the resource is instantiated in nonglobal zones. Required for some resource types that require global zone privileges in order to perform certain operations.
RT_system	true or false	If true, this resource type cannot be modified or taken offline.

You manage an RG with `clrg manage`, which moves it to the offline state:

```
# /usr/cluster/bin/clrg manage test-rg
# /usr/cluster/bin/clrg status test-rg

=== Cluster Resource Groups ===

Group Name        Node Name        Suspended        Status
----------        ---------        ---------        ------
test-rg           bird             No               Offline
                  dizzy            No               Offline
```

In the `offline` state, the resource group is not providing service, but is under cluster control. Upon certain events, such as a node joining the cluster, or other resource groups coming online, the cluster will try to bring a managed resource group online on one node (if it's a failover service) or on several nodes (if it's a scalable service). You can also order the cluster to bring it online with `clrg online`:

```
# /usr/cluster/bin/clrg online test-rg
# /usr/cluster/bin/clrg status test-rg

=== Cluster Resource Groups ===

Group Name        Node Name        Suspended        Status
----------        ---------        ---------        ------
test-rg           bird             No               Online
                  dizzy            No               Offline
```

Here, the cluster chose a node on which to bring the resource group online. If the resource group fails to start on the first node, usually because one of its resources fails to start, then the cluster automatically tries it on the remaining candidate nodes.

> **TIP** You can combine the manage and online steps with `clrg online -M`.

You can switch the resource group to a specific node with `clrg switch`:

```
# /usr/cluster/bin/clrg switch -n dizzy test-rg
# /usr/cluster/bin/clrg status test-rg

=== Cluster Resource Groups ===

Group Name        Node Name        Suspended        Status
----------        ---------        ---------        ------
test-rg           bird             No               Offline
                  dizzy            No               Online
```

To restart a resource group, use `clrg restart`. This command restarts all the resources within the group:

```
# /usr/cluster/bin/clrg restart test-rg
# /usr/cluster/bin/clrg status test-rg

=== Cluster Resource Groups ===

Group Name        Node Name        Suspended        Status
----------        ---------        ---------        ------
test-rg           bird             No               Offline
                  dizzy            No               Online
```

You can bring a resource group offline with `clrg offline`, unmanage it with `clrg unmanage`, and remove it with `clrg delete`:

```
# /usr/cluster/bin/clrg offline test-rg
# /usr/cluster/bin/clrg status test-rg

=== Cluster Resource Groups ===

Group Name        Node Name        Suspended        Status
----------        ---------        ---------        ------
test-rg           bird             No               Offline
                  dizzy            No               Offline

# /usr/cluster/bin/clrg unmanage test-rg
# /usr/cluster/bin/clrg status test-rg

=== Cluster Resource Groups ===

Group Name        Node Name        Suspended        Status
----------        ---------        ---------        ------
test-rg           bird             No               Unmanaged
                  dizzy            No               Unmanaged

# /usr/cluster/bin/clrg delete test-rg
# /usr/cluster/bin/clrg status test-rg
invalid resource group
clrg:  (C711394) Failed to access information for resource group "test-rg".

=== Cluster Resource Groups ===

Group Name        Node Name        Suspended        Status
----------        ---------        ---------        ------
```

Other useful resource group operations include suspending the group, with `clrg suspend`, which leaves it in its current state but tells the cluster not to perform any automatic recovery actions on it. Use `clrg resume` to unsuspend it.

`clrg evacuate` brings all resource groups offline on a specified node, attempting to bring them online on different nodes to maintain service availability.

Finally, `clrg quiesce` can "quiesce" a resource group that is failing to start but is taking a long time to completely fail, usually because the cluster is trying to start it on several nodes sequentially. The `quiesce` option will bring the resource group to a quiescent state. The resource group will probably not end up online and providing service.

Resource group properties

Resource groups contain both properties and resources. The properties are described in Table 16-2.

> **NOTE** The `rg_properties(5)` **man page describes the resource group properties.**

You can view the properties and resources of a resource group with `clrg show`:

```
# /usr/cluster/bin/clrg show -v test-rg

=== Resource Groups and Resources ===

Resource Group:                             test-rg
  RG_description:                           <NULL>
  RG_mode:                                  Failover
  RG_state:                                 Unmanaged
  RG_project_name:                          default
  RG_affinities:                            <NULL>
  RG_SLM_type:                              manual
  Auto_start_on_new_cluster:                True
  Failback:                                 False
  Nodelist:                                 bird dizzy
  Maximum_primaries:                        1
  Desired_primaries:                        1
  RG_dependencies:                          <NULL>
  Implicit_network_dependencies:            True
  Global_resources_used:                    <All>
  Pingpong_interval:                        3600
  Pathprefix:                               <NULL>
  RG_System:                                False
  Suspend_automatic_recovery:               False
```

This resource group has no resources, so you view only the properties.

TABLE 16-2

Resource Group Properties

Property	Value	Description
RG_Description	String	Human-readable description; unused by the cluster software
RG_mode	Failover or Scalable	Indicates whether the resource group is failover or scalable. Cannot be changed after resource group creation.
RG_state	Managed or Unmanaged	Read-only. Indicates whether the RG is currently managed.
RG_project_name	String	The OpenSolaris resource management project in which the processes under control of this resource group should run. See Chapter 18 for details about OpenSolaris resource management.
RG_affinities	Other resource groups with affinity modifiers +, ++, +++, -, or --.	Specifies other resource groups for which this group has positive or negative affinities. See below for details.
RG_dependencies	Other resource groups	Specifies other resource groups for which this group has a dependency. Unofficially deprecated in favor of resource dependencies.
RG_SLM_type	Manual or Automated	Indicates whether this resource group should use Open HA Cluster service-level management. If this property is set to automated, several other SLM-related properties become available. Service-level management is beyond the scope of this book; consult the official documentation for details.
Auto_start_on_new_cluster	True or False	Indicates whether the resource group should be brought online on a new cluster
Failback	True or False	Indicates whether the resource group should be switched from a less preferred node to a more preferred node if one joins the cluster

TABLE 16-2   *(continued)*

Property	Value	Description
Nodelist	Node names	The list of nodes on which this RG can run, in preference order
Maximum_primaries Desired_primaries	A number	The desired and maximum number of nodes on which the RG should run simultaneously. See below for details.
Implicit_network_ dependencies	True or False	If a resource specifies network_resources_used, the cluster can treat those as implicit strong dependencies, depending on the setting of this property.
Global_resources_used	* or "" (empty string)	A * indicates that resources in the resource group use the global file system.
Pingpong_interval	A number, in seconds	The cluster will refrain from attempting to start the resource group on a node within Pingpong_interval seconds after a failure to start on that node.
RG_system	True or False	If true, this resource group can't be brought offline or modified.
Pathprefix	A string	A directory for administrative files. Used only for resource groups containing NFS resources.
Suspend_automatic_ recovery	True or False	Read-only reflection of the current state of the resource group set with the clrg suspend command

One of the most important purposes of these properties is to control on which and how many nodes the cluster attempts to bring the resource group online. The nodelist property specifies the nodes, in preference order, on which the resource group should attempt to run. You can change this order at any time, but you can't remove a node from the nodelist on which the resource group is currently running. For example, you can change the order of the nodelist on test-rg to put dizzy first, using the clrg set command:

```
# /usr/cluster/bin/clrg set -p nodelist=dizzy,bird test-rg
# /usr/cluster/bin/clrg show -v test-rg

=== Resource Groups and Resources ===
```

```
Resource Group:                              test-rg
  RG_description:                            <NULL>
  RG_mode:                                   Failover
  RG_state:                                  Managed
  RG_project_name:                           default
  RG_affinities:                             <NULL>
  RG_SLM_type:                               manual
  Auto_start_on_new_cluster:                 True
  Failback:                                  False
  Nodelist:                                  dizzy bird
  Maximum_primaries:                         1
  Desired_primaries:                         1
  RG_dependencies:                           <NULL>
  Implicit_network_dependencies:             True
  Global_resources_used:                     <All>
  Pingpong_interval:                         3600
  Pathprefix:                                <NULL>
  RG_System:                                 False
  Suspend_automatic_recovery:                False
```

Now when you bring the resource group online, it starts on node `dizzy` instead of `bird`, because the cluster brings it online on the first node in the nodelist, if possible:

```
# /usr/cluster/bin/clrg online -M test-rg
# /usr/cluster/bin/clrg status test-rg

=== Cluster Resource Groups ===

Group Name      Node Name      Suspended      Status
----------      ---------      ---------      ------
test-rg         dizzy          No             Online
                bird           No             Offline
```

> **TIP** After changing the nodelist order, run `clrg remaster` to move the resource group to its preferred node or nodes.

The `maximum_primaries` and `desired_primaries` properties specify the number of nodes, or primaries, on which the resource group should run simultaneously. These values are constrained by the `rg_mode` property, which is read-only after resource group creation. If `rg_mode` is `failover`, then `maximum_primaries` and `desired_primaries` cannot be set to anything other than 1. However, you can set these values at resource group creation time to create a scalable resource group:

```
# /usr/cluster/bin/clrg set -p maximum_primaries=2 test-rg
clrg:  (C337559) test-rg: Maximum_Primaries must be 1 for a Failover type
  resource group
# /usr/cluster/bin/clrg create -p maximum_primaries=2 -p\
  desired_primaries=2 test-scal-rg
```

```
# /usr/cluster/bin/clrg show -v test-scal-rg

=== Resource Groups and Resources ===

Resource Group:                          test-scal-rg
  RG_description:                          <NULL>
  RG_mode:                                 Scalable
  RG_state:                                Unmanaged
  RG_project_name:                         default
  RG_affinities:                           <NULL>
  RG_SLM_type:                             manual
  Auto_start_on_new_cluster:               True
  Failback:                                False
  Nodelist:                                bird dizzy
  Maximum_primaries:                       2
  Desired_primaries:                       2
  RG_dependencies:                         <NULL>
  Implicit_network_dependencies:           True
  Global_resources_used:                   <All>
  Pingpong_interval:                       3600
  Pathprefix:                              <NULL>
  RG_System:                               False
  Suspend_automatic_recovery:              False
```

 Resource type, resource group, and resource property names are not case sensitive.

Another useful resource group property is RG_affinities. You can specify that a resource group has either a positive affinity or a negative affinity for one or more resource groups. A positive affinity means that it likes to run on the same node. A negative affinity means it likes to run on a different node. A strong affinity makes this desire a requirement, while a weak affinity requests "best effort." Use + for a weak positive affinity, ++ for strong positive, - for weak negative and -- for strong negative. For example, to set a strong positive affinity of test-rg on test-rg-1, use the following command:

```
# /usr/cluster/bin/clrg set -p rg_affinities=++test-rg-1 test-rg
```

With the affinity setting, test-rg cannot come online on a node unless test-rg-1 is online on that node:

```
# /usr/cluster/bin/clrg online test-rg
clrg:  (C135343) No primary node could be found for resource group test-rg; it
 remains offline
# /usr/cluster/bin/clrg online test-rg-1
# /usr/cluster/bin/clrg status test-rg test-rg-1

=== Cluster Resource Groups ===
```

```
Group Name        Node Name       Suspended       Status
----------        ----------      ----------      ------
test-rg           dizzy           No              Offline
                  bird            No              Online

test-rg-1         bird            No              Online
                  dizzy           No              Offline
```

```
# /usr/cluster/bin/clrg switch -n dizzy test-rg
clrg: (C406107) Cannot switch resource group test-rg online on node dizzy
  because it has strong positive affinities for resource group(s) {test-rg-1},
  which are not online on that node.
```

Negative affinities can be useful for a rudimentary load-balancing of services on different nodes of the cluster. For example, if you have one service that's much more important than another service, the less important service can declare a strong negative affinity for the more important service, ensuring that the more important one can always get a node to itself.

Resources

A resource represents an individual service on the cluster, such as the Apache web server, a highly available file system, or a logical hostname. Resources are always created inside a resource group, and are attached to that resource group for their lifetime. Resources must always be instantiated from a specific resource type.

You can manage resources on the cluster with the /usr/cluster/bin/clresource command, abbreviated /usr/cluster/bin/clrs. For example, you can view a list of the resources with clrs list:

```
# /usr/cluster/bin/clrs list
miles-rs
apache-scal-rs
azp-rs
coltrane-rs
apache-rs
```

Resource life cycles

Like resource groups, resources go through a life cycle. You can create a resource with clrs create, specifying the resource type to use as a template, the resource group that it lives in, and zero or more property values:

```
# /usr/cluster/bin/clrs create -g apache-scal-rg -t apache -p\
  Bin_dir=usr/apache2/2.2/bin -p Resource_dependencies=miles-rs -p\
  scalable=true -p port_list=80/tcp apache-scal-rs
```

A resource is created in the enabled mode, which means that it attempts to come online on any node on which its containing resource group is online. For example, because `apache-scal-rg` was already online, you can see that `apache-scal-rs` goes online as well:

```
# /usr/cluster/bin/clrs status apache-scal-rs

=== Cluster Resources ===

Resource Name        Node Name     State     Status Message
-------------        ---------     -----     --------------
apache-scal-rs       bird          Online    Online - Completed successfully.
                     dizzy         Online    Online - Completed successfully.
```

You can't bring the resource offline directly without bringing the whole resource group offline, but you can disable the resource, which forces it offline and sets it such that it won't be brought online, even if its containing resource group goes online. You can disable the resource with `clrs disable`:

```
# /usr/cluster/bin/clrs disable apache-scal-rs
# /usr/cluster/bin/clrs status apache-scal-rs

=== Cluster Resources ===

Resource Name        Node Name     State     Status Message
-------------        ---------     -----     --------------
apache-scal-rs       bird          Offline   Offline - Successfully stopped
 Apache Web Server.
                     dizzy         Offline   Offline - Successfully stopped
   Apache Web Server.

# /usr/cluster/bin/clrg status apache-scal-rg

=== Cluster Resource Groups ===

Group Name           Node Name     Suspended     Status
----------           ---------     ---------     ------
apache-scal-rg       bird          No            Online
                     dizzy         No            Online
```

Resource properties

Like resource groups, resources have properties. Resource properties, however, are more complicated. There are two types of resource properties: *standard properties*, which are the same for each resource, and *extension properties*, which are defined in the RTR file of the resource type. Table 16-3 lists the resource standard properties.

 **NOTE**   The `r_properties(5)` man page describes the resource properties.

TABLE 16-3

Standard Resource Properties

Property	Values	Description
Retry_interval Retry_count Thorough_probe_interval Cheap_probe_interval	Integers	Resource monitor settings, specifying the number of restarts to attempt on a failed resource within a specific interval before failing over the resource group to another node, and the amount of time between monitor probes
Load_balancing_weights Load_balancing_policy Affinity_timeout UDP_affinity Weak_affinity Generic_affinity Round_robin	Various	Network load balancing for scalable services. See the section on "Network load balancing" later in this Chapter for details.
Start_timeout Stop_timeout etc.	Integers, in seconds	Timeout values for the callback methods. If the method doesn't complete in that amount of time, the cluster infrastructure kills it and considers it a failure.
Port_list	Comma-separated list of `<port number>/protocol`	List of ports on which the service listens
Scalable	`true` or `false`	Indicates whether the resource is scalable or failover
Network_resources_used	List of resource names	Specifies logical hostname or shared address resources on which this resource depends
Failover_mode	NONE, SOFT, HARD, RESTART_ONLY, LOG_ONLY	Specifies the behavior on start and stop failures of the resource. Consult the documentation for details.

TABLE 16-3   *(continued)*

Property	Values	Description
R_description	string	Human-readable description of the resource. Ignored by the cluster.
Resource_dependencies Resource_dependencies_weak Resource_dependencies_restart Resource_dependencies_offline_ restart	Lists of other resources	Specifies dependencies of this resource on other resources.
Resource_project_name	String	The OpenSolaris resource management project in which the processes under control of this resource should run. See Chapter 18 for details about OpenSolaris resource management.
Type	String	Resource type
Type_version	String	Version of the resource type. Can be set to upgrade a resource to a new version of the resource type.

In addition to the standard properties, each resource type defines extension properties. You can view the properties of a resource with clrs show:

```
# /usr/cluster/bin/clrs show -v apache-scal-rs

=== Resources ===

Resource:                              apache-scal-rs
  Type:                                SUNW.apache:4.1
  Type_version:                        4.1
  Group:                               apache-scal-rg
  R_description:
  Resource_project_name:               default
  Enabled{bird}:                       False
  Enabled{dizzy}:                      False
  Monitored{bird}:                     True
  Monitored{dizzy}:                    True
```

```
Resource_dependencies:                              miles-rs
Resource_dependencies_weak:                         <NULL>
Resource_dependencies_restart:                      <NULL>
Resource_dependencies_offline_restart:              <NULL>

--- Standard and extension properties ---

Monitor_Uri_List:                                   <NULL>
    Class:                                          extension
    Description:                                    URI(s) that will be
monitored by the agent probe
    Per-node:                                       False
    Type:                                           stringarray

Probe_timeout:                                  90
    Class:                                          extension
    Description:                                    Time out value for the
probe (seconds)
    Per-node:                                       False
    Type:                                           int
...
```

Resource dependencies are some of the most interesting resource properties. With resource dependencies, you can specify that a resource depends on one or more other resources. The dependent resource will always start after, and stop before, the resource on which it depends. If the resource on which it depends is not online, the resource will not go online. Resource_dependencies_weak allows a weaker form of dependency in which the ordering is enforced only if both resources start simultaneously. This type of dependency is useful only for resources in the same resource group. The two forms of restart dependencies, resource_dependencies_restart, and resource_dependencies_offline_restart, enable a dependent resource to be restarted whenever a resource it depends on is restarted. To set resource dependencies, use clrs set:

```
# /usr/cluster/bin/clrs set -p Resource_dependencies=miles-rs apache-scal-rs
```

With this dependency, the apache-scal-rs resource cannot start unless the miles-rs resource is online. For example, if you disable miles-rs and then enable apache-scal-rs, apache-scal-rs will fail to go online. This leaves its containing resource group, apache-scal-rg in the PENDING_ONLINE_BLOCKED state, meaning that one or more of its resources (in this case, apache-scal-rs) is blocked, waiting for dependencies to be fulfilled:

```
# /usr/cluster/bin/clrs disable miles-rs
# /usr/cluster/bin/clrs enable apache-scal-rs
(C814348) WARNING: on node bird, resource group apache-scal-rg is in
 PENDING_ONLINE_BLOCKED state
(C814348) WARNING: on node dizzy, resource group apache-scal-rg is in
 PENDING_ONLINE_BLOCKED state
```

```
# /usr/cluster/bin/clrs status apache-scal-rs

=== Cluster Resources ===

Resource Name       Node Name    State     Status Message
-------------       ---------    -----     --------------
apache-scal-rs      bird         Offline   Offline - Successfully stopped
    Apache Web Server.
                    dizzy        Offline   Offline - Successfully stopped
    Apache Web Server.
```

Now if you enable miles-rs, apache-scal-rs will automatically come online because its
dependency is fulfilled:

```
# /usr/cluster/bin/clrs enable miles-rs
# /usr/cluster/bin/clrs status apache-scal-rs

=== Cluster Resources ===

Resource Name       Node Name    State     Status Message
-------------       ---------    -----     --------------
apache-scal-rs      bird         Online    Online - Completed successfully.
                    dizzy        Online    Online - Completed successfully.
```

Volume management

The examples so far in this chapter have used either UFS on raw devices or ZFS. However,
Open HA Cluster also supports volume management with the Solaris Volume Manager. You
can create disk sets on shared storage and register them as *device groups* with Open HA Cluster
using the metaset command. A device group is a highly available disk set that can be accessed
from any node of the cluster and is automatically failed over to a different node if its current
master dies.

CROSS-REF   The Solaris Volume Manager is discussed in Chapter 7.

You can create a global file system on top of a device group, rather than raw devices, to get
the benefits of volume management. See the Open HA Cluster/Sun Cluster documentation for
details.

Zones As Logical Nodes

Open HA Cluster provides two mechanisms for running services in OpenSolaris zones. The first
approach, *failover zones*, treats zones as a logical resource, just as storage is a logical resource
managed by the HAStoragePlus data service and IP addresses are logical resources managed by
the Logical Hostname and Shared Address data services. Zones are managed by the Solaris Containers data service. This approach treats the zones as black boxes, starting or stopping an entire

zone on the nodes on which it should run, similar to the way storage is mounted or network addresses are configured on nodes on which they are needed. The services that run in the zones are managed by separate resources with dependencies on the Solaris Containers resource. The main benefit of this approach is that it can be used with branded zones, such as zones running Linux. Thus, you can essentially create a virtual cluster of Linux nodes on top of an OpenSolaris installation. Consult the Solaris Containers Data Service documentation for details.

CROSS-REF   Zones, including branded zones, are discussed in Chapter 19.

The second approach treats zones as logical nodes, enabling you to specify the zones themselves in resource group nodelists. Although this approach can't support branded zones, it has the benefit of working with standard data services without modification. This feature is particularly useful for prototyping and testing on a single-node cluster.

As an example of the "zones as logical nodes" approach, suppose you want to run Apache in failover mode between zone mingus on node dizzy and zone brubeck on node bird.

You can use a configuration similar to that described previously in the section "Making Apache highly available." This configuration consists of a single failover resource group containing a logical hostname resource, an HAStoragePlus failover ZFS zpool resource, and the Apache resource itself. The principal difference is that the resource group specifies nonglobal zones in its nodelist, rather than physical nodes.

CAUTION   This example starts from scratch. If you configured the failover or scalable Apache as described earlier in this chapter, then first disable those resources, unmanage the resource groups, and destroy the zpool so they don't interfere with failover Apache:

```
# /usr/cluster/bin/clrg offline apache-scal-rg apache-sa
# /usr/cluster/bin/clrs disable miles-rs apache-scal-rs
# /usr/cluster/bin/clrg unmanage apache-scal-rg apache-sa
# /usr/cluster/bin/clrg offline apache-rg
# /usr/cluster/bin/clrs disable apache-rs azp-rs coltrane-rs
# /usr/cluster/bin/clrs delete apache-rs azp-rs coltrane-rs
# zpool destroy azp
# /usr/cluster/bin/clrg delete apache-rg
```

The HAStoragePlus resource is deleted before removing the zpool; and the logical hostname resource must be deleted to reuse the network address in the next example. Thus, the whole apache-rg is cleaned up.

Configuring failover storage

You configure failover storage for nonglobal zones similarly to configuring it for global zones. First, create the zpool:

```
# zpool create azpng /dev/did/dsk/d14
# zpool status
```

```
  pool: azpng
 state: ONLINE
 scrub: none requested
config:

        NAME                STATE    READ WRITE CKSUM
        azpng               ONLINE      0    0     0
          /dev/did/dsk/d14  ONLINE      0    0     0

errors: No known data errors
```

Next, create the resource group that will contain the Apache, HAStoragePlus, and logical host-name resources:

```
# /usr/cluster/bin/clrg create -n dizzy:mingus,bird:brubeck apache-ngz-rg
```

Note the `<nodename>:<zonename>` syntax for specifying nonglobal zones as logical nodes.

> **CAUTION** Nonglobal zones allow restricted access to some of the cluster administrative commands, but you should generally administer your cluster from the global zones so that you don't run into unexpected problems.

Now register the HAStoragePlus resource type and create the HAStoragePlus resource to manage the zpool:

```
# /usr/cluster/bin/clrt register HAStoragePlus
# /usr/cluster/bin/clrs create -g apache-ngz-rg -t HAStoragePlus -p\
  Zpools=azpng azp-ngz-rs
```

Bring the resource group online with `clrg online`:

```
# /usr/cluster/bin/clrg online -M apache-ngz-rg
# /usr/cluster/bin/clrg status apache-ngz-rg

=== Cluster Resource Groups ===

Group Name        Node Name        Suspended    Status
----------        ---------        ---------    ------
apache-ngz-rg     dizzy:mingus     No           Online
                  bird:brubeck     No           Offline
```

You can now verify that the cluster framework is importing the zpool on the physical node dizzy and making it available inside the nonglobal zone mingus on which the resource group is online. In the global zone on dizzy, you can see the zpool, but the azpng ZFS file system is not mounted in the usual place:

```
dizzy# hostname
dizzy
dizzy# zpool status
```

```
  pool: azp
 state: ONLINE
 scrub: none requested
config:

        NAME                                          STATE     READ WRITE CKSUM
        azp                                           ONLINE       0     0     0
          c4t600C0FF000000000092AFF00C5B5D70Bd0       ONLINE       0     0     0

errors: No known data errors
dizzy# ls /azpng
/azpng: No such file or directory
```

In fact, the file system is mounted in the nonglobal zone's root path, so it is accessible from the nonglobal zone:

```
mingus# hostname
mingus
mingus# ls /azpng
mingus#
```

Note that you don't need to do anything special to make the file system available in the nonglobal zone other than specify nonglobal zones in the resource group's nodelist. When bringing the resource group online on a logical node, the cluster framework automatically imports the zpool with an alternate root to make it available inside the nonglobal zone.

CROSS-REF   ZFS, including importing zpools with alternate roots, is discussed in Chapter 8.

Now that the failover storage is working, create your htdocs directory on it and configure Apache's DocumentRoot. First, create the htdocs and a dummy index.html. From the global zone on the node on which the zpool is imported, create the file system:

```
dizzy# zfs create azpng/htdocs
```

From the nonglobal zone, create index.html:

```
mingus# echo "hello, world, from ngzone" > /azpng/htdocs/index.html
mingus# chgrp bin /azpng/htdocs/index.html
```

Still in the nonglobal zone, change /etc/apache2/2.2/httpd.conf so that DocumentRoot points to the failover file system:

```
mingus# grep htdocs httpd.conf
DocumentRoot "/azpng/htdocs"
<Directory "/azpng/htdocs">
```

At this point, you should verify that Apache starts up and functions properly in the nonglobal zone mingus. See the instructions in the section "Making Apache highly available" earlier in the chapter.

Finally, on the second zone, `brubeck`, repeat the steps to configure `httpd.conf` and to test that Apache works. You can switch the resource group to that zone with `clrg switch` and the `<nodename>:<zonename>` notation:

```
# /usr/cluster/bin/clrg switch -n bird:brubeck apache-ngz-rg
```

Configuring logical hostname networking

Configuring networking for nonglobal zones is identical to configuring it for physical nodes. The cluster software takes care of the details of making the IP address accessible to processes running inside the zone. Simply create the logical hostname resource in the resource group as usual, from the global zone:

```
# /usr/cluster/bin/clrslh create -g apache-ngz-rg -h coltrane coltrane-rs
```

In each nonglobal zone, change the `ServerName` entry in `/etc/apache2/2.2/httpd.conf`:

```
# grep ServerName httpd.conf
# ServerName gives the name and port that the server uses to identify itself.
ServerName coltrane
```

Configuring failover Apache

The final step is to configure the Apache service itself. Once you've set up `httpd.conf` properly in each nonglobal zone, this step is identical to the physical node case:

```
# /usr/cluster/bin/clrt register apache
# /usr/cluster/bin/clrs create -g apache-ngz-rg -t apache -p\
  Bin_dir=/usr/apache2/2.2/bin -p Port_list=80/tcp -p\
  Resource_dependencies=azp-ngz-rs,coltrane-rs apache-ngz-rs
# /usr/cluster/bin/clrg status apache-ngz-rg

=== Cluster Resource Groups ===

Group Name        Node Name         Suspended    Status
----------        ---------         ---------    ------
apache-ngz-rg     dizzy:mingus      No           Offline
                  bird:brubeck      No           Online

# /usr/cluster/bin/clrs status apache-ngz-rs

=== Cluster Resources ===

Resource Name     Node Name         State      Status Message
-------------     ---------         -----      --------------
apache-ngz-rs     dizzy:mingus      Offline    Offline
                  bird:brubeck      Online     Online - Completed successfully.
```

Now that the service is configured and online, test it from any machine that can resolve coltrane through DNS:

```
$ /usr/sfw/bin/wget -q coltrane.sfbay
$ more index.html
hello, world, from ngzone
```

Network load balancing

When Open HA Cluster runs a service in scalable mode, it functions as a software load balancer, distributing network requests across the different nodes hosting the service. The scalable Apache example earlier in this chapter demonstrated how to set up a scalable service. This section shows how to tune the load balancing settings.

The Load_balancing_policy resource property determines the load balancing settings. The default value is LB_WEIGHTED, which distributes incoming network requests to the nodes hosting the service according to the Load_balancing_weights property. The default value for Load_balancing_weights is NULL, which means that requests are evenly distributed across the nodes:

```
# /usr/cluster/bin/clrs show -p Load_balancing_policy apache-scal-rs

=== Resources ===

Resource: apache-scal-rs

--- Standard and extension properties ---

Load_balancing_policy: LB_WEIGHTED
Class: standard
Description: Determines how the load is balanced across different nodes.
Type: string

# /usr/cluster/bin/clrs show -p Load_balancing_weights apache-scal-rs

=== Resources ===

Resource: apache-scal-rs

--- Standard and extension properties ---

Load_balancing_weights: <NULL>
Class: standard
Description: Indicates the weights taken by different nodes for balancing
 the load.
Type: stringarray
```

You can set the Load_balancing_weights property by specifying a weight for each node. The percentage of incoming requests directed to that node is the weight for that node divided by the total weights for all nodes:

```
# /usr/cluster/bin/clrs set -p Load_balancing_weights=1@dizzy,3@bird\
 apache-scal-rs
# /usr/cluster/bin/clrs show -p Load_balancing_weights apache-scal-rs
=== Resources ===

Resource: apache-scal-rs

--- Standard and extension properties ---

Load_balancing_weights: 1@dizzy 3@bird
Class: standard
Description: Indicates the weights taken by different nodes for balancing
 the load.
Type: stringarray
```

With these weight settings, node dizzy will get 1 divided by 4, or 25% of the network requests, and node bird will get 3 divided by 4, or 75% of the incoming requests. Note that you set the Load_balancing_policy and Load_balancing_weights on the Apache resource itself, not on the shared address network resource.

A weighted distribution policy is fine for simple services, but if your services have any sort of session state, client requests from the same IP address must be directed to the same physical host. You can set this *sticky* load balancing policy with the LB_STICKY policy.

NOTE The Load_balancing_policy is set at resource creation time, and cannot be subsequently changed:

```
# /usr/cluster/bin/clrs create -g apache-scal-rg -t apache -p\
 Bin_dir=/usr/apache2/2.2/bin -p Resource_dependencies=miles-rs -p\
 scalable=true -p Load_balancing_policy=Lb_sticky -p port_list=80/tcp apache-scal-rs
```

With this setting, incoming requests from the same client are directed to the same physical server.

Other cluster commands

Several other cluster commands, not yet mentioned in this chapter, can come in handy. In addition to the option to shut down the cluster, the /usr/cluster/bin/cluster command provides a summary of information about the cluster and its various subcomponents, with either the show or status options. Here's an example:

```
# /usr/cluster/bin/cluster show

=== Cluster ===
```

```
Cluster Name:                              jazz
  clusterid:                               0x480D02B8
  installmode:                             disabled
  heartbeat_timeout:                       10000
  heartbeat_quantum:                       1000
  private_netaddr:                         172.16.0.0
  private_netmask:                         255.255.248.0
  max_nodes:                               64
  max_privatenets:                         10
  udp_session_timeout:                     480
  global_fencing:                          pathcount
  Node List:                               bird, dizzy

  === Host Access Control ===

  Cluster name:                            jazz
    Allowed hosts:                         None
    Authentication Protocol:               sys
  ...
```

Much of the information about specific components can be obtained with the command for that area. For example, in addition to evacuating a node, the /usr/cluster/bin/clnode command provides information about cluster nodes with the show or status options, and can be used to add a node to or remove a node from a cluster:

```
# /usr/cluster/bin/clnode status

=== Cluster Nodes ===

--- Node Status ---

Node Name                                  Status
---------                                  ------
bird                                       Online
dizzy                                      Online
```

The /usr/cluster/bin/clquorum command provides information about and manages quorum devices:

```
# /usr/cluster/bin/clquorum list
d3
bird
dizzy
# /usr/cluster/bin/clquorum add d4
# /usr/cluster/bin/clquorum list
d3
d4
bird
dizzy
```

```
# /usr/cluster/bin/clquorum status

=== Cluster Quorum ===

--- Quorum Votes Summary ---

            Needed    Present    Possible
            ------    -------    --------
            3         4          4


--- Quorum Votes by Node ---

Node Name       Present       Possible       Status
---------       -------       --------       ------
bird            1             1              Online
dizzy           1             1              Online


--- Quorum Votes by Device ---

Device Name     Present       Possible       Status
-----------     -------       --------       ------
d3              1             1              Online
d4              1             1              Online

# /usr/cluster/bin/clquorum remove d4
```

Use the /usr/cluster/bin/clinterconnect command to obtain information about and manage the private interconnects:

```
# /usr/cluster/bin/clinterconnect show

=== Transport Cables ===

Transport Cable:                        bird:ce1,switch2@1
  Endpoint1:                              bird:ce1
  Endpoint2:                              switch2@1
  State:                                  Enabled

Transport Cable:                        bird:bge1,switch1@1
  Endpoint1:                              bird:bge1
  Endpoint2:                              switch1@1
  State:                                  Enabled

Transport Cable:                        dizzy:bge1,switch1@2
  Endpoint1:                              dizzy:bge1
  Endpoint2:                              switch1@2
  State:                                  Enabled
```

```
Transport Cable:                        dizzy:ce1,switch2@2
   Endpoint1:                              dizzy:ce1
   Endpoint2:                              switch2@2
   State:                                  Enabled

   ...
```

In addition to providing information about devices, the /usr/cluster/bin/cldevice command can manage the devices, including enabling and disabling monitoring of the disk paths.
Monitoring is enabled by default, but you can disable it if you want.

Finally, the /usr/cluster/bin/sccheck command checks a multitude of configuration settings on the cluster and reports any possible misconfigurations.

Making Custom Services Highly Available

Because Open HA Cluster is an application-agnostic platform for high availability, you can make
almost any off-the-shelf application highly available, even if there's no prebuilt data service for
that application. If SMF is already managing your service, then you can use the SMF Proxy data
service. Otherwise, you can use the generic data service (GDS).

> **CAUTION** Open HA Cluster does not provide session state failover, so interactive applications
> such as telnet or ssh are generally not good candidates for high availability on
> this platform. The *Solaris Cluster Data Service Developers Guide* listed in the "Resources" section
> at the end of this chapter contains a complete list of requirements that an application must meet
> in order to qualify for high availability with Open HA Cluster.

SMF Proxy

If SMF is already managing your service on a single node basis, then you can use an SMF Proxy
to turn it into a highly available service on the cluster by specifying only the Fault Managed
Resource Identifier (FMRI) of the service and the path to its manifest. For example, suppose you
have an application, myservice, that listens on port 1234, and is managed as an SMF service
on each node of your cluster:

```
# svcs myservice
STATE          STIME    FMRI
online         16:37:24 svc:/myservice:default
```

To turn this single-node service into a multi-node service, first create a text file listing the service
FMRI and the path to its manifest file:

```
# cat /opt/cluster/test/bin/psi
<svc:/myservice:default>,</opt/cluster/test/bin/myservice.xml>
```

CROSS-REF FMRIs and SMF are covered in Chapters 12 and 13, respectively.

Now you run just five cluster commands. First, create the resource group and network address resource:

```
# clrg create myservice-proxy-rg
# clrslh create -g myservice-proxy-rg -h coltrane coltrane-rs
```

Register the Proxy_SMF_failover resource type:

```
# clrt register Proxy_SMF_failover
```

NOTE There are actually three different SMF proxy resource types: Proxy_SMF_Failover, Proxy_SMF_Multimaster, and Proxy_SMF_Scalable, which turn an SMF service into an HA failover service, a multimaster service (running on more than one node simultaneously), or a network load-balanced service, respectively.

Finally, create the proxy resource that will manage the SMF service, specifying the path to the file containing the FMRI and manifest as the proxied_service_instances property:

```
# /usr/cluster/bin/clrs create -g myservice-proxy-rg -t Proxy_SMF_failover\
 -p proxied_service_instances=/opt/cluster/test/bin/psi -p\
 Resource_dependencies=coltrane-rs myservice-proxy-rs
```

Now you can bring the resource group online and verify its status:

```
# clrg online -M myservice-proxy-rg
# clrg status myservice-proxy-rg

=== Cluster Resource Groups ===

Group Name          Node Name   Suspended   Status
----------          ---------   ---------   ------
myservice-proxy-rg  bird        No          Online
                    dizzy       No          Offline
```

Because the resource group is running on node bird, you expect the underlying SMF service to be online on that node:

```
bird# hostname
bird
bird# svcs myservice
STATE       STIME      FMRI
online      16:45:28   svc:/myservice:default
```

The SMF service should be offline on the other node:

```
dizzy# hostname
dizzy
```

```
dizzy# svcs myservice
STATE          STIME        FMRI
offline        16:45:22     svc:/myservice:default
```

If you switch the resource group to dizzy, the underlying SMF service goes offline on bird and online on dizzy:

```
# clrg switch -n dizzy myservice-proxy-rg
# clrg status myservice-proxy-rg

=== Cluster Resource Groups ===

Group Name              Node Name    Suspended    Status
----------              ---------    ---------    ------
myservice-proxy-rg      bird         No           Offline
                        dizzy        No           Online
dizzy# hostname
dizzy
dizzy# svcs myservice
STATE          STIME        FMRI
online         16:46:41     svc:/myservice:default
bird# hostname
bird
bird# svcs myservice
STATE          STIME        FMRI
offline        16:46:40     svc:/myservice:default
```

Generic data service

The simplest way to make an application not managed by SMF highly available is to use the generic data service (GDS). This resource type provides a generic interface for managing applications as resources. At a minimum, you provide only a start command and listening port for your application. The GDS takes care of starting the application on the node(s) where it should run, stopping it with signals, and even monitoring it by attempting to connect to the listening port.

For example, suppose the myservice application introduced earlier was not being managed already by SMF. You can make this service highly available with only five cluster commands.

First, ensure that you've installed the application on both nodes of the cluster. In this example, the daemon lives in /opt/cluster/test/bin/.

Next, register the GDS resource type:

```
# /usr/cluster/bin/clrt register gds
```

633

Then create a resource group and a network address resource:

```
# /usr/cluster/bin/clrg create myservice-rg
# /usr/cluster/bin/clrslh create -g myservice-rg -h coltrane coltrane-rs
```

Add a resource of type generic data service, specifying the start command (simply the path to the daemon in this case), the listening port, the signal to be used to stop the daemon, and the network resources used:

```
# /usr/cluster/bin/clrs create -g myservice-rg -t gds -p\
  Start_command=/opt/cluster/test/bin/myservice -p\
  Resource_dependencies=coltrane-rs -p Stop_signal=15 -p port_list=1234/tcp\
  myservice-rs
```

Finally, bring the service online and verify its status:

```
# /usr/cluster/bin/clrg online -M myservice-rg
# /usr/cluster/bin/clrg status myservice-rg

=== Cluster Resource Groups ===

Group Name Node Name Suspended Status
---------- --------- --------- ------
myservice-rg bird    No Online
             dizzy   No Offline
```

If you want more control over how the cluster manages your service, GDS enables you to specify additional information, including a stop command (if you don't want to use signals), a validate command, a probe command for application-specific monitoring, and other settings.

Disaster Recovery with Open High Availability Cluster

As described earlier, the principal reason to consider using the Open High Availability Cluster software is to keep your business running, even in the face of a major catastrophe. The term *business continuity* derives from this requirement. Recovery from localized equipment failures can be handled by automatically failing over services to redundant systems in the same datacenter using the Open HA Cluster features described so far in this chapter. However, failing over to another machine in the same room is insufficient in the face of more widespread disasters, such as the floods that caused so much havoc in New Orleans after hurricane Katrina in 2005.

Recovering from disasters of that magnitude requires advance planning and a backup infrastructure at a geographic distance from the primary site. The Open HA Cluster Geographic Edition framework can provide a key part of the disaster recovery infrastructure and plan that you need.

FIGURE 16-4

RPO and RTO are objectives that address data loss and recovery time in a business continuity plan.

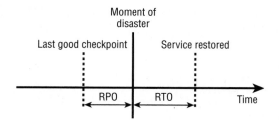

Terminology

Before looking at the Geographic Edition in detail, you should understand two common terms used in the context of business continuity: *recovery point objective* (RPO) and *recovery time objective* (RTO). These concepts are illustrated in Figure 16-4.

Recovery Point Objective

Put simply, RPO can be defined as "how much data can you afford to lose?" Your system must make regular copies of operating data in a safe place. If the primary data is lost, it will be necessary to restore from the most recent copy. The maximum permissible time between the time of the last copy and the time disaster strikes is the RPO.

Recovery Time Objective

The simple definition of RTO is "how long can you afford to be offline?" If the disaster is of such magnitude that the whole primary site is lost, what is the maximum time it will it take to get the data restored and made available from a secondary site elsewhere? That is the RTO.

Note that both RPO and RTO are *objectives*. After being defined in the plan, the system must be configured to achieve them. A common mistake is to start with the technology and then try to make the plan fit it. For a successful disaster recovery installation, the need for top-down design cannot be overstressed. Don't start with the software and then figure out what to do with it. Plan your disaster response, and let that guide the design of the Open HA Cluster installation.

Open HA Cluster Geographic Edition

In the past, a common approach to disaster recovery was to make regular backups onto tape and to store those at a remote site. This kind of backup is still important for archival purposes, but if such backups are made daily, then an RPO of less than 24 hours cannot be guaranteed, and the need to obtain new equipment prior to restoring the tapes could result in RTO measured in days or weeks. That might be acceptable for back-office operations such as payroll processing, but it is not suitable for online services such as banking and vending. For such services, RPO is often measured in minutes, and RTO in hours.

The solution to this problem is continuous replication of modified data to a remote site, managed together with the applications that use the data. By managing both data and application together in one framework, you can ensure continuous availability of the service offered by the application. Open HA Cluster Geographic Edition provides that coordinated management.

> **CAUTION**   Don't succumb to the temptation of specifying RPO as zero, which implies that data at the primary and secondary sites must always be identical in all circumstances. If the secondary site is unavailable, perhaps for maintenance or as a result of a network outage, then an RPO of zero could be achieved only if the primary site stopped writing to local storage. That would make the secondary site a single point of failure, which is unlikely to be what is required.

Setting up a Geographic Edition configuration

A single cluster, as described earlier in this chapter, provides a high degree of data integrity and availability through tight integration between servers and storage. As the distance between cluster components increases, however, the additional network delays involved can create performance problems. To protect against a citywide disaster, a redundant copy of data must be several hundred kilometers away, but the round-trip delay for a packet of data on a 100-km path is approximately 1 millisecond. Such a delay will severely slow down writes to storage. Stretching a single cluster between a primary and backup site over such a distance soon becomes impractical when good performance is required.

Open HA Cluster Geographic Edition combines two clusters, one at each location. These could be single-node clusters, although to provide maximum availability in normal operation it is advisable to use at least a two-node cluster at the primary site.

Application management

Both clusters are configured with the standard Open HA Cluster software to provide local application and storage management, as described earlier.

Heartbeat

Each cluster in a *partnership* monitors the connection to its partner by means of a heartbeat. By default, the standard configuration uses TCP/UDP messages, but you can add custom heartbeat modules for other network types.

Data replication

To provide rapid, continuous transfer of data changes from the primary site to the secondary site, you can use one of several kinds of data replication software. Some are commercial and others are available as open source. Open HA Cluster Geographic Edition supports a number of these products, and you can develop control modules for others.

Supplied replication control modules

Open HA Cluster Geographic Edition provides plug-ins for several implementations of data replication software. Many of these, such as StorageTek TrueCopy, Symmetrix Remote Data Replicator, and Oracle DataGuard, are commercial proprietary products. However, StorageTek Availability Suite (AVS) is open-source software available with OpenSolaris. AVS contains two software components: the StorageTek Network Data Replicator (SNDR) and Instant Image (II), a point-in-time snapshot utility. SNDR, which runs on one of the OpenSolaris cluster systems, intercepts writes to a local storage volume. It copies the writes across the network to a partner at the remote site, where they are applied to a storage volume. The two volumes are therefore kept in step at the block level. AVS does not require any specific storage hardware: It works with all local storage supported by Open Solaris.

Custom mechanisms

You can add support for other replication software by writing a Java MBean plug-in and associated control programs to control configuration, monitoring, and switchover of data replication.

An Open HA Cluster project is in progress to simplify this process through the use of the generic Script-Based Plug-in (SBP). Developers will be able to use the SBP to add support for other replication types, including custom one-off designs, by writing scripts in a manner similar to the GDS agent for Open HA Cluster described earlier in this chapter. It is not necessary to develop a new Java MBean if the SBP is used.

Topology and architecture

There are two principal ways to configure clusters for geographic protection: as an active-active pair, in which each site replicates to the other, or as a star, in which one or more remote sites replicate to a central disaster recovery location. The two topologies are shown in Figures 16-5 and 16-6, respectively.

FIGURE 16-5
_____

In an active-active topology, each site replicates to the other.

Active-Active Topology

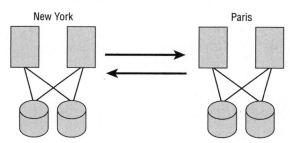

FIGURE 16-6

In a star topology, remote sites replicate to a central disaster recovery location.

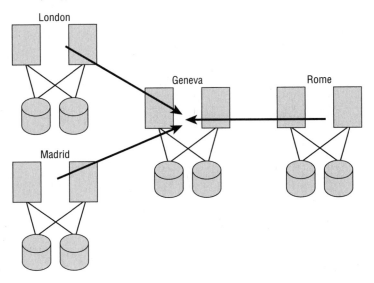

Star Topology

The Geographic Edition architecture maintains the hierarchical model of Open HA Cluster and extends it vertically. Just as a single-site configuration will group servers and storage into a cluster, a Geographic Edition configuration will group a pair of clusters into a *partnership*. One cluster can be a member of multiple partnerships, as shown in the star configuration.

Within each *partnership*, you define one or more *protection groups*, each of which contains cluster resource groups and data replication resources.

Installing and configuring Geographic Edition

Install Geographic Edition from the same medium from which you installed the main cluster software. If you're using Solaris Cluster Express (SCX), run the interactive installer script in the Solaris_<platform> subdirectory of the unzipped installation image, where <platform> is either sparc or x86:

```
# ./installer
```

Follow the onscreen instructions to select the following products from the Open High Availability Cluster Geographic Edition submenu:

■ Open High Availability Cluster Geographic Edition

■ The data replication software you want to use

■ (*Optional*) Open High Availability Cluster Geographic Edition Manager

You can install the software at the same time you install the main cluster software, but you must configure and create both clusters before activating the Geographic Edition software. The two clusters that make up a partnership must have compatible configurations. They don't need to be identical, but key managed resources, such as the names of application resource groups that are to be protected by the Geographic Edition, must be the same on both clusters.

NOTE The Geographic Edition software has been designed so that it can be added to a running cluster with no disruption to applications that are running on the cluster. If this is a requirement, refer to the full Solaris Cluster Geographic Edition documentation for detailed information on how to do this safely.

Cluster names

The names of the clusters in a partnership are used to derive the network hostnames for the clusters. This means that the names chosen for the clusters must correspond to the conventions for Internet hostnames as described in RFC952. Specifically, do not use the underscore (_) and period (.) characters. If you use invalid names, the Geographic Edition software displays an error and will not start.

Configuring a partnership

This section provides an example of the basic configuration steps for two clusters named newyork and paris. The first step is to start the framework on each cluster.

Starting the framework

Ensure that all the nodes are online and part of the cluster. To view the current status of the cluster, run the following command from any node:

```
# /usr/cluster/bin/cluster status
```

Then, on each cluster node, start the common agent container as root:

```
# /usr/sbin/cacaoadm enable
# /usr/sbin/cacaoadm start
```

On one node of each cluster, start the Geographic Edition framework with the following command:

```
# /usr/cluster/bin/geoadm start
```

Configuring trust between clusters

Communication between the clusters in a partnership must be secure. This requirement is particularly important when the two clusters are connected via a public network. The link between the clusters uses public key encryption to ensure this security, and the clusters must exchange public keys as part of the initial configuration.

On one node of one cluster, use the following command to import the keys from the remote cluster (paris in this example):

```
# /usr/cluster/bin/geops add-trust -c paris
```

Repeat this process on a node of the other cluster. You can confirm that the key import has been performed correctly by using the verify command:

```
# /usr/cluster/bin/geops verify-trust -c paris
```

Creating the partnership

After the framework is started on both clusters and trust has been established between them, create a partnership. A partnership is created on one cluster and then joined from the other cluster, using the geops command. In the example, the partnership is called ny-paris and is initially created from cluster newyork:

```
# /usr/cluster/bin/geops create -c paris -p\
   Notification_emailaddrs=admin@company.com ny-paris
```

This form of the command will use the default heartbeat to monitor the link between the clusters, and will send an e-mail message to the address admin@company.com if the connection is lost.

The partnership should then be joined from cluster paris:

```
# /usr/cluster/bin/geops join-partnership -c newyork ny-paris
```

Configuring a protection group

After the two clusters have been linked in a partnership, you can create one or more *protection groups* to manage applications and data replication. The following example creates a protection group for an Apache web server whose data is replicated using AVS. The data volumes used are managed by the Solaris Volume Manager, and must already exist. The example assumes that the resource group for the web server is initially offline.

You must define all required resources, such as logical hostnames used for replication, on both clusters before creating the protection group.

Creating the protection group

On one node of the cluster that will be the primary site, become superuser and create the protection group with the geopg command. In this example, the protection group is called apache-pg:

```
# /usr/cluster/bin/geopg create -s ny-paris -d avs -o primary apache-pg
```

Adding an AVS device group to the protection group

Before you add a device group to the protection group, use the geopg list command to ensure that the protection group is offline, and that the Nodelist property of the protection group has the same entries, in the same order, as the Nodelist property of the device group. If necessary, change one or both nodelists to ensure that this condition is met.

Create the file /var/cluster/geo/avs/<dgname>-volset.ini, where <dgname> is replaced by the name of the device group you are adding. This file must contain a valid SNDR volume set definition. The following example shows such a file entry for a Solaris Volume Manager volume named avsset. The entry must be on one line (ignore the line breaks in the example, which result from the page size for this book):

```
lh-paris-1 /dev/md/avsset/rdsk/d100 /dev/md/avsset/rdsk/d101 lh-newyork-1
  /dev/md/avsset/rdsk/d100 /dev/md/avsset/rdsk/d101 ip async C avsset
```

Add the device group to the protection group. This example adds a device group named apache-ds to the protection group apache-pg:

```
# /usr/cluster/bin/geopg add-device-group -p local_logical_host=lh-paris-1\
  -p remote_logical_host=lh-newyork-1 -p Enable_volume_set=True apache-ds apache-pg
```

The Enable_volume_set=True property instructs the command to use the volset.ini file that you created earlier, and automatically sets up replication of the volumes as defined in that file. Replication is configured between the logical hostname lh-paris-1 on the local cluster to lh-newyork-1 on the remote cluster.

Adding an application resource group to the protection group

Before you add an application resource group to the protection group, ensure that it exists on both clusters and that the Auto_start_on_new_cluster property of the resource group is set to False. In this example, the resource group name is apache-rg:

```
# /usr/cluster/bin/clrg show -p auto_start_on_new_cluster apache-rg
```

Setting the Auto_start_on_new_cluster property to False ensures that the Geographic Edition framework will not attempt to start the resource group automatically.

Add the application resource group to the protection group:

```
# /usr/cluster/bin/geopg add-resource-group apache-rg apache-pg
```

Copying the protection group information to the remote cluster

After creating the protection group on one cluster of the partnership, you must replicate it to the other cluster. On one node of the other cluster, become superuser and use the geopg get command:

```
# /usr/cluster/bin/geopg get -s ny-paris apache-pg
```

Activating the protection group

You can activate a protection group on only one cluster for maintenance purposes, but normally you will activate it on both clusters of a partnership:

```
# /usr/cluster/bin/geopg start -e global apache-pg
```

This will start the protection group and the data replication. The application resource group will be brought online on the cluster designated as the primary site.

Geographic Edition operations

After a partnership has been created, the two clusters use a heartbeat to monitor each other and the connection between them. If one site stops responding, the other will alert an administrator. This alert can be an e-mail message as described in the preceding example, or it can result in the execution of an arbitrary script. This script could, for example, trigger a pager message.

If the primary site is lost, then the secondary site will not automatically take over. This is intentional, as the recovery of the computer infrastructure should be just a part of a much larger reaction specified by the business continuity plan. Depending on the nature of the outage, other tasks may need to be performed first, or it may be preferable to repair the outage rather than experience the disruption of a transfer to a remote site. Consider, for example, a failure of a UPS protecting the primary site power supply. Bypassing the faulty unit and restarting the systems may be a preferable and more rapid solution to the outage.

If a transfer to the secondary site is required, two options are possible: *switchover* or *takeover*. These are performed at the protection-group level; it is not necessary to operate on all protection groups in a partnership together.

Switchover

A switchover is a managed swap of the roles within a protection group. The switchover operation is fully automated after it has been initiated by user command. The replicated copies of the data are synchronized and the replication is stopped. The cluster that was primary for the protection group is reconfigured as secondary, and the previous secondary is made primary. The replication is then restarted in the reverse direction, and the application resource group is brought online on the new primary. This operation can be performed to enable maintenance and upgrades on one cluster.

Takeover

A takeover is a unilateral promotion of the protection group secondary to the role of primary. Replication is stopped, and if the existing primary can be reached it is placed offline. The storage volumes are brought online on the new primary, and the application resource groups are started.

This is the emergency operation, normally used only when the primary site is no longer reachable and the secondary site must take over. It is not possible to guarantee that no data will be lost, because some replication updates may have been buffered for transmission at the primary site, and they will be lost. It is in this scenario that the designated RPO becomes significant.

Because this action is performed automatically, it can be designed and tested in advance. If a major disaster occurs, you don't need experts for the replication and application software on standby or have to worry about human error due to stress. A single command is sufficient to provide a managed transition to the secure remote site:

```
# /usr/cluster/bin/geopg takeover apache-pg
```

Customizing changeover functionality

You can specify a *role-change action script* as a property of a protection group. This script is executed when the primary or secondary role of a protection group changes. It can be used to update external services — for example, to remap entries in a naming service such as DNS so that client systems are redirected to the new primary site:

```
# /usr/cluster/bin/geopg set-prop -p RoleChange_ActionCmd=<script>\
 -p RoleChange_ActionArgs=<arguments>
```

Monitoring the framework

Use the following to check the status of all the entities within an Open HA Cluster Geographic Edition partnership:

```
# /usr/cluster/bin/geoadm status
# /usr/cluster/bin/geops list ny-paris
# /usr/cluster/bin/geopg list apache-pg
```

Resources

The first place to look for information on Open HA Cluster is the HA Clusters community group on OpenSolaris.org: http://opensolaris.org/os/community/ha-clusters. The community page contains links to all the active projects, documentation, presentations, an FAQ, and more.

Details of Project Colorado, the effort to run Open HA Cluster on the OpenSolaris binary distribution and to minimize the hardware requirements, can be found on the project web page at http://opensolaris.org/os/project/colorado.

For detailed instructions on using the cluster, consult the Solaris Cluster documentation from Sun. Although written for the enterprise product, the information is mostly applicable to Open HA Cluster, and provides the most detailed information available. The complete Sun Cluster Software Collection is available at http://docs.sun.com/app/docs/coll/1124.6. Some specific books of interest include the following:

- *Sun Cluster Concepts Guide*: Provides an overview of the software and various concepts (http://docs.sun.com/app/docs/doc/820-2554).

- *Sun Cluster Software Installation Guide*: How to install and configure the cluster (http://docs.sun.com/app/docs/doc/820-2555).

- *Sun Cluster System Administration Guide*: Covers administration of most aspects of the cluster other than service management (http://docs.sun.com/app/docs/doc/820-2558).

- *Sun Cluster Data Services Planning and Administration Guide*: The service management side of administration (http://docs.sun.com/app/docs/doc/820-2561).

- *Sun Cluster Data Service Developers Guide*: Everything you need to know to write your own agent (http://docs.sun.com/app/docs/doc/820-2559).

Sun also provides guidebooks specific to each data service. The x86 versions can be found at http://docs.sun.com/app/docs/coll/1573.1. Some books from this collection of particular interest include the following:

- *Sun Cluster Data Service for Apache*: Details on both failover and scalable Apache configurations (http://docs.sun.com/app/docs/doc/819-2975).

- *Sun Cluster Data Service for Solaris Containers*: Guidebook for using the HA Containers agent for failing over Zones as a black-box resource (http://docs.sun.com/app/docs/doc/819-3069).

A handy two-page quick reference guide to the Sun Cluster commands can be found at http://dlc.sun.com/pdf/819-6811/819-6811.pdf.

The Sun Cluster Geographic Edition documentation is a separate set, found at http://docs.sun.com/app/docs/coll/1191.4.

There are also two books on Sun Cluster 3.x:

- *Sun Cluster 3 Programming* by Joseph Bianco, Peter Lees, and Kevin Rabito (Prentice Hall, 2004).

- *Designing Enterprise Solutions with Sun Cluster 3.0* by Richard Elling and Tim Read (Prentice Hall, 2001).

The Sun Cluster Oasis group blog at http://blogs.sun.com/SC/ contains many practical articles on various aspects of Sun Cluster and Open HA Cluster, mostly written by the engineers directly working on the code.

The Sun Cluster wiki also provides a wealth of information about Sun Cluster and Open HA Cluster: http://wikis.sun.com/display/SunCluster/Home.

Finally, you can browse the source code for Open HA Cluster at http://src.opensolaris.org/source/xref/ohac, which includes subdirectories for Agents, Geographic Edition, and Core.

Summary

This chapter introduced the concept of high-availability clusters and introduced the Open High Availability Cluster software that can cluster multiple physical machines running OpenSolaris. You learned how to configure hardware for a cluster, how to install and configure the cluster software, and how to make Apache HTTP Server highly available in both failover and scalable mode. By reading this chapter, you also learned some advanced cluster administration, including details of resources, resource types, and resource groups. Also included were details about making your own custom services highly available with the generic data service and the SMF proxy, and you were introduced to Open HA Cluster Geographic Edition business continuity software.

This chapter concludes Part IV of this book. Part V switches gears to the important topic of virtualization. Chapter 17 provides an overview of the various virtualization technologies available on OpenSolaris, and the remaining chapters in the section delve into resource management, zones, xVM, LDoms, and VirtualBox.

Part V

OpenSolaris Virtualization

Chapter 17

Virtualization Overview

Running many applications and users on a single system has long been a common practice, particularly when computers were quite expensive. More recently, as the cost of a standalone system has fallen, it has become common to deploy each application stack on a dedicated machine, even though a majority of these systems are underutilized. In large enterprises, this has led to server-sprawl, with thousands of lightly used systems each running its own software stack. However, as other costs, such as space, power, and cooling, become more significant, this trend is reversing. This has led to a resurgence of interest in *virtualization* as a solution to consolidating these standalone applications onto shared machines.

Virtualization is a technique long used by operating systems to provide the illusion of exclusive access to shared system resources. For example, when running multiple processes on a single CPU, the operating system uses a form of virtualization to share the CPU among each process. A time-shared machine with multiple users provides another form of virtualization. These simple forms of virtualization are familiar, and largely taken for granted because an operating system such as OpenSolaris is inherently multi-tasking and multi-user. When you start to consolidate workloads and users onto a shared system this way, though, you soon find that, at a minimum, some form of resource management is necessary to provide control over the behavior of these competing consumers.

Running multiple applications and users on the same operating system is a familiar use of virtualization, however more sophisticated virtualization techniques provide additional isolation, up to the point of concurrently running multiple different operating systems on the same hardware. Simultaneously running

649

multiple operating systems has been used for decades, particularly on mainframes, but is now commonly used on all classes of machines.

In addition to resource management, OpenSolaris supports a variety of other virtualization techniques that enable greater isolation and flexibility. These techniques include *operating-system-level virtualization,* whereby the machine is still running a single OpenSolaris kernel, but the OS makes it appear as though multiple instances are running. OpenSolaris also provides support for simultaneously running more than one operating system. This is commonly called *full virtualization.* These different forms of virtualization are explained in more detail in this chapter.

OpenSolaris provides a range of virtualization solutions, each with advantages and disadvantages. Having a choice enables you to pick the best tool for the job at hand. In fact, these approaches are not mutually exclusive — it is possible to combine them to solve even more complex problems.

Benefits of Virtualization

In general, virtualization enables you to run multiple workloads on the same hardware in a predictable, secure, and isolated way. Depending on which virtualization solution you choose, there are different benefits, including the following:

- Higher utilization of the machine is possible through sharing of the system.
- Application stacks are completely isolated from each other.
- Misbehaving processes or malicious users in one instance cannot interfere with activities in another instance.
- Faults are isolated. This can include isolation of a complete crash of the operating system.
- Name conflicts, such as simultaneous use of a TCP port, are avoided.
- Security is improved. If the operating system instance is compromised, then only that instance is affected while the rest of the system remains secure.
- Administration can be delegated. The administrator for the specific instance can configure it as necessary and boot or reboot without affecting other instances.
- Cross-platform applications can be developed and tested on the same hardware, such as a developer's laptop.
- Consolidation is simplified. With the current focus on non-hardware related costs of running a machine, such as power or the high cost of expanding a datacenter, it makes economic sense to consolidate lightly used systems into fewer, better utilized machines.

The different virtualization solutions provided on OpenSolaris offer these benefits to varying degrees. The next section explains the different forms of virtualization, and later in the chapter you'll see a more detailed comparison of the strengths and weaknesses of the various alternatives.

Types of Virtualization

As previously described, OpenSolaris supports three primary types of virtualization: resource management, operating-system-level virtualization, and full virtualization.

Resource management

Once you start consolidating applications onto the same system, it's quickly apparent that you need some way to ensure that the appropriate resources are provided for each workload. You don't want a low-priority workload consuming most of the system's memory or CPU, starving a high-priority workload. Because this is a general problem, all forms of virtualization provide some way to control how resources are allocated to the different virtual machines. In this book, however, the term "resource management" is used specifically to describe OpenSolaris features that can be used to manage different workloads running directly on the same OS.

The OpenSolaris resource management capabilities provide a rich feature set that enables you to define workloads and then set limits and guarantees on the availability of the system's resources for each workload. Because these capabilities are built in to OpenSolaris itself, they are very lightweight.

CROSS-REF Resource management is the focus of Chapter 18.

Operating-system-level virtualization

Although running multiple workloads on the same OS is very efficient and provides the best possible performance for each workload, there is only minimal isolation of each workload, even when using resource management. For example, when two applications need to use the same network port, or a common configuration file needs to be set up differently for each workload, a namespace conflict results. Another limitation is that it is difficult to safely delegate administration of each workload. In many cases, privileges are required, but handing out those privileges allows access to other workloads that are owned by different users.

These sorts of problems are the reason why many sites originally deployed each workload on its own machine. In general, resource management, by itself, is insufficient in a complex environment. That's where operating-system-level virtualization comes in.

With operating-system-level virtualization, there is still only a single underlying operating system kernel, but on top of it you can create an environment for a workload that looks very much like its own standalone OS. On OpenSolaris this environment is called a *zone*. A zone provides a secure, isolated environment for running a workload. A zone boots and halts much like a standalone system, although these actions happen very quickly. Within the zone is a root user who can administer the zone, but that root user is distinct from the root user outside the zone. The root user inside the zone cannot see or affect anything outside of the zone. Within a zone, only processes running in the zone are visible. The zone provides a distinct namespace, so there are no conflicts on files or ports. For example, if an application opens port 80 in the zone, another application in a different zone can also open port 80.

CROSS-REF Zones are the focus of Chapter 19.

All of a zone's capabilities are inherently provided by the single, running version of OpenSolaris, so zones are very lightweight. There is no overhead for running inside a zone, meaning that application performance is just as fast as normal. In addition, the OpenSolaris resource management features should be applied to a zone, providing bounds for zone resource consumption. A zone and resource management used together is called a *container*.

Although having a single underlying kernel is a strength when it comes to performance, it can also be a limitation for zones. When the system reboots, all of the zones are also rebooted. Updating software on the system also has implications for the zones because some parts of the kernel and user-level libraries must stay in sync. Zones include the capability to run non-native environments, such as Linux, through the use of branded zones, but there is always only the single OpenSolaris kernel running on the machine.

Full virtualization

When you need more isolation and flexibility than zones provide, full virtualization is the next step. With full virtualization, multiple operating systems are actually running on the machine, with a thin layer underneath, the *hypervisor*, managing the system's physical resources. Each of the environments running a guest OS is called a *virtual machine*, or *domain*. These two terms basically mean the same thing, and which one is used tends to vary based on the specific hypervisor being used. With full virtualization, you can simultaneously run multiple instances of the same operating system or different operating systems.

NOTE The hypervisor is a software or firmware layer that sits underneath the operating system and manages access to the hardware. It acts like a simplified OS. It performs hardware resource allocation tasks similar to those performed by the guest operating system for processes. Instead of allocating the hardware resources to a process, the hypervisor allocates them to a virtual machine, and the guest OS in that virtual machine then allocates them to processes, just as it does when running on bare metal.

Types of hypervisors

Hypervisors are classified as either type 1 or type 2. A type 1 hypervisor runs directly on the bare hardware; a type 2 hypervisor runs on top of an underlying host operating system. The guest operating system then runs above the hypervisor. A type 2 hypervisor is different from operating-system-level virtualization. With a type 2 hypervisor, the base operating system does not know about the hypervisor and guest operating systems running above it — those simply appear as layered application software to the base operating system. With operating-system-level virtualization, the base OS inherently understands and manages the containers running within the OS.

OpenSolaris provides type 1 hypervisor virtualization through xVM Hypervisor on x86 hardware and Logical Domains (LDoms) on SPARC hardware. Type 2 hypervisor virtualization is provided through VirtualBox. Because they are just applications, other type 2 hypervisors can also run on OpenSolaris.

NOTE xVM Hypervisor is the name given to the port of the open source Xen project to run on OpenSolaris. In this book, xVM Hypervisor is usually shortened to xVM, unless the full name must be used to avoid confusion. Logical Domains is usually shortened to LDoms.

Although a type 1 hypervisor controls access to the hardware, it does not normally include support for the drivers for all of the devices supported by a full OS. Instead, the hypervisor works in conjunction with an OS running in a control domain to transform virtual I/O from a guest domain into physical I/O in the control domain. Both xVM and LDoms support this concept. A type 2 hypervisor just uses the I/O services of the underlying base OS.

Fully virtualized operating systems versus paravirtualization

The operating system running in a domain on top of a hypervisor can be categorized as either *fully virtualized* or *paravirtualized*.

A fully virtualized OS is completely unmodified and does not know that it is running on top of a hypervisor. Because of this, the OS assumes it can access hardware in a way that is incompatible with running in a virtualized environment. The underlying hypervisor software must be capable of detecting this, by either dynamically trapping into code to handle the access, or rewriting the guest OS code. In either case the hypervisor must manage these accesses in a way that is transparent to the running OS. This causes extra complexity in the hypervisor and extra overhead at runtime. A fully virtualized OS running on top of a hypervisor performs noticeably slower than if it were running on bare hardware. Depending on the processor architecture, supporting a fully virtualized OS within the hypervisor can be quite difficult. Newer processors include extensions, such as Intel VT-x or AMD-V, which provide hardware support to a hypervisor for managing a fully virtualized OS, but significant overhead still exists.

A paravirtualized OS has been modified to know when it is running on top of a hypervisor. When the OS detects this, it makes calls to the hypervisor instead of attempting to access the hardware directly. This is much more efficient in a virtual environment than running an unmodified OS, but it's also less flexible because the OS must be explicitly modified to work in conjunction with the specific hypervisor.

An alternative to these two options is a fully virtualized OS that is running with paravirtualized drivers. Device drivers are completely modular in a modern OS, making it possible to plug new drivers in to an otherwise unmodified OS. The new, paravirtualized drivers then interface with the hypervisor. This yields the I/O performance benefits of a paravirtualized OS, even though the rest of the OS is not hypervisor-aware. However, other hardware accesses, such as to the memory management unit (MMU), by the OS will still be slower compared to a fully paravirtualized OS.

The xVM Hypervisor is capable of running fully virtualized guest operating systems as long as the underlying processor includes support for virtualization extensions. It can also run paravirtualized guest operating systems and fully virtualized operating systems with paravirtualized drivers. LDoms only supports paravirtualized guest operating systems. OpenSolaris has been paravirtualized to run as a guest OS on top of both the xVM and LDoms hypervisors. It has also been enhanced to run as a control domain for both hypervisors. Operating systems running on top of VirtualBox always run as fully virtualized guests.

Comparison of virtualization layers

This discussion of the different types of virtualization may seem a bit daunting, as there are many new terms and several different layers with the various solutions. Figure 17-1 provides a side-by-side comparison of where the different components and layers exist in the different solutions.

FIGURE 17-1

Compare the different virtualization layers.

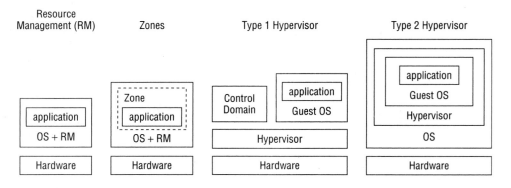

The first stack on the left, showing resource management, should look the most familiar. It is the typical configuration of an application running on the OS, which sits directly on bare metal. The key addition here is the use of resource management within the OS to set various limits on the application.

The Zones stack is very similar to the resource management case, except that zones provide an isolation boundary around the application environment. The zone is a boundary, not a layer.

In the type 1 hypervisor stack, the hypervisor acts as a layer between the guest OS and the hardware. The OS no longer directly manages the hardware, but works through the hypervisor. Alongside the guest OS is another OS instance, acting as the control domain for the system.

Finally, in the type 2 hypervisor stack you see that the hypervisor is really just an application running on the OS. Within that application is a running guest OS that in turn runs the application.

Study the layers with these different solutions and you can see how it is possible to mix and match various combinations. In the most extreme case, you could use a zone on a guest OpenSolaris instance running in a type 2 hypervisor such as VirtualBox on an OS running on a type 1 hypervisor such as xVM. Another possibility would be to run a type 2 hypervisor such as VirtualBox inside of a zone running on OpenSolaris on a type 1 hypervisor. Although such configurations are possible, they are virtualization overkill. Typically, you use only one type of virtualization or at most a combination of one of the hypervisors with zones.

Other virtualization solutions

QEMU is an open source type 2 hypervisor. OpenSolaris.org hosts a project to improve the support for OpenSolaris as both host and guest in that environment.

In addition to the open source hypervisors provided with OpenSolaris, several similar proprietary solutions are available from other vendors. Microsoft delivers its Hyper-V software, and VMware offers a suite of products in this area. VMware ESX Server is a type 1 hypervisor, and the low-end products, VMware Server and VMware Workstation, are type 2 hypervisors. Because VMware Server is both well established and freeware, it is a commonly deployed solution for users who want to run multiple virtual machines. OpenSolaris can run as a guest in this environment, but not as the host because this software is proprietary and VMware has not ported it to OpenSolaris. There are also a variety of other third-party, closed-source virtualization products from different sources. Because they aren't part of OpenSolaris, they aren't discussed in this book.

> **CROSS-REF** Chapter 2 describes how to install OpenSolaris under VMware Workstation.

Comparing Virtualization Solutions

Each of the virtualization solutions described here has various strengths and weaknesses. It is not always easy or obvious to determine which solution to use. This section provides a rough comparison between the various solutions to help you get a better sense of when it is appropriate to use one or the other.

From a performance perspective, both resource management and zones are built into Open-Solaris, so there is no additional layering that applications have to go through. Using either of these, or a combination of both, normally provides full performance. In addition, the degree of scaling will be higher than is possible with a hypervisor because the overhead of the hypervisor is not present. In general, a type 1 hypervisor should provide better performance than a type 2 hypervisor, although both solutions impart a performance hit compared to running OpenSolaris on bare metal. The kinds of performance impact seen when running on a hypervisor vary according to which hypervisor is used, the domain configuration, how I/O is set up, and whether the guest is paravirtualized or has to run in a fully virtualized domain.

Beyond the performance and overhead implications of using virtualization, other important factors include the level of isolation and the flexibility that is provided. For this, you are typically looking at either zones or one of the hypervisors, as resource management by itself doesn't provide much isolation.

Zones provide excellent isolation, as long as the single underlying kernel is not a limitation. Because some amount of code has to be in sync between the kernel and the user level, software management operations such as upgrading the base OS can impact all zones. With a hypervisor, each domain is running its own kernel, so software management can happen independently. In addition, if the kernel crashes, all zones stop running, but a kernel crash in a guest domain on a hypervisor is restricted to that domain. However, because the hypervisor is a small kernel in its own right, any problem in the hypervisor can still affect all domains. Likewise, domains on a hypervisor typically use I/O services from some other domain, so a disruption in that domain also causes problems. These factors are frequently overlooked with a hypervisor, but real-world examples are easy to find.

Flexibility can mean various things. A hypervisor provides the most flexibility for each domain because each is running its own, standalone operating system. This flexibility extends to concurrently running, dramatically different kernels such as Windows, Linux, and OpenSolaris. The Zones feature does provide the flexibility to run different user-level environments inside the zone using branded zones. Sun Microsystems provides Solaris 8 and Solaris 9 branded zones and OpenSolaris includes support for the 1x brand, which runs a Linux user-level environment.

In terms of portability, because zones are part of OpenSolaris, they run anywhere that Open-Solaris runs. Type 1 hypervisors tend to be more platform-specific and there are various limitations on where they can be used. For example, xVM only supports x86-based systems and requires certain hardware to support fully virtualized domains, whereas LDoms only runs on certain variants of the SPARC platform. A type 2 hypervisor such as VirtualBox is the most portable because it is primarily application software and runs on a wide variety of host operating systems, although it does not currently run on SPARC hardware.

Another important factor is how easy the different solutions are to set up, use, and manage. On its own, OpenSolaris resource management can actually be quite difficult to use, but when used in conjunction with zones, it is very easy. Setting up a zone is easier than one of the type 1 hypervisors, although setting up VirtualBox is probably the easiest of all because of its excellent GUI-based tools. Ease of use and manageability are two very active areas of development across the entire virtualization spectrum, so you should expect to see significant improvements in this area for all solutions.

Table 17-1 summarizes all these factors for the various solutions.

As you can see, one size does not fit all, so it may take some experimentation to determine which solution is best for your problem.

TABLE 17-1

Solution Factors

Factor	Resource Management	Zones	xVM	LDoms	VirtualBox
Performance	High	High	Medium	Medium	Low
Efficiency	High	High	Medium	Medium	Low
Scalability	High	High	Medium	Medium	Low
Isolation	Low	Medium	High	High	High
Flexibility	Low	Medium	High	High	High
Portability	Medium	Medium	Low	Low	High
Ease of Use	Low	Medium	Low	Low	High

Virtualization and a Graphical Display

If you are used to working on a laptop or workstation running a window system, you might be wondering how to use the window system of the various domains once each is consolidated onto the same system. For some configurations this won't be an issue if you are simply running a non-graphics based workload in the domain. However, in some cases it is important to run a particular graphical application, or perhaps you want to run an entire guest window system in the domain.

The techniques to run graphical applications vary with each virtualization solution. VirtualBox automatically provides a complete window environment for the guest OS, whereas the other solutions require some additional work. The steps to set up graphical access for either a zone or a guest instance of OpenSolaris running in a type 1 hypervisor domain are similar.

If you need only the capability to run specific graphical applications, the easiest solution is to leverage the capabilities of X11, the underlying window system technology on OpenSolaris, combined with ssh, the secure shell, to forward the application to your native display. That's done using the ssh -X command.

CROSS-REF X11 forwarding using ssh -X is covered in Chapter 11.

If you want to run the entire window system remotely displayed onto your native display, OpenSolaris enables this with support for VNC, the Virtual Network Computing protocol. Using a VNC client, such as vncviewer included in OpenSolaris, or a client for some other OS, you can display the entire desktop that is running in the zone or domain.

CROSS-REF See Chapter 4 for more information about setting up and using VNC on the desktop. Follow the steps provided to set up the zone or domain for remote display.

Virtualization Administration

When using virtualization to consolidate many systems into one, management problems typically do not diminish. Under a hypervisor approach, each virtual machine is administered like a standalone system, so the total number of entities to manage has not decreased. In addition, the hypervisor and control domain must be managed. With zones, there is only a single operating system to administer but each zone still requires a certain amount of management, so the overall level of work might still be comparable to a collection of standalone systems. In general, virtualization does not reduce the systems administration burden and might even increase it. A variety of open source projects and proprietary solutions are attempting to address this problem.

One project specifically targeting OpenSolaris, and working to address management issues with a focus on virtualization, is the xVM Ops Center. This project is still in the early stages but is targeted toward managing all aspects of virtualization on OpenSolaris, including zones, xVM Server, and LDoms.

NOTE xVM Hypervisor and xVM Ops Center are two different projects related to virtualization that share the xVM name. The umbrella xVM site is at http://openxvm.org/.

Summary

This chapter provided an overview of basic virtualization concepts, including resource management, operating-system-level virtualization using zones, and hypervisor-level virtualization with xVM, LDoms, or VirtualBox. Type 1 and 2 hypervisors, as well as paravirtualization and full virtualization, were explained. This chapter also compared the different virtualization solutions provided by OpenSolaris.

Resource Management

R esource Management is the collection of facilities in OpenSolaris that are used to configure, monitor, and control the system's resource allocation to running processes. In the context of this chapter, resources are predominantly CPU or memory. Using resource management to constrain multiple workloads running on the same system is the most basic form of virtualization available on OpenSolaris.

Introduction to Resource Management

When multiple users or software application stacks are sharing the same machine, it is possible for one of them to monopolize the system's resources. The resource management capabilities in OpenSolaris provide a variety of ways to specify how these resources should be allocated so that the system's overall objectives are met. For example, if the system runs a specific, business-critical application, along with other, less critical, applications, then the resource management capabilities can be used to ensure that the business-critical application always has the resources it needs when it is ready to run. The resource management features can be used to provide minimum or maximum guarantees for resource utilization as well as to partition those resources between consumers.

OpenSolaris resource management is not one single feature. Instead, it is a collection of different capabilities within the operating system. As such, resource management can seem confusing because some features are independent of the others. This chapter describes each of these individual capabilities and explains when they can be used on their own or combined with one of the other features.

Resource management encompasses the following individual OpenSolaris features:

- Projects and Tasks
- Resource Controls
- Resource Caps
- Resource Pools
- Processor Sets
- Scheduling
- Accounting

In addition to these facilities, OpenSolaris includes an operating system virtualization feature called *Zones*. Zones are discussed in detail in Chapter 19, but it is worth noting that they leverage, and are integrated with, many of the resource management features described in this chapter. In fact, zones provide a simplified and unified way to use many of the OpenSolaris resource management features without the need for some of the administrative complexity you'll see in this chapter.

Projects and Tasks

Projects and *tasks* are the mechanisms used to organize processes so that resource management settings can easily be applied to logical groups of processes. Every process running on the system is assigned to both a project and a task. This can be seen using the ps command with the options to display the project and task data:

```
$ ps -eo user,pid,project,taskid,args
    USER    PID  PROJECT      TASKID COMMAND
    root      0  system            0 sched
    root      1  system            1 /sbin/init
 ...
    sarah  3068  group.staff      82 -bash
 ...
```

Here, the first processes on the system, sched and init, are assigned to both the system project and their own tasks. The bash process for user sarah is in the group.staff project and task 82.

The id command can also show the current project:

```
$ id -p
uid=100(sarah) gid=10(staff) projid=10(group.staff)
```

A project within OpenSolaris is much like the corresponding concept in the real world. It has a name and it has certain attributes associated with it. Tasks are part of a project and inherit those attributes. Processes running on the system are always part of a task, so they are also part of a project. Each process can be associated with only a single task, which is, in turn, associated with a single project. However, there can be many tasks within a project and many processes within a task. Whenever a process forks, it inherits its project and task from the parent. This relationship is illustrated in Figure 18-1.

FIGURE 18-1

The relationship between processes, tasks, and projects

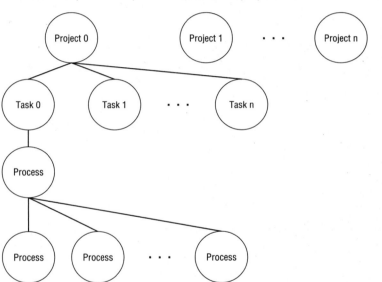

The project database

Projects are defined in the project database. This can be the /etc/project file on the local system or stored in a name service such as NIS or LDAP. Access to the project database is configured using the name service switch.

CROSS-REF NIS, LDAP, and the name service switch are described in Chapter 10 on network file systems and directory servers.

The format of the project database is described briefly here, and in full detail on the project(4) man page. The /etc/project file defines one project per line with a set of colon-delimited fields:

```
name:id:comment:user_list:group_list:attributes
```

The project name is the first field; the project ID is the second field, and so on. The user list, group list, and attributes are described later in this chapter, along with the commands used to manipulate the database.

Determining the default project

When a user logs in to the system, a default project must be assigned to the initial process for that user. The following procedure, which is documented on the getprojent(3PROJECT) man page, is used to assign the user's initial process to a project.

The getdefaultproj() function is used to determine the default project for a process. This function goes through the following steps:

1. Look for the project attribute for the user in the user_attr database. If the attribute is in the user_attr database, then the function will try to look up the project name in the project database. If the project is not found or the user is not a member of the project, then go to the next step.

CROSS-REF   The user_attr database is briefly described in Chapter 11, "Security."

2. Search the project database for the project user.{*username*}. For example, the project name field in the database for user name smith would be user.smith. If this project is not found or the user is excluded from that project, then go to the next step.

3. Using the user's default group ID, which is assigned in his or her passwd entry, search the project database for the project *group.groupname*. For example, if the user's default group ID were 10 and the group database mapped 10 to the staff group, the project name field would be group.staff. If no match is found or the user is excluded from that project, then go to the next step.

4. Use the project named default unless the user is excluded from that project, as described later in the "Configuring projects" section.

If a default project cannot be assigned, then the user cannot log in to the system. Once a project has been assigned, any subsequent processes created as children of the initial process will inherit that project, unless the project is changed using the procedures described later in this section.

Many of the basic system processes are started when the machine boots. These processes are not associated with a user login. Instead, there is a special project with ID 0, the system project, which is the project with which these processes are associated. You can see a few of those in the ps example earlier. If you look at the /etc/project file, you'll also notice that there is a project named user.root that is used for the system administrator. When you log in, or su, to root, the user.root project is the one that those processes will use. You can see how this default project is assigned to root based on step 2, as just described.

Changing tasks

Although your initial process is assigned to a default project and a new task when you log in, it is possible to change the task and project. The newtask command is used to start a process in a new task and project or to change the project of an existing process.

If you are allowed to join a project, described in the next section, then you can use the newtask command to start a new task in a different project, as this simple example using myproject shows:

```
$ id -p
uid=100(sarah) gid=10(staff) projid=10(group.staff)
$ newtask -p myproject id -p
uid=100(sarah) gid=10(staff) projid=100(myproject)
```

In this example, the newtask command is used just to run the id command in myproject. Of course, in normal usage the command would probably start a new stack of software running. If you need to change the project of a running process, you can also use the newtask command by specifying the pid of the process with the -c option:

```
$ newtask -c 5039 -p myproject
```

In addition to the id command, which shows the current project, the projects command shows all of the projects of which you are a member:

```
$ projects
default group.staff myproject
```

Configuring projects

Setting up membership in a project and defining the project's attributes are the two main configuration tasks.

Project membership

To join a project other than your default project, you must be configured as a member of that project. As previously described, the format of a project entry is as follows:

```
name:id:comment:user_list:group_list:attributes
```

The user_list or group_list fields are used to specify a list of users or groups that are members of the project. These are simple comma-delimited lists. You can also use an asterisk (*) as a wildcard, indicating any user or group is allowed, or an exclamation (!), indicating that the named user or group is not allowed.

Instead of directly editing the project database, the `projmod` command is used to make updates to existing projects, `projadd` adds a new project, and `projdel` deletes an existing project. The man pages for these commands describe the options in detail. The following example adds a user named `sarah` to an existing project named `myproject`:

```
# projmod -a -U sarah myproject
```

The next example defines a new project named `build` with a user named `sarah` as a member:

```
# projadd -U sarah build
```

Because an explicit project ID was not specified, one is automatically assigned. The `projects` command can be used to display the database:

```
$ projects -l
system
    projid : 0
    comment: ""
    users  : (none)
    groups : (none)
    attribs:
user.root
    projid : 1
    comment: ""
    users  : (none)
    groups : (none)
    attribs:
...
build
    projid : 100
    comment: ""
    users  : sarah
    groups : (none)
    attribs:
```

Project attributes

So far, you have seen the basics of projects, but until some attributes are defined for a project, it is only minimally useful. The project attributes actually specify the resource management settings that will be applied to processes in that project. The next few sections describe these resource management capabilities in more detail, so this example simply illustrates how to set some attributes on the `build` project you just created:

```
# projmod -K "rcap.max-rss=10000000" \
-K "project.max-lwps=(privileged,100,none)" build
```

This example defines two different attribute/value pairs for the project, replacing any attributes that had been defined. It is also possible to add or remove individual attributes using the `-a` or

-r options, respectively. These new resource management settings will be applied to any new tasks in that project. You can also cause these new settings to be applied to existing tasks in the project with the -A option.

The project attributes can be project-level resource controls, described in the "Resource Controls" section, a resource cap, described in the "Resource Caps" section, or a pool binding, described in the "Resource Pools" section.

Managing by project and task

In addition to the ps command, shown earlier, several other commands are project and task aware. The prstat command summarizes project information with the -J option:

```
$ prstat -J
PID USERNAME   SIZE    RSS STATE  PRI NICE      TIME  CPU PROCESS/NLWP
...
PROJID      NPROC  SWAP    RSS MEMORY      TIME  CPU PROJECT
    10         70 1110M 1063M    52%   5:43:02 2.8% group.staff
     1          2  572K 3408K   0.2%   0:00:00 0.0% user.root
     0         51   87M   39M   1.9%   0:07:14 0.0% system
Total: 123 processes, 359 lwps, load averages: 0.07, 0.05, 0.04
```

Likewise, the -T option summarizes by task. The prstat command can also be used with the -j projectname option to monitor processes within the specified project, or the -k taskid option to monitor processes in the specified task.

The pgrep and pkill proc tools also accept -J and -T options so that they can be used for projects or tasks.

CROSS-REF The proc tools are described in more detail in Chapter 14.

Using these commands, you can easily monitor and manage a collection of processes by project or task.

Resource Controls

Resource controls, or rctls, is the mechanism used within OpenSolaris to configure limits for processes, tasks, projects, or zones. Resource controls are values set within the kernel and applied to the associated object at runtime, controlling the behavior of that object. Rctls have replaced most of the configuration that used to be done in the /etc/system file in earlier releases of Solaris. Using rctls enables dynamic management of the system's limits, instead of the static boot-time configuration provided by /etc/system. In addition, rctls are always used within the kernel instead of the traditional limits managed by the setrlimit system call. Although the setrlimit and getrlimit system calls, as well as the plimit command, are still available for backward compatibility, rctls are the preferred interface for managing system limits.

CROSS-REF   **Zones and their interaction with rctls are explained in Chapter 19. The basic resource control concepts described here also apply to zone rctls.**

Using rctls

OpenSolaris provides a broad range of rctls, which are described shortly. This example illustrates one rctl: `process.max-file-descriptor`. This rctl sets the upper limit for the number of open file descriptors that a process can have. The `prctl` command is the CLI that is used to view and modify rctl settings. It is used for managing all types of rctls — process, task, project, or zone. By default, it is directed against a process. Using the pid for your login shell, you can see all of the rctl settings for that process:

```
$ prctl 11609
process: 11609: bash
NAME      PRIVILEGE        VALUE    FLAG    ACTION          RECIPIENT
...
process.max-file-descriptor
          basic            256       -      deny            11609
          privileged       65.5K     -      deny               -
          system           2.15G    max     deny               -
...
```

This indicates that the current basic value for the `process.max-file-descriptor` rctl is 256, which means that the process can have 256 open file descriptors. If it tried to open more than that, it would receive an error. Note that privilege levels, flags, and actions are associated with the rctl. Those are explained in the next section.

TIP   **Instead of looking up a process with `ps` and then using the pid, you can use `$$`, which the shell expands to your current pid, to see the rctl values for your process.**

Instead of looking at a single process, you can view the rctl settings for a specific project:

```
$ prctl -i project group.staff
project: 10: group.staff
NAME      PRIVILEGE        VALUE    FLAG    ACTION          RECIPIENT
...
project.max-lwps
          system           2.15G    max     deny               -
...
```

There is no `max-file-descriptor` rctl for a project, so this example was trimmed to show the `project.max-lwps` rctl instead. It also shows how to use the `-i` option with `prctl` to specify what you are interested in. The `-i` option accepts `process`, `task`, `project`, or `zone` as a parameter and defaults to `process`.

Some rctls can be specified at more than one level, with the system using the order process, task, project, and then zone, and the most constrained limit being applied.

The full rctl syntax is complex. It is explained in more detail in the next section, but this example shows how to set a new value for the process.max-file-descriptor rctl on process 11609:

```
$ prctl -r -n process.max-file-descriptor -v 512 11609
$ prctl -n process.max-file-descriptor 11609
process: 11609: bash
NAME      PRIVILEGE      VALUE     FLAG    ACTION      RECIPIENT
process.max-file-descriptor
          basic          512        -      deny         11609
          privileged     65.5K      -      deny           -
          system         2.15G     max     deny           -
```

The -r option means replace the current value with the new value, the -n option specifies the rctl name, and the -v option specifies a new value. This process will now be allowed to have 512 open file descriptors before receiving an error.

rctl Syntax

The preceding prctl output shows that an rctl can have multiple privileges, as well as a flag and action associated with each privilege level.

The PRIVILEGE specifies the value for the three possible levels:

Privilege	Definition
basic	The user can modify the value.
privileged	The superuser can modify the value.
system	The systems absolute limit

The basic value cannot exceed the privileged value, and the privileged value cannot exceed the system value.

The ACTION shows what action will be taken when the value is reached:

Action	Description
none	No action is taken. This can used to monitor when a value is exceeded.
deny	The request for more resources is denied.
signal=	The specified signal is sent to the process that exceeded the limit. The valid signals are SIGBART, SIGXRES, SIGHUP, SIGSTOP, SIGTERM, and SIGKILL.

The FLAG column can be either max, if the value represents the system's upper limit, or inf, if the value represents no limit. Otherwise, the field contains a dash (-) as a placeholder.

The prctl command can be used to set both the value and the action for a specific privilege level, as this example setting a task rctl shows:

```
# prctl -t basic -n task.max-lwps -v 25 -e signal=SIGXRES \
  -p 11609 -i task 79
# prctl -n task.max-lwps -i task 79
task: 79
NAME       PRIVILEGE      VALUE    FLAG   ACTION          RECIPIENT
task.max-lwps
           basic          25       -      signal=XRES     11609
           system         2.15G    max    deny            -
```

The preceding example shows that the task ID, 79, was specified using the -i option, but a pid within the task must also be specified using -p. A pid must always be provided when setting an rctl. You can also use the command to delete specific rctl values:

```
# prctl -t basic -n task.max-lwps -d signal -p 11609 -i task 79
```

The rctladm command is used to administer the global rctl facility. Use this command to set the logging behavior for a specific rctl or to enable and disable rctls. The -l option displays the current global configuration:

```
# rctladm -l
process.max-port-events    syslog=off    [ deny count ]
process.max-msg-messages   syslog=off    [ deny count ]
process.max-msg-qbytes     syslog=off    [ deny bytes ]
process.max-sem-ops        syslog=off    [ deny count ]
...
```

You may want to enable system logging for the rctls that you want to monitor. See the rctladm(1M) man page for more details if necessary.

rctl list

Table 18-1 briefly describes each of the current set of rctls in OpenSolaris. The name of the rctl indicates whether it specifies per-process, per-project, per-task, or per-zone limits.

Project rctls

Although resource controls can be set on a process dynamically, they are more useful when specified on a project. That way, all processes in the project use the specified rctls. This example sets both the task.max-lwps and project.max-lwps rctls for the build project:

```
# projmod -K "task.max-lwps=(basic,100,deny)" \
  -K "project.max-lwps=(privileged,500,deny)" build
```

TABLE 18-1

Current OpenSolaris rctls

rctl	Definition
`process.max-address-space`	Maximum address space for a process, in bytes
`process.max-core-size`	Maximum size of a core dump file, in bytes
`process.max-cpu-time`	Maximum CPU time, in seconds
`process.max-data-size`	Maximum heap size, in bytes
`process.max-file-descriptor`	Maximum number of file descriptors
`process.max-file-size`	Maximum file offset for writing, in bytes
`process.max-msg-messages`	Maximum number of messages in a message queue (see the `msg.h(3HEAD)` man page)
`process.max-msg-qbytes`	Maximum number of bytes in a message queue (see the `msg.h(3HEAD)` man page)
`process.max-port-events`	Maximum number of events per event port (see the `port_create(3C)` man page)
`process.max-sem-nsems`	Maximum number of semaphores per set (see the `semaphore(3C)` man page)
`process.max-sem-ops`	Maximum number of semaphore operations per `semop()` call (see the `semaphore(3C)` man page)
`process.max-stack-size`	Maximum stack size, in bytes
`project.cpu-cap`	Described in detail in the "CPU caps" section later in this chapter
`project.cpu-shares`	Described in detail in the "Fair Share Scheduler" section later in this chapter
`project.max-contracts`	Maximum number of contracts (see the `contract(4)` man page)
`project.max-crypto-memory`	Maximum amount of kernel memory that can be used for crypto operations
`project.max-locked-memory`	Maximum amount of physical memory that can be locked, in bytes

continued

TABLE 18-1	*(continued)*
rctl	**Definition**
project.max-lwps	Maximum number of lightweight processes. Each running process accounts for one or more LWPs.
project.max-msg-ids	Maximum number of message queue IDs (see the msg.h(3HEAD) man page)
project.max-port-ids	Maximum number of event ports (see the port_create(3C) man page)
project.max-sem-ids	Maximum number of semaphore IDs (see the semaphore(3C) man page)
project.max-shm-ids	Maximum number of shared memory IDs (see the shmop(2) man page)
project.max-shm-memory	Maximum amount of shared memory, in bytes (see the shmop(2) man page)
project.max-tasks	Maximum number of tasks
task.max-cpu-time	Maximum CPU time for all processes in the task, in seconds
task.max-lwps	Maximum number of lightweight processes for all processes in the task
zone.cpu-cap	CPU caps are described in detail in the "Scheduling" section, later in this chapter. That section applies to zones as well as to projects.
zone.cpu-shares	CPU shares are described in detail in the section "Fair Share Scheduler," later in this chapter. That section applies to zones as well as to projects.
zone.max-locked-memory	Maximum amount of physical memory that can be locked, in bytes
zone.max-lwps	Maximum number of lightweight processes. Each running process accounts for one or more LWPs.
zone.max-msg-ids	Maximum number of message queue IDs (see the msg.h(3HEAD) man page)
zone.max-sem-ids	Maximum number of semaphore IDs (see the semaphore(3C) man page)
zone.max-shm-ids	Maximum number of shared memory IDs (see the shmop(2) man page)
zone.max-shm-memory	Maximum amount of shared memory, in bytes (see the shmop(2) man page)
zone.max-swap	Maximum amount of swap space, in bytes

The projmod example and the values for these rctls should make more sense now. Tasks within the project will be limited to 100 lightweight processes, and the overall project is limited to 500. You can use multiple -K options to specify more than one rctl, and you can add, remove, or replace individual rctls on a project. The projmod(1M) man page describes all of the options in detail.

Resource Caps

Resource caps are another facility to control processes within OpenSolaris. Although the name makes it sound similar to rctls, this facility is actually quite different. Resource caps specify a soft limit on the amount of physical memory that can be used by a project or a zone. This is different from the max-locked-memory rctls because it relates to the total amount of physical memory a process should be allowed to use. You might have noticed that there is no rctl to set this kind of limit. Providing such an rctl is actually quite difficult with the current virtual memory implementation in OpenSolaris. Instead, the resource cap facility was created to solve this problem. Although the name sounds like a general-purpose subsystem, and it was probably intended that way when it was first designed, in reality its only use is to limit physical memory consumption.

Resource caps are implemented by a user-level daemon, rcapd, which will scan all processes in a project or zone that have a memory limit and attempt to page out pages from physical memory when the project or zone is over its limit. That is why this is a soft limit — the rcapd doesn't start working until the collection is over its limit, and it can take some time before it can bring the collection back under the limit.

The limit is configured for a project using the standard projmod syntax you have already seen, using the rcap.max-rss attribute:

```
# projmod -K "rcap.max-rss=10000000" build
```

In addition to configuring the limit for the project, you must also ensure that the SMF service that implements resource caps, svc:/system/rcap, is enabled.

NOTE Configuring the limit for a zone is described in Chapter 19. SMF is described in Chapter 13. When used with zones, the SMF service does not need to be manually enabled; the zone's infrastructure does that automatically. The rcap service in the global zone will cap any nonglobal zones that have a physical memory limit, along with any projects running in the global zone. If memory limits are configured on projects within a nonglobal zone, then that zone needs to run its own instance of the rcap service.

The rcapstat command is used to monitor the behavior of the rcap service:

```
# rcapstat
    id project      nproc    vm    rss    cap    at avgat    pg avgpg
   100 myproject      -      0K     0K    20K    0K    0K    0K    0K
   102 build          -    456K  3232K  9766K    0K    0K    0K    0K
    id project      nproc    vm    rss    cap    at avgat    pg avgpg
   100 myproject      -      0K     0K    20K    0K    0K    0K    0K
   102 build          -    456K  3232K  9766K    0K    0K    0K    0K
```

By default, the command outputs updated information every five seconds, although that can be changed by specifying the interval as a command-line argument. As shown in the example, the `build` project is using only 3,232KB, well under its 9,766KB limit. If the project exceeds its limit, the other statistics in the output will be updated as the `rcap` service starts scanning processes in the project and paging out memory. You can also use the `-z` option to monitor the behavior for nonglobal zones.

The `rcapadm` command is used to configure the behavior of the `rcap` service. You can set the scan parameters and minimum memory utilization, as well as dynamically change limits for zones. The `rcapadm(1M)` man page describes all of the options.

Resource Pools

Resource Pools enable you to partition a subset of the system's CPUs into *processor sets* and assign those pools to projects or zones. This setting restricts those projects or zones to using only the processors assigned to the pool. In this way, you can explicitly control and guarantee that specific processors will only be available for exclusive use by the specified workloads. Although pools currently work with only processor sets, the framework is extensible so that other types of sets, such as memory sets, can be added later.

Configuring a pool

Because the CLI syntax is complex, the procedures to configure a pool are fairly difficult and error-prone. This example walks through the basic steps to set up a pool and processor set with a range of 1–8 CPUs assigned to it. Start by enabling pools and discovering the current configuration:

```
# pooladm -e
# pooladm -s
```

You can now see the default pool configuration using the `pooladm` command:

```
# pooladm
system default
        string  system.comment
        int     system.version 1
        boolean system.bind-default true
        string  system.poold.objectives wt-load

        pool pool_default
                int     pool.sys_id 0
                boolean pool.active true
                boolean pool.default true
                int     pool.importance 1
                string  pool.comment
                pset    pset_default
```

```
pset pset_default
        int      pset.sys_id -1
        boolean  pset.default true
        uint     pset.min 1
        uint     pset.max 65536
        string   pset.units population
        uint     pset.load 22
        uint     pset.size 20
        string   pset.comment

        cpu
                int      cpu.sys_id 17
                string   cpu.comment
                string   cpu.status on-line

        cpu
                int      cpu.sys_id 16
                string   cpu.comment
                string   cpu.status on-line
        ...
        cpu
                int      cpu.sys_id 10
                string   cpu.comment
                string   cpu.status on-line
```

This output is explained in more detail later, but note a few items. There is one pool, pool_default, and one processor set, pset_default, which is associated with the default pool. You can see this binding with the pset property on the default pool. The default processor set shows that the system has a total of 20 CPUs (the pset_size property). Also note that the CPUs do not print out in any particular order. The other properties are explained later in this section.

Now you can create a new processor set and pool:

```
# poolcfg -c 'create pset mypset (uint pset.min=1; uint pset.max=8)'
# poolcfg -c 'create pool mypool'
# poolcfg -c 'associate pool mypool (pset mypset)'
# pooladm -c
```

This creates a pool named mypool and a processor set named mypset with a range of 1–8 CPUs. The -c option to poolcfg indicates that the argument is a command. Note that the command must be in quotes so that it is passed as a single argument, and that each parameter within the command has an explicit type associated with it. The poolcfg command syntax and parameters are explained in more detail next. The final pooladm -c command instantiates the configuration into the kernel, a process also explained below.

TIP   Although it is possible to associate a pset with more than one pool, it is usually simpler to have a one-to-one mapping. Sharing psets could be more useful in the future if memory sets are added.

You can see the new configuration using `pooladm`:

```
# pooladm
system default
        string   system.comment
        int      system.version 1
        boolean  system.bind-default true
        string   system.poold.objectives wt-load

        pool mypool
                int      pool.sys_id 1
                boolean  pool.active true
                boolean  pool.default false
                int      pool.importance 1
                string   pool.comment
                pset     mypset

        pool pool_default
                int      pool.sys_id 0
                boolean  pool.active true
                boolean  pool.default true
                int      pool.importance 1
                string   pool.comment
                pset     pset_default

        pset mypset
                int      pset.sys_id 1
                boolean  pset.default false
                uint     pset.min 1
                uint     pset.max 8
                string   pset.units population
                uint     pset.load 29
                uint     pset.size 8
                string   pset.comment

                cpu
                        int      cpu.sys_id 5
                        string   cpu.comment
                        string   cpu.status on-line
                ...
                cpu
                        int      cpu.sys_id 2
                        string   cpu.comment
                        string   cpu.status on-line

        pset pset_default
                int      pset.sys_id -1
                boolean  pset.default true
                uint     pset.min 1
                uint     pset.max 65536
                string   pset.units population
```

```
uint     pset.load 19
uint     pset.size 12
string   pset.comment
cpu
         int      cpu.sys_id 17
         string   cpu.comment
         string   cpu.status on-line
...
cpu
         int      cpu.sys_id 10
         string   cpu.comment
         string   cpu.status on-line
```

This output indicates that all eight CPUs were assigned to `mypset`. This is not guaranteed. When you specify a range of CPUs and instantiate the configuration, some number of CPUs within the range will be assigned, based on what is available in the default processor set and what can be taken from other processor sets. If the configuration cannot be instantiated, you will receive an error.

Binding a pool to a project

Now that you have configured a basic pool and processor set, you can update your project definition so that all of the new tasks in the project are bound to the pool:

```
# projmod -a -K project.pool=mypool build
# projects -l
...
build
        projid : 100
        comment: ""
        users  : sarah
        groups : (none)
        attribs: project.max-lwps=(privileged,100,none)
                 project.pool=mypool
                 rcap.max-rss=10000000
```

The `project.pool` attribute is used to specify a pool for the project.

Dynamically binding to a pool

The `poolbind` command is used to query pool bindings and to dynamically bind processes, tasks, projects, or zones to a pool. You can query the pool binding of a process using the `-q` option, and the resource, or pset, bindings using the `-Q` option:

```
$ newtask -p build
$ poolbind -q $$
4734    mypool
$ poolbind -Q $$
4734    pset    mypset
```

Here the shell variable $$, which represents the pid of the current process, is used to show the pool binding and processor set resource binding.

If you have administrative privileges, you can bind a running process to a pool using the -p option:

```
# poolbind -p mypool 4707
# poolbind -q 4707
4707    mypool
```

By default, poolbind works with processes, but you can also dynamically bind tasks, projects, or zones by specifying the type of object using the -i option. This example dynamically binds task 143 to mypool:

```
# poolbind -p mypool -i taskid 143
```

In addition, individual programs can be run within a pool using the -e option to poolbind:

```
# poolbind -p mypool -e make
```

Monitoring pools

The poolstat command displays the configured pools and the usage of the processor sets bound to the pool:

```
$ poolstat
                       pset
id pool           size used load
 1 mypool            8 0.00 0.00
 0 pool_default     12 0.00 0.02
```

The poolstat command includes several options to display various parts of the pool configuration as well as options to continuously display updated statistics. See its man page for further details.

Advanced pool configuration

Once you are familiar with the basic usage of pools, there are a variety of advanced features you may want to use.

Static versus dynamic configuration

The system's default pool configuration is stored in the /etc/pooladm.conf file. When the system boots, it reads this file to instantiate the pool configuration. The system also maintains the current dynamic configuration within the kernel. When you first set up the pool, the poolcfg commands committed the configuration to the pooladm.conf file, and then you instantiated the dynamic configuration using the following command:

```
# pooladm -c
```

You can dynamically change the current runtime configuration without saving the changes to the persistent configuration file by using the -d option on the poolcfg commands. This changes the kernel's pool configuration, but those changes will be lost when the system reboots. The pooladm -s command saves the current in-kernel configuration out to the default configuration file, making the current configuration persistent.

Modifying the configuration

The poolcfg command supports a variety of subcommands that are used to define or modify the pool configuration. In the original example, you used the create subcommand to define a pool and pset, then the associate subcommand to tie the two together. The poolcfg command also supports the info, destroy, modify, and transfer subcommands. This example modifies the configuration for mypset to use up to four CPUs instead of the range it was originally defined to use:

```
# poolcfg -c 'modify pset mypset (uint pset.min=1; uint pset.max=4)'
# pooladm -c
```

You can use the poolcfg -c info subcommand, pooladm, or the poolstat command to view the new configuration:

```
# poolstat -r pset
 id pool              type rid rset       min  max size used load
  1 mypool            pset  1 mypset        1    4    4 0.00 0.00
  0 pool_default      pset -1 pset_default  1  66K   16 0.00 0.01
```

There are various ways to move CPUs from one pset to another. This example transfers three CPUs from mypset back to the default processor set within the kernel pool configuration, leaving a single CPU in mypset:

```
# poolcfg -c 'transfer 3 from pset mypset to pset_default' -d
# poolstat -r pset
 id pool              type rid rset       min  max size used load
  1 mypool            pset  1 mypset        1    4    1 0.00 0.00
  0 pool_default      pset -1 pset_default  1  66K   19 0.00 0.01
```

Pool properties

In the pooladm output, you saw a variety of objects with different properties listed for each instance. The pools framework supports four different types of objects: system, pool, pset, and cpu. The properties are named after the associated object. Table 18-2 lists each property, its associated type, whether the user can set the property, and a brief definition. The full definition of each property is described on the libpool(3LIB) man page. The meaning of most of these properties is straightforward, but a few require further explanation. Many of them are specific to the dynamic pool daemon, poold, which is described in more detail in the next section.

TABLE 18-2

Pool Property Descriptions

Property	Type	Edit	Definition
system.allocate-method	string	yes	Method to allocate CPUs to psets. See explanation below for details.
system.bind-default	bool	yes	If the specified pool is not found, bind to the pool named pool.default. Defaults to true.
system.comment	string	yes	User-supplied comment
system.name	string	yes	User-supplied name
system.poold.history-file	string	yes	Poold decision history file used for tracking rebalancing decisions
system.poold.log-level	string	yes	Poold logging level. Values are ALERT, CRIT, ERR, WARNING, NOTICE, INFO, and DEBUG.
system.poold.log-location	string	yes	Poold logging location
system.poold.monitor-interval	uint64	yes	Poold monitoring sample interval, in milliseconds. Defaults to 15 seconds.
system.poold.objectives	string	yes	Poold objective for rebalancing. The value wt-load is the only valid objective for the system.
system.version	int64	no	libpool version required to manipulate the configuration
pool.active	bool	yes	Marks the pool as active
pool.comment	string	yes	User-supplied comment
pool.default	bool	no	The default pool
pool.importance	int64	yes	Pool importance for poold
pool.name	string	yes	User-supplied name
pool.scheduler	string	yes	Scheduling class for processes bound to the pool
pool.sys_id	int64	no	Pool ID
pool.temporary	bool	no	Pool definition exists only in-kernel; cannot be persistently saved
pset.comment	string	yes	User-supplied comment

Property	Type	Edit	Definition
pset.default	bool	no	The default pset
pset.load	uint64	no	The number of processes in the run queue for this pset
pset.max	uint64	yes	Maximum number of CPUs in the set
pset.min	uint64	yes	Minimum number of CPUs in the set
pset.name	string	yes	User-supplied name
pset.poold.objectives	string	yes	Pset objectives for poold
pset.size	uint64	no	Number of CPUs assigned to the pset
pset.sys_id	int64	no	Pset ID
pset.temporary	bool	no	Pset definition exists only in-kernel; cannot be persistently saved
pset.type	string	no	Type of resource. pset is the only valid value.
pset.units	string	no	Meaning of the size value. The only valid value is population.
cpu.comment	string	yes	User-supplied comment
cpu.pinned	bool	yes	CPU pinned to pset
cpu.status	string	yes	CPU status: online, offline, or no-intr
cpu.sys_id	int64	no	CPU ID

The system.allocate-method property is used to specify how CPUs are allocated across psets when a configuration is instantiated or updated. This property applies to psets only when a range is specified with the pset.min and pset.max properties. If the two properties have the same value, then the specified number of CPUs must be allocated to the pset. However, when a range is specified, the system must decide how CPUs should be allocated.

There are two valid values for the system.allocate-method property: importance based and surplus to default. The default is importance based, which means that pools with higher importance are favored when CPUs are allocated to psets. When surplus to default is used, only the minimum number of CPUs is allocated to each pset, and the rest are assigned to the default pset. As mentioned earlier, CPUs are only assigned to psets when a configuration is instantiated. It is up to the dynamic pool daemon (poold) to reassign CPUs after that.

A scheduling class can be assigned to a pool. That way, processes bound to the pool are scheduled using the pool's class, instead of the system's default scheduling class. The various OpenSolaris scheduling classes are described later in this chapter, but the following example demonstrates setting the Fair Share Scheduler (FSS) class on the pool:

```
# poolcfg -c 'modify pool mypool (string pool.scheduler="FSS")'
# pooladm -c
```

The cpu properties configure specific CPUs. This example shows pinning CPU 0 and configuring it so that it won't process interrupts:

```
# poolcfg -c 'modify cpu 0 (boolean cpu.pinned=true)'
# poolcfg -c 'modify cpu 0 (string cpu.status="no-intr")'
# pooladm -c
```

Here, CPU 0, which was already associated with mypset, will not be removed from the pset by the dynamic pool daemon, and will never be used for interrupt handling.

> **TIP**   Although it is possible to configure pools very specifically, as the example shows, it is rarely necessary. Normally, simply setting the pset processor range and pool importance, while leaving the rest of the configuration up to the system to manage, yields good results.

The dynamic pool daemon

As shown in the previous section, many of the pool properties are used to configure the behavior of the dynamic pool daemon (poold). The poold runs as a separate SMF service that monitors utilization of all of the psets and periodically rebalances CPUs between psets based on the configuration.

Use the following to enable poold:

```
# svcadm enable system/pools/dynamic
```

> **CAUTION**   Enabling the base pools service (system/pools) does not automatically enable the poold service (system/pools/dynamic). You must explicitly enable this service or there will be no dynamic rebalancing of CPUs between psets.

The utilization of a pset is defined as a percentage between 0 and 100. The poold implements a fairly sophisticated control program that uses feedback from the past utilization of each pset, as well as the history of reallocations, to determine how CPUs should be allocated. A brief spike in the utilization of a pset does not mean that CPUs are automatically moved to that pset. However, a sustained high utilization of a pset can cause CPUs to be moved, within the constraints imposed by the rest of the configuration. This becomes complicated when the sum of the pset maximums exceeds the number of CPUs available on the system. The sum of the pset minimums must be greater than or equal to the number of CPUs on the system or the configuration cannot be instantiated. In some cases, poold temporarily reallocates CPUs in such a way that utilization is reduced or objectives aren't actually being met, but through its history mechanism, it tracks those decisions as feedback for future reallocations.

The system.poold.objectives property is one input to the algorithm that poold uses to reassign CPUs. Only two values are valid: Either nothing is set or wt-load is used, which is also the default. The wt-load objective means that the system tries to reassign CPUs to pools that have a higher overall utilization.

The pool.importance property is another input to the poold algorithm. This property is used to specify the relative importance of the various pools.

The pset.poold.objectives property is yet another input. There are two valid values for this property: locality and utilization. The locality property means that poold will use locality group data, described in the liblgrp(3LIB) man page, as input. This can be specified as tight, loose, or none. The following example shows setting a locality to tight, which can improve the performance of some applications in the pset, but limits the ability of the poold to move CPUs around:

```
# poolcfg -c \
'modify pset mypset (string pset.poold.objectives="locality tight")'
```

The utilization property means that poold will try to match the CPUs to the utilization within the pset. This can be specified using the greater than (>) or less than (<) relational operators, as well as the approximate (~) operator, which means that utilization can fluctuate around the target value. This example sets the utilization objective to a range greater than 50% and less than 75%:

```
# poolcfg -c 'modify pset mypset
(string pset.poold.objectives="utilization > 50; utilization < 75")'
```

You can also specify an importance for specific objectives. This example combines both the locality and utilization objectives, with the utilization being five times as important as the locality:

```
# poolcfg -c 'modify pset mypset
(string pset.poold.objectives="locality tight; 5:utilization < 75")'
```

> **TIP** In most cases, you don't need to set pset objectives. It is usually sufficient to simply set the pool importance and let poold reallocate CPUs based on the system's wt-load objective.

The default poold log file is /var/log/pool/poold. You can check this file to understand the daemon's behavior and the decisions it makes.

Processor Sets

OpenSolaris includes another facility named *processor sets*. Although the name is the same as the one used within resource pools, this is actually a separate facility and is incompatible with resource pools. You must disable resource pools to use standalone processor sets.

The basic concept of processor sets is similar to that of the psets described within resource pools. This facility enables you to bind processes to a group of processors, and processors within the set can only run processes bound to that set. Because these two capabilities are so similar, they may be unified into one underlying implementation in the future.

> **TIP** In general, the processor set concept provided by the resource pools facility is more flexible and is usually preferable to using the standalone processor sets described in this section.

Processor sets are managed using the psrset command. You define a new processor set using the c option, specifying a list of processor IDs to assign to the set. The psrinfo command can be used to list the processor IDs for all of the processors on the system. This example creates a new set with processor IDs 6, 7, and 8 assigned:

```
# psrset -c 6 7 8
created processor set 1
processor 6: was not assigned, now 1
processor 7: was not assigned, now 1
processor 8: was not assigned, now 1
# psrset
user processor set 1: processors 6 7 8
```

Here, the new processor set ID — in this case, 1 — is printed when the set is created. You can use the psrset command with no options to list the sets. Note that processor set definitions are not persistent across reboots, and there is no way to associate a processor set with a project or task.

You can execute a command within a processor set using the -e option, as this example running make in set 1 shows:

```
# psrset -e 1 make
```

The psrset command also includes various options for displaying process to set bindings and for rebinding running processes to a set. The psrset(1M) man page describes all of the options.

Scheduling

Scheduling is the algorithm used by the kernel to determine which processes to run and for how long. OpenSolaris implements an extensible scheduling framework so that different algorithms, called *scheduling classes*, can be provided, and different groups of processes can be scheduled using these different classes.

The following classes are provided in OpenSolaris:

Abbreviation	Name
FSS	Fair Share Scheduler
FX	Fixed Priority
IA	Interactive
RT	Real Time
SYS	System
TS	Time Share

The Time Share (TS) class is the system's default class. This class provides the traditional Unix time-shared behavior in which all processes that are eligible to run are treated equally, and no single process will starve other runnable processes. The system time-slices across all of the runnable processes so that they all get a chance to run. The process' nice value is also used as an input into these scheduling decisions. See the nice(1) man page for more information. Based on various inputs, such as the nice value and the amount of recent CPU usage, the process priority is calculated to determine when it should run.

The Interactive (IA) class is a variation of the TS class. This class is used by processes running in the window system to give them a priority boost, in order to improve the user's interactive experience.

The System (SYS) class is a special class used only for kernel threads, which are allowed to run until they have finished their work. These processes have a higher priority range than processes in the FSS, FX, IA, or TS classes.

The Fixed Priority (FX) class overlaps the same overall priority range as processes in the FSS, IA, or TS classes, but processes in this class are assigned a priority that never changes, unlike processes in TS or IA. The FX class also has a priority range that exceeds FSS, IA, or TS by one, so processes in this class are ensured that they are always slightly higher in priority than processes in the other three classes.

The Real Time (RT) class is also a fixed-priority class, but the priority range is higher than the SYS class. That is, processes in this class will even preempt kernel threads.

You can use ps with the -c option to see the scheduling class that each process is using. On a typical desktop computer, you will normally observe a mix of FX, IA, SYS, and TS classes in the CLS column, and you might even notice the occasional RT class, as the example shows. You can also see the process' current priority in the PRI column:

```
$ ps -ecf
      UID   PID  PPID  CLS PRI    STIME TTY      TIME CMD
     root     0     0  SYS  96  Mar 03 ?       0:04 sched
     root     1     0   TS  59  Mar 03 ?       0:20 /sbin/init
```

```
    root     2     0  SYS  98  Mar 03 ?        0:07 pageout
    root     3     0  SYS  60  Mar 03 ?      193:22 fsflush
    root   149     1  TS   59  Mar 03 ?        0:00 /usr/lib/power/powerd
    root     7     1  TS   59  Mar 03 ?        0:22 /lib/svc/bin/svc.startd
...
    root 13531     1  RT  100  09:41:15 ?      0:01 /usr/lib/inet/xntpd
  daemon   595     1  FX   60  Mar 03 ?        0:00 /usr/lib/nfs/lockd
   sarah  2932  2930  IA   59  Mar 03 ?      142:15 /usr/X11/bin/Xorg :0
```

The Fair Share Scheduler

The final scheduling class is the Fair Share Scheduler (FSS). This class is more complex than the others and requires more explanation. Although this class shares the same priority range as the FX, IA, and TS classes, the way that processes are scheduled is calculated differently.

The FSS class enables you to configure the scheduling of CPU time to groups of processes based on their relative importance. This is configured through the use of projects or zones by defining the cpu-shares resource control (rctl). The cpu-shares setting defines the relative importance of the project or zone as compared to the other projects or zones. This section focuses on configuring projects; configuring zones is described in Chapter 19.

As described earlier, a project is used to group a collection of processes together and apply resource management settings to that group. The project.cpu-shares rctl enables you to specify the relative importance of the project compared to other projects. This example configures settings on two different projects:

```
# projmod -K "project.cpu-shares=(privileged,2,none)" myproject
# projmod -K "project.cpu-shares=(privileged,5,none)" build
```

Based on the relative numbers, you can see that the build project is more than twice as important as myproject.

The FSS uses these numbers to determine how processes in different projects should be scheduled. This calculation occurs only when there are more runnable processes than CPU resources. That is, if there are only a few runnable processes and many free CPUs, then all of the processes can be scheduled; but if there are more processes than available CPU time, then the FSS will allocate CPU resources across projects based on the share allotted to each project.

The allocation of CPU resources to a project is calculated as the number of shares for the project divided by the total number of shares among all active projects. Thus, as runnable processes appear within projects or as projects are created and destroyed, the total number of shares will change, affecting the allocation for each individual project.

This is easier to understand with an example. Assume there are four projects, A, B, C, and D, with the following shares, and each project has at least one runnable process:

```
A     1
B     1
```

```
C    2
D    5
```

Nine shares are allocated, so project A will get 11% (one-ninth) of the CPU resources, while project D will get 56% (five-ninths). If there were no runnable processes in project B, then it would not factor in to the calculation, so project A would get 13% (one-eighth) and project D would get 63% (five-eighths) of the CPU resources. Note that the total number of runnable processes within each project is not a factor, as long as there is at least one runnable process in each project.

There are a few special cases to consider as well. For example, on a two-processor system, if there are two projects, each with one runnable process, then the number of shares does not matter because each process can run on only one processor. There is a 1-to-1 mapping. However, if there is only one active project with many runnable processes, then it is free to use all of the available CPU resources. If a project is assigned 0 shares, the processes in the project will run only when there is no other work to do. If shares are combined with resource pools to partition workloads, the calculation is restricted to the set of projects assigned to each processor set. When zones are in use, the CPU allocation is first calculated for each zone, and then a second calculation is made across projects within each zone.

It is worth comparing the overall behavior of FSS to the TS class. For example, if there are two projects, each with an equal number of shares, the first with 99 runnable processes and the second with one runnable process, then the TS class would allocate only 1% of the CPU resources to the process in the second project (1/100). However, the FSS class would allocate 50% to the process in the second project (one-half). The cpu-shares indicate the relative importance of the collection of processes in each project, whereas the TS class simply treats all processes as equal. Using FSS means that a project with many active processes cannot hog the system's CPUs but is instead scheduled based on project priority, expressed through its cpu-shares, as compared with the other active projects on the system — hence, the name "Fair Share Scheduler."

Because the FSS class shares the same priority range with the FX, IA, and TS classes, you should not mix FSS processes with processes from these other classes. This can lead to unexpected scheduling decisions. There are two different ways to address this. One option is to use FSS for everything by setting it as the default system scheduling class, as described in the next section. The other option is to use resource pools to partition projects so that projects with shares are run in a different processor set from the rest of the processes. This example configures a project with shares in an explicit pool and pset:

```
# projmod -K \
"project.pool=mypool;project.cpu-shares=(privileged,5,none)" build
# newtask -p build bash
# ps -eo user,pid,project,taskid,class,args
    USER   PID  PROJECT TASKID  CLS COMMAND
...
   sarah   910    build     81  FSS bash
# poolbind -Q $$
910      pset    mypset
```

When processes are run in a project that has an explicit cpu-shares setting, the FSS class is automatically used. Thus, this configuration ensures that the project's processes are not mixed in with the rest of the processes on the system, which are running in the default pool and processor set.

Managing scheduling classes

The dispadmin command is used to manage the system's scheduling classes. You can use the -l option to see the available classes on the system:

```
# dispadmin -l
CONFIGURED CLASSES
==================
SYS     (System Class)
TS      (Time Sharing)
IA      (Interactive)
RT      (Real Time)
FX      (Fixed Priority)
FSS     (Fair Share)
```

The -d option is used to view or set the system's default scheduling class. This example sets it to FSS and then displays the default:

```
# dispadmin -d FSS
# dispadmin -d
FSS     (Fair Share)
```

When the system boots, this class will be used by default for all processes, unless an application explicitly sets its class to some other value (which requires administrative privileges).

You can also use the dispadmin command to view or change the class-specific options, although that is not normally done.

The priocntl command is used to dynamically change the scheduling parameters of a process or group of processes. This example moves pid 968 into the IA class:

```
# priocntl -s -c IA 968
```

The next example moves all of the processes in the build project, with project ID 100, to the RT class:

```
# priocntl -s -c RT -i projid 100
```

You can query a collection's scheduling parameters using the -d option:

```
# priocntl -d -i projid 100
REAL TIME PROCESSES:
    PID   RTPRI       TQNTM      TQSIG
    975       0        1000          0
```

You can also use `priocntl` to run a process in a specific class and to configure various scheduling parameters. The `priocntl(1)` man page provides details on all of the parameters, as well as a detailed explanation of each class and its class-specific options.

For more information on the implementation and overhead of the various scheduling classes, see *Solaris Internals* by Richard McDougall and Jim Mauro (Prentice Hall, 2006).

CPU caps

OpenSolaris includes one more scheduling-related feature that can be used to manage process scheduling: the `cpu-cap` resource control. The overall resource control capability was described earlier in this chapter.

The `cpu-cap` rctl enables you to set an upper limit on how much CPU can be used by processes within a project or zone. This limit should be set if you want to cap the amount of CPU being used even if the system has additional free CPU cycles. This is useful in certain cases, such as an environment in which users purchase a fixed amount of CPU, or if you want to set expectations such that users don't get used to better performance when the system is lightly loaded, and then complain later when more load is added. Think of the `cpu-cap` rctl as the opposite of the `cpu-shares` rctl used with FSS. While CPU shares guarantee a minimum amount of CPU when the system is heavily loaded, CPU caps guarantee a maximum amount of CPU, even when the system is lightly loaded.

The `cpu-cap` value is specified as a percentage of one CPU, so you can limit CPU usage in fractions of a CPU. This example sets the project `cpu-cap` to 150, which represents 100% of one CPU and 50% of a second CPU:

```
# projmod -a -K "project.cpu-cap=(privileged,150,deny)" myproject
```

The limit is calculated by keeping track of the CPU usage for all of the threads in the project over a short time interval, using the OpenSolaris micro-state accounting feature. When the cap is reached, the threads are not scheduled to run again until the limit calculation once again drops below the cap. CPU caps are not enforced for processes in the real-time scheduling class.

Accounting

OpenSolaris includes both a legacy and an extended accounting capability. Accounting can be used to maintain a historical record of resource usage, which is useful for basic record-keeping, capacity planning, or for usage charging. Both accounting facilities can be used at the same time.

Legacy accounting

The legacy accounting features in OpenSolaris are provided using a traditional implementation with a predefined accounting record that is written when a process terminates. The accounting records are stored in the /var/adm/pacct file. Legacy accounting can be used to record activity only at the user and process level.

Accounting can be enabled with the following command:

```
# /usr/lib/acct/startup
```

An SMF service for accounting has not yet been created, so you must manually set up a legacy rc script to cause accounting to be enabled when the system boots. You can do so as follows:

```
# cd /etc/rc2.d
# ln -s ../init.d/acct S15acct
```

The lastcomm command can be used to read the accounting data and print an abbreviated list of commands that have been executed on the system — in reverse order, with the most recent command first. This command will automatically work with either legacy or extended accounting records:

```
# lastcomm
who       root     pts/1       0.01 secs Sun Mar 30 15:04
ps        root     pts/1       0.03 secs Sun Mar 30 15:02
...
```

The lastcomm command prints the command, the user who executed the command, his or her terminal, the amount of CPU time used by the process, and the timestamp when the process terminated. You can also use various options to filter the data by terminal, command, or user. See the lastcomm(1) man page for more information.

The acctcom command prints accounting records in more detail but works only with the legacy accounting system. It prints the commands in order, so the most recent command is last. This command has a variety of options, described on the acctcom(1) man page:

```
# acctcom
COMMAND                    START    END      REAL     CPU    MEAN
NAME      USER   TTYNAME   TIME     TIME     (SECS)  (SECS) SIZE(K)
...
date      sarah  pts/2     16:05:06 16:05:06  0.01    0.01 3048.00
ls        sarah  pts/2     16:05:08 16:05:08  0.06    0.01 6936.00
```

You can use a variety of commands to prepare daily or monthly reports and to maintain the accounting files. To enable reporting, you need to set up a variety of cron jobs. The full procedure is described in the chapter "Managing System Accounting" in the *System Administration Guide: Advanced Administration*. You can also get more information on the acctsh(1M) man page.

Extended accounting

The extended accounting feature in OpenSolaris is much more flexible than legacy accounting. With extended accounting, activity can be tracked at the user, group, task, project, and zone levels. In addition, it provides both an extensible file format and an API that enables applications to generate interim, application-specific accounting data along with the default data collected when a process or task completes. The API is also used to read the accounting data for processing. The collected data can be configured to track activity at both the process level and the task level.

The `acctadm` command is used to manage the extended accounting subsystem. You must enable accounting for the resources you are interested in tracking. The `-r` option displays the valid resources by type: `process`, `task`, or `flow`:

```
# acctadm -r
process:
extended pid,uid,gid,cpu,time,command,tty,projid,taskid,ancpid,
wait-status,zone,flag,memory,mstate
basic    pid,uid,gid,cpu,time,command,tty,flag
task:
extended taskid,projid,cpu,time,host,mstate,anctaskid,zone
basic    taskid,projid,cpu,time
flow:
extended saddr,daddr,sport,dport,proto,dsfield,nbytes,npkts,action,
ctime,lseen,projid,uid
basic    saddr,daddr,sport,dport,proto,nbytes,npkts,action
```

The resources represent the specific data elements that can be stored in an accounting record. For convenience, these resources are grouped into `basic` and `extended` groups, or you can explicitly specify which pieces of data you want to record. Use the `-e` option to enable accounting for the specified resources and type of object:

```
# acctadm -e extended -f /var/adm/exacct/task task
# acctadm -e pid,uid,time,command,mstate -f /var/adm/exacct/proc \
  process
```

Here, the task-level accounting resource was specified using the `extended` group, which records all of the individual data elements contained in that group. You can also see that the process-level accounting was explicitly configured with a list of resources. The `-f` option specifies the file where the accounting data is stored. Looking at the various accounting resources, you can see how activity can be tracked at the user, group, task, project, or zone levels.

When you enable extended accounting using the `acctadm` command, the following SMF services are automatically enabled as well: `svc:/system/extended-accounting:task`, `svc:/system/extended-accounting:process`, and `svc:/system/extended-accounting:flow`.

The `acctadm` command with no argument shows the current accounting configuration:

```
# acctadm
            Task accounting: active
       Task accounting file: /var/adm/exacct/task
```

```
      Tracked task resources: extended
    Untracked task resources: none
         Process accounting: active
    Process accounting file: /var/adm/exacct/proc
   Tracked process resources: pid,uid,time,command,mstate
 Untracked process resources:gid,projid,taskid,cpu,tty,host,flag,
ancpid,wait-status,zone,memory
            Flow accounting: inactive
       Flow accounting file: none
      Tracked flow resources: none
    Untracked flow resources: extended
```

The accounting records can be summarized using the lastcomm command or accessed using the API described in the libexacct(3LIB) man page. There is also a demo program, delivered by the SUNWosdem package, that can be used to dump the accounting records. This program is installed in the /usr/demo/libexacct directory and must first be compiled. Once built, you can use it to display the accounting records, as this example shows:

```
# ./exdump /var/adm/exacct/task
  101   group-task              [group of 25 object(s)]
 2000   taskid                  91
 2001   projid                  100
 2009   cpu-sys-sec             0
 200a   cpu-sys-nsec            402654256
 2007   cpu-user-sec            0
 2008   cpu-user-nsec           514332004
 2003   start-sec               1206905248
 2004   start-nsec              505367312
 2005   finish-sec              1206905801
 2006   finish-nsec             884819412
 2002   hostname                "myhost"
 200b   faults-major            7
 200c   faults-minor            0
 200e   msgs-snd                0
 200d   msgs-recv               0
 200f   blocks-in               8
 2010   blocks-out              11
 2011   chars-rdwr              1021984
 2012   ctxt-vol                575
 2013   ctxt-inv                193
 2014   signals                 0
 2015   swaps                   0
 2016   syscalls                9481
 2018   anctaskid               90
 2019   zone                    "global"
```

Here, there is one task accounting record, consisting of 25 data elements. The number of elements in each record varies according to the resources you configured using acctadm. This demo program is not meant as a production-level accounting tool. Instead, use it as a starting point for creating your own accounting tools or you can use add-on software to process the accounting data. There is also a Perl module for accessing the accounting data. See the Exacct(3PERL), Project(3PERL), and Task(3PERL) man pages for more details.

You can use the wracct command to cause a partial or interval accounting record to be written for a long-running process or task that has not yet completed. This example causes a partial record to be written for the process with pid 857:

```
# wracct -i 857 -t partial process
```

These accounting records are tagged so that a program that is processing the accounting data can distinguish between a full record and a partial or interval record.

Resources

The Resource Management project, which encompasses most of the material in this chapter, is at http://opensolaris.org/os/project/rm.

If you are interested in the architecture and design of the various resource management subsystems, you can access the ARC cases on the ARC community website at http://opensolaris.org/os/community/arc/. In particular, the following cases are the most fundamental for resource management:

```
PSARC/1999/119 Tasks, projects, and extended accounting
PSARC/2000/136 Administrative support for processor sets and
               extensions
PSARC 2000/137 Resource Controls
PSARC/2000/452 Revised Share Scheduler
PSARC/2002/287 Dynamic Resource Pools
PSARC/2002/519 rcapd(1MSRM): resource capping daemon
PSARC/2004/402 CPU Caps
```

If you are interested in the implementation of resource management, source code for the various components is spread out between the kernel, libraries, and commands.

For projects and tasks, the main header is usr/src/uts/common/sys/project.h. The primary kernel code is in usr/src/uts/common/os/project.c, which includes detailed comments. The library is under usr/src/lib/libproject. The user-level commands are under usr/src/cmd/projadd and usr/src/cmd/projects.

For resource controls, the main header is usr/src/uts/common/sys/rctl.h. The primary kernel code is in usr/src/uts/common/os/rctl.c, which includes a detailed comment. The process (proc) library interface is in usr/src/lib/libproc/common/pr_getrctl.c. The user-level commands are under usr/src/cmd/prctl.

The resource capping daemon is under usr/src/cmd/rcap.

For pools, the main header is `usr/src/uts/common/sys/pool.h`. The primary kernel code is in `usr/src/uts/common/os/pool.c`, which includes detailed comments. The library is under `usr/src/lib/libpool`. The user-level commands are under `usr/src/cmd/pools`.

The dynamic pool daemon source code is under `usr/src/cmd/pools/poold`. This daemon is a mix of C and Java source, with most of the logic implemented in Java. The `usr/src/cmd/pools/poold/com/sun/solaris/domain/pools/Poold.java` file includes a detailed comment and is a good starting point.

The kernel scheduling code and various scheduling classes are under `usr/src/uts/common/disp`. The `dispadmin` command is under `usr/src/cmd/dispadmin`.

The legacy accounting header is `usr/src/uts/common/sys/acct.h`. The primary kernel code is in `usr/src/uts/common/os/acct.c`. The commands are under `usr/src/cmd/acct` and `usr/src/cmd/lastcomm`. The extended accounting header is in `usr/src/uts/common/sys/exacct.h`. The primary kernel code is in `usr/src/uts/common/os/exacct.c`. The library is under `usr/src/lib/libexacct`. The `acctadm` command is under `usr/src/cmd/acctadm`.

Solaris Internals by Richard McDougall and Jim Mauro (Prentice Hall, 2006) includes a discussion of scheduling in Solaris.

Summary

This chapter described the various mechanisms within OpenSolaris that can be used to control and monitor the system's resources. These resources are primarily the system's CPU and memory. Projects and tasks were described as a grouping mechanism to manage related workloads. The various system controls, including resource controls, resource caps, resource pools, processors sets, and scheduling, were covered, along with the ways to tie those capabilities into projects. The accounting facilities, which enable you to monitor overall usage of the system, were also described.

Chapter 19

Zones

As described in Chapter 17, zones are the operating system-level virtualization capability provided by OpenSolaris. This chapter focuses on zones and explains how resource management features, covered in Chapter 18, are used in conjunction with them. The combination of zones and resource management is called *containers*.

Introduction to Zones

The OpenSolaris zones capability is used to create a virtualized environment for running software in a secure and isolated way. Within the zone, it appears to users and applications that they are running on a standalone system. Users and processes outside of the zone cannot be seen or affected, there are no name conflicts on files or ports, and the behavior of software within the zone is contained to that zone. Because there are no name conflicts across zones, each zone has a unique user-ID namespace and its own root user. Administration within the zone is delegated to that zone's root user, who can configure and manage the zone almost as he or she sees fit. The various limitations are discussed in this chapter.

Although each zone appears as a standalone operating system from inside the zone, in reality there is a single instance of an OpenSolaris kernel running on the hardware. This kernel is inherently aware of zones and actively manages the containment of processes and actions within the zone. As described in Chapter 17, this type of virtualization is known as operating-system-level virtualization. Because the OS is actively involved in managing the containment of processes within the zone, the behavior and I/O of those processes does not go through an additional virtualization layer. Zones are very lightweight: All processes on the system are always executing within a zone and those processes always run at full speed. Because of this, you can run many zones on a single system, and you can realize all of the performance of the system, even when explicitly running in a zone.

The base operating system that is installed and running on the hardware is called the *global zone*. Additional instances of zones are called *non-global zones*. The global zone root user has ultimate authority and administrative control over all zones on the system. He or she can configure, create, destroy, and manage all aspects of each zone. Administrative actions within the global zone can impact the non-global zones. Actions within a non-global zone do not impact other zones.

Uses of Zones

Zones are an ideal solution for consolidating many standalone systems onto a single machine. This can increase the utilization of the hardware and decrease the number of physical systems to install, maintain, and manage. Because each zone is an isolated environment, the actions and configuration in one zone do not affect the other zones.

Another use for zones is to provide encapsulation of the application stack. Within the zone, modifications can be made without affecting the rest of the system. Once everything is completely set up, the zone can be treated as a container that can be cloned, used to provision other zones, and migrated from system to system. Even on a system that runs only a single application stack, installing and provisioning within a zone enables that environment to be virtualized away from the base system and treated as an independent entity. It also provides an extra level of security without imposing any overhead on performance.

Zones can also be used when there is a need to delegate administration to another user who should not have management access to the primary system. By giving that user a zone, he or she can perform their own system configuration and management in that zone without affecting other users or the global zone.

Getting Started with Zones

OpenSolaris provides three primary commands to administer zones: `zonecfg`, `zoneadm`, and `zlogin`. `zonecfg` is used to configure a zone. `zoneadm` is used for ongoing administration such as installation, booting, or halting the zone. `zlogin` is used to log in to the zone, including logging in to the zone's console.

Configuring a zone

The first step in setting up a new non-global zone is to configure it using the `zonecfg` command. You must be root or have root privileges in the global zone to configure and administer zones. To avoid having to be root, the Zone Management RBAC profile can be assigned to a user. This same RBAC profile is also used for the other management tasks related to zones.

CROSS-REF See Chapter 11, which discusses OpenSolaris security, for information on using RBAC.

The following example steps through the configuration, installation, and booting of a new zone named myzone:

```
# zonecfg -z myzone
myzone: No such zone configured
Use 'create' to begin configuring a new zone.
zonecfg:myzone> create
zonecfg:myzone> set zonepath=/pl/zones/myzone
zonecfg:myzone> add net
zonecfg:myzone:net> set physical=bge0
zonecfg:myzone:net> set address=192.168.0.92
zonecfg:myzone:net> end
zonecfg:myzone> exit
```

zonecfg provides an interactive command-line environment to configure a zone. To invoke the command, specify the zone name with the -z option. Because the zone does not yet exist, zonecfg tells you to create it, which is done with the create subcommand.

Next, a value for the zonepath property is specified using the set subcommand. This defines where in the file system the root directory tree for the zone will be placed. Each zone must have its own unique zonepath. In this example, myzone's root directory tree will reside under /pl/zones/myzone.

NOTE Each zone's root directory tree resides someplace in the file system of the global zone. Within this tree is a parallel installation of the system software that is unique to the zone. In this way, the zone has its own private copies of all system files and configuration data. The zonepath specifies where in the global zone's file system tree the non-global zone's root will live. On SXCE, it is common to configure the zone so that it shares most of the read-only portions of its file system with the global zone. This is described in the "Sparse root versus whole root" section later in this chapter. Depending on how the zone is configured, its root directory tree can consume a few tens of megabytes up to several gigabytes within the global zone's file system. The SXCE distribution is described in Chapter 2. Many of the SXCE-related topics described in this chapter are applicable to the Solaris 10 release.

Next, a net resource is added using the add subcommand. The net resource has two properties: physical and address. The physical property specifies the name of the network interface that will be virtualized for the zone. For now you can use the same primary NIC that is configured in the global zone. The address property specifies the IP address for the zone. Each zone should be assigned a unique IP address, just as you would with individual standalone systems. In this example, the bge0 network interface is used with an IP address of 192.168.0.92. You can specify the IP address as an IPv4 address, IPv6 address, literal address, or hostname.

CROSS-REF You can view all of the network interfaces configured in the global zone by running the `ifconfig -a` command in your shell in the global zone. Network commands are described in more detail in Chapter 9.

Finally, the end subcommand is used to finish the `net` resource you added and the `exit` subcommand is used to exit the `zonecfg` command itself.

At this point you have completed creating the new zone named `myzone`. The zone is configured but it is not yet installed. To see all zones and their states, use the `zoneadm` command:

```
$ zoneadm list -cv
   ID NAME          STATUS       PATH                    BRAND    IP
    0 global        running      /                       native   shared
    - myzone        configured   /pl/zones/myzone        native   shared
```

The `zoneadm` command supports several subcommands, which are discussed throughout this chapter. The example here uses the `list` subcommand. After a zone has been configured using `zonecfg`, you'll primarily use the `zoneadm` command for ongoing administration of the zone. For the `zoneadm list` subcommand, the `-c` option means to show all zones, not just running zones, and the `-v` option means verbose output. You can see the zone named `myzone` that you just created. It is in the `configured` state, which means it has been defined but not yet installed. You can also see where in the file system the zone will live, the `zonepath` that you specified in `zonecfg`. The Brand and IP columns are discussed later in the chapter. In this example, you can also see that the global zone is running. The global zone refers to the environment of the base operating system, which is itself a zone, and is always running. Each running zone has an ID assigned to it and the global zone always has zone ID 0. You can use the zone ID or zone name within various commands to get more information about the specific zone, as discussed later.

Installing a zone

After a zone has been configured, the next step is to install it. Installation will populate the zonepath with the operating system files, similar to installing a standalone system. Once again, you use the `zoneadm` command but this time with the `install` subcommand:

```
# zoneadm -z myzone install
A ZFS file system has been created for this zone.
Preparing to install zone <myzone>.
Creating list of files to copy from the global zone.
Copying <12458> files to the zone.
Initializing zone product registry.
Determining zone package initialization order.
Preparing to initialize <1194> packages on the zone.
Initialized <1194> packages on zone.
Zone <myzone> is initialized.

The file </pl/zones/myzone/root/var/sadm/system/logs/install_log>
contains a log of the zone installation.
```

The output from the `zoneadm install` subcommand shows the progress as the zone is installed. Depending on how the zone is configured, it can take several minutes or more to install the zone because it's essentially a second installation of OpenSolaris.

Note that the first output line says that a ZFS file system was created. In this example, assuming the `zonepath`, `/p1/zones/myzone`, resides within a ZFS file system, the zone installation process automatically creates a new ZFS file system for the zone, as shown here. This enables you to leverage the capabilities of ZFS for the zone as well as the integration between zones and ZFS, which is discussed further later in this chapter.

CROSS-REF The innovative features of the ZFS file system are discussed in detail in Chapter 8.

Now that the zone has been installed, you can check the status again using `zoneadm`:

```
$ zoneadm list -cv
    ID NAME            STATUS      PATH                    BRAND    IP
     0 global          running     /                       native   shared
     - myzone          installed   /p1/zones/myzone        native   shared
```

Note that listing zones does not require root privileges, but other `zoneadm` subcommands, such as booting or halting a zone, do require root privileges.

You can see the zone's status has changed from `configured` to `installed`.

Booting a zone

Once the zone has been installed, it can then be booted. A zone can boot, halt, and reboot much like a standalone system but the `zoneadm` command is used to initiate those tasks for the zone. To boot the zone, use the `zoneadm` command with the `boot` subcommand. Privileged users within a zone can reboot or halt only that zone.

TIP You might want to read ahead to the next section, which describes logging in to the zone's console, and do that in a second terminal window while booting the zone so that you can see the zone's console output as it boots.

```
# zoneadm -z myzone boot
```

As you work with zones, you'll notice that booting a zone takes only a few seconds, although the first boot takes longer due to the system configuration and SMF initialization process. Once you are logged into the zone, you halt or reboot the zone using the same commands you would use to manage the global zone (`shutdown`, `halt`, and `reboot`, for instance).

Check the zone's status and you can see it is now running:

```
$ zoneadm list -v
    ID NAME            STATUS      PATH                    BRAND    IP
     0 global          running     /                       native   shared
     1 myzone          running     /p1/zones/myzone        native   shared
```

The -c option isn't needed in this case because you are only looking at running zones. The zone has been assigned a zone ID of 1. A new ID is assigned each time a zone boots.

Logging in to a zone

Once a zone has been installed, you can use the zlogin command to log in to the zone. During the first boot of a zone, it must be configured with a host name, time zone, root password, and so on, just as with a standalone system.

> **CAUTION** A common mistake is to omit this step, which leaves your zone running but because it hasn't been configured yet, it is mostly unusable. For example, you can't log in to the zone over the network until you have completed configuration of the zone. For this reason, it is a good idea to log in to the zone's console while it is booting for the first time so that you can complete the steps to configure the zone. A technique to bypass this step is described later in the chapter.

To log in to the zone's console, use the -C option:

```
# zlogin -C myzone
[Connected to zone 'myzone' console]
```

At this point the command will just sit there until the zone is booted in another window. Once that is done, you'll start to see console output, just as you would on a standalone system:

```
[NOTICE: Zone booting up]

SunOS Release 5.11 Version snv_82 64-bit
Copyright 1983-2007 Sun Microsystems, Inc.  All rights reserved.
Use is subject to license terms.
Hostname: myzone
Loading smf(5) service descriptions: 148/148
...
```

Eventually the zone will finish initializing and, because this is the first boot, you'll see the system configuration prompts, as shown on a standalone system the first time it boots. Similarly, after you complete system configuration, the zone will reboot and you'll be presented with a login prompt:

```
myzone console login:
```

> **TIP** To drop off the zone console, type a ~. escape sequence, which returns you to your shell prompt in the global zone. This has no effect on the state of the zone, which continues to run.

The zlogin command can also be used to run commands within the zone without actually logging in to an interactive shell:

```
# zlogin myzone uptime
   5:24pm  up 1 min(s),  0 users,  load average: 0.38, 0.22, 0.14
```

Halting a zone

Use the `zoneadm halt` subcommand to halt a running zone, and the `reboot` subcommand to reboot the zone:

```
# zoneadm -z myzone halt
```

The root user within a non-global zone can also halt or reboot the zone at any time using the standard system commands such as `halt`, `shutdown`, or `reboot`. These commands executed in non-global zones have no effect on the global zone.

Advanced Zone Configuration

`zonecfg` provides many additional capabilities to configure a zone.

 **NOTE** Any changes you make through `zonecfg` for a running zone will not take effect until the zone reboots. Techniques to dynamically change the configuration of a zone, without rebooting, are described later in the chapter.

Within the `zonecfg` command, the attributes for the zone are specified using a combination of properties and resources. Properties are simple attributes for the zone. Resources represent a collection of properties that define an instance of a resource. You can specify one or more instances of most resources. You set the value of a property and you add an instance of a resource. In the previous example, you set the value of the `zonepath` property and you added one instance of the `net` resource. Within that instance of the `net` resource, you set the value of the two properties defined for that resource. As shown in this section, you can add additional instances of a specific resource. For example, you could add another instance of the `net` resource to the previous configuration if you wanted that zone to have two network interfaces defined.

NOTE Don't confuse the `zonecfg` resources with resource management. Although they have the same name, these are two different concepts. The `zonecfg` resources are used to specify a zone's configuration. Resource management is the collection of features used by the OS to define how the system's resources are allocated and controlled. *Resource controls* is yet another feature that uses the "resource" name, but it is also different. Resource controls are one component of resource management.

Resource management

The zone you set up in the previous example did not include any resource management settings, but it is critical to configure a zone with the correct resource management settings or the zone could disrupt the functioning of the entire system.

CROSS-REF The OpenSolaris resource management features are discussed in Chapter 18. These features have specific capabilities applicable to zones.

Resource controls

The kernel implements a set of zone-specific resource controls. The syntax for fully specifying a resource control within `zonecfg` is complex, so `zonecfg` allows these values to be set as simple properties, as Table 19-1 shows.

TABLE 19-1

Resource Control Properties

Property	Full Resource Control Name
cpu-shares	zone.cpu-shares
max-lwps	zone.max-lwps
max-msg-ids	zone.max-msg-ids
max-sem-ids	zone.max-sem-ids
max-shm-ids	zone.max-shm-ids
max-shm-memory	zone.max-shm-memory

This example shows how to set the resource control as a simple property:

```
zonecfg:myzone> set max-lwps=1000
```

The following shows how to set the same resource control using the fully specified syntax by adding an instance of the `zonecfg rctl` resource:

```
zonecfg:myzone> add rctl
zonecfg:myzone:rctl> set name=zone.max-lwps
zonecfg:myzone:rctl> add value (priv=privileged,limit=1000,action=deny)
zonecfg:myzone:rctl> end
```

The simplified syntax is preferable unless you need the capability to construct a complex resource control configuration.

> **CAUTION**   This example is another case demonstrating that it is easy to confuse the `zonecfg` resource with the resource control. Remember that these are two different concepts with the same name.

At a minimum, set `max-lwps` so that a malicious or compromised zone cannot consume all of the processes on the system. The `cpu-shares` resource control is described in the next section. The rest of the resource controls in Table 19-1 are used to set limits on the System V shared memory usage within the zone.

The fair share scheduler

Unless the zone is assigned to a pool, which is described later, it shares CPUs with the global zone and all other zones that are not assigned to a pool. Without the proper configuration, this sharing would allow a zone to monopolize the CPU cycles of the system. OpenSolaris includes the Fair Share Scheduling (FSS) class, which prevents this behavior. The FSS class ensures that all processes are given the proper share of CPU cycles, based upon the number of shares assigned. FSS comes into play only when the system is fully loaded. That is, if a single zone is busy with work but the rest of the zones are not doing anything, the busy zone is allowed to use all of the CPU cycles. However, if multiple zones have more work than available CPU cycles, the FSS allocates the CPU fairly, according to the number of CPU shares assigned to each zone.

This behavior is in contrast to the behavior of the default Time Sharing class (TS). The TS class attempts to ensure that all processes, independent of the zone they are in, are given a fair share of the system. If one zone has 100 processes that can run and another zone only has one process that can run, the first zone would get 100 times more CPU cycles than the second zone if the TS class were in use. This behavior can be prevented with FSS.

With FSS, each zone has a CPU share value assigned to it. As described in the previous section, the cpu-shares setting is a resource control that can be set as a simple property. By default, each zone has one share assigned, so if the FSS is in use and the cpu-shares resource control is not explicitly set, the zone still has one share.

The simplest way to understand shares is through an example. Assume you have three non-global zones, each with one share, and a global zone with one share. If all of the zones are busy with work, each zone gets an equal 25% of the CPU resources (1 share divided by 4 total shares). However, the cpu-shares setting is not an explicit percentage because the total number of outstanding shares can change dynamically. If another zone boots up and is also busy with work, then each zone now gets only 20% of the CPU resources because there are now five outstanding shares. If the fifth zone had 3 cpu-shares assigned instead of just 1, that fifth zone would get 43% of the CPU resource (3 shares divided by 7 total shares) and the other four zones would each get 14% (1 share divided by 7 total shares). If these five zones are running but only two of those zones, each with one share, are actually busy doing work, then only those two zones are competing for CPU cycles and each would get 50%.

The key point is that when the system is completely busy, each zone still gets its fair share of CPU resources if it has some work to do, no matter how many processes are runnable within each zone. Using FSS enables the system to be safely overprovisioned. A busy zone can use all of the available CPU resources to do work; but when other zones have work to do, they still get their share.

> **TIP** If the zones are not assigned to pools, as described in the next section, always use FSS to ensure that a single misbehaving or busy zone does not starve the other zones on the system. This is also critical for performing administration in the global zone because otherwise, a completely busy zone could significantly impact the capability to run processes in the global zone.

Explicitly setting a cpu-share on a zone does not automatically cause the system to use FSS as the default scheduling class. In almost every case it is best to set up the system with FSS as the default scheduling class when zones are in use. Use the dispadmin command in the global zone to set the class:

```
# dispadmin -d FSS
```

If cpu-shares is explicitly set but FSS is not the default scheduling class, a warning appears when the zone boots.

Pools

The zonecfg command enables you to set the pool property, which causes the zone to be bound to the specified pool when the zone boots. As shown in Chapter 18, setting up and managing a pool can be complex. A simpler alternative is to use the zonecfg dedicated-cpu resource:

```
zonecfg:myzone> add dedicated-cpu
zonecfg:myzone:dedicated-cpu> set ncpus=1-4
zonecfg:myzone:dedicated-cpu> set importance=5
zonecfg:myzone:dedicated-cpu> end
```

When a zone is configured this way, a pool is automatically created with the specified number or range of CPUs assigned to the pool when the zone boots. If necessary, the svc:/system/pools service in the global zone is also enabled. In this example, the number of CPUs assigned to the pool is a range of 1–4 and the importance property is set, although it is not required. If it's set, the property is used as input to the dynamic pool daemon (poold). The poold dynamically reallocates CPUs to different pools based on the ranges specified for each pool, how busy each pool is, and the pool importance.

As the dedicated-cpu resource name implies, the pool is dedicated to the zone. It is created when the zone boots, only that zone is assigned to the pool, and the pool is destroyed when the zone halts. This is in contrast to the behavior when a pool is assigned via the pool property. When you use the pool property, you must explicitly set up the pool, but you also have more control over how zones are allocated to a pool. For example, you could create a pool and assign more than one zone to it.

CROSS-REF   The procedures to manually configure a pool are described in Chapter 18.

Pools are particularly useful when a zone should be restricted to a subset of the total number of CPUs on the system. For example, if you have an application that is licensed to run on only two CPUs, you could run it on a 32-way machine using a dedicated-cpu configuration with ncpus set as 1–2. This would ensure that the zone can never see more than two CPUs, keeping the application within its license agreement. If this zone were not very busy, then it could actually be allocated only one CPU, as a range of 1–2 was specified.

When zones are configured to use pools, you can use the poolstat command in the global zone to monitor the pools. Pools that are dynamically created for zones with dedicated-cpu settings are named with the SUNWtmp_ prefix and the zone name, so that it is easy to correlate the pool to the zone:

```
$ poolstat
                          pset
 id pool          size used load
  0 pool_default     2 0.00 0.03
  2 SUNWtmp_myzone   2 0.00 0.83
```

CROSS-REF The poolstat output is described in Chapter 18.

When using pools, enable the dynamic pool daemon poold whenever possible so that it can dynamically rebalance CPUs across pools:

```
# svcadm enable system/pools/dynamic
```

This service is not enabled by default because the daemon is written in Java and some systems may not have Java installed. If poold is not enabled and you are using a pool configuration with a range of CPUs, the CPUs are not rebalanced after the zone boots. CPUs are assigned or moved around when the zone boots but not after. Thus, poold should always be enabled when using ranges to yield the expected behavior.

NOTE With respect to pools, two different SMF services are involved: the base pools service and the dynamic pools service, as described in Chapter 18.

The cpu-shares resource control cannot be used when a dedicated-cpu resource is set up because that configuration does not make sense. With a dedicated-cpu configuration, there is no possible CPU sharing among zones for FSS to manage.

Capped CPU usage

CPU caps are another feature that can be used to control how CPU resources are allocated to a zone. A CPU cap sets an upper limit on the amount of CPUs used by the zone, no matter how much work the zone has. That is, even if the system is idle except for the one zone, when the zone hits its CPU cap, it is not allowed to use more CPU cycles. CPU caps are useful in a charge-back environment where the user is only paying for so many CPUs. With a cap, users can't use more CPUs than they have paid for. Another use would be to set user expectations. For example, if the system only has a few zones and is lightly loaded but you know that more zones will be added later, you can use a CPU cap so that users don't complain later when there are fewer free CPU cycles.

CPU caps also can be used as an alternative to FSS if you know in advance how many zones you will have and you carve up all of the CPU cycles among those zones so that the total is less than or equal to the number of available cycles. For example, if you have seven non-global zones and eight CPUs, you could set a CPU cap of one CPU per zone, as described below, leaving one CPU free for the global zone. This way, a single zone could never monopolize the CPU cycles on the system, although neither could it use excess CPU cycles, as it could with the FSS.

A CPU cap can be specified using the `capped-cpu` resource within `zonecfg`. This resource is similar to, but mutually exclusive with, the `dedicated-cpu` resource described earlier because it doesn't make sense to use both on the same zone. However, different zones can use one or the other with no problem. This example sets a cap to 25% of one CPU:

```
zonecfg:myzone> add capped-cpu
zonecfg:myzone:capped-cpu> set ncpus=.25
zonecfg:myzone:capped-cpu> end
```

There is no `importance` property with the `capped-cpu` resource because that applies only to `poold` rebalancing CPUs across pools. Likewise, the `ncpus` property cannot be specified as a range for the same reason. However, unlike the `dedicated-cpu` resource, which must work in units of whole CPUs, in the `capped-cpu` resource you can set the `ncpus` property to a fraction, indicating that the zone is capped to a fraction of a CPU. In this example, the zone is limited to using 25% of a single CPU. If `ncpus` were set to 4.5, the zone would be limited to using four full CPUs and 50% of a fifth CPU.

Because CPU caps are implemented in the kernel as a resource control, an alternative to using the `capped-cpu` resource is to specify the cap using the full resource control syntax within `zonecfg`, although as described earlier, the simplified syntax is usually preferable. Here's the full syntax:

```
zonecfg:myzone> add rctl
zonecfg:myzone:rctl> set name=zone.cpu-cap
zonecfg:myzone:rctl> add value (priv=privileged,limit=25,action=deny)
zonecfg:myzone:rctl> end
```

This example also sets a limit of 25% of a CPU.

CROSS-REF As described in Chapter 18, explicit resource controls use integer values, so the `cpu-cap` limit is interpreted as a percent of CPU.

Although the `capped-cpu` and `dedicated-cpu` resources are mutually exclusive, you can use the `capped-cpu` resource with a `cpu-shares` setting for FSS. In this configuration, the FSS ensures a minimum allocation of the system when it is completely busy; and the CPU cap ensures a maximum allocation of the system even if it is idle. This enables you to overprovision the system with charge-back zones under the assumption that most of the time the zones will not be using all of their available CPU cycles, but if a zone is busy it will use only what was paid for.

Capped memory

As with CPU resource management, you should also configure limits on the memory that can be consumed by the zone. The `zonecfg` `capped-memory` resource is the simplest way to set memory limits:

```
zonecfg:myzone> add capped-memory
```

```
zonecfg:myzone:capped-memory> set physical=512m
zonecfg:myzone:capped-memory> set swap=1g
zonecfg:myzone:capped-memory> set locked=10m
zonecfg:myzone:capped-memory> end
```

This example limits the amount of physical memory that the zone can use to 512MB, the amount of swap space to 1GB, and the amount of physical memory that the zone can lock to 10MB. As the resource name implies, these are caps on, or upper limits to, the amount of memory that can be used.

As with the resource controls described earlier, the `swap` and `locked` properties are actually simplified names for the `zone.max-swap` and `zone.max-locked-memory` resource controls. You could set these limits using the full resource control syntax although that's rarely required.

CROSS-REF As described in Chapter 18, `rcapd` limits the amount of physical memory used by the zone.

Setting the physical property configures the `rcapd` in the global zone. When the `physical` property is set and the zone boots, the `system/rcap` service is automatically enabled in the global zone, if it is not already enabled. Unlike with projects, the `rcapd` running in the global zone caps the memory used by each of the non-global zones. You could also run an `rcapd` within the zone to cap projects defined within the zone.

Resource management example

This complete example shows how you can modify the zone you first created to add a useful resource management configuration to the zone:

```
# zonecfg -z myzone
zonecfg:myzone> set max-lwps=1000
zonecfg:myzone> set cpu-shares=1
zonecfg:myzone> add capped-memory
zonecfg:myzone:capped-memory> set physical=512m
zonecfg:myzone:capped-memory> set swap=1g
zonecfg:myzone:capped-memory> set locked=10m
zonecfg:myzone:capped-memory> end
zonecfg:myzone> exit
```

TIP Use `zonecfg` to configure resource management-related settings for the global zone, too. Run `zonecfg -z global` to customize the global zone. Most of the non-resource management-related settings are invalid for the global zone, and you will get an error if you try to set any of those.

Networking

Along with a good resource management configuration, almost every zone needs access to a network. Without a network configured, the zone behaves as an isolated, standalone system that can be logged into only from the global zone using the `zlogin` command by a user with root privileges. Thus, networking is fundamental to a typical zone configuration.

Zones support two different networking configuration models. The default model is a shared Internet Protocol (IP) stack; the alternative is an exclusive IP stack. In the `zoneadm list` output, the IP stack type for the zone is listed in the last column:

```
# zoneadm list -v
   ID NAME           STATUS      PATH                 BRAND   IP
    0 global         running     /                    native  shared
    1 myzone         running     /p1/zones/myzone     native  shared
```

With a shared IP stack, the global zone manages the network configuration on behalf of the non-global zone. A physical network interface can be shared by the global zone and any number of non-global zones. The zone's IP address is defined in the zone configuration and cannot be changed within the non-global zone. The non-global zone cannot use the `ifconfig` command to modify any settings on the network interface assigned to the zone, and all routing is managed by the global zone. Within the kernel is a single IP software stack that is shared by the global zone and all non-global zones configured with shared stacks. As a result, any packets sent between these zones are completely routed within the kernel and never leave the system.

With an exclusive IP stack, there is literally a complete IP software stack in the kernel dedicated to the zone. The zone is assigned a dedicated network interface, which is completely managed by the non-global zone. The zone sets its own IP address and manages its own routing. Any packets sent from this zone to the global zone or other non-global zones on the system must leave the machine to be routed externally. An exclusive stack zone behaves just like a standalone machine as far as networking is concerned.

There are various advantages and disadvantages to each approach:

- With a shared stack, many zones can share a single physical interface, which is then virtualized to each zone.

- With a shared stack, the global zone administrator controls the network configuration, which cannot be changed in the non-global zone by a malicious administrator or anyone else.

- With a shared stack, network traffic between zones on the same machine never leaves the system and runs at kernel speed. However, because of the complexity of the IP network stack, it is virtually impossible to guarantee that zones will not be able to see traffic that they should not see.

- With a shared stack, you can't plumb the same IP address on the loopback interface of different zones, a capability that is required in order to support the cluster scalable services feature described in Chapter 16.

- With an exclusive stack, the zone must have a dedicated physical interface or VLAN.

■ With an exclusive stack, network traffic is guaranteed to be isolated because the entire stack is dedicated to a single zone and all packets leave the machine for external routing. This guarantee is critical when a secure network configuration is required.

The following example shows how to configure the network for the default shared stack zone:

```
zonecfg:myzone> add net
zonecfg:myzone:net> set physical=bge0
zonecfg:myzone:net> set address=192.168.0.92
zonecfg:myzone:net> end
```

This configuration is identical to the one you set up in the initial example. Because net is a zonecfg resource, you can add additional network interfaces if needed. The following adds a second network interface to the same zone:

```
zonecfg:myzone> add net
zonecfg:myzone:net> set physical=bge1
zonecfg:myzone:net> set address=192.168.1.92
zonecfg:myzone:net> end
```

The physical network interface is virtualized when the zone boots. When the zone is running, you can see this using the ifconfig command in the global zone:

```
# ifconfig -a
lo0: flags=2001000849<UP,LOOPBACK,RUNNING,MULTICAST,IPv4,VIRTUAL>
 mtu 8232 index 1
    inet 127.0.0.1 netmask ff000000
lo0:1: flags=2001000849<UP,LOOPBACK,RUNNING,MULTICAST,IPv4,VIRTUAL>
 mtu 8232 index 1
    zone myzone
    inet 127.0.0.1 netmask ff000000
bge0: flags=201000843<UP,BROADCAST,RUNNING,MULTICAST,IPv4,CoS>
 mtu 1500 index 2
    inet 192.168.0.14 netmask ffffff00 broadcast 192.168.0.255
    ether 0:a:e4:30:6e:bb
bge0:1: flags=201000843<UP,BROADCAST,RUNNING,MULTICAST,IPv4,CoS>
 mtu 1500 index 2
    zone myzone
    inet 192.168.0.92 netmask ffffff00 broadcast 192.168.0.255
lo0: flags=2002000849<UP,LOOPBACK,RUNNING,MULTICAST,IPv6,VIRTUAL>
 mtu 8252 index 1
    inet6 ::1/128
```

Note that bge0:1 is the virtualized network interface, with the zone attribute set to myzone. In the non-global zone, you would see only the network interface that was configured on the zone:

```
myzone# ifconfig -a
lo0:1: flags=2001000849<UP,LOOPBACK,RUNNING,MULTICAST,IPv4,VIRTUAL>
 mtu 8232 index 1
```

```
        inet 127.0.0.1 netmask ff000000
bge0:1: flags=201000843<UP,BROADCAST,RUNNING,MULTICAST,IPv4,CoS>
 mtu 1500 index 2
        inet 192.168.0.92 netmask ffffff00 broadcast 192.168.0.255
```

This example shows how to configure an exclusive stack zone:

```
zonecfg:myzone> set ip-type=exclusive
zonecfg:myzone> add net
zonecfg:myzone:net> set physical=bge1
zonecfg:myzone:net> end
zonecfg:myzone> exit
```

You must first set the ip-type property for the zone. A zone ip-type can either be shared or exclusive. Within the same zone, you cannot have some interfaces shared and others exclusive. Additionally, the net resource only specifies the physical interface that is dedicated to the zone. You don't specify an IP address because that is managed within the zone itself. If you set up multiple exclusive IP stack zones to use the same physical NIC, the first zone that boots "owns" the NIC, and the other zones are denied access.

CROSS-REF   The procedures described in Chapter 9 to configure networking for a standalone system are also used to configure the network within an exclusive IP stack zone. To use an exclusive stack without dedicating a NIC to the zone, you can configure a VLAN on the NIC and then use that in the zone configuration. The steps to set up a VLAN are also described in Chapter 9.

Sparse root versus whole root

Non-global zones support the capability to share system software by sharing a portion of their file system with the global zone. The capability to configure a zone this way is directly related to how software is managed for both the global and non-global zone. This configuration is used when you want to ensure that a subset of the global zone's system software is kept in sync with the non-global zone. To simply share file system space with the zone, without consideration for software management within that space, use the fs resource, which is described in the Resources section later in this chapter.

Sparse and whole-root zones is a topic that highlights significant differences between the SXCE and OpenSolaris distributions. This section describes the concept of a *sparse-root zone* versus a *whole-root zone*. The Software management and Brand sections later in this chapter provide more information about those topics and how they relate to a sparse or whole-root zone.

As you have seen, the zonecfg command has an interactive interface for configuring a zone, but the subcommands can also be used directly on the command line. The info subcommand can be used interactively or as a subcommand at the shell prompt to print the configuration of the zone, as the following example shows:.

```
$ zonecfg -z myzone info
```

```
zonename: myzone
zonepath: /pl/zones/myzone
brand: native
autoboot: false
bootargs:
pool:
limitpriv:
scheduling-class:
ip-type: shared
inherit-pkg-dir:
    dir: /lib
inherit-pkg-dir:
    dir: /platform
inherit-pkg-dir:
    dir: /sbin
inherit-pkg-dir:
    dir: /usr
net:
    address: 192.168.0.92
    physical: bge0
```

Note in this output the four inherit-pkg-dir resources. By default, on SXCE or Solaris 10, a native-branded zone is configured with these four inherit-pkg-dir entries. A zone configured with any inherit-pkg-dir resources is called a sparse-root zone. These global zone directories are loopback mounted read-only within the zone when it boots, reducing the space overhead within the file system for the zone.

CROSS-REF **The loopback file system, lofs, is described in Chapter 7. The native brand, and branded zones in general, are discussed in the "Branded Zones" section later in this chapter.**

In addition to saving file system space, sparse-root zones have another advantage: The memory needed to run common programs can be shared among all zones. Because a common set of system processes is typically running in both the global zone and all sparse-root zones, only a single image of each program binary is paged in to memory, reducing the overall working set of the system.

Software installed into an inherit-pkg-dir must be managed from the global zone. It cannot be modified within a non-global zone; these directories are read-only in the non-global zone. When a new version of the software is installed in the global zone, each zone that inherits one of these directories has its package metadata updated. Likewise, if a patch is applied to this software in the global zone, the patch metadata for these non-global zones is also updated. Because the software is being managed in the global zone, no actual software installation takes place inside of the non-global zone. Instead, only the metadata that describes the software has to be updated.

A limitation of sparse-root zones is that the non-global zone administrator cannot install any additional software into these directories because they are mounted read-only within the zone. In some cases, add-on software needs to be installed into only one of these directories — typically, /usr. One alternative to address this problem is to create a whole-root zone. A whole-root zone is configured with no inherit-pkg-dirs. You can do this when creating the zone by using the zonecfg remove subcommand to delete all of the inherit-pkg-dir entries:

```
zonecfg:myzone> remove inherit-pkg-dir
Are you sure you want to remove ALL 'inherit-pkg-dir' resources (y/[n])?
```

Another way to set up a whole-root zone is to create it using the blank template:

```
zonecfg:myzone> create -t SUNWblank
```

NOTE A template is simply another zone configuration that is used as the starting point to create a new zone configuration. Any zone can be used as a template. A few special templates, such as SUNWblank, are predefined with the zones software.

Because the inherit-pkg-dir settings are fundamental to the way that software within the zone is installed, these settings cannot be modified on the zone after it has been installed.

If the zone needs limited write access to an inherited directory but you don't want to incur the overhead of a whole-root zone, an alternative is to configure a sparse-root zone with a writable file system mounted under the inherited directory. One common example is to set up a writable /usr/local directory for a sparse-root zone. Configuring these additional file systems into zones is described later in this chapter.

NOTE Not all types of brands support sparse-root zones. Some brands require the zone to be a whole-root zone because it doesn't make sense to share the system software and packaging information between the global and non-global zone.

Other zonecfg features

The preceding examples used many of the most common zonecfg capabilities. This section provides an overview of the remaining zonecfg features.

Editing properties and resources

You have seen and used several zonecfg resources so far, including net, rctl, inherit-pkg-dir, and capped-memory. Within zonecfg, resources are a group of simple properties. For example, the net resource includes two properties: physical and address. In general, you can have more than one instance of a resource, but within a resource, each property is unique. Thus, the default native zone configuration has four inherit-pkg-dir resource instances. There are a few exceptions, though. Specifically, the dedicated-cpu, capped-cpu, and capped-memory resources may have only a single instance. The dedicated-cpu and capped-cpu resources are also mutually exclusive. Aside from these restrictions, the other resources can have multiple instances and there are no mutual exclusion rules.

The `zonecfg` interactive user interface provides the capability to select a specific resource instance for modification. This is done by specifying enough properties and their values to unambiguously identify the specific instance to modify:

```
zonecfg:myzone> select net physical=bge0
```

This example shows how to select the net resource you created earlier. Once selected, you can then modify the property values for that resource.

Similarly, you can delete a specific resource instance by specifying it with the properties and their values:

```
zonecfg:myzone> remove net physical=bge0
```

You also can remove all of the instances of a specific resource by omitting any properties:

```
zonecfg:myzone> remove inherit-pkg-dir
Are you sure you want to remove ALL 'inherit-pkg-dir' resources (y/[n])?
```

To change a property's value, simply set a new value. Use the `clear` subcommand to remove a property's value altogether:

```
zonecfg:myzone> clear ip-type
```

This causes the property to either have no value or revert to its default value. In this example, the `ip-type` property reverted to the default shared stack value. Not all properties can be cleared; many of them are required. For example, in the net resource, the `physical` property requires a value, and attempting to clear it results in an error. In these cases, you can either set a new value for the property or remove the entire resource instance.

The `zonecfg` interactive environment offers a few additional capabilities that make it easier to configure zones. You can use tab-completion to avoid having to fully type out subcommands and properties. The environment maintains a command history, so you can use the up arrow on your keyboard to move to a previous command, and the left and right arrows to position the cursor for editing. You can also use `help` to see information about subcommands and properties, as shown here:

```
zonecfg:myzone> add capped-memory
zonecfg:myzone:capped-memory> help
The 'capped-memory' resource scope is used to set an upper limit (a cap) on the
amount of physical memory, swap space and locked memory that can be used by
this zone.
Valid commands:
    set physical=<qualified unsigned decimal>
    set swap=<qualified unsigned decimal>
    set locked=<qualified unsigned decimal>
And from any resource scope, you can:
    end    (to conclude this operation)
    cancel    (to cancel this operation)
```

```
    exit    (to exit the zonecfg utility)
zonecfg:myzone:capped-memory>
```

Additional properties and resources

Other zonecfg global properties and resources that have not yet been covered include the autoboot, bootargs, limitpriv, and scheduling-class properties, as well as the attr, dataset, device, and fs, resources. The brand property is discussed later in the chapter.

Global properties

The zone's autoboot property indicates whether the zone should boot automatically when the system boots. It is false by default. If you want the zone to automatically boot, set the property to true:

```
zonecfg:myzone> set autoboot=true
```

The bootargs property persistently configures a set of boot arguments to be passed to the zone when it boots. This property is rarely set; but as an example, if you wanted the zone to always boot to a specific SMF milestone, you could set the bootargs to indicate that:

```
zonecfg:myzone> set bootargs="-m milestone=none"
```

CROSS-REF   SMF milestones are described in Chapter 13.

In addition, a set of boot arguments can be passed to the zone through the zoneadm boot subcommand when you boot the zone, although those arguments only apply to that boot. You can boot the zone to single-user with the following zoneadm command:

```
# zoneadm -z myzone boot -- -s
```

The limitpriv property modifies the set of privileges available within the zone. This is another property that you will rarely change. By default, zones are restricted to a safe subset of the system privileges. The root user in a non-global zone has fewer privileges than the root user in the global zone, which prevents the zone's root user from modifying the system in potentially damaging ways. In some cases you may want to give additional or fewer privileges to a specific zone. You use the limitpriv property to specify that. There are currently about 70 different privileges in the system. Only a subset of them can be added to a non-global zone because the others would completely violate the containment that zones provide. Consult the zones manual for a complete list of privileges and a description of which ones can be added to a zone. One set of privileges that might be useful to add to zones in which users are doing development are the ones to enable DTrace. Users inside a zone cannot DTrace within the kernel because that requires the dtrace_kernel privilege, which cannot be granted to a zone for security reasons. However, with the dtrace_user and dtrace_proc privileges, they can DTrace user-level activity. This example adds the user-level DTrace privileges:

```
zonecfg:myzone> set limitpriv="default,dtrace_user,dtrace_proc"
```

When the keyword default is used as the first privilege, this implies a standard set of safe, default privileges. You can remove privileges from this set by preceding them with an exclamation point (!) or a minus sign (-). This example shows how to remove the proc_lock_memory privilege, which is required for processes to be able to lock memory within a zone:

```
zonecfg:myzone> set limitpriv="default,-proc_lock_memory"
```

Another global property is scheduling-class. You rarely need to set this property. Normally the zone simply uses the system's default scheduling class. However, one case where it is useful to set the zone's scheduling class is when the global zone is not using FSS but you'd like to use FSS for projects within the zone. In that case you would set the scheduling-class property:

```
zonecfg:myzone> set scheduling-class=FSS
```

The zonename is also a global property. You can set this property to rename the zone. The zone must not be running when you set this property. Here's an example:

```
zonecfg:myzone> set zonename=myzone2
zonecfg:myzone2> exit
# zoneadm list -cv
   ID NAME          STATUS     PATH                    BRAND    IP
    0 global        running    /                       native   shared
    - myzone2       installed  /pl/zones/myzone        native   shared
```

Resources

There are four resources yet to be discussed: attr, dataset, device, and fs.

attr

The attr resource can be used to add arbitrary attributes to a zone. The zones themselves do not generally use this information, but it could be useful to the zone administrator. One scenario might be to keep track of the person who has been granted root access within the zone:

```
zonecfg:myzone> add attr
zonecfg:myzone:attr> set name=root
zonecfg:myzone:attr> set type=string
zonecfg:myzone:attr> set value="Sarah Smith"
zonecfg:myzone:attr> end
zonecfg:myzone> add attr
zonecfg:myzone:attr> set name=phone
zonecfg:myzone:attr> set type=string
zonecfg:myzone:attr> set value=54321
zonecfg:myzone:attr> end
```

Using zone attributes enables you to keep track of any relevant information as part of the zone configuration.

dataset

Use the dataset resource to delegate administrative control of a ZFS dataset to a zone. Delegating a ZFS dataset is one way to add additional file system space to the zone, and it enables the administrator within the zone to perform her own management on the dataset. For example, she could create additional datasets within the delegated dataset, take her own snapshots, or make her own clones. Once a dataset has been delegated, the global zone can no longer mount the dataset. The ZFS `zoned` property is automatically set on delegated datasets. As the global zone administrator, be careful not to reset that property or try to mount any delegated datasets unless you know that the non-global zone has been deleted and is no longer using the dataset. To ensure that the non-global zone does not consume all of the space in the ZFS pool, set a quota on the delegated dataset. The following example shows how to set a 512MB quota on a dataset and delegate it to a zone:

```
# zfs set quota=512m pl/space/myzone
# zonecfg -z myzone
zonecfg:myzone> add dataset
zonecfg:myzone:dataset> set name=pl/space/myzone
zonecfg:myzone:dataset> end
```

CROSS-REF   ZFS is covered in depth in Chapter 8.

device

The `device` resource can be used to add device access to a zone. Normally a zone has access only to a limited set of safe pseudo-devices such as `/dev/null`, `/dev/zero`, and so on. Look under `/dev/dsk` within a zone and you won't see anything there. In some cases it is useful to add a device, such as a disk slice, to a zone. One case where that is common is with databases that need access to a raw disk partition. Another case is when you want the non-global zone administrator to be able to create and maintain his own file system on a disk partition. The following example adds both the block and raw `/dev/dsk/c0t0d0s7` and `/dev/rdsk/c0t0d0s7` partitions to the zone:

```
zonecfg:myzone> add device
zonecfg:myzone:device> set match=/dev/*dsk/c0t0d0s7
zonecfg:myzone:device> end
```

Here, a wildcard was used to match both dsk and rdsk. You can use wildcards anywhere in the match value, so to add all slices of a disk to a zone you would use something like `/dev/dsk/c0t1d0s*`. You can also add multiple device resources if the match property can't completely specify which devices you want to add. For instance, you might want to add access to both a disk slice and the audio device to a zone. (Disk slices are described in Chapter 7.)

CAUTION   Note that adding devices to zones represents a security hole. If a malicious user has root access to a device, even within a non-global zone, he could cause corruption, which might panic the system. In general, it is preferable to avoid adding disk devices to zones unless absolutely required. Instead, you can usually meet the storage needs of a zone by using the `fs` or `dataset` resources. Because file systems and datasets are managed outside of the zone, there is no way for a malicious user to cause a problem.

fs

The fs resource is used to add additional file systems to a zone. It is an alternative to the dataset resource as a way to add additional file system space to a zone. The fs resource can be used with a variety of file systems, whereas the dataset resource is used exclusively to delegate a ZFS dataset to a zone.

CROSS-REF The various OpenSolaris file systems are covered in Chapter 7, with the exception of ZFS, which is covered in Chapter 8.

A key difference between fs and inherit-pkg-dir resources is that the file systems mounted using the fs resource can be either read-only or read-write. In addition, inherit-pkg-dir resources explicitly require that the software installed in those directories be managed and maintained consistently across zones by the global zone administrator. There is no such requirement for software installed into file system space that is added using the fs resource.

The most common technique to add a file system to a zone is to use the lofs file system to loop-back mount a directory from the global zone into the non-global zone. When using lofs, an entire global zone file system does not have to be mounted into the zone; any subdirectory will work. In addition, when using lofs, the same directory can be safely mounted into multiple zones because there is only a single underlying file system that the kernel is managing. The following sets up a lofs mount:

```
zonecfg:myzone> add fs
zonecfg:myzone:fs> set dir=/export/projects
zonecfg:myzone:fs> set special=/pl/space/myzone
zonecfg:myzone:fs> set type=lofs
zonecfg:myzone:fs> end
```

Here, the dir property specifies where in the zone the file system should be mounted; the special property specifies the directory from the global zone that will be mounted into the zone; and the type property indicates that this is a lofs mount into the zone. This is a zonecfg resource, so you can set up as many additional fs mounts into the zone as needed.

As mentioned earlier, sometimes you want to make a subdirectory within an inherit-pkg-dir writable. This is easy to do by using a lofs mount of a writable file system under the read-only inherit-pkg-dir, as this example setting up /usr/local shows:

```
zonecfg:myzone> add fs
zonecfg:myzone:fs> set dir=/usr/local
zonecfg:myzone:fs> set special=/pl/space/myzone
zonecfg:myzone:fs> set type=lofs
zonecfg:myzone:fs> end
```

Using this configuration, any changes made to /usr/local within the zone will appear in the /pl/space/myzone subdirectory in the global zone.

The fs resource includes an additional property named raw and a nested resource named options. You use the options resource to specify the mount options for the file system that will be used when mounting into the zone. These options are file system specific and are the same options described in Chapter 7. You could change the first example so that /pl/space/myzone was read-only within the zone by adding the ro option to that instance:

```
zonecfg:myzone> select fs dir=/export/projects
zonecfg:myzone:fs> add options ro
zonecfg:myzone:fs> end
```

As with a top-level resource, you can add as many options resources as needed to specify all of the mount options for the file system.

The raw property is used when adding other file system types, such as UFS, to the zone. Other file systems don't have the same flexibility as lofs. In most cases you must dedicate those file systems to a specific zone and no sharing is allowed. That's because in most cases a file system can be mounted only once on the system. For some of those file systems you also need to set the raw property, which is used when the zone boots, so that the file system can be verified with fsck. This example shows adding a UFS file system to a zone:

```
zonecfg:myzone> add fs
zonecfg:myzone:fs> set dir=/export
zonecfg:myzone:fs> set special=/dev/dsk/c0d1s7
zonecfg:myzone:fs> set raw=/dev/rdsk/c0d1s7
zonecfg:myzone:fs> set type=ufs
zonecfg:myzone:fs> add options nodevices
zonecfg:myzone:fs> add options noatime
zonecfg:myzone:fs> end
```

You can see that the raw device is specified using the raw property, and you can see another example of adding mount options. File systems added to the zone using an fs resource are managed by the global zone when it boots the non-global zone. There is no entry for these file systems in the zone's vfstab. As an alternative, you could use the device resource to add /dev/*dsk/c0d1s7 to the zone, although that has the drawbacks mentioned earlier. With the device added this way, a UFS file system could be created on that slice and a vfstab entry made for the file system by the administrator within the zone.

One final example shows adding a ZFS file system using the fs resource. In the global zone you first create the ZFS dataset, and then add it in zonecfg:

```
# zfs create pl/sp/myzone
# zfs set mountpoint=legacy pl/sp/myzone
# zonecfg -z myzone
zonecfg:myzone> add fs
zonecfg:myzone:fs> set dir=/space
zonecfg:myzone:fs> set special=pl/sp/myzone
zonecfg:myzone:fs> set type=zfs
zonecfg:myzone:fs> end
zonecfg:myzone> exit
```

Note a few interesting points in this example. First, you must set the ZFS mountpoint property to legacy so that it is not automatically mounted in the global zone. This is required because a file system can be mounted only once and the global zone mounts the file system for the non-global zone when it boots. Second, the special property specifies the ZFS dataset name, unlike with UFS, for which a disk slice name is used. Finally, there is no raw property because ZFS file systems are not fsck-ed when mounted. Now you've seen three different ways that ZFS storage can be made available to a zone. The first, using delegated datasets, is useful when the non-global zone administrator needs control over his own dataset. The second, using lofs, is the most common approach when you just want to make some space available to a zone. That space can also be shared with other zones because there is only one underlying file system mount. The final example would not be commonly used but it illustrates the flexibility of the fs resource.

Summary of all zonecfg properties and resources

The zonecfg help subcommand can print a list of all the zonecfg properties and resources:

```
zonecfg:myzone> help set
usage:
set <property-name>=<property-value>
    Sets property values.

For resource type ... there are property types ...:
    (global)            zonename
    (global)            zonepath
    (global)            brand
    (global)            autoboot
    (global)            bootargs
    (global)            pool
    (global)            limitpriv
    (global)            scheduling-class
    (global)            ip-type
    (global)            max-lwps
    (global)            max-shm-memory
    (global)            max-shm-ids
    (global)            max-msg-ids
    (global)            max-sem-ids
    (global)            cpu-shares
    fs                  dir, special, raw, type
    inherit-pkg-dir     dir
    net                 address, physical
    device              match
    rctl                name, value
    attr                name, type, value
    dataset             name
    dedicated-cpu       ncpus, importance
    capped-cpu          ncpus
```

Additional zonecfg subcommands

A few additional zonecfg subcommands and options haven't been covered yet. When creating a zone, you can use the -t option on the create subcommand to specify the name of another existing zone to use as a template. This enables you to reuse one zone configuration when creating another:

```
# zonecfg -z myzone2
myzone2: No such zone configured
Use 'create' to begin configuring a new zone.
zonecfg:myzone2> create -t myzone
```

This example creates myzone2 with the same configuration as myzone, except that the zonepath is not set.

You can also use the export subcommand to output a zone configuration to a file and then create a new zone configuration from that file:

```
# zonecfg -z myzone export -f /tmp/config
# cat /tmp/config
create -b
set zonepath=/pl/zones/myzone
set autoboot=false
set ip-type=shared
add inherit-pkg-dir
set dir=/lib
end
add inherit-pkg-dir
set dir=/platform
end
add inherit-pkg-dir
set dir=/sbin
end
add inherit-pkg-dir
set dir=/usr
end
```

The output is simply the sequence of commands used to create the configuration. You could edit this file, update the zonepath, and create a new zone from the resulting command file, as shown in this example:

```
# zonecfg -z myzone2 </tmp/config
myzone2: No such zone configured
Use 'create' to begin configuring a new zone.
# zoneadm list -cv
  ID NAME       STATUS     PATH               BRAND    IP
   0 global     running    /                  native   shared
   - myzone     installed  /pl/zones/myzone   native   shared
   - myzone2    configured /pl/zones/myzone2  native   shared
```

You can redirect any set of zonecfg commands from an input file if you need to modify a zone in an automated fashion.

Finally, the `delete` subcommand is used to delete a zone configuration:

```
# zonecfg -z myzone2 delete -F
```

The `-F` option forces the deletion; otherwise, you are prompted to confirm that you really want to delete the configuration. After a zone has been installed, it cannot be deleted until it is first uninstalled.

> **CAUTION** Using the `-F` option uninstalls or deletes the zone with no confirmation. After these operations, there is no way to undo them, so be sure you want to do this when using `-F`.

Advanced zoneadm Features

You have already seen the `zoneadm install`, `boot`, `halt`, and `reboot` subcommands. This section describes the remaining subcommands.

Moving a zone on the same machine

Once a zone has been installed it may become necessary to relocate the zone within the local file system. This is accomplished with the `zoneadm move` subcommand:

```
# zoneadm -z myzone move /newpool/zones/myzone
```

> **NOTE** The zone must be halted before it can be moved.

This command causes the contents of the `zonepath` to be relocated to the new location. Depending on file system boundaries, this might be simply a rename or it could require actually transferring the contents of the `zonepath` from one file system to another. The `zoneadm` command handles both cases correctly. When the execution is complete, the `zonepath` property is updated to the new location. If the command fails for some reason, such as insufficient space in the new location, then the zone configuration is left as it was with the original `zonepath`.

Moving a zone from one machine to another

It is also possible to move a zone from one system to another. This is called *zone migration*, and is done in four steps:

1. Prepare the zone for migration by detaching it from the source system.
2. Physically move the zone data from the source to the destination system.
3. Configure the zone on the destination system.
4. Attach the zone on the destination system.

The zone cannot be running when it is migrated, unlike the xVM domains described in the next chapter.

It is important to remember that the zone depends on the operating system software installed in the global zone. This dependency is clearer with a sparse-root zone, but even a whole-root zone must have the correct version of the system libraries that interact with the kernel running on the machine. If these are out of sync, then applications running in the zone could exhibit incorrect behavior and obscure bugs. As a result, the attach process validates that the system software on the destination is an exact match for the system software on the original source system. If this is not the case, then the attach fails and an error list of out-of-sync software is output.

In the following example, the hostnames src and dst are used in the command prompts to make it clear where each step is performed:

```
src# zoneadm -z myzone halt
src# zoneadm -z myzone detach
```

The detach subcommand prepares the zone for migration. Once a zone has been detached, it is no longer in the installed state. It still exists on the source system but is now in the configured state:

```
src# zoneadm list -cv
  ID NAME             STATUS     PATH                     BRAND    IP
   0 global           running    /                        native   shared
   - myzone           configured /pl/zones/myzone         native   shared
```

The next step is to move the zone data from the source system to the destination. This step is deliberately left up to the system administrator because there are many different ways to relocate the zone. It could be copied using a tar or cpio archive, it could be written to tape and mailed to a remote site, or it might not move at all if the zone resides on a SAN that will be reconfigured such that the destination host can access the storage. This example creates a cpio archive which you can transfer to the destination host; just remember that this step can be done in many different ways:

```
src# cd /pl/zones
src# find myzone -depth | cpio -oP@0 myzone.cpio
1189888 blocks
```

The myzone.cpio archive now contains the complete image of the zone. You must now transfer this archive to the destination system. All further commands in this example are on the destination. The example also assumes that the zonepath will reside in /export/zones on the destination host, which is a different location from what was on the source system:

```
dst# cd /export/zones
dst# cpio -idmP@ <myzone.cpio
1189664 blocks
dst# rm myzone.cpio
```

Now that the zone data resides on the destination, the next step is to recreate the zone's configuration. This is done using the zonecfg create subcommand with the -a option, indicating that the creation is to be done using zone data that is being attached:

```
dst# zonecfg -z myzone
myzone: No such zone configured
```

```
Use 'create' to begin configuring a new zone.
zonecfg:myzone> create -a /export/zones/myzone
zonecfg:myzone> info
zonename: myzone
zonepath: /export/zones/myzone
brand: native
autoboot: false
bootargs:
pool:
limitpriv:
scheduling-class:
ip-type: shared
inherit-pkg-dir:
    dir: /lib
inherit-pkg-dir:
    dir: /platform
inherit-pkg-dir:
    dir: /sbin
inherit-pkg-dir:
    dir: /usr
net:
    address: 192.168.0.92
    physical: beg0
zonecfg:myzone> exit
```

The -a option on the create subcommand specifies the path where the zone data was installed on the destination host. The zonecfg command recreates the original zone configuration from that data, although the zonepath is modified to use the new location on the destination. It may be necessary to customize other parts of the configuration before the zone can be used. For example, the net resource still has the original physical NIC configured. If the destination has a different NIC, you might need to update that property. Likewise for the IP address, if the host was moved to a new subnet, or any other parts of the configuration that depended on the specifics of the source system.

TIP   When you use the create -a option to attach the configuration, check whether anything needs to be changed while you're still in the zonecfg session.

You can now see that the zone is configured on the new host:

```
dst# zoneadm list -cv
  ID NAME            STATUS      PATH                        BRAND   IP
   0 global          running     /                           native  shared
   - myzone          configured  /export/zones/myzone        native  shared
```

The final step in the migration is to attach the zone to the new host:

```
dst# zoneadm -z myzone attach
dst# zoneadm list -cv
  ID NAME            STATUS      PATH                        BRAND   IP
```

```
0 global          running    /                         native  shared
- myzone          installed  /export/zones/myzone      native  shared
```

Attaching the zone changes the state from configured to installed, and the zone can now be booted on the new host.

As previously mentioned, the attach process validates that the system software on the destination is an exact match for the system software on the original source system. You can use the dry-run options to the `detach` and `attach` subcommands to validate that a new machine can host the zone before you attempt to migrate it:

src# `zoneadm -z myzone detach -n | ssh dst zoneadm attach -n -`

With the `attach` dry-run option, the zone does not yet have to be configured on the destination machine.

If the destination is running newer software than the source, then it is possible to update the system software in the zone to match the system software on the new host using the `-u` option to `attach`:

dst# `zoneadm -z myzone attach -u`

This can be done only if all of the system software is newer. If the destination is running older system software or a mixture of older and newer software, the `attach` update will fail with an error. The process updates only the system software within the zone that must be in sync with the global zone. Other software within the zone is left alone. (The "Software management" section later in the chapter has more details about which software must remain in sync.)

If the source system dies but the storage on which the zone resides is still accessible, perhaps because it is on a SAN or the disks were recabled to a new host, it is possible to attach the zone to the new host without first detaching it. You cannot use the `zonecfg create -a` option described earlier because the zone metadata generated by the `detach` process does not exist. You have to manually recreate the zone configuration using `zonecfg`. However, once that's done, you can run the `attach` subcommand; the software validation takes place just as if the zone had been detached, and any inconsistencies are reported. If there are no inconsistencies or if you update the zone's software with the `-u` option, the zone is fully usable on the new host.

The multi-step zone migration enables different capabilities beyond simply migrating a zone from one host to another. Note that in this example the original source system still has all of the zone data available. There is nothing to prevent you from reattaching the zone to the source system. As long as there is no conflict with the networking or services provided by the zones on the source and destination hosts, this is an easy way to duplicate a zone configuration from one system to another. You can use the `attach -u` option to perform rolling upgrades of the zone by moving it from one machine to another, after you have validated the operating system release on the new host and are ready to run the zone there. You can archive a zone to tape and reattach it to the machine if you need to reactivate the zone for some reason.

Cloning a zone

The zoneadm command can be used to clone one zone installation to another. This capability is useful if you create a master zone with all of the add-on application software installed and configured that will be needed for another zone. After the second zone has been configured using zonecfg, you can use the zoneadm clone subcommand as an alternative to simply installing the zone:

```
# zoneadm -z myzone2 clone myzone
Cloning snapshot p1/zones/myzone@SUNWzone1
Instead of copying, a ZFS clone has been created for this zone.
sys-unconfig started Sat Feb 09 15:48:09 2008
sys-unconfig completed Sat Feb 09 15:48:09 2008
```

In this example you can see that both zones are installed on ZFS, so instead of having to make a full copy of the zone, the zoneadm command automatically creates a ZFS snapshot and ZFS clone that are used to install the second zone. This enables the second zone to be installed almost instantly. If both zones do not reside in the same ZFS zpool, or if they are not on ZFS at all, then a full copy of the zone's contents is made to install the second zone. This is still much faster than installing a fresh zone because all of the software metadata and customization is already complete. Depending on the hardware and whether the zone is sparse-root or whole-root, the full copy still only takes between a few seconds and a few minutes. The source zone must be halted when cloning, which ensures that the zone's files are in a consistent and stable state.

When using ZFS, in addition to speed, another advantage of cloning is that the space consumed by the ZFS clone is a fraction of the space needed for the original:

```
# zfs list
NAME                        USED   AVAIL  REFER  MOUNTPOINT
...
p1                          61.2G  12.4G  23K    /p1
p1/zones                    2.63G  12.4G  26K    /p1/zones
p1/zones/myzone             632M   12.4G  632M   /p1/zones/myzone
p1/zones/myzone@SUNWzone1   133K   -      632M   -
p1/zones/myzone2            240K   12.4G  632M   /p1/zones/myzone2
```

Note that the original zone, myzone, consumed 632MB of space in the pool, but the cloned zone consumes less than 256KB. As changes are made in the second zone, it's natural that the amount of space consumed increases because of the copy-on-write nature of ZFS, but there's almost always a significant amount of space that is common between the two zones and thus shared. The other interesting thing to note in the zfs list output is the snapshot, p1/zones/myzone@SUNWzone1, which was automatically created when the zone was cloned. Each time you clone a zone when using ZFS, a new snapshot is automatically created for the new clone. You can also reuse a snapshot from an earlier zone clone by using the -s option to the clone subcommand, like this:

```
# zoneadm -z myzone3 clone -s p1/zones/myzone@SUNWzone1 myzone
```

When attempting to reuse a snapshot, it is possible that the snapshot was taken before an update to the operating system software. If that is the case, the snapshot is out of date with respect to the current system and is no longer a valid starting point for installing a new zone. Before using an existing snapshot, the zoneadm command automatically validates that the system software in the snapshot is still current, similar to what is done when migrating a zone to a new host; and if the snapshot is out of date, zoneadm prevents you from reusing it. By default, when a snapshot is not explicitly specified on the command line, a new snapshot is taken each time you clone from a zone. If you specify a snapshot and it is out of date, you can simply omit the -s option and a new snapshot will be taken.

The final thing to notice in the example is that after the zone is cloned, it is unconfigured. This means that the zone's basic identity — hostname, nameservice configuration, root password, and so on — is cleared. This way, the new zone goes through the normal system configuration steps on the first boot, just as it would if it were freshly installed.

Uninstalling a zone

The zoneadm uninstall subcommand is used to remove the software from a zone in preparation for deleting the zone:

```
# zoneadm -z myzone2 uninstall -F
The ZFS file system for this zone has been destroyed.
# zonecfg -z myzone2 delete -F
```

If the zone was installed on ZFS, then the ZFS dataset that was automatically created when the zone was installed is now automatically destroyed. Otherwise, the zoneadm command removes all of the software that is installed. Once a zone is uninstalled, it is back in the configured state, and the zonecfg command can be used to delete the configuration.

Ongoing Zones Administration

So far, this chapter has focused on configuring a zone with zonecfg and the various features of the zoneadm command. This section covers the various aspects of managing a zone once it is installed and running.

Preconfiguring system identity

When a zone boots for the first time, it goes through the system configuration process, just as a freshly installed system does. This interactive process establishes the zone's identity, such as its hostname, time zone, and root password. When you first boot a zone, you must zlogin to the zone's console to answer these interactive questions. Omitting this step is a common mistake; and as a result, not all of the zone's SMF services will start correctly, leaving the zone in a state in which it appears to be running but the zone isn't usable.

It is possible to preconfigure the zone's identity so that the zone skips this interactive process and completely boots the first time. To do so, place a sysidcfg file in the zone's etc directory, which contains all of the system configuration information. See the `sysidcfg(4)` man page for a complete description of this file. The following shows an example for myzone:

```
# cat sysidcfg
system_locale=C
terminal=xterms
network_interface=primary {
                hostname=myzone
}
nfs4_domain=dynamic
security_policy=NONE
name_service=NONE
timezone=US/Mountain
root_password=fknhJhXYmdeKE
```

This file would be placed in the zone's `/etc` directory before the first boot so that none of the system identification questions are asked during the initial boot, as shown in this example:

```
# cp sysidcfg /pl/zones/myzone/root/etc
```

Zones-related processes

Once your zones are running, you may notice some extra processes associated with them. In particular, there are two administrative processes for each running zone: `zoneadmd` and `zsched`. The `zoneadmd` process runs in the global zone and is responsible for setting up the virtual platform for the zone. It also manages connections to the zone from `zlogin`. The `zsched` process runs within the zone and provides some of the same services to the zone that process 0 — the `sched` process — does in the global zone. Specifically, kernel threads for the zone are owned by the `zsched` process.

> **CAUTION** The `zoneadmd` and `zsched` processes are managed automatically by the system and should not be run by hand or killed.

Accessing a zone

After a zone has been booted for the first time, do not attempt to access files under the zonepath from the global zone. That's because it is possible for the zone's root to deliberately modify the zone's file system to leave Trojan horses for the superuser accessing the files from the global zone. A simple example is if the zone's `/etc/passwd` file were replaced with a symlink to `/etc/passwd`. The global zone administrator might attempt to edit this file, thinking she was modifying the zone's `/etc/passwd`, when in reality she would be editing the global zone's `/etc/passwd`. This is because the symlink is resolved in the context of the zone in which the command is running. If the edit were made in the non-global zone, the symlink would point to itself and there would be no way to harm the global zone.

This example is a simple one, but there are various other ways in which the zone's file systems could be corrupted by a zone administrator attempting to compromise the global zone. Even if you trust the non-global zone root user, it's still possible for the zone to be hacked by an attacker who could then lay a trap. This is only an issue for the root user in the global zone because only the root user can attempt to access the zone's file systems from the global zone. The permissions on the zonepath prevent a regular user from accessing the zone's file systems.

The key thing to remember is that the non-global zone administrator has root privileges within the zone, so she can make changes in the zone that a non-privileged user could never make. As a result, do not trust the contents of a zone once it has been booted. Instead, if you need to access files within the zone, do so using the zlogin command. The zlogin command runs your programs within the zone context and is safe. The software management commands that run in the global zone to access the non-global zone file systems also use specific, safe techniques to access the zone so that the global zone cannot be hacked by a compromised non-global zone.

Monitoring

There are a variety of tools you can use to monitor the status of zones, including zoneadm, various commands running in the global zone, and DTrace.

Zone states

The zoneadm list subcommand is one of the first commands to turn to when checking the status of a zone. As shown earlier, once a zone is created with zonecfg, it is in the configured state; after the zone is installed with the zoneadm install subcommand, it is in the installed state; and after the zone is booted, it is in the running state. In addition to these three states, zones can also be in the incomplete, ready, shutting down, or down states.

The incomplete state is used during zone installation. If the installation fails for any reason, then the zone is left in the incomplete state and must be uninstalled to return it to the configured state. The ready state is a transitional state during zone boot. In the ready state, the zone's virtual environment has been created but no processes are running in the zone. It is possible to put the zone into the ready state, although that is not common. The shutting down and down states are also transitional states when a zone is halting. A zone would not normally be in either of these states for very long, unless there is a bug in the system that prevents the zones from completely shutting down. Once a zone has been halted, it transitions through these states back to the installed state. If a zone is stuck in the down state, a bug somewhere in the system is preventing one or more processes in the zone from terminating.

CROSS-REF   If a zone is stuck in the down state and you are feeling adventurous, you might want to try some of the debugging techniques described in Chapter 24 to determine the problem.

When a zone is booted, it quickly transitions to the running state. Just because a zone shows up in the running state in the zoneadm list output doesn't mean that all of your applications are running in the zone. The zone running state does not correlate to the status of the software in the zone. Just as with a standalone system, the system is booted and some of the user-level system processes are running, but other processes might not be started yet because all of their SMF dependencies haven't been met or because the zone itself was booted to an SMF milestone where the applications won't be started. To monitor the status of processes within the zone, you'll use some of the techniques described in the next section.

Tools

This section discusses techniques you can use from the global zone to monitor the non-global zones.

CROSS-REF To monitor behavior within the zone, you can use many of the standard OpenSolaris tools described in Chapter 14.

The zlogin command can be used to run an application within the zone to check the zone's status. For example, after the zone has booted, you can check the status of SMF within the zone using the svcs command:

```
# zlogin myzone svcs -xv
svc:/system/avahi-bridge-dsd:default (Avahi Daemon Bridge to Bonjour)
 State: maintenance since Sat Feb 09 17:23:30 2008
Reason: Start method failed repeatedly, last exited with status 1.
   See: http://sun.com/msg/SMF-8000-KS
   See: man -M /usr/man -s 1M avahi-daemon-bridge-dsd
   See: /var/svc/log/system-avahi-bridge-dsd:default.log
Impact: This service is not running.
```

Many commands also have a zone option that enables you to target that command to a specific zone. In the global zone, the ps -e command lists all of the processes running on the system, including those in every zone. You can use the -Z option so that an extra column with the zonename is printed for each process, or you can use the -o option to customize the fields in which you are interested. To see what processes are running within a specific zone, use the -z option:

```
# ps -fz myzone
    UID   PID  PPID   C    STIME TTY          TIME CMD
   root 14827     1   0 17:23:27 ?           0:01 /usr/sbin/nscd
   root 14926     1   0 17:23:29 ?           0:00 /usr/lib/utmpd
...
```

In addition to the ps command, the ipcrm, ipcs, pgrep, pkill, prstat, ptree, and pkill commands accept a -z option to target a specific zone.

The prstat command with the -Z option reports a summary of all zone activity and is a useful tool to monitor the overall status of all the zones. This command clears the screen and produces a display like the following that updates every five seconds by default:

```
   PID USERNAME  SIZE   RSS STATE  PRI NICE      TIME  CPU PROCESS/NLWP
   387 daemon   8160K  824K sleep   59    0   3:13:22 0.8% rcapd/1
```

```
    15832 root      4720K 3036K cpu1    59    0   0:00:00 0.3% prstat/1
    ...
    ZONEID   NPROC SWAP  RSS MEMORY      TIME CPU ZONE
        0     128 1122M 592M   29%   5:32:55 2.4% global
       14      23  31M  29M  1.4%   0:00:08 0.0% myzone
    Total: 151 processes, 467 lwps, load averages: 0.06, 0.07, 0.13
```

The summary at the end of the screen lists the running zones, the number of processes, memory consumption, and CPU usage. With this overview you can quickly see if a zone is misbehaving and target that zone to determine the specific problem. The df and ipcs commands also accept a − Z option.

If a zone has a physical memory-cap set, it is enforced by the rcapd running in the global zone. You can monitor rcapd statistics for zones using the rcapstat -z option:

```
# rcapstat -z
    id zone              nproc   vm  rss   cap   at avgat   pg avgpg
    16 myzone              -    30M  37M  512M   0K    0K   0K    0K
```

This command lists each zone with a physical memory cap, the resident set size for the zone, and the current cap. If the zone is over its cap and rcapd is actively working to bring the zone back under the cap, additional statistics are printed; otherwise, those are 0.

If the zone is assigned to a pool, either explicitly with the pool property or implicitly with a dedicated-cpu resource, then poolstat can be used to monitor the pools. Recall that the dedicated-cpu's pool is named after the zone, so it is easy to see which pool is associated with which zone:

```
# poolstat
                           pset
    id pool             size used load
     0 pool_default        2 0.00 0.02
     3 SUNWtmp_myzone      2 0.00 0.21
```

You can also customize the poolstat output if you want to see the current min and max settings along with the size:

```
# poolstat -o pool,size,min,max,load -r all
pool            size  min  max load
pool_default       2    1  66K 0.01
SUNWtmp_myzone     2    1    4 0.00
```

Instead of a -z or -Z option, some commands accept an -i option indicating the type of object to which the command applies. The renice command is one of these. When used with the -i zoneid option, you can adjust the priority of all processes within a specific zone:

```
# renice -n 19 -i zoneid myzone
```

This example sets the priority of all the processes in myzone as low as possible so that they run only when there is nothing else to do on the system.

You can see the current resource control settings for a zone using the -i option on the prctl command:

```
# prctl -i zone myzone
zone: 16: myzone
NAME      PRIVILEGE     VALUE    FLAG   ACTION                        RECIPIENT
zone.max-swap
          privileged    1.00GB    -     deny                                  -
          system        16.0EB    max   deny                                  -
zone.max-locked-memory
          privileged    10.0MB    -     deny                                  -
          system        16.0EB    max   deny                                  -
...
```

Other commands that accept a -i option are described later in the section "Dynamically reconfiguring a zone."

DTrace

When using DTrace to monitor zones, it is often useful to limit the tracing to a specific zone using the curpsinfo->pr_zoneid member of the psinfo_t structure. This simple example uses pr_zoneid in the DTrace predicate to trace all of the system call entries from zoneid 14:

```
syscall:::entry
/curpsinfo->pr_zoneid == 14/
{
    printf("%s\n", probefunc);
}
```

An alternative is to check that the pr_zoneid is not 0, which would trace all system calls in all non-global zones because the global zone always has zoneid 0.

CROSS-REF Chapter 15 is devoted to the DTrace facility.

Dynamically reconfiguring a zone

In some cases it is desirable to update a running zone's configuration without rebooting the zone. Changes made using zonecfg don't take effect until the next time the zone boots. Not every attribute can be dynamically changed, but it is possible to update parts of the zone's state by using various system commands.

CAUTION Any changes made via system commands are only temporary and will be lost the next time the zone boots, unless the change is also made to the zone's configuration through zonecfg.

To add additional file system space to a zone, you can simply run the `mount` command to add the mount within the zone's root. First be sure to create the mount point in the zone, as this example using lofs shows:

```
# zlogin myzone mkdir /space
# mount -F lofs /p1/sp/myzone /p1/zones/myzone/root/space
# zlogin myzone df -hl
Filesystem              size  used  avail capacity  Mounted on
...
/space                  33G   20G   12G   63%       /space
```

You can dynamically add a network interface using the `zone` option to `ifconfig`:

```
# ifconfig bge0 addif 192.168.0.92 netmask 255.255.255.0 zone myzone
Created new logical interface bge0:1
```

The `-zone` option to `ifconfig` can be used to remove an interface from a zone.

A zone's pool binding can be changed using the `poolbind` command with the `-i` option:

```
# poolbind -p newpool -i zoneid myzone
```

CROSS-REF If the pool does not already exist, you have to create it first using the pool commands described in Chapter 18.

You can dynamically change the scheduling class for processes within a zone using the `priocntl` command. The following sets the zone to use the FSS class:

```
# priocntl -s -c FSS -i zoneid 18
```

Note that the `priocntl` command does not accept the zonename as the argument for the `-i zoneid` option, so you must use the zoneid, which you can obtain using the `zoneadm list` subcommand.

Likewise, a zone's resource control settings can be dynamically adjusted using the `prctl` command with the `-i` option. This example modifies the `max-lwps` resource control to 2000:

```
# prctl -r -n zone.max-lwps -v 2000 -i zone myzone
```

Because you are using the command line interface, the full resource control name, `zone.max-lwps`, must be spelled out. A resource control can also be removed with the `prctl` command:

```
# prctl -n zone.max-lwps -x -i zone myzone
```

To change the amount of physical memory that `rcapd` is capping for the zone, use the `rcapadm` command with the `-z` option. This example sets the new physical cap to 256MB:

```
# rcapadm -z myzone -m 256m
```

If you are monitoring a zone's physical caps using `rcapstat -z`, you might notice that it takes a few iterations of output before the new cap is updated. That's because the `rcapd` only updates its limits periodically.

SMF

The SMF service `svc:/system/zones` is used to boot zones whose `autoboot` property is set to `true` when the system boots. It also does an orderly shutdown of running zones when the system performs an orderly shutdown. This service must always be enabled in order for these two capabilities to work correctly. Other than knowing what it does, you won't normally have to do anything with this service.

CROSS-REF See Chapter 13 for more information on SMF.

Backup and restore

The actual details of the backup commands vary according to the software being used, so this section focuses on general issues. Because non-global zones fundamentally depend on the global zone and are part of the overall system configuration, they should be backed up from the global zone as part of the normal system backup strategy. This is straightforward because zones simply reside in the local file systems. You may need to take additional steps if you have added a raw device to a zone that it is using for data. In that case, be sure to back up the contents of those devices as well.

In some cases, the non-global zone administrator may want to run her own backups within the zone. This may be due to different backup policies between the global and non-global zone or because the file system paths appear differently between the two, or because the non-global zone has been changed by the zone administrator and she wants a new backup. Backing up in this situation can be more complex:

- If you're backing up to a local device, such as a tape drive, then it must be made available to the zone.

- If a network backup tool is being used, then the server must be accessible from the zone. This can be an issue if an exclusive IP stack zone is used and the networking in the zone is configured differently from the global zone.

- Not all file systems should be backed up because there is no way to restore them from the non-global zone. Any `inherit-pkg-dirs` or `lofs` mounts should be skipped because that data is backed up strictly from the global zone.

- Not all third-party backup tools are zone aware, so they might not work correctly in a zone. However, some tools have been enhanced to understand zones and work fine when run within a non-global zone.

It is best to check the capabilities of the tool you are using when you first deploy your zones so that you understand how the zones will interact with the backup strategy.

Because delegated ZFS datasets cannot be mounted in the global zone, either back up these datasets from within the non-global zone or use the ZFS `send` and `receive` subcommands in the global zone to back up and restore snapshots of these datasets. This example shows the use of the `send` subcommand to make a backup of a delegated dataset snapshot:

```
# zfs send rpool/export/zones/myds@mysnap1 >/export/sp/mydump
```

Software management

Software management on OpenSolaris is a rapidly evolving technology and it differs from earlier releases of Solaris. Basic software management for OpenSolaris uses the IPS system, described in Chapter 6, while the SXCE distribution uses the traditional SVR4 packaging system. These differences affect how software is managed for zones.

As mentioned earlier with respect to sparse-root zones and whole-root zones, the `inherit-pkg-dir` concept is fundamentally related to how software is managed between the global and non-global zones. In addition, the concept of a zone's brand, which is described further in the "Branded Zones" section later in this chapter, also affects how software is managed.

On systems running SXCE, for native-branded zones, the SVR4 packages are tagged with information that indicates whether the package must be the same for both the global and non-global zones. This information, in conjunction with the zone's `inherit-pkg-dir` configuration, is used to determine which software must stay in sync with the global zone. As you add packages, upgrade the system, or perform patching operations in the global zone, the system ensures that both the software and the information related to the installation of that software are maintained correctly inside the non-global zone as well. These concepts are applicable to OpenSolaris as well, but because OpenSolaris uses the IPS packaging system, the traditional SVR4 packaging, patching, and how this relates to zones are not discussed further here. If you need more information about SVR4 packaging, consult the legacy Solaris documentation.

Although system software is managed using the IPS packaging system on OpenSolaris, you can still install add-on software using the SVR4 system. Currently, IPS support for zones is under development, and support for zones is in transition to the new model. To support zones during this transition, a new brand, `ipkg`, has been defined. (See the "Branded Zones" section later in this chapter for more background on how branded zones work.) On OpenSolaris, newly created zones default to using the `ipkg` brand, which provides support for installing software into the zone using IPS. Only the whole-root model is supported because IPS does not yet support installing software using the sparse-root model in which only the package metadata is updated.

In addition, IPS does not yet have a mechanism to indicate that system software must be kept in sync between the global and non-global zones. Given that, when using zones on OpenSolaris, you must manually ensure that the system software stays in sync. More specifically, even though it is possible to install one version of OpenSolaris in the global zone and a different build in a non-global zone, be careful not to do this because it can easily lead to obscure failures that are difficult to diagnose.

All of these limitations are well understood and simply reflect the developmental state of IPS at the time of this writing. These limitations are being addressed and may very well be fixed by the time you read this. Check the documentation for the current release of OpenSolaris that you are using to determine exactly how zones behave with respect to software management using IPS. It is expected that the need for the ipkg brand will eventually disappear as IPS support for zones matures. When that happens, native-branded zones will simply use IPS on OpenSolaris, just as native-branded zones today use SVR4 on SXCE.

In addition to using IPS, ipkg-branded zones also use a ZFS root file system that is based on the ZFS-root model used in the global zone. This enables the dataset cloning and software backout capabilities that are provided by software management in the global zone. When the global zone is updated to a new boot environment using pkg image-update, a new ZFS clone for each zone is created at the same time. That way, each boot environment has the appropriate zone datasets associated with it and you can easily switch from one boot environment to another.

Other tools

This chapter has focused on the core system tools for configuring and managing zones, but other open source projects provide tools related to zones. Once you are familiar with the core tools, you might want to investigate some of these other projects:

- The webmin project is a popular tool for system management. It includes support for managing zones.

- The Zone Manager project on OpenSolaris.org attempts to simplify zone creation and management with a single non-interactive command line tool.

- As mentioned in the chapter introduction, the xVM OpsCenter project is working to provide a simplified and unified view of system management with a focus on virtualization.

Limitations to Zones

Because zones are an operating-system-level virtualization solution, they have certain limitations that other virtualization solutions don't have. There are also certain limitations with the current implementation that might change in the future.

There is a single kernel for the whole system, so non-global zones are not allowed to inspect data within the kernel. That would violate the encapsulation that zones provide. Nor are zones allowed to change data in the kernel. This includes actions such as installing a new driver or changing a kernel setting. In many cases this limitation can be worked around by installing the driver from the global zone or by making a global change to a system setting and using resource controls to limit individual zones. In general, zones cannot run different operating systems because there is only a single underlying kernel, but zones can run different user-level environments, as described in the following section.

As discussed earlier, processes within zones do not have all of the privileges that are available in the global zone. Some privileges simply cannot be given to a process within a zone. If those privileges are needed for some reason, then that application is unsuitable to run within a zone. For similar reasons, some commands do not work in a zone; and if an application depends on running one of those commands, it won't work.

You have already seen techniques to work around applications that need to access devices or write to file systems that might not normally be writable within a zone by configuring the zone to use either the `device` or `fs` resources.

Zones cannot currently be NFS servers for file systems within the zone, and zonepaths cannot reside on an NFS mounted file system. Because of the way that NFS and local file systems interact, zones should not be NFS clients of the global zone. Normally, when an NFS mount is attempted on the same system, the automounter detects this and transparently uses a lofs mount instead. The automounter cannot detect this within a zone because it appears that two different systems are involved. If a zone needs access to file systems from the global zone, an explicit lofs mount in the zone configuration should be used instead. Aside from that, there are no other limitations of zones as NFS clients.

In addition, there are the limitations described throughout this chapter and which typically relate to the zone configuration itself. For instance, as mentioned earlier, when using a sparse-root zone, those directories are not writable within the zone. Software installed in those directories must be managed by the global zone. Another example is the use of a shared IP stack zone, where the zone itself cannot reconfigure the network or use the network in an insecure way. These types of configuration limitations can also be viewed as a strength because the limits are often used to provide extra security beyond what is normally possible inside the zone.

Branded Zones

All zones have a brand associated with them. A zone's brand dictates the user-level environment installed and running within that zone.

Brands are a fundamental part of the zone infrastructure. Within the zone's implementation are a variety of hooks and mechanisms to modify the behavior of the zone so that it can be used with a different user-level environment. The amount of interpositioning delivered by a brand varies from simple to complex. A specific brand might hook into the zone's infrastructure at only a few points, perhaps by providing extensions for installing or booting the zone. Another brand might use a more sophisticated interpositioning mechanism whereby it intercepts system calls and modifies its behavior to emulate a completely different operating system within the zone. This type of brand has more overhead than a native zone because of the system call interpositioning, but this overhead is still usually much less than what is seen with hypervisor-based virtualization, so the scalability advantage of zones remains. Using this support, it is possible to run unmodified binaries that were built for another operating system, assuming the appropriate brand module has been implemented.

With the brand capability, zones can provide support for complex non-native environments and still maintain the advantage of low overhead and the simplicity of running a single kernel in the global zone.

In zonecfg you probably noticed the brand property, which you have also seen in the zoneadm list output:

```
$ zoneadm list -cv
  ID NAME            STATUS      PATH                        BRAND    IP
   0 global          running     /                           native   shared
  25 myzone          running     /export/zones/myzone        ipkg     shared
```

The ipkg brand

Until now the chapter has focused primarily on the native brand, although the ipkg brand was discussed earlier in the "Software management" section. On SXCE, the native brand uses the same system software environment as the global zone. That is, native-branded zones use the same release of SXCE that's installed in the global zone. Likewise, the ipkg brand represents the same version of OpenSolaris system software that's installed in the global zone. There is no system call interpositioning associated with this brand. Instead, the brand is used only to deliver the IPS support for the software management operations for zones, such as install, clone, or uninstall. As previously mentioned, this support is currently in transition, and the details of this brand will change in a future release — or it may disappear altogether.

The lx brand

The lx brand was the first non-native brand provided with zones. It provides an environment to execute an unmodified CentOS 3. *x* or Red Hat Enterprise Linux 3.x 32-bit distribution within the zone. This brand is delivered only for the x86 architecture.

To use the brand, you first configure the zone as an lx-branded zone. It is simplest to create the zone using the SUNWlx zone template provided with the brand:

```
# zonecfg -z mycentos
mycentos: No such zone configured
Use 'create' to begin configuring a new zone.
zonecfg:mycentos> create -t SUNWlx
zonecfg:mycentos> set zonepath=/pl/zones/mycentos
zonecfg:mycentos> add net
zonecfg:mycentos:net> set physical=bge0
zonecfg:mycentos:net> set address=192.168.0.95
zonecfg:mycentos:net> end
zonecfg:mycentos> add capped-memory
zonecfg:mycentos:capped-memory> set physical=512m
zonecfg:mycentos:capped-memory> set swap=1g
zonecfg:mycentos:capped-memory> set locked=0
zonecfg:mycentos> set max-lwps=1000
zonecfg:mycentos> set cpu-shares=1
```

```
zonecfg:mycentos> info
zonename: mycentos
zonepath: /pl/zones/mycentos
brand: lx
autoboot: false
bootargs:
pool:
limitpriv:
scheduling-class:
ip-type: shared
[max-lwps: 1000]
[cpu-shares: 1]
net:
    address: 192.168.0.95
    physical: bge0
capped-memory:
    physical: 512M
    [swap: 1G]
    [locked: 0]
rctl:
    name: zone.max-swap
    value: (priv=privileged,limit=1073741824,action=deny)
rctl:
    name: zone.max-locked-memory
    value: (priv=privileged,limit=0,action=deny)
rctl:
    name: zone.max-lwps
    value: (priv=privileged,limit=1000,action=deny)
rctl:
    name: zone.cpu-shares
    value: (priv=privileged,limit=1,action=none)
zonecfg:mycentos> exit
```

Creating the zone with the SUNWlx template sets the brand property to lx and excludes any inherit-pkg-dirs because those don't make sense in this case. Many non-native brands are whole-root zones. As shown in the example, most of the standard zonecfg properties and resources work just like they do with a native branded zone. Set the resource management capabilities, networking, and so on just as you normally would. The global zone manages these capabilities, so it doesn't matter what environment is running in the non-global zone. You can't delegate a ZFS dataset because this release of Linux doesn't know how to manage ZFS, but you can place the zone itself on ZFS or add a file system with the fs resource using lofs. For devices, such as the NIC assigned to the zone, it doesn't matter whether Linux has a driver for the device because the driver is actually running in the OpenSolaris kernel and is virtualized into the zone. The lx brand does not support exclusive stack zones.

Once the lx-branded zone has been created, you install it using the zoneadm command. The brand delivers hooks to enable installation from an ISO image of the CentOS or RedHat distribution. Alternatively, you can download a CentOS 3.x tarball linked off the BrandZ project page on OpenSolaris.org and install from that. This example installs the zone using that tarball:

```
# zoneadm -z mycentos install -d ~/zones/centos_fs_image.tar.bz2
A ZFS file system has been created for this zone.
Installing zone 'mycentos' at root directory '/pl/zones/mycentos'
from archive '/home/myhome/zones/centos_fs_image.tar.bz2'

This process may take several minutes.

Setting up the initial lx brand environment.
System configuration modifications complete.
Setting up the initial lx brand environment.
System configuration modifications complete.

Installation of zone 'mycentos' completed successfully.

Details saved to log file:
    "/pl/zones/mycentos/root/var/log/mycentos.install.23743.log"
```

As shown in this example, because the zonepath resides on ZFS, a ZFS dataset is automatically created, just as with native zones. Other zone features such as cloning or migration also work just as they do with a native zone. Once you are familiar with managing native zones, there is very little additional brand-specific information you need to learn.

Using the zoneadm list subcommand, you can see this zone is configured with the lx brand:

```
# zoneadm list -cv
  ID NAME          STATUS      PATH                    BRAND    IP
   0 global        running     /                       native   shared
  25 myzone        running     /pl/zones/myzone        ipkg     shared
   - mycentos      installed   /pl/zones/mycentos      lx       shared
```

Once a zone has been installed, you cannot change its brand.

Now that the zone has been installed, you can boot and zlogin just as you normally would. Use the zoneadm command to boot the zone:

```
# zoneadm -z mycentos boot
```

In another window, log in to the zone's console and watch it boot:

```
# zlogin -C mycentos
[Connected to zone 'mycentos' console]
[NOTICE: Zone booting up]
INIT: version 2.85 booting
        Welcome to CentOS
        Press 'I' to enter interactive startup.
Configuring kernel parameters: [ OK ]
```

```
Setting hostname mycentos:  [  OK  ]
Checking root filesystem
[  OK  ]
...
CentOS release 3.7 (Final)
Kernel 2.4.21 on an i686

mycentos login: root
Password:
...
-bash-2.05b# uname -a
Linux mycentos 2.4.21 BrandZ fake linux i686 athlon i386 GNU/Linux
-bash-2.05b# ps -aux
USER       PID %CPU %MEM   VSZ  RSS TTY   STAT START  TIME COMMAND
xfs      26009  0.0  0.2  8320 4244 ?     S    Feb20  0:00 xfs -droppriv -da
daemon   26019  0.0  0.0  4636 1732 ?     S    Feb20  0:00 /usr/sbin/atd
root     26074  0.0  0.1  5568 2484 ?     R    Feb20  0:00 ps -aux
root         1  0.0  0.1  4244 2148 ?     S    Feb20  0:00 /sbin/init
...
```

The zone runs through the normal Linux boot processing much like a standalone system would. All of the user-level processes are run in the normal sequence. Once you log in, you can see that the native Linux commands and environment are present.

> **TIP** Using the lx brand enables you to download Linux binary applications, built for CentOS 3.x or related distributions, and immediately run them with no additional work.

Experimental Linux 2.6 support

The lx brand has been extended to provide support for running a Linux 2.6-based distribution, although there is still additional work to do to complete that brand. To enable this support, configure an lx-branded zone as previously described. Add the following attribute to turn on the experimental 2.6 support:

```
zonecfg:mycentos5> add attr
zonecfg:mycentos5:attr> set name="kernel-version"
zonecfg:mycentos5:attr> set type=string
zonecfg:mycentos5:attr> set value="2.6"
zonecfg:mycentos5:attr> end
```

Now you can install the zone from a CentOS 5.x-based tarball. The zone will be bootable although there are certain known issues with the experimental support. A few applications are known not to work or have not been tested. Check the BrandZ community pages on opensolaris.org to determine the current status of this brand.

Other brands

In addition to the lx brand, the Open HA Cluster software uses parts of the brand infrastructure to hook into zones for failover. However, no system call interpositioning is needed for that brand. Sun Microsystems also offers `solaris8` and `solaris9` branded zones running on Solaris 10 for the SPARC architecture. Because those brands and operating system versions are not open source and don't run on OpenSolaris at this time, they are not described here.

Implementation

If a brand delivers system call interpositioning, the brand module installs into the kernel and dynamically enables interpositioning on a per-system-call basis. Thus, if a specific brand were to only interpose on a few system calls, the rest would still run at full speed. On the x86 architecture, interpositioning is enabled on a per-process basis, so only processes running in a branded zone incur any overhead for the brand's interpositioning. On the SPARC architecture, interpositioning is enabled when a branded zone boots, so there is some additional overhead when a branded zone is running, but typically only around 1–2%.

When a branded program that uses system call interpositioning runs, it is transparently linked with its brand library in addition to its other dependencies. Thus, each branded process has a copy of the brand library linked in. If the system call is interposed on, then when a system call is made, the kernel immediately redirects execution back out to the brand library in the process within its user-level code. The brand library then provides whatever behavior is needed to emulate the brand's environment. In complex cases this might entail making one or more native system calls and adjusting the results to correspond to what processes in the brand expect. In simple cases the brand library might return a result with no additional system call. Most of the emulation work is handled within the brand library in user-level code; the kernel module primarily redirects execution back out of the kernel when needed.

A brand can also provide other complex emulation if needed. For example, a non-native version of procfs can be emulated by a brand.

Resources

- The zones community is at `http://opensolaris.org/os/community/zones`. On the zones community page you can find links to an extensive FAQ, to project documents and plans, and to the Zones discussion where community members ask and answer questions.
- The Resource Management project is at `http://opensolaris.org/os/project/rm`.
- The BrandZ community is at `http://opensolaris.org/os/community/brandz`.
- The CentOS project is at `http://centos.org`.
- The sample CentOS 3.x tarball can be downloaded from `http://dlc.sun.com/osol/brandz/downloads/centos_fs_image.tar.bz2`.
- The experimental Linux 2.6 brand support is described at `http://opensolaris.org/os/community/brandz/todo/linux_2_6`.

Some of the other projects that work with zones are as follows:

- The zone manager project at `http://opensolaris.org/os/project/zonemgr`
- The webmin project at `http://webmin.com`
- The xVM OpsCenter project at `https://openxvm.dev.java.net`

If you are interested in the architecture and design of zones, BrandZ, and the 1x brand, the ARC cases are available on the ARC community at `http://opensolaris.org/os/community/arc`. In particular, the following two cases are the most fundamental:

```
PSARC/2002/174 Virtualization and Namespace Isolation in Solaris
PSARC/2005/471 BrandZ: Support for non-native zones
```

However, there are many smaller zones-related cases, subsequent to the original 2002/174 case, that document the architecture of specific enhancements.

If you are interested in the implementation of zones, BrandZ, and the 1x brand, the zones source code is spread out among the kernel, libraries, and commands. Within the source tree, the primary kernel module is at `usr/src/uts/common/os/zone.c`. This file begins with an extensive comment that explains many of the fundamentals of the zone implementation. Although the file contains much of the zones-related kernel code, the kernel fundamentally understands zones and there are various bits of zones-related checking throughout the kernel. The main zone header file is at `usr/src/head/libzonecfg.h` and the primary library source is under `usr/src/lib/libzonecfg`. The main zone commands are under `usr/src/cmd/zoneadm`, `usr/src/cmd/zoneadmd`, `usr/src/cmd/zonecfg`, and `usr/src/cmd/zlogin`. The BrandZ kernel code is primarily in `usr/src/uts/common/os/brand.c` and the library code is under `usr/src/lib/libbrand`. The 1x brand kernel code is under `usr/src/uts/common/brand/1x` and the 1x brand user-level code is under `usr/src/lib/brand/1x`.

Summary

This chapter described Zones, the OpenSolaris operating-system-level virtualization feature, and how it is integrated with resource management. The benefits, features, and management of zones were explored. Because zones are so lightweight, they are good choice for encapsulating or consolidating workloads onto a system where scalability or performance is critical. The limitations of the single kernel were explained, although through the use of branded zones, there is more flexibility than the single kernel might imply.

xVM Hypervisor

The xVM hypervisor is the type 1 hypervisor virtualization solution provided in OpenSolaris for the x86 hardware architecture. Using xVM, system resources can be shared among *domains*, each of which is an isolated environment that runs a standalone operating system. The OpenSolaris xVM hypervisor is based on the Xen open source project.

IN THIS CHAPTER

xVM concepts

Getting started with xVM

Advanced xVM administration

Live migration

Virtual devices

xVM troubleshooting

> **NOTE** The xVM name is used on a variety of OpenSolaris-related software components that work with virtualization. In this chapter, xVM is used specifically to refer to the hypervisor based on the Xen project. Sun Microsystems also offers their xVM Server product, which is a self-contained virtualization appliance built around the hypervisor and the xVM Ops Center management tools. This chapter focuses on interacting with the hypervisor directly, not as an appliance as offered by the xVM Server product.

xVM runs both paravirtualized and fully virtualized guest operating systems. OpenSolaris has been paravirtualized to run on the hypervisor as either the control domain or a guest OS. This paravirtualization provides better performance when interacting with the hypervisor than a domain running a fully virtualized OS.

In addition to the standard virtualization benefits provided by running an OS on a hypervisor, xVM offers features such as the capability to suspend and resume a running domain, as well as live migration of a running domain from one host to another.

> **CROSS-REF** Chapter 17 describes the benefits of virtualization and basic virtualization concepts such as a hypervisor, full virtualization, and paravirtualization. If you are unfamiliar with these concepts, refer to Chapter 17 before proceeding.

The xVM hypervisor is one of the fastest evolving technologies within OpenSolaris. By the time you read this, there will likely be new features and enhancements that were unavailable at the time this chapter was written, but the material here will get you started with xVM, and you can consult the documentation for your specific release of OpenSolaris to learn more about any additional features that might be available.

xVM Concepts

xVM introduces a variety of new concepts and terms that you'll encounter as you configure and manage domains. This section explains some of these concepts.

A new platform has been defined for OpenSolaris running in a paravirtualized domain on xVM: i86xpv. You will see this in the uname output:

```
$ uname -i
i86xpv
```

> **NOTE** Although you have seen the uname command in Chapters 3 and 14, the -i option has not been discussed. This option prints the system's platform name. The platform is used by the OpenSolaris kernel to determine which hardware-specific module the kernel will use to interact with the underlying system hardware. Previously, x86 systems didn't have multiple platforms because x86 hardware is fairly generic. However, on SPARC systems, a variety of platforms provide modules for the kernel, which enables the OS to use the hardware features properly and more efficiently.

For running on the xVM hypervisor, OpenSolaris delivers the i86xpv platform module. When OpenSolaris is booted on the hypervisor, or when OpenSolaris is running in a paravirtualized domain, the system platform is reported as i86xpv, causing that platform module to be used by the kernel. Instead of directly accessing the hardware, such as the Memory Management Unit (MMU), the i86xpv-specific portions of the kernel make explicit *hypercalls* to the xVM hypervisor. Because the platform-specific portion of the kernel is optimized to work directly with the hypervisor, paravirtualized domains are much more efficient than fully virtualized domains, in which the hypervisor must trap and manage every hardware access.

With xVM the control domain is called *dom0*. This is the domain that initially boots the host OS, which is used to configure and manage other domains, as well as to provide virtual I/O services. There is only one dom0 running on a system at a time. Within the various tools, dom0 is named Domain-0. The host OS running in dom0 must be paravirtualized to run on top of the xVM hypervisor. Because the OS must be modified to run as a paravirtualized OS, currently, only open source systems, such as OpenSolaris, Linux, or BSD, have been modified to run as dom0.

A domain that runs a guest OS is called a *domU*. Multiple domUs can be running at any time, each running a different installation of a guest OS. The number of domUs that can run concurrently is limited by the overall hardware resources available on the system, and the load in each domU.

This chapter focuses on using OpenSolaris as both the host OS in dom0 and as a guest OS in a domU, although some examples of running other operating systems in a domU are also provided.

xVM supports both paravirtualized and fully virtualized guest operating systems in a domU. As described in Chapter 17, a fully virtualized OS does not know it is running on a hypervisor. In xVM, a fully virtualized domU is also called a *hardware-assisted virtual machine* (HVM). xVM depends on the hardware virtualization features provided by the CPU, through either the Intel VT-x or AMD-V extensions, to run a fully virtualized guest domain. If your system's CPU does not include those extensions, then you will only be able to run paravirtualized guests. With xVM it is also possible to run an HVM domain that is set up to use paravirtualized drivers. This is sometimes known as HVM+PV. This configuration improves I/O performance over a standard HVM domain, although the rest of the guest OS kernel that interacts with the hardware will still not perform as well as a fully paravirtualized OS.

> **TIP** Some systems require the CPU virtualization extensions to be enabled in the BIOS. If you think your system has a CPU that supports these extensions but xVM won't let you install a fully virtualized domain, then first check your BIOS to determine whether this is configurable. Because each BIOS differs in how this is determined, consult your system documentation for specific instructions.

When running a paravirtualized domain, the I/O devices are virtualized using drivers that split the functionality between the guest OS and the host OS running in dom0. A *frontend* driver is used in the domU. This driver communicates, using shared memory, with a *backend* driver in dom0. The backend driver then talks to the physical device, which is accessible only from dom0. This structure, along with the various logical components and domains used in xVM, is shown in Figure 20-1. For example, the xdf driver is the frontend disk driver and the xdb driver is the backend disk driver — likewise for networking with the xnf and xnb drivers.

When running a fully virtualized domain, the hypervisor must trap any read or write operation, as well as any direct memory access (DMA) operation, to a physical device. The hypervisor then forwards those requests to a QEMU process running in dom0. QEMU is used to emulate devices at the physical layer and, in turn, talks to the real device drivers in dom0. This adds significant overhead to an HVM domain, causing it to be noticeably slower, because there are several expensive transitions between the domU, the dom0, the hypervisor, and the various subsystems, for each device access.

> **NOTE** The full set of QEMU software is a type 2 hypervisor in its own right, but in the context of xVM only a subset of QEMU is used to emulate physical devices for HVM domains.

Because the domUs depend on dom0 for I/O services, it is recommended that you avoid running applications in dom0. In general, when using xVM, it is best to only use dom0 for management, and I/O for domUs, because any disruption in dom0, such as a kernel panic, will bring down all of the domains. A kernel panic in a domU will bring down only that domU.

FIGURE 20-1

The relationship between hardware, hypervisor, domains, and drivers looks complicated.

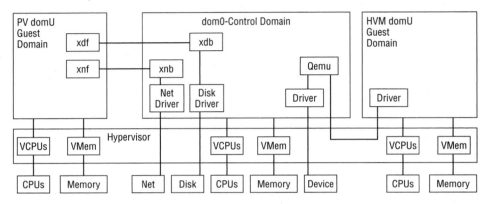

Although not shown in Figure 20-1, domain consoles are also virtualized through the `xencon-soled` daemon running in dom0.

Getting Started with xVM

This section focuses on the basics of getting a domU up and running. The xVM `virt-manager` GUI provides an easy way to create and manage domUs. Subsequent sections discuss many of the concepts introduced here in more detail, along with various command line interfaces (CLIs) that provide additional control over domU management.

Installing the xVM software and booting under the hypervisor

If you don't already have the xVM packages installed, the following command installs all of the necessary xVM packages:

```
# pkg install SUNWxvm SUNWlibvirt SUNWxvmdom SUNWxvmhvm \
SUNWvirt-manager SUNWvirtinst SUNWvdisk SUNWurlgrabber
```

If you intend to access a domain's graphical display, you need the `SUNWvncviewer` package, which is included in the default OpenSolaris installation. Once the packages are installed, update the GRUB menu to add the xVM hypervisor as a boot option:

```
# /boot/solaris/bin/update_grub
```

Use the `bootadm` command to manage your boot environments. To set up the system so that it always boots the xVM hypervisor, set your default GRUB entry as shown here. First, list your GRUB menu so that you can see which entry is the hypervisor:

```
# bootadm list-menu
The location for the active GRUB menu is: /rpool/boot/grub/menu.lst
default 6
timeout 10
0 OpenSolaris 2008.05 snv_86_rc3 X86
1 opensolaris-2
2 opensolaris-3
3 Solaris 2008.11 snv_91 X86
4 Solaris xVM
5 opensolaris-4
6 opensolaris-5
```

Here, the hypervisor is entry number 4, `Solaris xVM`. Use the `bootadm set-menu` subcommand to configure this as the default:

```
# bootadm set-menu default=4
```

Reboot the system so your OpenSolaris installation is running as dom0 on top of the hypervisor. After the system reboots, you can verify that you are running on the hypervisor, because your system should now be using the paravirtualized x86 platform kernel module:

```
$ uname -i
i86xpv
```

The last step before setting up domains is to enable the xVM SMF services:

```
# svcadm enable -r xvm/domains xvm/virtd
```

TIP You may also need to enable the `sysevent` handling for xVM. To determine whether the `sysevent` handler is already set up, use the following command:

```
# syseventadm list -c EC_xendev
```

If you don't see any output, use the following commands to install the `sysevent` handler:

```
# syseventadm add -c EC_xendev \
/usr/lib/xen/scripts/xpvd-event 'action=$subclass' \
'domain=$domain' 'vdev=$vdev' 'device=$device' \
'devclass=$devclass' 'febe=$fob'

# syseventadm restart
```

Configuring and installing a guest domain

The `virt-manager` GUI enables you to quickly configure a new domU:

```
# virt-manager &
```

Alternately, you can select the System Tools ➤ Virtual Machine Manager menu option. Figure 20-2 shows the initial dialog that you see when you start the GUI. In the future this window will allow you to select which system you want to manage, but for now you can just click the Connect button, which allows you to manage domains on the local host.

FIGURE 20-2

Click Connect in the Open Connection dialog.

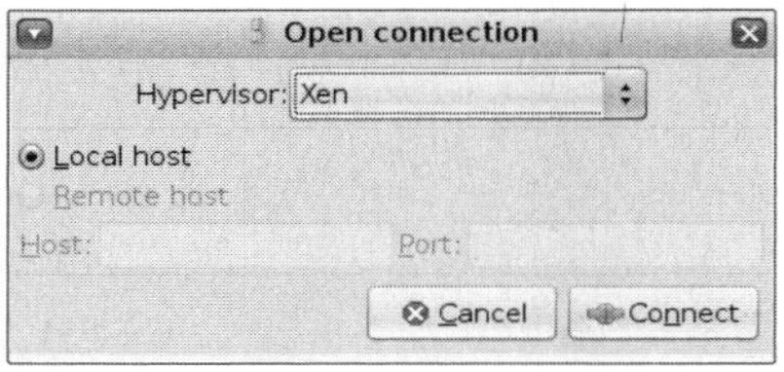

This brings up the main `virt-manager` window, shown in Figure 20-3.

FIGURE 20-3

Use the main Virtual Machine Manager window to monitor and manage domains.

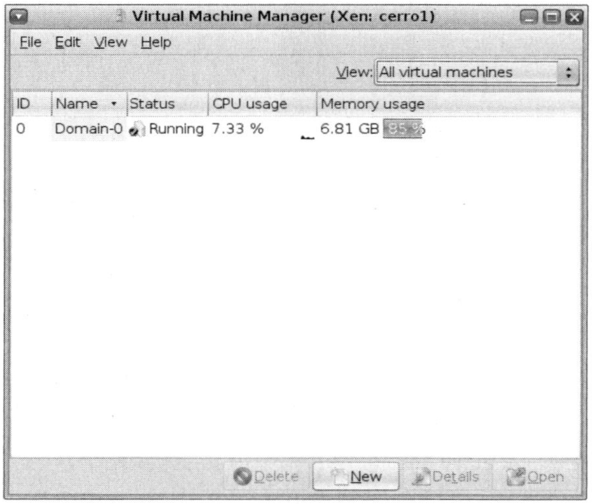

Select the New button to start a wizard that walks you through the steps to create a new domU. The GUI and its wizards are easy to use and understand, so each step is only summarized here. You create each new domU using a similar sequence.

First, you name the domU. In this example it is named mydomu. Next, you choose the virtualization method for the domain; this can be either paravirtualized or fully virtualized. You must make this choice based on what guest OS you intend to run in the domain and whether it has been paravirtualized. If you will be installing OpenSolaris as the guest, choose a paravirtualized domain.

NOTE For this example you install the Solaris Express Community Edition (SXCE) distribution as a paravirtualized domain because at the time of this writing, paravirtualized OpenSolaris domains do not support a graphical console, and the OpenSolaris distribution provides only a GUI-based installer. Instructions for configuring a GUI display for this domain once it has been installed, a discussion of GUI-based HVM installs, and a more complex procedure to install the OpenSolaris distribution as a paravirtualized domain are described later in the chapter. (See Chapter 2 for information about SXCE.)

The next step is to specify the location of the install media. You can enter either a URL that refers to the install media, or a Kickstart URL, which is a tool specific to installing Red Hat Linux. A technique to install SXCE using JumpStart is described later in this chapter. Enter the path to your SXCE ISO image.

On the next screen, assign disk storage space to the domain. You can use either a physical device, such as a free disk slice or ZFS zvol, or a simple file in the host file system that is used to emulate a disk drive for the VM. Because of the simplicity and generality of using a file, the initial examples in this chapter use a file; but for better performance, a physical device is the preferred option. If you choose a file, you must also specify the total size, in MB, and whether the file should be fully allocated up front. You don't need to allocate all of the space in advance, as long as you know there will be enough space should the virtual disk require it. This way, only the space that is actually needed by the domain will be used.

CROSS-REF Most systems do not normally have a free physical disk slice, but with ZFS, setting up a physical device as a zvol is easy, flexible, and provides the performance benefits of a physical device. Using a zvol is the recommended configuration for virtual disks.

Chapter 7 provides more information on OpenSolaris partitions and slices. Using a ZFS zvol for the virtual disk is described later in this chapter in the section "Virtual disks."

Next, specify how the domain connects to the network. You can choose a virtual network or a shared physical device. The shared physical device allows the domain to use the same network interface as the dom0. Currently, the virtual network option is not available and is grayed out.

Finally, allocate the memory and virtual CPUs available to the domain. For memory you can specify both the amount of memory available when the domain starts, as well as the maximum amount of memory the domain can use. One virtual CPU is allocated to the domain by default, but you can increase that if necessary. Memory and Virtual CPUs are discussed in more detail later in this chapter.

FIGURE 20-4

The virt-manager window shows both a dom0 and a domU.

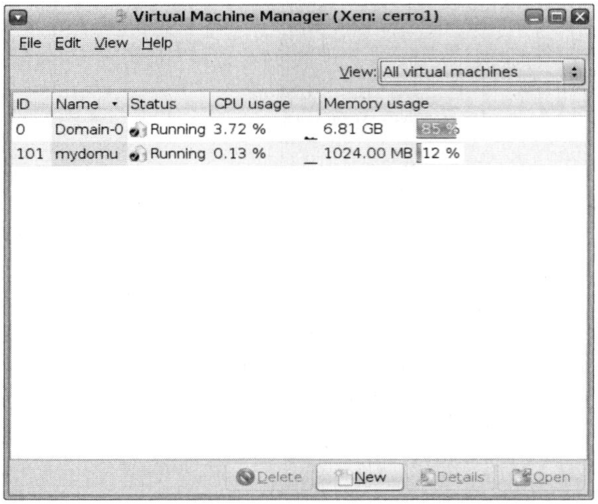

Review your configuration on the final screen and click Finish to create the new domain and bring up a text-based console window. At this point, you can respond to any prompts during the SXCE installation, and watch the installation of the guest OS. After you have completed the installation, the main virt-manager window will look similar to Figure 20-4.

Logging in to a guest domain

During domain installation, you interacted with the domU on its text-based console. You disconnect from the console using the Ctrl+] key combination. Within virt-manager, after you select a domU, the Open button will be enabled. This button brings up a console window for the domain.

In addition to accessing the domain on its console, you can always ssh into the domain, just as you would a standalone system. Using the ssh -X option enables you to run X11-based graphical applications remotely, assuming the guest OS supports ssh and X11.

Currently, creating a new domain within virt-manager does not set up a graphical display for the domain. Setting up a graphical display is described later in this chapter.

Basic management of a guest domain

The main window in virt-manager enables you to monitor and control the state and basic resource utilization of each domain.

In Figure 20-4 you can see the main window with the menu bar across the top, the domain display in the center, and various control buttons across the bottom. The center pane provides information about each domain, including its status, CPU, and memory utilization. In Figure 20-4, the status of mydomu is Running. If the domain were not running, the status would be Shutdown.

At the top of the window are File, Edit, View, and Help menus. The File menu items are Close, Quit, and the following three options:

File Menu Item	Description
New Machine	Same as the New button on the main window, which you used when you created the domain earlier
Restore Saved Machine	Brings up a file browser that you use to select a file that holds the state of a previously running domain. That will restart the domain at the point at which it was saved. Saving a domain's state into a file is described later.
Open Connection	Brings up the same window that you see when you first start virt-manager

Here are descriptions of the Edit menu items:

Edit Menu Item	Description
Host Details Machine Details	These options bring up the same window as the Details button at the bottom of the screen, depending on your selection of dom0 or one of the domUs.
Delete Machine	Same as the Delete button at the bottom of the screen. It's used to delete a domain. This option is grayed out if you have selected a running domain. Otherwise, if the domain is shut down, you can delete it.
Preferences	Enables you to configure the status update interval for the main window, as well as console behavior for a domain

The View menu enables you to select which domain attributes are displayed in the main window.

The four buttons on the bottom of the main window are Delete, New, Details, and Open. The first three have been described already. The Details button brings up a Virtual Machine Details window that provides additional information and controls for the selected domain (see Figure 20-5).

At the top of this window are Virtual Machine, View, and Help menus. The toolbar at the top of the main window has Run, Pause, and Shutdown buttons. The main body of the window has tabs that show either an overview of the domain or details about the domain's hardware configuration.

FIGURE 20-5

The Details window for this domU shows performance information as well as basic details.

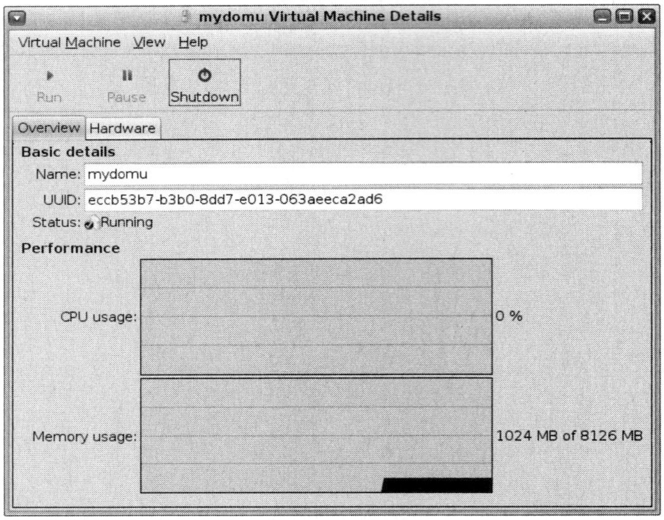

The Virtual Machine menu has options for Run, Pause, Shutdown, Save, Destroy, and Close. The Run, Pause, and Shutdown options provide the same functionality as the buttons with the same name in the toolbar at the top of the main window. They enable you to manage the state of the domain. If the domain is currently shut down, then Run is enabled, and you can start the domain. The other options are grayed out until the domain is running. Once the domain is running, Shutdown, Save, and Destroy are enabled, while Run is grayed out. The Shutdown option initiates a graceful shutdown of the running domain. The Save option brings up a file browser that enables you to specify a file, and then saves the state of the domain into the file. You can later use the Restore Saved Machine option, described earlier, to restart the domain at the saved point. The Destroy option immediately stops the running domain, although using Shutdown is the preferred way to stop a domain. Currently, the Pause option is always grayed out.

The View menu items are Graphical Console, Serial Console, and Toolbar. The two console options bring up the appropriate console window for the domain; Toolbar enables or disables the toolbar on the main window.

The main body of the window has Overview and Hardware tabs. The Overview tab shows performance graphs for CPU and memory usage over time. The Hardware tab's left pane enables selection of the processor, memory, disk, or NIC configuration for the domain. The right pane shows current settings for the selected item and, in the case of processor or memory, enables you to customize the setting.

Advanced xVM Administration

The previous section provided a quick overview of setting up a dom0 and a domU. As you saw, the `virt-manager` GUI provides an easy-to-use interface for basic management and monitoring of domains; but to perform more advanced administration tasks, you need the various xVM CLIs.

Command line interfaces

The CLIs provided with xVM are `virt-install`, `virsh`, and `xm`. The `virt-install` CLI can be used as an alternative to the `virt-manager` GUI for installing a domain. The `virsh` command is the preferred and primary CLI for ongoing management of your domains, but in some cases there are features still available only in the legacy `xm` CLI. An `xm` feature is described here only when there is no corresponding feature in `virsh`.

As its name implies, you can use the `virsh` command as an interactive shell. This chapter focuses on using `virsh` as a true CLI in its non-interactive mode, but see the `virsh(1M)` man page and experiment with the command to learn more about using it as a shell.

Installation

A variety of techniques can be used to install a domU, depending on which guest OS you are installing, whether the guest is paravirtualized or fully virtualized, and the requirements of the guest OS installation program.

Basic installation

The `virt-install` command first creates a new domain and then installs it, all from a single invocation. This CLI is useful if you want to automatically create domains from a script or you need to specify more information than the GUI supports. The following command performs the same installation that was done in the GUI example earlier:

```
# virt-install -p --nographics -n mydomu -f /xvm/mydomu.img \
-r 1024 -s 10 -l /export/iso/sxce.iso
```

The `-p` option indicates that `virt-install` should create a paravirtualized domain. The second option, `--nographics`, means that no graphical console will be used for the domain. Currently, paravirtualized domains do not support running with a graphical console, so this option must be used for these domains. A fully virtualized domain can use a graphical console. Creating and installing an HVM domain is shown in an example below. The `-f` option specifies the name of the domain's virtual disk file. The `-r` option specifies the amount of memory for the domain, in megabytes. The `-s` option specifies the size of the disk file, in gigabytes. The `-l` option specifies the URL of the ISO image to use to install the paravirtualized domain. This option is only used for paravirtualized domains.

An additional option that is useful for installing SXCE in a paravirtualized domain is `--autocf`, which specifies the path to a directory containing configuration data for `sysidtool(1M)`and a JumpStart profile. Using this enables you to configure a completely hands-off installation of SXCE in the domain.

If you need to install a domain that requires a graphical display during the installation, such as Windows, then you must install a fully virtualized domain, although a workaround for installing the OpenSolaris distribution into a paravirtualized domain, using the GUI, is described below.

The `virt-install` command can also be used to determine whether your system supports fully virtualized domains. When run without arguments, the command prompts for the input needed to create and install the domain. The first prompt gives an indication of whether the system supports HVM domains:

```
# virt-install
What is the name of your virtual machine?
```

The preceding prompt means that your system hardware is not capable of running a fully virtualized guest; but if you see the following, then it can:

```
# virt-install
Would you like a fully virtualized guest (yes or no)?  This will
 allow you to run unmodified operating systems
```

The following example shows how to install OpenSolaris in an HVM domain, using a graphical console:

```
# virt-install -v --vnc -n osoldomu -f /xvm/osoldomu.img \
-r 1024 -s 10 -c /export/iso/osol.iso --os-type=solaris \
--os-variant=opensolaris
```

The first option, `-v`, indicates that `virt-install` should create an HVM domain. The second option indicates that a graphical console, using VNC, should be configured. Note that the option specifying the path to the ISO, `-c`, is also different from the earlier example. The `-c` option specifies the virtual CD-ROM device for the domain. Use this option as an alternative to `-l` when installing HVM domains. The `--os-type` and `--os-variant` options enable you to specify which OS is installed in the domain. These options are only used for HVM domains and should always be specified in this case. They provide information that is used to optimize the device emulation for the given OS. Possible values for `os-type` are `solaris`, `unix`, `linux`, `windows`, or `other`. The possible `os-variant` values depend on the `os-type`. See the `virt-install(1M)` man page for a complete list.

Because the OpenSolaris distribution requires a graphical display to install, using an HVM domain is one option for getting OpenSolaris up and running within a domain, although performance will suffer. Another option is described later.

CROSS-REF You can find more information about using VNC in Chapter 4, in the virtualization overview in Chapter 17, and later in this chapter.

Once virt-install creates the new domain, it opens a VNC console window on the domain, and you will see the normal screen output for the guest OS you are installing. You can then follow the procedures outlined in Chapter 2 to install OpenSolaris in the domain.

> **TIP** When using a VNC console for the domain, you must be logged in on the dom0 graphical console, or be configured to use a remote display, so that the VNC window displays properly; otherwise, you will receive and error indicating that the window cannot be displayed.

You would use a similar virt-install invocation, specifying a different ISO, to install a different guest OS into an HVM domain. For example, the following installs Windows XP:

```
# virt-install -v --vnc -n winxpdomu -f /xvm/xp.img \
-r 1024 -s 10 -c /export/iso/winxp.iso --os-type=windows \
--os-variant=winxp
```

The virt-install command supports a variety of additional options that can be used when creating new domains. The --vcpus=N option enables you to specify the number of virtual CPUs to allocate to the domain. Use the -b ifname option to explicitly control which dom0 network interface to use for the domain's network traffic. In addition to these commonly used options, there are many others. The virt-install(1M) man page describes each option in detail.

Installing OpenSolaris in a paravirtualized domain

Although virt-install is the preferred CLI for installing domains, it cannot be used to install the OpenSolaris distribution in a paravirtualized domain, due to the lack of graphics support for paravirtualized domains. There is also a second limitation with virt-install: It always sets up the domain to use SATA-style disks, but as of this writing, the OpenSolaris Live CD can only run off of IDE-style virtual disks. In cases like this, you can use the legacy xm create subcommand to work around some of the virt-install limitations.

> **TIP** John Levon's blog at http://blogs.sun.com/levon/entry/opensolaris_ 2008_11_as_a describes an alternative technique to install OpenSolaris in a paravirtualized domain.

To install using xm create, you must create a python definition file that specifies the configuration of your new domain:

```
name="mydomu5"
vcpus=1
memory="1024"
bootloader="/usr/lib/xen/bin/pygrub"
kernel="/platform/i86xpv/kernel/amd64/unix"
ramdisk="/boot/x86.microroot"
extra="/platform/i86xpv/kernel/amd64/unix -B console=ttya,livemode=text"
disk=['file:/export/iso/osol.iso,6:cdrom,r',
'file:/xvm/disk1,0,w']
vif=['']
```

```
on_shutdown="destroy"
on_reboot="destroy"
on_crash="destroy"
```

Most of the entries in this file are either self-explanatory or don't need modification, but a few might not be obvious. The `extra` entry specifies additional boot arguments used to boot OpenSolaris for installation. It shows the correct boot arguments for the OpenSolaris distribution to boot to a text console. The `disk` entry specifies two disks. The order of these disks matters because the system will boot off of the first disk. In this example, the first disk refers to the ISO file that is used as the domain's virtual CD-ROM. You must set up your `disk` entry to refer to both the OpenSolaris ISO image and the virtual disk you want to install onto. The `vif` entry specifies the virtual network interface for the domain. If you leave this blank, the system uses the appropriate default. The `on_reboot` entry might not be obvious either. In this definition it is set to `destroy`, which means that once the domain installation is complete and the domain issues a reboot, the domain is left shut down. Otherwise, it would simply reboot back into the installation program again.

When you use `xm create` to install this image, OpenSolaris will boot from the Live CD image and present the initial prompts on the text-based console:

```
# xm create -c mydomu5.py
Using config file "./mydomu5.py".
Started domain mydomu5
                        v3.1.4-xvm chgset 'Mon Jul 07 23:58:09 2008
 -0700 15878:0caafd8ebef9'
SunOS Release 5.11 Version snv_86 64-bit
Copyright 1983-2008 Sun Microsystems, Inc.  All rights reserved.
Use is subject to license terms.
Hostname: opensolaris
Remounting root read/write
Probing for device nodes ...
Preparing live image for use
Done mounting Live image
USB keyboard
...
opensolaris console login: jack
Password:
```

At the login prompt, enter `jack` for the username, and enter `jack` again at the password prompt. You can now get the DHCP address on your domain's network using the `ifconfig` command, and, if necessary, enable the `sshd` service. From a different window in dom0, `ssh` with X redirection into the domain's IP address with the login `jack`:

```
% ssh -X jack@192.168.0.80
```

Once you have logged into the domain, you can start the graphical installer, which displays back onto the dom0 console:

```
jack@opensolaris:~$ pfexec gui-install
```

> **TIP** You can use a similar technique to install the SXCE distribution using its GUI installer, although you first need to set up a login because SXCE does not include the predefined `jack` login.

Once the installation has finished and the domain shuts down, note that it doesn't appear in the `virsh list` output anymore. The last step is to redefine the domain using a modified version of the earlier python definition:

```
name="mydomu5"
memory="1024"
disk=['file:/xvm/disk1,0,w']
vif=['']
on_shutdown="destroy"
on_reboot="restart"
on_crash="destroy"
```

In this definition you have removed the `kernel`, `ramdisk`, and `extra` properties because the system is able to boot from the installed virtual disk. The `disk` entry is also modified to remove the CD-ROM ISO file, and the `on_reboot` entry is modified to restart the domain. You can then define this domain using the `xm new` subcommand:

```
# xm new mydomu5 -f mydomu5.py
```

After you have done that, you can use the normal `virsh` commands to manage the domain.

> **TIP** OpenSolaris places its root file system on ZFS. A dom0 running OpenSolaris already knows how to boot a domU with a ZFS root file system, but a dom0 running a different OS might not have that capability. In that case, you need to specify an additional boot argument for the domU, as in the following example:
>
> ```
> <bootloader_args>--args="zfs-bootfs=rpool/ROOT/opensolaris"
> </bootloader_args>
> ```
>
> See the "Boot arguments" section later in the chapter for details on how to set this up.

Although it isn't the preferred way to install a domain, `xm create` is still useful in complex cases such as this. Another example would be if you need to install a domain onto multiple disks. With `virt-install`, you can only specify a single disk, so you would have to add the additional disks after the domain was installed. With `xm create` you can install the domain with all of the disks at once.

Cloning a domain

Once you have a domain configured, installed, and customized the way you like, you might want to clone that domain, rather than start from scratch on a new domain.

To create a new domain based on the configuration of an existing domain, you must first dump the domain's configuration. To do so, use the `virsh dumpxml` subcommand:

```
# virsh dumpxml mydomu >spec.xml
```

This creates a file containing an XML specification for `mydomu`. This is what the file looks like for the first domain you created:

```
# cat spec.xml
<domain type='xen' id='-1'>
  <name>mydomu</name>
  <uuid>62939af0-be9c-36bf-1d0c-4b54b725e3b6</uuid>
  <bootloader>/usr/lib/xen/bin/pygrub</bootloader>
  <os>
    <type>linux</type>
  </os>
  <memory>1048576</memory>
  <vcpu>1</vcpu>
  <on_poweroff>destroy</on_poweroff>
  <on_reboot>restart</on_reboot>
  <on_crash>restart</on_crash>
  <devices>
    <interface type='bridge'>
      <target dev='vif-1.0'/>
      <mac address='00:16:3e:08:bb:3d'/>
      <script path='vif-vnic'/>
    </interface>
    <disk type='file' device='disk'>
      <driver name='file'/>
      <source file='/xvm/mydomu.img'/>
      <target dev='xvda'/>
    </disk>
  </devices>
</domain>
```

To create a new domain from this file, edit the file to change various fields for the new domain. Update the `<name>` field with the name of the new domain and update the `<source file>` field to refer to the virtual disk file for the new domain. Then delete the `<uuid>` and `<mac address>` lines, which causes `virsh` to generate new values for these properties of the new domain.

Finally, use the `define` subcommand to create the new domain from the updated domain specification:

```
# virsh define spec.xml
```

Now that you have created the new domain, you need to copy the virtual disk from the original domain. The new virtual disk should be named with the same value used in the `<source file>` field in the XML file. If your virtual disks are ZFS zvols or are in their own ZFS datasets, then you can simply use zfs clone to instantaneously make a copy of the disk. Otherwise, you must fully copy the file.

CROSS-REF ZFS is discussed in Chapter 8.

The virsh create subcommand is similar to the define subcommand, except that the domain is started after being created. To use this subcommand, you need to ensure that the virtual disk was copied before creating the new domain.

TIP The cloned domain will have the same identity — such as hostname, IP address, name service configuration, and other attributes — as the original domain. You can run the sys-unconfig(1M) command after the new domain first boots or on the original domain before cloning. This clears the system identity properties from the domain and halts it. When you reboot the domain, you are prompted for new system identity information on the domain console.

When you are done with a domain, you can use the virsh undefine subcommand to delete an inactive domain.

CAUTION The undefine subcommand deletes a domain with no confirmation, so be sure that is what you want before running it. The undefine subcommand does not delete the domain's virtual disk file, so you should clean that up manually. If you accidentally undefine a domain but have a backup copy of the domain's XML definition, then you can just recreate the domain from the XML file, and the data will still be available on the virtual disk.

Monitoring

The virsh command provides a variety of subcommands for displaying data about domains. The nodeinfo subcommand provides basic CPU and memory information about the system. This can be used to help with capacity planning when determining how many domUs to configure on the host:

```
# virsh nodeinfo
CPU model:            i86pc
CPU(s):              4
CPU frequency:       2792 MHz
CPU socket(s):       2
Core(s) per socket:  2
Thread(s) per core:  1
NUMA cell(s):        1
Memory size:         8387584 kB
```

The list subcommand prints a list of domains and their states:

```
# virsh list
  Id Name                 State
----------------------------------
   0 Domain-0             running
   3 mydomu               running
```

The possible states are described in Table 20-1.

TABLE 20-1

Domain States

State	Description
blocked	The domain is blocked. This is a normal state for an active domain if the guest OS is waiting on I/O.
crashed	The domain crashed and is not configured to restart.
in shutdown	This is a transition state while shutting down (xm calls this state dying).
paused	The domain has been paused by the virsh suspend command.
running	The domain is running on a CPU.
shut off	The domain is shut off.

Use the domstate subcommand to get the state of a specific domain:

```
# virsh domstate mydomu
running
```

The dominfo subcommand displays information about the domain:

```
# virsh dominfo mydomu
Id:             3
Name:           mydomu
UUID:           21c6e7d5-45e7-6a72-8e21-03d1bc41a641
OS Type:        linux
State:          blocked
CPU(s):         1
CPU time:       102.4s
Max memory:     1048576 kB
Used memory:    1048576 kB
```

In this example, note that the OS Type shows linux even though OpenSolaris was installed in the domain. Calling this linux here is misleading because this field actually indicates whether the domain is paravirtualized or HVM. The value linux means this is a paravirtualized domain. An HVM domain would show the value as hvm.

> **TIP**   You can use some of the virsh subcommands, such as dominfo, on dom0 too. Use Domain-0 as the domain name.

There is no subcommand to display the full domain configuration with user-friendly output. You can use the virsh dumpxml command, shown earlier, to see most of the configuration details in

XML format. If you compare the XML output of a paravirtualized domain to an HVM domain, you will notice several key differences.

For a paravirtualized domain, you will see the following:

```
<bootloader>/usr/lib/xen/bin/pygrub</bootloader>
```

For an HVM domain, you will see entries similar to this in the XML output:

```
<os>
  <type>hvm</type>
  <loader>/usr/lib/xen/boot/hvmloader</loader>
  <boot dev='hd'/>
</os>
  <emulator>/usr/lib/xen/bin/qemu-dm</emulator>
  <disk type='file' device='disk'>
    <driver name='file'/>
    <source file='/export/xvm/osol.img'/>
    <target dev='hda'/>
  </disk>
```

The `<type>hvm</type>` entry tells you this is an HVM domain. Note also that qemu-dm is used for device emulation. This is only the case in HVM domains. One other key difference is in the `<disk>` entry. For an HVM domain, `<target dev>` uses a different naming scheme from a paravirtualized domain. This is important to remember if you later want to add an additional disk device to an HVM domain. Adding disk devices is described in more detail in the next section.

The xm list subcommand provides even more data:

```
# xm list -l mydomu
(domain
    (on_crash restart)
    (uuid 21c6e7d5-45e7-6a72-8e21-03d1bc41a641)
    (bootloader_args )
    (vcpus 1)
    (name mydomu)
    (on_poweroff destroy)
    (on_reboot restart)
    (bootloader /usr/lib/xen/bin/pygrub)
    (maxmem 1024)
    (memory 1024)
    (shadow_memory 0)
    (cpu_weight 256)
    (cpu_cap 0)
    (features )
    (on_xend_start ignore)
    (on_xend_stop shutdown)
    (start_time 1216677066.27)
```

```
(cpu_time 25.562737138)
(online_vcpus 1)
...
```

A monitoring feature, unavailable in virsh, is provided by the xentop command. Like the traditional top command, it shows a continuously updated, terminal-based display of domain activity:

```
# xentop
xentop - 08:46:57   Xen 3.1.4-xvm
2 domains: 2 running, 0 blocked, 0 paused, 0 crashed, 0 dying, 0 shutdown
Mem: 8388148k total, 7338708k used, 1049440k free     CPUs: 4 @ 2792MHz
      NAME   STATE   CPU(sec) CPU(%)     MEM(k) MEM(%)  MAXMEM(k) MAXMEM(%) VCPUS
  NETS NETTX(k) NETRX(k) VBDS    VBD_OO    VBD_RD    VBD_WR SSID
   Domain-0 -----r     14649   94.3    6170624   73.6   no limit       n/a      4
      0        0        0    0         0         0        0  0
      mydomu -----r      1512   74.9    1035264   12.3    1035264      12.3      1
      1      187    13757    1         0         1      297  0


 Delay   Networks   vBds   VCPUs   Repeat header   Sort order   Quit
```

The first line of output shows the system uptime and xVM version information. Line two shows the number of active domains and the number in each state. Line three shows overall memory statistics and CPU information. Lines four and five are header information for the domain statistics. These lines are followed by the data for each domain, with two lines of output per domain. The first line corresponds to the first line of the header; the second line corresponds to the second line. This example shows two domains, dom0 and mydomu.

The first status line for mydomu shows the state, the various fields for both CPU and memory utilization, and finally the number of virtual CPUs allocated to the domain.

The state column has six positions, with a letter or dash in each one. Each letter denotes one of the possible states for the domain: r is running, b is blocked, p is paused, s is shut down, c is crashed, and d is dying. The dying state is the same as the in shutdown state shown by the virsh list subcommand.

The second line of output for mydomu shows network and virtual block device (VBD) data. The network and disk I/O numbers will fluctuate, as there is I/O activity in the domain during the update interval. The first column (NETS) indicates there is one virtual network interface for the domain. The next two columns, NETTX(k) and NETRX(k), show network transmit and receive statistics, in kilobytes, that have occurred during the update interval. The (VBDS) column indicates there is a single virtual block device configured for the domain. The next column (VBD_OO) is the "out of order" statistic, which is not used on OpenSolaris. This column is always 0. This is followed by virtual block device read and write (VBD_RD, VBD_WR) statistics showing the virtual disk I/O that has occurred during the update interval. The last field (SSID) is the domain's security ID. This is set as part of labeled domains, which use access control, and is currently unused on OpenSolaris. This column is always 0.

The bottom line shows the runtime options for changing the displayed data. Each highlighted letter toggles either display or customization of the associated data. The domains can be sorted by each field. The sort field is highlighted and you can toggle through which field to sort using the S key (Sort order) key.

The xentop command also includes various options that you can specify on the command line to customize the display. See the xentop(1M) man page for details on the options.

Ongoing management

The virsh CLI is frequently used as an alternative to the virt-manager GUI because it provides more capabilities for managing a domain than the GUI.

Reconfiguration

Table 20-2 lists the virsh subcommands that are used to modify a domain's configuration.

TABLE 20-2

virsh Configuration Subcommands

Subcommand	Description
attach-device	Adds a device specified by an XML file to the domain. As of this writing, attaching an arbitrary device to a domain is not possible.
attach-disk	Adds a disk to the domain
attach-interface	Adds a network interface to the domain
detach-device	Removes a device specified by an XML file from the domain. As of this writing, detaching an arbitrary device from a domain is not possible.
detach-disk	Removes a disk from the domain.
detach-interface	Removes a network interface from the domain.
setmem	Changes the memory reservation for the domain. The value is in KB.
setmaxmem	Changes the maximum memory limit for the domain. The value is in KB.
setvcpus	Changes the number of virtual CPUs for the domain.

The following example illustrates creating a new virtual disk file and adding it to mydomu:

```
# mkfile 1g /xvm/disk2
# virsh attach-disk mydomu /xvm/disk2 xvdb --driver file
```

After the domain name, the next parameter is the path to either the virtual disk file or the physical device that you are attaching. In this case, a virtual disk file path, /xvm/disk2, is used. The following parameter, xvdb in this example, is the name of the target disk for the domain. The last two parameters specify that a virtual disk file is being configured for the domain. If you were adding a physical device, the --driver parameter would specify phy.

For a domain running OpenSolaris, the target disk name can be either a number or an xvd-style virtual disk name. Using either a number or an xvd name dictates whether the virtual disk will be treated as an IDE/ATA disk or as a SATA disk, respectively. If the target disk name on the attach-disk subcommand uses a number, then the numbers 0, 1, and 2 correspond to the IDE/ATA disk names /dev/dsk/c0d0, /dev/dsk/c0d1, and /dev/dsk/c0d2 in the OpenSolaris guest. When using an xvd-style target name, the names xvda, xvdb, and xvdc correspond to the SATA disk names /dev/dsk/c0t0d0, /dev/dsk/c0t1d0, and /dev/dsk/c0t2d0 in the OpenSolaris guest.

> **TIP** Use the xvd-style names so that the virtual disk is treated as a SATA device. This will provide a noticeable performance improvement.

For domains that are not running OpenSolaris, the target disk name syntax varies, although a Linux domain also supports xvd-style naming.

The target naming for an HVM domain follows a different convention. Instead of the targets using numbers or xvd-style names, they are named hda, hdb, hdc, and so on. Using the earlier example, if mydomu were an HVM domain instead of a paravirtualized domain, you would use the following command to attach the virtual disk:

```
# virsh attach-disk mydomu /xvm/disk2 hdb --driver file
```

Within an HVM domain, the disks follow the OpenSolaris IDE/ATA naming convention just described.

> **CROSS-REF** See Chapter 7 for more information on OpenSolaris disks and the commands you use within the domain to manage the new disks assigned to the domain.

To remove a disk from mydomu, specify the target name:

```
# virsh detach-disk mydomu xvdb
```

To add a new virtual network interface to mydomu, use the attach-interface subcommand:

```
# virsh attach-interface mydomu bridge e1000g0
```

The detach-interface subcommand removes the network interface from the domain.

This example sets the number of virtual CPUs for mydomu to 2 and changes the memory reservation to 786MB:

```
# virsh setvcpus mydomu 2
# virsh setmem mydomu 786432
```

TIP You can increase the number of virtual CPUs and the memory reservation while the domain is shut down; but once the domain is active, you can only decrease these settings below the initial value that was in effect when the domain started. After decreasing the value, you can increase the setting up to the initial value, but not above the initial value. If you plan to dynamically adjust the number of virtual CPUs or the memory reservation for an active domain, start the domain with the largest initial values that you expect to need, and then adjust these settings down once the domain is running. You can then increase the settings later, up to the initial values. Any changes you make this way while the domain is running are in effect only while the domain is active.

Virtual CPUs, memory, and managing the various devices for a domain are discussed in more detail later in this chapter.

Starting and stopping a domain

Table 20-3 lists the virsh subcommands that are used to manage the running state of a domain.

TABLE 20-3

virsh State Management Subcommands

Subcommand	Description
destroy	Immediately halts an active domain. The shutdown subcommand is generally a better alternative to the destroy subcommand.
reboot	Performs an orderly shutdown of an active domain, followed by restarting the domain
restore	Restores the domain from a saved state file
resume	Starts scheduling a suspended domain
save	Saves the domain state to a file. The domain is shut down once this command completes.
shutdown	Performs an orderly shutdown of an active domain
start	Starts running an inactive domain
suspend	Stops an active domain from being scheduled to run

The `start` and `shutdown` subcommands are used most often because they start an inactive domain and shut down an active domain:

```
# virsh start mydomu
# virsh shutdown mydomu
```

The `destroy` subcommand can be used instead of `shutdown`. This immediately brings the domain to the shut off state:

```
# virsh destroy mydomu
```

CAUTION The `destroy` subcommand is similar to a physical system losing power and may cause data loss or corruption within the domain.

The `suspend` subcommand will stop an active domain from being scheduled to run on the system, but any resources, such as memory, that have been allocated to the domain will remain in use by the domain. This moves the domain to the `paused` state:

```
# virsh suspend mydomu
# virsh list
 Id Name                      State
----------------------------------
  0 Domain-0                  running
 28 mydomu                    paused
```

The `resume` subcommand is used on a suspended domain to make it eligible for scheduling again:

```
# virsh resume mydomu
# virsh list
 Id Name                      State
----------------------------------
  0 Domain-0                  running
 28 mydomu                    blocked
```

The `save` subcommand saves a snapshot of an active domain into a file. After the image has been saved, the domain will be in the `shut off` state and all of the resources it was consuming are freed:

```
# virsh save mydomu /xvm/mysnapshot
Domain mydomu saved to /xvm/mysnapshot
# virsh list
 Id Name                      State
----------------------------------
  0 Domain-0                  running
  - mydomu                    shut off
```

The `restore` subcommand takes a preexisting domain snapshot and restores the state of the domain:

```
# virsh restore /xvm/mysnapshot
```

Because the `save` subcommand creates a snapshot of the full virtual machine state of the domain, the guest OS does not go through its normal shutdown procedures. For this reason, always use the `restore` subcommand to pick up where the guest OS left off. If you simply use the `start` subcommand, it is probable that the guest OS file system data won't be flushed to disk. This can lead to file system corruption or data loss in some cases. Likewise, if you restore the domain, run for a while, but then decide later to restore from the snapshot, the snapshot will probably again be out of sync with the file system, leading to the same problems. If you always save and restore the domain, then there is no issue. If you think you might want to revert to a saved snapshot later, save a copy of the virtual disk image that corresponds to the snapshot. This is particularly easy if you are using ZFS because you can take a ZFS snapshot of the virtual disk file that corresponds to the snapshot of the domain state.

Automatically starting and stopping a domain

For production domains, you will usually want the domUs to start automatically when the dom0 boots. Unfortunately, at the time of this writing, configuring this behavior is slightly complex because you must dump the configuration, edit it, and reload it. Recall that the `xm list` output shown earlier contained the following property;

```
(on_xend_start ignore)
```

The property controls the behavior of the domain when the `svc:/system/xvm/domains` SMF service starts.

CROSS-REF SMF is described in Chapter 13. The xVM-specific SMF services are described in the section "SMF services" later in this chapter.

The `on_xend_start` property defaults to `ignore`, which means the domain will not automatically start when the dom0 boots. Setting this value to `start` causes the domain to automatically boot. To change this value, use the `xm` command to dump the domain configuration to a file, edit the file to change the value, and then reload the file. This is shown in the following example:

```
# xm list -l mydomu > /tmp/mydomu.txt
```

Edit the `/tmp/mydomu.txt` file and change the `(on_xend_start ignore)` property to `(on_xend_start start)`. Now reload the domain configuration:

```
# xm new -F /tmp/mydomu.txt
```

In the `xm list` output you'll also see the following property:

```
(on_xend_stop shutdown)
```

This means that as the `svc:/system/xvm/domains` SMF service in dom0 is stopping, it will perform an orderly shutdown of any active domain. This is generally the desired behavior and normally you shouldn't need to change the value.

Boot arguments

Currently, xVM uses the `pygrub` bootloader to boot the guest OS in a paravirtualized domain. On OpenSolaris, `pygrub` does not use the GRUB `menu.lst` file from within the domain, so you need to modify the domain configuration if you wish to pass boot parameters into a paravirtualized domain.

The following procedure shows how to modify the `pygrub` parameters to pass boot options into the domain. In this example, the domain is booted with the `-k` option, which causes the kernel debugger, `kmdb`, to be loaded before the OpenSolaris kernel is loaded.

CROSS-REF   See Chapter 24 for more information on `kmdb`.

First, dump the XML domain definition to a file:

```
# virsh dumpxml mydomu >mydomu.xml
```

Within this file you should see the following line:

```
<bootloader>/usr/lib/xen/bin/pygrub</bootloader>
```

Edit the XML file, adding the following line immediately after the `<bootloader>` line:

```
<bootloader_args>--args="-k"</bootloader_args>
```

Use the XML file to update the domain definition:

```
# virsh define mydomu.xml
```

Now, when you start the domain, `pygrub` will first load `kmdb`.

You can also set xVM-related, dom0 boot arguments by modifying the GRUB `menu.lst` entry used when booting the system under the hypervisor. Update the GRUB entry so that the `kernel$` line includes the dom0 arguments:

```
kernel$ /boot/$ISADIR/xen.gz dom0_mem=1G dom0_max_vcpus=1 dom0_vcpus
_pin=true
```

This example shows setting all three possible dom0 boot arguments. The meaning of these arguments is explained later in the "Virtual Devices" section. To modify the GRUB entry, use the `bootadm list-menu` subcommand to get the location of the GRUB menu. As of this writing, it is at `/rpool/boot/grub/menu.lst`. Edit this file, updating the `kernel$` line on the appropriate menu entry. These settings will be in effect the next time the system boots.

Domain console

The domain's console provides access to the guest OS for system installation or administrative tasks, even when the guest OS is not accepting network connections.

Paravirtualized domain console access

As stated earlier, paravirtualized domains currently do not support installation using a graphical console. The `virsh console` subcommand is used to connect to the domain's text-based console. The `Ctrl+]` key combination will disconnect from the console. The `--verbose` option shows any console output that would have been displayed before you ran the command:

```
# virsh console --verbose mydomu
mydomu console login: ^]
#
```

Once OpenSolaris is installed in the domain, you can configure graphical access to the domain using VNC.

CROSS-REF Configuring and using VNC is described in Chapter 4, as well as in the introductory virtualization material in Chapter 17.

Once you have set up the VNC server in the domain, you should be able to run the `vncviewer` on a client system and see the normal OpenSolaris graphical login within the VNC window:

```
% vncviewer mydomu:0 &
```

HVM domain console access

Unlike paravirtualized domains, HVM domains can be configured and installed with a graphical console from the start. The previous HVM installation examples used the `virt-install --vnc` option to configure those domains using VNC for the display. When installing a domain, you can also provide the `--vncport` option to specify the VNC port number for the display.

Use the `virsh vncdisplay` subcommand to get the VNC port number for a domain:

```
# virsh vncdisplay osoldomu
:0
```

Unlike the guest OS-specific VNC configuration you set up for a paravirtualized domain, the VNC console for an HVM domain is virtualized and managed by xVM itself, through the `qemu-dm` process associated with that domain. When connecting to the domain console from a window on dom0's graphical console, you can simply connect to the local host and port:

```
# vncviewer :0 &
```

If you are not running `vncviewer` locally in dom0, you must configure the `xend vnc-listen` property to allow remote system access. By default, `vnc-listen` is set to 127.0.0.1, which restricts VNC access to the local host. Setting this to 0.0.0.0 allows any VNC client to connect to the HVM domU console, which might present a security issue that you should consider before enabling this access. You can set the config/vncpasswd property as well, although that doesn't provide true security because any user can view the SMF properties:

```
# svccfg -s xvm/xend setprop config/vnc-listen="0.0.0.0"
# svcadm refresh xvm/xend
# svcadm restart xvm/xend
```

You should make this change before starting the HVM domain because this setting is passed to the qemu-dm process and the service change doesn't propagate to running qemu-dm processes.

SMF services

The following SMF services run in dom0 and are used to manage xVM:

```
svc:/system/xvm/console:default
svc:/system/xvm/domains:default
svc:/system/xvm/store:default
svc:/system/xvm/virtd:default
svc:/system/xvm/xend:default
```

When setting up xVM in dom0, ensure that these services are enabled and online. Beyond that, there is little you need to do to configure these services, with the exception of the xend service, described shortly.

The svc:/system/xvm/console service manages the xenconsoled(1M). This is the daemon that coordinates domain console accesses made using the virsh console subcommand.

The svc:/system/xvm/domains service boots domains when the dom0 boots, and shuts down active domains when dom0 is shutting down.

The svc:/system/xvm/store service manages the xenstored(1M) daemon. This is the daemon that manages the domain configuration data.

The svc:/system/xvm/virtd service manages the libvirtd daemon. This daemon provides services for the libvirt library, used by the virsh command.

The svc:/system/xvm/xend service manages the xend(1M) daemon. This is the administrative daemon that manages xVM and domains on the system. Table 20-4 describes its properties.

These properties are described in more detail on the xend(1M) man page. The following example illustrates setting the default-nic property to use the network interface named nge0:

```
# svccfg -s svc:/system/xvm/xend setprop config/default-nic=nge0
# svcadm refresh svc:/system/xvm/xend
# svcadm restart svc:/system/xvm/xend
```

With this configuration, domU networking will run over the nge0 NIC unless the domain was explicitly configured to use a different dom0 NIC as its backend device.

TABLE 20-4

xend Service Properties

Property	Description
config/default-nic	Specifies the default dom0 network interface that domains use for networking. This is useful when the system has multiple NICs and you want to constrain domains to use a specific NIC by default.
config/dom0-cpus	The number of physical CPUs used by dom0. This property is discussed in more detail later.
config/dom0-min-mem	The minimum amount of memory for dom0, in MB. Defaults to 196.
config/enable-dump	Enables domain core dumps in /var/xen/dump. Defaults to true.
config/vnc-listen	Address to listen on for HVM domain console VNC sessions. Defaults to 127.0.0.1, which means only connections from the local host are allowed.
config/vncpasswd	Password used for connecting to HVM domain console VNC sessions. Defaults to an empty string, which means no password is required. VNC passwords are not secure and do not provide security over domain consoles.
config/xend-relocation-address	The address to listen on for domain migration requests. Defaults to 127.0.01.
config/xend-relocation-hosts-allow	Hosts allowed to make domain migration requests. Defaults to localhost.
config/xend-relocation-server	Enables live migration. Defaults to true.
config/xend-unix-server	Enables the legacy HTTP server interface. Defaults to true.

CAUTION Restarting the xend service will drop any open paravirtualized domain console sessions.

Live Migration

One of the compelling features of xVM, compared to many other virtualization solutions for OpenSolaris, is the capability to perform live migration of a running domain. This is useful if you need to dynamically rebalance workloads among systems, or you need to perform maintenance on a host system without disrupting the applications running in the domUs.

Enabling live migration

Before you can migrate a machine to a new host, that host must be configured to accept the migration of a domain. As mentioned earlier, the following SMF xvm/xend service properties are used to configure the system as the target of a migration:

```
config/xend-relocation-address      127.0.0.1
config/xend-relocation-hosts-allow  ^localhost$
config/xend-relocation-server       true
```

With these default property settings, even though xend-relocation-server is true, the host will not accept migration requests from any other system because it is configured to accept requests only from itself. You must update the other two properties to specify which hosts are allowed to migrate domains to this system. Setting xend-relocation-address to be blank means the host will listen for requests on all of the system's network interfaces. The xend-relocation-hosts-allow property specifies a space-separated list of machines that are allowed to initiate a migration to this host. The property value contains regular expressions for pattern matching on a variety of hostnames. The carrot (^) and dollar sign ($) are pattern-matching characters to ensure that the entire hostname matches exactly.

The following example configures the xend SMF service on a target machine to accept migrations from the system named myhost, on any network interface:

```
# svccfg -s svc:system/xvm/xend setprop config/xend-relocation-address='""'
# svccfg -s svc:system/xvm/xend setprop config/xend-relocation-hosts-allow=\
'"^myhost$ ^localhost$"'
# svcadm refresh svc:system/xvm/xend:default
# svcadm restart svc:system/xvm/xend:default
```

In addition to configuring the target system to accept migrations, you must also configure the domain that you want to migrate so that the domain's storage is accessible from both the target and the host. The easiest way to do this is to configure the domain with its virtual disk as a file, owned by the xvm user, that is stored on an NFS server that both hosts can access. Alternatively, you can install the domain on an iSCSI initiator that you can configure on both hosts. The following example shows a virt-install command in which the domain's virtual disk is an NFS file accessed through the automounter:

```
# virt-install --nographics -n mydomu2 -p \
-f /net/myhost/xvm/mydomu2.img -r 1024 -s 10 -l /export/iso/sxce.iso
```

You can specify the disk path this way even though the file lives on the local host. That way, the domain will be ready to migrate, even if you intend to run it locally most of the time. If you have already set up your domain without specifying the virtual disk file path this way, you can dump the definition to an XML file, update the file path, and redefine the domain, as described earlier. You must also ensure that xvm-user access to the file from the remote host is properly configured.

CROSS-REF NFS access control and management, as well as the automounter, are covered in Chapter 10. iSCSI is covered in Chapter 7, and configuring a virtual disk on an iSCSI initiator is covered later in this chapter.

Finally, a few basic conditions should be true for a successful migration. Both the host and the target should be on the same subnet in order for the domain's network connections to continue working correctly, and host and target should have similar CPUs. That is, migrating from a system with AMD CPUs to one with Intel CPUs can be problematic. Both systems should be running the same version of xVM, and there should be enough CPU and memory resources on the target system to host the domain.

Migrating a domain

Once everything is properly configured, migrating a running domain is straightforward, requiring only a single command, as the following example shows. The prompts indicate which system each command is run on. The example migrates the running domain from a system named myhost to a system named targethost. The xm -l flag indicates that a live migration should be performed:

```
myhost# virsh list
  Id Name                     State
----------------------------------
   0 Domain-0                 running
   9 mydomu                   blocked
myhost# xm migrate -l mydomu targethost
```

The migration command takes a few moments to run as the domain state is transferred to targethost. If you watch the domain status on both machines during the migration, you'll see something like the following. Initially, the target system only has dom0 defined and running:

```
targethost# virsh list
  Id Name                     State
----------------------------------
   0 Domain-0                 running
```

Once the migration has been initiated and is underway, you will see the following status on the target system:

```
targethost# virsh list
  Id Name                     State
----------------------------------
   0 Domain-0                 running
   1 mydomu                   no state
```

You can see that the target system now knows about mydomu, but the domain has no state yet. On the source system, the domain will transition to the shut off state:

```
myhost# virsh list
  Id Name                    State
----------------------------------
   0 Domain-0                running
   - mydomu                  shut off
```

Once the migration has completed, the target system will show the domain in its normal state, either running or blocked:

```
targethost# virsh list
  Id Name                    State
----------------------------------
   0 Domain-0                running
   1 mydomu                  blocked
```

If you used the virsh console command to connect to the domain console on the original system, you would see the following console message:

```
Aug  1 18:47:19 mydomu genunix: NOTICE: Domain suspending for save/migrate
```

The console session is eventually dropped on the source system as the domain shuts down, but if you connect to the console on the target system, you will see the following message:

```
Aug  1 18:47:53 mydomu unix: NOTICE: domain restore/migrate completed
```

Later, you can live-migrate the domain back to the original system or to yet a third machine. Once the domain is shut down or has been migrated off of the target system, the domain is no longer defined or visible there. The domain remains defined on the original host where it was created.

Virtual Devices

With xVM, the various physical system resources, such as CPUs, memory, disks, and NICs, are virtualized so they can be shared among domains.

CPUs

When running on the xVM hypervisor, CPUs are allocated and managed as virtual CPUs. A virtual CPU holds the state that is associated with a physical CPU, including the physical CPU registers, its flags, and so on. The xVM hypervisor manages virtual CPUs much like a traditional time-share OS schedules processes; when the hypervisor schedules a virtual CPU to run, the CPU state is loaded and runs on a physical CPU. The guest OS running in the domain associated with the virtual processor then does its own scheduling of that processor, just as it would when running on bare metal.

When configuring a domain, you specify the number of virtual CPUs allocated to that domain. With virt-install this is specified using the --vcpus=N option. The default is to assign one virtual CPU to the domain. The `--check-cpu` option checks whether the specified number of virtual CPUs exceeds the number of physical CPUs, printing a warning if that is the case.

As described earlier, the `virsh setvcpus` subcommand is used to assign a new number of virtual CPUs for a domain.

Monitoring

The `virsh vcpuinfo` subcommand prints status information about each of the virtual CPUs assigned to a domain. The following example shows the status with two virtual CPUs assigned to `mydomu`:

```
# virsh vcpuinfo mydomu
VCPU:           0
CPU:            0
State:          running
CPU time:       7.8s
CPU Affinity:   yyyy

VCPU:           1
CPU:            3
State:          blocked
CPU time:       7.3s
CPU Affinity:   yyyy
```

The `VCPU` and `CPU` fields print the ID of the associated CPU. The `State` field shows the same state, as described previously. The `CPU time` field shows the amount of time actually used by the virtual CPU. The `CPU Affinity` field uses a single letter, y, to show the affinity for each physical CPU on the system. Because this example was run on a four-processor system, four letters appear in the output. CPU affinity is described in more detail in the CPU affinity section.

The `xm vcpu-list` subcommand also shows similar information, but for all active domains:

```
# xm vcpu-list
Name              ID   VCPU   CPU  State    Time(s)  CPU Affinity
Domain-0          0    0      1    -b-      846.5    any cpu
Domain-0          0    1      2    -b-      342.0    any cpu
Domain-0          0    2      0    -b-      369.5    any cpu
Domain-0          0    3      3    r--      389.8    any cpu
mydomu            2    0      3    -b-       24.9    any cpu
mydomu            2    1      1    -b-       20.9    any cpu
```

Scheduling

The `virsh schedinfo` subcommand prints information about the xVM hypervisor scheduling configuration for a domain:

```
# virsh schedinfo mydomu
Scheduler     : credit
```

```
weight        : 256
cap           : 0
```

The default scheduler used by the xVM hypervisor is the *credit scheduler*. Other legacy schedulers are available with xVM, but because they are being phased out, only the credit scheduler is described here.

The xm sched-credit subcommand displays the credit scheduler parameters for all domains:

```
# xm sched-credit
Name                          ID Weight  Cap
Domain-0                       0    256    0
mydomu                         2    256    0
```

The credit scheduler is a fair-share scheduler that allocates virtual CPUs to physical CPUs based on the workload in each domain. If a domain has a runnable virtual CPU and a physical CPU is idle, then the domain's virtual CPU is allocated to a physical CPU; but if all of the physical CPUs are busy and other virtual CPUs are runnable, then the scheduler ensures that virtual CPUs are allocated to physical CPUs across domains so that each domain gets a fair share of the physical CPU resources.

The schedinfo example shows the configurable inputs to the credit scheduler. The weight sets the domain's importance relative to other domains. If a second domain had weight 128, then it would get half the physical CPU resources of mydomu, which has a weight of 256, when there are more runnable virtual CPUs than there are physical CPUs. The proportion of physical CPU resources that a domain receives is calculated across all of the active domains. The default domain weight is 256, and the value can be set in the range 1 to 65535.

In addition to configuring the fair-share weight of a domain, you can set a limit on CPU usage, as shown in the cap field of the schedinfo output. The default of 0 means there is no cap. When a cap is set and a domain reaches it, its virtual CPUs won't be scheduled to run even if there are idle physical CPUs. The cap value is set as a percentage of a CPU. A value of 100 represents 1 full CPU, 50 represents half of a CPU, and 200 represents two full CPUs. The usage against the cap is calculated over the fixed, 30-ms scheduling interval in the hypervisor.

The virsh sched-info subcommand is also used to configure the credit scheduler parameters for a domain. The following example sets the weight for mydomu to 512, which means that if both dom0 and mydomu need more physical CPU resources than are available, mydomu would get twice the CPU that dom0 would get:

```
# virsh schedinfo --weight 512 mydomu
# xm sched-credit
Name                          ID Weight  Cap
Domain-0                       0    256    0
mydomu                         2    512    0
```

You can read more about the credit scheduler at http://wiki.xensource.com/xenwiki/CreditScheduler.

CPU affinity

Configuring CPU affinity enables you to control on which physical CPUs a domain is scheduled. That may be useful in some cases, such as on a NUMA system, where the workload running in a domain performs noticeably better when all of the execution takes place on a specific subset of CPUs. By default, any virtual CPU can be scheduled to run on any physical CPU, as illustrated in the vcpuinfo example. Once you configure CPU affinity for a virtual CPU, it is only scheduled on the specified physical CPUs. The virsh vcpupin subcommand sets the CPU affinity for a virtual CPU in a domain.

> **TIP** You can use the lgrpinfo command to view CPU topology, and then use specific CPU IDs reported by lgrpinfo as physical CPU ID inputs for the vcpupin subcommand. See Chapter 14 for more information on the lgrpinfo command.

The next example sets the affinity for both of the virtual CPUs, 0 and 1, that are allocated to mydomu, so that they use only physical CPUs 2 and 3:

```
# virsh vcpupin mydomu 0 2,3
# virsh vcpupin mydomu 1 2,3
```

You can now see this affinity in the vcpuinfo subcommand:

```
# virsh vcpuinfo mydomu
VCPU:           0
CPU:            2
State:          blocked
CPU time:       56.1s
CPU Affinity:   --yy

VCPU:           1
CPU:            3
State:          blocked
CPU time:       32.9s
CPU Affinity:   --yy
```

The CPU Affinity field indicates that each virtual CPU will not use physical CPUs 0 or 1, indicated by the dash (-) in the first and second character, but that they will use physical CPUs 2 or 3, indicated by the y in the third and fourth characters.

The xm vcpu-list subcommand shows the same CPU affinity data alongside the other domains:

```
# xm vcpu-list
Name              ID   VCPU   CPU  State   Time(s)  CPU Affinity
Domain-0          0    0      3    r--     923.2    any cpu
Domain-0          0    1      2    -b-     378.0    any cpu
Domain-0          0    2      0    -b-     402.4    any cpu
Domain-0          0    3      1    -b-     426.9    any cpu
mydomu            2    0      2    -b-      91.9    2-3
mydomu            2    1      3    -b-      45.2    2-3
```

To clear the CPU affinity setting, specify all of the CPUs:

```
# virsh vcpupin mydomu 0 0,1,2,3
# virsh vcpupin mydomu 1 0,1,2,3
# xm vcpu-list
Name                       ID  VCPU   CPU State   Time(s) CPU Affinity
Domain-0                    0     0     2   -b-     927.6 any cpu
Domain-0                    0     1     1   -b-     380.2 any cpu
Domain-0                    0     2     3   r--     403.7 any cpu
Domain-0                    0     3     0   -b-     428.8 any cpu
mydomu                      2     0     0   -b-      95.7 any cpu
mydomu                      2     1     1   -b-      46.0 any cpu
```

Dom0 CPUs

As described earlier, the xend service property config/dom0-cpus enables you to configure the number of physical CPUs that are allocated to virtual CPUs for use by dom0. This property defaults to 0, which means that each virtual CPU will be allocated to a physical CPU if possible. Setting this to a non-zero value does not mean that physical CPUs are exclusively allocated to dom0; the physical CPUs can still also be used by virtual CPUs from another domain, unless you configured CPU affinity to prevent this, as described earlier. However, this does enable you to ensure that dom0 does not run on CPUs that you want only domU domains to use.

Memory

Recall that you can configure both the amount of memory reserved for a domain and the maximum amount of memory that a domain can use. virt-install does not allow setting these values separately; the -r option specifies both the reserved and maximum amount of memory. These two settings can be changed using the virsh setmem and setmaxmem subcommands.

virsh setmem reserves the given minimum amount of memory for the domain. This value cannot be greater than the value specified with the setmaxmem subcommand. As its name implies, setmaxmem specifies the largest amount of memory a domain can use. In this example, the maximum is set to 4GB, and 2GB is reserved:

```
# virsh setmaxmem mydomu 4194304
# virsh setmem mydomu 2097152
```

Changing the amount of memory available to the domain uses the *balloon driver*, which manages increasing or decreasing the domain's memory, much like a balloon can increase or decrease in size.

Currently, if you attempt to increase the amount of memory beyond the initial reservation set when the domain starts, the new reservation does not take effect, and you will see a warning similar to the following on the domain console:

```
Jul 29 18:49:54 mydomu unix: WARNING: New balloon target (0x80000
pages) is larger than original memory size (0x3f300 pages).
Ballooning beyond original memory size is not allowed.
```

The general way to handle this is to start the domain with the largest reservation of memory you expect the domain will need, and then reduce the reservation once the domain has started. Later, if necessary, you can increase the size anywhere in the range up to the value that was in effect when the domain started.

When the system initially boots, a small amount of memory is used by the hypervisor and the rest is available to dom0. As domUs start, they take their reserved amount of memory from the memory available to dom0. You can see this using the dominfo subcommand on dom0, after mydomu is running with a 2GB reservation. This system has 8GB of memory:

```
# virsh dominfo Domain-0
Id:               0
Name:             Domain-0
UUID:             00000000-0000-0000-0000-000000000000
OS Type:          linux
State:            running
CPU(s):           4
CPU time:         2397.9s
Max memory:       no limit
Used memory:      6151168 kB
```

Here, about 6GB remains available to dom0. The other 2GB is used by mydomu, with a small amount used by the hypervisor. Once memory has been taken from the dom0 pool, it is not automatically returned to dom0 when the domain shuts down or its reservation is reduced, although this free memory is available for use by other domains. To reclaim this memory for dom0, use setmem:

```
# virsh setmem Domain-0 9000000
```

TIP You can provide a large value for the amount of memory and dom0 will recover as much memory as possible, up to the amount you specified or up to the amount available, whichever is less.

Because domUs take memory from the total that dom0 initially starts with, ensure that dom0 retains enough memory for itself. As described earlier, you tune this with the config/dom0-min-mem property on the xvm/xend service. The property defaults to 196MB, so it should be tuned up to at least 1GB.

TIP Although you can allow domains to take memory from dom0 as needed, losing memory can adversely affect the performance of software running in dom0. This is a particular problem if you are using ZFS in dom0 to provide storage services for the other domains. In this case, it is better to run dom0 with a fixed amount of memory that doesn't shrink. When using ZFS, a recommended minimum for dom0 is 2GB, although more is generally better. You can configure this by setting a memory value for dom0 at boot time and configuring dom0-min-mem as well. Set the dom0_mem boot argument in GRUB, as shown in the following example:

```
kernel$ /boot/$ISADIR/xen.gz dom0_mem=2G
```

Set the `dom0-min-mem` SMF property, as shown in this example:

```
# svccfg -s svc:/system/xvm/xend setprop \
config/dom0-min-mem=2000
```

Virtual disks

Up to this point, the example domains have been configured using a file to represent the virtual disk device for the domain. A file is the most flexible because the space is easily allocated in the dom0 file system. A file is also the easiest solution for domain migration because it can be accessed over NFS from each of the dom0s that will host the domU. However, you can also directly use block devices for virtual disks. Using an iSCSI initiator as the block device is another alternative that works with domain migration.

With ZFS, you can create a zvol in your zpool that can then be used as a block device for your domain.

CROSS-REF   ZFS zvols are described in Chapter 8, and iSCSI is described in Chapter 7.

This example shows how to set up a 10GB zvol and install a domain using that block device:

```
# zfs create -V 10g rpool/export/myzvol
# virt-install -p --nographics -n mydomu3 \
-f /dev/zvol/dsk/rpool/export/myzvol -r 1024 -l /export/sp/nvdvd.iso
```

You still use the `-f` option to specify the file path for the domain, but this is now actually a device path. There is no `-s` option specifying the file size because the device size is used implicitly.

If you compare this domain's definition with the definition of a domain created using a simple file, you will see that this domain's virtual disk is configured as a physical device:

```
# virsh dumpxml mydomu3
...
    <disk type='block' device='disk'>
      <driver name='phy'/>
      <source dev='/dev/zvol/dsk/rpool/export/myzvol'/>
      <target dev='xvda'/>
    </disk>
...
```

Whether you use a simple file in its own ZFS dataset or a zvol, ZFS makes cloning domains fast because you can use the built-in clone capabilities provided by ZFS to instantly provision another virtual disk for a new domain.

This abbreviated example sets up dom0 and installs a domain onto an iSCSI initiator, using the iSCSI target configured in Chapter 7:

```
# iscsiadm add discovery-address 192.168.0.1
```

```
# iscsiadm modify discovery -t enable
# virt-install --nographics -n mydomu4 -p \
-f /dev/dsk/c1t01000003BA4E5E2000002A0047FA3E22d0s2 -r 1024 \
-l /export/sp/nvdvd.iso
```

The `virsh attach-disk` subcommand is used to attach an additional storage device to a domain. This subcommand accepts `--driver`, `--subdriver`, `--type`, and `--mode` parameters. The `driver` parameter arguments can be `file`, `tap`, or `phy`. The `type` parameter arguments can be `disk`, `floppy`, or `cdrom`. The mode parameter arguments can be `readonly` or `shareable`.

The `attach-disk` examples used so far have only shown the `--driver file` option. In addition to the raw file-based virtual disks seen so far, xVM also supports VMware vmdk format files and VirtualBox vdi format files. You can either use a preexisting virtual disk file created by one of those applications or you can create the file directly using the `vdiskadm` command. The following example creates a 10GB sparse vmdk formatted virtual disk file.

```
# vdiskadm create -t vmdk:sparse -s 10g /xvm/mydisk
```

The `-t` option specifies one of `vmdk:sparse`, `vmdk:fixed`, `vdi:sparse`, `vdi:fixed`, or `raw`.

The `tap` driver type is used to access these virtual disk files. This example attaches the vmdk file just created using the SATA style `xvdb` name.

```
# virsh attach-disk mydomu /xvm/mydisk xvdb --driver tap \
--subdriver vdisk
```

The following example adds a physical CD-ROM device to a domain:

```
# virsh attach-disk mydomu /dev/dsk/c6t0d0s2 2 \
--driver phy --type cdrom --mode readonly
```

Within the domain, you can now mount this device using the `/dev/dsk/c0d2` name:

```
# mount -F hsfs /dev/dsk/c0d2s2 /mnt
```

You can use the `xm block-list` subcommand to display information about the block devices configured on a domain, but most of the output is useful only for low-level xVM debugging. In general, the `virsh dumpxml` subcommand is better for viewing the block devices configured for a domain:

```
# virsh dumpxml xpdom
<domain type='xen' id='19'>
  <name>xpdom</name>
...
    <disk type='file' device='disk'>
      <driver name='file'/>
      <source file='/export/xvm/winxp'/>
      <target dev='hda'/>
```

```
        </disk>
        <disk type='file' device='cdrom'>
          <driver name='file'/>
          <source file='/export/sp/winxp_sp2.iso'/>
          <target dev='hdc'/>
          <readonly/>
        </disk>
        ...
```

To provide storage redundancy to a domain, you can set up a redundant disk configuration within either the domain or dom0. To set this up, simply allocate multiple virtual disks to the domain, and then it is up to the domain to install and configure the guest OS storage so that it is redundant. For OpenSolaris, this involves setting up a ZFS mirror or RAID Z configuration within the domain. Ensure that the devices you allocate to the domU do not have a single point of failure in dom0. For example, allocating two virtual disk files, both on the same physical disk in dom0, to the domU will not allow the domU to create a truly redundant storage configuration, although it might appear redundant from within the domain.

A better alternative is to configure storage redundancy in dom0 where you have full visibility over the physical storage configuration. For example, if you use ZFS and configure a redundant zpool using either mirroring or RAID Z, then you can allocate a single virtual disk file from that storage into the domU and it will automatically benefit from all of the ZFS features, including redundancy. In this way, guest operating systems that don't support ZFS can still transparently realize the benefits that ZFS provides.

Networking

Paravirtualized domains use the xnb backend driver in dom0 to communicate with a physical network interface.

Each network interface in a domU causes the dynamic creation of an xnb device instance and a virtual NIC (VNIC) in dom0. The VNICs are then layered on top of the physical NICs, which enables many domUs to share network access over a single physical NIC. Use the dladm command to monitor the VNICs in dom0. In this example, two VNICs are allocated to domains. Both of the VNICs are layered on top of the same physical e1000g0 NIC:

```
# dladm show-link
LINK        CLASS    MTU     STATE     OVER
e1000g0     phys     1500    up        --
vnic8       vnic     1500    unknown   e1000g0
vnic9       vnic     1500    unknown   e1000g0
# dladm show-link -s
LINK        IPACKETS    RBYTES       IERRORS  OPACKETS  OBYTES      OERRORS
e1000g0     3836794     4504511779   0        1848376   252952540   0
vnic8       5343        332430       0        140       5912        0
vnic9       905         55884        0        1         14          0
```

You can use the `virsh dumpxml` output to correlate an active domain's network interface with the VNIC assigned to the domain:

```
# virsh dumpxml mydomu
...
    <interface type='bridge'>
      <source bridge='e1000g0 '/>
      <target dev='vif9.0'/>
      <mac address='00:16:3e:1f:a0:8f'/>
      <script path='vif-vnic'/>
    </interface>
...
```

The `<target dev>` entry indicates that the network is using virtual interface 9, which corresponds to `vnic9` in dom0. You can also use the XML output to obtain the MAC address assigned to the interface.

The `xm network-list` subcommand can be used to display information about the network interfaces configured on a domain, but like the `block-list` subcommand, most of the output is useful only for low-level xVM debugging.

The `virsh attach-interface` subcommand is used to add network interfaces to a domain. This subcommand takes a type parameter of either `network` or `bridge`, although on OpenSolaris, `bridge` is the only valid value at this time.

To provide network redundancy to a domain, set up link aggregation in dom0, and then configure the domU network interfaces on top of that device:

```
# dladm create-aggr -1 e1000g0 -1 e1000g1 myaggr0
```

Next, plumb and configure the aggregation.

CROSS-REF You can find the complete procedure for setting up link aggregation in Chapter 9.

Once the aggregation is set up, you can configure a domain's virtual network on top of the aggregation:

```
# virsh attach-interface mydomu bridge myaggr0
```

As an alternative to using link aggregation in dom0, you could configure IP multipathing in the domU, as long as you set up the domU with multiple NICs. This moves the network management from dom0 into the domU. (The IPMP procedures are described in Chapter 9.)

Other devices

Currently, configuring other system hardware, such as USB, into a domain is not possible, although xVM is evolving rapidly in this area and this capability might exist by the time you read this. Check the xVM documentation for the OpenSolaris release you're running.

Devices in HVM domains

As noted earlier, HVM domains use a subset of QEMU, called qemu-dm, to provide device emulation for the domain. You saw qemu-dm in the example XML output for an HVM domain; there is also a qemu-dm process running in dom0 for each active HVM domain. This device emulation is used for both I/O devices and platform-specific hardware access. Every time the guest OS in an HVM domain attempts to access hardware, the hypervisor traps that access and forwards the request to the qemu-dm process in dom0. This accounts for the high overhead of an HVM domain as compared to a paravirtualized domain. For an HVM domain, QEMU is configured to emulate an Intel PIIX3 IDE chip set and a Realtek 8139 NIC. Thus, as described earlier, disks appear as IDE/ATA devices, and the network emulation provides very poor performance. Using paravirtualized device drivers in an HVM domain improves I/O performance, although all other low-level hardware access must still be emulated. As of this writing, you cannot tune the configuration of qemu-dm beyond using the os-type and os-varient options when installing the domain.

Because of the performance impact of fully emulated I/O, using paravirtualized drivers in an HVM domain is a necessity for a production system. OpenSolaris includes paravirtualized drivers for use in an HVM domain. Those drivers have been back-ported to the Solaris 10 release of the OS, which is not fully virtualized, and thus must run in an HVM domain. Sun also provides paravirtualized drivers for Windows at the Sun Download Center (www.sun.com/download), although these drivers are not open source. Configuring and managing these closed source operating systems is one of the many strengths of the xVM Server appliance.

Troubleshooting

A variety of tools — such as log files, core dumps, and DTrace — are available to assist in troubleshooting xVM-related problems.

Logs

The xVM log files are saved in the /var/log/xen directory. There are log files for xend, qemu-dm, and others. Although these logs are most useful for developers working on xVM, you might be able to spot an issue in the log file, or you might need to provide the logs to help in diagnosing a bug. You can also use the xm dmesg subcommand to print recent messages logged to the xVM message buffer:

```
# xm dmesg
xVM version 3.1.4-xvm
```

```
(xVM) Command line:
(xVM) Video information:
(xVM)  VGA is text mode 80x25, font 8x16
(xVM)  VBE/DDC methods: none; EDID transfer time: 2 seconds
(xVM)  EDID info not retrieved because no DDC retrieval method detected
(xVM) Disc information:
(xVM)  Found 2 MBR signatures
(xVM)  Found 2 EDD information structures
...
(xVM) Xen is relinquishing VGA console.
(xVM) *** Serial input -> DOM0 (type 'CTRL-a' three times to switch input
 to Xen).
(xVM) Freed 128kB init memory.

(xVM) Xen trace buffers: initialized
```

DomU core dumps

If a running OpenSolaris domU panics, it will dump core, just as it would on a standalone system. You can also take a core dump from dom0 using the `virsh dump` subcommand. The domU remains active after the dump is taken, so you can analyze the state of the domain while it continues to provide service. The dump directory must be world-writable or not owned by root:

```
# virsh dump mydomu /export/sp/mydump
Domain mydomu dumpd to /export/sp/mydump
# mdb /export/sp/mydump
> ::status
debugging domain crash dump /export/sp/mydump (64-bit) from mydomu
operating system: 5.11 snv_95 (i86pc)
>
```

Alternatively, you can use the `xm dump-core` subcommand, which has an option to crash the domain after the dump has been taken.

If the domU is paravirtualized, is running OpenSolaris, and was booted under `kmdb`, then you can use the `xm sysrq` subcommand in dom0 to force the domain to break into `kmdb`:

```
# xm sysrq mydomu b
```

If the domain was not booted under `kmdb`, then you will see a notice on the domain console but nothing else will happen:

```
External debug event received
evtchn_pending [ 0 0 0 0 0 0 0 ]
evtchn_mask [ ffffffffffffff81 ffffffffffffffff ffffffffffffffff
 ffffffffffffffff ffffffffffffffff ffffffffffffffff ffffffffffffffff
```

```
ffffffffffffffff ]
CPU0 pending 0 mask 0 sel 0
```

NOTE   Configuring an OpenSolaris domain to boot under kmdb was described in the section "Boot arguments" earlier in the chapter.

On the domain console you would see the following:

```
mydomu console login:
External debug event received

Welcome to kmdb
Loaded modules: [ scsi_vhci crypto neti ptm xpv_psm ufs unix zfs krtld s1394
sppp nca uhci hook lofs genunix ip usba specfs random sctp arp xpv_uppc ]
[0]>  $C
ffffff00018d1b50 kmdb_enter+0xb()
ffffff00018d1b80 debug_enter+0x37(fffffffffbc0dd98)
ffffff00018d1bc0 xen_debug_handler+0x1f(0)
ffffff00018d1c20 xen_sysrq_handler+0xa6(fffffffffbc415d0, ffffff00a83bb9a8, 2)
ffffff00018d1c60 xenwatch_thread+0xa8()
ffffff00018d1c70 thread_start+8()
[0]>
```

Dom0 core dump

Although the running dom0 cannot access the state of the hypervisor, when the hypervisor panics, the dom0 core dump includes the hypervisor state within the core file, as if the hypervisor were just another OpenSolaris kernel module. This module is named xpv. If the panic occurs in OpenSolaris itself, then the hypervisor state is not included in the dump. Debugging the hypervisor is outside of the scope of this book, but Nils Nieuwejaar's blog at http://blogs.sun.com/nilsn/entry/debugging_an_xvm_panic has an example of debugging a crash dump into the hypervisor.

DTrace

Although you cannot trace into the hypervisor code itself, the xpv provider can be used to trace the hypercalls between dom0 and the hypervisor. The details of these calls are primarily useful for developers working on xVM, but this provider does enable you to get an overview of the interaction of the OS with the hypervisor.

CROSS-REF   Chapter 15 covers DTrace.

Resources

The xVM hypervisor community is at `http://opensolaris.org/os/community/xen`. Here you can find links to download the software, articles, and documentation, as well as a link to the xVM discussion, where community members ask and answer questions. OpenSolaris also hosts a QEMU project at `http://opensolaris.org/os/project/qemu`.

Because xVM is based on the open source Xen project, the Xen site at `http://xen.org` is also a good resource for general Xen-related information.

Within the ON source tree, the hypervisor source is under `usr/src/uts/common/xen`. The i86xpv drivers are under `usr/src/uts/i86xpv`. The OpenSolaris paravirtualized drivers for use in an HVM domain are under `usr/src/uts/i86pc/i86hvm`. The user-level source code for the various commands can be downloaded from the `xen.org` website.

The initial ARC case for the xVM hypervisor is *PSARC 2006/260 Solaris on Xen*, although currently the case had not been opened. The case for paravirtualized drivers in HVM domains is at `http://opensolaris.org/os/community/arc/caselog/2007/664`.

The `http://wikis.sun.com/display/xVM/Sun+xVM` site provides information about both the xVM hypervisor and the xVM Ops Center management tools project, as does the `http://openxvm.org` website. You can also find other useful information, such as xVM Blueprints, on the `wikis.sun.com` website.

Professional Xen Virtualization by William von Hagen (Wrox, 2008) might be useful for general Xen background material, particularly if you are running Xen on a dom0 that is not running OpenSolaris.

Finally, xVM, and Xen in general, are very active areas of development and deployment, so you can find a lot of useful sites and blogs by searching on these topics.

Summary

This chapter described the xVM hypervisor, the OpenSolaris hypervisor-level virtualization feature for x86-based systems. Using the xVM hypervisor enables you to create isolated, independent domains and run different guest operating systems within each one, while sharing the underlying hardware resources. It also examined the features, configuration, and ongoing management of xVM.

Logical Domains (LDoms)

ogical Domains (LDoms) are the hypervisor-based virtualization
solution provided on the Chip Multi-Threading (CMT) versions of
the SPARC hardware architecture. LDoms can be used to partition
system resources into domains, each of which is an isolated environment
that can run a standalone OS. This provides virtualization capabilities
for SPARC similar to those described in the last chapter for the x86
architecture using the xVM hypervisor.

Introduction to LDoms

LDoms provide a type 1 hypervisor that is designed into the architecture
of the SPARC microprocessor itself. The hypervisor is implemented as a
firmware layer that supports running paravirtualized operating systems.
It does not allow running fully virtualized operating systems. LDoms are
supported on the CMT versions of the SPARC microprocessor, including
the T1, T2, and T2 Plus processors, which support 32 or 64 threads per
chip (the M-class SPARC machines do not support LDoms). This version of
the SPARC architecture is reported as sun4v by the uname -m command.
Earlier versions of SPARC processors, such as the common sun4u architecture, do not support LDoms. Because the hypervisor is part of the system
firmware and is closely tied to the CMT version of SPARC, this chapter is
more hardware specific than much of the rest of the material in this book.

CROSS-REF See Chapter 17 for background material on virtualization.

OpenSolaris has been paravirtualized to run on the sun4v architecture. Instead of accessing the hardware directly, the sun4v-specific portions of the kernel make explicit calls to the hypervisor in the system firmware. Like the paravirtualization support in xVM, this paravirtualization simultaneously abstracts the OS away from the physical hardware and provides better performance when interacting with the hypervisor, as compared to a fully virtualized OS. Because LDoms only support paravirtualized operating systems, earlier versions of Solaris — or other operating systems that run on SPARC — won't run on this hardware without first being ported to sun4v.

> **NOTE**   Currently, the OpenSolaris distribution has not been released on SPARC. Work is underway on that project, however, and it will likely be complete by the time you read this. The examples in this chapter use the SXCE distribution, but there is very little in this chapter that is specific to either of these distributions.

LDoms enable the system's physical hardware to be partitioned into separate domains, each of which can run a standalone operating system. Physical I/O devices are assigned to individual domains but LDoms also support virtual I/O from one domain to another, which transforms the virtual request into physical I/O. Although this enables physical I/O devices to be shared between domains, other hardware — such as CPUs or memory — is physically partitioned and allocated to a single domain.

LDom Concepts

The capabilities of LDoms are similar to xVM but the terminology differs. This section covers the concepts and terminology unique to LDoms.

Types of domains

LDoms support four different types of domains, defined by the roles that each domain can perform. Each domain is installed with a standalone operating system and acts as an independent entity on the system:

- The *control domain* manages all other domains and is the one in which the LDom Manager runs. This tool is used to create, configure, start, and stop the other domains. There can only be one control domain on the system. The initial installation of OpenSolaris becomes the first domain once you start using LDoms and it will be the control domain. This is similar to the xVM dom0 described in the previous chapter, but there is less dependence on the control domain with LDoms. For example, with LDoms you can reboot the control domain and the other domains will continue to run, which is not the case with xVM.

- An *I/O domain* has direct physical access to devices. The control domain is typically an I/O domain. The number of I/O domains on the system is limited by the number of system buses. For example, the T1000 system can split its bus into two, so it supports two I/O domains. Because an I/O domain has direct access to devices, its I/O can be faster than if it had to do virtual I/O. In most cases an I/O domain acts as a service domain as well.

- A *service domain* has physical access to devices, so it is usually also an I/O domain, and it thus provides virtual I/O services to other domains. Because the number of I/O domains is limited, most domains are configured with virtual devices using the services provided by a service domain.

- A *guest domain* uses services from a service domain but provides no services to any other domains on the system.

The number of configurable domains is limited by the number of threads on the processor, but there can be other platform-specific limitations as well. For example, the T5440 uses the T2 Plus processor and supports a total of 256 threads, but that system supports only 128 domains. Check the specifications for your system for any limitations related to the number of domains. Each domain must have at least one hardware thread bound to it, although it is common to allocate more. Configuring an entire CPU core's threads to a domain usually gives the best performance to software running in that domain, but allocating that many threads to each domain severely limits the total number of domains that can be used.

A typical, simple configuration consists of the control domain, which also acts as a service domain, providing virtual I/O services to all other domains on the system (guest domains). However, more complex configurations can be created to spread the I/O load among domains and provide redundancy. Although each domain is independent, a reboot of a service domain can affect the I/O of guest domains using those services. Configurations to avoid this single point of failure are described later in the chapter.

Types of services and devices

Because the number of I/O domains is limited, most domains will not have access to physical devices. Instead, guest domains will use virtual I/O services provided by a service domain. The virtual I/O includes support for storage, networking, and a system console. The following terminology and abbreviations are used to describe these virtual services and devices:

- A *Logical Domain Channel* (LDC) is a communication channel between a domain and the hypervisor. LDCs are also used for communication between a service domain and a guest domain, as well as to communicate system information such as FMA events or dynamic reconfiguration events to a domain.

- The *Virtual Disk Service* (VDS) provides virtual storage services from a service domain to guest domains. The *Virtual Disk Service Device* (VDSDEV) represents physical storage that is associated with a VDS instance in a service domain. A *Virtual Disk* (VDISK) in a guest domain connects to the VDS and maps to a VDSDEV instance in a service domain.

- The *Virtual Switch Service* (VSW) provides virtual network services from a service domain to guest domains. This service acts just like a physical, layer 2 network switch, also sometimes known as a *bridge*. Networking can be completely self-contained within the virtual switch or an external network can be configured to provide connectivity outside of the switch. A *Virtual Network* (VNET) is a network interface in a guest domain that connects to the VSW in a service domain.

- The *Virtual Console Concentrator Service* (VCC) provides a virtual console service from the service domain to each guest domain. The *Virtual Console* (VCONS) in a guest domain connects to the VCC service in the control domain.

- A *Virtual CPU* (VCPU) represents a hardware thread on the processor. The current generation of systems provides 32, 64, or 256 hardware threads, each of which can be bound to a VCPU. Each domain must have at least one VCPU assigned to it.

Depending on the processor, several *Cryptographic Mathematical Arithmetic Units* (MAUs) are available for use with encryption and decryption. The MAU is a special-purpose mathematical device that can be used to accelerate cryptographic processing. On the T1 processor, each core has an associated MAU, for a total of eight MAUs on that system. If the applications running within a domain will use this hardware, 0 or more MAUs can be bound to the domain as needed.

In addition to these virtual services and devices, each guest domain has access to virtual memory and its own instance of the *OpenBoot PROM* (OBP), provided by the hypervisor.

> **NOTE** The OBP is the firmware on SPARC systems. It initializes the hardware and boots the OS. If you are familiar with x86-based systems, the OBP provides functionality similar to the BIOS on x86, but with additional capabilities. In addition to its use on Sun SPARC platforms, OBP was standardized as IEEE 1275-1994 and is used on a variety of other systems.

To use LDoms, you define instances of the VDS, VSW, and VCC services in a service domain. For each guest domain, you define the VCPU, MAU, Memory, VDSDEV, VDISK, VNET, VCONS, and OBP resources.

Figure 21-1 shows the basic relationship between the physical hardware, the services running in the control domain, and the client devices in a guest domain. In all cases, the hypervisor mediates and manages the physical hardware used by each domain.

FIGURE 21-1

The relationship between hardware, hypervisor, domains, and services.

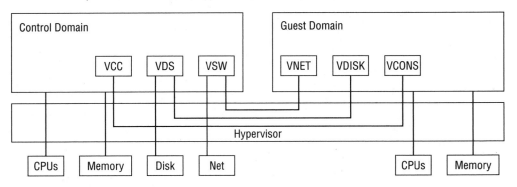

Getting Started with LDoms

The procedures and commands to administer LDoms are fairly complex. Layered tools, such as xVM Ops Center, will eventually simplify this process but this chapter presents the low-level CLIs you can use to administer LDoms. This section focuses on getting domains up and running. Subsequent sections discuss many of the concepts introduced here in more detail.

This chapter is based on the LDoms 1.0.3 software, but new versions are released regularly so check the LDoms community page at www.opensolaris.org to determine the latest version.

Checking the firmware

Because the hypervisor is part of the system firmware, make sure you have the latest firmware installed before configuring logical domains. Download the latest firmware patch for your hardware from the SunSolve website (sunsolve.sun.com) and follow the instructions to determine whether you already have the latest firmware installed. If you don't, you will be guided through the hardware-specific procedure to update the firmware.

> **CAUTION** If you have to install new firmware, carefully follow the instructions included with the firmware patch. It is best to be physically present at the machine in case you need to take administrative steps to reset the system controller.

The examples in this chapter use a T1000 running the LDoms 1.0.3 software. Some of the hardware-specific commands might differ across machines, so check the release notes and instructions for your specific platform.

First, connect to the system controller and check the firmware version:

```
sc> showhost version -v
Sun-Fire-T1000 System Firmware 6.6.1  2008/02/11 15:54

Host flash versions:
    OBP 4.28.1 2008/02/11 13:04
    Hypervisor 1.6.1 2008/02/11 12:15
    POST 4.28.1 2008/02/11 13:29
```

Here, the firmware release is 6.6.1, which is a valid version for the LDoms 1.0.3 software, so no further action is required. The following table shows the required firmware versions for use with LDoms 1.0.3, based on the system's processor.

Processor	Firmware Version
UltraSPARC T2 Plus	7.1.x
UltraSPARC T2	7.1.x
UltraSPARC T1	6.6.x

Installing the management software

The LDoms Manager software is currently delivered in the SVR4 `SUNWldm` package. The Logical Domains community on OpenSolaris.org has a link to the location to download this package (currently `http://sun.com/servers/coolthreads/ldoms/get.jsp`). The software installs into the `/opt/SUNWldm/bin` directory, so for simplicity you might want to add this directory to the path of the system administrator. The rest of the examples assume this directory is in the path. The download includes its own installer or you can simply add the package as follows:

```
# pkgadd -d . SUNWldm.v
```

TIP   If you don't use the installer, you need to manually enable the `svc:/ldoms/ldmd` SMF service before you can use LDoms. See Chapter 13 for more information on SMF. This example enables the service:

```
# svcadm enable svc:/ldoms/ldmd
```

Administrative privileges

You must be root or have root privileges in the control domain to configure and administer domains. To avoid having to be root, the `LDoms Management` or `LDoms Review` rights profile can be assigned to a user. The `LDoms Review` profile enables a user to view the configurations but not to modify them.

CROSS-REF   See Chapter 11, which discusses OpenSolaris security, for information on configuring rights profiles.

Configuring the control domain

The initial installation of OpenSolaris running on the system becomes the control domain once you have installed the domain manager and started to configure LDoms. Each domain can be given a name. The name *primary* is automatically used for the control domain.

The `ldm` command is used to manage LDoms. It has a variety of subcommands. Start by verifying that the domain state is `active` using the `list` subcommand. The `active` states means the domain is up and running. Other domain states and details of the `list` output are described in detail later in the chapter:

```
# ldm list

------------------------------------------------------------------------
Notice: the LDom Manager is running in configuration mode. Configuration and
resource information is displayed for the configuration under construction;
```

```
not the current active configuration. The configuration being constructed
will only take effect after it is downloaded to the system controller and
the host is reset.
-------------------------------------------------------------------------------
NAME            STATE     FLAGS    CONS    VCPU   MEMORY   UTIL   UPTIME
primary         active    -n-c-    SP      32     8064M    0.7%   23m
```

The primary domain initially has all of the system resources allocated to it. You need to de-allocate some of those resources from the primary domain so that they can be allocated to other domains. The following example allocates four hardware threads to the primary domain. It also allocates 4100MB — slightly more than half of the physical memory — to the primary domain. The rest of the system's hardware threads, memory, and MAU support will be available to allocate to other domains.

CAUTION You cannot dynamically reconfigure CPUs on the control domain if you have any MAUs assigned to it. If you don't need cryptographic units in the control domain, remove them:

```
# ldm set-mau 0 primary
-------------------------------------------------------------------------------
Notice: the LDom Manager is running in configuration mode. Any configuration
changes made will only take effect after the machine configuration is
downloaded to the system controller and the host is reset.
-------------------------------------------------------------------------------


# ldm set-vcpu 4 primary
# ldm set-memory 4100M primary
```

For most of the ldm subcommands, the last parameter (primary in this example) is the name of the domain to which the command applies. After each set subcommand you will see the reconfiguration warning, indicating that your changes won't take effect until the domain reboots. It is omitted in the example here, after the first command, for brevity.

Next, create the three services needed to support guest domains:

```
# ldm add-vds primary-vds0 primary
# ldm add-vsw net-dev=bge0 primary-vsw0 primary
# ldm add-vcc port-range=5000-5100 primary-vcc0 primary
```

The add-vds subcommand creates a Virtual Disk Service; add-vsw creates a Virtual Switch Service; and add-vcc creates a Virtual Console Concentrator service. The names of each of these services are primary-vds0, primary-vsw0, and primary-vcc0, respectively. The bge0 network interface is set as the physical NIC to use for external connectivity on the virtual switch using the net-dev option to the add-vsw subcommand. The port range 5000-5100 is set for virtual consoles as an option on the add-vcc subcommand.

 **NOTE** Here, the services are named after the domain providing the service (the primary domain) and the type of service, but you can name the services anything you like.

As shown after each command, the notice indicates that the primary domain has a reconfiguration in progress:

```
# ldm list

---------------------------------------------------------------------------
Notice: the LDom Manager is running in configuration mode. Configuration and
resource information is displayed for the configuration under construction;
not the current active configuration. The configuration being constructed
will only take effect after it is downloaded to the system controller and
the host is reset.
---------------------------------------------------------------------------
NAME           STATE     FLAGS   CONS   VCPU  MEMORY   UTIL   UPTIME
primary        active    -n-cv   SP     4     4100M    0.0%   42m
```

Now that the control domain has been reconfigured, save this configuration to the system controller. This example saves the new configuration using the name myconfig:

```
# ldm add-config myconfig
```

Finally, enable the virtual network terminal server daemon (vntsd). This daemon provides console services to all but the control domain and is not enabled by default. This SMF service should be enabled after you configure the virtual console service:

```
# svcadm enable svc:/ldoms/vntsd:default
```

CROSS-REF   See Chapter 13 for more information on SMF.

Now reboot the control domain to activate the new configuration:

```
# init 6
```

After the system reboots, log in and view the new configuration:

```
# ldm list
NAME           STATE     FLAGS   CONS   VCPU  MEMORY   UTIL   UPTIME
primary        active    -n-cv   SP     4     4100M    0.0%   2m

# ldm list -l
NAME           STATE     FLAGS   CONS   VCPU  MEMORY   UTIL   UPTIME
primary        active    -n-cv   SP     4     4100M    2.6%   2m

SOFTSTATE
Solaris running

VCPU
    VID    PID    UTIL  STRAND
    0      0      0.0%  100%
    1      1      0.0%  100%
    2      2      0.0%  100%
    3      3      0.0%  100%
```

```
MEMORY
     RA              PA              SIZE
     0x8000000       0x8000000       4100M

VARIABLES
     auto-boot?=false
     diag-switch?=true
     keyboard-layout=US-English

IO
     DEVICE          PSEUDONYM       OPTIONS
     pci@780         bus_a
     pci@7c0         bus_b

VCC
     NAME            PORT-RANGE
     primary-vcc0    5000-5100

VSW
     NAME            MAC                 NET-DEV   DEVICE      MODE
     primary-vsw0    00:14:4f:fb:fc:58   bge0      switch@0

VDS
     NAME            VOLUME          OPTIONS          DEVICE
     primary-vds0

VCONS
     NAME            SERVICE                          PORT
     SP
```

Note some key points in the detailed output:

- Four CPUs are now assigned to the control domain, and 4100MB of memory.
- The three services you configured, with their names and properties, are indicated.
- The virtual switch was automatically assigned a MAC address.
- A few additional properties and services — VARIABLES, IO, and VCONS — are listed that you didn't configure. Those are discussed later in the chapter.
- SOFTSTATE shows that the operating system is running in the control domain.

Configuring a guest domain

Now that some system resources have been freed up, you can configure a guest domain. In this example, the name of the domain is mydomain:

```
# ldm add-domain mydomain
# ldm set-vcpu 4 mydomain
```

```
# ldm set-memory 2048M mydomain
# ldm set-mau 0 mydomain
```

This assigns four virtual CPUs, 2GB of memory, and no MAUs to the new domain.

The next step is to assign a disk to the new domain. This example shows how you can leverage ZFS to create a file that you then use as a boot disk for the domain. The other options, using physical disks, is described later in the chapter. One of those options might be a better choice, depending on your configuration, but using ZFS files as virtual disks offers the most flexibility.

CROSS-REF Fully configuring ZFS is described in detail in Chapter 8.

The following example creates a ZFS dataset, and then a 10GB file within the dataset to use as the boot disk for the domain. As this example shows, you must physically allocate a file to use it as a boot disk for a domain:

```
# zfs create p1/myldom
# mkfile 10g /p1/myldom/zdisk
```

Now you can configure this file as a virtual disk for the domain:

```
# ldm add-vdsdev /p1/myldom/zdisk vol1@primary-vds0
# ldm add-vdisk vdisk1 vol1@primary-vds0 mydomain
```

A Virtual Disk Service Device (VDSDEV) named vol1 is defined for the zdisk file and is associated with the primary-vds0 service. Then a virtual disk named vdisk1 that uses the VDS-DEV is defined for mydomain.

Because systems supporting LDoms are servers that are usually managed remotely, you typically install the domain using an ISO image file of the install media, or over the network. This example uses an ISO image file, which enables the installation to be performed without anyone being physically present at the machine. Installing from a physical CD-ROM or DVD is described later in this chapter. To install from an ISO file, configure the file as another virtual disk for the domain, as shown in this example where the ISO file is named /p1/iso/solarisdvd.iso:

```
# ldm add-vdsdev /p1/iso/solarisdvd.iso solarisdvd@primary-vds0
# ldm add-vdisk dvd solarisdvd@primary-vds0 mydomain
```

See your distribution's documentation for the procedures to set up and use a network install server instead of a local ISO file.

Next, define a virtual network interface for the domain:

```
# ldm add-vnet vnet0 primary-vsw0 mydomain
```

Notice that this network interface uses the `primary-vsw0` virtual switch service that you created when you defined your control domain.

Finally, define some OBP settings for the domain:

```
# ldm set-var auto-boot\?=false mydomain
```

Here you set the `auto-boot` property to false, which means the domain won't automatically boot once it is started.

That completes the basic configuration of the guest domain. If you look at the configuration you can see that it is defined and in the `inactive` state:

```
# ldm list
NAME            STATE       FLAGS   CONS    VCPU  MEMORY    UTIL  UPTIME
primary         active      -n-cv   SP      4     4100M     0.3%  1d 1h 6m
mydomain        inactive    -----           4     2G
```

The `bind` command allocates, or binds, the specified resources to the new domain:

```
# ldm bind mydomain
```

Until that is done, the resources are available to be bound to other domains. You can use the `list` command to see the configuration of this new domain:

```
# ldm list -l mydomain
NAME            STATE       FLAGS   CONS    VCPU  MEMORY    UTIL  UPTIME
mydomain        bound       -----   5000    4     2G

VCPU
    VID    PID    UTIL STRAND
    0      4           100%
    1      5           100%
    2      6           100%
    3      7           100%

MEMORY
    RA                  PA                  SIZE
    0x8800000           0x108800000         2G

VARIABLES
    auto-boot?=false

NETWORK
    NAME                SERVICE                     DEVICE      MAC
    vnet0               primary-vsw0@primary        network@0   00:14:4f:fb:4d:cc

DISK
    NAME                VOLUME                      TOUT DEVICE  SERVER
```

```
      vdisk1          vol1@primary-vds0              disk@0  primary
      dvd             solarisdvd@primary-vds0        disk@1  primary

  VCONS
      NAME            SERVICE                   PORT
      mydomain        primary-vcc0@primary      5000
```

Note two things in this output. First, because you didn't specify a MAC address when you created the virtual network interface, one was automatically assigned. Similarly, you didn't configure a virtual console, so one was created and a port was also automatically assigned within the range you specified.

Logging in to a guest domain

Now that the guest domain has been defined, you can connect to its virtual console. Do this in a different window so you can watch the guest domain's console while you boot the domain. Use the port that was automatically assigned to this domain, shown in the preceding list output. You must do this from the control domain because this is a local connection:

```
# telnet localhost 5000
Trying 127.0.0.1...
Connected to localhost.
Escape character is '^]'.

Connecting to console "mydomain" in group "mydomain" ....
Press ~? for control options ..
```

Nothing happens on the console at this point because the guest domain isn't running yet.

Booting and installing a guest domain

Back in the control domain, you can now start the guest domain:

```
# ldm start mydomain
LDom mydomain started
# ldm list
NAME        STATE     FLAGS   CONS    VCPU   MEMORY   UTIL   UPTIME
primary     active    -n-cv   SP      4      4100M    0.6%   1d 1h 55m
mydomain    active    -t---   5000    4      2G       0.0%   1s
```

The list output indicates that the guest domain is now active. If you watch the window on the guest domain's console, you'll see something like the following output (it will vary slightly depending on your hardware):

```
Sun Fire(TM) T1000, No Keyboard
Copyright 2008 Sun Microsystems, Inc.  All rights reserved.

OpenBoot 4.28.1, 2048 MB memory available, Serial #66625424.
```

```
Ethernet address 0:14:4f:fb:ae:c9, Host ID: 83fbaec9.

{0} ok
```

On the guest domain console you are now sitting at the OBP prompt, just as you would be on a standalone SPARC system that was just powered on. Because you configured the domain with its OBP auto-boot as false, the domain did not try to boot. The OBP reports the amount of memory you configured for the domain, but it also reports the system's MAC address, not the MAC address that was previously shown in the ldm list output.

LDoms automatically sets up OBP device aliases for the domain. You can see this using the devalias command at the OBP prompt:

```
{0} ok devalias
dvd                 /virtual-devices@100/channel-devices@200/disk@1
vdisk1              /virtual-devices@100/channel-devices@200/disk@0
vnet0               /virtual-devices@100/channel-devices@200/network@0
net                 /virtual-devices@100/channel-devices@200/network@0
disk                /virtual-devices@100/channel-devices@200/disk@0
virtual-console     /virtual-devices/console@1
name                aliases
```

This shows that the logical names you used when you configured the virtual disks, vdisk1 and dvd, have been aliased to the full device path. You can use the path for the DVD to boot and install the domain from the ISO image file:

```
{0} ok boot /virtual-devices@100/channel-devices@200/disk@1
Boot device: /virtual-devices@100/channel-devices@200/disk@1 File
 and args:

SunOS Release 5.11 Version snv_100 64-bit
Copyright 1983-2008 Sun Microsystems, Inc.  All rights reserved.
Use is subject to license terms.
Configuring /dev
...
```

After the system boots from the ISO image, you can manually answer the questions about installing SXCE and the installation will begin. Once the domain has finished installing, you can log in on the console or over the network and run various commands to observe some of the LDoms-specific services and devices within the domain. This example uses ifconfig to show the network interface:

```
# ifconfig -a
lo0: flags=2001000849<UP,LOOPBACK,RUNNING,MULTICAST,IPv4,VIRTUAL> mtu 8232
 index 1
        inet 127.0.0.1 netmask ff000000
vnet0: flags=201000843<UP,BROADCAST,RUNNING,MULTICAST,IPv4,CoS> mtu 1500 index 2
```

```
       inet 10.4.235.46 netmask ffffff00 broadcast 10.4.235.255
       ether 0:14:4f:fb:4d:cc
```

You can see the virtual network interface in the ifconfig output. Use the format command to see the virtual disk:

```
# format
Searching for disks...done


AVAILABLE DISK SELECTIONS:
       0. c0d0 <SUN-DiskImage-10GB cyl 34950 alt 2 hd 1 sec 600>
          /virtual-devices@100/channel-devices@200/disk@0
Specify disk (enter its number):
```

Within the guest domain, you boot, reboot, or halt the domain just as you would a standalone system. From the control domain, you can also use the ldm command stop to halt the guest domain:

```
# ldm stop mydomain
LDom mydomain stopped
# ldm list
NAME          STATE     FLAGS    CONS    VCPU   MEMORY   UTIL   UPTIME
primary       active    -n-cv    SP      4      4100M    2.0%   1d 2h 4m
mydomain      bound     -----    5000    4      2G
```

The guest domain is no longer active at this point.

> **CAUTION** Shutting down the domain with ldm stop causes an orderly shutdown, but ldm stop -f is like turning off the power to a standalone system. Because the OS does not have a chance to do an orderly shutdown, file system corruption or data loss can occur within the guest domain.

Advanced LDom Administration

The ldm command is the primary CLI for configuring and managing domains. This section provides details about the various ldm subcommands and how to create more sophisticated domain configurations.

Monitoring

There are several ldm subcommands to display various parts of the domain configurations. You used the list subcommand, for instance, in earlier examples. The -l option provides a long listing with most of the relevant information. You can see information on all of the domains or provide the name of a specific LDom to only see information about that domain.

The `ls-bindings` subcommand lists the resources that have been bound to the domains. This information is a subset of the `list -l` output. The `ls-services` subcommand lists the services that have been defined, and the `ls-constraints` subcommand lists the definition of domains that act as constraints for the creation of a new domain. The `ls-devices` command is one of the more useful variations because it shows what devices have not been allocated to a domain and are therefore available for the creation of a new domain. Here's an example:

```
# ldm ls-devices
VCPU
     PID      %FREE
     8        100
     9        100
     ...
     30       100
     31       100

MAU

     ID       CPUSET
     0        (0, 1, 2, 3)
     1        (4, 5, 6, 7)
     2        (8, 9, 10, 11)
     3        (12, 13, 14, 15)
     4        (16, 17, 18, 19)
     5        (20, 21, 22, 23)
     6        (24, 24, 26, 27)
     7        (28, 29, 30, 31)

MEMORY
     PA                   SIZE
     0x108400000          4M
     0x188800000          1912M
```

ldm list output

The `ldm list` output provides a lot of information about a domain. Here is an example listing for the two domains you created:

```
# ldm list
NAME          STATE     FLAGS    CONS    VCPU    MEMORY    UTIL    UPTIME
primary       active    -n-cv    SP      4       4100M     0.3%    2d 45m
mydomain      active    -n---    5000    4       2G        0.2%    9h 36m
```

This section covers most of the values, beginning with states and flags.

Domain states and flags

The possible values for the STATE are described in the following table.

Value	Description
active	The domain is running.
binding	Transition state while resources are being bound
bound	Resources are bound to the domain. It is not running.
inactive	Domain is being configured but resources are not yet bound
starting	Transition state while domain is starting
stopping	Transition state while domain is stopping
unbinding	Transition state while resources are being unbound

FLAGS are reported in five columns within the field. A dash (-) is used as a placeholder if the flag in that column is not set:

```
Column 1        Column 2        Column 3        Column 4        Column 5
   s               n, t            d               c               v
```

The following table describes each flag.

Flag	Description
s	Starting or stopping
n	Normal — OS has booted
t	Transition — Domain started but OS has not yet booted
d	Delayed reconfiguration in progress
c	Control domain
v	Virtual I/O service domain

UTIL and UPTIME

The UTIL column reports on utilization of the virtual CPUs assigned to the domain. It can be used to monitor how busy the domain is, so that CPUs can be added or removed if necessary. This value is the percentage of time that the virtual CPUs assigned to the domain have spent running code in the domain. When the OS in the domain calls into the hypervisor, that time is not included in the utilization calculation. If the OS is mostly idle, perhaps because it is waiting for input, then that time is spent in the hypervisor and not counted in the utilization. This column is blank when the domain is not active.

Utilization will be high when the domain is in transition at the OBP prompt. Once the OS within the domain boots, the utilization should track the activity within the domain.

The UPTIME column shows the amount of time that the domain has been active. When the OS within the domain reboots, this value resets.

MIB

The LDoms software includes an SNMP agent that can be run in the control domain to provide status information to an SNMP management application. The agent is delivered in the SUNWldmib.v package, which is included as part of the download of the domain manager. The MIB for the agent provides information on each domain, including configuration and status. The full MIB is documented in the manual *Logical Domains (LDoms) MIB 1.0.3 Administration Guide: For the Control Domain*, which, along with other LDoms documentation, is linked from the LDoms community page on opensolaris.org.

Because there are no notification events from the domain manager, the agent polls the manager to update status. As a result, there can be a slight delay in the data provided by the agent. Most of the information provided by the agent is read-only, but domains can be started and stopped by setting a value in the ldomAdminState property within the ldomTable . SNMP traps can be sent when domains are created or destroyed, a configuration change is made, or a domain changes state.

CROSS-REF See Chapter 14 for more information on SNMP.

ldmd daemon

The Logical Domains Manager Daemon (ldmd) is part of the domain management infrastructure in the control domain. When you install the LDoms software, the svc:/ldoms/ldmd SMF service is installed and enabled. The daemon is required to manage domains from the control domain.

Delayed reconfiguration

With the exception of CPUs, dynamically changing other resources of an active domain is considered a delayed reconfiguration operation. The changes do not take effect until a reboot of the domain being reconfigured. A delayed reconfiguration operation also restricts configuration changes to other domains. The following changes the domain's amount of memory from 2GB to 3GB:

```
# ldm set-memory 3000m mydomain
Initiating delayed reconfigure operation on LDom mydomain.  All configuration
changes for other LDoms are disabled until the LDom reboots, at which time
```

```
the new configuration for LDom mydomain will also take effect.
# ldm list
NAME       STATE    FLAGS   CONS   VCPU  MEMORY   UTIL   UPTIME
primary    active   -n-cv   SP     4     4100M    0.3%   2d 1h 33m
mydomain   active   -nd--   5000   4     3000M    0.2%   10h 24m
```

If the domain is not active, you can change its configuration without causing a delayed reconfiguration to occur. Adding or removing CPUs from an active domain is not a delayed reconfiguration operation and happens immediately.

You might need to cancel a reconfiguration if it is blocking another more urgent reconfiguration on a different domain, or if the need for the new configuration changed before you had a chance to apply it. You can cancel delayed reconfiguration operations if necessary, as shown in this example:

```
# ldm rm-reconf mydomain
```

Virtual I/O services

The three virtual services that can be provided by a service domain — Virtual Disk Service (VDS), Virtual Switch Service (VSW), and Virtual Console Concentrator Service (VCC) — were briefly described earlier in this chapter. This section provides details about these services and their capabilities.

Here are the subcommands you initially used to create the services when setting up the control domain:

```
# ldm add-vds primary-vds0 primary
# ldm add-vsw net-dev=bge0 primary-vsw0 primary
# ldm add-vcc port-range=5000-5100 primary-vcc0 primary
```

The set-vsw and set-vcc subcommands can be used to modify the options on an existing service. (There is no set-vds subcommand because the VDS has no options.) For example, to narrow the range of ports configured on the primary-vcc0 service you could do the following:

```
# ldm set-vcc port-range=5000-5050 primary-vcc0
```

The rm-vds, rm-vsw, and rm-vcc subcommands remove the corresponding service.

The Virtual Disk Service

The VDS accepts disk I/O requests from virtual disk clients and passes them to the physical storage configured within the service domain.

When you set up the initial services and the guest domain, you configured a disk file within ZFS to use as a boot disk. It was added to the VDS service configuration using the following command:

```
# ldm add-vdsdev /p1/myldom/zdisk vol1@primary-vds0
```

The add-vdsdev subcommand is used to add a storage device to a VDS. Initially you used a file, but this can be a full disk, a disk slice, or a volume (that is, from a volume manager such as SVM or a ZFS zvol). You can add more storage to the service at any time. The following uses a disk slice to create a virtual disk device:

```
# ldm add-vdsdev /dev/dsk/c0t0d0s6 slice6@primary-vds0
# ldm list -l primary
...
VDS
    NAME            VOLUME          OPTIONS         DEVICE
    primary-vds0    slice6                          /dev/rdsk/c0t0d0s6
                    vol1                            /pl/myldom/zdisk

...
```

In the add-vdsdev command, the new volume was given a different name, slice6, from the volume that was already configured, vol1. Note that the name on the command line is composed of two components: the volume name itself and the VDS name. The volume name is slice6, and you are adding it to the VDS named primary-vds0. To add an entire disk, you would specify slice 2, which is partitioned across the whole disk by default.

Virtual disks can be configured in a domain so that they appear as either a full disk, supporting the standard eight slices, or as a single-slice disk. There are some limitations to virtual devices that can be used as boot disks within a domain. A file, volume, or full disk that was configured as a full disk can be partitioned within the domain and can be used as a boot disk. A single-slice disk cannot be partitioned within the domain. It appears as a single partition and cannot be used as a boot disk. Files, volumes, or entire disks are configured in a domain as full disks by default, although the slice option can be used on the add-vdsdev command to force them to appear as a single slice. A physical disk slice configured into a domain always appears as a single slice.

CROSS-REF Chapter 7 has more information about disk slices and how they are named.

Although there is more than one storage device in the service, this storage is not shared in a pool such as occurs with a ZFS pool. Instead, when you create a virtual disk for your guest domain, you specify which volume is associated with it. This command adds the virtual disk you just created to mydomain:

```
# ldm add-vdisk timeout=15 vdisk2 slice6@primary-vds0 mydomain
```

This virtual disk, named vdisk2, was associated with the slice6 volume in the primary-vds0 VDS. Although you may have configured only a single VDS, there can be many volumes within that service, each of which is associated with a virtual disk for a guest domain. Notice that this example specified an optional timeout property, which is the number of seconds before an error is returned if a connection cannot be established with the VDS. If no timeout is specified, the disk waits indefinitely to connect to the service. This value is displayed in the TOUT column in the list output:

```
# ldm list -l mydomain
...
DISK

    NAME            VOLUME                      TOUT DEVICE  SERVER
    vdisk1          vol1@primary-vds0                disk@0  primary
    vdisk2          slice6@primary-vds0         15   disk@1  primary
...
```

Once mydomain is rebooted, the new disk is available.

To remove a volume from the virtual disk service, use the rm-vdsdev subcommand:

```
# ldm rm-vdsdev vol2@primary-vds0
```

The volume cannot be in use when you attempt to remove it.

The initial volume you created was backed by a fully allocated file within a ZFS dataset. You created that file using the mkfile command, which physically allocated 10GB of space. As mentioned previously, a fully allocated file or full disk is required when you want to use the device as a boot disk. You can also add a ZFS volume, or zvol, to the VDS. The following commands create a ZFS volume that is 5GB in size and add it to the existing VDS with the name extraspace:

```
# zfs create -V 5G p1/ldomspace/mydomain
# ldm add-vdsdev /dev/zvol/rdsk/p1/ldomspace/mydomain extraspace@primary-vds0
# ldm list -l primary
...
VDS
    NAME            VOLUME       OPTIONS    DEVICE
    primary-vds0    extraspace              /dev/zvol/rdsk/p1/ldomspace/mydomain
                    vol1                    /p1/myldom/zdisk
...
```

The new volume can now be associated with a virtual disk in mydomain:

```
# ldm add-vdisk vdisk3 extraspace@primary-vds0 mydomain
```

To add a CD-ROM or DVD to a domain, you configure it just like a regular VDSDEV, specifying the whole disk using the device name for slice 2. That way, a CD-ROM or DVD drive can be used to install OpenSolaris, or another supported OS, from physical media.

The Virtual Switch Service

The VSW passes packets back and forth from the virtual network clients in the guest domains to the physical network interfaces. It also acts as a simple layer-2 switch, or bridge, for network traffic between domains.

For the `add-vsw` subcommand, you can specify a MAC address for the switch using the `mac-addr` parameter. This parameter is optional; if you do not specify a MAC address for the switch, one is automatically allocated from the range used by LDoms. The `net-dev` parameter is also optional. If you do not specify a physical NIC, the virtual switch only passes traffic between domains that are configured to use the switch. None of that network traffic leaves the system.

You can define more than one instance of these services so that you can assign different services to different domains. For example, you might want some domains to share one virtual switch with a physical NIC and another set of domains to share a different virtual switch with a different NIC. To create a new switch, simply define one with a different name:

```
# ldm add-vsw net-dev=bge1 primary-vsw1 primary
# ldm list -l primary
...
VSW
    NAME            MAC                 NET-DEV   DEVICE    MODE
    primary-vsw0    00:14:4f:fb:fa:49   bge0      switch@0  prog,promisc
    primary-vsw1    00:14:39:eb:fc:58   bge1      switch@1  prog,promisc
...
```

This new virtual switch is named `primary-vsw1`.

The Virtual Console Concentrator Service

The VCC service communicates with the virtual network terminal server daemon (`vntsd`) and handles all of the console I/O. The `vntsd` is managed by the `svc:/ldoms/vntsd` SMF service and is documented in the `vntsd(1M)` man page.

> **TIP** Create the VCC service before enabling the `vntsd` SMF service so that once the `vntsd` service starts, it can find the VCC service in the domain.

When you create a VCC service you must specify the port range to use — that's the range of TCP ports to use for the console connections. The `ldm list` subcommand shows which port is assigned to the console of each domain in the `CONS` column:

```
# ldm list
NAME        STATE     FLAGS   CONS   VCPU   MEMORY    UTIL   UPTIME
primary     active    -n-cv   SP     4      4100M     1.0%   17h 4m
mydomain    active    -t--v   5000   6      3000M     0.0%   4s
```

In this case the primary domain's console server is the service processor (SP), and mydomain's console is on port 5000, so you access its console using `telnet` to that port:

```
# telnet localhost 5000
```

You can also connect to domain consoles over the network if access is configured in the `vntsd` SMF manifest.

The vntsd service defaults to listening for connections on localhost (IP address 127.0.0.1), so you can only access domain consoles from the control domain by telnet to localhost. However, by changing the service configuration you can enable remote access. This example reconfigures the console service for remote access:

```
# svccfg
svc:> select ldoms/vntsd
svc:/ldoms/vntsd> listprop
vntsd                         application
vntsd/timeout_minutes         integer  0
vntsd/vcc_device              astring  virtual-console-concentrator@0
vntsd/listen_addr             astring  localhost
...
svc:/ldoms/vntsd> setprop vntsd/listen_addr = 192.168.0.21
svc:/ldoms/vntsd> exit
# svcadm refresh ldoms/vntsd
# svcadm restart ldoms/vntsd
```

You can now access domain consoles from a different machine by telnet-ing to the specified host, like this:

```
% telnet 192.168.0.21 5000
```

A hostname can also be used instead of an IP address.

The vntsd service also include two other properties: timeout_minutes and vcc_device. timeout_minutes controls how long a connection can be inactive before it is closed. A value of 0 means no timeout. The vcc_device property specifies which instance of the VCC service to use.

Physical I/O

When you initially set up the control domain you also configured it as an I/O and service domain. Until now you have only used the virtual I/O services provided by that single domain, but the PCI Express (PCI-E) bus on a T1000 server has two ports with different leaf nodes. These ports are named pci@780 (bus_a) and pci@7c0 (bus_b). The PCI-E bus can be configured to assign each leaf to a different domain. This enables you to have two domains with direct access to physical devices, as an alternative to using virtual I/O. The ldm list output shows the bus configuration in the IO section, as shown here:

```
# ldm list -l primary
...
IO
    DEVICE          PSEUDONYM         OPTIONS
    pci@780         bus_a
    pci@7c0         bus_b
...
```

The number of buses, and thus the number of I/O domains, varies by hardware platform. The procedure to configure a split PCI-E bus varies depending on the hardware so follow the procedure in the documentation for your specific hardware. The example in this section is for a T1000.

It is critical that you keep the system boot disk in the primary domain; otherwise, the system won't boot. First determine which leaf of the PCI-E bus the boot disk is on. The system used in the example booted from disk c0t0d0. You can use ls to look at the dev tree and determine which bus the boot disk is on, as shown in this example:

```
# ls -l /dev/dsk/c0t0d0s0
lrwxrwxrwx   1 root      root          49 Jan  7 11:55 /dev/dsk/c0t0d0s0 ->
  ../../devices/pci@7c0/pci@0/pci@8/scsi@2/sd@0,0:a
```

You can see from the device path that this disk is on the pci@7c0, or bus_b, leaf. Thus, bus_b must remain configured in the primary domain, but bus_a can be configured into a different domain. Now that you know which side of the bus the boot disk is on, you can remove the other side of the bus from the primary-domain:

```
# ldm rm-io pci@780 primary
```

At this point, save this new configuration to the system controller:

```
# ldm add-config split-bus
# ldm ls-config
factory-default
myconfig [current]
split-bus [next]
```

The add-config and ls-config subcommands are described in more detail in the section "Managing configurations on the system controller" later in this chapter.

Once the system has rebooted, you can observe the change to the I/O resource in the primary domain. Now, the other side of the bus is available to add to a different domain. In this example, only bus_b is currently configured in the primary domain, and bus_a is free for use in another domain:

```
# ldm ls -l primary
...
IO
    DEVICE            PSEUDONYM         OPTIONS
    pci@7c0           bus_b
...
# ldm ls-devices
...
IO
    DEVICE            PSEUDONYM
    pci@780           bus_a
```

You can now add this bus to a different domain using the add-io subcommand:

```
# ldm add-io pci@780 mydomain
Initiating delayed reconfigure operation on LDom mydomain.  All configuration
changes for other LDoms are disabled until the LDom reboots, at which time
the new configuration for LDom mydomain will also take effect.
# ldm list -l mydomain
NAME            STATE      FLAGS   CONS   VCPU  MEMORY   UTIL  UPTIME
mydomain        active     -nd--   5000   6     3000M    0.1%  6h 51m
...
IO
    DEVICE          PSEUDONYM        OPTIONS
    pci@780         bus_a
...
```

After rebooting mydomain to activate the configuration change, mydomain has physical access to the I/O devices on the bus. This domain is now considered an I/O domain and could also act as a service domain, providing virtual I/O services, to other domains, just as the primary domain does. Any NICs or HBAs on the bus are directly accessible, as shown with the primary domain.

Creating services in a different domain

Creating a service in a different domain causes that domain to assume the role of a service domain. This example adds a new instance of the Virtual Switch Service to mydomain:

```
# ldm add-vsw alternate-vsw0 mydomain
Initiating delayed reconfigure operation on LDom mydomain.  All configuration
changes for other LDoms are disabled until the LDom reboots, at which time
the new configuration for LDom mydomain will also take effect.
# ldm list
NAME        STATE      FLAGS   CONS   VCPU  MEMORY   UTIL  UPTIME
primary     active     -n-cv   SP     4     4100M    0.3%  11h 28m
mydomain    active     -nd-v   5000   6     3000M    0.1%  11h 25m
```

This defined an instance of a virtual switch service in mydomain. You can see that it is now a service domain by the v flag in the list output. Other guest domains can be configured to use that switch service instead of the switch service configured in the primary domain. Configuring services in different domains is useful if that domain has alternate physical devices configured, if you want to spread the service load for a fully virtual service, or if you want to provide redundancy in case one of the service domains reboots.

CPU, memory, and MAU

You set values for CPU and memory in the initial example using the set-vcpu and set-memory subcommands. There is also a set-mau subcommand to set the number of

MAUs assigned to the domain. The add-vcpu, add-memory, and add-mau subcommands enable you to increment these settings. The rm-vcpu, rm-memory, and rm-mau subcommands are used to remove these resources from the domain. Here, two virtual CPUs are removed from mydomain:

```
# ldm rm-vcpu 2 mydomain
```

The number of virtual CPUs that can be bound at any one time is limited by the number of hardware threads on the processor. You can allocate more virtual CPUs than there are threads, but you won't be able to bind all of the domains at the same time. To dynamically add or remove CPUs from a domain, the svc:/platform/sun4v/drd SMF service must be enabled within the domain. The following example enables the service:

```
# svcadm enable svc:/platform/sun4v/drd
```

> **TIP** The number of hardware threads in each core varies by processor model. When you bind virtual CPUs to hardware threads, the hypervisor assigns threads in order. That is, if you bind four threads to a domain, then those four threads would be on the same core, assuming that the core supports at least four threads and no other domain is bound. This has implications for how the common resources within a core, such as caches, are shared. Over time, if you reallocate virtual CPUs across domains, any sharing of the L1 cache within a core can be lost. This might affect the performance of the OS and applications running within a domain.

Memory can be assigned in units of bytes, kilobytes (k), megabytes (m) or gigabytes, with a granularity of 8KB.

While CPUs and memory are commonplace, the MAU is a device you might not be familiar with. The sun4v version of the SPARC architecture supports a special-purpose mathematical unit that is used to accelerate cryptographic processing. This is increasingly important for secure networked applications. Within the T1 processor, each CPU core also includes an MAU. The flexibility to configure the MAUs is limited by the hardware. While the T1 processor supports 32 threads, it only supports eight MAUs, one per CPU core. Other SPARC processors might have different limitations. Because of the hardware design regarding how the threads interact with the MAU, when an MAU is bound to a domain, at least one thread from the corresponding core must also be bound to that domain. This imposes some limitations on how virtual CPUs, which correspond to hardware threads, can be bound to domains because you must ensure that a thread from the core is bound to each domain that also has an MAU allocated. This complexity means that it's best not to allocate an MAU to a domain unless it is actually needed. As with threads, MAUs are allocated by the hypervisor, in order, as you bind domains. For simplicity when allocating an MAU to a domain, it is usually best to allocate all of the threads from the core to the domain as well.

The floating-point units (FPUs) on the system are handled differently and do not have the same limitations as the MAU.

Virtual Disks

Recall that virtual disks are added to a guest domain using the `add-vdisk` subcommand. Here's the command you used to add the virtual disk when you first configured `mydomain`:

```
# ldm add-vdisk vdisk1 vol1@primary-vds0 mydomain
```

The `add-visk` subcommand simply maps a virtual disk for the guest domain into a VDSDEV configured in the virtual disk service. Here the virtual disk is named `vdisk1` and the VDSDEV in the `primary-vds0` service is `vol1`. This command also accepts one option, a timeout:

```
# ldm add-vdisk timeout=10 vdisk2 vol2@primary-vds0 mydomain
```

The timeout specifies the number of seconds before the virtual disk times out if it cannot establish a connection to the associated virtual disk service. After the timeout, the application receives a disk error. Without a specific timeout, the virtual disk will not return an error to the application and waits forever. The timeout is shown in the `TOUT` column of the `list -l` subcommand output:

```
# ldm list -l mydomain
...
DISK
    NAME            VOLUME                      TOUT DEVICE  SERVER
    vdisk1          vol1@primary-vds0                disk@0  primary
    vdisk2          vol2@primary-vds0           10   disk@1  primary
...
```

Within the domain the virtual disks are assigned logical disk names in the order that they are configured:

```
# format
Searching for disks...done


AVAILABLE DISK SELECTIONS:
       0. c0d0 <SUN-DiskImage-10GB cyl 34950 alt 2 hd 1 sec 600>
          /virtual-devices@100/channel-devices@200/disk@0
       1. c0d1 <SUN-DiskImage-10GB cyl 34950 alt 2 hd 1 sec 600>
          /virtual-devices@100/channel-devices@200/disk@1
```

The disk names are listed in the `ldm list` output under the `DEVICE` column and you can see how those map to the device path in the guest domain. Here the `c0d0` disk maps to `vol1`, with the device name disk@0, and `c0d1` maps to `vol2`, with the device name disk@1.

Each virtual disk has a cndn style name. Virtual disks that support partitioning, such as a whole disk or a disk file, will have the full set of disk slices named within the domain. Virtual disks that only support a single slice, such as a corresponding physical slice, only have one slice named in devfs within the domain.

The `rm-vdisk` subcommand removes a virtual disk from the domain:

```
# ldm rm-vdisk vdisk2 mydomain
```

Disk Redundancy

Recall that if the service domain goes down or reboots, any virtual disk I/O using that domain pauses until the service is restored. This is much like a storage area network (SAN), where any interruption within the SAN affects the disk I/O. You can avoid the problem by configuring two service domains and a redundant disk service. Simply configure two virtual disks into the domain, each of which is bound to a different service domain, and then mirror the disks within the domain by using ZFS or SVM. A disk mirror is the simplest configuration, but more complex redundant configurations are possible.

See Chapter 7 for information on SVM, and Chapter 8 for information on ZFS.

Networking

Virtual network interfaces are configured for a guest domain using the `add-vnet` subcommand, as shown in the initial example using this command:

```
# ldm add-vnet vnet0 primary-vsw0 mydomain
```

This virtual network interface is bound to the `primary-vsw0` virtual switch, and within the guest domain it has the name `vnet0`. The `add-vnet` subcommand takes one optional argument that enables you to specify a MAC address for the interface. If you don't explicitly set the MAC address, one is automatically assigned. This example explicitly sets a MAC address on the interface:

```
# ldm add-vnet mac-addr=80:00:33:55:22:66 vnet0 primary-vsw0 mydomain
```

The `ldm list` subcommand shows the MAC address that was assigned:

```
# ldm list -l mydomain
...
NETWORK
    NAME            SERVICE                 DEVICE        MAC
    vnet0           primary-vsw0@primary    network@0     80:00:33:55:22:66
...
```

The `DEVICE` column shows the name in the device tree within the domain. You can see this by looking at the device tree with `ls`, as shown here:

```
# ls -l /devices/virtual-devices\@100/channel-devices\@200
...
drwxr-xr-x   2 root      sys           512 Feb 20 07:57 network@0
```

```
crw-rw-rw-  1 root    sys      289, 1 Feb 22 15:31 network@0:vnet0
...
```

Use the `set-vnet` subcommand to change the MAC address of an existing VNET, and the `rm-vnet` subcommand to remove the VNET:

```
# ldm rm-vnet vnet0 mydomain
```

Network Redundancy

As with virtual disks, virtual network interfaces depend on their service domain, and connectivity is interrupted if the service domain is unavailable. However, you can configure a redundant configuration, much like you did with virtual disks, by adding two different VNETs into the domain, each of which is provided by a different service domain, and then configuring those interfaces into an IP multi-pathing (IPMP) group.

See Chapter 9 for information on IPMP.

Console

For the initial example you created a virtual console concentrator (VCC) service in the primary domain but you never configured a console for the guest domain. Virtual consoles are made available over TCP using the port range specified when you configured the VCC. As you saw, if no console was explicitly configured for a domain, one is automatically allocated when the domain is started. The port number is shown in the `ldm list` output.

You can explicitly set a console port number for a domain using the `set-vcons` subcommand. This subcommand can be used only if the domain is not already bound to its resources. To change the console settings for an existing domain, first unbind it:

```
# ldm stop mydomain
LDom mydomain stopped
# ldm unbind mydomain
# ldm set-vcons port=5010 mydomain
# ldm bind mydomain
# ldm list
NAME        STATE    FLAGS   CONS   VCPU  MEMORY   UTIL  UPTIME
primary     active   -n-cv   SP     4     4100M    0.5%  17h 18m
mydomain    bound    -----   5010   6     3000M
```

The `list` output indicates in the CONS column that the domain is now using port 5010. The long listing shows the port, along with the VCC service that the domain's console is using:

```
# ldm list -l mydomain
...
VCONS
```

```
        NAME                    SERVICE                 PORT
        mydomain                primary-vcc0@primary    5010
```

The primary domain's console is provided by the system's service processor (SP), as shown in the VCONS section of the list output for the primary domain:

```
# ldm list -l primary
...
VCONS
        NAME                    SERVICE                 PORT
        SP
```

The set-vcons subcommand also enables you to set other options for the console. To specify a specific VCC, use the service option. If you had configured a second VCC service named alt-vcc, you could associate the domain's console to that service like this:

```
# ldm set-vcons service=alt-vcc mydomain
```

You can group more than one domain's console onto a single port using the group option:

```
# ldm set-vcons group=grp1 mydomain
# ldm list -l mydomain
...
VCONS
        NAME                    SERVICE                 PORT
        grp1                    primary-vcc0@primary    5010
```

The NAME for the virtual console is now the group name you assigned instead of the domain name. The vntsd, described earlier, manages the connections to the domain consoles. If there is only a single console in the group, the vntsd simply connects the telnet command to the console. However, if there is more than one console in the group, as the following example shows, you are prompted for the console to connect to:

```
# ldm set-vcons port=5010 group=grp1 mydomain2
# ldm bind mydomain2
# telnet localhost 5010
Trying 127.0.0.1...
Connected to localhost.
Escape character is '^]'.

myhost-vnts-grp1: h, l, c{id}, n{name}, q: nmydomain
Connecting to console "mydomain" in group "grp1" ....
Press ~? for control options ..
```

Here you bound a second domain to the same group and port. When you connect to the port, the vntsd prompts you to choose the domain you want to connect to. The example used the n option to specify mydomain. The l option shows a list of domains:

```
myhost-vnts-grp1: h, l, c{id}, n{name}, q:l
```

```
DOMAIN ID              DOMAIN NAME                 DOMAIN STATE
0                      mydomain                    online
1                      mydomain2                   online
```

The c option can be used instead of the n option if you want to specify the domain ID. The DOMAIN STATE column shows the status of the console. When the console is not in use, the state is online. If another user is already connected to the console, the state is connected. In the following example the c option is used to select the console for domain 0:

```
myhost-vnts-grp1: h, l, c{id}, n{name}, q:1
DOMAIN ID              DOMAIN NAME                 DOMAIN STATE
0                      mydomain                    connected
1                      mydomain2                   online

myhost-vnts-grp1: h, l, c{id}, n{name}, q: c0
Connecting to console "mydomain" in group "grp1" ....
Press ~? for control options ..
You do not have write access
```

More than one user can connect to a domain's console but only the first user to connect is given write access. Subsequent users connect read-only, as in the previous example. When the first user drops off the console, the next user in line is given write access. If necessary, you can use the ~w command as the first input on a line to force write-access, as shown here:

```
~w
Warning: another user currently has write permission
to this console and forcibly removing him/her will terminate
any current write action and all work will be lost.
Would you like to continue?[y/n] y
```

This action forces the original console connection that had read-write access into read-only mode.

> **TIP** You can use the special ~p or ~n commands to toggle to the previous or next console in the group. The ~# command sends a break to the domain, and ~. drops the connection.

Variables

You configure OBP variables for the domain using the add-var or set-var subcommands. These commands are essentially equivalent, although you can use the set-var subcommand to clear a variable's value by not providing a value for the variable. This is the setting you configured in the initial example:

```
# ldm set-var auto-boot\?=false mydomain
```

Use the rm-var subcommand to remove a variable from the configuration.

Other administrative subcommands

The previous sections described the various subcommands for creating and modifying the configuration of your domains. The final subcommand for managing the configuration is the destroy subcommand, which deletes a domain definition. You must first unbind the domain from its resources before you can destroy it:

```
# ldm unbind mydomain
# ldm destroy mydomain
# ldm list
NAME         STATE      FLAGS    CONS    VCPU    MEMORY    UTIL    UPTIME
primary      active     -n-cv    SP      4       4100M     0.3%    36m
```

In addition to the subcommands used for configuration, there are subcommands to manage the state of the domains themselves. You have used the bind, start, and stop subcommands in the examples. The start and stop commands take a -a option that applies the command to all domains:

```
# ldm stop -a
```

You do not specify a domain name in this case. You use the unbind command to detach a domain from its resources. You can also use the panic subcommand to cause a domain to panic and generate a crash dump:

```
# ldm panic mydomain
```

On the console of mydomain you would see the following.

```
#
panic[cpu0]/thread=2a10001fca0: Panic - Generated at user request

000002a10001f6a0 unix:process_nonresumable_error+2f8 (2a10001f890, 5, 40, 40,
  1, 100000000)
    %l0-3: 000000000180c5f0 0000000000000000 0000000000000000 000000000000ffff
    %l4-7: 0000000003000000 0000000000000000 0000000000000000 0000000000000000
000002a10001f7e0 unix:ktl0+64 (0, 3f, 185d4d0, 3c, 0, 12)
    %l0-3: 000000000180c000 0000000000000000 0000000001406 0000000001026d0c
    %l4-7: 0000000000000000 0000000000000000 0000000000000000 000002a10001f890
000002a10001f930 unix:cpu_halt+130 (0, 1, 180c000, 1875fd8, 0, 1)
    %l0-3: 000000000186faf4 0000000000000000 0000000000000000 000000000185d4d0
    %l4-7: 0000000000000000 0000000000000000 0000000000000016 0000000000000001
000002a10001f9e0 unix:idle+120 (30003dfcb60, 6, 180c000, ffffffffffffffff, 1,
  1829400)
    %l0-3: 000000000186fad0 000000000000001b ffffffffffffffff 0000000000000000
    %l4-7: 0000000000000000 0000000000000000 000000000103f6b8 000000000182a800

syncing file systems... 5 3 done
dumping to /dev/dsk/c0d0s1, offset 107413504, content: kernel
100% done: 55424 pages dumped, compression ratio 10.36, dump succeeded
rebooting...
```

Managing configurations on the system controller

When you set up the first example and when you created the split bus configuration, you saved those configurations to the system's service processor. On a T1000, the service processor can save eight different configurations. The capabilities vary by platform, so check the system documentation for your specific hardware. Each configuration represents the complete state for all of the domains when the configuration was saved, so you can easily revert to an earlier configuration or switch from one set of domain configurations to another.

The ls-config subcommand shows the set of configurations that have been defined:

```
# ldm ls-config
factory-default
myconfig
split-bus [current]
```

Here you see the two configurations that have been defined in the examples, along with the factory-default configuration, which represents the base system configuration with no domains defined and can be used to revert the machine to its initial state. The factory-default configuration does not count as one of the eight you can save. The split-bus configuration, defined earlier, is the current configuration and is used when the system boots. Use the set-config subcommand to switch to a different configuration:

```
# ldm set-config myconfig
# ldm ls-config
factory-default
myconfig [next]
split-bus [current]
```

The myconfig configuration will be the active one on the next boot.

CAUTION   After the control domain reboots, the new configuration will be in effect, although the ls-config command will not show the correct data until the system has been powered off and on from the service processor.

Use the add-config subcommand to save the current configuration to the service processor; the rm-config subcommand deletes a configuration. This example deletes the split-bus configuration you created earlier:

```
# ldm rm-config split-bus
```

Migrating a domain from one machine to another

LDoms can be migrated between machines, but as of this writing the domain cannot be running when it is moved, unlike xVM, which supports hot migration. Start by saving the domain configuration to a file using the ls-constraints subcommand with the -x option, which creates an XML description of the domain.

 Use the `ls-constraints` subcommand to save a backup of the domain definition at any time.

In the following example, the command prompts `src#` or `dst#` are used to indicate on which machine the command is being executed:

```
src# ldm ls-constraints -x mydomain >/domains/mydomain
src# cat /domains/mydomain

<?xml version="1.0"?>

<LDM_interface version="1.1" xmlns:xsi="http://www.w3.org/2001/XMLSchema
-instance" xsi:noNamespaceSchemaLocation="./schemas/combined-v3.xsd"
 xmlns:ovf="./schemas/envelope" xmlns:rasd="./schemas/CIM
_ResourceAllocationSettingData" xmlns:vssd="./schemas/CIM
_VirtualSystemSettingData" xmlns:gprop="./schemas/GenericProperty"
 xmlns:bind="./schemas/Binding">
  <data version="3.0">
    <Envelope>
      <References/>
      <Content xsi:type="ovf:VirtualSystem_Type" ovf:id="mydomain">
        <Section xsi:type="ovf:ResourceAllocationSection_Type">
          <Item>
            <rasd:OtherResourceType>ldom_info</rasd:OtherResourceType>
            <rasd:Address>auto-allocated</rasd:Address>
          </Item>
...
</LDM_interface>
```

Now you must copy this file to the new host and recreate the domain on that system. If the new host is not already set up to support guest domains, free resources and create the required services, just as you did in the initial example when you set up the control domain, and as shown here on the `dst` system:

```
dst# ldm list
NAME           STATE    FLAGS    CONS    VCPU   MEMORY    UTIL   UPTIME
primary        active   -n-cv    SP      32     8000M     0.1%   36m

dst# ldm set-mau 0 primary
dst# ldm set-vcpu 8 primary
dst# ldm add-vds primary-vds0 primary
dst# ldm add-vsw net-dev=bge0 primary-vsw0 primary
dst# ldm add-vcc port-range=5000-5100 primary-vcc0 primary
dst# ldm add-vdsdev /p1/myldom/zdisk vol1@primary-vds0
dst# ldm add-config myconfig
```

After rebooting to activate the new configuration, you can enable the `vntsd` service and complete the setup for the guest domain:

```
dst# svcadm enable svc:/ldoms/vntsd:default
```

Make sure a copy of the disk image is available on the new host. Because the original domain simply used a file for the boot disk, you can copy that file to the new host, as shown here:

```
dst# cd /p1/myldom
dst# scp src:/p1/myldom/zdisk .
...
dst# chmod 1600 zdisk
```

For a physical disk slice or disk, you may need to copy the data from one disk to another, physically recable the disk to the new host, or perhaps reconfigure your SAN. The exact procedure varies depending on how the storage is configured between the two machines.

Now create the domain from the XML file that you copied from the source system:

```
dst# ldm create -i /tmp/mydomain
dst# ldm list
NAME            STATE      FLAGS   CONS    VCPU   MEMORY   UTIL   UPTIME
primary         active     -n-cv   SP      4      4100M    0.5%   17m
mydomain        inactive   -----           4      2G
```

Here you use the -i option on the create subcommand to define the domain using the XML specification that was saved on the first machine. Depending on the configuration of the virtual services on the new host, you may need to make adjustments to the new guest domain configuration. Check the service names and the associations between the guest domain and the control domain to ensure that all of the virtual services that the guest is defined to use are correctly set up in the control domain.

Finally, you can bind the domain to its resources and start it:

```
dst# ldm bind mydomain
dst# ldm start mydomain
```

Hardening the control domain

Because the control domain has complete administrative control over all domains on the system, it is important to limit access and lock down the security of the control domain. The LDom management software that you downloaded includes plug-ins for the Solaris Security Toolkit, delivered in the SUNWjass package. Because that software is not part of OpenSolaris, it is not discussed in detail here, but you should consider consulting the *LDoms Administration Guide* for information on using that toolkit with LDoms. In addition, Chapter 11 describes OpenSolaris security in detail, explaining how to configure and improve the security of OpenSolaris.

Resources

The LDoms community is at http://opensolaris.org/os/community/ldoms. On the LDoms community page are links to download the hypervisor firmware, management software, articles, and documentation, as well as a link to the LDoms discussion where community members ask and answer questions.

The Solaris Security Toolkit can be downloaded at `http://sun.com/download`.

The SPARC architecture and processor definitions that support the `sun4v` hypervisor have been open-sourced under the GPLv2 license. The documentation and specifications can be found at `www.opensparc.net`.

One of the other projects that works with LDoms is the xVM OpsCenter project at `openxvm.org` and `xvmserver.org`.

If you are interested in the architecture and design of LDoms, the ARC cases are available on the ARC community at `http://opensolaris.org/os/community/arc`, although not all of the cases have been opened up yet. In particular, the umbrella case for LDoms is *FWARC/2005/633 LDoms: Project Q Logial Domaining Umbrella (sun4v/hypervisor/LDoms)*.

However, there are many other LDom-related cases, subsequent to the original 2005/633 case, that document the architecture of specific subsystems.

If you are interested in the source code, the paravirtualization of OpenSolaris to work with LDoms is in the platform-specific kernel modules, and the code is under `usr/src/uts/sun4v`. The `vntsd` daemon is under `usr/src/cmd/vntsd`.

Summary

This chapter explored LDoms, the OpenSolaris type 1 hypervisor virtualization feature for SPARC. Using LDoms enables you to create isolated, independent environments and run different operating systems in each one, while sharing the same underlying hardware resources. The features, configuration, and management of LDoms were detailed.

VirtualBox

VirtualBox is an open source type 2 hypervisor that can be used on OpenSolaris and a variety of other systems. As described in Chapter 17, a type 2 hypervisor runs on top of the *host* operating system, so it is extremely easy to install, set up, and use. However, performance is usually not as good as with a type 1 hypervisor. Given these trade-offs, VirtualBox is an excellent solution for users, such as software developers, who need the capability to easily and concurrently run different operating systems, but it might not be the right solution for deploying a production system.

One of the advantages of VirtualBox is that it runs on many different host operating systems, including OpenSolaris, Mac OS, Windows, and various distributions of Linux, such as Debian, Fedora, Red Hat, SUSE, Ubuntu, and others. Because of this, it provides an attractive way to start using OpenSolaris, even if your system has no free partition to install and run on bare metal.

To run VirtualBox, you need an x86-based system running one of the supported host operating systems, and you should have enough extra memory and disk space, and a fairly powerful CPU to support running the hypervisor.

As shown in this chapter, a VirtualBox virtual machine (VM) can be configured to emulate many different facets of a modern x86-based PC. This enables a wide variety of guest operating systems to run, including DOS, many flavors of Windows, from 3.1 through Vista, different versions of Linux, different versions of BSD, Netware, and, of course, OpenSolaris.

This chapter focuses primarily on using OpenSolaris as both the host OS and guest OS, but you can consult the VirtualBox manual for specifics on using different operating systems as either the host or the guest.

Getting Started

Download and install the VirtualBox software from the Downloads link at `http://virtualbox.org`. You can choose prebuilt software for the host operating system you are using. For OpenSolaris, there is both a 32-bit and a 64-bit download, so be sure to select the correct one based on which kernel you are running. If you are running a different host OS, select the appropriate download and, if necessary, read the manual for details on installing and using the software on your system.

> **NOTE** You can also download the source code and build it yourself, if you prefer. The source download links are also on the `virtualbox.org` web page.

After the software has been downloaded and unpacked, install the package. As of this writing, only traditional SVR4 packages are available.

This example installs VirtualBox 2.0.4, although new versions are released regularly, and there will certainly be a newer version available by the time you read this:

```
# pkgadd -d VirtualBox-2.0.4-SunOS-amd64-r36488.pkg
```

> **NOTE** Also available is a second package that delivers an OpenSolaris kernel driver, which provides an abstraction layer for the kernel services used by VirtualBox. Newer versions of OpenSolaris already include the driver, but you need to install it on older versions. The `ReadMe.txt` file included with the download explains how to determine whether your system needs the extra package.

Configuring and installing a virtual machine

Once VirtualBox is installed, a nonprivileged user can start it and manage his or her personal VMs. The following command starts VirtualBox (or you can use the Gnome menu System Tools ➤ Sun xVM VirtualBox):

```
$ VirtualBox &
```

VirtualBox provides a simple, easy-to-use GUI that enables you to create and manage your VMs. Figure 22-1 shows the first VirtualBox window you'll see.

This is the primary management window for your VMs. It is mostly empty because you don't have any VMs yet; when you create a new VM, it will show up in the panel on the left. The panel on the right shows information about the selected VM, and the controls across the top enable you to manage the VM.

FIGURE 22-1

Main VirtualBox window

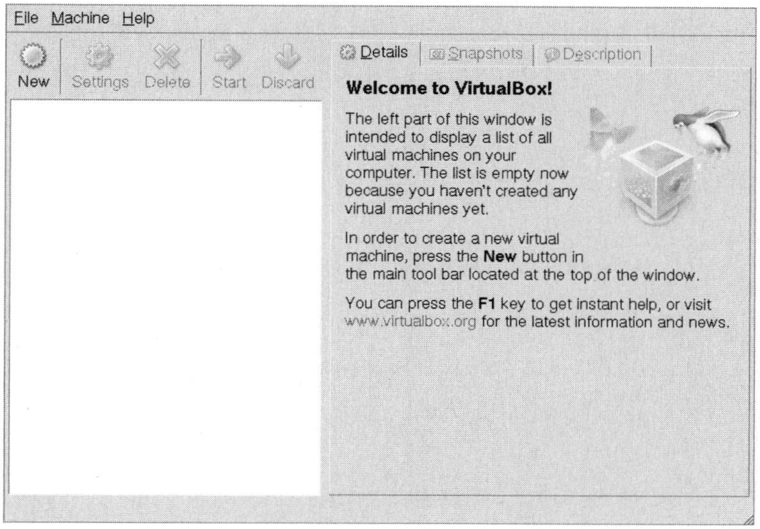

As the GUI instructs, click the New button to create a new VM. This brings up a wizard that walks you through the steps to create the VM. The GUI and its wizards are easy to use and understand, so each step is only summarized here. You create each new VM using a similar sequence.

1. Name the VM and choose what guest OS will run in the VM. In this example, the VM is named `myvb` and the guest OS is OpenSolaris.

2. Pick the base memory size for the VM. This can range from 4MB to 2GB. You can always change this later, so don't worry too much about what value you choose now. For running OpenSolaris, 1GB is a reasonable value. 512MB is the minimum required to install OpenSolaris.

3. Set up a virtual hard disk for the VM. This will be a file on the host OS that is used to emulate a disk drive for the VM. You can create a new virtual disk file or use an existing one. Because this is the first VM you're creating, choose New. That brings up a second wizard to help you create the disk file. You can choose a dynamically expanding or fixed-size file. Dynamically expanding is usually a good choice because only the space that is actually needed is used. Specify a filename and location in the file system. The default location is in your home directory under `.VirtualBox/VDI`, but you can place the file anywhere. You also need to set a size limit — anywhere from 4MB to 2TB — for the file. For this example, use 10GB, which is more than enough to install OpenSolaris and store additional

data files. A minimum of 4GB is recommended for an OpenSolaris guest. This completes the steps in the virtual disk wizard.

Now you're back in the VM creation wizard and are ready to finish. The wizard shows a summary screen and if everything looks correct, you can complete creating the VM.

Figure 22-2 shows the main window once the VM has been created.

FIGURE 22-2

Updated main window

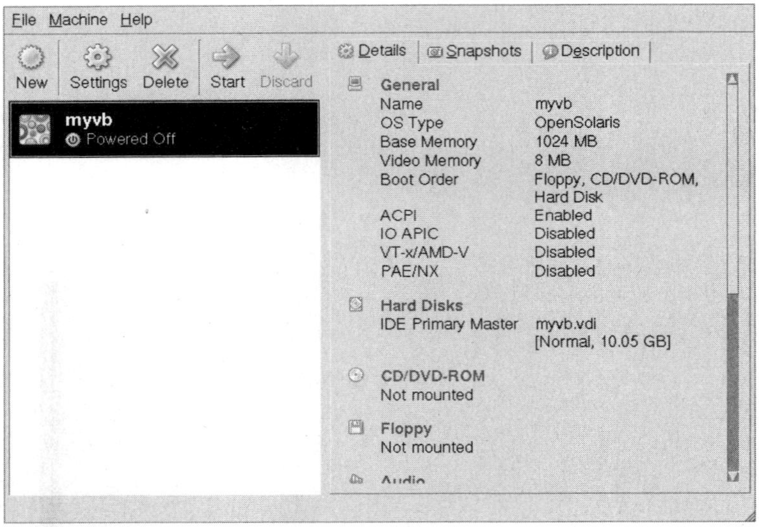

The new VM appears in the left panel, and details about its configuration are in the right panel. When multiple VMs are configured, details for the selected VM are displayed on the right. The newly enabled buttons across the top enable you to modify the selected VM configuration, delete the selected VM, or start it.

Booting and installing the guest OS

The next step is to boot the new VM and install the guest OS. To boot the VM, click the Start button. The first time you boot a new VM, VirtualBox opens the First Run Wizard. This wizard sets up the VM so that it is easy to install the guest OS. Within the wizard, you select the installation media, which can be a physical CD-ROM/DVD in the host's drive, or an ISO image file. In this example, you can install from the same ISO image file described in Chapter 2 — the OpenSolaris distribution image that you can download from OpenSolaris.com. If you are installing a different open source guest OS, you can usually download an ISO image from the site hosting that project. If you have physical media containing the guest OS, you could choose to install using the host system's CD-ROM/DVD drive, or, if you are running OpenSolaris, you can make an ISO file from the media by using the dd command, described in Chapter 7. This frees up the host's CD-ROM/DVD drive and enables you to keep the image file online for use in subsequent installs.

With the install media selected, finish the wizard and the VM will boot from that media. During the boot, a terminal console pops up and you get the grub menu, just as you would on a standalone system (and as described in Chapter 2). When the default grub entry starts to boot, VirtualBox switches from using a terminal-based console to running the guest OS window system embedded within a window on the host OS window system (see Figure 22-3).

FIGURE 22-3

OpenSolaris VM running within a window

TIP You can also find guest OS images for VirtualBox on the web. These VirtualBox disk images are pre-installed with a guest OS and therefore ready to run. One site hosting a variety of images is http://virtualbox.wordpress.com, although you can easily find others by searching for "vitualbox images." Instructions for installing these images are available on the various download sites, or you can usually just set up the virtual disk as described in the "Storage" section later in this chapter, which also explains how you can directly use VMware VMDK images.

If you have already installed OpenSolaris on a standalone system, this screen will look familiar because the VM window is the same screen you saw when you booted the Live CD to perform the installation. To proceed with installing OpenSolaris in the VM at this point, simply follow the procedures outlined in Chapter 2.

NOTE If you have never used a VM before, this window may seem a little strange. When your focus is outside of the window, you are interacting with your host OS window system. However, when your focus shifts inside of the window, you are interacting with the guest OS window system running inside the window. This can be a big adjustment when you are running a different OS as the host and guest because the behavior changes based on the window system that has the focus.

Look closely at Figure 22-3 to see the window border with the usual Gnome window controls. (The window border will have the normal controls for the specific host OS that you're running.) Immediately within the Gnome window border you can see the VirtualBox menus in the control bar at the top, and various informative icons in the strip along the bottom. These are described in greater detail in the next section. Finally, the guest OS occupies the body of the window.

Once your mouse focus is captured in the VirtualBox window, the physical mouse will control the mouse cursor for the guest OS and you won't be able to use the mouse for the host OS window system. This normally happens once you click within the window. VirtualBox uses a special key — the *Host Key* — to release the mouse from the guest OS window system back to the host OS. This key is shown in bottom, right corner of the VirtualBox icon strip at the bottom of the window. By default, the Host Key is the right Ctrl key, but in Figure 22-4 you can see that the Host Key is currently configured to be F10. Before running a VM, either confirm that the right Ctrl key exists on your keyboard or change the setting to use a different key. Configuring the Host Key is described in the next section.

FIGURE 22-4

Host Key location

Host Key

CAUTION You used the VirtualBox First Run Wizard to temporarily configure the VM to boot from the OpenSolaris ISO image. If you stop the VM before installing OpenSolaris, the next time you try to start the VM, there won't be any installed OS for the VM to run. The next section describes how you can manually configure the VM to boot from the ISO image.

Managing VirtualBox

The basic controls for managing an individual VM are available on the running VM window, and the management GUI enables you to manage all of the virtual machines.

The running VM window

Each running VM appears in its own window (refer to Figure 22-3). This window includes a variety of controls and status indicators.

Menus

Figure 22-5 shows the VirtualBox top-level menus across the top of the guest OS window.

FIGURE 22-5

VirtualBox top-level menus

The Machine menu enables you to control the size of the window, disable the mouse, insert special key sequences such as Ctrl+Alt+Delete, take a snapshot, and control the VM. With a snapshot, you can save the state of the VM so that it can be restored to the same point the next time you start it. The VM controls enable you to reset the running VM, just as if you had reset a physical system, pause the VM so that it is not consuming any CPU resources on the host OS, and issue an ACPI (Advanced Configuration and Power Interface) shutdown. This is the same as pressing the power button on a physical system. The guest OS detects this and normally performs an orderly shutdown. If you select the Close option, you can choose to save the VM state, send the ACPI shutdown, or simply power off the VM.

NOTE Advanced Configuration and Power Interface (ACPI) is an industry standard interface used on modern x86-based hardware.

The Devices menu enables you to control the devices available to the running VM. You can mount or unmount CD/DVD or floppy drives, choose a network adapter, configure USB drives, configure shared folders, set up a remote display, or install VirtualBox guest additions. Shared folders require the guest additions, described later in the "Advanced Features" section. The remote display option enables the VirtualBox VRDP server so that you can connect to the VM from a remote machine, as discussed in more detail later in this chapter.

> **NOTE** VRDP is the VirtualBox implementation of RDP, the Remote Desktop Protocol. RDP enables clients to connect to a system running Microsoft Terminal Services and remotely use the graphical user interface. VirtualBox implements the VRDP server so that you can remotely access the VM using any RDP client.

The Help menu provides help and other information about VirtualBox.

Icons

Figure 22-6 points out the VirtualBox status icons across the bottom-right of the guest OS window. These icons show the status of the Virtual Disks, CD/DVD, Floppy, Network, USB, Shared Folders, Mouse, and Host Key. If the corresponding device is not configured for the VM, the icon is grayed out. The disk or CD icons blink as the underlying device is being accessed in the VM. You can mouse-over each icon to see a pop-up showing more information about how that item is configured.

FIGURE 22-6

VirtualBox status icons

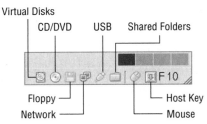

The VirtualBox management GUI

Across the top of the VirtualBox primary management GUI are the File, Machine, and Help menus. This is the GUI that enables you to create a new VM and manage existing VMs.

The File menu enables you to manage various properties of VirtualBox as a whole. It includes the Virtual Disk Manager and Preferences items. You can use the Virtual Disk Manager to browse, create, and delete your virtual disks, CD/DVD images, and floppy images. Using Preferences, you can configure the default location for various files, enable VT-x/AMD-V support, set the Host Key, and set the language in which the GUI will display.

> **NOTE** VT-x/AMD-V support enables use of the hardware virtualization features available on newer x86 CPUs. Normally you leave this disabled because VirtualBox uses fast software techniques to provide virtualization. However, you need to enable this feature to run 64-bit guest operating systems. OpenSolaris automatically runs in either 32-bit or 64-bit mode, depending on the hardware, so you don't need a CPU with virtualization support to run OpenSolaris as a guest. See the VirtualBox manual for recommendations on other situations in which to use this feature. On OpenSolaris, the manual is installed at /opt/VirtualBox/UserManual.pdf.

The Machine menu includes the same five controls that are displayed in the main window: New, Settings, Delete, Start, and Discard. It also has a Pause item that you use to pause the selected VM when it is running, and a Show Log item you can use to view the VirtualBox log file.

The Help menu offers the same help options as the Help menu on the running VM window.

Recall that the left pane in the main window lists your VMs. When you select one of those VMs, data about it is displayed in the right pane, which has three tabs:

- **Details** — Displays information about the VM configuration
- **Snap** — Lists the snapshots for the VM
- **Description** — Shows your description of the VM

As previously mentioned, snapshots are used to save the state of a VM so that you can restart the VM at the same point. Because the complete state of the VM is saved, all of the running processes within it, along with their data, including the state of persistent data on the virtual disks, are saved. When you close a VM, one option is to save its state as a snapshot. You can also take a snapshot of the VM while it is running.

> **NOTE** See the "Storage" section later in this chapter for details on how to configure virtual disks so that persistent data is not lost if you roll back to an earlier snapshot.

If you take a snapshot when you shut down the VM, restarting the VM will resume at the same point; but if you take a snapshot while the VM is running, the VM state changes immediately as the guest continues to run. This changed status is displayed in the Snapshot pane. When taking a snapshot of a running VM, you can specify a name for the snapshot and provide a description of the VM's state, which is useful if you need to revert to the snapshot later. As you continue to take snapshots of the running VM, you can see your tree of named snapshots within the Snapshot pane.

If you took a snapshot of the VM while it was running and later shut down the VM, restarting the VM can't use that snapshot because the state changed. To address this situation, you can either take a final snapshot before closing the VM, or use the management GUI to revert to an earlier snapshot. You use the Revert to Current Snapshot button in the Snapshot pane to cause the VM to start with the latest snapshot. Deleting the latest snapshot with the Discard Current Snapshot and State button enables you to restart using the previous snapshot in the tree. Each time you do this, you step back earlier in the history of your VM execution.

The VM status in the left pane shows Saved if the VM is powered off, but the latest snapshot will be used to resume the VM. Otherwise, the state will be Powered Off. The Snapshots pane also indicates whether the VM state has changed since the snapshot was taken.

You have already seen that the New button is used to create a new VM, and the Start button is used to begin running a VM. The Delete button enables you to delete the VM. If you have a saved snapshot, this button is grayed out. The Discard button can be used to remove the snapshot in this case. If the VM won't be restarted with a snapshot, the Discard button is grayed out instead. When a VM is running, the Start button is replaced by the Show button, which opens the VM window in cases when it is not currently displayed.

The last major control button is Settings (see Figure 22-7). This button is grayed out when the VM is running or will be restarted from a snapshot. If neither of these conditions holds, then the button is enabled and you can change the configuration of the VM.

FIGURE 22-7

The Settings button

FIGURE 22-8

Settings control panel

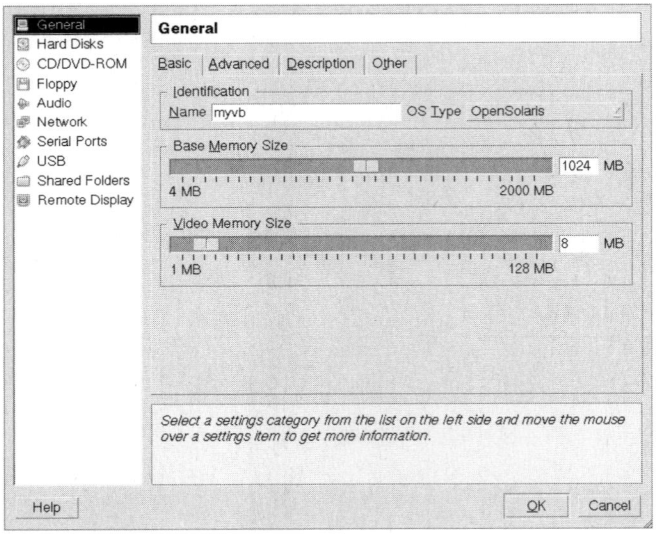

Figure 22-8 shows the Settings control panel. The various options in this control panel enable you to customize the system emulation provided by the VM. In most cases you won't need to change the settings because the defaults are appropriate for running most guests.

The different groups of settings that can be configured are listed in the left pane; select one and the options for that group are shown in the right pane. Most of the settings are either obvious or not typically changed, so only some of them are described here. The built-in help, which appears at the bottom of the right pane as you mouse over the controls, describes each control, or the VirtualBox manual can be used if you need more information.

In the General section's Advanced tab, you can select the devices that appear in the VM and change the boot order. This is similar to setting the device boot order in a standalone machine BIOS. The First Boot Wizard temporarily sets up the VM to boot from your install media, but if you later need to boot from the CD/DVD, you can set that here. You can also enable use of the VT-x/AMD-V hardware virtualization settings for the VM if you are running a 64-bit guest OS. VirtualBox requires all running VMs to use the same VT-x/AMD-V setting, so the setting for the first VM you start will dictate the behavior for any other running VMs.

In the Hard Disks settings, you can add or delete virtual disks. You can also configure the disk as the IDE primary master, IDE primary slave, or IDE secondary slave. The CD/DVD-ROM settings enable you to configure the virtual CD/DVD drive to use either the physical system drive or an ISO file. The Floppy settings provide the same capability for the virtual floppy drive.

In the Network settings you configure networking for the VM. You can configure up to four NICs for the VM. By default, a newly created VM has one NIC configured. In most cases you won't need to modify the network configuration, but networking is described in more detail later in the chapter. You can also configure the VM to emulate several different popular NIC types, in case your guest OS only has drivers for a certain NIC.

The Shared Folders and Remote Display settings are described in more detail in the following section. The Audio, Serial Ports, and USB settings are self-explanatory.

Advanced Features

VirtualBox includes several advanced features that improve the ease of use and flexibility of virtual machines.

Guest additions

The VirtualBox guest additions are a set of enhancements that can be installed in a guest OS to provide better integration between it and the host OS. The guest additions are device drivers and other applications that improve the behavior of the guest when running under VirtualBox. Guest additions are currently available for OpenSolaris, Windows, and Linux guests. It is generally recommended that you install the guest additions if you are going to be using the guest for any serious work.

TABLE 22-1

Guest Addition Features

Feature	Description
Mouse Pointer Integration	The mouse is no longer captured when you click in the guest OS window. Instead, the mouse works on windows in the guest OS when over the window.
Video Support	Window resizing works automatically. A full-screen guest OS window assumes the full resolution of the host OS window. More generally, resizing the guest OS window automatically changes the screen resolution for the guest OS.
Seamless Windows	The guest OS window background is removed and the display is enlarged to full-screen. This enables the guest windows to be displayed on the host OS desktop side by side with the host windows. You toggle this mode by pressing the Host Key + L.
Shared Clipboard	Enables copy/paste operations between host and guest. Once the guest additions are installed, this is configured under the Advanced tab in General Settings.
Time Synchronization	Enables VirtualBox to keep the VM time in sync with the actual time maintained by the host
Shared Folders	Enables sharing of files between the host and the guest. As of this writing, this feature is not yet implemented in the OpenSolaris guest additions.
Automated Login for Windows Guests	See the VirtualBox manual for details.

Table 22-1 describes these features.

The following procedure installs the guest additions for an OpenSolaris guest OS:

1. Use the GUI to configure the VM CD/DVD to use the ISO image for the guest additions. On an OpenSolaris host the default location for the VirtualBox software installation is /opt/VirtualBox and the guest additions ISO is /opt/VirtualBox/additions/VBoxGuestAdditions.iso. The location will vary if the host is running a different OS. Alternatively, in a running VM you can select Devices ➤ Install Guest Additions to immediately mount the ISO. On some guests, but not OpenSolaris, this also starts the installation of the guest additions.

2. Boot the VM and install the package in the guest OS using the following command. For OpenSolaris, the CD media will be mounted at /media:

   ```
   # pkgadd -d /media/VBOXADDITIONS_2.0.4_38405/VBoxSolarisAdditions.pkg
   ```

3. Restart the guest OS window system to activate the new features.

See the VirtualBox manual for procedures on installing the additions on a different guest OS.

Although Shared Folders are not currently available in the OpenSolaris guest additions, you can use Shared Folders in other guest operating systems that are hosted on both OpenSolaris as well as other host operating systems.

Within the Settings control panel, under Shared Folders, you can select a directory on the host OS that should be shared into the VM. You also specify a name for the shared folder and whether it should be read-only. Using a shared folder varies based upon the guest OS. For example, in a Windows-based VM file browser, you can find shared folders under My Network Places ➤ Entire Network ➤ VirtualBox Shared Folder. You can also use the Windows command prompt to set up access to the folder as follows:

```
> net use d: \\vboxsvr\myshare
```

Replace the *myshare* string with the name you assigned to the share in the VM configuration. For a Linux-based VM, the following example sets up access to a shared folder:

```
# mount -t vboxsf myshare /mnt
```

The management CLI

Until now, you've used the GUI to configure and manage your VMs. However, some of the advanced features in VirtualBox can only be configured using the command line interface (CLI). In addition, the CLI is useful for various tasks, such as scripting, which cannot be performed using a GUI. VBoxManage is the CLI and you can see its various subcommands in the following example running on the host OS:

```
$ VBoxManage -\?
VirtualBox Command Line Management Interface Version 2.0.4
(C) 2005-2008 Sun Microsystems, Inc.
All rights reserved.

Usage:
VBoxManage [-v|-version]     print version number and exit
VBoxManage -nologo ...       suppress the logo
VBoxManage -convertSettings ...       allow to auto-convert settings files
VBoxManage -convertSettingsBackup ...  allow to auto-convert settings files
                                       but create backup copies before
...
VBoxManage vmstatistics    <vmname>|<uuid> [-reset]
                           [-pattern <pattern>] [-descriptions]
```

The list vms subcommand lists each VM and its configuration data:

```
$ VBoxManage list vms
VirtualBox Command Line Management Interface Version 2.0.4
(C) 2005-2008 Sun Microsystems, Inc.
All rights reserved.
```

```
Name:          myvb
Guest OS:      OpenSolaris
UUID:          62652c41-1a7d-4cb6-71a8-15c33b4830f9
Config file:   /home/sarah/.VirtualBox/Machines/myvb/myvb.xml
Memory size:   1024MB
VRAM size:     64MB
...
```

You can use the modifyvm subcommand to change a VM configuration, the startvm subcommand to start a VM, and so on. Each VBoxManage subcommand and its options are fully described in the VirtualBox user manual.

Networking

VM network configuration was briefly described earlier in the chapter. By default, VirtualBox configures Network Address Translation (NAT) for a VM. This is the simplest form of network configuration and it usually works well between the VM and host OS. With this configuration, VirtualBox behaves like a router and automatically translates network packets between the virtual network used by the VM and the physical network configured on the host OS. The NAT configuration is a good solution if applications running in the VM only initiate access to the Internet, but it is not a good solution if you want to run a server, such as a web server, in the VM. In that case, connections must be initiated externally, but because of the NAT the server in the VM will be invisible to the outside world.

If you need to run an externally visible server within the VM, you can still use NAT, but you need to configure the network to use port forwarding for the VM. That enables VirtualBox to monitor the specified ports on the host OS side and pass that traffic along to the VM. One drawback with this configuration is that it is no longer possible to run the same service, on the same ports, in the host OS, because that would result in a port conflict.

The following example forwards ssh traffic between host port 2048 and VM port 22 (the default ssh port):

```
$ VBoxManage setextradata myvb \
       ''VBoxInternal/Devices/pcnet/0/LUN#0/Config/myforward/Protocol'' TCP
$ VBoxManage setextradata myvb \
       ''VBoxInternal/Devices/pcnet/0/LUN#0/Config/myforward/GuestPort'' 22
$ VBoxManage setextradata myvb \
       ''VBoxInternal/Devices/pcnet/0/LUN#0/Config/myforward/HostPort'' 2048
```

With this configuration, you can ssh from the host OS into the guest OS, as shown here.

```
$ ssh -p 2048 localhost
```

This configuration also allows you to scp files between the host OS and the guest OS.

CROSS-REF   The ssh and scp commands are described in Chapter 11.

The `setextradata` subcommand enables you to associate arbitrary key/value pairs with a VM. In the previous example, the key is a special string that corresponds to the name of the network interface configured on the VM. That setting works if the VM is configured with either the PCnet-PCI II or PCnet-Fast III adapter emulation. If the VM is configured to use the Intel PRO adapters, then the `e1000` name is used instead of `pcnet`, as the following commands illustrate:

```
$ VBoxManage setextradata myvb \
       ''VBoxInternal/Devices/e1000/0/LUN#0/Config/myforward/Protocol'' TCP
$ VBoxManage setextradata myvb \
       ''VBoxInternal/Devices/e1000/0/LUN#0/Config/myforward/GuestPort'' 22
$ VBoxManage setextradata myvb \
       ''VBoxInternal/Devices/e1000/0/LUN#0/Config/myforward/HostPort'' 2048
```

The `myforward` portion of the name is an arbitrary string that you can choose to name the configuration.

Host ports lower than 1024 are privileged on OpenSolaris, so forwarding any of those ports requires that root run the VM. Various other limitations with using NAT and port forwarding with VirtualBox are described in the manual.

To clear these settings, simply rerun the three commands without the final parameter.

In addition to NAT, you can configure the VM to use either Host Interface networking or Internal networking. With Host Interface networking, VirtualBox uses a virtual NIC configured in the host OS to provide network access to the VM. Configuring Host Interface networking varies according to the host OS, and the steps can be complex. For more details consult the VirtualBox manual. With Internal networking, VirtualBox creates a virtual network within the host OS. VMs can communicate with each other over the virtual network, but no network traffic ever leaves the host. You can configure Internal networking in the GUI under Network settings.

Storage

When you first installed the VM, you used the New Virtual Disk wizard to set up on the host OS a file that is used to emulate a disk drive for the VM. These files are called *Virtual Disk Image (VDI)* files. In the Hard Disks settings, you can bring up the Virtual Disk Manager (see Figure 22-9) to create, manage, and delete VDI files for your VMs. The New button enables you to define a new virtual disk, bringing up the same New Virtual Disk wizard that you used when you created the first virtual disk for the VM. Once the virtual disk has been defined, it can be associated with a specific VM. You can also release virtual disks from one VM and then reuse them later on a different VM.

VDI files are the most common way to provide storage to the VM, although shared folders, described earlier in the chapter, are also used.

VirtualBox supports using VDI files as *normal* images, *immutable* images, or *write-through* images. A normal image is the default. It can only be used by a single VM at any one time, and when you snapshot the VM, the image is also snapshotted, so that it reverts if you revert the VM to the snapshot. Immutable images are essentially read-only and can be shared by multiple VMs. VirtualBox does allow you to write to an immutable image, but all changes are tracked separately for each VM using the image, and are discarded when the VM shuts down. Because modifications are not persistent, you must start with a normal image and switch it to immutable once it is in the desired state. You cannot currently change the type on a registered image, so you must first remove it from the VM, unregister the image, re-register it as immutable, and then reattach it to the VM.

FIGURE 22-9

Virtual Disk Manager

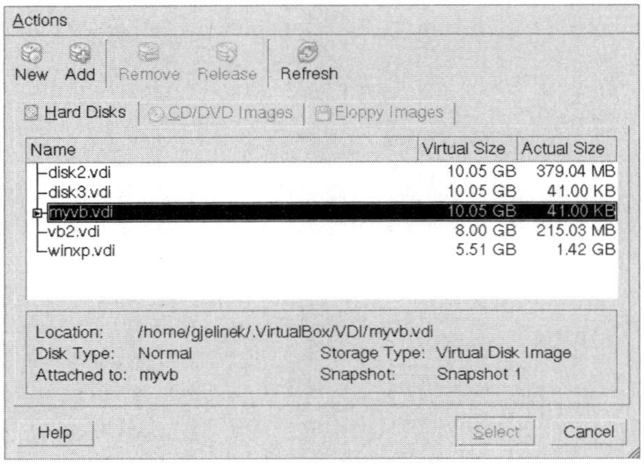

```
Actions

  New   Add   Remove  Release   Refresh

  ☐ Hard Disks  │ ⊙ CD/DVD Images │ ☐ Floppy Images

  Name                      Virtual Size  Actual Size
  ├disk2.vdi                  10.05 GB    379.04 MB
  ├disk3.vdi                  10.05 GB     41.00 KB
  ├myvb.vdi                   10.05 GB     41.00 KB
  ├vb2.vdi                     8.00 GB    215.03 MB
  └winxp.vdi                   5.51 GB      1.42 GB


  Location:   /home/gjelinek/.VirtualBox/VDI/myvb.vdi
  Disk Type:  Normal           Storage Type:  Virtual Disk Image
  Attached to: myvb            Snapshot:      Snapshot 1


  Help                                 Select     Cancel
```

The following example shows the necessary commands to change the type on an image:

```
$ VBoxManage unregisterimage disk ~/.VirtualBox/VDI/disk2.vdi
$ VBoxManage registerimage disk ~/.VirtualBox/VDI/disk2.vdi -type immutable
```

A write-through image is similar to a normal image except that the state is not saved when you snapshot, so the disk does not revert if you go back to an earlier snapshot. This is useful for application data that you don't want to lose. You can set up an existing disk as write-through using the same sequence described in the previous example, but with -type writethrough. To create a disk as write-through from the beginning, use the createvdi subcommand, as the following example, which creates a 1GB sparse image, shows:

```
$ VBoxManage createvdi -filename ~/.VirtualBox/VDI/disk4.vdi \
-size 1000 -register -type writethrough
```

Virtual disks can be configured to appear connected to the VM using either a traditional IDE disk controller or a more modern Serial ATA (SATA) controller. The VirtualBox SATA emulation is faster and more lightweight than the IDE emulation, but not every guest OS supports SATA, or it might support SATA, but not support booting from a SATA disk. In addition, IDE supports a maximum of three virtual disks, whereas the SATA emulation supports up to 30. By default, the first disk set up for a VM is configured to appear as the IDE master. To configure the VM to use the disk as a SATA device, change the VM configuration before you first boot and install the guest in the VM.

By default, the SATA emulation presents the first four SATA ports in IDE compatibility mode. This improves the chance that the guest OS can boot from the disk. OpenSolaris falls into this category; for the VirtualBox SATA emulation, you can configure the VM so the first disk is a SATA disk, but leave it in IDE compatibility mode so that OpenSolaris can boot from the disk. Depending on your hardware, OpenSolaris can boot from some physical SATA disks when run on bare metal.

TIP The following command remaps the SATA IDE compatibility mode from the first port to the last port:

```
$ VBoxManage modifyvm myvb -sataideemulation1 30
```

This causes the VM to present the disk on the first port as a native SATA device. Do this only if your VM is not booting from the disk or you are sure that the guest OS will boot correctly from a SATA disk.

VirtualBox supports cloning of VDI disks using the following command:

```
$ VBoxManage clonevdi myvb.vdi disk2.vdi
```

This enables you to quickly create a copy of a virtual disk for a second VM. Once the cloned disk has been created, you can use the Existing button when creating a new VM to configure it to use the clone. Always use the clonevdi command instead of simply copying the file because VirtualBox keeps track of VDIs using a unique identifier and it won't run if two VDIs have the same ID.

In addition to VDI files, you can configure the VM to either use iSCSI disks or directly access a local, physical disk.

CROSS-REF See Chapter 7 for information on iSCSI and an example showing how to set up an iSCSI target under OpenSolaris.

While you could configure an iSCSI initiator under OpenSolaris, set up a file system on the target, and then use that file system to hold VDI files, VirtualBox includes a built-in iSCSI initiator that can be used to directly access iSCSI targets as virtual disks. You can configure it within VirtualBox using the following command, which uses the iSCSI target created in Chapter 7:

```
$ VBoxManage addiscsidisk -server 192.168.0.1 \
-target iqn.1986-03.com.sun:02:8f23a58f-337f-6989-d09f-d4fb7bb3dfae.mytarget
```

The target value is the iSCSI Name printed by the OpenSolaris iscsitadm command when you list the targets that are configured. Other operating systems have different ways to configure a target and get this data.

Additional options to the addiscsidisk subcommand, such as a port or a password, can also be used for more advanced iSCSI configurations. Once the iSCSI disk has been defined, you can use the Virtual Disk Manager to configure the disk in a VM.

The VBoxManage unregisterimage disk subcommand can be used to delete the iSCSI disk from VirtualBox, although it will still exist as a valid target on the server.

In addition to supporting VDI files for virtual disks, VirtualBox also supports Virtual Machine DisK (VMDK) files.

> **NOTE** VMDK is the disk format defined and used by the popular VMware virtual machine software. VMware has opened this file format and it appears to be turning into a de facto standard for virtual disk images.

You can add existing VMDK files to a VM using the Virtual Disk Manager. Note that when using VMDK files, VirtualBox currently cannot create snapshots and will only write-through to the image.

Finally, VirtualBox enables you to allocate an entire raw disk or raw disk partition to a VM but because the configuration procedure is complex, there are security implications associated with accessing a raw disk. A misconfiguration could corrupt the entire system, so carefully read the manual to be sure you fully understand the procedures before attempting to use raw disks with VirtualBox. In most cases, using standard VDI files or iSCSI suffices.

Remote access

As previously mentioned, VirtualBox includes a built-in RDP server that enables you to remotely connect to a VM's window. When running a VM on a server with no local display, you can ssh into the system, and use either the VirtualBox GUI with remote display or the VBoxManage CLI to fully configure the VM. Then you can use the VBoxHeadless command to start the VM with the VDRP server enabled and with no local window.

On the server, run the following:

```
myhost$ VBoxHeadless -startvm myvb
VirtualBox Headless Interface 2.0.4
(C) 2008 Sun Microsystems, Inc.
All rights reserved

Listening on port 3389
```

The -vrdpport option enables you to specify a different port. Additional options are available for recording data and specifying screen properties.

OpenSolaris includes an RDP client, although you may need to first install it:

```
# pkg install SUNWrdesktop
```

Then you can connect to the server and you should see the initial screen for the VM:

```
$ rdesktop myhost
```

You don't have to start the VM using VBoxHeadless. You can start it under the normal GUI and use the Devices ➢ Remote Display control to enable remote access. In this case, the VM window is usable on both the server and client. That can be useful if you want to concurrently share access to the VM between two machines for some reason, such as troubleshooting.

The VRDP server can also be enabled under the Settings ➢ Remote Display control so that you don't have to enable it every time the VM starts; and you can use this control to change some of the RDP properties, such as the port or authentication method, if necessary. The authentication method settings are described in the VirtualBox manual. Only the Null authentication setting is currently supported on OpenSolaris, although the other settings work on other host operating systems.

CAUTION Running with the Remote Display option enabled and the Null authentication setting enables any client to connect to the VM. This may pose a security risk. It is recommended that you only enable the VRDP server if necessary.

Programmatic interfaces

This book does not focus on programming, but it is worth noting that VirtualBox includes a public API that you can use to write your own interface. In most cases, the GUI or VBoxManage CLI is sufficient, but the API is described in the VirtualBox manual if needed.

Running within a zone

VirtualBox can be combined with another OpenSolaris virtualization feature — zones — to provide enhanced capabilities. Because there is essentially no overhead associated with running applications in a zone, you can run a VM within a zone with no additional performance penalty. The benefit of running a VM inside a zone is the additional encapsulation the zone provides. For example, you can configure the zone to use OpenSolaris resource management features so that the VM only uses the configured resources. One possibility is to set up the zone in conjunction with the Fair Share Scheduler so that VMs running in different zones don't starve each other or any other applications on the system. Another benefit is use of the migration capabilities provided by zones.

CROSS-REF Resource management is described in Chapter 18. Zones, and configuring zones to use resource management, are described in Chapter 19.

To configure a zone so that it can run VirtualBox, the zone configuration should include the vboxdrv device:

```
zonecfg:myzone> add device
zonecfg:myzone:device> set match=/dev/vboxdrv
zonecfg:myzone:device> end
```

Once a zone is installed, install the VirtualBox packages, as described earlier. After the zone is properly set up, you can either create VMs within the zone or, if file system sharing is properly configured between the global and nonglobal zone, run a VM from inside the zone that was originally configured in the global zone.

This example shows logging in to a zone named `myzone` and running VirtualBox inside the zone:

```
$ ssh -X myzone
Password:
Last login: Wed Jun 25 18:35:47 2008 from 192.168.0.11
Sun Microsystems Inc.   SunOS 5.11      snv_91   January 2008
myzone$ VirtualBox&
```

CAUTION If you are running VirtualBox from within a zone using a shared directory with the global zone, make sure you don't try to also run VirtualBox from the global zone. VirtualBox cannot track the status of each VM in this case because it looks like you are running on two different systems. You could corrupt your configuration or data if you change the configuration or run the same VM multiple times.

Resources

The VirtualBox home page (`http://virtualbox.org`) is the primary starting point for more information about VirtualBox. The left column links to end-user documentation, which includes the manual, FAQs, and various tutorials. The technical documentation describes the implementation and source code. The Downloads link leads to prebuilt binaries as well as a link to the source code. Finally, the Community link leads to user forums, mailing lists, IRC, and bug reporting.

Summary

This chapter provided an introduction to VirtualBox, a popular open source type 2 hypervisor for x86-based systems running OpenSolaris or many other host operating systems. Setting up and managing VirtualBox is easy using the simple GUI features provided by the software. VirtualBox provides a good virtualization solution when you need to run different operating systems for various tasks such as software development or testing. With the guest additions, you can achieve seamless integration between applications concurrently running on a variety of guest operating systems, as well as the host operating system.

Part VI

Deploying and Developing on OpenSolaris

Deploying a Web Stack on OpenSolaris

It almost goes without saying that contemporary computer use revolves around the World Wide Web. From games, social networking, and blogs to news and e-commerce, web-based services are indispensable. Each of those services, from your friend's personal blog to your favorite online vendor, is running on one or more servers called a *web server*. If you are considering deploying a web server, whether you're starting a personal web page or blog or setting up a multimillion-dollar e-commerce site, the OpenSolaris operating system is a great choice to run it. Open-Solaris is also an excellent platform for developing web-based applications. This chapter describes how to deploy a web stack on OpenSolaris; Chapter 24 covers developing on OpenSolaris.

The Web Stack on OpenSolaris

The traditional web stack consists of a web server frontend and a database backend, connected with a scripting language. One of the most popular combinations of these three components, the Apache HTTP server, the MySQL database, and the PHP scripting language, are together referred to by their acronym: the *AMP* stack.

> **NOTE** Although the Apache HTTP Server is not the only application from Apache, it is often called just "Apache." This book follows that usage.

Because the AMP stack is so popular, many platforms are optimized for that configuration, even giving it a customized name. For example, when running on Linux, the AMP stack is expanded as LAMP. When running on Windows, it's called WAMP. On Solaris or OpenSolaris, it's the SAMP stack.

There are, of course, many variations on the AMP stack. For example, the PostgreSQL database can be used instead of MySQL, and some web applications are written in Ruby, Python, Java, or Perl instead of PHP. Furthermore, most Java-based applications require an additional *servlet container*. Apache Tomcat is probably the best-known example of a servlet container.

Another popular form of web services software is the *application server*. An application server combines the web server, servlet container, and business logic (usually in the form of Enterprise JavaBeans) into one integrated environment. Two examples of application servers are GlassFish and JBoss.

This chapter first walks you through the steps to install and configure a basic AMP stack on OpenSolaris. Then it describes how to substitute various components, such as PostgreSQL and the Sun Java System Web Server in place of MySQL and the Apache HTTP Server, respectively. Finally, it explains how to run Java-based web applications with Apache Tomcat and the GlassFish application server.

HTTP Servers, Servlet Containers, and Application Servers: What's Right for You?

If you're new to web stacks and web services, you might be confused by the various options. In brief, an HTTP server provides web pages to web browsers, such as Mozilla Firefox. The network communication between the browser and the server uses the Hypertext Transfer Protocol (HTTP). A web server can *serve* static Hypertext Markup Language (HTML) pages or it can run scripts in PHP, Perl, or other languages, to generate dynamic content. An HTTP server can also serve different kinds of content, such as flash applications.

A web application is generally a collection of scripts that the HTTP server runs to generate dynamic content. The scripts usually interact with a database backend, so if you just want to set up a blog, wiki, or similar script-based web application, you can probably use a standard HTTP server. Common examples of these kinds of web applications include WordPress and MediaWiki. One caveat, however, is that Java-based web applications generally require a slightly different kind of HTTP server called a *servlet container*. A servlet container, or servlet engine, is an HTTP server that knows how to run special Java programs called *servlets*. A popular Java-based web application is the Apache Roller blogging software.

An application server is sort of a combination of a full-fledged software application and an HTTP server. An application server can provide the *business logic*, such as implementing a shopping cart for an online vendor, along with the web-based user interaction provided by the HTTP server. An

continued

continued

application server usually includes capabilities to run Java servlets and Enterprise JavaBeans. These application servers are generally useful for sophisticated web applications that have many users. If you haven't heard of an application server before now, you probably don't need to use one.

The AMP Stack

The OpenSolaris Web Stack project has made the AMP stack trivially easy to install and use.

Installing the AMP stack

The OpenSolaris binary distribution doesn't include the AMP stack components on the Live CD, but they are easy to obtain from the package repositories. The default repository at `pkg.opensolaris.org/release` contains most of the components. The additional Web Stack repository, `pkg.opensolaris.org/webstack`, contains some software not in the core repository, such as phpMyAdmin and Drupal, as well as early access to newer versions of components. For example, as of this writing, `pkg.opensolaris.org/release` contains MySQL server version 5.0.45, whereas `pkg.opensolaris.org/webstack` contains MySQL server version 5.1.25. Unless otherwise stated, the examples in this chapter use the release repository as the source for the packages.

The simplest way to get the AMP stack on your system is to install the `amp-dev` group package, which provides Apache, MySQL, and PHP, among other components. Note that the versions of Apache, MySQL, and PHP installed by `amp-dev` are expected to change over time:

```
# pkg install amp-dev
```

Installing `amp-dev` provides hundreds of megabytes of software, including the following:

- Apache HTTP Server, including the Tomcat connector plug-in, the PHP5 module, and other extensions
- MySQL
- PHP, including PHP modules for MySQL and PostgreSQL
- Python (another scripting language)
- Apache Tomcat
- The NetBeans Integrated Development Environment
- The web stack GUI (a graphical interface for managing web stack components)
- Squid Web Proxy Cache (proxy server and web cache daemon for improving web server performance)

- memcached (memory caching system for improving performance)
- Subversion, Mercurial, and CVS version control systems

CROSS-REF Chapters 3 and 6 cover the Image Packaging System (IPS), package installation, and network package repositories. See Chapter 24 for a discussion of the OpenSolaris development tools and languages, including Python, NetBeans, Subversion, Mercurial, and CVS.

If you're short on disk space, you may want to install only Apache, MySQL, and PHP. As the following example shows, several packages are involved in installing Apache and PHP (note that the output from `pkg install` is omitted for brevity):

```
# pkg install SUNWapch22 SUNWapch22m-jk SUNWapch22m-security SUNWapch22d\
SUNWapch22m-php5 SUNWapch22m-fcgid SUNWapch22m-dtrace
# pkg install SUNWmysql5
# pkg install SUNWphp524 SUNWphp524doc SUNWphp524man SUNWphp524-pgsql\
SUNWphp524-mysql
```

Now that the packages are installed, you can configure the applications. If you installed the `webstackui` package, which is part of the `amp-dev` package, you can configure the applications from the Applications ➤ Developer Tools menu option. Alternatively, you can use the command line. The examples in this chapter use the command line.

Web Services in Zones

Apache HTTP Server, Apache Tomcat, GlassFish, and the rest of the servers discussed in this chapter can run in nonglobal zones as well as the global zone. In fact, combining nonglobal zones with resource management features such as resource caps, resource pools, and CPU caps gives you multiple virtual hosts in which to run a web stack. This configuration can be useful for both prototyping and deploying. For example, zones give you a convenient way to experiment with different web stacks without worrying about port binding conflicts. For deployment, zones enable you to run several unrelated web services on the same physical machine, or even to set up a web hosting service to provide dedicated virtual servers for clients. Resource management is described in Chapter 18, and zones are covered in Chapter 19.

Configuring Apache

OpenSolaris runs Apache as a service under SMF, which means that instead of running the `apachectl` script directly to start, stop, or restart Apache, you use SMF commands such as `svcadm`.

CROSS-REF SMF and its commands, such as `svcadm`, are described in Chapter 13.

To configure Apache, simply enable the Apache service:

```
# /usr/sbin/svcadm enable network/http:apache22
```

```
# svcs apache22
STATE          STIME    FMRI
online         15:16:45 svc:/network/http:apache22
```

You can test that Apache is up and running by opening a web browser on the local machine and navigating to `http://localhost`. You should see something like Figure 23-1.

FIGURE 23-1

The default web page after starting Apache on your system.

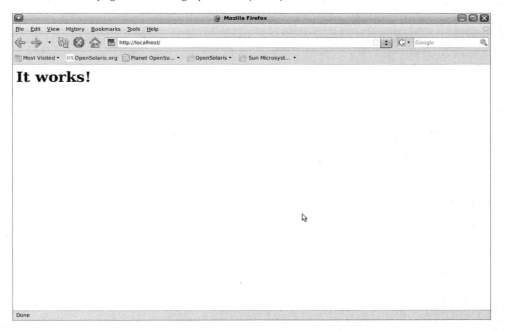

To finish a simple configuration for one domain name, set the `ServerAdmin` and `ServerName` properties in `/etc/apache2/2.2/httpd.conf` to your e-mail address and to the domain name, respectively.

You then need to restart Apache:

```
# svcadm restart apache22
```

TIP   In order for clients to access the domain name served by Apache, that domain name must be resolvable by DNS or some other mechanism from those client machines. Most domain name registrars, such as `GoDaddy.com`, provide DNS services free. Contact your registrar for more information. DNS is covered in Chapter 9.

Advanced Apache configuration is the same as on other platforms. Consult the "Resources" section later in this chapter for more details.

Configuring PHP

If you've installed the SUNWapch22-php5 package or the amp-dev group package, OpenSolaris requires no additional steps to configure PHP to work with Apache. You can test your Apache/PHP configuration by creating a test script in /var/apache2/2.2/htdocs, such as:

```
# cat /var/apache2/2.2/htdocs/test.php
<?php
        phpinfo();
?>
```

After pointing your browser from the local machine to http://localhost/test.php, you should see something like what is shown in Figure 23-2.

FIGURE 23-2

The PHP test page verifies that your Apache and PHP configurations are correct.

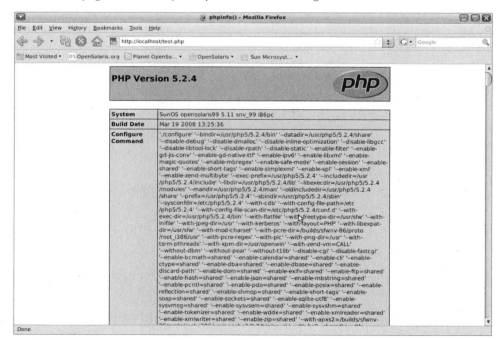

Configuring MySQL

Like Apache, MySQL is a service managed by SMF. To configure MySQL, just enable the service:

```
# svcadm enable mysql
# svcs mysql
STATE          STIME     FMRI
online         15:49:06  svc:/application/database/mysql:version_50
```

That's it! MySQL is now ready to use.

 **CAUTION** By default, MySQL has no root password. You should set a password immediately, as described below.

Installing phpMyAdmin

MySQL comes with a command-line client, /usr/mysql/bin/mysql. If you prefer using a graphical user interface to administer your databases, you can install a GUI client. One of the most popular GUI administrative software for MySQL is phpMyAdmin, which is available from the Web Stack repository. To install it, first add the webstack repository as an authority, if you haven't already done so:

```
# pkg set-authority -O http://pkg.opensolaris.org:80/webstack webstack
# pkg authority
AUTHORITY                      URL
webstack                       http://pkg.opensolaris.org:80/webstack/
opensolaris.org (preferred)    http://pkg.opensolaris.org/release/
```

Next, install the phpmyadmin package (output omitted for brevity):

```
# pkg install phpmyadmin
```

Finally, copy the configuration file from the samples-conf.d directory to the conf.d directory and restart Apache:

```
# cp /etc/apache2/2.2/samples-conf.d/phpmyadmin.conf /etc/apache2/2.2/conf.d
# svcadm restart apache22
```

Now you can use phpMyAdmin by pointing your browser at http://localhost/phpmyadmin. Once logged in, you will see something similar to what is shown in Figure 23-3.

TIP Remember to log in to phpMyAdmin with your MySQL root account, not your machine root account.

Subsequent examples in this chapter use the mysql command-line client but if you install php-MyAdmin, you can use that instead.

FIGURE 23-3

phpMyAdmin provides a graphical user interface for managing MySQL.

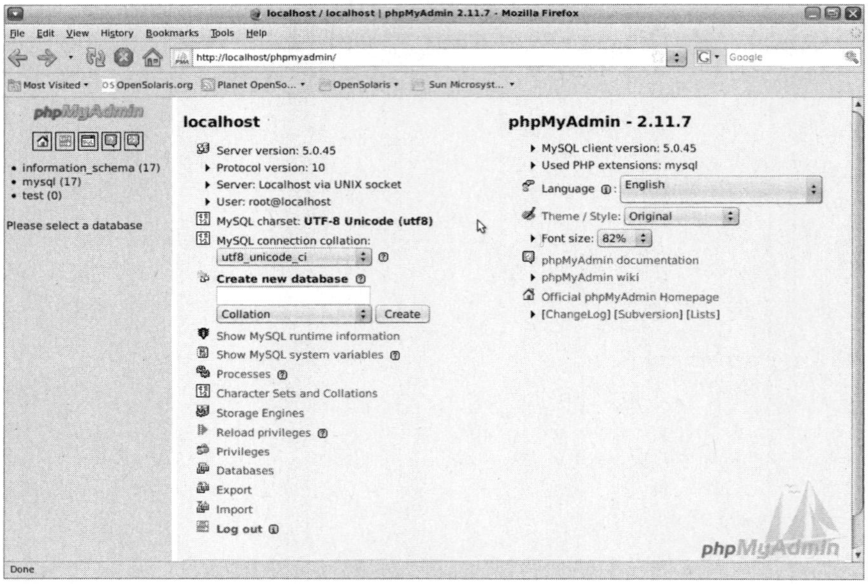

Changing the root password

The first thing you should do once the MySQL service is enabled is set a root password:

```
# /usr/mysql/bin/mysql -u root
Welcome to the MySQL monitor.  Commands end with ; or \g.
Your MySQL connection id is 3
Server version: 5.0.45 Source distribution

Type 'help;' or '\h' for help. Type '\c' to clear the buffer.

Mysql> SET PASSWORD FOR root@localhost=PASSWORD('goodpass');
Query OK, 0 rows affected (0.01 sec)

mysql> quit
Bye
#
```

The password in this example is "goodpass," but you should choose a more secure password. Once you have a root password, run mysql with the -p option:

```
# /usr/mysql/bin/mysql -u root -p
Enter password: <password>
Welcome to the MySQL monitor.  Commands end with ; or \g.
```

```
Your MySQL connection id is 5
Server version: 5.0.45 Source distribution

Type 'help;' or '\h' for help. Type '\c' to clear the buffer.

Mysql>
```

Beyond setting the password and installing phpMyAdmin, advanced MySQL configuration is the same as on other platforms. See the "Resources" section at the end of the chapter for more details.

Web applications

Now that you have a working AMP stack, you can install open-source or proprietary web applications or write your own. This section demonstrates how to install and configure WordPress, the popular open source blogging software. Most web applications have similar steps.

CROSS-REF To develop your own web applications on OpenSolaris, consult Chapter 24 for details on the OpenSolaris Development Platform.

To install WordPress, follow these steps:

1. Download the WordPress zip file from `http://wordpress.org`. This example installs version 2.6.2, which is the latest version as of this writing.

2. Unzip and untar the file under the `/var/apache2/2.2/htdocs` directory. The contents are put in a wordpress subdirectory.

```
# cd <directory where wordpress was downloaded>
# mv wordpress-2.6.2.tar.gz /var/apache2/2.2/htdocs
# cd /var/apache2/2.2/htdocs
# tar -xzf wordpress-2.6.2.tar.gz
# ls -d wordpress
wordpress
# rm wordpress-2.6.2.tar.gz
```

3. Create a database and user for WordPress in MySQL:

```
# /usr/mysql/bin/mysql -u root -p
Enter password: <password>
Welcome to the MySQL monitor.  Commands end with ; or \g.
Your MySQL connection id is 4
Server version: 5.0.45 Source distribution

Type 'help;' or '\h' for help. Type '\c' to clear the buffer.

Mysql> CREATE DATABASE wordpress;
Query OK, 1 row affected (0.00 sec)
mysql> GRANT ALL PRIVILEGES ON wordpress.* TO "wordpress"@"localhost"-
  IDENTIFIED BY "insecurepassword";
```

```
Query OK, 0 rows affected (0.00 sec)

mysql> FLUSH PRIVILEGES;
Query OK, 0 rows affected (0.06 sec)

mysql> quit
Bye
#
```

4. Rename wp-config-sample.php to wp-config.php:

```
# cd /var/apache2/2.2/htdocs/wordpress
# mv wp-config-sample.php wp-config.php
```

5. Edit wp-config.php to set the DB_NAME, DB_USER, and DB_PASSWORD you created in step 3. The settings should look something like this:

```
# cat wp-config.php
...
define('DB_NAME', 'wordpress');      // The name of the database
define('DB_USER', 'wordpress');       // Your MySQL username
define('DB_PASSWORD', 'insecurepassword'); // ...and password
...
```

6. Run the WordPress install script from your web browser by navigating to http://<yourdomain>/wordpress/wp-admin/install.php. This is a one-step process. On the first screen, which looks something like Figure 23-4, enter the requested information.

   You'll then see the result screen, shown in Figure 23-5.

That's it! To use your blog, navigate to http://yourdomain/wordpress.

Alternatives to Apache, MySQL, and PHP

Although Apache, MySQL, and PHP make up the "official" AMP stack, you may prefer to substitute one or more components. The Sun Java System Web Server and the PostgreSQL database are popular alternatives for the Apache HTTP Server and MySQL database, respectively.

Sun Java System Web Server

The Sun Java System Web Server from Sun Microsystems is an alternative to the Apache HTTP Server. One benefit of the Sun Java System Web Server over Apache is that it's also a servlet container, eliminating the need for a separate application such as Apache Tomcat. Servlet containers are described in more detail later in this chapter.

The Sun Java System Web Server is available from the webstack repository in the sun-webserver7 package. If you haven't already added a webstack authority, you must

FIGURE 23-4

The WordPress installation requires only two pieces of information.

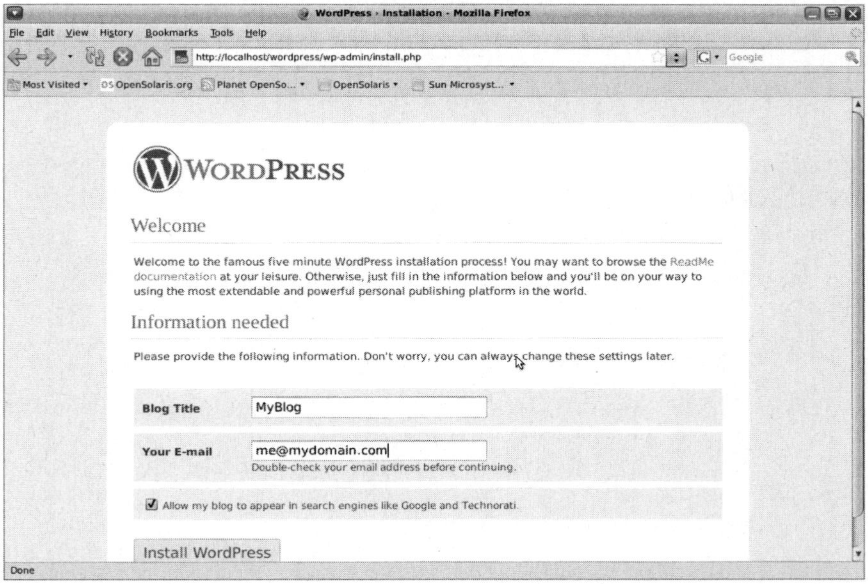

do that before installing the web server. As usual, the example omits the output from `pkg install`:

```
# pkg set-authority -O http://pkg.opensolaris.org:80/webstack webstack
# pkg install sun-webserver7
```

The web server is installed into `/opt/webserver7`. Before starting the web server, you need to set up a default `webserver` instance by running the `configureServer` command (output is omitted for brevity):

```
# cd /opt/webserver7
# ./lib/configureServer -i ./setup/configureServer.properties
```

You now have a `webserver` instance configured in `/var/opt/webserver7/https-localhost`.

CAUTION Before starting the Sun Java System Web Server, disable the Apache HTTP Server so that they don't interfere with each other:

```
# svcadm disable apache22
```

The web server is not managed by SMF, so you need to start it manually by running the `startserv` command:

```
# /var/opt/webserver7/https-localhost/bin/startserv
Sun Java System Web Server 7.0U3 B06/16/2008 10:24
info: CORE5076: Using [Java HotSpot(TM) Server VM, Version 1.6.0_07]
from [Sun Microsystems Inc.]
info: HTTP3072: http-listener-1: http://localhost:8080 ready to accept requests
info: CORE3274: successful server startup
```

FIGURE 23-5

The installation result screen confirms that the blog has been created.

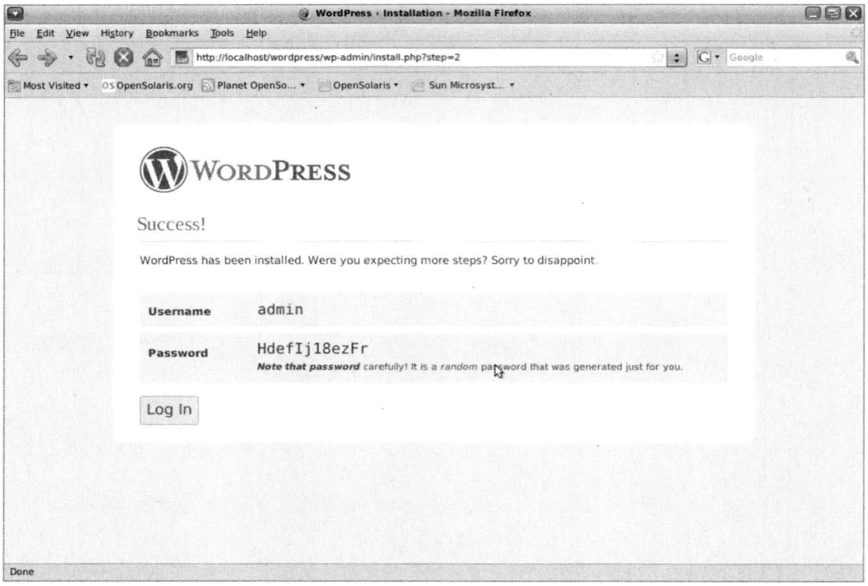

Your web server is now running and ready to serve pages on port 8080. When you connect to port 8080 on your machine, your screen will be similar to the one shown in Figure 23-6.

By default, static web pages are served out of the `/var/opt/webserver-7/https-localhost/docs` directory. You can shut down the web server with `/var/opt/webserver7/https-localhost/bin/stopserv`.

PostgreSQL

The open source PostgreSQL database, also available on OpenSolaris, is a popular alternative to MySQL. As of this writing, there is no group package for PostgreSQL. Instead, you need to explicitly install all eight packages. This example installs version 8.3, which is the latest version available as of this writing:

```
# pkg install SUNWpostgr-83-libs SUNWpostgr-83-devel SUNWpostgr-83-docs
 SUNWpostgr-83-tcl SUNWpostgr-83-pl SUNWpostgr-83-client SUNWpostgr-83
-contrib SUNWpostgr-83-server
```

TIP To find later versions of PostgreSQL, use `pkg search -r` to find packages containing "postgres."

Because the PostgreSQL database administration uses RBAC, it must be administered by the `postgres` role or by someone with the "Postgres Administration" profile, both of which are created at OpenSolaris installation time. Give the `postgres` role a password and assign it to at least one user, as shown here:

```
# passwd postgres
New Password:
Re-enter new Password:
passwd: password successfully changed for postgres
# usermod -R postgres test
```

FIGURE 23-6

The Sun Java System Web Server default page confirms that the server is configured properly.

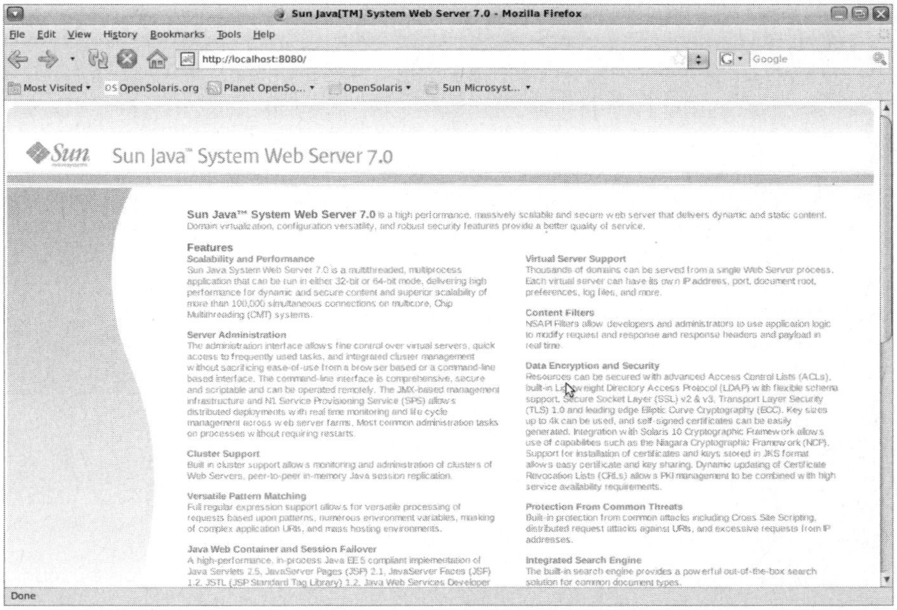

CROSS-REF   Role-based access control (RBAC) is discussed in Chapter 11.

Now the user — in this case, test — who has been assigned the postgres role can assume it and initialize the server. As of this writing, the postgres role is assigned a non-existent shell: pfksh. Change the shell to something else before assuming the postgres role. See Chapter 3 for instructions on switching shells.

```
$ su postgres
Password:
$ /usr/postgres/8.3/bin/initdb /var/postgres/8.3/data
The files belonging to this database system will be owned by user "postgres".
This user must also own the server process.

The database cluster will be initialized with locale en_US.UTF-8.
The default database encoding has accordingly been set to UTF8.
The default text search configuration will be set to "english".

fixing permissions on existing directory /var/postgres/8.3/data ... ok
creating subdirectories ... ok
selecting default max_connections ... 100
selecting default shared_buffers/max_fsm_pages ... 32MB/204800
creating configuration files ... ok
creating template1 database in /var/postgres/8.3/data/base/1 ... ok
initializing pg_authid ... ok
initializing dependencies ... ok
creating system views ... ok
loading system objects' descriptions ... ok
creating conversions ... ok
creating dictionaries ... ok
setting privileges on built-in objects ... ok
creating information schema ... ok
vacuuming database template1 ... ok
copying template1 to template0 ... ok
copying template1 to postgres ... ok

WARNING: enabling "trust" authentication for local connections
You can change this by editing pg_hba.conf or using the -A option the
next time you run initdb.

Success. You can now start the database server using:

    /usr/postgres/8.3/bin/postgres -D /var/postgres/8.3/data
or
    /usr/postgres/8.3/bin/pg_ctl -D /var/postgres/8.3/data -l logfile start
```

Ignore the output from initdb about starting the database server with a command from /usr/postgres/8.3/bin. Because PostgreSQL is managed by SMF on OpenSolaris, you simply need to enable the service. The PostgreSQL 8.3 manifest defines two different postgres instances for 32-bit and 64-bit; enable only one of those instances depending on the architecture of your platform. This example enables the 32-bit instance because it is run on a 32-bit platform:

```
$ svcs postgresql_83
STATE          STIME   FMRI
disabled      6:40:35 svc:/application/database/postgresql_83:default_64bit
disabled      6:40:35 svc:/application/database/postgresql_83:default_32bit
$ svcadm enable postgresql_83:default_32bit
$ svcs postgresql_83
STATE          STIME   FMRI
disabled      6:40:35 svc:/application/database/postgresql_83:default_64bit
online        6:54:22 svc:/application/database/postgresql_83:default_32bit
```

PostgreSQL is now ready to use.

Languages other than PHP

You can, of course, use and write web applications that use languages other than PHP. If you installed the amp-dev package, you already have PHP and Python. To install a different language, find the package in the repository and install it. This example installs Ruby:

```
# pkg install SUNWruby18
```

With Ruby installed, you can use web applications that depend on Ruby. One of the most popular languages for web services is, of course, Java. Java-based web services are covered in detail in the next section.

Java-based Web Services

Java-based web services deserve special attention because they generally require a Java servlet engine, such as Apache Tomcat, or an integrated application server, such as GlassFish. As described earlier, the Sun Java System Web Server has a built-in servlet engine.

Apache Tomcat

Apache Tomcat is a servlet container, or servlet engine, that enables you to run Java Servlet or Java Server Pages (JSPs). Many popular web applications, such as the Apache Roller blogging software, use these technologies. It's also a popular development environment.

You can run Tomcat in standalone mode, in which it handles all incoming HTTP requests, or you can connect it through the Apache HTTP Server, such that the HTTP server triages incoming HTTP requests and directs a subset of those requests to Tomcat. This book explains how to configure Tomcat in standalone mode on OpenSolaris. To connect it through Apache, consult the Apache HTTP Server and Apache Tomcat references listed in the "Resources" section at the end of this chapter.

Installing Apache Tomcat

If you installed the amp-dev package, you already have the SUNWtcat package installed. Otherwise, you need to install the SUNWtcat package explicitly:

```
# pkg install SUNWtcat
```

As of this writing, this package contains Apache Tomcat 5.5.26.

Configuring Apache Tomcat in stand-alone mode

You can get Apache Tomcat up and running in two simple steps after installing the package. First, copy the server.xml-example file to server.xml in /var/apache/tomcat/conf:

```
# cp /var/apache/tomcat/conf/server.xml-example /var/apache/tomcat/conf/server.xml
```

> **CAUTION**   Before starting Tomcat, stop the Apache HTTP Server and the Sun Java System Web Server so they won't interfere with Tomcat.

```
# svcadm disable apache22
# /var/opt/webserver7/https-localhost/bin/stopserv
```

Now you can start Tomcat by running the startup.sh script:

```
# /usr/apache/tomcat/bin/startup.sh
Using CATALINA_BASE:   /var/apache/tomcat
Using CATALINA_HOME:   /usr/apache/tomcat
Using CATALINA_TMPDIR: /var/apache/tomcat/temp
Using JRE_HOME:        /usr/java
```

Tomcat should now be up and running, listening on port 8080. If you point your web browser at that port on the domain, you should see something similar to Figure 23-7.

Unfortunately, Tomcat on OpenSolaris doesn't run as an SMF service by default, which means it won't start automatically when the system boots, won't be restarted if it encounters a failure, and won't receive any of the other benefits of being under SMF control. Consider doing a web search for a Tomcat SMF service, or writing an SMF service yourself for Tomcat if you intend to deploy it.

To deploy Java-based web applications on Tomcat that use MySQL, you need the MySQL JDBC driver. Download the latest version of Connector/J from the MySQL website: http://dev.mysql.com/downloads/connector/j/5.1.html. Next, untar/unzip the download file and copy mysql-connector-java-5.1.7-bin.jar to /usr/apache/tomcat/common/lib:

```
# cd <download directory>
# tar -xzf mysql-connector-java-5.1.7.tar.gz
```

```
# cp mysql-connector-java-5.1.7/mysql-connector-java-5.1.7-bin.jar\
  /usr/apache/tomcat/common/lib
```

FIGURE 23-7

The Apache Tomcat default page confirms that Tomcat is configured correctly.

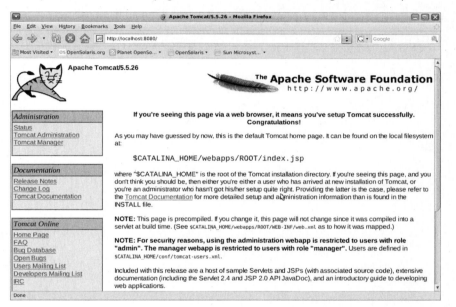

Some applications also need the Java Mail API. You can download it from `http://java`
`.sun.com/products/javamail`. After unzipping the download file, copy `mail.jar` to
`/usr/apache/tomcat/common/lib`:

```
# cd <download directory>
# unzip -q javamail-1_4_1.zip
# cp javamail-1.4.1/mail.jar /usr/apache/tomcat/common/lib
```

NOTE You need to restart Tomcat in order for it to use the new jar files you installed. Run
the `shutdown.sh` script followed by the `startup.sh` script:

```
# /usr/apache/tomcat/bin/shutdown.sh
Using CATALINA_BASE:   /var/apache/tomcat
Using CATALINA_HOME:   /usr/apache/tomcat
Using CATALINA_TMPDIR: /var/apache/tomcat/temp
Using JRE_HOME:        /usr/java
# /usr/apache/tomcat/bin/startup.sh
```

```
Using CATALINA_BASE:   /var/apache/tomcat
Using CATALINA_HOME:   /usr/apache/tomcat
Using CATALINA_TMPDIR: /var/apache/tomcat/temp
Using JRE_HOME:        /usr/java
```

Example: Apache Roller

Now that you have Tomcat running, you can install Java-based web applications such as the Apache Roller blogging software web application. This example requires MySQL and the MySQL JDBC driver, as well as the Java Mail API:

1. Create a database for Roller:

    ```
    # /usr/mysql/bin/mysql -u root -p
    Enter password: <password>
    Welcome to the MySQL monitor.  Commands end with ; or \g.
    Your MySQL connection id is 2
    Server version: 5.0.45 Source distribution

    Type 'help;' or '\h' for help. Type '\c' to clear the buffer.

    mysql> CREATE DATABASE roller;
    Query OK, 1 row affected (0.01 sec)

    mysql> GRANT ALL on roller.* to roller@localhost IDENTIFIED by
     'rollerpass';
    Query OK, 0 rows affected (0.33 sec)

    mysql> quit
    Bye
    ```

2. Create a properties file, roller-custom.properties, in /usr/apache/tomcat/common/classes, with the following entries (substituting your database username and password, and your mail hostname, username, and password):

    ```
    # cat /usr/apache/tomcat/common/classes/roller-custom.properties
    installation.type=auto
    database.configurationType=jdbc
    database.jdbc.driverClass=com.mysql.jdbc.Driver
    database.jdbc.connectionURL=jdbc:mysql://localhost:3306/roller
    database.jdbc.username=roller
    database.jdbc.password=rollerpass
    mail.configurationType=properties
    mail.hostname=smtp-server.example.com
    mail.username=nsolter
    mail.password=nick
    ```

3. Download Apache Roller from http://roller.apache.org.

4. Unzip the downloaded zip file and deploy the Roller web application. This example simply copies the entire roller directory as is to /var/apache/tomcat/webapps. If you

prefer using WAR files, then create a WAR file from the Roller directory and let Tomcat explode it:

```
# cd <download directory>
# unzip -q apache-roller-4.0.zip
# cp -r apache-roller-4.0/webapp/roller /var/apache/tomcat/webapps
```

5. Restart Tomcat:

```
# /usr/apache/tomcat/bin/shutdown.sh
Using CATALINA_BASE:   /var/apache/tomcat
Using CATALINA_HOME:   /usr/apache/tomcat
Using CATALINA_TMPDIR: /var/apache/tomcat/temp
Using JRE_HOME:        /usr/java
# /usr/apache/tomcat/bin/startup.sh
Using CATALINA_BASE:   /var/apache/tomcat
Using CATALINA_HOME:   /usr/apache/tomcat
Using CATALINA_TMPDIR: /var/apache/tomcat/temp
Using JRE_HOME:        /usr/java
```

6. Point your browser at `http://<yourdomain>:8080/roller`. You should see something similar to Figure 23-8.

7. Follow the instructions to create the tables and complete the installation process. Then you can follow the onscreen instructions to create users and weblogs. Happy blogging!

FIGURE 23-8

The Apache Roller initial page prompts you to create the database tables.

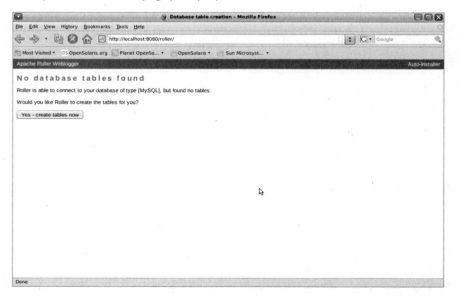

GlassFish Application Server

For more complicated Java web applications, you can run a full-fledged application server instead of a servlet engine. GlassFish is an open-source application server that can run Java-based web applications. You can find it in the glassfishv2 package in the pkg.opensolaris.org/release repository. To run GlassFish on your system, first install the glassfishv2 package. Note that it includes several other packages on which it depends, including the JavaDB database:

```
# pkg install glassfishv2
```

Now that the packages are installed, you can configure and start the GlassFish server.

NOTE If you installed and configured Apache Tomcat on your system, shut it down before trying to start GlassFish because they bind to the same port by default:

```
# /usr/apache/tomcat/bin/shutdown.sh
```

As of this writing, installing the IPS version of GlassFish does not create any *administrative domains*. A domain is the administrative boundary in GlassFish, and at least one is required to run the server. See the GlassFish documentation for more details on administrative domains. You can create a domain manually with the asadmin create-domain command:

```
# /usr/appserver/bin/asadmin create-domain --adminport 4848 mydomain
Please enter the admin user name>nsolter
Please enter the admin password>mynewpassword
Please enter the admin password again>mynewpassword
Please enter the master password [Enter to accept the default]:>masterpass
Please enter the master password again [Enter to accept the default]:>masterpass
Using port 4848 for Admin.
Using default port 8080 for HTTP Instance.
Using default port 7676 for JMS.
Using default port 3700 for IIOP.
Using default port 8181 for HTTP_SSL.
Using default port 3820 for IIOP_SSL.
Using default port 3920 for IIOP_MUTUALAUTH.
Using default port 8686 for JMX_ADMIN.
Domain being created with profile:developer, as specified by variable
 AS_ADMIN_PROFILE in configuration file.
Security Store uses: JKS
Domain mydomain created.
```

Now you can start the application server in that domain:

```
# /usr/appserver/bin/asadmin start-domain mydomain
Starting Domain mydomain, please wait.
Log redirected to /var/appserver/domains/mydomain/logs/server.log.
Please enter the master password>masterpass
Redirecting output to /var/appserver/domains/mydomain/logs/server.log
Domain mydomain is ready to receive client requests. Additional services are
```

```
being started in background.
Domain [mydomain] is running [Sun Java System Application Server 9.1_01 (build
    b09d-fcs)] with its configuration and logs at: [/var/appserver/domains].
Admin Console is available at [http://localhost:4848].
Use the same port [4848] for "asadmin" commands.
User web applications are available at these URLs:
[http://localhost:8080 https://localhost:8181 ].
Following web-contexts are available:
[/web1  /__wstx-services ].
Standard JMX Clients (like JConsole) can connect to JMXServiceURL:
[service:jmx:rmi:///jndi/rmi://OS0805:8686/jmxrmi] for domain management
    purposes.
Domain listens on at least following ports for connections:
[8080 8181 4848 3700 3820 3920 8686 ].
Domain does not support application server clusters and other standalone
    instances.
```

Now GlassFish is running on port 8080. When you connect your browser to that port, you should see something similar to Figure 23-9.

At this point, you can deploy Java-based web applications, such as Apache Roller.

FIGURE 23-9

The GlassFish default page confirms that your domain is configured correctly.

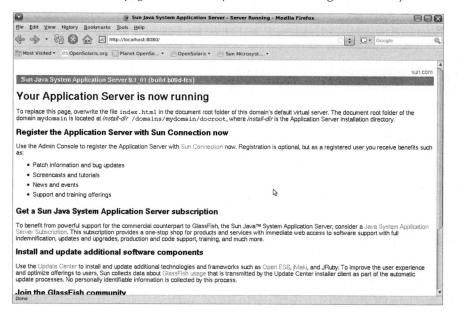

Resources

Resources for general web stack information on OpenSolaris include the following:

- The OpenSolaris Web Stack project: `http://opensolaris.org/os/project/webstack`.
- *Web Stack Getting Started Guide*: `http://dlc.sun.com/osol/docs/content/WEBSTACK/webstackgsg.html`.
- *OpenSolaris 2008.05 Development Environment*: `http://dlc.sun.com/osol/docs/content/OSDEV/chapterid.html`.

There is a plethora of online documentation about Apache, but, surprisingly, not a lot of books. The best place to start is with the Apache HTTP Server project at `apache.org`: `http://httpd.apache.org`. For specific configuration information, your best bet is to do a web search on the area of interest and explore the many tutorials, forums, and other pages that come up.

PHP and MySQL have more books written about them, including *Beginning PHP 5 and MySQL: From Novice to Professional*, by W. Jason Gilmore (Apress, 2004). This book is a great starting point for PHP and MySQL in general.

The best place to look for documentation about the Sun Java System Web Server is Sun's official docs: `http://docs.sun.com/app/docs/coll/1653.2`.

For PostgreSQL on OpenSolaris, consult the article "PostgreSQL in the OpenSolaris OS" by Zdenek Kotala at `http://sun.com/bigadmin/features/articles/postgresql_opensolaris.jsp`.

For Java-based web services, Apache Tomcat, and GlassFish, consult the following:

- *Core Servlets and JavaServer Pages Volume 1: Core Technologies*, by Marty Hall and Larry Brown (Prentice Hall, 2003).
- *Head First Servlets and JSP*, by Bryan Basham, Kathy Sierra, and Bert Bates (O'Reilly, 2004).
- *Professional Apache Tomcat 5*, by Vivek Chopra, et al. (Wrox, 2004).
- `https://glassfish.dev.java.net`.

To learn more about WordPress and Roller, start with their websites, `http://wordpress.org` and `http://roller.apache.org`, respectively.

Summary

This chapter described how to install and configure the basic AMP stack on OpenSolaris, consisting of the Apache HTTP Server, MySQL, and PHP, and how to deploy web applications, such as WordPress, using the AMP stack. You learned how to substitute the Sun Java System Web Server for the Apache HTTP Server, PostgreSQL for MySQL, and other scripting languages, such as Ruby, for PHP. Finally, you learned how to install and configure Apache Tomcat and the GlassFish application server, and to deploy Java-based web applications such as Apache Roller.

Developing on OpenSolaris

This book has focused on managing OpenSolaris as a day-to-day desktop and a platform for deploying services, but it's important not to overlook its suitability as a development platform. Whether you want to write web applications, enterprise systems software, scientific programs, or desktop applications, OpenSolaris provides a complete development environment to fit your needs. Programming language support from C and C++ to Java to PHP, Python, and Ruby enables you to develop, compile, and debug virtually any type of software on OpenSolaris.

Additionally, the NetBeans Integrated Development Environment (IDE) enables programming ease and comfort, while source code management software such as CVS, Mercurial, and Subversion support development teams. Finally, the Image Packaging System (IPS) enables you to easily make your developed software available on the OpenSolaris platform. Although most of these tools are available on other platforms too, the wide variety of virtualization options on OpenSolaris, combined with its sophisticated debugging and observability tools, such as DTrace and MDB, provide a great incentive to choose OpenSolaris as your development platform.

Java Development

Given the ties of both OpenSolaris and Java to Sun Microsystems, and the ubiquity of Java, it should be no surprise that OpenSolaris supports Java development quite well.

Compilers and tools

OpenSolaris includes the Java 6 runtime for running Java programs but because of the Open-Solaris philosophy to install by default only the functionality needed by most users, it doesn't include the Java Development Kit (JDK). To obtain the `javac` compiler, `jar` archiver, and other utilities, you need to install the JDK. If you're running the OpenSolaris distribution, you can obtain the JDK by installing the `SUNWj6dev` (32-bit) or `SUNWj6dvx` (64-bit) package.

CROSS-REF You can use the `isainfo` command to determine whether your system is running in 32-bit or 64-bit mode. See Chapters 3 and 14 for details.

For example, use the following on a 32-bit system:

```
# pkg install SUNWj6dev
```

CAUTION Although appealingly named, the `java-dev` group package is probably not what you want if you're just doing Java development because it includes a lot of extraneous software, such as Mercurial, Subversion, MySQL, Sun Studio Express, Glassfish, CVS, NetBeans, and Firefox.

If you're using a different distribution of OpenSolaris that doesn't support IPS packaging, you can download the JDK from `http://java.sun.com/javase/downloads/index.jsp`.

With the JDK installed, Java development on OpenSolaris is just like Java development on other Linux or UNIX platforms. The JDK installs the Java commands such as `javac` in `/usr/java/bin` but puts symbolic links to them in `/usr/bin`, so you should find them in your default path. For example, you can compile and run Java programs as follows:

```
$ cat JavaTest.java
class JavaTest
{
    public static void main(String args[])
    {
        System.out.println("Hello, world!");
    }
}
$ javac JavaTest.java
$ java JavaTest
Hello, world!
```

Java Development Environments

Although you can certainly write your Java programs with any of the text editors described in Chapter 3, such as `vim` and `emacs`, and compile them by hand with `javac`, command-line Java programming can quickly become tiresome. If you have more than a few source files to manage,

continued

continued
then you'll probably want to work with an Integrated Development Environment (IDE), or at least set up an automated build system with Apache Ant or Make. The NetBeans IDE, Ant, and Make are covered later in this chapter.

Debugging with JDB

Although you'll probably prefer to do your Java debugging through an IDE such as NetBeans, the JDK does include a command-line symbolic debugger, the Java Debugger (JDB). JDB uses the same commands as dbx, the symbolic debugger for C and C++ included in Sun Studio, so if you're familiar with dbx, you'll be right at home with JDB.

CROSS-REF Chapter 15 discusses the DTrace support for Java, another useful observability and debugging tool.

Introduction to JDB

The best way to explore JDB is to jump in with an example. Suppose you want to write a simple spell-check program similar to the standard UNIX spell command. The program's behavior is to take words to be checked on the command line and write them out if they are misspelled. If a word is correctly spelled, it is not written out. The program works by first importing correctly spelled words from a dictionary file and then checking each user-specified word against its dictionary of correctly spelled words. Here's a first stab at the program:

CAUTION The following program listing is buggy!

```java
import java.util.*;
import java.io.*;

class Spell
{
    public static void main(String args[])
    {
        SpellChecker myChecker = null;
        try {
            myChecker = new SpellChecker();
        } catch (Exception e) {
            System.out.println(e.toString());
            System.exit(1);
        }

        for (int i = 0; i < args.length; i++) {
            if (!myChecker.checkWord(args[i])) {
                System.out.println(args[i]);
            }
        }
    }
}
```

```
class SpellChecker
{
    private static String dictFile = "dict.txt";
    private HashSet<String> words;

    SpellChecker() throws Exception
    {
        BufferedReader input = null;
        words = new HashSet<String>();

        input = new BufferedReader (new FileReader(dictFile));
        if (input == null) {
            throw new Exception ("Cannot open " + dictFile);
        }

        String line = null;
        while ((line = input.readLine()) != null) {
            words.add(line.toLowerCase());
        }
        input.close();
    }

    boolean checkWord(String word)
    {
        return (words.contains(word.toLowerCase()));
    }
}
```

For testing, keep the dictionary file small:

```
aardvark
abacus
abaft
abalone
abandon
abandoned
abase
abash
abasia
abate
```

Now compile and test the program:

```
$ javac Spell.java
$ java Spell notaword
notaword
```

So far, so good. The program correctly printed the misspelled word, notaword. Now try a real word:

```
$ java Spell abandon
abandon
```

That's not right! The word is spelled correctly, so it shouldn't be printed. Time for some debugging. First, you need to compile your class with the `-g` option to `javac`, specifying that it should include symbolic debugging info:

```
$ javac -g Spell.java
```

Now you can start the JDB debugger with the `jdb` command:

```
$ jdb
Initializing jdb ...
>
```

The debugger gives you a command prompt. Before running the program, you can set a breakpoint near the location where you think the problem is so that the debugger stops the program execution there, enabling you to explore. In this case, it makes sense to explore the `checkWord()` method of the `SpellChecker` class:

```
> stop in SpellChecker.checkWord
Deferring breakpoint SpellChecker.checkWord.
It will be set after the class is loaded
```

Now you can run the program:

```
> run Spell abandon
run  Spell abandon
Set uncaught java.lang.Throwable
Set deferred uncaught java.lang.Throwable
>
VM Started: Set deferred breakpoint SpellChecker.checkWord

Breakpoint hit: "thread=main", SpellChecker.checkWord(),
 line=48 bci=0
48       return (words.contains(word.toLowerCase()));

main[1]
```

At this point, you can check out the state of the variables in the program with the `print` command:

```
main[1] print word
 word = "abandon"
main[1] print words
 words = "[aardvark     , abacus                , abalone
  , abandon         , abate       , abase      , abandoned
    , abash      , abasia            , abaft        ]"
main[1]
```

Evidently, the words stored in the `HashMap` have extra white space at the end, so the string comparison to the entered word always fails. Trim the strings before adding them to the `HashMap`:

```
words.add(line.trim().toLowerCase());
```

Now the program works as expected:

```
$ javac Spell.java
$ java Spell abandon
$
```

JDB commands

Table 24-1, while not comprehensive, lists the most useful JDB commands, which enable you to do almost all the debugging you need. For more details on JDB, see the references listed in the "Resources" section. These commands are all run from the JDB command prompt.

TABLE 24-1

JDB Commands

Command	Behavior
help	Prints a list of commands
run <classname> <arguments>	Runs the named class, passing it the specified command-line arguments
stop in <class name> .<method name>	Sets a breakpoint to stop program execution at the specified spot
stop at <class name>:<line>	
cont	Runs the stopped program to the next breakpoint
step	Runs the next line, stepping into function/method calls; If the next line contains a function or method call, the debugger will stop such that the next line to be executed is the first line of the nested function/method.
next	Runs the next line, stepping over function/method calls. The debugger will stop such that the next line to be executed is the subsequent line in the same function/method, having executed all nested function/method calls in between.
clear <class name> .<method name>	Clears the specified breakpoint
clear <class name>:<line>	
print <expr>	Prints the value of an expression, such as a variable
list	Shows the code at this point in the program

C and C++ Development

UNIX has a long history of supporting C and C++ programming, and OpenSolaris is no exception. Both the Sun Studio and GNU compilers are readily accessible from the package repository, along with all the tools you need, such as `make`, `autoconf`, `flex`, and `bison`. In addition, the NetBeans IDE, covered later in this chapter, supports the C and C++ compilers. Finally, OpenSolaris contains sophisticated C and C++ debugging tools, including symbolic debuggers, Modular Debugger (MDB), and a memory error-detection library called `libumem`.

Compilers and tools

Two popular sets of compilers and tools are available for C and C++ development: Sun Studio and the GNU Compiler Collection (GCC).

Sun Studio

Sun Studio is a full-fledged development environment including C, C++, and Fortran compilers, an IDE, a debugger, Distributed Make (`dmake`), a performance analyzer, and other helpful tools. The Sun Studio compilers have better performance in many cases than do the GCC compilers. As a testament to their capabilities, the Sun Studio compilers are used to compile most of OpenSolaris itself. As of this writing, the latest product release is Sun Studio 12, available from the Sun Download Center, `http://developers.sun.com/sunstudio/`.

The OpenSolaris package repository contains a version of Sun Studio called Sun Studio Express, which is a snapshot of the ongoing Sun Studio development. This chapter shows you how to install and use Sun Studio Express. If you would prefer the more stable Sun Studio commercial release, simply download and install it from the Sun Download Center.

The easiest way to set up a Sun Studio Express development environment is to install the `ss-dev` group package, which includes the following:

- Sun Studio Express
- Java Development Kit (JDK) 6 (required for the Sun Studio IDE)
- Mercurial, Subversion, and CVS source code management
- GNU Make, Automake, and Autoconf
- Bison and Flex parser and lexer
- Solaris header files

You can install the package with the following:

```
# pkg install ss-dev
```

Alternately, install just the `sunstudioexpress` package:

```
# pkg install sunstudioexpress
```

Be aware that some open source projects depend on the GNU build tools even when using the Sun Studio compiler. Now that Sun Studio Express is installed, you can compile C programs with `/opt/SunStudioExpress/bin/cc`:

```
$ cat test.c
#include <stdio.h>

int main (int argc, char **argv)
{
        printf("Hello, world\n");
        return (0);
}
$ /opt/SunStudioExpress/bin/cc -o test test.c
$ ./test
Hello, world
```

TIP When configured for Solaris or OpenSolaris, most open source projects look for the cc compiler in your path, so to compile open source code bases (and for your own convenience), add `/opt/SunStudioExpress/bin` to your path.

For a list of compiler options, run `/opt/SunStudioExpress/bin/cc -flags`.

NOTE If you've installed the Sun Studio product instead of Sun Studio Express, you'll find the compiler binaries in `/opt/SUNWspro/bin` instead of `/opt/SunStudioExpress/bin`.

The C++ compiler is `/opt/SunStudioExpress/bin/CC`:

```
$ cat test.cc
#include <iostream>
using namespace std;

int main(int argc, char **argv)
{
  cout << "hello, world" << endl;
  return (0);
}
$ /opt/SunStudioExpress/bin/CC -o testcc test.cc
$ ./testcc
hello, world
```

As with Java programming, command-line C and C++ development can quickly become tiresome. You probably want to either use an IDE such as NetBeans, or set up build automation with Make or GNU Make. Both of these options are explored later in this chapter.

GNU tools

If you prefer or require the GNU Compiler Collection (GCC) compiler and tools, you can install and use those instead of Sun Studio. The easiest way to obtain GCC is to install the gcc-dev group package, which contains the following:

- gcc, g++, and gdb
- Mercurial, Subversion, and CVS source code management
- GNU Make, Automake, and Autoconf
- Bison and Flex parser and lexer

Install the package with the following:

```
# pkg install gcc-dev
```

The GNU C compiler driver, gcc, installs into /usr/sfw/bin, with symbolic links from /usr/gnu/bin and /usr/bin. Because /usr/bin should be in your path by default, you can use gcc without specifying the path. For example, use the following to compile the C program listed earlier in the Sun Studio section:

```
$ gcc -o test test.c
$ ./test
Hello, world
```

> **NOTE** The symbolic link to gcc in /usr/gnu/bin is named cc, not gcc.

Similarly, the GNU C++ compiler driver, g++, installs into /usr/sfw/bin, with a symbolic link from /usr/bin. You can compile C++ programs with g++. For example, use the following to compile the C++ program listed earlier in the Sun Studio section:

```
$ g++ -o testcc test.cc
$ ./testcc
hello, world
```

gcc, g++, and c++: Which binary do I use?

Both gcc and g++ are simply driver programs that call the compiler and linker for you. There is only one compiler, which compiles both C and C++ code, so you could compile C++ code with gcc and C code with g++. The difference is that g++ links your program with the required

continued

continued

C++ libraries automatically. If you use gcc to compile C++ code, you need to link with the C++ libraries explicitly on the command line. It's easiest to use g++ for C++ code and gcc for C code.

Confusingly, the GNU Compiler Collection also provides a binary named c++ in /usr/bin and /usr/sfw/bin, which is a hard link to g++.

OpenSolaris C APIs

OpenSolaris contains a rich environment for programming in C. In addition to the C standard library, OpenSolaris supports the POSIX APIs, as well as some additional functionality not part of POSIX. In fact, most of the shell commands in OpenSolaris have C API equivalents. Details of the various APIs are beyond the scope of this book. For that level of programming detail, consult one of the UNIX or Solaris systems programming books listed in the "Resources" section. *Solaris Systems Programming* by Rich Teer is a particularly good place to start. This section lists some of the most useful application programming interfaces (APIs) that you might want to explore further:

- C standard library
- Additional string manipulation
- Low-level I/O (creat, open, close, etc.)
- File and directory manipulations
- File system manipulations
- Date and time (time, etc.)
- Users and groups (setuid, etc.)
- Signals
- Process control (fork, exec, etc.)
- Networking with sockets
- Interprocess communication (such as pipes, FIFOs, and message queues)
- Remote procedure calls (RPC)
- Doors
- Threads and synchronization primitives (mutexes, semaphores, etc.)
- Logging and events (syslog and sysevents)

TIP   Most of the C header files are in the SUNWhea package, which is not installed by default. This package contains even the C standard library headers; without it, you can't do much C programming. Both ss-dev and gcc-dev are dependent on SUNWhea, so if you install the compilers that way, you'll get the headers; but if you install the compilers another way, then you may need to install the SUNWhea package explicitly.

Debugging

If you've done any C and C++ programming, you've almost certainly had to do some debugging. Sun Studio and GCC include the symbolic command-line debuggers dbx and GDB, respectively. These are not OpenSolaris-specific. OpenSolaris also includes the Modular Debugger (MDB), which is powerful even when symbolic information is not available, and the memory debugging library libumem.

dbx and GDB

GDB and dbx are *symbolic debuggers* for the GNU Compiler Collection and Sun Studio, respectively. A symbolic debugger is one that enables you to access the symbols in your program, such as variable and class names. Let's first look at symbolic debugging with an example, and then examine a summary of the commands in both dbx and GDB.

Suppose you're writing the software for an electronic voting machine in C. To keep things simple, the ballot questions are stored in a text file called ballot.txt, with each question on a single line. All ballot questions are yes or no, so the possible answers don't need to be stored in the file.

For the design of the program, one approach is to store the ballot questions in a linked list for easy iteration when presenting the ballot to voters. The first chunk of the functionality you might choose to implement is reading the text file questions into the linked list. The following buggy program is an attempt to perform this task:

CAUTION Remember that the following program listing is buggy!

```c
#include <stdio.h>
#include <stdlib.h>
#include <string.h>

#define BALLOT_FILE "ballot.txt"

typedef struct BallotList
{
  char *question;
  struct BallotList *next;
} BallotList;

void readBallot(BallotList **ballot);
int main(int argc, char **argv)
{
  BallotList *ballot = NULL;
  readBallot(&ballot);
  if (ballot == NULL) {
    printf("Error reading ballot!\n");
    exit(1);
  }
```

```
    printf("Ballot read successfully\n");
}

void
readBallot(BallotList **ballot)
{
  char buf[1012];
  BallotList *first = NULL;
  BallotList *cur = NULL;
  FILE *ballotFile = NULL;

  if ((ballotFile = fopen(BALLOT_FILE, "r")) == NULL) {
    return;
  }

  while (fgets(buf, 1011, ballotFile) != NULL) {
    BallotList *next = malloc(sizeof(BallotList));
    next->next = NULL;
    strcpy(next->question, buf);

    if (first == NULL) {
      first = cur = next;
    } else {
      cur->next = next;
      cur = next;
    }
  }

  *ballot = first;
}
```

As a sample ballot file, you might use something like this:

```
$ cat ballot.txt
Test question one?
Test question two?
Test question three?
```

This program compiles fine, but it doesn't run particularly well, as shown in the following example:

```
$ /opt/SunStudioExpress/bin/cc -o voting voting.c
$ ./voting
Segmentation Fault (core dumped)
```

A segmentation fault usually signals some sort of memory error, but the output doesn't indicate where it occurred. Time for a debugger!

dbx example

You can use dbx to debug this program.

NOTE You can use dbx to debug C and C++ programs compiled with Sun Studio or GCC. You can use GDB to debug C and C++ programs compiled with GCC, and C programs compiled with dbx, but it might not work properly on C++ programs compiled with Sun Studio. That's because the C++ debugging information and Application Binary Interface (ABI) are not standard across compilers, and GDB doesn't understand the Sun Studio debugging information and ABI. Sun Studio, however, understands the GCC C++ debugging information and ABI.

To take advantage of symbolic debugging, you need to compile the program with the -g flag:

```
$ /opt/SunStudioExpress/bin/cc -o voting -g voting.c
```

Now you can run it under dbx:

```
$ /opt/SunStudioExpress/bin/dbx voting
For information about new features see `help changes'
To remove this message, put `dbxenv suppress_startup_message 7.7'
 in your .dbxrc
Reading voting
Reading ld.so.1
Reading libc.so.1
(dbx) run
Running: voting
(process id 1078)
signal SEGV (no mapping at the fault address) in strcpy at 0xd1297134
0xd1297134: strcpy+0x0024:       movl      %eax,(%edi)
Current function is readBallot
   49          strcpy(next->question, buf);
(dbx)
```

NOTE In some cases, it isn't practical to rerun the buggy program to reproduce the problem. See the "Debugging core files" section later in this chapter for alternatives.

You already have more information than before because you can see exactly where the SEGV occurred. One of the first things to do is view a full stack trace using the where command:

```
(dbx) where
  [1] strcpy(0x8050bc9, 0x6f697473), at 0xd1297134
=>[2] readBallot(ballot = 0x8047d00), line 49 in "voting.c"
  [3] main(argc = 1, argv = 0x8047d38), line 19 in "voting.c"
```

Because you have symbolic information, you can print the contents of variables in memory. The SEGV occurred on a strcpy, so you can start with the two arguments to that function call:

```
(dbx) print buf
buf = "Test question two?\n"
(dbx) print next->question
next->question = 0x6f697473 "<bad address 0x6f697473>"
```

It looks like there's a problem with the question field of the next struct. To see where the problem might come from, look at the code in readBallot right before the strcpy function call using the list - command in dbx:

```
(dbx) list -
   31     BallotList *cur = NULL;
   32     FILE *ballotFile = NULL;
   33
   34     if ((ballotFile = fopen(BALLOT_FILE, "r")) == NULL) {
   35       return;
   36     }
   37
   38     while (fgets(buf, 1011, ballotFile) != NULL) {
   39       BallotList *next = malloc(sizeof(BallotList));
   40       next->next = NULL;
```

It looks like space is allocated for the BallotList structure, but take another look at the structure definition:

```
(dbx) whatis -t struct BallotList
struct BallotList {
    char *question;
    struct BallotList *next;
};
```

It looks like there's no space allocated for the question field of the BallotList structure. You need to replace the strcpy with strdup(), which allocates memory appropriately:

```
BallotList *next = malloc(sizeof(BallotList));
next->next = NULL;
next->question = strdup(buf);
```

Now the program works fine:

```
$ /opt/SunStudioExpress/bin/cc -o voting -g voting.c
$ ./voting
Ballot read successfully
```

GDB example

Debugging the program in GDB is almost identical to debugging it in dbx:

```
$ gcc -o voting -g voting.c
$ gdb voting
GNU gdb 6.3.50_2004-11-23-cvs
Copyright 2004 Free Software Foundation, Inc.
GDB is free software, covered by the GNU General Public License, and you are
welcome to change it and/or distribute copies of it under certain conditions.
Type "show copying" to see the conditions.
There is absolutely no warranty for GDB.  Type "show warranty" for details.
This GDB was configured as "i386-pc-solaris2.11"...
(gdb) run
Starting program: /export/home/nsolter/cdbg/voting
```

```
Program received signal SIGSEGV, Segmentation fault.
0xd1297134 in store () from /lib/libc.so.1
(gdb) where
#0  0xd1297134 in store () from /lib/libc.so.1
#1  0x08047e04 in ?? ()
#2  0x08050e4c in readBallot (ballot=0x8047d88) at voting.c:41
#3  0x08050d6f in main (argc=1, argv=0x8047db4) at voting.c:18
(gdb) up
#1  0x08047e04 in ?? ()
(gdb) up
#2  0x08050e4c in readBallot (ballot=0x8047d88) at voting.c:41
41              strcpy(next->question, buf);
(gdb) print buf
```

$1 = "Test question two?\n", '\0' <repeats 33 times>, "½·/Ñ\200\202:Ñ\000\000
\000\000\000\000\000\000\001\000\000\000\000*%Ñ\000@:Ñ‚y\004\b½·/Ñ\000*%Ñ\200
\202:Ñ\000\000\000\000\000*%Ñ\200\202:Ñ\000@:ÑÕ:=Ñ½·/Ñ\203¹0Ñ\000@:Ñy\004\b
\000*%Ñ\000z\004\b\"¹0Ñ\000*%ÑÿÿÿÿpÁ?ÑÜÇ?Ñ$r=Ñ\bz\004\b®\t=Ñ\003\000\000\000
\030z\004\b½\004=Ñ\003\000\000\000ÜÇ?Ñ9s=ÑxÁ?ÑDz\004\bjx=Ñ\003\000\000\000xÁ
?Ñxî?ÑÜÇ?"...

```
(gdb) print next->question
$2 = 0x6f697473 <Address 0x6f697473 out of bounds>
(gdb) list
36          }
37
38          while (fgets(buf, 1011, ballotFile) != NULL) {
39             BallotList *next = malloc(sizeof(BallotList));
40             next->next = NULL;
41             strcpy(next->question, buf);
42
43             if (first == NULL) {
44                first = = next;
      } else {
(gdb) ptype BallotList
type = struct BallotList {
    char *question;
    struct BallotList *next;
}
```

Attaching to live processes

You can use dbx and GDB to debug a live process even if you didn't start the process under the debugger by attaching to the process. The only catch is that you must have access to the executable file for the process. For example, here's how to attach to the process named long-running with pid 1336 and the executable in the working directory:

```
$ pgrep long-running
1336
$ /opt/SunStudioExpress/bin/dbx long-running 1336
For information about new features see `help changes'
To remove this message, put `dbxenv suppress_startup_message 7.7'
  in your .dbxrc
```

```
Reading long-running
Reading ld.so.1
Reading libc.so.1
Attached to process 1336
stopped in __nanosleep at 0xd1310ad5
0xd1310ad5: __nanosleep+0x0015: jae        __nanosleep+0x23
[ 0xd1310ae3, .+0xe ]
Current function is main
    4        sleep (10);
(dbx)
```

After attaching to the process, you can set breakpoints, using the cont command to continue executing the program until it hits the next one:

```
(dbx) stop in sleep
dbx: warning: 'sleep' has no debugger info -- will trigger on first
 instruction
(2) stop in _sleep
(dbx) cont
stopped in _sleep at 0xd12ff932
0xd12ff932: _sleep        :        pushl    %ebp
Current function is main
sleep (10);
```

CROSS-REF Proc tools such as pstack and pflags and the truss command are also quite useful for debugging live processes and core files. These tools are discussed in Chapter 14.

Debugging core files

Bugs aren't always easily reproducible. Some bugs are timing or user-input dependent. Furthermore, running through a debugger might change the behavior or timing. OpenSolaris includes a facility that enables *post mortem debugging* of a process that terminated abnormally. By default, if OpenSolaris terminates a process because of a segmentation violation or another signal with the disposition to dump a core file, then it dumps the process' current address space and some extra debugging information into a *core file*. You can open the core file in a debugger just as you would attach to a live process, and examine the state of its memory. If the program was compiled with debugging information, you need access to all the symbolic information as well. For example, when the voting program from the previous section terminated with a SEGV, it output this message:

```
$ ./voting
Segmentation Fault (core dumped)
```

The "core dumped" after the notification of the segmentation fault means that the process' memory was saved to a core file. Unless you've configured it otherwise, the core file is named core in the working directory. The details of core file naming and using coreadm to tune core file settings are discussed later in this chapter. You can open the core file in GDB or dbx. Unlike with a live process, of course, you can't actually execute the program:

```
$ file core
core:            ELF 32-bit LSB core file 80386 Version 1, from 'voting'
```

```
$ gdb voting core
GNU gdb 6.3.50_2004-11-23-cvs
Copyright 2004 Free Software Foundation, Inc.
GDB is free software, covered by the GNU General Public License, and you are
welcome to change it and/or distribute copies of it under certain conditions.
Type "show copying" to see the conditions.
There is absolutely no warranty for GDB. Type "show warranty" for details.
This GDB was configured as "i386-pc-solaris2.11"...
Core was generated by `./voting'.
Program terminated with signal 11, Segmentation fault.
Reading symbols from /lib/libc.so.1...done.
Loaded symbols for /lib/libc.so.1
#0  0xd1297134 in store () from /lib/libc.so.1
(gdb) where
#0  0xd1297134 in store () from /lib/libc.so.1
#1  0x08047e30 in ?? ()
#2  0x08050e4c in readBallot (ballot=0x8047db8) at voting.c:41
#3  0x08050d6f in main (argc=1, argv=0x8047de4) at voting.c:18
(gdb) up
#1  0x08047e30 in ?? ()
(gdb) up
#2  0x08050e4c in readBallot (ballot=0x8047db8) at voting.c:41
41              strcpy(next->question, buf);
(gdb) print buf
$1 = "Test question two?\n", '\0' <repeats 33 times>, ''½·/Ñ\200\202:Ñ\000\000
\000\000\000\000\000\000\000\001\000\000\000\000*%Ñ\000@:Ñey\004\b½·/Ñ\000*%Ñ\200
\202:Ñ\000\000\000\000\000*%Ñ\200\202:Ñ\000@:ÑÕ;=Ñ½·/Ñ\203¹0Ñ\000@:Ñ\034z\004\b
\000*%ÑOz\004\b\"¹0Ñ\000*%ÑÿÿÿÿpÁ?ÑÜÇ?Ñ$r=Ñ8z\004\b®\t=Ñ\003\000\000\000Hz\004
\b½\004=Ñ\003\000\000\000ÜÇ?Ñ9s=ÑxÁ?Ñtz\004\bjx=Ñ\003\000\000\000xÁ?Ñxî?ÑÜÇ?"...
(gdb)
```

dbx and GDB command summary

Table 24-2 summarizes the most useful dbx and GDB commands. The dbx and GDB command sets are quite similar, but there are some important differences.

MDB

OpenSolaris includes another debugger called Modular Debugger (MDB). Unlike GDB and dbx, MDB is designed for low-level debugging, in which symbolic information might not be available. This means you can run MDB on a live process, on a core file, or even on the running kernel itself, without access to the executable files. This debugger is particularly useful for diagnosing problems that are not easily reproducible or that have occurred outside your environment (such as at a customer site), where only the core file is available.

To get a feel for MDB, start with a simple example. Suppose the voting program in the previous section was compiled without debugging information and all you have is the core file. You can still get some information with MDB:

```
$ mdb core
Loading modules: [ libc.so.1 ld.so.1 ]
```

```
> ::status
debugging core file of voting (32-bit) from OS0805
file: /export/home/nsolter/cdbg/voting
initial argv: ./voting
threading model: native threads
status: process terminated by SIGSEGV (Segmentation Fault)
> ::stack
libc.so.1`strcpy+0x24(8047db0, 0)
main+0x18(1, 8047de4, 8047dec, 80509cf)
_start+0x7d(1, 8047e98, 0, 8047ea1, 8047eac, 8047ebc)
> $q

$
```

TABLE 24-2

dbx and GDB Commands

dbx Command	GDB Command	Behavior
help	help	Displays a list of commands
where	where or bt	Prints a stack trace
up/down	up/down	Moves up or down the stack
run	run	Runs the program
list	list	Prints the lines of high-level code at the current spot
print	print	Prints the value of an expression, such as a variable
whatis	ptype	Prints the definition of a type
stop <arg>	break <arg>	Sets breakpoints
cont	cont	Continues running the program after stopping at a breakpoint
step	step	Runs the next line, stepping into function/method calls. If the next line contains a function or method call, then the debugger will stop such that the next line to be executed is the first line of the nested function/method.
next	next	Runs the next line, stepping over function/method calls. The debugger will stop such that the next line to be executed is the subsequent line in the same function/method, having executed all nested function/method calls in between.
clear	clear	Clears breakpoints

The stack trace shows that it failed inside `strcpy`. Your next steps might be to print the variables and arguments to the functions or to disassemble the code around the problem area to try to track down the source of the bug. (These investigations require knowledge of your target platform's assembly, register usage, and stack memory layout, and so are beyond the scope of this book.)

As you can see, debugging a random program with MDB without symbolic information can be somewhat painful. MDB's built-in debugging commands are mostly limited to examining memory and providing the basic debugging functionality for setting breakpoints and stepping through programs; but the real power of MDB lies, as its name implies, in its modularity and extensibility. MDB enables application and kernel developers to write commands, called *dcmds* and *walkers*, that can utilize specific information about the application being debugged. These custom commands can help you extract information about the program without needing to understand the program's memory layout. To see a list of dcmds available at any point in MDB, run `::dcmds`. To see a list of walkers, run `::walkers`.

> **NOTE** Many useful dcmds and walkers are available for kernel debugging. Using MDB for kernel debugging is described later in this chapter.

You can write your own module for MDB, containing dcmds and walkers specific to your application. Consult the references in the "Resources" section near the end of this chapter for details.

Libumem

MDB is particularly useful when combined with the userland memory allocation library `libumem`. This library is a port of the kernel memory allocator, known as the *slab allocator*, to userland. It interposes on the memory allocation routines such as `malloc` and `free`, providing a safer memory allocation library than that implemented in `libc`. In particular, it detects common errors such as reading previously freed memory, writing to unallocated memory, and the like. To run a program under `libumem`, set the shell environment variable `LD_PRELOAD` to `libumem.so`, and provide options to it via the `UMEM_DEBUG` and `UMEM_LOGGING` variables.

> **TIP** The `umem_debug(3MALLOC)` man page describes the various options for the `UMEM_DEBUG` and `UMEM_LOGGING` flags.

`libumem` works by putting extra space and debugging information around each user-requested allocation, and by setting the uninitialized memory to recognizable byte patterns. Specifically, each memory allocation starts with eight bytes of metadata, followed by the user data, then the *redzone* and some debug metadata. Because `libumem` uses caches of pre-allocated memory chunks, the user data is a chunk of memory that is at least as large as requested by the user. The portion of memory that the user can use ends with the `0xbb` value. Each word of uninitialized memory in the user allocation is set to `0xbaddcafe`. The redzone marks the end of the user-allocated chunk, and is marked with the `0xfeedface` indicator. For the purposes of this example, that's all you need to know. For details, see the references in the "Resources" section.

For example, consider this trivial program that overflows a memory allocation in the heap:

```
$ cat mem-error.c
#include <stdlib.h>
#include <stdio.h>
#include <string.h>

int main(int argc, char **argv)
{
        char *ptr;
        ptr = (char *)malloc(10);
        strcpy(ptr, "Hello, world!");

        printf("%s", ptr);
        free(ptr);
}
```

When you run it under libumem, libumem detects the memory error and aborts the program to generate a core file:

```
$ LD_PRELOAD=libumem.so UMEM_DEBUG=default UMEM_LOGGING=transaction,contents,fail\
  ./mem-error
Abort (core dumped)
```

Now you can examine this core file with MDB, or one of the other debuggers described previously:

```
$ mdb core
Loading modules: [ libumem.so.1 libc.so.1 ld.so.1 ]
```

Note that the libumem MDB module is loaded because the program was run with libumem. As usual, first check the status, although in this case it doesn't tell you anything you don't already know:

```
> ::status
debugging core file of mem-error (32-bit) from OS0805
file: /export/home/nsolter/cdbg/mem-error
initial argv: ./mem-error
threading model: native threads
status: process terminated by SIGABRT (Abort)
```

Next, find all the dcmds and walkers in the libumem module:

```
> ::dmods -l libumem.so.1

libumem.so.1
  dcmd allocdby          - given a thread, print its allocated buffers
  dcmd bufctl            - print or filter a bufctl
  dcmd bufctl_audit      - print a bufctl_audit
```

```
dcmd findleaks          - search for potential memory leaks
dcmd freedby            - given a thread, print its freed buffers
dcmd ugrep              - search user address space for a pointer
dcmd umalog             - display umem transaction log and stack traces
dcmd umastat            - umem allocator stats
dcmd umausers           -
display current medium and large users of the umem allocator
dcmd umem_cache         - print a umem cache
dcmd umem_debug         - toggle umem dcmd/walk debugging
dcmd umem_log           - dump umem transaction log
dcmd umem_malloc_dist   - report distribution of outstanding malloc()s
dcmd umem_malloc_info   - report information about malloc()s by cache
dcmd umem_status        - Print umem status and message buffer
dcmd umem_verify        - check integrity of umem-managed memory
dcmd vmem               - print a vmem_t
dcmd vmem_seg           - print or filter a vmem_seg
dcmd whatis             - given an address, return information
walk allocdby           - given a thread, walk its allocated bufctls
walk bufctl             - walk a umem cache's bufctls
walk bufctl_history     - walk the available history of a bufctl
walk freectl            - walk a umem cache's free bufctls
walk freedby            - given a thread, walk its freed bufctls
walk freemem            - walk a umem cache's free memory
walk leak               -
given a leak ctl, walk other leaks w/ that stacktrace
walk leakbuf            -
given a leak ctl, walk addr of leaks w/ that stacktrace
walk umem               - walk a umem cache
walk umem_alloc_112     - walk the umem_alloc_112 cache
...
```

Generally, the dcmd to start with is ::umem_status. This command returns the memory error:

```
> ::umem_status
Status:          ready and active
Concurrency:     2
Logs:            transaction=64k content=64k fail=64k (inactive)
Message buffer:
umem allocator: redzone violation: write past end of buffer
buffer=80a8fd0  bufctl=80aee30  cache: umem_alloc_24
previous transaction on buffer 80a8fd0:
thread=1  time=T-0.000055947  slab=80a9f98  cache: umem_alloc_24
libumem.so.1'umem_cache_alloc_debug+0x14f
libumem.so.1'umem_cache_alloc+0x180
libumem.so.1'umem_alloc+0xc5
libumem.so.1'malloc+0x27
mem-error'main+0xf
mem-error'_start+0x7d
umem: heap corruption detected
```

```
stack trace:
libumem.so.1'umem_err_recoverable+0x39
libumem.so.1'umem_error+0x47f
libumem.so.1'umem_free+0xf7
libumem.so.1'process_free+0x55
libumem.so.1'free+0x17
mem-error'main+0x42
mem-error'_start+0x7d
```

Here, the detected error was a redzone violation. Based on libumem's memory layout, described earlier, that means the program wrote past the end of its allocated memory into the redzone. With such a simple program, it's immediately obvious based on the stack trace of the buffer allocation which allocation it was (the only one in the program), but in a more complicated program you might need to disassemble the code to figure out where the allocation occurred:

```
> main+0xf::dis
main:                   pushl   %ebp
main+1:                 movl    %esp,%ebp
main+3:                 subl    $0x8,%esp
main+6:                 pushl   $0x0
main+8:                 pushl   $0xa
main+0xa:               call    -0x173     <PLT=libumem.so.1`malloc>
main+0xf:               addl    $0x8,%esp
main+0x12:              movl    %eax,-0x8(%ebp)
main+0x15:              pushl   $0x8050af0
main+0x1a:              movl    -0x8(%ebp),%eax
main+0x1d:              pushl   %eax
main+0x1e:              call    -0x177     <PLT=libc.so.1`strcpy>
main+0x23:              addl    $0x8,%esp
main+0x26:              movl    -0x8(%ebp),%eax
main+0x29:              pushl   %eax
main+0x2a:              pushl   $0x8050b00
main+0x2f:              call    -0x178     <PLT=libc.so.1`printf>
```

This discussion of libumem and MDB is really just a taste of their true power. For example, another useful libumem dcmd not demonstrated here is findleaks, which detects memory leaks in C and C++ programs. For more details see the references listed in the "Resources" section. Although the overhead of learning the somewhat arcane commands and studying your assembly and memory layout might seem prohibitive, a one-time investment can quickly pay off with reduced debugging time.

CAUTION Because libumem is implemented as an interposed memory allocator, it detects only heap-based memory errors, not stack-based problems. To detect stack-based problems, you need to use another tool. Unfortunately, some of the best tools, such as Rational Purify, are not open source, so you need to purchase a license to use them.

Other Languages

If Java, C, and C++ aren't your thing, don't worry! OpenSolaris provides development environments for almost any programming or scripting language. This section shows you how to set up your system to code in a few of the most popular ones, including Perl, Python, Ruby, PHP, and good old shell scripting.

Perl

The OpenSolaris default installation includes Perl in /usr/perl5. As of this writing, the exact version is 5.8.4. /usr/bin/perl is a symbolic link to /usr/perl5/5.8.4/bin/perl, so it should be in your default path.

For example, you can run a Perl script as follows:

```
$ cat test.pl
#!/usr/bin/perl

print "hello, world!\n";
$ perl test.pl
hello, world!
```

Use the following if the file is executable:

```
$ ./test.pl
hello, world!
```

Python

Like Perl, Python is also in the default OpenSolaris installation. In fact, it's used to implement some significant pieces of OpenSolaris such as the installer and Image Packaging System. The command /usr/bin/python is a symbolic link to the latest version, which, as of this writing, is 2.4.4. You can run Python scripts in the usual way:

```
$ cat test.py
#!/usr/bin/python

print "Hello, world!"
$ python test.py
Hello, world!
```

Or, if the file is executable:

```
$ ./test.py
Hello, world!
```

Ruby on Rails

Ruby is not included by default on OpenSolaris, but it is available from the package repository. As described in Chapter 23, you can install the SUNWruby18 package:

```
# pkg install SUNWruby18
```

Alternatively, you can install the SUNWruby-dev group package:

```
# pkg install SUNWruby-dev
```

In addition to Ruby itself, SUNWruby-dev pulls in the following:

- Java Development Kit (JDK) 6
- NetBeans IDE
- Mercurial, Subversion, and CVS source code management
- Firefox web browser
- Squid and memcached (mentioned in Chapter 23).

After installation of either SUNWruby18 directly or the SUNWruby-dev group package, /usr/bin/ruby is a symbolic link to the latest version of Ruby (1.8.6 as of this writing). You can run Ruby scripts in the usual way:

```
$ cat test.rb
#!/usr/bin/ruby

puts 'Hello, world!'
$ ruby test.rb
Hello, world!
```

Or, if the file is executable:

```
$ ./test.rb
Hello, world!
```

> **TIP**   If you prefer JRuby, you can find it in the SUNWjruby package.

The SUNWruby18 package also includes the RubyGem package manager for Ruby in /usr/bin/gem. You can use gem to install Rails:

```
# gem update
Updating installed gems...
Bulk updating Gem source index for: http://gems.rubyforge.org
Gems: [] updated
# gem install rails --include-dependencies
Bulk updating Gem source index for: http://gems.rubyforge.org
Successfully installed rails-2.1.0
```

```
Successfully installed rake-0.8.1
Successfully installed activesupport-2.1.0
Successfully installed activerecord-2.1.0
Successfully installed actionpack-2.1.0
Successfully installed actionmailer-2.1.0
Successfully installed activeresource-2.1.0
Installing ri documentation for rake-0.8.1...
Installing ri documentation for activesupport-2.1.0...
Installing ri documentation for activerecord-2.1.0...
Installing ri documentation for actionpack-2.1.0...
Installing ri documentation for actionmailer-2.1.0...
Installing ri documentation for activeresource-2.1.0...
Installing RDoc documentation for rake-0.8.1...
Installing RDoc documentation for activesupport-2.1.0...
Installing RDoc documentation for activerecord-2.1.0...
Installing RDoc documentation for actionpack-2.1.0...
Installing RDoc documentation for actionmailer-2.1.0...
Installing RDoc documentation for activeresource-2.1.0...
```

Note that Rails is installed in /usr/ruby/1.8/bin, without symbolic links in /usr/bin. For example:

```
$ /usr/ruby/1.8/bin/rails myapp
      create
      create  app/controllers
      create  app/helpers
      create  app/models
  ...
```

If you'll be using Rails a lot, you can create your own symlink in /usr/bin. You can also develop Ruby on Rails applications with the NetBeans IDE, described later in this chapter.

PHP

Like Ruby, PHP is not installed by default on OpenSolaris, but it is readily available from the package repository. Because PHP is typically used as part of the Apache, MySQL, and PHP (AMP) stack, it's included in the amp-dev group package.

CROSS-REF Chapter 23 describes the contents of the amp-dev package and how to install it, how to install just the PHP packages, and how to use PHP with Apache and MySQL.

Shell scripting

As discussed in Chapter 3, OpenSolaris contains all the standard shells, including bash, csh, and ksh. If you're familiar with Linux, you're probably most comfortable scripting with bash, which is the default user shell. Many of the scripts in OpenSolaris, however, are written using the Korn Shell.

893

> CAUTION   OpenSolaris includes `ksh93`, which is slightly different from the `ksh88` that is the
> default Korn shell in Solaris 10 and Solaris Express.

Build Automation

OpenSolaris supports both Apache Ant and Make for configuring an automated build environment for your software projects. Ant is available in the `SUNWant` package, Solaris Make is in the `SUNWsprot` package, and GNU Make is in `SUNWgmake`. The `SUNWsprot` package should be installed by default. You can install the other two as follows:

```
# pkg install SUNWant
# pkg install SUNWgmake
```

If you're unfamiliar with Ant or Make, consult one of the references in the "Resources" section.

> CAUTION   Solaris Make and GNU Make differ from each other and from the base System V
> Make. For example, conditional or target-specific macro definitions in Solaris Make
> look like this:
>
> ```
> target := MYMACRO=myvalue
> ```
>
> The equivalent in GNU Make looks like this:
>
> ```
> target : MYMACRO=myvalue
> ```
>
> Consult the documentation for whichever variant of Make you choose to ensure that you're using
> it correctly.

NetBeans

NetBeans is an open source, cross-platform integrated development environment (IDE) written in Java. If you're running the OpenSolaris distribution, you can obtain NetBeans from the package repository:

```
# pkg install netbeans
```

If you're using a different distribution, you can download NetBeans from `www.netbeans.org/`.

Once you've installed NetBeans, you can launch the IDE by selecting Applications ➤ Developer Tools ➤ NetBeans IDE, or by running `/usr/netbeans/bin/netbeans` from the command line. When the application starts, a window like the one shown in Figure 24-1 appears.

What about Eclipse?

If you've done much development on Linux or other platforms, you may be more familiar with the Eclipse IDE. You can install Eclipse from the package repository with `pkg install eclipse`, then launch it by running `/usr/eclipse/eclipse`.

FIGURE 24-1

NetBeans is a full-featured IDE.

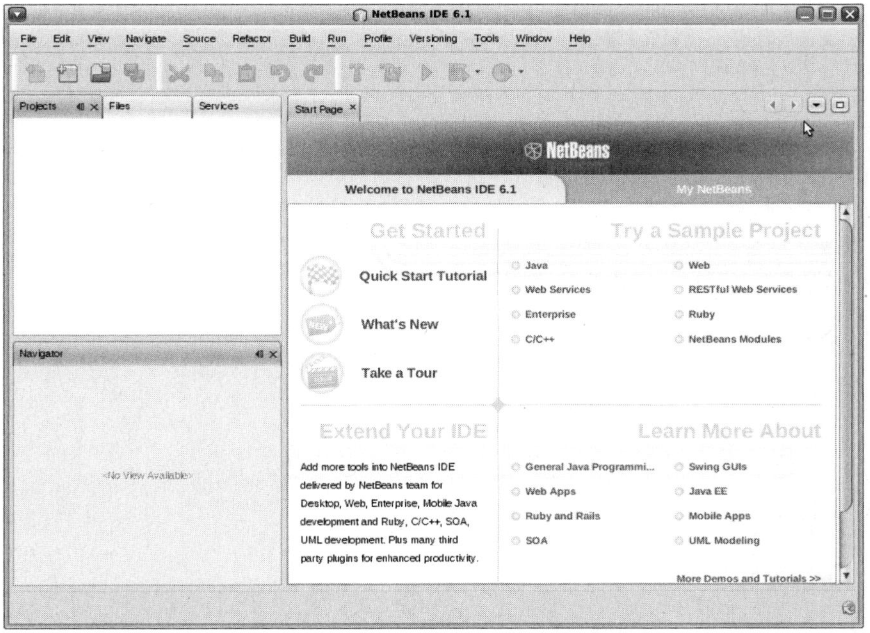

NetBeans overview

NetBeans provides support for several different programming languages, including Java, C/C++, and Ruby; but before diving into the language-specific features of NetBeans, it's useful to get an overview of the functionality. This section uses the Java programming language, but the functionality applies to projects of any type.

FIGURE 24-2

Use the New Project dialog to create a Java Application project.

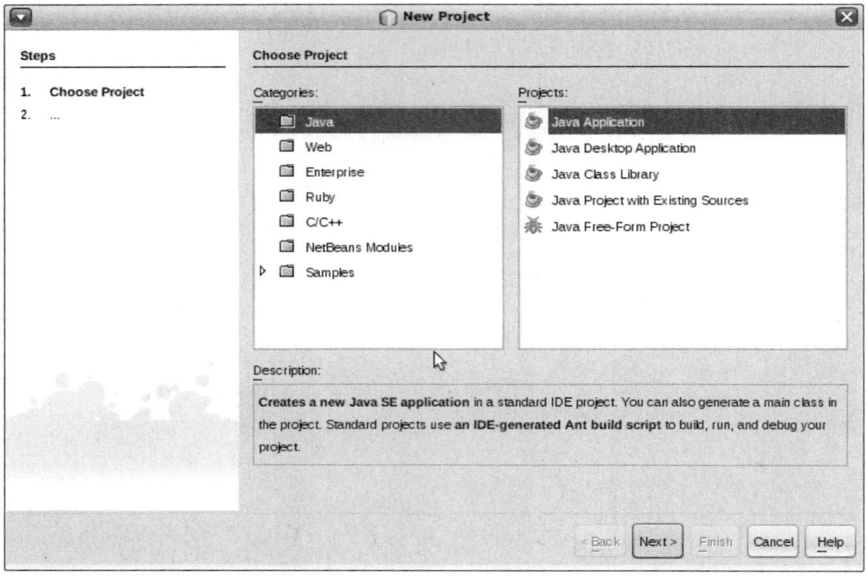

If you've never used NetBeans, a good place to familiarize yourself with the application is a basic console application. To create a Java console application, select File ➤ New Project. Select Java in the Categories list and Java Application in the Projects list (see Figure 24-2).

In the next screen, choose your project name, project location, the name of your main class, and other settings. After you click Finish, you'll see a window like the one shown in Figure 24-3 (minus the Output pane at the bottom).

Note that NetBeans creates a source file for you, `Main.java`. You can edit the file to put some code application logic inside the main method. For example, you could add the following:

```
System.out.println("Hello, world");
```

You can then compile and run the program by selecting Run ➤ Run Main Project. This command compiles the program and then runs it, returning the output in an Output pane at the bottom of the screen, as shown in Figure 24-3.

You can add more files to your project via File ➤ New File. The pop-up window provides a choice of file types. For basic Java console applications, you'll probably use only Java Class and Java Interface. When you're done with the project, close it by selecting File ➤ Close *<project name>*.

FIGURE 24-3

Running the new Java Application project brings up an Output pane.

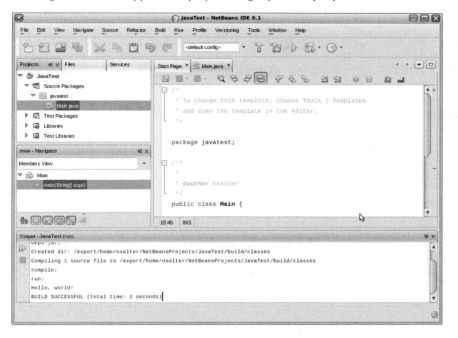

NetBeans for Java

Now that you've seen how to create, modify, and run a project in NetBeans, it's time to step back and get an overview of the Java development features. NetBeans comes with some sample projects, which make it easy to explore the full capabilities and features of NetBeans Java development. This section uses the AnagramGame sample. First, close the project you created earlier. Then create a new AnagramGame project based on the sample by choosing File ➤ New Project and then selecting Samples ➤ Java in the Categories list and Anagram Game in the Projects list, as shown in Figure 24-4.

On the next screen, accept the defaults and click Finish. Now that you have a project open, you can explore the Files, Navigation, Building, and Debugging features of the IDE.

Files

There are a few different ways you can explore the files in your project (see Figure 24-5). You can open a file by selecting File ➤ Open File, or you can click the Files tab. If the Files tab is not visible, select Window ➤ Files. From the Files tab you can explore the source of your project. Double-click a file to open it in the editing pane on the right.

FIGURE 24-4

Use the New Project dialog to create an Anagram Game sample project.

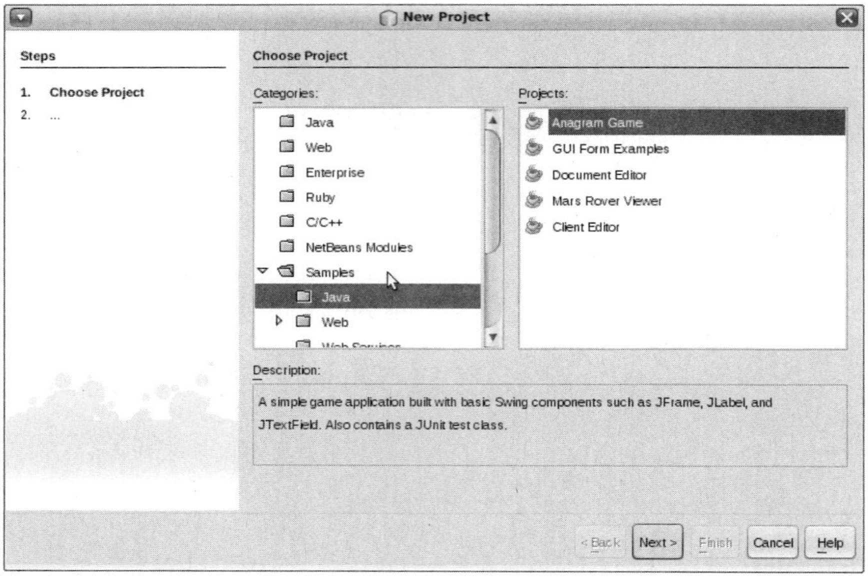

In addition to editing as you would in any text editor, NetBeans provides some sophisticated editing tools, most of which are under the Source and Refactor menus. For example, you can select a chunk of code and then choose Refactor ➤ Introduce Method to move it into a new method. In addition, the editor provides suggestions for you as you type, such as for method names that a given object could call.

You can add a new file with the File ➤ New File menu option, which brings up a wizard to help you choose the kind of file, such as a Java class file, a Java interface file, and so on. You can also select the project to which the source file should be added.

To add an existing file to a project, right-click on Source Files in the Projects tab of the top, left window and select Add Existing Item. Similarly, you can remove a file from the project or delete it by right-clicking on it in the Source Files list and selecting Remove From Project or Delete.

Navigation

With a large project, it's often difficult to find the specific method or class that you need. Net-Beans provides several quick ways to jump around within the project. One of these is the Navigator, which sits below the File browser (refer to Figure 24-5). If it doesn't show up when a file is opened, select Window ➤ Navigating ➤ Navigator. The Navigator shows all the definitions in the global and class scope in the currently open file. Double-clicking on a name immediately puts the cursor at that definition in the source file.

FIGURE 24-5

NetBeans provides tools for browsing files.

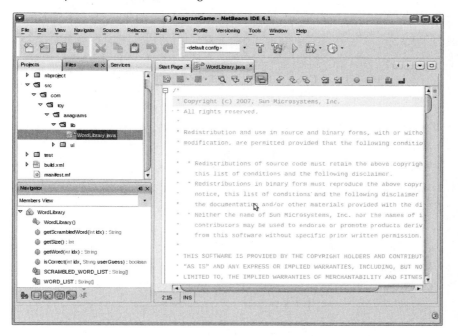

You can also use the Navigate ➢ Go to File and Navigate ➢ Go to Type menu options to jump to files and type definitions.

Finally, you can right-click on any name in a file, select Navigate in the pop-up menu, and select one of the options. For example, clicking on an object name gives you the option to jump to the source, declaration, Super implementation, and so on. One interesting option is to Inspect Members. Selecting this option brings up a nifty browser that enables you to explore the class interface, as shown in Figure 24-6.

> **TIP** The navigation facilities work for classes in the Java libraries as well as your own classes.

NetBeans contains other navigation features, which you can explore on your own as you start to use it.

Building and running

From the Build menu you can build your application and change build options. When you build a project, the build output appears in the Output pane at the bottom of the window. If the Output pane isn't open, select Window ➢ Output ➢ Output from the menu.

FIGURE 24-6

NetBeans provides a useful tool for inspecting class members.

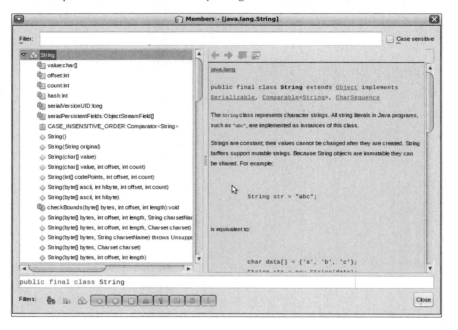

To change build options, select File ➤ <project name> Properties. Here you can add source files and libraries and set other configuration options, such as whether to build a Jar file or generate debugging information.

To run the project, select Run ➤ Run Main Project. If the project build is not up-to-date, selecting the Run menu item forces the project to rebuild before running. For a command-line program, the program output shows up in the Output pane.

Debugging

NetBeans enables you to debug Java programs directly within the IDE, providing the same functionality available in JDB, but in graphical form. You can set breakpoints by clicking on the left column of the editor. Breakpoints are designated by a red square. Figure 24-7 shows a breakpoint in the one line in Main.

Once you've set your breakpoints, select Run ➤ Debug Main Project. A Debugger Console appears in the Output pane, and a debugging pane on the right shows the value of local variables, the call stack, breakpoints, and watchpoints (watches). Figure 24-8 shows these features.

FIGURE 24-7

You can debug Java programs with breakpoints.

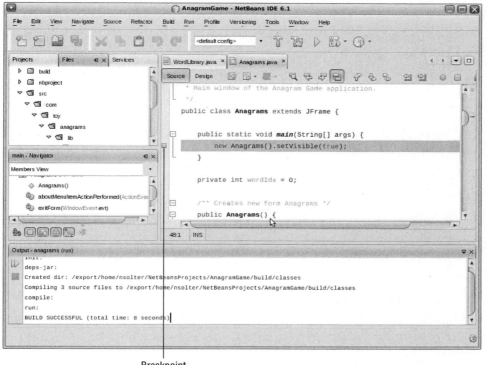

Breakpoint

At this point, you can step through the program by selecting Step Over and Step Into from the Run menu (the equivalent of step and next in JDB). You can also Continue the program to the next breakpoint, or set breakpoints and watchpoints.

Profiling

To analyze the performance of your Java program, select Profile ➤ Profile Main Project. The first time you select it, you'll be asked to enable profiling for the project. Click OK and the Profile window pops up, providing the options shown in Figure 24-9.

Click Run and agree to let it calibrate your system. The first time you profile an application, you need to click through a few screens before the program starts. When the application completes, choose Yes in the pop-up window that asks whether you want to take a snapshot of the collected results. You'll be presented with information in the editor window, as shown in Figure 24-10.

FIGURE 24-8

During a debugging session, a pane on the lower right provides detailed information.

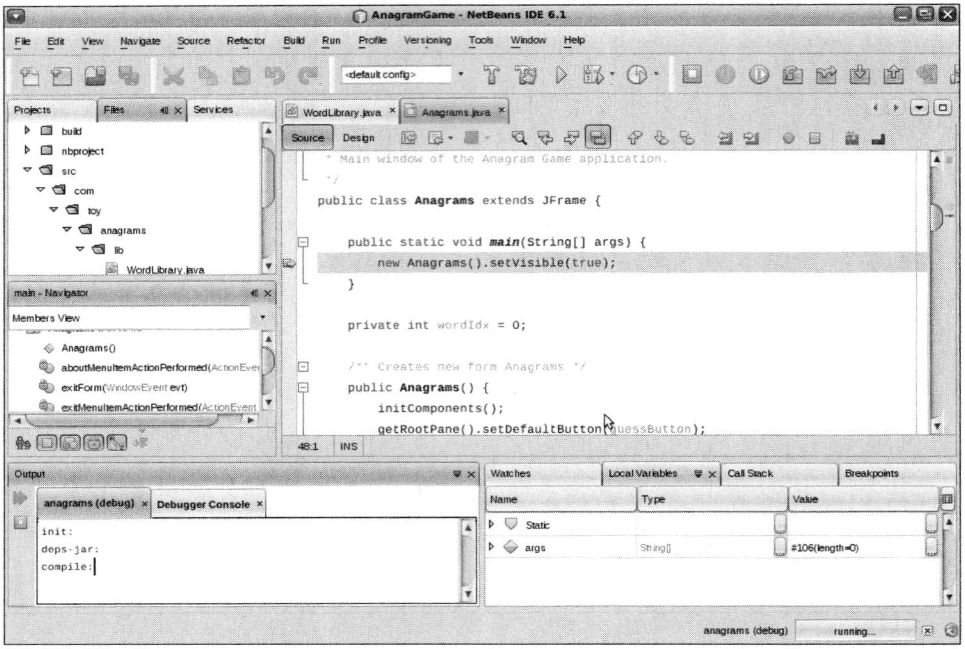

As shown by the amount of data available for even a small program, profiling can be a powerful tool.

Java GUI applications

In addition to the Java Console application projects shown earlier, NetBeans contains extensive support for developing Java applications with graphical user interfaces. To create such a program, select File ➤ New Project, and then choose Java in the Categories list and Java Desktop Application in the Projects list. The project contains a complete skeleton application using the Swing framework. The nifty thing about using NetBeans to develop a Swing application is that it provides a graphical editor for the GUI components. To select the graphical tool, click the Design tab in the text editor for a class that implements a graphical object. For example, in the skeleton project just created, the DesktopApplication1View.java class (the class name will vary according to whatever name you gave your project) enables you to use the graphical design tool, as shown in Figure 24-11.

You can drag and drop GUI components from the Palette on the right onto the frame in the editor window.

Starting a profiling session brings up this initial window.

NetBeans C and C++ development

NetBeans supports C and C++ development with either the GNU compiler set or the Sun Studio Express compiler set described earlier. You can create a C/C++ project by selecting C/C++ from the Categories list and C/C++ Application from the Projects list in the New Project dialog. Unlike a Java project, a C/C++ project is initially empty, other than the makefile.

Files

You can create a file using File ➤ New File. Note that you can select the project to which the file should be added at file creation time. As with Java projects, you can add and remove files from the project at any time. The Source and Refactor menu items can be used on C and C++ source files as well. See the previous section for Java development.

Navigation

The navigation support for C and C++ projects is similar to that for Java projects. One useful feature that applies only to C and C++ is the capability to view or inspect the Include Hierarchy, available by right-clicking anywhere in the editor and selecting either Navigate ➤ View Includes Hierarchy or Navigate ➤ Inspect Includes Hierarchy from the pop-up menu. That brings up either a new window on the right or a pop-up window (see Figure 24-12) that enables you to transitively explore the header files included in the selected source or header file.

FIGURE 24-10

The profiling results generate data in the editor window.

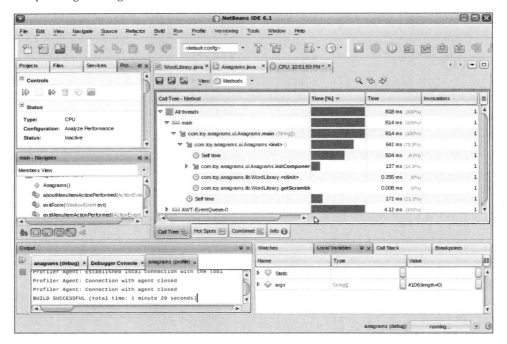

Building and running

By default, NetBeans uses the GNU compiler collection (GCC) if it can find it in your path. If you've installed GCC as described earlier in this chapter, NetBeans should find it automatically.

You can also use the Sun Studio Express compiler collection, but you need to add it manually. Select Tools ➤ Options, and click the C/C++ tab (second from the right on the top panel). Click the Add button. In the Add New Tool Collection window that appears, enter the path to the Sun Studio Express compiler collection and select Sun Studio 12 as the Tool Collection Family. Unfortunately, as of this writing, NetBeans doesn't recognize the Sun Studio Express `dbx` debugger.

Alternatively, Sun Studio Express comes with its own IDE, launched with `/opt/SunStudioExpress/bin/sunstudio`. This IDE is built on NetBeans, so it works almost identically, but it is configured to use the Sun Studio Express compilers and debuggers. Figure 24-13 shows the Sun Studio Express IDE.

The Sun Studio IDE also enables you to use GCC, so for C and C++ development you should generally use the Sun Studio version of NetBeans, rather than NetBeans itself. For simplicity, the remainder of this discussion refers to the IDE as Sun Studio.

FIGURE 24-11

Use Java's graphical design tool to visually edit your graphical layout.

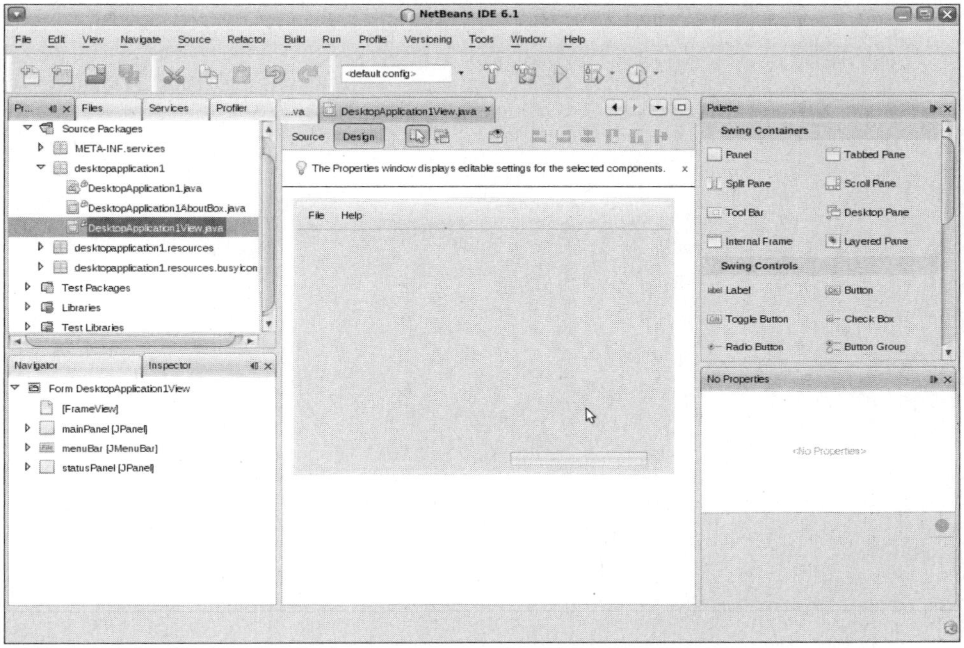

Building and running C and C++ programs in Sun Studio generally works the same for C and C++ applications as for Java applications. As with Java projects, you can adjust the build configuration through File ➤ <project name> Properties. There you can select the compiler collection, target platform, include directories, and so on.

> **TIP** When running a console application, the IDE brings up a new window to show the output, running with the working directory as the top-level directory of your project. Therefore, that's the place to put configuration files or any other files the program expects to find.

Debugging

Sun Studio provides a GUI interface to either GDB or dbx, depending on the compiler collection. You can run the program through the debugger just as you would a Java program, selecting Run ➤ Debug Main Project. Like the graphical Java debugger, the C++ debugger brings up a window with the local variables, call stack, breakpoints, watchpoints, and so on. For example, Figure 24-14 shows what the IDE looks like when debugging the voting program introduced earlier in this chapter.

FIGURE 24-12

Inspecting the include hierarchy is one of the useful navigation tools for C and C++ in NetBeans.

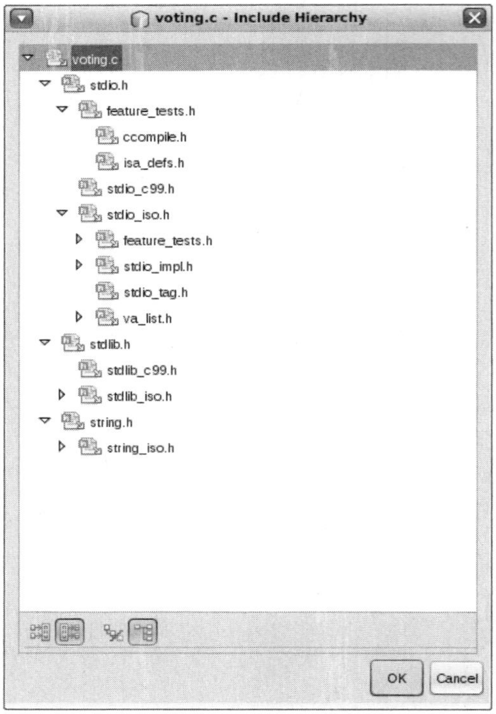

> **NOTE**   Profiling C and C++ programs is not supported in Sun Studio or NetBeans, so the Sun Studio IDE omits the Profile menu altogether. However, DTrace, discussed in Chapter 15, provides significant profiling capabilities for any application running on OpenSolaris. In fact, there is a DTrace plug-in available for the IDE that works with both NetBeans and Sun Studio Express. The next section has details on installing plug-ins.

NetBeans plug-ins

In addition to its core functionality, NetBeans is extensible with plug-ins. These enhancements range from support for the Mercurial SCM and DTrace to jMaki AJAX and PHP. Some of the plug-ins are community contributed.

To install a plug-in, select Tools ➤ Plugins. The Plugins pop-up window opens (see Figure 24-15).

FIGURE 24-13

The Sun Studio IDE is built on NetBeans.

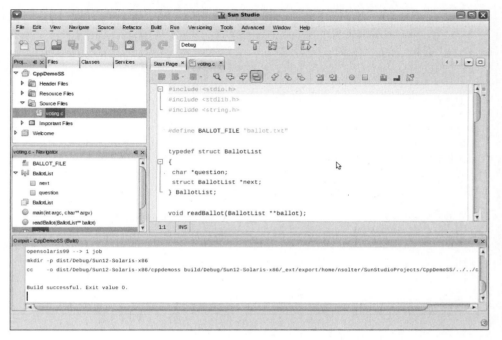

You can update your already installed plug-ins from the Updates menu. The more interesting area is the Available Plugins tab, which enables you to select and install any of the 80 or so plug-ins available.

NetBeans web application development

In addition to supporting standalone Java, C, and C++ applications, NetBeans provides an environment for developing various kinds of web applications.

To start a web application, create a new project and from the New Project window, select Web as the Category and Web Application as the Project. On the next screen, select a development server, such as GlassFish or Apache Tomcat, that is installed on your system. The examples in this chapter use Apache Tomcat 5.5, and assume that it has already been installed and configured.

CROSS-REF See Chapter 23 for instructions on installing and configuring GlassFish, Tomcat, and other web servers, servlet engines, and application servers.

FIGURE 24-14

You can debug a C project with the Sun Studio IDE.

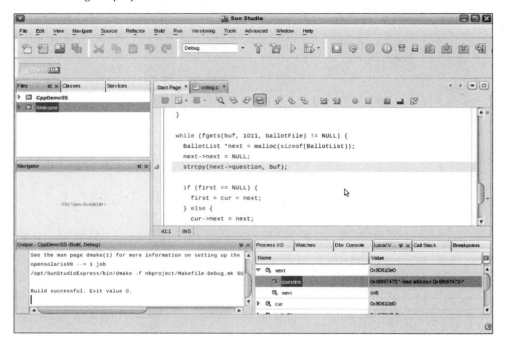

The first time you create a web application you need to register a server with the IDE. To do so, select the Add button to the right of the Server box. Select Tomcat 5.5 (or whichever server you want to use). On the next screen, fill in the server details, as shown in Figure 24-16.

NOTE This screen requires the name and password of a Tomcat user in the "manager" role. The option to "Create user if it does not exist" doesn't seem to work, so you need to add the user and role yourself. To do so, edit the file /var/apache/tomcat/conf/tomcat-users.xml to add the following two lines (substituting your desired username and password):

```
<role rolename="manager"/>
<user username="netbeans" password="netbeans" roles="manager"/>
```

Then restart Tomcat:

```
# /usr/apache/tomcat/bin/shutdown.sh
Using CATALINA_BASE:   /var/apache/tomcat
Using CATALINA_HOME:   /usr/apache/tomcat
Using CATALINA_TMPDIR: /var/apache/tomcat/temp
Using JRE_HOME:        /usr/java
# /usr/apache/tomcat/bin/startup.sh
```

```
Using CATALINA_BASE:    /var/apache/tomcat
Using CATALINA_HOME:    /usr/apache/tomcat
Using CATALINA_TMPDIR:  /var/apache/tomcat/temp
Using JRE_HOME:         /usr/java
```

FIGURE 24-15

Many plug-ins are available for NetBeans.

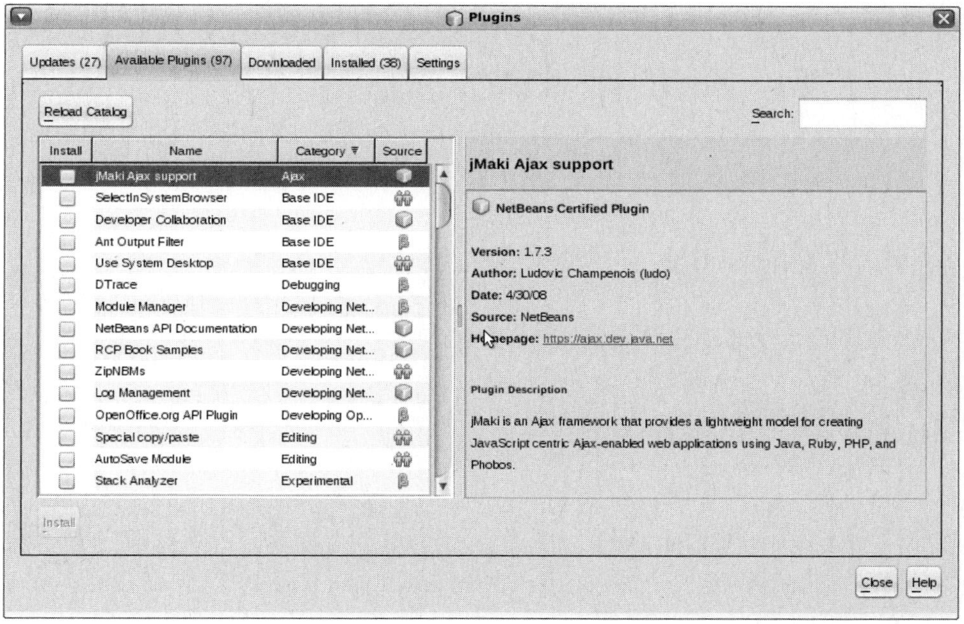

After adding the server, click Next to select frameworks such as Java Server Faces or Struts, or click Finish if you don't want to use any frameworks.

> **TIP** You can edit the Tomcat server configuration within NetBeans by selecting Tools ➢ Servers.

The project starts you off with a skeleton index.jsp and all the configuration files necessary to run the service under a server such as Tomcat. Running the project from the IDE causes Net-Beans to build a Web Archive (WAR) file, deploy it to Tomcat, and open Firefox to test the web application (which in this case is just a Hello, World), as shown in Figure 24-17.

You can add various types of files to the project, including JSP pages and Java Servlets, HTML, CSS, JavaScript, and many others, as shown in Figure 24-18.

FIGURE 24-16

You must specify some configuration options when adding the Apache server.

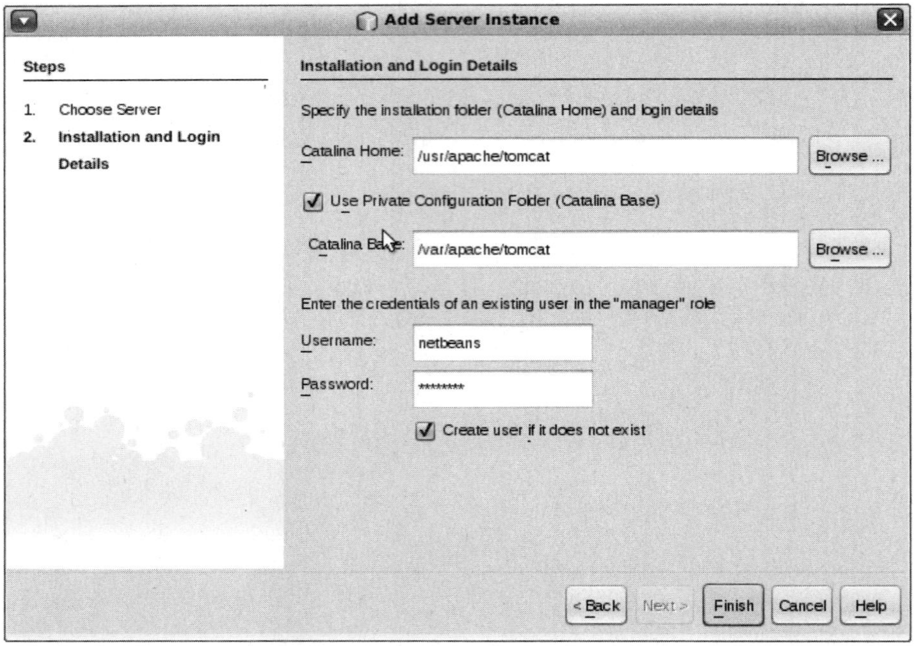

Plug-ins for web applications

Many of the available NetBeans plug-ins are for web development. For example, you can add the GWT4NB plug-in to provide support for the Google Web Toolkit within your web applications. Once you've added the plug-in, a GWT RPC Service is included as a possible file type when you add a file.

Web application Palette

As with a Java GUI application, a web application project enables you to drag and drop HTML and other elements from the Palette pane to your JSP, HTML, and other file types, as shown in Figure 24-19.

Debugging and profiling web applications

You can debug web applications, which among other features enables you to place breakpoints in servlet code and step through the application as it's being run through Tomcat. It also places the Tomcat logs in the Output pane, as shown in Figure 24-20.

FIGURE 24-17

Testing the web application opens the Firefox browser.

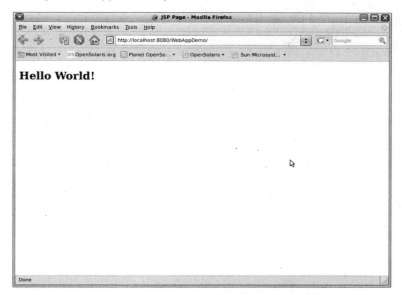

FIGURE 24-18

You can add files of many different types to a web application project.

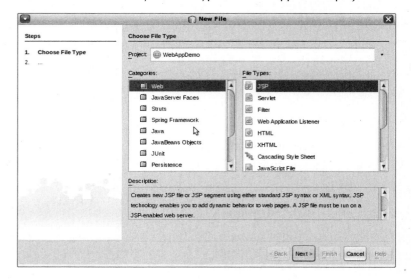

FIGURE 24-19

Use the web application Palette to edit your layout visually.

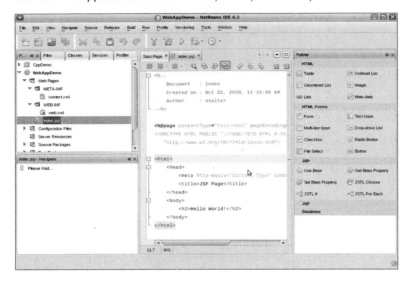

FIGURE 24-20

Debugging a web application is similar to debugging a C or Java application.

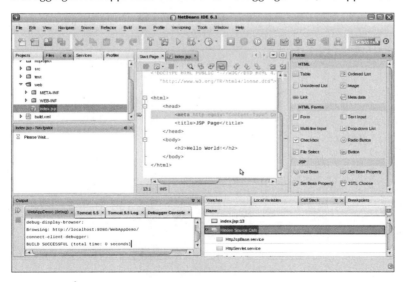

You can profile web applications as well using the Profile menu. See the NetBeans documentation for details.

More for NetBeans

In addition to the Java, C, C++, and web application development environments described so far, NetBeans supports a wide variety of other development environments and tools. For example, you can create Ruby, JRuby, and Ruby on Rails projects, which can integrate directly from NetBeans with a database. NetBeans also includes support for both CVS and Subversion Source Code Management systems. You can check out and commit files directly from the Versioning menu. Support for Mercurial is available as a plug-in. Consult the NetBeans documentation at http://netbeans.org for more details.

Source Code Management

Any development project involving more than one person or intended as more than a one-off prototype needs some form of *version control*, also known as *source code management* (SCM). SCM software supports two tasks: enabling multiple authors to work on the project simultaneously, and keeping revision history and versioning information about the source code files. There are two major types of SCM software: *centralized*, whereby the code is kept in a central *repository*, and *distributed*, whereby each developer has one or more copies of the complete repository.

OpenSolaris includes several different SCM systems, including CVS, Subversion, and Mercurial, all of which are open source. These SCMs enable concurrent editing of files by multiple developers — resolved by merging, rather than requiring specific exclusive locking of files for editing.

NOTE The original Source Code Control System (SCCS) is also still available in OpenSolaris, but it's not suitable for multi-person developer projects because it doesn't support concurrent editing or merging very well. Use one of the newer SCM systems instead.

CVS

The Concurrent Versions System (CVS) is an open source SCM system that has been around since the 1980s. It's a centralized SCM that has decreased in popularity recently in favor of newer systems such as Subversion and Mercurial. Nonetheless, it has the benefit of being familiar to many developers, so it might be a reasonable choice for your projects.

OpenSolaris includes CVS in the SUNWcvs package. If you've installed java-dev, ss-dev, gcc-dev, amp-dev, or ruby-dev, you already have it. Otherwise, you can install it as follows:

```
# pkg install SUNWcvs
```

To access all the CVS functionality, use the /usr/bin/cvs command.

Creating a repository

As a centralized SCM, CVS uses a single central repository. You should create this repository on a server machine to which all the development machines can connect via NFS or SSH. You can create the actual repository in a single cvs init command, which creates a CVSROOT subdirectory in the specified directory containing the administrative files:

```
$ mkdir myproj
$ cvs -d /export/home/nsolter/myproj init
$ ls myproj
CVSROOT
```

Next, add at least one directory to the repository with the cvs import command:

```
$ mkdir devdir
$ cd devdir
$ export CVSROOT=/export/home/nsolter/myproj
$ cvs import -m "created devdir" devdir myvendortag myreleasetag

No conflicts created by this import
```

The strings myvendortag and myreleasetag can be set to whatever is appropriate for your project. Now your repository is ready to use, although it doesn't contain any source files yet.

> **CAUTION** With the default configuration, all users who access the repository must have write access to create lock files. If there's a default group, such as staff, of which all users are members, then you can give the group write access.

Checking out a repository

Never work directly in the repository. To do any development work, check out a working copy of the repository, even if it's on the same machine. To do so, use the cvs checkout command.

TIP The `cvs` command uses the `CVSROOT` environment variable to find the repository. You can override that variable with the `-d` option to `cvs`.

For example, to check out a repository to which you have direct file system access (e.g., via NFS), you can simply set `CVSROOT` to the path to the repository and issue the `cvs checkout` command:

```
$ mkdir mycopy
$ cd mycopy
$ export CVSROOT=/export/home/nsolter/myproj
$ cvs checkout devdir
cvs checkout: Updating devdir
```

You now have a working copy of the `devdir` directory in the repository.

NOTE You can also, of course, access CVS remotely without direct file system access. See the documentation for details.

Working with a repository

Once you've checked out a repository, you can create and modify files in your working directory as usual. However, those changes don't propagate to the repository unless you specifically commit them.

NOTE The commands in this section all use the `CVSROOT` environment variable. This section assumes you've set that variable to point to the `CVSROOT`.

To add a file, use `cvs add`:

```
$ cvs add test.c
cvs add: scheduling file `test.c' for addition
cvs add: use `cvs commit' to add this file permanently
```

To check in changes (additions, deletions, and modifications), use `cvs commit`:

```
$ cvs commit
cvs commit: Examining .
/export/home/nsolter/myproj/devdir/test.c,v  <--  test.c
initial revision: 1.1
```

`cvs commit` brings up your default editor, where you can add your comments for this revision. After you exit the editor, CVS commits the changes.

To refresh your working copy with the latest changes in the repository, run `cvs update`:

```
$ cvs update
cvs update: Updating .
U test2.c
```

As shown here, the `update` command lists all the files that it is updating.

> **NOTE** There is no symmetric equivalent to the `checkout` subcommand, such as `checkin`. Once you've checked out your files, you check in changes with `commit` and refresh your working copy with `update`.

Handling conflicts

Always update your repository before committing. Otherwise, if there is a conflict, then CVS issues an error:

```
$ cvs commit
cvs commit: Examining .
cvs commit: Up-to-date check failed for `test.c'
cvs [commit aborted]: correct above errors first!
```

The update flags files with conflicts:

```
$ cvs update
cvs update: Updating .
RCS file: /export/home/nsolter/myproj/devdir/test.c,v
retrieving revision 1.1
retrieving revision 1.2
Merging differences between 1.1 and 1.2 into test.c
rcsmerge: warning: conflicts during merge
cvs update: conflicts found in test.c
C test.c
```

It's your responsibility to fix the conflicts manually. When you open the merged file, you can see that CVS has put the merge output directly in the file:

```
        printf("Hello, world!\n");
<<<<<<< test.c
        return (0);
=======
        printf("And hello, universe!\n");
>>>>>>> 1.2
```

After fixing the file (in this case accepting both changes), you can then commit:

```
$ cvs commit
cvs commit: Examining .
/export/home/nsolter/myproj/devdir/test.c,v  <--  test.c
new revision: 1.3; previous revision: 1.2
```

Viewing history

You can view the revision history of each file with `cvs annotate` and `cvs log`:

```
$ cvs annotate test.c

Annotations for test.c
***************
1.1         (test      07-Jul-08): #include <stdio.h>
1.1         (test      07-Jul-08):
1.1         (test      07-Jul-08): int main(int argc, char **argv)
1.1         (test      07-Jul-08): {
1.1         (test      07-Jul-08):     printf("Hello, world!\n");
1.3         (test      07-Jul-08):     return (0);
1.2         (nsolter   07-Jul-08):     printf("And hello, universe!\n");
1.1         (test      07-Jul-08): }
$ cvs log test.c

RCS file: /export/home/nsolter/myproj/devdir/test.c,v
Working file: test.c
head: 1.3
branch:
locks: strict
access list:
symbolic names:
keyword substitution: kv
total revisions: 3;     selected revisions: 3
description:
----------------------------
revision 1.3
date: 2008-07-07 11:58:22 -0600;  author: test;  state: Exp;  lines: +1 -0;
  commitid: 3UbdDsW5rzpMNT9t;
Added exit and fixed merge
----------------------------
revision 1.2
date: 2008-07-07 11:54:25 -0600;  author: nsolter;  state: Exp;  lines: +1 -0;
  commitid: Kdnr7fOLUyVoMT9t;
Added line to test.c
----------------------------
revision 1.1
date: 2008-07-07 11:43:46 -0600;  author: test;  state: Exp;  commitid:
  wr3qeF5u6ccJIT9t;
Added test.c
```

These examples just scratch the surface of CVS. It supports more advanced features as well, such as rolling back to previous versions of files. Consult the documentation for details.

Subversion

Although historically popular, CVS is somewhat creaky. For example, it lacks file groupings or atomic commit, treating changes to each file separately. Subversion SCM is intended to be a replacement for CVS, and is available on OpenSolaris in the SUNWsvn package. If you've installed java-dev, ss-dev, gcc-dev, amp-dev, or ruby-dev, then you have the package. Otherwise, you can install it explicitly:

```
# pkg install SUNWsvn
```

Subversion is designed to have the same look and feel as CVS, so if you're familiar with CVS, switching to Subversion should be fairly easy.

Creating a repository

The first thing you need to do to use Subversion is create a repository. To do so, use the svnadmin command. Note that you do not need to create the directory beforehand:

```
$ svnadmin create /export/home/nsolter/mysvnproj
```

Next, you need to import at least one directory. This example imports the empty devdir directory from the CVS example earlier:

```
$ svn import devdir file:///export/home/nsolter/mysvnproj/devdirproj/
\-m "initial import"

Committed revision 1.
```

The first argument to svn import, devdir, is the directory to be imported, and the second argument, file:///export/home/nsolter/mysvnproj/devdirproj/, is the path within the repository in which to import it. Now your repository is ready to use, although it doesn't contain any source files yet.

Configuring a Subversion server

Subversion supports several different methods for clients to access the server, including the lightweight Subversion server daemon, the Apache web server, SSH, and direct file system access. The configuration for each of these is different. The examples in this book use the svnserver daemon because it is the simplest to configure, but consider using SSH for more security in your real deployments. Consult the documentation for details on the other methods.

To configure the Subversion server, simply run the svnserve command. You can run it as a nonprivileged user because it listens on the nonprivileged port 3690 by default:

```
$ svnserve -d
```

The server is now ready to serve the repository to clients; but before clients can access the repository, you need to configure the authentication. Edit the

<svnroot>/conf/svnserve.conf file to uncomment the password-db line and the realm line. You can use a different realm name — the name is irrelevant to the authentication. In the mysvnproj repository created in the previous section, the absolute path of this file is /export/home/nsolter/ mysvnproj/conf/svnserver.conf. The two lines in the file should look something like this:

```
password-db = passwd
...
realm = My Realm
```

Next, add the passwords in plaintext to the passwd file in the same directory. For the test user, this could look like the following:

```
test = testpass
```

Checking out a repository

Never work directly in the repository. For any development work, check out a working copy of the repository, even if it's on the same machine. To check out a repository, use svn checkout. For example, the following checks out the repository created in the previous section from the same host, assuming you've started the Subversion server:

```
$ svn checkout svn://localhost/export/home/nsolter/mysvnproj/devdirproj/
Checked out revision 1.
```

> **NOTE** Subversion doesn't use an environment variable to point to the repository. Instead, the initial checkout command takes a URL. If you're using the Subversion server instead of HTTP, use the svn prefix to the URL. Subsequent Subversion commands in the working copy of the repository remember the URL of the repository, so you don't need to specify it again.

Checking out from a different host uses the same command but with the server hostname or IP address in the URL instead of localhost.

You now have a working copy of the devdirproj directory in the repository. Note that Subversion creates the devdirproj directory locally in your working directory:

```
$ ls -l devdirproj
total 0
```

Working with a repository

Once you've checked out a repository, you can create and modify files in your working directory. However, those changes don't propagate to the repository unless you specifically commit them.

To add a file, use svn add:

```
$ cd devdirproj
$ vi test.c
```

```
$ svn add test.c
A        test.c
```

To check in changes (additions, deletions, and modifications), use svn commit:

```
$ svn commit -m "created test.c"
Authentication realm: <svn://localhost:3690> My Realm
Password for 'test':
Adding        test.c
Transmitting file data .
Committed revision 2.
```

The commit action prompts the user for a password, which you should have configured earlier. You only need to enter the password once per login session, the first time you attempt an action that requires write privileges.

By using -m, you avoid opening an editor during the commit operation to enter the comment. This is useful because Subversion doesn't use the default editor — it requires you to set the separate SVN_EDITOR environment variable.

To refresh your working copy with the latest changes in the repository, run svn update:

```
$ svn update
A   test2.c
Updated to revision 3.
```

As you can see, the update command lists the files that it is updating.

> **NOTE** There is no symmetric equivalent in Subversion to the checkout subcommand, such as checkin. Once you've checked out your files, you check in changes with commit and refresh your working copy with update.

Handling conflicts

Always update your repository before committing. If you haven't, and there is a conflict, Subversion issues an error:

```
$ svn commit -m "added return line"
Sending        test2.c
Transmitting file data .svn: Commit failed (details follow):
svn: Out of date: '/devdirproj/test2.c' in transaction '4-1'
```

An update will bring over conflicting files, but it marks them with a C in the output to indicate that they conflict:

```
$ svn update
C   test2.c
Updated to revision 4.
```

If there's a conflict, Subversion also adds three files to your working directory:

```
$ ls test2.*
test2.c         test2.c.mine  test2.c.r3     test2.c.r4
```

test2.c is the file under Subversion control, with the merge output directly in the file:

```
        printf("Hello, world!\n");
<<<<<<< .mine
        return (0);
=======
        printf("Hello, universe!\n");
>>>>>>> .r4
```

test2.c.mine is your version of the file, test2.c.r3 is the base version of the file against which both revisions were made, and test2.c.r4 is the modified version of the file by another commit action.

Before committing, you need to fix the test2.c file and remove the three additional files. Until you remove the files, Subversion considers the file in conflict. You can check the status with svn status:

```
$ svn status
?       test2.c.r3
?       test2.c.r4
?       test2.c.mine
C       test2.c
$ rm test2.c.mine test2.c.r3 test2.c.r4
$ svn status
M       test2.c
```

Now you can commit:

```
$ svn commit -m "added return line"
Sending         test2.c
Transmitting file data .
Committed revision 5.
```

Viewing history

The equivalent of cvs annotate is svn blame (although annotate is an alias for it):

```
$ svn blame test2.c
    3    nsolter #include <stdio.h>
    3    nsolter
    3    nsolter int main(int argc, char **argv)
    3    nsolter {
    3    nsolter         printf("Hello, world!\n");
    5      test         return (0);
```

```
        4    nsolter       printf("Hello, universe!\n");
nsolter }
```

svn log is similar to cvs log, but note that in Subversion, the revisions are on a project basis, not on an individual file basis:

```
$ svn log
------------------------------------------------------------------------
r4 | nsolter | 2008-07-07 14:31:03 -0600 (Mon, 07 Jul 2008) | 1 line

added line
------------------------------------------------------------------------
r3 | nsolter | 2008-07-07 14:27:12 -0600 (Mon, 07 Jul 2008) | 1 line

added test2.c
------------------------------------------------------------------------
r2 | test | 2008-07-07 14:15:58 -0600 (Mon, 07 Jul 2008) | 1 line

created test.c
------------------------------------------------------------------------
r1 | nsolter | 2008-07-07 12:41:44 -0600 (Mon, 07 Jul 2008) | 1 line

initial import
------------------------------------------------------------------------
```

These examples have just scratched the surface of Subversion. It supports more advanced features as well, such as rolling back to previous versions of files. Consult the documentation for details.

Mercurial

Unlike CVS and Subversion, Mercurial is a distributed SCM. As a selling point, it's the SCM of choice for much of the OpenSolaris source code itself, and was used by the authors of this book to manage the chapters and other files! If you want to use Mercurial, the first thing you need to do is to install the SUNWmercurial package. If you've installed any of the java-dev, ss-dev, gcc-dev, or ruby-dev group packages, you already have it. If not, you can install it explicitly:

```
# pkg install SUNWmercurial
```

You access all the Mercurial functionality via the /usr/bin/hg command (hg being the chemical symbol for mercury).

Mercurial uses a distributed model, so conceptually it is somewhat different from CVS and Subversion. Specifically, instead of requiring a single central repository to which all changes are committed, every developer has a copy of the repository to which he or she commits changes. These changes can then be *pushed* and *pulled* between repositories. Most projects, however, still use a master repository.

Creating a repository

To kick off a project with Mercurial, create an initial repository using `hg init`:

```
$ mkdir myhgproj
$ cd myhgproj
$ hg init
```

The repository is now available for your project. Unlike CVS and Subversion, you don't need to do any extra configuration steps to enable the repository to be accessed read-only over SSH, assuming that all users who will access it have an account on the machine. For truly distributed work, read-only access to each repository might be sufficient; but if you want a centralized repository, then you should provide read/write access to it. The details are beyond the scope of this book, but the Mercurial website has a good tutorial at `http://selenic.com/mercurial/wiki/index.cgi/SharedSSH`.

Cloning a repository

Each developer who wants to work on the project must make a copy or *clone* of the repository with `hg clone`:

```
$ hg clone ssh://test@localhost//export/home/nsolter/myhgproj
Password:
destination directory: myhgproj
no changes found
updating working directory
0 files updated, 0 files merged, 0 files removed, 0 files unresolved
```

The URL in the `hg clone` command deserves a bit of explication. It starts with `ssh://` followed by `username@hostname`. This example shows the `test` user at `localhost`. To connect to a remote host, substitute the remote host's name or IP address. Following the URL is the path to the repository on the remote machine. To specify an absolute path, use `//` between the hostname and the path. You now have a working copy of the `myhgproj` directory in the repository.

Working with a repository

Once you've cloned a repository, you can create and modify files in it, and you must explicitly commit these changes for them to take effect. Unlike CVS and Subversion, however, an additional step is needed to share these changes with other developers. Because Mercurial is decentralized, you must explicitly push the changes to other repositories. For example, to add a file, use `hg add`:

```
$ cd myhgproj
$ vi test.c
$ hg add test.c
```

This file is now added to your working directory but not to your local copy of the repository. To add it to your clone of the repository, use hg commit:

```
$ hg commit
No username found, using 'test@localhost' instead
```

The commit action brings up your default editor to enter comments for this *changeset*, or set of changes committed simultaneously (similar to a revision in Subversion).

> **TIP** You can use the -m option to hg commit to supply a comment for the changeset.

The new file is now committed to your clone of the repository, but not propagated to any other repositories. To propagate the changes yourself, you need write access to a master repository. If you have write access, you can use hg push:

```
$ hg push ssh://nsolter@localhost//export/home/nsolter/myhgproj
Password:
pushing to ssh://nsolter@localhost//export/home/nsolter/myhgproj
searching for changes
remote: adding changesets
remote: adding manifests
remote: adding file changes
remote: added 1 changesets with 1 changes to 1 files
```

> **TIP** Use hg outgoing to see what changes will be pushed without actually pushing them. Use hg incoming to see what changes will be pulled without actually pulling them.

Alternatively, users can pull changes from other developers' repositories to their own, without requiring anyone to give write permission to anyone else:

```
$ hg pull ssh://test@localhost//export/home/nsolter/myhgproj
Password:
pulling from ssh://test@localhost//export/home/nsolter/myhgproj
requesting all changes
adding changesets
adding manifests
adding file changes
added 1 changesets with 1 changes to 1 files
(run 'hg update' to get a working copy)
$ hg update
1 files updated, 0 files merged, 0 files removed, 0 files unresolved
```

You now have a working copy of the updated file in your working directory.

> **TIP** If you omit the URL from an hg command, Mercurial defaults to the URL of the repository from which you cloned your local repository.

Handling conflicts

If you've committed a change to your repository that conflicts with a change that you pull from a repository, Mercurial detects and flags it:

```
$ hg pull
Password:
pulling from ssh://test@localhost//export/home/nsolter/myhgproj
searching for changes
adding changesets
adding manifests
adding file changes
added 1 changesets with 1 changes to 1 files (+1 heads)
(run 'hg heads' to see heads, 'hg merge' to merge)
```

Here, Mercurial is indicating that you've caused a *branch* (a *head* is the latest revision of a branch). The usual action is to merge the changes:

```
$ hg merge
merging test.c
warning: conflicts during merge.
merging test.c failed!
0 files updated, 0 files merged, 0 files removed, 1 files unresolved
There are unresolved merges, you can redo the full merge using:
  hg update -C 1
  hg merge 2
```

At this point, because you haven't specified a merge tool, Mercurial requires you to fix the conflicts manually. Like Subversion and CVS, Mercurial placed the diff output in the file itself:

```
        printf("Hello, world!\n");
<<<<<<< local
        printf("Hello, universe!\n");
=======
        return (0);
>>>>>>> other
```

Mercurial has also added a file, test.c.orig, which you can delete. After fixing the file, you need to commit your merged changes:

```
$ hg commit -m "merged test.c"
```

 Mercurial enables you to specify a more sophisticated merge tool in the HGMERGE environment variable or in your .hgrc configuration file. Consult the documentation for details.

Viewing history

Like Subversion and CVS, Mercurial supports an `annotate` command to see the history of a file, as shown in this example:

```
$ hg annotate test.c
0: #include <stdio.h>
0:
0: int main(int argc, char **argv)
0: {
0:         printf("Hello, world!\n");
1:       printf("Hello, universe!\n");
2:       return (0);
0: }
0:
```

The `log` command shows you the history of the changesets:

```
$ hg log
changeset:    3:405f51993a1b
tag:          tip
parent:       1:e306ad43e764
parent:       2:4ace9f1a6f16
user:         test@localhost
date:         Mon Jul 07 16:42:40 2008 -0600
summary:      merged test.c

changeset:    2:4ace9f1a6f16
parent:       0:06b161b135ff
user:         nsolter@localhost
date:         Mon Jul 07 16:32:36 2008 -0600
summary:      Added return line

changeset:    1:e306ad43e764
user:         test@localhost
date:         Mon Jul 07 16:34:38 2008 -0600
summary:      Added printf line

changeset:    0:06b161b135ff
user:         nsolter@localhost
date:         Mon Jul 07 16:26:59 2008 -0600
summary:      Added test.c
```

Like the examples for CVS and Subversion, these examples just scratch the surface of Mercurial. It supports more advanced features as well, such as rolling back to previous versions of files and branching. Consult the documentation for details.

Building IPS Packages

As described in Chapter 6, the OpenSolaris distribution uses the new Image Packaging System (IPS). The best way to deploy applications on OpenSolaris is to distribute them as IPS packages.

IPS actions

Recall from Chapter 6 that an IPS package is a collection of *actions* of different types. Unlike with traditional System V packages, as a developer, you don't build the package yourself. Instead, you send the actions and data to an IPS repository. You can then install the package from the repository, which is the only way to install an IPS package.

IPS package example

Suppose you've developed a new command, `mycmd`, that you want to make available in an IPS package, `mypkg`. You want to install this command in `/opt/mypkg`, with a symbolic link in `/usr/bin`. Your command depends on `gzip` to function properly.

This example assumes you have an IPS repository running on your localhost on port 1234. (See Chapter 6 for details on setting up a repository.)

Preparing the IPS package

To send a package to an IPS repository, you need two things: the files and the actions.

Although not required, it's generally useful to put the files in a directory tree identical to what the directory tree of your files on the installed system will look like. This tree in your development directory is called a *proto* area. For example, your proto area for the `mypkg` package would consist of a single directory `opt/mypkg` with a single binary `opt/mypkg/mycmd`.

To accomplish the goals described earlier for your new package, you need four actions: a `dir` action to create the `/opt/mypkg` directory, a `file` action to install `mycmd` in `/opt/mypkg`, a `link` action to create the symlink in `/usr/bin`, and a `depend` action to specify the dependency on `gzip`. You can collect these actions together in an IPS manifest file (not to be confused with an SMF manifest file). The manifest file for the `mypkg` package looks like this:

```
$ cat mypkg.ips
dir mode=0755 owner=root group=bin path=/opt/mypkg
file opt/mypkg/mycmd mode=0555 owner=root group=bin path=/opt/mypkg/mycmd
link path=/usr/bin/mycmd target=/opt/mypkg/mycmd
depend type=require fmri=SUNWgzip
```

Each action is specified on a single line, starting with the action keyword, such as `file` or `path`, and each action has several properties. For example, the `dir` action has a `mode`, `owner`, `group`, and `path` property. Some actions, such as `file`, have a *payload*, which is sent to the repository, and must be specified first. The file payload is the actual file path relative to the working directory for the file that will be sent to the package repository as part of that action.

Sending the IPS package

Now that you have your files and actions ready, you send the package to the repository with a sequence of pkgsend commands. The first task is to open the transaction, providing the name of the package:

```
$ eval `pkgsend -s http://localhost:1234 open mypkg@1.0-1`
```

This command looks a little strange. First of all, why the eval? The reason is that the pkgsend open command returns environment settings that can be evaluated in the shell to set up your environment for the rest of the pkgsend commands. The -s option specifies the URL of the repository. The final argument is the name of your package, including the version number.

The next step is to send the actions defined in your IPS manifest file. Be sure to run this command in the root of your proto area:

```
$ pkgsend -s http://localhost:1234 include mypkg.ips
```

> **NOTE** You can send each action individually with pkgsend add instead of collecting the actions in a manifest, but that method is painstaking, and we do not recommend it. Alternatively, you can use the Directory Bundle support in pkgsend import to generate file and directory actions automatically for all files under a given directory, although this technique can't generate all your dependencies automatically.

Finally, close the transaction:

```
$ pkgsend -s http://localhost:1234 close
PUBLISHED
pkg:/mypkg@1.0,5.11-1:20081107T213417Z
```

Your package is now available in the local IPS repository.

Installing the package

To interact with your package in the IPS repository, first set the authority and refresh the catalog:

```
# pkg set-authority -O http://localhost:1234 local
# pkg refresh
```

Now you can browse the package contents:

```
# pkg contents -r mypkg
PATH
opt/mypkg
opt/mypkg/mycmd
usr/bin/mycmd
```

Finally, you can install the package and use my cmd:

```
# pkg install mypkg
DOWNLOAD                              PKGS       FILES      XFER (MB)
Completed                             1/1        1/1        0.00/0.00

PHASE                               ACTIONS
Install Phase                         6/6
PHASE                                ITEMS
Reading Existing Index                9/9
Indexing Packages                     1/1
# which mycmd
/usr/bin/mycmd
# ls -l /usr/bin/mycmd
lrwxrwxrwx 1 root root 16 2008-11-07 14:37 /usr/bin/mycmd -> /opt/mypkg/mycmd
```

This section provides only an introduction to building IPS packages. For details, consult the references listed in the "Resources" section later in this chapter.

Crash Dumps and Kernel Debugging

Crash dumps and core files are an important aspect of both process and kernel debugging. Be sure to read the section on configuring process core files even if you're not interested in doing any kernel debugging yourself.

Core files and crash dumps

A core file is a snapshot of the address space of a process at a point in time. A crash dump is the same thing but for the entire physical memory of the system. OpenSolaris enables you to configure both process core file and kernel crash dump behavior.

Process core files

As shown in the discussion of C and C++ debugging earlier in this chapter, the default configuration for process core files is to create a file named core in the working directory. This configuration can be set on both a global basis and a per-process basis with the coreadm command. Only users with the sys_admin privilege can set the global configuration.

The coreadm command without any arguments lists the current settings:

```
$ coreadm
     global core file pattern:
     global core file content: default
       init core file pattern: core
       init core file content: default
```

```
             global core dumps: disabled
        per-process core dumps: enabled
       global setid core dumps: disabled
  per-process setid core dumps: disabled
       global core dump logging: disabled
```

A typical configuration is to save all process core files in /var/core, using the executable name and process ID in the filename, so subsequent cores don't clobber old ones very often. You can use coreadm to configure core dumps with those settings:

```
# mkdir /var/core
# coreadm -g /var/core/core.%f.%p -e global
# coreadm
       global core file pattern: /var/core/core.%f.%p
       global core file content: default
         init core file pattern: core
         init core file content: default
             global core dumps: enabled
        per-process core dumps: enabled
       global setid core dumps: disabled
  per-process setid core dumps: disabled
       global core dump logging: disabled
```

Because per-process core dumps are still enabled, you now get two core files: one in the working directory and one in /var/core with 600 permissions. The global core file pattern doesn't apply to the core file generated in the working directory, so users might want to set their own pattern with something like the following:

```
$ coreadm -p core.%f.%p
```

> **TIP**   Use the gcore command to force a process to dump a core file of its current state without killing the process. gcore uses its own naming pattern for core files, not the pattern specified with coreadm.

Crash dumps

A crash dump is similar to a process core file, except for the system kernel itself at the time of the dump. This way, you can get a snapshot of the kernel state and, if configured to include it, all the process states. As mentioned in Chapters 3 and 7, crash dumps are generally saved to a dedicated dump device or a shared swap device. After dumping the memory, the system usually reboots. Upon reboot, you need to run the savecore utility, which extracts the dump from the dump device, saving it on the file system in the files unix.<number> and vmcore.<number>, where <number> is the number of the crash dump, starting with 0. You can also configure savecore to run automatically on reboot.

You can set the crash dump configuration with `dumpadm`. Without any arguments, `dumpadm` lists the current configuration. The `dumpadm` output in the following example is the default configuration in OpenSolaris:

```
# dumpadm
      Dump content: kernel pages
       Dump device: /dev/zvol/dsk/rpool/dump (dedicated)
Savecore directory: /var/crash/opensolaris99
  Savecore enabled: no
```

As shown here, crash dumps are dumped to `/dev/zvol/dsk/rpool/dump`, which is a dedicated dump device. The `savecore` command is not run automatically on reboot, but when you run it by hand the crash dump is saved to `/var/crash/opensolaris99`. (Note that `opensolaris99` is the hostname of the machine). You need to create the `/var/crash/opensolaris99` directory by hand before running `savecore` the first time.

With the `dumpadm` settings shown in the previous example, crash dumps are generated automatically for any kernel panic, disk space permitting. Note that the dump content contains kernel pages only. You can adjust these settings — to include process memory pages, for instance — with `dumpadm`, but you usually won't need to. Consult the `dumpadm(1M)` man page for details.

> **TIP** Run `reboot -d` to force a crash dump of the system. If you have a dedicated dump device configured, you can use `savecore -L` to generate a crash dump of the current system without rebooting.

Kernel debugging

OpenSolaris enables you to examine a crash dump or the live kernel with Modular Debugger (MDB), described earlier, for user processes. OpenSolaris also provides `kmdb` for advanced, possibly destructive, debugging of the live system.

mdb -k

You can examine a system crash dump with `mdb -k`:

```
# ls
bounds  unix.0  vmcore.0
# mdb -k unix.0 vmcore.0
Loading modules: [ unix genunix specfs dtrace cpu.generic uppc
 pcplusmp scsi_vhci zfs ip hook neti sctp arp usba uhci s1394 lofs
 random audiosup sd sppp ipc ptm crypto ]
>
```

You can also attach to the live system by running mdb -k without additional arguments:

```
# mdb -k
Loading modules: [ unix genunix specfs dtrace cpu.generic uppc
 pcplusmp scsi_vhci zfs ip hook neti sctp arp usba uhci s1394 lofs
 random sd audiosup sppp ipc ptm crypto ]
>
```

Once in MDB, a plethora of dcmds and walkers enable you to examine almost any aspect of the kernel. Kernel development and debugging aren't the focus of this book, so this section provides only a hint of the capabilities. Consult one of the MDB references listed later in the "Resources" section for more detail.

You can, for example, list all the threads and processes on the system with the threadlist and ps commands, respectively:

```
> ::threadlist
      ADDR      PROC       LWP CMD/LWPID
fec1e7e0 fec1df50 fec20110 sched/1
d2bf1de0 fec1df50         0 idle()
d2beede0 fec1df50         0 thread_reaper()
d2bebde0 fec1df50         0 tq:kmem_move_taskq
d2be8de0 fec1df50         0 tq:kmem_taskq
d2be5de0 fec1df50         0 tq:pseudo_nexus_enum_tq
  ...
> ::ps
S    PID   PPID   PGID    SID    UID     FLAGS     ADDR NAME
R      0      0      0      0      0 0x00000001 fec1df50 sched
R      3      0      0      0      0 0x00020001 d46d6338 fsflush
R      2      0      0      0      0 0x00020001 d46d6bc0 pageout
R      1      0      0      0      0 0x4a004000 d46d7448 init
R    589      1    589    589      0 0x42000000 d8f62ac8 fmd
R    561      1    558    558      0 0x4a004000 dcb67be8 intrd
R    531      1    531    531      0 0x52010000 db771ad0 sendmail
R    527      1    527    527     25 0x52010000 db76f028 sendmail
R    510      1    510    510      0 0x42000000 db772358 sshd
R    601    510    510    510      0 0x42010000 dcb66ad8 sshd
R    603    601    510    510    101 0x52010000 dcb67360 sshd
R    604    603    604    604    101 0x4a014000 dcb66250 bash
  ...
```

Using the address from a process, you can get more information about it with the ptools dcmds. For example, using the address of the first sshd process listed:

```
> db772358::ptree
fec1df50  sched
    d46d7448  init
        db772358  sshd
            dcb66ad8  sshd
```

```
                    dcb67360  sshd
                      dcb66250  bash
                        dcb659c8  bash
                          dcb58bf0  mdb
               d8f70128  sshd
               d67ddab8  sshd
                  db770138  bash
```

You can also examine the network activity and CPUs:

```
> ::netstat
TCPv4    St   Local Address          Remote Address        Stack       Zone
d3fb5980  0   192.168.1.103.22       192.168.1.105.4013      0     0
d3fb5e40  0   192.168.1.103.22       192.168.1.105.4014      0     0
TCPv6    St          Local Address                Remote Address          Stack
         Zone
UDPv4    St   Local Address          Remote Address        Stack       Zone
db64a0c0  3        0.0.0.0.514           0.0.0.0.0           0     0
db64a340  3        0.0.0.0.520           0.0.0.0.0           0     0
db64a840  3        0.0.0.0.38022         0.0.0.0.0           0     0
db64ad40  3        0.0.0.0.111           0.0.0.0.0           0     0
dc124d80  3        0.0.0.0.514           0.0.0.0.0           0     0
d795e080  3        0.0.0.0.57671         0.0.0.0.0           0     0
d795e580  3   192.168.1.103.68          0.0.0.0.0           0     0
d795e800  3        0.0.0.0.68            0.0.0.0.0           0     0
d795ea80  3        0.0.0.0.546           0.0.0.0.0           0     0
d795ed00  3        0.0.0.0.111           0.0.0.0.0           0     0
UDPv6    St          Local Address                Remote Address          Stack
         Zone
db64a0c0  3                  ::.514                      ::.0            0
    0
d795e080  3                  ::.57671                    ::.0            0
    0
d795ea80  3                  ::.546                      ::.0            0
    0
...
> ::cpuinfo -v
 ID ADDR     FLG NRUN BSPL PRI RNRN KRNRN SWITCH THREAD    PROC
  0 fec1fa38  1b    1    0  59  no    no  t-0    d7961600 mdb
                     |    |
     RUNNING <--+    +--> PRI THREAD     PROC
     READY             59 db055e00 sshd
     EXISTS
     ENABLE
```

kmdb

kmdb provides capabilities similar to mdb -k on the live system, with the additional feature of enabling you to actually control the live execution. You can attach to the live kernel with mdb -K (capital K).

> **CAUTION**   kmdb temporarily halts the system, and is only safe to run from the console.

You can also boot with kmdb. On a GRUB-based system, you can add the -k flag to the boot options. On a SPARC system, use boot -k from the ok prompt.

kmem_flags

Running the kernel with kmem_flags set is a great way to detect memory problems. This provides behavior in the kernel memory allocator that is similar to running with libumem in the userland. You can set kmem_flags in /etc/system:

```
set kmem_flags=0xf
```

You need to reboot for the setting to take effect.

> **CAUTION**   Running with kmem_flags has a significant impact on system performance.

Resources

The Java programming language is one of the most well-documented languages around. Any visit to a bookstore gives you a plethora of titles from which to choose. Here are a few suggestions:

- *Head First Java*, by Kathy Sierra and Bert Bates (O'Reilly, 2005). A good choice if you're new to the language.
- *Professional Java JDK, Sixth Edition*, by W. Clay Richardson, et al (Wrox, 2006).
- *Core Java, Volume I, Eighth Edition*, by Cay S. Horstmann and Gary Cornell (Prentice Hall, 2007).
- *Core Java, Volume II, Eighth Edition*, by Cay S. Horstmann and Gary Cornell (Prentice Hall, 2007).

The most useful Java information is available online at http://java.sun.com, including the complete Java SE 6 API reference at http://java.sun.com/javase/6/docs/api.

JDB is documented at http://java.sun.com/javase/6/docs/technotes/tools/solaris/jdb.html.

As with Java, there are a multitude of general C and C++ programming books, including the following:

- *C Programming Language, Second Edition* by Brian W. Kernighan and Dennis M. Ritchie (Prentice Hall, 1988). Although more than 20 years old, this book is the definitive C programming guide.

- *Professional C++*, by Nicholas A. Solter and Scott J. Kleper (Wrox, 2005).

- *Effective C++, Third Edition*, by Scott Meyers (Addison-Wesley, 2005).

There are also a few useful books on UNIX and Solaris systems programming in C, including these:

- *Solaris Systems Programming*, by Rich Teer (Prentice Hall, 2004).

- *UNIX Systems Programming for System VR4*, by David A. Curry (O'Reilly, 1996).

- *Advanced Programming in the UNIX Environment, Second Edition*, by W. Richard Stevens and Stephen A. Rago (Addison-Wesley, 2005).

- *Unix Network Programming, Volume 1: The Sockets Networking API, Third Edition*, by W. Richard Stevens, Bill Fenner, and Andrew M. Rudoff (Addison Wesley, 2003).

- *Unix Network Programming Volume 2: Interprocess Communication, Second Edition*, by W. Richard Stevens (Addison-Wesley, 1999) .

The Sun Studio compiler collection, including `dbx`, is documented extensively at `http://docs.sun.com/app/docs/coll/771.8`. Additional documentation can be found at `http://developers.sun.com/sunstudio/documentation`.

The GNU Compiler Collection documentation is linked off the main GCC page at `http://gcc.gnu.org`.

GDB is documented at its page, `http://gnu.org/software/gdb`.

There are a few good references for MDB and KMDB:

- *Solaris Performance and Tools: DTrace and MDB Techniques for Solaris 10 and OpenSolaris*, by Richard McDougall, Jim Mauro, and Brendan Gregg (Prentice Hall, 2006).

- The MDB Community on `OpenSolaris.org`, `http://opensolaris.org/os/community/mdb`.

- The *Solaris Modular Debugger Guide*, `http://docs.sun.com/app/docs/doc/816-5041`.

For information on `libumem`, consult the following:

- "Identifying Memory Management Bugs Within Applications Using the libumem Library," by Robert Benson, `http://access1.sun.com/techarticles/libumem.html`.

- Jonathan Adams' blog, `http://blogs.sun.com/jwadams`.

The Korn shell website contains quite a bit of information on ksh93: `http://kornshell.com/doc`.

The NetBeans web page, `http://netbeans.org`, contains documentation, tutorials, and many other useful resources.

Resources on source code management are a bit scarcer. Here are a few useful ones:

- "Subversion or CVS, Bazaar or Mercurial?" by John Ferguson Smart, `http://javaworld.com/javaworld/jw-09-2007/jw-09-versioncontrol.html?page=1`. This article is a good comparison of CVS, Subversion, and Mercurial.

- *Essential CVS*, by Jennifer Vesperman (O'Reilly, 2006).

- *Version Control with Subversion*, by C. Michal Pilato, Ben Collins-Sussman, and Brian W. Fitzpatrick. Available free online at `http://svnbook.red-bean.com`.

- *Distributed Revision Control with Mercurial*, by Bryan O'Sullivan, `http://hgbook.red-bean.com/hgbook.html`.

- Mercurial Usage (cheat sheet), `http://ivy.fr/mercurial/ref/v1.0/Mercurial-Usage-v1.0.pdf`.

- The Mercurial page, `http://selenic.com/mercurial/wiki`.

Additional information on IPS can be found at the Image Packaging System project page on OpoenSolaris.org, `http://opensolaris.org/os/project/pkg`, and on the "Getting Started with the Image Packaging System" user documentation at `http://dlc.sun.com/osol/docs/content/IPS/ggcph.html`.

Summary

This chapter examined the full-featured development and debugging environment offered by OpenSolaris for many kinds of applications. It explored the tools available for writing code in Java, C, C++, Perl, Python, Ruby, PHP, and shell, and described the Java and C/C++ debugging support on OpenSolaris, including the Java Debugger, the GNU Debugger, `dbx`, and MDB. This chapter also presented a tutorial on using the NetBeans IDE for developing Java, C/C++, and web applications. Additionally, the chapter covered three source code management solutions (CVS, Subversion, and Mercurial) and provided a brief discussion of core file and crash dump management and kernel debugging.

Index

Note to the Reader: Throughout this index **boldfaced** page numbers indicate primary discussions of a topic. *Italicized* page numbers indicate illustrations.

The books you
read to succeed.

Get the most out of the latest software and leading-edge technologies
with a Wiley Bible—your one-stop reference.

0-471-78886-4
978-0-471-78886-7

0-470-04030-0
978-0-470-04030-0

0-7645-4256-7
978-0-7645-4256-5

0-470-10089-3
978-0-470-10089-9

WILEY
Now you know.
wiley.com